Gillette®

LEAGUE
Publications Ltd

RUGBY LEAGUE 2005-06
Tales of the unexpected

League Publications Ltd

First published in Great Britain in 2005 by
League Publications Ltd
Wellington House
Briggate
Brighouse
West Yorkshire HD6 1DN

A CIP catalogue record for this book is available from the British Library
ISBN 1-901347-15-X

Designed and Typeset by League Publications Limited
Printed by ColourBooks Ltd, Dublin, Eire

Contributing Editor	Tim Butcher
Statistics, production and design	Daniel Spencer
Contributors	Gareth Walker
	Malcolm Andrews
	Mike Latham
	Raymond Fletcher
	Tony Hannan
	Phil Caplan
	Steve Kilgallon
	Mike Sterriker
	Alex Shirvani
	Martyn Sadler
	Steve Mascord
	Paul English
	Gavin Willacy
	Neil Barraclough
Pictures	Varley Picture Agency
	Action Photographics, Australia
	Vicky Matthers
	Graham Lynch
	Dave Williams
	Sig Kasatkin
	Max Flego
	Gordon Clayton
	Peter Morley

CONTENTS

FOREWORD

2005 was the year that international Rugby League exploded back to life. The 2005 Gillette Tri-Nations was a tremendous success that began with New Zealand's first victory in Sydney for nearly 50 years, and culminated in another famous Kiwi victory in the final at Leeds. In-between, we were treated to some fantastic Rugby League by all three nations, and whilst Great Britain couldn't improve on 2004, the overall success of the tournament far outweighed any disappointment.

The competition is clearly established in the sporting calendar, and I for one look forward to the 2006 tournament down under. The prospect of seeing the Lions on tour again is one that all League followers are rightly excited by.

From a Gillette perspective, 2005 saw our partnership with Rugby League evolve on several levels. In addition to our continued support for the International game, we opened the Gillette Rugby League Heritage centre at the George Hotel in Huddersfield. Whilst it is right and fitting that we look forward, it is also important that we celebrate the sport's rich history, and I thank Mike Stephenson for his vision and guidance on the project.

We hosted the second Gillette International Rugby League Awards, an event which is also now firmly established. We also extended our relationship with Paul Sculthorpe, as Gillette's ambassador for Rugby League. It has been a frustrating injury-plagued season for Paul, but he continues to be a wonderful ambassador for Gillette within the sport, and we thank him for his professionalism and support shown to Gillette.

I would also like to thank Graham Clay of Impress Sport and Adrian Smith of Touch Media for their hard work during 2005 to ensure that our association with Rugby League continues to be a successful one.

And, as we sponsor this yearbook for the third year I would also like to thank everyone at League Publications for their support.

Rugby League is regaining credibility at international level. I am confident that this will continue in 2006.

Enjoy the read and keep watching the great game of Rugby League.

Best wishes
TONY COLQUITT
Customer Development Director, Gillette Group UK

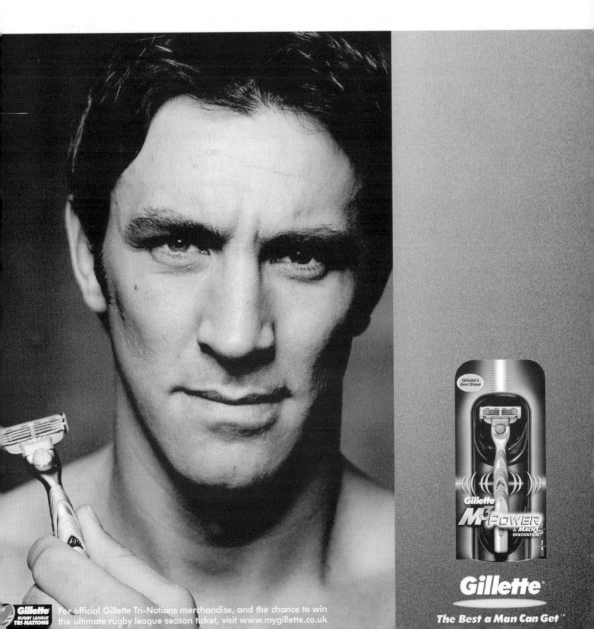

ACKNOWLEDGEMENTS

Rugby League 2005-2006 is the tenth in League Publications Ltd's annual series of Rugby League Yearbooks, the third year with the backing of Gillette.

Without the hard work and dedication of all the contributors to *Rugby Leaguer & Rugby League Express* and *Rugby League World* magazine, who provide such a tremendous service to the game of Rugby League, there could be no yearbook of this stature.

We are also fortunate to be able to include some wonderful action photography provided by, in particular, Varley Picture Agency, Col Whelan of Action Photographics in Sydney, Dave Williams of Rugby League Photos, and Peter Morley.

Co-editor Daniel Spencer has once again handled the statistical sections and the design. And Colourbooks of Dublin deserve some mention for the speed with which they produce the hard copies of the book.

Special mentions for Gareth Walker, Malcolm Andrews, Raymond Fletcher, Phil Caplan, Tony Hannan, Alex Shirvani, Steve Kilgallon, Steve Mascord, Paul English and Mike Latham, who have contributed to the writing of this book; and to Opta Index, who provided the Opta Index Analysis in our mind-boggling statistical section.

And a special thankyou to Mike Latham for his invaluable help with proofing much of the text.

TIM BUTCHER
Contributing Editor
Rugby League 2005-2006

INTRODUCTION

It's surprising what a difference eighty minutes of Rugby League can make.

After Great Britain came up short, again, against Australia at the KC Stadium, most British Rugby League supporters got that sinking feeling, the one where utter disappointment sits in the pit of your stomach.

Then we had those amazing events at Elland Road in Leeds a week later, and suddenly the outlook didn't seem so bad. And for that we have to thank Brian McClennan and his Kiwis of 2005. New Zealand had looked ominous in the first two games of the Gillette Tri-Nations that, this year, were played down under. But after Britain gave them a thrashing at Huddersfield in Game Five, it was safe to assume they had done their usual trick of starting strong and then disintegrating as the tour wore on.

How wrong we were. Not only did they beat Australia in the final, they absolutely hammered them, roared on by nearly all the 28,000 people present that night, to invigorate international Rugby League. Suddenly it all fell into place, the 2006 Tri-Nations, the 2007 'All Golds' Centenary tour, the 2008 World Cup. There was even talk of a Lions tour down under in 2010!

It would be fair to say that 2005 had indeed ended on a very positive note, despite the inability of our own national side to master the Kangaroos.

And what went before then wasn't bad either. In fact when you read through the story of 2005 in the pages ahead, you will realise you might have forgotten much of the drama that evolved over the months - from the saga that was the Gareth Ellis transfer as 2005 began right through to that magnificent late charge by Bradford Bulls that saw them create history by becoming the first team to win the Super League Grand Final from third place in the table.

It was obviously not a great year for some people, and there will be twice as many disappointed supporters this year because twice as many teams have endured relegation – two down from both Super League and NL1 as the League restructures itself to accommodate new clubs Les Catalans and Celtic Crusaders.

Leigh Centurions' Super League adventure proved to be short-lived, with coach Darren Abram, and indeed the whole club, faced with an impossible task to get their team and club up to speed in the space of weeks. It proved unachievable, although there was a handful of good times along the way, not least the 40-18 thrashing of Wakefield in front of the Sky TV cameras.

Leigh's experience at last made League bosses realise that automatic promotion and relegation are not necessarily ideal, such is the gulf between part-time and fully professional League. The result was a Super League strategy

Introduction

announced in mid-season to take effect in 2009, which will involve Super League clubs needing to fulfil minimum criteria and other clubs allowed a lead-in time to prepare before promotion – even though that might take place every three years. One of the effects of that policy should be to see National League One develop into a full-time competition – and next season three clubs, Leigh, Widnes and Hull Kingston Rovers will operate on that basis. A rise in standards off the field to match those on it will surely help secure television exposure that the National Leagues deserve.

Super League will of course feature Castleford Tigers again in 2006 after their one-year stay in NL1, which should be a boost to the competition. They are making one or two close-season signings to suggest they should be more competitive than Leigh last year.

But they will need to be as every other side has strengthened from what was a terrific Super League X.

The Bulls had a patchy year by their standards but came good when it mattered most, with Shontayne Hape and Lesley Vainikolo two of the dominant figures of the season. With a major change around in personnel, including the loss of their captain Jamie Peacock to arch-rivals Leeds, 2006 will be very interesting indeed down Odsal way.

The Rhinos, after a fantastic start to the year with their World Club Challenge win over Canterbury Bulldogs, proceeded to dominate Super League for almost all the season, before losing in dramatic fashion in the Powergen Challenge Cup final to an inspired Hull; being pipped to the Minor Premiership by St Helens; and then falling to an agonising defeat at Old Trafford.

Saints themselves were denied a crack at the Grand Final by an injury list that included three of their brightest stars in Paul Sculthorpe, Sean Long and Darren Albert. But they provided us with one of the dramas of the year when they sacked and suspended the coach who had brought them so much success in recent years, Ian Millward. It seemed almost inevitable that Millward would end up at Wigan. And it only took about two weeks.

The Warriors missed out on the play-offs for the first time, suffered record defeats in consecutive weeks, had an injury list as long as the A49, and recorded their best ever attendances. Somebody must be doing something right in Wigan.

Ditto Warrington, whose early play-off exit to Hull was a disappointment. But the Wolves fans, and indeed Rugby League as a whole thanked them for a wonderful few weeks of Joeymania.

Hull made a humbling exit themselves at Bradford the following week, but they had already won their silverware at Cardiff with that 25-24 win over Leeds. And in Danny Brough, a rags to riches story of sorts, they had one of the tales of the year. And coach John Kear was always good for a quote.

The story of Rugby League in London has been one of many twists and turns and 2005 certainly didn't disappoint on that front. The Broncos came within an inch of being thrown out of Super League – and probably would have faced extinction. But they still managed to turn in some of the most entertaining performances of the year and finish sixth. Their re-birth as Harlequins at the end of the year has set up one of the more interesting scenarios of Super League XI.

Which leaves Huddersfield, Salford and Wakefield, who all had play-off aspirations, with the Giants getting the closest, Brad Drew, Eorl Crabtree and

Chris Thorman the stars of a much-improved campaign.

The Wildcats suffered injuries and got rid of their coach in time-honoured fashion before the season was finished. But they finished on an optimistic note, with their big names signed up for the next year or two. Salford coach Karl Harrison wore his heart on his sleeve and produced a competitive Reds outfit which wasn't that far away from the shake-up.

Another fine season then? I'll leave that up to you and hope you enjoy this, the tenth yearbook produced by League Publications.

The Gillette Rugby League Yearbook 2005-2006 has an in-depth statistical section, featuring every team in the Rugby Football League, chapters on all the major competitions both here and abroad and a record of every game in Super League and the National Leagues One and Two.

It also contains details of the international season, with full coverage of the Gillette Tri-Nations and other international fixtures during the season.

And this year we have included an historical record of all the Grand Finals played since they were introduced in 1998, and a comprehensive list of players who made their debut in 2005.

Once again we have selected five individuals who we judge to have made the biggest impact on Rugby League this year.

And looking forward - you can find your club's fixtures for next season at the back of the yearbook.

TIM BUTCHER
Contributing Editor
Rugby League 2005-2006

League Publications produces the weekly newspaper 'Rugby Leaguer & Rugby League Express', as well as the monthly glossy magazine 'Rugby League World' and the website 'totalrugbyleague.com'.

1
PERSONALITIES OF 2005

Stacey Jones celebrates New Zealand's Tri-Nations victory with coach Brian McClennan

Who is the best scrum-half in the world?

Stacey Jones

Most people would suggest that Andrew Johns deserves that title, but after the 2005 Gillette Tri-Nations Final there will be plenty of observers who will put their hands up for Stacey Jones. Jones didn't only play in the game and play a part in all four tries in the Kiwis' shock 24-0 victory against Australia. He travelled from Auckland after witnessing the birth of his son just two days before the game, arriving at the Kiwis' Leeds hotel at 4.00pm on the day before the game.

Jones, who will lead the challenge of the new Super League club Les Catalans in 2006, had officially retired from international Rugby League when he refused to play for the Kiwis in the 2004 Tri-Nations tournament. But in 2005, with his replacement Thomas Leuluai recovering from a leg injury, he was persuaded to come out of international retirement, initially to play for the Kiwis in the first two games of the tournament against the

Australians in Sydney and Auckland.

But all along there was a suspicion that the Kiwis had persuaded Jones to play throughout the tournament, despite his commitments to his new club and his wife's impending labour. Jones confirmed after the Tri-Nations Final that he had been unable to resist the temptation to play in probably the biggest and most historic game in New Zealand Rugby League history, and, in describing the New Zealanders' motivation against Australia, he came out with the *Rugby Leaguer & League Express* quote of the week after the Kiwis' triumph. "They have been dominant for so long," said Jones. "They have been bullying us for a number of years, so it's about time we got one over them."

The British supporters among the Tri-Nations Final crowd knew exactly what he was talking about.

Jamie Lyon

If you want to know who was the outstanding player in Super League in 2005, just check out the major awards.

Man of Steel – Jamie Lyon. Rugby League Writers' Player of the Year – Jamie Lyon.

Super League X could very easily be described as the year of Jamie Lyon, the boy from the Australian bush town of Wee Waa who rejected the high life in Sydney with Parramatta to return home, before sensationally signing with St Helens on a two-year contract.

And what a signing he proved to be. If you were looking for thrills, Knowsley Road was the place to be, and Lyon was the player to watch. Probably no other player in the history of St Helens has demonstrated such wonderful handling skills as Lyon, and few players have been more adept at scoring or creating tries. Lyon's form also ensured big viewing audiences for Saints matches whenever they featured on Sky Sports. And Lyon was a particularly welcome member of the Saints squad in a season when two linchpins of the side – Paul Sculthorpe and Sean Long – had seasons which were wrecked by injury.

Lyon's partnership with his winger Darren Albert was one of the highlights of Super League X - between them they scored 47 tries in Super League alone - ranking alongside the pairing of Hape and Vainikolo at Bradford.

Saints became the first club in the history of Super League to fail to qualify for the Grand Final after finishing in first position. But Lyon's almost superhuman effort in dragging them back from a 19-0 deficit in the qualifying semi-final against Leeds Rhinos almost got them to Old Trafford, as he scored two tries and brilliantly created one for his teammate Ian Hardman.

Saints may have lost, but, with Lyon in their side, there are sure to be many more memorable occasions at Knowsley Road in 2006.

Danny Brough

At one time scrum-halves always used to be little cocky guys.

Players who had lots of confidence in their own ability, who used to love nothing more than to taunt opposing forwards, who would tackle men twice their size, and who would think nothing of landing a crucial drop goal to win tight games for their side.

Think of Alex Murphy, Tommy Bishop and Andy Gregory from days gone by. And now you can think of Hull's Danny Brough, the player with the outrageous hairstyle who joined the Super League club from National League 2 club York City Knights for not much more than a song at the start of the season, and whose drop goal and nerveless goalkicking (with four successful conversions) were key factors in Hull's 25-24 Powergen Challenge Cup Final victory against Leeds Rhinos.

Brough had given up a career as a plumber to take a gamble on his ability to make the grade as a Super League player, accepting a two-year contract at the start of the season that saw him halve his income, and didn't even place him in Hull's 20-man Super League squad.

By the end of the season Hull had agreed a new two-year contract with Brough that saw him firmly established as a first-team regular.

It was that Challenge Cup Final – possibly the last to be played at Cardiff's Millennium Stadium, and the first to be played on the August Bank Holiday weekend – that sealed Brough's reputation.

At a crucial point in the game Brough's one-pointer established a 19-12 lead for Hull, and although the Rhinos looked as though they had taken the spoils with two late converted tries, Brough's nerve held as he converted Paul Cooke's late try for Hull to win the match.

Brough had developed a top kicking game as the season unfolded, and ousted his teammate Cooke as the club's first-choice goalkicker. And his value to Hull was emphasised even more when he was surprisingly dropped from Hull's team for their final play-off game of the season, as Hull went down 71-0 to the rampant Bradford Bulls.

16

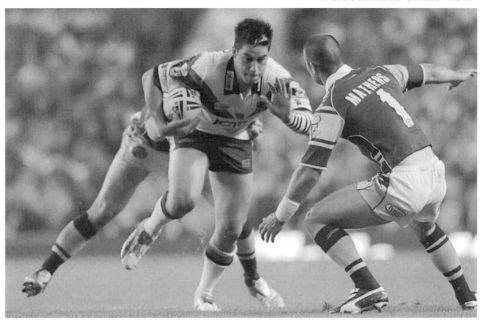

Shontayne Hape

Shontayne Hape has a unique record in 2005. He is the only leading Super League player to have played more than ten matches in this season's competition without losing a single game.

And he is the only player to win a Super League Grand Final and the Gillette Tri-Nations Grand Final in the 2005 season.

But for most of the season both objectives would have seemed distant possibilities. For the first 20 rounds of Super League the Bradford Bulls star was out injured after undergoing knee ligament surgery following an injury sustained in the 2004 Tri-Nations competition. The Bulls, having to get by without the partnership between Hape and the Volcano, Lesley Vainikolo, were struggling in fifth place in the Super League table when Hape returned to action in July in a game against strugglers Leigh Centurions.

But from that point the Bulls' season was transformed, and they wouldn't lose another match. Winning their last eight games of the regular season, with Hape and Vainikolo firing together once again, they finished third in the table, and then won four play-off matches to become the first club to finish outside the top two to win the Super League title.

But the glory wasn't over for Hape. The week after the Grand Final he was called into the New Zealand team for their Tri-Nations clash against Australia in Auckland, and although his winning run came to an end in that game, he impressed sufficiently to secure selection in the Kiwis' Tri-Nations final team, although selected at loose forward, rather than in his usual position at centre.

It didn't prevent Hape having a blinder, however, along with the rest of the Kiwis. "Everyone had belief going into the game, and everyone wanted to work hard, and when they do this is what we can achieve," said Hape, after the climax to his wonderful year.

One of the finest careers in modern Rugby League finally came to an end on the second Sunday in October, when Brad Davis, who had turned 37 in March, helped Castleford Tigers seal their return to Super League with a stunning 36-8 National League One Grand Final victory over Whitehaven at the Halton Stadium.

Davis, playing one of the finest games of his long career, earned the *Rugby Leaguer & League Express* Gamestar award. "His kicking pinned Whitehaven back, his promoting took Castleford forward, and he snared two interception tries for good measure," read the citation. Davis contributed much more than his two interception tries in the Grand Final, playing a major role in each of the Tigers' other four tries.

So a player who first appeared in British Rugby League in 1992, when he paid his own fare to this country to turn out with Nottingham City in the lower reaches of professional Rugby

Brad Davis

League, finally achieved his objective of taking the Tigers back into Super League thirteen years later.

During that time he has also played with Huddersfield, York, Wakefield and Villeneuve, but Castleford is the club with which he will be most strongly identified when his career is recalled, and the Grand Final will always be the game that defines his contribution to the Tigers' cause.

"At the start of the season it was my goal to get Castleford back into Super League, and to achieve that is a wonderful feeling. It was the most important game I have ever played in," said Davis after the final whistle.

You would have to go a long way to find a Tigers supporter who would be prepared to disagree with that judgement.

2
THE 2005 SEASON

DECEMBER 2004
Ellis in Wonderland

After the Aussies had blown away Great Britain's Tri-Nations dream, there was little panic from the Rugby Football League, which, led by its Executive Chairman Richard Lewis, preferred to focus on the profit of £750,000 the tournament had generated.

Most players were enthusiastic about repeating the exercise in 2005, though the Australians were keen to shorten their stay in the UK by playing two games down under before coming over to take on the Poms. That ambition was strengthened when the Kangaroos, on their way home after the Tri-Nations, took on the US Tomahawks in Philadelphia and only squeezed past the hosts 36-24, after trailing 24-6 at half-time. On the face of it, that looked like a major advance for the international game. But a serious injury to Willie Mason had Aussie administrators and commentators slamming the value of the fixture, guaranteeing that there would be no more development games for the full international side in the near future.

Australian champions, the Bulldogs, announced that they were facing an injury crisis ahead of their World Club Challenge clash with Leeds Rhinos. Mason was joined by eight other players on the Bulldogs' treatment table.

Meanwhile, Great Britain team doctor Chris Brookes hit back at claims that Paul Sculthorpe had been unfit to play in the Gillette Tri-Nations final. "It's our job to give players the chance to play in the game," said Dr Brookes. "Paul felt fine during the warm-up, but during the game he started to feel his injury. His back was twisted in a tackle, he tried his best to keep going, but couldn't carry on any longer after half-time."

Leeds Rhinos duo Keith Senior and Ryan Bailey both escaped suspension despite breaching Rugby League's doping control regulations after taking the banned substance ephedrine. The Rugby League's Advisory Panel accepted that they had taken the substance, which is contained in some over-the-counter cold cures by mistake, and not to enhance their performance.

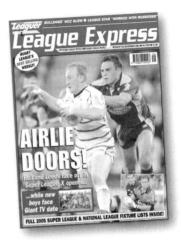

The RFL Executive Chairman Richard Lewis slammed Bradford chairman Chris Caisley over comments attributed to him in the local Telegraph and Argus newspaper. In an article entitled "Caisley calls on RFL to come clean", Caisley hit out at what was described as "the circumstances surrounding the positive drugs tests of Leeds Rhinos' Great Britain internationals Keith Senior and Ryan Bailey....We don't want it to appear as if it's a case of sour grapes, but we would like to know when the tests were done."

"That's an extraordinary comment," said Lewis.

"We have never specified before when tests are done. When tests are done has never been an issue; suffice to say it was in the latter part of the season. To say anything was being hidden is absolute nonsense."

The RFL appointed a serious injury consultant in David Phillips to co-ordinate the game's response and care for players injured playing the game. And the game's governing body introduced new regulations that required Super League clubs to name 20-man squads four days in advance of the weekend matches. The regulation was intended to prevent insider betting on matches, which had led to hefty suspensions for Sean Long and Martin Gleeson earlier in the year.

Newcomers Blackpool revealed that they would be playing under the name of the 'Panthers'. Coach Mark Lee was joined by his former Salford teammate Steve Blakeley on the Panthers staff with Willie Swann named as captain and former Oldham player-coach Steve Molloy joining as the pack leader. "We want to be in the first division in the first year," said club spokesman Dave Rowland.

With the Challenge Cup moved to an August final in 2005, December was a rest period for Rugby League, at least on the field. Off it there was plenty of activity, with Widnes welcoming new coach Frank Endacott after he was granted a work permit, and stand-off Owen Craigie, with ten years' experience of the NRL, despite only being 26 years of age.

Widnes, already frustrated in their chase for Kiwi scrum-half Thomas Leuluai, pulled out of a deal for Frenchman Maxime Greseque in a week that Super League rivals Huddersfield Giants announced the capture of Castleford prop Paul Jackson on a one-year deal.

St Helens, meanwhile, were beaten in the final of the Dubai rugby union sevens, but chairman Eamonn McManus thought it likely they would return the next year. And London Broncos - who had recruited Melbourne forward Danny Williams, despite his having nine games of an NRL suspension still to run, and South Sydney prop Filimone Lolohea - hinted that Shane Webcke could be a target for 2006.

Former London Broncos scrum-half Dennis Moran revealed that he "couldn't wait" to leave the Griffin Park club and would have probably returned to Australia if he hadn't been able to join Wigan during the close season. "I just wanted to come to a club that was a lot more stable, and that has good players who can stand

up to the job," said Moran. One of Moran's new teammates, Andy Farrell, was named Super League Player of the Year by readers of *Rugby Leaguer & League Express.*

Promoted Leigh - riding high on the securing of a 12-month shirt sponsorship deal with Emirate Airlines - signed PNG international John Wilshere when he was released by Warrington after only playing eight games for the Wolves. Centurions coach Darren Abram considered the risk of Wilshere's injury record one worth taking.

But the transfer story that dominated the headlines for the whole of December was the scramble for the services of Wakefield's Gareth Ellis. The story went something like this: Ellis likely to stay at Wakefield...Bulls offer Ellis swap deal...Ellis agrees Bradford deal...Ellis deal collapses...Ellis likely to stay at Wakefield...Leeds Rhinos get their man.

The Great Britain player had already been the subject of a £125,000 offer from ambitious Warrington Wolves when Bradford moved in as favourites for Ellis's signature. Ellis had one year remaining of his contract with the Wildcats, and after that would be a free agent. Wakefield had already offered their captain a new three-year contract, which he had refused. And Ellis had rejected a lesser contract offer from Leeds. So when the Bulls arrived on the scene with a deal that involved Jamie Langley and Stuart Reardon coming to Belle Vue, Wakefield looked like they would take the bait, and Ellis agreed personal terms with Bradford.

But the deal hit a stumbling block when Reardon and Langley both declined to join the Wildcats, and Ellis was expected to see out his time at Wakefield. He was on the team bus for their Boxing Day friendly with Leeds at Headingley (in which they were hammered 46-6) and Ellis's agent David Howes, the former RFL administrator, said in *Rugby Leaguer & League Express* on 27th December: "He will be staying with Trinity under the terms of his existing contract which expires at the end of next season," concluding that Bradford would be the club most likely to then sign him.

But when the Wildcats headed for their warm-weather training camp in Portugal on New Year's Day, four days later, Gareth Ellis was a Leeds Rhinos player.

Leeds - who claimed they had made an enquiry to Bradford for Jamie Langley, although the Bulls denied it - stepped in with a four-year deal for Ellis, and the transfer took less than 24 hours to complete. "I'd had a few meetings with

Gareth Ellis receives his Leeds shirt for 2005 and meets the Rhinos fans

Leeds, and I was always impressed with what they had to offer," said Ellis. "The atmosphere at Headingley, and seeing the Super League trophy on Boxing Day was a big thing. I suppose I thought to myself that if I had the opportunity, why not take it? After all, a Rugby League career is not a long one."

Wakefield chief executive Diane Rogerson claimed everyone at Wakefield was glad that the saga was finally over. "It got to a stage where everybody wanted to bring the process to a conclusion," she said. "We will never please everybody, though. Some supporters were very happy that we have realised our asset for a very good price (estimated at around the £200,000 mark), whereas if Gareth had stayed we would also have been very happy; it was a win-win situation.

"And I have to give Gary Hetherington (Leeds chief executive) credit, he handled everything very well. We spoke to him on Tuesday morning, and by Wednesday morning (29th December) we had agreed the deal. With Bradford everything was dragging on, and everybody was getting very frustrated. We had an agreement with them, but they couldn't deliver what they agreed."

Jamie Langley thanked the Bulls supporters who campaigned for him and his teammate Stuart Reardon not to move to Wakefield as part of the Ellis deal. "It's great when you know the fans want you to stay with the club," said Langley. It was a dramatic end to the year, but it was all put into perspective by the Asian tsunami that hit the Indian Ocean on Boxing Day, killing hundreds of thousands of people.

Bradford and Great Britain star Stuart Fielden was on holiday on the Thai island of Phuket with his friend, Keighley Cougars player Danny Ekis, at the time the tsunami struck. Both he and Ekis were lucky to escape with their lives. A decision not to get up early on Boxing Day morning almost certainly saved them.

JANUARY
Crowded house

The club-versus-country debate began to surface in the New Year. Great Britain coach Brian Noble, speaking publicly for the first time since his side lost the Gillette Tri-Nations final 44-4 to Australia the previous November, asked the British game to throw more support behind international football. Noble admitted the result had been a "huge blow in the guts", but pledged his renewed enthusiasm for the Great Britain coaching job, and said lessons had been learned from the result.

But he pointed to the limited time the British players spend together, saying: "The debate needs to be about how we can improve the concept of Great Britain, because the facts are very plain - we are given less preparation time, the toughest agenda, and we have less players playing in our competition. There are 13 or 14 reasons (why Great Britain lost). There is a State of Origin series that teaches their players a higher threshold of rugby, and we just need to find that higher threshold for ourselves in the big games. We are a great nation for just believing in Great Britain for six weeks. It's something I have to look at with the right authorities and as a sport as a whole. The international calendar shouldn't just sneak up on us after the last game of the season."

RFL Executive Chairman Richard Lewis accepted that it would be ideal to give Noble more time with the Great Britain squad, perhaps combined with a restriction on the number of games a Super League player can play, but that it would depend on funding being available to compensate the clubs.

As if to emphasise the difficulties involved in building international Rugby League, the 2005 Tri-Nations competition, barely nine moths away, was thrown into doubt as the Australian and New Zealand authorities were reported to have failed to reach agreement on where the games between the two countries would be played. The disagreement stemmed from New Zealand's desire to host both games, with NZRL chairman Selwyn Pearson saying: "We want both Tests here. Australia have plenty of big League – city-versus-country matches and three State of Origin games each year. We want something for League fans in this country."

Meanwhile the chairman of the Rugby League International Federation,

Colin Love, said he believed that the 2008 World Cup, to be played in Australia to celebrate the centenary of the game in that country, was likely to be contested by just twelve teams, and a final decision would be made early in the year. Love also announced a plan to strengthen the Polynesian nations before the World Cup. "I think you might be surprised at the quality of teams that will represent some of the nations involved in the tournament," he said. "Samoa and Tonga will be forces to be reckoned with in that time. We are already embarking on programmes whereby we are identifying elite youth in those nations and putting them into training squads through the Australian Rugby League...And we can only see a country like France going forward from here."

Homeowners Friendly Society, under their 'engage' banner were to replace Tetley's as the naming-rights sponsor of Super League, with Super League having negotiated a £100,000 per annum increase on the £700,000 per annum paid by the brewing giant.

Andy Farrell was awarded the OBE in the New Year honours list with local MP Ian McCartney saying: "This is tremendous recognition for the game of Rugby League. Andy Farrell is an outstanding athlete, as good as anyone in any sport in the world. And it is typical of the man that he has said he is taking this for the sport of Rugby League, rather than for himself."

Farrell flew home from Wigan's training camp in Florida carrying an injury, and was thought likely to miss the first four months of the season after knee surgery, with club chairman Maurice Lindsay demanding action to protect players. "I think that Rugby League should take the responsibility to examine the real health of the game, and by that I mean the health and physical state of the players," Lindsay told *Rugby Leaguer & League Express*. "Andy Farrell is only the tip of the iceberg, and I really am concerned about this. But there are no statistics available indicating how many players have needed end-of-season operations. There should be some research done by the RFL so that we would know what we are doing to our athletes. Burnout, fatigue and the possible effects on players after their retirement are a cause of great concern for me, and should be for the game as a whole. At Wigan we had seven players, apart from Andy, who required surgery at the end of the season. And when you think that we are going to go right through to the end of November without a break, you can only see the situation getting even worse.

"Andrew picked up his injury in the Tri-Nations Final, and he hoped that rest would cure it, but he has ultimately needed surgery. It is a heavy price that he and the club have had to pay for giving all to their country. The Tri-Nations was a massive drain upon the players following a long season. Andrew is irreplaceable, and with the restrictions of the rule limiting squads to 20 players, it means we will be drafting teenagers into our squad before we even kick off the season."

Another player struggling with injury couldn't put it down to the Tri-Nations. The Warriors were waiting to determine the exact extent of new signing Luke Davico's worrying pectoral injury sustained in the midweek friendly at Salford - a recurrence of an injury he suffered in Australia.

Hull's major signing of the off-season, Stephen Kearney, came back from

January

Hull's training camp in Spain carrying a pectoral injury similar to Davico's. Paul King - in the middle of rehabilitation following a knee reconstruction that kept him out of Tri-Nations reckoning - didn't even make it to Spain. For the second consecutive year, the Hull prop was forced to stay at home because of an acute fear of flying - he suffers from severe claustrophobia that means he struggles to even get on a bus. The previous season he had boarded the plane before suffering a panic attack. Hypnotherapy had failed to cure his fear.

King wasn't the only one. Warrington Wolves flew to their pre-season camp in Lanzarote without star centre signing Toa Kohe-Love, who also couldn't overcome his fear of flying.

St Helens prop forward Keith Mason also missed the club's pre-season trip to Portugal but claustrophobia was not to blame, an internal ulcer in his leg seeing him rushed to hospital before the team flew out. Coach Ian Millward wasn't having a great deal of luck with one of his close-season signings, Michael Smith. The big Kiwi, who joined Saints from Castleford, played just one trial match for the club, but was reluctant to re-locate from his Hull base, despite a move being part of his two-year contract. He was made available to other clubs.

One player who did make the trip was Saints' new Australian signing Jamie Lyon, with whom Millward admits he was delighted. "Jamie has probably settled in better than any Australian has every settled in at St Helens," explained Millward. "We are very impressed with everything about him, including his manners, and it's as though he's been here for five years." Lyon made his first appearance in a Saints shirt in the 22-16 friendly win over Widnes Vikings. And comedian Johnny Vegas made a late cameo appearance for Saints in a pre-season 28-18 home win over Hull, which doubled as a testimonial game for Keiron Cunningham.

There were several player movements as clubs fine-tuned their squads for the big kick-off in February. Bradford off-loaded two of their young players - prop Richard Moore to Leigh Centurions, and stand-off Chris Bridge to Warrington. But cross-code starlet Matt Cook pledged the next three years to Rugby League by signing a new contract with the Bulls, after playing in the union under-19 Six Nations and for the England under-18 League Academy the previous year.

The Bulls' signing from Castleford, Ryan Hudson, was threatening to take his former club to a tribunal to try and recoup unpaid monies.

The Tigers terminated the contracts of 15 players in mid-October, rather than the end of November, after their relegation was guaranteed. A tribunal had already come down in favour of former Castleford Tigers stars Paul Mellor and Motu Tony, who were the first players to ask the RFL for a ruling against the Tigers. The Tigers eventually settled with all the players.

Hudson, though, had bigger things to worry about, as he was suspended by the Bulls, for disciplinary reasons, with the RFL confirming he was under investigation by the doping control panel.

London Broncos - whose final two squad members, prop Filimone Lolohea and halfback Thomas Leuluai, arrived in the capital early on New Year's Eve morning - looked destined for a company voluntary agreement (CVA), while club sources continued to deny the Broncos had a done deal with the New Zealand millionaire Eric

Settling in well - Jamie Lyon

Watson. London enjoyed a ten-day pre-season camp in Canet, a beach resort ten miles from Perpignan, concluding the visit with a 28-24 defeat to UTC.

Salford City Reds admitted they might not move to their new Barton stadium until 2007 with chief executive Dave Tarry saying the delay was no cause for concern. And Leigh Centurions, meanwhile, took the unusual decision to hand out their squad numbers in alphabetical order.

Outside Super League, the Hull Daily Mail issued a full apology to Doncaster Dragons coach St John Ellis following an article they had published after a controversial match between Hull Kingston Rovers and Doncaster in July 2004. Ellis also collected a five-figure payout from the newspaper following claims about his post-match conduct. Hull KR signed Scottish rugby union international winger Jonathan Steel.

And as Leeds Rhinos prepared for the World Club Challenge clash with the Bulldogs, they held a joint training session with the England rugby union team. "The fact that they wanted to come and train with us is humbling," said Rhinos captain Kevin Sinfield. "They are the world champions, and they are the best at what they do, so to rub shoulders with them is a great experience from our point of view."

POWERGEN CHALLENGE CUP PRELIMINARY ROUND

Saturday 15th January 2005
Castleford Lock Lane 30 Ideal Isberg 0; Castleford Panthers 28 Ovenden 24; Cottingham Tigers 2 Barrow Island 8; Crosfields 10 Illingworth 22; Cutsyke 16 Shaw Cross Sharks 14; East Leeds 22 Waterhead 29; Heworth 6 Loughborough University 21; Huddersfield Sharks 14 Stanningley 19; Hull Wyke 30 Embassy 36; Hunslet Warriors 6 Halton Simms Cross 38; Ince Rosebridge 17 Hensingham 18; Normanton Knights 17 Seaton Rangers 16; Rochdale Mayfield 21 Featherstone Lions 16; Stanley Rangers 15 Eastmoor Dragons 14; West London 42 Fife Lions 10; Widnes St Maries 52 Saddleworth Rangers 0; York Acorn 12 East Hull 64

Sunday 16th January 2005
Cardiff Demons 12 Walney Central 28

FEBRUARY
World party

The biggest crowd ever for the World Club Challenge on British soil, 37,028, massed at Elland Road to see 'home' team Leeds Rhinos beat Australian champions Canterbury Bulldogs 39-32 in magnificent style.

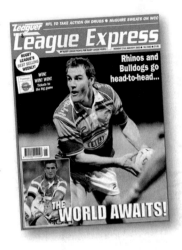

A blistering first-half performance from Leeds saw them build a 20-point lead which proved just enough to hold off the never-say-die Bulldogs. Two tries that helped the Rhinos get the upper hand were out of the top drawer. First Danny McGuire scored a sensational solo effort, off a superb, low slipped pass from Barrie McDermott. Then a magnificent team effort finished off by Rob Burrow in the 38th minute had the Rhinos 26-6 up at the break.

Luke Patten scored a superbly-worked try five minutes into the second half, but Richie Mathers and Jamie-Jones Buchanan tries had Leeds 38-12 in front. It looked like game over, but four more Bulldogs tries in 15 whirlwind minutes had them only six points behind with eight minutes to go, until a late Kevin Sinfield field goal saw the Rhinos home.

At the heart of the Bulldogs comeback was the most prodigious talent seen

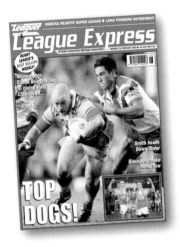

for years - second-rower Sonny Bill Williams. The teenager's stunning array of offloads and bone-shattering defence – Marcus Bai the victim of one creasing shoulder charge – was a highlight of a highly-entertaining clash. Williams' performance had a queue of British clubs, including Leeds, forming for his services - he was out of contract at the end of this season - almost before the final whistle had sounded.

The aftermath had officials at both ends of the world suggesting the possibility of a WCC staged in Australia next year. Leeds chief executive Gary Hetherington claimed that the Rhinos would like to travel to Australia to defend their crown if they were to win the Super League title for the second year in a row. "We are

Kevin Sinfield leaves Sonny Bill Williams
grounded as Braith Anasta moves in

keen to win Super League again, and if we do we would like to play it in Australia or New Zealand next year," said Hetherington. Leeds had made only one major signing in the off-season - that of Gareth Ellis - and he made his senior debut in the WCC. And on their form seven days before the start of Super League X, they looked well capable of retaining their crown. William Hill made them 11/10 favourites, with Bradford 5/2, St Helens 9/2, Wigan 6/1 and Leigh the rank outsiders at 1000/1.

CARNEGIE WORLD CLUB CHALLENGE

Friday 4th February 2005

LEEDS RHINOS 39 BULLDOGS 32

RHINOS: 1 Richard Mathers; 2 Mark Calderwood; 3 Chev Walker; 4 Keith Senior; 5 Marcus Bai; 13 Kevin Sinfield (C); 6 Danny McGuire; 8 Ryan Bailey; 14 Andrew Dunemann; 15 Danny Ward; 18 Jamie Jones-Buchanan; 12 Chris McKenna; 20 Gareth Ellis (D). Subs (all used): 10 Barrie McDermott; 11 Ali Lauitiiti; 7 Rob Burrow; 16 Willie Poching.
Tries: Walker (5), Calderwood (9), McGuire (22), Poching (31), Burrow (39), Mathers (51), Jones-Buchanan (54);
Goals: Sinfield 5/7; **Field goal:** Sinfield.
BULLDOGS: 1 Luke Patten; 2 Hazem El Masri; 3 Jamaal Lolesi; 4 Willie Tonga; 5 Trent Cutler; 6 Braith Anasta; 7 Corey Hughes; 8 Chris Armit; 9 Adam Perry; 10 Roy Asotasi; 11 Reni Maitua; 12 Sonny Bill Williams; 13 Tony Grimaldi (C). Subs (all used): 14 Brett Oliver; 15 Ben Czislowski; 16 Nate Myles; 17 Adam Brideson.
Tries: El Masri (19, 57), Patten (45), Lolesi (62, 72), Grimaldi (67); **Goals:** El Masri 4/6.
Rugby Leaguer & League Express Men of the Match:
Rhinos: Kevin Sinfield; *Bulldogs:* Sonny Bill Williams.
Penalty count: 6-6; **Half time:** 26-6;
Referee: Sean Hampstead (Australia);
Attendance: 37,028 *(at Elland Road, Leeds).*

February

Super League X enjoyed a great opening weekend to the season, although as far as the national media was concerned the only story in town was the Rugby Football Union's pursuit of the Wigan and Great Britain captain Andy Farrell - the player who won the Rugby League World magazine's Gillette Golden Boot as the best player in the world in 2004.

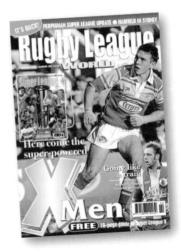

Wigan coach Denis Betts declined to talk about the potential loss of Farrell, beyond admitting he had not been in the stadium during the Friday night 15-4 victory over Salford City Reds. The Warriors, with four players - David Vaealiki, Dennis Moran, Wayne Godwin and Jerry Seuseu, who was placed on report for lifting his knees in the tackle - on debut, put any off-field distractions firmly behind them, as they began their Super League campaign with a hard-fought victory in atrociously wet conditions. Danny Tickle led from the front with an outstanding display in attack and defence, as the Warriors dominated large portions of the game, but weren't safe until David Allen went over for his first senior try with eight minutes remaining. Winger Brian Carney missed the game, and was expected to miss two to three more weeks after having a plate removed from his arm.

Moran scored the first Wigan try after seven minutes and his price for finishing as top try-scorer was cut from 12/1 to 8/1. The bookies also reported betting interest in Mark Calderwood, who was backed down from 20/1 to 14/1, although he didn't score in round one. Leeds Rhinos began the Super League season as 11/10 favourites and after their opening night 16-12 win at Hull, combined with Bradford Bulls' shock 16-28 defeat at home to Wakefield Trinity Wildcats the following Sunday, they went odds on. Leeds' win made it a club record 14 successive rounds of Super League without defeat.

Motu Tony was the most impressive of Hull's four debutants, although another former Castleford player, Tom Saxton grabbed a try, Nathan Blacklock almost snatched a match-winning interception and Jamie Thackray played solidly off the bench. A Keith Senior try put Leeds 16-2 up early in the second half and the Rhinos, with Richard Mathers solid at the back in testing wet conditions, just held off a late Hull comeback.

Leigh Centurions' 30-12 defeat to Huddersfield Giants in the Saturday TV game was not only a disappointing result for the game's newest Super League club, but the Centurions' crowd of 4,042 was well below expectations, especially after the club actually sold more than 5,000 tickets in the period leading up to the game. More than a thousand fans bought tickets but failed to turn out for the game on what was one of the wettest nights of the year. Problems with the Hilton Park floodlights saw them switched on only ten minutes before kick-off, with both sides having had to work through their pre-game warm-ups in the dark.

"It seems unkind to say it after just one round, but the evidence is undeniable. Surely, only a miracle can ensure Leigh's Super League survival", wrote Tony Hannan in *Rugby Leaguer & League Express*, as a constant concession of penalties, often for technical offences, ensured that the home side were always up against it. And Leigh provided the first dismissal of the season on 50 minutes, when second-rower Oliver Wilkes - until then having a big game - was dismissed for felling Huddersfield substitute Eorl Crabtree with a high tackle. He got one match the following Tuesday.

Leigh had little or no answer to new boy Brad Drew's constant metre-making from dummy-half, Sean Penkywicz's exceptional support play, and returning prop Paul Jackson's powerhouse effort at the heart of a dominant Giants pack.

London Broncos, with a huge turnaround of players and the departures of Jim Dymock and Dennis Moran were many people's favourites to accompany Leigh into NL1 at the end of the season. But the Broncos' all-new combination of Luke Dorn at stand-off, Thomas Leuluai at scrum-half and new skipper Mark McLinden at hooker was enough to conjure a 28-24 win over Warrington Wolves at Griffin Park. Another debutant - there were ten in all - Aussie second-rower Lee Hopkins, made a big impression.

Jamie Lyon managed to provide some sparkle in the mud as Saints eased to a 40-18 victory over Widnes at Knowsley Road. New prop Paul Anderson, brought in from Bradford in the close season, also impressed. Widnes, despite being able to field just one recognised prop in Julian O'Neill and losing Owen Craigie to injury midway through the second half, never gave up the fight. Second-rower Matthew Whitaker was pushed up to the front row and was the Vikings' best overall performer. "I was disappointed with the result, but I'm certainly not disappointed with the effort that went in," coach Endacott reflected.

Wakefield looked like they were to carry on from their whirlwind finish to 2004 as they recorded their first ever win - by 28-16 - at Odsal in the Super League era. Bradford appeared lacklustre from the start and missed the incisive edge of Shontayne Hape, who had undergone a knee reconstruction after an injury sustained in training during the Tri-Nations. But Trinity had heroes all over the park. Darrell Griffin and Michael Korkidas led the forward charge, while 16-point Jamie Rooney and halfback partner Ben Jeffries orchestrated the threequarter line. The absence of last season's top scorer Sid Domic (groin), Rob Spicer (hip) and Duncan MacGillivray (shoulder), were hardly noticed. The strong-running David Solomona, having not played pre-season and having only been back in full training for a fortnight due to a quad muscle injury, and new signing Julian O'Neill also impressed.

An Owen Craigie-inspired Widnes enjoyed their first ever Super League win over Bradford Bulls to give hometown hero Terry O'Connor the perfect debut at Halton Stadium in round two. Captain Shane Millard burrowed over in the 78th minute to complete a stunning 31-22 victory that left the Bulls joint bottom of the table. "We are a team that wants to work hard for each other. The mood here is excellent. Even Gary Connolly is doing extras in training and I've never seen that before," quipped O'Connor.

Leigh remained the only other team without a league point, but the Centurions led at half way and competed well before being edged 26-22 by the

February

Wolves at the Halliwell Jones Stadium. Chris Leikvoll, a superb display of hard-running from centre-cum-prop Ben Westwood, and the incisive kicking game of captain Lee Briers were enough to get Warrington home in front of a bumper 11,412 crowd.

A sell-out Headingley crowd on the Friday saw Leeds continue the defence of their title with a 30-18 win over St Helens. The Rhinos needed a second-half shut out of Saints to stay on course, with Danny McGuire, who that week signed a two-year extension to his contract to keep him at Leeds until the end of 2009, typifying the doggedness of the Rhinos defence. Paul Sculthorpe said in the lead-up to the game that he would relish the GB captain's armband should Andy Farrell move to union. And he staked a massive claim as he single-handedly dragged his side back into the game after Leeds had gone 12 points up in as many minutes.

But Kevin Sinfield's touchline conversion of Mark Calderwood's second try, which opened up a three-score lead, gave Saints too much to make up.

Wakefield Trinity Wildcats remained the only other side with two wins after their home 18-16 Saturday night TV win over Wigan, who, after Trinity's win at Odsal the week before, remained the one side they had never beaten in Super League. "I thought Wakefield were great," said Wigan coach Denis Betts. "They were well organised. They've got a lot of big strong lads who are willing to run the ball fast and at the back of that, there's Jeffries and Rooney who can open a team up, along with Solomona. They're a good side and it's going to be hard to pick up wins down here for the opposition."

Jamie Rooney scored the most spectacular try of the game, picking off Dennis Moran's stray pass, showing exceptional speed over 80 metres and holding off Liam Colbon's attempted tackle to plant the ball by the corner flag.

Salford got off the mark as fullback Karl Fitzpatrick produced two tries out of nowhere to edge the Reds home against London at the Willows, 20-16. After the game, Reds boss Karl Harrison singled out his skipper Malcolm Alker for some special praise, pointing out that his attacking game had improved considerably after working with former Great Britain hooker Jimmy Lowes, who joined the Reds' coaching staff in the close season. "He was sensational tonight," said Harrison. "His game has always been about defence. He's known as a tackling machine. But now he's building the full package."

And Hull got off the mark with a 36-28 win at Huddersfield as Nathan Blacklock opened his British scoring account with a hat-trick of tries, including two from stunning interceptions. They were to prove match-winners as the Giants pulled back from being 36-10 down going into the last quarter to almost snatch an incredible victory.

That weekend St Helens coach Ian Millward called for referees in Super League to be full-time to reduce inconsistent interpretations by officials. The RFL had already lost top whistler Russell Smith, who had decided to referee in Australia. And Referees Controller Stuart Cummings was recovering at home after suffering a heart attack. The referees' boss was rushed to hospital, but was allowed home after the diagnosis revealed that he hadn't suffered a major health crisis.

The longest-priced winning bet in Rugby League history came in for one lucky punter on the Friday night of round three, when Bradford Bulls recovered from a seemingly impossible position to win their engage Super League match against Wigan by 28-27. With the Bulls trailing 27-12 with only ten minutes to go, the odds against their victory went out to 499/1 on Betfair, and they were snapped up by one punter who refused to write off the Bulls' chances of winning the game. Nine minutes, three tries and two conversions later, the punter had scooped almost £2,500 for his £5 staked.

Wigan's defeat was their first at home since July 2003 and there were overnight MRI scans for Terry Newton (knee), Gareth Hock (knee), Bob Beswick (knee), while Danny Sculthorpe suffered a hamstring injury, and Danny Orr suffered concussion. Jerome Guisset came through a solid debut safely after signing from French rugby union in midweek.

The Bulls players celebrated their first win of the season wildly after the hooter sounded, a triumph for their never-say-die attitude epitomised by workaholic and inspiring skipper Jamie Peacock. And Robbie Paul's return after warming the bench on a bitterly cold night was timely. Paul sparked the Bulls' fightback with the assist for Peacock's strong charge that pierced the close-range Wigan defence. He was then twice involved in a flowing move that led to Stuart Reardon crossing, his

Wigan's Kevin Brown looks for support against Bradford during a thriller in Round Three

initial cross-field run creating space where none existed.

And then with one minute 49 seconds remaining on the big screen, Iestyn Harris's long pass sent Michael Withers gliding over as David Vaealiki made a vain attempt at an intercept. Paul Deacon kept his nerve to land the angled conversion attempt and seal the Bulls' late victory.

London Broncos put a difficult week behind them with a record 72-8 victory over Wakefield at Griffin Park. News broke on the same Sunday morning that the Broncos' new signing from Melbourne Storm, forward Danny Williams, had allegedly refused to take an RFL doping test, and was face a Rugby Football League tribunal on 9 March. Broncos chief executive Nic Cartwright explained that the Williams debate was whether the Ireland international had refused or forgotten about the test. "Danny has taken about 30 drugs tests in his career and never failed one," said Cartwright.

The RFL refused to accept the registration of the Broncos' contract with New Zealand international Vinnie Anderson. With London poised to announce an agreement with creditors over a voluntary agreement to pay back their mounting debts, one other club who were keen on signing Anderson – believed to be Bradford Bulls – had objected to the RFL over the Broncos spending money they may not have.

On the field Paul Sykes broke the club record for goals in a game, with twelve goals as the rampant Broncos ended Wakefield's 100 per cent start.

Which left Leeds Rhinos with the only perfect record after they hammered Widnes 66-8 at Headingley. Widnes captain Shane Millard had to leave the pitch with a suspected broken jaw in the 17th minute, before Leeds produced a blitz of seven tries and 42-unanswered points in the opening 23 minutes of the second half. Mark Calderwood raced in for four touchdowns.

At Hull, Warrington lost halfback Nathan Wood and forward Paul Noone, both with knee injuries, as the Wolves went down 32-10. Great Britain aspirant Richard Horne put in another masterly performance and opposite number Lee Briers matched him throughout in the creative stakes. Winger Gareth Raynor collected two tries.

St Helens got back to winning form with a 34-24 win over the Giants at Knowsley - but the scoreline flattered them. Ian Millward backed up his call for full-time officials with another pop at current refereeing standards after a game in which an unlikely five penalties went against the side in possession. "I have to say again, that I am a bit confused with the refereeing. The coaches want a meeting but Richard Lewis and the RFL have told us we can't have one."

At the beginning of February, Sport England, the government body responsible for coordinating the development of sport in England, announced that Rugby League would receive £3,240,557 during the 2005/6 financial year, and £11,546,373 over the next four years. The funding had been allocated by Sport England's National Investment Panel, of which RFL Executive Chairman Richard Lewis himself was a member.

"It's a very good deal for Rugby League, and the good thing about having secure funding such as this, with an assured cash flow, is that it allows you to plan properly for the future," Lewis told 'Rugby Leaguer & League Express'.

SUPER LEAGUE TABLE - *Sunday 27th February*

	P	W	D	L	F	A	D	PTS
Leeds Rhinos	3	3	0	0	112	38	74	6
London Broncos	3	2	0	1	116	52	64	4
Hull FC	3	2	0	1	80	54	26	4
St Helens	3	2	0	1	92	72	20	4
Salford City Reds	3	2	0	1	56	37	19	4
Wakefield T Wildcats	3	2	0	1	54	104	-50	4
Wigan Warriors	3	1	0	2	58	50	8	2
Huddersfield Giants	3	1	0	2	82	82	0	2
Bradford Bulls	3	1	0	2	66	86	-20	2
Warrington Wolves	3	1	0	2	60	82	-22	2
Widnes Vikings	3	1	0	2	57	128	-71	2
Leigh Centurions	3	0	0	3	40	88	-48	0

POWERGEN CHALLENGE CUP FIRST ROUND

Saturday 5th February 2005
Barrow Island 16 Skirlaugh 12; Blackbrook 6 Oulton Raiders 9; Castleford Panthers 10 East Hull 20; Clayton 20 Leigh Miners Rangers 42 (aet); Essex Eels 12 Elland 44; Gateshead Storm 10 Wath Brow Hornets 66; Halton Simms Cross 23 Widnes St Maries 14; Haydock 46 Cutsyke 12; Hull Dockers 46 Dudley Hill 16; Illingworth 20 Stanley Rangers 18; Milford Marlins 42 Huddersfield Underbank Rangers 20; Oldham St Annes 52 Loughborough University 10; Queens 22 Millom 24; Royal Navy 16 Normanton Knights 18; South London Storm 24 West London Sharks 20; St Albans Centurions 14 Thatto Heath 48; Stanningley 40 Walney Central 16; Warrington Wizards 16 Sharlston Rovers 22; Waterhead 36 Askam 24; West Bowling 12 Leigh East 10; West Hull 8 The Army 38; Westgate Redoubt 6 Eccles & Salford Juniors 26; Wigan St Judes 68 Embassy 0; Wigan St Patricks 58 Hensingham 6

Sunday 6th February 2005
Bramley Buffaloes 31 Thornhill Trojans 10; Royal Air Force 8 Castleford Lock Lane 44; Siddal 26 Coventry Bears 4

POWERGEN CHALLENGE CUP SECOND ROUND

Saturday 19th February 2005
Barrow Island 10 Elland 14; Castleford Lock Lane 50 South London Storm 24; Halton Simms Cross 16 Thornhill Trojans 24; Haydock 48 Normanton Knights 30; Illingworth 28 Eccles and Salford Juniors 26; Milford Marlins 14 Wath Brow Hornets 34; Oldham St Annes 18 Leigh Miners Rangers 12; Rochdale Mayfield 14 Stanningley 19; Sharlston Rovers 31 Oulton Raiders 21; Siddal 29 Wigan St Patricks 26; Thatto Heath 26 East Hull 38; Waterhead 15 the Army 12; West Bowling 26 Hull Dockers 27 (aet); Wigan St Judes 22 Millom 6

MARCH
Capital decision

Friday 4th March 2005 turned out to be one of the most crucial dates in the ten-year history of Super League. It emerged that on 26th November the previous year London Broncos had been presented with a petition by the Inland Revenue for the compulsory winding-up of the company. The Inland Revenue refused to accept a proposal to pay off part of the debt under a CVA, and on Wednesday 2nd March London Broncos Limited was finally wound up in a hearing at the Royal Courts of Justice on the Strand.

By then, however, a new company had been formed to run the club, and the issue at stake for the Super League clubs at an emergency meeting at the Galpharm Stadium the following Friday was whether they were prepared to approve the new company to take over the old company's membership of Super League, while abandoning the club's creditors.

After four-and-a-half hours of argument they finally agreed to back the Broncos' future in the competition. Richard Lewis had to return early from his holiday in Tenerife to chair the meeting, facing a group of clubs that were determined to eject the London club - which was admitted to Super League in the first season of the competition in 1996.

The five clubs that reportedly voted to accept the Broncos as continuing members of Super League were: Huddersfield Giants, Hull FC, Leeds Rhinos, St Helens and Warrington Wolves. The clubs who opposed the Broncos were reported as being: Bradford Bulls, Leigh Centurions, Salford City Reds and Wigan Warriors, with Wigan proposing that if the Broncos stayed in the competition they should be deducted ten points from that season's league table. Wakefield and Widnes abstained.

A relieved Broncos chief executive Nic Cartwright was confident the Broncos could face the future with optimism. "All the conditions are in place to make sure we don't get into this position again," he said. "We are now operating as a debt-free organisation and a stable club. We have a business plan approved by the RFL, and that will take us forward."

Nigel Wood, the RFL's Chief Operating Officer, said: "While London Broncos are undoubtedly relieved to have been saved, it cannot be allowed to mask the very serious issue that this unacceptable episode has raised. I fully expect the RFL to review its rules concerning circumstances such as these and make appropriate recommendations for the future."

The Broncos were now expected to come back to the RFL with a proposal to sign New Zealand Test star Vinnie Anderson under the terms of a three-year contract, while the following Sunday they travelled to Odsal and found the Bulls approaching their best form, with Iestyn Harris and Leon Pryce - filling in at fullback for the injured Michael Withers - the standouts.

Wakefield made it three wins out of four games at home to Leigh, but there was no backlash from the club's record defeat by London the week before. Sid Domic returned to the Wakefield side for his seasonal debut and scored two tries. But Leigh, who were briefly ahead midway through the first half, showed plenty of tenacity in a 38-26 defeat, Julian O'Neill's try twelve minutes from the end deciding the outcome.

Wigan blitzed Widnes with a devastating ten-minute spell which yielded three tries just after the hour mark at Halton Stadium, to avoid a third successive defeat. Up to then they trailed 20-12 on the back of a towering performance from Terry O'Connor, playing against the club that had released him the season before. Danny Tickle was once again impressive for the Warriors and Kevin Brown helped himself to two late tries.

A Paul Cooke-inspired Hull continued their recent domination over Salford to move into second place in the table after a 22-12 success at the Willows. The East Yorkshire side's tenth successive victory over the City Reds - the fifth at the Willows - since 2000 was also their third win on the bounce since the rain-sodden opening night defeat against Leeds. Cooke had a major hand in all four Hull tries - scoring one and providing the passes that created the other three, while earning additional post-match praise from coach John Kear for his unsung defensive work.

Everyone was still chasing the Rhinos though after they extended their club record unbeaten Super League run to 17 matches, beating the Giants 54-10 at the Galpharm Stadium. Every Leeds player played his part in this scoring spectacular, but the inspiration was Kevin Sinfield. Huddersfield put in plenty of effort, but were outclassed in every department after Mark Calderwood's try after 46 seconds. The attendance of 10,088 was Huddersfield's biggest home crowd since 12,417 saw their first Super League match, against Bradford Bulls, in 1998.

The game of the round had already been played on the Friday night as St Helens came back from the dead at Warrington to win 18-16. Leading 16-4 after Graham Appo's 71st minute try, the Halliwell Jones Stadium was in a frenzy. Nine minutes later the Wolves fans were reflecting again on their side's jinxed record against Saints in Super League that now stretched to just one win in 24 encounters.

Saints, lacking the injured Paul Sculthorpe, Sean Long and Jason Hooper, launched their amazing recovery with Darren Albert's 73rd minute try, the Australian marking his 100th club appearance. Then Keiron Cunningham's flat pass from dummy-half was brilliantly timed for Micky Higham to crash over. Paul Wellens had missed the first but added that conversion. As the last seconds were shouted down by the anxious Wolves faithful, there was just time for one last play. Paul Anderson's charge down the left channel was halted with three seconds left, and stand-in tactical kicker Jamie Lyon launched one last high kick into the right corner. The range was perfect as Albert timed his run and leap to perfection, knocking the ball backwards as Brent Grose challenged, for the waiting Cunningham to grab the loose ball and fall over the line.

Ryan Hudson's career at Bradford was over before he had even worn a Bulls shirt as his contract was terminated after he was found guilty of testing positive for the banned steroid stanozolol. "We are saddened for Ryan Hudson and the dreadful impact his action has had on a burgeoning career, but our position on these matters is absolutely definite and he left us with no room for manoeuvre," said Bulls chairman Chris Caisley.

It also emerged that the Bulls could lose winger Lesley Vainikolo to Gloucester rugby union club when his contract at Odsal ran out at the end of the season. According to some sources Gloucester had already agreed terms with Vainikolo for a cross-code switch, with the offer of a £200,000-a-season, three-year deal.

On the Friday night of round five the Bulls scored seven second-half tries at the Coliseum, four of which came in the last eight minutes, to record their third successive Super League victory, by 46-6, and condemn Leigh to a fifth straight defeat. Karl Pryce and Iestyn Harris scored two tries each, while Leigh lost their captain Jason Ferris with a worrying-looking facial injury.

Vinnie Anderson slotted in nicely on his debut after his midweek signing for St Helens and Jamie Lyon, who formed a potent right-wing partnership with Darren Albert, notched the first two tries of his Saints career in a 46-12 home win over Salford. Without a win at Knowsley Road for 25 years, Salford were trailing 36-0 at the interval.

Sean Penkywicz was a late withdrawal from the Giants side that went on to record a 34-18 win over Widnes at the Galpharm Stadium. Paul Reilly returned from injury with an impressive game, and Paul White scored two electric tries after coming off the bench. Aaron Moule scored two tries for the Vikings, who suffered a further blow when stand-off Owen Craigie limped off with a knee injury in the 33rd minute.

Keeping the Vikings company on two points in the league standings were neighbours Warrington. The Wolves suffered their fourth defeat, at Headingley by 38-6, but a three-try-in-eight-minutes blitz gave the score a lopsided look. Keith Senior was back to his rampaging best with a superb three-try show.

London Broncos' exciting attacking machine was at full throttle in the Saturday TV game as they beat Wigan, lacking the injured Brian Carney, Danny Orr, Gareth Hock and the soon-to-depart Andy Farrell, 34-20 at Griffin Park. London had been given a boost in the week leading up to the game when Danny Williams - who hadn't yet played a game for the club - was cleared of wrongdoing by a RFL Advisory Panel. The 30-year-old back-rower had been charged with failing to provide a urine sample when requested by doping officers on 10th December 2004, when they visited the Broncos on the first day of their pre-season training.

Paul Sykes score two tries and kicked seven goals as London led Wigan 34-8 at one stage. Coach Tony Rea revealed he had spent the night before pondering whether this was the best ever Broncos team. "We always had a reputation for being tradesman-like, hard to beat, heads down. But these guys have more speed, creativity and play at a different level. It's good for growing the game in London."

A last-gasp try from man of the match Jamie Thackray kept Hull in the top three - although they dropped below St Helens on points difference after their 36-33 victory - denying unlucky Wakefield a deserved win in the KC sunshine, a dubious forward-pass decision against them giving Hull the position for the winning score.

March

Rochdale Hornets defeated Pennine League amateur side Illingworth 120 points to 4 in the third round of the Powergen Challenge Cup - the highest ever points total to be achieved in the Challenge Cup, surpassing the 119-2 victory by Huddersfield in 1914 against amateur team Swinton Park Rangers. Only one amateur club survived the third round of the Powergen Challenge Cup - Wath Brow Hornets, from the National Conference Premier Division, recording a 32-30 victory over Dewsbury Rams.

Lesley Vainikolo hinted he would be staying at Odsal after the Friday round six 32-22 win over Hull at Odsal. Vainikolo had been linked with Gloucester, with the union club confirming that talks about a switch of codes were at an advanced stage. "I'll probably stay at the Bulls, we'll just have to wait and see over the next couple of weeks," said Vainikolo. "Bradford came back with a pretty good deal. I'm happy where I am and my heart's here."

Vainikolo had a fitness test on a strained hamstring before the game against Hull, and Paul Johnson missed the clash with a shoulder injury. Hull coach John Kear called for a time limit on video referee decisions after it took almost three minutes for David Campbell to rule that Bradford Bulls' Andy Lynch had scored a crucial late try. With both sides scoring four tries, Paul Deacon's five penalties in an eight-goal tally proved decisive.

Stephen Kearney made his long-delayed Hull debut, with the former New Zealand Test forward appearing to have fully recovered from the pectoral injury that caused him to miss the first five rounds.

Meanwhile the Bulls Chairman Chris Caisley, writing in the club's match programme, criticised the decision of the other Super League clubs to allow London Broncos to go into liquidation with £3 million debts and yet remain in Super League. "I never cease to be amazed by the 'goings-on' in league," wrote Caisley.

The Broncos - who had lost Neil Budworth for the season with a knee injury picked up the week before against Wigan - were back in entertainment mode on the Sunday, and Widnes were the victims of a 66-8 mauling at Griffin Park. The win, with man of the match Luke Dorn scoring two tries - put London in third spot. "We are in a hole, there's no hiding from that," admitted Widnes coach Frank Endacott after this annihilation. "It's not that big a hole that we can't get out of it but, jeez, we've got to get out of it quick."

Chris Bridge made a lively impact on his first start for the Wolves in a dogged 14-8 home win over Huddersfield, which left Leigh as the only team keeping Widnes off the bottom of the table. The Centurions were no match for Wigan, Kris Radlinski scoring a Friday night hat-trick in front of a 15,000-plus crowd at the JJB Stadium. Danny Tickle confirmed his outstanding start to the season with another top display in the Warriors pack.

There were a couple of tries apiece for Darren Albert, Willie Talau, James Roby and Keiron Cunningham as on-fire St Helens humbled Wakefield 64-16 at Knowsley Road. Roby's second try turned into Super League's first eight-pointer as in the act of scoring, the youngster was needlessly pushed by David Solomona.

Meanwhile the Rhinos were closing in fast on Bradford Bulls' record of 21 consecutive regular round victories in Super League after cruising home 30-12, their 19th in a row, against Salford City Reds at the Willows.

Round 7 of this season's Super League competition broke attendance records on two fronts.

The six matches played on Easter Thursday and Good Friday attracted an aggregate of 69,830 supporters, which beat the previous all-time record aggregate of 69,499 set by Round 1 of Super League IX in 2004, with a Super League record average crowd of 11,638 also being generated.

And the game between Wigan and St Helens at the JJB Stadium on Friday afternoon drew a sell-out crowd of 25,004. That figure beat the previous record for a Super League regular season match of 24,020, set by the Bulls v Rhinos at Odsal in Super League IV in 1999.

There were just under 23,000 in Odsal on Easter Thursday as five tries in the last half hour took Leeds to a 42-12 victory. Kevin Sinfield, who also kicked seven goals out of seven attempts, just edged Keith Senior for the gamestar award in the week that Lesley Vainikolo signed a four-year contract extension.

After Good Friday, Leeds were four points ahead of the pack at the top of the table, as Wigan beat St Helens 22-20. It was a stunning result, as the long-running saga of Andy Farrell's move to rugby union was finally brought to a conclusion the day before. Though the saving on his salary, plus the signing fee from the RFU, was thought to release something in the region of £800,000 for team strengthening, just how would Wigan face up to life without a player who had dominated their side for a decade?

All the seven tries came in the first half, with St Helens outscoring the home team by four to three, as Danny Tickle's goalkicking proved decisive in the end, his penalty from in front of the posts nine minutes from time splitting the teams.

Saints' Australian centre Jamie Lyon spent two nights in hospital after collapsing in the dressing room due to dehydration after the game, and prop forward Mark Edmondson also collapsed, and later on had to go to hospital for an operation on his hand, where it was discovered that he had snapped a tendon and broken a finger.

Wigan's Sean O'Loughlin suffered a serious knee injury which ruled him out for the rest of the season, along with Gareth Hock, who suffered a similar fate in the round three defeat by Bradford.

Widnes Vikings moved four points above point-less Leigh as they beat them 35-28 at the Halton Stadium. Stand-off Paul Crook's 74th minute field goal - Owen Craigie was due to see a specialist to determine the extent a knee injury - finally edged the win.

Elsewhere on Good Friday, there were some calls for the head of coach Paul Cullen after the Reds hammered Warrington 42-10 at the Willows, Stuart Littler scoring a hat-trick, with GB hopeful Malcolm Alker again in superb form.

Hull captain Richard Swain suffered a broken arm just six minutes before the end of the 20-16 win in London, Danny Brough making his debut at scrum-half. And at Belle Vue, Huddersfield Giants blitzed Wakefield in the second half to leapfrog the Wildcats into seventh pace with a 42-20 win.

March

On Easter Monday, Leeds Rhinos had to complete a victory over Wakefield Trinity Wildcats at Headingley - which seemed a formality after Wakefield's capitulation on Good Friday against the Giants - to equal Bradford Bulls' 1997 feat of going 21 successive regular season Super League matches undefeated.

Danny McGuire was back after an operation on a groin injury but it couldn't stop Wakefield winning 44-28 - Leeds' first defeat for 19 months at home - with David Solomona, playing with a broken hand, and David March the pick of an inspired Wildcats side.

Round eight was also significant for Leigh Centurions as they recorded their first Super League points with a 24-22 win over London Broncos - who had been pressing for third spot, and had Danny Williams on debut - at Hilton Park. Local hero Neil Turley's 72nd-minute touchline conversion to a Rob Jackson try was the difference between the two sides as Leigh fully deserved their first win. In the absence of Darren Fleary, scrum-half John Duffy put in a captain's knock and typified Leigh's never-say-die attitude.

The win was all the more surprising, as in the previous week, Centurions' executive director Derek Beaumont and football director Steve Blakeley sensationally quit the club's board of directors. It brought to a close a torrid four days in which Leigh were hammered 64-6 at Wigan; revealed that new signing Dom Feaunati needed a hernia operation; lost an appeal case that left them having to pay £30,000 to a player who hadn't played a game for them; and saw club captain Jason Ferris walk out of the club.

Wigan, despite a mounting injury-list - missing seven regular first-teamers - moved into third as they leapfrogged Hull with a 21-15 victory at the KC Stadium. The Warriors came from 14-0 down at half-time, Liam Colbon's interception try setting them on the way to a memorable comeback. Brett Dallas's 74th minute try finally sealed the two points.

Michael De Vere made his Super League debut, landing five out of five goal attempts, as the Stanley Gene-inspired Giants moved into seventh place with a 26-12 win over Salford City Reds. De Vere became the first Australian international to play for the club since Pat Devery in 1948.

Jon Clarke led the Wolves to a vital derby 44-12 home victory over their old rivals Widnes with a try hat-trick. Lee Briers, despite an off night with the boot, led from the front after signing a two-year extension to his Wolves contract the previous week.

Paul Wellens also scored a hat-trick as St Helens beat Bradford in a classic encounter at Knowsley Road, by 34-27. Paul Deacon, thinking the scores were level when in fact Saints held a two-point advantage, made it 28-27 with a field goal five minutes from time. Deacon's second field-goal attempt flew wide of the posts with a minute to go, Saints marched upfield to play out time, and Wellens' third try brought down the curtain on an exhausting Bank Holiday weekend.

SUPER LEAGUE TABLE - *Tuesday 29th March*

	P	W	D	L	F	A	D	PTS
Leeds Rhinos	8	7	0	1	304	122	182	14
St Helens	8	6	0	2	274	165	109	12
Wigan Warriors	8	5	0	3	215	145	70	10
Hull FC	8	5	0	3	195	168	27	10
London Broncos	8	4	0	4	276	172	104	8
Bradford Bulls	8	4	0	4	231	212	19	8
Huddersfield Giants	8	4	0	4	202	200	2	8
Wakefield T Wildcats	8	4	0	4	205	300	-95	8
Salford City Reds	8	3	0	5	146	171	-25	6
Warrington Wolves	8	3	0	5	150	200	-50	6
Widnes Vikings	8	2	0	6	150	332	-182	4
Leigh Centurions	8	1	0	7	130	291	-161	2

APRIL
Storm in the C-Cup

The first weekend in April marked the entry of the big guns into the rescheduled Powergen Challenge Cup - after eight clear rounds of Super League.

One of the most competitive ties of the fourth round was at the Galpharm Stadium where St Helens edged a fiery encounter with the Giants 26-22.

The match was overshadowed by controversy even before the kick-off when the original referee, Ian Smith, was switched from officiating the game after an appearance at a Fans' Forum event in Huddersfield the previous Thursday. It wouldn't have been that important but Giants' boss Jon Sharp publicly slammed Smith's replacement Ronnie Laughton, turning his post-match press conference into a video analysis session designed to prove Laughton had made two incorrect decisions that cost Huddersfield the match.

Leeds Rhinos edged through 26-22 at home to Warrington and were installed as strong favourites for the Cup following the draw for the fifth round which was made on BBC television on the Sunday afternoon, after they were drawn at home against French club Pia.

Amateurs Wath Brow Hornets fell on their great adventure to France, defeated at Toulouse 60-12, while Hull KR met a similar fate at UTC, losing 32-18. And Hull beat Wakefield 36-12 in the Sunday TV game, with Paul Cooke the key figure.

The two teams at the bottom of the Super League table were in the news that week. Leigh Centurions prop forward Richard Moore was hit by a five-match suspension (reduced to four on appeal) by the RFL Disciplinary Committee - three games for the illegal use of his forearm in a tackle, and another two matches for using his knees whilst running into a tackle.

Widnes completed the triple loan signings of Jamie Durbin, Gray Viane and Richie Barnett amidst an injury crisis that had swallowed up half of the first-team squad.

And on a sad note, Bradford legend Trevor Foster died at the age of 90 on Saturday morning, 2nd April, only three days after attending the launch of his biography at Odsal Stadium.

April

After Round Nine, Leigh and Widnes were looking increasingly isolated in the bottom two Super League positions.

Leigh, as expected, got little joy at St Helens on the Friday night. Sean Long scored 18 points for Saints from two tries and five goals, giving him a club and representative career total of 2,005 points. Long achieved the milestone despite spending only 27 minutes on the pitch after sustaining a knee injury.

But Widnes pushed Hull all the way before succumbing to a cruel 32-28 defeat at the KC Stadium. Vikings held leads in both halves, and were still pressing for a match-winning try when the hooter sounded. But Hull just hung on to climb to third in the table, Nathan Blacklock's 71st minute try proving decisive in a see-saw encounter.

With veteran pack men Terry O'Connor and Mick Cassidy leading from the front, Owen Craigie - a surprise returnee from injury - providing the craft at halfback, and Aaron Moule outstanding in the centres, Widnes had threatened to chalk up a desperately-needed victory. But quickfire tries to Richard Whiting and Blacklock gave Hull a vital eight-point cushion going into the last five minutes, while man of the match Danny Brough's faultless six goals proved crucial as the teams scored five tries each.

Warrington Wolves coach Paul Cullen pointed to a relaxed build-up to match day as a significant factor in his side's improved form after the Wolves picked up their fourth win from five home games - meaning they moved out of tenth position in the table - when they defeated Bradford Bulls 35-32 at the Halliwell Jones Stadium.

Iestyn Harris hinted at a return to the dominating figure of his first spell in Rugby League, but the Wolves led 29-4 at one stage in the second half, too much for the Bulls to make up.

Leeds stayed two points ahead of St Helens at the top of the table with a 64-6 thrashing of London Broncos. The match was billed as a battle of two of the most attractive attacking sides in the competition. But Leeds were the only side to exhibit their skills in a second half that saw them run in eight of their 13 tries almost at will. Rhinos captain Kevin Sinfield went past the 1,000-career points mark, after kicking six goals.

Wakefield Wildcats' on-loan Leeds prop Chris Feather suffered a knee injury during Wakefield's 16-14 defeat at Salford, while coach Shane McNally denied rumours doing the rounds that the missing Sid Domic was unhappy at the Atlantic Solutions Stadium. "I hate to mention injuries, but in all we've got eight players out who would have made our 17, including David Solomona and Sid Domic, and that has to tell," said McNally.

That week Salford chief executive David Tarry confirmed that the lack of a casino at the Reds' proposed stadium development - the government had decided to scale down the number of 'super casinos' being built to just one, likely to be in Blackpool - would not impact on the building of the stadium, or the club's spending plans.

The Giants moved into fifth spot in the table with a 24-16 win over third-placed Wigan at the Galpharm. Sixteen points in the closing stages couldn't cloud the fact that Huddersfield had dominated the previous 67 minutes of a match played in bitterly cold conditions. Brad Drew's 90-metre breakout try as

The late, great Trevor Foster

Wigan dominated the early stages of the second half, clinched the Huddersfield win.

And that week the news broke that Kiwi Test scrum-half Stacey Jones was poised to link up with French side Perpignan for their Super League bow. Perpignan also tied up French international forward Djamel Fakir in the face of competition from several English clubs, reported to include Bradford Bulls.

After Saints' Saturday night 30-20 win at London Broncos coach Ian Millward told St Helens supporters to not believe rumours suggesting that captain Paul Sculthorpe - who had missed the last four matches with hamstring and back problems - had a serious injury.

With scrum-half Sean Long having had an operation the previous week to remove a floating bone in his knee, Saints fielded a makeshift halfback pair of hooker Mick Higham at scrum-half and Vinnie Anderson at stand-off against the Broncos, with Jason Hooper continuing his comeback after a long-term knee injury at right centre.

Straight after the game, 19-year-old Broncos scrum-half Thomas Leuluai - the only British-based player to be selected for the New Zealand team for the following Friday's Anzac Test against Australia in Brisbane - dashed to the airport to catch a plane down under. The match-up produced the Broncos' biggest crowd of the season, as they sank to their fourth straight defeat.

St Helens were still two points adrift of Leeds, who on the Friday night recorded their highest ever win at Wigan, by 38-14. Trailing 6-12 after 22 minutes - opposing props Jerry Seuseu and McDermott were sin-binned after an altercation at a scrum in the opening stages - the Rhinos went on to dominate the rest of the game, scoring 32 points with just a Danny Tickle penalty in reply. Leeds winger Mark Calderwood touched down for a try - giving him a club and representative career total of 100 tries.

April

Salford moved into the top-six with a significant 22-6 win at the Halton Stadium. "It's a massive result for us, it shapes the season for us now," said coach Karl Harrison, as reports emerged from down under that Salford were poised to sign South Sydney captain Bryan Fletcher within the next fortnight. "We're in sixth spot which is where we're aiming to be." Stuart Littler scored twice immediately after Widnes lost Terry O'Connor to the sin bin, and Luke Robinson added two more tries.

"I think that was the most confident I've been all year about a victory," said Frank Endacott afterwards. "Either they're (his players) great actors or I'm a poor judge." Widnes - who lost Owen Craigie to mumps - remained four points adrift of safety, with Leeds, Wigan and St Helens awaiting in the next month. Endacott said he would be ready to make a move for New Zealand Warriors halfback Stacey Jones - strongly linked to a move to French club Perpignan - if the Kiwi nalfback were to become available.

Widnes' nerves weren't helped by Leigh - with Jason Duffy and Nick Owen on debut - moving one point closer to them with a shock 22-all home draw with third-placed Hull. Hull only drew level two minutes from the end when Richard Horne broke for Nathan Blacklock to finish a stunning 60-metre counter attack in the corner.

Bradford leapfrogged Huddersfield into fifth spot after a commanding ten-try 54-10 win over the Giants at Odsal, a hat-trick from Lesley Vainikolo one highlight. The game was dedicated to the memory of the late Trevor Foster MBE.

By the Sunday night there were five teams, from positions four to eight, on ten league points. One of them was Warrington, as captain Lee Briers scored two tries and had a say in five others in a 40-28 win at Wakefield. Trailing 40-16 at one stage, Wakefield regained some pride with late tries from Mark Applegarth and Olivier Elima. Coach Shane McNally admitted he could not explain how Wakefield could beat champions Leeds Rhinos and then lose three matches in a row.

After the first ten games of the season *Rugby Leaguer & League Express* calculated that attendances had risen significantly in Super League X, the average crowd being 9,463, compared to a final average crowd for the previous season of 8,833.

Off the field, Wigan were in fine shape, and had enjoyed the biggest rise in attendances over the first ten rounds, with an average home crowd of over 16,000. But on the field, the cracks were beginning to show in a squad stretched by injury and the departure of Andy Farrell.

In the Friday night TV game they were on the end of a 40-8 beating by Bradford at Odsal, Bradford's biggest ever win - excluding war-time - against Wigan. Brian Noble persisted with swapping scrum-half Paul Deacon and hooker Robbie Paul around and it paid dividends for the second week running, against a Warriors side lacking captain Kris Radlinski. On-loan signing Wayne McDonald from Leeds Rhinos made an impact in the first of his substitute stints, but two-try Brett Dallas provided their only finishing edge on the night. For the Bulls, Brad Meyers was tremendous, and was rewarded with two tries.

"If we go any higher we'll get vertigo," was Karl Harrison's response as his

Reds side moved into fifth position after a 42-6 Friday night win over Leigh at the Willows. Former Wigan halfback Luke Robinson collected two tries - making it seven in the last four games - and Leigh product Stuart Littler collected a hat-trick. The Centurions - who had loan signing from Warrington, Warren Stevens on debut, were well in the game at half-time, but folded in the second half.

In the Saturday TV game Widnes rubbished pre-match predictions of a points-riot, but still ended up on the wrong end of a 42-20 scoreline against Leeds at the Halton Stadium. A personal haul of 22 points took Kevin Sinfield past 1,000 for the Rhinos.

Widnes had Warrington halfback Jamie Durbin on debut and another loan-signing, winger Richie Barnett from Hull, provided the talking point of the match when he scored a try in the 68th minute, video referee Steve Cross taking three frustrating minutes to decide on the try. Refs boss Stuart Cummings, back at his desk after a heart scare earlier in the season, rejected the suggestion to put a time limit on video refereeing decisions.

St Helens kept the pressure up on leaders Leeds with their fourth successive victory, this one at the Galpharm but, not for the first time this season, they had to repeatedly shake off a determined Huddersfield outfit to ensure the spoils 36-22.

That week, Keiron Cunningham ended months of speculation by finally putting pen to paper on a new two-year contract to keep him at St Helens until the end of 2007. And Saints welcomed the return of Sean Long, on the bench, and new father Jamie Lyon, back from Australia after attending the birth of his first child.

Lee Gilmour collared by Huddersfield's Eorl Crabtree as St Helens edge out the Giants

Saints' three tries in nine minutes midway through the second half and Paul Wellens' try-saving stop of Paul Smith in the 64th minute decided the outcome. "Overall I thought it was a great contest - I think the scoreline was flattering," was Giants coach Jon Sharp's reaction. "It's an indication of how far we've come after conceding nearly 200 points in our four games against Saints last year, we have now pushed them close on all three occasions this season."

That week the Giants had terminated the contract of 23-year-old halfback Sean Penkywicz, who was suspended for two years by a RFL Advisory Panel, after he had tested positive for the banned substance stanozolol in a test taken

April

at a Huddersfield training session on 17th December the previous year.

A dramatic game at the Halliwell Jones ended with the Wolves going into the top six for the first time in SLX after a 36-34 win over Hull. Warrington surrendered a 30-12 lead to trail 30-34, before clinching the game with a Chris Bridge-converted Graham Appo try, created by Nat Wood's brilliance, three minutes from time. Henry Fa'afili grabbed a hat-trick for the Wolves, with a towering performance from Danny Lima off the bench leaving Hull's stirring second-half comeback in vain.

Prop forward Paul King - out of action after undergoing a knee reconstruction following his injury at Salford in September 2004 - played his first game of the season off the bench for Hull, whose star player, Paul Cooke, had been linked with a move to Bradford. Despite being in the final year of his contract, Cooke hadn't yet received an offer of a new deal from Hull to stay at the KC Stadium, but he denied he had received an offer to join the Bulls next season. "I gather I'm signing for Bradford, and they are going to pay me around £130,000 a year - I wish," he said. "It has also been suggested I am earning £90,000-per-year at Hull - again, I wish. If I was on that kind of money here do you think I would be driving around in a Fiat Punto?"

Wakefield coach Shane McNally was understandably relieved after his injury-ravaged side hauled themselves into mid-table comfort courtesy of a scrappy 29-18 home win over down-in-the-dumps London. Jamie Rooney's 55th-minute try ensured a disappointing London had too much to do as former Broncos prop Darrell Griffin won the official man of the match award with a gutsy display.

'On the evidence of this largely inept display, it would take a brave soul indeed to bet on this most maddening of teams (London) still being in Super League this time next year', wrote *Rugby Leaguer & League Express* reporter Tony Hannan. Eight rounds earlier, London had recorded a 72-8 win over the Wildcats.

That week Super League-bound Perpignan launched their recruitment drive for 2006 by signing Kiwi scrum-half Stacey Jones from the New Zealand Warriors, Canberra Raiders second-rower Ian Hindmarsh, brother of Test forward Nathan, and Wests Tigers loose forward John Wilson.

SUPER LEAGUE TABLE - *Sunday 24th April*

	P	W	D	L	F	A	D	PTS
Leeds Rhinos	11	10	0	1	448	162	286	20
St Helens	11	9	0	2	400	223	177	18
Hull FC	11	6	1	4	283	254	29	13
Bradford Bulls	11	6	0	5	357	265	92	12
Salford City Reds	11	6	0	5	226	197	29	12
Warrington Wolves	11	6	0	5	261	294	-33	12
Wigan Warriors	11	5	0	6	253	247	6	10
Huddersfield Giants	11	5	0	6	258	306	-48	10
Wakefield T Wildcats	11	5	0	6	276	374	-98	10
London Broncos	11	4	0	7	320	295	25	8
Widnes Vikings	11	2	0	9	204	428	-224	4
Leigh Centurions	11	1	1	9	174	415	-241	3

At the end of April the RFL announced it had toughened up the criteria for National League clubs who want to gain promotion to Super League. After a review of stadium facilities among National League clubs, the RFL informed the ten member clubs in LHF Healthplan National League One of the improvements they needed to undertake before being considered for promotion. In previous seasons admission to the elite competition had been granted if any club expressed an intention to undertake improvements. But now, any work had to be completed by 31st August 2005, 38 days before the LHF Healthplan Grand Final.

MAY
A touch of Basil

At the start of May Great Britain coach Brian Noble selected 40 players for his train-on squad for the autumn's Gillette Tri-Nations series, and unveiled St Helens skipper Paul Sculthorpe as the new captain of Great Britain, with Bradford captain Jamie Peacock to be his deputy. He also included Leeds Rhinos captain Kevin Sinfield, a shock omission from the 2004 Tri-Nations, but whose form and leadership had been key to the Rhinos near-perfect season so far.

After Round 12 of Super League, Leeds stayed top after an eight-try 44-14 win over Huddersfield at Headingley. Rob Burrow scored his first hat-trick at club level as Barrie McDermott was in a virtually unstoppable mood. Ryan Clayton made his debut from the bench for the Giants after signing for the rest of the season, and Chris Nero signed a new two-year contract that week.

Leigh provided the result of the weekend when they hammered Wakefield at home in the Saturday TV game by 40-18. Phil Jones became the first Leigh player to score a Super League hat-trick as the Centurions moved off the bottom of the table for the first time, one point above Widnes. Five tries in the final 24 minutes saw the Centurions crush the tame Wildcats who had no answer to a fourth-quarter onslaught. Former Leeds Aussie hooker Robbie Mears made an eye-catching debut for the Centurions.

The night before, the Vikings had fallen to a cruel 23-22 defeat at the JJB Stadium, a 75th-minute field goal from Dennis Moran seeing Wigan narrowly escape a fourth consecutive loss for the first time in 20 years. The crucial moment came five minutes after the Vikings - who trailed 18-6 at the break - fought back to level the scores at 22-22, thanks to a try from centre Gray Viane and a towering touchline conversion from Stephen Myler.

Even after Moran's decisive interjection, Widnes had the chance to snatch a draw. But on the last play of a heart-stopping game, with a field-goal attempt begging, they instead went for a try and, after Simon Finnigan was tackled short, Wigan centre David Vaealiki defused an Owen Craigie kick to the corner.

Wigan were back in sixth after Warrington's St Helens hoodoo continued at Knowsley Road on the Friday. In a game in which Paul Sculthorpe made his Saints return after a six-week injury lay-off, the Wolves led 30-28 with time ticking down. Just two minutes remained when they conceded only their fifth penalty of the evening, as Brent Grose was pulled up on the intervention of a touch-judge for raking Jamie Lyon's face in the tackle. Sean Long kept his nerve from 28 metres out and tied the scores.

A draw would have been a fair result, but after a Paul Wellens run down centre-field, a Keiron Cunningham pass from dummy-half saw Long land the match-winning field goal with just 26 seconds to play. The hooter sounded before the Wolves could re-start, and their losing run at Knowsley Road in Super League was extended to eleven games. Better news for the Wolves was that fullback Grose had snubbed approaches from NRL clubs by signing a three-year extension to his contract at the Halliwell Jones Stadium.

In one of the more uninspiring contests of the year, Hull fought back from an early deficit at the KC Stadium to grind out a 20-6 victory over a Salford side that had looked capable of recording a shock in the opening half-hour. And on a baking afternoon in Brentford, London ran out of energy, and the Bulls won 41-26, after being 18-0 down at half-time.

And that weekend, Rugby League's international profile rose another notch as Georgia won a 34-14 victory over the Netherlands in the Hook of Holland in the first European Nations Cup qualifying match.

The second weekend of May featured Powergen Challenge Cup Round Five, but only one story dominated the headlines.

On Wednesday 4th May St Helens released a statement announcing that coach Ian Millward had been suspended with immediate effect pending disciplinary proceedings. At a Knowsley Road press conference, chief executive Sean McGuire cited legal reasons for saying little, but the following day - as the country went to the polls on the day of the general election - the details of three charges dribbled out, all involving allegations of Millward swearing.

On the Friday night St Helens supporters demonstrated at Knowsley Road against their chairman Eamonn McManus and chief executive McGuire as Saints, with Millward's assistant Dave Rotheram in charge, defeated York City Knights 62-0 in the Cup.

The day after, St Helens legend, and director, Eric Ashton MBE, let it be known that Millward's sacking was nothing to do with him. Millward fulfilled a commitment as the BBC's summariser for the Hull-Bradford and Salford-London Challenge Cup ties, and promised on air he had a story to tell. He refused to discuss the specific nature of the allegations, but McManus was unhappy with a statement that Millward's solicitor Richard Cramer had issued, and countered with his own statement. It read: "The detailed disciplinary charges against Ian Millward are being considered by me, and I anticipate that I will conclude my decision within the next couple of days. The charges are being grossly and irresponsibly trivialised in the press, and in particular by Ian's solicitor Richard Cramer, who should not be speaking on the matter at all under the legal disciplinary procedures".

Millward was sacked the following Tuesday, as McManus released an 18-point statement running to 1,200 words. Cramer promised an immediate appeal, a necessary first step before a claim for unfair dismissal. But McManus added: "We are very confident he would be wasting his money." Two days later Millward's appeal was rejected.

Toulouse became only the second French club to reach the quarter-finals of the Challenge Cup after overcoming Doncaster 32-18 in an ill-tempered, full-blooded home tie, with centre Fabrice Estebanez the star. They were rewarded with a home tie against Widnes Vikings, who proved far too strong for NL1 Barrow at Craven Park. The other French clubs' Cup runs came to an end in the fifth round, Pia winning many friends in their 70-0 mismatch at Leeds, and UTC unlucky to be edged out at Wigan 16-10, Kevin Brown's last-gasp try breaking French hearts.

St Helens drew Wigan Warriors, London, who had a fine win at Salford landed Leeds away and Hull versus Leigh completed the quarter-final line-up. The Centurions had to come from behind to beat Halifax 40-20 at Hilton Park, while Hull saved their best performance of the year to knock out Bradford at the KC Stadium, holding off a magnificent late Bulls rally to win 26-24.

It was unlucky Friday the 13th for St Helens caretaker coach Dave Rotheram, as Saints ran into a red-hot Hull team at the KC Stadium in the first game of the post-Millward era. Some rated the 44-6 win the best performance ever given by a Hull team in Super League. Led by halfbacks Paul Cooke and man of the match Richard Horne they were virtually faultless. Jamie Thackray - who had agreed a new two-year contract that week - Ewan Dowes and Shayne McMenemy were towering in the pack. Shaun Briscoe's two tries either side of the half-hour mark had the game wrapped up as Hull led 22-0.

The following Tuesday, New Zealand national coach Daniel Anderson was confirmed as the new head coach of St Helens.

Widnes Vikings, who admitted they had rekindled their interest in scrum-half Maxime Greseque, got themselves back off the bottom of the table with a convincing 47-34 win at struggling Wakefield, to end a nightmare run of five straight defeats. The Vikings scored seven tries, with Stephen Myler piling up a personal haul of 22 points from a try and nine goals from as many attempts. Coach Frank Endacott also singled out Terry O'Connor for praise.

Wildcats captain Jason Demetriou that week agreed a contract extension to keep him at the club until the end of the 2007 season.

Bradford Bulls denied suggestions that coach Brian Noble was ready to leave the club at the end of the season to concentrate on his Great Britain job, and signed centre Ben Harris, 21, from NRL club Canterbury Bulldogs.

Reports also surfaced that captain Jamie Peacock had been offered a new deal by the Bulls, but had not yet accepted it. Other Super League clubs were thought to be ready to jump, but would have to wait until the September 1st deadline for players coming out of contract.

An 11-try 58-0 trouncing of Salford at the Willows that included a hat-trick apiece for centre Karl Pryce and hooker Paul Deacon, who also kicked seven goals in a personal 26-point haul, kept the Bulls in fourth position.

Leigh were back in bottom spot as Mark Calderwood scored a hat-trick in Leeds' comprehensive 60-4 win at the Coliseum. The Centurions admitted that week that prop forward Richard Moore, who had last played in Leigh's maiden Super League win over London Broncos on 28th March, hadn't been seen since his suspension after that game.

London Broncos - just two points above the relegation zone - denied that they were about to forge a link with the Harlequins rugby union club that would see the Broncos return to one of their former homes, the Stoop Memorial Ground. "We haven't agreed anything with them," Broncos chief executive Nic Cartwright claimed. Scrum-half Thomas Leuluai agreed to a new deal to keep him in the capital until the end of the 2006 season, and centre Tyrone Smith also signed a contract extension to the end of 2007.

A seventh successive Super League defeat - this one by 34-24 at Huddersfield - had the Broncos as many people's favourites to join Leigh in NL1 next year. Chris Nero, playing in the centre, scored a fine hat-trick for the Giants, although a game of many twists was never settled until Chris Thorman scored the final try in the 77th minute.

Warrington Wolves had signalled their ambition to join the big-hitters of the game with a mammoth offer to Melbourne scrum-half Matt Orford for 2006. And they also brought back former player Mike Forshaw as assistant coach from his role as Performance Lifestyle Advisor with the RFL.

And after round 13 they moved in to fifth position with a 28-22 win over Wigan at the Halliwell Jones Stadium, as they shrugged off a ten-point second-half deficit to overcome the Warriors in a tense finish to an absorbing struggle.

Nathan Wood's 50-metre interception try off Dennis Moran's pass finally sealed victory on 78 minutes to move Warrington into the top-six. But the drama was far from over as Brett Dallas looked certain to snatch a draw for the Warriors with a try in the dying seconds, only to be denied by a last-ditch tackle from Ben Westwood that was deemed to have jarred the ball loose before Dallas grounded it.

To have had yet another victory cruelly snatched from their grasp would have been an injustice to Warrington, who had been behind from the 11th minute to the 72nd minute, but refused to give in. Wigan coach Denis Betts was phlegmatic over the last-second decision that denied his team the chance of a draw saying: "That's the nature of sport."

That weekend Wigan chairman Maurice Lindsay dampened speculation about a possible takeover bid for the club. With Wigan owner Dave Whelan celebrating the promotion of Wigan Athletic FC into the Premiership, rumours that he would be prepared to sell the Warriors had grown steadily in the town. "If there was any real interest it has not materialised into any form of offer," said Lindsay, who was in Australia at the time.

Just twelve days after he was sacked by St Helens, Ian Millward was put in charge of his former club's biggest rival. The affable 44-year old Australian was unveiled to the media by Wigan owner Dave Whelan at a JJB Stadium conference on Monday 23rd May, with Warriors coach Denis Betts taking an assistant's role after an injury-blighted run had seen the Cherry & Whites slide out of the top-six.

"I am over the moon," grinned an obviously delighted Millward. "I've known the depths of despair and then sheer elation over the past couple of weeks after the bombshell was dropped on me at St Helens. But when I got a call from Maurice Lindsay on Saturday morning, all the dark clouds lifted away. Maurice asked me when I would like to start, and I said 'probably November, then we could have pre-season, assess the players and look where we need to strengthen'. And Maurice's reply was 'How about Monday'?"

The deluge of pro-Millward/anti-Saints directors letters from St Helens supporters to the *Rugby Leaguer & League Express* Mailbag suddenly dried up. Wigan fans' reactions were mixed in their acceptance of a man who had given them so much misery in his five seasons

in charge of their arch rivals. Some thought it was a superb move to sign on the best trophy winner in Super League, whilst others were threatening to rip up their season tickets in protest.

It all added incredible extra spice to the Powergen Challenge Cup quarter-final between the two great foes at Knowsley Road scheduled for June 26th.

Betts' last game in charge proved a sad end to his tenure, as Huddersfield completed their first double over Wigan since the 1941/2 season - their first win in Wigan for 48 years - with a 26-24 victory at the JJB Stadium, after trailing 20-4 at half-time. More injury worries for Wigan came as centre David Vaealiki sprung a shoulder, but there was some good long-term news as former Kangaroo second-rower Bryan Fletcher was announced as a 2006 signing.

Leeds maintained their four-point lead at the top of Super League with a second win over Leigh in a week, but at one stage the Centurions were level at 24-all before falling to a 42-24 defeat at Headingley. Danny McGuire scored the crucial try on the hour mark.

St Helens, still reeling from the hammering at Hull eight days before, won a 29-22 victory at the Halton Stadium. Paul Sculthorpe produced a superb break to lay on Mick Higham's decisive try 12 minutes from time, before rubber stamping the win with a late field goal.

London's seven-game losing streak - a run which had seen them go from play-off contenders to relegation candidates - finally came to an end with an exciting 34-18 win against Salford at Griffin Park. Dave Highton's tackle on Luke Robinson in the 77th minute was crucial, as it forced a fumble which Rob Purdham and Jon Wells turned into six points at the other end.

A late Danny Brough field goal cemented Hull's third-place spot with a 35-28 win at Belle Vue after a still out-of-sorts Wakefield twice threatened to spring a surprise. Despite being 24-12 behind at the break, the Wildcats fought back to run in three tries in seven minutes for a four-point lead after 48 minutes, as Brough's sin-binning left his side short of numbers at the start of the second half. But Hull gamestar Shayne McMenemy crossed for a 61st-minute try to once again level the scores in an entertaining, topsy-turvy encounter, and John Kear's men had more than enough in the tank to go on and finish the job.

In an amazing game at Odsal, a 36-point scoring burst without reply swept Warrington to a first league double over Bradford for 25 years and their first win there since 1993. Chris Bridge showed just what a talent the Bulls let go at the end of the previous season with a 24-point haul after the Wolves trailed 24-8 with only half-an-hour left. Bridge, at stand-off because of an injury to captain Lee Briers, scored two tries and eight goals from as many attempts.

The following morning, *Rugby Leaguer & League Express* revealed that Warrington had signed New Zealand Test star and North Queensland Cowboys captain Paul Rauhihi.

Daniel Anderson couldn't have hoped for a better start to his St Helens career, as his new charges inflicted Leeds' second defeat of the season in round 15 - a 38-24 win at Knowsley Road.

The former New Zealand international coach declared himself "exhilarated" after watching his new charges reduce the gap at the top of the table to two points with a wonderful display packed with pride and intensity. Leading 26-6 after 39 minutes of the first half, even when a largely outfought Leeds eventually got around to staging a gallant rearguard action, with second rower Jamie Jones-Buchanan completing a hat-trick in defeat, this was never going to be anything other than Saints' night.

That night Saints announced that star winger Darren Albert, 29, had signed a new two-year contract. "I'm delighted to have signed a new deal, and confirmed my commitment to the club," said Albert.

Hull conceded the most points at the KC Stadium since moving there in 2003 when they lost 42-24 to Bradford. Paul Deacon's nine goals helped him to get the gamestar award ahead of Leon Pryce. Hull coach John Kear did not seek to make excuses, despite his obvious disappointment, and gave due credit to the Bulls. "Bradford came here very determined after the defeat against Warrington. They were very physical and I think might have out-muscled us. We have had a tough run with Salford, Bradford in the Cup and League, St Helens and Wakefield. Generally, I think we have come through very well indeed and it has hardened us up for the Challenge Cup and Super League."

The Bulls were missing Lesley Vainikolo, who had been told to expect at least six weeks out of action after suffering a medial ligament strain in the 24-44 defeat to Warrington Wolves.

But coach Brian Noble was celebrating a new two-year contract at Odsal. "I am delighted to be able to commit my future to the Bulls," he said. "This club has been a big part of my life, and I am very happy here. The main thing is to continue the stability and continuity that has served this club so well over the past decade. I would not have accepted this offer if I didn't feel confident that I can continue to bring success to the club, both this season and over the next two years."

Widnes Vikings moved three points clear of Leigh with an impressive 40-12 home win over Huddersfield, to confirm their mid-season resurgence. Gray Viane, whose 80-metre try late in the first half had sent in his side on level terms at the break, completed a hat-trick with two of the Vikings five second-half touchdowns - Simon Finnigan, Shane Millard and Mark Smith adding the others in an inspired attacking purple patch covering 16 minutes.

The Australian Julian O'Neill made his third debut - coming off the bench after 53 minutes - for Widnes after being released by Wakefield. Coach Frank Endacott was confident that the Vikings had enough time to climb clear of the bottom two. "I don't think it's too late at all. It can all turn around very quickly, we've had a horrific run this year with injuries, and signing Julian gives us a bit more player depth - and a lot more experience. We've got a lot of confidence and a lot of spirit in our squad at the moment - with an ounce of luck we can turn our season around in the next few weeks."

London Broncos played their last game at Griffin Park for seven weeks as they thrashed Leigh Centurions 70-16, giving a debut off the bench to new signing, former Junior Kangaroo Feleti Mateo, who joined the club on loan from Parramatta.

Wakefield were new relegation fancies after Warrington cemented their top-five spot with a 38-30 home win over the Wildcats, though it took an incisive break from the indomitable Nathan Wood in the 75th minute to finally kill off the Wildcats' challenge in a thrilling see-saw clash.

And on the Spring Bank Holiday Monday, Ian Millward got his Wigan career off to a winning start with a 34-20 win at the Willows. The City Reds led twice in the first half thanks to two tries from prop Andy Coley - before four unanswered touchdowns either side of the interval put the Warriors in command.

Salford coach Karl Harrison hit out at referee Richard Silverwood after seeing his side sink to a fifth straight defeat. "I thought we had some really tough calls against us today and I'm not happy with the performance of Mr Silverwood, but that's as much as I can say about that. Certain teams get away with certain things, which is wrong," he said, highlighting the referee's decision to place Danny Sculthorpe on report after he caught Mark Shipway with an elbow, rather than sending him off. Sculthorpe got two matches from the RFL Disciplinary.

SUPER LEAGUE TABLE - *Monday 30th May*

	P	W	D	L	F	A	D	PTS
Leeds Rhinos	15	13	0	2	618	242	376	26
St Helens	15	12	0	3	504	343	161	24
Hull FC	15	9	1	5	406	336	70	19
Bradford Bulls	15	9	0	6	522	359	163	18
Warrington Wolves	15	9	0	6	401	401	0	18
Wigan Warriors	15	7	0	8	356	343	13	14
Huddersfield Giants	15	7	0	8	344	438	-94	14
London Broncos	15	6	0	9	474	404	70	12
Salford City Reds	15	6	0	9	270	343	-73	12
Wakefield T Wildcats	15	5	0	10	386	534	-148	10
Widnes Vikings	15	4	0	11	335	526	-191	8
Leigh Centurions	15	2	1	12	258	605	-347	5

At the end of May, the RFL unveiled its strategy for Super League at a press conference in the Holiday Inn at Brighouse.

Many media outlets latched onto plans to 'scrap' promotion and relegation at the start of the 2009 Super League season, after Super League is expanded from 12 to 14 clubs but the substance of the strategy wasn't quite that straightforward.

By 2009 - when a new TV contract would have to be in place - the RFL hope to have identified two new clubs, most likely from outside the game's traditional heartland. And from then on they will only consider admitting new teams on a three-yearly basis.

Before then, a review of current Super League clubs would be carried out in 2006, with clubs having to meet as yet undecided criteria - although one of these is an annual turnover of at least three million pounds.

JUNE
Nothing Toulouse

"Rout 66" was the headline on the front page of *Rugby Leaguer & League Express* on Monday morning June 6th, and that said it all about St Helens' 66-4 win at Odsal. Saints ran in 12 tries, including a hat-trick for Vinnie Anderson and braces for Jon Wilkin, Jamie Lyon and Ade Gardner, as a hapless Bulls' outfit conceded over 40 points at Odsal for the third time in 2005.

Leon Pryce was sent off in the 28th minute for a high shot on Lyon - but even without the extra man, Saints had already proved too good for the hosts. And they were without their captain Paul Sculthorpe due to a recurrence of his persistent hamstring problems. Lyon was brilliant, and was involved in the first four of Saints' second-half efforts. Twice he beat Karl Pratt - once to send Sean Long over and once to race clear himself - before going over again after good work from Long and then providing an amazing final pass that saw Vinnie Anderson crash over after Wilkin intercepted Iestyn Harris's long pass.

"We started poorly and got worse," Bulls coach Brian Noble said. "We've got six days to turn it around. It's a huge test of our character. Some things out there were just not acceptable."

With doubts around several Bradford players' futures at Odsal, the club's fans were given a boost when Stuart Fielden revealed he did not have a clause enabling him to leave Bradford Bulls before his contract expires at the end of 2007, despite suggestions to the contrary in the Australian press. Fielden was named along with Great Britain teammates Martin Gleeson and Brian Carney as targets for the new NRL club to be based on the Gold Coast from 2007. But he admitted that he would consider heading down under when his current deal with the Bulls ran out.

Hull slipped out of the top three, as they fell at Headingley 34-14. Keith Senior was voted the official man of the match. The Rhinos centre had an outstanding game with a hat-trick of tries, but the crucial player for Leeds was again Kevin Sinfield, the outstanding player in Super League so far. A commanding second-half performance saw Leeds post three tries in eight minutes to win a highly-physical encounter.

There was a highly unusual incident late in the match when referee Richard Silverwood penalised Sinfield after the Leeds skipper indicated that he intended to kick for goal after being awarded a penalty. Instead he aimed the place kick for the left corner of the ground, with Rob Burrow following the ball up to touch down. "Once the touch judges have been sent behind the posts, the only option is to kick at goal. If the ref then thinks it is a deliberate attempt not to kick at goal, then it's a penalty. Richard Silverwood gave the right decision," explained refs' boss Stuart Cummings.

The Wolves slid up to third, but only just, after a 24-22 win at Huddersfield, their eighth victory in nine matches, with hooker Jon Clarke epitomising the Wolves' fighting spirit. Wayne McDonald made his first start in the Claret and Gold after signing from Leeds on an 18-month contract.

Leigh's outside chances of avoiding an immediate return to NL1 faded as Widnes Vikings moved five points clear of them with a 34-14 win at the Coliseum. The relegation showdown brought the best out of Owen Craigie - who scored a hat-trick of tries - and Vikings captain Shane Millard, who both made huge contributions to the flattering 20-point victory, with John Wilshere once again impressing for Leigh.

On the Friday night Ian Millward's honeymoon period at Wigan came to an end, as London edged the Warriors 22-18 - the Broncos' first away win of the season, and their first double over Wigan in the Super League era. Wigan out-scored the Broncos by four tries to three, but Paul Sykes' goal-kicking eventually proved crucial. The Broncos' centre kicked five from five attempts, including two penalties, whereas Danny Tickle was unable to find his customary accuracy to mark his 100th appearance for Wigan.

Wigan also had a helping hand from a controversial score that handed them a lifeline going into the break. As Wayne Godwin and Brian Carney tried to break a stern Broncos defence, with the visitors leading 20-10, the hooter clearly sounded from the timekeepers located in the press-box as Carney was tackled. But referee Karl Kirkpatrick failed to hear it and Wigan scored on the next play, as Kris Radlinski sent the almost apologetic Brett Dallas over in the left corner.

That week Wigan announced they had signed Wests Tigers winger Pat Richards on a three-year contract from 2006.

Four tries in the last 19 minutes swept Wakefield Trinity Wildcats to a remarkable 36-24 home victory over Salford City Reds. With Luke Robinson leading the way, the Reds seemed to be heading for victory at 24-14 on the hour, but then Wakefield ran amok to end a four-match losing run, with David Solomona making a rapid impact after making a return from an eight-match injury lay-off.

Ali Lauitiiti become the eighth Super League player - and the first substitute - to score five tries in a match in the Rhinos' 70-6 demolition of Wakefield Trinity Wildcats on the Friday night of Round 17. Mike Umaga, Jason Robinson, Tony Smith, Anthony Sullivan, Kevin Iro, Lesley Vainikolo and Danny McGuire were the other to have achieved the feat. Four of Lauitiiti's tries came in a devastating eleven-minute spell after the break before Wakefield's biggest Super League home attendance of 9,457.

Meanwhile the Rhinos signed Rob Burrow to a new five-year contract, and announced that injured hooker Matt Diskin was ready for his

London's Mark Tookey splits the Widnes defence as the Broncos see off the Vikings

first runout of the year in the Senior Academy.

The Bulls got back on track on the Saturday night with a 20-38 victory at Huddersfield Giants, although they had to win without their Great Britain star Leon Pryce, who was suspended for three matches after being found guilty of a reckless high tackle on St Helens' Jamie Lyon the week before. The Giants were well in the contest during a see-saw first hour in which the lead changed hands five times. But a second try from Robbie Paul, an impressive contributor from the bench, put two scores between the sides for the first time, and the Bulls finished much the stronger.

Maurice Lindsay admitted he was in the dark about reports that his captain Kris Radlinski was the subject of a bid from Sale rugby union club. A crowd of 12,125 was Wigan's highest against Hull in the Super League era, just as it had been against London the week previously, but it couldn't prevent the Warriors slipping to a 28-24 defeat, leaving them with just two wins from their last nine league games. When Kirk Yeaman swooped for his second try with just three minutes to go after Richie Barnett hacked on a Danny Washbrook kick in a classic counter-attack, Wigan were contemplating a third successive home defeat for the first time since they lost four home games in a row at Central Park in 1983. Wigan gave a debut to Liam Botham, released by Leeds and signed on a short-term contract until the end of the season.

Former Wigan utility Chris Chester joined Hull teammates Graeme Horne and Kirk Dixon in penning new contracts to keep the trio at the KC Stadium until the end of 2007.

Jamie Lyon's hat-trick thwarted a courageous Salford victory at the Willows on the Friday night, as St Helens roared back to overturn a 22-12 deficit in the final quarter to clinch a 33-22 victory, securing Daniel Anderson a third successive Super League win. The Reds' halfbacks Tim Hartley and Luke Robinson played a huge part in building Salford's deserved lead, but in the end the class of Lyon and the cruel bounce of the ball took its toll on a courageous home defence.

The Broncos midfield trio of Thomas Leuluai – a man the Vikings had coveted in the off-season – Luke Dorn and outstanding captain Mark McLinden excelled as London consolidated their top-six position with a 24-10 win at error-prone Widnes. Only late tries to Gary Connolly and Owen Craigie prevented a whitewash.

A three-try burst just after half-time helped Warrington retain third place after they trailed 7-4 at the break to a courageous Leigh side. Brent Grose's 43rd-minute try got the ball rolling before two quickfire follow-ups from Henry Fa'afili emphasised the visitors' superiority. From there it was Warrington all the way with the Wolves running in an eventual eight tries.

That weekend Maurice Oldroyd stood down as chairman of the British Amateur Rugby League Association, marking the end of a 32-year involvement with the association - he was a founding father of the amateur arm of the game in 1973.

Wigan chairman Maurice Lindsay sprung to the defence of his coach Ian Millward after a Saturday night record 70-0 defeat by Leeds at Headingley in Round 18. "The truth is that Ian has got very few players to pick from," said Lindsay, who spoke to a group of Wigan fans after the match.

The Rhinos had swooped to sign Manly Sea Eagles winger Scott Donald for 2006 after revealing that current winger Mark Calderwood would be leaving Headingley at the end of this season. Again the Warriors were forced to look to youth, with teenager James Coyle the latest to be given a Super League start, in a 13-try humiliation, with Calderwood getting two of them.

Such was the Broncos' recent resurgence that they were disappointed with only taking a point from a thriller at Knowsley Road on the same Friday evening, with a 28-all draw. The Broncos recovered from a nightmare start, conceding two early tries to a Saints side that began in rampant form, to take a shock 20-8 lead at the interval. Willie Talau's hat-trick try left honours even two minutes from the end.

A superb hat-trick by Nathan Blacklock and two excellently-taken tries by opposite winger Richie Barnett took Hull to an otherwise forgettable 30-16 home win over Leigh.

June

Warrington - who confirmed the signing of Paul Rauhihi on a two-year contract - sealed their sixth consecutive victory as a blistering second-half performance blew away Salford's dogged resistance in a 48-14 success. Leading by a slender two points as the final quarter approached, the Wolves ripped 32 points in the final 22 minutes, with Ben Westwood grabbing a hat-trick.

Wakefield went close to pulling off an amazing fightback at the Galpharm. They looked to be down and out as Huddersfield Giants raced to a 28-0 lead in the opening half-hour. But with only six minutes to go it was 30-22 with Wakefield piling on the pressure. Then Huddersfield's Paul March moved smartly from a scrum inside his own quarter to find Paul White coming through on the burst and there was

Salford's Karl Fitzpatrick halts a charging Martin Gleeson as Warrington blow away the City Reds

never any chance of anyone stopping him as he streaked 80 metres to the posts. Chris Nero added a last-minute try for a deceptive 40-22 scoreline.

The following Wednesday Wakefield coach Shane McNally was sacked, assistant Tony Smith taking over in a caretaker capacity.

A late Paul Deacon field goal - one minute and four seconds into injury time - earned Bradford a last-gasp draw with relegation battlers Widnes Vikings, as Odsal officials were left seething at referee Steve Ganson's handling of the game. Frank Endacott was happy though. "The home fans were going on (about the refereeing) behind me. To be honest, I don't know what the hell they were going on about. I thought he (Ganson) had a very good game. If we got a performance like that every week I'd be more than happy."

The Bulls, too, could find plenty to hearten them after clawing their way back into a 24-21 lead thanks to three tries in five minutes, having trailed 21-6 with less than 15 minutes to go. That week they signed Torquay-born 22 year old Parramatta hooker Ian Henderson, the younger brother of Castleford captain Andy, to the end of the 2007 season.

A priceless away point was a more than satisfactory outcome for Frank Endacott's Vikings. With ten games to go in the regular season, the Vikings now had eleven points, one behind Salford and Wakefield, with Wigan another two points ahead on 14.

SUPER LEAGUE TABLE - *Sunday 19th June*

	P	W	D	L	F	A	D	PTS
Leeds Rhinos	18	16	0	2	792	262	530	32
St Helens	18	14	1	3	631	397	234	29
Warrington Wolves	18	12	0	6	515	444	71	24
Hull FC	18	11	1	6	478	410	68	23
Bradford Bulls	18	10	1	7	589	470	119	21
London Broncos	18	8	1	9	548	460	88	17
Huddersfield Giants	18	8	0	10	426	522	-96	16
Wigan Warriors	18	7	0	11	398	463	-65	14
Salford City Reds	18	6	0	12	330	460	-130	12
Wakefield T Wildcats	18	6	0	12	450	668	-218	12
Widnes Vikings	18	5	0	12	404	589	-185	11
Leigh Centurions	18	2	1	15	295	711	-416	5

Vinnie Anderson dives over during St Helens' Challenge Cup massacre of Wigan

Toulouse Olympique celebrated a historic day for French Rugby League, as the French Elite club became the first club from across the Channel to reach the semi-final of the Powergen Challenge Cup, defeating Widnes Vikings 40-24 at the Stade des Minimes in Toulouse in front of the BBC cameras

The Vikings were totally outplayed in temperatures that reached 35 degrees Celsius, and they were 20-0 down inside as many minutes. Toulouse stand-off Dave Mulhall earned the official man-of-the-match award, but there were several contenders. Hooker Cédric Gay, with his two vital individual tries and constant probing of the Widnes defence, certainly deserved a share of the plaudits, as did centre Damien Couturier with his eight goals from as many attempts. And Toulouse's ex-Widnes front-rower Tommy Gallagher's 72nd minute touchdown ensured that there was no way back for the Super League side.

Wigan, who suffered a club-record defeat for the second week in a row, with their 75-0 Cup-hammering against St Helens at Knowsley Road, saw their odds against being relegated shorten from 50/1 to 33/1. Their 70-0 capitulation against Leeds the week before was heartbreaking for the Warriors faithful but this 13-try humiliation against their oldest enemies was even worse.

Saints - in a week when they announced the signing of Kiwi Test prop Jason Cayless on a four-year contract - ran amok on a hot afternoon to leave Ian Millward's homecoming in tatters. Playing a brilliant style of attacking football and displaying an equally-impressive defence Saints ran in their highest ever score against Wigan,

Mark Calderwood loses possession under pressure from Jon Wells as Leeds deny London

before a capacity crowd. Prop Mark Edmondson helped himself to a second-half hat-trick and fellow front-rower Nick Fozzard to two tries in a man of the match display.

The only downside for St Helens was that Sean Long was expected to be out of action for up to six weeks after suffering a broken wrist in training the previous Friday, and stand-off Jason Hooper suffered a dislocated shoulder just before half-time.

Kevin Sinfield - at loose forward for the first time this season - guided the Rhinos into the last four with a 32-12 win over London at Headingley. The Leeds skipper produced the six key moments in a dazzling nine-minute second-half spell that finally turned a gripping encounter - dominated by persistent drizzle - the favourites' way.

Leeds were tenuously hanging on to a 16-12 lead just after the hour, Thomas Leuluai's ricocheting grubber seeing highly impressive fullback Richard Mathers trapped in-goal.

From the drop out, Sinfield produced the first of his game-breaking moments, sending his low-trajectory kick torpedoing past Nick Bradley-Qalilawa and into touch for a Rhinos scrum.

At the end of the subsequent set, with Leeds menacing the visiting quarter, Sinfield's perfectly-executed grubber to the wing forced Lee Hopkins to pick up, the chase bundling him over the touchline for a second Leeds feed, this time on the Broncos ten-metre line.

Taking the ball from the base of the scrum, Sinfield committed two defenders on a storming dart and produced a perfect flat pass for Danny McGuire to scamper over for a crucial score that established a ten-point margin.

John Kear's Hull seemed to be saving their best for the Challenge Cup and they duly hammered Leigh 46-14 on the Saturday TV game. A near-perfect first 40 minutes had the Centurions a hopeless 34-0 down at half-time, with Richard Horne dominant, scoring two first-half tries.

Hull were still third favourites to win the Cup and those odds lengthened when they drew the seemingly-unstoppable St Helens in the semi-finals.

JULY
To Hull and back

Leeds coach Tony Smith described the Rhinos' 36-26 defeat of Bradford at a sold-out Headingley as a "poor performance. Bradford played exceptionally well, better than I've seen them play for quite some time. But to give away as much opportunity to the opposition as we did is what I'm disappointed with."

Smith produced a masterstroke by sending captain Kevin Sinfield back onto the pitch in the 63rd minute, with ten points separating the sides after Ben Harris had hauled the Bulls back into the contest with a try made by namesake Iestyn. With his first touch, Sinfield took Gareth Ellis's pass in the centre position and glided in and away from a bemused defence, before a perfectly-timed inside ball sent Keith Senior powering clear for his second touchdown.

Sinfield converted - part of an exemplary kicking performance which was again a crucial difference, as the sides were only one try apart at the finish.

The Bulls closed the gap at the end with two touchdowns in the closing eight minutes. At the heart of the strong finish was Iestyn Harris, for whom the match started and ended ignominiously. He came off the bench and then returned to it with a late sin-binning, but in between he was a dominant figure in a welcome return to form at his old stamping ground.

St Helens overcame another injury blow to Paul Sculthorpe with a hard earned 38-26 away victory over Wakefield Trinity Wildcats, who showed signs of a revival under new coach Tony Smith. Sculthorpe had been an influential figure in the first half when he scored a try, created another and kicked three goals to help the Saints to a 24-14 lead. But their captain did not return for the second half because of a hamstring injury.

Despite not picking up a win in his first match as a senior coach, Tony Smith looked as if he was still enjoying the experience at the post-match press conference. "I wasn't nervous," he said. "More excited than anything. I said to the groundsman before the game that I've been to Wembley three times and played in two Grand Finals, but I was more excited about today than I was when I played in any of those, or even when I made my debut as a 17-year-old. I hope the excitement and enthusiasm was passed on to the players."

If it hadn't been for the boot of Lee Briers, the Wildcats could well have slipped into the bottom two. Briers rose from the treatment bench to break a deadlocked Mersey derby at Halton Stadium, kicking the field goal which separated Warrington from their local rivals.

The Wolves captain had spent most of the second half sitting on the bench with a thigh strain before Paul Cullen pushed him back on the field with 11 minutes to go, purely for his value in a drop-goal shootout. It took two attempts, his first fading short of the posts. But with seven minutes to go Ben Westwood broke through the Widnes half, Mick Cassidy downed him with an ankle tap and Briers made no mistake with the shot from in front of the posts off the next play. Frank Endacott described the 25-24 defeat as "heartbreaking", at the end of a week in which the Vikings signed Cronulla fullback David Peachey subject to them staying in Super League.

And the Wolves confirmed they had signed Cronulla halfback Michael Sullivan, who the previous month had admitted that an addiction to gambling had cost him over A$100,000, telling the Australian Daily Telegraph that he was interested in a move to Super League to "further my career and atone for some of the mistakes I have made financially".

On the Saturday night, Huddersfield's play-off hopes took a heavy blow with a 24-16 defeat at the Willows. "It was an ugly win," Reds coach Karl Harrison admitted, after watching his side collect their first victory after seven straight league defeats and move further away from the relegation zone. "But an ugly win is better than a pretty loss."

The previous night, a crowd of almost seven and a half thousand squeezed into Hilton Park to see Wigan win the local derby 30-22, stand-in skipper Dennis Moran and substitutes Danny Tickle and Terry Newton inspiring a second-half revival. Trailing 10-4 late in the first half to a Centurions side that dominated possession and field position, Wigan were staring down the barrel of their fifth successive defeat. But Martin Aspinwall's second try just before the break, and Moran's close-range effort shortly after, wrested control of the game. Leigh prop Craig Stapleton and raw-boned Cumbrian Oliver Wilkes, back from injury, were both to the fore in a go-forward pack.

Warriors winger Brian Carney - who confirmed he would be joining new club Gold Coast for the 2007 NRL season - picked up a hamstring problem. Wigan also announced the signing of tough New Zealand prop Iafeta 'Feca' Palea'aesina for 2006.

Nearly 4,000 fans made their way to a drizzly Brewery Field for the first of London Broncos' "on the road" matches and both the capital city side and Hull served up a feast in a 24-24 draw, Danny Brough's late penalty earning Hull a point.

And at the start of July the RFL appointed Simon Malcolm to the newly created post of Director of Marketing and Corporate Communications.

Leeds coach Tony Smith was of the opinion that the new French Super League club to be based in Perpignan would mount a more formidable challenge than some observers anticipated, after the Rhinos had gone down 32-24 to London Broncos in Round 20 at the Stade Aime Giral.

About 1,000 Leeds fans in a 7,000 crowd watched the Rhinos, playing without skipper Kevin Sinfield, who dislocated a thumb against Bradford, but with Matt Diskin making his first appearance of the season from the bench, throw away a 24-8 second-half lead. The Broncos hit back with four converted tries without reply in the last quarter to snatch a surprise win - their seventh undefeated game on the trot.

St Helens - without seven first-choice players - moved to within a point of leaders Leeds with an 18-10 home win over Hull at Knowsley Road. Paul Sculthorpe, Sean Long, Jason Hooper, James Graham, Vinnie Anderson, Lee Gilmour and Mick Higham were all sat in the stands as Paul Wellens scored a crucial second-half try and 17-year-old scrum-half Scott Moore created two more.

A 5,000-strong travelling army of Warrington supporters were hopeful of a first win on Wigan soil since January 1993, but left reflecting on only their second defeat - by 36-17 - in their last 13 games. The Wolves had looked the likelier winners, spurning a host of clear-cut openings before Wigan, facing up to the prospect of their fourth successive home defeat, put on a battling second-half display to score five tries. Dennis Moran again led from the front as Wigan captain, narrowly edging out a host of worthy candidates for the gamestar award.

The turnout of 14,162 fans at the JJB Stadium on the Saturday night, coming so soon after Wigan suffered record defeats to Leeds and St Helens, was a real fillip for Wigan. As was the decision of Kris Radlinski to turn his back on rugby union and extend his contract with Wigan until the end of 2007. "The signing of Kris was an indication of what the club is all about," said Maurice Lindsay. "I am certain that his signing was an inspiration that led to the team's defeat of Warrington." On the contra side Brian Carney had asked Wigan to release him from the final year of his contract to allow him to play with Newcastle Knights.

Hefin O'Hare's last-minute interception and 50-metre sprint for a try clinched a 32-22 home win for 12-man Huddersfield over Leigh in a penalty-riddled game. The Giants were hanging on to a 26-22 lead when Leigh Centurions made a last desperate bid for victory. But as they quickly moved the ball wide Oliver Wilkes' pass to the wing was pounced on by substitute O'Hare and there was no one to stop him haring for the posts.

Huddersfield were reduced to 12 men in the 15th minute when fullback Paul Reilly was sent off for an alleged elbow to the face of Danny Halliwell after he had kicked ahead. He later got a three-match suspension. Chris Thorman was once again the Giants main man with eight goals, a try and a hand in another.

Widnes didn't get going at the Willows until they were 24-0 down and they ended up 34-16 losers as Chris Charles collected a special mention from his coach. "He worked his socks off for the team," said Karl Harrison. "He's one of those guys who doesn't get recognised by the paying public a lot but he does so much for a team."

A Karl Pratt hat-trick could not stop Tony Smith's rejuvenated Wildcats turning up the heat on Widnes with a scintillating seven-try victory over fifth-placed Bradford. In sweltering temperatures, the Bulls edged an entertaining first half 24-20, thanks to a couple of Pratt tries in the last three minutes before the break. By then, a back on-form Wakefield produced a great second-half performance, topped off by the 61st-minute introduction of double try-scorer Jamie Rooney. Gamestar Ben Jeffries also touched down twice.

Widnes coach Frank Endacott admitted that his side was in big trouble, after their 18-44 Round 21 home defeat by Wakefield Trinity Wildcats, leaving the Vikings second from bottom of the Super League table on eleven points, five points behind the Wildcats, with just seven games to play. "We should all go to church this week and pray - we have tried everything else," said Endacott. One gleam of light for the Vikings was a hat-trick of tries by Gray Viane, in reply to a hat-trick by Wakefield winger Semi Tadulala.

A tense, bad tempered game at the Halton Stadium saw three incidents placed on report, with four players yellow-carded, with David March having two separate spells in the sin bin. And Jamie Rooney suffered a knee injury that was to rule him out for the rest of the season.

Leigh Centurions meanwhile were already planning for National League One, with director Keith Freer hitting out at fans who were suggesting the club would go into liquidation in the event of relegation. "It is utter rubbish," said Freer.

After over a month without a win Bradford got their hopes of a respectable play-off place back on track with a comfortable 58-12 success over Leigh. Ben Harris scored three tries and created one in a prominent display alongside Ian Henderson and Stuart Fielden. Centre Shontayne Hape emerged unscathed from his first Super League appearance since limping out of the Gillette Tri-Nations tournament the previous autumn with a knee injury.

The sending off of Paul Cooke cast a shadow over Hull FC's 34-24 home win over the Giants. The in-form stand off was dismissed in the 66th minute for a head-butt on Huddersfield Giants hooker Brad Drew. He was banned for a match, meaning he would be available for the Powergen Challenge semi-final on the last weekend of July.

Despite the flow of penalties spoiling much of the game a number of players managed to rise above it all. Hull's Kirk Yeaman had an outstanding all-round game in the centre, scoring a couple of tries and having a hand in another. Prop Ewan Dowes also had another storming game and captain Richard Swain made his first appearance since breaking his arm on Good Friday at London.

Winger Lee Greenwood, in his first match since joining the Giants from London Broncos, marked his debut with a superb try, being involved early on in the spectacular 90-metre move before finishing it off with a 40-metre sprint to the line. But once Hull scored their final try in the 59th minute to make it 34-20 the result was decided.

Warrington retained third spot and brought the Broncos' seven-match unbeaten run to an end with a performance full of character on a hot afternoon at the Halliwell Jones. Brent Grose was coolness itself in defence and capped an outstanding display with the game's clinching try.

The Broncos lost their inspirational scrum-half Thomas Leuluai with what was thought to be a sprained ankle midway through the first half, but turned out to be a triple fracture, ruling him out of the rest of Super League and the Gillette Tri-Nations.

Leeds decisively swept away the overwhelmed City Reds, registering seven first-half touchdowns in a point-a-minute blitz to finish 54-14 victors at Headingley. Although Leeds lost a 16-point lead the week before in France, when Mark Calderwood put them a similar margin ahead in as many minutes this time, a repeat looked highly unlikely. Calderwood had that week resisted an eleventh hour attempt by the Rhinos to persuade him to re-sign at Headingley in order to finalise his move to Wigan Warriors for 2006.

Wigan's mini winning run was ended at Knowsley Road as St Helens beat them 40-18 with plenty to spare. Paul Sculthorpe returned and was back to his inspirational best as Willie Talau scored Saints' first and last try.

That week the RFL revealed that no Super League club had breached the salary cap regulations in 2004. "The salary cap and the '20/20' rule has played a pivotal role in ensuring that the season's engage Super League is the most competitive to date," said the RFL's Director of Finance and Chief Operating Officer Nigel Wood. "This is reflected in increased attendances and television viewing figures."

As the Broncos, under the new chairmanship of Ian Lenagan, prepared to announce a return to The Stoop in a tie-up with Harlequins rugby union club, they consolidated their play-off spot in Round 22 with a 36-26 victory over Huddersfield Giants on their return to Griffin Park after two months on the road.

Wigan-born Lenagan, a company director who became a millionaire when his software company was floated on the Stock Exchange in 2000, was finally persuaded to take on his new role when he visited Perpignan earlier that month for the Broncos' 'home' game against Leeds Rhinos.

Meanwhile the Giants were now staring at a four-point gap between them and a first play-off campaign, with just the six 'add-on' games remaining.

Leeds Rhinos confirmed they would be seeking compensation from Iestyn Harris and Bradford Bulls, following the decision by a High Court judge, Mr Justice Gray, that Harris had a contractual obligation to play for the Rhinos in 2004, and therefore broke the terms of his contract to sign a three-and-a-half-year deal, thought to be worth £200,000 per year, with the Bulls in July of that year. The Rhinos alleged that the Bulls enticed Harris to break his agreement with them.

The Bulls and Harris were ordered to pay the Rhinos £64,000, which represented the legal costs they had incurred so far, and they were now to seek compensation for the losses they claimed to have suffered by Harris not fulfilling his side of the deal. Harris originally left Headingley in the autumn of 2001 to play for Wales in the 2003 rugby union World Cup.

The two clubs both issued official statements. Leeds chief executive Gary Hetherington said: "We are naturally pleased that Mr Justice Gray has upheld the validity of the contract between Leeds Rhinos and Iestyn Harris and legal proceedings will continue."

A Bradford spokesman said: "We have received the decision handed down in the High Court on Wednesday and, with our legal representatives, are looking at the implications of the decision. We will not be commenting further."

Wakefield Wildcats' third victory in four games under Tony Smith took them seven points clear of the relegation zone. David Solomona followed up his three-year contract extension with the match-winning try against Wigan at the JJB Stadium in the Friday TV game - Trinity's first win at Wigan since 1994 - when he somehow got the ball down in a massed tackle as the referee called 'last'. The Wildcats also announced the re-signing of Fijian winger Semi Tadulala for the next two seasons, and Australian halfback Ben Jeffries for the next three years.

Bradford prop Stuart Fielden stood tall as the Bulls came away with a hard-fought 24-18 win from Salford. The Reds could have snatched a draw in a late rally that included two tries in three minutes from Andy Coley and Karl Fitzpatrick, against a Bulls side that had second-half sin-binnings for Michael Withers and Stuart Reardon.

The Bulls were expected to announce the following week that they had signed Leeds Rhinos winger Marcus Bai.

Leeds, who were also resigned to losing Chris McKenna at the end of the season, showed their determination to hang onto pole position in Super League, a proud record stretching back to the start of the previous season, as they maintained their one-point advantage over Saints with a blistering eight-try 44-22 victory over Warrington at the Halliwell Jones Stadium. Gamestar Rob Burrow sparked their victory march with a try and also kicked seven goals from eight attempts for a personal points-tally of 18 in the absence of injured skipper Kevin Sinfield.

Hull had an eye on the following weekend's Powergen Challenge Cup semi-final, but they had enough to repel a committed Widnes performance, seizing third place from Warrington with a confidence-boosting 40-20 win at the Halton Stadium.

Despite the result, and a five-point gap to tenth-placed Salford, Vikings' coach Frank Endacott was happier with the commitment of his team, and refused to accept relegation. "We've a week off now and we need it. But we'll come back refreshed and ready to give it all we've got in the final six rounds. If we are going to go down then we'll go down fighting," he said.

The Centurions were all but relegated to NL1, but looked like bowing out of the engage Super League with all guns blazing on the evidence of a 27-20 home defeat by high-flying St Helens. The heartening home display included a hat-trick from centre Danny Halliwell. For Saints there were two-try contributions from Darren Albert and Jamie Lyon, whose second try, seven minutes from the end, sealed a flattering victory. St Helens were reported to be in a chase for New Zealand Warriors winger Francis Meli, along with Bradford and Warrington.

SUPER LEAGUE TABLE - *Sunday 24th July*

	P	W	D	L	F	A	D	PTS
Leeds Rhinos	22	19	0	3	952	356	596	38
St Helens	22	18	1	3	754	471	283	37
Hull FC	22	13	2	7	586	496	90	28
Warrington Wolves	22	14	0	8	605	564	41	28
Bradford Bulls	22	12	1	9	731	580	151	25
London Broncos	22	10	2	10	653	560	93	22
Wigan Warriors	22	9	0	13	510	576	-66	18
Huddersfield Giants	22	9	0	13	524	637	-113	18
Wakefield T Wildcats	22	9	0	13	598	786	-188	18
Salford City Reds	22	8	0	14	420	570	-150	16
Widnes Vikings	22	5	1	16	482	732	-250	11
Leigh Centurions	22	2	1	19	371	858	-487	5

Coach John Kear celebrates Hull's Challenge Cup semi-final defeat of St Helens

Leeds Rhinos were quoted by the bookies at 7 to 2 on, and Hull at 5 to 2 against to lift the Challenge Cup after the semi-finals, both played at the Galpharm Stadium Huddersfield on the last weekend in July.

Leeds eventually eased through to the final by 56-18 against Toulouse Olympique on the Sunday. But the Rhinos' 22-18 half-time lead flattered them as the French side played with great adventure. But when Rob Burrow's 40/20 set up Mark Calderwood for the try that opened up a 16-point lead early in the second half, Toulouse had given their all.

Paul Cooke was not a member of the initial 40-man Great Britain Tri-Nations squad that went into training camp at the University of Bath on the first day of August, despite being man of the match in Hull's outstanding 34-8 victory against St Helens at the Galpharm Stadium on the Saturday. It had been 69 years since Hull beat St Helens in the Challenge Cup, and it was Daniel Anderson's first defeat in ten matches since taking charge at Knowsley Road.

"Nobody gave us a chance on Saturday, and when people write you off it brings out that extra special effort in the team," said Cooke. "Everybody says a Challenge Cup Final is a great day out win, lose or draw.

"I don't think that's the right attitude to have. A 'day out' is no good for the players - if we wanted a great day out, we'd go to Blackpool! It's not a great day out in Cardiff unless you win, and we've got this far now, why shouldn't we go on and win it? I honestly don't want to know what it feels like to lose a final."

As July came to a close, Warrington Wolves were awaiting the outcome of their application for a work permit for Andrew Johns, and for the approval of the Australian Rugby League, before they could confirm the capture of the player widely regarded as the best in the world.

AUGUST
Saints above

Salford City Reds Football Director Steve Simms applauded Warrington Wolves' signing of Andrew Johns for the final two games of the regular Super League season and the play-offs beyond. But, as speculation grew that Adrian Morley would be the next big-name NRL player to take up a short-term contract in England, Simms also demanded that rule changes be put in place to stop wholesale imports and the devaluation of the English play-off series.

"I applaud Warrington for making the signing that they hope will enhance their chances of making the Grand Final, but I don't think it is fair for clubs to be able to do this at this stage of the competition," said Simms. "I believe it devalues the play-offs when one club suddenly brings in a player of his stature to try and improve their Grand Final prospects.

"Joey is an outstanding talent, and it says volumes for the British game that he is prepared to come and play over here. But it could start an avalanche. For instance, Canterbury Bulldogs are running ninth in the NRL, and if they don't make the play-offs they have five Kolpak players who could come straight into a top-six side - without overseas quota problems. What would that say about our game and the players in it? Warrington haven't broken any rules, and in no way am I knocking them for what they have done. In fact you have to commend them for their enterprise. But it is an issue that must be looked at."

One of the three players on Warrington Wolves' overseas quota would have to be deregistered to make way for the arrival of Johns - with Graham Appo the likely candidate.

With Lee Briers absent with a thigh injury Warrington dominated large parts of their second home game, in Round 23, against St Helens, but still went down 30-10, with Paul Wellens outstanding. Great Britain Test halfback Sean Long was reported in Sydney as wanting Saints to release him from the final two years of his contract so he could join Souths in the NRL. St Helens rejected any idea that they would be prepared to allow him to go. Sydney Roosters confirmed they were negotiating with Saints' second-rower Mark Edmondson over a possible two-year contract.

Leigh Centurions' relegation to National League One was officially confirmed when they lost to champions Leeds Rhinos at the Coliseum, the Rhinos scoring 14 tries in a 74-0 romp. The result capped off a particularly turbulent week for the Leigh club which saw the departure of head coach Darren Abram, injury and illness affecting a number of players and also caretaker coach Tommy Martyn who was only able to take one training session in the build-up to the game. Martyn admitted in the post-game press conference that he would be interested in the vacant coaching position. Rhinos youngster Ashley Gibson scored three tries and five goals on his debut off the bench.

Widnes were looking increasingly isolated in eleventh place. Former Australian Test captain Gorden Tallis had revealed he rejected a mammoth offer from Widnes to come out of retirement and play six matches. But the Vikings did make two short-term Australian signings - South Sydney's Brad Watts and St George halfback Keiran Kerr. Both players made their debuts in the 74-24 defeat against Bradford Bulls at Odsal Stadium - the most points Widnes had conceded in a match in their long history.

There was an impressive and often explosive return by Lesley Vainikolo. "The Volcano" had missed eight matches because of a knee injury, but he immediately showed all his old power to go over for two tries. The Bulls strongly denied a story in The Sun newspaper at the weekend that they had signed Australian Test star Brett Kimmorley on a two-year deal from next season. "That is absolute garbage," said Bulls' Media Manager Stuart Duffy.

The only good news for the Vikings was that Terry O'Connor looked set to delay his retirement if Widnes were relegated from Super League at the end of the season.

Wigan maintained their outside hopes of a top-six finish with their third league victory of the campaign over the Reds, at the JJB Stadium on the Friday evening. Skipper Terry Newton, fit-again Brian Carney and second-rower Danny Tickle each scored two tries. But Kris Radlinski was ruled out of the Tri -Nations as well as the rest of the Super League season after undergoing surgery for a knee injury. And new Super League club Les Catalans were hoping to sign Wigan forward Jerome Guisset for their inaugural season in 2006.

Salford were understood to be interested in taking Danny Orr to the Willows, with Cliff Beverley returning to New Zealand at the end of the season, and were also targeting Widnes Vikings' Australian centre Aaron Moule.

Chris Thorman's 20 points from eight goals and an individual try sparked Huddersfield's 44-12 win at Wakefield - who lost captain Jason Demetriou for the rest of the season with a dislocated shoulder - and kept the Giants' play-off ambitions simmering. Stanley Gene also played a key role on his return from a knee injury. The Giants were thought to be making a bid to sign Wigan stars Martin Aspinwall and Stephen Wild and the following Wednesday the Wildcats appointed Tony Smith as head coach on a permanent basis on a two-year contract.

Hull suffered a Challenge Cup semi-final hangover as London came away from the KC Stadium with a 17-16 win to maintain a crucial four-point lead over Huddersfield and Wigan in the race for sixth place. Paul Sykes' cool-headed field goal broke the deadlock in the 76th minute.

After round 24 the bookies were quoting the Rhinos, still at the top of the pile, but only by one point, as hot favourites, at 4/5 to win the Grand Final for the second year in succession.

A Danny McGuire-inspired Leeds won an ultimately comprehensive Saturday night 44-24 victory over the Broncos with four second-half tries, as London led 12-4 after 17 minutes. "Danny's getting back to his best," said McGuire's coach

August

Tony Smith, reflecting on a season in which his young playmaker had failed to hit previous heights, largely due to niggling injury. The Rhinos announced they had signed Shane Millard on a one-year contract for the 2006 season. The 30 year-old Widnes hooker was de-registered from the Vikings' roster in July because of surgery on a knee injury.

St Helens prop Mark Edmondson signed a two-year contract to play with the Sydney Roosters and he was missing, along with Paul Sculthorpe - ruled out for the season as he awaited knee surgery - as Saints hammered Wakefield for the second time at Knowsley Road, by 60-4. Sean Long, chosen to wear the captain's armband, accumulated a 24-point haul from a try and ten goals from as many attempts as Saints completed a club record win over Wakefield. Darren Albert scored a hat-trick.

Wigan's horrific run with injuries ran true to form when they defeated Widnes Vikings 48-24 at the Halton Stadium. After the news that Liam Botham was to miss the rest of the season, and subsequently retire on medical advice, with a neck injury, 17-year-old centre Daryl Goulding, making his Super League debut, suffered a suspected broken ankle.

Widnes outlined plans to make an immediate return to Super League in the event of the growing likelihood of their relegation to National League One after their ninth home defeat of the season.

An emphatic Friday night 38-22 defeat of Warrington kept the Giants hot on the heels of London Broncos as they both challenged for a top-six spot. Brad Drew produced one of the best all-round performances by a hooker in 2005, as the Wolves slipped out of the top four.

As well as still chasing the SLX play-offs, the Giants were looking to the future and were set to move for Wakefield Trinity Wildcats' forward Steve Snitch, as well as re-signing second rower Paul Smith on a two-year deal.

Former Bulls hooker James Lowes highlighted Malcolm Alker's performance in the Reds' 58-12 hammering at Bradford: "I would put Malcolm in the Great Britain team without any hesitation. He has consistently been the best number nine in the competition this year." Alker scored one of Salford's two tries, a spectacular 75-metre interception, as they slipped to a fourth successive defeat - their 11th in 13 matches. Shontayne Hape and Iestyn Harris each collected two tries as the Bulls eased into fourth spot. The hapless Reds were not helped by a series of injuries - all serious - which virtually deprived them of their entire front row before the game was through. Sean Rutgerson limped out after barely two minutes with a hamstring pull and was followed by Gareth Haggerty (concussion) and Mitchell Stringer, who was whisked away by ambulance with a suspected lower leg fracture.

NL-bound Leigh Centurions - who announced they were to remain a full-time professional club next season - found Challenge Cup finalists Hull in sensational form at the KC Stadium, losing 70-20. Hull may have been without their playmaking halfbacks Paul Cooke and Richard Horne - Cooke missed out with an eye injury and Horne pulled out of the side on the Saturday with an elbow problem - but they were awesome in the opening quarter. Gareth Raynor opened the scoring in only the second minute, and six more tries followed - in the next 20 minutes! Danny Brough converted them all and John Kear's side led 42-0 with barely the first quarter of the match completed. Brough at scrum-half and debutant 17-year-old Tommy Lee at stand-off had a field day. Mercifully Leigh finished with a flourish with two late tries. First Craig Stapleton produced a brilliant side-step and weaving run to beat three Hull defenders down the left. Then Paul Rowley's chip through and chase - plus Nick Owen's conversion completed the scoring.

Then, almost suddenly, Leeds Rhinos weren't top of the Super League table any more. The round 25 Leeds-Bradford re-run turned the competition upside down as the Bulls ran in 30-unanswered points in a second-half super show to complete a 42-10 victory.

Bradford had served notice of intent with their second-half display at Headingley six rounds before, the catalyst for their current unbeaten run that started in round 21 with the home win over Leigh. And they now had last season's most potent left-sided pairing in the competition - Shontayne Hape and Lesley Vainikolo - back, along with the under-rated Paul Johnson.

While Hape took the scoring plaudits with a sharp hat-trick – taking his try-tally to seven in the last three starts – it was the incisive decision making from Paul Deacon that chiseled out the chances and significantly gave time and space for Iestyn Harris to control the game. Skipper Jamie Peacock and livewire Ian Henderson had the home defence constantly back-pedalling.

Leeds' night was summed up by teenage winger Lee Smith, drafted in for his fourth start after previous ever-present Mark Calderwood failed to shake off a dead leg. When the Rhinos were at their dominant best, dictating the tempo in the early stages, he superbly read Kevin Sinfield's last-tackle dink over to the wing, whipping the ball away from the menacing advance of Vainikolo before spinning and skipping his way into the corner. Smith's experience at fullback saw him cope magnificently with two towering high kicks but when the Bulls varied the tactic in the second half to attack him along the ground, they twice gained match-winning reward.

The events around the 25th minute of the game were perhaps the most crucial of the season for Leeds. First Ben Harris's uncompromising dumping of Danny McGuire immediately spilt possession and led to the double whammy of Hape's first try and McGuire's withdrawal with a compounded shoulder injury. Worse was to follow for Leeds in their next possession, Keith Senior landing awkwardly and badly spraining his ankle in a double Joe Vagana tackle.

It meant Senior and McGuire were huge doubts for the following Saturday's Powergen Challenge Cup Final, while Willie Poching was rated as a 50/50 chance as he recovered from an operation on a fractured cheekbone.

Hull fell to a 24-28 defeat by Wigan at the KC Stadium, but they came through the game without any serious injuries, playmakers Paul Cooke and Richard Horne fit for the final despite missing the clash with the Warriors. The win kept Wigan's top-six chances alive with halfbacks Danny Orr, back after injury, and Dennis Moran keeping the youthful Warriors going forward, despite early injuries to Terry Newton (hip) and Brian Carney (hamstring). At one stage they led 26-8 before a Danny Tickle penalty halted a stirring Hull comeback.

St Helens capitalised on the Rhinos' slip-up against the Bulls to seize top spot with a 50-4 win at Knowsley Road over London Broncos. Jamie Lyon was again in magical form and Sean Long, Keiron Cunningham and Paul Anderson other stand-outs. They lost Australia-bound prop Mark Edmondson inside the opening 31 minutes - with a season-ending shoulder injury - and utility man Jason Hooper - who had signed for another year that week - was also sidelined though with a less serious injury in the second half.

Lee Gilmour on the burst as St Helens go top following a big win over London

Huddersfield ran up a club record Super League score - beating Leigh 68-16 at the Galpharm - with Chris Thorman scoring 36 points from four tries and ten goals, all Huddersfield Super League records, and Chris Nero getting a hat-trick of tries. Michael De Vere made a return after a seven-match absence with a broken hand.

An Anthony Stewart second-half hat-trick ensured another season in Super League for Salford City Reds and a 37-0 win over Wakefield, as Karl Harrison's scrappers ended a four-match losing streak to leap above their opponents on points difference.

And a home 60-16 humiliation by local rivals Warrington confirmed Widnes's eleventh-placed finish, ending their four-year stint in Super League. But the Vikings were still hoping that the winners of the NL1 Grand Final would not meet the criteria for Super League - giving Widnes the opportunity to remain in the top flight.

Though the relegation positions had been decided, no fewer than eight of the remaining Super League clubs were involved in a struggle for play-off positions. Only Salford and Wakefield, mathematically safe from relegation but unable to reach the top six, had no incentive other than pride to play for in the final three rounds of the season.

Bradford's resurgence had seen them cruise into third spot, a point above Hull and Warrington, with a better points difference than the teams immediately below them.

The fight for sixth spot was closer still, with three teams level on 24 points, though London were in the best position. Their points difference (+28) was well ahead of Wigan (-10) and Huddersfield (-13), and they had a theoretically easier run-in, with games to come against lower-ranked Widnes and Salford. Wigan had a daunting run home with their next two fixtures against the top two sides in the table, though they were both at the JJB Stadium. Huddersfield had their destiny in their own hands, still to play both of their top-six rivals. But that week all eyes were focused on Cardiff.

SUPER LEAGUE TABLE - *Sunday 21st August*

	P	W	D	L	F	A	D	PTS
St Helens	25	21	1	3	894	489	405	43
Leeds Rhinos	25	21	0	4	1080	422	658	42
Bradford Bulls	25	15	1	9	905	626	279	31
Hull FC	25	14	2	9	702	561	141	30
Warrington Wolves	25	15	0	10	697	648	49	30
London Broncos	25	11	2	12	698	670	28	24
Wigan Warriors	25	12	0	13	626	636	-10	24
Huddersfield Giants	25	12	0	13	674	687	-13	24
Salford City Reds	25	9	0	16	481	668	-187	18
Wakefield T Wildcats	25	9	0	16	614	927	-313	18
Widnes Vikings	25	5	1	19	546	914	-368	11
Leigh Centurions	25	2	1	22	407	1076	-669	5

CHALLENGE CUP FINAL
Farewell Cardiff?

It was rated as the final with everything as Hull won their first Challenge Cup for 23 years with a breathless 25-24 win over red-hot favourites Leeds at the Millennium Stadium. Paul Cooke and Danny Brough wrote themselves into the history books with the match-winning combination with 191 seconds to go, as Hull came from 19-24 down to snatch a victory that, on the hour-mark, was theirs for the taking. The Rhinos - led magnificently by Kevin Sinfield, with blood soaking through a dressing covering a gashed eyebrow that needed ten stitches after a collision of heads - had come back magnificently from 19-12 behind to post two converted tries in the space of four minutes through Mark Calderwood and Marcus Bai. But Hull re-grouped and their bravery and persistence were rewarded.

Shayne McMenemy made his second telling tactical kick of the afternoon - his grubber to the corner forcing a Calderwood error, giving his side another set of six tackles. Within seconds Richard Horne switched the attack back to the left for Cooke to dummy to the outside and cut between Sinfield and Danny Ward before crossing jubilantly behind the posts, nearly over-running the in-goal area in the process. Brough safely negotiated the conversion from in front of the sticks.

Hull FC - 2005 Challenge Cup Winners

Challenge Cup Final

Still the drama continued, as Sinfield's swirling and bouncing kick-off forced an error out of Jamie Thackray and gave the Rhinos one last chance with 70 seconds to go. The Rhinos were able to work the position for one last pot-shot at goal, only for inspirational Hull captain Richard Swain to race 20 metres to charge down Kevin Sinfield's attempted field goal. "At the end I was just thinking 'I don't want to have to go to a replay'," Swain said after the final whistle

The game was another tactical triumph for Hull's head coach John Kear. Hull's forward pack never allowed the Rhinos to set a platform up front, and they had an array of creative and kicking options in Horne, Cooke and Brough.

"This is the best win I've been associated with, no doubt about it," said Kear, who joined a select group of coaches to guide two clubs to Challenge Cup wins, having coached Sheffield to a 17-8 Wembley success in 1998. "And the reason for that is because we've knocked out Wakefield, Bradford, Leigh, St Helens and now the world champions.

It's been such a tough campaign, and the players have rightly reaped the benefits of it."

Kear sprung a surprise as the teams lined up, selecting Nathan Blacklock at fullback to replace Shaun Briscoe, ruled out on the eve of the final through appendicitis, and playing Motu Tony on the right wing. Blacklock more than justified Kear's faith in him, while Tony was another Hull hero with a classy try. "We were all very upset that Shaun Briscoe missed out on this," said Kear. "At 12.00pm on Friday he was playing in a Challenge Cup Final, and at 4.00pm he was under the surgeon's knife, so I think that indicates the serious nature of the situation. He will obviously get a winners' medal for his contribution in the earlier rounds."

The Rhinos' three injury doubts -

POWERGEN CHALLENGE CUP FINAL

Saturday 27th August 2005

HULL FC 25 LEEDS RHINOS 24

HULL: 2 Nathan Blacklock; 14 Motu Tony; 30 Richard Whiting; 3 Kirk Yeaman; 5 Gareth Raynor; 6 Richard Horne; 21 Danny Brough; 8 Ewan Dowes; 9 Richard Swain (C); 20 Garreth Carvell; 11 Shayne McMenemy; 12 Stephen Kearney; 13 Paul Cooke. Subs (all used): 10 Paul King for Carvell (19); 17 Chris Chester for Kearney (25); 15 Jamie Thackray for Dowes (28); Carvell for King (32); Dowes for Carvell (50); Kearney for McMenemy (50); King for Thackray (50); McMenemy for Chester (61); 16 Tom Saxton for Kearney (70); Thackray for King (71); Carvell for Dowes (72).
Tries: Tony (20), Raynor (46), Whiting (53), Cooke (77);
Goals: Brough 4/4; **Field goal:** Brough.
RHINOS: 1 Richard Mathers; 2 Mark Calderwood; 3 Chev Walker; 4 Keith Senior; 5 Marcus Bai; 13 Kevin Sinfield (C); 7 Rob Burrow; 8 Ryan Bailey; 9 Matt Diskin; 15 Danny Ward; 11 Ali Lauitiiti; 12 Chris McKenna; 20 Gareth Ellis. Subs (all used): 18 Jamie Jones-Buchanan for Ward (17); 16 Willie Poching for McKenna (19); 6 Danny McGuire for Ellis (25); 14 Andrew Dunemann for Diskin (27); Ward for Bailey (30); McKenna for Senior (41); Bailey for Jones-Buchanan (47); Diskin for Burrow (54); Ellis for Lauitiiti (56); Jones-Buchanan for Poching (58); Lauitiiti for McKenna (64); Poching for Lauitiiti (78).
Tries: Calderwood (12, 65), Ward (50), Bai (68);
Goals: Sinfield 4/4.
Rugby Leaguer & League Express Men of the Match:
Hull: Richard Swain; *Rhinos:* Kevin Sinfield.
Penalty count: 3-3; **Half-time:** 6-6;
Referee: Steve Ganson (St Helens);
Attendance: 74,213 *(at Millennium Stadium, Cardiff).*

Keith Senior, Danny McGuire and Willie Poching - were all in the side, with Barrie McDermott the unlucky player to be omitted, ultimately leaving Leeds short of firepower up front. A disconsolate Senior blamed himself for the defeat. Carrying an ankle injury into the game, he never looked comfortable, struggling for position as Tony scored Hull's opener down his flank, and he watched the second half from the Leeds dug-out after describing the final ten minutes of the first half as just too painful. Leeds coach Tony Smith staunchly defended his decision to play Senior, just eight days after the Great Britain centre was stretchered from the field with the injury against Bradford.

Sinfield took the Lance Todd Trophy as man of the match, although the vote was taken with ten minutes to go, and a host of Hull players would have

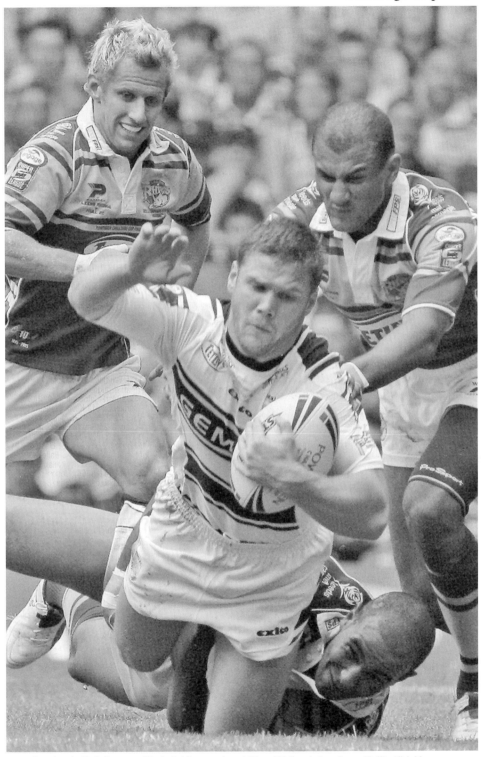

Leeds trio Rob Burrow, Mark Calderwood and Chev Walker bring down Hull's Kirk Yeaman

A diving Marcus Bai denies Nathan Blacklock

deserved the ultimate personal accolade, including Swain, Cooke and Brough. Twelve months before, Brough had been playing for York City Knights in NL2, and it was his 58th-minute field goal that proved the difference between the sides. "It's a dream come true," he said.

'If this was to be the last Challenge Cup Final in Cardiff, it was a fitting way to go' wrote *Rugby Leaguer & League Express* reporter Mike Latham. 'The stadium was a magnificent sporting cathedral, and Rugby League fans, with their impeccable behaviour and passion for the greatest game of all, made the occasion one to savour. Rugby League's ability to put on spectacles like this on the most important stage must be envied across the sporting world.'

RFL Executive Chairman Richard Lewis admitted it would be a wrench to leave Cardiff when the next season's Challenge Cup returned to Wembley, and he would like to play other games at the Millennium Stadium. "It has been a very popular stadium, and if we had a major match to schedule we would love to do it in Cardiff, which has been a great success," said Lewis. "But it is right that the Challenge Cup Final goes back to Wembley."

SEPTEMBER
Six appeal

Lesley Vainikolo set a Super League record by scoring six tries - the first coming after just 29 seconds, the last an exhilarating 80-metre breakaway in the closing moments - in their 49-6 victory against Hull on the Friday night of round 26. The last time more than five tries were scored in a match between two top division sides was when Martin Offiah scored ten for Wigan in the 1992 Premiership semi-final against Leeds.

"It feels good when people come up and congratulate me for the record. But it is a team effort, and luckily my centre partner Shontayne (Hape) was in a good mood as well," said the New Zealand Test winger.

The Bulls' new signing - Great Britain Test star Adrian Morley - arrived at Bradford the following Wednesday, while Salford City Reds rejected an approach from the Bulls for fullback Karl Fitzpatrick.

St Helens announced the signing of Leon Pryce for 2006 on a three-year deal, to bring the curtain down on his seven-year career at Bradford Bulls.

Hull also signed a player for the remainder of the season - Sione Faumuina, due to arrive from Auckland later that weekend. And Hull were about to sign Wakefield Trinity Wildcats' centre or loose forward Sid Domic for the following season, having already snapped up Bulls Hull-born back-rower Lee Radford.

Bradford's recent run of form, and their recruitment of Morley, had seen the odds against the Bulls winning their fourth Super League title tumble to 11/4 with bookmakers William Hill, behind St Helens (5/4) and Leeds Rhinos (2/1).

Warrington coach Paul Cullen allayed any fears after the Wolves' 32-22 win over Salford that Andrew Johns would not be fit to make his Wolves debut against Leeds the following Saturday night, after he sustained a shin injury in Newcastle Knights' narrow NRL defeat to St George-Illawarra. As expected Graham Appo was deregistered from the Wolves roster to make way for Johns.

Nathan Wood demonstrated he wasn't going to step aside and offer the scrum-half berth to Johns. The Wolves' veteran was the key factor in a hard-fought, if unimpressive win that lifted them back into the top four, with Hull slipping out. The 33-year-old scored one length-of-the-field try and had a hand in two others as the Wolves eventually found their form to battle past stubborn opponents.

David Solomona charges through the Widnes defence during a comprehensive win for the Wildcats

Wakefield Trinity Wildcats signed Kiwi Monty Betham and were linked with Paul White, set to leave Huddersfield Giants after rejecting an improved contract offer from the club. The Wildcats ended a run of three defeats with a 46-6 home thrashing of Widnes.

The Vikings' only hope of Super League survival was if the winner of the NL1 Grand Final failed to satisfy RFL criteria. And in Monday's *Rugby Leaguer & League Express* RFL Executive Chairman Richard Lewis denied a story that appeared in a national newspaper the previous Friday claiming that Whitehaven had been told their application to enter Super League would be rejected. The story claimed that Haven had been told that a proposal to play their early season games next year at Carlisle United's Brunton Park ground, while the Recreation Ground was being brought up to the required standard, was not acceptable.

The Vikings were still waiting for a decision on their Super League future before advertising for a new head coach. Current coach Frank Endacott had another year to run on his contract, but it would become void if the Vikings dropped to National League One.

And Widnes second-rower John Stankevitch said he would be taking legal advice after he was forced to retire from the game at the age of 25. He claimed an incident involving former Wigan Warriors prop Craig Smith had led to his career ending. While playing for St Helens in the 2003 Super League play-off against Wigan, Stankevitch dislocated his shoulder in a clash with Smith, which put him out of action for nine months. Smith received a letter from the RFL advising him to change his running style after catching Stankevitch with his knees.

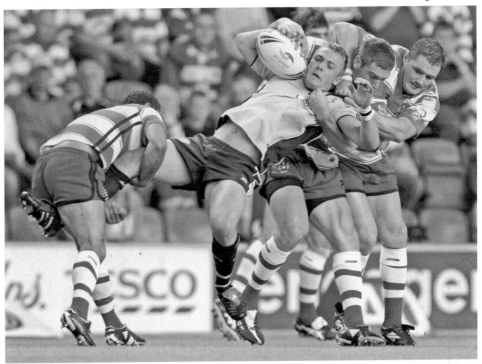

Dennis Moran, Stephen Wild and Terry Newton halt Lee Smith as Wigan come out on top against Leeds

Wigan confirmed their resurgence under new coach Ian Millward, beating Leeds 24-22 at the JJB Stadium, less than three months after losing at Headingley 70-0. Without the injured Chris McKenna and Keith Senior from their Cup final line-up, the Rhinos were forced into a late re-jig when Richard Mathers went down with gastric flu. And they thought they had won it at the death when Willie Poching pounced after Kevin Brown fumbled Danny McGuire's high kick, only for referee Ronnie Laughton to disallow Leeds claims and award them a scrum feed instead. Before that Harrison Hansen's late try, converted by Danny Orr, sealed the Wigan win.

A one-sided game saw Leigh slump to their heaviest ever home defeat - by 78-4 - and a 15th straight loss, as Saints showed their relegated hosts no mercy to take a major step towards securing the Minor Premiership. Leigh's new boss for 2006, New Zealander Tony Benson, watched on from the stands.

Wigan's shock win over Leeds on the Friday night cranked up the pressure on London and Huddersfield who met at Griffin Park the following day, with the Broncos gaining a controversial 16-12 win. Match Officials Director Stuart Cummings admitted that referee Richard Silverwood made a crucial error that could have cost Huddersfield Giants the game. The Giants had gone ahead with an early penalty, and, as the Broncos re-started the game with a kick from the centrespot, Eorl Crabtree caught the restart within the Giants' in-goal area, having put his back foot over the dead-ball line. The laws of the game state that the kick should therefore have been adjudged to have gone straight out on the full, and a Giants penalty at the centre spot should have been awarded. Instead referee Silverwood ruled a goal-line drop-out, and from it London went ahead and on course for a crucial win.

Andrew Johns leads out Warrington for the Wolves' clash with Leeds

Andrew Johns credited the Warrington defence as the main reason for the Wolves' 33-16 victory over Leeds Rhinos on his Super League debut in the Saturday TV game as 'Joeymania' gripped the town of Warrington. The Newcastle Knights halfback enjoyed a winning start to his short-term stint with the Wolves, scoring thirteen points and collecting the man of the match award against the reigning Super League champions.

Johns was delighted with the ease in which he was able to adapt to the Wolves' style of play, despite having only had three days training with the rest of the squad. But he didn't have everything his own way, as Leeds dominated much of the first-half territory.

Twice he kicked dead from deep, misjudging the pace of the Halliwell Jones outfield. And when he had another clearance charged down by Ali Lauitiiti, it prompted the predictable chants of "what a waste of money" from the Leeds supporters. Johns produced his best individual moment at the most crucial stage of the game – when the Rhinos were back to 18-16 early in the second half. A lethal sidestep took him through and his animated reaction, airborne with fists pumping even before Logan Swann had grounded the ball, showed how pumped up he was for this game.

Hysteria was the only way to describe the scenes at the final whistle. The Wolves' signature of wingers Stuart Reardon from Bradford and Richie Barnett from Hull for 2006 almost went unnoticed.

St Helens pair Sean Long and Darren Albert suffered serious facial injuries in the bruising battle with Wigan Warriors at the JJB Stadium on the Friday night of round 27, which Saints won 38-12. And Lee Gilmour was stretchered off with concussion after being knocked unconscious.

Gilmour and Long were both injured in incidents involving Wigan hooker Terry Newton, whilst Albert suffered an accidental clash of heads with Brett Dallas. Newton was that week banned for a total of ten games for the first two incidents. The game confirmed Saints as Minor Premiers, but coach Daniel Anderson was far from happy. "It came at a cost," he said.

Saints denied reports that they would try to bring Francis Meli, the New Zealand Warriors winger they had signed for the 2006 season, to this country for the rest of this season to replace the injured Albert.

Wigan chairman Maurice Lindsay refuted reports that Newton would be leaving the JJB Stadium at the end of the season. Reports had linked Newton to Bradford Bulls, but Lindsay claimed that he would be staying at Wigan.

Adrian Morley made little impact after going on as a 17th minute substitute in a 52-34 Bradford home win over Huddersfield - his first stint since joining the Bulls on a short-term contract from Sydney Roosters. The Great Britain forward played for 43 minutes before retiring to the bench and Bradford went from 34-18 down to 48-34 up before he made a last-minute return.

Huddersfield kept a close watch on Lesley Vainikolo, making his 100th appearance for Bradford, until the big winger broke free to score two tries in a late fling to take his tally to 11 in five matches since his return from injury.

London's 26-18 defeat at Salford kept both the Giants and Wigan's hopes of making the play-offs alive, although the Broncos just needed to beat Widnes at Griffin Park in the final round to qualify.

It was a clash of two losing runs at the Halton Stadium, where Widnes marked the official opening of their new east stand - to make the ground four-sided - by ending a nine-game losing sequence against the Centurions 36-20, Leigh's 16th straight loss.

A killer try by Hull's new signing Sione Faumuina in the final seconds of a pulsating match at Belle Vue put paid to a lively Wakefield performance in their last home outing of the season. Faumuina, at centre in place of the suspended Kirk Yeaman - two matches for a dangerous tackle in the defeat at Bradford - dived over from a pass flipped back by Nathan Blacklock at the corner flag to seal a 32-30 victory. If Hull could beat Warrington at the KC Stadium in round 28, they would have home advantage over the Wolves in the Elimination Play-off.

St Helens were presented with the League Leaders' Shield on the last Saturday of the regular season but Bradford spoiled the Knowsley Road party with a 32-18 win.

The Bulls turned around the game, and the whole complexion of the Super League play-offs, with a devastating five-try burst in the space of 12 minutes late in the game. When they trailed 8-18 with 13 minutes to go of a rugged and scrappy encounter the Bulls looked set to have to settle for a fourth-placed finish and a home tie against Hull FC, with Warrington retaining third spot.

But two tries by gamestar Paul Johnson, a second from Lesley Vainikolo, a 70-metre spectacular from Saints-bound Leon Pryce and a late effort from Ben

September

Harris shattered Saints and left the Bulls looking forward to the prospect of two home play-off ties and then a trip to Saints or Leeds if they could extend their winning run beyond the current eight games.

St Helens fans said farewell to Darren Albert, whose season, along with Sean Long's had been ended the week before at Wigan, after four seasons at Knowsley Road. Albert was to return to the NRL after signing a two-year deal with Cronulla Sharks.

The Rhinos got a morale–boosting win in before the play-offs with a 34-26 success over Wakefield at Headingley. It was Leeds' first win in a month, and the game also saw Mark Calderwood, with a brace of touchdowns, emerge as Super League's top try scorer. And a crowd of over 17,500 ensured a seasonal average that was a new competition high and the best at Headingley since 1951.

A brace of converted tries in the closing minutes of an otherwise tight and evenly-matched first half put Wigan on their way to ending the regular season with a 36-22 victory at Huddersfield, although the success proved too little too late for the battered 2005 Warriors. London's emphatic home 68-10 victory over Widnes made the result largely meaningless in terms of league standing and left the Warriors without a place in the play-offs for the first time in Super League history.

London Broncos bade farewell to Griffin Park with a comprehensive 12-try demolition of Widnes. Star of the show was scrum-half Luke Dorn, who ran in four tries, as the club soon to be known as 'Quins built up an unbridgeable 38-0 half-time lead.

Leigh bowed out of Rugby League's top echelon with a 25th league defeat, a 17th consecutive defeat, but pride restored in a 14-20 home loss to Salford.

The Andrew Johns effect continued to fire Warrington Wolves as they won at Hull 30-16. There was less of the euphoria that surrounded the Australian superstar's debut a week earlier, but his colleagues remained on a high. And it was more than Hull's blood and guts effort could cope with. Victory for Warrington meant they would have home advantage when the two teams met again in the following weekend's play-offs.

FINAL SUPER LEAGUE TABLE - Sunday 18th September

	P	W	D	L	F	A	D	PTS
St Helens	28	23	1	4	1028	537	491	47
Leeds Rhinos	28	22	0	6	1152	505	647	44
Bradford Bulls	28	18	1	9	1038	684	354	37
Warrington Wolves	28	18	0	10	792	702	90	36
Hull FC	28	15	2	11	756	670	86	32
London Broncos	28	13	2	13	800	718	82	28
Wigan Warriors	28	14	0	14	698	718	-20	28
Huddersfield Giants	28	12	0	16	742	791	-49	24
Salford City Reds	28	11	0	17	549	732	-183	22
Wakefield T Wildcats	28	10	0	18	716	999	-283	20
Widnes Vikings	28	6	1	21	598	1048	-450	13
Leigh Centurions	28	2	1	25	445	1210	-765	5

3
SUPER LEAGUE PLAY-OFFS 2005

Super League Play-offs

WEEK ONE

Elimination Play-offs

Warrington Wolves had no regrets about signing Andrew Johns at the end of the Super League season, despite their early play-off exit to Hull.

The Wolves' 40-6 home reversal on the Saturday night at the Halliwell Jones Stadium meant that Johns left the club after only three appearances. "He's feeling the same as the other sixteen players, very disappointed to have been beaten by that score in what was a very big game for us," said Wolves coach Paul Cullen. "But bringing him over was worth every penny, every second and every ounce of effort. There are no guarantees in sport. If there were, then every Tom, Dick and Harry could do it. You have to factor in that there are many variables, and some went against us."

The Wolves had achieved their highest home gate of the season when Johns made his club debut against Leeds Rhinos in round 27 of Super League, enabling them to finish the year with an average of 11,003 for the season, the club's first five-figure average gate in the Super League era.

But the Elimination play-off proved a harrowing night for the Wolves, who saw their whole year lost in the blink of a Nathan Blacklock hat-trick. 'Tingha' scored his third right on half-time to give Hull an 18-0 lead which put Warrington virtually out of the game, as for the first fifteen minutes the black and white defence had held out against a wave of Warrington attacks. But the Martin Gleeson-Henry Fa'afili partnership, which had devastated teams down the right edge all season, lost its cohesion in the face of some superb defence by Kirk Yeaman. Toa Kohe-Love burned up the opposite side with regularity, but he never found the same wavelength as wingman Chris Bridge.

Early on Fa'afili dropped a Martin Gleeson pass close to the Hull line when he could have scored; Brent Grose kicked to the corner for Bridge, who touched the ball down on the dead-ball line; Paul Wood made a great break, but Kohe-Love dropped the ball in a crucial position; Lee Briers kicked a '40/20', and the Wolves looked almost certain to score. Then up stepped Richard Whiting, virtually on the Hull line, to intercept a pass from Nathan Wood to Andrew Johns. Whiting charged down the field, and although he was tackled, Hull had gained the momentum for Whiting to put Nathan Blacklock over in the corner for their first try. Hull were leading 4-0 when Warrington could have been 18-0 in front.

Bridge dropped a crucial pass, Martin Gleeson knocked on in a Kirk Yeaman tackle, and then Hull got a fortunate penalty when Tom Saxton was adjudged to have been obstructed by Mark Hilton after he kicked the ball over the defence. The once-again excellent Danny Brough - who was carried from the field a week

Hull's Ewan Dowes looks for a way past Warrington duo Jon Clarke and Logan Swann

before with a suspected broken leg - kicked the penalty, and when Johns dropped a Nathan Wood pass, it was almost a confirmation that this wasn't going to be Warrington's night.

Richard Horne kicked a bomb towards Bridge's corner, the Wolves winger couldn't collect it, and Blacklock nipped in for his second try. Then Fa'afili appeared to touch down a Briers kick to the corner, but the video showed he'd put an arm and foot on the touch-in-goal line, before Blacklock scored his third try, the video showing that Whiting hadn't knocked on in the build-up. Johns scored a superbly taken try after 62 minutes, but Hull had a stranglehold on the game by then.

The seven-try masterclass was the first play-off game Hull had won in five attempts since they broke into the upper echelons of the Super League.

Bradford's Jamie Peacock heads for the tryline, leaving London's Jon Wells trailing in his wake

'There was no happy ending or glowing sunset for the London Broncos to gallop into, but the spirit of the ghost riders in the sky remains with the club. They will re-emerge as Harlequins next season, still battling to make the breakthrough that has eluded them for a quarter of a century. This play-off eliminator was a summary of those 25 years. They began well and promised much until going into a second-half depression. Then they fought back with a spirit that augurs well for the future.' That was *Rugby Leaguer & League Express* reporter Raymond Fletcher's appraisal of London after their 44-22 Elimination Play-off defeat at Odsal on the Friday night.

After struggling to take a four-point interval lead the Bulls stampeded to 36-8 within the hour and finished with eight tries to make it nine victories in a row. A significant reason for Bradford's strong finish to the season had been the return after injury of left-wing duo Shontayne Hape and Lesley Vainikolo. Three more tries brought the New Zealanders' combined total in seven matches to 24, with Vainikolo's two giving him 15 during the post-injury period.

Bradford were forced to make a late change when Paul Deacon withdrew because of sickness and missed his first game of the season. Robbie Paul - strongly linked with a move to Huddersfield Giants - stepped up to regain his scrum-half role and produce the odd reminder of what a great asset he had been to the club over 12 seasons.

Solomon Haumono's second try was worthy of being the last ever by a Bronco. Pouncing on a Bradford error near half way he brushed past two defenders as he pounded 40 metres for a wonderful try. But London were well beaten, lestyn Harris capping another fine game with two smart solo tries and five goals.

Leeds' Marcus Bai takes on St Helens' Lee Gilmour as Jon Wilkin moves in

WEEK TWO

Qualifying Semi-final

Leeds Rhinos took the shortest possible route to Old Trafford and earned themselves a little more rest after their arduous season, as they warded off a sensational Saints comeback inspired by Jamie Lyon in a dramatic game at rain-soaked Knowsley Road.

Leading 19-0 with eleven minutes remaining of a pulsating game played at a punishingly high pace, the Rhinos looked home if not dry, until the brilliant Australian centre finally escaped the defensive shackles of his fellow countryman Chris McKenna.

McKenna had made an important early contribution with a shuddering tackle on Lyon that set up Danny McGuire's opening try. With Danny Ward ploughing over, and Ali Lauitiiti scoring perhaps the try of his life - an 80-metre spectacular - the Rhinos had taken command, with their outstanding skipper Kevin Sinfield adding three conversions and a field goal. But Lyon scored two tries, set up another for wing partner Ian Hardman, and kicked two touch-line conversions before time ran out on Saints' brave revival after Chev Walker brilliantly dealt with a towering Lyon kick with just three seconds left on the clock.

Super League Play-offs

Only then could Tony Smith's men begin to prepare for their second successive Grand Final and enjoy the prospect of another week off. Smith felt that the two-week preparation time the Rhinos earned by virtue of their top-two finish had been beneficial, and that a similar break would be equally advantageous. "The two weeks were fantastic for us, perfect," Smith said.

"It freshened us all up. It has been a very long campaign, week-in and week-out, starting with the World Club Championship and continuing with the Super League and Challenge Cup every week. It has been a long and intense season, especially as the competition as a whole has got a lot closer. I am fearful of burn-out, especially with some of the representative players, and that is something that needs to be considered."

With Keith Senior, according to his coach, in contention for a final place after injury, the Rhinos were looking forward to having a fully-fit squad from which to select for the most important game of the season.

Saints, on the other hand, had seen injuries mount in the closing weeks of the season, as Jason Hooper joined long-term casualties Paul Sculthorpe, Sean Long, Mark Edmondson and Darren Albert in missing the rest of the season, after retiring with a dislocated shoulder midway through the second half.

Elimination Semi-final

"We've fallen flat on our faces." Hull FC coach John Kear summed up perfectly his side's stunning fall from grace. Just five weeks after reaching the heights with their Powergen Challenge Cup final victory they crashed to the widest margin defeat in their long history - a 71-0 Saturday night hammering by the Bulls at Odsal.

Kear refused to make the dismissal of Stephen Kearney for a high tackle on Stuart Fielden after only seven minutes - Bradford were already 6-0 up and in total command when Kearney was sent off - an excuse for the abysmal performance, although he was not happy with referee Steve Ganson's sending-off decision. "I've seen much worse actions put on report and much worse actions escape punishment," said Kear. "But we are not hiding behind that. Steve Ganson didn't miss a tackle, didn't cough the ball up cheaply or kick poorly. The people I feel sorry for are the spectators who came along expecting a pulsating contest and ended up with 13 players playing at the top of their form playing against 12 players playing poorly." Kearney, retiring from playing anyway, was suspended for two games the following Tuesday.

Having done so much right this season, Kear also admitted getting it wrong in leaving out Danny Brough. One of Hull's Cup final heroes, scrum-half Brough was dropped and short-term New Zealand recruit, centre or second row, Sione Faumuina brought in at stand-off.

"The decision was made because we felt we would try to match Bradford's physical presence with a physical presence," Kear explained. "But anybody who looks at the scoreboard can see that it didn't work. I'll hold my hand up and say I got the decision wrong. It's easy to look back with hindsight. There are loads of Monday morning coaches and they tend not to get it wrong. But unfortunately we have to be Thursday afternoon coaches."

This was the Bulls at their rampaging best and out for revenge after their Challenge Cup knockout at Hull. It resulted in a succession of Super League play-off records falling. The 71 points was a team record, while Lesley Vainikolo's four tries and Paul Deacon's ten goals were both individual bests.

Bradford's Lesley Vainikolo celebrates his fourth try against Hull with Michael Withers

Vainikolo scored a Super League record six tries against Hull last month and they were powerless to stop him once again. Centre partner Shontayne Hape who had just signed a new contract to keep him at Odsal until the end of the 2008 season - also got one and since they had returned from injury the pair had totalled 29 tries in eight matches. But the man of the match award went to hooker Ian Henderson, who was irrepressible, especially in the first half when his darting runs had Hull in a tangle and had much to do with their eventual disintegration.

Stuart Fielden completed the try scoring in the 76th minute and Robbie Paul stepped up to kick only the third goal of his Bradford career. A suggestion that it was a 'farewell to Odsal goal' was dismissed by coach Brian Noble, although it was generally accepted Paul was heading for Huddersfield Giants.

WEEK THREE

Final Eliminator

With three out of the previous four play-off games having been decided by margins of more than 20 points, culminating in the Bulls' 71 points margin of victory over Hull, it was hardly surprising that some observers were labelling the 2005 play-off series a let-down.

But on Friday night 7th October St Helens and Bradford produced a classic final eliminator as the Bulls hung on to enter their fifth successive Grand Final.

It was their eleventh victory in a row, and it was appropriate that Shontayne Hape, who played his first game of the season in the first of those victories against Leigh Centurions in July, should score the Bulls' first and last tries. Saints became the first side to finish as minor premiers and not reach the Grand Final and lost their third successive game at Knowsley Road - where they were previously unbeaten in 2005 - for the first time since 1997.

Saints may have lost, but they were still magnificent, despite their big-name absentees. The loss through injury of Paul Sculthorpe, Mark Edmondson, Sean Long, Jason Hooper and Darren Albert left Saints severely depleted at the pivotal time of the season. They had hit their peak in mid-summer, inflicting a 66-4 defeat on the Bulls at Odsal, as part of a 13- match unbeaten league run under Daniel Anderson. The events at the JJB in their penultimate league game, when Saints lost Long and Albert for the season, will ultimately be judged as

St Helens' James Graham stopped by Bradford's Iestyn Harris

defining moments in deciding their destiny. A Saints performance oozing with character, fight and spirit - and no little skill - epitomised by three-try Jon Wilkin's stand-out performance - was of little consolation.

But they could have won the eliminator if they had been a little less frenetic at crucial times in the second half, particularly when Mickey Higham dropped a pass from James Roby that would surely have seen him touching down for the winning try just after Paul Deacon's field goal had put Bradford one point ahead.

After storming to a 12-0 lead after 12 minutes, Paul Johnson getting their second try, the Bulls had to survive a thrilling Saints fightback, with Keiron Cunningham on top form, that could have sunk them. Half-time came at just the right time for Bradford, with Saints' young halfback Scott Moore landing a '40/20' just as the hooter went, as Wilkin's first two tries and three Jamie Lyon goals had put St Helens 14-12 ahead.

The Bulls regrouped, and took the lead again early in the second-half with Jamie Langley's try. Wilkin scored his third try of the game to put Saints ahead, before a high tackle by Nick Fozzard on Adrian Morley allowed Paul Deacon to level the scores and steady Bradford's nerves.

Deacon, with a coolly-struck field goal nine minutes and 48 seconds from time edged the Bulls in front again before Hape sealed it with his second try three minutes from time.

It had been an exhausting game for a side coming from third position to make the Grand Final, but when asked if the Bulls still had enough petrol in the tank for one more game, coach Brian Noble was defiant. "Definitely," he said. "We are not satisfied with this and can still finish strongly."

SUPER LEAGUE GRAND FINAL
Unbeata-Bull

Bradford Bulls became the first club to win the Super League title from third place in the table when they completed a 15-6 victory over Leeds Rhinos at Old Trafford.

"To complete a season on a twelve-match winning run says a lot about the character and desire of these players," said coach Brian Noble. "They decided to close the door on everyone else and found a way to win every week. They did it the hard way and deserve all the plaudits you can give them. The spirit in this team is second to none, better than anything else I have experienced before.

"From the position we were in we couldn't finish top of the league ladder, but we knew that if everyone was fit and we could get ourselves into contention, and into the play-offs, then we had a chance, because this is a very special team.

"It was another scruffy-type game, but certain individuals stood up, as they have done every week. It wasn't pretty at times, but you can't always win trophies by playing open, off-the-cuff stuff, you have to be prepared to roll your sleeves up and tough it out."

Noble rubbished reports that he had seriously considered giving up as Bulls coach in mid-season after the home drubbing by St Helens.

"There have been one or two tough times during the season, but at no stage have I considered quitting," he said. "We had players out because of injury, and once the likes of Les and Shontayne came back I always felt we could turn things around."

When the chips were down Noble's big-game players came up trumps. Lesley Vainikolo, Shontayne Hape and Paul Johnson made timely returns from injury to help shape what became an irresistible force in the closing months of the campaign as the Bulls juggernaut gathered force.

The late-season acquisition of Adrian Morley, heart-breaking though it may have been to previously ever-present Andy Lynch, added steel to the pack and gave invaluable support to captain Jamie Peacock and Stuart Fielden, while the signing of hooker Ian Henderson from Parramatta was a masterstroke.

Rhinos coach Tony Smith was left to reflect on losing two major finals in the course of less than two months. While the Challenge Cup Final could have gone either way right up to the hooter, this game gradually drifted away from his side in the second half, as Leeds lost their cohesion and threat in attack and had no answer to the Bulls' magnificently resolute defence.

Though Danny McGuire tried everything he knew, Rob Burrow was busy in attack, and fullback Richard Mathers put in another top performance, the Rhinos failed to recreate the magnificent support play and offloading game they displayed for much of the season, and simply ran out of ideas about how to break down an effective Bulls rearguard.

The understandable decision to risk the fitness of key strike player Keith Senior at Cardiff ultimately backfired on the Rhinos twice. Not only did it contribute to their Cup Final defeat, but it put back Senior's recovery and left Leeds short of a major attacking weapon in the most important game of the season. A thigh injury to Ryan Bailey also reduced their pack options, as virtually every Leeds forward was outplayed on the night by his opposite number.

The teams made a spectacular entrance down a red carpet onto the magnificent Old Trafford stage in front of another colourful, expectant sell-out crowd on a mild, dry and still evening.

The Bulls set the agenda from the start, Paul Deacon's deep kick-off towards the old scoreboard end forcing a handling error out of Willie Poching, who knocked on in the shadow of his own posts. Mark Calderwood, who got precious few opportunities on his final Rhinos appearance, then conceded the first goal-line drop-out from Deacon's follow-up kick.

The Rhinos survived the initial onslaught, Brad Meyers being held up in a massed tackle involving Mathers and Chev Walker as the Bulls sought the early breakthrough. They lost Johnson after his tackle on Mathers went wrong, but happily the Bulls second-rower was soon fit to resume.

Rhinos captain Kevin Sinfield hoisted a testing kick in his side's first attacking threat, forcing Michael Withers to concede a drop-out after McGuire's sharp follow-up tackle. A Sinfield kick forced Deacon to concede another, but a Gareth Ellis knock-on released the pressure valve on the Bulls.

Leon Pryce conceded the first penalty of the evening for interference on Sinfield after Mathers made an outstanding kick return from Deacon. Bailey charged for the line, and McGuire then put through a testing kick, but Vainikolo set the standard for an immaculate personal display by safely gathering. Andrew Dunemann, in his last Leeds game, was a vital steadying influence in the early stages as the sparring continued.

Barrie McDermott's entry raised the intensity a notch or two, and was greeted with huge cheers by the Rhinos fans. Twice more Vainikolo dealt safely with McGuire's testing kicks as the Bulls stood firm.

Pryce won the Bulls' first penalty after Dunemann was pinged for holding down, and the stalemate was broken seconds later when McDermott's high tackle on Morley left Deacon with a straightforward 21-metre penalty midway through the first half.

Marcus Bai and Michael Withers contest a high ball as Iestyn Harris and Lee Radford look on

93

Super League Grand Final

But when the Bulls lost possession from the re-start the Rhinos took full advantage, Dunemann evading Morley's challenge to stab through a close range kick from dummy-half, and McGuire triumphantly swallow-diving on the loose ball over the Bulls line. Sinfield failed with the conversion attempt from wide out on the left.

The Bulls responded with a triple substitution and stepped up the pressure. Dunemann twice conceded penalties, and from the second Deacon levelled the scores from in front of the posts for a ball-stripping offence on Henderson.

The Bulls were growing in self-belief, and took advantage after Ali Lauitiiti put down McGuire's pass 20-metres from his own line. Iestyn Harris, growing in influence, was held up on the right before supplying a long pass that hit the predatory Pryce at pace. Pryce, revelling in his roaming role from the wing in his last Bulls appearance, cut between Walker and Sinfield from 20 metres after dummying a pass outside, and went over for the Bulls' first try that Deacon, unusually, was unable to convert.

Morley, one eye blackened from the brutal skirmishes in the forwards, then conceded a 33rd-minute penalty in possession for leading with the elbow on McDermott, and Sinfield's angled 15-metre kick left the Rhinos two points adrift.

But the Bulls went closest to another try before the break as Ben Harris was held up short by Chris McKenna's excellent close-range tackle, while attacking kicks by Pryce and Deacon lacked the necessary accuracy to turn possession into points.

The intense forward-dominated style of the first half continued on the resumption with little sign of a let-up. Robbie Paul's offload to Michael Withers 40 metres out almost created something, but was deemed forward. McGuire's chip was then well taken by Pryce, and the livewire Rhinos' stand-off was then denied by a sharp Ben Harris tackle 30 metres out after Jamie Jones-Buchanan's offload created an opportunity.

There followed two contentious video referee's decisions that ultimately shaped the contest. After more than two minutes' deliberation Hape had claims for a 45th-minute try denied after Vainikolo was ruled to have impeded the Rhinos' defence after he competed with Calderwood and Mathers for Deacon's hoisted kick.

In the 50th minute Fielden lost possession 25 metres out in a massed tackle, and Leeds almost took advantage. Dunemann's clever pass gave Walker

ENGAGE SUPER LEAGUE GRAND FINAL

Saturday 15th October 2005

BRADFORD BULLS 15 LEEDS RHINOS 6

BULLS: 6 Michael Withers; 3 Leon Pryce; 13 Ben Harris; 4 Shontayne Hape; 5 Lesley Vainikolo; 18 Iestyn Harris; 7 Paul Deacon; 12 Jamie Peacock (C); 9 Ian Henderson; 29 Stuart Fielden; 16 Paul Johnson; 10 Brad Meyers; 11 Lee Radford. Subs (all used): 24 Adrian Morley for Johnson (5); 19 Jamie Langley for Peacock (24); 8 Joe Vagana for Fielden (24); Johnson for Radford (24); 1 Robbie Paul for Henderson (31); Peacock for Vagana (45); Fielden for Morley (49); Henderson for Paul (54); Radford for Meyers (60); Morley for Peacock (62); Meyers for Langley (73); Peacock for Johnson (74). **Tries:** L Pryce (29), Vainikolo (53); **Goals:** Deacon 3/5; **Field goal:** I Harris.
RHINOS: 1 Richard Mathers; 2 Mark Calderwood; 3 Chev Walker; 12 Chris McKenna; 5 Marcus Bai; 6 Danny McGuire; 7 Rob Burrow; 8 Ryan Bailey; 14 Andrew Dunemann; 15 Danny Ward; 20 Gareth Ellis; 16 Willie Poching; 13 Kevin Sinfield (C). Subs (all used): 10 Barrie McDermott for Ward (17); 11 Ali Lauitiiti for Poching (21); 18 Jamie Jones-Buchanan for Bailey (31); Ward for McDermott (34); 9 Matt Diskin for Ellis (48); Poching for Lauitiiti (48); McDermott for Ward (54); Ellis for Poching (61); Lauitiiti for McDermott (61); Poching for Dunemann (65); Ward for Jones-Buchanan (68); Dunemann for Ellis (71). **Try:** McGuire (22); **Goals:** Sinfield 1/2.
Rugby Leaguer & League Express Men of the Match: *Bulls:* Leon Pryce; *Rhinos:* Danny McGuire.
Penalty count: 6-8; **Half-time:** 8-6;
Referee: Ashley Klein (Keighley);
Attendance: 65,537 *(at Old Trafford, Manchester).*

an opportunity close to the line. But as Withers came in with a last-ditch tackle, he caused the Rhinos' centre to momentarily lose possession before seeming to regain control as he tried to ground the ball one-handed over the whitewash. Another marginal decision went against the attacking team.

Two minutes later came the decisive try, Deacon's huge kick forcing Marcus Bai to concede a goal-line drop-out. In the follow-up attack, Jamie Langley went close after a powerful surge, and Vainikolo, after dummying to pass to the left, forced his way through the attempted tackles of three Leeds defenders to notch his side's second try. Deacon converted, and almost immediately reinforced the Bulls' dominance with a long raking kick to touch.

Many of the Leeds attacks now lacked conviction, and they failed to profit from a loose Fielden offload when Walker kicked the ball dead. Withers then made an important tackle on Calderwood, after Ellis and Burrow sparked a breakaway from deep, only for Dunemann to ruin the momentum of the attack with a costly knock-on.

Lauitiiti's flailing arm then conceded a 65th-minute penalty for a high tackle on the rampaging Morley, but Deacon hit the 30-metre attempt wide of the upright. Johnson then went close, and Vainikolo was held up just short after Henderson's clever inside pass.

The Rhinos' last real chance was gone after Sinfield's long pass was seized upon by Hape with nine minutes remaining, and the Bulls broke away for Iestyn Harris to set the seal on their hard-earned triumph with a coolly-struck field goal with five minutes to go. When Dunemann knocked on a pass with 40 seconds left on the clock, the Bulls' celebrations could finally begin.

Pryce won the Harry Sunderland Trophy and looked one of the few backs capable of making a clean break. Vainikolo, Withers, Morley and Langley were other stand-out Bulls performers in what was a terrific team effort. McGuire, Mathers, Burrow and Dunemann were Leeds' best.

While the Bulls' victory was well deserved, for the neutral supporter this was perhaps the least memorable of the eight Grand Finals of the summer era.

Jamie Peacock bursts past Matt Diskin and Danny Ward

MAN OF STEEL AWARD WINNERS

MAN OF STEEL
Jamie Lyon (St Helens)

PLAYERS' PLAYER OF THE YEAR
Jamie Lyon (St Helens)

COACH OF THE YEAR
Tony Smith (Leeds Rhinos)

YOUNG PLAYER OF THE YEAR
Richard Whiting (Hull FC)

REFEREE OF THE YEAR
Ashley Klein

TOP TRY SCORER
Mark Calderwood (Leeds Rhinos)
for scoring 27 regular season tries

METRE MAKER
Terry O'Connor (Widnes Vikings)
for making 4250 regular season metres

HIT MAN
Malcolm Alker (Salford City Reds)
for making 938 regular season tackles

ENGAGE SUPER LEAGUE
DREAM TEAM 2005
1 Paul Wellens (St Helens)
2 Mark Calderwood (Leeds Rhinos)
3 Jamie Lyon (St Helens)
4 Martin Gleeson (Warrington Wolves)
5 Darren Albert (St Helens)
6 Paul Cooke (Hull FC)
7 Rob Burrow (Leeds Rhinos)
8 Jamie Thackray (Hull FC)
9 Keiron Cunningham (St Helens)
10 Paul Anderson (St Helens)
11 Jamie Peacock (Bradford Bulls)
12 Ali Lauitiiti (Leeds Rhinos)
13 Kevin Sinfield (Leeds Rhinos)

The 2005 Super League Dream Team

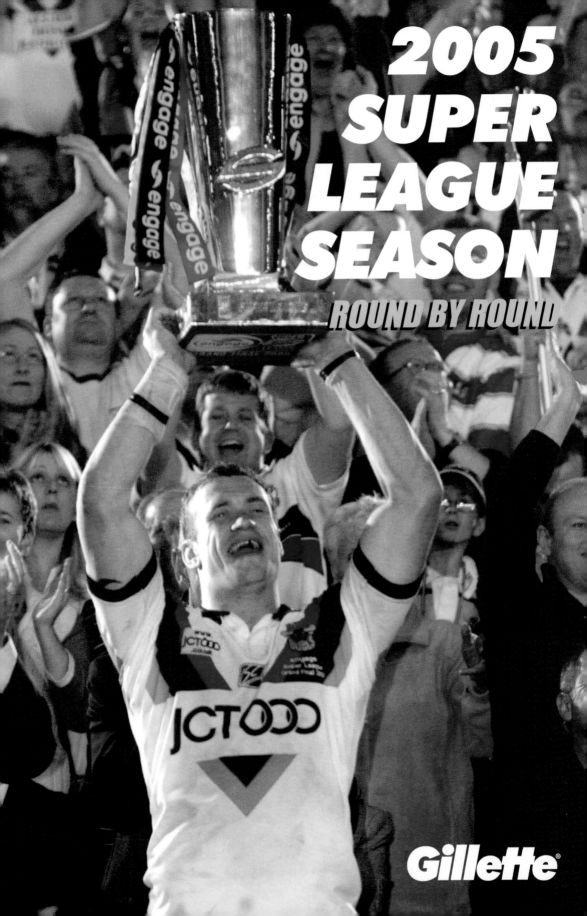

2005 SUPER LEAGUE SEASON

ROUND BY ROUND

Gillette®

LEFT: Leigh's John Duffy passes to Neil Turley as the Centurions make their Super League bow in defeat against Huddersfield

ABOVE: Bradford's Lesley Vainikolo looks on as Jamie Rooney dives over to score during Wakefield's flying start at Odsal

ROUND 4

ROUND 1

RIGHT: Ryan Bailey and Jamie-Jones Buchanan halt Kirk Yeaman as Hull and Leeds kick off Super League X

ABOVE: James Roby brought down by Warrington's Warren Stevens as St Helens score three late tries to snatch victory

ROUND 2

LEFT: Leeds captain Kevin Sinfield leaves Willie Talau grounded as the Rhinos race past St Helens

ROUND 3

ABOVE: London's Anthony Armour is mobbed by teammates after scoring during the Broncos' mauling of Wakefield

RIGHT: London's Lee Hopkins looks for support during the Broncos' home win over Wigan

ABOVE: Brent Grose halted by Stuart Jones and Jim Gannon as Warrington see off Huddersfield in a low-scoring encounter

ROUND 5

ROUND 6

ROUND 7

BELOW: Brad Meyers can't stop Chev Walker scoring as Leeds inflict a big Easter defeat on Bradford at Odsal

RIGHT: Kris Radlinski celebrates a try with Terry Newton as Wigan edge out St Helens in front of a Super League regular season record crowd

RIGHT: Leigh's Steve Maden collared by London's Joe Mbu as the Centurions get their first Super League win

ROUND 8

ABOVE: Wakefield's David March beats Leeds trio Danny McGuire, Gareth Ellis and Richard Mathers to score as the Wildcats stun the Rhinos

CHALLENGE CUP ROUND 4

ABOVE: Stephen Kearney and Ewan Dowes put in a big hit on Wakefield's Michael Korkidas as Hull set off on the Cardiff trail

ABOVE: Bradford's Lee Radford gets to grips with Warrington's Henry Fa'afili as the Wolves just hold off a Bulls comeback

ROUND 9

ROUND 10

BELOW: Bradford's Lesley Vainikolo crosses to score as the Bulls defeat Huddersfield

ROUND 11

LEFT: St Helens' Jason Hooper goes past Warrington's Brent Grose as the Saints snatch another last-gasp win over the Wolves

ROUND 12

RIGHT: Warrington duo Danny Lima and Mark Hilton ground Richard Horne during the Wolves' narrow win against Hull

LEFT: Leigh skipper Darren Fleary takes on Wakefield's Sam Obst as the Centurions thrash the Wildcats

ROUND 14

ABOVE: Huddersfield's Chris Thorman gets a pass away during the Giants' memorable away win at Wigan

BELOW: Warrington's Nathan Wood flings a pass over the head of Wigan's Brian Carney as the Wolves edge a thriller

CHALLENGE CUP ROUND 5

BELOW: Motu Tony goes in under the posts as Hull see off Bradford at the KC Stadium

ROUND 13

ABOVE: Paul Sculthorpe congratulates Vinnie Anderson on scoring as Daniel Anderson's reign as St Helens coach begins with victory over Leeds

ROUND 15

ROUND 17

RIGHT: Salford's Stuart Littler halted by Lee Gilmour and Paul Anderson as the City Reds run St Helens close

ABOVE: Widnes' Terry O'Connor tackled by Huddersfield's Stuart Jones as the Vikings defeat the Giants

ROUND 16

ROUND 20

RIGHT: Jon Wilkin dives over during St Helens' big win over twelve-man Bradford at Odsal

ROUND 18

BELOW: Leeds' Barrie McDermott crashes through Stephen Wild and Kevin Brown to score during the Rhinos' 70-0 mauling of Wigan

LEFT: Bradford's Karl Pryce and Widnes' Andrew Emelio compete for a high ball as the Bulls and Vikings fight out a controversial draw

CHALLENGE CUP QUARTER FINALS

RIGHT: Stephen Wild can't stop Paul Wellens from scoring as St Helens inflict a record 75-0 defeat on bitter rivals Wigan

LEFT: Wakefield's Michael Korkidas tackled by Bradford's Paul Johnson as the Wildcats beat the Bulls again

ROUND 19

RIGHT: Salford's Chris Charles celebrates scoring with Stuart Littler and Andy Coley as the City Reds down Huddersfield

ROUND 21

RIGHT: Wakefield's Jamie Field on the charge as the Wildcats inflict a major blow on Widnes' survival hopes

LEFT: Shontayne Hape makes his Bradford comeback as the Bulls start their remarkable end of season winning run with victory over Leigh

RIGHT: Ewan Dowes looks to escape the clutches of St Helens' Nick Fozzard as Hull turn in a stunning semi-final performance

LEFT: Hull celebrate reaching the Challenge Cup Final

BELOW: Leeds' Mark Calderwood goes in at the corner as the Rhinos book their Challenge Cup Final place with a hard-fought victory over Toulouse

CHALLENGE CUP SEMI-FINALS

ABOVE: Toulouse take the acclaim of the crowd at the end of their memorable Challenge Cup campaign

BELOW: Hull's Paul King outnumbered by the London defence as the Broncos edge a close one

ROUND 23

BELOW: Leeds' Danny McGuire weaves past Bradford's Michael Withers as the Bulls enjoy a big defeat of the Rhinos

ABOVE: Leeds' Chev Walker tries to escape from Mark Gleeson as the Rhinos turn on the style against Warrington

ROUND 22

BELOW: Wigan's Bob Beswick stretches out to score as the Warriors defeat Widnes

ROUND 24

ROUND 25

CLOCKWISE, FROM TOP:

Richard Horne looks for support as Ryan Bailey moves in

Gareth Raynor, Nathan Blacklock and Mark Calderwood chase a loose ball

Paul Cooke shows his jubilation at scoring the winning try

Richard Horne, flanked by Nathan Blacklock and Motu Tony, lifts the Challenge Cup

ROUND 27

ABOVE: Andrew Johns gets a pass away during a dream debut as Warrington defeat Leeds

ABOVE: Adrian Morley in action during his Bradford debut as the Bulls power past Huddersfield

RIGHT: Lesley Vainikolo on the rampage as he sets new Super League tries in a match record.

ROUND 26

RIGHT: Brian Carney touches down during his farewell Wigan appearance as the Warriors defeat Huddersfield

ROUND 28

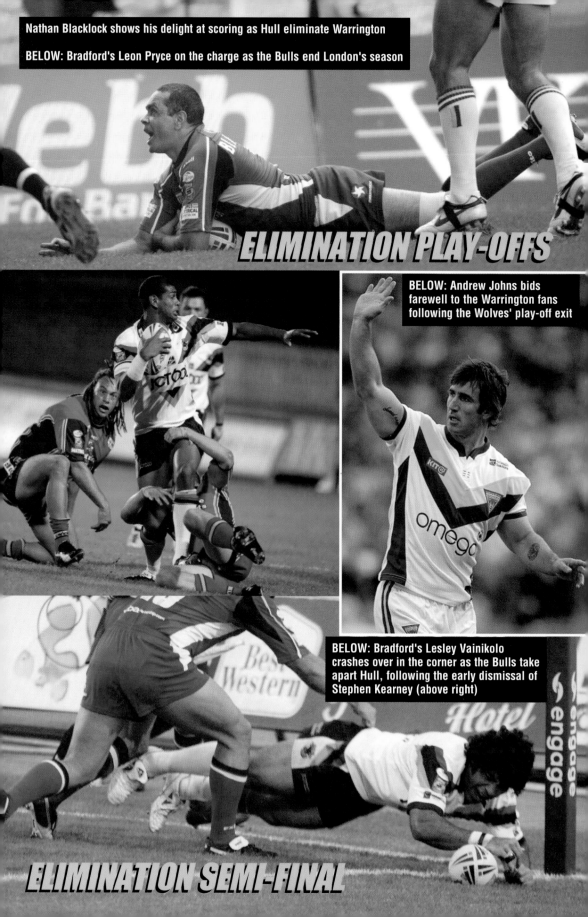

Nathan Blacklock shows his delight at scoring as Hull eliminate Warrington

BELOW: Bradford's Leon Pryce on the charge as the Bulls end London's season

ELIMINATION PLAY-OFFS

BELOW: Andrew Johns bids farewell to the Warrington fans following the Wolves' play-off exit

BELOW: Bradford's Lesley Vainikolo crashes over in the corner as the Bulls take apart Hull, following the early dismissal of Stephen Kearney (above right)

ELIMINATION SEMI-FINAL

QUALIFYING SEMI-FINAL

ABOVE: Leeds' Ali Lauitiiti races away from St Helens' Paul Wellens to score as the Rhinos become the first side to reach the 2005 Grand Final

BELOW: Bradford's Shontayne Hape dives over to score the winning try against St Helens as the Bulls book their fifth successive Grand Final appearance

FINAL ELIMINATOR

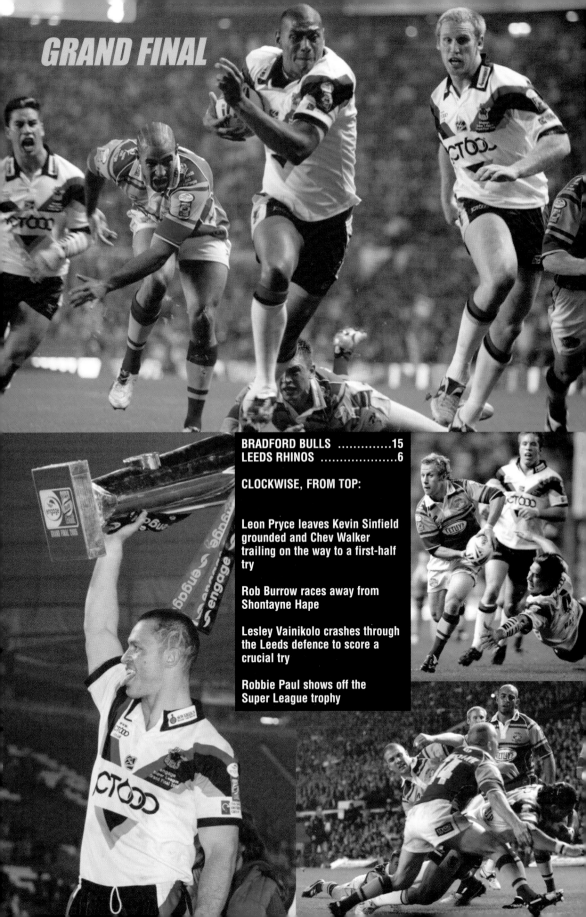

GRAND FINAL

BRADFORD BULLS 15
LEEDS RHINOS 6

CLOCKWISE, FROM TOP:

Leon Pryce leaves Kevin Sinfield grounded and Chev Walker trailing on the way to a first-half try

Rob Burrow races away from Shontayne Hape

Lesley Vainikolo crashes through the Leeds defence to score a crucial try

Robbie Paul shows off the Super League trophy

4
NATIONAL LEAGUE 2005

NATIONAL LEAGUE ONE SEASON
History makers

CASTLEFORD TIGERS' first ever stint outside the top flight since their entry into the RFL in 1926 ended up being a short one, as they made an immediate return to Super League after a colourful campaign.

Brad Davis

Red hot favourites to win the NL1 Grand Final at the beginning of the season, the Tigers set off at a terrific pace, before a stumble mid-season, which included losing a gripping Northern Rail Cup Final against Hull KR at Blackpool.

But despite missing out to Whitehaven for the Minor Premiership, then going down at the Recreation Ground in the Qualifying semi-final, Cas recovered sufficiently to record a stunning Grand Final win when it mattered most. With Castleford legend Brad Davis producing the kind of performance that dreams are made of in his final outing as a professional player, the Tigers totally outplayed Haven in a comprehensive 36-8 win at the Halton Stadium.

It provided a personal triumph for Australian coach Dave Woods, who was plagued by speculation surrounding his future throughout the season, and was subsequently not handed a new contract despite earning promotion.

But Woods could reflect on a successful year in which he had several stand-out players, including NL1 Dream Team members Andy Kain, Steve Crouch and Waine Pryce. Stand-off Kain was also crowned NL1 Young Player of the Year, while Pryce was the competition's top try-scorer. Captain and hooker/scrum half Andrew Henderson was among the most consistent performers in NL1, while Michael Platt, Michael Shenton and Craig Huby were the pick of a tremendous crop of rising young stars.

Andrew
Henderson

Despite their Grand Final heartache, the 2005 season will forever go down in **WHITEHAVEN's** history. For the first time in their 57-year existence, Haven lifted a trophy when they were crowned League Leaders by winning at Rochdale on the final day of the NL1 season.

It was a magnificent achievement for their coach Steve McCormack and his committed squad of players, with their only real disappointment being that they failed to do themselves justice against Castleford at Widnes. McCormack was crowned NL1 Coach of the Year for the second season running, though at the end of the season, he would end his three-year

Gary
Broadbent

stint in Cumbria to join Widnes Vikings, and be replaced by St Helens assistant Dave Rotheram.

He leaves behind a remarkable legacy, and a squad packed with players that did their town and club proud during the 2005 campaign. None were better than fullback Gary Broadbent, whose unstinting efforts earned him a nomination for the NL1 Player of the Year prize.

He was joined in the competition's Dream Team by free-scoring threequarters Craig Calvert and Mick Nanyn, while hooker Carl Sice and prop David Fatialofa were among those unlucky to miss out. Australian scrum-half Joel Penny also did an admirable job of filling the sizeable boots of Sam Obst, while fellow countryman Ryan Tandy had a storming end to the season after rejoining the club from Barrow. The hope now for Haven was that they could kick onto the next level and realise their Super League dream.

Top-flight ambitions have been long held and well documented for **HULL KINGSTON ROVERS** in recent years, and midway through the 2005 season, they looked perfectly placed to make those dreams reality. After securing a thrilling 19-18 Northern Rail Cup Final win over Castleford, the Robins then thrashed the Tigers in the league at Craven Park and were many people's favourites to go all the way.

But as has so often been the case for Rovers in recent times, they tripped up in the closing stages of the campaign, and their season ended on an ignominious note when they were soundly beaten at home by Halifax in the play-offs.

That constituted a considerable disappointment for young coach Justin Morgan, who joined the club in July following the departure of Harvey Howard for reasons that never came fully to light. Morgan has since overseen an eye-catching close-season

Andy Raleigh

recruitment drive that will see the Robins start the 2006 season as one of the favourites for promotion.

Rovers had two of NL1's outstanding players in the shape of halfback James Webster and second-rower Andy Raleigh, who was crowned the competition's Player of the Year. Australian Webster also had a lengthy and impressive spell as caretaker-coach which included being in charge for the NRC Final.

Those two were joined in the NL1 Dream Team by blockbusting prop Makali Aizue for the second year running, and he was part of a formidable set of front-rowers in which David Tangata-Toa and James Garmston also shone. With hooker Andy Ellis earning a nomination for the Young Player of the Year, Hull KR weren't short of impressive individuals. The target for Morgan was to mould them into a Grand Final-winning unit.

HALIFAX had only survived in NL1 by the skin of their teeth and a blade of grass in 2004 - but went on to make significant progress under coach Anthony Farrell. A league campaign that was plagued by injuries and inconsistencies ended on a high note when they secured fourth place on the final day of the season - but it was in the play-offs when they really impressed.

A total demolition of Doncaster at the Shay was followed by a stunning win at Hull KR, and Fax were then within a whisker of toppling Castleford for a place in the Grand Final. They fell just short - but there was still much to be positive about for former prop Farrell. Australian hooker Ben Fisher proved one of the

117

shrewdest captures of the season, and earned a Dream Team place alongside Australian loose forward Pat Weisner, who rarely allowed his standards to slip.

Rikki Sheriffe

With winger Rikki Sheriffe and scrum-half Ben Black running in 54 tries between them, Fax were not short of firepower, and also had one of the most promising young players outside the top flight in the shape of threequarter James Haley. Back-rower Damian Ball provided a massive late season boost, while forwards Dave Larder and Ryan McDonald gave terrific support.

Unfortunately for Fax, several of those players left for pastures new at the end of the season - but the former Super League club still appears to be on the rise after sorting out the financial legacies of past regimes.

DONCASTER DRAGONS enjoyed mixed fortunes in 2005 - finishing fifth in the league without ever fully realising the potential that their squad undoubtedly had.

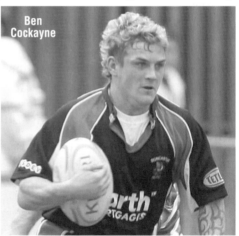

Ben Cockayne

On their day, the Dragons - under the game's longest serving coach St John Ellis - could be a match for anyone in the division.

But they were too inconsistent, and the campaign finished on a major low with a heavy play-off defeat at Halifax.

Ellis unearthed one of the best amateur signings in recent memory in Eastmoor halfback-turned-fullback Ben Cockayne, who narrowly missed out on a Dream Team place before switching close season to Hull KR.

Forwards Craig Lawton and Peter Green were models of consistency in the second row, while three-quarter Craig Farrell and stand-off Graham Holroyd also had their moments.

The year ended with a major overhaul at the club, with chairman John Wright overseeing a change of name and club colours, ahead of the now Doncaster Lakers' move to a new stadium for the 2007 season.

Wright was hopeful that the amendments will help the club earn a Super League franchise in 2009.

After surviving relegation against the odds in 2004, **ROCHDALE HORNETS** move on to finish sixth and make the play-offs, taking the impressive scalps of Castleford, Hull KR and Halifax (twice) along the way. But hopes of progressing further were ended emphatically in the play-offs at Hull KR, with the loss of three scrum-halves through injury - including player-coach Bobbie Goulding - proving too much to overcome.

Chris Giles

Still, Goulding's achievements earned him a second consecutive Coach of the Year nomination, and he had plenty of eye-catching performers in his squad. Former Widnes threequarter Chris Giles excelled when switched to fullback, while forwards Gareth Price and Lee Doran both had mighty seasons. Goulding also rolled back the clock on a handful of occasions, including a virtuoso display in Castleford's first league defeat of the season, a match that effectively ended his year when he suffered a torn bicep.

But another year of progression for the club was tinged with sadness by the deaths of long-serving directors Ray Taylor and Paul Reynolds. The pair had been instrumental in turning the club around at the end of 2003, and will be greatly missed at Spotland.

OLDHAM's achievement in avoiding relegation ranks alongside those of many of the teams above them, after a hugely challenging campaign for the Roughyeds. Coach Gary Mercer was well behind his rivals in terms of recruitment when he took over before the start of the season, and a poor Northern Rail Cup campaign appeared to signal a fall from grace for a club that was one game away from Super League just four years earlier.

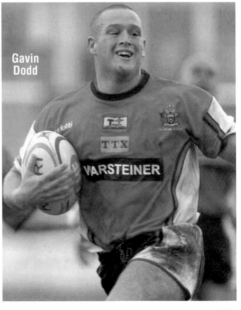
Gavin Dodd

When details of an unpaid tax bill of £180,000 emerged, the club looked as though it might not last until the end of the season. But directors Chris Hamilton and Sean Whitehead, after what seemed like endless meetings, finally agreed a deal to repay the Inland Revenue, and Mercer began to turn matters around on the field to the extent that they were still in with a chance of the play-offs until the closing weekends.

They eventually missed out, but not through a lack of effort from the likes of excellent New Zealand scrum-half Marty Turner, fullback Gavin Dodd, and prop Ricky Bibey. Mercer turned down the offer of a new contract at the end of the year and has since been replaced by former Halifax coach John Pendlebury.

BATLEY BULLDOGS' rollercoaster of a season ended with a dramatic 28-26 NL1 Qualifying Final win over local rivals Dewsbury, preserving their NL1 status. Up until then, the Bulldogs had been a model of inconsistency, mixing performances of promise with defeats to clubs they feel they should have beaten.

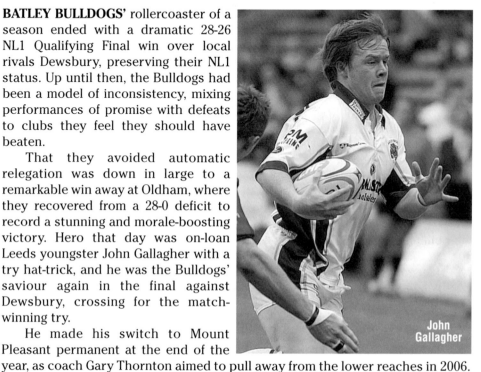

John Gallagher

That they avoided automatic relegation was down in large to a remarkable win away at Oldham, where they recovered from a 28-0 deficit to record a stunning and morale-boosting victory. Hero that day was on-loan Leeds youngster John Gallagher with a try hat-trick, and he was the Bulldogs' saviour again in the final against Dewsbury, crossing for the match-winning try.

He made his switch to Mount Pleasant permanent at the end of the year, as coach Gary Thornton aimed to pull away from the lower reaches in 2006.

Thornton's captain and on-field leader, Barry Eaton, had another top season at scrum-half, along with Batley's other key players including centre Iain Marsh, Aussie packman Dane Morgan, and livewire hooker Kris Lythe, who had an excellent game in that crucial win over the Rams. Late-season additions Stephen Jones and Darren Robinson also played important roles in the run-in.

FEATHERSTONE ROVERS' slide to the lowest tier of the professional game was a painful one for their supporters, who saw their team fall from being one match from the 2004 Grand Final to relegation to NL2. Coach Gary Price left the club mid-season amid accusations that his family were abused in the Northern Rail Cup defeat at Swinton, and he was later replaced by Rovers' 1983 Wembley hero David Hobbs.

Price - a Coach of the Year nominee in 2004 - suffered from an injury hoodoo, worse than anybody else in the competition, with key loose forward Richard Blakeway just one of a host of stars to pick up season-ending problems. That put Rovers up against it almost from the off, and though Hobbs oversaw an improvement in performance late in the campaign, it was not enough to save this proud old club.

The progress that Featherstone made off the field in recent years made the decline harder to stomach, though they were keen to bounce back at the first attempt.

Aussie halfback Josh Weeden showed flashes of brilliance before his campaign was ended by an horrific broken ankle, as did Liam Finn, while fullbacks Nathan Batty and Craig Moss had their moments. Prop Stuart Dickens returned to the club from Salford and put in some storming performances as Rovers sought to stave off the drop. But they fell short on the final day of the season, and Rovers must now rebuild.

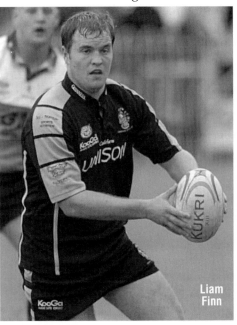

Liam Finn

BARROW RAIDERS looked relegation candidates from day one, and lived up to their billing by winning just one league game all season. That victory, at home to Rochdale, raised early hopes of survival, but the departure of their two most experienced players, Simon Knox and later Andy Fisher, hit them hard.

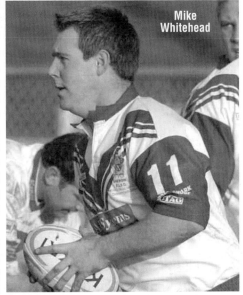

Mike Whitehead

Coach Peter Roe admitted that the Raiders had failed to recruit a big enough squad to compete, and he was struggling to find 17 fit players on a regular basis as injuries hit home. Still, the well-liked Roe was considered to be doing a good enough job to be handed a new contract towards the end of the season, before his full-time position was made redundant due to financial problems at the club. He has since been replaced by local coach Paul Crarey, but the Raiders' main focus towards the end of the year was ensuring their immediate future.

The Raiders' best performers on the field in 2005 included Australian fullback Joel Osborn, and hard-working pack members Mike Whitehead and Paul Wilcock. French threequarter Freddie Zitter and local hero Darren Holt also troubled opposition teams on a regular basis, but as a collective, Barrow fell below their NL1 peers.

NATIONAL LEAGUE TWO SEASON
Boogie Knights

YORK CITY KNIGHTS had encountered desperate disappointment by losing out on promotion in the most heart-breaking of circumstances in 2004 - but more than made up for it the following year. Led by new coach Mick Cook, the Knights secured the NL2 title and automatic promotion with three games to spare, after a season of outstanding consistency. Such was their impact, that five Knights were named in the NL2 Dream Team and former Sheffield forward Cook was crowned Coach of the Year.

York's shining quartet were the competition's leading try-scorer, Peter Fox, centres Dan Potter and Neil Law, prop Adam Sullivan, and loose forward Lee Patterson, who was also nominated for the Player of the Year prize. The likes of hooker Jim Elston, fullback Matt Blaymire and second-rower John Smith also provided considerable contributions in a memorable campaign.

With the visionary club continuing to make huge strides off the field and regularly attracting bumper attendances, the fledgling club looked set to be a real asset to National League One the following season.

Dan Potter

Certainly, under Cook, chairman Roger Dixon and chief executive John Guilford, they looked far better equipped to compete than their promotion predecessors Keighley and Barrow.

Adam
Sullivan

A head-turning close-season recruitment drive saw **DEWSBURY RAMS** installed as many people's favourites to earn promotion, but Andy Kelly's side fell just short. Losing home and away to both eventual champions York and the less successful Sheffield all but ruled out their title hopes, and though they recovered to make the NL1 Qualifying Final, defeat against local rivals Batley meant they would be back in NL2 in 2006.

Still, there was so much to be positive about for a club that finished second bottom of the whole pile just a year earlier. Recruiting the likes of Ryan Sheridan, Francis Maloney, Warren Jowitt, Darren Rogers and Richard Chapman gave the Rams a massive boost, with all of those staying for the following year.

Surprisingly, Jowitt was the only

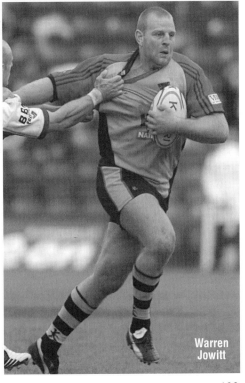

Warren
Jowitt

one to make the Dream Team, though promising fullback Ian Preece was nominated for the Young Player award. Chris Hall, Alex Bretherton and Paul Hicks were among other players to impress at various times, and the Rams appeared well placed to continue their revival.

The popular Kelly was relishing the task following his battle against renal cancer in the later stages of the season, news that brought perspective to Dewsbury's disappointing defeat to Batley at the Halton Stadium.

John Tuimaualuga

WORKINGTON TOWN's recent resurgence continued in 2005, though hopes of earning promotion were dashed with a play-off defeat at Dewsbury. Coach Ged Stokes, developing into a local hero in West Cumbria, had to battle against injury problems for much of the campaign, but Town still finished third, thanks in large to their excellent Kiwi contingent.

Second-rower or prop John Tuimualuga was named NL2 Player of the Year, while hooker Jonny Limmer was again outstanding and fullback Lusi Sione among the most dangerous runners of the ball outside Super League. With halfbacks Tane Manihera and Lee Kiddie providing guidance in the middle of the field, Town were a tough side to beat, especially at their Derwent Park home, where they went undefeated.

And the off-field work that the club had put so much time into in recent seasons was recognised when Town were awarded the National League Community Programme of the Year prize. With talk of a new stadium on the horizon, the future appeared rosy for Workington. But the key to their future could be their request to have the overseas quota extended for Cumbrian clubs, allowing them to import more Kiwis that can oversee their impressive development schemes, as well as providing quality on the field on Sunday afternoons.

Phil Joseph

SWINTON LIONS had some of National League Two's outstanding performers in their ranks. Hooker or loose forward Phil Joseph won the Young Player of the Year award, and was joined in the NL2 Dream Team by rock-solid fullback Wayne English, powerful winger Marlon Billy, and free-scoring stand off Lee Marsh, who broke the club's points-in-a-season record. With experienced scrum-half Ian Watson central to most things the Lions did well, and prop or second-rower Danny Heaton a real handful for opposition defences, Swinton were a match for any side on their day.

But their promotion hopes were dashed by a one-point play-off defeat at Workington Town. A mini mid-season slump when they lost four out of five games also dented aspirations of finishing higher than fourth.

Still, the Lions and young coach Paul Kidd made genuine progress on their 2004 season - the target now will be continuing that ascent. Several key players have left the Lions during the close season, but with the likes of Watson, English and Billy committing their futures to the club, they could again be contenders the next term.

HUNSLET HAWKS exceeded most people's expectations by finishing fifth, level on points with Swinton. Roy Sampson was nominated for the Coach of the Year after guiding the unfancied Hawks into the play-offs. Sampson made some shrewd additions to his squad, not least experienced twins Anthony and David Gibbons, who added both steel and class to Hunslet's backline. George Rayner was again outstanding at fullback, while Chris Redfearn rarely let his side down from loose forward,

George Rayner

and Mark Moxon was a willing worker at scrum-half.

But the Hawks' stand-out performer was undoubtedly hooker Jamaine Wray, who can count himself unlucky to have been pipped to both the Young Player award and the Dream Team by Swinton's Phil Joseph. Wray's busy work around the play-the-balls was a major reason for the Hawks' success, which ended with a play-off defeat against the Lions. And Wray's decision to stay at the club, alongside Rayner, Redfearn, Moxon and the Gibbons brothers, should have seen Hunslet remain a force.

Arguably the biggest strides of the whole league were made by **GATESHEAD THUNDER** and their impressive rookie coach Dean Thomas. The former York and Barrow threequarter took Thunder to their first ever play-off finish - a remarkable achievement for the perennial strugglers.

Chris Birch

Thomas brought in a host of excellent overseas players and blended them into an impressive unit that shocked more than a handful of their NL2 contemporaries. Australian scrum-half Chris Birch was the pick, breaking several club records and making the NL2 Dream Team. He was well supported by halfback partner Mike Hobbs, fullback Wade Liddell, and mighty Fijian second-rower Tabua Cakacaka. And of Thunder's English contingent, young forward Rob Line and centre or second row Ian Brown also caught the eye.

Thomas was deservedly nominated for the Coach of the Year award, though in typical Gateshead style, the year ended with serious doubts being raised over their financial position, despite the team's success. Chairman Bill Midgley insisted that Thunder needed more support from the terraces and sponsors if they were to build on the undoubted strides of 2005.

Missing out on the NL2 play-offs constituted a significant disappointment for **SHEFFIELD EAGLES**, whose progression in recent season appeared to have stalled. But a close-season overhaul, in which former Hull KR coach Gary Wilkinson was brought in to work alongside football director Mark Aston and a host of impressive signings were made, has indicated the Eagles might be poised to soar again in 2006.

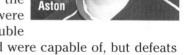

Mark Aston

Still, Aston will have been disappointed with the overall outcome of 2005, in which the Eagles were inconsistent, at times infuriatingly so. A league double over high-flying Dewsbury showed what Sheffield were capable of, but defeats against Blackpool and Keighley also illustrated their Jekyll and Hyde qualities.

Hooker Liam Brentley was one player to escape that inconsistency, and cleaned up at the Eagles' end of season awards. Sheffield-born 'Australian' John Crawford also had an excellent year in his debut campaign at the Don Valley Stadium, but on the whole, the Eagles were keen to put last season behind them and kick on.

Less than two years earlier, **KEIGHLEY COUGARS** had earned promotion from NL2 with a tremendous Grand Final win over Sheffield - so to finish eighth on their return to the competition illustrated their fall from grace.

Danny Murgatroyd

Coach Gary Moorby, who had masterminded that promotion season, put the decline down in large to a lack of investment at first-team level, with the departure of several key players that were never replaced. Moorby believed that the addition of just two signings could have made the Cougars promotion challengers again, as they often competed with the best in the division without recording sufficient wins.

Moorby left the club at the end of the season and was replaced by Cougar hero Peter Roe, returning for a second spell at the club. He had to pick up a squad that often flattered to deceive, despite strong performances from a handful of players.

Prop Danny Murgatroyd was the pick, earning a place in the NL2 Dream Team and a subsequent move to Dewsbury, while Keighley legend Phil Stephenson was always a tower of strength. Centre David Foster rarely let anyone down, while fullback Matt Bramald was among the tries, despite the Cougars' problems.

No-one could label **BLACKPOOL PANTHERS'** first season as uneventful. With their original chairman walking out on the club before the start of the season, director of rugby Dave Rowland took control and oversaw a colourful campaign.

The pre-season promise that had surrounded coach Mark Lee and an impressive list of recruits evaporated when Lee was surprisingly sacked, and then replaced by former Great Britain international Kevin Ashcroft. Ashcroft then took a team manager role, with loose forward Willie Swann assuming the coaching reins with help from fellow player Liam Bretherton. Between them, they helped the Panthers avoid the NL2 wooden spoon, as they finished the year on a high with an away day win at London Skolars. But that fell some way short of the pre-season predictions of some at the Panthers.

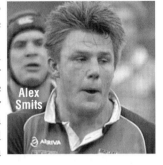

Liam Bretherton

Australian utility back Glen Godbee was superb throughout the first half of the season, before returning home after a mix-up saw him arrive late for a match at Hunslet. Young halfback Liam McGovern also caught the eye at times, while Blackpool's most dependable performer was undoubtedly second-rower Gary Smith, who has since left for Batley.

There off season saw a new coach and board in place at the Panthers, with Rowland handing over control to the other board members, who have appointed experienced prop Simon Knox in charge of first team affairs. Whether that adds up to more stable, successful times in 2006 remained to be seen - but it promised to be as interesting as always for League fans by the seaside.

Collecting the wooden spoon and recording just two league wins may seem like a step backwards for **LONDON SKOLARS**, but the capital club continued to push forward in their attempts to establish themselves as a competitive force. The 2005 season was undoubtedly disappointing for the Skolars. It wasn't that they received regular hidings from rivals clubs - they rarely failed to compete - but they never looked likely to replicate the six league victories they achieved the previous year.

Coaches Marcus Tobin and Alex Smits battled on admirably with limited resources, but when the pair decided to head for pastures new at the end of the season, the club made a major statement of intent by appointing experienced scrum-half Latham Tawhai in a full-time capacity. He inherited a squad that had undoubted talent, even if they failed to kick on from 2004.

Among their best performers were utility back Tim Gee and the Pittman brothers Kurt and especially Matt. Outside back Austin Aggrey was also a handful for opposition defenders when not sidelined through injury, and there could have been enough signs there for Tawhai to re-ignite the Skolars' fire.

NORTHERN RAIL CUP FINAL
Blackpool rocks

Hull Kingston Rovers proved the fallibility of promotion favourites Castleford as caretaker player-coach James Webster guided them to a thrilling Northern Rail Cup Final win.

In front of a full house at Blackpool's Bloomfield Road, second-half tries from the outstanding Andy Raleigh and Cook Island international Byron Ford saw the Robins lift their first trophy for eight years.

Despite falling short of their best, the Tigers had led 10-2 at the interval. Rovers had a try to Dwayne Barker controversially disallowed, and moments later Castleford fullback Michael Platt supported a Paul Handforth break to stride under the posts. But six minutes after half-time, Rovers burst into life when Raleigh forced his way over from close range.

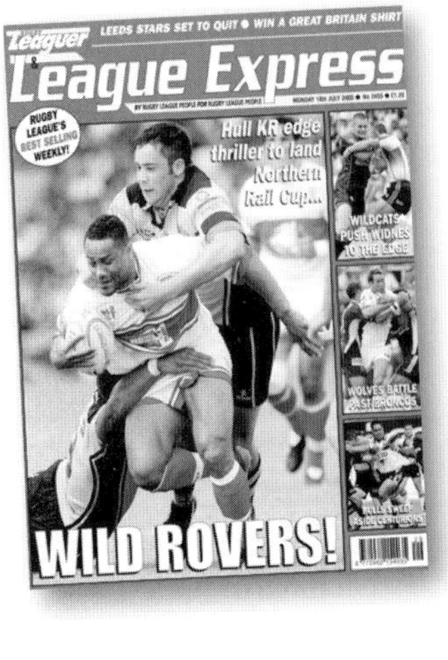

With 12 minutes remaining and the game delicately poised at 12-10 in Rovers' favour, Ford then plucked a wayward Brad Davis pass out of the air and sprinted 80 metres to the line for a try that was converted by the faultless Gareth Morton. And though Jon Hepworth gave the Tigers hope with his late score, the Robins held firm for a memorable victory.

"They threw a lot at us in the first half, but we withstood it and came out on top," said Webster, who also took the official man of the match award.

"We were under no illusions that if we didn't come out firing in the second half they

NORTHERN RAIL CUP FINAL

Sunday 17th July 2005

CASTLEFORD TIGERS 16 HULL KINGSTON ROVERS 18

TIGERS: 1 Michael Platt; 2 Waine Pryce; 3 Deon Bird; 4 Jon Hepworth; 5 Michael Shenton; 6 Paul Handforth; 7 Brad Davis; 8 Adam Watene; 9 Andrew Henderson; 10 Andy Bailey; 11 Tom Haughey; 13 Craig Huby; 12 Steve Crouch. Subs (all used): 14 Andy Kain; 15 Richard Fletcher; 16 Byron Smith; 17 Frank Watene.
Tries: Platt (32), Hepworth (73); **Goals:** Huby 4/4.
On report: Platt (50) - spear tackle on Ford.
ROVERS: 1 Leroy Rivett; 2 Jon Steel; 3 Kane Epati; 4 Gareth Morton; 5 Byron Ford; 6 Paul Mansson; 7 James Webster; 8 James Garmston; 9 Andy Ellis; 10 David Tangata-Toa; 11 Andy Raleigh; 12 Jason Netherton; 13 Dale Holdstock. Subs (all used): 14 Paul Pickering; 15 Dwayne Barker; 16 Jamie Bovill; 17 Makali Aizue.
Tries: Raleigh (46), Ford (68); **Goals:** Morton 5/5.
Rugby Leaguer & League Express Men of the Match: *Tigers:* Andrew Henderson; *Rovers:* Andy Raleigh.
Penalty count: 7-10; **Half-time:** 10-2;
Referee: Ben Thaler (Wakefield);
Attendance: 9,400 *(at Bloomfield Road, Blackpool).*

David Tangata-Toa looks for a way past Tom Haughey

could skip away and that would be the end of it."

"We've backed ourselves against every single team we've played against," Webster continued. "We just felt confident today. We trained enormous on Saturday - probably the best all year - and we just had that feeling."

It was one of Webster's last games in charge, as he stepped aside for the arrival of fellow Australian Justin Morgan, who watched the clash from the Robins bench.

Castleford coach Dave Woods felt his team were the better side, and was far from happy with the performances of the officials on the day

"At half-time we were real confident," Woods said.

"I thought we were the better team all over, the whole day. But we didn't play smart with the ball in the second half.

"A good ten metres would have helped us, but that wasn't to be.

"Fifty-fifty calls went their way, and calls that were probably 70/30 our way went their way as well. What do you do about it?

"But we will regroup. We're disappointed that we couldn't take the trophy back for the fans, but we're still working towards the end of the year - that was always our aim."

NATIONAL LEAGUE PLAY-OFFS
Haven scent glory

Rochdale Hornets and Doncaster Dragons were the first casualties of the NL1 play-offs after being soundly beaten at Hull KR and Halifax respectively.

Rochdale, shorn of three scrum-halves, were little match for the Robins at Craven Park, where James Webster inspired a 45-4 win after Byron Ford scored two well-taken early tries.

Second-half tries from Andy Raleigh – a stunning breakaway effort – Michael Smith, Paul Parker and Makali Aizue completed the win, with Hornets' misery compounded when prop Rob Ball was sent off for dissent four minutes from the end.

The Dragons found themselves on the end of a real hiding at Halifax, who racked up a 64-10 win at the Shay. Doncaster were hindered by the 31st-minute dismissal of Martin Ostler for a spear tackle, though in truth they were

Hull KR's Makali Aizue hauled back by Rochdale's Gareth Price

already facing a thumping, as Ben Black finished with a hat-trick for Fax.

Damian Gibson, Andy Kirk and Rikki Sheriffe all grabbed try doubles, with Pat Weisner finished with 20 points through a try and eight goals.

That set up a Craven Park clash with Hull KR, and underdogs Halifax triumphed again. With hooker Ben Fisher - who would later sign for the Robins - outstanding, Fax built up a 20-0 half-time lead, and held on in the second half to record a memorable 36-22 win.

Rovers did fight back well in the second half, with winger Ford again recording two tries to raise hopes of a famous comeback. But when second rower Dave Larder crashed over for Fax in the dying stages, the Robins had again fallen at the play-offs hurdle.

Whitehaven's Ryan Tandy finds his progress halted by Castleford duo Adrian Vowles and Adam Watene

The same weekend, Whitehaven were booking their place in the Grand Final with a thrilling 32-22 win over Castleford at the Recreation Ground. The Tigers looked certain winners when leading 18-0 after less than a quarter of the game – Waine Pryce, Michael Eagar and Deon Bird all crossing.

But the second-half sin-binning of Bird proved crucial, and a stunning Haven fight-back was completed when centre Mick Nanyn stormed over for two tries in the closing six minutes.

That meant Castleford needed a home victory over Halifax to be assured of their Grand Final place - and they managed it, though not before an almighty late Fax surge in the 15-12 Tigers win.

The Tigers had looked in complete control when Damien Blanch's 56th minute saw them lead 15-2. But two tries in the space of six minutes from Rikki Sheriffe and Kirk set up a pulsating finish, with Cas' grateful to fullback Michael Platt for a handful of try-saving interventions.

NATIONAL LEAGUE ONE QUALIFYING SERIES

Workington Town endured a determined Gateshead Thunder effort before pulling away in the second half to record a 47-12 Elimination play-off win.

Town led just 16-12 at the interval, as Thunder threatened despite being without key scrum-half Chris Birch through suspension. But a second-half Neil Frazer hat-trick helped Town to an eventually comfortable win.

Other Town tries came courtesy of Lusi Sione, Tane Manihera, Martyn Wilson, Tani Lavulavu and Brett Smith, with Jon Roper contributing 11 points with the boot.

Workington celebrate as Tane Manihera (7) crashes over to score against Swinton

Prop Lee Williamson's hat-trick proved to be in vain as Hunslet Hawks crashed out of the play-offs 40-28 at Swinton.

The Lions trailed 10-12 at half-time, before second-rower Danny Heaton helped inspire a second-half charge to victory. Heaton was one of seven Lions try scorers, with two in five minutes from Andy Crabtree – who was later sent off for a late tackle – and Lee Patterson proving vital against the gallant Hawks. Anthony Gibbons' late score was scant consolation for ending a season of promise.

That result set up an Elimination semi-final at Workington, and after a dramatic finale, Town emerged 17-16 winners.

Tries from Wilson and Sione, against a sole effort from Marlon Billy, had seen Town edge 10-8 in front at half-time. But the sides were locked together when Lions centre Dave Llewellyn crossed on the hour mark, only for halfback Lee Kiddie's field goal to prove the difference between two-well matched sides.

Meanwhile, Batley Bulldogs ensured their place in the final with an accomplished win 40-20 win over Dewsbury Rams at Mount Pleasant.

Neil Roden's quickfire double and early tries to Barry Eaton, Craig Lingard and Darren Robinson proved crucial as Batley established a formidable 30-4 half-time lead. Dewsbury battled back after the break with winger Darren Rogers completing a try double, but it wasn't enough.

The Rams then had to face Workington to book a Bulldogs rematch, and with Rogers again crossing twice, Andy Kelly's team recorded a gritty 26-18 win.

Town were still fully in the game at half-time, trailing by six points despite being without key playmaker Manihera, a loss which forced them to field loose forward Brett Smith at scrum-half. But Rogers' second, on 56 minutes, booked the Rams' progression to the Halton Stadium.

The bottom two sides in NL1 in 2005 - which were Featherstone and Barrow - were automatically relegated, and the seventh-placed side, Batley, entered the NL1 Qualifying play-offs with sides 2-6 in NL2 to decide the final NL1 berth for 2006. York, who finished in first place in NL2, were automatically promoted.

NATIONAL LEAGUE GRAND FINALS
Brad all over

Brad Davis provided a fairytale ending to his playing career as he guided Castleford Tigers back into Super League at the first attempt.

The veteran Australian halfback had already signalled his intentions to hang up his boots after the Grand Final, but even he could not had dreamt up a more perfect script for his finale. Davis snared two interception tries and helped create the Tigers' other four, as they totally overwhelmed a disappointing Haven outfit. With outstanding support from the likes of Andrew Henderson, Tommy Haughey and Damien Blanch, 37-year-old Davis deservedly took the man of the match award. It also proved to be a fitting farewell for Australian coach Dave Woods, who was not handed a new contract despite guiding the Tigers back into Super League.

After a furious opening 15 minutes, the contest turned on the sin-binning of Haven stand-off Leroy Joe for a late hit on Davis. With Joe off the field, Cas' scored twice through Craig Huby and Steve Crouch to establish their grip on the game. Davis's pinpoint wide kick then laid on a try for Aussie winger Blanch just after Joe's return, and by the time the Tigers number six had intercepted Joel Penny's pass to score just before the break, the match was all but over.

Davis repeated his trick from a stray Spencer Miller ball straight after half-time, and when he was involved in the build-up to Haughey's try, a landslide Cas' win looked on the cards at 36-0.

To their credit, the Cumbrians restored some lost pride with late tries from David Seeds and Craig Calvert, but for their coach Steve McCormack and the thousands of fans that had travelled south, this was a day of immense disappointment.

"You don't like losing any game, never mind a Grand Final, but this year I don't think we've done ourselves justice in the game," said McCormack, who would later join Widnes Vikings. "I'm disappointed - I think everybody is. We haven't performed anything like we can."

Castleford players and fans celebrate Craig Huby's try

His counterpart Woods couldn't hide his delight. "We've copped criticism all year, people telling us we're not good enough because we're not winning games easily," he reflected. "The media saying we should be running past sides because we're full-time. I don't think enough credit is given to the opposition teams we play. I'm really pleased for the boys because they've worked hard all season."

Woods also had a final word on Davis's display. "He's not bad for an old fella is he? He was great - I told him this would be his game today and it was. Brad is a big-game player and he's done a great job all year for us. It was his last game today and he goes out a winner."

LHF HEALTHPLAN NATIONAL LEAGUE ONE GRAND FINAL

Sunday 9th October 2005

CASTLEFORD TIGERS 36 WHITEHAVEN 8

TIGERS: 1 Michael Platt; 2 Waine Pryce; 3 Michael Shenton; 4 Jon Hepworth; 5 Damien Blanch; 6 Brad Davis; 7 Andrew Henderson; 8 Adam Watene; 9 Aaron Smith; 10 Richard Fletcher; 11 Tom Haughey; 12 Steve Crouch; 13 Deon Bird. Subs (all used): 14 Paul Handforth; 15 Craig Huby; 16 Adrian Vowles; 17 Frank Watene.
Tries: Huby (22), Crouch (24), Blanch (26), Davis (33, 45), Haughey (52); **Goals:** Fletcher 2/3, Huby 3/4, Hepworth 1/1.
WHITEHAVEN: 1 Gary Broadbent; 2 Craig Calvert; 3 David Seeds; 4 Mick Nanyn; 5 Wesley Wilson; 6 Leroy Joe; 7 Joel Penny; 8 Ryan Tandy; 9 Carl Sice; 10 David Fatialofa; 11 Spencer Miller; 12 Howard Hill; 13 Aaron Lester. Subs (all used): 14 Carl Rudd; 15 Aaron Summers; 16 Craig Chambers; 17 Marc Jackson.
Tries: Nanyn (56), Calvert (78); **Goals:** Nanyn 0/2.
Sin bin: Joe (16) - late tackle on Davis.
On report: Joe (16) - late tackle on Davis; Sice (40) - alleged biting.
Rugby Leaguer & League Express Men of the Match: *Tigers:* Brad Davis; *Whitehaven:* Wesley Wilson.
Penalty count: 4-9; **Half-time:** 26-0;
Referee: Steve Ganson (St Helens);
Attendance: 13,300 *(at Halton Stadium, Widnes).*

NATIONAL LEAGUE ONE QUALIFYING SERIES - FINAL

A 66th minute try from stand-off John Gallagher proved the difference, as local rivals Batley Bulldogs and Dewsbury Rams fought out a genuine classic for a place in NL1. After a stirring start from the Bulldogs, Dewsbury had battled back to lead by four points midway through the second half, and thought they had extended that advantage when Kevin Crouthers claimed his second try.

But after lengthy deliberations, the score was ruled out by video referee Steve Presley, and man of the match Gallagher stepped forward to provide his match-winning intervention.

The game had started at breakneck speed, with Iain Marsh crossing in the fifth minute for Batley, and Mark Sibson then finishing a length-of-the-field move for Batley to lead 10-0. The

Kevin Crouthers grabbed by Dane Morgan

Bulldogs scored further first-half tries from Stephen Jones and Barry Eaton, though Dewsbury kept in touch courtesy of a brilliant Darren Rogers score and further efforts from Ryan Sheridan and Chris Hall.

Crouthers' first try then edged the Rams ahead 13 minutes after the break, as the incessant scoring eased somewhat. But Gallagher - who had joined Batley on loan before making the move permanent - then took on the defence from close range and stretched out for the all-important score.

"It was a great advert for National League rugby," Bulldogs coach Gary Thornton said. "Both sides were a credit - there weren't that many penalties or errors in the game."

His opposite number Andy Kelly added: "With so much at stake you have to acknowledge the effort of both sides. For our club to be here in a final is testimony to the foresight of our chairman (Mark Sawyer) 12 months ago. Promotion was the ultimate goal this season so it's disappointing to fall at the final hurdle. But I was happy with the efforts of the players."

NATIONAL LEAGUE ONE QUALIFYING SERIES - FINAL

Sunday 9th October 2005

BATLEY BULLDOGS 28 DEWSBURY RAMS 26

BULLDOGS: 1 Craig Lingard; 2 Jamie Stokes; 3 Iain Marsh; 4 Stephen Jones; 5 Mark Sibson; 6 John Gallagher; 7 Barry Eaton; 8 Dane Morgan; 9 Kris Lythe; 10 Joe Berry; 11 Sean Richardson; 12 Tim Spears; 13 Darren Robinson. Subs (all used): 14 Aiden Lister; 15 David Rourke; 16 Gary Shillabeer; 17 Martin McLoughlin.
Tries: Marsh (5), Sibson (15), Jones (26), Eaton (38), Gallagher (66); **Goals:** Eaton 4/5.
Sin bin: Robinson (38) - striking.
RAMS: 1 Ian Preece; 2 Darren Rogers; 3 Chris Hall; 4 Kevin Crouthers; 5 Richard Tillotson; 6 Francis Maloney; 7 David Mycoe; 8 Paul Hicks; 9 Richard Chapman; 10 Matt Walker; 11 Warren Jowitt; 12 Ged Corcoran; 13 Kurt Rudder. Subs (all used): 14 Ryan Sheridan; 15 Wayne McHugh; 16 James Walker; 17 Jonlee Lockwood.
Tries: Rogers (17), Sheridan (21), Hall (31), Crouthers (53); **Goals:** Maloney 5/5.
Sin bin: J Walker (38) - retaliation.
Rugby Leaguer & League Express Men of the Match:
Bulldogs: John Gallagher; *Rams:* Francis Maloney.
Penalty count: 3-3; **Half-time:** 22-18; **Referee:** Ben Thaler (Wakefield). *(at Halton Stadium, Widnes).*

LHF HEALTHPLAN NATIONAL LEAGUE AWARDS

NATIONAL LEAGUE ONE

PLAYER OF THE YEAR
Andy Raleigh (Hull Kingston Rovers)
Nominees:
Gary Broadbent (Whitehaven)
James Webster (Hull Kingston Rovers)

YOUNG PLAYER OF THE YEAR
Andy Kain (Castleford Tigers)
Nominees:
Andy Ellis (Hull Kingston Rovers)
James Haley (Halifax)

COACH OF THE YEAR
Steve McCormack (Whitehaven)
Nominees:
Bobbie Goulding (Rochdale Hornets)
Dave Woods (Castleford Tigers)

GMB RLPA PLAYERS'
PLAYER OF THE YEAR
Andy Raleigh (Hull Kingston Rovers)

RUGBY LEAGUE WORLD
ALL-STARS TEAM
1 Gary Broadbent (Whitehaven)
2 Craig Calvert (Whitehaven)
3 Jon Goddard (Oldham)
4 Mick Nanyn (Whitehaven)
5 Waine Pryce (Castleford Tigers)
6 Andy Kain (Castleford Tigers)
7 James Webster (Hull Kingston Rovers)
8 Makali Aizue (Hull Kingston Rovers)
9 Ben Fisher (Halifax)
10 Ryan Tandy (Barrow/Whitehaven)
11 Andy Raleigh (Hull Kingston Rovers)
12 Steve Crouch (Castleford Tigers)
13 Pat Weisner (Halifax)

NATIONAL LEAGUE TWO

PLAYER OF THE YEAR
John Tuimaualuga (Workington Town)
Nominees:
Chris Birch (Gateshead Thunder)
Lee Patterson (York City Knights)

Andy Raleigh shows off his awards

YOUNG PLAYER OF THE YEAR
Phil Joseph (Swinton Lions)
Nominees:
Ian Preece (Dewsbury Rams)
Jamaine Wray (Hunslet Hawks)

COACH OF THE YEAR
Mick Cook (York City Knights)
Nominees:
Roy Sampson (Hunslet Hawks)
Dean Thomas (Gateshead Thunder)

RUGBY LEAGUE WORLD
ALL-STARS TEAM
1 Wayne English (Swinton Lions)
2 Peter Fox (York City Knights)
3 Dan Potter (York City Knights)
4 Neil Law (York City Knights)
5 Marlon Billy (Swinton Lions)
6 Lee Marsh (Swinton Lions)
7 Chris Birch (Gateshead Thunder)
8 Danny Murgatroyd (Keighley Cougars)
9 Phil Joseph (Swinton Lions)
10 Adam Sullivan (York City Knights)
11 John Tuimaualuga (Workington Town)
12 Warren Jowitt (Dewsbury Rams)
13 Lee Patterson (York City Knights)

NATIONAL LEAGUE CLUB OF THE YEAR
Hull Kingston Rovers

NATIONAL LEAGUE COMMUNITY
PROGRAMME OF THE YEAR
Workington Town

NATIONAL LEAGUE
REFEREE OF THE YEAR
Ben Thaler

5
INTERNATIONAL YEAR

GILLETTE TRI-NATIONS
Black & white revolution

New Zealand's success in the 2005 Gillette Tri-Nations overturned League's world order. The final at Elland Road provided an incredible climax for New Zealand's Brian McClennan in his first year in the job, and he declared the Kiwis to be the "world champions" after their 24-0 win ended Australia's 27-year reign without a loss in a series. Iconic scrum-half Stacey Jones insisted the black and whites would have to beat their trans-Tasman rivals a few more times to secure top ranking, but McClennan was unequivocal. "It's the best moment in sport for all of us to be rated as the best team in the world," he said. "That's what this is all about - yup, we're world champions alright."

TRI-NATIONS SQUADS

GREAT BRITAIN
Rob Burrow (Leeds Rhinos), Brian Carney (Wigan Warriors), Keiron Cunningham (St Helens), Paul Deacon (Bradford Bulls), Gareth Ellis (Leeds Rhinos), Stuart Fielden (Bradford Bulls), Nick Fozzard (St Helens), Lee Gilmour (St Helens), Martin Gleeson (Warrington Wolves), Iestyn Harris (Bradford Bulls), Mick Higham (St Helens), Richard Horne (Hull FC), Paul Johnson (Bradford Bulls), Adrian Morley (Sydney Roosters), Jamie Peacock (Bradford Bulls) (C), Leon Pryce (Bradford Bulls), Gareth Raynor (Hull FC), Keith Senior (Leeds Rhinos), Kevin Sinfield (Leeds Rhinos), Jamie Thackray (Hull FC), Chev Walker (Leeds Rhinos), Paul Wellens (St Helens), Stephen Wild (Wigan Warriors), Jon Wilkin (St Helens)

Mark Calderwood (Leeds Rhinos) was called into the squad after Game Five, but did not play.

AUSTRALIA
Anthony Minichiello (Sydney Roosters); Matt King (Melbourne Storm); Timana Tahu (Parramatta Eels); Brent Tate (Brisbane Broncos); Matt Cooper (St George-Illawarra Dragons); Mark Gasnier (St George-Illawarra Dragons); Darren Lockyer (Brisbane Broncos) (C); Trent Barrett (St George-Illawarra Dragons); Andrew Johns (Newcastle Knights); Scott Prince (Wests Tigers); Craig Gower (Penrith Panthers); Jason Ryles (St George-Illawarra Dragons); Mark O'Meley (Bulldogs); Steve Price (New Zealand Warriors); Petero Civoniceva (Brisbane Broncos); Danny Buderus (Newcastle Knights); Craig Fitzgibbon (Sydney Roosters); Nathan Hindmarsh (Parramatta Eels); Luke O'Donnell (North Queensland Cowboys); Willie Mason (Bulldogs); Andrew Ryan (Bulldogs); Ben Kennedy (Manly Sea Eagles); Trent Waterhouse (Penrith Panthers)

Nathan Hindmarsh withdrew with a knee injury and was replaced by Ben Creagh (St George-Illawarra Dragons). Andrew Johns needed knee surgery after game two and Eric Grothe (Parramatta Eels) was called in to travel to England. Timana Tahu was injured in game one.

NEW ZEALAND
Brent Webb (NZ Warriors); Manu Vatuvei (NZ Warriors); Paul Whatuira (Wests Tigers); Clinton Toopi (NZ Warriors); Iosia Soliola (Sydney Roosters); Nigel Vagana (Cronulla Sharks); Motu Tony (Hull FC); Lance Hohaia (NZ Warriors); Stacey Jones (NZ Warriors); Roy Asotasi (Bulldogs); Nathan Cayless (Parramatta Eels); Iafeta Palea'aesina (NZ Warriors); Paul Rauhihi (North Queensland Cowboys); Ruben Wiki (NZ Warriors) (C); David Solomona (Wakefield Trinity Wildcats); Louis Anderson (NZ Warriors); David Faiumu (North Queensland Cowboys); David Kidwell (Melbourne Storm); Frank Pritchard (Penrith Panthers); Tony Puletua (Penrith Panthers); Wairangi Koopu (NZ Warriors)

Iosia Soliola was ruled out with a leg injury; Nathan Cayless played in game one and then left camp for birth of a child; Wairangi Koopu played no part in the Tri-Nations. Shontayne Hape (Bradford Bulls) and Ali Lauitiiti (Leeds Rhinos) were added to the initial squad.

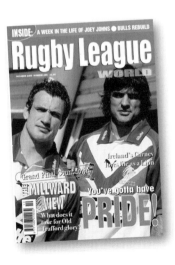

The result marked:
- Australia's first series loss since 1978;
- Their first series loss to New Zealand since 1953;
- First time Australia have been held scoreless since 1985;
- Equalled biggest losing margin of 24 points in the 49-25 loss to New Zealand in 1952.

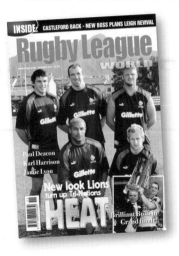

GAME ONE

An ancient Samurai war cry was one of the inspirations behind New Zealand's unforgettable triumph over Australia.

In their first victory in Sydney since 1959, Brian McLennan's Kiwis watched as the world champions ate up their 18-0 lead in just seven minutes and gathered under the posts after a 45th minute try to Australian debutant Matt King that gave his side the lead for the first time.

In front of an encouraging 28,255 crowd at Telstra, they then mustered one of the great Kiwi efforts of the modern era to claw their way back to the front, stand-off Nigel Vagana beating Anthony Minichiello and Danny Buderus on a magnificent run from halfway to score the clincher with 14 minutes left.

"A champion team can beat a team of champions, and that's what we did tonight," said McClennan

The bookmakers had treated the Kiwis with disdain. They were missing so many of their stars. Boom youngsters Sonny Bill Williams, Benji Marshall, Iosia Soliola and Thomas Leuluai, the dependable Matt Utai and Dene Halatau and the ever-consistent Jason Cayless were just some of those injured.

And Lesley Vainikolo, Shontayne Hape and Ali Lauitiiti were playing in the Super League Grand Final instead of representing their country. But the Kiwis pride carried them through. "We went to war today," said New Zealand captain Ruben Wiki. "It was all from the heart. That's what we're about."

From the start the Kiwis caught their opponents on the hop, with fine defence cutting off promising Australian moves. Seven minutes into the game a solid burst by back-rower Frank Pritchard had them in good field position. Stacey Jones, back in the Test side after a two-year self-imposed exile, darted towards the Australian tryline. He dummied towards Wiki, who was running a decoy, before turning the ball back inside to a trailing Clinton Toopi, who was over for the first try of the match.

Two and a half minutes later and Toopi was in again. From the restart the big Kiwi forwards had barrelled their way up the pitch. Then in a 60-metre move the ball passed through four or five sets of hands before Toopi touched down. Fullback Brent Webb, who only qualifies for New Zealand because of the residency rule, made a try-saving tackle on veteran loose forward Ben Kennedy, rolling him over on the tryline and forcing the ball from his hands.

Webb then picked up his own try, skirting wide from a scrum on the 20-metre line and fooling centre Brent Tate with a perfect dummy. The Kiwis led 18-nil after just 18 minutes.

And they could very well have been further ahead when debutant winger Jake Webster narrowly missed a try – with ref Steve Ganson overlooking the fact that the man who tackled him, Trent Waterhouse, was a mile offside.

Yet, one can never write off a team with such greats of the game as Darren Lockyer and Andrew Johns. They are always ready to inspire those around them. It was Tate who made up for his lapse and started the Australian resurgence. He took a pass near his own line and weaved his way 88 metres through some sloppy defence to score Australia's first try.

Pritchard erred in kicking out on the full from the restart. And within a minute Johns was over off a clever pass from substitute hooker Craig Gower.

The onslaught continued. Less than three minutes later and the video referees gave Mark Gasnier the green light after he was tackled by Manu Vatuvei and Jones wide out and the corner post was flattened. Another two minutes passed and Tate was in a second time after a movement that stretched over 70 metres, Johns finally flinging a basketball pass to the Aussie centre after attracting three defenders.

It was 18-all with only seconds of the half remaining.

Yet that was almost enough time for the home side to score again, Lockyer dropping a pass with the tryline at his mercy.

Most spectators expected Australia to go on with the job in the second stanza, especially when they hit the lead for the first time after debutant winger King scored with 47

minutes on the clock. But Wiki and Jones rallied their troops.

Midway through the half, the Kiwis scored twice within a matter of seven minutes. Nathan Cayless finished off some good lead-up work by David Kidwell, Nigel Vagana and Toopi. Then Vagana himself ran 55 metres from dummy-half to give the New Zealanders an eight-point buffer. Jones booted a penalty goal to stretch the lead to ten.

However when Gasnier scored his second try with some fancy footwork, the Australians trailed by just four points, with six minutes remaining. It was perhaps fitting that Gaz should get a second – because when the Kiwis last won in Sydney his uncle Reg Gasnier scored a brace of tries for Australia, too.

It was left to the Man of the Moment, Clinton Toopi, to seal the victory when

---

GILLETTE TRI-NATIONS - GAME ONE

Saturday 15th October 2005

AUSTRALIA 28 NEW ZEALAND 38

AUSTRALIA: 1 Anthony Minichiello (Sydney Roosters); 2 Timana Tahu (Parramatta Eels); 3 Brent Tate (Brisbane Broncos); 4 Mark Gasnier (St George-Illawarra Dragons); 5 Matt King (Melbourne Storm); 6 Darren Lockyer (Brisbane Broncos) (C); 7 Andrew Johns (Newcastle Knights); 8 Steve Price (New Zealand Warriors); 9 Danny Buderus (Newcastle Knights); 10 Petero Civoniceva (Brisbane Broncos); 11 Luke O'Donnell (North Queensland Cowboys); 12 Craig Fitzgibbon (Sydney Roosters); 13 Ben Kennedy (Manly Sea Eagles). Subs (all used): 14 Craig Gower (Penrith Panthers); 15 Jason Ryles (St George-Illawarra Dragons); 16 Andrew Ryan (Bulldogs); 17 Trent Waterhouse (Penrith Panthers). **Tries:** Tate (30, 38), Johns (33), Gasnier (36, 73), King (47); **Goals:** Fitzgibbon 1/4, Johns 1/2.
NEW ZEALAND: 1 Brent Webb (New Zealand Warriors); 2 Jake Webster (Melbourne Storm); 3 Paul Whatuira (Wests Tigers); 4 Clinton Toopi (New Zealand Warriors); 5 Manu Vatuvei (New Zealand Warriors); 6 Nigel Vagana (Cronulla Sharks); 7 Stacey Jones (New Zealand Warriors); 8 Paul Rauhihi (North Queensland Cowboys); 9 Lance Hohaia (New Zealand Warriors); 10 Ruben Wiki (New Zealand Warriors) (C); 11 David Kidwell (Melbourne Storm); 12 Frank Pritchard (Penrith Panthers); 13 Louis Anderson (New Zealand Warriors). Subs (all used): 14 David Faiumu (North Queensland Cowboys); 15 Roy Asotasi (Bulldogs); 16 Nathan Cayless (Parramatta Eels); 17 David Solomona (Wakefield Trinity Wildcats). **Tries:** Toopi (7, 10, 76), Webb (18), Cayless (59), Vagana (66); **Goals:** Jones 7/7.
On report: Vagana & Pritchard (44) - alleged dangerous tackle on Waterhouse.
Rugby Leaguer & League Express Men of the Match: *Australia:* Petero Civoniceva; *New Zealand:* Clinton Toopi. **Penalty count:** 7-7; **Half-time:** 18-18; **Referee:** Steve Ganson (England); **Attendance:** 28,255 *(at Telstra Stadium, Sydney).*

he was tackled by Waterhouse but reached out with his right arm to plant the ball firmly over the tryline. Toopi was in raptures and blew kisses to the adoring New Zealand fans in the cavernous stadium.

Australia lost threequarter Timana Tahu after he tore his hamstring in the Saturday night epic, while scans cleared Kiwis' hooker Lance Hohaia of a broken leg.

There was outrage in the Australian media when Nigel Vagana was cleared of a controversial spear tackle on Waterhouse because judiciary officials believed the wrong player had been charged.

GAME TWO

Australian captain Darren Lockyer scored two tries and had a hand in three others as the Kangaroos edged the Kiwis on a wild and wet evening at Ericsson Stadium.

And, while he may not have been as dominant as he was in the 2004 Gillette Tri-Nations final at Elland Road the previous November, he was certainly inspirational, as Australia recovered from the previous weekend's loss to post a narrow, but important 28-26 victory over the Kiwis.

Lockyer was delighted to taste victory again. It had been a long drought for the Aussie skipper. He had not been on a winning side for almost three months – since the Broncos beat Canberra 24-18 on July 30. And, ironically, he had scored two tries on that occasion, too.

The Kiwis started with commitment, a powerful gang-hit forcing Steve Price backwards in the first tackle of the match. It was to be a feature of the New Zealanders' play all evening. But the Australians were first to put points on the board. Matt Cooper got to an Andrew Johns bomb, flung the ball overhead to Anthony Minichiello, who in turn sent it on to Lockyer, who outpaced the cover defence to score.

It took the Kiwis less than two and a half minutes to reply. An overhead pass from Stacey Jones gave winger Jake Webster an open run for the line.

Jones began the move that led to the Kiwis' second try, sending fullback Brent Webb heading towards the line. Webb dummied to pass, before eventually doing so. And Nigel Vagana managed to touch down before three Australian defenders barrelled him over the sideline in the corner. It was Vagana's 17th try in Test matches, equalling Sean Hoppe's New Zealand record. A penalty goal by Jones in the 30th minute was the first successful kick of the night – and the home side led 10-4.

Kiwi centre Paul Whatuira knocked on from a Johns kick. And moments later Cooper was over to score wide out on the left after good lead-up work by Lockyer and Barrett, who was working well in the unfamiliar role as substitute hooker.

But the New Zealanders were not finished. Webb made a long run. Vagana continued the drive towards the line, and from the next ruck David Kidwell gave Motu Tony a sniff and the Hull half ducked under a would-be tackle to score.

Jones' conversion sent the home side to the break with a handy 16-8 lead.

But this was wiped out in less than five minutes of Aussie magic soon after the struggle resumed in the second half. The players had been back on the pitch for less than four minutes when Mark O'Meley, Barrett and Lockyer positioned Gasnier perfectly. Shontayne Hape was left grasping at thin air as Gaz danced past him. No sooner had play restarted than Barrett flung a long pass to Minichiello, whose inside pass sent Lockyer past Webb and over for his second try. But more was to follow, with Barrett and Lockyer setting up Cooper for him to claim a brace of tries, too.

In total – three tries in the space of 4 minutes 42 seconds. Has any Test blitz been more pronounced?

Australia led 24-16, but they realised this Kiwi side, with its new-found spirit, would not cower like some of those in the past. And they were proved right, when Webster went over for his second try with 17 minutes left.

It stirred the Aussies. Ben Kennedy took the ball from deep within his half and, with a miracle one-handed pass as he was being tackled, sent Minichiello racing to the line to score. Minichiello got across the line but English referee Steve Ganson referred the decision to the video referee, who ruled he was held up.

Then, with just over three minutes remaining, the Kiwis were given a lifeline. Substitute David Faiumu took a quick tap kick from a penalty near the line and, catching the Australians unawares, was over to score. Jones

GILLETTE TRI-NATIONS - GAME TWO

Friday 21st October 2005

NEW ZEALAND 26 AUSTRALIA 28

NEW ZEALAND: 1 Brent Webb (New Zealand Warriors); 2 Jake Webster (Melbourne Storm); 3 Paul Whatuira (Wests Tigers); 4 Shontayne Hape (Bradford Bulls); 5 Manu Vatuvei (New Zealand Warriors); 6 Nigel Vagana (Cronulla Sharks); 7 Stacey Jones (New Zealand Warriors); 8 Paul Rauhihi (North Queensland Cowboys); 9 Motu Tony (Hull FC); 10 Ruben Wiki (New Zealand Warriors) (C); 11 David Kidwell (Melbourne Storm); 12 David Solomona (Wakefield Trinity Wildcats); 13 Louis Anderson (New Zealand Warriors). Subs (all used): 14 David Faiumu (North Queensland Cowboys); 15 Roy Asotasi (Bulldogs); 16 Iafeta Palea'aesina (New Zealand Warriors); 17 Tony Puletua (Penrith Panthers).
Tries: Webster (15, 63), Vagana (26), Tony (38), Faiumu (77); **Goals:** Jones 3/6.
AUSTRALIA: 1 Anthony Minichiello (Sydney Roosters); 2 Matt King (Melbourne Storm); 3 Mark Gasnier (St George-Illawarra Dragons); 4 Matt Cooper (St George-Illawarra Dragons); 5 Brent Tate (Brisbane Broncos); 6 Darren Lockyer (Brisbane Broncos) (C); 7 Andrew Johns (Newcastle Knights); 8 Petero Civoniceva (Brisbane Broncos); 9 Danny Buderus (Newcastle Knights); 10 Steve Price (New Zealand Warriors); 11 Luke O'Donnell (North Queensland Cowboys); 12 Craig Fitzgibbon (Sydney Roosters); 13 Ben Kennedy (Manly Sea Eagles). Subs (all used): 14 Trent Barrett (St George-Illawarra Dragons); 15 Jason Ryles (St George-Illawarra Dragons); 16 Mark O'Meley (Bulldogs); 17 Trent Waterhouse (Penrith Panthers).
Tries: Lockyer (12, 46), Cooper (34, 48), Gasnier (44), Minichiello (68); **Goals:** Fitzgibbon 2/5, Johns 0/1.
Rugby Leaguer & League Express Men of the Match: *New Zealand:* Ruben Wiki; *Australia:* Darren Lockyer.
Penalty count: 7-4; **Half-time:** 16-8; **Referee:** Steve Ganson (England); **Attendance:** 15,400 *(at Ericsson Stadium, Auckland).*

kicked the conversion and there were only two points between the two sides. But Australia defended that slender lead for the remaining two minutes.

Despite the defeat, New Zealand firmly believed they would keep getting better as the Gillette Tri-Nations continued, despite mystery surrounding the likelihood of their star halfback Stacey Jones appearing in the Kiwi line-up against Great Britain at Loftus Road the following Saturday.

The Kiwis travelled without Jones, who said he would "probably not" play the third game, and would definitely be unavailable for the tournament final due to the expected birth of his third child on 24 November.

Andrew Johns needed medical scans on his right knee after he hobbled off the plane at Sydney Airport, and was informed he needed urgent surgery on the injury. Penrith's Craig Gower, Clive Churchill medallist Scott Prince and Trent Barrett were thought to provide adequate cover, while Parramatta winger Eric Grothe was drafted into the squad that flew out to England.

GAME THREE

Stacey Jones did play against Great Britain, and directed the Kiwis to a seven-try 42-26 success at Loftus Road. With a hand in four of his side's tries, including the gamebreaking effort by prop Paul Rauhihi eight minutes from time, and a flawless haul of seven goals, Jones once again stamped his authority on proceedings to take the Kiwis closer to the Tri-Nations final. Coach Brian McClennan hoped Jones could be persuaded to make the journey to Elland Road at the end of November should the Kiwis make the decider, but said he was not putting any pressure on his key man.

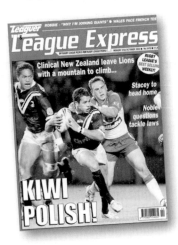

With record-breaking captain Ruben Wiki, making his 47th Test appearance, and two-try Brent Webb and Clinton Toopi also enjoying top games, the Kiwis had too much firepower up front, organisation in midfield and incisive attacking skills out wide for a Great Britain side that began the game looking decidedly ring-rusty.

After two back-to-back Tests against Australia, the Kiwis looked honed to perfection, despite their gruelling flight from Auckland. And Great Britain prop Stuart Fielden, who had an outstanding game, called on the Rugby Football League to give Great Britain "a fair crack of the whip" by ensuring they didn't go into the following year's Tri-Nations series "cold" against match-hardened opposition.

Defeat was tough on several home players, with Paul Johnson becoming the first British forward to score a Test match hat-trick since Oldham's Albert Avery in Auckland way back in 1910. Hunslet's Bill Jukes scored a hat-trick from the pack against Australia earlier on that pioneering tour, and is the only other Great Britain forward to achieve that feat. Keiron Cunningham revelled on his return to the international stage after a three-year injury-enforced absence.

But Brian Noble faced a selection dilemma after vice-captain Brian Carney endured a nightmare game, and was finally relieved of his torment when Johnson switched out of the pack with fifteen minutes to go. Carney's error-ridden performance was ruthlessly exploited by the Kiwis.

Noble sprang a pre-match surprise by naming captain Jamie Peacock in the front row, and brought in Rob Burrow and Nick Fozzard for their Test debuts off the bench. Toopi, the Kiwis' hat-trick hero of their win in Sydney, returned after injury.

Though Britain won two early penalties, both for transgressions on Fielden, with David Solomona being placed on report - subsequently getting a one-match ban - for a dangerous throw that allowed Paul Deacon to kick his side into a second-minute lead, the Kiwis forced the pace.

Webb sliced over for his first try from a scrum after Peacock's costly knock-on trying to take a misdirected pass by Kevin Sinfield from the deep re-start kick. Jones ushered the fullback expertly over after running around the base of the scrum with the use of Nigel Vagana as a dummy runner proving effective.

Solomona, first receiver from Motu Tony's pass from dummy-half, then sent Manu Vatuvei cutting inside Carney's attempted tackle as the Kiwis extended their lead to 12-2 in their next attack. Vatuvei was then denied a second on the first of several marginal video referee's decisions after Solomona's kick to the corner.

Carney then dropped Jones's high kick, but Solomona was unable to pick up the loose ball and Britain escaped. Keith Senior, making his first appearance since the Challenge Cup Final, then made a timely interception close to his own line, Webb preventing a superb counter-attack with a sharp tackle on the supporting Leon Pryce on halfway.

Paul Whatuira ended Britain's first real attack with an interception close to his own line, but Fielden tracked back brilliantly to overhaul him on halfway with a stunning cover tackle. Carney was held up close to the line by Vatuvei and Cunningham, attempting to burrow over from dummy half, was held up in a massed tackle over the line. In the follow-up attack Senior's pass that squeezed Pryce over by the flag was forward, and the Kiwis escaped.

Carney's miserable night continued as he dropped another Jones kick, and Sinfield was penalised for picking up the ball in an offside position. The Kiwis took full advantage, Jones hoisting an inch-perfect kick from ten metres out in front of the British posts to the other wing for Jake Webster to leap high and collect to score.

Finally the home fans had something to cheer with Johnson's first try - an exceptional finish down the right after superb approach work by Cunningham. The British hooker feigned to pass from dummy-half, and then threw out a pass that hit his target at full pace, Johnson doing the rest as he cut between Jones and Vatuvei in a spearing 40-metre run to the corner. Lee Gilmour was then held up short on the crash ball after some more clever prompting by Cunningham.

But the Kiwis survived to post a seemingly impregnable 24-8 interval score-line. Toopi was denied by Paul Wellens' sharp tackle after Vatuvei's inside pass, before Jones' one-handed pass out of the tackle allowed Webb to combine with Whatuira and cut over for his second try just before the break.

In the second half Britain's stirring revival was built on Senior slicing over from Chev Walker's pass after Toopi had fumbled Sinfield's kick to the corner. And when, two minutes later, another mighty charge from Fielden, and

GILLETTE TRI-NATIONS - GAME THREE

Saturday 29th October 2005

GREAT BRITAIN 26 NEW ZEALAND 42

GREAT BRITAIN: 1 Paul Wellens (St Helens); 2 Brian Carney (Wigan Warriors); 3 Martin Gleeson (Warrington Wolves); 4 Keith Senior (Leeds Rhinos); 5 Leon Pryce (Bradford Bulls); 6 Kevin Sinfield (Leeds Rhinos); 7 Paul Deacon (Bradford Bulls); 8 Stuart Fielden (Bradford Bulls); 9 Keiron Cunningham (St Helens); 10 Jamie Peacock (Bradford Bulls) (C); 11 Lee Gilmour (St Helens); 12 Paul Johnson (Bradford Bulls); 13 Gareth Ellis (Leeds Rhinos). Subs (all used): 14 Rob Burrow (Leeds Rhinos); 15 Adrian Morley (Sydney Roosters); 16 Chev Walker (Leeds Rhinos); 17 Nick Fozzard (St Helens).
Tries: Johnson (28, 47, 60), Senior (45);
Goals: Deacon 1/1, Sinfield 4/4.
NEW ZEALAND: 1 Brent Webb (New Zealand Warriors); 2 Jake Webster (Melbourne Storm); 3 Paul Whatuira (Wests Tigers); 4 Clinton Toopi (New Zealand Warriors); 5 Manu Vatuvei (New Zealand Warriors); 6 Nigel Vagana (Cronulla Sharks); 7 Stacey Jones (New Zealand Warriors); 8 Paul Rauhihi (North Queensland Cowboys); 9 Motu Tony (Hull FC); 10 Ruben Wiki (New Zealand Warriors) (C); 11 David Kidwell (Melbourne Storm); 12 David Solomona (Wakefield Trinity Wildcats); 13 Awen Guttenbeil (New Zealand Warriors). Subs (all used): 14 Louis Anderson (New Zealand Warriors); 15 Roy Asotasi (Bulldogs); 16 Frank Pritchard (Penrith Panthers); 17 Ali Lauitiiti (Leeds Rhinos).
Tries: Webb (3, 38), Vatuvei (6), Webster (23), Toopi (53, 75), Rauhihi (72); **Goals:** Jones 7/7.
On report: Solomona (2) - alleged dangerous tackle on Fielden.
Rugby Leaguer & League Express Men of the Match:
Great Britain: Paul Johnson; *New Zealand:* Stacey Jones.
Penalty count: 7-7; **Half-time:** 8-24; **Referee:** Glen Black (New Zealand); **Attendance:** 15,568 *(at Loftus Road, London).*

Cunningham's artistry from dummy-half, set up Johnson for his second, the home side trailed by only four points.

But Jones again stamped his authority on proceedings, forcing Wellens to concede the game's first goal-line drop-out after a towering bomb from 40 metres out. The Kiwis took advantage in the follow-up, Webb, Jones and Awen Guttenbeil combining in a sweeping attack to get Toopi over after Whatuira was held up short. Wellens then kept Britain in the game with a try-saving tackle on Toopi after another high-speed attack.

On the hour-mark, though, Britain again closed the gap to four, again from a surging Fielden run and magical hands from Cunningham seeing Johnson spinning out of Ali Lauitiiti's attempted tackle to score by the posts. Carney's miserable evening was ended early after he conceded another goal-line drop-out, leading to Vatuvei being denied by the video referee as he tried to plant the ball down one-handed in Carney's tackle by the flag. Britain almost took advantage of the let-off when Lauitiiti's crucial tackle halted Fozzard's charge, only for Burrow to make a crucial knock-on as he took on the close-range defence.

With that, home hopes disappeared, as Jones' cleverly-disguised pass sent Rauhihi - a stand-out even without his luminous green boots - over with Wiki the dummy runner that again left the British defence confused. Tony and Louis Anderson then combined at the end of another high-speed handling attack to get Toopi safely over for his second to conclude the evening's rich entertainment.

Coach McClennan was at the centre of some more rare scenes at full-time, when he joined in on a haka as the Kiwis formed a guard of honour for skipper Ruben Wiki after his world record Test appearance.

Wiki was visibly touched by the gesture, and was using his own video camera as he was interviewed afterwards to ensure he would always have a record of the evening. "After Friday night's game I reflected on what that meant when I equalled the record - it was a pretty powerful feeling," he said. "I'm up there with some great company in Gary Freeman, Mal Meninga, Gilbert Benausse, Mick Sullivan and Garry Schofield, and it's a great privilege to be there."

New Zealand were to press the Rugby League International Federation for new rules over international player releases after Lesley Vainikolo was withdrawn by the Bulls in the week leading up to the Test so he could undergo surgery.

GAME FOUR

Great Britain were the rank outsiders to win the Gillette Tri-Nations tournament after their 20-6 defeat by Australia at the JJB Stadium, which left them with no points from two matches, and a negative points difference of 30 after two defeats. Bookmakers William Hill were making Australia the hot favourites at 1/3, with the Kiwis at 9/4, and Britain on the market at 33/1.

The Kangaroos ruthlessly applied the killer punches late in the day to condemn Great Britain to another Tri-Nations heartbreak on a murky night in Wigan. Leading 8-6 with just five minutes remaining of an authentic Test Match, the Australians had enough in the tank to come up with two late tries.

Three of the survivors from the 2004 Tri-Nations Final romp, skipper Darren Lockyer, fullback Anthony Minichiello and second row Craig Fitzgibbon, all played crucial roles in inflicting another devastating blow to British hopes.

Lockyer came up with the crucial plays when it mattered, and gave his side a creativity and threat from halfback that Britain lacked. Minichiello's unerringly outstanding positional play in defence, and his ability to pop up at the right time in attack, were demonstrated once again as he grabbed the gamebreaking try, while Fitzgibbon, who kicked four goals, was the pick of a typically industrious though unspectacular Kangaroos pack.

Standout home performances from props Stuart Fielden and Adrian Morley, hooker Keiron Cunningham and fullback Paul Wellens went unrewarded and counted for nothing. They should have capitalised on their second-half dominance long before Minichiello's try, cruelly against the run of play, sealed Australia's victory five minutes from time.

Britain, who conceded an unfortunate 80-metre interception try to Matt Cooper when Cunningham's telegraphed pass was brilliantly anticipated by the Kangaroos' centre, fought back as Morley capped his display with a close-range score. Late tries by Minichiello and Cooper rewarded the Kangaroos' staying power in the dreadfully wet and cold conditions.

Fitzgibbon's fourth-minute penalty, struck on the angle from 27 metres after Paul Deacon was penalised for a tackle in an offside position, got the Kangaroos off the mark. They almost added to their tally two minutes later, as Scott Prince's kick to the wing was knocked in-field by Brent Tate for the unmarked Luke O'Donnell, but the assist was plainly forward.

Paul Deacon's grubber forced a rare error out of Minichiello, who knocked on five metres from his own line. From the scrum move Martin Gleeson, on the crash ball, was hauled down just short of the line, but Fielden's spillage then let the Kangaroos off the hook.

As Britain continued to pound the line Cunningham, so impressive in the early exchanges, threw out a long pass to the right wing that was cleverly anticipated by Cooper, who raced 80 metres for an opportunist try just before the midway point of the first half. Fitzgibbon converted as the home crowd was suddenly deflated.

Despite that body blow Britain, sustained by an impressive stint off the bench from debutant Jamie Thackray, had most of the pressure.

As the conditions deteriorated Britain survived a Wellens knock-on straight from the re-start kick-off to again take the game to Australia. After Brian Carney was crowded out on the right, Cunningham cleverly created a reviving try for Morley with his dummy-half skills. Morley, timing his angled run to perfection, spun out of two tackles and crashed over the line, Sinfield adding the conversion. In the build-up Ryles had lost possession driving out the ball from his own line.

Minichiello steadied the ship for his side with two great takes from testing kicks by Deacon and Cunningham. A Fitzgibbon knock-on in Sinfield's tackle with fifteen minutes remaining could have proved costly for the Kangaroos, but after Wellens was held up short Gleeson lost possession in the shadow of the posts and the chance was gone.

A debatable penalty against Leon Pryce for a ball-steal in the tackle piggy-backed the Kangaroos up-field, and then Johnson was pinged in the tackle 25 metres out, only for Fitzgibbon to miss the penalty attempt with seven minutes remaining.

But the Kangaroos had broken the siege and, with five minutes left, they applied the crucial blow. Lockyer's artistry on the last tackle from first receiver created the opening for Minichiello to burst over on the angle, despite an attempted double tackle by Wellens and Sinfield.

Fitzgibbon's conversion ended British hopes, and when Deacon's re-start kick failed to go ten metres the Kangaroos took full advantage. Ben Kennedy's magical offload after he had taken Minichiello's pass broke the defence, and Gasnier sent Cooper over for his second try of the evening.

Britain now needed to win their remaining pool games against Australia and New Zealand by an aggregate margin of up to 30 points or more to make the November 26 final at Elland Road.

GILLETTE TRI-NATIONS - GAME FOUR

Saturday 5th November 2005

GREAT BRITAIN 6 AUSTRALIA 20

GREAT BRITAIN: 1 Paul Wellens (St Helens); 2 Brian Carney (Wigan Warriors); 3 Martin Gleeson (Warrington Wolves); 4 Keith Senior (Leeds Rhinos); 5 Leon Pryce (Bradford Bulls); 6 Iestyn Harris (Bradford Bulls); 7 Paul Deacon (Bradford Bulls); 8 Stuart Fielden (Bradford Bulls); 9 Keiron Cunningham (St Helens); 10 Adrian Morley (Sydney Roosters); 11 Jamie Peacock (Bradford Bulls) (C); 12 Paul Johnson (Bradford Bulls); 13 Kevin Sinfield (Leeds Rhinos). Subs (all used): 14 Lee Gilmour (St Helens); 15 Chev Walker (Leeds Rhinos); 16 Jamie Thackray (Hull FC); 17 Mick Higham (St Helens).
Try: Morley (49); **Goals:** Sinfield 1/1.
AUSTRALIA: 1 Anthony Minichiello (Sydney Roosters); 5 Brent Tate (Brisbane Broncos); 3 Mark Gasnier (St George-Illawarra Dragons); 4 Matt Cooper (St George-Illawarra Dragons); 2 Matt King (Melbourne Storm); 7 Scott Prince (Wests Tigers); 8 Petero Civoniceva (Brisbane Broncos); 9 Danny Buderus (Newcastle Knights); 10 Steve Price (New Zealand Warriors); 11 Luke O'Donnell (North Queensland Cowboys); 12 Craig Fitzgibbon (Sydney Roosters); 13 Ben Kennedy (Manly Sea Eagles). Subs (all used): 14 Trent Barrett (St George-Illawarra Dragons); 15 Jason Ryles (St George-Illawarra Dragons); 16 Mark O'Meley (Bulldogs); 17 Willie Mason (Bulldogs).
Tries: Cooper (19, 78), Minichiello (75); **Goals:** Fitzgibbon 4/5.
Rugby Leaguer & League Express Men of the Match:
Great Britain: Adrian Morley; *Australia:* Anthony Minichiello.
Penalty count: 6-7; **Half-time:** 0-8; **Referee:** Tim Mander (Australia); **Attendance:** 25,004 *(at JJB Stadium, Wigan).*

GAME FIVE

Great Britain's incredible 38-12 victory over New Zealand in Huddersfield blew the Gillette Tri-Nations tournament wide open. Britain had been written off as no-hopers, but in just two weeks they went from conceding a record 42 points against New Zealand on home soil to scoring the most points against the Kiwis at home.

It was the best display by Great Britain for many a year. But coach Brian Noble also shared in the accolades after making some controversial changes, including the surprise late dropping of Kevin Sinfield.

The width of Britain's victory was all the more remarkable for overcoming a series of injuries during the match that forced them into make-do-and-mend changes on the run. At regular intervals they lost scrum-half Paul Deacon, winger Brian Carney and fullback Paul Wellens.

The loss of Deacon was the most serious as he departed after an opening 22 minutes in which he answered the critics who expressed surprise that he had retained his place after two uninspiring performances. Deacon was heading for his best ever display in a Great Britain jersey when he fell to a tackle by Nigel Vagana that left him with horrific facial injuries. The Kiwi stand-off was placed on report, and received a one-match ban later in the week. Just eight minutes before departing, Deacon had scored a gem of a try when he jinked and spun round to touch down near the posts.

Carney's hamstring injury, sustained when scoring his second try in the 33rd minute, cut short another display that struck back at those who demanded his head after a nightmare game against New Zealand two weeks before.

Both of Carney's tries were the result of top-class wing play. The first came in the 25th minute, when Chev Walker's pass had the winger almost tight-roping the touchline before sprinting in from 20 metres. The sight of Manu Vatuvei floundering in his wake completed Carney's rehabilitation, for the big Kiwi winger had been his chief tormentor a fortnight earlier.

Much better followed eight minutes later, after centre partner Martin Gleeson's whipped-out pass unleashed Carney near half way. Lightning acceleration left Clinton Toopi pawing thin air near the touchline, before Carney cut inside fullback Brent Webb for the sort of try wingers dream about.

Leon Pryce had been comparatively quiet in the previous two matches, but this time he reverted to the roving role that won him the Harry Sunderland Trophy in the previous month's Grand Final, and came up with another outstanding performance.

GILLETTE TRI-NATIONS - GAME FIVE

Saturday 12th November 2005

GREAT BRITAIN 38 NEW ZEALAND 12

GREAT BRITAIN: 1 Paul Wellens (St Helens); 2 Brian Carney (Wigan Warriors); 3 Martin Gleeson (Warrington Wolves); 4 Keith Senior (Leeds Rhinos); 5 Leon Pryce (Bradford Bulls); 6 Iestyn Harris (Bradford Bulls); 7 Paul Deacon (Bradford Bulls); 8 Stuart Fielden (Bradford Bulls); 9 Keiron Cunningham (St Helens); 10 Adrian Morley (Sydney Roosters); 11 Jamie Peacock (Bradford Bulls) (C); 12 Paul Johnson (Bradford Bulls); 13 Gareth Ellis (Leeds Rhinos). Subs (all used): 14 Mick Higham (St Helens); 15 Chev Walker (Leeds Rhinos); 16 Jamie Thackray (Hull FC); 17 Richard Horne (Hull FC).
Tries: Fielden (5), Deacon (14), Carney (25, 33), Walker (43), Senior (54); **Goals:** Deacon 2/2, Harris 5/5.
NEW ZEALAND: 1 Brent Webb (New Zealand Warriors); 2 Jake Webster (Melbourne Storm); 3 Shontayne Hape (Bradford Bulls); 4 Clinton Toopi (New Zealand Warriors); 5 Manu Vatuvei (New Zealand Warriors); 6 Nigel Vagana (Cronulla Sharks); 7 Stacey Jones (New Zealand Warriors); 8 Paul Rauhihi (North Queensland Cowboys); 9 Motu Tony (Hull FC); 10 Ruben Wiki (New Zealand Warriors) (C); 11 David Kidwell (Melbourne Storm); 12 David Solomona (Wakefield Trinity Wildcats); 13 Awen Guttenbeil (New Zealand Warriors). Subs (all used): 14 David Faiumu (North Queensland Cowboys); 15 Roy Asotasi (Bulldogs); 16 Louis Anderson (New Zealand Warriors); 17 Ali Lauitiiti (Leeds Rhinos).
Tries: Webster (48, 77), Lauitiiti (72); **Goals:** Jones 0/3.
Sin bin: Hape (39) – holding down.
On report: Vagana (22) – alleged high tackle on Deacon.
Rugby Leaguer & League Express Men of the Match:
Great Britain: Chev Walker; *New Zealand:* Ali Lauitiiti.
Penalty count: 10-9; **Half-time:** 26-0;
Referee: Tim Mander (Australia);
Attendance: 19,232 *(at Galpharm Stadium, Huddersfield).*

There was not a better solo effort in the whole game than Pryce's superb run that set up Walker's 43rd minute try. Having moved in midfield, the left winger shot away from a play-the-ball before high-stepping his way past a couple of defenders, and sending Walker pounding for the corner.

Stuart Fielden received the official man of the match award. The Bradford prop began Britain's six-try charge when he powered over after only five minutes, and continued to be a driving force up front.

Keiron Cunningham, who provided the pass for Fielden's try, was also a strong contender for match honours. In fact, all the British forwards made a

Iestyn Harris steps his way through the New Zealand defence

huge contribution, with Jamie Thackray again standing out, in only his second Great Britain appearance.

After a less than ordinary match against Australia, Iestyn Harris justified his retention at stand-off with a much-improved performance that included the neat pass that got Walker away on his try-making run, and a faultless five-goal kicking display.

New Zealand began the match knowing they could afford to lose by 23 points and still qualify for the final, though coach Brian McClennan denied that affected their approach. None of their players repeated the form that brought

such high praise following victories over Britain and Australia. That included Stacey Jones, who was the inspiration behind the comprehensive defeat of Britain. Called out of international retirement yet again - Lance Hohaia had aggravated an ankle injury against England the previous Sunday - the scrum-half fell well short of his brilliant best. The look of despair on the Kiwis' faces when the final hooter sounded suggested they thought they might have blown it.

● Great Britain's previous highest home score against New Zealand came with the 35-19 victory at Swinton in 1961, and their widest margin was 26-6 at Elland Road, Leeds, in 1989. Their biggest win of all against New Zealand is 53-19 in the 1972 World Cup at Pau, France.

The Kangaroos warmed up for the Tri-Nations climax with a solid, eight-try, 44-12 win over France in Perpignan.

The exact mathematics of qualification going into the last GB-Australia clash had many pundits in a tizz.

If Great Britain lost or drew, the final at Elland Road would be between Australia and New Zealand.

The complications would set in if Great Britain won, as each team would finish with four points in the Tri-Nations table, and the order in which they finished would be decided by points difference.

As things currently stood, Australia has a points difference of +6, New Zealand -2, and Great Britain -4.

If Great Britain won by just one point, the Aussies and Kiwis would make the final.

If the margin was two points, both New Zealand and Great Britain would have a points difference of minus 2, but the Kiwis for/against percentage of 98.33 would be better than Great Britain's, unless the scoreline on Saturday was 48-46 or higher in Britain's favour.

If Great Britain won by three to seven points, the Kiwis would be out, and the final would be between Australia and Great Britain.

If the British defeated Australia by eight points, however, the Kiwis and Aussies would both end the tournament with a points difference of minus 2, and the Aussies would go out of the competition on a for/against percentage, unless they scored 42 points or more in defeat.

If Great Britain beat the Australians by nine or more, however, the Australians would automatically go out of the competition.

GAME SIX

All the numerical calculations proved to be of little value. It was much the same old story for Great Britain as Australia's 26-14 victory took them through to the Gillette Tri-Nations Final and a meeting with New Zealand.

Britain had managed just one win in their last eleven clashes with Australia and this game followed the same pattern as most of the other defeats. They battled bravely, competed throughout and scored a couple of good tries. But

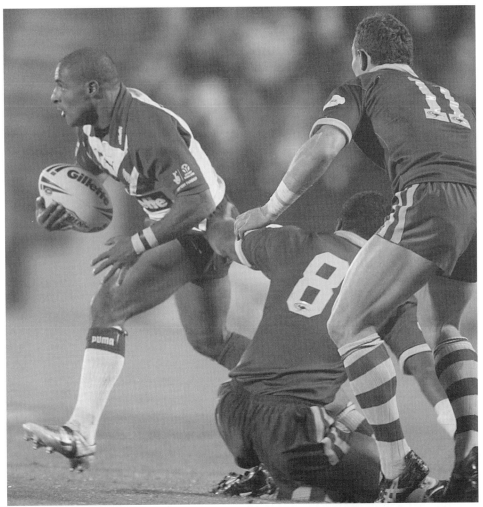

Gareth Raynor goes past Petero Civoniceva and Luke O'Donnell

when it came to finding that bit extra to turn effort into class they were found wanting.

Despite being without the world's two greatest halfbacks, Darren Lockyer - who had broken a foot in Paris in training for the Test against France - and Andrew Johns, the Aussies ruled the middle with stand-ins Trent Barrett and Craig Gower. One or the other had a part in all four of their tries with Gower's performance extraordinary considering he suffered a thigh injury in the warm up.

Gower had the thigh strapped and showed little sign of the injury until going off late on. The scrum-half struck the first telling blow in the 20th minute when his perfectly-placed high

kick led to Matt Cooper opening the try scoring. Matt King out-jumped Brian Carney to knock the ball down to Cooper, who strode in for the touchdown.

Barrett then took over as the provider to have a hand in Australia's next three tries. He combined with Anthony Minichiello, who sent Mark O'Meley over for a crucial try seconds before the interval. Then Barrett whipped out the pass that launched Brent Tate on a marvellous 80-metre run for Australia's third try in the 50th minute and ten minutes later he produced the pass that enabled Mark Gasnier to finish off Britain with a try on the hour.

Barrett's contribution was all the more impressive for having spent two spells in the sin bin. He made his first walk in the 28th minute when referee Steve Ganson sent him packing for not releasing Stuart Fielden when the tackle was deemed to have been completed. And in the 70th minute he was on his way again after obstructing Iestyn Harris as the Great Britain stand-off chased his own fly kick and was brought down just short of the posts.

Despite the halfbacks' contribution, the official man of the match award went to Minichiello for another outstanding fullback display. He had been impressive throughout the tournament and the following Monday was awarded the Gillette Golden Boot, presented by Rugby League World magazine to the world's best player in 2005. In addition to his part in O'Meley's try, Minichiello went close to scoring a superb solo try. Only a great smother tackle by his opposite number, Leon Pryce, stopped him in full cry for the line.

Australia also had a big advantage in the threequarter line with only King failing to get among the try scorers.

GILLETTE TRI-NATIONS - GAME SIX

Saturday 19th November 2005

GREAT BRITAIN 14 AUSTRALIA 26

GREAT BRITAIN: 1 Leon Pryce (Bradford Bulls); 2 Brian Carney (Wigan Warriors); 3 Martin Gleeson (Warrington Wolves); 4 Keith Senior (Leeds Rhinos); 5 Gareth Raynor (Hull FC); 6 Iestyn Harris (Bradford Bulls); 7 Richard Horne (Hull FC); 8 Stuart Fielden (Bradford Bulls); 9 Keiron Cunningham (St Helens); 10 Adrian Morley (Sydney Roosters); 11 Jamie Peacock (Bradford Bulls) (C); 12 Paul Johnson (Bradford Bulls); 13 Gareth Ellis (Leeds Rhinos). Subs (all used): 14 Mick Higham (St Helens); 15 Chev Walker (Leeds Rhinos); 16 Jamie Thackray (Hull FC); 17 Kevin Sinfield (Leeds Rhinos).
Tries: Carney (33), Horne (73); **Goals:** Harris 3/4.
AUSTRALIA: 1 Anthony Minichiello (Sydney Roosters); 2 Matt King (Melbourne Storm); 3 Mark Gasnier (St George-Illawarra Dragons); 4 Matt Cooper (St George-Illawarra Dragons); 5 Brent Tate (Brisbane Broncos); 6 Trent Barrett (St George-Illawarra Dragons); 7 Craig Gower (Penrith Panthers); 8 Petero Civoniceva (Brisbane Broncos); 9 Danny Buderus (Newcastle Knights) (C); 10 Jason Ryles (St George-Illawarra Dragons); 11 Luke O'Donnell (North Queensland Cowboys); 12 Craig Fitzgibbon (Sydney Roosters); 13 Ben Kennedy (Manly Sea Eagles). Subs (all used): 14 Craig Wing (Sydney Roosters); 15 Willie Mason (Bulldogs); 16 Mark O'Meley (Bulldogs); 17 Trent Waterhouse (Penrith Panthers).
Tries: Cooper (20), O'Meley (40), Tate (50), Gasnier (60); **Goals:** Fitzgibbon 5/5, Gower 0/1.
Sin bin: Barrett (28) – professional foul; (70) - obstruction.
Rugby Leaguer & League Express Men of the Match:
Great Britain: Mick Higham; *Australia:* Anthony Minichiello.
Penalty count: 10-6; **Half-time:** 8-14;
Referee: Steve Ganson (England); **Attendance:** 25,150
(at Kingston Communications Stadium, Hull).

Tate's try was the gamebreaker and deserved to win any match. When Barrett's pass set him off, the winger swept easily past Keith Senior before moving out to the touchline. When Pryce tried to cut him off, Tate powered through his diving tackle to race clear for a glorious 80-metre try.

Gasnier was another Australian to have an impressive series and marked his performance with an excellent try. Barrett provided the pass for Gasnier to shrug off Jamie Peacock, make light of Richard Horne's effort and plunge over with Keiron Cunningham hanging on to him.

Although Britain's overall performance left much to be desired, they had their moments. None better than when they at least had some satisfaction in scoring the last try of the match, brilliantly inspired by substitute Mick Higham, who pushed Minichiello close for individual honours after having a major role in both of Britain's tries.

The one he cut out for Horne in the 70th minute was as good as anything Australian produced. From acting halfback at a play-the-ball ten metres inside the home half, Higham moved smartly away before handing on to Peacock. When Peacock was held, Higham backed up to make a second penetrative dash that led to Horne bursting on to his pass and sprinting 40 metres to the posts.

Stuart Fielden struggled with a back injury but Britain's entire front row was again one of their major strengths without being able to subdue an Aussie pack that was out to answer questions about any supposed inferiority.

With Britain needing to win by three points to reach the final and Australia having to avoid defeat by more eight points or more to go through, both teams showed signs of the pressure and each knocked on within the first minute on a freezing night. Further signs of the tension was that both teams settled for an easy two points from penalties given in good attacking positions. Iestyn Harris put Britain ahead after 12 minutes and Fitzgibbon equalised four minutes later.

Australia went ahead in the 20th minute with Cooper's try and Fitzgibbon added the goal. Harris pulled back two points with another penalty goal following Barrett's first sin bin departure before Carney's try put the Lions level and the vast majority of the capacity crowd in a hopeful mood. They certainly got behind Britain and things were looking good until, as so often happens, Australia upped the tempo and scored with a late burst before the interval.

When Fitzgibbon's touchdown effort was disallowed Australia maintained the pressure for O'Meley to go over. Fitzgibbon's goal made it 8-14 at half-time and within three minutes of the restart he tagged on another penalty from 35 metres. The visitors began to take more control by the minute and they opened up with Tate's stunning try followed by Gasnier's. At 8-26 it was as good as over.

Britain had their final fling with Horne's try and a couple of near misses, but they struggled to make a significant impact and Australia finished worthy winners.

TEST MATCHES

Saturday 12th November 2005

FRANCE 12 AUSTRALIA 44

FRANCE: 1 Renaud Guigue; 2 Freddie Zitter; 3 Christophe Moly; 4 Jerome Hermet; 5 Olivier Charles; 6 Laurent Frayssinous; 7 Julien Rinaldi; 8 David Ferriol; 9 David Berthezene; 10 Jerome Guisset; 11 Djamel Fakir; 12 Sebastien Raguin; 13 Gregory Mounis. Subs (all used): 14 Maxime Greseque; 15 Adel Fellous; 16 Aurelien Cologni; 17 Jean-Christophe Borlin.
Tries: Frayssinous (17), Greseque (57); **Goals:** Frayssinous 2/2.
AUSTRALIA: 1 Anthony Minichiello (Sydney Roosters); 2 Eric Grothe (Parramatta Eels); 3 Mark Gasnier (St George-Illawarra Dragons); 4 Matt Cooper (St George-Illawarra Dragons); 5 Brent Tate (Brisbane Broncos); 6 Scott Prince (Wests Tigers); 7 Craig Gower (Penrith Panthers) (C); 8 Mark O'Meley (Bulldogs); 9 Craig Wing (Sydney Roosters); 10 Jason Ryles (St George-Illawarra Dragons); 11 Willie Mason (Bulldogs); 12 Ben Creagh (St George-Illawarra Dragons); 13 Trent Waterhouse (Penrith Panthers). Subs (all used): 14 Steve Price (New Zealand Warriors); 15 Petero Civoniceva (Brisbane Broncos); 16 Andrew Ryan (Bulldogs); 17 Matt King (Melbourne Storm).
Tries: Minichiello (5, 23), Mason (8), Waterhouse (30, 76), Prince (49), Gower (61), Cooper (68); **Goals:** Prince 6/8.
Rugby Leaguer & League Express Men of the Match:
France: Djamel Fakir; *Australia:* Craig Gower.
Penalty count: 6-7; **Half-time:** 6-22; **Referee:** Ashley Klein (England); **Attendance:** 7,500 *(at Stade Aime Giral, Perpignan).*

Friday 18th November 2005

FRANCE 22 NEW ZEALAND 38

FRANCE: 1 Adam Innes; 2 Olivier Charles; 3 Jerome Hermet; 4 Teddy Saddaoui; 5 Freddie Zitter; 6 Laurent Frayssinous; 7 Julien Rinaldi; 8 David Ferriol; 9 David Berthezene; 10 Jerome Guisset; 11 Laurent Carrasco; 12 Sebastien Raguin; 13 Christophe Moly. Subs (all used): 14 Maxime Greseque; 15 Aurelien Cologni; 16 Adel Fellous; 17 Djamel Fakir.
Tries: Raguin (3, 59), Ferriol (17), Charles (53);
Goals: Frayssinous 2/2, Greseque 1/2.
NEW ZEALAND: 1 Brent Webb (New Zealand Warriors); 2 Jake Webster (New Zealand Warriors); 3 Shontayne Hape (Bradford Bulls); 4 Clinton Toopi (New Zealand Warriors); 5 Paul Whatuira (Wests Tigers); 6 David Solomona (Wakefield Trinity Wildcats); 7 Stacey Jones (New Zealand Warriors); 8 Iafeta Palea'aesina (New Zealand Warriors); 9 David Faiumu (North Queensland Cowboys); 10 Ruben Wiki (New Zealand Warriors) (C); 11 Frank Pritchard (Penrith Panthers); 12 Ali Lauitiiti (Leeds Rhinos); 13 Bronson Harrison (Wests Tigers). Subs (all used): 14 Motu Tony (Hull FC); 15 Tony Puletua (Penrith Panthers); 16 David Kidwell (Melbourne Storm); 17 Louis Anderson (New Zealand Warriors).
Tries: Palea'aesina (8), Kidwell (15), Hape (34), Lauitiiti (54), Anderson (72), Jones (73), Webb (79); **Goals:** Jones 4/6, Tony 1/1.
Rugby Leaguer & League Express Men of the Match:
France: Sebastien Raguin; *New Zealand:* Brent Webb.
Penalty count: 11-7; **Half-time:** 12-16; **Referee:** Karl Kirkpatrick (England); **Attendance:** 8,013 *(at Stade Ernest Wallon, Toulouse).*

Gillette Tri-Nations 2005

New Zealand trailed France in Toulouse with nine minutes left before scoring three late tries through substitute Louis Anderson, scrum-half Stacey Jones - making yet another 'surprise appearance' - and fullback Brent Webb for a 38-22 win.

GILLETTE TRI-NATIONS FINAL

GILLETTE TRI-NATIONS - FINAL TABLE								
	P	W	D	L	F	A	D	Pts
Australia	4	3	0	1	102	84	18	6
New Zealand	4	2	0	2	118	120	-2	4
Great Britain	4	1	0	3	84	100	-16	2

Stacey Jones flew 12,000 miles home for the birth of his son, and back to arrive a day before the kick-off to inspire New Zealand to a remarkable 24-0 win over Australia at Elland Road.

The jet-lagged scrum-half helped end Australia's 27-year world dominance with a masterful display that saw him involved in all 24 of New Zealand's points. Two superbly-judged kicks brought tries, he was a key link in a passing move that brought another, and he sent in Brent Webb for the final touchdown. Add four goals, and there was no doubting his immense contribution.

The little general may have seemed to be sleep-walking at times, and rarely broke into more than a trot, but he was wide awake enough to plot Australia's downfall. It completed a great series for Jones, who was coaxed out of international retirement to replace the injured Thomas Leuluai.

But this was also a great all-round performance by New Zealand, full of pride, passion and power. And though Australia had finished on top of the Gillette Tri-Nations table, two points ahead of New Zealand, no one was doubting the Kiwis' right to be hailed as the world's best.

After all, this was their second defeat of Australia in this year's competition, following a 38-28 victory that was their first in Sydney for 46 years.

Australia were 5-1 on red hot favourites to lift the trophy, with the Kiwis given a ten-point start on the handicap coupons. Australia had not lost a Test series or world competition since losing twice to France in 1978. Australia had not lost twice to New Zealand in the same year since 1953.

Then, pow! New Zealand equalled their widest margin victory over the Aussies, and nilled them for the first time since they scored an 18-0 victory in 1985. It doesn't come much more convincing than that.

Australia never looked like winning – or scoring, apart from a near miss by Trent Barrett. Even after New Zealand stormed to a 16-0 interval lead there was a general feeling that Australia would reply with a typical match-winning late rush. It never came. Nor did the habitual New Zealand collapse.

This was the most controlled performance from a New Zealand side for many years. Full credit went to coach Brian McClennan.

In his first year in charge of New Zealand, McClennan allied their natural flair and skills to a more disciplined and methodical approach. Apart from their "holiday break" against Great Britain, when they lost 38-12, they applied themselves monastically to his gameplan.

Magnificently led by Ruben Wiki, the Kiwis' pack completely dominated the opposition. Wiki took the official man of the match award, but it could have been given as a token nomination for the whole pack.

The surprise switching of Bradford Bulls centre Shontayne Hape to loose forward was another shrewd move by McClennan. Hape looked a natural in the

The champagne flows as New Zealand celebrate their Tri-Nations success

role, and even outshone his opposite number, Ben Kennedy, who until Saturday had been one of Australia's best players during the series. "It's more embarrassing than disappointing," said Kennedy. "We never really gave ourselves a chance."

On a bitterly cold night, New Zealand must have been warmed by the great support they received from the vast majority of the 26,534 crowd. It only emphasised their role as clear underdogs. But they came out with the ferocity of Rottweilers, and within minutes a pack of them had rushed Australia winger Matt King into touch. The pattern was set. The Aussies were not to be allowed an inch.

Even before that New Zealand had taken the lead, with Paul Whatuira touching down Jones's perfectly-placed long cross-field kick. Jake Webster got to it first ahead of King, before Whatuira dived for the touchdown after the ball bounced loose. It was a 50-50 video decision,

GILLETTE TRI-NATIONS - FINAL

Saturday 26th November 2005

AUSTRALIA 0 NEW ZEALAND 24

AUSTRALIA: 1 Anthony Minichiello (Sydney Roosters); 2 Matt King (Melbourne Storm); 3 Mark Gasnier (St George-Illawarra Dragons); 4 Matt Cooper (St George-Illawarra Dragons); 5 Brent Tate (Brisbane Broncos); 6 Trent Barrett (St George-Illawarra Dragons); 7 Craig Gower (Penrith Panthers); 8 Petero Civoniceva (Brisbane Broncos); 9 Danny Buderus (Newcastle Knights) (C); 10 Jason Ryles (St George-Illawarra Dragons); 11 Luke O'Donnell (North Queensland Cowboys); 12 Craig Fitzgibbon (Sydney Roosters); 13 Ben Kennedy (Manly Sea Eagles). Subs (all used): 14 Craig Wing (Sydney Roosters) for Buderus (32); 15 Willie Mason (Bulldogs) for O'Donnell (31); 16 Mark O'Meley (Bulldogs) for Civoniceva (26); 17 Steve Price (New Zealand Warriors) for Ryles (26); Buderus for Tate (53); Ryles for Mason (53); O'Donnell for Kennedy (55); Civoniceva for O'Meley (58); Kennedy for Fitzgibbon (64); Mason for Price (66); O'Meley for Civoniceva (72).
NEW ZEALAND: 1 Brent Webb (New Zealand Warriors); 2 Jake Webster (Melbourne Storm); 3 Paul Whatuira (Wests Tigers); 4 Clinton Toopi (New Zealand Warriors); 5 Manu Vatuvei (New Zealand Warriors); 6 Nigel Vagana (Cronulla Sharks); 7 Stacey Jones (New Zealand Warriors); 8 Paul Rauhihi (North Queensland Cowboys); 9 Motu Tony (Hull FC); 10 Ruben Wiki (New Zealand Warriors) (C); 11 David Kidwell (Melbourne Storm); 12 Louis Anderson (New Zealand Warriors); 13 Shontayne Hape (Bradford Bulls). Subs (all used): 14 David Faiumu (North Queensland Cowboys) for Tony (24); 15 Roy Asotasi (Bulldogs) for Rauhihi (17); 16 David Solomona (Wakefield Trinity Wildcats) for Rauhihi (49); 17 Ali Lauitiiti (Leeds Rhinos) for Asotasi (57); Rauhihi for Wiki (31); Wiki for Kidwell (49); Tony for Faiumu (57); Faiumu for Vagana (62); Kidwell for Hape (72); Asotasi for Anderson (72); Rauhihi for Lauitiiti (75).
Tries: Whatuira (4), Vatuvei (20, 26), Webb (52);
Goals: Jones 4/7.
Rugby Leaguer & League Express Men of the Match: *Australia:* Trent Barrett; *New Zealand:* Stacey Jones.
Penalty count: 8-11; **Half-time:** 0-16; **Referee:** Steve Ganson (England); **Attendance:** 26,534 *(at Elland Road, Leeds).*

155

and it went in favour of New Zealand.

The powder keg atmosphere eventually exploded with a brawl in the 19th minute. It followed David Kidwell's interception of Craig Gower's pass as Australia threatened danger near the Kiwi line. Kidwell galloped to midfield before being smashed down by Brent Tate. When Luke O'Donnell was penalised for interference after the tackle, Kidwell threw the ball at him, and the Australian retaliated with a lunge that sparked off the brawl.

After the smoke cleared New Zealand took advantage of the territory gained from the penalty to mount a raid that ended with Jones, Louis Anderson and Clinton Toopi combining to send Manu Vatuvei over in the corner. Five minutes later the big winger was in again, when he touched down another accurate kick by Jones. It was a superbly-taken try by Vatuvei, as he jumped to snatch the ball from Tate's grasp and wrench himself away for the touchdown. The video again confirmed the score.

Jones had failed to convert any of the three tries from wide out, but he was spot on with penalty kicks in the 35th and 37th minute, both for interference after the tackle, to give New Zealand a totally unexpected 16-0 interval lead. It might have been more had not Vatuvei lost the ball as he cut inside near the opposition line.

The second half began with an air of anticipation that Australia would come out with all guns blazing in an attempt to achieve one of their famed late rush victories. But the more they tried the more desperate they became, and the mistakes followed.

In contrast, New Zealand remained totally focused on their objective, and made certain of it in the 51st minute when fullback Brent Webb burst on to Jones's pass and charged in from close range. There was a suggestion of an obstruction by Anderson on Barrett, but the video referee saw nothing wrong. Jones added the simple goal, and a penalty from 30 metres six minutes later following Steve Price's high tackle on Webb.

Webster almost got another Kiwi try in the 69th minute, only for Whatuira's pass to be ruled marginally forward. Jones had also been off target with a field goal that would have resulted in them breaking the record for Australia's widest margin defeat in any international match. That has stood since 1953 when New Zealand beat them 49-25 at Brisbane.

Australia tried desperately to avoid the ignominy of failing to score a try for the first

Roy Asotasi reaces away from Craig Wing

time in 20 years, but New Zealand defended as if the result was still in doubt, and came up with a series of magnificent last-ditch tackles that kept out the opposition. The final hooter heralded a historic victory for New Zealand and a great night for international Rugby League.

"We didn't give ourselves a chance," said Australian coach Wayne Bennett. "They played tremendously well, and coming into half-time their ball control was almost 100 per cent. We were 50."

Asked if he expected recriminations, Bennett answered: "What are they going to do? Stop us from going back to Australia? "Life will go on. We're a big enough country, a big enough nation to take a loss. We've had a lot of success over a long period of time in our sport. It was going to happen one day, it just happens to be today unfortunately."

OTHER INTERNATIONALS
Test crowds flock back

ANZAC TEST

Without Tony Puletua, Joe Galuvao and a host of 'retired' stars like Stacey Jones, Stephen Kearney and Awen Guttenbeil, the Kiwis found themselves 22-4 down a couple of minutes before half-time at Suncorp Stadium and seemingly headed for a flogging. But impressive debutant Jerome Ropati scored after a Jason Cayless offload and winger Jamaal Lolesi kicked his first top-grade goal to put Daniel Anderson's men back into the game at 10-22.

After half-time, they should have really put the wind up the Australians. Instead, they repeatedly failed to finish off breaks and spilt the ball. Needing no further invitation, the World Cup holders resumed normal service with centre Willie Tonga crossing in the 56th minute and fullback Anthony Minichiello in the 62nd.

The result was comfortable for Australia; not without hope for the Kiwis. "It's frustrating for the team," said Anderson afterwards. "We know we have to be very good to beat the Kangaroos. The Australians were a little too classy on the night but there were some signs there that were a little bit pleasing for us."

From Australia's point of view, the most important statistic was the crowd: 40,317. It was the highest attendance for a trans-Tasman Test in Brisbane ever and the highest for any of the green-and-golds' home games in more than three decades.

Australia coach Wayne Bennett told some First World War stories before kick-off, with the ANZAC long weekend one of remembrance on both sides of the Tasman.

ANZAC TEST

Friday 22nd April 2005

AUSTRALIA 32 NEW ZEALAND 16

AUSTRALIA: 1 Anthony Minichiello (Sydney Roosters); 2 Luke Rooney (Penrith Panthers); 3 Shaun Berrigan (Brisbane Broncos); 4 Willie Tonga (Bulldogs); 5 Matt Sing (North Queensland Cowboys); 6 Darren Lockyer (Brisbane Broncos) (C); 7 Brett Kimmorley (Cronulla Sharks); 8 Steve Price (New Zealand Warriors); 9 Luke Priddis (Penrith Panthers); 10 Petero Civoniceva (Brisbane Broncos); 11 Nathan Hindmarsh (Parramatta Eels); 12 Craig Fitzgibbon (Sydney Roosters); 13 Tonie Carroll (Brisbane Broncos). Subs (all used): 14 Craig Wing (Sydney Roosters); 15 Ben Kennedy (Manly Sea Eagles); 16 Mark O'Meley (Bulldogs); 17 Trent Waterhouse (Penrith Panthers).
Tries: Sing (10), Berrigan (16), Carroll (27), Lockyer (35), Tonga (55), Minichiello (61); **Goals:** Fitzgibbon 4/6.
NEW ZEALAND: 1 Jerome Ropati (New Zealand Warriors); 2 Jamaal Lolesi (Bulldogs); 3 Nigel Vagana (Cronulla Sharks); 4 Paul Whatuira (Wests Tigers); 5 Matt Utai (Bulldogs); 6 Benji Marshall (Wests Tigers); 7 Thomas Leuluai (London Broncos); 8 Paul Rauhihi (North Queensland Cowboys); 9 Louis Anderson (New Zealand Warriors); 10 Ruben Wiki (New Zealand Warriors) (C); 11 Frank Pritchard (Penrith Panthers); 12 Wairangi Koopu (New Zealand Warriors); 13 David Kidwell (Melbourne Storm). Subs (all used): 14 Dene Halatau (Wests Tigers); 15 Jason Cayless (Sydney Roosters); 16 Roy Asotasi (Bulldogs); 17 Clinton Toopi (New Zealand Warriors).
Tries: Utai (21), Ropati (39, 71); **Goals:** Lolesi 2/3.
Rugby Leaguer & League Express Men of the Match:
Australia: Steve Price; *New Zealand:* Benji Marshall.
Half-time: 22-10; **Referee:** Russell Smith (England);
Attendance: 40,317 *(at Suncorp Stadium, Brisbane).*

EUROPEAN NATIONS CHAMPIONSHIP

France continued their upward trend when they wrapped up the 2005 European Nations Championship with a 38-16 win over Wales in Carcassonne. The win marked their first victory over Wales in 24 years, and a further step along the way to France's rehabilitation as a senior League-playing nation.

The Euro Nations - which excluded England who had easily won the previous two year's competitions - was hailed a success by the man responsible for the competition, tournament director Graeme Thompson, especially the opportunity to ease Georgia into the family of League-nations.

"They've come a long, long way this year," he says. "They might have lost 60-nil to France, but they had some very good spells in that game, considering their lack of technical knowledge. I think they have a long-term commitment. We had a little bit of political unrest just before the tournament, and the people in charge now had to put up a fight to get where they are - so they have already shown their commitment.

Having marched into the final with an 80-0 crushing of Russia, and then an historic 60-0 win over Georgia in Tbilisi, the French found the mix of Super League, National League and Welsh Conference experience harder to overcome. The success was built on a solid pack performance, allied to a busy display by Catalans scrum-half Julien Rinaldi, and some fine wing play from Olivier Charles and Frédéric Zitter, who scored the first two French tries.

GROUP ONE

WALES 22 SCOTLAND 14

In a closely fought encounter at the home of the Celtic Crusaders, a crowd of well over a thousand saw Wales beat Scotland for the first time. With a five-try to two superiority the scoreline should have been bigger but the Welsh failed to convert any of their tries. The experience of captain Lee Briers was crucial to Wales' win and after the game he was optimistic about making the final in Carcassonne.

SCOTLAND 6 IRELAND 12

Constant drizzle accentuated the errors in Glasgow but didn't prevent a bruising encounter as Karl Fitzpatrick opened the scoring when he picked up a neat inside switch to score five metres from touch and then intercepted a Scottish pass and made 60 metres before offloading to Dean Gaskell who made no mistake by scoring under the posts. Paul Handforth slotted home the conversion to give Ireland a 10-0 lead going into the interval. The old heads of McDermott and skipper Terry O'Connor ensured the Irish remained cool under pressure, and a Billy Treacy penalty extended their lead. Scotland's persistent efforts were rewarded in the dying minutes of the game when Dave McConnell scored a fine individual try, Gareth Morton converting.

IRELAND 10 WALES 31

Ireland's hopes of progressing to the European Nations Cup final were blown away by a ferocious wind and a highly-charged Welsh side at a cold and wet Terenure.

As the rain pelted down, Lee Briers was outstanding as Wales marched to a 19-0 lead at the interval. Within one minute of the restart Michael Platt, playing on the wing, scored three metres from touch, though Paul Handforth missed the conversion.

But centre Anthony Blackwood's second try and then a penalty try on 70 minutes when Welsh hooker Ian Watson tried a chip and chase made it 31-4 going into the last ten minutes before Francis Cummins scored on 79 minutes, and Handforth had the final kick of the game with his successful conversion.

GROUP TWO

FRANCE 80 RUSSIA 0

France completely outclassed Russia - suffering from a political fall out in Moscow -in a one-sided European Nations opener. With John Monie in charge for the first time, the French ran in 14 tries and kicked 12 goals, virtually booking their place in the final. From the third minute, when Villeneuve winger Jérôme Hermet went over, it was all one-way. Hull KR centre Damien Couturier finished a dazzling handling move to score the game's most spectacular try but the opposition was too often found wanting.

RUSSIA 48 GEORGIA 14

Seven days after their humiliation in the south of France, two-try Russian hooker Roman Ovchinnikov led the Bears to an overwhelming win over a Georgian side containing several rugby union internationals. Ovchinnikov ran the show with his searing darts and clever distribution as the Russians were given too much latitude to display their skills by an inexperienced side, the opening quarter seeing the hosts race away to a decisive lead in the heavy Moscow rain. The first ever international Eastern European derby was played out in front of an enthusiastic crowd which included RFL Development Director Gary Tasker.

GEORGIA 0 FRANCE 60

Ten-try France were given a more than useful workout in preparation for the final in a cold and wet Tbilisi by a committed and enthusiastic Georgian side who have made impressive strides in their debut campaign.

Unlike the previous week in Russia, when the 'Lelos' seemed overawed by their more experienced opponents, the Georgians were highly competitive early on and were eventually undone by the sublime talents of stand-off Maxime Greseque, who posted 32 of Les Chanticleers points courtesy of three tries and an impeccable ten goals.

EUROPEAN NATIONS CHAMPIONSHIP - FINAL STANDINGS

Group One

	P	W	D	L	F	A	D	PTS
Wales	2	2	0	0	53	24	29	4
Ireland	2	1	0	1	22	37	-15	2
Scotland	2	0	0	2	20	34	-14	0

Group Two

	P	W	D	L	F	A	D	PTS
France	2	2	0	0	140	0	140	4
Russia	2	1	0	1	48	94	-46	2
Georgia	2	0	0	2	14	108	-94	0

EUROPEAN NATIONS CHAMPIONSHIP

Sunday 16th October 2005

GROUP ONE

WALES 22 SCOTLAND 14

WALES: 1 Damian Gibson (Halifax); 2 Bryn Powell (Featherstone Rovers); 3 Adam Hughes (Widnes Vikings); 4 Aled James (Sheffield Eagles); 5 Richard Johnson (Aberavon Fighting Irish); 6 Lee Briers (Warrington Wolves) (C); 7 Mark Lennon (Manly Sea Eagles); 8 David Mills (Widnes Vikings); 9 Ian Watson (Swinton Lions); 10 Gareth Dean (Carcassonne); 11 Anthony Blackwood (Halifax); 12 Jordan James (Castleford Tigers); 13 Phil Joseph (Swinton Lions). Subs (all used): 14 Karl Hocking (Bridgend Blue Bulls); 15 Byron Smith (Castleford Tigers); 16 Jon Breakingbury (Valley Cougars); 17 Neil Davies (Aberavon Fighting Irish).
Tries: Powell (10, 19), Hughes (55), James (61), Briers (80);
Goals: Briers 0/2, Lennon 1/4.
SCOTLAND: 1 Wade Liddell (Gateshead Thunder); 2 Jon Steel (Hull Kingston Rovers); 3 Dougie Flockhart (Clyde Bulls); 4 Gareth Morton (Hull Kingston Rovers); 5 Andy McPhail (Clyde Bulls); 6 Dave McConnell (Rochdale Hornets) (C); 7 Danny Brough (Hull FC); 8 Oliver Wilkes (Leigh Centurions); 9 Andrew Henderson (Castleford Tigers); 10 Richard Fletcher (Castleford Tigers); 11 Iain Marsh (Batley Bulldogs); 12 Alex Szostak (Bradford Bulls); 13 Mike Wainwright (Warrington Wolves). Subs (all used): 14 Ben Fisher (Halifax); 15 Andy Brown (Fife Lions); 16 Ian Sinfield (Swinton Lions); 17 Nick Surtees (St Albans Centurions).
Tries: Brough (24, 65); **Goals:** Morton 3/3.
Rugby Leaguer & League Express Men of the Match:
Wales: Lee Briers; *Scotland:* Danny Brough.
Half-time: 8-6; **Referee:** Thierry Alibert (France); **Attendance:** 1,176
(at Brewery Field, Bridgend).

GROUP TWO

FRANCE 80 RUSSIA 0

FRANCE: 1 Renaud Guigue; 2 Olivier Charles; 3 Adam Innes; 4 Damien Couturier; 5 Jerome Hermet; 6 Laurent Frayssinous; 7 Maxime Gresèque; 8 David Ferriol; 9 Cedric Gay; 10 Jerome Guisset; 11 Laurent Carrasco; 12 Gregory Mounis; 13 Christophe Moly. Subs (all used): 14 Julien Rinaldi; 15 Djamel Fakir; 16 Sebastien Raguin; 17 Freddie Zitter.
Tries: Hermet (3, 58), Charles (8), Couturier (14), Mounis (23), Ferriol (33, 46), Innes (38), Rinaldi (43), Raguin (54), Moly (61), Guigue (68), Gresèque (72, 78);
Goals: Frayssinous 8/9, Gresèque 4/5.
RUSSIA: 30 Oleg Sokolov; 2 Rinat Chamsoutdinov; 3 Sergei Dobrynin; 4 Artem Grigoryan; 5 Valentin Baskakov; 6 Viktor Nechaev; 7 Igor Gavrilin; 8 Jan Gvozdev; 9 Roman Ovchinnikov; 10 Andrey Dumalkin; 11 Alexander Lysenkov; 12 Irakli Schikvadze; 13 Evgeny Bouzhukov. Subs (all used): 8 Andrey Kuzovkov; 15 Denis Korolev; 16 Alexander Chulkov; 20 Nikolay Zagoskin.
Rugby Leaguer & League Express Men of the Match:
France: Maxime Gresèque; *Russia:* N/A.
Half-time: 34-0; **Referee:** Julian King (England); **Attendance:** 1,000
(at Stade Fournier, Arles).

Sunday 23rd October 2005

GROUP ONE

SCOTLAND 6 IRELAND 12

SCOTLAND: 1 Wade Liddell (Gateshead Thunder); 2 Jon Steel (Hull Kingston Rovers); 3 Mick Nanyn (Whitehaven); 4 Gareth Morton (Hull Kingston Rovers); 5 Dougie Flockhart (Clyde Bulls); 6 Dave McConnell (Rochdale Hornets) (C); 7 Andrew Henderson (Castleford Tigers); 8 Ryan McDonald (Halifax); 9 Ben

Fisher (Halifax); 10 Richard Fletcher (Castleford Tigers); 11 Iain Morrison (Huddersfield Giants); 12 Oliver Wilkes (Leigh Centurions); 13 Iain Marsh (Batley Bulldogs). Subs (all used): 14 Danny Brough (Hull FC); 15 Alex Szostak (Bradford Bulls); 16 Nick Surtees (St Albans Centurions); 17 Andy McPhail (Clyde Bulls).
Try: McConnell (76); **Goals:** Morton 1/1.
IRELAND: 1 Francis Cummins (Leeds Rhinos); 2 Michael Platt (Castleford Tigers); 3 Stuart Littler (Salford City Reds); 4 Anthony Stewart (Salford City Reds); 5 Dean Gaskell (Warrington Wolves); 6 Karl Fitzpatrick (Salford City Reds); 7 Martin Gambles (Blackpool Panthers); 8 Terry O'Connor (Widnes Vikings) (C); 15 Paul Handforth (Castleford Tigers); 10 Barrie McDermott (Leeds Rhinos); 11 Paul McNicholas (Hull FC); 12 Ged Corcoran (Dewsbury Rams); 14 Simon Finnigan (Widnes Vikings). Subs (all used): 13 Gareth Haggerty (Salford City Reds); 9 Philip Purdue (East Coast Eagles); 16 Billy Treacy (Treaty City Titans); 17 Kevin O'Riordan (Treaty City Titans).
Tries: Fitzpatrick (10), Gaskell (27);
Goals: Handforth 1/2, Treacy 1/1.
Rugby Leaguer & League Express Men of the Match:
Scotland: Ryan McDonald; *Ireland:* Dean Gaskell.
Half-time: 0-10; **Referee:** Jason Robinson (Australia); **Attendance:** 1,276
(at Old Anniesland, Glasgow).

GROUP TWO

RUSSIA 48 GEORGIA 14

RUSSIA: 1 Oleg Logunov; 2 Denis Korolev; 3 Sergei Dobrynin; 27 Oleg Smirnov; 5 Valentin Baskakov; 16 Viktor Nechaev; 7 Andrey Kuzovkov; 8 Jan Gvozdev; 9 Roman Ovchinnikov; 10 Andrey Dumalkin; 11 Alexander Lysenkov; 12 Irakli Schikvadze; 13 Evgeny Bouzhukov. Subs (all used): 4 Artem Grigoryan; 14 Alexander Chulkov; 18 Nikolay Zagoskin; 25 Rinat Chamsoutdinovv.
Tries: Kuzovkov, Ovchinnikov 2, Dobrynin, Nechaev, Schikvadze, Korolev, Grigoryan, Bouzhukov;
Goals: Kuzovkov 1/2, Logunov 5/7.
GEORGIA: 1 Giorgi Assatiani; 2 Zviad Koberidze; 3 Revaz Guigauri; 4 Aleksander Guilauri; 5 David Jhamutashvili; 6 Lekso Gugava; 7 Bidzina Samkharadze; 8 Giorgi Mtchedlishvili; 9 Nodar Andghuladze; 10 David Gasviani; 11 Giorgi Trapaidze; 12 Nikoloz Mkheidze; 13 Vakhtang Akhvlediani. Subs (all used): 14 Fridon Udessiani; 15 Vakhtang Tskhadadze; 16 Beka Qurashvili; 17 George Maisuradze.
Tries: Jhamutashvili 2, Maisuradze;
Goals: Udessiani 1/3.
Rugby Leaguer & League Express Men of the Match:
Russia: Roman Ovchinnikov;
Georgia: David Jhamutashvili.
Half-time: 32-4; **Referee:** Thierry Alibert (France). *(at Luzhniki Arena, Moscow).*

Sunday 30th October 2005

GROUP ONE

IRELAND 10 WALES 31

IRELAND: 1 Francis Cummins (Leeds Rhinos); 2 Michael Platt (Castleford Tigers); 4 Anthony Stewart (Salford City Reds); 3 Stuart Littler (Salford City Reds); 5 Dean Gaskell (Warrington Wolves); 6 Karl Fitzpatrick (Salford City Reds); 7 Paul Handforth (Castleford Tigers); 8 Terry O'Connor (Widnes Vikings) (C); 15 Martin Gambles (Blackpool Panthers); 10 Barrie McDermott (Leeds Rhinos); 11 Paul McNicholas (Hull FC); 12 Ged Corcoran (Dewsbury Rams); 14 Simon Finnigan (Widnes Vikings). Subs (all used): 13 Gareth Haggerty (Salford City Reds); 16 Billy Treacy (Treaty City Titans); 17 Kevin O'Riordan (Treaty City Titans); 18 Mike Brodie (Treaty City Titans).
Tries: Platt (41), Cummins (79);
Goals: Handforth 1/2.
Sin bin: O'Connor (32) - fighting.
WALES: 1 Damian Gibson (Halifax); 2 Bryn Powell (Featherstone Rovers); 3 Anthony Blackwood (Halifax); 4 Adam Hughes (Widnes

Vikings); 5 Richard Johnson (Aberavon Fighting Irish); 6 Lee Briers (Warrington Wolves) (C); 7 Mark Lennon (Manly Sea Eagles); 8 David Mills (Widnes Vikings); 9 Ian Watson (Swinton Lions); 10 Gareth Dean (Carcassonne); 11 Chris Morley (Halifax); 12 Jordan James (Castleford Tigers); 13 Phil Joseph (Swinton Lions). Subs (all used): 14 Paul Morgan (Bridgend Blue Bulls); 15 Lenny Woodard (Bridgend Blue Bulls); 16 Byron Smith (Castleford Tigers); 17 Gareth Price (Rochdale Hornets).
Tries: Blackwood (3, 55), Johnson (7), Hughes (25), Watson (70, pen);
Goals: Briers 5/6; **Field goal:** Briers.
Rugby Leaguer & League Express Men of the Match:
Ireland: Paul McNicholas; *Wales:* Lee Briers.
Half-time: 0-19; **Referee:** Tim Mander (Australia). *(at Terenure RFC, Dublin).*

GROUP TWO

GEORGIA 0 FRANCE 60

GEORGIA: 1 Giorgi Assatiani; 2 Zviad Koberidze; 3 Nodar Andghuladze; 4 Sandro Guilauri; 5 David Jhamutashvili; 6 Revaz Guigauri; 7 Irakli Ghvinjilia; 8 Beka Qurashvili; 9 Bidzina Samkharadze; 10 Giorgi Trapaidze; 11 Nikoloz Mkheidze; 12 Vakso Axvlediaki; 13 Vakhtang Akhvlediani. Subs (all used): 14 Fridon Udessiani; 15 David Gasviani; 16 Gregory Nishnianidze; 17 Mamuka Tskhadadze.
FRANCE: 1 Adam Innes; 2 Freddie Zitter; 3 Teddy Saddaoui; 4 Jerome Hermet; 5 Olivier Charles; 6 Maxime Gresèque; 7 Julien Rinaldi; 8 Sebastien Raguin; 9 David Berthezene; 10 Adel Fellous; 11 Laurent Carrasco; 12 Aurelien Cologni; 13 Christophe Moly. Subs (all used): 14 Gregory Mounis; 15 Thomas Bosc; 16 Cedric Gay; 17 Jean-Christophe Borlin.
Tries: Gresèque (7, 23, 74), Saddaoui (23, 70), Zitter (39, 76), Charles (46, 58), Mounis (53);
Goals: Gresèque 10/10.
Rugby Leaguer & League Express Men of the Match:
Georgia: Vakhtang Akhvlediani;
France: Maxime Gresèque.
Half-time: 0-24; **Referee:** Ben Thaler (England). *(at Vake Stadium, Tbilisi).*

Saturday 5th November 2005

FINAL

FRANCE 38 WALES 16

FRANCE: 1 Renaud Guigue; 2 Freddie Zitter; 3 Teddy Saddaoui; 4 Jerome Hermet; 5 Olivier Charles; 6 Laurent Frayssinous; 7 Julien Rinaldi; 8 David Ferriol; 9 David Berthezene; 10 Jerome Guisset; 11 Gregory Mounis; 12 Djamel Fakir; 13 Christophe Moly. Subs (all used): 14 Laurent Carrasco; 15 Maxime Gresèque; 16 Adel Fellous; 17 Sebastien Raguin.
Tries: Zitter (2, 16), Rinaldi (20), Saddaoui (33), Guisset (39, 66), Charles (77);
Goals: Frayssinous 5/7.
WALES: 1 Damian Gibson (Halifax); 2 Bryn Powell (Featherstone Rovers); 3 Aled James (Sheffield Eagles); 4 Adam Hughes (Widnes Vikings); 5 Richard Johnson (Aberavon Fighting Irish); 6 Lee Briers (Warrington Wolves); 7 Mark Lennon (Manly Sea Eagles); 8 David Mills (Widnes Vikings); 9 Ian Watson (Swinton Lions); 10 Gareth Dean (Carcassonne); 11 Anthony Blackwood (Halifax); 12 Jordan James (Castleford Tigers); 13 Phil Joseph (Swinton Lions). Subs (all used): 14 Paul Morgan (Bridgend Blue Bulls); 15 Lenny Woodard (Bridgend Blue Bulls); 16 Byron Smith (Castleford Tigers); 17 Gareth Price (Rochdale Hornets).
Tries: Hughes (29, 41), Briers (47);
Goals: Briers 2/3.
Sin bin: Dean (16) - high tackle;
Briers (53) - dissent.
Rugby Leaguer & League Express Men of the Match:
France: Julien Rinaldi; *Wales:* Ian Watson.
Half-time: 26-6; **Referee:** Glen Black (New Zealand); **Attendance:** 4,000
(at Stade Albert Domec, Carcassonne).

INTERNATIONAL FRIENDLIES

ENGLAND 22 FRANCE 12

France produced a spirited display at the scene of their last international victory over England in 1981, giving an experienced Great Britain aspirants side a real run for their money. Although playing the majority of the flowing rugby in the first half, the French showed that their defensive organisation had improved immensely under John Monie.

On a dank Headingley evening, the hosts took the lead; Malcolm Alker beginning the charge before fine passes from Richard Mathers and Eorl Crabtree allowed Chris Thorman to easily step Renaud Guigue for the opening score between the posts which he converted.

With second-rowers Sebastien Raguin and Djamel Fakir setting a fine lead, the French hit back as hooker David Berthezene scooted clear to burrow over and level. Laurent Frayssinous released Gregory Mounis, who was a creative thorn throughout the first half, and his magnificent cut-out pass set Olivier Charles clear. He kicked round Mathers but was obstructed and, from the penalty, typical Gallic flair produced a wonderful score as the ball rippled across the backline, Damien Couturier, Frayssinous and Julien Rinaldi allowing Mounis to send Zitter over in the corner.

The Barrow winger had another try effort disallowed two minutes later when Ade Gardner just forced him into touch after more great work from Berthezene and Mounis. A Frayssinous penalty made it 12-6.

England turned the match within 15 minutes of the re-start, as Luke Robinson dummied to Mark Gleeson before scrambling over past Berthezene and Guigue, and a clever grubber from Thorman allowed Jamie Jones-Buchanan pounce to put England back in front.

Victory was secured in the closing stages when Crabtree's offload was again the catalyst and on the last tackle Paul Sykes, who impressed throughout with his dogged defence and option taking, sent the big Huddersfield prop sliding over out wide on the blind side.

ENGLAND 22 NEW ZEALAND 30

Lance Hohaia's 79th minute try secured a 30-22 victory over England at Warrington, the day after Britain had lost their first Gillette Tri-Nations encounter with Australia. It put Hohaia, who ran the Kiwis' attack, in pole position to stand in for Stacey Jones, not expected to play in the following Saturday's GB re-match. But subsequently Hohaia was found to have further damaged ankle ligaments he had injured in the Tri-Nations opener in Sydney, and was withdrawn from the New Zealand party.

Mark Calderwood scored England's first two tries to strengthen support for his call-up to the Great Britain squad. The second was a beauty, coming two minutes after Manu Vatuvei had levelled the scores at 6-6. Calderwood appeared on the opposite wing and, released by Paul Sykes just inside his own half, he raced clear and cruised around stand-in fullback Henry Fa'afili. It was level at half-time after Shontayne Hape took two men with him after collecting captain

England's Ben Westwood finds his progress halted against New Zealand

Ali Lauitiiti's pass, before Chris Thorman kicked a penalty for an incorrect play-the-ball.

Within two minutes of the restart substitute Joe Vagana charged up the middle and one play later, Jake Webster took Hohaia's kick to score. But David Hodgson scored after Luke Robinson's dart from a scrum, then within a minute, Thorman pressed his own GB claim with a lovely little burst and delicate back-flick for Eorl Crabtree to sidestep his way under the posts.

New Zealand fought back well though, with Fa'afili, Paul Whatuira and Hohaia tries taking them home.

And elsewhere....

● A Cumbria select side defeated Ireland 64-4, during the Wolfhounds' preparation for the European Nations Championship.

● The Lebanon Cedars won the inaugural International Orara Valley Sevens, easily defeating the Sydney Metro All-Stars 44-16 in the final.

● Argentina hosted the Australian Police side in April, losing 40-4 and 50-6.

● In May Georgia brushed off a 2,000-mile trip from Tblisi to make a winning start to its Rugby League life, beating Holland 34-14 in the seaside town of Hook of Holland.

● Shaw Cross Sharks completed a successful tour of Serbia, winning a round robin sevens tournament involving locals Vojvodina and Morava, before going on to beat a Belgrade Select XIII 48-10.

● The Tupapa Panthers became 2005 Cook Islands premiers after beating the Titikaveka Bulldogs 24-12 in the grand final.

Other Internationals

● Holland defeated Serbia 26-10 at the FC Radnicki Stadium in Belgrade.

● In July over 8,000 fans attended the Euro Nations qualifier decider in Dynamo Stadium, Tblisi, as Georgia beat Serbia 44-12.

● Heidelberg Sharks beat StuSta München 72-64 on Saturday 23rd July in a 9-a-side game - the first ever League match between two German sides.

● The Vauxhall Vultures beat Olympic Angels 44-22 in the first game in the Jamaica National Rugby League.

● The Royal Scots won the Scotland RL Grand Final 56-46 over the Fife Lions at Glasgow's GHA Club.

● Liban Espoirs lost 26-0 to England Lionhearts at Lancaster in August.

● The Mu'a Saints won the 2005 Tongan championship, beating Nakolo Bulls 38-20 in the grand final.

● Australia won the World Youth under-16s Championship, thrashing France 62-6 in the final at the Olympic Stadium in Moscow.

● Mount Albert secured a 24-22 victory over Canterbury Bulls in the Bartercard Cup grand final.

● In Australia in October, Tonga beat Samoa 34-20; Fiji A beat Portugal 40-4; and Malta beat Greece 24-22 in Sydney; PNG beat the Junior Kangaroos 24-16 at Richardson Park in Darwin.

● The 2005 Mediterranean Cup was cancelled at the eleventh hour because of the reluctance of some sides to travel to Lebanon.

INTERNATIONAL FRIENDLIES

Sunday 16th October 2005

CUMBRIA 64 IRELAND 4

CUMBRIA: 1 Gary Broadbent (Whitehaven); 2 Craig Calvert (Whitehaven); 3 David Seeds (Whitehaven); 4 Wesley Wilson (Whitehaven); 5 Matt Gardner (Leeds Rhinos); 6 Lee Kiddie (Workington Town); 7 Liam Campbell (Wakefield Trinity Wildcats); 8 Mark Cox (Whitehaven); 9 Carl Sice (Whitehaven); 10 Dean Vaughan (Workington Town); 11 Spencer Miller (Whitehaven); 12 Howard Hill (Whitehaven); 13 Carl Rudd (Whitehaven). Subs (all used): 14 Brett McDermott (Whitehaven); 15 Matthew Tunstall (Workington Town); 16 Ryan McDonald (Halifax); 17 Craig Chambers (Whitehaven).
Tries: Gardner (1, 25), Broadbent (5, 32), Sice (20, 36), Vaughan (54), Calvert (62), Miller (65), McDonald (69), Campbell (72, 74), Wilson (79); **Goals:** Rudd 3/5, McDonald 2/4, Campbell 1/3, Tunstall 0/1.
IRELAND: 1 Michael Platt (Castleford Tigers); 2 Mike Brodie (Treaty City Titans); 3 Kevin O'Riordan (Treaty City Titans); 4 Anthony Stewart (Salford City Reds); 5 Carl De Chenu (Sheffield Eagles); 6 Billy Treacy (Treaty City Titans); 7 Martin Gambles (Treaty City Titans); 8 Philip Purdue (East Coast Eagles); 9 Eric Roberts (Kildare Dragons); 10 David Bates (York City Knights); 11 Eoin Power (Kildare Dragons); 12 Barry Sweeney (Waterford Vikings); 13 Wayne Corcoran (Halifax). Subs (all used): 14 Paul Handforth (Castleford Tigers); 15 Simon Finnigan (Widnes Vikings); 16 Stuart Littler (Salford City Reds); 17 Gareth Haggerty (Salford City Reds).
Try: Littler (45); **Goals:** Treacy 0/1.
Rugby Leaguer & League Express Men of the Match:
Cumbria: Liam Campbell; *Ireland:* Stuart Littler.
Penalty count: 7-7; **Half-time:** 30-0; **Referee:** Ben Thaler (England); **Attendance:** 1,216 *(at Recreation Ground, Whitehaven).*

Sunday 23rd October 2005

ENGLAND 22 FRANCE 12

ENGLAND: 1 Richard Mathers (Leeds Rhinos); 2 Mark Calderwood (Leeds Rhinos); 3 Paul Sykes (London Broncos); 4 Stuart Reardon (Bradford Bulls); 5 Ade Gardner (St Helens); 6 Chris Thorman (Huddersfield Giants) (C); 7 Luke Robinson (Salford City Reds); 8 Eorl Crabtree (Huddersfield Giants); 9 Malcolm Alker (Salford City Reds); 10 Paul Wood (Warrington Wolves); 11 Lee Radford (Bradford Bulls); 12 Jamie Jones-Buchanan (Leeds Rhinos); 13 Chris Charles (Salford City Reds). Subs (all used): 14 Mark Gleeson (Warrington Wolves); 15 Mike Bennett (St Helens); 16 Darrell Griffin (Wakefield Trinity Wildcats); 17 Andy Lynch (Bradford Bulls).
Tries: Thorman (6), Robinson (46), Jones-Buchanan (55), Crabtree (77); **Goals:** Thorman 3/4.
FRANCE: 1 Renaud Guigue; 2 Freddie Zitter; 3 Jerome Hermet; 4 Damien Couturier; 5 Olivier Charles; 6 Laurent Frayssinous; 7 Julien Rinaldi; 8 Jerome Guisset; 9 David Berthezene; 10 Adel Fellous; 11 Sebastien Raguin; 12 Djamel Fakir; 13 Gregory Mounis. Subs (all used): 14 Maxime Greseque; 15 Laurent Carrasco; 16 David Ferriol; 17 Christophe Moly.
Tries: Berthezene (16), Zitter (26); **Goals:** Frayssinous 2/3.
Rugby Leaguer & League Express Men of the Match:
England: Paul Sykes; *France:* Gregory Mounis.
Penalty count: 4-5; **Half time:** 4-6; **Referee:** Glen Black (New Zealand); **Attendance:** 2,609 *(at Headingley, Leeds).*

Sunday 6th November 2005

ENGLAND 22 NEW ZEALAND 30

ENGLAND: 1 Richard Mathers (Leeds Rhinos); 2 Mark Calderwood (Leeds Rhinos); 3 Paul Sykes (London Broncos); 4 Ben Westwood (Warrington Wolves); 5 David Hodgson (Salford City Reds); 6 Chris Thorman (Huddersfield Giants) (C); 7 Luke Robinson (Salford City Reds); 8 Eorl Crabtree (Huddersfield Giants); 9 Malcolm Alker (Salford City Reds); 10 Paul Wood (Warrington Wolves); 11 Stephen Wild (Wigan Warriors); 12 Lee Radford (Bradford Bulls); 13 Jon Wilkin (St Helens). Subs (all used): 14 Stuart Reardon (Bradford Bulls); 15 Jamie Jones-Buchanan (Leeds Rhinos); 16 Darrell Griffin (Wakefield Trinity Wildcats); 17 Andy Lynch (Bradford Bulls).
Tries: Calderwood (4, 17), Hodgson (58), Crabtree (59); **Goals:** Thorman 3/5.
NEW ZEALAND: 1 Henry Fa'afili (Warrington Wolves); 2 Jake Webster (Melbourne Storm); 3 Paul Whatuira (Wests Tigers); 4 Shontayne Hape (Bradford Bulls); 5 Manu Vatuvei (New Zealand Warriors); 6 Motu Tony (Hull FC); 7 Lance Hohaia (New Zealand Warriors); 8 Iafeta Palea'aesina (New Zealand Warriors); 9 David Faiumu (North Queensland Cowboys); 10 Tony Puletua (Penrith Panthers); 11 Louis Anderson (New Zealand Warriors); 12 Ali Lauitiiti (Leeds Rhinos) (C); 13 Bronson Harrison (Wests Tigers). Subs (all used): 14 Robbie Paul (Bradford Bulls); 15 Joe Vagana (Bradford Bulls); 16 Willie Poching (Leeds Rhinos); 17 Frank Pritchard (Penrith Panthers).
Tries: Vatuvei (15), Hape (31), Webster (42), Fa'afili (66), Whatuira (68), Hohaia (79); **Goals:** Hohaia 3/5, Poching 0/1.
Rugby Leaguer & League Express Men of the Match:
England: Chris Thorman; *New Zealand:* Lance Hohaia.
Penalty count: 6-3; **Half-time:** 12-12; **Referee:** Jason Robinson (Australia); **Attendance:** 7,298 *(at Halliwell Jones Stadium, Warrington).*

SEASON DOWN UNDER
Against all odds

'Fairytales can come true,
It can happen to you,
If you're young at heart.
For it's hard you will find,
To be narrow of mind,
If you're young at heart.'

Frank Sinatra sang the lyrics so well. And Wests Tigers coach Tim Sheens understood them even better. Sheens, young at heart but old in the wisdom gained in 22 years as a senior coach, took a side that bookmakers were suggesting might finish stone motherless last in the 2005 NRL Premiership to success in the final week of the race for the NRL crown.

The Tiger cubs – for that is what they were, mostly kids hardly out of nappies – shocked everyone, even probably Sheens himself, by beating the North Queensland Cowboys 30-16 in the Grand Final in front of 82,453 excited fans at Homebush on the first Sunday in October.

They were 75-1 outsiders to win the crown at the start of the season. Midway through the year their form was such that the bookmakers were offering odds of 150-1. If you haggled they'd feel pity and give you a juicy 200-1. And even as they started to peg back the leaders, they were still looked upon with disdain. After all, how could this team of 'no names' ever hope to compete with the likes of Brisbane (with nine internationals in their ranks), the Bulldogs (nine), St George Illawarra (six), and Parramatta (five).

In the words of the old Australian expression (a word play on the name of a famous old department store) – Wests Tigers had two chances of winning the Premiership, Buckleys and none!

In its five-year history, the club forged by a forced merger between two pioneering sides, Western Suburbs Magpies and Balmain Tigers, had never even reached the final eight for the end-of-season play-offs. They were completely written-off as potential challengers when thrashed 30-14 by the Melbourne Storm at Leichhardt in early June. But then came a remarkable winning streak of eight straight matches. And suddenly the ugly ducklings were a chance for the Minor Premiership.

Then the Storm broke again – Melbourne hammering the Tigers in the penultimate round of the season proper. And the following week, Penrith (out of the race for a spot in the play-offs) smacked their bottoms, too, on the Sunday before the finals.

In hindsight, the losses were seen as the wake-up call Wests needed. On the opening weekend of the play-offs they gave North Queensland a dreadful pounding, 50-6. Next to fall were the Brisbane Broncos (34-6) and, in the biggest surprise of all, the Tigers were outstanding in a 20-12 success over St George Illawarra Dragons. This set up a return bout with the Cowboys, who had regrouped after their embarrassing loss to Wests to overcome the Storm 24-16 before putting Parramatta Eels to the sword 29-0. The much-maligned Wests were favourites for the season finale. But they still had to wait for the fat lady to sing.

The Grand Final was going to make history even before the kick-off. Neither side had ever previously made it to the season decider. And when Wests Tigers eventually emerged triumphant they were the first of the NRL merged clubs to have achieved the ultimate prize. A long wait for the fans of the two merged sides was over. Balmain had last won the Premiership in 1969. For the Wests' fans it was a much longer wait – right back to 1952.

Pat Richards and Paul Whatuira savour Wests' Grand Final victory

The Cowboys were first on the scoreboard eight minutes into the encounter. Matt Bowen was in to touch down after a sensational passing movement, with Origin centre Paul Bowman flinging the ball blindly over his head and Johnathan Thurston grasping it with glee before slipping the ball on to the Cowboys' fullback.

The Tigers came back after a mistake by Bowman, who threw a loose pass behind his own line in the direction of Bowen. But it was instead snapped up by young substitute Wests prop Bryce Gibbs who, with his first touch of the ball, grabbed the try.

The Cowboys appeared to have replied almost immediately when Ty Williams was over the line. But Matt Cecchin, a late replacement as a touch judge, suggested there may have been an illegal tackle in the lead-up. And he was proved right with the video referees ruling Steve Southern had taken out Dene Halatau when he was about to make a tackle.

The Wigan-bound Wests winger Pat Richards had a try disallowed, too. He made a remarkable lunge for the line, with his legs in the air as the corner post was taken out by defenders. But the video replays showed the ball had slipped out of his hands when he tried to force it behind the tryline. Richards was lucky to even be playing after tearing ankle ligaments the previous weekend. But, with hours of recuperation in a hyperbaric chamber and pain-killing injections, he made it onto the pitch.

He was rewarded soon after when the Tigers scored one of the best tries of

Daniel Fitzhenry dives past the despairing challenge of Ty Williams to score

the season – maybe even the decade. Brett Hodgson took the ball deep in Wests territory and passed to Marshall. From just two metres out from his own line, Marshall tip-toed his way through the defence until he had reached the 40-metre line in the Cowboys' half. There he flicked a blind pass to a limping Richards who set off for the line. But his injured ankle slowed him down. As Richards looked like being caught he pushed away Rod Jensen with a disdainful fend and continued on to score.

Eventually, with the pain-killers wearing off, Richards was forced from the field. However, by this time he had done his job and helped establish a winning lead.

Another player who had gone into the Grand Final with injury doubts, Cowboys captain Travis Norton, gave his side a glimmer of hope when he collected a splendid reverse pass from Thurston to score in the 55th minute. But the Tigers replied with a try to Daniel Fitzhenry, set up by Prince and Shane Elford. Each team scored a late touchdown. But nothing was going to prevent a Wests win.

Scott Prince, named as NRL Captain of the Year in the Dally M Awards, won the Clive Churchill Medal as Man of the Match. But any one of the 17 Tigers could have been so honoured.

Sheens – and, for that matter, opposition coach Murray – heralded in a new era in Rugby League. The pair proved that young players, given the chance to use their innovative talents, will beat the older experienced stars who play the safe, dependable style of Rugby League demanded of coaches no longer young at heart.

More than 4.1 million Australians watched the NRL Grand Final on television – up almost 25 per cent on the previous year. In both Sydney and Brisbane it was the most-watched television programme of any kind for 2005. And in the NSW capital it was biggest Grand Final television audience in history.

And what about the sides that didn't make it to the Grand Final?

PARRAMATTA EELS (3rd)

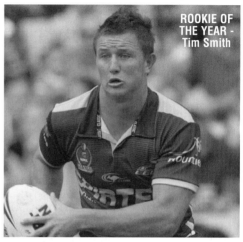

ROOKIE OF THE YEAR - Tim Smith

Brian Smith's Premiership hoodoo continued. Parramatta, the team he had coached to win the NRL Minor Premiership and favourite to take out the major crown, crashed at the second-last hurdle, steam-rolled in their preliminary final by an enthusiastic North Queensland Cowboys outfit. It was the latest in a succession of disappointments for the respected coach – from defeats by St George and the Bradford Bulls to a shock loss in the 2001 NRL Grand Final with the Eels.

Parramatta's loss was even more dramatic in that it was the only occasion in 2005 that the Eels had failed to get on the scoreboard.

The bright spot was the emergence of 20-year-old scrum-half Tim Smith, who was named Rookie of the Year at the annual Dally M Awards night.

ST GEORGE-ILLAWARRA DRAGONS (4th)

When the Dragons lost five of their first six matches there was a chorus of calls for coach Nathan Brown to be axed. But then St George Illawarra found the form that had been missing. And by the time the finals were played the Dragons were disputing Premiership favouritism with Parramatta.

And with good reason. They had no less than six internationals in their side – centres Mark Gasnier and Matt Cooper, stand-off Trent Barrett, props Jason Ryles and Luke Bailey, utility star Shaun Timmins. And in October a seventh would make the grade – 20-year-old centre turned second-rower Ben Creagh, seconded to Australia's Tri-Nations squad.

But the Dragons left their worst form for the match that counted – the preliminary final against subsequent champions Wests Tigers.

Brown was heartbroken.

"You blokes [journalists] don't realise how hard it is to win a comp," he noted.

"They're bloody hard to win. It's not anyone's God-given right to win a Grand Final or even get there."

BRISBANE BRONCOS (5th)

Once again the Broncos promised so much and failed to deliver at the business end of the season. They sat at the top of the NRL Ladder for most of the season. But then they lost their last seven games, to forego the Minor Premiership when beaten by Parramatta in the final round and then go down to Melbourne and Wests Tigers in their two finals' appearances.

Coach Wayne Bennett reacted by sacking the three highest profile members of his coaching staff – former internationals Kevin Walters, Gary Belcher and Glenn Lazarus.

Whether that will be enough to change the Broncos' fortunes in 2006 only time will tell. But a side led by Australian Test captain Darren Lockyer and with internationals Shane Webcke, Petero Civoniceva, Shaun Berrigan, Brent Tate, Brad Thorn, Tonie Carroll, Darren Smith and Dane Carlaw in its ranks shouldn't cave in when the going gets tough.

MELBOURNE STORM (6th)

Another team to falter when the chips were down was the Melbourne Storm. The Storm reached the play-offs where they beat a disappointing Brisbane outfit only to fall in the second week to the Cowboys. But they did manage to produce two Tri-Nations debutants – centre Matt King (Australia) and winger Jake Webster (New Zealand).

Melbourne could find the going tougher in 2006 with the retirement of long-serving captain Robbie Kearns and the defection of playmaker Matt Orford and centre Steve Bell to Manly. Kiwi international prop Alex Chan has also departed to join Les Catalans in their first season in Super League.

CRONULLA SHARKS (7th)

After winning eight of their first 10 matches, the Sharks were looking to have a feeding frenzy at the expense of the other NRL sides. Then everything went pear-shaped with thrashings at the hands of the Eels, Cowboys and Tigers. And Cronulla never recovered.

They were given a lift in Round 24 at Brookvale when they posted a record 68-6 victory over Manly. That afternoon captain Brett Kimmorley thumbed his nose at critics who had attacked him since NSW's Origin I defeat with a hat-trick and a hand in many of the other nine Cronulla tries.

But the hoped-for revival never came and the Sharks were eliminated in the first week of the play-offs.

MANLY SEA EAGLES (8th)

The Sea Eagles achieved more than most critics expected in 2005. This was thanks largely to the inspirational efforts of veteran backrower Ben Kennedy, who joined the club from Newcastle and figured prominently in almost every Player of the Year Award, including the Dally Ms.

They won five of their first six games to lead the Premiership race. But eventually they ran out of petrol and were unceremoniously bundled out of the play-offs in the first week, beaten 46-22 by Parramatta.

Kennedy and that other stalwart Steve Menzies were NSW Origin regulars and young second-rower Anthony Watmough made his inter-state debut.

Manly will be boosted in 2006 by the signings from Melbourne, Matt Orford and Steve Bell.

SYDNEY ROOSTERS (9th)

One of the great disappointments of 2005. Here was a side that had played in four of the previous five Grand Finals and boasted no less than seven Test and World Cup stars in its ranks (Luke Ricketson, Anthony Minichiello, Adrian Morley, Jason Cayless, Craig Wing, Craig Fitzgibbon and Michael Crocker).

Yet the Roosters failed to make the play-offs. They sorely missed the genius of retired captain Brad Fittler. Players of that calibre are never easy to replace. But there was also some hint of internal dissention, especially concerning Crocker, who will team up with Melbourne next season.

A plus for the Roosters is the recruitment for 2006 of former Test stand-off Braith Anasta and hard-working Souths skipper Ashley Harrison.

PENRITH PANTHERS (10th)

It was a year the Panthers would rather forget. After figuring prominently for three seasons (highlighted by their Premiership success in 2003), the side from the foot of the Blue Mountains never really looked like setting the competition on fire (despite an impressive 38-22 victory over the eventual champions Wests Tigers in the final round of the home-and-away games).

And the disappointments were magnified when only Trent Waterhouse and Craig Gower made Australia's side for the Tri-Nations opener and Frank Pritchard the Kiwi line-up.

NEW ZEALAND WARRIORS (11th)

Coach Tony Kemp was shown the door after an unsatisfactory 2005 and former Roosters and Warriors fullback Ivan Cleary will be at the helm next season.

The Warriors' problem was their inability to get home in the tight clashes. They lost five of the eight encounters that were decided by six points or less. Had they won another two they would have figured in the finals series.

They did miss new captain Steve Price who was out for a couple of months after being injured in the first State of Origin clash. But he and Kiwi Test captain Ruben Wiki did provide some much-needed spirit in the Warriors pack.

The big question mark for 2006 is who will step into the shoes of departing veteran half Stacey Jones who has left to join Les Catalans in Perpignan. And the Warriors will also miss the exciting play of Iafeta Palea'aesina who has accepted big bucks on offer at Wigan.

BULLDOGS (12th)

What a fall from grace! Premiers one year – able to beat home only three clubs the next.

They started the Premiership with a real growl, savaging St George Illawarra 46-28 in the opening round. But from then on it was all downhill. Granted the Bulldogs had a horror run of injuries, but they still had enough stars in action to have given a better account of themselves.

Here are how many games each of the Tests stars missed – Sonny Bill Williams (21), Willie Tonga (18), Willie Mason (17), Mark O'Meley (12) and Hazem El Masri (eight). Playmaker Brent Sherwin, fullback Luke Patten and tough forward Rene Maitua each also missed a significant part of the season.

SOUTH SYDNEY RABBITOHS (13th)

Poor old Souths. At last they have some money to spend on some half-decent stars. And they have managed to attract a world-renowned coach in Shaun McRae to the Rabbits' burrow.

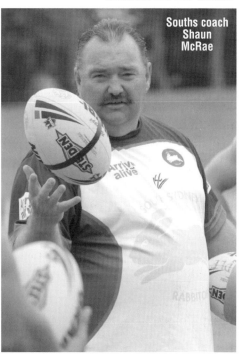

Souths coach Shaun McRae

But the big name players still don't want to play in a team bereft of other achievers and with little on the scoreboard to suggest that a renaissance is on its way. Matt Orford (Storm) and Braith Anasta (Bulldogs) each rejected megabucks to join the Rabbitohs next year. And to rub salt into the wound, Souths' best in 2005, Ashley Harrison, departed for greener pastures at Bondi.

On the positive side, Souths do have a few exciting youngsters in Yileen 'Buddy' Gordon, Beau Champion and John Sutton coming through the ranks.

CANBERRA RAIDERS (14th)

Four straight wins to start the season had former Bulls coach Matthew Elliott in an excited frame of mind. But then his Raiders side hit the wall. Cursed by a record number of injuries, Canberra were never really in the hunt for success.

One can only wonder how much worse the record may have been but for the return to Australia from Super League of the aging Hull stand-off Jason Smith and Rhino forward Matt Adamson. And then they were out injured, too, and the side looked rudderless.

NEWCASTLE KNIGHTS (15th)

For a while it looked as if Newcastle could go through the entire season without a win (the most recent side to be so embarrassed was Eastern Suburbs back in 1967). The Knights were suffering from the absence of injured superstars Andrew Johns and Danny Buderus and lost their first 13 encounters.

Then Johns returned from his broken jaw, weaved his magic and...hey presto...Newcastle started knocking off the top teams. Even though they couldn't avoid the wooden spoon they went into the history books with the best record of any side to finish last – eight victories. And included in those wins were successes over Grand Finalists, the North Queensland Cowboys, and Minor Premiers, the Parramatta Eels.

With the arrival of Wigan star Brian Carney for the 2006 season, things are looking rosy at EnergyAustralia Stadium, where packed houses will frighten even the best of opponents in 2006.

NRL SCOREBOARD

FINAL NRL PREMIERSHIP TABLE

	P	W	L	D	B	F	A	Pts
Parramatta Eels	24	16	8	0	2	704	456	36
St George-Illawarra Dragons	24	16	8	0	2	655	510	36
Brisbane Broncos	24	15	9	0	2	597	484	34
Wests Tigers	24	14	10	0	2	676	575	32
North Queensland Cowboys	24	14	10	0	2	639	563	32
Melbourne Storm	24	13	11	0	2	640	462	30
Cronulla Sharks	24	12	12	0	2	550	564	28
Manly Sea Eagles	24	12	12	0	2	554	632	28
Sydney Roosters	24	11	13	0	2	488	487	26
Penrith Panthers	24	11	13	0	2	554	554	26
New Zealand Warriors	24	10	14	0	2	515	528	24
Bulldogs	24	9	14	1	2	472	670	23
South Sydney Rabbitohs	24	9	14	1	2	482	700	23
Canberra Raiders	24	9	15	0	2	465	606	22
Newcastle Knights	24	8	16	0	2	467	667	20

(Eels won JJ Giltinan Shield as the NRL Minor Premiers)

QUALIFYING FINALS

WESTS TIGERS 50 ....**NORTH QUEENSLAND COWBOYS 6**
Tigers: T – Shane Elford (15), Brett Hodgson (29, 44, 72), Daniel Fitzhenry (47), Paul Whatuira (65), Liam Fulton (69), Pat Richards (78); G – Brett Hodgson 9/9
Cowboys: T – Matt Sing (36); G – Josh Hannay 1/1
Half-time: 14-6; **Referee:** Paul Simpkins
Video referees: Graeme West & Mick Stone
Attendance: 26,463 *at Telstra Stadium (September 9)*

BRISBANE BRONCOS 18 ....**MELBOURNE STORM 24**
Broncos: T – Scott Minto (19), Darren Smith (42), Brett Seymour (75); G – Brett Seymour 3/4
Storm: T – Jake Webster (14), Billy Slater (30), Matt King (35), Greg Inglis (67); G – Cameron Smith 2/2, Matt Orford 2/2
Half-time: 4-18; **Referee:** Steve Clark
Video referee: Chris Ward
Attendance: 25,193 *at Suncorp Stadium (September 10)*

ST GEORGE-ILLAWARRA DRAGONS 28 ....**CRONULLA SHARKS 22**
Dragons: T – Colin Best (17, 47), Dean Young (52), Trent Barrett (55), Wes Naiqama (74); G – Michael Ennis 4/4, Wes Naiqama 0/1
Sharks: T – Beau Scott (11), David Simmons (44), Nigel Vagana (65), Paul Gallen (78); G – Luke Covell 3/4
Half-time: 4-6; **Referee:** Tony Archer
Video referees: Phil Cooley & Steve Nash
Attendance: 19,608 *(Ground record) at WIN Stadium (September 10)*

PARRAMATTA EELS 46 ....**MANLY SEA EAGLES 22**
Eels: T – Timana Tahu (8, 50), Chad Robinson (11), Mark Riddell (17), Eric Grothe (27), Luke Burt (35), Daniel Wagon (68), Adam Peek (79); G – Luke Burt 7/8
Sea Eagles: T – Anthony Watmough (46), Ben Kennedy (73, 75); G – Michael Witt 0/1, Michael Monaghan 1/1, Luke Williamson 2/2
Half-time: 28-0; **Referee:** Tim Mander
Video referees: Mick Stone & Graeme West
Attendance: 19,710 *at Parramatta Stadium (September 11)*

SEMI-FINALS

MELBOURNE STORM 16 ....**NORTH QUEENSLAND COWBOYS 24**
Storm: T – Steve Bell (46), Matt King (63), Matt Orford (69); G – Cameron Smith 1/1, Matt Orford 1/2
Cowboys: T – Matt Bowen (10), Ty Williams (18, 22), David Faiumu (77); G – Josh Hannay 2/2, Johnathan Thurston 2/2
Half-time: 0-16; **Referee:** Paul Simpkins
Video referees: Chris Ward & Mick Stone
Attendance: 16,810 *at Aussie Stadium (September 17)*

WESTS TIGERS 34 ....**BRISBANE BRONCOS 6**
Tigers: T – Benji Marshall (15), Daniel Fitzhenry (40, 68), Scott Prince (44), Mark O'Neill (63), Brett Hodgson (76); G – Brett Hodgson 5/6
Broncos: T – Darren Lockyer (47); G – Brett Seymour 1/1
Half-time: 10-0; **Referee:** Tim Mander
Video referees: Graeme West & Phil Cooley
Attendance: 36,563 *at Aussie Stadium (September 18)*

PRELIMINARY FINALS

ST GEORGE-ILLAWARRA DRAGONS 12 ....**WESTS TIGERS 20**
Dragons: T – Wes Naiqama (26), Trent Barrett (52); G – Michael Ennis 2/2
Tigers: T – Benji Marshall (3), Dean Halatau (22, 56), Chris Heighington (34); G – Brett Hodgson 2/4
Half-time: 6-16; **Referee:** Tim Mander
Video referees: Mick Stone & Chris Ward
Attendance: 41,260 *at Aussie Stadium (September 24)*

PARRAMATTA EELS 0 ....**NORTH QLD COWBOYS 29**
Cowboys: T – Matt Bowen (23), Rod Jensen (38), Brett Firman (38), Ty Williams (54), Josh Hannay (65); G – Josh Hannay 4/5; FG – Johnathan Thurston (60)
Half-time: 0-18; **Referee:** Steve Clark
Video referee: Phil Cooley & Graeme West
Attendance: 44,327 *at Telstra Stadium (September 25)*

GRAND FINAL

WESTS TIGERS 30 ....**NORTH QUEENSLAND COWBOYS 16**
Tigers: T – Gibbs (17), Richards (35), Laffranchi (45), Fitzhenry (62), Payten (79); G – Hodgson 5/6
Cowboys: T – Bowen (8), Norton (55); G – Hannay 2/3
Tigers: 1 Brett Hodgson; 2 Daniel Fitzhenry; 3 Shane Elford; 4 Paul Whatuira, 5 Pat Richards; 6 Benji Marshall, 7 Scott Prince (c); 8 Anthony Laffranchi, 9 Robbie Farah, 10 John Skandalis, 11 Ben Galea, 12 Mark O'Neill, 13 Dene Halatau. Subs: 14 Liam Fulton, 15 Chris Heighington, 16 Bryce Gibbs, 17 Todd Payten.
Cowboys: 1 Matt Bowen; 2 Ty Williams, 3 Josh Hannay, 4 Paul Bowman, 5 Matt Sing; 16 Justin Smith, 6 Johnathan Thurston; 8 Paul Rauhihi, 9 Aaron Payne, 10 Shane Tronc, 11 Steve Southern, 12 Luke O'Donnell, 13 Travis Norton (c). Subs: 7 Brett Firman, 14 Rod Jensen, 15 David Faiumu, 17 Mitchell Sargent.
Rugby Leaguer & League Express Men of the Match:
Tigers: Scott Prince; *Cowboys:* Johnathan Thurston
Clive Churchill Medal: Scott Prince (Wests Tigers)
Referee: Tim Mander; **Video referees:** Graeme West & Mick Stone
Half-time: 12-6; **Attendance:** 82,453 *at Telstra Stadium (October 2)*

TOP POINTSCORERS

	T	G	FG	Pts
Brett Hodgson (Wests Tigers)	15	124	0	308
Luke Burt (Parramatta Eels)	11	85	0	214
Preston Campbell (Penrith Panthers)	11	73	0	190
Luke Covell (Cronulla Sharks)	9	75	0	186
Hazem El Masri (Bulldogs)	11	68	0	180
Matt Orford (Melbourne Storm)	10	63	2	172

TOP TRYSCORERS

Matt Bowen (North Queensland Cowboys)	21
Colin Best (St George-Illawarra Dragons)	20
Pat Richards (Wests Tigers)	20
Billy Slater (Melbourne Storm)	20
Shaun Berrigan (Brisbane Broncos)	19
Paul Whatuira (Wests Tigers)	18
Ty Williams (North Queensland Cowboys)	18

MINOR GRADES GRAND FINALS

NSWRL PREMIER LEAGUE

PARRAMATTA EELS 31 ....**SYDNEY ROOSTERS 12**
Eels: T – Joel Reddy (24), Jarryd Hayne (32, 36), Ashley Graham (45), Drew Dalton (75); G – Brett Delaney 5/5; FG – Marcus Perenara (73)
Roosters: T – Nigel Plum (50), Michael Lett (55); G – Jamie Soward
Half-time: 18-0; **Referee:** Ben Cummins

NSWRL JERSEY FLEGG TROPHY *(Under-20s)*

ST GEORGE-ILLAWARRA DRAGONS 30............**PARRAMATTA EELS 20**
Dragons: T – Tom Hewitt (5, 47), Josh Lewis (33), Chris Houston (51), Jason Nightingale (56), Beau Ryan (66); G – Josh Lewis 3/6
Eels: T – Michael Bason (17), Simon Micallef (22), Krisnan Inu (36), Weller Hauraki (68); G – David Williams 2/4
Half-time: 10-10; **Referee:** Jason Robinson

DALLY M AWARDS

Dally M Medal (Player of the Year):
Johnathan Thurston (North Queensland Cowboys)
Coach of the Year: Tim Sheens (Wests Tigers)
Captain of the Year: Scott Prince (Wests Tigers)
Rookie of the Year: Tim Smith (Parramatta Eels)
Summons-Provan Medal (Fans' choice):
Nathan Hindmarsh (Parramatta Eels)
Representative Player of the Year: Andrew Johns (Newcastle Knights)

POSITIONAL WINNERS

Fullback: Brett Hodgson (Wests Tigers)
Wing: Eric Grothe (Parramatta Eels)
Centre: Mark Gasnier (St George-Illawarra Dragons)
Stand-off: Braith Anasta (Bulldogs)
Scrum half: Andrew Johns (Newcastle Knights)
Prop: Luke Bailey (St George-Illawarra Dragons)
Hooker: Danny Buderus (Newcastle Knights)
Second row: Nathan Hindmarsh (Parramatta Eels)
Loose forward: Ben Kennedy (Manly Sea Eagles)

STATE OF ORIGIN SERIES

If they ever need evidence that Andrew Johns is one of the greatest players in the modern era, Rugby League historians should look no further than his displays in the 2005 State of Origin series. It was Johns who turned the series New South Wales' way with two of the most dominant performances seen in the quarter-of-a-century of Origin encounters. Yet, he should not have even been playing.

Wind back time to April 17. Johns was leading his beloved Knights against the New Zealand Warriors on a day that was supposed to be one of celebration, as the Newcastle club unveiled their new grandstand. Joey had only been back in action for six weeks after missing most of the previous season recovering from a knee reconstruction. Some 14 minutes from full-time he went in for a tackle on one of the Warriors and reeled away with a badly-broken jaw.

Critics thought it may be the end of Johns' illustrious career. But, with only one game under his belt he was drafted into the NSW side for Origin II after Trent Barrett had failed a fitness test. The selectors were not without their critics. But history shows how Johns turned in a five-star performance to inspire NSW to a victory that squared up the series. And in another superb display he helped the Blues to success in the third and deciding encounter.

The Queenslanders have always been opponents of the idea of 'golden point' extra time. It was forced upon them by the officials in Sydney. But in the opening Origin encounter at Suncorp Stadium (Lang Park) the system worked in their favour. And what a finish it provided!

The Blues had staged a remarkable comeback from 19-0 down with 32 minutes left on the clock to momentarily hit the lead before seeing the clash head into extra time. Then, after three minutes of spine-tingling excitement, NSW scrum half Brett Kimmorley threw a desperation pass, hoping to break the deadlock. He certainly did – but not in the way he had expected. Like a thief in the night, will-o'-the-wisp Queensland substitute Matt Bowen plucked the ball out of the air and sped 40 metres to the tryline to steal the game 24-20 for the Maroons.

In truth, the old system in which the game would have ended in a draw would have been a much fairer result. For in the words of the cliché, neither side deserved to lose. This opener of the 25th anniversary Origin series was a spectacular demonstration of why Rugby League is 'The Greatest Game Of All'. The record Brisbane crowd of 52,484 was enthralled for the 83 minutes and 19 seconds of the encounter. So, too, were the 3.1 million Australians who watched it on television (and the figure would have been higher had the blinkered hierarchy on the Nine Network had the courage to show it live in the Australian Rules strongholds of Melbourne, Adelaide and Perth).

Two Cameron Smith penalties had the home side ahead 2-0. Then came a controversial decision that affected the final result. Queensland captain Darren Lockyer flung a pass at fullback Billy Slater who was charging into the backline at speed. It appeared to have been knocked forward. Queensland debutant winger Ty Williams pounced on the ball and touched down. In a shock ruling video referee Graeme West ruled the ball had missed Slater's hands and had come off the fullback's knees (or at least one knee).

After the now traditional melee, with Carl Webb taking on Luke Bailey and putting the big Test prop off his game, the Queenslanders continued to dominate. Another Smith penalty goal stretched the lead to 12-0. And in the closing seconds of the first half, Lockyer calmly potted a field goal.

Soon after play resumed for the second half there was a magic long pass from Lockyer. Second-rower Michael Crocker hit the ball at full speed and, running at a wonderful angle that bamboozled the NSW defence, he was over the tryline before the Blues could blink. Smith's conversion had the Maroons looking good at 19-0.

What followed was a miraculous transformation of the match.

Penrith's Test winger Luke Rooney finished off a crisp backline movement with a try. Ten minutes later Minichiello broke through and Mark Gasnier scored. The New South Welshmen were on a roll. Craig Fitzgibbon won the race for the ball after a cross-field kick from Cooper. And just two and a half minutes later NSW captain Danny Buderus started and finished a 60-metre movement and the Blues were in front for the first time, 20-19, with less than nine minutes left on the clock.

Lockyer should have given Queensland victory with three and a half minutes remaining, but he missed a relatively simple attempt at a penalty goal from in front (first-choice kicker Smith was having a breather on the bench). Then with just over two minutes until full-time, Thurston snapped the field goal that locked up the scores. All that remained was for Bowen to score his wonderful intercept try in 'golden point' time.

The thrilling finish to Origin I ensured there was not a vacant seat in the cavernous Telstra Stadium when the gladiators resumed their battle in Sydney. A sell-out crowd of 82,389 packed the Homebush arena and there would not have been one among their number who wouldn't have been wondering if Johns could make a successful comeback at the elite level.

Even though he had played just one game for Newcastle after recovering from the smashed jaw, NSW coach Ricky Stuart had wanted him in his side. But the selectors were not convinced and chose Dragons captain Trent Barrett out of position at No 7. When Barrett was forced out through injury, the selectors bowed to Stuart's wishes. It was defining moment in the history of the State of Origin.

Johns turned in a performance that only the great players can produce. As the Blues triumphed 32-22, he had a hand in all five NSW tries. And his kicking had to be seen to be believed. Long kicks, including a vital 40/20 that helped swing the game. Banana kicks. Chip kicks. Bombs. Three out of three attempts at conversion. He displayed his whole perfect repertoire.

Then there was his passing game. Long cut-out passes and short, crisp flicks to catch the Queensland defences unawares. And when he decided to run the ball ... well, Johns has no peer at that.

"It was outstanding for a bloke who has been out of the game for so long," said Stuart. "We all talk about champions who come back and play Origin football ... but he's not making a comeback, Joey. He's just re-igniting his representative career. For a player to come back and have that bearing on a game of football ... he's an extremely gifted footy player."

Without Johns NSW would probably have been beaten and the series wrapped up by Queensland. Instead the Blues dominated a game that continued Queensland's awful record at the old Olympic stadium. Ten matches, nine losses and one lone draw.

The Maroons were ahead at half-time even though NSW dominated early. NSW winger Rooney looked like scoring but Billy Slater punched the ball out of his hands. Matt King was close to scoring on the other flank. When caught he sent a basketball pass inside towards an unmarked Minichiello only to see it intercepted by the hard-working Michael Crocker. A kick by Johns bore fruit, bouncing off the left goalpost to be scooped up by Minichiello, who fell over the line to score. And a penalty goal stretched the lead to eight before Queensland hit back.

Lockyer put up a cross-field bomb and big Brad Thorn leaped high to take the ball and touch down. A length of the field move by Crocker and Lockyer gave them a further tryscoring opportunity, but King saved the day for the Blues. Then just before half-time, Minichiello spilled a pass from Braith Anasta. Slater pounced on the loose ball and sped 85 metres to score. It was 12-8 to the Queenslanders at the break.

They looked to have gone further ahead soon after play resumed in the second stanza when referee Steve Clark was ready to rule a try to winger Ty Williams. But a touch judge ruled he had taken a forward pass.

It was crucial decision. Moments later Johns booted his 40/20. And after two sets of six, Johns threw a long pass to Anasta who put Minichiello over for his second try. Then, within a period of just 23 seconds, Danny Buderus and Luke Bailey were tackled short of the line before Johns set up a try for veteran Steve Menzies. At 20-12 the Blues were looking good. Their prospects were even better when Johns began a long move that included Anasta and Gasnier, with Cooper handling twice before scoring.

A Bowen solo effort from halfway gave the Queenslanders some semblance of hope. But in their hearts they must have known they were doomed. Buderus and Johns combined for the Newcastle hooker to score and even a consolation try to Petero Civoniceva right on full-time made no difference.

After victory in Origin II Johns had warned about NSW becoming overconfident. But Johns and his teammates in the blue strip aimed up. NSW became only the second side from the southern state to come from one match down in an Origin series and win the decider in Brisbane. And their 32-10 hammering of Queensland set the scene for the international demise of several of their top players. When Australia's Tri-Nations squad was named later in the year Matt Bowen, Matt Sing, Shaun Berrigan, Tonie Carroll and Michael Crocker, all Test players in 2004 and/or 2005, were to miss out.

Johns was again dominant in a side that had a host of stars, whose stoicism was never more evident that in the first five and a half minutes. In that period the Blues turned in one of the greatest defensive efforts in the history of the Origin clashes. For no less than 27 tackles, in five sets of six, the Queenslanders hammered the NSW tryline. Yet they were repelled each and every time. Johns and the pack's back three of Ben Kennedy, Nathan Hindmarsh and Fitzgibbon were prominent.

In the end it was an uncharacteristic gentle kick from Lockyer that turned the tide. Minichiello pounced on the ball, split the Queensland defence and then ran some 85 metres. He was caught by fullback Bowen in a desperation tackle, but the mental damage had been done. The Maroons were never the same again.

A penalty goal booted by Fitzgibbon gave the visitors a slender lead before the Blues settled in to wear down their opponents. Johns helped set up the first try, delaying a pass with a clever dummy before sending stand-off Anasta through a gap between Berrigan and Lockyer.

Around six minutes later Johns put up a high kick. NSW centre Gasnier was first to reach the ball and the Blues had scored again. It was fast becoming a procession. As half-time approached Johns slipped a reverse pass to Minichiello, who in turn delayed a cut-out pass to King, for the winger to score the first try of a hat-trick. With an 18-0 lead at half-time the Blues were looking good.

The second half was only six minutes old when Johns slipped an inside pass to King for the easiest of tries. And when Timana Tahu touched down and King scored his third try, the Blues led 32-0.

At that stage Stuart took pity and rested playmaker Johns. It was perhaps significant that with Joey out of the equation, the Maroons were able to salvage a semblance of pride with two consolation tries – to Johnathan Thurston and Bowen.

The Queensland selectors must have rued their decision to drop Billy Slater, one of the few players who can turn a game in the twinkling of an eye, for the deciding match. And there was also the way they had ignored Scott Prince, the 2004 scrum-half, who was playing brilliantly for the Wests Tigers as they methodically journeyed towards the 2005 NRL Premiership. How the Maroons could have used him!

The Wally Lewis Medal (as Man of the Series) went to Minichiello. But there would not be one Australian who would argue against Johns being the man who inspired the Blues' victory in the silver anniversary series.

176

ORIGIN I

QUEENSLAND 24 . . . . **NEW SOUTH WALES 20**
Queensland: T – Williams (19), Crocker (48), Bowen (83);
G – Smith 5; FG – Lockyer, Thurston
NSW: T – Rooney (51), Gasnier (61), Fitzgibbon (68), Buderus (70);
G – Fitzgibbon 2

Queensland: 1 Billy Slater (Storm); 2 Ty Williams (Cowboys), 3 Shaun Berrigan (Broncos), 4 Paul Bowman (Cowboys), 5 Matt Sing (Cowboys); 6 Darren Lockyer (Broncos) (c), 7 Johnathan Thurston (Cowboys); 8 Petero Civoniceva (Broncos), 9 Cameron Smith (Storm), 10 Steve Price (Warriors), 11 Michael Crocker (Roosters), 12 Brad Thorn (Broncos), 13 Chris Flannery (Roosters). Subs: 14 Ben Ross (Panthers), 15 Carl Webb (Cowboys), 16 Casey McGuire (Broncos), 17 Matt Bowen (Cowboys).
NSW: 1 Anthony Minichiello (Roosters); 2 Matt King (Storm), 3 Mark Gasnier (Dragons), 4 Matt Cooper (Dragons), 5 Luke Rooney (Panthers); 6 Trent Barrett (Dragons), 7 Brett Kimmorley (Sharks); 8 Luke Bailey (Dragons), 9 Danny Buderus (Knights) (c), 10 Jason Ryles (Dragons), 11 Nathan Hindmarsh (Eels), 12 Craig Fitzgibbon (Roosters), 13 Ben Kennedy (Sea Eagles). Subs: 14 Craig Wing (Roosters), 15 Steve Simpson (Knights), 16 Andrew Ryan (Bulldogs), 17 Anthony Watmough (Sea Eagles).
Rugby Leaguer & League Express Men of the Match:
Queensland: Steve Price; *NSW:* Anthony Minichiello.
Half-time: 13-0; **Referee:** Paul Simpkins; **Video referee:** Chris Ward
Attendance: 52,482 (ground record) *at Suncorp Stadium (May 25)*

Tonie Carroll (Broncos) was originally selected for Queensland but was ruled out injured and replaced by McGuire.

ORIGIN II

NEW SOUTH WALES 32 . . . . **QUEENSLAND 22**
NSW: T – Minichiello (14, 44), Menzies (48), Cooper (59), Buderus (76); G – Fitzgibbon 3, Johns 3
Queensland: T – Thorn (22), Slater (32), Bowen (68), Civoniceva (80); G – Smith 3

NSW: 1 Anthony Minichiello (Roosters); 2 Matt King (Storm), 3 Mark Gasnier (Dragons), 4 Matt Cooper (Dragons), 5 Luke Rooney (Panthers); 6 Braith Anasta (Bulldogs), 7 Andrew Johns (Knights); 15 Steve Simpson (Knights), 9 Danny Buderus (Knights) (c), 10 Jason Ryles (Dragons), 11 Nathan Hindmarsh (Eels), 12 Craig Fitzgibbon (Roosters), 13 Ben Kennedy (Sea Eagles). Subs: 8 Luke Bailey (Dragons), 14 Craig Wing (Roosters), 16 Andrew Ryan (Bulldogs), 17 Steve Menzies (Sea Eagles).
Queensland: 1 Billy Slater (Storm); 2 Ty Williams (Cowboys), 3 Shaun Berrigan Broncos), 4 Paul Bowman (Cowboys), 5 Matt Sing (Cowboys); 6 Darren Lockyer (Broncos) (c), 7 Johnathan Thurston (Cowboys); 8 Brad Thorn (Broncos), 9 Cameron Smith (Storm), 10 Petero Civoniceva (Broncos), 11 Michael Crocker (Roosters), 12 Carl Webb (Cowboys), 13 Chris Flannery (Roosters). Subs: 14 Ben Ross (Panthers), 15 Dane Carlaw (Broncos), 16 Casey McGuire (Broncos), 17 Matt Bowen (Cowboys).
Rugby Leaguer & League Express Men of the Match:
NSW: Andrew Johns; *Queensland:* Michael Crocker.
Half-time: 6-12; **Referee:** Steve Clarke; **Video referee:** Graeme West
Attendance: 82,389 *at Telstra Stadium (June 15)*

Trent Barrett (Dragons) was originally chosen at scrum half for NSW but withdrew through injury and was replaced by Johns.

ORIGIN III

QUEENSLAND 10 . . . . **NEW SOUTH WALES 32**
Queensland: T – Thurston (73), Bowen (77); G – Smith
NSW: T – Anasta (20), Gasnier (27), King (30, 47, 63), Tahu (53); G – Fitzgibbon, Johns 3

Queensland: 1 Matt Bowen (Cowboys); 2 Ty Williams (Cowboys), 3 Shaun Berrigan (Broncos), 4 Paul Bowman (Cowboys), 5 Matt Sing (Cowboys); 6 Darren Lockyer (Broncos) (c), 7 Johnathan Thurston (Cowboys); 8 Danny Nutley (Sharks), 9 Cameron Smith (Storm), 10 Petero Civoniceva (Broncos), 11 Michael Crocker (Roosters), 12 Brad Thorn (Broncos), 17 Tonie Carroll (Broncos). Subs: 13 Chris Flannery (Roosters), 14 Ben Ross (Panthers), 15 Corey Parker (Broncos), 16 Ashley Harrison (Rabbitohs).
NSW: 1 Anthony Minichiello (Roosters); 2 Matt King (Storm), 3 Mark Gasnier (Dragons), 4 Matt Cooper (Dragons), 5 Timana Tahu (Eels); 6 Braith Anasta (Bulldogs), 7 Andrew Johns (Knights); 15 Steve Simpson (Knights), 9 Danny Buderus (Knights) (c), 10 Jason Ryles (Dragons), 11 Nathan Hindmarsh (Eels), 12 Craig Fitzgibbon (Roosters), 13 Ben Kennedy (Sea Eagles). Subs: 8 Luke Bailey (Dragons), 14 Craig Gower (Panthers), 16 Andrew Ryan (Bulldogs), 17 Steve Menzies (Sea Eagles).
Rugby Leaguer & League Express Men of the Match:
Queensland: Danny Nutley; *NSW:* Andrew Johns
Half-time: 0-18; **Referee:** Paul Simpkins; **Video referee:** Graeme West
Attendance: 52,496 *at Suncorp Stadium (July 6)*

Wally Lewis Medal (Man of the Series): Anthony Minichiello (NSW)

Gillette
RUGBY LEAGUE
TRI-NATIONS

FINAL

AUSTRALIA........................0
NEW ZEALAND 24

ABOVE: Ali Lauitiiti, Ruben Wiki, Motu Tony and Shontayne Hape show off the Tri-Nations trophy

RIGHT: Manu Vatuvei shows his delight at scoring his first try

GAME SIX

GREAT BRITAIN 14
AUSTRALIA 26

CLOCKWISE, FROM TOP:
Great Britain reflect on their
Tri-Nations exit;
Adrian Morley loses possession
under pressure from Danny
Buderus and Craig Fitzgibbon;
Brent Tate shows his delight at
scoring a great individual try

GAME FIVE

GREAT BRITAIN 38
NEW ZEALAND 12

CLOCKWISE, FROM RIGHT:
Shontayne Hape collars Paul
Wellens; Jamie Peacock halts
Manu Vatuvei; Stuart Fielden
applauds the Great Britain fans

GILLETTE RUGBY LEAGUE TRI-NATIONS

GAME FOUR

GREAT BRITAIN 6
AUSTRALIA 20

CLOCKWISE, FROM TOP:
Adrian Morley goes over to score;
Stuart Fielden tackled by
Luke O'Donnell; Martin Gleeson
grounds Anthony Minichiello

GAME THREE

GREAT BRITAIN 26
NEW ZEALAND 42

CLOCKWISE, FROM TOP:
New Zealand celebrate victory
with their fans; Awen Guttenbeil
dumped by Gareth Ellis and
Jamie Peacock; Stacey Jones
takes on Lee Gilmour

Gillette RUGBY LEAGUE TRI-NATIONS

GAME TWO

NEW ZEALAND 26
AUSTRALIA 28

RIGHT: Matt Cooper beats
Jake Webster to score;
BELOW: Darren Lockyer slides
over; BOTTOM: David Kidwell on
the charge

TEST MATCHES

BELOW RIGHT: Eorl Crabtree
looks to offload as New
Zealand edge out England

RIGHT: Ben Creagh and Willie
Mason lift David Ferriol as
Australia defeat France

BELOW: Jerome Guisset
brought down as France run
New Zealand close

GAME ONE

AUSTRALIA 28
NEW ZEALAND 38

LEFT: Ruben Wiki leads the haka;
BELOW: David Kidwell leads the
Kiwi celebrations; BOTTOM: Brent
Webb races away for a try

ABOVE: Wales' Phil Joseph looks to break free against Scotland

LEFT: Ireland's Anthony Stewart tackled by Wales' Bryn Powell

BELOW: Karl Fitzpatrick dives over to score for Ireland against Scotland

TEST MATCH

RIGHT: England's Jamie Jones-Buchanan in the thick of the action against France

REPRESENTATIVE MATCH

RIGHT: Cumbria's Carl Rudd swamped by the Ireland defence

FRANCE **38**
WALES **16**

Action from the European Nations
Cup Final, David Ferriol grounded
by Anthony Blackwood (top),
Renaud Guigue tackled by
Damian Gibson (above)

BELOW: St George-Illawarra's Trent Barrett hauls down Newcastle's Andrew Johns

RIGHT: Manly's Shayne Dunley evades Cronulla's David Peachey

BELOW: Nathan Cayless offloads for Minor Premiers Parramatta against New Zealand Warriors

NRL SEASON

ANZAC TEST

ABOVE: Australia's Steve Price tries to break free against New Zealand

STATE OF ORIGIN

ABOVE: New South Wales celebrate their Origin success

LEFT: Matt Bowen scores the winning try in Origin I

RIGHT: Steve Menzies looks for support in Origin III

WESTS TIGERS 30
NORTH QUEENSLAND............16

LEFT: Benji Marshall leaves Matt Sing grounded on the way to setting up a try for Pat Richards (below)

NRL GRAND FINAL

LEFT: Scott Prince lifts the NRL Premiership trophy

RIGHT: Matt Bowen tries to break free

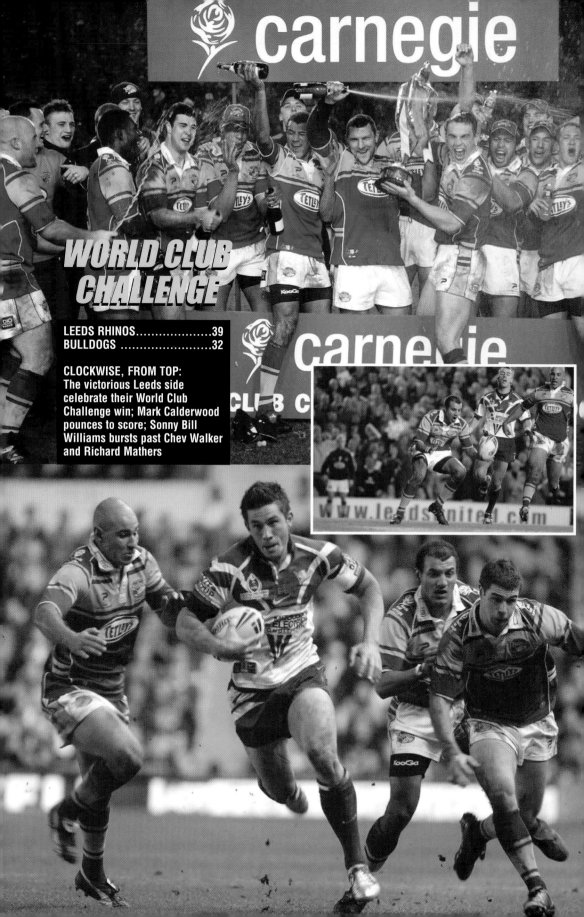

carnegie

WORLD CLUB CHALLENGE

LEEDS RHINOS....................39
BULLDOGS 32

CLOCKWISE, FROM TOP:
The victorious Leeds side
celebrate their World Club
Challenge win; Mark Calderwood
pounces to score; Sonny Bill
Williams bursts past Chev Walker
and Richard Mathers

CASTLEFORD TIGERS...........36
WHITEHAVEN 8

LEFT: Steve Crouch crashes past Aaron Lester for a try

BELOW LEFT: Man of the match Brad Davis celebrates

BELOW: Castleford show their jubilation at returning to Super League

NATIONAL LEAGUE ONE GRAND FINAL

National League 2005 Grand Final WINNERS

NATIONAL LEAGUE CUP FINAL

ABOVE: Hull KR celebrate winning the Northern Rail Cup after defeating Castleford

RIGHT: Byron Ford races away from Brad Davis

NATIONAL LEAGUE ONE SEASON

LEFT: Whitehaven's David Seeds lifts the League Leaders Trophy

RIGHT: Ben Fisher on the burst for Halifax against Doncaster in the play-offs

LEFT: Danny Maun in action for relegated Featherstone

BELOW: York celebrate winning the National League Two title

NATIONAL LEAGUE TWO SEASON

LEFT: Workington's Taani Lavulavu looks to offload against Swinton

RIGHT: Gateshead's Steven Bradley bursts through the Dewsbury defence

NATIONAL LEAGUE ONE QUALIFYING FINAL

BATLEY BULLDOGS 28
DEWSBURY RAMS 26

ABOVE: An airborne Stephen Jones scores for Batley

ABOVE: Barry Eaton goes past Richard Chapman

RIGHT: Craig Lingard leads the celebrations as Batley survive in NL1

NATIONAL LEAGUE THREE GRAND FINAL

ABOVE: Bramley's Scott Pendlebury tackled by Marco Rossi

RIGHT: Bradford-Dudley Hill celebrate victory

LHF National League 3 2005 Grand Final WINNERS

BARLA NATIONAL CUP

RIGHT: Wath Brow's Mark Troughton lifts the National Cup

BELOW: Wath Brow's Andrew Hocking looks for a way through against Skirlaugh

BARLA NATIONAL CONFERENCE

BELOW: Leigh Miners Rangers - National Conference Grand Final winners

LEFT: Miners Rangers' Tommy Goulden on the charge against Wath Brow

ABOVE: Bridgend Blue Bulls - Harry Jepson Trophy winners
BELOW: Blackpool Sea Eagles - Conference Shield winners
BOTTOM RIGHT: Wetherby Bulldogs - Conference Regional winners

TOTALRL.COM CONFERENCE

Bridgend's Hywel Davies takes on the Leeds Akkies defence during the Conference Grand Final

6
STATISTICAL REVIEW

SUPER LEAGUE PLAYERS
1996-2005

PLAYER	CLUB	YEAR	APP	TRIES	GOALS	FG	PTS
Carl Ablett	London	2005	3(2)	0	0	0	0
	Leeds	2004	(1)	0	0	0	0
Darren Abram	Oldham	1996-97	25(2)	11	0	0	44
Darren Adams	Paris	1996	9(1)	1	0	0	4
Guy Adams	Huddersfield	1998	1(2)	0	0	0	0
Matt Adamson	Leeds	2002-04	54(8)	9	0	0	36
Phil Adamson	St Helens	1999	(1)	0	0	0	0
Ade Adebisi	London	2004	(1)	0	0	0	0
Jamie Ainscough	Wigan	2002-03	30(2)	18	0	0	72
Glen Air	London	1998-2001	57(13)	27	0	1	109
Darren Albert	St Helens	2002-05	105	77	0	0	308
Paul Alcock	Widnes	2003, 2005	1(7)	1	0	0	4
Neil Alexander	Salford	1998	(1)	0	0	0	0
Malcolm Alker	Salford	1997-2002, 2004-05	173(1)	37	0	1	149
Chris Allen	Castleford	1996	(1)	0	0	0	0
David Allen	Wigan	2003, 2005	6(15)	2	0	0	8
Gavin Allen	London	1996	10	0	0	0	0
John Allen	Workington	1996	20(1)	6	0	0	24
Ray Allen	London	1996	5(3)	3	0	0	12
Richard Allwood	Gateshead	1999	(4)	0	0	0	0
Sean Allwood	Gateshead	1999	3(17)	1	0	0	4
David Alstead	Warrington	2000-02	23(10)	3	0	0	12
Asa Amone	Halifax	1996-97	32(7)	10	0	0	40
Grant Anderson	Castleford	1996-97	15(6)	3	0	0	12
Paul Anderson	St Helens	2005	26(2)	6	0	0	24
	Bradford	1997-2004	74(104)	30	0	0	120
	Halifax	1996	5(1)	1	0	0	4
Paul Anderson	Sheffield	1999	3(7)	1	0	0	4
	St Helens	1996-98	2(28)	4	1	0	18
Vinnie Anderson	St Helens	2005	17(2)	9	0	0	36
Phil Anderton	St Helens	2004	1	0	0	0	0
Eric Anselme	Halifax	1997	(2)	0	0	0	0
Mark Applegarth	Wakefield	2004-05	18(1)	3	0	0	12
	Huddersfield	2001	7	4	0	0	16
Graham Appo	Warrington	2002-05	60(13)	35	80	0	300
Anthony Armour	London	2005	11(7)	1	0	0	4
Colin Armstrong	Workington	1996	11(2)	1	0	0	4
Richard Armswood	Workington	1996	5(1)	1	0	0	4
Danny Arnold	Salford	2001-02	26(13)	13	0	0	52
	Huddersfield	1998-2000	55(7)	26	0	0	104
	Castleford	2000	(4)	0	0	0	0
	St Helens	1996-97	40(1)	33	0	0	132
Chris Ashton	Wigan	2005	1	2	0	0	8
Martin Aspinwall	Wigan	2001-05	85(13)	27	0	0	108
Mark Aston	Sheffield	1996-99	67(6)	6	243	6	516
Paul Atcheson	Widnes	2002-04	16(35)	4	0	0	16
	St Helens	1998-2000	58(4)	18	0	0	72
	Oldham	1996-97	40	21	0	0	84
David Atkins	Huddersfield	2001	26(1)	4	0	0	16
Brad Attwood	Halifax	2003	(3)	0	0	0	0
Warren Ayres	Salford	1999	2(9)	1	2	0	8
Jerome Azema	Paris	1997	(1)	0	0	0	0
Marcus Bai	Leeds	2004-05	57	42	0	0	168
David Baildon	Hull	1998-99	26(2)	4	0	0	16
Andy Bailey	Hull	2004-05	2(8)	1	0	0	4
Julian Bailey	Huddersfield	2003-04	47	13	0	0	52
Ryan Bailey	Leeds	2002-05	61(19)	3	0	0	12
Simon Baldwin	Salford	2004-05	13(26)	3	0	0	12
	Sheffield	1999	7(15)	2	0	0	8
	Halifax	1996-98	41(15)	16	0	1	65
Rob Ball	Wigan	1998-2000	3(4)	0	0	0	0
Paul Ballard	Widnes	2005	3(1)	2	0	0	8
Darren Bamford	Salford	2005	2(1)	0	0	0	0
Michael Banks	Bradford	1998	(1)	0	0	0	0
Frederic Banquet	Paris	1996	16(2)	7	4	0	36
Lee Bardauskas	Castleford	1996-97	(2)	0	0	0	0
Craig Barker	Workington	1996	(2)	0	0	0	0
Dwayne Barker	London	2004	3	1	0	0	4
	Hull	2003	(1)	0	0	0	0
Mark Barlow	Wakefield	2002	(1)	0	0	0	0
Danny Barnes	Halifax	1999	2	0	0	0	0
Richie Barnett	Hull	2004-05	21(5)	21	0	0	84
	Widnes	2005	4	2	0	0	8
Richie Barnett	Hull	2003-04	31(1)	17	0	0	68
	London	2001-02	31(4)	13	0	0	52
David Barnhill	Leeds	2000	20(8)	5	0	0	20
Paul Barrow	Warrington	1996-97	1(10)	1	0	0	4
Scott Barrow	St Helens	1997-2000	9(13)	1	0	0	4
Steve Barrow	London	2000	2	0	0	0	0
	Hull	1998-99	4(17)	1	0	0	4
	Wigan		(8)	3	0	0	12
Ben Barton	Huddersfield	1998	1(6)	1	0	0	4
Danny Barton	Salford	2001	(1)	0	0	0	0
Wayne Bartrim	Castleford	2002-03	41(2)	9	157	0	350
Greg Barwick	London	1996-97	30(4)	21	110	2	306
David Bastian	Halifax	1996	(2)	0	0	0	0
David Bates	Castleford	2001-02	(4)	0	0	0	0
	Warrington	2001	1(2)	0	0	0	0
Nathan Batty	Wakefield	2001	1(1)	0	0	0	0
Russell Bawden	London	1996-97, 2002-04	50(49)	15	0	0	60
Neil Baxter	Salford	2001	1	0	0	0	0
Neil Baynes	Salford	1999-2002, 2004	84(19)	10	0	0	40
	Wigan	1996-98	(10)	1	0	0	4
Robbie Beazley	London	1997-99	48(15)	13	0	0	52
Robbie Beckett	Halifax	2002	27	15	0	0	60
Dean Bell	Leeds	1996	1	1	0	0	4
Ian Bell	Hull	2003	(1)	0	0	0	0
Mark Bell	Wigan	1998	22	12	0	0	48
Paul Bell	Leeds	2000	1	0	0	0	0
Troy Bellamy	Paris	1997	5(10)	0	0	0	0
Adrian Belle	Huddersfield	1998	10(2)	0	0	0	0
	Oldham	1996	19	8	0	0	32
Jamie Benn	Castleford	1998, 2000	3(8)	1	15	0	34
Andy Bennett	Warrington	1996	6(5)	1	0	0	4
Mike Bennett	St Helens	2000-05	47(52)	10	0	0	40
John Bentley	Huddersfield	1999	13(4)	3	0	0	12
	Halifax	1996, 1998	22(3)	24	0	0	96
Phil Bergman	Paris	1997	20(1)	14	0	0	56
Joe Berry	Huddersfield	1998-99	25(14)	3	0	0	12
Colin Best	Hull	2003-04	57	34	0	0	136
Roger Best	London	1997-98	1(5)	1	0	0	4
Bob Beswick	Wigan	2004-05	5(14)	2	0	0	8
Mike Bethwaite	Workington	1996	17(3)	1	0	0	4
Denis Betts	Wigan	1998-2001	82(24)	33	0	0	132
Cliff Beverley	Salford	2004-05	47(1)	14	0	0	56
Adam Bibey	Widnes	2004	(1)	0	0	0	0
Ricky Bibey	St Helens	2004	4(14)	0	0	0	0
	Wigan	2001-03	5(29)	0	0	0	0
Chris Birchall	Halifax	2002-03	24(22)	4	0	0	16
	Bradford	2000	(1)	0	0	0	0
Deon Bird	Widnes	2003-04	39(6)	9	0	0	36
	Wakefield	2002	10(1)	1	0	0	4
	Hull	2000-02	37(22)	20	0	0	80
	Gateshead	1999	19(3)	13	0	0	52
	Paris	1996-97	30	12	2	0	52
Nathan Blacklock	Hull	2005	25(1)	20	0	0	80
Richie Blackmore	Leeds	1997-2000	63	25	0	0	100
Matthew Blake	Wakefield	2003-04	1(5)	0	0	0	0
Steve Blakeley	Salford	1997-2002	103(5)	26	241	2	588
	Warrington	2000	4(3)	1	9	0	22
Richard Blakeway	Castleford	2002-04	1(14)	0	0	0	0
Ian Blease	Salford	1997	(1)	0	0	0	0
Jamie Bloem	Huddersfield	2003	18(4)	3	11	0	34
	Halifax	1998-2002	82(25)	25	100	2	302
Vea Bloomfield	Paris	1996	4(14)	3	0	0	12
Pascal Bomati	Paris	1996	17(1)	10	0	0	40
Simon Booth	Hull	1998-99	15(9)	2	0	0	8
	St Helens	1996-97	10(4)	1	0	0	4
Steve Booth	Huddersfield	1998-99	16(4)	2	3	0	14
Alan Boothroyd	Halifax	1997	2(3)	0	0	0	0
John Boslem	Paris	1996	(5)	0	0	0	0
Liam Bostock	St Helens	2004	1	0	0	0	0
Liam Botham	Wigan	2005	5	0	0	0	0
	Leeds	2003-05	2(11)	4	0	0	16
	London	2004	6(2)	3	6	0	24
Frano Botica	Castleford	1996	21	5	84	2	190
Matthew Bottom	Leigh	2005	(1)	0	0	0	0
Hadj Boudebza	Paris	1996	(2)	0	0	0	0
David Boughton	Huddersfield	1999	26(1)	4	0	0	16
David Bouveng	Halifax	1997-99	66(2)	19	0	0	76
Tony Bowes	Huddersfield	1998	3(2)	0	0	0	0
Radney Bowker	London	2004	3	1	0	0	4
	St Helens	2001	(1)	0	0	0	0
David Boyle	Bradford	1999-2000	36(13)	15	0	1	61
Andy Bracek	Warrington	2005	(7)	0	0	0	0
	St Helens	2004	(1)	0	0	0	0
David Bradbury	Hudds-Sheff	2000	21(2)	1	0	0	4
	Salford	1997-99	23(10)	6	0	0	24
	Oldham	1996-97	19(6)	9	0	0	36
John Braddish	St Helens	2001-02	1(5)	0	3	0	6
Graeme Bradley	Bradford	1996-98	62(1)	29	0	0	116
Nick Bradley-Qalilawa	London	2005	28	19	0	0	76
Darren Bradstreet	London	1999-2000	1(3)	0	0	0	0
Dominic Brambani	Castleford	2004	2(2)	0	0	0	0
Liam Bretherton	Wigan	1999	(5)	2	0	0	8
	Warrington	1997	(1)	0	0	0	0
Johnny Brewer	Halifax	1996	4(2)	2	0	0	8
Chris Bridge	Warrington	2005	18(3)	8	57	1	147
	Bradford	2003-04	2(14)	4	6	0	28
Lee Briers	Warrington	1997-2005	189(11)	60	522	41	1325
	St Helens	1997	3	0	11	0	22

PLAYER	CLUB	YEAR	APP	TRIES	GOALS	FG	PTS
Carl Briggs	Salford	1999	8(5)	3	0	1	13
	Halifax	1996	5(3)	1	0	0	4
Mike Briggs	Widnes	2002	1(2)	1	0	0	4
Shaun Briscoe	Hull	2004-05	49(1)	35	0	0	140
	Wigan	2002-03	23(5)	11	0	0	44
Darren Britt	St Helens	2002-03	41	3	0	0	12
Gary Broadbent	Salford	1997-2002	117(2)	22	0	0	88
Paul Broadbent	Wakefield	2002	16(5)	0	0	0	0
	Hull	2000-01	40(9)	3	0	0	12
	Halifax	1999	26(1)	2	0	0	8
	Sheffield	1996-98	63(1)	6	0	0	24
Andrew Brocklehurst	Salford	2004-05	7(12)	1	0	0	4
	London	2004	12(6)	2	0	0	8
	Halifax	2001-03	37(8)	2	0	0	8
Justin Brooker	Wakefield	2001	25	9	0	0	36
	Bradford	2000	17(4)	11	0	0	44
Danny Brough	Hull	2005	18(5)	2	60	1	129
Darren Brown	Salford	1999-2001	47(9)	11	6	0	56
Gavin Brown	Leeds	1996-97	5(2)	1	2	0	8
Kevin Brown	Wigan	2003-05	38(15)	24	0	0	96
Lee Brown	Hull	1999	(1)	0	0	0	0
Michael Brown	London	1996	(2)	0	0	0	0
Todd Brown	Paris	1996	8(1)	2	0	0	8
Adrian Brunker	Wakefield	1999	17	6	0	0	24
Justin Bryant	Paris	1996	4(1)	0	0	0	0
	London	1996	7(8)	1	0	0	4
Austin Buchanan	Wakefield	2005	3	2	0	0	8
	London	2003	3(1)	2	0	0	8
Neil Budworth	London	2002-05	59(11)	4	1	0	18
James Bunyan	Huddersfield	1998-99	8(7)	2	0	0	8
Andy Burgess	Salford	1997	3(12)	0	0	0	0
Darren Burns	Warrington	2002-04	66(6)	19	0	0	76
Gary Burns	Oldham	1996	6	1	0	0	4
Paul Burns	Workington	1996	5(2)	1	0	0	4
Rob Burrow	Leeds	2001-05	64(66)	59	59	1	355
Dean Busby	Warrington	1999-2002	34(34)	7	0	0	28
	Hull	1998	8(6)	0	0	0	0
	St Helens	1996-98	1(7)	0	0	0	0
Ikram Butt	London	1996	5(1)	0	0	0	0
Shane Byrne	Huddersfield	1998-99	1(5)	0	0	0	0
Didier Cabestany	Paris	1996-97	20(6)	2	0	0	8
Joel Caine	Salford	2004	24	8	13	0	58
	London	2003	6	4	1	0	18
Mark Calderwood	Leeds	2001-05	117(9)	88	0	0	352
Mike Callan	Warrington	2002	(4)	0	0	0	0
Matt Calland	Huddersfield	2003	2	0	0	0	0
	Hull	1999	1	0	0	0	0
	Bradford	1996-98	44(5)	24	0	0	96
Dean Callaway	London	1999-2000	26(24)	12	0	0	48
Laurent Cambres	Paris	1996	(1)	0	0	0	0
Chris Campbell	Warrington	2000	7(1)	2	0	0	8
Liam Campbell	Wakefield	2005	(1)	0	0	0	0
Logan Campbell	Hull	1998-99, 2001	70(13)	14	0	0	56
	Castleford	2000	14(2)	3	0	0	12
	Workington	1996	7(1)	1	0	0	4
Blake Cannova	Widnes	2002	(1)	0	0	0	0
Phil Cantillon	Widnes	2002-03	27(21)	18	0	0	72
	Leeds	1997	(1)	0	0	0	0
Daryl Cardiss	Warrington	2003-04	23(2)	3	4	0	20
	Halifax	1999-2003	91(8)	39	4	0	164
	Wigan	1996-98	12(6)	4	0	0	16
Dale Cardoza	Warrington	2002	5	1	0	0	4
	Halifax	2001	3	1	0	0	4
	Huddersfield	2000-01	20(9)	11	0	0	44
	Sheffield	1998-99	11(7)	3	0	0	12
Paul Carige	Salford	1999	24(1)	7	0	0	28
Jim Carlton	Huddersfield	1999	3(11)	2	0	0	8
Brian Carney	Wigan	2001-05	91(10)	42	1	0	170
	Hull	2000	13(3)	7	0	0	28
	Gateshead	1999	3(2)	2	0	0	8
Martin Carney	Warrington	1997	(1)	0	0	0	0
Paul Carr	Sheffield	1996-98	45(5)	15	0	0	60
Bernard Carroll	London	1996	2(1)	1	0	0	4
Mark Carroll	London	1998	15(3)	1	0	0	4
Tonie Carroll	Leeds	2001-02	42(2)	30	0	0	120
Darren Carter	Workington	1996	10(3)	0	1	0	2
Steve Carter	Widnes	2002	14(7)	4	0	0	16
John Cartwright	Salford	1997	9	0	0	0	0
Garreth Carvell	Hull	2001-05	27(69)	18	0	0	72
	Leeds	1997-2000	(4)	0	0	0	0
	Gateshead	1999	4(4)	1	0	0	4
Garen Casey	Salford	1999	13(5)	3	23	0	58
Mick Cassidy	Widnes	2005	24	0	0	0	0
	Wigan	1996-2004	184(36)	30	0	0	120
Chris Causey	Warrington	1997-99	(18)	1	0	0	4
Arnaud Cervello	Paris	1996	4	4	0	0	16
Gary Chambers	Warrington	1996-2000	65(28)	2	0	0	8
Pierre Chamorin	Paris	1996-97	27(3)	8	3	0	38
Chris Chapman	Leeds	1999	(1)	0	0	0	0
Damien Chapman	London	1998	6(2)	3	4	1	21
David Chapman	Castleford	1996-98	24(6)	8	0	0	32
Jaymes Chapman	Halifax	2002-03	5(8)	1	0	0	4
Richard Chapman	Sheffield	1996	1	2	0	0	8
Chris Charles	Salford	2004-05	51(3)	5	133	0	286
	Castleford	2001	1(4)	1	0	0	4
Andy Cheetham	Huddersfield	1998-99	30	11	0	0	44
Kris Chesney	London	1998	1(2)	0	0	0	0
Chris Chester	Hull	2002-05	60(18)	13	0	0	52
	Wigan	1999-2001	21(22)	5	0	0	20
	Halifax	1996-99	47(14)	16	15	1	95
Lee Chilton	Workington	1996	10(3)	6	0	0	24
Gary Christie	Bradford	1996-97	4(7)	1	0	0	4
Dean Clark	Leeds	1996	11(2)	3	0	0	12
Des Clark	St Helens	1999	4	0	0	0	0
	Halifax	1998-99	35(13)	6	0	0	24
Greg Clarke	Halifax	1997	1(1)	0	0	0	0
John Clarke	Oldham	1996-97	27(4)	5	0	0	20
Jon Clarke	Warrington	2001-05	126(2)	26	1	0	106
	London	2000-01	19(11)	2	0	0	8
	Wigan	1997-99	13(10)	3	0	0	12

PLAYER	CLUB	YEAR	APP	TRIES	GOALS	FG	PTS
Ryan Clayton	Huddersfield	2005	4(6)	0	0	0	0
	Castleford	2004	11(6)	3	0	0	12
	Halifax	2000, 2002-03	28(12)	6	0	0	24
Gavin Clinch	Salford	2004	21(1)	1	0	1	5
	Halifax	1998-99, 2001-02	88(2)	26	45	5	199
	Hudds-Sheff	2000	18(2)	5	0	1	21
	Wigan	1999	10(2)	4	12	0	40
John Clough	Salford	2004-05	1(9)	0	0	0	0
Paul Clough	St Helens	2005	(1)	0	0	0	0
Bradley Clyde	Leeds	2001	7(5)	1	0	0	4
Evan Cochrane	London	1996	5(1)	1	0	0	4
Liam Colbon	Wigan	2004-05	5(6)	1	0	0	4
Anthony Colella	Huddersfield	2003	5(1)	2	0	0	8
Liam Coleman	Leigh	2005	1(4)	0	0	0	0
Andy Coley	Salford	2001-02, 2004-05	60(34)	18	0	0	72
Richard Colley	Bradford	2004	1	0	0	0	0
Steve Collins	Hull	2000	28	17	0	0	68
	Gateshead	1999	20(4)	13	0	0	52
Wayne Collins	Leeds	1997	21	3	0	0	12
Gary Connolly	Widnes	2005	20	4	1	0	18
	Wigan	1996-2002, 2004	168(10)	70	5	0	290
	Leeds	2003-04	27	6	0	0	24
Matt Cook	Bradford	2005	(7)	0	0	0	0
Mick Cook	Sheffield	1996	9(10)	2	0	0	8
Paul Cook	Huddersfield	1998-99	11(6)	2	13	0	34
	Bradford	1996-97	14(8)	7	38	1	105
Peter Cook	St Helens	2004	(1)	0	0	0	0
Paul Cooke	Hull	1999-2005	143(27)	29	232	1	581
Ben Cooper	Leigh	2005	25(1)	5	0	0	20
	Huddersfield	2000-01, 2003-04	28(12)	3	0	0	12
Ged Corcoran	Halifax	2003	1(11)	0	0	0	0
Wayne Corcoran	Halifax	2003	4(2)	0	0	0	0
Mark Corvo	Salford	2002	7(5)	0	0	0	0
Brandon Costin	Huddersfield	2001, 2003-04	69	42	93	3	357
	Bradford	2002	20(1)	8	0	0	32
Wes Cotton	London	1997-98	12	3	0	0	12
Phil Coussons	Salford	1997	7(2)	3	0	0	12
Alex Couttet	Paris	1997	1	0	0	0	0
Nick Couttet	Paris	1997	1	0	0	0	0
Jamie Coventry	Castleford	1996	1	0	0	0	0
Jimmy Cowan	Oldham	1996-97	2(8)	0	0	0	0
Will Cowell	Warrington	1998-2000	6(8)	1	0	0	4
Neil Cowie	Wigan	1996-2001	116(27)	10	0	1	41
Mark Cox	London	2003	(3)	0	0	0	0
James Coyle	Wigan	2005	2(3)	1	0	0	4
Eorl Crabtree	Huddersfield	2001, 2003-05	30(37)	10	0	0	40
Andy Craig	Halifax	1999	13(7)	1	3	0	10
	Wigan	1996	5(5)	2	0	0	8
Owen Craigie	Widnes	2005	15	7	0	2	30
Scott Cram	London	1999-2002	65(7)	4	0	0	16
Steve Craven	Hull	1998-2003	53(42)	4	0	0	16
Nicky Crellin	Workington	1996	(2)	0	0	0	0
Jason Critchley	Wakefield	2000	7(1)	4	0	0	16
	Castleford	1997-98	27(3)	11	0	0	44
Martin Crompton	Salford	1998-2000	30(6)	11	6	2	58
	Oldham	1996-97	36(1)	16	0	3	67
Paul Crook	Widnes	2005	2(2)	0	5	1	11
Paul Crook	Oldham	1996	4(9)	0	3	0	6
Lee Crooks	Castleford	1996-97	27(2)	2	14	0	36
Alan Cross	St Helens	1997	(2)	0	0	0	0
Steve Crouch	Castleford	2004	4(1)	2	0	0	8
Kevin Crouthers	Warrington	2001-03	12(1)	4	0	0	16
	London	2000	6(4)	1	0	0	4
	Wakefield	1999	4(4)	1	0	0	4
	Bradford	1997-98	3(9)	2	0	0	8
Matt Crowther	Hull	2001-03	48	20	166	0	412
	Hudds-Sheff	2000	10(4)	5	22	0	64
	Sheffield	1996-99	43(4)	22	10	0	108
Heath Cruckshank	Halifax	2003	19(1)	0	0	0	0
	St Helens	2001	1(12)	0	0	0	0
Paul Cullen	Warrington	1996	19	3	0	0	12
Francis Cummins	Leeds	1996-2005	217(13)	120	26	2	534
Keiron Cunningham	St Helens	1996-2005	240(9)	110	0	0	440
Andy Currier	Warrington	1996-97	(2)	1	0	0	4
Joe Dakuitoga	Sheffield	1996	6(3)	0	0	0	0
Brett Dallas	Wigan	2000-05	135	79	0	0	316
Paul Darbyshire	Warrington	1997	(6)	0	0	0	0
Maea David	Hull	1998	1	0	0	0	0
Paul Davidson	Halifax	2001-03	22(30)	10	0	0	40
	London	2000	6(10)	4	0	0	16
	St Helens	1998-99	27(16)	7	0	0	28
	Oldham	1996-97	17(18)	14	0	1	57
Gareth Davies	Warrington	1996-97	1(6)	0	0	0	0
Wes Davies	Wigan	1998-2001	22(22)	11	0	0	44
Brad Davis	Castleford	1997-2000, 2004	96	29	41	10	208
	Wakefield	2001-03	51(12)	15	22	5	109
Matt Daylight	Hull	2000	17(1)	7	0	0	28
	Gateshead	1999	30	25	0	0	100
Michael De Vere	Huddersfield	2005	14	1	25	0	54
Paul Deacon	Bradford	1998-2005	167(43)	54	645	19	1525
	Oldham	1997	(2)	0	0	0	0
Craig Dean	Halifax	1996-97	25(11)	12	1	1	51
Gareth Dean	London	2002	(4)	0	0	0	0
Yacine Dekkiche	Hudds-Sheff	2000	11(3)	3	0	0	12
Jason Demetriou	Wakefield	2004-05	52(1)	22	2	0	92
	Widnes	2002-03	47(1)	15	1	0	62
Martin Dermott	Warrington	1997	1	0	0	0	0
David Despin	Paris	1996	(1)	0	0	0	0
Fabien Devecchi	Paris	1996-97	17(10)	2	0	0	8
Paul Devlin	Widnes	2002-04	32	16	0	0	64
Stuart Dickens	Salford	2005	4(5)	0	4	0	8
Matt Diskin	Leeds	2001-05	94(15)	22	0	0	88
Kirk Dixon	Hull	2004-05	2(4)	4	0	0	16
Paul Dixon	Sheffield	1996-97	5(9)	1	0	0	4
Gareth Dobson	Castleford	1998-2000	(10)	0	0	0	0
Michael Docherty	Hull	2000-01	(6)	0	0	0	0

Super League Players 1996-2005

PLAYER	CLUB	YEAR	APP	TRIES	GOALS	FG	PTS
Sid Domic	Wakefield	2004-05	48	30	0	0	120
	Warrington	2002-03	41(4)	17	0	0	68
Glen Donkin	Hull	2002-03	(10)	1	0	0	4
Stuart Donlan	Huddersfield	2004-05	38(2)	6	0	0	24
	Halifax	2001-03	65(2)	22	0	0	88
Jason Donohue	Bradford	1996	(4)	0	0	0	0
Jeremy Donougher	Bradford	1996-99	40(21)	13	0	0	52
Justin Dooley	London	2000-01	37(18)	2	0	0	8
Dane Dorahy	Halifax	2003	20	7	45	0	118
	Wakefield	2000-01	16(2)	4	19	1	55
Luke Dorn	London	2005	28	23	0	0	92
Ewan Dowes	Hull	2003-05	58(18)	8	0	0	32
	Leeds	2001-03	1(9)	0	0	0	0
Adam Doyle	Warrington	1998	9(3)	4	0	0	16
Rod Doyle	Sheffield	1997-99	52(10)	10	0	0	40
Brad Drew	Huddersfield	2005	28	5	1	0	22
Damien Driscoll	Salford	2001	23(1)	1	0	0	4
Jason Duffy	Leigh	2005	3(1)	0	0	0	0
John Duffy	Leigh	2005	21	6	0	0	24
	Salford	2000	3(11)	0	1	1	3
	Warrington	1997-99	12(12)	0	0	0	0
Andrew Duncan	London	1997	2(4)	2	0	0	8
	Warrington	1997	(1)	0	0	0	0
Andrew Dunemann	Leeds	2003-05	76(4)	11	0	2	46
	Halifax	1999-2002	68	19	0	1	77
Matt Dunford	London	1997-98	18(20)	3	0	1	13
Jamie Durbin	Widnes	2005	1	0	0	0	0
	Warrington	2003	(1)	0	0	0	0
James Durkin	Paris	1997	(5)	0	0	0	0
Bernard Dwyer	Bradford	1996-2000	65(10)	14	0	0	56
Jim Dymock	London	2001-04	94(1)	15	0	1	61
Leo Dynevor	London	1996	8(11)	5	7	0	34
Jason Eade	Paris	1997	9	4	0	0	16
Michael Eagar	Hull	2004-05	12	4	0	0	16
	Castleford	1999-2003	130(2)	60	0	0	240
	Warrington	1998	21	6	0	0	24
Barry Eaton	Widnes	2002	25	2	49	4	110
	Castleford	2000	1(4)	0	3	0	6
Greg Ebrill	Salford	2002	15(6)	1	0	0	4
Cliff Eccles	Salford	1997-98	30(5)	1	0	0	4
Chris Eckersley	Warrington	1996	1	0	0	0	0
Steve Edmed	Sheffield	1997	15(1)	0	0	0	0
Mark Edmondson	St Helens	1999-2005	27(75)	10	0	0	40
Diccon Edwards	Castleford	1996-97	10(5)	1	0	0	4
Peter Edwards	Salford	1997-98	35(2)	4	0	0	16
Shaun Edwards	London	1997-2000	32(8)	16	1	0	66
	Bradford	1998	8(2)	4	0	0	16
	Wigan	1996	17(3)	12	1	0	50
Danny Ekis	Halifax	2001	(1)	0	0	0	0
Abi Ekoku	Bradford	1997-98	21(4)	6	0	0	24
	Halifax	1996	15(1)	5	0	0	20
Olivier Elima	Wakefield	2003-05	16(31)	10	0	0	40
	Castleford	2002	(1)	1	0	0	4
Abderazak Elkhalouki	Paris	1997	(1)	0	0	0	0
Gareth Ellis	Leeds	2005	27	8	0	0	32
	Wakefield	1999-2004	86(17)	21	2	0	88
Danny Ellison	Castleford	1998-99	7(16)	6	0	0	24
	Wigan	1996-97	15(1)	13	0	0	52
Andrew Emelio	Widnes	2005	22(2)	8	0	0	32
Patrick Entat	Paris	1996	22	2	0	0	8
Jason Erba	Sheffield	1997	1(4)	0	0	0	0
James Evans	Huddersfield	2004-05	38	15	0	0	60
Paul Evans	Paris	1997	18	8	0	0	32
Wayne Evans	London	2002	11(6)	2	0	0	8
Richie Eyres	Warrington	1997	2(5)	0	0	0	0
	Sheffield	1997	2(3)	0	0	0	0
Henry Fa'afili	Warrington	2004-05	36	27	0	0	108
Sala Fa'alogo	Widnes	2004-05	8(15)	2	0	0	8
Maurie Fa'asavalu	St Helens	2004-05	4(34)	5	0	0	20
Bolouagi Fagborun	Huddersfield	2004-05	3(2)	1	0	0	4
Esene Faimalo	Salford	1997-99	23(25)	2	0	0	8
	Leeds	1996	3(3)	0	0	0	0
Joe Faimalo	Salford	1998-2000	23(47)	7	0	0	28
	Oldham	1996-97	37(5)	7	0	0	28
Karl Fairbank	Bradford	1996	17(2)	4	0	0	16
David Fairleigh	St Helens	2001	26(1)	8	0	0	32
Jim Fallon	Leeds	1996	10	5	0	0	20
Danny Farrar	Warrington	1998-2000	76	13	0	0	52
Andy Farrell	Wigan	1996-2004	230	77	1026	16	2376
Anthony Farrell	Widnes	2002-03	24(22)	4	1	0	18
	Leeds	1997-2001	99(23)	18	0	0	72
	Sheffield	1996	14(5)	5	0	0	20
Craig Farrell	Hull	2000-01	1(3)	0	0	0	0
Abraham Fatnowna	London	1997-98	7(2)	2	0	0	8
	Workington	1996	5	2	0	0	8
Sione Faumuina	Hull	2005	3	1	0	0	4
Vince Fawcett	Wakefield	1999	13(1)	2	0	0	8
	Warrington	1998	4(7)	1	0	0	4
	Oldham	1997	5	3	0	0	12
Danny Fearon	Huddersfield	2001	(1)	0	0	0	0
	Halifax	1999-2000	5(6)	0	0	0	0
Chris Feather	Wakefield	2001-02, 2004-05	29(32)	9	0	0	36
	Leeds	2003-04	10(29)	5	0	0	20
Dom Feaunati	Leigh	2005	4	1	0	0	4
	St Helens	2004	10(7)	7	0	0	28
Luke Felsch	Hull	2000-01	46(6)	7	0	0	28
	Gateshead	1999	28(1)	2	0	0	8
Leon Felton	Warrington	2002	4(2)	0	0	0	0
	St Helens	2001	1(1)	0	0	0	0
Brett Ferres	Bradford	2005	(7)	1	0	0	4
Jason Ferris	Leigh	2005	4	1	0	0	4
Jamie Field	Wakefield	1999-2005	124(52)	17	0	0	68
	Huddersfield	1998	15(5)	0	0	0	0
	Leeds	1996-97	3(11)	0	0	0	0
Mark Field	Wakefield	2003-05	27(6)	3	0	0	12
Jamie Fielden	London	2003	(1)	0	0	0	0
	Huddersfield	1998-2000	4(8)	0	0	0	0
Stuart Fielden	Bradford	1998-2005	125(78)	37	0	0	148
Lafaele Filipo	Workington	1996	15(4)	3	0	0	12
Salesi Finau	Warrington	1996-97	16(15)	8	0	0	32
Liam Finn	Wakefield	2004	1(1)	0	1	0	2
	Halifax	2002-03	16(5)	2	30	1	69
Lee Finnerty	Halifax	2003	18(2)	5	2	0	24
Phil Finney	Warrington	1998	1	0	0	0	0
Simon Finnigan	Widnes	2003-05	51(19)	21	0	0	84
Matt Firth	Halifax	2000-01	12(2)	0	0	0	0
Andy Fisher	Wakefield	1999-2000	31(8)	4	0	0	16
Karl Fitzpatrick	Salford	2004-05	30(10)	11	2	0	48
Darren Fleary	Leigh	2005	24	1	0	0	4
	Huddersfield	2003-04	43(8)	4	0	0	16
	Leeds	1997-2002	98(9)	3	0	0	12
Greg Fleming	London	1999-2001	64(1)	40	2	0	164
Richard Fletcher	Hull	1999-2004	11(56)	5	0	0	20
Greg Florimo	Halifax	2000	26	6	4	0	32
	Wigan	1999	18(2)	7	1	0	30
Jason Flowers	Salford	2004	6(1)	0	0	0	0
	Halifax	2002	24(4)	4	0	0	16
	Castleford	1996-2001	119(19)	33	0	1	133
Stuart Flowers	Castleford	1996	(3)	0	0	0	0
Adrian Flynn	Castleford	1996-97	19(2)	10	0	0	40
Wayne Flynn	Sheffield	1997	3(5)	0	0	0	0
Adam Fogerty	Warrington	1998	4	0	0	0	0
	St Helens	1996	13	1	0	0	4
Carl Forber	Leigh	2005	4	1	0	0	4
	St Helens	2004	1(1)	0	6	0	12
Paul Forber	Salford	1997-98	19(12)	4	0	0	16
Mike Ford	Castleford	1997-98	25(12)	5	0	3	23
	Warrington	1996	3	0	0	0	0
Jim Forshaw	Salford	1999	(1)	0	0	0	0
Mike Forshaw	Warrington	2004	20(1)	5	0	0	20
	Bradford	1997-2003	162(7)	32	0	0	128
	Leeds	1996	11(3)	5	0	0	20
Mark Forster	Warrington	1996-2000	102(1)	40	0	0	160
David Foster	Halifax	2000-01	4(9)	0	0	0	0
Nick Fozzard	St Helens	2004-05	52(2)	3	0	0	12
	Warrington	2002-03	43(11)	2	0	0	8
	Huddersfield	1998-2000	24(8)	2	0	0	8
	Leeds	1996-97	6(16)	3	0	0	12
David Fraisse	Workington	1996	8	0	0	0	0
Daniel Frame	Widnes	2002-05	100(6)	24	0	0	96
Andrew Frew	Halifax	2003	17	5	0	0	20
	Wakefield	2002	21	8	0	0	32
	Huddersfield	2001	26	15	0	0	60
Dale Fritz	Castleford	1999-2003	120(4)	9	0	0	36
David Furner	Leeds	2003-04	45	8	23	0	78
	Wigan	2001-02	51(2)	21	13	0	110
David Furness	Castleford	1996	(1)	0	0	0	0
Tommy Gallagher	Widnes	2004	(6)	0	0	0	0
	London	2003	1(9)	1	0	0	4
Mark Gamson	Sheffield	1996	3	0	0	0	0
Jim Gannon	Huddersfield	2003-05	63(14)	10	0	0	40
	Halifax	1999-2002	83(4)	14	0	0	56
Steve Garces	Salford	2001	(1)	0	0	0	0
Jean-Marc Garcia	Sheffield	1996-97	35(3)	22	0	0	88
Ade Gardner	St Helens	2002-05	76(11)	34	0	0	136
Matt Gardner	Castleford	2004	1	1	0	0	4
Steve Gartland	Oldham	1996	1(1)	0	1	0	2
Daniel Gartner	Bradford	2001-03	74(1)	26	0	0	104
Dean Gaskell	Warrington	2002-05	58(1)	10	0	0	40
Richard Gay	Castleford	1996-2002	94(16)	39	0	0	156
Andrew Gee	Warrington	2000-01	33(1)	4	0	0	16
Stanley Gene	Huddersfield	2001, 2003-05	70(6)	27	0	0	108
	Hull	2000-01	5(23)	6	0	0	24
Steve Georgallis	Warrington	2001	5(1)	2	0	0	8
Shaun Geritas	Warrington	1997	(5)	1	0	0	4
Anthony Gibbons	Leeds	1996	9(4)	2	0	1	9
David Gibbons	Leeds	1996	3(4)	2	0	0	8
Scott Gibbs	St Helens	1996	9	3	0	0	12
Ashley Gibson	Leeds	2005	(1)	3	5	0	22
Damian Gibson	Castleford	2003-04	40(3)	5	0	0	20
	Salford	2002	28	3	0	0	12
	Halifax	1998-2001	104(1)	39	0	0	156
	Leeds	1997	18	3	0	0	12
Ian Gildart	Oldham	1996-97	31(7)	0	0	0	0
Chris Giles	Widnes	2003-04	35	12	0	0	48
	St Helens	2002	(1)	0	0	0	0
Peter Gill	London	1996-99	75(6)	20	0	0	80
Carl Gillespie	Halifax	1996-99	47(36)	13	0	0	52
Michael Gillett	London	2001-02	23(21)	12	2	0	52
Simon Gillies	Warrington	1999	28	6	0	0	24
Lee Gilmour	St Helens	2004-05	50(1)	14	0	0	56
	Bradford	2001-03	44(31)	20	0	0	80
	Wigan	1997-2000	44(39)	22	0	0	88
Marc Glanville	Leeds	1998-99	43(3)	5	0	0	20
Eddie Glaze	Castleford	1996	1	0	0	0	0
Paul Gleadhill	Leeds	1996	4	0	0	0	0
Mark Gleeson	Warrington	2000-05	17(60)	9	0	0	36
Martin Gleeson	Warrington	2005	28	17	0	0	68
	St Helens	2002-04	56(1)	25	0	0	100
	Huddersfield	1999-2001	47(9)	18	0	0	72
Sean Gleeson	Wigan	2005	2(3)	0	0	0	0
Jonathan Goddard	Castleford	2000-01	(2)	0	0	0	0
Richard Goddard	Castleford	1996-97	11(3)	2	10	0	28
Brad Godden	Leeds	1998-99	47	15	0	0	60
Wayne Godwin	Wigan	2005	5(18)	2	0	0	8
	Castleford	2001-04	30(33)	18	56	0	184
Marvin Golden	Widnes	2003	4	1	0	0	4
	London	2001	17(2)	1	0	0	4
	Halifax	2000	20(2)	5	0	0	20
	Leeds	1996-99	43(11)	19	0	0	76
Brett Goldspink	Halifax	2000-02	64(5)	2	0	0	8
	Wigan	1999	6(16)	1	0	0	4
	St Helens	1998	19(4)	2	0	0	8
	Oldham	1997	13(2)	0	0	0	0
Luke Goodwin	London	1998	9(2)	3	1	1	15
	Oldham	1997	16(4)	10	17	2	76
Andy Gorski	Salford	2001-02	(2)	0	0	0	0
Bobbie Goulding	Salford	2001-02	31(1)	2	56	4	124
	Wakefield	2000	12	3	25	3	65
	Huddersfield	1998-99	27(1)	3	65	4	146
	St Helens	1996-98	42(2)	9	210	4	460
Darrell Goulding	Wigan	2005	1	0	0	0	0

PLAYER	CLUB	YEAR	APP	TRIES	GOALS	FG	PTS
Mick Govin	Leigh	2005	5(6)	4	0	0	16
James Graham	St Helens	2003-05	8(23)	4	0	0	16
Nathan Graham	Bradford	1996-98	17(28)	4	0	1	17
Nick Graham	Wigan	2003	13(1)	2	0	0	8
Jon Grayshon	Huddersfield	2003-05	6(42)	5	0	0	20
Brett Green	Gateshead	1999	10(2)	0	0	0	0
Toby Green	Huddersfield	2001	3(1)	1	0	0	4
Craig Greenhill	Castleford	2004	21(4)	1	0	0	4
	Hull	2002-03	56	3	2	0	16
Brandon Greenwood	Halifax	1996	1	0	0	0	0
Gareth Greenwood	Huddersfield	2003	(1)	0	0	0	0
	Halifax	2002	1	0	0	0	0
Lee Greenwood	Huddersfield	2005	7	3	0	0	12
	London	2004-05	30(2)	19	0	0	76
	Halifax	2000-03	38(2)	17	0	0	68
	Sheffield	1999	1(1)	0	0	0	0
Darrell Griffin	Wakefield	2003-05	48(20)	8	3	0	38
Jonathan Griffiths	Paris	1996	(4)	1	0	0	4
Andrew Grima	Workington	1996	2(9)	2	0	0	8
Tony Grimaldi	Hull	2000-01	56(1)	14	0	0	56
	Gateshead	1999	27(2)	10	0	0	40
Danny Grimley	Sheffield	1996	4(1)	1	0	0	4
Simon Grix	Halifax	2003	2(4)	0	0	0	0
Brett Grogan	Gateshead	1999	14(7)	3	0	0	12
Brent Grose	Warrington	2003-05	83	41	0	0	164
Jerome Guisset	Wigan	2005	20(2)	3	0	0	12
	Warrington	2000-04	59(65)	21	0	0	84
Reece Guy	Oldham	1996	3(4)	0	0	0	0
Gareth Haggerty	Salford	2004-05	1(50)	9	0	0	36
	Widnes	2002	1(2)	1	0	0	4
Andy Haigh	St Helens	1996-98	20(16)	11	0	0	44
Carl Hall	Leeds	1996	7(2)	3	0	0	12
Martin Hall	Halifax	1998	2(10)	0	0	0	0
	Hull	1999	7	0	0	0	0
	Castleford	1998	4	0	0	0	0
	Wigan	1996-97	31(5)	7	6	0	40
Steve Hall	Widnes	2004	1	0	0	0	0
	London	2002-03	35(3)	10	0	0	40
	St Helens	1999-2001	36(22)	19	0	0	76
Graeme Hallas	Huddersfield	2001	1	0	0	0	0
	Hull	1998-99	30(10)	6	39	1	103
	Halifax	1996	11(4)	5	0	0	20
Danny Halliwell	Leigh	2005	5	3	0	0	12
	Halifax	2000-03	17(8)	4	0	0	16
	Warrington	2002	9(1)	8	0	0	32
	Wakefield	2002	3	0	0	0	0
Colum Halpenny	Wakefield	2003-05	75(1)	28	0	0	112
	Halifax	2002	22	12	0	0	48
Jon Hamer	Bradford	1996	(1)	0	0	0	0
Andrew Hamilton	London	1997, 2003	1(20)	3	0	0	12
John Hamilton	St Helens	1998	3	0	0	0	0
Karle Hammond	Halifax	2002	10(2)	2	14	0	36
	Salford	2001	2(3)	1	0	0	4
	London	1999-2000	47	23	2	3	99
	St Helens	1996-98	58(8)	28	0	4	116
Anthony Hancock	Paris	1997	8(6)	1	0	0	4
Michael Hancock	Salford	2001-02	12(24)	7	0	0	28
Gareth Handford	Castleford	2001	7(2)	0	0	0	0
	Bradford	2000	1(1)	0	0	0	0
Paul Handforth	Wakefield	2000-04	17(44)	10	13	0	66
Paddy Handley	Leeds	1996	1(1)	2	0	0	8
Dean Hanger	Warrington	1999	7(11)	3	0	0	12
	Huddersfield	1998	20(1)	5	0	0	20
Harrison Hansen	Wigan	2004-05	18(13)	5	0	0	20
Lee Hansen	Wigan	1997	10(5)	0	0	0	0
Shontayne Hape	Bradford	2003-05	65(2)	47	0	0	188
Lionel Harbin	Wakefield	2001	(1)	0	0	0	0
Ian Hardman	St Helens	2003-05	24(9)	7	5	0	38
Jeff Hardy	Hudds-Sheff	2000	20(5)	6	0	1	25
	Sheffield	1999	22(4)	7	0	0	28
Spencer Hargrave	Castleford	1996-99	(6)	0	0	0	0
Bryn Hargreaves	Wigan	2004-05	10(6)	1	0	0	4
Lee Harland	Castleford	1996-2004	148(35)	20	0	0	80
Neil Harmon	Halifax	2003	13(3)	0	0	0	0
	Salford	2001	6(5)	0	0	0	0
	Bradford	1998-2000	15(13)	2	0	0	8
	Huddersfield	1998	12	1	0	0	4
	Leeds	1996	10	1	0	0	4
Ben Harris	Bradford	2005	18(1)	6	0	0	24
Iestyn Harris	Bradford	2004-05	43(2)	23	20	2	134
	Leeds	1997-2001	111(7)	57	490	6	1214
	Warrington	1996	16	4	63	2	144
Karl Harrison	Hull	1999	26	2	0	0	8
	Halifax	1996-98	60(2)	2	0	0	8
Andrew Hart	London	2004	12(1)	2	0	0	8
Tim Hartley	Salford	2004-05	6(7)	5	0	0	20
Carlos Hassan	Bradford	1996	6(4)	2	0	0	8
Phil Hassan	Wakefield	2002	9(1)	0	0	0	0
	Halifax	2000-01	25(4)	3	0	0	12
	Salford	1998	15	2	0	0	8
	Leeds	1996-97	38(4)	12	0	0	48
Tom Haughey	London	2003-04	10(8)	1	0	0	4
	Wakefield	2001-02	5(12)	0	0	0	0
Simon Haughton	Wigan	1996-2002	63(46)	32	0	0	128
Solomon Haumono	London	2005	24(5)	8	0	0	32
Andy Hay	Widnes	2003-04	50(2)	7	0	0	28
	Leeds	1997-2002	112(27)	43	0	0	172
	Sheffield	1996-97	17(3)	5	0	0	20
Adam Hayes	Hudds-Sheff	2000	2(1)	0	0	0	0
Joey Hayes	Salford	1999	9	2	0	0	8
	St Helens	1996-98	11(6)	7	0	0	28
Mitch Healey	Castleford	2001-03	68(1)	10	16	0	72
Ricky Helliwell	Salford	1997-99	(2)	0	0	0	0
Tom Hemingway	Huddersfield	2005	2(1)	0	0	0	0
Bryan Henare	St Helens	2000-01	4(12)	1	0	0	4
Richard Henare	Warrington	1996-97	28(2)	24	0	0	96
Ian Henderson	Bradford	2005	14	5	0	0	20
Kevin Henderson	Wakefield	2005	5	1	0	0	4
	Leigh	2005	(1)	0	0	0	0
Brad Hepi	Castleford	1999, 2001	9(21)	3	0	0	12
	Salford	2000	3(5)	0	0	0	0
	Hull	1998	15(1)	3	0	0	12
Jon Hepworth	Castleford	2003-04	19(23)	7	8	0	44
	Leeds	2003	(1)	0	0	0	0
	London	2002	(2)	0	0	0	0
Ian Herron	Hull	2000	9	1	17	0	38
	Gateshead	1999	25	4	105	0	226
Jason Hetherington	London	2001-02	37	9	0	0	36
Gareth Hewitt	Salford	1999	2(1)	0	0	0	0
Andrew Hick	Hull	2000	9(9)	1	0	0	4
	Gateshead	1999	12(5)	2	0	0	8
Paul Hicks	Wakefield	1999	(1)	0	0	0	0
Darren Higgins	London	1998	5(6)	2	0	0	8
Iain Higgins	London	1997-98	1(7)	2	0	0	8
Liam Higgins	Hull	2003-05	1(29)	0	0	0	0
Mick Higham	St Helens	2001-05	43(56)	32	0	0	128
Chris Highton	Warrington	1997	1(1)	0	0	0	0
David Highton	London	2004-05	21(24)	2	0	0	8
	Salford	2002	4(5)	2	0	0	8
	Warrington	1998-2001	18(14)	2	0	0	8
Paul Highton	Salford	1998-2002, 2004-05	93(62)	10	0	0	40
	Halifax	1996-97	12(18)	2	0	0	8
Andy Hill	Huddersfield	1999	(4)	0	0	0	0
	Castleford	1999	4(4)	0	0	0	0
Chris Hill	Leigh	2005	(1)	0	0	0	0
Danny Hill	Hull	2004-05	(5)	0	0	0	0
Howard Hill	Oldham	1996-97	22(12)	4	0	0	16
John Hill	St Helens	2003	(1)	0	0	0	0
	Halifax	2003	1(2)	0	0	0	0
	Warrington	2001-02	(4)	0	0	0	0
Mark Hilton	Warrington	1996-2000, 2002-05	138(35)	7	0	0	28
Andy Hobson	Widnes	2004	5(13)	0	0	0	0
	Halifax	1998-2003	51(85)	8	0	0	32
Gareth Hock	Wigan	2003-05	34(28)	11	0	0	44
Andy Hodgson	Wakefield	1999	14(2)	2	1	0	10
	Bradford	1997-98	8(2)	4	0	0	16
David Hodgson	Salford	2005	28	10	0	0	40
	Wigan	2000-04	90(19)	43	0	0	172
	Halifax	1999	10(3)	5	0	0	20
Darren Hogg	London	1996	(1)	0	0	0	0
Michael Hogue	Paris	1997	5(7)	0	0	0	0
Chris Holden	Warrington	1996-97	2(1)	0	0	0	0
Stephen Holgate	Halifax	2000	1(10)	0	0	0	0
	Hull	1999	1	0	0	0	0
	Wigan	1997-98	11(26)	2	0	0	8
	Workington	1996	19	3	0	0	12
Martyn Holland	Wakefield	2000-03	52(3)	6	0	0	24
Tim Holmes	Widnes	2004-05	15(4)	0	0	0	0
Graham Holroyd	Huddersfield	2003	3(5)	0	0	0	0
	Salford	2000-02	40(11)	8	75	5	187
	Halifax	1999	24(2)	3	74	5	165
	Leeds	1996-98	40(26)	22	101	8	298
Dallas Hood	Wakefield	2003-04	18(9)	1	0	0	4
Jason Hooper	St Helens	2003-05	64(4)	28	23	0	158
Lee Hopkins	London	2005	29	6	0	0	24
Sean Hoppe	St Helens	1999-2002	69(16)	32	0	0	128
Graeme Horne	Hull	2003-05	13(38)	8	0	0	32
Richard Horne	Hull	1999-2005	162(9)	58	12	2	258
John Hough	Warrington	1996-97	9	2	0	0	8
Sylvain Houles	Wakefield	2003, 2005	8(1)	1	0	0	4
	London	2001-02	17(10)	11	0	0	44
	Hudds-Sheff	2000	5(2)	1	0	0	4
Harvey Howard	Wigan	2001-02	25(27)	1	0	0	4
	Bradford	1998	4(2)	1	0	0	4
	Leeds	1996	8	0	0	0	0
Kim Howard	London	1997	4(5)	0	0	0	0
Stuart Howarth	Workington	1996	(2)	0	0	0	0
Phil Howlett	Bradford	1999	5(1)	2	0	0	8
Craig Huby	Castleford	2003-04	(12)	0	3	0	6
Ryan Hudson	Castleford	2002-04	73(6)	21	0	0	84
	Wakefield	2000-01	42(9)	11	0	1	45
	Huddersfield	1998-99	12(7)	0	0	0	0
Adam Hughes	Widnes	2002-05	89(2)	45	51	0	282
	Halifax	2001	8(8)	8	0	0	32
	Wakefield	1999-2000	43(3)	21	34	0	152
	Leeds	1996-97	4(5)	4	0	0	16
Ian Hughes	Sheffield	1996	9(8)	4	0	0	16
Steffan Hughes	London	1999-2001	1(13)	1	0	0	4
David Hulme	Salford	1997-99	53(1)	5	0	0	20
	Leeds	1996	8(1)	2	0	0	8
Paul Hulme	Warrington	1996-97	23(1)	2	0	0	8
Gary Hulse	Widnes	2005	12(5)	2	0	0	8
	Warrington	2001-04	20(28)	8	0	1	33
Alan Hunte	Salford	2002	19(2)	9	0	0	36
	Warrington	1999-2001	83	49	0	0	196
	Hull	1998	21	7	0	0	28
	St Helens	1996-97	30(2)	28	0	0	112
Nick Hyde	Paris	1997	5(5)	1	0	0	4
Andy Ireland	Hull	1998-99	22(15)	0	0	0	0
	Bradford	1996	1	0	0	0	0
Kevin Iro	St Helens	1999-2001	76	39	0	0	156
	Leeds	1996	16	9	0	0	36
Andrew Isherwood	Wigan	1998-99	(5)	0	0	0	0
Olu Iwenofu	London	2000-01	2(1)	0	0	0	0
Chico Jackson	Hull	1999	(4)	0	0	0	0
Lee Jackson	Hull	2001-02	37(9)	12	1	0	50
	Leeds	1999-2000	28(24)	7	0	0	28
Michael Jackson	Sheffield	1998-99	17(17)	2	0	0	8
	Halifax	1996-97	27(6)	11	0	0	44
Paul Jackson	Huddersfield	1998, 2005	15(22)	0	0	0	0
	Castleford	2003-04	7(21)	0	0	0	0
	Wakefield	1999-2002	57(41)	2	0	0	8
Rob Jackson	Leigh	2005	20(3)	5	0	0	20
	London	2002-04	26(14)	9	0	0	36
Wayne Jackson	Halifax	1996-97	17(5)	2	0	0	8
Aled James	Widnes	2003	3	0	0	0	0
Andy James	Halifax	1996	(4)	0	0	0	0
Pascal Jampy	Paris	1996-97	3(2)	0	0	0	0
Ben Jeffries	Wakefield	2003-05	76(6)	47	1	4	194
Mick Jenkins	Hull	2000	24	2	0	0	8
	Gateshead	1999	16	3	0	0	12
Ed Jennings	London	1998-99	1(2)	0	0	0	0
Lee Jewitt	Wigan	2005	(2)	0	0	0	0

Super League Players 1996-2005

PLAYER	CLUB	YEAR	APP	TRIES	GOALS	FG	PTS
Andrew Johns	Warrington	2005	3	1	12	1	29
Matthew Johns	Wigan	2001	24	3	0	1	13
Andy Johnson	Salford	2004-05	8(26)	7	0	0	28
	Castleford	2002-03	32(16)	11	0	0	44
	London	2000-01	24(21)	12	0	0	48
	Huddersfield	1999	5	1	0	0	4
	Wigan	1996-99	24(20)	19	0	0	76
Bruce Johnson	Widnes	2004-05	(4)	0	0	0	0
Jason Johnson	St Helens	1997-99	2	0	0	0	0
Mark Johnson	Salford	1999-2000	22(9)	16	0	0	64
	Hull	1998	10(1)	4	0	0	16
	Workington	1996	12	4	0	0	16
Nick Johnson	London	2003	(1)	0	0	0	0
Paul Johnson	Bradford	2004-05	37(5)	18	0	0	72
	Wigan	1996-2003	74(46)	54	0	0	216
Chris Jones	Leigh	2005	1(1)	0	0	0	0
Danny Jones	Halifax	2003	1	0	0	0	0
David Jones	Oldham	1997	14(1)	5	0	0	20
Mark Jones	Warrington	1996	8(11)	2	0	0	8
Phil Jones	Leigh	2005	16	8	31	0	94
	Wigan	1999-2001	14(7)	6	25	0	74
Stephen Jones	Huddersfield	2005	(1)	0	0	0	0
Stuart Jones	Huddersfield	2004-05	42(6)	6	0	0	24
	St Helens	2003	(18)	2	0	0	8
	Wigan	2002	5(3)	1	0	0	0
Jamie Jones-Buchanan	Leeds	1999-2005	29(48)	16	0	0	64
Tim Jonkers	Salford	2004-05	5(10)	0	0	0	0
	St Helens	1999-2004	41(64)	12	0	0	48
Darren Jordan	Wakefield	2003	(1)	0	0	0	0
Phil Joseph	Huddersfield	2004	7(6)	0	0	0	0
Warren Jowitt	Hull	2003	(2)	0	0	0	0
	Salford	2001-02	17(4)	2	0	0	8
	Wakefield	2000	19(3)	8	0	0	32
	Bradford	1996-99	13(25)	5	0	0	20
Chris Joynt	St Helens	1996-2004	201(14)	68	0	0	272
Gregory Kacala	Paris	1996	7	1	0	0	4
Andy Kain	Castleford	2004	2(2)	1	0	0	4
Mal Kaufusi	London	2004	1(3)	0	0	0	0
Stephen Kearney	Hull	2005	22(2)	5	0	0	20
Damon Keating	Wakefield	2002	7(17)	1	0	0	4
Shaun Keating	London	1996	1(3)	0	0	0	0
Mark Keenan	Workington	1996	3(4)	1	0	0	4
Tony Kemp	Wakefield	1999-2000	15(5)	2	0	1	9
	Leeds	1996-98	23(2)	5	0	2	22
Damien Kennedy	London	2003	5(11)	1	0	0	4
Ian Kenny	St Helens	2004	(1)	0	0	0	0
Jason Kent	Leigh	2005	23	1	0	0	4
Shane Kenward	Wakefield	1999	28	6	0	0	24
	Salford	1998	1	0	0	0	0
Jason Keough	Paris	1997	2	1	0	0	4
Keiran Kerr	Widnes	2005	6	2	0	0	8
Martin Ketteridge	Halifax	1996	7(5)	0	0	0	0
Ronnie Kettlewell	Warrington	1996	(1)	0	0	0	0
David Kidwell	Warrington	2001-02	14(12)	9	0	0	36
Andrew King	London	2003	23(1)	15	0	0	60
Dave King	Huddersfield	1998-99	11(17)	2	0	0	8
James King	Leigh	2005	5(7)	0	0	0	0
Kevin King	Wakefield	2005	8(1)	2	0	0	8
	Castleford	2004	(1)	0	0	0	0
Paul King	Hull	1999-2005	103(53)	18	0	1	73
Andy Kirk	Wakefield	2005	6(3)	1	0	0	4
	Salford	2004	20	5	0	0	20
	Leeds	2001-02	4(4)	0	0	0	0
John Kirkpatrick	London	2004-05	18(1)	5	0	0	20
	St Helens	2001-03	10(11)	10	0	0	40
	Halifax	2003	4	1	0	0	4
Wayne Kitchin	Workington	1996	11(6)	3	17	1	47
Ian Knott	Leigh	2005	8(1)	2	0	0	8
	Wakefield	2002-03	34(5)	7	79	0	186
	Warrington	1996-2001	68(41)	24	18	0	132
Matt Knowles	Wigan	1996	(3)	0	0	0	0
Phil Knowles	Salford	1997	1	0	0	0	0
Simon Knox	Halifax	1999	(6)	0	0	0	0
	Salford	1998	1(1)	0	0	0	0
	Bradford	1996-98	9(19)	7	0	0	28
Toa Kohe-Love	Warrington	1996-2001, 2005	141(2)	79	0	0	316
	Bradford	2004	1(1)	0	0	0	0
	Hull	2002-03	42	19	0	0	76
Paul Koloi	Wigan	1997	1(2)	1	0	0	4
Michael Korkidas	Wakefield	2003-05	71(10)	10	0	0	40
David Krause	London	1996-97	22(1)	7	0	0	28
Ben Kusto	Huddersfield	2001	21(4)	9	0	1	37
Adrian Lam	Wigan	2001-04	105(2)	40	1	9	171
Mark Lane	Paris	1996	(2)	0	0	0	0
Allan Langer	Warrington	2000-01	47	13	4	0	60
Kevin Langer	London	1996	12(4)	2	0	0	8
Junior Langi	Salford	2005	13(2)	2	0	0	8
Chris Langley	Huddersfield	2000-01	18(1)	3	0	0	12
Jamie Langley	Bradford	2002-05	25(46)	20	0	0	80
Andy Last	Hull	1999-2005	16(10)	4	0	0	16
Dale Laughton	Warrington	2002	15(1)	0	0	0	0
	Huddersfield	2000-01	36(2)	4	0	0	16
	Sheffield	1996-99	48(22)	5	0	0	20
Ali Lauitiiti	Leeds	2004-05	27(20)	22	0	0	88
Jason Laurence	Salford	1997	1	0	0	0	0
Graham Law	Wakefield	1999-2002	34(30)	6	40	0	104
Neil Law	Wakefield	1999-2002	83	39	0	0	156
	Sheffield	1998	1(1)	1	0	0	4
Dean Lawford	Widnes	2003-04	17(1)	5	2	4	28
	Halifax	2001	1(1)	0	0	0	0
	Leeds	1997-2000	15(8)	2	3	0	14
	Huddersfield	1999	6(1)	0	6	1	13
	Sheffield	1996	9(5)	2	1	1	11
Johnny Lawless	Halifax	2001-03	73(1)	10	0	0	40
	Hudds-Sheff	2000	19(6)	3	0	0	12
	Sheffield	1996-99	76(4)	11	0	0	44
Mark Leafa	Leigh	2005	28	2	0	0	8
Leroy Leapai	London	1996	2	0	0	0	0
Jim Leatham	Hull	1998-99	20(18)	4	0	0	16
	Leeds	1997	(1)	0	0	0	0

PLAYER	CLUB	YEAR	APP	TRIES	GOALS	FG	PTS
Andy Leathem	Warrington	1999	2(8)	0	0	0	0
	St Helens	1996-98	20(1)	1	0	0	4
Danny Lee	Gateshead	1999	16(2)	0	0	0	0
Jason Lee	Halifax	2001	10(1)	2	0	0	8
Mark Lee	Salford	1997-2000	25(11)	1	0	4	8
Robert Lee	Hull	1999	4(3)	0	0	0	0
Tommy Lee	Hull	2005	2	0	0	0	0
Matthew Leigh	Salford	2000	(6)	0	0	0	0
Chris Leikvoll	Warrington	2004-05	38(7)	2	0	0	8
Jim Lenihan	Huddersfield	1999	19(1)	10	0	0	40
Mark Lennon	Castleford	2001-03	30(21)	10	21	0	82
Gary Lester	Hull	1998-99	46	17	0	0	68
Stuart Lester	Wigan	1997	1(3)	0	0	0	0
Afi Leuila	Oldham	1996-97	17(3)	2	0	0	8
Thomas Leuluai	London	2005	20	13	0	0	52
Simon Lewis	Castleford	2001	4	3	0	0	12
Jon Liddell	Leeds	2001	1	0	0	0	0
Jason Lidden	Castleford	1997	15(1)	7	0	0	28
Danny Lima	Warrington	2004-05	15(39)	9	0	0	36
Stuart Littler	Salford	1998-2002, 2004-05	127(12)	47	0	0	188
Peter Livett	Workington	1996	3(1)	0	0	0	0
Scott Logan	Hull	2001-03	27(20)	5	0	0	20
Filimone Lolohea	London	2005	8(15)	0	0	0	0
David Lomax	Huddersfield	2000-01	45(9)	4	0	0	16
	Paris	1997	19(2)	1	0	0	4
Dave Long	London	1999	(1)	0	0	0	0
Karl Long	London	2003	(1)	0	0	0	0
	Widnes	2002	4	1	0	0	4
Sean Long	St Helens	1997-2005	165(7)	101	652	10	1718
	Wigan	1996-97	1(5)	0	0	0	0
Davide Longo	Bradford	1996	1(3)	0	0	0	0
Gary Lord	Oldham	1996-97	28(12)	3	0	0	12
Paul Loughlin	Huddersfield	1998-99	34(2)	4	4	0	24
	Bradford	1996-97	36(4)	15	8	0	76
Karl Lovell	Hudds-Sheff	2000	14	5	0	0	20
	Sheffield	1999	22(4)	8	0	0	32
James Lowes	Bradford	1996-2003	205	84	2	2	342
Laurent Lucchese	Paris	1996	13(5)	2	0	0	8
Zebastian Luisi	London	2004-05	21(1)	7	0	0	28
Peter Lupton	Hull	2003-05	18(22)	9	3	0	42
	London	2000-02	10(15)	2	2	0	12
Andy Lynch	Bradford	2005	2(27)	6	0	0	24
	Castleford	1999-2004	78(48)	15	0	0	60
Jamie Lyon	St Helens	2005	27(1)	22	42	0	172
Duncan MacGillivray	Wakefield	2004-05	13(10)	3	0	0	12
Brad Mackay	Bradford	2000	24(2)	8	0	0	32
Graham Mackay	Hull	2002	27	18	24	0	120
	Bradford	2001	16(3)	12	1	0	50
	Leeds	2000	12(8)	10	2	0	44
Keiron Maddocks	Leigh	2005	1(3)	0	0	0	0
Steve Maden	Leigh	2005	23	9	0	0	36
	Warrington	2002	3	0	0	0	0
Mateaki Mafi	Warrington	1996-97	7(8)	7	0	0	28
Brendan Magnus	London	2000	3	1	0	0	4
Mark Maguire	London	1996-97	11(4)	7	13	0	54
Adam Maher	Hull	2000-03	88(4)	24	0	0	96
	Gateshead	1999	21(5)	3	0	0	12
Lee Maher	Leeds	1996	4(1)	0	0	0	0
Shaun Mahony	Paris	1997	5	0	0	0	0
David Maiden	Hull	2000-01	32(10)	11	0	0	44
	Gateshead	1999	5(16)	8	0	0	32
Craig Makin	Salford	1999-2001	24(20)	2	0	0	8
Brady Malam	Wigan	2000	5(20)	1	0	0	4
Francis Maloney	Castleford	1998-99, 2003-04	71(7)	24	33	3	165
	Salford	2001-02	45(1)	26	5	0	114
	Wakefield	2000	11	1	1	0	6
	Oldham	1996-97	39(2)	12	91	2	232
George Mann	Warrington	1997	14(5)	1	0	0	4
	Leeds	1996	11(4)	2	0	0	8
Misili Manu	Widnes	2005	1	0	0	0	0
David March	Wakefield	1999-2005	143(17)	33	112	0	356
Paul March	Huddersfield	2003-05	64(10)	16	36	1	137
	Wakefield	1999-2001	32(23)	14	18	0	92
Nick Mardon	London	1997-98	14	2	0	0	8
Oliver Marns	Halifax	1996-2002	54(19)	23	0	0	92
Paul Marquet	Warrington	2002	23(2)	0	0	0	0
Iain Marsh	Salford	1998-2001	1(4)	0	0	0	0
Lee Marsh	Salford	2001-02	3(4)	0	0	0	0
Richard Marshall	Leigh	2005	4(16)	0	0	0	0
	London	2002-03	33(11)	1	0	0	4
	Huddersfield	2000-01	35(14)	1	0	0	4
	Halifax	1996-99	38(34)	2	0	0	8
Jason Martin	Paris	1997	15(2)	3	0	0	12
Scott Martin	Salford	1997-99	32(18)	8	0	0	32
Tony Martin	London	1996-97, 2001-03	97(1)	36	170	1	485
Mick Martindale	Halifax	1996	(4)	0	0	0	0
Tommy Martyn	St Helens	1996-2003	125(20)	87	63	12	486
Dean Marwood	Workington	1996	9(6)	0	22	0	44
Martin Masella	Warrington	2001	10(14)	5	0	0	20
	Wakefield	2000	14(8)	4	0	0	16
	Leeds	1997-1999	59(5)	1	0	0	4
Colin Maskill	Castleford	1996	8	1	1	0	6
Keith Mason	St Helens	2003-05	33(23)	4	0	0	16
	Wakefield	2000-01	5(17)	0	0	0	0
Vila Matautia	St Helens	1996-2001	31(68)	9	0	0	36
Feleti Mateo	London	2005	4(10)	1	0	0	4
Barrie-Jon Mather	Castleford	1998, 2000-02	50(12)	21	0	0	84
Richard Mathers	Leeds	2002-05	71(2)	22	0	0	88
	Warrington	2002	4(3)	0	0	0	0
Jamie Mathiou	Leeds	1997-2001	31(82)	3	0	0	12
Terry Matterson	London	1996-98	46	15	90	6	246
Casey Mayberry	Halifax	2000	1(1)	0	0	0	0
Chris Maye	Halifax	2003	3(4)	0	0	0	0
Joe Mbu	London	2003-05	29(19)	4	0	0	16
Danny McAllister	Gateshead	1999	3(3)	1	0	0	4
	Sheffield	1996-97	33(7)	10	0	0	40
John McAtee	St Helens	1996	2(1)	0	0	0	0

PLAYER	CLUB	YEAR	APP	TRIES	GOALS	FG	PTS
Nathan McAvoy	Salford	1997-98, 2004-05	57(4)	18	0	0	72
	Bradford	1998-2002	67(22)	45	0	0	180
Dave McConnell	London	2003	(4)	0	0	0	0
	St Helens	2001-02	3(2)	4	0	0	16
Robbie McCormack	Wigan	1998	24	2	0	0	8
Steve McCurrie	Leigh	2005	7(3)	1	0	0	4
	Widnes	2002-04	55(22)	10	0	0	40
	Warrington	1998-2001	69(26)	31	0	0	124
Barrie McDermott	Leeds	1996-2005	163(69)	28	0	0	112
Brian McDermott	Bradford	1996-2002	138(32)	33	0	0	132
Ryan McDonald	Widnes	2002-03	6(4)	0	0	0	0
Wayne McDonald	Huddersfield	2005	8(5)	0	0	0	0
	Wigan	2005	(4)	0	0	0	0
	Leeds	2002-05	34(47)	14	0	0	56
	St Helens	2001	7(11)	4	0	0	16
	Hull	2000	5(8)	4	0	0	16
	Wakefield	1999	9(17)	8	0	0	32
Craig McDowell	Huddersfield	2003	(1)	0	0	0	0
	Warrington	2002	(1)	0	0	0	0
	Bradford	2000	(1)	0	0	0	0
Wes McGibbon	Halifax	1999	1	0	0	0	0
Billy McGinty	Workington	1996	1	0	0	0	0
Kevin McGuinness	Salford	2004-05	29(1)	4	0	0	16
Danny McGuire	Leeds	2001-05	58(32)	76	0	1	305
Gary McGuirk	Workington	1996	(4)	0	0	0	0
Richard McKell	Castleford	1997-98	22(7)	2	0	0	8
Chris McKenna	Leeds	2003-05	65(4)	18	0	0	72
Phil McKenzie	Workington	1996	4	0	0	0	0
Chris McKinney	Oldham	1996-97	4(9)	2	0	0	8
Mark McLinden	London	2005	22(3)	8	0	0	32
Shayne McMenemy	Hull	2003-05	59(3)	9	0	0	36
	Halifax	2001-03	63	11	0	0	44
Andy McNally	London	2004	5(3)	0	0	0	0
	Castleford	2001, 2003	2(5)	1	0	0	4
Steve McNamara	Huddersfield	2001, 2003	41(9)	3	134	1	281
	Wakefield	2000	15(2)	2	32	0	72
	Bradford	1996-99	90(3)	14	348	7	759
Paul McNicholas	Hull	2004-05	28(12)	4	0	0	16
Neil McPherson	Salford	1997	(1)	0	0	0	0
Duncan McRae	London	1996	11(2)	3	0	1	13
Derek McVey	St Helens	1996-97	28(4)	6	1	0	26
Dallas Mead	Warrington	1997	2	0	0	0	0
Robbie Mears	Leigh	2005	8(6)	0	0	0	0
	Leeds	2001	23	6	0	0	24
Paul Medley	Bradford	1996-98	6(35)	9	0	0	36
Chris Melling	Wigan	2004-05	8(2)	1	3	0	10
Paul Mellor	Castleford	2003-04	36(3)	18	0	0	72
Craig Menkins	Paris	1997	4(5)	0	0	0	0
Gary Mercer	Castleford	2002	(1)	0	0	0	0
	Leeds	1996-97, 2001	40(2)	9	0	0	36
	Warrington	2001	18	2	0	0	8
	Halifax	1998-2001	73(2)	16	0	0	64
Tony Mestrov	London	1996-97, 2001	59(8)	4	0	0	16
	Wigan	1998-2000	39(39)	3	0	0	12
Keiran Meyer	London	1996	4	1	0	0	4
Brad Meyers	Bradford	2005	23(6)	9	0	0	36
Gary Middlehurst	Widnes	2004	(2)	0	0	0	0
Simon Middleton	Castleford	1996-97	19(3)	8	0	0	32
Shane Millard	Widnes	2003-05	69	23	0	0	92
	London	1998-2001	72(14)	11	1	0	46
David Mills	Widnes	2002-05	17(77)	8	0	0	32
Lee Milner	Halifax	1999	(1)	0	0	0	0
John Minto	London	1996	13	4	0	0	16
Martin Moana	Salford	2004	6(3)	1	0	0	4
	Halifax	1996-2001, 2003	126(22)	62	0	1	249
	Wakefield	2002	19(2)	10	0	0	40
	Huddersfield	2001	3(3)	2	0	0	8
Steve Molloy	Huddersfield	2000-01	26(20)	3	0	0	12
	Sheffield	1998-99	32(17)	3	0	0	12
Chris Molyneux	Huddersfield	2000-01	1(18)	0	0	0	0
	Sheffield	1999	1(2)	0	0	0	0
Adrian Moore	Huddersfield	1998-99	1(4)	0	0	0	0
Danny Moore	London	2000	7	0	0	0	0
	Wigan	1998-99	49(3)	18	0	0	72
Jason Moore	Workington	1996	(5)	0	0	0	0
Richard Moore	Leigh	2005	2(5)	0	0	0	0
	Bradford	2002-04	1(26)	0	0	0	0
	London	2002, 2004	5(9)	2	0	0	8
Scott Moore	St Helens	2004-05	5(2)	1	0	0	4
Dennis Moran	Wigan	2005	25	15	0	1	61
	London	2001-04	107(2)	74	2	5	305
Willie Morganson	Sheffield	1997-98	18(12)	5	3	0	26
Paul Moriarty	Halifax	1996	3(2)	0	0	0	0
Adrian Morley	Bradford	2005	2(4)	0	0	0	0
	Leeds	1996-2000	95(14)	25	0	0	100
Chris Morley	Salford	1999	3(5)	0	0	0	0
	Warrington	1998	2(8)	0	0	0	0
	St Helens	1996-97	21(16)	4	0	0	16
Iain Morrison	Huddersfield	2003-05	11(23)	0	0	0	0
	London	2001	(1)	0	0	0	0
Gareth Morton	Leeds	2001-02	1(1)	0	0	0	0
Aaron Moule	Widnes	2004-05	29	12	0	0	48
Wilfried Moulinec	Paris	1996	1	0	0	0	0
Mark Moxon	Huddersfield	1998-2001	20(5)	1	0	1	5
Brett Mullins	Leeds	2001	5(3)	1	0	0	4
Damian Munro	Widnes	2002	8(2)	1	0	0	4
	Halifax	1996-97	9(6)	8	0	0	32
Matt Munro	Oldham	1996-97	26(5)	8	0	0	32
Craig Murdock	Salford	2000	(2)	0	0	0	0
	Hull	1998-99	21(6)	8	0	2	34
	Wigan	1996-98	18(17)	14	0	0	56
Justin Murphy	Widnes	2004	5	1	0	0	4
Doc Murray	Warrington	1997	(2)	0	0	0	0
	Wigan	1997	6(2)	0	0	0	0
Scott Murrell	Leeds	2005	(1)	0	0	0	0
	London	2004	3(3)	2	0	0	8
David Mycoe	Sheffield	1996-97	12(13)	1	0	0	4
Rob Myler	Oldham	1996-97	19(2)	6	0	0	24
Stephen Myler	Widnes	2003-05	35(14)	8	74	0	180

PLAYER	CLUB	YEAR	APP	TRIES	GOALS	FG	PTS
Vinny Myler	Salford	2004	(4)	0	0	0	0
	Bradford	2003	(1)	0	0	0	0
Matt Nable	London	1997	2(2)	1	0	0	4
Brad Nairn	Workington	1996	14	4	0	0	16
Frank Napoli	London	2000	14(6)	2	0	0	8
Carlo Napolitano	Salford	2000	(3)	1	0	0	4
Stephen Nash	Widnes	2005	4(1)	0	0	0	0
Jim Naylor	Halifax	2000	7(6)	2	0	0	8
Scott Naylor	Salford	1997-98, 2004	30(1)	9	0	0	36
	Bradford	1999-2003	127(1)	51	0	0	204
Mike Neal	Salford	1998	(1)	0	0	0	0
	Oldham	1996-97	6(4)	3	0	0	12
Jonathan Neill	Huddersfield	1998-99	20(11)	0	0	0	0
	St Helens	1996	1	0	0	0	0
Chris Nero	Huddersfield	2004-05	48(4)	20	0	0	80
Jason Netherton	London	2003-04	6	0	0	0	0
	Halifax	2002	2(3)	0	0	0	0
	Leeds	2001	(3)	0	0	0	0
Paul Newlove	Castleford	2004	5	1	0	0	4
	St Helens	1996-2003	162	106	0	0	424
Richard Newlove	Wakefield	2003	17(5)	8	0	0	32
Terry Newton	Wigan	2000-05	157(9)	62	0	0	248
	Leeds	1996-1999	55(14)	4	0	0	16
Gene Ngamu	Huddersfield	1999-2000	29(2)	9	67	0	170
Sonny Nickle	St Helens	1999-2002	86(18)	14	0	0	56
	Bradford	1996-98	25(16)	9	0	0	36
Jason Nicol	Salford	2000-02	52(7)	11	0	0	44
Tawera Nikau	Warrington	2000-01	51	7	0	0	28
Rob Nolan	Hull	1998-99	20(11)	6	0	0	24
Paul Noone	Warrington	2000-05	55(52)	12	19	0	86
Chris Norman	Halifax	2003	13(3)	2	0	0	8
Paul Norman	Oldham	1996	(1)	0	0	0	0
Andy Northey	St Helens	1996-97	8(17)	2	0	0	8
Danny Nutley	Warrington	1998-2001	94(1)	3	0	0	12
Tony Nuttall	Oldham	1996-97	1(7)	0	0	0	0
Clinton O'Brien	Wakefield	2003	(2)	0	0	0	0
Sam Obst	Wakefield	2005	14(12)	9	0	0	36
Matt O'Connor	Paris	1997	11(4)	1	26	2	58
Terry O'Connor	Widnes	2005	25	2	0	0	8
	Wigan	1996-2004	177(45)	9	0	0	36
Jarrod O'Doherty	Huddersfield	2003	26	3	0	0	12
David O'Donnell	Paris	1997	21	3	0	0	12
Martin Offiah	Salford	2000-01	41	20	0	2	82
	London	1996-99	29(3)	21	0	0	84
	Wigan	1996	8	7	0	0	28
Mark O'Halloran	London	2004-05	34(3)	10	0	0	40
Hefin O'Hare	Huddersfield	2001, 2003-05	72(10)	27	0	0	108
Hitro Okesene	Hull	1998	21(1)	0	0	0	0
Anderson Okiwe	Sheffield	1997	1	0	0	0	0
Jamie Olejnik	Paris	1997	11	8	0	0	32
Kevin O'Loughlin	Halifax	1997-98	2(4)	0	0	0	0
	St Helens	1997	(3)	0	0	0	0
Sean O'Loughlin	Wigan	2002-05	70(18)	16	0	2	66
Jules O'Neill	Widnes	2003-05	57(3)	14	158	7	379
	Wakefield	2005	10(2)	2	4	0	16
	Wigan	2002-03	29(1)	12	72	0	192
Julian O'Neill	Widnes	2002-05	57(39)	3	0	0	12
	Wakefield	2001	24(1)	2	0	0	8
	St Helens	1997-2000	95(8)	5	0	0	20
Steve O'Neill	Gateshead	1999	1(1)	0	0	0	0
Tom O'Reilly	Warrington	2001-02	8(6)	1	0	0	4
Chris Orr	Huddersfield	1998	19(3)	2	0	0	8
Danny Orr	Wigan	2004-05	42	12	10	0	68
	Castleford	1997-2003	150(18)	65	279	3	821
Nick Owen	Leigh	2005	8(1)	1	11	0	26
Jason Palmada	Workington	1996	12	2	0	0	8
Junior Paramore	Castleford	1996	5(5)	3	0	0	12
Paul Parker	Hull	1999-2002	23(18)	9	0	0	36
Rob Parker	Bradford	2000, 2002-05	19(76)	14	0	0	56
	London	2001	9	1	0	0	4
Wayne Parker	Halifax	1996-97	12(1)	0	0	0	0
Ian Parry	Warrington	2001	(1)	0	0	0	0
Jules Parry	Paris	1996	10(2)	0	0	0	0
Regis Pastre-Courtine	Paris	1996	4(3)	4	0	0	16
Andrew Patmore	Oldham	1996	8(5)	3	0	0	12
Henry Paul	Bradford	1999-2001	81(5)	29	350	6	822
	Wigan	1996-98	60	37	23	0	194
Junior Paul	London	1996	3	1	0	0	4
Robbie Paul	Bradford	1996-2005	198(31)	121	3	0	490
Danny Peacock	Bradford	1997-99	32(2)	15	0	0	60
Jamie Peacock	Bradford	1999-2005	163(25)	38	0	0	152
Martin Pearson	Wakefield	2001	21(1)	3	60	3	135
	Halifax	1997-98, 2000	55(6)	24	181	0	458
	Sheffield	1999	17(6)	9	36	2	110
Jacques Pech	Paris	1996	16	0	0	0	0
Mike Pechey	Warrington	1998	6(3)	2	0	0	8
Bill Peden	London	2003	21(3)	7	0	0	28
Sean Penkywicz	Huddersfield	2004-05	21(11)	7	0	0	28
	Halifax	2000-03	29(27)	8	0	0	32
Julian Penni	Salford	1998-99	4	0	0	0	0
Lee Penny	Warrington	1996-2003	140(5)	54	0	0	216
Paul Penrice	Workington	1996	11(2)	2	0	0	8
Chris Percival	Widnes	2002-03	26	6	0	0	24
Apollo Perelini	St Helens	1996-2000	103(16)	27	0	0	108
Mark Perrett	Halifax	1996-97	15(4)	4	0	0	16
Adam Peters	Paris	1997	16(3)	0	0	0	0
Dominic Peters	London	1998-2003	58(11)	12	0	0	48
Mike Peters	Warrington	2000	2(12)	1	0	0	4
	Halifax	2000	1	0	0	0	0
Willie Peters	Widnes	2004	9	3	0	2	14
	Wigan	2000	29	15	5	6	76
	Gateshead	1999	27	11	1	6	52
Adrian Petrie	Workington	1996	(1)	0	0	0	0
Rowland Phillips	Workington	1996	22	1	0	0	4
Nathan Picchi	Leeds	1996	(1)	0	0	0	0
Ian Pickavance	Hull	1999	4(2)	2	0	0	8
	Huddersfield	1999	3(14)	0	0	0	0
	St Helens	1996-98	12(44)	6	0	0	24

Super League Players 1996-2005

PLAYER	CLUB	YEAR	APP	TRIES	GOALS	FG	PTS
James Pickering	Castleford	1999	1(19)	0	0	0	0
Steve Pickersgill	Warrington	2005	(6)	0	0	0	0
Nick Pinkney	Salford	2000-02	64	29	0	0	116
	Halifax	1999	26(2)	13	0	0	52
	Sheffield	1997-98	33	10	0	0	40
Mikhail Piskunov	Paris	1996	1(1)	1	0	0	4
Darryl Pitt	London	1996	2(16)	4	0	1	17
Andy Platt	Salford	1997-98	20(3)	1	0	0	4
Michael Platt	Salford	2001-02	3	1	0	0	4
Willie Poching	Leeds	2002-05	46(64)	38	0	0	152
	Wakefield	1999-2001	65(4)	20	0	0	80
Quentin Pongia	Wigan	2003-04	15(10)	0	0	0	0
Dan Potter	Widnes	2002-03	34(2)	6	0	0	24
	London	2001	1(3)	1	0	0	4
Craig Poucher	Hull	1999-2002	31(5)	5	0	0	20
Bryn Powell	Salford	2004	1(1)	0	0	0	0
Daio Powell	Sheffield	1999	13(1)	2	0	0	8
	Halifax	1997-98	30(3)	17	0	0	68
Daryl Powell	Leeds	1998-2000	49(30)	12	0	2	50
Karl Pratt	Bradford	2003-05	35(19)	18	0	0	72
	Leeds	1999-2002	62(12)	33	0	0	132
Paul Prescott	Wigan	2004-05	1(4)	0	0	0	0
Steve Prescott	Hull	1998-99, 2001-03	99	46	191	3	569
	Wakefield	2000	22(1)	3	13	0	38
	St Helens	1996-97	32	15	17	0	94
Lee Prest	Workington	1996	(1)	0	0	0	0
Gareth Price	Salford	2002	(2)	0	0	0	0
	London	2002	2(2)	3	0	0	12
	St Helens	1999	(11)	2	0	0	8
Gary Price	Wakefield	1999-2001	55(13)	11	0	0	44
Richard Price	Sheffield	1996	1(2)	0	0	0	0
Tony Priddle	Paris	1997	11(7)	3	0	0	12
Karl Pryce	Bradford	2003-05	16(7)	16	1	0	66
Leon Pryce	Bradford	1998-2005	159(29)	86	0	0	344
Waine Pryce	Castleford	2000-04	81(12)	39	0	0	156
Andrew Purcell	Castleford	2000	15(5)	3	0	0	12
	Hull	1999	27	4	0	0	16
Rob Purdham	London	2002-05	53(15)	16	2	1	69
Scott Quinnell	Wigan	1996	6(3)	1	0	0	4
Lee Radford	Bradford	1999-2005	79(65)	18	12	0	96
	Hull	1998	(7)	2	0	0	8
Kris Radlinski	Wigan	1996-2005	231	134	1	0	538
Adrian Rainey	Castleford	2002	4(7)	1	0	0	4
Jean-Luc Ramondou	Paris	1996	1(1)	1	0	0	4
Craig Randall	Halifax	1999	8(11)	4	0	0	16
	Salford	1997-98	12(18)	4	0	0	16
Scott Ranson	Oldham	1996-97	19(2)	7	0	0	28
Aaron Raper	Castleford	1999-2001	48(4)	4	2	1	21
Ben Rauter	Wakefield	2001	15(6)	4	0	0	16
Gareth Raynor	Hull	2001-05	101	63	0	0	252
	Leeds	2000	(3)	0	0	0	0
Tony Rea	London	1996	22	4	0	0	16
Stuart Reardon	Bradford	2003-05	62(11)	32	0	0	128
	Salford	2002	7(1)	3	0	0	12
Mark Reber	Wigan	1999-2000	9(9)	5	0	0	20
Alan Reddicliffe	Warrington	2001	1	0	0	0	0
Tahi Reihana	Bradford	1997-98	17(21)	0	0	0	0
Paul Reilly	Huddersfield	1999-2001, 2003-05	104(7)	24	0	0	96
Robert Relf	Widnes	2002-04	68(2)	5	0	0	20
Steve Renouf	Wigan	2000-01	55	40	0	0	160
Steele Retchless	London	1998-2004	177(6)	13	0	0	52
Scott Rhodes	Hull	2000	2	0	0	0	0
Phillipe Ricard	Paris	1996-97	2	0	0	0	0
Andy Rice	Huddersfield	2000-01	2(13)	1	0	0	4
Basil Richards	Huddersfield	1998-99	28(17)	1	0	0	4
Craig Richards	Oldham	1996	1	0	0	0	0
Andy Richardson	Hudds-Sheff	2000	(2)	0	0	0	0
Sean Richardson	Widnes	2002	2(18)	1	0	0	4
	Wakefield	1999	5(1)	0	0	0	0
	Castleford	1996-97	3(8)	1	0	0	4
Shane Rigon	Bradford	2001	14(11)	12	0	0	48
Craig Rika	Halifax	1996	2	0	0	0	0
Chris Riley	Warrington	2005	1(2)	1	0	0	4
Peter Riley	Workington	1996	7(5)	0	0	0	0
Julien Rinaldi	Wakefield	2002	(3)	1	0	0	4
Dean Ripley	Castleford	2004	3(4)	1	0	0	4
Leroy Rivett	Warrington	2002	9	1	0	0	4
	Hudds-Sheff	2000	5(1)	1	0	0	4
	Leeds	1996-2000	39(15)	21	0	0	84
Jason Roach	Warrington	1998-99	29(7)	15	0	0	60
	Castleford	1997	7	4	0	0	16
Ben Roarty	Huddersfield	2003-05	52	5	0	0	20
Mark Roberts	Wigan	2003	(3)	0	0	0	0
Robert Roberts	Huddersfield	2001	(1)	0	0	0	0
	Halifax	2000	(3)	0	0	0	0
	Hull	1999	24(2)	4	13	4	46
Craig Robinson	Wakefield	2005	(1)	0	0	0	0
Jason Robinson	Wigan	1996-2000	126(1)	87	0	1	349
Jeremy Robinson	Paris	1997	10(3)	1	21	0	46
John Robinson	Widnes	2003-04	7	1	0	0	4
Luke Robinson	Salford	2005	28	11	7	1	59
	Wigan	2002-04	17(25)	9	6	1	49
	Castleford	2004	9	4	3	0	22
Will Robinson	Hull	2000	22	4	0	0	16
	Gateshead	1999	28	9	0	0	36
James Roby	St Helens	2004-05	19(23)	14	0	0	56
Mike Roby	St Helens	2004	(1)	0	0	0	0
Carl Roden	Warrington	1997	1	0	0	0	0
Matt Rodwell	Warrington	2002	10	3	0	0	12
Darren Rogers	Castleford	1999-2004	162(1)	81	0	0	324
	Salford	1997-98	42	16	0	0	64
Jamie Rooney	Wakefield	2003-05	45(4)	24	165	12	438
	Castleford	2001	2(1)	0	6	0	12
Jonathan Roper	Castleford	2001	13	7	12	0	52
	Salford	2000	1(4)	1	3	0	10
	London	2000	4	0	0	0	0
	Warrington	1996-2000	75(8)	33	71	0	274
Scott Roskell	London	1996-97	30(2)	16	0	0	64
Steve Rosolen	London	1996-98	25(9)	10	0	0	40
Adam Ross	London	1996	(1)	0	0	0	0
Paul Round	Castleford	1996	(3)	0	0	0	0
Steve Rowlands	Widnes	2004-05	18(3)	2	15	0	38
	St Helens	2003	(1)	0	0	0	0
Paul Rowley	Leigh	2005	15(7)	3	0	0	12
	Huddersfield	2001	24	3	0	0	12
	Halifax	1996-2000	107(3)	27	1	3	113
Nigel Roy	London	2001-04	100	39	0	0	156
Nicky Royle	Widnes	2004	13	7	0	0	28
Chris Rudd	Warrington	1996-98	31(17)	10	16	0	72
Sean Rudder	Castleford	2004	9(3)	2	0	0	8
James Rushforth	Halifax	1997	(4)	0	0	0	0
Danny Russell	Huddersfield	1998-2000	50(13)	8	0	0	32
Ian Russell	Oldham	1997	1(3)	1	0	0	4
	Paris	1996	3	0	0	0	0
Richard Russell	Castleford	1996-98	37(4)	2	0	0	8
Robert Russell	Salford	1998-99	2(1)	0	1	0	2
Sean Rutgerson	Salford	2004-05	46(4)	3	0	0	12
Chris Ryan	London	1998-99	44(3)	17	10	0	88
Sean Ryan	Castleford	2004	11(5)	2	0	0	8
	Hull	2002-03	53	8	0	0	32
Justin Ryder	Wakefield	2004	19(3)	11	0	0	44
Matt Salter	London	1997-99	14(34)	0	0	0	0
Ben Sammut	Hull	2000	20	4	67	0	150
	Gateshead	1999	26(2)	6	17	0	58
Dean Sampson	Castleford	1996-2003	124(28)	24	0	0	96
Paul Sampson	London	2004	1(2)	1	0	0	4
	Wakefield	2000	17	8	0	0	32
Lee Sanderson	London	2004	1(5)	1	7	0	18
Jason Sands	Paris	1996-97	28	0	0	0	0
Lokeni Savelio	Halifax	2000	2(11)	0	0	0	0
	Salford	1997-98	18(20)	0	0	0	0
Tom Saxton	Hull	2005	19(8)	3	0	0	12
	Castleford	2002-04	37(12)	11	0	0	44
Jonathan Scales	Halifax	2000	1	0	0	0	0
	Bradford	1996-98	46(4)	24	0	0	96
Andrew Schick	Castleford	1996-98	45(13)	10	0	0	40
Garry Schofield	Huddersfield	1998	(2)	0	0	0	0
Gary Schubert	Workington	1996	(1)	0	0	0	0
Matt Schultz	Hull	1998-99	23(9)	2	0	0	8
	Leeds	1996	2(4)	0	0	0	0
John Schuster	Halifax	1996-97	31	9	127	3	293
Nick Scruton	Leeds	2002, 2004-05	(17)	0	0	0	0
	Hull	2004	2(16)	3	0	0	12
Danny Sculthorpe	Wigan	2002-05	13(49)	7	0	0	28
Paul Sculthorpe	St Helens	1998-2005	186(1)	86	311	7	973
	Warrington	1996-97	40	6	0	0	24
Mick Seaby	London	1997	3(2)	1	0	0	4
Danny Seal	Halifax	1996-99	8(17)	3	0	0	12
Matt Seers	Wakefield	2003	11(1)	2	0	0	8
Anthony Seibold	London	1999-2000	33(19)	5	0	0	20
Keith Senior	Leeds	1999-2005	165(1)	99	0	0	396
	Sheffield	1996-99	90(2)	40	0	0	160
Fili Seru	Hull	1998-99	37(1)	13	0	0	52
Anthony Seuseu	Halifax	2003	1(11)	1	0	0	4
Jerry Seuseu	Wigan	2005	21(2)	0	0	0	0
Darren Shaw	Salford	2002	5(9)	1	0	0	4
	London	1996, 2002	22(8)	3	0	0	12
	Castleford	2000-01	50(6)	1	0	0	4
	Sheffield	1998-99	51(1)	3	0	1	13
Mick Shaw	Halifax	1999	5	1	0	0	4
	Leeds	1996	12(2)	7	0	0	28
Phil Shead	Paris	1996	3(2)	0	0	0	0
Richard Sheil	St Helens	1997	(1)	0	0	0	0
Kelly Shelford	Warrington	1996-97	25(3)	4	0	2	18
Michael Shenton	Castleford	2004	1(2)	0	0	0	0
Ryan Sheridan	Castleford	2004	2	0	0	0	0
	Widnes	2003	14(3)	2	0	0	8
	Leeds	1997-2002	123(7)	46	0	1	185
	Sheffield	1996	9(3)	5	0	1	21
Rikki Sheriffe	Halifax	2003	6(1)	3	0	0	12
Ian Sherratt	Oldham	1996	5(3)	1	0	0	4
Peter Shiels	St Helens	2001-02	44(3)	11	0	0	44
Gary Shillabeer	Huddersfield	1999	(2)	0	0	0	0
Mark Shipway	Salford	2004-05	30(12)	3	0	0	12
Ian Sibbit	Salford	2005	20(1)	6	0	0	24
	Warrington	1999-2001, 2003-04	63(18)	24	0	0	96
Mark Sibson	Huddersfield	1999	2	2	0	0	8
Jon Simms	St Helens	2002	(1)	0	0	0	0
Craig Simon	Hull	2000	23(2)	8	0	0	32
	Gateshead	1999	25(4)	6	0	0	24
Darren Simpson	Huddersfield	1998-99	17(1)	5	0	0	20
Robbie Simpson	London	1999	6(7)	0	0	0	0
Kevin Sinfield	Leeds	1997-2005	163(25)	32	454	7	1043
Wayne Sing	Paris	1997	18(1)	2	0	0	8
Fata Sini	Salford	1997	22	7	0	0	28
Ben Skerrett	Castleford	2003	(1)	0	0	0	0
Kelvin Skerrett	Halifax	1997-99	31(6)	2	0	0	8
	Wigan	1996	1(8)	0	0	0	0
Troy Slattery	Wakefield	2002-03	33(5)	4	0	0	16
	Huddersfield	1999	3	1	0	0	4
Mick Slicker	Huddersfield	2001, 2003-05	17(48)	2	0	0	8
	Sheffield	1999	(3)	1	0	0	4
	Halifax	1997	2(5)	0	0	0	0
Ian Smales	Castleford	1996-97	10(8)	5	0	0	20
Aaron Smith	Bradford	2003-04	12(1)	3	0	0	12
Andy Smith	Salford	2005	4	1	0	0	4
	Bradford	2004-05	8(5)	3	0	0	12
Byron Smith	Castleford	2004	(9)	0	0	0	0
	Halifax	2003	6(1)	0	0	0	0
Chris Smith	Hull	2001-02	12	3	0	0	12
	St Helens	1998-2000	62(9)	26	0	0	104
	Castleford	1996-97	36(1)	12	0	0	48
Craig Smith	Wigan	2002-04	77(3)	10	0	0	40
Damien Smith	St Helens	1998	21(1)	8	0	0	32
Danny Smith	Paris	1996	10(2)	1	15	0	34
	London	1996	2(1)	1	0	0	4
Darren Smith	St Helens	2003	25(1)	14	0	0	56
Gary Smith	Castleford	2001	(1)	0	0	0	0
Hudson Smith	Bradford	2000	8(22)	2	0	0	8
	Salford	1999	23(2)	5	0	0	20
James Smith	Salford	2000	23(3)	6	0	0	24

PLAYER	CLUB	YEAR	APP	TRIES	GOALS	FG	PTS
Jamie Smith	Hull	1998-99	24(6)	6	12	0	48
	Workington	1996	5(3)	0	1	0	2
Jason Smith	Hull	2001-04	61(3)	17	0	1	69
Kris Smith	London	2001	(1)	0	0	0	0
	Halifax	2001	(1)	0	0	0	0
Lee Smith	Leeds	2005	5(4)	6	4	0	32
Leigh Smith	Workington	1996	9	4	0	0	16
Mark Smith	Widnes	2005	12(15)	4	0	0	16
	Wigan	1999-2004	35(77)	8	0	0	32
Michael Smith	Castleford	1998, 2001-04	86(33)	32	0	0	128
	Hull	1999	12(6)	3	0	0	12
Paul Smith	Huddersfield	2004-05	37(10)	10	0	0	40
Paul Smith	Warrington	2001	(1)	0	0	0	0
	Castleford	1997-2000	6(37)	3	0	0	12
Paul Smith	London	1997	7(1)	2	0	0	8
Peter Smith	Oldham	1996	2	0	0	0	0
Richard Smith	Wakefield	2001	8(1)	1	0	0	4
	Salford	1997	(1)	1	0	0	4
Tony Smith	Hull	2001-03	43(5)	26	0	0	104
	Wigan	1997-2000	66(5)	46	0	0	184
	Castleford	1996-97	18(2)	10	0	0	40
Tony Smith	Workington	1996	9	1	0	0	4
Tyrone Smith	London	2005	20(4)	11	0	0	44
Rob Smyth	Leigh	2005	15(1)	4	0	0	16
	Warrington	2000-03	65	35	20	0	180
	London	1998-2000	32(2)	9	15	0	66
	Wigan	1996	11(5)	16	0	0	64
Steve Snitch	Wakefield	2002-05	10(53)	4	0	0	16
Bright Sodje	Wakefield	2000	15	4	0	0	16
	Sheffield	1996-99	54	34	0	0	136
David Solomona	Wakefield	2004-05	47(2)	18	0	0	72
Alfred Songoro	Wakefield	1999	8(5)	4	0	0	16
Romain Sort	Paris	1997	(1)	0	0	0	0
Paul Southern	Salford	1997-2002	79(33)	6	13	0	50
	St Helens	2002	1(1)	0	0	0	0
Roy Southernwood	Wakefield	1999	1	0	0	0	0
	Halifax	1996	2	0	0	0	0
Jason Southwell	Huddersfield	2004	(1)	0	0	0	0
Waisale Sovatabua	Wakefield	2001-03	44(3)	19	0	0	76
	Hudds-Sheff	2000	23(1)	8	0	0	32
	Sheffield	1996-99	56(17)	19	0	1	77
Yusef Sozi	London	2000-01	(5)	0	0	0	0
Andy Speak	Castleford	2001	4(4)	0	0	0	0
	Wakefield	2000	6(5)	2	0	0	8
	Leeds	1999	4	1	0	0	4
Tim Spears	Castleford	2003	(3)	0	0	0	0
Ady Spencer	London	1996-99	8(36)	5	0	0	20
Rob Spicer	Wakefield	2002-05	28(18)	4	0	0	16
Stuart Spruce	Widnes	2002-03	45(4)	19	0	0	76
	Bradford	1996-2001	107(2)	57	0	0	228
Lee St Hilaire	Castleford	1997	4(2)	0	0	0	0
Marcus St Hilaire	Huddersfield	2003-05	72(2)	30	0	0	120
	Leeds	1996-2002	59(33)	31	0	0	124
Dylan Stainton	Workington	1996	2(3)	0	0	0	0
Mark Stamper	Workington	1996	(1)	0	0	0	0
John Stankevitch	Widnes	2005	17(5)	0	0	0	0
	St Helens	2000-04	74(40)	25	0	0	100
Gareth Stanley	Bradford	2000	1	1	0	0	4
Craig Stapleton	Leigh	2005	27(1)	4	0	0	16
Graham Steadman	Castleford	1996-97	11(17)	5	0	0	20
Jamie Stenhouse	Warrington	2000-01	9(3)	3	0	0	12
Gareth Stephens	Sheffield	1997-99	23(6)	2	0	0	8
David Stephenson	Hull	1998	11(7)	3	0	0	12
	Oldham	1997	10(8)	2	0	0	8
Francis Stephenson	London	2002-05	42(34)	5	0	0	20
	Wigan	2001	2(9)	0	0	0	0
	Wakefield	1999-2000	50(1)	6	0	0	24
Paul Sterling	Leeds	1997-2000	79(12)	50	0	0	200
Paul Stevens	Oldham	1996	2(1)	0	0	0	0
	London	1996	(1)	0	0	0	0
Warren Stevens	Leigh	2005	4(14)	1	0	0	4
	Warrington	1996-99, 2002-05	17(66)	1	0	0	4
	Salford	2001	(8)	0	0	0	0
Anthony Stewart	Salford	2004-05	48	15	0	0	60
	St Helens	1997-2003	93(23)	44	0	0	176
Troy Stone	Widnes	2002	18(6)	1	0	0	4
	Huddersfield	2001	12(1)	1	0	0	4
Lynton Stott	Wakefield	1999	21	4	6	1	29
	Sheffield	1996-98	40(4)	15	0	0	60
Mitchell Stringer	Salford	2005	11(3)	0	0	0	0
	London	2004-05	10(19)	0	0	0	0
Graham Strutton	London	1996	9(1)	2	0	0	8
Matt Sturm	Leigh	2005	8(19)	3	0	0	12
	Warrington	2002-04	1(18)	0	0	0	0
	Huddersfield	1998-99	46	8	0	0	32
Anthony Sullivan	St Helens	1996-2001	137(2)	105	0	0	420
Phil Sumner	Warrington	1996	(5)	0	0	0	0
Simon Svabic	Salford	1998-2000	13(5)	3	19	0	50
Richard Swain	Hull	2004-05	46	4	0	0	16
Anthony Swann	Warrington	2001	3	1	0	0	4
Logan Swann	Warrington	2005	25	10	0	0	40
	Bradford	2004	25	6	0	0	24
Willie Swann	Warrington	1996-97	25(2)	6	0	0	24
Nathan Sykes	Castleford	1996-2004	158(52)	3	0	0	12
Paul Sykes	London	2001-05	95(1)	26	220	3	547
	Bradford	1999-2002	5(4)	2	3	0	14
Wayne Sykes	London	1999	(2)	0	0	0	0
Semi Tadulala	Wakefield	2004-05	52	18	0	0	72
Whetu Taewa	Sheffield	1997-98	33(7)	8	0	0	32
Alan Tait	Leeds	1996	3(3)	1	0	0	4
Willie Talau	St Helens	2003-05	58(1)	24	0	0	96
Ian Talbot	Wakefield	1999	9(5)	2	31	0	70
	Wigan	1997	3	1	0	0	4
Albert Talipeau	Wakefield	2004	2(3)	0	0	0	0
Gael Tallec	Halifax	2000	5(19)	3	0	0	12
	Castleford	1998-99	19(21)	3	0	0	12
	Wigan	1996-97	8(12)	3	0	0	12
Joe Tamani	Bradford	1996	11(3)	4	0	0	16
Andrew Tangata-Toa	Huddersfield	1999	15	2	0	0	8
Kris Tassell	Wakefield	2002	24	10	0	0	40
	Salford	2000-01	35(10)	12	0	0	48
Shem Tatupu	Wigan	1996	(3)	0	0	0	0
Tony Tatupu	Wakefield	2000-01	20	2	0	0	8
	Warrington	1997	21(1)	6	0	0	24
James Taylor	Leigh	2005	(4)	0	0	0	0
Joe Taylor	Paris	1997	9(5)	2	0	0	8
Lawrence Taylor	Sheffield	1996	(1)	0	0	0	0
Frederic Teixido	Sheffield	1999	(4)	0	0	0	0
	Paris	1996-97	2(3)	1	0	0	4
Karl Temata	London	2005	1(2)	1	0	0	4
Jason Temu	Hull	1998	13(2)	1	0	0	4
	Oldham	1996-97	25(3)	1	0	0	4
Paul Terry	London	1997	(1)	0	0	0	0
Jamie Thackray	Hull	2005	16(14)	3	0	0	12
	Castleford	2003-04	7(11)	3	0	0	12
	Halifax	2000-02	10(38)	3	0	0	12
Adam Thaler	Castleford	2002	(1)	0	0	0	0
Giles Thomas	London	1997-99	1(2)	0	0	0	0
Steve Thomas	London	2004	4(2)	0	0	0	0
	Warrington	2001	2	0	0	0	0
Alex Thompson	Sheffield	1997	4(11)	0	0	0	0
Bobby Thompson	Salford	1999	28	5	2	0	24
Chris Thorman	Huddersfield	2000-01, 2005	64(14)	29	101	0	318
	London	2003	26(1)	7	81	1	191
	Sheffield	1999	5(13)	2	8	1	25
Tony Thorniley	Warrington	1997	(5)	0	0	0	0
Danny Tickle	Wigan	2002-05	82(22)	33	171	2	476
	Halifax	2000-02	25(17)	10	91	2	224
Kris Tickle	Warrington	2001	(1)	0	0	0	0
John Timu	London	1998-2000	57(3)	11	0	0	44
Kerrod Toby	London	1997	2(2)	0	0	0	0
Tulsen Tollett	London	1996-2001	105(5)	38	49	1	251
Joel Tomkins	Wigan	2005	5(8)	3	0	0	12
Glen Tomlinson	Wakefield	1999-2000	41(5)	8	0	0	32
	Hull	1998	5	1	0	0	4
	Bradford	1996-97	27(13)	12	0	0	48
Ian Tonks	Castleford	1996-2001	32(50)	11	13	0	70
Motu Tony	Hull	2005	14(7)	1	0	0	4
	Castleford	2004	8(1)	1	0	0	4
Mark Tookey	London	2005	13(14)	5	0	0	20
	Castleford	2004	2(8)	1	0	0	4
Paul Topping	Oldham	1996-97	23(10)	1	19	0	42
Patrick Torreilles	Paris	1996	9(1)	1	25	0	54
Mat Toshack	London	1998-2004	120(21)	24	0	0	96
Darren Treacy	Salford	2002	24(1)	6	1	0	26
Dean Treister	Hull	2003	16(1)	3	0	0	12
Steve Trindall	London	2003-05	40(20)	3	0	0	12
George Truelove	Wakefield	2002	2	1	0	0	4
	London	2000	5	1	0	0	4
Va'aiga Tuigamala	Wigan	1996	21	10	3	0	46
Fereti Tuilagi	St Helens	1999-2000	43(15)	21	0	0	84
	Halifax	1996-98	55(3)	27	0	0	108
Sateki Tuipulotu	Leeds	1996	6(3)	1	2	0	8
Neil Turley	Leigh	2005	6(3)	2	20	1	49
Darren Turner	Huddersfield	2000-01, 2003-04	42(13)	13	0	0	52
	Sheffield	1996-99	41(29)	15	0	0	60
Ian Turner	Paris	1996	1(1)	1	0	0	4
Gregory Tutard	Paris	1996	1(1)	0	0	0	0
Brendon Tuuta	Warrington	1998	18(2)	4	0	0	16
	Castleford	1996-97	41(1)	3	0	0	12
Mike Umaga	Halifax	1996-97	38(1)	16	5	0	74
Kava Utoikamanu	Paris	1996	6(3)	0	0	0	0
David Vaealiki	Wigan	2005	21	6	0	0	24
Joe Vagana	Bradford	2001-05	123(22)	10	0	0	40
Nigel Vagana	Warrington	1997	20	17	0	0	68
Tevita Vaikona	Bradford	1998-2004	145(2)	89	0	0	356
Lesley Vainikolo	Bradford	2002-05	91(4)	102	0	0	408
Eric Van Brussell	Paris	1996	2	0	0	0	0
Richard Varkulis	Warrington	2004	4(1)	3	0	0	12
Marcus Vassilakopoulos	Sheffield	1997-99	15(11)	3	10	2	34
	Leeds	1996-97	1(3)	0	0	0	0
Phil Veivers	Huddersfield	1998	7(6)	1	0	0	4
	St Helens	1996	(1)	1	0	0	4
Eric Vergniol	Paris	1996	14(1)	6	0	0	24
Gray Viane	Widnes	2005	20	13	0	0	52
	St Helens	2004	4	1	0	0	4
Adrian Vowles	Castleford	1997-2001, 2003	125(1)	29	1	1	119
	Wakefield	2002-03	24(3)	6	1	0	26
	Leeds	2002	14(3)	2	0	0	8
Michael Wainwright	Wakefield	2004-05	21(10)	8	0	0	32
Mike Wainwright	Warrington	1996-99, 2003-05	122(13)	19	0	0	76
	Salford	2000-02	72(3)	9	0	0	36
Ben Walker	Leeds	2002	23(1)	8	100	0	232
Chev Walker	Leeds	1999-2005	120(17)	67	0	0	268
Matt Walker	Huddersfield	2001	3(6)	0	0	0	0
Anthony Wall	Paris	1997	9	3	3	0	18
Mark Wallace	Workington	1996	14(1)	3	0	0	12
Kerrod Walters	Gateshead	1999	10(12)	2	1	0	10
Kevin Walters	Warrington	2001	1	0	0	0	0
Barry Ward	St Helens	2002-03	20(30)	4	0	0	16
Danny Ward	Leeds	1999-2005	70(48)	9	0	1	37
Phil Waring	Salford	1997-99	6(8)	2	0	0	8
Brett Warton	London	1999-2001	49(7)	14	133	0	322
Kyle Warren	Castleford	2002	13(14)	3	0	0	12
Danny Washbrook	Hull	2005	(4)	0	0	0	0
Frank Watene	Wakefield	1999-2001	24(37)	6	0	0	24
Dave Watson	Sheffield	1998-99	41(4)	4	0	0	16
Ian Watson	Salford	1997, 2002	24(17)	8	3	5	43
	Workington	1996	4(1)	1	15	0	34
Kris Watson	Warrington	1996	11(2)	2	0	0	8
Brad Watts	Widnes	2005	6	3	0	0	12
Michael Watts	Warrington	2002	3	0	0	0	0
Jason Webber	Salford	2000	25(1)	10	0	0	40
Paul Wellens	St Helens	1998-2005	177(23)	75	20	1	341
Jon Wells	London	2004-05	42(2)	19	0	0	76
	Wakefield	2003	22(1)	1	0	0	4
	Castleford	1996-2002	114(14)	49	0	0	196

Super League Players 1996-2005

PLAYER	CLUB	YEAR	APP	TRIES	GOALS	FG	PTS
Dwayne West	St Helens	2000-02	8(16)	6	0	0	24
	Wigan	1999	1(1)	0	0	0	0
Craig Weston	Widnes	2002, 2004	23(9)	2	1	2	12
	Huddersfield	1998-99	46(1)	15	15	0	90
Ben Westwood	Warrington	2002-05	75(4)	35	0	0	140
	Wakefield	1999-2002	31(7)	8	1	0	34
Andrew Whalley	Workington	1996	(2)	0	0	0	0
Matt Whitaker	Widnes	2004-05	10(20)	9	0	0	36
	Huddersfield	2003-04	3(14)	0	0	0	0
David White	Wakefield	2000	1(2)	0	0	0	0
Josh White	Salford	1998	18(3)	5	5	1	31
	London	1997	14(2)	8	0	1	33
Paul White	Huddersfield	2003-05	11(32)	17	16	0	100
Richard Whiting	Hull	2004-05	37(11)	21	3	2	92
Danny Whittle	Warrington	1998	(2)	0	0	0	0
David Whittle	St Helens	2002	1(2)	0	0	0	0
	Warrington	2001	1(2)	0	0	0	0
Jon Whittle	Widnes	2005	13	2	0	0	8
	Wigan	2003	1	0	0	0	0
Stephen Wild	Wigan	2001-05	67(20)	24	0	0	96
Oliver Wilkes	Leigh	2005	13(1)	1	0	0	4
	Huddersfield	2000-01	1(6)	0	0	0	0
	Sheffield	1998	(1)	0	0	0	0
Jon Wilkin	St Helens	2003-05	45(13)	20	0	1	81
Alex Wilkinson	Hull	2003-04	11(4)	1	0	0	4
	Huddersfield	2003	8	4	0	0	16
	London	2002	5(1)	0	0	0	0
	Bradford	2000-01	3(3)	1	0	0	4
Bart Williams	London	1998	5(3)	1	0	0	4
Danny Williams	London	2005	1(16)	0	0	0	0
Desi Williams	Wigan	2004	2	0	0	0	0
Jonny Williams	London	2004	(4)	0	0	0	0
John Wilshere	Leigh	2005	26	8	6	0	44
	Warrington	2004	5	2	0	0	8
Craig Wilson	Hull	2000	2(16)	1	0	1	5
	Gateshead	1999	17(11)	5	0	1	21
George Wilson	Paris	1996	7(2)	3	0	0	12
Richard Wilson	Hull	1998-99	(13)	0	0	0	0
Scott Wilson	Warrington	1998-99	23(2)	6	0	0	24
Johan Windley	Hull	1999	2(2)	1	0	0	4
Paul Wingfield	Warrington	1997	5(3)	6	1	0	26
Michael Withers	Bradford	1999-2005	131(4)	83	15	4	366
Jeff Wittenberg	Huddersfield	1998	18(1)	1	0	0	4
	Bradford	1997	8(9)	4	0	0	16
Martin Wood	Sheffield	1997-98	24(11)	4	18	2	54
Nathan Wood	Warrington	2002-05	90	38	0	3	155
	Wakefield	2002	11	2	0	0	8
Paul Wood	Warrington	2000-05	51(71)	21	0	0	84
Phil Wood	Widnes	2004	2(1)	0	0	0	0
Darren Woods	Widnes	2005	(1)	0	0	0	0
David Woods	Halifax	2002	18(2)	8	0	0	32
Rob Worrincy	Castleford	2004	1	0	0	0	0
Troy Wozniak	Widnes	2004	13(7)	1	0	0	4
Matthew Wray	Wakefield	2002-03	13(3)	2	0	0	8
David Wrench	Wakefield	2002-05	25(49)	6	0	0	24
	Leeds	1999-2001	7(17)	0	0	0	0
Craig Wright	Castleford	2000	1(9)	0	0	0	0
Nigel Wright	Huddersfield	1999	4(6)	1	0	0	4
	Wigan	1996-97	5(5)	2	0	1	9
Ricky Wright	Sheffield	1997-99	2(13)	0	0	0	0
Vincent Wulf	Paris	1996	13(4)	4	0	0	16
Andrew Wynyard	London	1999-2000	34(6)	4	0	0	16
Bagdad Yaha	Paris	1996	4(4)	2	4	0	16
Malakai Yasa	Sheffield	1996	1(3)	0	0	0	0
Kirk Yeaman	Hull	2001-05	73(17)	41	0	0	164
Grant Young	London	1998-99	22(2)	2	0	0	8
Ronel Zenon	Paris	1996	(4)	0	0	0	0
Nick Zisti	Bradford	1999	6(1)	0	0	0	0

OLD FACES - Players making their debuts for new clubs in 2005

PLAYER	CLUB	DEBUT vs	ROUND	DATE
Carl Ablett	London	St Helens (a)	25	20/8/05
Paul Anderson	St Helens	Widnes (h)	1	11/2/05
Richie Barnett	Widnes	Hull (a)	9	10/4/05
Liam Botham	Wigan	Hull (h)	17	10/6/05
Andy Bracek	Warrington	Hull (a)	3	27/2/05
Chris Bridge	Warrington	Huddersfield (h)	6	20/3/05
Austin Buchanan	Wakefield	Widnes (h)	26	4/9/05
Mick Cassidy	Widnes	St Helens (a)	1	11/2/05
Ryan Clayton	Huddersfield	Leeds (a)	12	29/4/05
Gary Connolly	Widnes	St Helens (a)	1	11/2/05
Jamie Durbin	Widnes	Leeds (h)	11	23/4/05
Gareth Ellis	Leeds	Hull (a)	1	11/2/05
		(first team debut: Bulldogs, WCC, 4/2/05)		
Chris Feather	Wakefield	Bradford (a)	1	13/2/05
Darren Fleary	Leigh	Wakefield (a)	4	6/3/05
Carl Forber	Leigh	Huddersfield (a)	25	21/8/05
Martin Gleeson	Warrington	London (a)	1	13/2/05
Wayne Godwin	Wigan	Salford (h)	1	11/2/05
Lee Greenwood	Huddersfield	Hull (a)	21	16/7/05
Jerome Guisset	Wigan	Bradford (a)	3	25/2/05
Kevin Henderson	Wakefield	St Helens (a)	24	12/8/05
David Hodgson	Salford	Wigan (a)	1	11/2/05
Sylvain Houles	Wakefield	Leeds (a)	8	28/3/05
Gary Hulse	Widnes	St Helens (a)	1	11/2/05
Paul Jackson	Huddersfield	Leigh (a)	1	12/2/05
Rob Jackson	Leigh	Huddersfield (h)	1	12/2/05
Kevin King	Wakefield	Bradford (a)	1	13/2/05
Andy Kirk	Wakefield	London (a)	3	27/2/05
Toa Kohe-Love	Warrington	London (a)	1	13/2/05
Andy Lynch	Bradford	Wakefield (h)	1	13/2/05
Steve McCurrie	Leigh	Huddersfield (h)	1	12/2/05
Wayne McDonald	Wigan	Bradford (a)	11	22/4/05
	Huddersfield	Warrington (h)	16	5/6/05
Robbie Mears	Leigh	Wakefield (h)	12	30/4/05
Richard Moore	Leigh	Huddersfield (h)	1	12/2/05
Dennis Moran	Wigan	Salford (h)	1	11/2/05
Adrian Morley	Bradford	Huddersfield (h)	27	11/9/05
Scott Murrell	Leeds	Leigh (h)	14	20/5/05
Terry O'Connor	Widnes	Bradford (h)	2	20/2/05
Jules O'Neill	Wakefield	Bradford (a)	1	13/2/05
	Widnes	Huddersfield (h)	15	29/5/05
Luke Robinson	Salford	Wigan (a)	1	11/2/05
Tom Saxton	Hull	Leeds (h)	1	11/2/05
Ian Sibbit	Salford	Wigan (a)	1	11/2/05
Andy Smith	Salford	Huddersfield (h)	19	2/7/05
Mark Smith	Widnes	St Helens (a)	1	11/2/05
John Stankevitch	Widnes	St Helens (a)	1	11/2/05
Warren Stevens	Leigh	Salford (a)	11	22/4/05
Mitchell Stringer	Salford	Leeds (h)	6	18/3/05
Logan Swann	Warrington	London (a)	1	13/2/05
Jamie Thackray	Hull	Leeds (h)	1	11/2/05
Chris Thorman	Huddersfield	Leigh (a)	1	12/2/05
Motu Tony	Hull	Leeds (h)	1	11/2/05
Mark Tookey	London	Warrington (h)	1	13/2/05
Gray Viane	Widnes	Hull (a)	9	10/4/05
Jon Whittle	Widnes	St Helens (a)	1	11/2/05
John Wilshere	Leigh	Huddersfield (h)	1	12/2/05

NEW FACES - Players making their Super League debuts in 2005

PLAYER	CLUB	DEBUT vs	ROUND	DATE
Vinnie Anderson	St Helens	Salford (h)	5	11/3/05
Anthony Armour	London	Warrington (h)	1	13/2/05
Chris Ashton	Wigan	Huddersfield (a)	28	18/9/05
Paul Ballard	Widnes	Leigh (h)	7	25/3/05
Darren Bamford	Salford	St Helens (a)	5	11/3/05
Nathan Blacklock	Hull	Leeds (h)	1	11/2/05
Matthew Bottom	Leigh	Hull (a)	18	17/6/05
Nick Bradley-Qalilawa	London	Warrington (h)	1	13/2/05
Danny Brough	Hull	London (a)	7	25/3/05
Liam Campbell	Wakefield	Leeds (a)	28	16/9/05
Paul Clough	St Helens	Hull (h)	20	8/7/05
Liam Coleman	Leigh	Leeds (h)	23	7/8/05
Matt Cook	Bradford	St Helens (a)	8	28/3/05
James Coyle	Wigan	Hull (a)	8	28/3/05
Owen Craigie	Widnes	St Helens (a)	1	11/2/05
Paul Crook	Widnes	London (a)	6	20/3/05
Michael De Vere	Huddersfield	Salford (h)	8	28/3/05
Stuart Dickens	Salford	Hull (h)	4	5/3/05
Luke Dorn	London	Warrington (h)	1	13/2/05
Brad Drew	Huddersfield	Leigh (a)	1	12/2/05
Jason Duffy	Leigh	Hull (h)	10	17/4/05
Andrew Emelio	Widnes	St Helens (a)	1	11/2/05
Sione Faumuina	Hull	Wakefield (a)	27	11/9/05
Brett Ferres	Bradford	Hull (h)	6	18/3/05
Jason Ferris	Leigh	Huddersfield (h)	1	12/2/05
Ashley Gibson	Leeds	Leigh (a)	23	7/8/05
Sean Gleeson	Wigan	Salford (a)	15	30/5/05
Darrell Goulding	Wigan	Widnes (a)	24	14/8/05
Ben Harris	Bradford	Warrington (h)	14	22/5/05
Solomon Haumono	London	Warrington (h)	1	13/2/05
Tom Hemingway	Huddersfield	Warrington (h)	16	5/6/05
Ian Henderson	Bradford	Leeds (a)	19	1/7/05
Kevin Henderson	Leigh	Warrington (a)	2	20/2/05
Chris Hill	Leigh	St Helens (h)	26	4/9/05
Lee Hopkins	London	Warrington (h)	1	13/2/05
Lee Jewitt	Wigan	St Helens (h)	27	9/9/05
Andrew Johns	Warrington	Leeds (h)	27	10/9/05
Chris Jones	Leigh	Huddersfield (a)	20	10/7/05
Stephen Jones	Huddersfield	London (a)	22	24/7/05
Stephen Kearney	Hull	Bradford (a)	6	18/3/05
Jason Kent	Leigh	Huddersfield (h)	1	12/2/05
Keiran Kerr	Widnes	Bradford (a)	23	7/8/05
James King	Leigh	Huddersfield (h)	1	12/2/05
Junior Langi	Salford	Wakefield (h)	9	8/4/05
		(first team debut: Rochdale (a), CCR4, 3/4/05)		
Mark Leafa	Leigh	Huddersfield (h)	1	12/2/05
Tommy Lee	Hull	Leigh (h)	24	14/8/05
Thomas Leuluai	London	Warrington (h)	1	13/2/05
Filimone Lolohea	London	Warrington (h)	1	13/2/05
Jamie Lyon	St Helens	Widnes (h)	1	11/2/05
Keiron Maddocks	Leigh	St Helens (a)	9	8/4/05
Misili Manu	Widnes	Leigh (a)	16	5/6/05
		(first team debut: Swinton (h), CCR4, 3/4/05)		
Feleti Mateo	London	Leigh (h)	15	29/5/05
Mark McLinden	London	Warrington (h)	1	13/2/05
Brad Meyers	Bradford	Wakefield (h)	1	13/2/05
Stephen Nash	Widnes	Wigan (h)	24	14/8/05
Sam Obst	Wakefield	Bradford (a)	1	13/2/05
Nick Owen	Leigh	Hull (h)	10	17/4/05
Steve Pickersgill	Warrington	Leeds (a)	5	11/3/05
Chris Riley	Warrington	Huddersfield (a)	24	12/8/05
Craig Robinson	Wakefield	London (h)	11	24/4/05
Jerry Seuseu	Wigan	Salford (h)	1	11/2/05
Lee Smith	Leeds	Wakefield (h)	8	28/3/05
Tyrone Smith	London	Warrington (h)	1	13/2/05
Craig Stapleton	Leigh	Huddersfield (h)	1	12/2/05
James Taylor	Leigh	London (h)	8	28/3/05
Karl Temata	London	Salford (a)	27	9/9/05
Joel Tomkins	Wigan	Widnes (a)	4	6/3/05
David Vaealiki	Wigan	Salford (h)	1	11/2/05
Danny Washbrook	Hull	St Helens (a)	13	13/5/05
Brad Watts	Widnes	Bradford (a)	23	7/8/05
Danny Williams	London	Leigh (a)	8	28/3/05
Darren Woods	Widnes	London (a)	28	18/9/05

SUPER LEAGUE X
Club by Club

1 December 2004 - Bulls announce they will bring forward their kick-off times for all Sunday games from 6.00pm to 3.00pm in 2005.

13 December 2004 - Wakefield offered swap deal for Gareth Ellis, with Jamie Langley and Stuart Reardon the players offered.

23 December 2004 - Leeds Rhinos contact Bradford to check on the availability and valuation of Jamie Langley.

5 January 2005 - prop Richard Moore signs for Leigh Centurions.

10 January 2005 - Jamie Peacock is new team captain for Super League X. Robbie Paul remains as club captain.

23 January 2005 – Bulls Academy lose to London Skolars 20-28 in Dublin, as Matt Cook signs a new three-year contract.

24 January 2005 - Bulls suspend new signing from Castleford, Ryan Hudson, for disciplinary reasons. RFL confirm he is under investigation by the doping control panel.

25 January 2005 – centre Shontayne Hape to miss the first six months of Super League X following a knee reconstruction, after a training injury in the Gillette Tri-Nations.

7 March 2005 – Bulls lose out to London Broncos in chase for Kiwi international Vinnie Anderson, although he eventually signs for St Helens.

11 March 2005 - Bulls terminate the three-year contract of Ryan Hudson after the 25-year-old pleaded guilty to providing a urine sample containing the banned steroid Stanozolol.

22 March 2005 - Lesley Vainikolo signs a new four-year contract that will keep him at Odsal until the end of the 2009 Super League season, ending speculation that he may switch codes.

1 April 2005 - Ryan Hudson loses his appeal against a two-year drugs ban.

17 April 2005 – Bulls dedicate their game against Huddersfield to club legend Trevor Foster, who died aged 90, after 67 years of involvement at Odsal.

KEY DATES - BRADFORD BULLS

10 May 2005 - Bulls sign 21-year-old Canterbury Bulldogs centre Ben Harris.

16 May 2005 - Bulls deny suggestions that coach Brian Noble could be ready to leave the club at the end of the season to concentrate on his Great Britain role.

24 May 2005 - Lesley Vainikolo suffers a knee injury in the game against Warrington and is forecast to be sidelined for eight weeks.

26 May 2005 - Bulls extend Brian Noble's contract for a further two years.

6 June 2005 – Stuart Fielden confirms to Rugby Leaguer & League Express he does not have a clause enabling him to leave Bradford Bulls before his contract expires at the end of 2007, despite suggestions to the contrary in the Australian press.

7 June 2005 - Leon Pryce is suspended for three matches for a reckless high tackle in the Bulls' 66-4 engage Super League defeat at the hands of St Helens at Odsal.

1 July 2005 - Salford City Reds sign 20-year-old winger Andy Smith on loan until the end of the season.

4 July 2005 – St Helens deny they have signed Leon Pryce.

20 July 2005 – Leeds win their high court action against the Bulls and their former player Iestyn Harris.

8 August 2005 - Bulls strongly deny they have signed Australian Test star Brett Kimmorley on a two-year deal from next season.

10 August 2005 - Leon Pryce to leave Odsal at the end of the season after he rejects an improved contract offer.

25 August 2005 – Stuart Reardon will also leave at the end of the season.

31 August 2005 - Bulls confirm both Jamie Peacock and Lee Radford will leave the club at the end of the season.

1 September 2005 - Leeds Rhinos confirm signing of Great Britain international Jamie Peacock on a four-year contract.

1 September 2005 - Sydney Roosters prop Adrian Morley signs for the Bulls on a short-term contract to the end of the season.

1 September 2005 - St Helens announce signing of Leon Pryce on a three-year contract.

2 September 2005 - Lesley Vainikolo breaks the Super League tries-in-a-match record with six tries in Bradford's 49-6 home win over Hull.

5 September 2005 - Bulls rubbish claims that they want to sign Cronulla fullback David Peachey.

8 September 2005 - Warrington Wolves announce signing of Stuart Reardon on a three-year deal.

15 September 2005 – Leeds centre/second row Chris McKenna is announced as the Bulls' first signing for the 2006 season.

17 September 2005 - Bulls seal third spot with 32-18 win at St Helens.

21 September 2005 – Jamie Langley signs new two-year deal.

10 October 2005 – Stanley Gene revealed by Rugby Leaguer & League Express as new Bradford signing, as Bulls march to Old Trafford with 23-18 final eliminator win at St Helens.

15 October 2005 – Bulls win Super League Grand Final 15-6

17 October 2005 – Rob Parker signs for Warrington Wolves.

20 October 2005 – Bulls sign Mick Higham from St Helens and immediately swap him with Wigan for Terry Newton.

25 October 2005 – Robbie Paul signs for Huddersfield, and Stanley Gene signs for the Bulls.

BRADFORD BULLS

DATE	FIXTURE	RESULT	SCORERS	LGE	ATT
13/2/05	Wakefield (h)	L16-28	t:K Pryce,I Harris,Langley g:Deacon(2)	10th	15,137
20/2/05	Widnes (a)	L31-22	t:L Pryce,Smith,I Harris,K Pryce g:Deacon(3)	11th	7,230
25/2/05	Wigan (a)	W27-28	t:Langley,I Harris,Peacock,Reardon,Withers g:Deacon(4)	9th	13,111
6/3/05	London (h)	W48-22	t:Vainikolo(2),Johnson,Langley,Deacon(2),K Pryce,Meyers,Paul g:Deacon(6)	8th	11,282
11/3/05	Leigh (a)	W6-46	t:I Harris(2),K Pryce(2),Vainikolo,Parker,L Pryce,Deacon,Langley g:Deacon(5)	5th	4,241
18/3/05	Hull (h)	W32-22	t:I Harris,L Pryce,Lynch,K Pryce g:Deacon(8)	4th	13,394
24/3/05	Leeds (h)	L12-42	t:K Pryce,Reardon g:Deacon(2)	6th	22,843
28/3/05	St Helens (a)	L34-27	t:Lynch(2),K Pryce,Paul g:Deacon(5) fg:Deacon	6th	12,364
3/4/05	Featherstone (a) (CCR4)	W14-80	t:Paul(3),Parker,Fielden,L Pryce,I Harris(2),Smith(3),Ferres(2),Pratt g:Deacon(11),Vagana	N/A	3,355
10/4/05	Warrington (a)	L35-32	t:Meyers,Vainikolo(2),Langley(2),Withers g:Deacon(4)	7th	10,654
17/4/05	Huddersfield (h)	W54-10	t:Vainikolo(3),Reardon(2),Pratt,Paul,Langley,Radford,Fielden g:Deacon,I Harris(6)	4th	13,481
22/4/05	Wigan (h)	W40-8	t:Reardon,Vainikolo,Withers,Meyers(2),Fielden,Paul g:Deacon(6)	4th	13,527
1/5/05	London (a)	W26-41	t:I Harris,Reardon,Fielden,Peacock,Langley,L Pryce,K Pryce g:Deacon(6) fg:Deacon	4th	3,879
7/5/05	Hull (a) (CCR5)	L26-24	t:Peacock,Vainikolo(2),K Pryce g:Deacon(4)	N/A	11,350
13/5/05	Salford (a)	W0-58	t:L Pryce,K Pryce(3),Pratt,Deacon(3),Parker,Vainikolo(2) g:Deacon(7)	4th	4,102
22/5/05	Warrington (h)	L24-44	t:Vainikolo,Peacock,Reardon,I Harris g:Deacon(4)	4th	14,428
28/5/05	Hull (a)	W24-42	t:Meyers,Ferres,L Pryce(2),Reardon,K Pryce g:Deacon(9)	4th	11,563
5/6/05	St Helens (h)	L4-66	t:Reardon	5th	15,260
11/6/05	Huddersfield (a)	W20-38	t:B Harris,Paul(2),K Pryce,Parker,Radford,Reardon g:Deacon(5)	5th	6,022
19/6/05	Widnes (h)	D25-25	t:Deacon,Paul(2),Radford g:Deacon(4) fg:Deacon	5th	10,715
1/7/05	Leeds (a)	L36-26	t:Peacock,Johnson(2),B Harris,Meyers g:Deacon(3)	5th	21,225
10/7/05	Wakefield (a)	L44-34	t:Withers,Deacon,Pratt(3),Meyers g:Deacon(5)	5th	5,954
17/7/05	Leigh (a)	W58-12	t:Fielden,Henderson,I Harris,B Harris(3),Pratt,L Pryce,Withers,Meyers g:Deacon(6),I Harris(3)	5th	10,294
22/7/05	Salford (a)	W18-24	t:K Pryce,Deacon,I Harris,L Pryce g:Deacon(3),I Harris	5th	3,684
7/8/05	Widnes (h)	W74-24	t:Fielden,Peacock,Withers(2),Vainikolo(2),Hape(2),I Harris,L Pryce,Lynch,Reardon(2) g:Deacon(11)	5th	10,128
14/8/05	Salford (h)	W58-12	t:Hape(2),Peacock,I Harris(2),L Pryce,Lynch,Johnson,Deacon,Vainikolo g:Deacon(7),I Harris(2)	4th	10,113
19/8/05	Leeds (a)	W10-42	t:Hape(3),Lynch,Langley,Deacon,Paul,I Harris g:Deacon(5)	3rd	20,220
2/9/05	Hull (h)	W49-6	t:Vainikolo(6),Hape,Fielden,Vagana,Peacock g:Deacon(4) fg:Deacon	3rd	13,326
11/9/05	Huddersfield (h)	W52-34	t:Henderson,Johnson(2),Deacon,Vainikolo(2),Fielden,Meyers,Radford g:Deacon(8)	3rd	13,207
17/9/05	St Helens (a)	W18-32	t:Vainikolo(2),Johnson(2),L Pryce,B Harris g:Deacon(4)	3rd	11,064
23/9/05	London (h) (EPO)	W44-22	t:I Harris(2),Vainikolo(2),Peacock,Hape,Henderson,K Pryce g:I Harris(5),K Pryce	N/A	9,167
1/10/05	Hull (h) (ESF)	W71-0	t:Henderson(2),Peacock,Withers,Vainikolo(4),Johnson,Hape,I Harris,Fielden g:Deacon(10),Paul fg:I Harris	N/A	13,148
7/10/05	St Helens (a) (FE)	W18-23	t:Hape(2),Johnson,Langley g:Deacon(3) fg:Deacon	N/A	11,604
15/10/05	Leeds (GF) ●	W15-6	t:L Pryce,Vainikolo g:Deacon(3) fg:I Harris	N/A	65,537

● Played at Old Trafford, Manchester

			APP		TRIES		GOALS		FG		PTS	
	D.O.B.	ALL	SL	ALL	SL	ALL	SL	ALL	SL	ALL	SL	
Ryan Atkins	7/10/85	(1)	0	0	0	0	0	0	0	0	0	
Matt Cook	14/11/86	(8)	(7)	0	0	0	0	0	0	0	0	
Paul Deacon	13/2/79	33	31	12	12	168	153	5	5	389	359	
Brett Ferres	17/4/86	(9)	(7)	3	1	0	0	0	0	12	4	
Stuart Fielden	14/9/79	34	32	9	8	0	0	0	0	36	32	
Shontayne Hape	30/1/82	10(2)	10(2)	12	12	0	0	0	0	48	48	
Ben Harris	24/9/83	18(1)	18(1)	6	6	0	0	0	0	24	24	
Iestyn Harris	25/6/76	33(1)	31(1)	19	17	17	17	2	2	112	104	
Ian Henderson	23/4/83	14	14	5	5	0	0	0	0	20	20	
Paul Johnson	25/11/78	19	19	10	10	0	0	0	0	40	40	
Jamie Langley	21/12/83	17(11)	15(11)	10	10	0	0	0	0	40	40	
Andy Lynch	20/10/79	2(29)	2(27)	6	6	0	0	0	0	24	24	
Brad Meyers	5/1/80	24(6)	23(6)	9	9	0	0	0	0	36	36	
Adrian Morley	10/5/77	2(4)	2(4)	0	0	0	0	0	0	0	0	
Rob Parker	5/9/81	9(16)	7(16)	4	3	0	0	0	0	16	12	
Robbie Paul	3/2/76	19(12)	17(12)	12	9	1	1	0	0	50	38	
Jamie Peacock	14/12/77	33	32	10	9	0	0	0	0	40	36	
Karl Pratt	18/7/80	14(6)	12(6)	7	6	0	0	0	0	28	24	
Karl Pryce	27/7/86	15(6)	14(5)	17	16	1	1	0	0	70	66	
Leon Pryce	9/10/81	24(6)	23(6)	14	13	0	0	0	0	56	52	
Lee Radford	26/3/79	32	30	4	4	0	0	0	0	16	16	
Stuart Reardon	13/10/81	25	23	12	12	0	0	0	0	48	48	
Andy Smith	6/7/84	3(3)	2(3)	4	1	0	0	0	0	16	4	
Joe Vagana	21/1/75	18(15)	17(14)	1	1	0	0	0	0	6	4	
Lesley Vainikolo	4/5/79	23	22	34	32	0	0	0	0	136	128	
Michael Withers	16/5/76	20	20	8	8	0	0	0	0	32	32	

Stuart Fielden

LEAGUE RECORD
P28-W18-D1-L9
(3rd, SL/Grand Final Winners,
Champions)
F1038, A684, Diff+354
37 points.

CHALLENGE CUP
Round Five

ATTENDANCES
Best - v Leeds (SL - 22,843)
Worst - v London (EPO - 9,167)
Total (SL, inc play-offs) - 209,446
Average (SL, inc play-offs) - 13,090
(Down by 410 on 2004)

30 November 2004 - Giants sign Castleford Tigers' former Huddersfield Academy prop Paul Jackson on a one-year deal.

3 January 2005 – Giants hand trial to Newcastle rugby union centre Stephen Jones.

15 January 2005 – squad heads for warm-weather training camp in Portugal.

1 February 2005 – Ben Roarty appointed captain.

28 March 2005 – Michael De Vere makes his Huddersfield debut against Salford.

3 April 2005 - Giants hit out at RFL's decision to swap referee Ian Smith from the Cup game with St Helens after he appears at a supporter's forum

11 April 2005 - Sean Penkywicz is called to appear before the Rugby Football League's Advisory Panel following alleged breaches of the RFL's Doping Control regulations.

19 April 2005 – Ryan Clayton signed until end of season.

21 April 2005 - Sean Penkywicz is suspended for two years after being found guilty of providing a sample containing the prohibited substance Stanozolol. His suspension is back-dated to start on 11 March 2005.

5 May 2005 – coach Jon Sharp is referred to the RFL's Disciplinary Commissioner for comments allegedly made following the Powergen Challenge Cup fourth round game.

3 June 2005 - Giants sign 29-year-old Leeds Rhinos prop forward Wayne McDonald – on loan at Wigan - on an 18-month deal.

KEY DATES - HUDDERSFIELD GIANTS

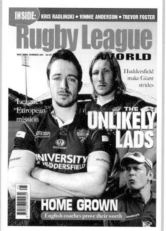

16 June 2005 - James Evans signs a new two-year deal.

22 June 2005 - prop forward Mick Slicker, 26, is forced to retire due to chronic and persistent knee problems.

7 July 2005 - Australian back-row forward Chris Nero signs a new-two year deal.

13 July 2005 - fullback Paul Reilly cops a three-match ban after he was red-carded 15 minutes into the Giants' 32-22 win over Leigh for an elbow in a challenge on Centurions centre Danny Halliwell.

22 August 2005 - winger Hefin O'Hare announces he will leave the Galpharm Stadium at the end of the season, his fifth at the Giants, to join the Glasgow rugby union club on a two-year contract.

1 September 2005 - Giants award full-time contract to 18-year-old back-rower Simon George.

3 September 2005 – play-off hopes take fatal blow after controversial 16-12 defeat to London Broncos at Griffin Park.

6 September 2005 - Giants extend contract of head coach Jon Sharp for a further three seasons to the end of season 2008.

9 September 2005 – sign NL1 player of the year Andy Raleigh from Hull KR on a two-year deal, with Paul White to leave for Wakefield at end of season.

15 September 2005 – Giants announce re-signing of 18-year-old halfback Thomas Hemingway on a two-year deal, but release Ben Roarty

19 September 2005 – Giants linked with Robbie Paul.

21 September 2005 – Giants sign Stephen Wild from Wigan and Steve Snitch from Wakefield.

29 September 2005 – sign 20-year-old Leeds Rhinos winger Mat Gardner on a two-year deal.

30 September 2005 – Stuart Donlan and Bolu Fagborun both re-sign on one-year contracts.

13 October 2005 – Giants sign St George Illawarra winger Albert Torrens on a one-year deal, and Wigan back Martin Aspinwall on a two-year contract.

25 October 2005 – Robbie Paul signs for Giants on two-year contract.

25 October 2005 – Stanley Gene joins Bradford.

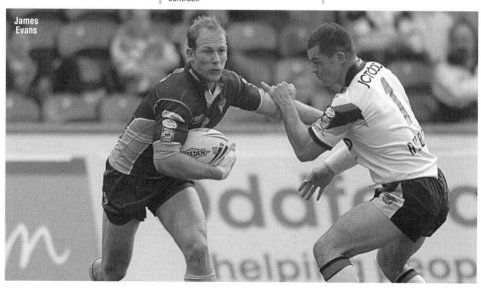

James Evans

HUDDERSFIELD GIANTS

DATE	FIXTURE	RESULT	SCORERS	LGE	ATT
12/2/05	Leigh (a)	W12-30	t:Gene,Penkywicz,Stuart Jones,White g:Thorman(7)	2nd	4,042
20/2/05	Hull (h)	L28-36	t:Crabtree,White(2),Thorman,Donlan g:Thorman(4)	4th	6,610
25/2/05	St Helens (a)	L34-24	t:Evans(2),Crabtree,Grayshon g:Thorman(4)	8th	9,507
6/3/05	Leeds (h)	L10-54	t:O'Hare,Gannon g:Thorman	10th	10,088
11/3/05	Widnes (h)	W34-18	t:Crabtree,White(2),Reilly,St Hilaire(2) g:Thorman(5)	9th	3,383
20/3/05	Warrington (a)	L14-8	t:Gene g:Thorman(2)	8th	9,014
25/3/05	Wakefield (a)	W20-42	t:O'Hare,Thorman,Grayshon,White,Roarty,Gene g:Thorman(9)	8th	5,288
28/3/05	Salford (h)	W26-12	t:St Hilaire(2),Smith,Gene g:De Vere(5)	7th	4,760
3/4/05	St Helens (h) (CCR4)	L22-26	t:Gene,St Hilaire,Nero,White g:De Vere(3)	N/A	7,105
8/4/05	Wigan (h)	W24-16	t:Reilly(3),Drew g:De Vere(4)	5th	5,288
17/4/05	Bradford (a)	L54-10	t:De Vere,Gene g:De Vere	7th	13,481
24/4/05	St Helens (h)	L22-36	t:Thorman(2),Smith,Nero g:Thorman(3)	8th	7,432
29/4/05	Leeds (a)	L44-14	t:Fagborun,Drew g:Thorman(2),Drew	8th	15,514
15/5/05	London (h)	W34-24	t:Nero(3),Donlan,O'Hare,Thorman g:De Vere(5)	8th	3,682
20/5/05	Wigan (a)	W24-26	t:St Hilaire,Thorman(2),O'Hare,Nero g:De Vere(3)	6th	10,057
29/5/05	Widnes (a)	L40-12	t:March,Smith g:De Vere(2)	7th	5,946
5/6/05	Warrington (h)	L22-24	t:Drew,St Hilaire(2),Reilly g:De Vere(3)	8th	6,162
11/6/05	Bradford (h)	L20-38	t:Thorman,St Hilaire,Donlan,Smith g:De Vere(2)	8th	6,022
19/6/05	Wakefield (h)	W40-22	t:Crabtree,Reilly,Thorman,Nero(2),White g:Thorman(8)	7th	4,544
2/7/05	Salford (a)	L24-16	t:St Hilaire,Donlan,Thorman g:Thorman(2)	8th	2,682
10/7/05	Leigh (h)	W32-22	t:Evans,Thorman,Grayshon,O'Hare g:Thorman(8)	8th	3,889
16/7/05	Hull (a)	L34-24	t:Smith,Greenwood,Nero,Crabtree g:Thorman(4)	8th	7,962
24/7/05	London (a)	L35-26	t:Drew,Thorman,Gannon,Nero g:Thorman(5)	8th	3,221
7/8/05	Wakefield (a)	W12-44	t:Nero,Thorman,March(2),St Hilaire,Grayshon,Smith g:Thorman(8)	8th	4,476
12/8/05	Warrington (h)	W38-22	t:Reilly,Drew,Crabtree(2),Nero(2),Gannon g:Thorman(5)	8th	4,077
21/8/05	Leigh (h)	W68-16	t:Thorman(4),O'Hare,March(2),Nero(3),Greenwood,White g:Thorman(10)	8th	3,902
3/9/05	London (a)	L16-12	t:Thorman g:Thorman(4)	8th	2,877
11/9/05	Bradford (a)	L52-34	t:St Hilaire,Evans,Gene,March,Crabtree,Greenwood g:Thorman(5)	8th	13,207
18/9/05	Wigan (h)	L22-36	t:Smith,Evans,White,Thorman g:Thorman(3)	8th	5,917

		APP		TRIES		GOALS		FG		PTS	
	D.O.B.	ALL	SL	ALL	SL	ALL	SL	ALL	SL	ALL	SL
Ryan Clayton	22/11/82	4(6)	4(6)	0	0	0	0	0	0	0	0
Eorl Crabtree	2/10/82	19(10)	19(9)	8	8	0	0	0	0	32	32
Michael De Vere	11/12/76	15	14	1	1	28	25	0	0	60	54
Stuart Donlan	29/8/78	14	14	4	4	0	0	0	0	16	16
Brad Drew	25/8/75	29	28	5	5	1	1	0	0	22	22
James Evans	5/11/78	22	21	5	5	0	0	0	0	20	20
Bolouagi Fagborun	28/3/86	1(1)	1(1)	1	1	0	0	0	0	4	4
Jim Gannon	16/6/77	20(6)	19(6)	3	3	0	0	0	0	12	12
Stanley Gene	11/5/74	19(2)	18(2)	7	6	0	0	0	0	28	24
Jon Grayshon	10/5/83	3(20)	3(20)	4	4	0	0	0	0	16	16
Lee Greenwood	28/9/80	7	7	3	3	0	0	0	0	12	12
Tom Hemingway	6/12/86	2(1)	2(1)	0	0	0	0	0	0	0	0
Paul Jackson	29/9/78	16(11)	15(11)	0	0	0	0	0	0	0	0
Stephen Jones	9/1/83	(1)	(1)	0	0	0	0	0	0	0	0
Stuart Jones	7/12/81	17(4)	17(3)	1	1	0	0	0	0	4	4
Paul March	25/7/79	21(6)	20(6)	6	6	0	0	0	0	24	24
Wayne McDonald	3/9/75	8(5)	8(5)	0	0	0	0	0	0	0	0
Iain Morrison	6/5/83	(5)	(5)	0	0	0	0	0	0	0	0
Chris Nero	14/2/81	27(1)	26(1)	16	15	0	0	0	0	64	60
Hefin O'Hare	2/6/79	21(2)	20(2)	6	6	0	0	0	0	24	24
Sean Penkywicz	18/5/82	2(2)	2(2)	1	1	0	0	0	0	4	4
Paul Reilly	10/5/76	16(1)	15(1)	7	7	0	0	0	0	28	28
Ben Roarty	5/2/75	15	14	1	1	0	0	0	0	4	4
Mick Slicker	16/8/78	1(8)	1(7)	0	0	0	0	0	0	0	0
Paul Smith	17/5/77	24(4)	23(4)	7	7	0	0	0	0	28	28
Marcus St Hilaire	26/1/77	23(1)	22(1)	12	11	0	0	0	0	48	44
Chris Thorman	26/9/80	26(1)	26(1)	19	19	99	99	0	0	274	274
Paul White	7/12/82	5(18)	5(17)	10	9	0	0	0	0	40	36

Brad Drew

LEAGUE RECORD
P28-W12-D0-L16
(8th, SL)
F742, A791, Diff-49
24 points.

CHALLENGE CUP
Round Four

ATTENDANCES
Best - v Leeds (SL - 10,088)
Worst - v Widnes (SL - 3,383)
Total (SL only) - 75,756
Average (SL only) - 5,411
(Up by 1,049 on 2004)

TOUCHDOWN!

Blacklock hits the ground running in Hull

KEY DATES - HULL F.C.

24 June 2005 - Paul Cooke signs a three-year extension to his current contract that will keep him at Hull until at least 2008.

25 June 2005 - Hull stroll into the last four of the Powergen Challenge Cup with a 46-14 win over Leigh at the KC

13 July 2005 – Hull release Michael Eagar from the remainder of his contract by mutual consent.

16 July 2005 - Paul Cooke is sent off in the 67th minute of Hull's home 34-24 win over Huddersfield - the first red card of his career - for an attempted head-butt on Brad Drew.

15 November 2004 – Hull give injury-hit Richard Fletcher six months notice of termination on the two years remaining on his contract, and he heads to play with Brisbane Easts.

24 January 2005 – Stephen Kearney picks up pectoral injury in training camp in Portugal.

12 March 2005 – form prop Jamie Thackray - originally signed on a one-year contract - signs a new two-year deal.

18 March 2005 – former Kiwi captain Stephen Kearney finally makes his Hull FC debut at Bradford.

7 June 2005 - Richard Horne and coach John Kear win the Super League Player and Coach of the Month awards for May.

9 June 2005 – Chris Chester, Graeme Horne and Kirk Dixon extend contracts to end of 2007.

22 June 2005 - Hull forward Chris Chester set to miss the Powergen Challenge Cup quarter-final against Leigh after being banned for one match for a high tackle in the 30-16 Super League win over Leigh.

22 June 2005 - Kiwi Tri-Nations centre Jamaal Lolesi tipped to join Hull next season.

Paul Cooke

20 July 2005 - Cooke given one match ban, making him available to play in Hull's Challenge Cup semi-final against St Helens.

30 July 2005 - Paul Cooke is man of the match in Hull's convincing 34-8 victory over St Helens in the Powergen Challenge Cup semi-final.

27 August 2005 - a field goal by Danny Brough proves the difference, as Hull hold off Leeds Rhinos to win the Cup for the first time since 1982, by 25-24.

31 August 2005 - teenagers Louis McCarthy-Scarsbrook and Ade Adebisi recalled from loan by London to join the senior Quins RL squad in 2006.

5 September 2005 – announce signing of Wakefield centre Sid Domic and Bradford's Lee Radford on two year-deals.

6 September 2005 - Kirk Yeaman misses last two rounds of the regular season after being suspended for two games for a dangerous tackle in the away defeat by Bradford Bulls.

11 September 2005 – short-term signing Sione Faumuina scores late winning try on debut in 32-30 win at Wakefield.

24 September 2005 – Hull stun Warrington in Elimination play-off with 40-6 win at Halliwell Jones

1 October 2005 – Hull crash out of play-offs with 71-0 defeat to Bulls at Odsal.

17 October 2005 – Paul King, Garreth Carvell (both wrist), Graeme Horne (back), Richard Whiting, Chris Chester (both shoulder), Shayne McMenemy, Nathan Blacklock, Shaun Briscoe (all knee), Ewan Dowes, Kirk Yeaman (both hernias) all undergo surgery.

25 October 2005 – Leeds make bid for Paul King.

HULL F.C.

DATE	FIXTURE	RESULT	SCORERS	LGE	ATT
11/2/05	Leeds (h)	L12-16	t:Saxton,Raynor g:Cooke(2)	8th	17,080
20/2/05	Huddersfield (a)	W28-36	t:Blacklock(3),Saxton,Chester,Yeaman g:Cooke(6)	6th	6,610
27/2/05	Warrington (h)	W32-10	t:Raynor(2),Briscoe,Lupton,Thackray g:Cooke(6)	3rd	10,169
5/3/05	Salford (a)	W12-22	t:Raynor(2),Yeaman,Cooke g:Cooke(3)	2nd	3,568
13/3/05	Wakefield (h)	W36-33	t:Cooke,Swain,Raynor,Briscoe,Tony,Yeaman,Thackray g:Cooke(4)	3rd	10,805
18/3/05	Bradford (a)	L32-22	t:Blacklock(2),Eagar,Raynor g:Cooke(3)	5th	13,394
25/3/05	London (a)	W16-20	t:Raynor,Yeaman,Kearney g:Brough(4)	3rd	4,665
28/3/05	Wigan (h)	L15-21	t:Chester,Kearney g:Brough(3) fg:Whiting	4th	14,172
3/4/05	Wakefield (a) (CCR4)	W12-36	t:Raynor,McMenemy,Briscoe(2),Yeaman,Thackray,Tony g:Brough(2),Cooke(2)	N/A	4,866
10/4/05	Widnes (h)	W32-28	t:R Horne,Yeaman(2),Whiting,Blacklock g:Brough(6)	3rd	9,078
17/4/05	Leigh (a)	D22-22	t:Whiting,McMenemy,Yeaman,Blacklock g:Brough(3)	3rd	3,427
24/4/05	Warrington (a)	L36-34	t:Briscoe,Eagar,Whiting,Cooke,Kearney,King g:Brough,Cooke(4)	3rd	10,383
1/5/05	Salford (h)	W20-6	t:Briscoe,Yeaman,Cooke g:Cooke(2),Brough(2)	3rd	8,929
7/5/05	Bradford (h) (CCR5)	W26-24	t:Blacklock,Whiting,Cooke,Chester,Tony g:Cooke(3)	N/A	11,350
13/5/05	St Helens (h)	W44-6	t:Whiting(2),Blacklock,Briscoe(2),McMenemy,R Horne,McNicholas g:Cooke(5),Brough	3rd	10,862
22/5/05	Wakefield (a)	W28-35	t:King,Briscoe(2),Brough,R Horne,McMenemy g:Cooke(5) fg:Brough	3rd	5,194
28/5/05	Bradford (h)	L24-42	t:Carvell,Raynor(2),Blacklock g:Cooke(3),Brough	3rd	11,563
3/6/05	Leeds (a)	L34-14	t:Briscoe,Blacklock g:Brough(2),Cooke	4th	17,427
10/6/05	Wigan (h)	W24-28	t:Briscoe,Barnett(2),Yeaman g:Cooke(2),Brough(2)	4th	12,125
17/6/05	Leigh (h)	W30-16	t:Barnett(2),Blacklock(3),Carvell g:Cooke(2),Brough	4th	7,949
25/6/05	Leigh (h) (CCQF)	W46-14	t:McMenemy,Saxton,R Horne(2),Thackray,Blacklock,Barnett,Cooke g:Cooke(7)	N/A	10,447
2/7/05	London (a) ●	D24-24	t:Chester,Barnett,Blacklock,Briscoe g:Cooke(3),Brough	4th	3,775
8/7/05	St Helens (a)	L18-10	t:Whiting,Yeaman g:Cooke	4th	9,199
16/7/05	Huddersfield (h)	W34-24	t:Barnett(2),R Horne,Yeaman(2),Whiting g:Cooke(5)	4th	7,962
24/7/05	Widnes (a)	W20-40	t:Dixon(3),R Horne,Kearney,G Horne,Carvell g:Brough(6)	3rd	5,378
30/7/05	St Helens (CCSF) ●●	W34-8	t:McMenemy(2),Cooke,Tony,R Horne g:Cooke(5),Brough(2)	N/A	16,171
7/8/05	London (h)	L16-17	t:Dowes,Cooke,McMenemy g:Cooke(2)	3rd	8,109
14/8/05	Leigh (h)	W76-20	t:Raynor(2),Carvell(2),Briscoe(2),Brough,Whiting,Thackray,Dixon,Dowes,Yeaman(2) g:Brough(12)	3rd	6,576
21/8/05	Wigan (h)	L24-28	t:Blacklock,G Horne,Saxton,Raynor g:Brough(4)	4th	9,935
27/8/05	Leeds (CCF) ●●●	W25-24	t:Tony,Raynor,Whiting,Cooke g:Brough(4) fg:Brough	N/A	74,213
2/9/05	Bradford (h)	L49-6	t:Raynor g:Brough	5th	13,326
11/9/05	Wakefield (a)	W30-32	t:Carvell,Swain,Raynor,Chester,Cooke,Faumuina g:Brough(4)	5th	5,721
16/9/05	Warrington (h)	L16-30	t:Kearney,Blacklock(2) g:Cooke(2)	5th	15,763
24/9/05	Warrington (a) (EPO)	W6-40	t:Blacklock(3),Chester,Yeaman,Whiting,Raynor g:Brough(6)	N/A	12,243
1/10/05	Bradford (a) (ESF)	L71-0		N/A	13,148

● Played at Brewery Field, Bridgend
●● Played at Galpharm Stadium, Huddersfield
●●● Played at Millennium Stadium, Cardiff

	D.O.B.	APP		TRIES		GOALS		FG		PTS	
		ALL	SL	ALL	SL	ALL	SL	ALL	SL	ALL	SL
Andy Bailey	15/10/82	(1)	(1)	0	0	0	0	0	0	0	0
Richie Barnett	26/4/81	8	6	8	7	0	0	0	0	32	28
Nathan Blacklock	4/4/76	29(1)	25(1)	22	20	0	0	0	0	88	80
Shaun Briscoe	23/2/83	24(1)	20(1)	15	13	0	0	0	0	60	52
Danny Brough	15/1/83	22(6)	18(5)	2	2	68	60	2	1	146	129
Garreth Carvell	21/4/80	11(15)	8(13)	6	6	0	0	0	0	24	24
Chris Chester	8/10/78	17(7)	15(6)	6	5	0	0	0	0	24	20
Paul Cooke	17/4/81	32	27	10	6	78	61	0	0	196	146
Kirk Dixon	19/7/84	2(4)	2(3)	4	4	0	0	0	0	16	16
Ewan Dowes	4/3/81	33(2)	28(2)	2	2	0	0	0	0	8	8
Michael Eagar	15/8/73	6	6	2	2	0	0	0	0	8	8
Sione Faumuina	27/3/81	3	3	1	1	0	0	0	0	4	4
Liam Higgins	19/7/83	1(13)	1(13)	0	0	0	0	0	0	0	0
Danny Hill	31/10/84	(2)	(2)	0	0	0	0	0	0	0	0
Graeme Horne	22/3/85	6(17)	5(14)	2	2	0	0	0	0	8	8
Richard Horne	16/7/82	29	24	8	5	0	0	0	0	32	20
Stephen Kearney	12/6/72	27(2)	22(2)	5	5	0	0	0	0	20	20
Paul King	28/6/79	7(13)	7(9)	2	2	0	0	0	0	8	8
Andy Last	25/3/81	1	1	0	0	0	0	0	0	0	0
Tommy Lee	1/2/88	2	2	0	0	0	0	0	0	0	0
Peter Lupton	7/3/82	4(3)	4(3)	1	1	0	0	0	0	4	4
Shayne McMenemy	19/7/76	33(1)	28(1)	8	4	0	0	0	0	32	16
Paul McNicholas	26/5/75	5(10)	5(9)	1	1	0	0	0	0	4	4
Gareth Raynor	24/2/78	25	21	18	16	0	0	0	0	72	64
Tom Saxton	3/10/83	20(9)	19(8)	4	3	0	0	0	0	16	12
Richard Swain	2/7/75	19	17	2	2	0	0	0	0	8	8
Jamie Thackray	30/9/79	18(17)	16(14)	5	3	0	0	0	0	20	12
Motu Tony	29/5/81	16(10)	14(7)	5	1	0	0	0	0	20	4
Danny Washbrook	18/9/85	(4)	(4)	0	0	0	0	0	0	0	0
Richard Whiting	20/12/84	24(1)	20(1)	11	9	0	0	1	1	45	37
Kirk Yeaman	15/9/83	31(1)	26(1)	17	16	0	0	0	0	68	64

Ewan Dowes

LEAGUE RECORD
P28-W15-D2-L11
(5th, SL/Elimination Semi Finalists)
F756, A670, Diff+86
32 points.

CHALLENGE CUP
Winners

ATTENDANCES
Best - v Leeds (SL - 17,080)
Worst - v Leigh (SL - 6,576)
Total (SL only) - 148,952
Average (SL only) - 10,639
(Down by 758 on 2004)

8 November 2004 – coach Tony Smith signs one-year extension to his contract to end of 2006 season.

20 November 2004 – Matt Diskin sustains serious knee injury on his Great Britain debut against New Zealand at Hull.

8 December 2004 - Francis Cummins – still sidelined after a knee reconstruction - agrees a one-year deal which will see him take up a role in the club's backroom staff.

13 December 2004 - Leeds in chase for Gareth Ellis, although Bradford thought to be favourites.

23 December 2004 - Keith Senior and Ryan Bailey escape suspension after being found guilty of taking ephedrine in a cold cure.

23 December 2004 - Rhinos contact Bradford to check on the availability of Jamie Langley.

26 December 2004 – Rhinos beat Wakefield 46-6 in the Boxing Day friendly at Headingley.

29 December 2004 - Wakefield confirm sale of Gareth Ellis to Leeds on a four-year contract.

17 January 2005 – Three-day cross code training session with England rugby union at Headingley.

4 February 2005 - Leeds win World Club Challenge, beating Canterbury Bulldogs 39-32 at Elland Road.

11 February 2005 – Leeds kick off Super League with a 16-12 win at Hull.

15 February 2005 - Danny McGuire signs a new five-year contract at Headingley, keeping him at the Rhinos at least until the 2009 season.

21 February 2005 - Danny McGuire has an operation on a groin injury and is ruled out for up to six weeks.

23 March 2005 - Matt Diskin, Danny Ward and Jamie Jones-Buchanan agree one-year extensions to their contracts.

6 April 2005 - Ali Lauitiiti returns from two-game absence after returning home to New Zealand following a family bereavement.

KEY DATES - LEEDS RHINOS

13 April 2005 - Danny Ward handed one-match ban for a reckless high tackle during 64-6 win over London.

19 April 2005 - Danny McGuire out for a month after suffering a broken bone in his left hand in Leeds' win at Wigan.

21 April 2005 - Wayne McDonald goes on loan to Wigan.

27 May 2005 – Leeds lose 38-24 at St Helens.

3 June 2005 - Huddersfield Giants sign Wayne McDonald on an 18-month deal.

7 June 2005 - Rob Burrow signs new five-year contract extension which will see him remain at Headingley until at least the end of the 2010 season.

8 June 2005 - Rhinos release Liam Botham from the remaining six months of his contract, to join Wigan on loan.

10 June 2005 - Ali Lauitiiti equals Super League record with five tries in 70-6 win at Wakefield.

14 June 2005 - Nick Scruton (three years) and Lee Smith (four) sign long-term contracts.

15 June 2005 – Mark Calderwood set to leave Leeds at the end of the season.

18 June 2005 – Rhinos inflict record 70-0 defeat on Wigan

20 June 2005 – Leeds announce signing of Manly winger Scott Donald on three-year contract.

1 July 2005 - Kevin Sinfield out with a dislocated thumb sustained in 36-26 win over Bradford.

6 July 2005 - Barrie McDermott announces he will retire at the end of season.

9 July 2005 - Matt Diskin makes long-awaited return in Leeds' 32-24 defeat by London Broncos in Perpignan.

18 July 2005 – Chris McKenna and Marcus Bai reported to have turned down contract offers.

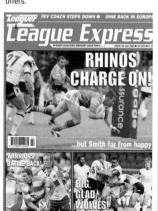

20 July 2005 – High Court rules in favour of Rhinos in their action against Bradford Bulls and former player Iestyn Harris.

31 July 2005 – Leeds quoted at 2/7 to win the Powergen Challenge Cup after their 56-18 semi-final defeat of Toulouse Olympique at the Galpharm Stadium.

9 August 2005 - Willie Poching undergoes corrective minor surgery to mend a fracture in his cheekbone suffered in the 74-0 win over Leigh.

10 August 2005 - Rhinos announce signing of hooker Shane Millard from Widnes Vikings on a one-year contract, as Kevin Sinfield returns after five-game absence for clash against London Broncos at Headingley.

17 August 2005 - Liam Botham forced to retire from the game at the age of 27 with a neck injury.

19 August 2005 - Keith Senior suffers ankle injury in 42-10 defeat by Bradford Bulls at Headingley.

27 August 2005 - a field goal by Danny Brough proves the difference, as Hull hold off Leeds to win the Cup by 25-24.

1 September 2005 - Leeds confirm signing of Jamie Peacock on a four-year contract from Bradford Bulls.

14 September 2005 – Ali Lauitiiti signs new two-year deal with Rhinos, as Chris McKenna joins Bulls

15 October 2005 – lose 15-6 to Bradford in Grand Final

16 October 2005 – Francis Cummins announces retirement

18 October 2005 – Andrew Dunemann joins Salford

25 October 2005 – Rhinos make approach to Hull for Paul King

LEEDS RHINOS

DATE	FIXTURE	RESULT	SCORERS	LGE	ATT
4/2/05	Bulldogs (WCC) ●	W39-32	t:Walker,Calderwood,McGuire,Poching,Burrow,Mathers,Jones-Buchanan g:Sinfield(5) fg:Sinfield	N/A	37,028
11/2/05	Hull (a)	W12-16	t:Bai,Walker,Senior g:Sinfield(2)	6th	17,080
18/2/05	St Helens (h)	W30-18	t:Calderwood(2),Walker,Mathers,Poching g:Sinfield(5)	1st	21,225
27/2/05	Widnes (a)	W66-8	t:Calderwood(4),Lauitiiti,Ellis(2),Bai,McDermott,Burrow(2),Poching g:Sinfield(9)	1st	17,307
6/3/05	Huddersfield (a)	W10-54	t:Calderwood,Mathers(2),McKenna(2),Walker(2),Burrow,Jones-Buchanan g:Sinfield(9)	1st	10,088
11/3/05	Warrington (h)	W38-6	t:Calderwood,Senior(3),Mathers,Ward,Bai g:Sinfield(5)	1st	15,637
18/3/05	Salford (a)	W12-30	t:Bai,Lauitiiti,McDermott,Senior,Burrow g:Sinfield(5)	1st	5,118
24/3/05	Bradford (a)	W12-42	t:Walker,Ellis,Senior,Burrow(2),Sinfield,Calderwood g:Sinfield(7)	1st	22,843
28/3/05	Wakefield (h)	L28-44	t:Burrow(2),Ellis,Botham,Senior g:Sinfield(4)	1st	18,257
2/4/05	Warrington (h) (CCR4)	W26-22	t:Burrow(2),McKenna,Calderwood,Walker g:Sinfield(3)	N/A	8,215
9/4/05	London (h)	W64-6	t:Lauitiiti,Poching,Senior(2),McGuire(2),Walker,Burrow,Mathers(2),Bai(3) g:Sinfield(6)	1st	14,235
15/4/05	Wigan (a)	W14-38	t:Senior(2),Poching,Botham,Bai,Lauitiiti,Calderwood g:Sinfield(4),Burrow	1st	16,022
23/4/05	Widnes (a)	W20-42	t:Jones-Buchanan(2),Sinfield(2),Botham,Senior,Ellis g:Sinfield(7)	1st	6,524
29/4/05	Huddersfield (h)	W44-14	t:Walker(3),Ellis,Botham,Poching(2),Lauitiiti g:Sinfield(6)	1st	15,514
6/5/05	Pia (h) (CCR5)	W70-0	t:Calderwood(3),Burrow(2),Ellis,Mathers(2),McKenna,Smith(2),Scruton,Jones-Buchanan g:Sinfield(4),Burrow(5)	N/A	7,705
13/5/05	Leigh (h)	W4-60	t:Calderwood(3),Smith(2),Burrow(2),McDermott,Sinfield(2),Walker g:Sinfield(8)	1st	5,200
20/5/05	Leigh (h)	W42-24	t:Mathers,McGuire(2),McKenna,Ellis,Calderwood(2) g:Sinfield(7)	1st	14,026
27/5/05	St Helens (a)	L38-24	t:Bai,Jones-Buchanan,Burrow(2) g:Burrow(2)	1st	13,236
3/6/05	Hull (h)	W34-14	t:Senior(3),Bai,Burrow,Mathers g:Sinfield(5)	1st	17,427
10/6/05	Wakefield (a)	W6-70	t:Mathers(2),Bai,Senior,Lauitiiti(5),Poching,Burrow,McDermott,Ellis g:Sinfield(6),Burrow(3)	1st	9,457
18/6/05	Wigan (h)	W70-0	t:Burrow(2),Walker(2),Dunemann,McDermott(2),Calderwood(2),McGuire(2),Senior,Lauitiiti g:Sinfield(8),Burrow	1st	18,177
24/6/05	London (h) (CCQF)	W32-12	t:McGuire(2),Walker,Burrow,Senior,Bai g:Sinfield(4)	N/A	9,444
1/7/05	Bradford (h)	W36-26	t:Senior(2),Jones-Buchanan,McGuire(2),Lauitiiti g:Sinfield(6)	1st	21,225
9/7/05	London (a) ●●	L32-24	t:Bai,Mathers,McGuire,Calderwood,Senior g:Burrow(2)	1st	7,000
15/7/05	Salford (a)	W54-14	t:McGuire,Burrow(2),Calderwood(3),Mathers(2),Dunemann,Poching g:Burrow(7)	1st	13,904
23/7/05	Warrington (a)	W22-46	t:Walker,Diskin,Burrow,Senior,Bai(2),Calderwood g:Burrow(7)	1st	11,036
31/7/05	Toulouse (CCSF) ●●●	W56-18	t:McKenna,Ellis,McGuire(2),Lauitiiti,Bai,Calderwood,Burrow,Walker,Poching g:Burrow(8)	N/A	10,553
7/8/05	Leigh (a)	W0-74	t:Bailey(2),Smith,Ward,Calderwood(2),Senior,Walker,Gibson(3),McKenna,McGuire(2) g:Smith(4),Gibson(5)	1st	4,922
13/8/05	London (h)	W44-24	t:Bai,Calderwood,McKenna,Senior(2),McGuire(4) g:Sinfield(3),Burrow	1st	13,318
19/8/05	Bradford (h)	L10-42	t:Smith,Sinfield g:Sinfield	2nd	20,220
27/8/05	Hull (CCF) ●●●●	L25-24	t:Calderwood(2),Ward,Bai g:Sinfield(4)	N/A	74,213
2/9/05	Wigan (a)	L24-22	t:Smith(2),Walker,Dunemann g:Sinfield(3)	2nd	14,158
10/9/05	Warrington (a)	L33-16	t:Mathers,Diskin,Bai g:Sinfield(2)	2nd	13,024
16/9/05	Wakefield (h)	W34-26	t:Walker,McKenna,Poching(2),Calderwood(2) g:Sinfield(5)	2nd	17,619
30/9/05	St Helens (a) (QSF)	W16-19	t:McGuire,Ward,Lauitiiti g:Sinfield(3) fg:Sinfield	N/A	13,209
15/10/05	Bradford (GF) ●●●●●	L15-6	t:McGuire g:Sinfield	N/A	65,537

● Played at Elland Road, Leeds ●● Played at Stade Aime Giral, Perpignan
●●● Played at Galpharm Stadium, Huddersfield ●●●● Played at Millennium Stadium, Cardiff
●●●●● Played at Old Trafford, Manchester

		APP		TRIES		GOALS		FG		PTS	
	D.O.B.	ALL	SL	ALL	SL	ALL	SL	ALL	SL	ALL	SL
Marcus Bai	11/10/72	33	28	19	16	0	0	0	0	76	64
Ryan Bailey	11/11/83	30(1)	25	2	2	0	0	0	0	8	8
Liam Botham	26/8/77	1(12)	1(10)	4	4	0	0	0	0	16	16
Rob Burrow	26/9/82	29(5)	24(4)	28	21	37	24	0	0	186	132
Mark Calderwood	25/10/81	35	29	35	27	0	0	0	0	140	108
Francis Cummins	12/10/76	(3)	(3)	0	0	0	0	0	0	0	0
Matt Diskin	27/1/82	8(5)	6(5)	2	2	0	0	0	0	8	8
Andrew Dunemann	10/6/76	31(4)	27(2)	3	3	0	0	0	0	12	12
Gareth Ellis	3/5/81	33	27	10	8	0	0	0	0	40	32
Ashley Gibson	25/9/86	(1)	(1)	3	3	5	5	0	0	22	22
Jamie Jones-Buchanan	1/8/81	24(6)	20(5)	9	7	0	0	0	0	36	28
Ali Lauitiiti	13/7/79	15(18)	13(15)	14	13	0	0	0	0	56	52
Richard Mathers	24/10/83	35	29	17	14	0	0	0	0	68	56
Barrie McDermott	22/7/72	6(26)	5(23)	6	6	0	0	0	0	24	24
Wayne McDonald	3/9/75	1(5)	1(5)	0	0	0	0	0	0	0	0
Danny McGuire	6/12/82	15(12)	12(10)	23	18	0	0	0	0	92	72
Chris McKenna	29/10/74	29(1)	23(1)	9	6	0	0	0	0	36	24
Scott Murrell	5/9/85	(1)	(1)	0	0	0	0	0	0	0	0
Willie Poching	30/8/73	15(18)	14(13)	12	10	0	0	0	0	48	40
Nick Scruton	24/12/84	(19)	(15)	1	0	0	0	0	0	4	0
Keith Senior	24/4/76	29	23	25	24	0	0	0	0	100	96
Kevin Sinfield	12/9/80	31	26	6	6	149	129	2	1	324	283
Lee Smith	8/8/86	6(4)	5(4)	8	6	4	4	0	0	40	32
Chev Walker	9/10/82	33(1)	28(1)	18	14	0	0	0	0	72	56
Danny Ward	15/6/80	29(2)	24(2)	4	3	0	0	0	0	16	12

Mark Calderwood

LEAGUE RECORD
P28-W22-D0-L6
(2nd, SL/Grand Final Runners-Up)
F1152, A505, Diff+647
44 points.

CHALLENGE CUP
Runners-Up

ATTENDANCES
Best - v Bradford/St Helens
(SL - 21,225)
Worst - v Pia (CC - 7,705)
Total (SL only) - 238,091
Average (SL only) - 17,006
(Up by 398 on 2004)

20 October 2004 – Leigh sign Steve McCurrie, Rob Jackson and James King.

22 October 2004 – net Aussies Craig Stapleton and Kevin Henderson and Darren Fleary, and retain Neil Turley, Paul Rowley, Steve Maden and Danny Halliwell.

2 November 2004 – sign Cronulla utility back Jason Kent and Academy players Jason Duffy from Wigan and Nick Owen from Warrington.

5 November 2004 – announce signing of Jason Ferris from Manly and Mark Leafa from South Sydney.

15 November 2004 – Richard Marshall signs new contract, while Heath Cruckshank joins coaching staff.

8 December 2004 - Leigh sign Papua New Guinea International wingman John Wilshere, released by the Wolves at the end of the 2004 season after an injury-hit year.

29 December 2004 – club secures new 12-month shirt sponsorship deal with Emirates Airlines.

5 January 2005 - sign prop Richard Moore from Bradford Bulls.

8 February 2005 - Darren Fleary appointed team captain, with Jason Ferris named club captain.

12 February 2005 – lose 30-12 to Huddersfield Giants in Super League opener at he Coliseum, with second row forward Oliver Wilkes suspended for one match after being sent off for a high tackle.

KEY DATES - LEIGH CENTURIONS

28 February 2005 – coach Darren Abram insists he has full support of Leigh board after three straight losses.

22 March 2005 – new signing from St Helens, Dom Feaunati needs surgery on a hernia before he can make his Leigh debut.

23 March 2005 - Centurions terminate home-sick Jason Ferris's contract with immediate effect. Executive Director Derek Beaumont and Football Director Steve Blakeley both quit the club.

28 March 2005 – gain first Super League win on Easter Monday, beating London at the Coliseum in round eight 24-22.

31 March 2005 - Richard Moore banned for five games after being found guilty of illegal use of the forearm and raising a leg in the tackle against London.

4 April 2005 - Richard Moore has his suspension reduced from five to four matches on appeal.

13 April 2005 - halfback John Duffy undergoes surgery on his thumb, ruling him out for around six weeks.

19 April 2005 - Warrington Wolves prop Warren Stevens joins on loan.

20 April 2005 - Leigh fined £100 with £10 costs following 'breaches of the RFL's Operational Rules concerning entry on to the field of play by trainers'.

20 April 2005 – Centurions sign former Leeds hooker Robbie Mears for the remainder of the engage Super League X campaign, with an option for 2006.

30 April 2005 – move above Widnes into 11th place after 40-18 televised hammering of Wakefield.

5 June 2005 – 34-14 home defeat by Widnes leaves Leigh five points adrift at the bottom of Super League.

24 June 2005 – Richard Moore suspended by the club for 'personal reasons'.

25 June 2005 – go out of Powergen Challenge Cup at quarter-final stage with a 46-14 defeat by Hull at the KC Stadium.

18 July 2005 – Ian Knott out for season with back problem as club admits it is already planning for life in National League One in 2006.

2 August 2005 – coach Darren Abram's contract terminated with immediate effect by mutual consent. Assistant Tommy Martyn takes over as caretaker.

7 August 2005 – 74-0 home defeat by Leeds confirms relegation

1 September 2005 – New Zealander Tony Benson appointed as coach on a two-year contract, as Tommy Martyn quits the club.

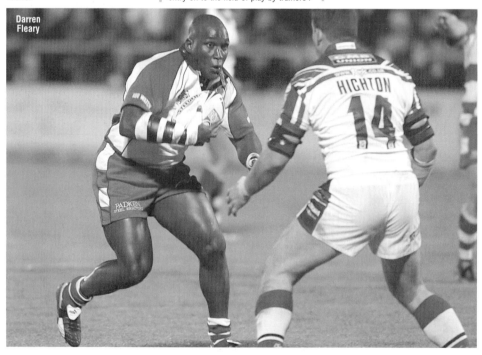

Darren Fleary

LEIGH CENTURIONS

DATE	FIXTURE	RESULT	SCORERS	LGE	ATT
12/2/05	Huddersfield (h)	L12-30	t:Sturm,Smyth g:Turley,Wilshere	11th	4,042
20/2/05	Warrington (a)	L26-22	t:Kent,Smyth,Ferris g:P Jones(5)	12th	11,412
26/2/05	Salford (h)	L6-32	t:P Jones g:Turley	12th	4,180
6/3/05	Wakefield (a)	L38-26	t:Maden,Turley,Fleary,Govin g:Turley(3),P Jones(2)	12th	4,814
11/3/05	Bradford (h)	L6-46	t:Knott g:P Jones	12th	4,241
18/3/05	Wigan (a)	L62-6	t:Wilkes g:P Jones	12th	15,089
25/3/05	Widnes (a)	L35-28	t:Knott,Wilshere(2),Stapleton,Leafa g:Turley(4)	12th	6,026
28/3/05	London (h)	W24-22	t:Turley,John Duffy,Wilshere,Jackson g:Turley(4)	12th	3,201
3/4/05	Batley (a) (CCR4)	W8-25	t:Turley,Knott,King(2),Wilshere g:Turley,Wilshere fg:Marshall	N/A	1,661
8/4/05	St Helens (a)	L60-16	t:Maden,John Duffy,Wilshere g:Wilshere(2)	12th	10,444
17/4/05	Hull (h)	D22-22	t:Jackson,Maden(2),Smyth g:Owen(3)	12th	3,427
22/4/05	Salford (a)	L42-6	t:Cooper g:Owen	12th	5,021
30/4/05	Wakefield (h)	W40-18	t:Rowley,P Jones(3),Maden,Cooper,Smyth g:P Jones(6)	11th	3,213
8/5/05	Halifax (h) (CCR5)	W40-20	t:Cooper(2),Wilshere,Rowley(2),P Jones,Fleary g:P Jones(6)	N/A	3,255
13/5/05	Leeds (h)	L4-60	t:P Jones	12th	5,200
20/5/05	Leeds (a)	L42-24	t:Leafa,P Jones,Feaunati,Wilshere g:P Jones(4)	12th	14,026
29/5/05	London (a)	L70-16	t:P Jones,Cooper,John Duffy g:Turley(2)	12th	3,522
5/6/05	Widnes (h)	L14-34	t:Maden,Sturm,Wilshere g:Wilshere	12th	5,170
12/6/05	Warrington (h)	L7-42	t:Stapleton g:Turley fg:Turley	12th	7,249
17/6/05	Hull (a)	L30-16	t:Maden,McCurrie g:Turley(4)	12th	7,949
25/6/05	Hull (a) (CCQF)	L46-14	t:Marshall,Jackson,Halliwell g:Wilshere	N/A	10,447
1/7/05	Wigan (h)	L22-30	t:Wilshere,Govin,Sturm g:P Jones(5)	12th	7,458
10/7/05	Huddersfield (a)	L32-22	t:Govin,Maden,Wilshere g:P Jones(5)	12th	3,889
17/7/05	Bradford (a)	L58-12	t:P Jones,Cooper g:P Jones(2)	12th	10,294
22/7/05	St Helens (h)	L20-27	t:Halliwell(3),John Duffy g:Wilshere(2)	12th	5,142
7/8/05	Leeds (a)	L0-74		12th	4,922
14/8/05	Hull (a)	L76-20	t:Jackson,Govin,Stapleton,Rowley g:Owen(2)	12th	6,576
21/8/05	Huddersfield (a)	L68-16	t:Stapleton,Stevens,Jackson g:Owen(2)	12th	3,902
4/9/05	St Helens (h)	L4-78	t:Cooper	12th	5,534
11/9/05	Widnes (a)	L36-20	t:Owen,John Duffy,Jackson,Forber g:Owen(2)	12th	5,293
16/9/05	Salford (h)	L14-20	t:Rowley,John Duffy,Maden g:Owen	12th	3,519

		APP		TRIES		GOALS		FG		PTS	
	D.O.B.	ALL	SL	ALL	SL	ALL	SL	ALL	SL	ALL	SL
Matthew Bottom	2/1/86	(2)	(1)	0	0	0	0	0	0	0	0
Liam Coleman	17/6/86	1(4)	1(4)	0	0	0	0	0	0	0	0
Ben Cooper	8/10/79	28(1)	25(1)	7	5	0	0	0	0	28	20
Jason Duffy	16/4/87	3(1)	3(1)	0	0	0	0	0	0	0	0
John Duffy	2/7/80	24	21	6	6	0	0	0	0	24	24
Dom Feaunati	14/6/78	4(1)	4	1	1	0	0	0	0	4	4
Jason Ferris	6/7/76	4	4	1	1	0	0	0	0	4	4
Darren Fleary	2/12/72	27	24	2	1	0	0	0	0	8	4
Carl Forber	17/3/85	4	4	1	1	0	0	0	0	4	4
Mick Govin	5/11/84	6(7)	5(6)	4	4	0	0	0	0	16	16
Danny Halliwell	23/3/81	6	5	4	3	0	0	0	0	16	12
Kevin Henderson	1/10/81	(1)	(1)	0	0	0	0	0	0	0	0
Chris Hill	3/11/87	(1)	(1)	0	0	0	0	0	0	0	0
Rob Jackson	4/9/81	23(3)	20(3)	6	5	0	0	0	0	24	20
Chris Jones	27/5/82	1(1)	1(1)	0	0	0	0	0	0	0	0
Phil Jones	30/9/77	18	16	9	8	37	31	0	0	110	94
Jason Kent	21/4/80	26	23	1	1	0	0	0	0	4	4
James King	12/12/80	5(9)	5(7)	2	0	0	0	0	0	8	0
Ian Knott	2/10/76	10(1)	8(1)	3	2	0	0	0	0	12	8
Mark Leafa	4/12/80	31	28	2	2	0	0	0	0	8	8
Keiron Maddocks	26/10/84	1(3)	1(3)	0	0	0	0	0	0	0	0
Steve Maden	13/9/82	26	23	9	9	0	0	0	0	36	36
Richard Marshall	9/10/75	4(19)	4(16)	1	0	0	0	1	0	5	0
Steve McCurrie	1/6/73	8(4)	7(3)	1	1	0	0	0	0	4	4
Robbie Mears	25/9/74	8(6)	8(6)	0	0	0	0	0	0	0	0
Richard Moore	2/2/81	2(5)	2(5)	0	0	0	0	0	0	0	0
Nick Owen	16/10/84	8(1)	8(1)	1	1	11	11	0	0	26	26
Paul Rowley	12/3/75	17(7)	15(7)	5	3	0	0	0	0	20	12
Rob Smyth	22/2/77	15(2)	15(1)	4	4	0	0	0	0	16	16
Craig Stapleton	13/8/78	30(1)	27(1)	4	4	0	0	0	0	16	16
Warren Stevens	4/10/78	4(14)	4(14)	1	1	0	0	0	0	4	4
Matt Sturm	13/12/72	10(20)	8(19)	3	3	0	0	0	0	12	12
James Taylor	11/9/84	(5)	(4)	0	0	0	0	0	0	0	0
Neil Turley	15/3/80	7(3)	6(3)	3	2	21	20	1	1	55	49
Oliver Wilkes	2/5/80	13(1)	13(1)	1	1	0	0	0	0	4	4
John Wilshere	5/5/78	29	26	10	8	8	6	0	0	56	44

Mark Leafa

LEAGUE RECORD
P28-W2-D1-L25
(12th, SL)
F445, A1210, Diff-765
5 points.

CHALLENGE CUP
Quarter Finalists

ATTENDANCES
Best - v Wigan (SL - 7,458)
Worst - v London (SL - 3,201)
Total (SL only) - 66,498
Average (SL only) - 4,750
(Up by 2,584 on 2004, NL1)

KEY DATES - LONDON BRONCOS

28 March 2005 – Danny Williams makes his debut in the 24-22 Easter Monday defeat at Leigh.

25 April 2005 - Broncos reported to be in battle to keep their halfback Thomas Leuluai, following Leuluai's appearance in New Zealand' 32-16 defeat in the Anzac Test in Brisbane.

5 May 2005 - Tyrone Smith signs a contract extension which will see him remain in the capital at least until the end of 2007.

6 May 2005 - Thomas Leuluai agrees a new deal to keep him at London until the end of the 2006 season.

11 May 2005 - Danny Williams suspended for one game after being found guilty of a reckless high tackle in the the Broncos' 26-12 Powergen Challenge Cup fifth-round win over Salford.

9 July 2005 - beat Leeds Rhinos 32-24 at the Stade Aime Giral in Perpignan.

17 July 2005 - Thomas Leuluai set to miss the remainder of the engage Super League season after breaking an ankle in three places early in the first half of the 26-14 defeat at Warrington.

24 July 2005 - Broncos back at Griffin Park against Huddersfield Giants after seven weeks on the road, as club unveil new owner, Ian Lenagan.

26 July 2005 - the Broncos set to return to the Stoop and become Harlequins RL as soon as the 2005 Super League season is over.

18 August 2005 - Zebastian Luisi and assistant coach Rohan Smith both agree to contract extensions at London Broncos/Harlequins for the 2006 season.

2 November 2004 – Kiwi international scrum-half Thomas Leuluai joins from NZ Warriors on one-year deal, while takeover of club by Warriors owner Eric Watson is denied.

8 November 2004 – Broncos sign Roosters reserve stand-off Luke Dorn.

15 November 2004 – announce signing of Solomon Haumono, Mark McLinden and Tyrone Smith.

29 November 2004 – Broncos sign Manly centre Nick Bradley-Qalilawa and Melbourne forward Danny Williams, currently serving an 18-match suspension.

29 December 2005 - Broncos secure signing of South Sydney prop Filimone Lolohea, a Tonga representative in the 2000 World Cup.

19 January 2005 – edged 28-24 in pre-season warm up by Union Treiziste Catalane in St Estève.

9 February 2005 – Jon Wells signs new contract up to 2008.

14 February 2005 - Broncos announce signing of Kiwi International Vinnie Anderson, released from his contract at NZ Warriors, on a three-year deal. The RFL decline to register the contract because of financial uncertainties.

3 March 2005 - Mitchell Stringer is released just three games into the Super League season, and rejoins his old club Sheffield, before moving onto Salford.

4 March 2005 - meeting of Super League clubs at Huddersfield approves a financial re-structuring of the Broncos after Inland Revenue refuses settlement of historic debt.

8 March 2005 – Vinnie Anderson signs a three-year contract with St Helens.

9 March 2005 - Danny Williams found not guilty of refusing to provide a sample on 10 December 2004

21 March 2005 – hooker Neil Budworth requires a knee reconstruction which will sideline him for the full season.

19 August 2005 - Filimone Lolohea agrees a new one-year deal for the 2006 season.

31 August 2005 - Broncos recall Louis McCarthy-Scarsbrook and Ade Adebisi, both of whom have been on loan at Hull FC in 2005.

3 September 2005 - Broncos edge Huddersfield 16-12 in controversial game to all but tie up sixth spot.

23 September 2005 – go out of play-offs in 44-22 defeat at Bradford.

5 October 2005 - Broncos sign 24-year old hooker Chad Randall from Manly, while Neil Budworth extends contract to end of the 2006 season.

5 October 2005 - Broncos confirm release of Francis Stephenson, Steve Trindall, Anthony Armour, Dave Highton, Mark O'Halloran, John Kirkpatrick, Lee Sanderson and Feleti Mateo.

17 October 2005 – club officially becomes Harlequins RL.

4 November 2005 – announce signings of Widnes prop forward David Mills, and Halifax pair Rikki Sheriffe and Pat Weisner.

Danny Williams

LONDON BRONCOS

DATE	FIXTURE	RESULT	SCORERS	LGE	ATT
13/2/05	Warrington (h)	W28-24	t:Dorn,Sykes,Haumono,McLinden,Purdham g:Sykes(4)	5th	4,179
18/2/05	Salford (a)	L20-16	t:Wells,Leuluai,Dorn g:Sykes(2)	8th	3,315
27/2/05	Wakefield (h)	W72-8	t:Purdham,Dorn(2),Hopkins(2),Smith(2),Armour,Greenwood(2),		
			McLinden,Leuluai g:Sykes(12)	2nd	2,854
6/3/05	Bradford (a)	L48-22	t:Haumono,Dorn,Smith,Sykes g:Sykes(3)	5th	11,282
12/3/05	Wigan (h)	W34-20	t:Tookey,Haumono,Sykes(2),Hopkins g:Sykes(7)	4th	5,057
20/3/05	Widnes (h)	W66-8	t:Bradley-Qalilawa(2),Luisi,Kirkpatrick(2),Haumono,Dorn(2),		
			Smith,Tookey,Wells,Trindall g:Sykes(9)	3rd	3,365
25/3/05	Hull (h)	L16-20	t:Bradley-Qalilawa,Dorn,Mbu g:Sykes(2)	4th	4,665
28/3/05	Leigh (a)	L24-22	t:Wells,Sykes,McLinden,Bradley-Qalilawa g:Sykes(3)	5th	3,201
3/4/05	Hunslet (a) (CCR4)	W4-70	t:Kirkpatrick(3),O'Halloran(2),Haumono,Sykes,Wells,Hopkins,		
			Greenwood(4),Dorn g:Sykes(7)	N/A	450
9/4/05	Leeds (a)	L64-6	t:Leuluai g:Sykes	6th	14,235
16/4/05	St Helens (h)	L20-30	t:Bradley-Qalilawa(2),Leuluai,Dorn g:Sykes(2)	9th	5,261
24/4/05	Wakefield (a)	L29-18	t:O'Halloran,Luisi,Bradley-Qalilawa,Dorn g:Sykes	10th	3,258
1/5/05	Bradford (h)	L26-41	t:Sykes,Hopkins,Wells,Smith,Bradley-Qalilawa g:Sykes(3)	10th	3,879
8/5/05	Salford (a) (CCR5)	W12-26	t:Sykes,Leuluai,McLinden,Smith g:Sykes(5)	N/A	2,339
15/5/05	Huddersfield (a)	L34-24	t:Wells,Smith,Bradley-Qalilawa(2),Leuluai g:Sykes(2)	10th	3,682
22/5/05	Salford (h)	W34-18	t:Dorn,Purdham,Smith,Haumono,Tookey,Wells g:Sykes(5)	9th	2,997
29/5/05	Leigh (h)	W70-16	t:Purdham(4),McLinden(2),Highton,Leuluai(3),Sykes,Dorn		
			g:Sykes(11)	8th	3,522
3/6/05	Wigan (a)	W18-22	t:Dorn,Bradley-Qalilawa,Smith g:Sykes(5)	6th	10,262
12/6/05	Widnes (a)	W10-24	t:Dorn,Purdham,McLinden,Leuluai g:Sykes(4)	6th	5,996
17/6/05	St Helens (a)	D28-28	t:Wells,Leuluai,Luisi,Bradley-Qalilawa,Purdham g:Sykes(4)	6th	8,521
24/6/05	Leeds (a) (CCQF)	L32-12	t:Bradley-Qalilawa,Haumono g:Sykes(2)	N/A	9,444
2/7/05	Hull (h) ●	D24-24	t:Hopkins,Dorn,Bradley-Qalilawa,McLinden g:Sykes(4)	6th	3,775
9/7/05	Leeds (h) ●●	W32-24	t:Bradley-Qalilawa(2),Leuluai(2),Dorn,O'Halloran g:Sykes(4)	6th	7,000
17/7/05	Warrington (a)	L26-14	t:Bradley-Qalilawa,Hopkins g:Sykes(2),Purdham	6th	10,146
24/7/05	Huddersfield (h)	W35-26	t:Sykes,Purdham,Bradley-Qalilawa,Tookey,Smith,Dorn		
			g:Sykes(5) fg:Sykes	6th	3,221
7/8/05	Hull (a)	W16-17	t:Smith,Sykes,Dorn g:Sykes(2) fg:Sykes	6th	8,109
13/8/05	Leeds (a)	L44-24	t:Wells,Dorn,Sykes(2) g:Sykes(4)	6th	13,318
20/8/05	St Helens (a)	L50-4	t:Bradley-Qalilawa	6th	7,604
3/9/05	Huddersfield (h)	W16-12	t:Bradley-Qalilawa,Luisi,Wells g:Sykes(2)	6th	2,877
9/9/05	Salford (a)	L26-18	t:Sykes,Haumono,Wells g:Sykes(3)	6th	2,683
18/9/05	Widnes (h)	W68-10	t:Smith,McLinden,Tookey,Dorn(4),Luisi(2),Mateo,Wells,Temata		
			g:Sykes(10)	6th	3,885
23/9/05	Bradford (a) (EPO)	L44-22	t:Wells,Haumono(2),Luisi g:Sykes(3)	N/A	9,167

● Played at Brewery Field, Bridgend
●● Played at Stade Aime Giral, Perpignan

		APP		TRIES		GOALS		FG		PTS	
	D.O.B.	ALL	SL	ALL	SL	ALL	SL	ALL	SL	ALL	SL
Carl Ablett	19/12/85	3(2)	3(2)	0	0	0	0	0	0	0	0
Anthony Armour	12/10/82	12(7)	11(7)	1	1	0	0	0	0	4	4
Nick Bradley-Qalilawa											
	28/3/80	31	28	20	19	0	0	0	0	80	76
Neil Budworth	10/3/82	3(1)	3(1)	0	0	0	0	0	0	0	0
Luke Dorn	2/7/82	30(1)	28	24	23	0	0	0	0	96	92
Lee Greenwood	28/9/80	5(2)	5(1)	6	2	0	0	0	0	24	8
Solomon Haumono	13/10/75	26(6)	24(5)	10	8	0	0	0	0	40	32
David Highton	31/1/80	19(6)	16(6)	1	1	0	0	0	0	4	4
Lee Hopkins	17/2/78	31(1)	29	7	6	0	0	0	0	28	24
John Kirkpatrick	3/1/79	5	4	5	2	0	0	0	0	20	8
Thomas Leuluai	22/6/85	22	20	14	13	0	0	0	0	56	52
Filimone Lolohea	31/1/79	9(15)	8(15)	0	0	0	0	0	0	0	0
Zebastian Luisi	22/12/84	18(1)	17(1)	6	6	0	0	0	0	24	24
Feleti Mateo	2/5/85	4(10)	4(10)	1	1	0	0	0	0	4	4
Joe Mbu	6/11/83	16(7)	14(7)	1	1	0	0	0	0	4	4
Mark McLinden	8/7/79	24(3)	22(3)	9	8	0	0	0	0	36	32
Mark O'Halloran	6/3/81	14(4)	12(3)	4	2	0	0	0	0	16	8
Rob Purdham	14/4/80	17(5)	15(5)	10	10	1	1	0	0	42	42
Tyrone Smith	12/5/83	21(5)	20(4)	12	11	0	0	0	0	48	44
Francis Stephenson	20/1/76	9(7)	7(6)	0	0	0	0	0	0	0	0
Mitchell Stringer	1/11/83	(2)	(2)	0	0	0	0	0	0	0	0
Paul Sykes	11/8/81	32	29	14	12	133	119	2	2	324	288
Karl Temata	12/7/78	1(2)	1(2)	1	1	0	0	0	0	4	4
Mark Tookey	9/3/77	13(17)	13(14)	5	5	0	0	0	0	20	20
Steve Trindall	23/4/73	22(5)	20(5)	1	1	0	0	0	0	4	4
Jon Wells	23/9/78	26(1)	23(1)	13	12	0	0	0	0	52	48
Danny Williams	4/9/73	2(18)	1(16)	0	0	0	0	0	0	0	0

Paul Sykes

LEAGUE RECORD
P28-W13-D2-L13
(6th, SL/Elimination Play-Off)
F800, A718, Diff+82
28 points.

CHALLENGE CUP
Quarter Finalists

ATTENDANCES
Best - v St Helens (SL - 5,261)
Worst - v Wakefield (SL - 2,854)
Total (SL only) - 56,537
Average (SL only) - 4,038
(Up by 580 on 2004)

Karl
Fitzpatrick

KEY DATES -
SALFORD CITY REDS

8 November 2004 – football manager Steve Simms in Sydney for talks with Kangaroo halfback Craig Gower.

22 November 2004 – Reds open talks with Kiwi international prop Paul Rauhihi.

9 January 2005 – Reds head for warm-weather training camp in Florida and rising star Tim Hartley returns with broken wrist.

10 January 2005 - new stadium put back a year to start of 2007 season.

31 January 2005 – Adrian Morley hints in Australian press that he might join home-town Salford when his his Sydney Roosters contract runs out at the end of 2007.

11 February 2005 – Paul Highton breaks arm in 15-4 opening night defeat at Wigan.

26 February 2005 - Tim Jonkers suffers suspected broken bone in his foot in 32-6 Super League victory at Leigh.

4 March 2005 – Craig Gower signs long-term contract at Penrith.

10 March 2005 – Reds sign former London prop Mitchell Stringer for the remainder of the season, and dismiss reports that Gareth Haggerty is to leave the Willows.

14 April 2005 - coach Karl Harrison escapes censure from the RFL after an investigation by the Disciplinary Commissioner. Assistant coach Scott Naylor issued with a formal written warning for 'alleged breaches of technical area rules and alleged use of foul and abusive language'.

18 April 2005 – Reds forecast to sign former Kangaroo Bryan Fletcher in next fortnight.

18 May 2005 - Bryan Fletcher signs for Wigan.

10 June 2005 – a hat-trick of tries by Jamie Lyon denies Salford a shock win over St Helens.

1 July 2005 – Reds sign 20-year-old winger Andy Smith from Bradford on loan until the end of the season.

11 July 2005 – club denies reports they have made an approach to St Helens stand-off Jason Hooper.

18 July 2005 – Reds are linked with Leigh's John Wilshere and Warrington's Nathan Wood.

1 August 2005 – Widnes centre Aaron Moule targeted, as prop Neil Baynes moves to Whitehaven on permanent deal.

5 September 2005 – Reds reject approach from Bradford for Karl Fitzpatrick, and tie up Luke Robinson until end of 2008.

13 September 2005 – Mark Shipway released, as club confirm they will play their home games in 2006 on Fridays.

5 October 2005 – Reds sign three Widnes players – Stephen Myler, one year, Aaron Moule for two years and Simon Finnigan for three years.

14 October 2005 – Simon Baldwin signs new 12-month contract.

18 October 2005 – Andrew Dunemann, released by Leeds, signs a 12-month contract.

Gareth
Haggerty

SALFORD CITY REDS

DATE	FIXTURE	RESULT	SCORERS	LGE	ATT
11/2/05	Wigan (a)	L15-4	t:Alker	9th	13,687
18/2/05	London (h)	W20-16	t:Stewart,Fitzpatrick(2),Sibbit g:Charles(2)	9th	3,315
26/2/05	Leigh (a)	W6-32	t:Hodgson,Shipway,Fitzpatrick,McGuinness,Haggerty,Sibbit g:Charles(3),Robinson	5th	4,180
5/3/05	Hull (h)	L12-22	t:Stewart,Hodgson,Haggerty	7th	3,568
11/3/05	St Helens (a)	L46-12	t:Baldwin,Alker g:Charles,Dickens	8th	9,971
18/3/05	Leeds (h)	L12-30	t:Baldwin,Hodgson g:Dickens,Robinson	9th	5,118
25/3/05	Warrington (h)	W42-10	t:McAvoy,Littler(3),Hodgson,Robinson,Sibbit g:Charles(4),Dickens(2),Robinson	7th	6,004
28/3/05	Huddersfield (a)	L26-12	t:McGuinness,Beverley g:Charles(2)	9th	4,760
3/4/05	Rochdale (a) (CCR4)	W24-30	t:Sibbit(2),Dickens,Baldwin,Alker,Robinson g:Charles(3)	N/A	1,971
8/4/05	Wakefield (h)	W16-14	t:Robinson(2),Hodgson g:Charles(2)	8th	3,378
17/4/05	Widnes (a)	W6-22	t:Littler(2),Robinson(2) g:Charles(3)	6th	5,878
22/4/05	Leigh (h)	W42-6	t:Sibbit,Littler(3),Robinson(2),Coley,Haggerty g:Charles(2),Robinson(3)	5th	5,021
1/5/05	Hull (a)	L20-6	t:Beverley g:Charles	5th	8,929
8/5/05	London (h) (CCR5)	L12-26	t:McGuinness,Bamford g:Charles(2)	N/A	2,339
13/5/05	Bradford (h)	L0-58		7th	4,102
22/5/05	London (a)	L34-18	t:Rutgerson,McAvoy,Haggerty g:Charles(3)	8th	2,997
30/5/05	Wigan (h)	L20-34	t:Coley(2),Stewart,Alker g:Charles(2)	9th	5,526
5/6/05	Wakefield (a)	L36-24	t:Hodgson,Hartley,Rutgerson,Robinson g:Charles(4)	9th	3,536
10/6/05	St Helens (h)	L22-33	t:Hartley(2),Littler,Charles g:Charles(3)	9th	4,704
19/6/05	Warrington (a)	L48-14	t:Shipway,Hartley,Beverley g:Charles	9th	10,925
2/7/05	Huddersfield (h)	W24-16	t:Beverley,Robinson,Charles g:Charles(6)	9th	2,682
8/7/05	Widnes (h)	W34-16	t:Littler,Sibbit,Robinson,Hodgson(2),Haggerty g:Charles(5)	9th	4,507
15/7/05	Leeds (a)	L54-14	t:Littler(2),Hartley g:Charles	9th	13,904
22/7/05	Bradford (h)	L18-24	t:Langi,Coley,Fitzpatrick g:Charles(3)	10th	3,684
5/8/05	Wigan (a)	L40-12	t:Littler,Brocklehurst g:Charles(2)	10th	10,156
14/8/05	Bradford (a)	L58-12	t:Smith,Alker g:Charles(2)	10th	10,113
19/8/05	Wakefield (h)	W37-0	t:Coley,Robinson,Stewart(3),Fitzpatrick g:Charles(5),Robinson fg:Robinson	9th	3,005
4/9/05	Warrington (a)	L32-22	t:Stewart,Sibbit,Littler,Fitzpatrick g:Charles(3)	10th	9,619
9/9/05	London (h)	W26-18	t:Stewart,Langi,Fitzpatrick,Littler,Haggerty g:Charles(3)	9th	2,683
16/9/05	Leigh (a)	W14-20	t:Hodgson(2),Littler,Stewart g:Charles(2)	9th	3,519

		APP		TRIES		GOALS		FG		PTS	
	D.O.B.	ALL	SL	ALL	SL	ALL	SL	ALL	SL	ALL	SL
Malcolm Alker	4/11/78	30	28	5	4	0	0	0	0	20	16
Simon Baldwin	31/3/75	5(15)	5(13)	3	2	0	0	0	0	12	8
Darren Bamford	8/8/86	2(2)	2(1)	1	0	0	0	0	0	4	0
Cliff Beverley	25/3/77	27	26	4	4	0	0	0	0	16	16
Andrew Brocklehurst	6/3/83	6(8)	6(8)	1	1	0	0	0	0	4	4
Chris Charles	7/3/76	29	27	2	2	70	65	0	0	148	138
John Clough	13/9/84	1(8)	1(8)	0	0	0	0	0	0	0	0
Andy Coley	7/7/78	18(9)	16(9)	5	5	0	0	0	0	20	20
Stuart Dickens	23/3/80	5(5)	4(5)	1	0	4	4	0	0	12	8
Karl Fitzpatrick	13/9/80	15(1)	14(1)	7	7	0	0	0	0	28	28
Gareth Haggerty	8/9/81	(27)	(26)	6	6	0	0	0	0	24	24
Tim Hartley	2/1/86	6(4)	6(4)	5	5	0	0	0	0	20	20
Paul Highton	10/11/76	8(6)	8(6)	0	0	0	0	0	0	0	0
David Hodgson	8/8/81	30	28	10	10	0	0	0	0	40	40
Andy Johnson	14/6/74	1(7)	1(6)	0	0	0	0	0	0	0	0
Tim Jonkers	3/7/81	5(7)	5(5)	0	0	0	0	0	0	0	0
Junior Langi	2/8/81	13(3)	13(2)	2	2	0	0	0	0	8	8
Stuart Littler	19/2/79	30	28	16	16	0	0	0	0	64	64
Nathan McAvoy	31/12/76	15(4)	14(4)	2	2	0	0	0	0	8	8
Kevin McGuinness	10/11/76	14(1)	12(1)	3	2	0	0	0	0	12	8
Luke Robinson	25/7/84	30	28	12	11	7	7	1	1	63	59
Sean Rutgerson	19/2/76	25(2)	23(2)	2	2	0	0	0	0	8	8
Mark Shipway	3/5/76	14(6)	12(6)	2	2	0	0	0	0	8	8
Ian Sibbit	15/10/80	22(1)	20(1)	8	6	0	0	0	0	32	24
Andy Smith	6/7/84	4	4	1	1	0	0	0	0	4	4
Anthony Stewart	5/3/79	24	22	9	9	0	0	0	0	36	36
Mitchell Stringer	1/11/83	11(3)	11(3)	0	0	0	0	0	0	0	0

Malcolm Alker

LEAGUE RECORD
P28-W11-D0-L17
(9th, SL)
F549, A732, Diff-183
22 points.

CHALLENGE CUP
Round Five

ATTENDANCES
Best - v Warrington (SL - 6,004)
Worst - v London (CC - 2,339)
Total (SL only) - 57,297
Average (SL only) - 4,093
(Up by 99 on 2004)

KEY DATES - ST HELENS

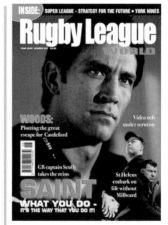

20 April 2005 - Ian Millward found guilty of breaching the RFL's regulations concerning coaching technical areas at the Powergen Challenge Cup win at Huddersfield Giants on April 3.

3 May 2005 - Paul Sculthorpe named as captain of Great Britain.

4 May 2005 - St Helens suspend Ian Millward. Assistant coach Dave Rotheram to cover coaching duties. Millward attends disciplinary hearing in Chester.

6 May 2005 - St Helens supporters demonstrate against their chairman and chief executive at Knowsley Road, as Saints defeat York City Knights 62-0.

7 December 2004 – Saints lose in final of Dubai International Invitation Rugby Union Sevens.

8 February 2005 – close-season signing Michael Smith quits St Helens.

11 February 2005 – prop Ricky Bibey released.

21 February 2005 – Saints make offer to Sonny Bill Williams.

8 March 2005 - Vinnie Anderson signs three-year contract with St Helens after the Kiwi's recently-signed contract London was turned down by the RFL.

8 March 2005 - former Castleford Tigers forward Michael Smith signs for Hull KR.

14 March 2005 – Saints fume at 'fake letter' in Australian press detailing huge offer to Sonny Bill Williams.

1 April 2005 - Widnes Vikings sign Gray Viane, who joined Saints at the end of the 2004 season from Wests Tigers.

5 April 2005 - coach Ian Millward referred to the RFL's Disciplinary Commissioner for an 'off-field incident' during Easter Monday's engage Super League fixture between St Helens and Bradford Bulls.

19 April 2005 - Keiron Cunningham extends contract for a further two years to the end of 2007.

10 May 2005 – Ian Millward, the longest-serving coach in Super League, is sacked for 'gross misconduct' on three charges of swearing and abuse.

17 May 2005 - St Helens appoint Daniel Anderson as their new head coach until December 2007.

23 May 2005 – Ian Millward starts his new job as head coach of Wigan Warriors.

27 May 2005 - Daniel Anderson gets off to a dream start with a 38-24 win over Super League leaders Leeds at Knowsley Road.

28 May 2005 - Darren Albert signs a contract extension to keep him at Knowsley Road until the end of 2007.

5 June 2005 – Saints, without captain Paul Sculthorpe, hammer Bradford 66-4 at Odsal.

24 June 2005 – Sean Long breaks wrist in training and is out for up to six weeks.

26 June 2005 - St Helens make the Powergen Challenge Cup semi-finals as they humiliate Wigan 75-0 at Knowsley Road - a record defeat for the second week in a row for the Warriors. Jason Hooper faces up to six weeks out of action with a shoulder injury.

29 June 2005 - announce signing of Sydney Roosters and New Zealand international prop forward Jason Cayless for 2006 on a four-year contract.

4 July 2005 - chief executive Sean McGuire denies St Helens have signed Bradford Bulls' Great Britain star Leon Pryce.

8 July 2005 - Saints tie up Jon Wilkin and Maurie Fa'asavalu on new three-year deals.

30 July 2005 – exit Powergen Challenge Cup after 34-8 semi-final defeat by Hull at the Galpharm Stadium.

3 August 2005 - Saints sign New Zealand international winger Francis Meli on a three-year contract from 2006.

3 August 2005 - St Helens agree in principle to release Darren Albert from his contract at the end of this season for him to join Cronulla.

8 August 2005 – Saints reject any idea that they would be prepared to allow Sean Long to join South Sydney, though Mark Edmondson joins the Roosters on two-year contract.

9 August 2005 – Paul Sculthorpe out for the season after surgery on long-standing knee problem.

16 August 2005 – Jason Hooper and Paul Anderson sign one-year contracts.

20 August 2005 - Saints go top of the table after 50-4 home win over London, Mark Edmondson ruled out for rest of season with shoulder injury.

1 September 2005 - the signing of Leon Pryce on a three-year contract is announced.

9 September 2005 - St Helens are minor premiers after a convincing 38-12 win at arch rivals Wigan, although Saints captain Sean Long and leading tryscorer Darren Albert taken to hospital with suspected broken cheekbones.

30 September 2005 – Jason Hooper out with shoulder injury sustained in 19-16 Qualifying semi-final defeat to Leeds.

7 October 2005 – Saints lose 18-23 to Bradford in Final Eliminator.

20 October 2005 – Mick Higham sold to Bradford.

ST HELENS

DATE	FIXTURE	RESULT	SCORERS	LGE	ATT
11/2/05	Widnes (h)	W40-18	t:Fozzard,Long,Higham,Wellens,Albert,Roby,Edmondson g:Sculthorpe(6)	1st	12,935
18/2/05	Leeds (a)	L30-18	t:Albert,Cunningham,Talau g:Sculthorpe(3)	3rd	21.225
25/2/05	Huddersfield (h)	W34-24	t:Gilmour(2),P Anderson,Talau,Albert(2),Wellens g:Sculthorpe(2),Wellens	4th	9,507
4/3/05	Warrington (a)	W16-18	t:Graham,Albert,Higham,Cunningham g:Wellens	3rd	12,098
11/3/05	Salford (h)	W46-12	t:Lyon(2),Talau,Long(2),Albert,Gardner,Cunningham g:Sculthorpe(7)	2nd	9,971
19/3/05	Wakefield (h)	W64-16	t:Talau(2),Gardner,Roby(2),Albert(2),Edmondson,Cunningham(2), V Anderson g:Sculthorpe(4),Lyon(6)	2nd	9,321
25/3/05	Wigan (a)	L22-20	t:Cunningham(2),Lyon,Wilkin g:Lyon(2)	2nd	25,004
28/3/05	Bradford (h)	W34-27	t:Wellens(3),Bennett,Roby,Albert g:Hardman(5)	2nd	12,364
3/4/05	Huddersfield (a) (CCR4)	W22-26	t:Gilmour,Albert(2),V Anderson g:Lyon(5)	N/A	7,105
8/4/05	Leigh (h)	W60-16	t:Lyon(3),Long(2),Wellens,Gardner(2),V Anderson,Hooper(2) g:Long(5),Lyon(3)	2nd	10,444
16/4/05	London (a)	W20-30	t:Roby,Albert,Edmondson,V Anderson,Bennett g:Hooper(4),Wellens	2nd	5,261
24/4/05	Huddersfield (a)	W22-36	t:Albert(2),Wellens,Higham(2),V Anderson g:Lyon(6)	2nd	7,432
29/4/05	Warrington (h)	W31-30	t:Long,Albert,Lyon(2),Higham g:Long(5) fg:Long	2nd	12,666
6/5/05	York (h) (CCR5)	W62-0	t:P Anderson,Gardner,Long(2),Wellens,Hardman(2),Hooper(2),Wilkin, Albert,Graham g:Long(7)	N/A	6,640
13/5/05	Hull (a)	L44-6	t:Fa'asavalu g:Long	2nd	10,862
21/5/05	Widnes (a)	W22-29	t:Sculthorpe,Albert(2),Wellens,Higham g:Long(3),Sculthorpe fg:Sculthorpe	2nd	7,641
27/5/05	Leeds (h)	W38-24	t:P Anderson,Albert,Long,V Anderson,Hardman,Sculthorpe g:Long(7)	2nd	13,236
5/6/05	Bradford (a)	W4-66	t:Wilkin(2),V Anderson(3),Gilmour,Long,Lyon(2),Gardner(2),Roby g:Long(7),Lyon,Hooper	2nd	15,260
10/6/05	Salford (a)	W22-33	t:Lyon(3),Wilkin,Wellens,Long g:Long(4) fg:Long	2nd	4,704
17/6/05	London (h)	D28-28	t:Talau(3),Cunningham,Long,Lyon g:Long(2)	2nd	8,521
26/6/05	Wigan (h) (CCQF)	W75-0	t:Gilmour,V Anderson,Fozzard(2),Hooper,Talau,Wellens,Edmondson(3), Lyon,Gardner,Graham g:Sculthorpe(9),Lyon(2) fg:Sculthorpe	N/A	17,100
3/7/05	Wakefield (a)	W26-38	t:Lyon,Sculthorpe,Wilkin(2),Wellens,V Anderson g:Lyon(4),Sculthorpe(3)	2nd	5,323
8/7/05	Hull (h)	W18-10	t:Bennett,Wellens,Lyon g:Lyon(3)	2nd	9,199
15/7/05	Wigan (h)	W40-18	t:Talau(2),Albert,Gilmour,Roby,Gardner,Edmondson g:Sculthorpe(6)	2nd	13,281
22/7/05	Leigh (a)	W20-27	t:Albert(2),Hooper,Lyon(2) g:Lyon(3) fg:Wilkin	2nd	5,142
30/7/05	Hull (CCSF) ●	L34-8	t:Lyon g:Sculthorpe(2)	N/A	16,171
5/8/05	Warrington (a)	W10-30	t:Bennett,Graham,Long,Gardner,Wellens g:Sculthorpe(5)	2nd	12,762
12/8/05	Wakefield (h)	W60-4	t:P Anderson,Albert(3),Long,Wellens,Lyon(2),Roby,Graham g:Long(10)	2nd	8,153
20/8/05	London (h)	W50-4	t:Albert(2),Hooper,Long,Gilmour,P Anderson,Wilkin,Cunningham,Wellens g:Long(6),Lyon	1st	7,604
4/9/05	Leigh (a)	W4-78	t:Bennett,Long(2),Wellens,Albert,Higham,Roby,P Anderson(2),Gardner(2), Cunningham,Graham,Fa'asavalu g:Long(6),Lyon(2),Hooper(3)	1st	5,534
9/9/05	Wigan (a)	W12-38	t:Cunningham(2),Wellens,Gardner,Wilkin,Fa'asavalu g:Long(3),Hooper,Lyon(3)	1st	20,274
17/9/05	Bradford (h)	L18-32	t:Talau(2),Wellens g:Lyon(3)	1st	11,064
30/9/05	Leeds (h) (QSF)	L16-19	t:Lyon(2),Hardman g:Lyon(2)	N/A	13,209
7/10/05	Bradford (h) (FE)	L18-23	t:Wilkin(3) g:Lyon(3)	N/A	11,604

● Played at Galpharm Stadium, Huddersfield

		APP		TRIES		GOALS		FG		PTS	
	D.O.B.	ALL	SL	ALL	SL	ALL	SL	ALL	SL	ALL	SL
Darren Albert	28/2/76	28	24	28	25	0	0	0	0	112	100
Paul Anderson	25/10/71	30(2)	26(2)	7	6	0	0	0	0	28	24
Vinnie Anderson	14/2/79	20(2)	17(2)	11	9	0	0	0	0	44	36
Mike Bennett	9/5/80	17(13)	15(12)	5	5	0	0	0	0	20	20
Paul Clough	27/9/87	(1)	(1)	0	0	0	0	0	0	0	0
Keiron Cunningham	28/10/76	30(4)	26(4)	12	12	0	0	0	0	48	48
Mark Edmondson	3/11/79	1(18)	1(16)	7	4	0	0	0	0	28	16
Maurie Fa'asavalu	12/1/80	1(24)	1(21)	3	3	0	0	0	0	12	12
Nick Fozzard	22/7/77	31(1)	28(1)	3	1	0	0	0	0	12	4
Ade Gardner	24/6/83	32	28	13	11	0	0	0	0	52	44
Lee Gilmour	12/3/78	29(1)	25(1)	7	5	0	0	0	0	28	20
James Graham	10/9/85	7(20)	7(16)	6	4	0	0	0	0	24	16
Ian Hardman	8/12/84	15(1)	14(1)	4	2	5	5	0	0	26	18
Mick Higham	18/9/80	8(10)	8(8)	7	7	0	0	0	0	28	28
Jason Hooper	14/10/77	21	18	7	4	9	9	0	0	46	34
Sean Long	24/9/76	22(1)	19(1)	17	15	66	59	2	2	202	180
Jamie Lyon	24/1/82	30(1)	27(1)	24	22	49	42	0	0	194	172
Keith Mason	20/1/82	4(12)	3(11)	0	0	0	0	0	0	0	0
Scott Moore	23/1/88	3(2)	3(2)	0	0	0	0	0	0	0	0
James Roby	22/11/85	12(17)	11(15)	9	9	0	0	0	0	36	36
Paul Sculthorpe	22/9/77	16	13	3	3	48	37	2	1	110	87
Willie Talau	25/1/76	27	25	13	12	0	0	0	0	52	48
Paul Wellens	27/2/80	31	27	19	17	3	3	0	0	82	74
Jon Wilkin	11/1/83	27(3)	24(2)	12	11	0	0	1	1	49	45

Keiron Cunningham

LEAGUE RECORD
P28-W23-D1-L4
(1st, SL/Final Eliminator)
F1028, A537, Diff+491
47 points.

CHALLENGE CUP
Semi Finalists

ATTENDANCES
Best - v Wigan (CC - 17,100)
Worst - v York (CC - 6,640)
Total (SL, inc play-offs) - 173,079
Average (SL, inc play-offs) - 10,817
(Up by 1,310 on 2004)

KEY DATES - WAKEFIELD T WILDCATS

1 February 2005 – Wildcats sign Julian O'Neill, Andy Kirk from Salford and Chris Feather on a season's loan from Leeds.

14 February 2005 – Trinity reject reports they are to sign former Castleford forward Michael Smith.

27 February 2005 - unbeaten start to Super League X ends in round three in London with 72-8 defeat.

28 March 2005 - David Solomona breaks hand in shock 44-28 win over leaders Leeds at Headingley and is then banned for two games after being found guilty of punching in the Round 7 game against Huddersfield Giants.

20 April 2005 - Wildcats fined £100 with £10 costs following 'breaches of the RFL's Operational Rules concerning entry on to the field of play by trainers'.

6 May 2005 - captain Jason Demetriou agrees a contract extension which will keep him at the club until the end of the 2007 season.

28 May 2005 - utility back Julian O'Neill leaves and re-joins Widnes Vikings.

22 June 2005 – Wildcats, a point above the relegation zone, after winning just one of their last seven Super League matches, sack coach Shane McNally, Super League coach of the year in 2004.

9 July 2005 – sign Steve Booth from Halifax for rest of season.

13 December 2004 – Bradford propose swap deal for skipper Gareth Ellis, with Jamie Langley and Stuart Reardon offered in exchange for the Great Britain star.

14 December 2004 - sign NL1 player of the year Sam Obst and offer three-month trial to former centre Sylvain Houles.

26 December 2004 - Ellis deal collapses as Wildcats go down 46-6 to Leeds Rhinos in the Boxing Day friendly at Headingley. Ellis tipped to stay at Belle Vue.

29 December 2004 – Gareth Ellis joins Leeds on a four-year contract with a fee in excess of £200,000 involved.

24 January 2005 – Rob Spicer sidelined for at least ten weeks with hip injury.

14 July 2005 - David Solomona extends his contract until the end of the 2008 season.

17 July 2005 – 44-18 win at Halton Stadium puts five points between 11th-placed Widnes and the Wildcats with seven games to play.

21 July 2005 - Fijian winger Semi Tadulala signs new two-year contract.

4 August 2005 – Andy Kirk released from his contract.

10 August 2005 – caretaker coach Tony Smith handed two-year contract

24 August 2005 – York winger Austin Buchanan arrives on loan until end of season.

13 September 2005 – Jamie Field and Colum Halpenny sign new one-year contracts.

20 September 2005 – Widnes centre Jon Whittle signs on one-year contract

30 September 2005 – Sam Obst signs new two-year contract.

12 October 2005 – Wildcats sign Newcastle Knights winger Craig Hall, of Scottish ancestry, on a 12-month deal.

David Solomona

WAKEFIELD T WILDCATS

DATE	FIXTURE	RESULT	SCORERS	LGE	ATT
13/2/05	Bradford (a)	W16-28	t:Rooney,Halpenny,Jeffries,Griffin g:Rooney(5) fg:Rooney(2)	3rd	15,137
19/2/05	Wigan (h)	W18-16	t:Demetriou,Rooney,Tadulala g:Rooney(3)	2nd	6,196
27/2/05	London (a)	L72-8	t:Griffin,Jeffries	6th	2,854
6/3/05	Leigh (h)	W38-26	t:Jeffries(2),Domic(2),Obst,Demetriou,O'Neill g:Rooney(5)	4th	4,814
13/3/05	Hull (a)	L36-33	t:King,Halpenny,Demetriou,Jeffries,Obst,Tadulala g:Rooney(4) fg:Rooney	6th	10,805
19/3/05	St Helens (a)	L64-16	t:Snitch,Kirk,Halpenny g:Rooney(2)	7th	9,321
25/3/05	Huddersfield (h)	L20-42	t:Halpenny,Tadulala,M Field g:Rooney(4)	9th	5,288
28/3/05	Leeds (a)	W28-44	t:Snitch,Demetriou(2),Halpenny,March(2),Tadulala,Griffin g:Rooney(6)	8th	18,257
3/4/05	Hull (h) (CCR4)	L12-36	t:Halpenny,Snitch g:Rooney(2)	N/A	4,866
8/4/05	Salford (a)	L16-14	t:Elima,O'Neill g:Rooney(3)	10th	3,378
17/4/05	Warrington (h)	L28-40	t:King,Jeffries(2),Applegarth,Elima g:O'Neill(4)	10th	5,129
24/4/05	London (h)	W29-18	t:Demetriou,Tadulala,Wrench,Jeffries,Rooney g:Rooney(4) fg:Rooney	9th	3,258
30/4/05	Leigh (a)	L40-18	t:Rooney,Domic,Applegarth g:Rooney(3)	9th	3,213
15/5/05	Widnes (h)	L34-47	t:Halpenny(2),Elima,Rooney,Demetriou,Jeffries g:Rooney(5)	9th	3,802
22/5/05	Hull (h)	L28-35	t:Demetriou,Griffin,March,Domic,Rooney g:Rooney(4)	10th	5,194
29/5/05	Warrington (a)	L38-30	t:March,Tadulala,Halpenny,Obst,Jeffries g:Rooney(5)	10th	10,113
5/6/05	Salford (h)	W36-24	t:Solomona,Feather,Halpenny,March,Rooney,J Field g:Rooney(6)	10th	3,536
10/6/05	Leeds (h)	L6-70	t:Rooney g:Rooney	10th	9,457
19/6/05	Huddersfield (a)	L40-22	t:Jeffries(2),MacGillivray,Obst g:Rooney(3)	10th	4,544
3/7/05	St Helens (h)	L26-38	t:Elima,Jeffries(2),Demetriou g:Rooney(5)	10th	5,323
10/7/05	Bradford (h)	W44-34	t:MacGillivray,Halpenny,Jeffries(2),Korkidas,Rooney(2) g:March(8)	10th	5,954
17/7/05	Widnes (a)	W18-44	t:Obst(2),Solomona,Tadulala(3),Jeffries g:March(7),Rooney	10th	6,116
22/7/05	Wigan (a)	W28-34	t:Halpenny(2),Obst,Jeffries,Spicer,Solomona g:March(5)	9th	9,021
7/8/05	Huddersfield (h)	L12-44	t:J Field,Solomona g:March(2)	9th	4,476
12/8/05	St Helens (a)	L60-4	t:Wainwright	9th	8,153
19/8/05	Salford (a)	L37-0		10th	3,005
4/9/05	Widnes (h)	W46-6	t:Obst,Elima(2),J Field,Domic(2),Henderson,Griffin g:March(7)	9th	3,234
11/9/05	Hull (h)	L30-32	t:Wainwright,Jeffries,Domic,Elima,Buchanan g:March(5)	10th	5,721
16/9/05	Leeds (a)	L34-26	t:Spicer,Jeffries,Buchanan,Domic,Obst g:March,Griffin(2)	10th	17,619

		APP		TRIES		GOALS		FG		PTS	
	D.O.B.	ALL	SL	ALL	SL	ALL	SL	ALL	SL	ALL	SL
Mark Applegarth	10/12/84	7	6	2	2	0	0	0	0	8	8
Austin Buchanan	22/5/84	3	3	2	2	0	0	0	0	8	8
Liam Campbell	5/6/86	(1)	(1)	0	0	0	0	0	0	0	0
Jason Demetriou	13/1/76	24	23	9	9	0	0	0	0	36	36
Sid Domic	8/2/75	18	18	8	8	0	0	0	0	32	32
Olivier Elima	19/5/83	13(9)	12(9)	7	7	0	0	0	0	28	28
Chris Feather	7/12/81	9(12)	9(11)	1	1	0	0	0	0	4	4
Jamie Field	12/12/76	16(9)	16(8)	3	3	0	0	0	0	12	12
Mark Field	21/3/84	18(2)	17(2)	1	1	0	0	0	0	4	4
Darrell Griffin	19/6/81	22(6)	21(6)	5	5	2	2	0	0	24	24
Colum Halpenny	25/4/79	24	23	13	12	0	0	0	0	52	48
Kevin Henderson	1/10/81	5	5	1	1	0	0	0	0	4	4
Sylvain Houles	3/8/81	5(1)	4(1)	0	0	0	0	0	0	0	0
Ben Jeffries	4/9/80	28	27	20	20	0	0	0	0	80	80
Kevin King	18/1/85	8(1)	8(1)	2	2	0	0	0	0	8	8
Andy Kirk	2/8/82	6(3)	6(3)	1	1	0	0	0	0	4	4
Michael Korkidas	12/1/81	21(7)	20(7)	1	1	0	0	0	0	4	4
Duncan MacGillivray	25/10/76	8(3)	8(3)	2	2	0	0	0	0	8	8
David March	25/7/79	25(4)	24(4)	5	5	35	35	0	0	90	90
Sam Obst	26/11/80	14(12)	14(12)	9	9	0	0	0	0	36	36
Julian O'Neill	14/10/72	10(3)	10(2)	2	2	4	4	0	0	16	16
Craig Robinson	30/7/85	(1)	(1)	0	0	0	0	0	0	0	0
Jamie Rooney	17/3/80	19(2)	18(2)	10	10	71	69	4	4	186	182
Steve Snitch	22/2/83	6(14)	6(13)	3	2	0	0	0	0	12	8
David Solomona	26/1/78	18(2)	18(2)	4	4	0	0	0	0	16	16
Rob Spicer	22/9/84	10(4)	10(4)	2	2	0	0	0	0	8	8
Semi Tadulala	3/3/78	27	26	9	9	0	0	0	0	36	36
Michael Wainwright	4/11/80	8(3)	8(3)	2	2	0	0	0	0	8	8
David Wrench	3/1/79	5(17)	4(17)	1	1	0	0	0	0	4	4

Semi Tadulala

LEAGUE RECORD
P28-W10-D0-L18
(10th, SL)
F716, A999, Diff-283
20 points.

CHALLENGE CUP
Round Four

ATTENDANCES
Best - v Leeds (SL - 9,457)
Worst - v Widnes (SL - 3,234)
Total (SL only) - 71,382
Average (SL only) - 5,099
(Up by 295 on 2004)

KEY DATES - WARRINGTON WOLVES

8 November 2004 – pay transfer fee to St Helens for 17-year-old Andy Bracek.

13 December 2004 – Wolves make offer to Wakefield for Gareth Ellis but Bradford rated as favourites.

6 January 2005 - Wolves close to completing signing of Bradford utility back Chris Bridge after agreeing terms with the player.

21 February 2005 – Warrington flag interest in Sonny Bill Williams.

24 March 2005 - Lee Briers signs a two-year extension to his contract which will keep him at the Halliwell Jones Stadium until the end of 2007.

11 April 2005 – 19-year-old winger Phil Berry, yet to make a Super League appearance, is summoned to appear before the RFL's Advisory Panel following alleged breaches of the RFL's Doping Control regulations.

19 April 2005 - prop Warren Stevens joins Leigh Centurions on loan.

21 April 2005 - Phil Berry suspended, back dated to start on 11 March 2005, for two years after being found guilty of providing a sample containing the prohibited substance Nandrolone.

27 April 2005 - Wolves sack Berry.

29 April 2005 - Brent Grose signs three-year extension to his contract to keep him at The Halliwell Jones Stadium until 2008.

12 May 2005 - Mike Wainwright signs a new contract that will keep him at Warrington until the end of the 2006 season.

12 May 2005 - Mike Forshaw to leave the RFL to take up a position on the Warrington Wolves coaching staff.

19 May 2005 - Mark Gleeson signs a new two-year contract to run to November 2007.

16 June 2005 - Wolves confirm signing of New Zealand and North Queensland Cowboys prop forward Paul Rauhihi on a two-year deal from 2006.

30 June 2005 - Wolves confirm signing of Cronulla Sharks hooker Michael Sullivan on a two-year contract, with a one-year option, for the Super League XI campaign.

1 August 2005 - Wolves await outcome of their application for a work permit for Andrew Johns, and for the approval of the Australian Rugby League, before confirming his capture for the season's run-in.

21 August 2005 – Wolves' 60-16 win at Halton Stadium condemns Widnes to relegation.

8 September 2005 - Wolves sign Stuart Reardon from Bradford Bulls on a three-year contract and Richie Barnett from Hull FC on a two-year deal.

10 September 2005 – Andrew Johns is man of the match as Warrington defeat Leeds Rhinos 33-16 at an emotional Halliwell Jones Stadium.

15 September 2005 - Daryl Cardiss set to leave the club at the end of the season by mutual agreement.

24 September 2005 – eliminated at first stage in home 40-8 defeat by Hull.

30 September 2005 – winger Dean Gaskell released to join Leigh.

17 October 2005 – Rob Parker signs from Bradford Bulls on a two-year contract.

WARRINGTON WOLVES

DATE	FIXTURE	RESULT	SCORERS	LGE	ATT
13/2/05	London (a)	L28-24	t:Hilton,N Wood,Westwood,Martin Gleeson(2) g:Briers(2)	7th	4,179
20/2/05	Leigh (h)	W26-22	t:Clarke(2),Martin Gleeson,N Wood,Briers g:Briers(3)	7th	11,412
27/2/05	Hull (a)	L32-10	t:Briers,Fa'afili g:Briers	10th	10,169
4/3/05	St Helens (h)	L16-18	t:Fa'afili,Appo g:Briers(2)	9th	12,098
11/3/05	Leeds (a)	L38-6	t:Martin Gleeson g:Briers	10th	15,637
20/3/05	Huddersfield (h)	W14-8	t:Kohe-Love,Grose g:Briers(3)	10th	9,014
25/3/05	Salford (a)	L42-10	t:Fa'afili,Bridge g:Briers	10th	6,004
29/3/05	Widnes (h)	W44-12	t:Clarke(3),Wainwright,Westwood,Martin Gleeson,Briers,Fa'afili(2) g:Briers(2),Bridge(2)	10th	10,061
2/4/05	Leeds (a) (CCR4)	L26-22	t:N Wood(2),Clarke,Westwood g:Bridge(3)	N/A	8,215
10/4/05	Bradford (h)	W35-32	t:N Wood,Grose(2),Fa'afili,Martin Gleeson(2) g:Briers(5) fg:Briers	9th	10,654
17/4/05	Wakefield (a)	W28-40	t:Westwood(2),Wainwright,N Wood,Briers(2),Clarke,Fa'afili g:Briers(3),Bridge	8th	5,129
24/4/05	Hull (h)	W36-34	t:Fa'afili(3),Grose,Westwood,Appo(2) g:Appo,Bridge(3)	6th	10,383
29/4/05	St Helens (a)	L31-30	t:Kohe-Love,N Wood(2),Westwood,Fa'afili g:Appo(5)	7th	12,666
15/5/05	Wigan (h)	W28-22	t:Wainwright,Lima(2),Swann,N Wood g:Bridge(4)	5th	12,790
22/5/05	Bradford (a)	W24-44	t:Bridge(2),Noone,Kohe-Love,P Wood,Lima,Fa'afili g:Bridge(8)	5th	14,428
29/5/05	Wakefield (h)	W38-30	t:Swann(2),Martin Gleeson,Fa'afili,Grose,N Wood(2) g:Bridge(5)	5th	10,113
5/6/05	Huddersfield (a)	W22-24	t:Clarke,Fa'afili,Westwood,Bridge g:Bridge(4)	3rd	6,162
12/6/05	Leigh (a)	W7-42	t:Westwood,Grose,Fa'afili(2),N Wood,Clarke,Bridge,Appo g:Bridge(5)	3rd	7,249
19/6/05	Salford (h)	W48-14	t:Swann(2),Kohe-Love(2),Martin Gleeson(2),Westwood(3) g:Bridge(4),Briers(2)	3rd	10,925
3/7/05	Widnes (a)	W24-25	t:Clarke,Martin Gleeson,Lima,N Wood,Appo g:Noone(2) fg:Briers	3rd	9,825
9/7/05	Wigan (a)	L36-17	t:Grose,Kohe-Love,Bridge g:Bridge(2) fg:Bridge	3rd	14,162
17/7/05	London (h)	W26-14	t:Martin Gleeson,Gaskell,Fa'afili(2),Grose g:Bridge(3)	3rd	10,146
23/7/05	Leeds (h)	L22-46	t:Grose,Swann,Fa'afili(2) g:Appo(2),Briers	4th	11,036
5/8/05	St Helens (h)	L10-30	t:Martin Gleeson,Noone g:Bridge	4th	12,762
12/8/05	Huddersfield (a)	L38-22	t:Martin Gleeson,Swann,N Wood,Bridge g:Bridge(3)	5th	4,077
21/8/05	Widnes (a)	W16-60	t:Fa'afili(2),Westwood,Lima,Mark Gleeson,Kohe-Love(2),Grose,Martin Gleeson,P Wood,Riley g:Bridge(8)	5th	7,878
4/9/05	Salford (h)	W32-22	t:Westwood,N Wood,Martin Gleeson,Bridge,Briers,Leikvoll g:Bridge(4)	4th	9,619
10/9/05	Leeds (h)	W33-16	t:Fa'afili,Martin Gleeson,Grose,Swann,N Wood g:Johns(6) fg:Johns	4th	13,024
16/9/05	Hull (a)	W16-30	t:Swann(2),Grose,Kohe-Love(2) g:Johns(5)	4th	15,763
24/9/05	Hull (h) (EPO)	L6-40	t:Johns g:Johns	N/A	12,243

		APP		TRIES		GOALS		FG		PTS	
	D.O.B.	ALL	SL	ALL	SL	ALL	SL	ALL	SL	ALL	SL
Graham Appo	11/7/74	9(9)	9(8)	5	5	8	8	0	0	36	36
Andy Bracek	21/3/84	(7)	(7)	0	0	0	0	0	0	0	0
Chris Bridge	5/7/84	19(3)	18(3)	8	8	60	57	1	1	153	147
Lee Briers	14/6/78	23	22	6	6	28	28	2	2	82	82
Jon Clarke	4/4/79	30	29	10	9	0	0	0	0	40	36
Henry Fa'afili	30/5/80	30	29	23	23	0	0	0	0	92	92
Dean Gaskell	12/4/83	15(1)	14(1)	1	1	0	0	0	0	4	4
Mark Gleeson	16/6/82	11(17)	10(17)	1	1	0	0	0	0	4	4
Martin Gleeson	28/5/80	29	28	17	17	0	0	0	0	68	68
Brent Grose	11/9/79	30	29	12	12	0	0	0	0	48	48
Mark Hilton	31/3/75	23(4)	22(4)	1	1	0	0	0	0	4	4
Andrew Johns	19/5/74	3	3	1	1	12	12	1	1	29	29
Toa Kohe-Love	2/12/76	27	27	10	10	0	0	0	0	40	40
Chris Leikvoll	4/12/75	25(1)	25	1	1	0	0	0	0	4	4
Danny Lima	27/7/75	2(28)	2(27)	5	5	0	0	0	0	20	20
Paul Noone	22/4/81	9(11)	9(11)	2	2	2	2	0	0	12	12
Steve Pickersgill	28/11/85	(6)	(6)	0	0	0	0	0	0	0	0
Chris Riley	22/2/88	1(2)	1(2)	1	1	0	0	0	0	4	4
Warren Stevens	4/10/78	(8)	(7)	0	0	0	0	0	0	0	0
Logan Swann	10/2/75	25	25	10	10	0	0	0	0	40	40
Mike Wainwright	25/2/75	22	21	3	3	0	0	0	0	12	12
Ben Westwood	25/7/81	25(3)	24(3)	14	13	0	0	0	0	56	52
Nathan Wood	24/1/72	24	23	16	14	0	0	0	0	64	56
Paul Wood	10/10/81	8(17)	7(17)	2	2	0	0	0	0	8	8

Brent Grose

LEAGUE RECORD
P28-W18-D0-L10
(4th, SL/Elimination Play-Off)
F792, A702, Diff+90
36 points.

CHALLENGE CUP
Round Four

ATTENDANCES
Best - v Leeds (SL - 13,024)
Worst - v Huddersfield (SL - 9,014)
Total (SL, inc play-offs) - 166,280
Average (SL, inc play-offs) - 11,085
(Up by 1,196 on 2004)

25 October 2004 – Vikings ready to confirm signing of Kiwi halfback Thomas Leuluai.

10 November 2004 - sign hooker Mark Smith, released by Wigan.

6 December 2004 – pull out of bid to sign French scrum-half Maxime Greseque.

16 December 2004 – coach Frank Endacott arrives in Widnes after gaining work permit.

23 December 2004 – turn down £35,000 offer for Shane Millard from Leeds.

28 December 2004 – Vikings beat Wolves 12-6 in friendly.

1 January 2005 - New Zealander Karl Guttenbeil offered month's trial.

13 January 2005 - Vikings appoint former Kiwi prop Quentin Pongia as assistant conditioner.

20 February 2005 – beat Bradford 31-22 in first home game.

8 March 2005 - captain Shane Millard ruled out of action for at least six weeks after sustaining a broken jaw in the 32-20 Super League defeat by Wigan.

1 April 2005 - Vikings sign Gray Viane from St Helens.

28 May 2005 - Vikings re-sign Australian utility back Julian 'Jules' O'Neill after he was released by Wakefield Trinity Wildcats.

KEY DATES - WIDNES VIKINGS

22 June 2005 - Mick Cassidy agrees one-year extension to his contract, conditional on Widnes preserving their Super League status.

24 June 2005 - Cronulla fullback David Peachey reported to be a Widnes target.

26 June 2005 – Vikings make Challenge Cup exit in south of France heat-wave after televised 40-24 defeat to Toulouse.

28 June 2005 - Vikings secure the signature of David Peachey on a two-year contract starting in 2006 with help from supporters group Vikings Quids In.

17 July 2005 - coach Frank Endacott admits 'as a team we are not up to it' after the Vikings 18-44 home defeat by Wakefield Trinity Wildcats. Vikings remain second from bottom of the Super League table on eleven points, five points behind their the Wildcats, with just seven games to play.

10 August 2005 - Leeds Rhinos announce signing of Widnes captain Shane Millard on a one-year contract.

21 August 2005 - Vikings' crushing 16-60 defeat against Warrington confirms their place in Super League's bottom two - but the club is still hoping that the winners of the NL1 Grand Final do not meet the criteria for Super League.

1 September 2005 – Terry O'Connor, Mick Cassidy and Mark Smith sign contracts to stay with the Vikings even if their relegation to National League One is confirmed. Tim Holmes and Paul Crook also re-sign.

5 September 2005 - David Peachey deal looks unlikely to go ahead if the Vikings are relegated from Super League at the end of the season. Bradford Bulls deny they are interested in signing the Aussie.

14 September 2005 - coach Frank Endacott decides to return home to New Zealand after the final match of the season at London.

30 September 2005 – David Peachey vows to honour his contract even if Widnes are relegated.

9 October 2005 – Castleford Tigers win LHF NL1 Grand Final and gain promotion, relegating Widnes.

Gray Viane

WIDNES VIKINGS

DATE	FIXTURE	RESULT	SCORERS	LGE	ATT
11/2/05	St Helens (a)	L40-18	t:Moule,Whitaker g:Rowlands(5)	12th	12,935
20/2/05	Bradford (h)	W31-22	t:Craigie(2),Moule,Whitaker,Whittle,Millard g:Rowlands(3) fg:Craigie	10th	7,230
27/2/05	Leeds (a)	L66-8	t:Emelio g:Rowlands(2)	11th	17,307
6/3/05	Wigan (h)	L20-32	t:Rowlands,Finnigan,Emelio g:Rowlands(4)	11th	9,004
11/3/05	Huddersfield (a)	L34-18	t:Finnigan(2),Moule(2) g:Rowlands	11th	3,383
20/3/05	London (a)	L66-8	t:Moule(2)	11th	3,365
25/3/05	Leigh (h)	W35-28	t:Hughes,Moule,Emelio(2),Whitaker,Hulse g:Crook(5) fg:Crook	11th	6,026
29/3/05	Warrington (a)	L44-12	t:Moule,Whitaker g:Myler(2)	11th	10,061
3/4/05	Swinton (h) (CCR4)	W32-18	t:Frame(2),Manu(2),Cassidy,Holmes g:Crook(3),Rowlands	N/A	2,263
10/4/05	Hull (a)	L32-28	t:Finnigan(2),Moule,Frame,Emelio g:Myler(4)	11th	9,078
17/4/05	Salford (h)	L6-22	t:O'Connor g:Myler	11th	5,878
23/4/05	Leeds (h)	L20-42	t:Millard(2),Frame,Barnett g:Myler(2)	11th	6,524
29/4/05	Wigan (a)	L23-22	t:Frame,Millard,Hulse,Viane g:Myler(3)	12th	11,390
8/5/05	Barrow (a) (CCR5)	W8-50	t:Mills,Myler,Holmes,Whitaker(2),Manu,Hughes,Fa'alogo,Hulse g:Myler(7)	N/A	2,599
15/5/05	Wakefield (a)	W34-47	t:O'Connor,Finnigan,Hughes,Myler,Moule,Smith(2) g:Myler(9) fg:Craigie	11th	3,802
21/5/05	St Helens (h)	L22-29	t:Millard,Connolly,Whitaker,Emelio g:Myler(3)	11th	7,641
29/5/05	Huddersfield (h)	W40-12	t:Frame,Viane(3),Finnigan,Millard,Smith g:Myler(6)	11th	5,946
5/6/05	Leigh (a)	W14-34	t:Finnigan,Craigie(3),Millard g:Myler(6),Connolly	11th	5,170
12/6/05	London (h)	L10-24	t:Connolly,Craigie g:Jules O'Neill	11th	5,996
19/6/05	Bradford (a)	D25-25	t:Hulse,Connolly,Craigie,Emelio g:Jules O'Neill(4) fg:Jules O'Neill	11th	10,715
26/6/05	Toulouse (a) (CCQF)	L40-24	t:Emelio,Johnson,Smith,Manu g:Myler(4)	N/A	4,500
3/7/05	Warrington (h)	L24-25	t:Emelio,Viane(2),Julian O'Neill g:Jules O'Neill(4)	11th	9,825
8/7/05	Salford (a)	L34-16	t:Whittle,Finnigan,Viane g:Jules O'Neill(2)	11th	4,507
17/7/05	Wakefield (h)	L18-44	t:Viane(3),Fa'alogo g:Jules O'Neill	11th	6,116
24/7/05	Hull (h)	L20-40	t:Hughes,Millard,Viane(2),Frame	11th	5,378
7/8/05	Bradford (a)	L74-24	t:Finnigan,Hughes,Smith,Viane g:Jules O'Neill(2),Myler(2)	11th	10,128
14/8/05	Wigan (h)	L24-48	t:Kerr,Myler,Hughes,Watts g:Myler(4)	11th	6,384
21/8/05	Warrington (h)	L16-60	t:Hughes,Kerr,Finnigan g:Myler(2)	11th	7,878
4/9/05	Wakefield (a)	L46-6	t:Myler g:Myler	11th	3,234
11/9/05	Leigh (h)	W36-20	t:Ballard(2),Connolly,Jules O'Neill,Watts,Finnigan g:Myler(6)	11th	5,293
18/9/05	London (a)	L68-10	t:Alcock,Watts g:Jules O'Neill	11th	3,885

		APP		TRIES		GOALS		FG		PTS	
	D.O.B.	ALL	SL	ALL	SL	ALL	SL	ALL	SL	ALL	SL
Paul Alcock	12/11/82	(5)	(4)	1	1	0	0	0	0	4	4
Paul Ballard	4/9/84	3(1)	3(1)	2	2	0	0	0	0	8	8
Richie Barnett	26/4/81	4	4	2	2	0	0	0	0	8	8
Mick Cassidy	8/7/73	26	24	1	0	0	0	0	0	4	0
Gary Connolly	22/6/71	21	20	4	4	1	1	0	0	18	18
Owen Craigie	19/4/78	17	15	7	7	0	0	2	2	30	30
Paul Crook	28/8/86	3(2)	2(2)	0	0	8	5	1	1	17	11
Jamie Durbin	7/9/84	1	1	0	0	0	0	0	0	0	0
Andrew Emelio	18/10/81	25(2)	22(2)	9	8	0	0	0	0	36	32
Sala Fa'alogo	20/9/77	9(13)	8(12)	2	1	0	0	0	0	8	4
Simon Finnigan	8/12/81	24(4)	22(4)	12	12	0	0	0	0	48	48
Daniel Frame	7/6/75	28(2)	25(2)	7	5	0	0	0	0	28	20
Michael Gill	27/12/83	(1)	0	0	0	0	0	0	0	0	0
Tim Holmes	29/9/82	10(5)	8(4)	2	0	0	0	0	0	8	0
Adam Hughes	1/10/77	12(1)	10(1)	7	6	0	0	0	0	28	24
Gary Hulse	20/1/81	14(6)	12(5)	3	2	0	0	0	0	12	8
Bruce Johnson	26/1/84	(2)	(1)	1	0	0	0	0	0	4	0
Keiran Kerr	8/10/79	6	6	2	2	0	0	0	0	8	8
Misili Manu	4/3/80	4	1	4	0	0	0	0	0	16	0
Shane Millard	30/7/75	18	16	8	8	0	0	0	0	32	32
David Mills	1/6/81	3(20)	1(19)	1	0	0	0	0	0	4	0
Aaron Moule	20/6/77	15	13	10	10	0	0	0	0	40	40
Stephen Myler	21/7/84	17(4)	15(4)	4	3	62	51	0	0	140	114
Stephen Nash	14/1/86	4(2)	4(1)	0	0	0	0	0	0	0	0
Terry O'Connor	13/10/71	26	25	2	2	0	0	0	0	8	8
Jules O'Neill	14/10/72	12(2)	12(2)	1	1	15	15	1	1	35	35
Julian O'Neill	24/7/73	12(13)	10(13)	1	1	0	0	0	0	4	4
Steve Rowlands	9/9/84	10	9	1	1	16	15	0	0	36	34
Mark Smith	18/8/81	13(17)	12(15)	5	4	0	0	0	0	20	16
John Stankevitch	6/11/79	17(5)	17(5)	0	0	0	0	0	0	0	0
Gray Viane	19/2/82	20	20	13	13	0	0	0	0	52	52
Brad Watts	13/3/80	6	6	3	3	0	0	0	0	12	12
Matt Whitaker	6/3/82	10(15)	8(14)	7	5	0	0	0	0	28	20
Jon Whittle	9/9/82	13	13	2	2	0	0	0	0	8	8
Darren Woods	24/3/84	(1)	(1)	0	0	0	0	0	0	0	0

Mark Smith

LEAGUE RECORD
P28-W6-D1-L21
(11th, SL)
F598, A1048, Diff-450
13 points.

CHALLENGE CUP
Quarter Finalists

ATTENDANCES
Best - v Warrington (SL - 9,825)
Worst - v Swinton (CC - 2,263)
Total (SL only) - 95,119
Average (SL only) - 6,794
(Up by 627 on 2004)

KEY DATES - WIGAN WARRIORS

21 April 2005 – sign Wayne McDonald on loan from Leeds Rhinos.

27 April 2005 - Harrison Hansen signs new two-year deal until the end of the 2007 season.

12 May 2005 - chairman, Maurice Lindsay puts an end to recent rumours of a takeover bid for the club.

18 May 2005 - Bryan Fletcher signs for the 2006 and 2007 seasons from South Sydney.

23 May 2005 – Wigan cautious on reports they have signed Kiwi Test back-rower Joe Galuvao from Penrith Panthers.

23 May 2005 – Ian Millward, sacked by St Helens, starts new job as head coach of the Warriors. Current coach Denis Betts set to stay at the JJB Stadium as Millward's assistant.

31 May 2005 - prop Danny Sculthorpe suspended for two games for use of the forearm in Bank Holiday Monday Super League win against Salford City Reds.

3 June 2005 – on-loan Wayne McDonald joins Huddersfield Giants.

3 June 2005 - Wigan sign Wests Tigers 23-year-old winger Pat Richards for the 2006 and 2007 seasons.

8 June 2005 – Wigan take Liam Botham on loan after he is released by Leeds.

18 June 2005 – Leeds Rhinos inflict record 70-0 defeat on Wigan at Headingley.

26 June 2005 - St Helens inflict record 75-0 defeat on Wigan in Powergen Challenge Cup quarter-final.

28 June 2005 - New Zealand Warriors prop Iafeta Palea'aesina joins Wigan for next season.

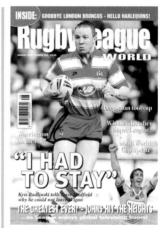

8 July 2005 - Wigan sign South Sydney's former Hull prop Scott Logan on a two-year contract from the 2006 season.

11 July 2005 - winger Brian Carney asks Wigan to release him from the final year of his contract to allow him to play next year with the Newcastle Knights, having already signed with the new Gold Coast franchise for their debut season in 2007.

19 July 2005 – Wigan agree to Carney's request.

22 July 2005 - Kevin Brown extends his contract at Wigan Warriors until the end of 2007.

1 August 2005 – new Super League club Les Catalans confirm they want to sign Wigan forward Jerome Guisset for their inaugural season in 2006.

8 August 2005 – captain Kris Radlinski will miss the Tri Nations as well as the rest of the Super League season after undergoing surgery for a knee injury.

17 August 2005 - Liam Botham forced to retire from the game at the age of 27 after picking up a neck injury.

29 August 2005 - Jerome Guisset says he is '99 per cent certain' to leave Wigan at the end of the season to join Les Catalans.

13 September 2005 - hooker Terry Newton suspended for ten matches - the heaviest suspension of the Super League era - for his part in Wigan's defeat by St Helens at the JJB Stadium.

18 September 2005 – seventh place finish despite last-day 36-22 win at Huddersfield.

26 October 2005 – prop Danny Sculthorpe joins promoted Castleford Tigers on loan for 2006.

31 October 2005 – Adrian Lam leaves to become assistant to former Wigan coach Stuart Raper at Cronulla.

8 November 2004 – complete signing of Dennis Moran from London on a two-year contract.

31 December 2004 - Andy Farrell awarded an OBE in the New Year's Honours List, two days after being named as Super League Player of the Year by readers of 'Rugby Leaguer & League Express'.

18 January 2005 - Farrell, forced to return home early from the club's pre-season training camp in Florida, set to miss start of Super League X with knee injury suffered during the Tri-Nations Series.

1 February 2005 – former centre Andrew Farrar joins coaching staff

9 February 2005 - Wigan confirm they have terminated close-season signing Luke Davico's contract after the former Canberra Raiders prop damaged a pectoral muscle in his one appearance, the pre-season friendly at Salford in January.

14 February 2005 – Wigan deny media reports a deal is in place to bring New Zealand sensation Sonny Bill Williams to the JJB Stadium for 2006.

22 February 2005 – Warriors complete signing of former Warrington prop Jerome Guisset on a two-year deal after a short spell in French rugby union.

25 February 2005 – Gareth Hock's season is ended with knee injury sustained in 28-27 round three home defeat by Bradford.

14 March 2005 – Andy Farrell's move to rugby union confirmed by the club.

18 March 2005 - Brian Carney sidelined for up to six weeks with a knee injury picked up in the final minute of the 62-6 home win against Leigh.

25 March 2005 – Sean O'Loughlin ruled out for season with knee injury suffered in 22-20 Good Friday home win over St Helens.

12 April 2005 - Wigan announce six-figure profit for 2004.

WIGAN WARRIORS

DATE	FIXTURE	RESULT	SCORERS	LGE	ATT
11/2/05	Salford (h)	W15-4	t:Moran,Allen g:Tickle(3) fg:O'Loughlin	4th	13,687
19/2/05	Wakefield (a)	L18-16	t:Vaealiki,Hock,Newton g:Tickle(2)	5th	6,196
25/2/05	Bradford (h)	L27-28	t:Vaealiki(2),Newton,Brown g:Tickle(5) fg:O'Loughlin	7th	13,111
6/3/05	Widnes (a)	W20-32	t:Beswick,Aspinwall,Newton,Brown(2) g:Tickle(6)	6th	9,004
12/3/05	London (a)	L34-20	t:Radlinski,Wild,Vaealiki g:Tickle(4)	7th	5,057
18/3/05	Leigh (h)	W62-6	t:Tickle,Carney,Dallas(2),Godwin,Radlinski(3),Moran,Vaealiki,Brown g:Tickle(9)	6th	15,089
25/3/05	St Helens (h)	W22-20	t:Tickle,Radlinski,Dallas g:Tickle(5)	5th	25,004
28/3/05	Hull (a)	W15-21	t:Colbon,Hansen,Dallas g:Tickle(4) fg:Tickle	3rd	14,172
3/4/05	Whitehaven (h) (CCR4)	W42-4	t:Godwin,Radlinski,Wild(2),Dallas,Allen(2) g:Tickle(5),Melling(2)	N/A	6,974
8/4/05	Huddersfield (a)	L24-16	t:Hansen,Guisset(2) g:Melling(2)	4th	5,288
15/4/05	Leeds (h)	L14-38	t:Radlinski(2) g:Tickle(3)	5th	16,022
22/4/05	Bradford (a)	L40-8	t:Dallas(2)	7th	13,527
29/4/05	Widnes (h)	W23-22	t:Brown,Carney,Wild,Tickle g:Tickle(3) fg:Moran	6th	11,390
6/5/05	Union Treiziste Catalane (h) (CCR5)	W16-10	t:Melling,Wild,Brown g:Melling(2)	N/A	5,906
15/5/05	Warrington (a)	L28-22	t:Aspinwall,Tickle,Moran g:Tickle(5)	6th	12,790
20/5/05	Huddersfield (h)	L24-26	t:Tickle,Dallas,Moran,Brown g:Tickle(4)	7th	10,057
30/5/05	Salford (a)	W20-34	t:Tickle,Dallas(2),Brown,Radlinski,Wild g:Tickle(5)	6th	5,526
3/6/05	London (h)	L18-22	t:Radlinski,Tickle,Dallas,Wild g:Tickle	7th	10,262
10/6/05	Hull (h)	L24-28	t:Moran(2),Tickle,Tomkins g:Tickle(4)	7th	12,125
18/6/05	Leeds (a)	L70-0		8th	18,177
26/6/05	St Helens (a) (CCQF)	L75-0		N/A	17,100
1/7/05	Leigh (a)	W22-30	t:Aspinwall(2),Moran,Tickle,Newton g:Tickle(5)	7th	7,458
9/7/05	Warrington (h)	W36-17	t:Moran,Melling,Dallas,Godwin,Tickle,Newton g:Tickle(6)	7th	14,162
15/7/05	St Helens (a)	L40-18	t:Aspinwall,Hargreaves,Guisset g:Tickle(3)	7th	13,281
22/7/05	Wakefield (h)	L28-34	t:Moran(2),Orr(2),Tickle g:Tickle(4)	7th	9,021
5/8/05	Salford (h)	W40-12	t:Tickle(2),Carney(2),Newton(2),Tomkins g:Tickle(4),Orr(2)	7th	10,156
14/8/05	Widnes (a)	W24-48	t:Brown,Sculthorpe,Wild,Allen,Coyle,Newton,Hansen,Beswick,Moran g:Tickle(6)	7th	6,384
21/8/05	Hull (a)	W24-28	t:Wild,Newton,Orr,Brown,Moran g:Tickle(4)	7th	9,935
2/9/05	Leeds (h)	W24-22	t:Moran(2),Orr,Hansen g:Tickle(3),Orr	7th	14,158
9/9/05	St Helens (h)	L12-38	t:Vaealiki,Tomkins g:Tickle(2)	7th	20,274
18/9/05	Huddersfield (a)	W22-36	t:Moran,Ashton(2),Orr,Brown,Sculthorpe,Carney g:Tickle(3),Carney	7th	5,917

		APP		TRIES		GOALS		FG		PTS	
	D.O.B.	ALL	SL	ALL	SL	ALL	SL	ALL	SL	ALL	SL
David Allen	15/9/85	8(15)	6(14)	4	2	0	0	0	0	16	8
Chris Ashton	29/3/87	1	1	2	2	0	0	0	0	8	8
Martin Aspinwall	21/10/81	29(1)	26(1)	5	5	0	0	0	0	20	20
Bob Beswick	8/12/84	7(9)	5(8)	2	2	0	0	0	0	8	8
Liam Botham	26/8/77	5	5	0	0	0	0	0	0	0	0
Kevin Brown	2/10/84	23(4)	20(4)	11	10	0	0	0	0	44	40
Brian Carney	23/7/76	16	15	5	5	1	1	0	0	22	22
Liam Colbon	30/9/84	4(5)	4(3)	1	1	0	0	0	0	4	4
James Coyle	28/12/85	3(3)	2(3)	1	1	0	0	0	0	4	4
Brett Dallas	18/10/74	28	25	12	11	0	0	0	0	48	44
Sean Gleeson	29/11/87	3(3)	2(3)	0	0	0	0	0	0	0	0
Wayne Godwin	13/3/82	6(20)	5(18)	3	2	0	0	0	0	12	8
Darrell Goulding	3/3/88	1	1	0	0	0	0	0	0	0	0
Jerome Guisset	29/8/78	22(3)	20(2)	3	3	0	0	0	0	12	12
Harrison Hansen	26/10/85	20(8)	18(7)	4	4	0	0	0	0	16	16
Bryn Hargreaves	14/11/85	9(8)	9(5)	1	1	0	0	0	0	4	4
Gareth Hock	5/9/83	3	3	1	1	0	0	0	0	4	4
Lee Jewitt	14/2/87	(2)	(2)	0	0	0	0	0	0	0	0
Wayne McDonald	3/9/75	(4)	(4)	0	0	0	0	0	0	0	0
Chris Melling	21/9/84	8(2)	7(1)	2	1	6	2	0	0	20	8
Dennis Moran	22/1/77	27	25	15	15	0	0	1	1	61	61
Terry Newton	7/11/78	25(3)	23(3)	9	9	0	0	0	0	36	36
Sean O'Loughlin	24/11/82	7	7	0	0	0	0	2	2	2	2
Danny Orr	17/5/78	18	18	5	5	3	3	0	0	26	26
Paul Prescott	1/1/86	(2)	(2)	0	0	0	0	0	0	0	0
Kris Radlinski	9/4/76	15	14	10	9	0	0	0	0	40	36
Danny Sculthorpe	8/9/79	6(17)	4(17)	2	2	0	0	0	0	8	8
Jerry Seuseu	19/4/74	24(2)	21(2)	0	0	0	0	0	0	0	0
Danny Tickle	10/3/83	28(2)	26(2)	13	13	108	103	1	1	269	259
Joel Tomkins	21/3/87	5(8)	5(8)	3	3	0	0	0	0	12	12
David Vaealiki	13/11/80	23	21	6	6	0	0	0	0	24	24
Stephen Wild	26/4/81	29(2)	26(2)	9	6	0	0	0	0	36	24

Danny Tickle

LEAGUE RECORD
P28-W14-D0-L14
(7th, SL)
F698, A718, Diff-20
28 points.

CHALLENGE CUP
Quarter Finalists

ATTENDANCES
Best - v St Helens (SL - 25,004)
Worst - v UTC (CC - 5,906)
Total (SL only) - 194,518
Average (SL only) - 13,894
(Up by 561 on 2004)

SUPER LEAGUE X
Round by Round

ROUND 1

Friday 11th February 2005

HULL FC 12 LEEDS RHINOS 16

HULL: 14 Motu Tony (D); 2 Nathan Blacklock (D); 16 Tom Saxton (D); 3 Kirk Yeaman; 5 Gareth Raynor; 6 Richard Horne; 7 Peter Lupton; 8 Ewan Dowes; 9 Richard Swain (C); 23 Paul McNicholas; 11 Shayne McMenemy; 17 Chris Chester; 13 Paul Cooke. Subs (all used): 15 Jamie Thackray (D); 18 Liam Higgins; 24 Graeme Horne; 31 Danny Hill.
Tries: Saxton (62), Raynor (74); **Goals:** Cooke 2/4.
RHINOS: 1 Richard Mathers; 2 Mark Calderwood; 3 Chev Walker; 4 Keith Senior; 5 Marcus Bai; 13 Kevin Sinfield (C); 6 Danny McGuire; 8 Ryan Bailey; 14 Andrew Dunemann; 12 Chris McKenna; 20 Gareth Ellis. Subs (all used): 10 Barrie McDermott; 11 Ali Lauitiiti; 7 Rob Burrow; 16 Willie Poching.
Tries: Bai (19), Walker (31), Senior (52); **Goals:** Sinfield 2/4.
Rugby Leaguer & League Express Men of the Match: *Hull:* Richard Swain; *Rhinos:* Richard Mathers.
Penalty count: 4-8; **Half-time:** 2-12; **Referee:** Karl Kirkpatrick (Warrington); **Attendance:** 17,080.

ST HELENS 40 WIDNES VIKINGS 18

SAINTS: 1 Paul Wellens; 2 Ade Gardner; 3 Jamie Lyon (D); 4 Willie Talau; 5 Darren Albert; 13 Paul Sculthorpe (C); 7 Sean Long; 8 Nick Fozzard; 14 Mick Higham; 17 Paul Anderson (D); 11 Lee Gilmour; 19 James Graham; 12 Jon Wilkin. Subs (all used): 15 Mike Bennett; 10 Mark Edmondson; 9 Keiron Cunningham; 21 James Roby.
Tries: Fozzard (4), Long (18, pen), Higham (20), Wellens (49), Albert (55), Roby (67), Edmondson (75);
Goals: Sculthorpe 6/8.
Sin bin: Graham (14) - holding down.
VIKINGS: 1 Gary Connolly (D); 5 Andrew Emelio (D); 3 Aaron Moule; 21 Jon Whittle (D); 19 Steve Rowlands; 6 Owen Craigie (D); 14 Gary Hulse (D); 15 Matt Whitaker; 9 Shane Millard (C); 10 Julian O'Neill; 11 Mick Cassidy (D); 12 John Stankevitch (D); 16 Daniel Frame. Subs (all used): 4 Adam Hughes; 13 Simon Finnigan; 20 Mark Smith (D); 18 Sala Fa'alogo.
Tries: Moule (24), Whitaker (60); **Goals:** Rowlands 5/5.
Rugby Leaguer & League Express Men of the Match: *Saints:* Paul Sculthorpe; *Vikings:* Matt Whitaker.
Penalty count: 8-9; **Half-time:** 20-12; **Referee:** Richard Silverwood (Dewsbury); **Attendance:** 12,935.

WIGAN WARRIORS 15 SALFORD CITY REDS 4

WARRIORS: 1 Kris Radlinski (C); 3 Martin Aspinwall; 19 Stephen Wild; 4 David Vaealiki (D); 2 Brett Dallas; 6 Danny Orr; 7 Dennis Moran (D); 8 Jerry Seuseu (D); 9 Terry Newton; 16 Danny Sculthorpe; 11 Gareth Hock; 12 Danny Tickle; 15 Sean O'Loughlin. Subs (all used): 14 Kevin Brown; 18 Wayne Godwin (D); 20 Harrison Hansen; 22 David Allen.
Tries: Moran (7), Allen (72); **Goals:** Tickle 3/3;
Field goal: O'Loughlin.
On report: Seuseu (58) - raising knees in tackle.
CITY REDS: 15 Karl Fitzpatrick; 2 David Hodgson (D); 3 Stuart Littler; 16 Nathan McAvoy; 5 Anthony Stewart; 1 Cliff Beverley; 7 Luke Robinson (D); 14 Paul Highton; 9 Malcolm Alker (C); 10 Sean Rutgerson; 12 Ian Sibbit (D); 20 Tim Jonkers; 13 Chris Charles. Subs (all used): 17 Gareth Haggerty; 33 Kevin McGuinness; 23 Andrew Brocklehurst; 8 Andy Coley.
Try: Alker (59); **Goals:** Charles 0/2.
Rugby Leaguer & League Express Men of the Match: *Warriors:* Danny Tickle; *City Reds:* Malcolm Alker.
Penalty count: 12-11; **Half-time:** 6-0;
Referee: Ashley Klein (Keighley); **Attendance:** 13,687.

Saturday 12th February 2005

LEIGH CENTURIONS 12 HUDDERSFIELD GIANTS 30

CENTURIONS: 22 Neil Turley; 24 John Wilshere (D); 9 Phil Jones; 1 Ben Cooper; 19 Rob Smyth; 10 Jason Kent (D); 2 John Duffy; 25 Richard Moore (D); 18 Paul Rowley; 16 Steve McCurrie (D); 12 Oliver Wilkes; 13 Mark Leafa (D); 3 Jason Ferris (C) (D). Subs (all used): 8 Rob Jackson (D); 20 Craig Stapleton; 11 James King (D); 21 Matt Sturm.
Tries: Sturm (75), Smyth (80);
Goals: Turley 1/1, Wilshere 1/2.
Dismissal: Wilkes (50) - high tackle on Crabtree.
Sin bin: Kent (35) - interference.
On report: Brawl (50).
GIANTS: 5 Stuart Donlan; 2 Hefin O'Hare; 3 James Evans; 13 Stanley Gene; 34 Marcus St Hilaire; 6 Chris Thorman (D2); 15 Sean Penkywicz; 21 Paul Jackson (D2); 9 Brad Drew (D); 10 Jim Gannon; 11 Chris Nero; 14 Stuart Jones; 12 Ben Roarty (C). Subs (all used): 1 Paul Reilly; 20 Paul White; 18 Eorl Crabtree; 17 Paul Smith.
Tries: Gene (10), Penkywicz (22), Stuart Jones (44), White (61); **Goals:** Thorman 7/8.
On report: Brawl (50).
Rugby Leaguer & League Express Men of the Match: *Centurions:* Jason Ferris; *Giants:* Chris Thorman.
Penalty count: 9-14; **Half-time:** 2-16;
Referee: Ian Smith (Oldham); **Attendance:** 4,042.

Sunday 13th February 2005

BRADFORD BULLS 16 WAKEFIELD TRINITY WILDCATS 28

BULLS: 17 Stuart Reardon; 22 Karl Pryce; 3 Leon Pryce;

---

16 Paul Johnson; 5 Lesley Vainikolo; 18 Iestyn Harris; 7 Paul Deacon; 8 Joe Vagana; 1 Robbie Paul; 29 Stuart Fielden; 10 Brad Meyers (D); 12 Jamie Peacock (C); 11 Lee Radford. Subs (all used): 19 Jamie Langley; 32 Andy Smith; 14 Andy Lynch (D); 27 Rob Parker.
Tries: K Pryce (14), I Harris (16), Langley (53);
Goals: Deacon 2/3.
WILDCATS: 21 Mark Field; 1 Colum Halpenny; 3 Jason Demetriou (C); 19 Kevin King (D); 5 Semi Tadulala; 6 Jamie Rooney; 7 Ben Jeffries; 8 Darrell Griffin; 9 David March; 10 Michael Korkidas; 18 Olivier Elima; 12 Jamie Field; 26 Julian O'Neill (D). Subs (all used): 14 Sam Obst (D); 15 David Wrench; 27 Chris Feather (D3); 11 David Solomona.
Tries: Rooney (6), Halpenny (30), Jeffries (44), Griffin (69); **Goals:** Rooney 5/6; **Field goals:** Rooney 2.
Rugby Leaguer & League Express Men of the Match: *Bulls:* Joe Vagana; *Wildcats:* Jamie Rooney.
Penalty count: 6-7; **Half-time:** 10-14;
Referee: Steve Ganson (St Helens); **Attendance:** 15,137.

LONDON BRONCOS 28 WARRINGTON WOLVES 24

BRONCOS: 25 Zebastian Luisi; 2 Jon Wells; 1 Paul Sykes; 4 Mark O'Halloran; 3 Nick Bradley-Qalilawa (D); 21 Luke Dorn (D); 7 Thomas Leuluai (D); 17 Mark Tookey (D); 6 Mark McLinden (C) (D); 10 Steve Trindall; 11 Solomon Haumono (D); 12 Lee Hopkins (D); 13 Rob Purdham. Subs (all used): 15 Mitchell Stringer; 18 Anthony Armour; 20 Filimone Lolohea (D); 24 Tyrone Smith (D).
Tries: Dorn (1), Sykes (36), Haumono (44), McLinden (54), Purdham (58); **Goals:** Sykes 4/5.
WOLVES: 1 Brent Grose; 5 Dean Gaskell; 3 Martin Gleeson (D); 4 Toa Kohe-Love (D2); 2 Henry Fa'afili; 6 Lee Briers (C); 7 Nathan Wood; 8 Chris Leikvoll; 14 Mark Gleeson; 10 Mark Hilton; 11 Logan Swann (D); 12 Mike Wainwright; 9 Jon Clarke. Subs (all used): 15 Ben Westwood; 16 Paul Wood; 17 Danny Lima; 18 Graham Appo.
Tries: Hilton (7), N Wood (11), Westwood (32), Martin Gleeson (48, 66); **Goals:** Briers 2/5.
Rugby Leaguer & League Express Men of the Match: *Broncos:* Mark McLinden; *Wolves:* Martin Gleeson.
Penalty count: 6-10; **Half-time:** 12-16; **Referee:** Ronnie Laughton (Barnsley); **Attendance:** 4,179.

ROUND 2

Friday 18th February 2005

LEEDS RHINOS 30 ST HELENS 18

RHINOS: 1 Richard Mathers; 2 Mark Calderwood; 3 Chev Walker; 4 Keith Senior; 5 Marcus Bai; 13 Kevin Sinfield (C); 6 Danny McGuire; 8 Ryan Bailey; 14 Andrew Dunemann; 15 Danny Ward; 18 Jamie Jones-Buchanan; 12 Chris McKenna; 20 Gareth Ellis. Subs (all used): 17 Wayne McDonald; 11 Ali Lauitiiti; 16 Willie Poching; 7 Rob Burrow.
Tries: Calderwood (3, 68), Walker (10), Mathers (28), Poching (42); **Goals:** Sinfield 5/5.
SAINTS: 5 Darren Albert; 2 Ade Gardner; 3 Jamie Lyon; 4 Willie Talau; 20 Ian Hardman; 13 Paul Sculthorpe (C); 7 Sean Long; 8 Nick Fozzard; 14 Mick Higham; 17 Paul Anderson; 19 James Graham; 11 Lee Gilmour; 12 Jon Wilkin. Subs (all used): 9 Keiron Cunningham; 10 Mark Edmondson; 15 Mike Bennett; 21 James Roby.
Tries: Albert (17), Cunningham (19), Talau (33);
Goals: Sculthorpe 3/3.
Rugby Leaguer & League Express Men of the Match: *Rhinos:* Kevin Sinfield; *Saints:* Paul Sculthorpe.
Penalty count: 9-5; **Half-time:** 18-18;
Referee: Ashley Klein (Keighley); **Attendance:** 21,225.

SALFORD CITY REDS 20 LONDON BRONCOS 16

CITY REDS: 15 Karl Fitzpatrick; 2 David Hodgson; 3 Stuart Littler; 33 Kevin McGuinness; 5 Anthony Stewart; 1 Cliff Beverley; 7 Luke Robinson; 8 Andy Coley; 9 Malcolm Alker (C); 10 Sean Rutgerson; 12 Ian Sibbit; 20 Tim Jonkers; 13 Chris Charles. Subs (all used): 11 Mark Shipway; 17 Gareth Haggerty; 24 Andy Johnson; 23 Andrew Brocklehurst.
Tries: Stewart (11), Fitzpatrick (29, 65), Sibbit (75);
Goals: Charles 2/4.
Sin bin: Rutgerson (56) - dissent.
BRONCOS: 25 Zebastian Luisi; 2 Jon Wells; 3 Nick Bradley-Qalilawa; 1 Paul Sykes; 23 Lee Greenwood; 21 Luke Dorn; 7 Thomas Leuluai; 10 Steve Trindall; 6 Mark McLinden (C); 17 Mark Tookey; 11 Solomon Haumono; 12 Lee Hopkins; 13 Rob Purdham. Subs (all used): 9 Neil Budworth; 15 Mitchell Stringer; 18 Anthony Armour; 24 Tyrone Smith.
Tries: Wells (35), Leuluai (44), Dorn (80);
Goals: Sykes 2/3.
Rugby Leaguer & League Express Men of the Match: *City Reds:* Karl Fitzpatrick; *Broncos:* Luke Dorn.
Penalty count: 9-5; **Half-time:** 8-4; **Referee:** Karl Kirkpatrick (Warrington); **Attendance:** 3,315.

Saturday 19th February 2005

WAKEFIELD TRINITY WILDCATS 18 WIGAN WARRIORS 16

WILDCATS: 21 Mark Field; 1 Colum Halpenny; 3 Jason Demetriou; 19 Kevin King; 5 Semi Tadulala; 6 Jamie Rooney; 7 Ben Jeffries; 8 Darrell Griffin; 9 David March; 10 Michael Korkidas; 18 Olivier Elima; 12 Jamie Field; 26 Julian O'Neill. Subs (all used): 14 Sam Obst; 15 David Wrench; 27 Chris Feather; 11 David Solomona.
Tries: Demetriou (29), Rooney (33), Tadulala (63);
Goals: Rooney 3/6.

WARRIORS: 1 Kris Radlinski (C); 3 Martin Aspinwall; 19 Stephen Wild; 4 David Vaealiki; 23 Liam Colbon; 6 Danny Orr; 7 Dennis Moran; 8 Jerry Seuseu; 9 Terry Newton; 12 Danny Tickle; 11 Gareth Hock; 20 Harrison Hansen; 15 Sean O'Loughlin. Subs (all used): 14 Kevin Brown; 18 Wayne Godwin; 22 David Allen; 27 Bryn Hargreaves.
Tries: Vaealiki (45), Hock (61), Newton (77);
Goals: Tickle 2/4.
Sin bin: Godwin (53) - interference.
On report: Seuseu (41) - late tackle on O'Neill.
Rugby Leaguer & League Express Men of the Match: *Wildcats:* Jamie Rooney; *Warriors:* Sean O'Loughlin.
Penalty count: 11-10; **Half-time:** 12-2; **Referee:** Richard Silverwood (Dewsbury); **Attendance:** 6,196.

Sunday 20th February 2005

HUDDERSFIELD GIANTS 28 HULL FC 36

GIANTS: 1 Paul Reilly; 2 Hefin O'Hare; 3 James Evans; 13 Stanley Gene; 5 Stuart Donlan; 6 Chris Thorman; 15 Sean Penkywicz; 21 Paul Jackson; 9 Brad Drew; 10 Jim Gannon; 11 Chris Nero; 14 Stuart Jones; 12 Ben Roarty (C). Subs (all used): 7 Paul March; 20 Paul White; 18 Eorl Crabtree; 17 Paul Smith.
Tries: Crabtree (34), White (47, 77), Thorman (59), Donlan (72); **Goals:** Thorman 4/5.
HULL: 14 Motu Tony; 2 Nathan Blacklock; 16 Tom Saxton; 3 Kirk Yeaman; 5 Gareth Raynor; 6 Richard Horne; 7 Peter Lupton; 8 Ewan Dowes; 9 Richard Swain (C); 18 Liam Higgins; 11 Shayne McMenemy; 17 Chris Chester; 13 Paul Cooke. Subs (all used): 15 Jamie Thackray; 1 Shaun Briscoe; 24 Graeme Horne; 31 Danny Hill.
Tries: Blacklock (5, 49, 53), Saxton (9), Chester (13), Yeaman (24); **Goals:** Cooke 6/7.
Sin bin: Swain (71) - dissent.
Rugby Leaguer & League Express Men of the Match: *Giants:* Chris Nero; *Hull:* Nathan Blacklock.
Penalty count: 8-5; **Half-time:** 6-22; **Referee:** Ronnie Laughton (Barnsley); **Attendance:** 6,610.

WARRINGTON WOLVES 26 LEIGH CENTURIONS 22

WOLVES: 1 Brent Grose; 2 Henry Fa'afili; 3 Martin Gleeson; 4 Toa Kohe-Love; 5 Dean Gaskell; 6 Lee Briers (C); 7 Nathan Wood; 8 Chris Leikvoll; 14 Mark Gleeson; 10 Mark Hilton; 11 Logan Swann; 12 Mike Wainwright; 9 Jon Clarke. Subs (all used): 15 Ben Westwood; 17 Danny Lima; 13 Paul Noone; 20 Warren Stevens.
Tries: Clarke (9, 70), Martin Gleeson (36), N Wood (42), Briers (73); **Goals:** Briers 3/5.
CENTURIONS: 1 Ben Cooper; 24 John Wilshere; 8 Rob Jackson; 9 Phil Jones; 19 Rob Smyth; 10 Jason Kent; 2 John Duffy; 20 Craig Stapleton; 3 Jason Ferris (C); 21 Matt Sturm; 11 James King; 16 Steve McCurrie; 13 Mark Leafa. Subs (all used): 18 Paul Rowley; 7 Kevin Henderson (D); 25 Richard Moore; 23 Ian Knott.
Tries: Kent (23), Smyth (26), Ferris (77);
Goals: P Jones 5/6.
Rugby Leaguer & League Express Men of the Match: *Wolves:* Lee Briers; *Centurions:* Mark Leafa.
Penalty count: 6-7; **Half-time:** 10-14;
Referee: Steve Ganson (St Helens); **Attendance:** 11,412.

WIDNES VIKINGS 31 BRADFORD BULLS 22

VIKINGS: 1 Gary Connolly; 5 Andrew Emelio; 3 Aaron Moule; 21 Jon Whittle; 19 Steve Rowlands; 6 Owen Craigie; 14 Gary Hulse; 8 Terry O'Connor (D); 9 Shane Millard (C); 15 Matt Whitaker; 11 Mick Cassidy; 12 John Stankevitch; 16 Daniel Frame. Subs (all used): 13 Simon Finnigan; 18 Sala Fa'alogo; 20 Mark Smith; 17 David Mills.
Tries: Craigie (7, 64), Moule (23), Whitaker (26), Whittle (59), Millard (78); **Goals:** Rowlands 3/7;
Field goal: Craigie.
Sin bin: Emelio (48) - professional foul.
BULLS: 17 Stuart Reardon; 22 Karl Pryce; 3 Leon Pryce; 16 Paul Johnson; 32 Andy Smith; 18 Iestyn Harris; 7 Paul Deacon; 8 Joe Vagana; 1 Robbie Paul; 29 Stuart Fielden; 10 Brad Meyers; 12 Jamie Peacock (C); 11 Lee Radford. Subs (all used): 14 Andy Lynch; 19 Jamie Langley; 27 Rob Parker; 15 Karl Pratt.
Tries: L Pryce (17), Smith (48), I Harris (51), K Pryce (68); **Goals:** Deacon 3/4.
Rugby Leaguer & League Express Men of the Match: *Vikings:* Owen Craigie; *Bulls:* Karl Pryce.
Penalty count: 7-10; **Half-time:** 16-6;
Referee: Ian Smith (Oldham); **Attendance:** 7,230.

ROUND 3

Friday 25th February 2005

ST HELENS 34 HUDDERSFIELD GIANTS 24

SAINTS: 1 Paul Wellens; 2 Ade Gardner; 3 Jamie Lyon; 4 Willie Talau; 5 Darren Albert; 13 Paul Sculthorpe (C); 14 Mick Higham; 8 Nick Fozzard; 9 Keiron Cunningham; 17 Paul Anderson; 19 James Graham; 11 Lee Gilmour; 12 Jon Wilkin. Subs: 10 Mark Edmondson; 15 Mike Bennett; 20 Ian Hardman (not used); 21 James Roby.
Tries: Gilmour (1, 12), Anderson (8), Talau (33), Albert (58, 63), Wellens (80); **Goals:** Sculthorpe 2/2, Wellens 1/5.
On report: Brawl (73).
GIANTS: 5 Stuart Donlan; 2 Hefin O'Hare; 3 James Evans; 13 Stanley Gene; 20 Paul White; 6 Chris Thorman; 7 Paul March; 21 Paul Jackson; 9 Brad Drew; 10 Jim Gannon; 11 Chris Nero; 14 Stuart Jones; 12 Ben Roarty (C). Subs (all used): 15 Sean Penkywicz; 17 Paul Smith; 18 Eorl Crabtree; 19 Jon Grayshon.
Tries: Evans (16, 75), Crabtree (48), Grayshon (51);
Goals: Thorman 4/5.
On report: Brawl (73).

Super League X - Round by Round

Rugby Leaguer & League Express Men of the Match:
Saints: Paul Wellens; *Giants:* Chris Thorman.
Penalty count: 8-8; **Half-time:** 20-6; **Referee:** Karl Kirkpatrick (Warrington); **Attendance:** 9,507.

WIGAN WARRIORS 27 BRADFORD BULLS 28

WARRIORS: 1 Kris Radlinski (C); 3 Martin Aspinwall; 19 Stephen Wild; 4 David Vaealiki; 2 Brett Dallas; 6 Danny Orr; 7 Dennis Moran; 16 Danny Sculthorpe; 9 Terry Newton; 10 Jerome Guisset (D); 11 Gareth Hock; 12 Danny Tickle; 15 Sean O'Loughlin. Subs (all used): 14 Kevin Brown; 22 David Allen; 18 Wayne Godwin; 24 Bob Beswick.
Tries: Vaealiki (8, 46), Newton (19), Brown (62);
Goals: Tickle 5/6; **Field goal:** O'Loughlin.
Sin bin: O'Loughlin (26) - dissent.
BULLS: 6 Michael Withers; 17 Stuart Reardon; 16 Paul Johnson; 3 Leon Pryce; 5 Lesley Vainikolo; 18 Iestyn Harris; 7 Paul Deacon; 8 Joe Vagana; 1 Robbie Paul; 29 Stuart Fielden; 12 Jamie Peacock (C); 11 Lee Radford; 19 Jamie Langley. Subs (all used): 15 Karl Pratt; 10 Brad Meyers; 27 Rob Parker; 14 Andy Lynch.
Tries: Langley (27), I Harris (54), Peacock (70), Reardon (75), Withers (80); **Goals:** Deacon 4/5.
Sin bin: Johnson (45) - holding down.
Rugby Leaguer & League Express Men of the Match:
Warriors: Dennis Moran; *Bulls:* Jamie Peacock.
Penalty count: 10-0; **Half-time:** 15-6;
Referee: Steve Ganson (St Helens); **Attendance:** 13,111.

Saturday 26th February 2005

LEIGH CENTURIONS 6 SALFORD CITY REDS 32

CENTURIONS: 1 Ben Cooper; 24 John Wilshere; 9 Phil Jones; 8 Rob Jackson; 19 Rob Smyth; 10 Jason Kent; 2 John Duffy; 20 Craig Stapleton; 3 Jason Ferris (C); 16 Steve McCurrie; 13 Mark Leafa; 12 Oliver Wilkes; 23 Ian Knott. Subs (all used): 22 Neil Turley; 25 Richard Moore; 18 Paul Rowley; 11 James King.
Try: P Jones (46); **Goals:** Turley 1/2.
On report: Moore (43) - alleged use of knees.
CITY REDS: 15 Karl Fitzpatrick; 2 David Hodgson; 3 Stuart Littler; 33 Kevin McGuinness; 5 Anthony Stewart; 1 Cliff Beverley; 7 Luke Robinson; 8 Andy Coley; 9 Malcolm Alker (C); 10 Sean Rutgerson; 12 Ian Sibbit; 20 Tim Jonkers; 13 Chris Charles. Subs (all used): 17 Gareth Haggerty; 24 Andy Johnson; 23 Andrew Brocklehurst; 11 Mark Shipway.
Tries: Hodgson (16), Shipway (30), Fitzpatrick (38), McGuinness (58), Haggerty (67), Sibbit (73);
Goals: Charles 3/4, Robinson 1/2.
Rugby Leaguer & League Express Men of the Match:
Centurions: Oliver Wilkes; *City Reds:* Malcolm Alker.
Penalty count: 6-8; **Half-time:** 0-16; **Referee:** Ronnie Laughton (Barnsley); **Attendance:** 4,180.

Sunday 27th February 2005

LEEDS RHINOS 66 WIDNES VIKINGS 8

RHINOS: 1 Richard Mathers; 2 Mark Calderwood; 3 Chev Walker; 4 Keith Senior; 5 Marcus Bai; 13 Kevin Sinfield (C); 7 Rob Burrow; 8 Ryan Bailey; 14 Andrew Dunemann; 15 Danny Ward; 18 Jamie Jones-Buchanan; 12 Chris McKenna; 20 Gareth Ellis. Subs (all used): 10 Barrie McDermott; 11 Ali Lauitiiti; 16 Willie Poching; 17 Wayne McDonald.
Tries: Calderwood (10, 15, 57, 61), Lauitiiti (30), Ellis (37, 46), Bai (41), McDermott (49), Burrow (52, 63), Poching (78); **Goals:** Sinfield 9/12.
VIKINGS: 1 Gary Connolly; 5 Andrew Emelio; 3 Aaron Moule; 21 Jon Whittle; 19 Steve Rowlands; 6 Owen Craigie; 14 Gary Hulse; 8 Terry O'Connor; 9 Shane Millard (C); 15 Matt Whitaker; 11 Mick Cassidy; 12 John Stankevitch; 10 Julian O'Neill; 13 Simon Finnigan; 18 Sala Fa'alogo.
Try: Emelio (4); **Goals:** Rowlands 2/3.
Rugby Leaguer & League Express Men of the Match:
Rhinos: Rob Burrow; *Vikings:* Terry O'Connor.
Penalty count: 4-8; **Half-time:** 18-8; **Referee:** Richard Silverwood (Dewsbury); **Attendance:** 17,307.

LONDON BRONCOS 72 WAKEFIELD TRINITY WILDCATS 8

BRONCOS: 25 Zebastian Luisi; 23 Lee Greenwood; 24 Tyrone Smith; 1 Paul Sykes; 3 Nick Bradley-Qalilawa; 21 Luke Dorn; 7 Thomas Leuluai; 11 Solomon Haumono; 9 Neil Budworth; 10 Steve Trindall; 13 Rob Purdham; 12 Lee Hopkins; 20 Filimone Lolohea. Subs (all used): 16 Joe Mbu; 17 Mark Tookey; 18 Anthony Armour; 6 Mark McLinden (C).
Tries: Purdham (10), Dorn (17, 69), Hopkins (21, 29), Smith (26, 60), Armour (32), Greenwood (48, 74), McLinden (67), Leuluai (75); **Goals:** Sykes 12/12.
WILDCATS: 21 Mark Field; 25 Andy Kirk; 3 Jason Demetriou (C); 19 Kevin King; 5 Semi Tadulala; 4 Jamie Rooney; 7 Ben Jeffries; 8 Darrell Griffin; 9 David March; 10 Michael Korkidas; 18 Olivier Elima; 12 Jamie Field; 26 Julian O'Neill. Subs (all used): 14 Sam Obst; 15 David Wrench; 16 Steve Snitch; 27 Chris Feather.
Tries: Griffin (65), Jeffries (80); **Goals:** Rooney 0/2.
Rugby Leaguer & League Express Men of the Match:
Broncos: Luke Dorn; *Wildcats:* Michael Korkidas.
Penalty count: 6-12; **Half-time:** 36-0;
Referee: Ian Smith (Oldham); **Attendance:** 2,854.

HULL FC 32 WARRINGTON WOLVES 10

HULL: 1 Shaun Briscoe; 2 Nathan Blacklock; 16 Tom Saxton; 3 Kirk Yeaman; 5 Gareth Raynor; 6 Richard Horne; 14 Motu Tony; 8 Ewan Dowes; 9 Richard Swain (C); 23 Paul McNicholas; 11 Shayne McMenemy; 17 Chris Chester; 13 Paul Cooke. Subs (all used): 7 Peter Lupton; 15 Jamie Thackray; 18 Liam Higgins; 24 Graeme Horne.
Tries: Raynor (6, 40), Briscoe (11), Lupton (67), Thackray (80); **Goals:** Cooke 6/6.
WOLVES: 1 Brent Grose; 2 Henry Fa'afili; 3 Martin Gleeson; 15 Ben Westwood; 5 Dean Gaskell; 6 Lee Briers (C); 7 Nathan Wood; 8 Chris Leikvoll; 9 Jon Clarke; 10 Mark Hilton; 13 Paul Noone; 12 Mike Wainwright; 11 Logan Swann. Subs (all used): 14 Mark Gleeson; 17 Danny Lima; 20 Warren Stevens; 23 Andy Bracek (D).
Tries: Briers (16), Fa'afili (23); **Goals:** Briers 1/2.
Rugby Leaguer & League Express Men of the Match:
Hull: Richard Horne; *Wolves:* Lee Briers.
Penalty count: 6-5; **Half-time:** 20-10;
Referee: Ashley Klein (Keighley); **Attendance:** 10,169.

ROUND 4

Friday 4th March 2005

WARRINGTON WOLVES 16 ST HELENS 18

WOLVES: 1 Brent Grose; 2 Henry Fa'afili; 3 Martin Gleeson; 4 Toa Kohe-Love; 5 Dean Gaskell; 6 Lee Briers (C); 18 Graham Appo; 8 Chris Leikvoll; 9 Jon Clarke; 10 Mark Hilton; 11 Logan Swann; 12 Mike Wainwright; 15 Ben Westwood. Subs (all used): 14 Mark Gleeson; 20 Warren Stevens; 23 Andy Bracek; 17 Danny Lima.
Tries: Fa'afili (14), Appo (71); **Goals:** Briers 4/4.
On report: Kohe-Love (28) - flopping.
SAINTS: 1 Paul Wellens; 20 Ian Hardman; 5 Darren Albert; 4 Willie Talau; 2 Ade Gardner; 3 Jamie Lyon; 14 Mick Higham; 8 Nick Fozzard; 9 Keiron Cunningham (C); 17 Paul Anderson; 11 Lee Gilmour; 15 Mike Bennett; 12 Jon Wilkin. Subs (all used): 17 Mark Edmondson; 21 James Roby; 24 Maurie Fa'asavalu; 19 James Graham.
Tries: Graham (39), Albert (73), Higham (77), Cunningham (80); **Goals:** Wellens 1/4.
Rugby Leaguer & League Express Men of the Match:
Wolves: Mark Gleeson; *Saints:* Mick Higham.
Penalty count: 7-9; **Half-time:** 8-4;
Referee: Ian Smith (Oldham); **Attendance:** 12,098.

Saturday 5th March 2005

SALFORD CITY REDS 12 HULL FC 22

CITY REDS: 15 Karl Fitzpatrick; 2 David Hodgson; 3 Stuart Littler; 33 Kevin McGuinness; 5 Anthony Stewart; 1 Cliff Beverley; 7 Luke Robinson; 18 Stuart Dickens (C); 9 Malcolm Alker; 10 Sean Rutgerson; 12 Ian Sibbit; 11 Mark Shipway; 13 Chris Charles. Subs (all used): 8 Andy Coley; 17 Gareth Haggerty; 23 Andrew Brocklehurst; 24 Andy Johnson.
Tries: Stewart (49), Hodgson (70), Haggerty (77);
Goals: Charles 0/3.
HULL: 1 Shaun Briscoe; 2 Nathan Blacklock; 16 Tom Saxton; 3 Kirk Yeaman; 5 Gareth Raynor; 14 Motu Tony; 6 Richard Horne; 8 Ewan Dowes; 9 Richard Swain (C); 23 Paul McNicholas; 11 Shayne McMenemy; 17 Chris Chester; 13 Paul Cooke. Subs (all used): 7 Peter Lupton; 18 Liam Higgins; 15 Jamie Thackray; 24 Graeme Horne.
Tries: Raynor (9, 79), Yeaman (35), Cooke (55);
Goals: Cooke 3/5.
Rugby Leaguer & League Express Men of the Match:
City Reds: Cliff Beverley; *Hull:* Paul Cooke.
Penalty count: 10-4; **Half-time:** 0-10; **Referee:** Karl Kirkpatrick (Warrington); **Attendance:** 3,568.

Sunday 6th March 2005

BRADFORD BULLS 48 LONDON BRONCOS 22

BULLS: 3 Leon Pryce; 17 Stuart Reardon; 16 Paul Johnson; 22 Karl Pryce; 5 Lesley Vainikolo; 18 Iestyn Harris; 7 Paul Deacon; 8 Joe Vagana; 1 Robbie Paul; 29 Stuart Fielden; 11 Lee Radford; 12 Jamie Peacock (C); 19 Jamie Langley. Subs (all used): 10 Brad Meyers; 15 Karl Pratt; 14 Andy Lynch; 27 Rob Parker.
Tries: Vainikolo (5, 77), Johnson (18), Langley (22), Deacon (32, 62), K Pryce (38), Meyers (52), Paul (58); **Goals:** Deacon 6/9.
Sin bin: L Pryce (73) - holding down.
BRONCOS: 25 Zebastian Luisi; 23 Lee Greenwood; 24 Tyrone Smith; 1 Paul Sykes; 3 Nick Bradley-Qalilawa; 21 Luke Dorn; 7 Thomas Leuluai; 20 Filimone Lolohea; 9 Neil Budworth; 10 Steve Trindall; 13 Rob Purdham; 12 Lee Hopkins; 11 Solomon Haumono. Subs (all used): 8 Francis Stephenson; 17 Mark Tookey; 18 Anthony Armour; 6 Mark McLinden (C).
Tries: Haumono (9), Dorn (13), Smith (45), Sykes (73);
Goals: Sykes 3/4.
Rugby Leaguer & League Express Men of the Match:
Bulls: Iestyn Harris; *Broncos:* Thomas Leuluai.
Penalty count: 6-9; **Half-time:** 26-12; **Referee:** Ronnie Laughton (Barnsley); **Attendance:** 11,282.

HUDDERSFIELD GIANTS 10 LEEDS RHINOS 54

GIANTS: 5 Stuart Donlan; 2 Hefin O'Hare; 3 James Evans; 13 Stanley Gene; 20 Paul White; 6 Chris Thorman (C); 7 Paul March; 8 Mick Slicker; 9 Brad Drew; 11 Chris Nero; 10 Jim Gannon; 17 Paul Smith; 14 Stuart Jones. Subs (all used): 15 Sean Penkywicz; 34 Marcus St Hilaire; 18 Eorl Crabtree; 19 Jon Grayshon.
Tries: O'Hare (27), Gannon (46); **Goals:** Thorman 1/2.
Sin bin: Gannon (52) - holding down.
RHINOS: 1 Richard Mathers; 2 Mark Calderwood; 12 Chris McKenna; 4 Keith Senior; 5 Marcus Bai; 13 Kevin Sinfield (C); 7 Rob Burrow; 8 Ryan Bailey; 14 Andrew

---

Dunemann; 15 Danny Ward; 18 Jamie Jones-Buchanan; 11 Ali Lauitiiti; 20 Gareth Ellis. Subs (all used): 10 Barrie McDermott; 3 Chev Walker; 17 Wayne McDonald; 16 Willie Poching.
Tries: Calderwood (1), Mathers (15, 79), McKenna (22, 48), Walker (38, 53), Burrow (60), Jones-Buchanan (76); **Goals:** Sinfield 9/9.
Rugby Leaguer & League Express Men of the Match:
Giants: Sean Penkywicz; *Rhinos:* Kevin Sinfield.
Penalty count: 6-8; **Half-time:** 4-24;
Referee: Steve Ganson (St Helens); **Attendance:** 10,088.

WIDNES VIKINGS 20 WIGAN WARRIORS 32

VIKINGS: 1 Gary Connolly; 3 Aaron Moule; 21 Jon Whittle; 19 Steve Rowlands; 6 Owen Craigie; 14 Gary Hulse; 8 Terry O'Connor; 9 Shane Millard (C); 10 Julian O'Neill; 11 Mick Cassidy; 13 Simon Finnigan; 16 Daniel Frame. Subs (all used): 15 Matt Whitaker; 18 Sala Fa'alogo; 20 Mark Smith; 12 John Stankevitch.
Tries: Rowlands (7), Finnigan (44), Emelio (53);
Goals: Rowlands 4/6.
WARRIORS: 1 Kris Radlinski (C); 3 Martin Aspinwall; 14 Kevin Brown; 4 David Vaealiki; 2 Brett Dallas; 6 Danny Orr; 7 Dennis Moran; 8 Jerry Seuseu; 9 Terry Newton; 10 Jerome Guisset; 24 Bob Beswick; 12 Danny Tickle; 15 Sean O'Loughlin. Subs (all used): 19 Stephen Wild; 18 Wayne Godwin; 16 Danny Sculthorpe; 29 Joel Tomkins (D).
Tries: Beswick (16), Aspinwall (29), Newton (64), Brown (67, 72); **Goals:** Tickle 6/7.
Rugby Leaguer & League Express Men of the Match:
Vikings: Terry O'Connor; *Warriors:* Danny Tickle.
Penalty count: 8-12; **Half-time:** 10-12; **Referee:** Richard Silverwood (Dewsbury); **Attendance:** 9,004.

WAKEFIELD TRINITY WILDCATS 38 LEIGH CENTURIONS 26

WILDCATS: 1 Colum Halpenny; 25 Andy Kirk; 3 Jason Demetriou (C); 4 Sid Domic; 5 Semi Tadulala; 6 Jamie Rooney; 7 Ben Jeffries; 27 Chris Feather; 9 David March; 10 Michael Korkidas; 11 David Solomona; 12 Jamie Field; 26 Julian O'Neill. Subs (all used): 14 Sam Obst; 15 David Wrench; 16 Steve Snitch; 8 Darrell Griffin.
Tries: Jeffries (5, 73), Domic (22, 24), Obst (37), Demetriou (42), O'Neill (68); **Goals:** Rooney 5/7.
CENTURIONS: 22 Neil Turley; 14 Steve Maden; 24 John Wilshere; 1 Ben Cooper; 19 Rob Smyth; 9 Phil Jones; 2 John Duffy; 4 Darren Fleary (D); 18 Paul Rowley (C); 20 Craig Stapleton; 12 Oliver Wilkes; 13 Mark Leafa; 10 Jason Kent. Subs (all used): 5 Mick Govin; 21 Matt Sturm; 11 James King; 15 Richard Marshall.
Tries: Maden (19), Turley (34), Fleary (50), Govin (71);
Goals: Turley 3/3, P Jones 2/2.
Sin bin: Fleary (58) - late tackle.
On report: Wilkes (67) - alleged spear tackle.
Rugby Leaguer & League Express Men of the Match:
Wildcats: Sid Domic; *Centurions:* Neil Turley.
Penalty count: 5-3; **Half-time:** 24-14;
Referee: Ashley Klein (Keighley); **Attendance:** 4,814.

ROUND 5

Friday 11th March 2005

HUDDERSFIELD GIANTS 34 WIDNES VIKINGS 18

GIANTS: 1 Paul Reilly; 2 Hefin O'Hare; 3 James Evans; 13 Stanley Gene; 34 Marcus St Hilaire; 6 Chris Thorman (C); 7 Paul March; 21 Paul Jackson; 9 Brad Drew; 18 Eorl Crabtree; 11 Chris Nero; 17 Paul Smith; 14 Stuart Jones. Subs (all used): 8 Mick Slicker; 16 Iain Morrison; 20 Paul White; 19 Jon Grayshon.
Tries: Crabtree (11), White (20, 32), Reilly (38), St Hilaire (40, 79); **Goals:** Thorman 5/6.
VIKINGS: 1 Gary Connolly; 5 Andrew Emelio; 3 Aaron Moule; 21 Jon Whittle; 19 Steve Rowlands; 6 Owen Craigie; 14 Gary Hulse; 8 Terry O'Connor (C); 20 Mark Smith; 15 Matt Whitaker; 11 Mick Cassidy; 16 Daniel Frame; 13 Simon Finnigan. Subs (all used): 10 Julian O'Neill; 18 Sala Fa'alogo; 17 David Mills; 12 John Stankevitch.
Tries: Finnigan (5, 49), Moule (54, 69);
Goals: Rowlands 1/4.
Rugby Leaguer & League Express Men of the Match:
Giants: Paul Reilly; *Vikings:* Simon Finnigan.
Penalty count: 9-8; **Half-time:** 22-4;
Referee: Ian Smith (Oldham); **Attendance:** 3,383.

LEEDS RHINOS 38 WARRINGTON WOLVES 6

RHINOS: 1 Richard Mathers; 2 Mark Calderwood; 3 Chev Walker; 4 Keith Senior; 5 Marcus Bai; 13 Kevin Sinfield (C); 7 Rob Burrow; 8 Ryan Bailey; 14 Andrew Dunemann; 11 Ali Lauitiiti; 12 Chris McKenna; 20 Gareth Ellis. Subs (all used): 18 Jamie Jones-Buchanan; 10 Barrie McDermott; 17 Wayne McDonald; 21 Liam Botham.
Tries: Calderwood (12), Senior (23, 59, 67), Mathers (44), Ward (65), Bai (79); **Goals:** Sinfield 5/6, Botham 0/1.
WOLVES: 1 Brent Grose; 5 Dean Gaskell; 3 Martin Gleeson; 4 Toa Kohe-Love; 2 Henry Fa'afili; 6 Lee Briers (C); 18 Graham Appo; 17 Danny Lima; 14 Mark Gleeson; 10 Mark Hilton; 12 Mike Wainwright; 15 Ben Westwood; 9 Jon Clarke. Subs (all used): 23 Andy Bracek; 22 Steve Pickersgill (D); 20 Warren Stevens; 26 Nicky Royle (not used).
Try: Martin Gleeson (18); **Goals:** Briers 1/1.
Rugby Leaguer & League Express Men of the Match:
Rhinos: Ali Lauitiiti; *Wolves:* Mark Gleeson.
Penalty count: 4-6; **Half-time:** 12-6;
Referee: Ashley Klein (Keighley); **Attendance:** 15,637.

LEIGH CENTURIONS 6 BRADFORD BULLS 46

CENTURIONS: 1 Ben Cooper; 8 Rob Jackson; 10 Jason Kent; 9 Phil Jones; 14 Steve Maden; 2 John Duffy; 3 Jason Ferris; 20 Craig Stapleton; 18 Paul Rowley; 4 Darren Fleary (C); 12 Oliver Wilkes; 13 Mark Leafa; 23 Ian Knott. Subs (all used): 21 Matt Sturm; 25 Richard Moore; 15 Richard Marshall; 5 Mick Govin.
Try: Knott (54); **Goals:** P Jones 1/1.
BULLS: 3 Leon Pryce; 17 Stuart Reardon; 16 Paul Johnson; 22 Karl Pryce; 5 Lesley Vainikolo; 18 Iestyn Harris; 7 Paul Deacon; 8 Joe Vagana; 1 Robbie Paul; 29 Stuart Fielden; 12 Jamie Peacock (C); 11 Lee Radford; 19 Jamie Langley. Subs (all used): 32 Andy Smith; 10 Brad Meyers; 27 Rob Parker; 14 Andy Lynch.
Tries: I Harris (18, 47), K Pryce (35, 72), Vainikolo (43), Parker (53), L Pryce (74), Deacon (76), Langley (80);
Goals: Deacon 5/9.
Rugby Leaguer & League Express Men of the Match:
Centurions: John Duffy; *Bulls:* Jamie Langley.
Penalty count: 5-9; **Half-time:** 0-10; **Referee:** Karl Kirkpatrick (Warrington); **Attendance:** 4,241.

ST HELENS 46 SALFORD CITY REDS 12

SAINTS: 1 Paul Wellens; 5 Darren Albert; 3 Jamie Lyon; 4 Willie Talau; 2 Ade Gardner; 13 Paul Sculthorpe (C); 7 Sean Long; 17 Paul Anderson; 14 Mick Higham; 8 Nick Fozzard; 11 Lee Gilmour; 27 Vinnie Anderson (D); 9 Keiron Cunningham. Subs (all used): 12 Jon Wilkin; 19 James Graham; 21 James Roby; 15 Mike Bennett.
Tries: Lyon (2, 30), Talau (15), Long (21, 40), Albert (23), Gardner (47), Cunningham (69);
Goals: Sculthorpe 7/8.
CITY REDS: 1 Cliff Beverley; 2 David Hodgson; 3 Stuart Littler; 24 Andy Johnson; 5 Anthony Stewart; 33 Kevin McGuinness; 7 Luke Robinson; 18 Stuart Dickens; 9 Malcolm Alker (C); 10 Sean Rutgerson; 20 Tim Jonkers; 8 Andy Coley; 13 Chris Charles. Subs (all used): 17 Gareth Haggerty; 23 Andrew Brocklehurst; 22 Simon Baldwin; 26 Darren Bamford (D).
Tries: Baldwin (54), Alker (59);
Goals: Charles 1/1, Dickens 1/1.
Rugby Leaguer & League Express Men of the Match:
Saints: Jamie Lyon; *City Reds:* Malcolm Alker.
Penalty count: 5-6; **Half-time:** 36-0; **Referee:** Richard Silverwood (Dewsbury); **Attendance:** 9,971.

Saturday 12th March 2005

LONDON BRONCOS 34 WIGAN WARRIORS 20

BRONCOS: 25 Zebastian Luisi; 2 Jon Wells; 24 Tyrone Smith; 1 Paul Sykes; 3 Nick Bradley-Qalilawa; 21 Luke Dorn; 7 Thomas Leuluai; 8 Francis Stephenson; 9 Neil Budworth; 10 Steve Trindall; 11 Solomon Haumono; 12 Lee Hopkins; 20 Filimone Lolohea. Subs (all used): 6 Mark McLinden (C); 16 Joe Mbu; 17 Mark Tookey; 18 Anthony Armour.
Tries: Tookey (22), Haumono (30), Sykes (53, 71), Hopkins (70); **Goals:** Sykes 7/7.
WARRIORS: 1 Kris Radlinski (C); 2 Brett Dallas; 3 Martin Aspinwall; 4 David Vaealiki; 19 Stephen Wild; 14 Kevin Brown; 7 Dennis Moran; 8 Jerry Seuseu; 9 Terry Newton; 10 Jerome Guisset; 12 Danny Tickle; 24 Bob Beswick; 13 Sean O'Loughlin. Subs (all used): 16 Danny Sculthorpe; 18 Wayne Godwin; 22 David Allen; 29 Joel Tomkins.
Tries: Radlinski (7), Wild (74), Vaealiki (77);
Goals: Tickle 4/4.
Rugby Leaguer & League Express Men of the Match:
Broncos: Paul Sykes; *Warriors:* Brett Dallas.
Penalty count: 9-5; **Half-time:** 14-6;
Referee: Steve Ganson (St Helens); **Attendance:** 5,057.

Sunday 13th March 2005

HULL FC 36 WAKEFIELD TRINITY WILDCATS 33

HULL: 1 Shaun Briscoe; 2 Nathan Blacklock; 4 Michael Eagar; 3 Kirk Yeaman; 5 Gareth Raynor; 24 Graeme Horne; 7 Peter Lupton; 8 Ewan Dowes; 9 Richard Swain (C); 15 Jamie Thackray; 11 Shayne McMenemy; 17 Chris Chester; 13 Paul Cooke. Subs (all used): 14 Motu Tony; 16 Tom Saxton; 18 Liam Higgins; 23 Paul McNicholas.
Tries: Cooke (2), Swain (8), Raynor (13), Briscoe (50), Tony (53), Yeaman (72), Thackray (79); **Goals:** Cooke 4/7.
WILDCATS: 1 Colum Halpenny; 25 Andy Kirk; 3 Jason Demetriou (C); 19 Kevin King; 5 Semi Tadulala; 6 Jamie Rooney; 7 Ben Jeffries; 27 Chris Feather; 9 David March; 10 Michael Korkidas; 11 David Solomona; 15 David Wrench; 12 Jamie Field. Subs (all used): 8 Darrell Griffin; 14 Sam Obst; 16 Steve Snitch; 26 Julian O'Neill.
Tries: King (23), Halpenny (25), Demetriou (35), Jeffries (42), Obst (59), Tadulala (67);
Goals: Rooney 4/6; **Field goal:** Rooney.
Rugby Leaguer & League Express Men of the Match:
Hull: Jamie Thackray; *Wildcats:* Sam Obst.
Penalty count: 10-8; **Half-time:** 16-16; **Referee:** Ronnie Laughton (Barnsley); **Attendance:** 10,805.

ROUND 6

Friday 18th March 2005

BRADFORD BULLS 32 HULL FC 22

BULLS: 3 Leon Pryce; 17 Stuart Reardon; 19 Jamie Langley; 22 Karl Pryce; 5 Lesley Vainikolo; 18 Iestyn Harris; 7 Paul Deacon; 8 Joe Vagana; 1 Robbie Paul; 29 Stuart Fielden; 12 Jamie Peacock (C); 10 Brad Meyers; 11 Lee Radford. Subs (all used): 25 Brett Ferres (D); 15 Karl Pratt; 27 Rob Parker; 14 Andy Lynch.
Tries: I Harris (6), L Pryce (43), Lynch (67), K Pryce (77);
Goals: Deacon 8/10.
HULL: 1 Shaun Briscoe; 2 Nathan Blacklock; 4 Michael Eagar; 3 Kirk Yeaman; 5 Gareth Raynor; 13 Paul Cooke; 6 Richard Horne; 8 Ewan Dowes; 9 Richard Swain (C); 15 Jamie Thackray; 11 Shane McMenemy; 12 Stephen Kearney (D); 17 Chris Chester. Subs (all used): 29 Andy Bailey; 16 Tom Saxton; 18 Liam Higgins; 7 Peter Lupton.
Tries: Blacklock (18, 47), Eagar (22), Raynor (52);
Goals: Cooke 3/5.
Rugby Leaguer & League Express Men of the Match:
Bulls: Stuart Fielden; *Hull:* Nathan Blacklock.
Penalty count: 7-6; **Half-time:** 14-10;
Referee: Ashley Klein (Keighley); **Attendance:** 13,394.

SALFORD CITY REDS 12 LEEDS RHINOS 30

CITY REDS: 26 Darren Bamford; 2 David Hodgson; 3 Stuart Littler; 12 Ian Sibbit; 5 Anthony Stewart; 33 Kevin McGuinness; 7 Luke Robinson; 18 Stuart Dickens; 9 Malcolm Alker (C); 10 Sean Rutgerson; 8 Andy Coley; 22 Simon Baldwin; 20 Tim Jonkers. Subs (all used): 17 Gareth Haggerty; 21 John Clough; 23 Andrew Brocklehurst; 27 Mitchell Stringer (D).
Tries: Baldwin (20), Hodgson (75);
Goals: Dickens 1/1, Robinson 1/1.
RHINOS: 1 Richard Mathers; 2 Mark Calderwood; 3 Chev Walker; 4 Keith Senior; 5 Marcus Bai; 13 Kevin Sinfield (C); 7 Rob Burrow; 8 Ryan Bailey; 14 Andrew Dunemann; 15 Danny Ward; 11 Ali Lauitiiti; 16 Willie Poching; 18 Jamie Jones-Buchanan. Subs (all used): 10 Barrie McDermott; 17 Wayne McDonald; 22 Nick Scruton; 21 Liam Botham.
Tries: Bai (6), Lauitiiti (18), McDermott (34), Senior (54), Burrow (66); **Goals:** Sinfield 5/5.
Rugby Leaguer & League Express Men of the Match:
City Reds: Simon Baldwin; *Rhinos:* Ali Lauitiiti.
Penalty count: 9-6; **Half-time:** 6-18;
Referee: Ian Smith (Oldham); **Attendance:** 5,118.

WIGAN WARRIORS 62 LEIGH CENTURIONS 6

WARRIORS: 1 Kris Radlinski (C); 5 Brian Carney; 19 Stephen Wild; 4 David Vaealiki; 2 Brett Dallas; 14 Kevin Brown; 7 Dennis Moran; 8 Jerry Seuseu; 9 Terry Newton; 10 Jerome Guisset; 20 Harrison Hansen; 12 Danny Tickle; 15 Sean O'Loughlin. Subs (all used): 3 Martin Aspinwall; 16 Danny Sculthorpe; 18 Wayne Godwin; 24 Bob Beswick.
Tries: Tickle (7), Carney (21), Dallas (26, 55), Godwin (32), Radlinski (39, 43, 76), Moran (64), Vaealiki (73), Brown (80); **Goals:** Tickle 9/11.
CENTURIONS: 24 John Wilshere; 14 Steve Maden; 10 Jason Kent; 1 Ben Cooper; 19 Rob Smyth; 9 Phil Jones; 2 John Duffy; 20 Craig Stapleton; 18 Paul Rowley; 4 Darren Fleary (C); 13 Mark Leafa; 23 Ian Knott; 12 Oliver Wilkes. Subs (all used): 21 Matt Sturm; 25 Richard Moore; 5 Mick Govin; 15 Richard Marshall.
Try: Wilkes (50); **Goals:** P Jones 1/2.
Rugby Leaguer & League Express Men of the Match:
Warriors: Danny Tickle; *Centurions:* Oliver Wilkes.
Penalty count: 11-6; **Half-time:** 28-0;
Referee: Julian King (St Helens); **Attendance:** 15,089.

Saturday 19th March 2005

ST HELENS 64 WAKEFIELD TRINITY WILDCATS 16

SAINTS: 1 Paul Wellens; 5 Darren Albert; 3 Jamie Lyon; 4 Willie Talau; 2 Ade Gardner; 21 James Roby; 7 Sean Long; 8 Nick Fozzard; 9 Keiron Cunningham; 17 Paul Anderson; 11 Lee Gilmour; 27 Vinnie Anderson; 13 Paul Sculthorpe (C). Subs (all used): 10 Mark Edmondson; 15 Mike Bennett; 16 Keith Mason; 19 James Graham.
Tries: Talau (4, 24), Gardner (22), Roby (28, 55), Albert (43, 51), Edmondson (47), Cunningham (61, 80), V Anderson (73); **Goals:** Sculthorpe 4/4; Lyon 6/8.
WILDCATS: 1 Colum Halpenny; 25 Andy Kirk; 3 Jason Demetriou (C); 19 Kevin King; 5 Semi Tadulala; 6 Jamie Rooney; 14 Sam Obst; 8 Darrell Griffin; 9 David March; 16 Steve Snitch; 11 David Solomona; 12 Jamie Field; 26 Julian O'Neill. Subs (all used): 10 Michael Korkidas; 15 David Wrench; 21 Mark Field; 27 Chris Feather.
Tries: Snitch (10), Kirk (37), Halpenny (65);
Goals: Rooney 2/3.
Rugby Leaguer & League Express Men of the Match:
Saints: Keiron Cunningham; *Wildcats:* Jamie Rooney.
Penalty count: 8-6; **Half-time:** 24-12; **Referee:** Karl Kirkpatrick (Warrington); **Attendance:** 9,321.

Sunday 20th March 2005

LONDON BRONCOS 66 WIDNES VIKINGS 8

BRONCOS: 25 Zebastian Luisi; 3 Nick Bradley-Qalilawa; 24 Tyrone Smith; 1 Paul Sykes; 5 John Kirkpatrick; 21 Luke Dorn; 7 Thomas Leuluai; 8 Francis Stephenson; 6 Mark McLinden (C); 10 Steve Trindall; 11 Solomon Haumono; 12 Lee Hopkins; 16 Joe Mbu. Subs (all used): 17 Mark Tookey; 18 Anthony Armour; 19 David Highton; 2 Jon Wells.
Tries: Bradley-Qalilawa (7, 14), Luisi (20), Kirkpatrick (29, 59), Haumono (35), Dorn (38, 64), Smith (40), Tookey (43), Wells (47), Trindall (62); **Goals:** Sykes 9/12.
VIKINGS: 24 Tim Holmes; 5 Andrew Emelio; 3 Aaron Moule; 21 Jon Whittle; 19 Steve Rowlands; 13 Simon Finnigan; 14 Gary Hulse; 8 Terry O'Connor (C); 20 Mark Smith; 10 Julian O'Neill; 11 Mick Cassidy; 12 John Stankevitch; 16 Daniel Frame. Subs (all used): 15 Matt Whitaker; 17 David Mills; 18 Sala Fa'alogo; 27 Paul Crook (D).
Tries: Moule (52, 70); **Goals:** Rowlands 0/2.
Rugby Leaguer & League Express Men of the Match:
Broncos: Mark Tookey; *Vikings:* Aaron Moule.
Penalty count: 9-8; **Half-time:** 36-0; **Referee:** Richard Silverwood (Dewsbury); **Attendance:** 3,365.

WARRINGTON WOLVES 14 HUDDERSFIELD GIANTS 8

WOLVES: 1 Brent Grose; 2 Henry Fa'afili; 3 Martin Gleeson; 4 Toa Kohe-Love; 5 Dean Gaskell; 6 Lee Briers (C); 25 Chris Bridge (D); 15 Ben Westwood; 14 Mark Gleeson; 10 Mark Hilton; 11 Logan Swann; 12 Mike Wainwright; 9 Jon Clarke. Subs (all used): 18 Graham Appo; 23 Andy Bracek; 20 Warren Stevens; 17 Danny Lima.
Tries: Kohe-Love (6), Grose (38); **Goals:** Briers 3/5.
GIANTS: 1 Paul Reilly; 2 Hefin O'Hare; 3 James Evans; 13 Stanley Gene; 34 Marcus St Hilaire; 6 Chris Thorman (C); 7 Paul March; 21 Paul Jackson; 9 Brad Drew; 10 Jim Gannon; 11 Chris Nero; 17 Paul Smith; 14 Stuart Jones. Subs (all used): 8 Mick Slicker; 16 Iain Morrison; 18 Eorl Crabtree; 20 Paul White.
Try: Gene (68); **Goals:** Thorman 2/3.
Sin bin: Drew (74) - dissent.
On report: Gene (25) - leading with the elbow.
Rugby Leaguer & League Express Men of the Match:
Wolves: Ben Westwood; *Giants:* Brad Drew.
Penalty count: 10-9; **Half-time:** 12-4; **Referee:** Ronnie Laughton (Barnsley); **Attendance:** 9,014.

ROUND 7

Thursday 24th March 2005

BRADFORD BULLS 12 LEEDS RHINOS 42

BULLS: 3 Leon Pryce; 17 Stuart Reardon; 19 Jamie Langley; 22 Karl Pryce; 5 Lesley Vainikolo; 18 Iestyn Harris; 7 Paul Deacon; 8 Joe Vagana; 1 Robbie Paul; 29 Stuart Fielden; 12 Jamie Peacock (C); 10 Brad Meyers; 11 Lee Radford. Subs (all used): 25 Brett Ferres; 15 Karl Pratt; 27 Rob Parker; 14 Andy Lynch.
Tries: K Pryce (7), Reardon (42); **Goals:** Deacon 2/3.
On report: L Pryce (59) - late challenge on Ellis.
RHINOS: 1 Richard Mathers; 2 Mark Calderwood; 3 Chev Walker; 4 Keith Senior; 5 Marcus Bai; 13 Kevin Sinfield (C); 7 Rob Burrow; 8 Ryan Bailey; 14 Andrew Dunemann; 15 Danny Ward; 11 Ali Lauitiiti; 12 Chris McKenna; 20 Gareth Ellis. Subs (all used): 10 Barrie McDermott; 16 Willie Poching; 22 Nick Scruton; 21 Liam Botham.
Tries: Walker (21), Ellis (38), Senior (48), Burrow (50, 75), Sinfield (59), Calderwood (72); **Goals:** Sinfield 7/7.
Rugby Leaguer & League Express Men of the Match:
Bulls: Stuart Fielden; *Rhinos:* Kevin Sinfield.
Penalty count: 6-3; **Half-time:** 6-12; **Referee:** Karl Kirkpatrick (Warrington); **Attendance:** 22,843.

Friday 25th March 2005

WIGAN WARRIORS 22 ST HELENS 20

WARRIORS: 1 Kris Radlinski (C); 2 Brett Dallas; 19 Stephen Wild; 4 David Vaealiki; 3 Martin Aspinwall; 14 Kevin Brown; 6 Danny Orr; 8 Jerry Seuseu; 9 Terry Newton; 10 Jerome Guisset; 12 Danny Tickle; 20 Harrison Hansen; 15 Sean O'Loughlin. Subs (all used): 16 Danny Sculthorpe; 24 Bob Beswick; 18 Wayne Godwin; 22 David Allen.
Tries: Tickle (8), Radlinski (10), Dallas (20);
Goals: Tickle 5/6.
SAINTS: 1 Paul Wellens; 2 Ade Gardner; 11 Lee Gilmour; 3 Jamie Lyon; 5 Darren Albert; 21 James Roby; 7 Sean Long; 8 Nick Fozzard; 9 Keiron Cunningham (C); 17 Paul Anderson; 19 James Graham; 27 Vinnie Anderson; 12 Jon Wilkin. Subs (all used): 16 Keith Mason; 26 Scott Moore; 10 Mark Edmondson; 15 Mike Bennett.
Tries: Cunningham (20, 36), Lyon (30), Wilkin (33);
Goals: Lyon 2/4.
Rugby Leaguer & League Express Men of the Match:
Warriors: Terry Newton; *Saints:* Keiron Cunningham.
Penalty count: 5-6; **Half-time:** 18-20;
Referee: Ian Smith (Oldham); **Attendance:** 25,004.

WIDNES VIKINGS 35 LEIGH CENTURIONS 28

VIKINGS: 19 Steve Rowlands; 5 Andrew Emelio; 1 Gary Connolly; 3 Aaron Moule; 4 Adam Hughes; 27 Paul Crook; 14 Gary Hulse; 8 Terry O'Connor (C); 20 Mark Smith; 10 Julian O'Neill; 12 John Stankevitch; 16 Daniel Frame; 13 Simon Finnigan. Subs (all used): 15 Matt Whitaker; 18 Sala Fa'alogo; 17 David Mills; 23 Paul Ballard (D).
Tries: Hughes (4), Moule (13), Emelio (27, 64), Whitaker (34), Hulse (55); **Goals:** Crook 5/6; **Field goal:** Crook.
CENTURIONS: 22 Neil Turley; 14 Steve Maden; 8 Rob Jackson; 1 Ben Cooper; 24 John Wilshere; 10 Jason Kent; 2 John Duffy; 20 Craig Stapleton; 18 Paul Rowley; 4 Darren Fleary (C); 13 Mark Leafa; 23 Ian Knott; 12 Oliver Wilkes. Subs (all used): 21 Matt Sturm; 25 Richard Moore; 5 Mick Govin; 16 Steve McCurrie.
Tries: Knott (9), Wilshere (23, 70), Stapleton (60), Leafa (71); **Goals:** Turley 4/5.
Rugby Leaguer & League Express Men of the Match:
Vikings: Terry O'Connor; *Centurions:* Craig Stapleton.
Penalty count: 10-10; **Half-time:** 22-12;
Referee: Ashley Klein (Keighley); **Attendance:** 6,026.

LONDON BRONCOS 16 HULL FC 20

BRONCOS: 25 Zebastian Luisi; 2 Jon Wells; 24 Tyrone Smith; 1 Paul Sykes; 3 Nick Bradley-Qalilawa; 21 Luke Dorn; 7 Thomas Leuluai; 8 Francis Stephenson; 6 Mark McLinden (C); 10 Steve Trindall; 11 Solomon Haumono; 12 Lee Hopkins; 16 Joe Mbu. Subs (all used): 17 Mark Tookey; 20 Filimone Lolohea; 19 David Highton; 23 Lee Greenwood.
Tries: Bradley-Qalilawa (2), Dorn (7), Mbu (75);
Goals: Sykes 2/3.
HULL: 14 Motu Tony; 26 Richie Barnett; 3 Kirk Yeaman; 4 Michael Eagar; 5 Gareth Raynor; 6 Richard Horne; 21

Danny Brough (D); 8 Ewan Dowes; 9 Richard Swain (C); 15 Jamie Thackray; 11 Shayne McMenemy; 23 Paul McNicholas; 13 Paul Cooke. Subs (all used): 12 Stephen Kearney; 18 Liam Higgins; 20 Garreth Carvell; 30 Richard Whiting.
Tries: Raynor (14), Yeaman (19), Kearney (26);
Goals: Brough 4/5.
Rugby Leaguer & League Express Men of the Match: *Broncos:* Lee Hopkins; *Hull:* Stephen Kearney.
Penalty count: 9-7; **Half-time:** 10-16; **Referee:** Ronnie Laughton (Barnsley); **Attendance:** 4,665.

SALFORD CITY REDS 42 WARRINGTON WOLVES 10

CITY REDS: 2 David Hodgson; 16 Nathan McAvoy; 3 Stuart Littler; 1 Cliff Beverley; 5 Anthony Stewart; 33 Kevin McGuinness; 7 Luke Robinson; 10 Sean Rutgerson; 9 Malcolm Alker (C); 18 Stuart Dickens; 12 Ian Sibbit; 8 Andy Coley; 13 Chris Charles. Subs (all used): 23 Andrew Brocklehurst; 17 Gareth Haggerty; 27 Mitchell Stringer; 22 Simon Baldwin.
Tries: McAvoy (10), Littler (18, 56, 74), Hodgson (35), Robinson (71), Sibbit (80);
Goals: Charles 4/4, Dickens 2/2, Robinson 1/1.
WOLVES: 1 Brent Grose; 5 Dean Gaskell; 4 Toa Kohe-Love; 3 Martin Gleeson; 2 Henry Fa'afili; 6 Lee Briers (C); 25 Chris Bridge; 17 Danny Lima; 14 Mark Gleeson; 15 Ben Westwood; 11 Logan Swann; 9 Jon Clarke; 12 Mike Wainwright. Subs (all used): 18 Graham Appo; 20 Warren Stevens; 16 Paul Wood; 22 Steve Pickersgill.
Tries: Fa'afili (22), Bridge (46); **Goals:** Briers 1/2.
Rugby Leaguer & League Express Men of the Match: *City Reds:* Malcolm Alker; *Wolves:* Brent Grose.
Penalty count: 5-6; **Half-time:** 18-4;
Referee: Julian King (St Helens); **Attendance:** 6,004.

WAKEFIELD TRINITY WILDCATS 20 HUDDERSFIELD GIANTS 42

WILDCATS: 21 Mark Field; 1 Colum Halpenny; 3 Jason Demetriou (C); 19 Kevin King; 5 Semi Tadulala; 6 Jamie Rooney; 7 Ben Jeffries; 8 Darrell Griffin; 9 David March; 10 Michael Korkidas; 11 David Solomona; 16 Steve Snitch; 26 Julian O'Neill. Subs (all used): 12 Jamie Field; 14 Sam Obst; 15 David Wrench; 27 Chris Feather.
Tries: Halpenny (3), Tadulala (22), M Field (43);
Goals: Rooney 4/4.
Dismissal: Solomona (78) - punching.
GIANTS: 5 Stuart Donlan; 2 Hefin O'Hare; 3 James Evans; 13 Stanley Gene; 34 Marcus St Hilaire; 6 Chris Thorman; 7 Paul March; 10 Jim Gannon; 9 Brad Drew; 18 Eorl Crabtree; 11 Chris Nero; 17 Paul Smith; 12 Ben Roarty (C). Subs (all used): 8 Mick Slicker; 19 Jon Grayshon; 20 Paul White; 21 Paul Jackson.
Tries: O'Hare (17), Thorman (19), Grayshon (48), White (60), Roarty (63), Gene (72); **Goals:** Thorman 9/9.
Rugby Leaguer & League Express Men of the Match: *Wildcats:* Ben Jeffries; *Giants:* Chris Thorman.
Penalty count: 7-7; **Half-time:** 14-14; **Referee:** Richard Silverwood (Dewsbury); **Attendance:** 5,288.

ROUND 8

Monday 28th March 2005

ST HELENS 34 BRADFORD BULLS 27

SAINTS: 1 Paul Wellens; 2 Ade Gardner; 11 Lee Gilmour; 5 Darren Albert; 20 Ian Hardman; 21 James Roby; 7 Sean Long; 8 Nick Fozzard; 9 Keiron Cunningham (C); 16 Keith Mason; 27 Vinnie Anderson; 15 Mike Bennett; 12 Jon Wilkin. Subs: 19 James Graham; 17 Paul Anderson; 24 Maurie Fa'asavalu; 26 Scott Moore (not used).
Tries: Wellens (24, 52, 80), Bennett (31), Roby (37), Albert (63); **Goals:** Hardman 5/8.
BULLS: 3 Leon Pryce; 17 Stuart Reardon; 19 Jamie Langley; 22 Karl Pryce; 32 Andy Smith; 18 Iestyn Harris; 7 Paul Deacon; 8 Joe Vagana; 1 Robbie Paul; 29 Stuart Fielden; 12 Jamie Peacock (C); 10 Brad Meyers; 11 Lee Radford. Subs (all used): 15 Karl Pratt; 20 Matt Cook (D); 27 Rob Parker; 14 Andy Lynch.
Tries: Lynch (22, 59), K Pryce (40), Paul (56);
Goals: Deacon 5/6; **Field goal:** Deacon.
Rugby Leaguer & League Express Men of the Match: *Saints:* Paul Wellens; *Bulls:* Stuart Fielden.
Penalty count: 5-5; **Half-time:** 16-6; **Referee:** Richard Silverwood (Dewsbury); **Attendance:** 12,364.

HULL FC 15 WIGAN WARRIORS 21

HULL: 1 Shaun Briscoe; 2 Nathan Blacklock; 30 Richard Whiting; 16 Tom Saxton; 5 Gareth Raynor; 6 Richard Horne (C); 21 Danny Brough; 8 Ewan Dowes; 7 Peter Lupton; 15 Jamie Thackray; 17 Chris Chester; 12 Stephen Kearney; 13 Paul Cooke. Subs (all used): 3 Kirk Yeaman; 11 Shayne McMenemy; 18 Liam Higgins; 20 Garreth Carvell.
Tries: Chester (2), Kearney (13); **Goals:** Brough 3/3;
Field goal: Whiting.
WARRIORS: 1 Kris Radlinski (C); 2 Brett Dallas; 4 David Vaealiki; 19 Stephen Wild; 3 Martin Aspinwall; 21 Chris Melling; 18 Wayne Godwin; 8 Jerry Seuseu; 9 Terry Newton; 10 Jerome Guisset; 20 Harrison Hansen; 12 Danny Tickle; 24 Bob Beswick. Subs (all used): 22 David Allen; 23 Liam Colbon; 25 James Coyle (D); 26 Paul Prescott.
Tries: Colbon (52), Hansen (70), Dallas (74);
Goals: Tickle 4/4; **Field goal:** Tickle.
Rugby Leaguer & League Express Men of the Match: *Hull:* Danny Brough; *Warriors:* Kris Radlinski.
Penalty count: 7-12; **Half-time:** 14-0;
Referee: Ashley Klein (Keighley); **Attendance:** 14,172.

LEIGH CENTURIONS 24 LONDON BRONCOS 22

CENTURIONS: 22 Neil Turley; 24 John Wilshere; 8 Rob Jackson; 1 Ben Cooper; 14 Steve Maden; 10 Jason Kent; 2 John Duffy (C); 21 Matt Sturm; 5 Mick Govin; 25 Richard Moore; 20 Craig Stapleton; 12 Oliver Wilkes; 13 Mark Leafa. Subs (all used): 29 James Taylor (D); 19 Rob Smyth; 15 Richard Marshall; 11 James King.
Tries: Turley (33), John Duffy (53), Wilshere (57), Jackson (72); **Goals:** Turley 4/5.
BRONCOS: 2 Jon Wells; 5 John Kirkpatrick; 24 Tyrone Smith; 1 Paul Sykes; 3 Nick Bradley-Qalilawa; 21 Luke Dorn; 7 Thomas Leuluai; 20 Filimone Lolohea; 6 Mark McLinden (C); 10 Steve Trindall; 11 Solomon Haumono; 12 Lee Hopkins; 16 Joe Mbu. Subs (all used): 8 Francis Stephenson; 19 David Highton; 14 Danny Williams (D); 18 Anthony Armour.
Tries: Wells (16), Sykes (27), McLinden (28), Bradley-Qalilawa (64); **Goals:** Sykes 3/4.
Sin bin: McLinden (71) - professional foul.
Rugby Leaguer & League Express Men of the Match: *Centurions:* John Duffy; *Broncos:* Paul Sykes.
Penalty count: 8-10; **Half-time:** 8-16;
Referee: Steve Ganson (St Helens); **Attendance:** 3,201.

HUDDERSFIELD GIANTS 26 SALFORD CITY REDS 12

GIANTS: 1 Paul Reilly; 2 Hefin O'Hare; 3 James Evans; 4 Michael De Vere (D); 34 Marcus St Hilaire; 6 Chris Thorman; 7 Paul March; 21 Paul Jackson; 9 Brad Drew; 10 Jim Gannon; 11 Chris Nero; 17 Paul Smith; 12 Ben Roarty (C). Subs (all used): 8 Mick Slicker; 19 Jon Grayshon; 13 Stanley Gene; 18 Eorl Crabtree.
Tries: St Hilaire (5, 40), Smith (20), Gene (58);
Goals: De Vere 5/5.
CITY REDS: 2 David Hodgson; 16 Nathan McAvoy; 3 Stuart Littler; 1 Cliff Beverley; 5 Anthony Stewart; 33 Kevin McGuinness; 7 Luke Robinson; 27 Mitchell Stringer; 9 Malcolm Alker (C); 8 Andy Coley; 23 Andrew Brocklehurst; 22 Simon Baldwin; 13 Chris Charles. Subs (all used): 18 Stuart Dickens; 17 Gareth Haggerty; 20 Tim Jonkers; 24 Andy Johnson.
Tries: McGuinness (38), Beverley (54); **Goals:** Charles 2/2.
Rugby Leaguer & League Express Men of the Match: *Giants:* Stanley Gene; *City Reds:* Malcolm Alker.
Penalty count: 8-12; **Half-time:** 20-6; **Referee:** Karl Kirkpatrick (Warrington); **Attendance:** 4,760.

LEEDS RHINOS 28 WAKEFIELD TRINITY WILDCATS 44

RHINOS: 1 Richard Mathers; 2 Mark Calderwood; 3 Chev Walker; 4 Keith Senior; 5 Marcus Bai; 13 Kevin Sinfield (C); 7 Rob Burrow; 8 Ryan Bailey; 16 Willie Poching; 17 Wayne McDonald; 21 Liam Botham; 12 Chris McKenna; 20 Gareth Ellis. Subs (all used): 10 Barrie McDermott; 6 Danny McGuire; 22 Nick Scruton; 23 Lee Smith (D).
Tries: Burrow (7, 79), Ellis (50), Botham (65), Senior (69); **Goals:** Sinfield 4/5.
WILDCATS: 21 Mark Field; 1 Colum Halpenny; 3 Jason Demetriou (C); 24 Sylvain Houles (D2); 5 Semi Tadulala; 6 Jamie Rooney; 7 Ben Jeffries; 8 Darrell Griffin; 9 David March; 10 Michael Korkidas; 11 David Solomona; 18 Olivier Elima; 22 Mark Applegarth. Subs (all used): 16 Steve Snitch; 27 Chris Feather; 15 David Wrench; 25 Andy Kirk.
Tries: Snitch (15), Demetriou (22, 72), Halpenny (24), March (38, 44), Tadulala (53), Griffin (60);
Goals: Rooney 6/8.
Rugby Leaguer & League Express Men of the Match: *Rhinos:* Rob Burrow; *Wildcats:* Mark Field.
Penalty count: 5-5; **Half-time:** 6-22;
Referee: Ian Smith (Oldham); **Attendance:** 18,257.

Tuesday 29th March 2005

WARRINGTON WOLVES 44 WIDNES VIKINGS 12

WOLVES: 1 Brent Grose; 2 Henry Fa'afili; 3 Martin Gleeson; 4 Toa Kohe-Love; 5 Dean Gaskell; 6 Lee Briers (C); 25 Chris Bridge; 10 Mark Hilton; 14 Mark Gleeson; 15 Ben Westwood; 16 Paul Wood; 12 Mike Wainwright; 9 Jon Clarke. Subs (all used): 18 Graham Appo; 22 Steve Pickersgill; 20 Warren Stevens; 17 Danny Lima.
Tries: Clarke (8, 53, 59), Wainwright (19), Westwood (30), Martin Gleeson (39), Briers (65), Fa'afili (72, 77);
Goals: Briers 2/7, Bridge 2/3.
VIKINGS: 19 Steve Rowlands; 5 Andrew Emelio; 3 Aaron Moule; 21 Jon Whittle; 23 Paul Ballard; 7 Stephen Myler; 14 Gary Hulse; 8 Terry O'Connor (C); 20 Mark Smith; 17 David Mills; 11 Mick Cassidy; 12 John Stankevitch; 13 Simon Finnigan. Subs (all used): 27 Paul Crook; 10 Julian O'Neill; 15 Matt Whitaker; 16 Daniel Frame.
Tries: Moule (15), Whitaker (43); **Goals:** Myler 2/3.
Rugby Leaguer & League Express Men of the Match: *Wolves:* Jon Clarke; *Vikings:* Mick Cassidy.
Penalty count: 6-9; **Half-time:** 18-8; **Referee:** Ronnie Laughton (Barnsley); **Attendance:** 10,061.

ROUND 9

Friday 8th April 2005

HUDDERSFIELD GIANTS 24 WIGAN WARRIORS 16

GIANTS: 1 Paul Reilly; 2 Hefin O'Hare; 3 James Evans; 4 Michael De Vere; 34 Marcus St Hilaire; 13 Stanley Gene; 7 Paul March; 21 Paul Jackson; 9 Brad Drew; 10 Jim Gannon; 11 Chris Nero; 17 Paul Smith; 12 Ben Roarty (C). Subs (all used): 8 Mick Slicker; 18 Eorl Crabtree; 19 Jon Grayshon; 20 Paul White.
Tries: Reilly (15, 39, 61), Drew (52); **Goals:** De Vere 4/4.
WARRIORS: 1 Kris Radlinski (C); 3 Martin Aspinwall; 19 Stephen Wild; 4 David Vaealiki; 2 Brett Dallas; 14 Kevin Brown; 6 Danny Orr; 8 Jerry Seuseu; 18 Wayne Godwin; 10 Jerome Guisset; 12 Danny Tickle; 20 Harrison Hansen; 24 Bob Beswick. Subs (all used): 27 Bryn Hargreaves; 22 David Allen; 23 Liam Colbon; 21 Chris Melling.
Tries: Hansen (67), Guisset (76, 78); **Goals:** Melling 2/3.
Rugby Leaguer & League Express Men of the Match: *Giants:* Paul Reilly; *Warriors:* Jerome Guisset.
Penalty count: 6-6; **Half-time:** 12-0;
Referee: Ashley Klein (Keighley); **Attendance:** 5,288.

SALFORD CITY REDS 16 WAKEFIELD TRINITY WILDCATS 14

CITY REDS: 2 David Hodgson; 4 Junior Langi; 3 Stuart Littler; 33 Kevin McGuinness; 5 Anthony Stewart; 1 Cliff Beverley; 7 Luke Robinson; 27 Mitchell Stringer; 9 Malcolm Alker (C); 10 Sean Rutgerson; 8 Andy Coley; 12 Ian Sibbit; 13 Chris Charles. Subs (all used): 17 Gareth Haggerty; 18 Stuart Dickens; 11 Mark Shipway; 22 Simon Baldwin.
Tries: Robinson (2, 28), Hodgson (10);
Goals: Charles 2/4.
WILDCATS: 21 Mark Field; 25 Andy Kirk; 3 Jason Demetriou (C); 24 Sylvain Houles; 5 Semi Tadulala; 6 Jamie Rooney; 7 Ben Jeffries; 27 Chris Feather; 9 David March; 10 Michael Korkidas; 18 Olivier Elima; 19 Kevin King; 22 Mark Applegarth. Subs (all used): 12 Jamie Field; 14 Sam Obst; 15 David Wrench; 26 Julian O'Neill.
Tries: Elima (14), O'Neill (58); **Goals:** Rooney 3/3.
Rugby Leaguer & League Express Men of the Match: *City Reds:* Mark Shipway; *Wildcats:* Oliver Elima.
Penalty count: 7-12; **Half-time:** 16-8;
Referee: Steve Ganson (St Helens); **Attendance:** 3,378.

ST HELENS 60 LEIGH CENTURIONS 16

SAINTS: 1 Paul Wellens; 20 Ian Hardman; 6 Jason Hooper; 5 Darren Albert; 2 Ade Gardner; 3 Jamie Lyon; 7 Sean Long (C); 8 Nick Fozzard; 9 Keiron Cunningham; 16 Keith Mason; 27 Vinnie Anderson; 11 Lee Gilmour; 21 James Roby. Subs (all used): 14 Mick Higham; 24 Maurie Fa'asavalu; 19 James Graham; 15 Mike Bennett.
Tries: Lyon (2, 13, 45), Long (5, 25), Wellens (22), Gardner (32, 42), V Anderson (35), Hooper (39, 77);
Goals: Long 5/5, Lyon 3/6.
CENTURIONS: 24 John Wilshere; 14 Steve Maden; 1 Ben Cooper; 8 Rob Jackson; 19 Rob Smyth; 10 Jason Kent; 2 John Duffy; 21 Matt Sturm; 5 Mick Govin; 4 Darren Fleary (C); 20 Craig Stapleton; 13 Mark Leafa; 23 Ian Knott. Subs (all used): 29 James Taylor; 30 Keiron Maddocks (D); 15 Richard Marshall; 11 James King.
Tries: Maden (51), John Duffy (60), Wilshere (65);
Goals: Wilshere 2/2, Smyth 0/1.
Rugby Leaguer & League Express Men of the Match: *Saints:* Jamie Lyon; *Centurions:* John Duffy.
Penalty count: 4-5; **Half-time:** 46-0; **Referee:** Karl Kirkpatrick (Warrington); **Attendance:** 10,444.

Saturday 9th April 2005

LEEDS RHINOS 64 LONDON BRONCOS 6

RHINOS: 1 Richard Mathers; 2 Mark Calderwood; 3 Chev Walker; 4 Keith Senior; 5 Marcus Bai; 13 Kevin Sinfield (C); 7 Rob Burrow; 8 Ryan Bailey; 14 Andrew Dunemann; 15 Danny Ward; 11 Ali Lauitiiti; 16 Willie Poching; 18 Jamie Jones-Buchanan. Subs (all used): 10 Barrie McDermott; 6 Danny McGuire; 21 Liam Botham; 22 Nick Scruton.
Tries: Lauitiiti (4), Poching (23), Senior (26, 64), McGuire (37, 45), Walker (39), Burrow (54), Mathers (60, 66), Bai (62, 68, 79);
Goals: Sinfield 6/9, Botham 0/3, Burrow 0/1.
On report: Ward (17) – high tackle.
BRONCOS: 25 Zebastian Luisi; 3 Nick Bradley-Qalilawa; 1 Paul Sykes; 4 Mark O'Halloran; 2 Jon Wells; 21 Luke Dorn; 7 Thomas Leuluai; 10 Steve Trindall; 6 Mark McLinden (C); 18 Anthony Armour; 11 Solomon Haumono; 12 Lee Hopkins; 20 Filimone Lolohea. Subs (all used): 17 Mark Tookey; 16 Joe Mbu; 19 David Highton; 14 Danny Williams.
Try: Leuluai (29); **Goals:** Sykes 1/1.
Rugby Leaguer & League Express Men of the Match: *Rhinos:* Ali Lauitiiti; *Broncos:* Thomas Leuluai.
Penalty count: 6-5; **Half-time:** 26-6; **Referee:** Richard Silverwood (Dewsbury); **Attendance:** 14,235.

Sunday 10th April 2005

WARRINGTON WOLVES 35 BRADFORD BULLS 32

WOLVES: 1 Brent Grose; 2 Henry Fa'afili; 3 Martin Gleeson; 4 Toa Kohe-Love; 18 Graham Appo; 6 Lee Briers (C); 7 Nathan Wood; 8 Chris Leikvoll; 14 Mark Gleeson; 10 Mark Hilton; 15 Ben Westwood; 12 Mike Wainwright; 9 Jon Clarke. Subs: 13 Paul Noone; 16 Paul Wood; 17 Danny Lima; 22 Steve Pickersgill (not used).
Tries: N Wood (7), Grose (13, 20), Fa'afili (27), Martin Gleeson (46, 69); **Goals:** Briers 5/7; **Field goal:** Briers.
BULLS: 6 Michael Withers; 17 Stuart Reardon; 19 Jamie Langley; 3 Leon Pryce; 5 Lesley Vainikolo; 18 Iestyn Harris; 7 Paul Deacon; 8 Joe Vagana; 1 Robbie Paul; 29 Stuart Fielden; 12 Jamie Peacock (C); 10 Brad Meyers; 11 Lee Radford. Subs (all used): 22 Karl Pryce; 25 Brett Ferres; 14 Andy Lynch; 27 Rob Parker.
Tries: Meyers (10), Vainikolo (50, 52), Langley (62, 79), Withers (71); **Goals:** Deacon 4/6, I Harris 0/1.
Rugby Leaguer & League Express Men of the Match: *Wolves:* Chris Leikvoll; *Bulls:* Iestyn Harris.
Penalty count: 7-4; **Half-time:** 23-4;
Referee: Ian Smith (Oldham); **Attendance:** 10,654.

HULL FC 32 WIDNES VIKINGS 28

HULL: 1 Shaun Briscoe; 2 Nathan Blacklock; 30 Richard Whiting; 3 Kirk Yeaman; 16 Tom Saxton; 6 Richard Horne (C); 21 Danny Brough; 8 Ewan Dowes; 27 Andy Last; 15 Jamie Thackray; 11 Shayne McMenemy; 23 Paul McNicholas; 13 Paul Cooke. Subs (all used): 14 Motu Tony; 18 Liam Higgins; 20 Garreth Carvell; 24 Graeme Horne.
Tries: R Horne (21), Yeaman (30, 40), Whiting (64), Blacklock (71); **Goals:** Brough 6/6.
VIKINGS: 24 Tim Holmes; 30 Richie Barnett (D); 28 Gray Viane (D); 3 Aaron Moule; 5 Andrew Emelio; 6 Owen Craigie; 7 Stephen Myler; 15 Matt Whitaker; 20 Mark Smith; 8 Terry O'Connor (C); 11 Mick Cassidy; 16 Daniel Frame; 13 Simon Finnigan. Subs (all used): 12 John Stankevitch; 14 Gary Hulse; 17 David Mills; 18 Sala Fa'alogo.
Tries: Finnigan (13, 53), Moule (37), Frame (46), Emelio (79); **Goals:** Myler 4/6.
Rugby Leaguer & League Express Men of the Match: *Hull:* Danny Brough; *Vikings:* Aaron Moule.
Penalty count: 9-6; **Half-time:** 20-12;
Referee: Ronnie Laughton (Barnsley); **Attendance:** 9,078.

ROUND 10

Friday 15th April 2005

WIGAN WARRIORS 14 LEEDS RHINOS 38

WARRIORS: 1 Kris Radlinski (C); 3 Martin Aspinwall; 14 Kevin Brown; 4 David Vaealiki; 2 Brett Dallas; 6 Danny Orr; 7 Dennis Moran; 8 Jerry Seuseu; 9 Terry Newton; 10 Jerome Guisset; 20 Harrison Hansen; 12 Danny Tickle; 19 Stephen Wild. Subs (all used): 18 Wayne Godwin; 22 David Allen; 23 Liam Colbon; 27 Bryn Hargreaves.
Tries: Radlinski (7, 22); **Goals:** Tickle 3/3.
Sin bin: Seuseu (12) - fighting.
RHINOS: 1 Richard Mathers; 2 Mark Calderwood; 3 Chev Walker; 4 Keith Senior; 5 Marcus Bai; 13 Kevin Sinfield (C); 7 Rob Burrow; 8 Ryan Bailey; 14 Andrew Dunemann; 10 Barrie McDermott; 11 Ali Lauitiiti; 16 Willie Poching; 18 Jamie Jones-Buchanan. Subs (all used): 6 Danny McGuire; 22 Nick Scruton; 23 Lee Smith; 21 Liam Botham.
Tries: Senior (19, 29), Poching (26), Botham (60), Bai (64), Lauitiiti (72), Calderwood (78);
Goals: Sinfield 4/6, Burrow 1/1.
Sin bin: McDermott (12) - fighting.
Rugby Leaguer & League Express Men of the Match: *Warriors:* Kris Radlinski; *Rhinos:* Rob Burrow.
Penalty count: 4-3; **Half-time:** 12-16; **Referee:** Karl Kirkpatrick (Warrington); **Attendance:** 16,022.

Saturday 16th April 2005

LONDON BRONCOS 20 ST HELENS 30

BRONCOS: 25 Zebastian Luisi; 3 Nick Bradley-Qalilawa; 1 Paul Sykes; 4 Mark O'Halloran; 23 Lee Greenwood; 21 Luke Dorn; 7 Thomas Leuluai; 8 Francis Stephenson; 6 Mark McLinden (C); 17 Mark Tookey; 11 Solomon Haumono; 12 Lee Hopkins; 20 Filimone Lolohea. Subs (all used): 10 Steve Trindall; 13 Rob Purdham; 19 David Highton; 14 Danny Williams.
Tries: Bradley-Qalilawa (29, 32), Leuluai (58), Dorn (72);
Goals: Sykes 2/4.
SAINTS: 1 Paul Wellens; 5 Darren Albert; 6 Jason Hooper; 4 Willie Talau; 21 James Roby; 27 Vinnie Anderson; 14 Mick Higham; 8 Nick Fozzard; 9 Keiron Cunningham (C); 17 Paul Anderson; 11 Lee Gilmour; 15 Mike Bennett; 12 Jon Wilkin. Subs: 10 Mark Edmondson; 16 Keith Mason; 24 Maurie Fa'asavalu; 26 Scott Moore (not used).
Tries: Roby (4), Albert (40), Edmondson (43), V Anderson (63), Bennett (75);
Goals: Hooper 4/5, Wellens 1/1.
Rugby Leaguer & League Express Men of the Match: *Broncos:* Luke Dorn; *Saints:* Jon Wilkin.
Penalty count: 8-9; **Half-time:** 8-14;
Referee: Ian Smith (Oldham); **Attendance:** 5,261.

Sunday 17th April 2005

BRADFORD BULLS 54 HUDDERSFIELD GIANTS 10

BULLS: 6 Michael Withers; 15 Karl Pratt; 17 Stuart Reardon; 3 Leon Pryce; 5 Lesley Vainikolo; 18 Iestyn Harris; 1 Robbie Paul; 12 Jamie Peacock (C); 7 Paul Deacon; 29 Stuart Fielden; 27 Rob Parker; 11 Lee Radford; 19 Jamie Langley. Subs (all used): 22 Karl Pryce; 8 Joe Vagana; 14 Andy Lynch; 10 Brad Meyers.
Tries: Vainikolo (3, 12, 68), Reardon (23, 78), Pratt (26), Paul (41), Langley (44), Radford (51), Fielden (74);
Goals: Deacon 1/3, I Harris 6/7.
GIANTS: 1 Paul Reilly; 20 Paul White; 3 James Evans; 4 Michael De Vere; 34 Marcus St Hilaire; 13 Stanley Gene; 7 Paul March; 21 Paul Jackson; 9 Brad Drew; 10 Jim Gannon; 11 Chris Nero; 17 Paul Smith; 12 Ben Roarty (C). Subs (all used): 14 Stuart Jones; 18 Eorl Crabtree; 19 Jon Grayshon; 6 Chris Thorman.
Tries: De Vere (60), Gene (71); **Goals:** De Vere 1/2.
Rugby Leaguer & League Express Men of the Match: *Bulls:* Iestyn Harris; *Giants:* Chris Nero.
Penalty count: 5-1; **Half-time:** 20-0; **Referee:** Richard Silverwood (Dewsbury); **Attendance:** 13,481.

LEIGH CENTURIONS 22 HULL FC 22

CENTURIONS: 26 Nick Owen (D); 19 Rob Smyth; 8 Rob Jackson; 1 Ben Cooper; 14 Steve Maden; 24 John Wilshere; 28 Jason Duffy (D); 21 Matt Sturm; 18 Paul Rowley; 4 Darren Fleary (C); 13 Mark Leafa; 20 Craig Stapleton; 23 Ian Knott. Subs (all used): 15 Richard Marshall; 11 James King; 29 James Taylor; 16 Steve McCurrie.
Tries: Jackson (34), Maden (38, 50), Smyth (58);
Goals: Owen 3/5.
Sin bin: Leafa (44) - late tackle on R Horne.
On report: Leafa (37) - late tackle on Whiting.
HULL: 1 Shaun Briscoe; 16 Tom Saxton; 4 Michael Eagar; 3 Kirk Yeaman; 2 Nathan Blacklock; 30 Richard Whiting; 6 Richard Horne (C); 8 Ewan Dowes; 21 Danny Brough; 15 Jamie Thackray; 11 Shayne McMenemy; 12 Stephen Kearney; 13 Paul Cooke. Subs (all used): 24 Graeme Horne; 23 Paul McNicholas; 20 Garreth Carvell; 14 Motu Tony.
Tries: Whiting (2), McMenemy (11), Yeaman (24), Blacklock (79); **Goals:** Brough 3/5.
Rugby Leaguer & League Express Men of the Match: *Centurions:* Ian Knott; *Hull:* Ewan Dowes.
Penalty count: 7-8; **Half-time:** 12-18;
Referee: Steve Ganson (St Helens); **Attendance:** 3,427.

WIDNES VIKINGS 6 SALFORD CITY REDS 22

VIKINGS: 1 Gary Connolly; 5 Andrew Emelio; 28 Gray Viane; 3 Aaron Moule; 30 Richie Barnett; 7 Stephen Myler; 14 Gary Hulse; 8 Terry O'Connor; 9 Shane Millard (C); 15 Matt Whitaker; 11 Mick Cassidy; 16 Daniel Frame; 13 Simon Finnigan. Subs (all used): 17 David Mills; 12 John Stankevitch; 18 Sala Fa'alogo; 20 Mark Smith.
Try: O'Connor (68); **Goals:** Myler 1/1.
Sin bin: O'Connor (17) - ungentlemanly conduct.
CITY REDS: 2 David Hodgson; 4 Junior Langi; 3 Stuart Littler; 33 Kevin McGuinness; 5 Anthony Stewart; 1 Cliff Beverley; 7 Luke Robinson; 27 Mitchell Stringer; 9 Malcolm Alker (C); 10 Sean Rutgerson; 8 Andy Coley; 12 Ian Sibbit; 13 Chris Charles. Subs (all used): 17 Gareth Haggerty; 18 Stuart Dickens; 11 Mark Shipway; 21 John Clough.
Tries: Littler (18, 22), Robinson (28, 59);
Goals: Charles 3/5.
Rugby Leaguer & League Express Men of the Match: *Vikings:* David Mills; *City Reds:* Stuart Littler.
Penalty count: 8-4; **Half-time:** 0-14;
Referee: Ashley Klein (Keighley); **Attendance:** 5,878.

WAKEFIELD TRINITY WILDCATS 28 WARRINGTON WOLVES 40

WILDCATS: 21 Mark Field; 24 Sylvain Houles; 3 Jason Demetriou (C); 19 Kevin King; 5 Semi Tadulala; 26 Julian O'Neill; 7 Ben Jeffries; 8 Darrell Griffin; 14 Sam Obst; 10 Michael Korkidas; 18 Olivier Elima; 22 Mark Applegarth; 12 Jamie Field. Subs (all used): 9 David March; 15 David Wrench; 16 Steve Snitch; 25 Andy Kirk.
Tries: King (2), Jeffries (21, 23), Applegarth (72), Elima (78); **Goals:** O'Neill 4/5.
WOLVES: 1 Brent Grose; 2 Henry Fa'afili; 3 Martin Gleeson; 4 Toa Kohe-Love; 18 Graham Appo; 6 Lee Briers (C); 7 Nathan Wood; 8 Chris Leikvoll; 9 Jon Clarke; 10 Mark Hilton; 15 Ben Westwood; 12 Mike Wainwright; 13 Paul Noone. Subs (all used): 25 Chris Bridge; 16 Paul Wood; 17 Danny Lima; 22 Steve Pickersgill.
Tries: Westwood (17, 50), Wainwright (27), N Wood (35), Briers (37, 44), Clarke (61), Fa'afili (66);
Goals: Briers 3/7, Bridge 1/1.
Sin bin: Grose (75) - holding down.
Rugby Leaguer & League Express Men of the Match: *Wildcats:* Ben Jeffries; *Wolves:* Lee Briers.
Penalty count: 10-5; **Half-time:** 16-18;
Referee: Ronnie Laughton (Barnsley); **Attendance:** 5,129.

ROUND 11

Friday 22nd April 2005

BRADFORD BULLS 40 WIGAN WARRIORS 8

BULLS: 6 Michael Withers; 15 Karl Pratt; 17 Stuart Reardon; 3 Leon Pryce; 5 Lesley Vainikolo; 18 Iestyn Harris; 1 Robbie Paul; 12 Jamie Peacock (C); 7 Paul Deacon; 29 Stuart Fielden; 27 Rob Parker; 11 Lee Radford; 19 Jamie Langley. Subs (all used): 22 Karl Pryce; 8 Joe Vagana; 10 Brad Meyers; 14 Andy Lynch.
Tries: Reardon (3), Vainikolo (25), Withers (32), Meyers (54, 74), Fielden (66), Paul (80);
Goals: Deacon 6/7, I Harris 0/1.
WARRIORS: 21 Chris Melling; 23 Liam Colbon; 3 Martin Aspinwall; 4 David Vaealiki; 2 Brett Dallas; 14 Kevin Brown; 7 Dennis Moran; 8 Jerry Seuseu; 9 Terry Newton (C); 10 Jerome Guisset; 20 Harrison Hansen; 19 Stephen Wild; 12 Danny Tickle. Subs (all used): 18 Wayne Godwin; 16 Danny Sculthorpe; 24 Bob Beswick; 17 Wayne McDonald (D).
Tries: Dallas (18, 39); **Goals:** Tickle 0/2.
On report: Guisset (65) - high tackle on K Pryce.
Rugby Leaguer & League Express Men of the Match: *Bulls:* Robbie Paul; *Warriors:* Terry Newton.
Penalty count: 5-5; **Half-time:** 14-8;
Referee: Steve Ganson (St Helens); **Attendance:** 13,527.

SALFORD CITY REDS 42 LEIGH CENTURIONS 6

CITY REDS: 2 David Hodgson; 4 Junior Langi; 3 Stuart Littler; 33 Kevin McGuinness; 5 Anthony Stewart; 1 Cliff Beverley; 7 Luke Robinson; 10 Sean Rutgerson; 9 Malcolm Alker (C); 27 Mitchell Stringer; 12 Ian Sibbit; 8 Andy Coley; 13 Chris Charles. Subs (all used): 11 Mark Shipway; 17 Gareth Haggerty; 20 Tim Jonkers; 22 Simon Baldwin.
Tries: Sibbit (24), Littler (34, 54, 73), Robinson (46, 64), Coley (68), Haggerty (76);
Goals: Charles 2/3, Robinson 3/6.
Sin bin: Littler (79) - fighting.
CENTURIONS: 26 Nick Owen; 19 Rob Smyth; 8 Rob Jackson; 1 Ben Cooper; 14 Steve Maden; 9 Phil Jones; 24 John Wilshere; 4 Darren Fleary (C); 18 Paul Rowley; 21 Matt Sturm; 20 Craig Stapleton; 13 Mark Leafa; 23 Ian Knott. Subs (all used): 31 Warren Stevens (D); 29 James Taylor; 15 Richard Marshall; 16 Steve McCurrie.
Try: Cooper (12); **Goals:** P Jones 0/1, Owen 1/1.
Sin bin: Rowley (79) - fighting.
Rugby Leaguer & League Express Men of the Match: *City Reds:* Luke Robinson; *Centurions:* John Wilshere.
Penalty count: 9-5; **Half-time:** 12-6;
Referee: Ronnie Laughton (Barnsley); **Attendance:** 5,021.

Saturday 23rd April 2005

WIDNES VIKINGS 20 LEEDS RHINOS 42

VIKINGS: 14 Gary Hulse; 28 Gray Viane; 1 Gary Connolly; 3 Aaron Moule; 30 Richie Barnett; 7 Stephen Myler; 29 Jamie Durbin (D); 8 Terry O'Connor; 9 Shane Millard (C); 12 John Stankevitch; 11 Mick Cassidy; 16 Daniel Frame; 13 Simon Finnigan. Subs (all used): 17 David Mills; 31 Paul Alcock; 10 Julian O'Neill; 20 Mark Smith.
Tries: Millard (15, 64), Frame (19), Barnett (68);
Goals: Myler 2/4.
Sin bin: Julian O'Neill (32) - fighting.
RHINOS: 1 Richard Mathers; 5 Marcus Bai; 4 Keith Senior; 3 Chev Walker; 2 Mark Calderwood; 13 Kevin Sinfield (C); 7 Rob Burrow; 8 Ryan Bailey; 14 Andrew Dunemann; 18 Jamie Jones-Buchanan; 11 Ali Lauitiiti; 16 Willie Poching; 20 Gareth Ellis. Subs (all used): 15 Danny Ward; 22 Nick Scruton; 23 Lee Smith; 21 Liam Botham.
Tries: Jones-Buchanan (3, 73), Sinfield (7, 58), Botham (33), Senior (40), Ellis (46); **Goals:** Sinfield 7/7.
Sin bin: Sinfield (18) - interference;
Bailey (32) - fighting.
Rugby Leaguer & League Express Men of the Match: *Vikings:* Mick Cassidy; *Rhinos:* Kevin Sinfield.
Penalty count: 7-4; **Half-time:** 12-24;
Referee: Ian Smith (Oldham); **Attendance:** 6,524.

Sunday 24th April 2005

HUDDERSFIELD GIANTS 22 ST HELENS 36

GIANTS: 1 Paul Reilly; 20 Paul White; 11 Chris Nero; 4 Michael De Vere; 34 Marcus St Hilaire; 13 Stanley Gene; 6 Chris Thorman; 18 Eorl Crabtree; 9 Brad Drew; 10 Jim Gannon; 14 Stuart Jones; 17 Paul Smith; 12 Ben Roarty (C). Subs (all used): 7 Paul March; 8 Mick Slicker; 16 Iain Morrison; 21 Paul Jackson.
Tries: Thorman (22, 35), Smith (48), Nero (77);
Goals: Thorman 3/3, Drew 0/1.
SAINTS: 1 Paul Wellens; 5 Darren Albert; 3 Jamie Lyon; 4 Willie Talau; 20 Ian Hardman; 6 Jason Hooper; 14 Mick Higham; 8 Nick Fozzard; 9 Keiron Cunningham (C); 17 Paul Anderson; 27 Vinnie Anderson; 11 Lee Gilmour; 12 Jon Wilkin. Subs (all used): 7 Sean Long; 15 Mike Bennett; 16 Keith Mason; 24 Maurie Fa'asavalu.
Tries: Albert (8, 42), Wellens (15), Higham (57, 65), V Anderson (68); **Goals:** Lyon 6/6.
Rugby Leaguer & League Express Men of the Match: *Giants:* Chris Thorman; *Saints:* Nick Fozzard.
Penalty count: 6-3; **Half-time:** 12-12; **Referee:** Karl Kirkpatrick (Warrington); **Attendance:** 7,432.

WARRINGTON WOLVES 36 HULL FC 34

WOLVES: 1 Brent Grose; 2 Henry Fa'afili; 3 Martin Gleeson; 4 Toa Kohe-Love; 18 Graham Appo; 6 Lee Briers (C); 7 Nathan Wood; 8 Chris Leikvoll; 9 Jon Clarke; 10 Mark Hilton; 11 Logan Swann; 12 Mike Wainwright; 15 Ben Westwood. Subs (all used): 25 Chris Bridge; 14 Mark Gleeson; 16 Paul Wood; 17 Danny Lima.
Tries: Fa'afili (8, 13, 53), Grose (25), Westwood (32), Appo (43, 77); **Goals:** Briers 0/2, Appo 1/2, Bridge 3/3.
HULL: 1 Shaun Briscoe; 16 Tom Saxton; 4 Michael Eagar; 3 Kirk Yeaman; 2 Nathan Blacklock; 30 Richard Whiting; 6 Richard Horne (C); 8 Ewan Dowes; 21 Danny Brough; 15 Jamie Thackray; 11 Shayne McMenemy; 12 Stephen Kearney; 13 Paul Cooke. Subs (all used): 24 Graeme Horne; 14 Motu Tony; 10 Paul King; 23 Paul McNicholas.
Tries: Briscoe (3), Eagar (37), Whiting (55), Cooke (57), Kearney (60), King (66); **Goals:** Brough 1/1, Cooke 4/6.
Rugby Leaguer & League Express Men of the Match: *Wolves:* Henry Fa'afili; *Hull:* Richard Whiting.
Penalty count: 4-6; **Half-time:** 18-12;
Referee: Ashley Klein (Keighley); **Attendance:** 10,383.

WAKEFIELD TRINITY WILDCATS 29 LONDON BRONCOS 18

WILDCATS: 21 Mark Field; 24 Sylvain Houles; 3 Jason Demetriou (C); 25 Andy Kirk; 5 Semi Tadulala; 6 Jamie Rooney; 7 Ben Jeffries; 8 Darrell Griffin; 14 Sam Obst; 16 Steve Snitch; 22 Mark Applegarth; 15 David Wrench; 26 Julian O'Neill. Subs (all used): 2 Michael Wainwright; 9 David March; 19 Kevin King; 28 Craig Robinson (D).
Tries: Demetriou (6), Tadulala (22), Wrench (28), Jeffries (50), Rooney (55); **Goals:** Rooney 4/7;
Field goal: Rooney.
BRONCOS: 25 Zebastian Luisi; 5 John Kirkpatrick; 3 Nick Bradley-Qalilawa; 4 Mark O'Halloran; 23 Lee Greenwood; 21 Luke Dorn; 1 Paul Sykes; 8 Francis Stephenson; 6 Mark McLinden (C); 17 Mark Tookey; 11 Solomon Haumono; 12 Lee Hopkins; 16 Joe Mbu. Subs (all used): 13 Rob Purdham; 14 Danny Williams; 20 Filimone Lolohea; 10 Steve Trindall.
Tries: O'Halloran (40), Luisi (59), Bradley-Qalilawa (63), Dorn (75); **Goals:** Sykes 1/4.
Sin bin: Luisi (37) - high tackle.
Rugby Leaguer & League Express Men of the Match: *Wildcats:* Darrell Griffin; *Broncos:* Mark O'Halloran.
Penalty count: 13-6; **Half-time:** 14-4; **Referee:** Richard Silverwood (Dewsbury); **Attendance:** 3,258.

ROUND 12

Friday 29th April 2005

LEEDS RHINOS 44 HUDDERSFIELD GIANTS 14

RHINOS: 1 Richard Mathers; 2 Mark Calderwood; 3 Chev Walker; 4 Keith Senior; 5 Marcus Bai; 13 Kevin Sinfield (C); 7 Rob Burrow; 18 Jamie Jones-Buchanan; 14 Andrew Dunemann; 15 Danny Ward; 11 Ali Lauitiiti; 16 Willie Poching; 20 Gareth Ellis. Subs (all used): 10 Barrie McDermott; 12 Chris McKenna; 22 Nick Scruton; 21 Liam Botham.
Tries: Burrow (8, 15, 64), Ellis (32), Botham (39), Poching (55, 61), Lauitiiti (77); **Goals:** Sinfield 6/8.
GIANTS: 34 Marcus St Hilaire; 24 Bolouagi Fagborun; 11 Chris Nero; 4 Michael De Vere; 20 Paul White; 6 Chris Thorman; 7 Paul March; 18 Eorl Crabtree; 9 Brad Drew; 10 Jim Gannon; 14 Stuart Jones; 17 Paul Smith; 12 Ben Roarty (C). Subs (all used): 21 Paul Jackson; 19 Jon Grayshon; 8 Mick Slicker; 22 Ryan Clayton (D).
Tries: Fagborun (19), Drew (50);
Goals: Thorman 2/2, Drew 1/1.
Rugby Leaguer & League Express Men of the Match: *Rhinos:* Rob Burrow; *Giants:* Stuart Jones.
Penalty count: 4-5; **Half-time:** 22-8;
Referee: Steve Ganson (St Helens); **Attendance:** 15,514.

ST HELENS 31 WARRINGTON WOLVES 30

SAINTS: 1 Paul Wellens; 5 Darren Albert; 3 Jamie Lyon; 11 Lee Gilmour; 2 Ade Gardner; 6 Jason Hooper; 7 Sean Long; 8 Nick Fozzard; 9 Keiron Cunningham; 15 Mike Bennett; 27 Vinnie Anderson; 12 Jon Wilkin; 13 Paul Sculthorpe (C). Subs (all used): 17 Paul Anderson; 14 Mick Higham; 16 Keith Mason; 10 Mark Edmondson.
Tries: Long (5), Albert (16), Lyon (34, 38), Higham (55);
Goals: Long 5/6; **Field goal:** Long.
WOLVES: 1 Brent Grose; 2 Henry Fa'afili; 3 Martin Gleeson; 4 Toa Kohe-Love; 18 Graham Appo; 6 Lee Briers (C); 7 Nathan Wood; 8 Chris Leikvoll; 9 Jon Clarke; 10 Mark Hilton; 11 Logan Swann; 12 Mike Wainwright; 15 Ben Westwood. Subs (all used): 14 Mark Gleeson; 17 Danny Lima; 16 Paul Wood; 25 Chris Bridge.
Tries: Kohe-Love (10), N Wood (22, 68), Westwood (25), Fa'afili (52); **Goals:** Appo 5/6.
Rugby Leaguer & League Express Men of the Match: *Saints:* Paul Wellens; *Wolves:* Jon Clarke.
Penalty count: 5-5; **Half-time:** 24-20; **Referee:** Richard Silverwood (Dewsbury); **Attendance:** 12,666.

WIGAN WARRIORS 23 WIDNES VIKINGS 22

WARRIORS: 21 Chris Melling; 5 Brian Carney; 3 Martin Aspinwall; 4 David Vaealiki; 2 Brett Dallas; 14 Kevin Brown; 7 Dennis Moran; 8 Jerry Seuseu; 9 Terry Newton (C); 10 Jerome Guisset; 20 Harrison Hansen; 12 Danny Tickle; 19 Stephen Wild. Subs (all used): 16 Danny Sculthorpe; 17 Wayne McDonald; 18 Wayne Godwin; 24 Bob Beswick.
Tries: Brown (7), Carney (23), Wild (27), Tickle (65);
Goals: Tickle 3/4; **Field goal:** Moran.
VIKINGS: 1 Gary Connolly; 5 Andrew Emelio; 28 Gray Viane; 3 Aaron Moule; 30 Richie Barnett; 6 Owen Craigie; 7 Stephen Myler; 8 Terry O'Connor; 9 Shane Millard (C); 12 John Stankevitch; 11 Mick Cassidy; 16 Daniel Frame; 13 Simon Finnigan. Subs (all used): 14 Gary Hulse; 18 Sala Fa'alogo; 10 Julian O'Neill; 20 Mark Smith.
Tries: Frame (19), Millard (47), Barnett (61), Viane (70);
Goals: Myler 3/4.
Rugby Leaguer & League Express Men of the Match: *Warriors:* Harrison Hansen; *Vikings:* Simon Finnigan.
Penalty count: 3-8; **Half-time:** 18-6; **Referee:** Karl Kirkpatrick (Warrington); **Attendance:** 11,390.

Saturday 30th April 2005

**LEIGH CENTURIONS 40
WAKEFIELD TRINITY WILDCATS 18**

CENTURIONS: 24 John Wilshere; 19 Rob Smyth; 8 Rob Jackson; 9 Phil Jones; 14 Steve Maden; 10 Jason Kent; 2 John Duffy; 4 Darren Fleary (C); 18 Paul Rowley; 31 Warren Stevens; 20 Craig Stapleton; 13 Mark Leafa; 23 Ian Knott. Subs (all used): 21 Matt Sturm; 15 Richard Marshall; 32 Robbie Mears (D); 1 Ben Cooper.
Tries: Rowley (15), P Jones (33, 66, 72), Maden (56), Cooper (75), Smyth (79); **Goals:** P Jones 6/8.
On report: Marshall and Kent (62) - high tackle.
WILDCATS: 21 Mark Field; 2 Michael Wainwright; 3 Jason Demetriou (C); 4 Sid Domic; 5 Semi Tadulala; 6 Jamie Rooney; 7 Ben Jeffries; 8 Darrell Griffin; 14 Sam Obst; 18 Olivier Elima; 15 David Wrench; 22 Mark Applegarth; 26 Julian O'Neill. Subs (all used): 9 David March; 10 Michael Korkidas; 12 Jamie Field; 24 Sylvain Houles.
Tries: Rooney (20), Domic (43), Applegarth (51);
Goals: Rooney 3/4.
Sin bin: Wainwright (30) - holding down.
Rugby Leaguer & League Express Men of the Match: *Centurions:* Phil Jones; *Wildcats:* David Wrench.
Penalty count: 6-5; **Half-time:** 12-8;
Referee: Ashley Klein (Keighley); **Attendance:** 3,213.

Sunday 1st May 2005

LONDON BRONCOS 26 BRADFORD BULLS 41

BRONCOS: 1 Paul Sykes; 2 Jon Wells; 6 Mark McLinden (C); 4 Mark O'Halloran; 3 Nick Bradley-Qalilawa; 21 Luke Dorn; 7 Thomas Leuluai; 10 Steve Trindall; 19 David Highton; 20 Filimone Lolohea; 12 Lee Hopkins; 13 Rob Purdham; 11 Solomon Haumono. Subs (all used): 8 Francis Stephenson; 14 Danny Williams; 17 Mark Tookey; 24 Tyrone Smith.
Tries: Sykes (8), Hopkins (30), Wells (39), Smith (48), Bradley-Qalilawa (79); **Goals:** Sykes 3/6.
BULLS: 3 Leon Pryce; 15 Karl Pratt; 17 Stuart Reardon; 19 Jamie Langley; 5 Lesley Vainikolo; 18 Iestyn Harris; 1 Robbie Paul; 12 Jamie Peacock (C); 7 Paul Deacon; 29 Stuart Fielden; 10 Brad Meyers; 27 Rob Parker; 11 Lee Radford. Subs (all used): 8 Joe Vagana; 14 Andy Lynch; 22 Karl Pryce; 25 Brett Ferres.
Tries: I Harris (41), Reardon (52), Fielden (59), Peacock (65), Langley (68), L Pryce (74), K Pryce (76);
Goals: Deacon 6/7; **Field goal:** Deacon.
Rugby Leaguer & League Express Men of the Match: *Broncos:* Lee Hopkins; *Bulls:* Stuart Fielden.
Penalty count: 8-11; **Half-time:** 18-0;
Referee: Ronnie Laughton (Barnsley); **Attendance:** 3,879.

HULL FC 20 SALFORD CITY REDS 6

HULL: 1 Shaun Briscoe; 2 Nathan Blacklock; 3 Kirk Yeaman; 4 Michael Eagar; 16 Tom Saxton; 30 Richard Whiting; 6 Richard Horne (C); 8 Ewan Dowes; 14 Motu Tony; 10 Paul King; 11 Shayne McMenemy; 12 Stephen Kearney; 13 Paul Cooke. Subs (all used): 15 Jamie Thackray; 17 Chris Chester; 20 Garreth Carvell; 21 Danny Brough.
Tries: Briscoe (29), Yeaman (37), Cooke (46);
Goals: Cooke 2/2, Brough 2/3.
CITY REDS: 2 David Hodgson; 4 Junior Langi; 3 Stuart Littler; 16 Nathan McAvoy; 5 Anthony Stewart; 1 Cliff Beverley; 7 Luke Robinson; 27 Mitchell Stringer; 9 Malcolm Alker (C); 10 Sean Rutgerson; 8 Andy Coley; 12 Ian Sibbit; 13 Chris Charles. Subs: 11 Mark Shipway; 17 Gareth Haggerty; 18 Stuart Dickens; 26 Darren Bamford (not used).
Try: Beverley (7); **Goals:** Charles 1/1.
Rugby Leaguer & League Express Men of the Match: *Hull:* Shayne McMenemy; *City Reds:* Malcolm Alker.
Penalty count: 9-7; **Half-time:** 12-6;
Referee: Ian Smith (Oldham); **Attendance:** 8,929.

ROUND 13

Friday 13th May 2005

HULL FC 44 ST HELENS 6

HULL: 1 Shaun Briscoe; 2 Nathan Blacklock; 16 Tom Saxton; 3 Kirk Yeaman; 5 Gareth Raynor; 13 Paul Cooke; 6 Richard Horne (C); 8 Ewan Dowes; 10 Paul King; 15 Jamie Thackray; 11 Shayne McMenemy; 12 Stephen Kearney; 30 Richard Whiting. Subs (all used): 20 Garreth Carvell; 21 Danny Brough; 23 Paul McNicholas; 28 Danny Washbrook (D).
Tries: Whiting (16, 45), Blacklock (22), Briscoe (29, 31), McMenemy (61), R Horne (65), McNicholas (71);
Goals: Cooke 5/7, Brough 1/1.
On report: McMenemy (11) - alleged biting.
SAINTS: 1 Paul Wellens; 5 Darren Albert; 3 Jamie Lyon; 11 Lee Gilmour; 2 Ade Gardner; 6 Jason Hooper; 7 Sean Long; 8 Nick Fozzard; 9 Keiron Cunningham; 17 Paul Anderson; 12 Jon Wilkin; 15 Mike Bennett; 13 Paul Sculthorpe (C). Subs (all used): 10 Mark Edmondson; 14 Mick Higham; 16 Keith Mason; 24 Maurie Fa'asavalu.
Try: Fa'asavalu (55); **Goals:** Long 1/1.
Rugby Leaguer & League Express Men of the Match: *Hull:* Richard Horne; *Saints:* Paul Wellens.
Penalty count: 4-8; **Half-time:** 22-0; **Referee:** Karl Kirkpatrick (Warrington); **Attendance:** 10,862.

LEIGH CENTURIONS 4 LEEDS RHINOS 60

CENTURIONS: 26 Nick Owen; 1 Ben Cooper; 8 Rob Jackson; 9 Phil Jones; 27 Dom Feaunati; 24 John Wilshere; 2 John Duffy; 4 Darren Fleary (C); 18 Paul Rowley; 31 Warren Stevens; 20 Craig Stapleton; 13 Mark Leafa; 10 Jason Kent. Subs (all used): 32 Robbie Mears; 21 Matt Sturm; 15 Richard Marshall; 11 James King.
Try: P Jones (16); **Goals:** P Jones 0/1.
RHINOS: 1 Richard Mathers; 2 Mark Calderwood; 3 Chev Walker; 12 Chris McKenna; 23 Lee Smith; 13 Kevin Sinfield (C); 7 Rob Burrow; 8 Ryan Bailey; 14 Andrew Dunemann; 15 Danny Ward; 18 Jamie Jones-Buchanan; 16 Willie Poching; 20 Gareth Ellis. Subs (all used): 11 Ali Lauitiiti; 10 Barrie McDermott; 22 Nick Scruton; 21 Liam Botham.
Tries: Calderwood (7, 29, 60), Smith (20, 42), Burrow (24, 65), McDermott (35), Sinfield (56, 75), Walker (68);
Goals: Sinfield 8/10, Smith 0/1.
Rugby Leaguer & League Express Men of the Match: *Centurions:* John Wilshere; *Rhinos:* Kevin Sinfield.
Penalty count: 7-12; **Half-time:** 4-28;
Referee: Ronnie Laughton (Barnsley); **Attendance:** 5,200.

SALFORD CITY REDS 0 BRADFORD BULLS 58

CITY REDS: 2 David Hodgson; 5 Anthony Stewart; 3 Stuart Littler; 33 Kevin McGuinness; 26 Darren Bamford; 1 Cliff Beverley; 7 Luke Robinson; 10 Sean Rutgerson; 9 Malcolm Alker (C); 27 Mitchell Stringer; 8 Andy Coley; 12 Ian Sibbit; 13 Chris Charles. Subs (all used): 24 Andy Johnson; 14 Paul Highton; 18 Stuart Dickens; 20 Tim Jonkers.
Goals: Charles 0/1.
BULLS: 17 Stuart Reardon; 15 Karl Pratt; 19 Jamie Langley; 22 Karl Pryce; 5 Lesley Vainikolo; 18 Iestyn Harris; 1 Robbie Paul; 8 Joe Vagana; 7 Paul Deacon; 29 Stuart Fielden; 12 Jamie Peacock (C); 27 Rob Parker; 11 Lee Radford. Subs (all used): 3 Leon Pryce; 14 Andy Lynch; 32 Andy Smith; 20 Matt Cook.
Tries: L Pryce (28), K Pryce (35, 49, 77), Pratt (39), Deacon (46, 52, 79), Parker (58), Vainikolo (61, 74);
Goals: Deacon 7/11.
Rugby Leaguer & League Express Men of the Match: *City Reds:* Sean Rutgerson; *Bulls:* Paul Deacon.
Penalty count: 5-6; **Half-time:** 0-16;
Referee: Ian Smith (Oldham); **Attendance:** 4,102.

Sunday 15th May 2005

HUDDERSFIELD GIANTS 34 LONDON BRONCOS 24

GIANTS: 34 Marcus St Hilaire; 2 Hefin O'Hare; 11 Chris Nero; 4 Michael De Vere; 5 Stuart Donlan; 6 Chris Thorman; 13 Stanley Gene; 18 Eorl Crabtree; 9 Brad Drew; 21 Paul Jackson; 14 Stuart Jones; 17 Paul Smith; 12 Ben Roarty (C). Subs (all used): 7 Paul March; 10 Jim Gannon; 19 Jon Grayshon; 22 Ryan Clayton.
Tries: Nero (4, 49, 56), Donlan (32), O'Hare (69), Thorman (77); **Goals:** De Vere 5/7.
BRONCOS: 6 Mark McLinden (C); 2 Jon Wells; 1 Paul Sykes; 4 Mark O'Halloran; 3 Nick Bradley-Qalilawa; 21 Luke Dorn; 7 Thomas Leuluai; 17 Mark Tookey; 19 David Highton; 18 Anthony Armour; 11 Solomon Haumono; 12 Lee Hopkins; 13 Rob Purdham. Subs (all used): 16 Joe Mbu; 10 Steve Trindall; 24 Tyrone Smith; 20 Filimone Lolohea.
Tries: Wells (11), Smith (25), Bradley-Qalilawa (39, 64), Leuluai (73); **Goals:** Sykes 2/5.
Rugby Leaguer & League Express Men of the Match: *Giants:* Chris Nero; *Broncos:* Mark McLinden.
Penalty count: 6-7; **Half-time:** 12-16; **Referee:** Richard Silverwood (Dewsbury); **Attendance:** 3,682.

WARRINGTON WOLVES 28 WIGAN WARRIORS 22

WOLVES: 1 Brent Grose; 2 Henry Fa'afili; 3 Martin Gleeson; 4 Toa Kohe-Love; 5 Dean Gaskell; 25 Chris Bridge; 7 Nathan Wood (C); 8 Chris Leikvoll; 9 Jon Clarke; 10 Mark Hilton; 11 Logan Swann; 12 Mike Wainwright; 15 Ben Westwood. Subs (all used): 13 Paul Noone; 14 Mark Gleeson; 16 Paul Wood; 17 Danny Lima.
Tries: Wainwright (20), Lima (31, 72), Swann (63), N Wood (78); **Goals:** Bridge 4/5.
WARRIORS: 14 Kevin Brown; 2 Brett Dallas; 4 David Vaealiki; 3 Martin Aspinwall; 5 Brian Carney; 6 Danny Orr; 7 Dennis Moran; 8 Jerry Seuseu; 9 Terry Newton (C); 10 Jerome Guisset; 20 Harrison Hansen; 19 Stephen Wild; 12 Danny Tickle. Subs (all used): 16 Danny Sculthorpe; 18 Wayne Godwin; 22 David Allen; 17 Wayne McDonald.
Tries: Aspinwall (11), Tickle (23), Moran (59);
Goals: Tickle 5/5.
Rugby Leaguer & League Express Men of the Match: *Wolves:* Mark Gleeson; *Warriors:* Dennis Moran.
Penalty count: 7-5; **Half-time:** 12-12;
Referee: Ashley Klein (Keighley); **Attendance:** 12,790.

**WAKEFIELD TRINITY WILDCATS 34
WIDNES VIKINGS 47**

WILDCATS: 21 Mark Field; 1 Colum Halpenny; 3 Jason Demetriou (C); 4 Sid Domic; 5 Semi Tadulala; 6 Jamie Rooney; 7 Ben Jeffries; 8 Darrell Griffin; 9 David March; 10 Michael Korkidas; 15 David Wrench; 18 Olivier Elima; 13 Rob Spicer. Subs (all used): 12 Jamie Field; 16 Steve Snitch; 25 Andy Kirk; 27 Chris Feather.
Tries: Halpenny (9, 12), Elima (30), Rooney (45), Demetriou (67), Jeffries (69); **Goals:** Rooney 5/6.
Sin bin: Griffin (22) - holding down;
Korkidas (64) - holding down.
VIKINGS: 1 Gary Connolly; 5 Andrew Emelio; 4 Adam Hughes; 3 Aaron Moule; 28 Gray Viane; 6 Owen Craigie; 7 Stephen Myler; 8 Terry O'Connor; 9 Shane Millard (C); 12 John Stankevitch; 18 Sala Fa'alogo; 16 Daniel Frame; 13 Simon Finnigan. Subs (all used): 10 Julian O'Neill; 14 Gary Hulse; 15 Matt Whitaker; 20 Mark Smith.
Tries: O'Connor (5), Finnigan (8), Hughes (18), Myler (24), Moule (33), Smith (51, 65);
Goals: Myler 9/9; **Field goal:** Craigie.
Sin bin: Stankevitch (2) - dissent.
Rugby Leaguer & League Express Men of the Match: *Wildcats:* Jamie Rooney; *Vikings:* Stephen Myler.
Penalty count: 10-9; **Half-time:** 16-32;
Referee: Steve Ganson (St Helens); **Attendance:** 3,802.

ROUND 14

Friday 20th May 2005

LEEDS RHINOS 42 LEIGH CENTURIONS 24

RHINOS: 1 Richard Mathers; 2 Mark Calderwood; 3 Chev Walker; 12 Chris McKenna; 5 Marcus Bai; 13 Kevin Sinfield (C); 6 Danny McGuire; 18 Jamie Jones-Buchanan; 14 Andrew Dunemann; 10 Barrie McDermott; 11 Ali Lauitiiti; 16 Willie Poching; 20 Gareth Ellis. Subs (all used): 22 Nick Scruton; 15 Danny Ward; 21 Liam Botham; 24 Scott Murrell (D).
Tries: Mathers (8), McGuire (10, 59), McKenna (19), Ellis (26), Calderwood (68, 73); **Goals:** Sinfield 7/7.
CENTURIONS: 24 John Wilshere; 14 Steve Maden; 1 Ben Cooper; 8 Rob Jackson; 27 Dom Feaunati; 9 Phil Jones; 10 Jason Kent; 4 Darren Fleary (C); 32 Robbie Mears; 20 Craig Stapleton; 16 Steve McCurrie; 11 James King; 13 Mark Leafa. Subs (all used): 31 Warren Stevens; 18 Paul Rowley; 15 Richard Marshall; 21 Matt Sturm.
Tries: Leafa (15), P Jones (43), Feaunati (46), Wilshere (56); **Goals:** P Jones 4/4.
Rugby Leaguer & League Express Men of the Match: *Rhinos:* Willie Poching; *Centurions:* James King.
Penalty count: 10-7; **Half-time:** 24-6;
Referee: Ashley Klein (Keighley); **Attendance:** 14,026.

WIGAN WARRIORS 24 HUDDERSFIELD GIANTS 26

WARRIORS: 1 Kris Radlinski (C); 5 Brian Carney; 3 Martin Aspinwall; 4 David Vaealiki; 2 Brett Dallas; 6 Danny Orr; 7 Dennis Moran; 8 Jerry Seuseu; 9 Terry Newton; 10 Jerome Guisset; 20 Harrison Hansen; 19 Stephen Wild; 12 Danny Tickle. Subs (all used): 14 Kevin Brown; 16 Danny Sculthorpe; 17 Wayne McDonald; 18 Wayne Godwin.
Tries: Tickle (4), Dallas (10), Moran (16), Brown (77);
Goals: Tickle 4/5.
GIANTS: 34 Marcus St Hilaire; 2 Hefin O'Hare; 11 Chris Nero; 4 Michael De Vere; 5 Stuart Donlan; 6 Chris Thorman; 13 Stanley Gene; 21 Paul Jackson; 9 Brad Drew; 18 Eorl Crabtree; 14 Stuart Jones; 17 Paul Smith; 12 Ben Roarty (C). Subs (all used): 7 Paul March; 10 Jim Gannon; 19 Jon Grayshon; 22 Ryan Clayton.
Tries: St Hilaire (29), Thorman (42, 68), O'Hare (52), Nero (58); **Goals:** De Vere 3/5.
Sin bin: Gannon (40) - dissent.
Rugby Leaguer & League Express Men of the Match:
Warriors: Terry Newton; *Giants:* Brad Drew.
Penalty count: 5-6; **Half-time:** 20-4;
Referee: Ian Smith (Oldham); **Attendance:** 10,057.

Saturday 21st May 2005

WIDNES VIKINGS 22 ST HELENS 29

VIKINGS: 24 Tim Holmes; 5 Andrew Emelio; 4 Adam Hughes; 1 Gary Connolly; 28 Gray Viane; 6 Owen Craigie; 7 Stephen Myler; 8 Terry O'Connor; 9 Shane Millard (C); 12 John Stankevitch; 11 Mick Cassidy; 16 Daniel Frame; 13 Simon Finnigan. Subs (all used): 10 Julian O'Neill; 15 Matt Whitaker; 18 Sala Fa'alogo; 20 Mark Smith.
Tries: Millard (15), Connolly (20), Whitaker (40), Emelio (50); **Goals:** Myler 3/5.
SAINTS: 1 Paul Wellens; 2 Ade Gardner; 3 Jamie Lyon; 4 Willie Talau; 5 Darren Albert; 6 Jason Hooper; 7 Sean Long; 17 Paul Anderson; 9 Keiron Cunningham; 24 Maurie Fa'asavalu; 12 Jon Wilkin; 27 Vinnie Anderson; 13 Paul Sculthorpe (C). Subs (all used): 15 Mike Bennett; 14 Mick Higham; 16 Keith Mason; 8 Nick Fozzard.
Tries: Sculthorpe (5), Albert (11, 56), Wellens (27), Higham (68); **Goals:** Long 3/3, Sculthorpe 1/3;
Field goal: Sculthorpe.
Rugby Leaguer & League Express Men of the Match:
Vikings: Shane Millard; *Saints:* Paul Wellens.
Penalty count: 7-3; **Half-time:** 18-18; **Referee:** Richard Silverwood (Dewsbury); **Attendance:** 7,641.

Sunday 22nd May 2005

BRADFORD BULLS 24 WARRINGTON WOLVES 44

BULLS: 6 Michael Withers; 15 Karl Pratt; 17 Stuart Reardon; 22 Karl Pryce; 5 Lesley Vainikolo; 18 Iestyn Harris; 1 Robbie Paul; 8 Joe Vagana; 7 Paul Deacon; 29 Stuart Fielden; 27 Rob Parker; 12 Jamie Peacock (C); 11 Lee Radford. Subs (all used): 3 Leon Pryce; 13 Ben Harris (D); 19 Jamie Langley; 14 Andy Lynch.
Tries: Vainikolo (5), Peacock (31), Reardon (44), I Harris (47); **Goals:** Deacon 4/4.
WOLVES: 1 Brent Grose; 2 Henry Fa'afili; 3 Martin Gleeson; 4 Toa Kohe-Love; 5 Dean Gaskell; 25 Chris Bridge; 7 Nathan Wood (C); 8 Chris Leikvoll; 9 Jon Clarke; 10 Mark Hilton; 11 Logan Swann; 12 Mike Wainwright; 15 Ben Westwood. Subs (all used): 13 Paul Noone; 14 Mark Gleeson; 16 Paul Wood; 17 Danny Lima.
Tries: Bridge (26, 73), Noone (50), Kohe-Love (54), P Wood (57), Lima (66), Fa'afili (79); **Goals:** Bridge 8/8.
Rugby Leaguer & League Express Men of the Match:
Bulls: Iestyn Harris; *Wolves:* Chris Bridge.
Penalty count: 2-5; **Half-time:** 12-8;
Referee: Steve Ganson (St Helens); **Attendance:** 14,428.

LONDON BRONCOS 34 SALFORD CITY REDS 18

BRONCOS: 6 Mark McLinden (C); 2 Jon Wells; 24 Tyrone Smith; 1 Paul Sykes; 4 Mark O'Halloran; 21 Luke Dorn; 7 Thomas Leuluai; 17 Mark Tookey; 19 David Highton; 18 Anthony Armour; 12 Lee Hopkins; 13 Rob Purdham; 16 Joe Mbu. Subs (all used): 10 Steve Trindall; 11 Solomon Haumono; 14 Danny Williams; 20 Filimone Lolohea.
Tries: Dorn (14), Purdham (24), Smith (28), Haumono (40), Tookey (64), Wells (77); **Goals:** Sykes 5/6.
CITY REDS: 2 David Hodgson; 25 Tim Hartley; 3 Stuart Littler; 16 Nathan McAvoy; 5 Anthony Stewart; 33 Kevin McGuinness; 7 Luke Robinson; 27 Mitchell Stringer; 9 Malcolm Alker (C); 10 Sean Rutgerson; 12 Ian Sibbit; 11 Mark Shipway; 13 Chris Charles. Subs (all used): 8 Andy Coley; 14 Paul Highton; 17 Gareth Haggerty; 21 John Clough.
Tries: Rutgerson (3), McAvoy (38), Haggerty (69);
Goals: Charles 3/3.
On report:
Haggerty (27) - alleged dangerous tackle on Smith.
Rugby Leaguer & League Express Men of the Match:
Broncos: David Highton; *City Reds:* John Clough.
Penalty count: 4-8; **Half-time:** 22-12; **Referee:** Karl Kirkpatrick (Warrington); **Attendance:** 2,997.

WAKEFIELD TRINITY WILDCATS 28 HULL FC 35

WILDCATS: 21 Mark Field; 1 Colum Halpenny; 3 Jason Demetriou (C); 4 Sid Domic; 5 Semi Tadulala; 6 Jamie Rooney; 7 Ben Jeffries; 27 Chris Feather; 9 David March; 10 Michael Korkidas; 18 Olivier Elima; 13 Rob Spicer; 26 Julian O'Neill. Subs (all used): 8 Darrell Griffin; 12 Jamie Field; 16 Steve Snitch; 14 Sam Obst.
Tries: Demetriou (18), Griffin (29), March (41), Domic (44), Rooney (48); **Goals:** Rooney 4/5.
HULL: 1 Shaun Briscoe; 2 Nathan Blacklock; 16 Tom Saxton; 3 Kirk Yeaman; 5 Gareth Raynor; 13 Paul Cooke; 6 Richard Horne (C); 8 Ewan Dowes; 10 Paul King; 15 Jamie Thackray; 12 Stephen Kearney; 11 Shayne McMenemy; 30 Richard Whiting. Subs (all used): 20 Garreth Carvell; 17 Chris Chester; 23 Paul McNicholas; 21 Danny Brough.
Tries: King (4), Briscoe (9, 64), Brough (31), R Horne (33), McMenemy (61); **Goals:** Cooke 5/6;
Field goal: Brough.
Sin bin: Brough (38) - persistent interference.
Rugby Leaguer & League Express Men of the Match:
Wildcats: Julian O'Neill; *Hull:* Shane McMenemy.
Penalty count: 10-5; **Half-time:** 12-24;
Referee: Ronnie Laughton (Barnsley); **Attendance:** 5,194.

ROUND 15

Friday 27th May 2005

ST HELENS 38 LEEDS RHINOS 24

SAINTS: 20 Ian Hardman; 5 Darren Albert; 3 Jamie Lyon; 4 Willie Talau; 2 Ade Gardner; 6 Jason Hooper; 7 Sean Long; 17 Paul Anderson; 9 Keiron Cunningham; 8 Nick Fozzard; 27 Vinnie Anderson; 11 Lee Gilmour; 13 Paul Sculthorpe (C). Subs (all used): 21 James Roby; 19 James Graham; 15 Mike Bennett; 24 Maurie Fa'asavalu.
Tries: P Anderson (8), Albert (13), Long (20), V Anderson (30), Hardman (44), Sculthorpe (50);
Goals: Long 7/7.
RHINOS: 1 Richard Mathers; 2 Mark Calderwood; 12 Chris McKenna; 4 Keith Senior; 5 Marcus Bai; 13 Kevin Sinfield (C); 7 Rob Burrow; 8 Ryan Bailey; 14 Andrew Dunemann; 15 Danny Ward; 16 Willie Poching; 18 Jamie Jones-Buchanan; 20 Gareth Ellis. Subs (all used): 6 Danny McGuire; 11 Ali Lauitiiti; 10 Barrie McDermott; 21 Liam Botham.
Tries: Bai (3), Jones-Buchanan (39, 66, 70);
Goals: Sinfield 2/3, Burrow 2/2.
Rugby Leaguer & League Express Men of the Match:
Saints: Sean Long; *Rhinos:* Jamie Jones-Buchanan.
Penalty count: 7-5; **Half-time:** 26-12; **Referee:** Karl Kirkpatrick (Warrington); **Attendance:** 13,236.

Saturday 28th May 2005

HULL FC 24 BRADFORD BULLS 42

HULL: 1 Shaun Briscoe; 2 Nathan Blacklock; 3 Kirk Yeaman; 30 Richard Whiting; 5 Gareth Raynor; 13 Paul Cooke; 6 Richard Horne (C); 8 Ewan Dowes; 10 Paul King; 15 Jamie Thackray; 17 Chris Chester; 12 Stephen Kearney; 11 Shayne McMenemy. Subs (all used): 16 Tom Saxton; 23 Paul McNicholas; 20 Garreth Carvell; 21 Danny Brough.
Tries: Carvell (43), Raynor (59, 62), Blacklock (75);
Goals: Cooke 3/4, Brough 1/1.
BULLS: 6 Michael Withers; 17 Stuart Reardon; 13 Ben Harris; 3 Leon Pryce; 22 Karl Pryce; 18 Iestyn Harris; 7 Paul Deacon; 14 Andy Lynch; 15 Karl Pratt; 29 Stuart Fielden; 12 Jamie Peacock (C); 10 Brad Meyers; 11 Lee Radford. Subs (all used): 1 Robbie Paul; 8 Joe Vagana; 25 Brett Ferres; 20 Matt Cook.
Tries: Meyers (22), Ferres (27), L Pryce (38, 73), Reardon (54), K Pryce (56); **Goals:** Deacon 9/10.
Rugby Leaguer & League Express Men of the Match:
Hull: Paul Cooke; *Bulls:* Paul Deacon.
Penalty count: 11-8; **Half-time:** 2-22;
Referee: Ashley Klein (Keighley); **Attendance:** 11,563.

Sunday 29th May 2005

LONDON BRONCOS 70 LEIGH CENTURIONS 16

BRONCOS: 6 Mark McLinden (C); 2 Jon Wells; 1 Paul Sykes; 4 Mark O'Halloran; 3 Nick Bradley-Qalilawa; 21 Luke Dorn; 7 Thomas Leuluai; 17 Mark Tookey; 19 David Highton; 18 Anthony Armour; 13 Rob Purdham; 12 Lee Hopkins; 16 Joe Mbu. Subs (all used): 11 Solomon Haumono; 14 Danny Williams; 20 Filimone Lolohea; 30 Feleti Mateo (D).
Tries: Purdham (6, 34, 39, 46), McLinden (19, 40), Highton (21), Leuluai (44, 48, 57), Sykes (64), Dorn (79); **Goals:** Sykes 11/12.
Sin bin: Highton (75) - retaliation.
CENTURIONS: 24 John Wilshere; 14 Steve Maden; 1 Ben Cooper; 9 Phil Jones; 27 Dom Feaunati; 10 Jason Kent; 2 John Duffy; 4 Darren Fleary (C); 32 Robbie Mears; 31 Warren Stevens; 20 Craig Stapleton; 11 James King; 13 Mark Leafa. Subs (all used): 15 Richard Marshall; 18 Paul Rowley; 21 Matt Sturm; 22 Neil Turley.
Tries: P Jones (10), Cooper (13), John Duffy (80);
Goals: Turley 2/3.
Sin bin: Stapleton (75) - high tackle on Highton.
On report: Fleary (48) - late tackle on McLinden.
Rugby Leaguer & League Express Men of the Match:
Broncos: Thomas Leuluai; *Centurions:* Robbie Mears.
Penalty count: 12-5; **Half-time:** 36-10;
Referee: Ben Thaler (Wakefield); **Attendance:** 3,522.

WARRINGTON WOLVES 38
WAKEFIELD TRINITY WILDCATS 30

WOLVES: 1 Brent Grose; 2 Henry Fa'afili; 3 Martin Gleeson; 4 Toa Kohe-Love; 25 Chris Bridge; 6 Lee Briers (C); 7 Nathan Wood; 8 Chris Leikvoll; 9 Jon Clarke; 10 Mark Hilton; 11 Logan Swann; 12 Mike Wainwright; 15 Ben Westwood. Subs (all used): 13 Paul Noone; 14 Mark Gleeson; 16 Paul Wood; 17 Danny Lima.
Tries: Swann (16, 39), Martin Gleeson (22), Fa'afili (27), Grose (32), N Wood (60, 75); **Goals:** Bridge 5/8.
WILDCATS: 21 Mark Field; 1 Colum Halpenny; 3 Jason Demetriou (C); 4 Sid Domic; 5 Semi Tadulala; 6 Jamie Rooney; 7 Ben Jeffries; 8 Darrell Griffin; 9 David March; 27 Chris Feather; 12 Jamie Field; 16 Steve Snitch; 13 Rob Spicer. Subs (all used): 10 Michael Korkidas; 14 Sam Obst; 17 Duncan MacGillivray; 18 Olivier Elima.
Tries: March (5), Tadulala (10), Halpenny (42), Obst (47), Jeffries (54); **Goals:** Rooney 5/6.
Rugby Leaguer & League Express Men of the Match:
Wolves: Martin Gleeson; *Wildcats:* Jamie Rooney.
Penalty count: 5-7; **Half-time:** 24-12;
Referee: Ian Smith (Oldham); **Attendance:** 10,113.

WIDNES VIKINGS 40 HUDDERSFIELD GIANTS 12

VIKINGS: 24 Tim Holmes; 5 Andrew Emelio; 1 Gary Connolly; 18 Sala Fa'alogo; 28 Gray Viane; 6 Owen Craigie; 7 Stephen Myler; 8 Terry O'Connor; 9 Shane Millard (C); 12 John Stankevitch; 11 Mick Cassidy; 16 Daniel Frame; 13 Simon Finnigan. Subs (all used): 10 Julian O'Neill; 17 David Mills; 33 Jules O'Neill (D3); 20 Mark Smith.
Tries: Frame (11), Viane (34, 59, 61), Finnigan (49), Millard (52), Smith (65); **Goals:** Myler 6/8.
GIANTS: 34 Marcus St Hilaire; 2 Hefin O'Hare; 11 Chris Nero; 4 Michael De Vere; 5 Stuart Donlan; 6 Chris Thorman; 7 Paul March; 21 Paul Jackson; 9 Brad Drew; 18 Eorl Crabtree; 14 Stuart Jones; 17 Paul Smith; 12 Ben Roarty (C). Subs (all used): 20 Paul White; 10 Jim Gannon; 19 Jon Grayshon; 22 Ryan Clayton.
Tries: March (3), Smith (21); **Goals:** De Vere 2/3.
Rugby Leaguer & League Express Men of the Match:
Vikings: Simon Finnigan; *Giants:* Paul March.
Penalty count: 7-6; **Half-time:** 12-12;
Referee: Ronnie Laughton (Barnsley); **Attendance:** 5,946.

Monday 30th May 2005

SALFORD CITY REDS 20 WIGAN WARRIORS 34

CITY REDS: 2 David Hodgson; 5 Anthony Stewart; 3 Stuart Littler; 16 Nathan McAvoy; 25 Tim Hartley; 1 Cliff Beverley; 7 Luke Robinson; 27 Mitchell Stringer; 9 Malcolm Alker (C); 8 Andy Coley; 10 Sean Rutgerson; 11 Mark Shipway; 13 Chris Charles. Subs (all used): 14 Paul Highton; 17 Gareth Haggerty; 21 John Clough; 4 Junior Langi.
Tries: Coley (5, 25), Stewart (48), Alker (70);
Goals: Charles 2/4.
WARRIORS: 1 Kris Radlinski (C); 5 Brian Carney; 19 Stephen Wild; 3 Martin Aspinwall; 2 Brett Dallas; 14 Kevin Brown; 7 Dennis Moran; 8 Jerry Seuseu; 9 Terry Newton; 16 Danny Sculthorpe; 10 Jerome Guisset; 12 Danny Tickle; 20 Harrison Hansen. Subs (all used): 18 Wayne Godwin; 27 Bryn Hargreaves; 29 Joel Tomkins; 30 Sean Gleeson (D).
Tries: Tickle (10), Dallas (33, 63), Brown (36), Radlinski (43), Wild (47); **Goals:** Tickle 5/7.
On report: Sculthorpe (72) - leading with the elbow.
Rugby Leaguer & League Express Men of the Match:
City Reds: David Hodgson; *Warriors:* Dennis Moran.
Penalty count: 7-10; **Half-time:** 10-16; **Referee:** Richard Silverwood (Dewsbury); **Attendance:** 5,526.

ROUND 16

Friday 3rd June 2005

LEEDS RHINOS 34 HULL FC 14

RHINOS: 1 Richard Mathers; 2 Mark Calderwood; 3 Chev Walker; 4 Keith Senior; 5 Marcus Bai; 13 Kevin Sinfield (C); 7 Rob Burrow; 8 Ryan Bailey; 14 Andrew Dunemann; 15 Danny Ward; 12 Chris McKenna; 18 Jamie Jones-Buchanan; 20 Gareth Ellis. Subs (all used): 16 Willie Poching; 11 Ali Lauitiiti; 6 Danny McGuire; 10 Barrie McDermott.
Tries: Senior (7, 59, 67), Bai (39), Burrow (50), Mathers (62); **Goals:** Sinfield 5/6.
HULL: 1 Shaun Briscoe; 2 Nathan Blacklock; 3 Kirk Yeaman; 16 Tom Saxton; 5 Gareth Raynor; 6 Richard Horne (C); 13 Paul Cooke; 10 Paul King; 21 Danny Brough; 8 Ewan Dowes; 24 Graeme Horne; 12 Stephen Kearney; 11 Shayne McMenemy. Subs (all used): 20 Garreth Carvell; 15 Jamie Thackray; 22 Kirk Dixon; 28 Danny Washbrook.
Tries: Briscoe (19), Blacklock (25);
Goals: Brough 2/3, Cooke 1/1.
Rugby Leaguer & League Express Men of the Match:
Rhinos: Kevin Sinfield; *Hull:* Danny Brough.
Penalty count: 10-8; **Half-time:** 12-12; **Referee:** Richard Silverwood (Dewsbury); **Attendance:** 17,427.

WIGAN WARRIORS 18 LONDON BRONCOS 22

WARRIORS: 1 Kris Radlinski (C); 5 Brian Carney; 21 Chris Melling; 3 Martin Aspinwall; 2 Brett Dallas; 14 Kevin Brown; 7 Dennis Moran; 8 Jerry Seuseu; 9 Terry Newton; 27 Bryn Hargreaves; 20 Harrison Hansen; 19 Stephen Wild; 12 Danny Tickle. Subs (all used): 18 Wayne Godwin; 26 Paul Prescott; 10 Jerome Guisset; 29 Joel Tomkins.
Tries: Radlinski (9), Tickle (22), Dallas (40), Wild (60);
Goals: Tickle 1/4.
BRONCOS: 6 Mark McLinden (C); 3 Nick Bradley-Qalilawa; 24 Tyrone Smith; 1 Paul Sykes; 2 Jon Wells; 21 Luke Dorn; 7 Thomas Leuluai; 18 Anthony Armour; 19 David Highton; 10 Steve Trindall; 13 Rob Purdham; 12 Lee Hopkins; 4 Mark O'Halloran. Subs (all used): 14 Danny Williams; 20 Filimone Lolohea; 11 Solomon Haumono; 30 Feleti Mateo.
Tries: Dorn (13), Bradley-Qalilawa (18), Smith (28);
Goals: Sykes 5/5.
Rugby Leaguer & League Express Men of the Match:
Warriors: Wayne Godwin; *Broncos:* Thomas Leuluai.
Penalty count: 9-6; **Half-time:** 14-20; **Referee:** Karl Kirkpatrick (Warrington); **Attendance:** 10,262.

Sunday 5th June 2005

HUDDERSFIELD GIANTS 22 WARRINGTON WOLVES 24

GIANTS: 1 Paul Reilly; 34 Marcus St Hilaire; 22 Ryan Clayton; 4 Michael De Vere; 5 Stuart Donlan; 6 Chris Thorman; 7 Paul March; 18 Eorl Crabtree; 9 Brad Drew; 10 Jim Gannon; 14 Stuart Jones; 17 Paul Smith; 12 Ben Roarty (C). Subs (all used): 19 Jon Grayshon; 21 Paul Jackson; 23 Tom Hemingway (D); 27 Wayne McDonald (D).
Tries: Drew (19), St Hilaire (54, 80), Reilly (71);
Goals: De Vere 3/5.
Sin bin: Gannon (65) - professional foul.
WOLVES: 1 Brent Grose; 2 Henry Fa'afili; 3 Martin Gleeson; 4 Toa Kohe-Love; 18 Graham Appo; 6 Lee Briers (C); 25 Chris Bridge; 8 Chris Leikvoll; 9 Jon Clarke; 10 Mark Hilton; 11 Logan Swann; 12 Mike Wainwright; 15 Ben Westwood. Subs (all used): 14 Mark Gleeson; 16 Paul Wood; 17 Danny Lima; 13 Paul Noone.
Tries: Clarke (14), Fa'afili (34), Westwood (62), Bridge (67); **Goals:** Bridge 4/5.
Rugby Leaguer & League Express Men of the Match:
Giants: Brad Drew; *Wolves:* Jon Clarke.
Penalty count: 6-6; **Half-time:** 6-10;
Referee: Ben Thaler (Wakefield); **Attendance:** 6,162.

LEIGH CENTURIONS 14 WIDNES VIKINGS 34

CENTURIONS: 24 John Wilshere; 14 Steve Maden; 1 Ben Cooper; 9 Phil Jones; 19 Rob Smyth; 10 Jason Kent; 2 John Duffy; 4 Darren Fleary (C); 32 Robbie Mears; 20 Craig Stapleton; 16 Steve McCurrie; 11 James King; 13 Mark Leafa. Subs (all used): 31 Warren Stevens; 21 Matt Sturm; 15 Richard Marshall; 22 Neil Turley.
Tries: Maden (42), Sturm (53), Wilshere (68);
Goals: Wilshere 1/2, P Jones 0/1.
Sin bin: Stapleton (79) – fighting.
On report: King (39) – use of forearm.
VIKINGS: 33 Jules O'Neill; 2 Misili Manu; 1 Gary Connolly; 18 Sala Fa'alogo; 28 Gray Viane; 6 Owen Craigie; 7 Stephen Myler; 8 Terry O'Connor; 9 Shane Millard (C); 12 John Stankevitch; 11 Mick Cassidy; 16 Daniel Frame; 13 Simon Finnigan. Subs (all used): 20 Mark Smith; 10 Julian O'Neill; 17 David Mills; 24 Tim Holmes.
Tries: Finnigan (11), Craigie (20, 76, 79), Millard (58);
Goals: Myler 6/6, Connolly 1/1.
Sin bin: Julian O'Neill (79) – fighting.
On report: Viane and Fa'alogo (25) – late tackle on Turley.
Rugby Leaguer & League Express Men of the Match:
Centurions: John Wilshere; *Vikings:* Shane Millard.
Penalty count: 6-9; **Half-time:** 0-16;
Referee: Ian Smith (Oldham); **Attendance:** 5,170.

WAKEFIELD TRINITY WILDCATS 36 SALFORD CITY REDS 24

WILDCATS: 21 Mark Field; 1 Colum Halpenny; 3 Jason Demetriou (C); 4 Sid Domic; 5 Semi Tadulala; 6 Jamie Rooney; 7 Ben Jeffries; 8 Darrell Griffin; 9 David March; 27 Chris Feather; 11 David Solomona; 16 Steve Snitch; 13 Rob Spicer. Subs (all used): 10 Michael Korkidas; 14 Sam Obst; 17 Duncan MacGillivray; 12 Jamie Field.
Tries: Solomona (2), Feather (16), Halpenny (61), March (64), Rooney (73), J Field (80); **Goals:** Rooney 6/7.
CITY REDS: 2 David Hodgson; 25 Tim Hartley; 3 Stuart Littler; 16 Nathan McAvoy; 5 Anthony Stewart; 1 Cliff Beverley; 7 Luke Robinson; 22 Simon Baldwin; 21 John Clough; 10 Sean Rutgerson; 9 Malcolm Alker (C); 11 Mark Shipway; 13 Chris Charles. Subs (all used): 4 Junior Langi; 14 Paul Highton; 17 Gareth Haggerty; 20 Tim Jonkers.
Tries: Hodgson (10), Hartley (22), Rutgerson (43), Robinson (54); **Goals:** Charles 4/4.
Sin bin: Charles (28) – holding down.
Rugby Leaguer & League Express Men of the Match:
Wildcats: Jamie Rooney; *City Reds:* Luke Robinson.
Penalty count: 9-8; **Half-time:** 14-12;
Referee: Ashley Klein (Keighley); **Attendance:** 3,536.

BRADFORD BULLS 4 ST HELENS 66

BULLS: 1 Robbie Paul; 17 Stuart Reardon; 13 Ben Harris; 3 Leon Pryce; 22 Karl Pryce; 18 Iestyn Harris; 7 Paul Deacon; 14 Andy Lynch; 15 Karl Pratt; 29 Stuart Fielden; 12 Jamie Peacock (C); 10 Brad Meyers; 11 Lee Radford. Subs (all used): 20 Matt Cook; 27 Rob Parker; 8 Joe Vagana; 25 Brett Ferres.
Try: Reardon (21); **Goals:** Deacon 0/1.
Dismissal: L Pryce (27) - high tackle on Lyon.
SAINTS: 1 Paul Wellens; 5 Darren Albert; 3 Jamie Lyon; 4 Willie Talau; 2 Ade Gardner; 6 Jason Hooper; 7 Sean Long (C); 17 Paul Anderson; 9 Keiron Cunningham; 8 Nick Fozzard; 12 Jon Wilkin; 11 Lee Gilmour; 27 Vinnie Anderson. Subs (all used): 21 James Roby; 19 James Graham; 10 Mark Edmondson; 24 Maurie Fa'asavalu.
Tries: Wilkin (3, 39), V Anderson (18, 57, 74), Gilmour (30), Long (42), Lyon (45, 50), Gardner (60, 76), Roby (63); **Goals:** Long 7/8, Lyon 1/1, Hooper 1/3.
Sin bin: Talau (34) - professional foul.
Rugby Leaguer & League Express Men of the Match:
Bulls: Karl Pryce; *Saints:* Jamie Lyon.
Penalty count: 8-3; **Half-time:** 4-24; **Referee:** Ronnie Laughton (Barnsley); **Attendance:** 15,260.

ROUND 17

Friday 10th June 2005

SALFORD CITY REDS 22 ST HELENS 33

CITY REDS: 2 David Hodgson; 5 Anthony Stewart; 3 Stuart Littler; 1 Cliff Beverley; 4 Junior Langi; 25 Tim Hartley; 7 Luke Robinson; 10 Sean Rutgerson; 9 Malcolm Alker (C); 22 Simon Baldwin; 16 Nathan McAvoy; 11 Mark Shipway; 13 Chris Charles. Subs (all used): 17 Gareth Haggerty; 20 Tim Jonkers; 21 John Clough; 27 Mitchell Stringer.
Tries: Hartley (9, 39), Littler (23), Charles (49);
Goals: Charles 3/4.
SAINTS: 1 Paul Wellens; 20 Ian Hardman; 3 Jamie Lyon; 4 Willie Talau; 2 Ade Gardner; 6 Jason Hooper; 7 Sean Long (C); 17 Paul Anderson; 9 Keiron Cunningham; 16 Keith Mason; 11 Lee Gilmour; 12 Jon Wilkin; 27 Vinnie Anderson. Subs (all used): 10 Mark Edmondson; 21 James Roby; 19 James Graham; 24 Maurie Fa'asavalu.
Tries: Lyon (15, 57, 63), Wilkin (28), Wellens (65), Long (75); **Goals:** Long 4/6; **Field goal:** Long.
Rugby Leaguer & League Express Men of the Match:
City Reds: Tim Hartley; *Saints:* Jamie Lyon.
Penalty count: 5-5; **Half-time:** 18-12; **Referee:** Ian Smith (Oldham); **Attendance:** 4,704.

WAKEFIELD TRINITY WILDCATS 6 LEEDS RHINOS 70

WILDCATS: 21 Mark Field; 1 Colum Halpenny; 3 Jason Demetriou (C); 4 Sid Domic; 5 Semi Tadulala; 6 Jamie Rooney; 7 Ben Jeffries; 8 Darrell Griffin; 9 David March; 27 Chris Feather; 11 David Solomona; 16 Steve Snitch; 13 Rob Spicer. Subs (all used): 10 Michael Korkidas; 14 Sam Obst; 17 Duncan MacGillivray; 12 Jamie Field.
Try: Rooney (28); **Goals:** Rooney 1/2.
RHINOS: 1 Richard Mathers; 2 Mark Calderwood; 3 Chev Walker; 4 Keith Senior; 5 Marcus Bai; 13 Kevin Sinfield (C); 7 Rob Burrow; 8 Ryan Bailey; 14 Andrew Dunemann; 15 Danny Ward; 12 Chris McKenna; 18 Jamie Jones-Buchanan; 20 Gareth Ellis. Subs (all used): 16 Willie Poching; 11 Ali Lauitiiti; 6 Danny McGuire; 10 Barrie McDermott.
Tries: Mathers (4, 48), Bai (23), Senior (33), Lauitiiti (36, 51, 55, 59, 62), Poching (39), Burrow (43), McDermott (65), Ellis (74); **Goals:** Sinfield 6/9, Burrow 3/4.
Rugby Leaguer & League Express Men of the Match:
Wildcats: Jamie Rooney; *Rhinos:* Ali Lauitiiti.
Penalty count: 2-4; **Half-time:** 6-28; **Referee:** Karl Kirkpatrick (Warrington); **Attendance:** 9,457.

WIGAN WARRIORS 24 HULL FC 28

WARRIORS: 7 Dennis Moran; 5 Brian Carney; 19 Stephen Wild; 3 Martin Aspinwall; 2 Brett Dallas; 14 Kevin Brown; 6 Danny Orr; 8 Jerry Seuseu; 9 Terry Newton (C); 10 Jerome Guisset; 20 Harrison Hansen; 12 Danny Tickle; 32 Liam Botham (D). Subs: 18 Wayne Godwin; 27 Bryn Hargreaves; 29 Joel Tomkins; 31 Chris Ashton (not used).
Tries: Moran (14, 37), Tickle (59), Tomkins (79);
Goals: Tickle 4/4.
HULL: 1 Shaun Briscoe; 2 Nathan Blacklock; 16 Tom Saxton; 3 Kirk Yeaman; 26 Richie Barnett; 13 Paul Cooke; 6 Richard Horne (C); 8 Ewan Dowes; 21 Danny Brough; 10 Paul King; 24 Graeme Horne; 12 Stephen Kearney; 11 Shayne McMenemy. Subs (all used): 22 Kirk Dixon; 28 Danny Washbrook; 20 Garreth Carvell; 15 Jamie Thackray.
Tries: Briscoe (4), Barnett (27, 49), Yeaman (32, 77);
Goals: Cooke 2/3, Brough 2/3.
Sin bin: Cooke (71) - holding down.
Rugby Leaguer & League Express Men of the Match:
Warriors: Dennis Moran; *Hull:* Kirk Yeaman.
Penalty count: 12-5; **Half-time:** 12-14; **Referee:** Ronnie Laughton (Barnsley); **Attendance:** 12,125.

Saturday 11th June 2005

HUDDERSFIELD GIANTS 20 BRADFORD BULLS 38

GIANTS: 1 Paul Reilly; 34 Marcus St Hilaire; 3 James Evans; 4 Michael De Vere; 5 Stuart Donlan; 6 Chris Thorman; 23 Tom Hemingway; 18 Eorl Crabtree; 9 Brad Drew; 10 Jim Gannon; 14 Stuart Jones; 17 Paul Smith; 12 Ben Roarty (C). Subs (all used): 11 Chris Nero; 20 Paul White; 21 Paul Jackson; 27 Wayne McDonald.
Tries: Thorman (15), St Hilaire (22), Donlan (42), Smith (45); **Goals:** De Vere 2/4.
BULLS: 6 Michael Withers; 17 Stuart Reardon; 13 Ben Harris; 19 Jamie Langley; 22 Karl Pryce; 18 Iestyn Harris; 7 Paul Deacon; 8 Joe Vagana; 15 Karl Pratt; 29 Stuart Fielden; 12 Jamie Peacock (C); 10 Brad Meyers; 11 Lee Radford. Subs (all used): 1 Robbie Paul; 14 Andy Lynch; 20 Matt Cook; 27 Rob Parker.
Tries: B Harris (4), Paul (26, 59), K Pryce (34), Parker (57), Radford (64), Reardon (72); **Goals:** Deacon 5/7.
Rugby Leaguer & League Express Men of the Match:
Giants: Brad Drew; *Bulls:* Jamie Peacock.
Penalty count: 7-9; **Half-time:** 10-16;
Referee: Ashley Klein (Keighley); **Attendance:** 6,022.

Sunday 12th June 2005

LEIGH CENTURIONS 7 WARRINGTON WOLVES 42

CENTURIONS: 24 John Wilshere; 14 Steve Maden; 8 Rob Jackson; 10 Jason Kent; 19 Rob Smyth; 22 Neil Turley; 2 John Duffy; 4 Darren Fleary (C); 32 Robbie Mears; 20 Craig Stapleton; 11 James King; 16 Steve McCurrie; 13 Mark Leafa. Subs (all used): 15 Richard Marshall; 21 Matt Sturm; 31 Warren Stevens; 18 Paul Rowley.
Try: Stapleton (6); **Goals:** Turley 1/2; **Field goal:** Turley.
Sin bin: Jackson (56) - fighting.
WOLVES: 1 Brent Grose; 5 Dean Gaskell; 15 Ben Westwood; 4 Toa Kohe-Love; 2 Henry Fa'afili; 25 Chris Bridge; 7 Nathan Wood (C); 10 Mark Hilton; 9 Jon Clarke; 8 Chris Leikvoll; 11 Logan Swann; 12 Mike Wainwright; 13 Paul Noone. Subs (all used): 18 Graham Appo; 14 Mark Gleeson; 16 Paul Wood; 17 Danny Lima.
Tries: Westwood (2), Grose (43), Fa'afili (48, 52), N Wood (62), Clarke (68), Bridge (71), Appo (79);
Goals: Bridge 5/8.
Sin bin: Kohe-Love (56) - fighting.
Rugby Leaguer & League Express Men of the Match:
Centurions: John Wilshere; *Wolves:* Chris Bridge.
Penalty count: 9-8; **Half-time:** 7-4;
Referee: Steve Ganson (St Helens); **Attendance:** 7,249.

WIDNES VIKINGS 10 LONDON BRONCOS 24

VIKINGS: 33 Jules O'Neill; 5 Andrew Emelio; 1 Gary Connolly; 18 Sala Fa'alogo; 28 Gray Viane; 6 Owen Craigie; 7 Stephen Myler; 8 Terry O'Connor; 9 Shane Millard (C); 12 John Stankevitch; 11 Mick Cassidy; 15 Matt Whitaker; 16 Daniel Frame. Subs (all used): 10 Julian O'Neill; 17 David Mills; 24 Tim Holmes; 20 Mark Smith.
Tries: Connolly (74), Craigie (80); **Goals:** Jules O'Neill 1/2.
BRONCOS: 6 Mark McLinden (C); 2 Jon Wells; 1 Paul Sykes; 24 Tyrone Smith; 3 Nick Bradley-Qalilawa; 21 Luke Dorn; 7 Thomas Leuluai; 17 Mark Tookey; 19 David Highton; 10 Steve Trindall; 13 Rob Purdham; 12 Lee Hopkins; 4 Mark O'Halloran. Subs (all used): 11 Solomon Haumono; 14 Danny Williams; 20 Filimone Lolohea; 30 Feleti Mateo.
Tries: Dorn (12), Purdham (21), McLinden (34), Leuluai (38); **Goals:** Sykes 4/5.
On report: Smith (44) – high tackle on Holmes.
Rugby Leaguer & League Express Men of the Match:
Vikings: Jules O'Neill; *Broncos:* Mark McLinden.
Penalty count: 11-10; **Half-time:** 0-22; **Referee:** Richard Silverwood (Dewsbury); **Attendance:** 5,996.

ROUND 18

Friday 17th June 2005

HULL FC 30 LEIGH CENTURIONS 16

HULL: 1 Shaun Briscoe; 2 Nathan Blacklock; 3 Kirk Yeaman; 16 Tom Saxton; 26 Richie Barnett; 13 Paul Cooke; 6 Richard Horne (C); 8 Ewan Dowes; 21 Danny Brough; 20 Garreth Carvell; 17 Chris Chester; 12 Stephen Kearney; 11 Shayne McMenemy. Subs (all used): 15 Jamie Thackray; 18 Liam Higgins; 24 Graeme Horne; 28 Danny Washbrook.
Tries: Barnett (3, 17), Blacklock (33, 53, 57), Carvell (64); **Goals:** Cooke 2/3, Brough 1/3.
On report: Chester (13) - alleged high tackle on Jackson.
CENTURIONS: 1 Ben Cooper; 27 Dom Feaunati; 6 Danny Halliwell; 8 Rob Jackson; 14 Steve Maden; 22 Neil Turley; 2 John Duffy; 4 Darren Fleary (C); 32 Robbie Mears; 21 Matt Sturm; 20 Craig Stapleton; 16 Steve McCurrie; 13 Mark Leafa. Subs (all used): 5 Mick Govin; 15 Richard Marshall; 31 Warren Stevens; 34 Matthew Bottom (D).
Tries: Maden (6), McCurrie (73); **Goals:** Turley 4/4.
Rugby Leaguer & League Express Men of the Match:
Hull: Nathan Blacklock; *Centurions:* John Duffy.
Penalty count: 9-7; **Half-time:** 16-10;
Referee: Ashley Klein (Keighley); **Attendance:** 7,949.

ST HELENS 28 LONDON BRONCOS 28

SAINTS: 1 Paul Wellens; 20 Ian Hardman; 3 Jamie Lyon; 4 Willie Talau; 2 Ade Gardner; 6 Jason Hooper; 7 Sean Long; 8 Nick Fozzard; 9 Keiron Cunningham; 17 Paul Anderson; 11 Lee Gilmour; 12 Jon Wilkin; 13 Paul Sculthorpe (C). Subs (all used): 10 Mark Edmondson; 15 Mike Bennett; 21 James Roby; 24 Maurie Fa'asavalu.
Tries: Talau (3, 59, 78), Cunningham (8), Long (45), Lyon (72); **Goals:** Long 2/6.
BRONCOS: 25 Zebastian Luisi; 3 Nick Bradley-Qalilawa; 24 Tyrone Smith; 1 Paul Sykes; 2 Jon Wells; 21 Luke Dorn; 7 Thomas Leuluai; 17 Mark Tookey; 19 David Highton; 20 Filimone Lolohea; 13 Rob Purdham; 12 Lee Hopkins (C); 16 Joe Mbu. Subs (all used): 11 Solomon Haumono; 14 Danny Williams; 10 Steve Trindall; 4 Mark O'Halloran.
Tries: Wells (25), Leuluai (36, 54), Bradley-Qalilawa (40), Purdham (75); **Goals:** Sykes 4/6.
Rugby Leaguer & League Express Men of the Match:
Saints: Willie Talau; *Broncos:* Luke Dorn.
Penalty count: 6-3; **Half-time:** 8-20; **Referee:** Karl Kirkpatrick (Warrington); **Attendance:** 8,521.

Saturday 18th June 2005

LEEDS RHINOS 70 WIGAN WARRIORS 0

RHINOS: 1 Richard Mathers; 2 Mark Calderwood; 3 Chev Walker; 4 Keith Senior; 5 Marcus Bai; 13 Kevin Sinfield (C); 7 Rob Burrow; 8 Ryan Bailey; 14 Andrew Dunemann; 15 Danny Ward; 12 Chris McKenna; 18 Jamie Jones-Buchanan; 20 Gareth Ellis. Subs (all used): 16 Willie Poching; 11 Ali Lauitiiti; 6 Danny McGuire; 10 Barrie McDermott.
Tries: Burrow (15, 78), Walker (20, 55), Dunemann (25), McDermott (34, 60), Calderwood (47, 64), McGuire (49, 67), Senior (51), Lauitiiti (70);
Goals: Sinfield 8/9, Burrow 1/3, McGuire 0/1.
WARRIORS: 14 Kevin Brown; 5 Brian Carney; 3 Martin Aspinwall; 32 Liam Botham; 21 Chris Melling; 7 Dennis Moran; 25 James Coyle; 10 Jerome Guisset; 9 Terry Newton (C); 16 Danny Sculthorpe; 20 Harrison Hansen; 12 Danny Tickle; 22 David Allen. Subs (all used): 18 Wayne Godwin; 8 Jerry Seuseu; 19 Stephen Wild; 29 Joel Tomkins.
On report:
Seuseu (59) - late challenge on Jones-Buchanan.
Rugby Leaguer & League Express Men of the Match:
Rhinos: Ali Lauitiiti; *Warriors:* Danny Sculthorpe.
Penalty count: 7-5; **Half-time:** 24-0;
Referee: Ian Smith (Oldham); **Attendance:** 18,177.

Sunday 19th June 2005

BRADFORD BULLS 25 WIDNES VIKINGS 25

BULLS: 6 Michael Withers; 17 Stuart Reardon; 13 Ben Harris; 19 Jamie Langley; 22 Karl Pryce; 18 Iestyn Harris; 7 Paul Deacon; 8 Joe Vagana; 15 Karl Pratt; 29 Stuart Fielden; 12 Jamie Peacock (C); 27 Rob Parker; 11 Lee Radford. Subs (all used): 20 Matt Cook; 25 Brett Ferres; 14 Andy Lynch; 1 Robbie Paul.
Tries: Deacon (56), Paul (68, 73), Radford (71);
Goals: Deacon 4/4; **Field goal:** Deacon.
On report: Vagana (12) - late tackle on Cassidy.
VIKINGS: 14 Gary Hulse; 5 Andrew Emelio; 1 Gary Connolly; 18 Sala Fa'alogo; 28 Gray Viane; 33 Jules O'Neill; 6 Owen Craigie; 8 Terry O'Connor; 9 Shane Millard (C); 12 John Stankevitch; 11 Mick Cassidy; 15 Matt Whitaker; 16 Daniel Frame. Subs (all used): 7 Stephen Myler; 17 David Mills; 10 Julian O'Neill; 20 Mark Smith.
Tries: Hulse (15), Connolly (28), Craigie (43), Emelio (78); **Goals:** Jules O'Neill 4/5; **Field goal:** Jules O'Neill.
Rugby Leaguer & League Express Men of the Match: *Bulls:* Jamie Peacock; *Vikings:* Mick Cassidy.
Penalty count: 3-5; **Half-time:** 0-13;
Referee: Steve Ganson (St Helens); **Attendance:** 10,715.

HUDDERSFIELD GIANTS 40
WAKEFIELD TRINITY WILDCATS 22

GIANTS: 1 Paul Reilly; 5 Stuart Donlan; 3 James Evans; 11 Chris Nero; 34 Marcus St Hilaire; 6 Chris Thorman (C); 7 Paul March; 18 Eorl Crabtree; 9 Brad Drew; 10 Jim Gannon; 19 Jon Grayshon; 17 Paul Smith; 14 Stuart Jones. Subs (all used): 27 Wayne McDonald; 22 Ryan Clayton; 20 Paul White; 21 Paul Jackson.
Tries: Crabtree (12), Reilly (23), Thorman (27), Nero (30, 79), White (74); **Goals:** Thorman 8/9.
WILDCATS: 21 Mark Field; 1 Colum Halpenny; 3 Jason Demetriou (C); 4 Sid Domic; 5 Semi Tadulala; 6 Jamie Rooney; 7 Ben Jeffries; 8 Darrell Griffin; 9 David March; 27 Chris Feather; 11 David Solomona; 17 Duncan MacGillivray; 13 Rob Spicer. Subs (all used): 10 Michael Korkidas; 14 Sam Obst; 18 Olivier Elima; 16 Steve Snitch.
Tries: Jeffries (34, 54), MacGillivray (37), Obst (42);
Goals: Rooney 3/4.
Rugby Leaguer & League Express Men of the Match: *Giants:* Chris Nero; *Wildcats:* Sam Obst.
Penalty count: 9-6; **Half-time:** 28-10; **Referee:** Richard Silverwood (Dewsbury); **Attendance:** 4,544.

WARRINGTON WOLVES 48 SALFORD CITY REDS 14

WOLVES: 1 Brent Grose; 2 Henry Fa'afili; 3 Martin Gleeson; 4 Toa Kohe-Love; 25 Chris Bridge; 6 Lee Briers (C); 7 Nathan Wood; 8 Chris Leikvoll; 9 Jon Clarke; 10 Mark Hilton; 11 Logan Swann; 15 Ben Westwood; 13 Paul Noone. Subs (all used): 5 Dean Gaskell; 18 Graham Appo; 16 Paul Wood; 17 Danny Lima.
Tries: Swann (3, 68), Kohe-Love (35, 75), Martin Gleeson (39, 79), Westwood (58, 63, 70);
Goals: Bridge 4/6, Briers 2/3.
CITY REDS: 15 Karl Fitzpatrick; 2 David Hodgson; 3 Stuart Littler; 1 Cliff Beverley; 4 Junior Langi; 25 Tim Hartley; 7 Luke Robinson; 10 Sean Rutgerson; 9 Malcolm Alker (C); 22 Simon Baldwin; 11 Mark Shipway; 16 Nathan McAvoy; 13 Chris Charles. Subs (all used): 8 Andy Coley; 17 Gareth Haggerty; 14 Paul Highton; 24 Andy Johnson.
Tries: Shipway (17), Hartley (30), Beverley (47);
Goals: Charles 1/3.
Rugby Leaguer & League Express Men of the Match: *Wolves:* Ben Westwood; *City Reds:* Luke Robinson.
Penalty count: 4-3; **Half-time:** 16-8; **Referee:** Ronnie Laughton (Barnsley); **Attendance:** 10,925.

ROUND 19

Friday 1st July 2005

LEEDS RHINOS 36 BRADFORD BULLS 26

RHINOS: 1 Richard Mathers; 2 Mark Calderwood; 3 Chev Walker; 4 Keith Senior; 5 Marcus Bai; 13 Kevin Sinfield (C); 7 Rob Burrow; 8 Ryan Bailey; 14 Andrew Dunemann; 15 Danny Ward; 18 Jamie Jones-Buchanan; 12 Chris McKenna; 20 Gareth Ellis. Subs (all used): 16 Willie Poching; 11 Ali Lauitiiti; 6 Danny McGuire; 10 Barrie McDermott.
Tries: Senior (2, 63), Jones-Buchanan (22), McGuire (35, 51), Lauitiiti (68); **Goals:** Sinfield 6/6.
BULLS: 6 Michael Withers; 17 Stuart Reardon; 13 Ben Harris; 16 Paul Johnson; 15 Karl Pratt; 1 Robbie Paul; 7 Paul Deacon; 8 Joe Vagana; 9 Ian Henderson (D); 29 Stuart Fielden; 19 Jamie Langley; 12 Jamie Peacock (C); 11 Lee Radford. Subs (all used): 14 Andy Lynch; 18 Iestyn Harris; 27 Rob Parker; 10 Brad Meyers.
Tries: Peacock (14), Johnson (29, 75), B Harris (61), Meyers (72); **Goals:** Deacon 3/5.
Sin bin: I Harris (78) – foul play.
Rugby Leaguer & League Express Men of the Match: *Rhinos:* Chev Walker; *Bulls:* Iestyn Harris.
Penalty count: 7-9; **Half-time:** 18-10;
Referee: Ashley Klein (Keighley); **Attendance:** 21,225.

LEIGH CENTURIONS 22 WIGAN WARRIORS 30

CENTURIONS: 24 John Wilshere; 14 Steve Maden; 6 Danny Halliwell; 9 Phil Jones; 8 Rob Jackson; 5 Mick Govin; 2 John Duffy; 4 Darren Fleary (C); 18 Paul Rowley; 20 Craig Stapleton; 12 Oliver Wilkes; 13 Mark Leafa; 10 Jason Kent. Subs (all used): 31 Warren Stevens; 21 Matt Sturm; 15 Richard Marshall; 32 Robbie Mears.
Tries: Wilshere (5), Govin (77), Sturm (80);
Goals: P Jones 5/5.
WARRIORS: 30 Sean Gleeson; 5 Brian Carney; 3 Martin Aspinwall; 4 David Vaealiki; 2 Brett Dallas; 22 David Allen; 7 Dennis Moran (C); 27 Bryn Hargreaves; 18 Wayne Godwin; 8 Jerry Seuseu; 19 Stephen Wild; 20 Harrison Hansen; 32 Liam Botham. Subs (all used): 9 Terry Newton; 16 Danny Sculthorpe; 12 Danny Tickle; 25 James Coyle.
Tries: Aspinwall (9, 34), Moran (44), Tickle (64), Newton (67); **Goals:** Botham 0/1, Tickle 5/6.
Rugby Leaguer & League Express Men of the Match: *Centurions:* John Wilshere; *Warriors:* Dennis Moran.
Penalty count: 8-9; **Half-time:** 10-8; **Referee:** Karl Kirkpatrick (Warrington); **Attendance:** 7,458.

Saturday 2nd July 2005

LONDON BRONCOS 24 HULL FC 24

BRONCOS: 6 Mark McLinden (C); 2 Jon Wells; 13 Rob Purdham; 1 Paul Sykes; 3 Nick Bradley-Qalilawa; 21 Luke Dorn; 7 Thomas Leuluai; 10 Steve Trindall; 19 David Highton; 11 Solomon Haumono; 12 Lee Hopkins; 14 Danny Williams; 16 Joe Mbu. Subs (all used): 17 Mark Tookey; 20 Filimone Lolohea; 4 Mark O'Halloran; 30 Feleti Mateo.
Tries: Hopkins (6), Dorn (14), Bradley-Qalilawa (36), McLinden (69); **Goals:** Sykes 4/5.
HULL: 1 Shaun Briscoe; 2 Nathan Blacklock; 30 Richard Whiting; 3 Kirk Yeaman; 26 Richie Barnett; 13 Paul Cooke; 6 Richard Horne (C); 8 Ewan Dowes; 21 Danny Brough; 15 Jamie Thackray; 17 Chris Chester; 12 Stephen Kearney; 11 Shayne McMenemy. Subs (all used): 14 Motu Tony; 24 Graeme Horne; 20 Garreth Carvell; 18 Liam Higgins.
Tries: Chester (20), Barnett (23), Blacklock (41), Briscoe (65); **Goals:** Cooke 3/4, Brough 1/1.
Rugby Leaguer & League Express Men of the Match: *Broncos:* Thomas Leuluai; *Hull:* Paul Cooke.
Penalty count: 4-4; **Half-time:** 16-10;
Referee: Ben Thaler (Wakefield);
Attendance: 3,775 *(at Brewery Field, Bridgend).*

SALFORD CITY REDS 24 HUDDERSFIELD GIANTS 16

CITY REDS: 15 Karl Fitzpatrick; 4 Junior Langi; 3 Stuart Littler; 2 David Hodgson; 28 Andy Smith (D); 1 Cliff Beverley; 7 Luke Robinson; 10 Sean Rutgerson; 9 Malcolm Alker (C); 14 Paul Highton; 11 Mark Shipway; 16 Nathan McAvoy; 13 Chris Charles. Subs (all used): 8 Andy Coley; 12 Ian Sibbit; 17 Gareth Haggerty; 22 Simon Baldwin.
Tries: Beverley (12), Robinson (48), Charles (56);
Goals: Charles 6/7.
On report: Spear tackle (69) on Gene.
GIANTS: 1 Paul Reilly; 34 Marcus St Hilaire; 3 James Evans; 22 Ryan Clayton; 5 Stuart Donlan; 6 Chris Thorman (C); 7 Paul March; 18 Eorl Crabtree; 9 Brad Drew; 10 Jim Gannon; 11 Chris Nero; 17 Paul Smith; 19 Jon Grayshon. Subs (all used): 2 Hefin O'Hare; 13 Stanley Gene; 21 Paul Jackson; 27 Wayne McDonald.
Tries: St Hilaire (9), Donlan (61), Thorman (69);
Goals: Thorman 2/3.
Rugby Leaguer & League Express Men of the Match: *City Reds:* Luke Robinson; *Giants:* Paul March.
Penalty count: 9-5; **Half-time:** 8-6; **Referee:** Richard Silverwood (Dewsbury); **Attendance:** 2,682.

Sunday 3rd July 2005

WIDNES VIKINGS 24 WARRINGTON WOLVES 25

VIKINGS: 24 Tim Holmes; 5 Andrew Emelio; 21 Jon Whittle; 18 Sala Fa'alogo; 28 Gray Viane; 6 Owen Craigie; 33 Jules O'Neill; 8 Terry O'Connor (C); 20 Mark Smith; 12 John Stankevitch; 11 Mick Cassidy; 16 Daniel Frame; 13 Simon Finnigan. Subs (all used): 10 Julian O'Neill; 17 David Mills; 7 Stephen Myler; 15 Matt Whitaker.
Tries: Emelio (15), Viane (45, 61), Julian O'Neill (69);
Goals: Jules O'Neill 4/6.
WOLVES: 1 Brent Grose; 2 Henry Fa'afili; 3 Martin Gleeson; 4 Toa Kohe-Love; 5 Dean Gaskell; 6 Lee Briers (C); 7 Nathan Wood; 8 Chris Leikvoll; 9 Jon Clarke; 10 Mark Hilton; 11 Logan Swann; 13 Paul Noone; 15 Ben Westwood. Subs (all used): 16 Paul Wood; 17 Danny Lima; 18 Graham Appo; 14 Mark Gleeson.
Tries: Clarke (1), Martin Gleeson (35), Lima (38), N Wood (49), Appo (57);
Goals: Noone 2/3, Briers 0/2; **Field goal:** Briers.
Rugby Leaguer & League Express Men of the Match: *Vikings:* Mark Smith; *Wolves:* Nathan Wood.
Penalty count: 6-8; **Half-time:** 8-14;
Referee: Ian Smith (Oldham); **Attendance:** 9,825.

WAKEFIELD TRINITY WILDCATS 26 ST HELENS 38

WILDCATS: 1 Colum Halpenny; 21 Mark Field; 3 Jason Demetriou (C); 13 Rob Spicer; 5 Semi Tadulala; 6 Jamie Rooney; 7 Ben Jeffries; 8 Darrell Griffin; 14 Sam Obst; 10 Michael Korkidas; 11 David Solomona; 17 Duncan MacGillivray; 4 Sid Domic. Subs (all used): 9 David March; 2 Michael Wainwright; 18 Olivier Elima; 16 Steve Snitch.
Tries: Elima (21), Jeffries (30, 66), Demetriou (64);
Goals: Rooney 5/5.
SAINTS: 1 Paul Wellens; 20 Ian Hardman; 3 Jamie Lyon; 4 Willie Talau; 2 Ade Gardner; 12 Jon Wilkin; 13 Paul Sculthorpe (C); 8 Nick Fozzard; 9 Keiron Cunningham; 17 Paul Anderson; 11 Lee Gilmour; 19 James Graham; 27 Vinnie Anderson. Subs (all used): 21 James Roby; 15 Mike Bennett; 16 Keith Mason; 10 Mark Edmondson.
Tries: Lyon (1), Sculthorpe (14), Wilkin (24, 46), Wellens (38), V Anderson (49);
Goals: Lyon 4/4, Sculthorpe 3/3.
Rugby Leaguer & League Express Men of the Match: *Wildcats:* David Solomona; *Saints:* Keiron Cunningham.
Penalty count: 10-6; **Half-time:** 14-24;
Referee: Ronnie Laughton (Barnsley); **Attendance:** 5,323.

ROUND 20

Friday 8th July 2005

SALFORD CITY REDS 34 WIDNES VIKINGS 16

CITY REDS: 15 Karl Fitzpatrick; 2 David Hodgson; 3 Stuart Littler; 12 Ian Sibbit; 28 Andy Smith; 1 Cliff Beverley; 7 Luke Robinson; 10 Sean Rutgerson; 9 Malcolm Alker (C); 14 Paul Highton; 11 Mark Shipway; 16 Nathan McAvoy; 13 Chris Charles. Subs (all used): 8 Andy Coley; 17 Gareth Haggerty; 22 Simon Baldwin; 25 Tim Hartley.
Tries: Littler (30), Sibbit (34), Robinson (40), Hodgson (50, 73), Haggerty (68); **Goals:** Charles 5/6.
VIKINGS: 24 Tim Holmes; 5 Andrew Emelio; 18 Sala Fa'alogo; 21 Jon Whittle; 28 Gray Viane; 6 Owen Craigie; 33 Jules O'Neill; 8 Terry O'Connor; 20 Mark Smith; 12 John Stankevitch; 11 Mick Cassidy; 9 Shane Millard (C); 13 Simon Finnigan. Subs (all used): 14 Gary Hulse; 15 Matt Whitaker; 16 Daniel Frame; 17 David Mills.
Tries: Whittle (56), Finnigan (62), Viane (70);
Goals: Jules O'Neill 2/3.
Rugby Leaguer & League Express Men of the Match: *City Reds:* Chris Charles; *Vikings:* Jon Whittle.
Penalty count: 5-8; **Half-time:** 18-0; **Referee:** Ronnie Laughton (Barnsley); **Attendance:** 4,507.

ST HELENS 18 HULL FC 10

SAINTS: 1 Paul Wellens; 5 Darren Albert; 3 Jamie Lyon; 4 Willie Talau; 2 Ade Gardner; 20 Ian Hardman; 26 Scott Moore; 8 Nick Fozzard; 9 Keiron Cunningham (C); 17 Paul Anderson; 10 Mark Edmondson; 15 Mike Bennett; 12 Jon Wilkin. Subs (all used): 16 Keith Mason; 21 James Roby; 24 Maurie Fa'asavalu; 28 Paul Clough (D).
Tries: Bennett (15), Wellens (50), Lyon (52);
Goals: Lyon 3/3.
HULL: 1 Shaun Briscoe; 2 Nathan Blacklock; 3 Kirk Yeaman; 30 Richard Whiting; 14 Motu Tony; 13 Paul Cooke; 6 Richard Horne (C); 8 Ewan Dowes; 21 Danny Brough; 15 Jamie Thackray; 17 Chris Chester; 12 Stephen Kearney; 11 Shayne McMenemy. Subs (all used): 10 Paul King; 16 Tom Saxton; 20 Garreth Carvell; 24 Graeme Horne.
Tries: Whiting (1), Yeaman (58);
Goals: Brough 0/1, Cooke 1/1.
Rugby Leaguer & League Express Men of the Match: *Saints:* Paul Wellens; *Hull:* Jamie Thackray.
Penalty count: 9-8; **Half-time:** 6-4;
Referee: Ian Smith (Oldham); **Attendance:** 9,199.

Saturday 9th July 2005

LONDON BRONCOS 32 LEEDS RHINOS 24

BRONCOS: 6 Mark McLinden (C); 4 Mark O'Halloran; 24 Tyrone Smith; 1 Paul Sykes; 3 Nick Bradley-Qalilawa; 21 Luke Dorn; 7 Thomas Leuluai; 10 Steve Trindall; 19 David Highton; 18 Anthony Armour; 11 Solomon Haumono; 12 Lee Hopkins; 13 Rob Purdham. Subs (all used): 20 Filimone Lolohea; 17 Mark Tookey; 30 Feleti Mateo; 16 Joe Mbu.
Tries: Bradley-Qalilawa (25, 68), Leuluai (37, 75), Dorn (61), O'Halloran (64); **Goals:** Sykes 4/6.
RHINOS: 1 Richard Mathers; 2 Mark Calderwood; 3 Chev Walker; 4 Keith Senior (C); 5 Marcus Bai; 6 Danny McGuire; 7 Rob Burrow; 8 Ryan Bailey; 14 Andrew Dunemann; 15 Danny Ward; 18 Jamie Jones-Buchanan; 12 Chris McKenna; 20 Gareth Ellis. Subs (all used): 16 Willie Poching; 11 Ali Lauitiiti; 10 Barrie McDermott; 9 Matt Diskin.
Tries: Bai (5), Mathers (16), McGuire (19), Calderwood (32), Senior (55); **Goals:** Burrow 2/5.
Rugby Leaguer & League Express Men of the Match: *Broncos:* Luke Dorn; *Rhinos:* Richard Mathers.
Penalty count: 10-6; **Half-time:** 8-20;
Referee: Ashley Klein (Keighley);
Attendance: 7,000 *(at Stade Aime Giral, Perpignan).*

WIGAN WARRIORS 36 WARRINGTON WOLVES 17

WARRIORS: 21 Chris Melling; 23 Liam Colbon; 3 Martin Aspinwall; 4 David Vaealiki; 2 Brett Dallas; 6 Danny Orr; 7 Dennis Moran (C); 27 Bryn Hargreaves; 18 Wayne Godwin; 10 Jerome Guisset; 22 David Allen; 19 Stephen Wild; 32 Liam Botham. Subs (all used): 12 Danny Tickle; 8 Jerry Seuseu; 9 Terry Newton; 20 Harrison Hansen.
Tries: Moran (11), Melling (49), Dallas (57), Godwin (66), Tickle (71), Newton (80);
Goals: Botham 0/1, Tickle 6/6.
WOLVES: 1 Brent Grose; 2 Henry Fa'afili; 3 Martin Gleeson; 4 Toa Kohe-Love; 5 Dean Gaskell; 25 Chris Bridge; 7 Nathan Wood (C); 16 Paul Wood; 9 Jon Clarke; 8 Chris Leikvoll; 12 Mike Wainwright; 11 Logan Swann; 15 Ben Westwood. Subs (all used): 14 Mark Gleeson; 17 Danny Lima; 13 Paul Noone; 22 Steve Pickersgill.
Tries: Grose (8), Kohe-Love (30), Bridge (60);
Goals: Bridge 2/3; **Field goal:** Bridge.
Rugby Leaguer & League Express Men of the Match: *Warriors:* Dennis Moran; *Wolves:* Chris Bridge.
Penalty count: 7-5; **Half-time:** 4-11; **Referee:** Richard Silverwood (Dewsbury); **Attendance:** 14,162.

Sunday 10th July 2005

HUDDERSFIELD GIANTS 32 LEIGH CENTURIONS 22

GIANTS: 1 Paul Reilly; 5 Stuart Donlan; 3 James Evans;

22 Ryan Clayton; 34 Marcus St Hilaire; 6 Chris Thorman (C); 7 Paul March; 27 Wayne McDonald; 9 Brad Drew; 10 Jim Gannon; 11 Chris Nero; 17 Paul Smith; 18 Eorl Crabtree. Subs (all used): 2 Hefin O'Hare; 19 Jon Grayshon; 20 Paul White; 21 Paul Jackson.
Tries: Evans (1), Thorman (29), Grayshon (46), O'Hare (79); **Goals:** Thorman 8/10.
Dismissal: Reilly (15) – use of the elbow.
CENTURIONS: 24 John Wilshere; 1 Ben Cooper; 6 Danny Halliwell; 9 Phil Jones; 14 Steve Maden; 5 Mick Govin; 2 John Duffy; 4 Darren Fleary (C); 18 Paul Rowley; 20 Craig Stapleton; 12 Oliver Wilkes; 13 Mark Leafa; 10 Jason Kent. Subs (all used): 35 Chris Jones (D); 31 Warren Stevens; 32 Robbie Mears; 21 Matt Sturm.
Tries: Govin (38), Maden (64), Wilshere (73);
Goals: P Jones 5/6.
Sin bin: Wilkes (45) - holding down.
Rugby Leaguer & League Express Men of the Match: *Giants:* Chris Thorman; *Centurions:* Steve Maden.
Penalty count: 15-9; **Half-time:** 16-10;
Referee: Steve Ganson (St Helens); **Attendance:** 3,889.

WAKEFIELD TRINITY WILDCATS 44 BRADFORD BULLS 34

WILDCATS: 1 Colum Halpenny; 21 Mark Field; 3 Jason Demetriou (C); 4 Sid Domic; 5 Semi Tadulala; 7 Ben Jeffries; 14 Sam Obst; 8 Darrell Griffin; 9 David March; 10 Michael Korkidas; 11 David Solomona; 17 Duncan MacGillivray; 12 Jamie Field. Subs (all used): 6 Jamie Rooney; 16 Steve Snitch; 18 Olivier Elima; 15 David Wrench.
Tries: MacGillivray (7), Halpenny (21), Jeffries (30, 67), Korkidas (48), Rooney (70, 80); **Goals:** March 8/8.
BULLS: 6 Michael Withers; 17 Stuart Reardon; 13 Ben Harris; 16 Paul Johnson; 15 Karl Pratt; 18 Iestyn Harris; 7 Paul Deacon; 8 Joe Vagana; 9 Ian Henderson; 29 Stuart Fielden; 12 Jamie Peacock (C); 10 Brad Meyers; 11 Lee Radford. Subs (all used): 3 Leon Pryce; 19 Jamie Langley; 27 Rob Parker; 14 Andy Lynch.
Tries: Withers (2), Deacon (27), Pratt (37, 40, 61), Meyers (79); **Goals:** Deacon 5/6.
Rugby Leaguer & League Express Men of the Match: *Wildcats:* Ben Jeffries; *Bulls:* Jamie Peacock.
Penalty count: 4-1; **Half-time:** 20-24; **Referee:** Karl Kirkpatrick (Warrington); **Attendance:** 5,954.

ROUND 21

Friday 15th July 2005

LEEDS RHINOS 54 SALFORD CITY REDS 14

RHINOS: 1 Richard Mathers; 2 Mark Calderwood; 3 Chev Walker; 4 Keith Senior (C); 5 Marcus Bai; 6 Danny McGuire; 7 Rob Burrow; 11 Ali Lauitiiti; 9 Matt Diskin; 10 Barrie McDermott; 18 Jamie Jones-Buchanan; 12 Chris McKenna; 20 Gareth Ellis. Subs (all used): 22 Nick Scruton; 16 Willie Poching; 14 Andrew Dunemann; 27 Francis Cummins.
Tries: McGuire (2), Burrow (8, 71), Calderwood (16, 39, 63), Mathers (27, 37), Dunemann (33), Poching (65); **Goals:** Burrow 7/10.
CITY REDS: 15 Karl Fitzpatrick; 2 David Hodgson; 3 Stuart Littler; 12 Ian Sibbit; 28 Andy Smith; 1 Cliff Beverley; 7 Luke Robinson; 10 Sean Rutgerson; 9 Malcolm Alker (C); 14 Paul Highton; 16 Nathan McAvoy; 11 Mark Shipway; 13 Chris Charles. Subs (all used): 8 Andy Coley; 17 Gareth Haggerty; 22 Simon Baldwin; 25 Tim Hartley.
Tries: Littler (42, 55), Hartley (53); **Goals:** Charles 1/3.
Rugby Leaguer & League Express Men of the Match: *Rhinos:* Rob Burrow; *City Reds:* Malcolm Alker.
Penalty count: 7-7; **Half-time:** 42-0; **Referee:** Karl Kirkpatrick (Warrington); **Attendance:** 13,904.

ST HELENS 40 WIGAN WARRIORS 18

SAINTS: 1 Paul Wellens; 5 Darren Albert; 3 Jamie Lyon; 4 Willie Talau; 2 Ade Gardner; 12 Jon Wilkin; 21 James Roby; 8 Nick Fozzard; 9 Keiron Cunningham; 17 Paul Anderson; 11 Lee Gilmour; 15 Mike Bennett; 13 Paul Sculthorpe (C). Subs (all used): 26 Scott Moore; 10 Mark Edmondson; 24 Maurie Fa'asavalu; 19 James Graham.
Tries: Talau (4, 55), Albert (7), Gilmour (21), Roby (39), Gardner (48), Edmondson (52); **Goals:** Sculthorpe 6/7.
Sin bin: Lyon (45) - interference.
WARRIORS: 21 Chris Melling; 23 Liam Colbon; 19 Stephen Wild; 4 David Vaealiki; 3 Martin Aspinwall; 6 Danny Orr; 7 Dennis Moran; 27 Bryn Hargreaves; 9 Terry Newton (C); 10 Jerome Guisset; 12 Danny Tickle; 22 David Allen; 32 Liam Botham. Subs (all used): 16 Danny Sculthorpe; 18 Wayne Godwin; 20 Harrison Hansen; 29 Joel Tomkins.
Tries: Aspinwall (31), Hargreaves (71), Guisset (75);
Goals: Tickle 3/3.
Sin bin: Aspinwall (20) - professional foul; Sculthorpe (46) - interference.
Rugby Leaguer & League Express Men of the Match: *Saints:* Paul Sculthorpe; *Warriors:* Danny Orr.
Penalty count: 9-15; **Half-time:** 24-6; **Referee:** Ronnie Laughton (Barnsley); **Attendance:** 13,281.

Saturday 16th July 2005

HULL FC 34 HUDDERSFIELD GIANTS 24

HULL: 14 Motu Tony; 16 Tom Saxton; 30 Richard Whiting; 3 Kirk Yeaman; 26 Richie Barnett; 13 Paul Cooke; 6 Richard Horne; 8 Ewan Dowes; 9 Richard Swain (C); 15 Jamie Thackray; 11 Shayne McMenemy; 12 Stephen Kearney; 17 Chris Chester. Subs (all used): 10 Paul King; 20 Garreth Carvell; 21 Danny Brough; 24 Graeme Horne.
Tries: Barnett (6, 16), R Horne (42), Yeaman (50, 59), Whiting (56); **Goals:** Cooke 5/6, Brough 0/1.
Dismissal: Cooke (66) – head-butt.
Sin bin: Tony (26) – interference.
GIANTS: 34 Marcus St Hilaire; 28 Lee Greenwood (D); 3 James Evans; 22 Ryan Clayton; 5 Stuart Donlan; 6 Chris Thorman (C); 7 Paul March; 27 Wayne McDonald; 9 Brad Drew; 21 Paul Jackson; 11 Chris Nero; 17 Paul Smith; 2 Hefin O'Hare. Subs (all used): 10 Jim Gannon; 18 Eorl Crabtree; 19 Jon Grayshon; 20 Paul White.
Tries: Smith (25), Greenwood (37), Nero (46), Crabtree (75); **Goals:** Thorman 4/5.
On report: Nero and Evans (80) – alleged spear tackle.
Rugby Leaguer & League Express Men of the Match: *Hull:* Kirk Yeaman; *Giants:* Chris Thorman.
Penalty count: 13-12; **Half-time:** 12-14; **Referee:** Richard Silverwood (Dewsbury); **Attendance:** 7,962.

Sunday 17th July 2005

BRADFORD BULLS 58 LEIGH CENTURIONS 12

BULLS: 6 Michael Withers; 17 Stuart Reardon; 13 Ben Harris; 16 Paul Johnson; 15 Karl Pratt; 18 Iestyn Harris; 7 Paul Deacon; 8 Joe Vagana; 9 Ian Henderson; 29 Stuart Fielden; 12 Jamie Peacock (C); 10 Brad Meyers; 19 Jamie Langley. Subs (all used): 3 Leon Pryce; 4 Shontayne Hape; 14 Andy Lynch; 27 Rob Parker.
Tries: Fielden (2), Henderson (10), I Harris (21), B Harris (26, 37, 79), Pratt (41), L Pryce (49), Withers (66), Meyers (77); **Goals:** Deacon 6/7, I Harris 3/3.
CENTURIONS: 24 John Wilshere; 19 Rob Smyth; 6 Danny Halliwell; 9 Phil Jones; 1 Ben Cooper; 5 Mick Govin; 10 Jason Kent; 4 Darren Fleary (C); 18 Paul Rowley; 20 Craig Stapleton; 35 Chris Jones; 12 Oliver Wilkes; 13 Mark Leafa. Subs (all used): 8 Rob Jackson; 31 Warren Stevens; 32 Robbie Mears; 21 Matt Sturm.
Tries: P Jones (31), Cooper (60); **Goals:** P Jones 2/2.
Rugby Leaguer & League Express Men of the Match: *Bulls:* Ben Harris; *Centurions:* Mark Leafa.
Penalty count: 8-4; **Half-time:** 30-6;
Referee: Ashley Klein (Keighley); **Attendance:** 10,294.

WARRINGTON WOLVES 26 LONDON BRONCOS 14

WOLVES: 1 Brent Grose; 2 Henry Fa'afili; 3 Martin Gleeson; 15 Ben Westwood; 5 Dean Gaskell; 25 Chris Bridge; 7 Nathan Wood (C); 8 Chris Leikvoll; 9 Jon Clarke; 10 Mark Hilton; 11 Logan Swann; 12 Mike Wainwright; 13 Paul Noone. Subs (all used): 18 Graham Appo; 14 Mark Gleeson; 16 Paul Wood; 17 Danny Lima.
Tries: Martin Gleeson (12), Gaskell (35), Fa'afili (57, 80), Grose (64); **Goals:** Bridge 3/5.
Sin bin: Clarke (69) - pushing off the ball.
BRONCOS: 1 Paul Sykes; 3 Nick Bradley-Qalilawa; 24 Tyrone Smith; 4 Mark O'Halloran; 2 Jon Wells; 6 Mark McLinden (C); 7 Thomas Leuluai; 10 Steve Trindall; 19 David Highton; 18 Anthony Armour; 11 Solomon Haumono; 12 Lee Hopkins; 13 Rob Purdham. Subs (all used): 14 Danny Williams; 17 Mark Tookey; 20 Filimone Lolohea; 30 Feleti Mateo.
Tries: Bradley-Qalilawa (40), Hopkins (71);
Goals: Sykes 2/3, Purdham 1/1.
Sin bin: Sykes (45) - holding down.
Rugby Leaguer & League Express Men of the Match: *Wolves:* Brent Grose; *Broncos:* Lee Hopkins.
Penalty count: 9-8; **Half-time:** 8-6;
Referee: Ian Smith (Oldham); **Attendance:** 10,146.

WIDNES VIKINGS 18 WAKEFIELD TRINITY WILDCATS 44

VIKINGS: 24 Tim Holmes; 5 Andrew Emelio; 21 Jon Whittle; 18 Sala Fa'alogo; 28 Gray Viane; 33 Jules O'Neill; 14 Gary Hulse; 8 Terry O'Connor; 9 Shane Millard (C); 12 John Stankevitch; 11 Mick Cassidy; 16 Daniel Frame; 13 Simon Finnigan. Subs (all used): 10 Julian O'Neill; 20 Mark Smith; 7 Stephen Myler; 15 Matt Whitaker.
Tries: Viane (49, 58, 73), Fa'alogo (68);
Goals: Jules O'Neill 1/4.
Sin bin: Smith (56) - fighting; Stankevitch (56) - fighting.
On report: Millard (51) - late tackle on Elima; Brawl (56).
WILDCATS: 1 Colum Halpenny; 2 Michael Wainwright; 3 Jason Demetriou (C); 4 Sid Domic; 5 Semi Tadulala; 7 Ben Jeffries; 14 Sam Obst; 8 Darrell Griffin; 9 David March; 10 Michael Korkidas; 11 David Solomona; 17 Duncan MacGillivray; 12 Jamie Field. Subs (all used): 6 Jamie Rooney; 15 David Wrench; 18 Olivier Elima; 16 Steve Snitch.
Tries: Obst (5, 37), Solomona (27), Tadulala (32, 42, 45), Jeffries (63); **Goals:** March 7/7, Rooney 1/1.
Sin bin: March (12) - persistent holding down, (56) - fighting; Korkidas (56) - fighting.
On report: Alleged biting incident (16); Brawl (56).
Rugby Leaguer & League Express Men of the Match: *Vikings:* Gray Viane; *Wildcats:* Semi Tadulala.
Penalty count: 11-9; **Half-time:** 0-24;
Referee: Steve Ganson (St Helens); **Attendance:** 6,116.

ROUND 22

Friday 22nd July 2005

LEIGH CENTURIONS 20 ST HELENS 27

CENTURIONS: 24 John Wilshere; 14 Steve Maden; 1 Ben Cooper; 6 Danny Halliwell; 19 Rob Smyth; 9 Phil Jones; 2 John Duffy; 4 Darren Fleary (C); 32 Robbie Mears; 20 Craig Stapleton; 15 Richard Marshall; 13 Mark Leafa; 10 Jason Kent. Subs (all used): 21 Matt Sturm; 31 Warren Stevens; 18 Paul Rowley; 8 Rob Jackson.
Tries: Halliwell (4, 21, 24), John Duffy (51);
Goals: Wilshere 2/4.
Sin bin: Mears (37) - holding down.
SAINTS: 20 Ian Hardman; 5 Darren Albert; 27 Vinnie Anderson; 4 Willie Talau; 2 Ade Gardner; 26 Scott Moore; 6 Jason Hooper; 8 Nick Fozzard; 21 James Roby; 19 James Graham; 11 Lee Gilmour; 15 Mike Bennett; 12 Jon Wilkin. Subs (all used): 3 Jamie Lyon; 24 Maurie Fa'asavalu; 9 Keiron Cunningham (C); 16 Keith Mason.
Tries: Albert (15, 46), Hooper (38), Lyon (54, 73);
Goals: Hooper 0/1, Lyon 3/4; **Field goal:** Wilkin.
Sin bin: Wilkin (35) - deliberate offside.
Rugby Leaguer & League Express Men of the Match: *Centurions:* John Duffy; *Saints:* Jamie Lyon.
Penalty count: 6-9; **Half-time:** 14-8;
Referee: Ian Smith (Oldham); **Attendance:** 5,142.

SALFORD CITY REDS 18 BRADFORD BULLS 24

CITY REDS: 15 Karl Fitzpatrick; 2 David Hodgson; 3 Stuart Littler; 12 Ian Sibbit; 4 Junior Langi; 1 Cliff Beverley; 7 Luke Robinson; 10 Sean Rutgerson; 9 Malcolm Alker (C); 27 Mitchell Stringer; 11 Mark Shipway; 16 Nathan McAvoy; 13 Chris Charles. Subs (all used): 8 Andy Coley; 17 Gareth Haggerty; 22 Simon Baldwin; 25 Tim Hartley.
Tries: Langi (24), Coley (72), Fitzpatrick (74);
Goals: Charles 3/4.
BULLS: 6 Michael Withers; 17 Stuart Reardon; 13 Ben Harris; 16 Paul Johnson; 22 Karl Pryce; 18 Iestyn Harris; 7 Paul Deacon; 8 Joe Vagana; 9 Ian Henderson; 29 Stuart Fielden; 12 Jamie Peacock (C); 10 Brad Meyers; 27 Rob Parker. Subs (all used): 4 Shontayne Hape; 3 Leon Pryce; 14 Andy Lynch; 20 Matt Cook.
Tries: K Pryce (8), Deacon (11), I Harris (51), L Pryce (58); **Goals:** Deacon 3/3, I Harris 1/1.
Sin bin: Withers (54) - professional foul; Reardon (71) - obstruction.
Rugby Leaguer & League Express Men of the Match: *City Reds:* Malcolm Alker; *Bulls:* Stuart Fielden.
Penalty count: 8-8; **Half-time:** 4-12; **Referee:** Richard Silverwood (Dewsbury); **Attendance:** 3,684.

WIGAN WARRIORS 28 WAKEFIELD TRINITY WILDCATS 34

WARRIORS: 1 Kris Radlinski (C); 2 Brett Dallas; 14 Kevin Brown; 19 Stephen Wild; 3 Martin Aspinwall; 6 Danny Orr; 7 Dennis Moran; 27 Bryn Hargreaves; 18 Wayne Godwin; 8 Jerry Seuseu; 22 David Allen; 12 Danny Tickle; 20 Harrison Hansen. Subs (all used): 16 Danny Sculthorpe; 9 Terry Newton; 10 Jerome Guisset; 30 Sean Gleeson.
Tries: Moran (12, 54), Orr (30, 64), Tickle (60);
Goals: Tickle 4/5.
WILDCATS: 1 Colum Halpenny; 2 Michael Wainwright; 3 Jason Demetriou (C); 4 Sid Domic; 5 Semi Tadulala; 7 Ben Jeffries; 14 Sam Obst; 8 Darrell Griffin; 9 David March; 10 Michael Korkidas; 11 David Solomona; 17 Duncan MacGillivray; 12 Jamie Field. Subs (all used): 13 Rob Spicer; 15 David Wrench; 18 Olivier Elima; 16 Steve Snitch.
Tries: Halpenny (18, 21), Obst (38), Jeffries (51), Spicer (72), Solomona (80); **Goals:** March 5/6.
Rugby Leaguer & League Express Men of the Match: *Warriors:* Dennis Moran; *Wildcats:* David Solomona.
Penalty count: 7-5; **Half-time:** 12-16; **Referee:** Karl Kirkpatrick (Warrington); **Attendance:** 9,021.

Saturday 23rd July 2005

WARRINGTON WOLVES 22 LEEDS RHINOS 46

WOLVES: 1 Brent Grose; 2 Henry Fa'afili; 3 Martin Gleeson; 4 Toa Kohe-Love; 18 Graham Appo; 6 Lee Briers (C); 7 Nathan Wood; 8 Chris Leikvoll; 14 Mark Gleeson; 10 Mark Hilton; 11 Logan Swann; 15 Ben Westwood; 9 Jon Clarke. Subs (all used): 22 Steve Pickersgill; 13 Paul Noone; 16 Paul Wood; 17 Danny Lima.
Tries: Grose (16), Swann (38), Fa'afili (67, 78);
Goals: Appo 2/4, Briers 1/1.
RHINOS: 1 Richard Mathers; 2 Mark Calderwood; 3 Chev Walker; 4 Keith Senior (C); 5 Marcus Bai; 6 Danny McGuire; 7 Rob Burrow; 15 Danny Ward; 9 Matt Diskin; 10 Barrie McDermott; 11 Ali Lauitiiti; 12 Chris McKenna; 20 Gareth Ellis. Subs (all used): 16 Willie Poching; 14 Andrew Dunemann; 22 Nick Scruton; 27 Francis Cummins.
Tries: Walker (3, 26), Diskin (20), Burrow (47), Senior (60), Bai (71, 80), Calderwood (74); **Goals:** Burrow 7/8.
Rugby Leaguer & League Express Men of the Match: *Wolves:* Logan Swann; *Rhinos:* Rob Burrow.
Penalty count: 7-6; **Half-time:** 12-18;
Referee: Steve Ganson (St Helens); **Attendance:** 11,036.

Sunday 24th July 2005

LONDON BRONCOS 35 HUDDERSFIELD GIANTS 26

BRONCOS: 25 Zebastian Luisi; 2 Jon Wells; 24 Tyrone Smith; 1 Paul Sykes; 3 Nick Bradley-Qalilawa; 21 Luke Dorn; 6 Mark McLinden (C); 10 Steve Trindall; 19 David Highton; 11 Solomon Haumono; 12 Lee Hopkins; 13 Rob Purdham; 16 Joe Mbu. Subs (all used): 17 Mark Tookey; 20 Filimone Lolohea; 30 Feleti Mateo; 4 Mark O'Halloran.
Tries: Sykes (6), Purdham (25), Bradley-Qalilawa (29), Tookey (34), Smith (55), Dorn (61); **Goals:** Sykes 5/6;
Field goal: Sykes.
GIANTS: 23 Tom Hemingway; 2 Hefin O'Hare; 3 James Evans; 11 Chris Nero; 28 Lee Greenwood; 6 Chris Thorman (C); 7 Paul March; 27 Wayne McDonald; 9 Brad Drew; 21 Paul Jackson; 19 Jon Grayshon; 17 Paul Smith; 18 Eorl Crabtree. Subs (all used): 10 Jim Gannon; 20 Paul White; 22 Ryan Clayton; 26 Stephen Jones (D).
Tries: Drew (3), Thorman (10), Gannon (73), Nero (80);

Goals: Thorman 5/6.
Rugby Leaguer & League Express Men of the Match: *Broncos:* Luke Dorn; *Giants:* Chris Thorman.
Penalty count: 3-6; **Half-time:** 22-14;
Referee: Ashley Klein (Keighley); **Attendance:** 3,221.

WIDNES VIKINGS 20 HULL FC 40

VIKINGS: 24 Tim Holmes; 5 Andrew Emelio; 21 Jon Whittle; 4 Adam Hughes; 28 Gray Viane; 7 Stephen Myler; 33 Jules O'Neill; 8 Terry O'Connor; 9 Shane Millard (C); 10 Julian O'Neill; 11 Mick Cassidy; 16 Daniel Frame; 13 Simon Finnigan. Subs (all used): 15 Matt Whitaker; 20 Mark Smith; 17 David Mills; 18 Sala Fa'alogo.
Tries: Hughes (17), Millard (23), Viane (43, 74), Frame (77); **Goals:** Myler 0/5.
HULL: 14 Motu Tony; 16 Tom Saxton; 22 Kirk Dixon; 3 Kirk Yeaman; 5 Gareth Raynor; 6 Richard Horne; 21 Danny Brough; 8 Ewan Dowes; 9 Richard Swain (C); 20 Garreth Carvell; 17 Chris Chester; 12 Stephen Kearney; 30 Richard Whiting. Subs (all used): 15 Jamie Thackray; 18 Liam Higgins; 24 Graeme Horne; 23 Paul McNicholas.
Tries: Dixon (14, 28, 65), R Horne (19), Kearney (47), G Horne (64), Carvell (70); **Goals:** Brough 6/9.
Rugby Leaguer & League Express Men of the Match: *Vikings:* Shane Millard; *Hull:* Danny Brough.
Penalty count: 9-6; **Half-time:** 8-18;
Referee: Ronnie Laughton (Barnsley); **Attendance:** 5,378.

ROUND 23

Friday 5th August 2005

WARRINGTON WOLVES 10 ST HELENS 30

WOLVES: 1 Brent Grose; 2 Henry Fa'afili; 3 Martin Gleeson; 4 Toa Kohe-Love; 18 Graham Appo; 25 Chris Bridge; 7 Nathan Wood (C); 8 Chris Leikvoll; 9 Jon Clarke; 10 Mark Hilton; 11 Logan Swann; 12 Mike Wainwright; 15 Ben Westwood. Subs (all used): 14 Mark Gleeson; 13 Paul Noone; 16 Paul Wood; 17 Danny Lima.
Tries: Martin Gleeson (47), Noone (53);
Goals: Bridge 1/2.
Sin bin: Clarke (28) - professional foul.
SAINTS: 1 Paul Wellens; 5 Darren Albert; 3 Jamie Lyon; 4 Willie Talau; 2 Ade Gardner; 6 Jason Hooper; 7 Sean Long; 8 Nick Fozzard; 9 Keiron Cunningham; 17 Paul Anderson; 15 Mike Bennett; 12 Jon Wilkin; 13 Paul Sculthorpe (C). Subs (all used): 21 James Roby; 19 James Graham; 24 Maurie Fa'asavalu; 10 Mark Edmondson.
Tries: Bennett (5), Graham (29), Long (36), Gardner (59), Wellens (70); **Goals:** Sculthorpe 5/6.
On report:
Fa'asavalu (72) - dangerous challenge on Grose.
Rugby Leaguer & League Express Men of the Match: *Wolves:* Ben Westwood; *Saints:* Paul Wellens.
Penalty count: 8-9; **Half-time:** 0-18;
Referee: Ian Smith (Oldham); **Attendance:** 12,762.

WIGAN WARRIORS 40 SALFORD CITY REDS 12

WARRIORS: 2 Brett Dallas; 5 Brian Carney; 14 Kevin Brown; 4 David Vaealiki; 3 Martin Aspinwall; 6 Danny Orr; 7 Dennis Moran; 8 Jerry Seuseu; 9 Terry Newton (C); 27 Bryn Hargreaves; 19 Stephen Wild; 12 Danny Tickle; 20 Harrison Hansen. Subs (all used): 22 David Allen; 16 Danny Sculthorpe; 29 Joel Tomkins; 30 Sean Gleeson.
Tries: Tickle (10, 75), Carney (18, 54), Newton (25, 40), Tomkins (61); **Goals:** Tickle 4/6, Orr 2/2.
CITY REDS: 15 Karl Fitzpatrick; 2 David Hodgson; 3 Stuart Littler; 12 Ian Sibbit; 4 Junior Langi; 1 Cliff Beverley; 7 Luke Robinson; 10 Sean Rutgerson; 9 Malcolm Alker (C); 27 Mitchell Stringer; 11 Mark Shipway; 16 Nathan McAvoy; 13 Chris Charles. Subs (all used): 14 Paul Highton; 23 Andrew Brocklehurst; 22 Simon Baldwin; 25 Tim Hartley.
Tries: Littler (7), Brocklehurst (48); **Goals:** Charles 2/2.
Rugby Leaguer & League Express Men of the Match: *Warriors:* Terry Newton; *City Reds:* Stuart Littler.
Penalty count: 5-3; **Half-time:** 24-6;
Referee: Steve Ganson (St Helens); **Attendance:** 10,156.

Sunday 7th August 2005

BRADFORD BULLS 74 WIDNES VIKINGS 24

BULLS: 6 Michael Withers; 17 Stuart Reardon; 13 Ben Harris; 4 Shontayne Hape; 5 Lesley Vainikolo; 18 Iestyn Harris; 7 Paul Deacon; 12 Jamie Peacock (C); 9 Ian Henderson; 29 Stuart Fielden; 16 Paul Johnson; 10 Brad Meyers; 11 Lee Radford. Subs (all used): 1 Robbie Paul; 3 Leon Pryce; 14 Andy Lynch; 27 Rob Parker.
Tries: Fielden (1), Peacock (12), Withers (16, 53), Vainikolo (18, 31), Hape (29, 59), I Harris (35), L Pryce (49), Lynch (56), Reardon (67, 70);
Goals: Deacon 11/13.
VIKINGS: 35 Brad Watts (D); 5 Andrew Emelio; 21 Jon Whittle; 4 Adam Hughes; 28 Gray Viane; 33 Jules O'Neill; 36 Keiran Kerr (D); 8 Terry O'Connor (C); 20 Mark Smith; 10 Julian O'Neill; 11 Mick Cassidy; 16 Daniel Frame; 13 Simon Finnigan. Subs (all used): 15 Matt Whitaker; 7 Stephen Myler; 17 David Mills; 12 John Stankevitch.
Tries: Finnigan (24), Hughes (39), Smith (63), Viane (74); **Goals:** Jules O'Neill 2/3, Myler 2/2.
Rugby Leaguer & League Express Men of the Match: *Bulls:* Paul Deacon; *Vikings:* Mark Smith.
Penalty count: 6-3; **Half-time:** 40-12;
Referee: Glen Black (New Zealand); **Attendance:** 10,128

LEIGH CENTURIONS 0 LEEDS RHINOS 74

CENTURIONS: 24 John Wilshere; 14 Steve Maden; 8 Rob Jackson; 1 Ben Cooper; 19 Rob Smyth; 10 Jason Kent; 28 Jason Duffy; 4 Darren Fleary (C); 30 Keiron Maddocks; 20 Craig Stapleton; 15 Richard Marshall; 12 Oliver Wilkes; 13 Mark Leafa. Subs (all used): 31 Warren Stevens; 21 Matt Sturm; 33 Liam Coleman (D); 26 Nick Owen.
On report:
Jackson and Stapleton (20) - spear tackle on Dunemann.
RHINOS: 1 Richard Mathers; 2 Mark Calderwood; 3 Chev Walker; 4 Keith Senior (C); 23 Lee Smith; 6 Danny McGuire; 14 Andrew Dunemann; 8 Ryan Bailey; 9 Matt Diskin; 15 Danny Ward; 16 Willie Poching; 12 Chris McKenna; 20 Gareth Ellis. Subs (all used): 10 Barrie McDermott; 11 Ali Lauitiiti; 22 Nick Scruton; 29 Ashley Gibson (D).
Tries: Bailey (16, 78), Smith (21), Ward (26), Calderwood (34, 53), Senior (40), Walker (44), Gibson (47, 66, 68), McKenna (62), McGuire (74, 76);
Goals: Smith 4/8, Gibson 5/6.
Rugby Leaguer & League Express Men of the Match: *Centurions:* Warren Stevens; *Rhinos:* Matt Diskin.
Penalty count: 6-6; **Half-time:** 0-26; **Referee:** Ronnie Laughton (Barnsley); **Attendance:** 4,922.

WAKEFIELD TRINITY WILDCATS 12 HUDDERSFIELD GIANTS 44

WILDCATS: 1 Colum Halpenny; 2 Michael Wainwright; 3 Jason Demetriou (C); 4 Sid Domic; 5 Semi Tadulala; 7 Ben Jeffries; 14 Sam Obst; 8 Darrell Griffin; 9 David March; 10 Michael Korkidas; 11 David Solomona; 17 Duncan MacGillivray; 12 Jamie Field. Subs (all used): 13 Rob Spicer; 15 David Wrench; 16 Steve Snitch; 18 Olivier Elima.
Tries: J Field (60), Solomona (64); **Goals:** March 2/3.
Sin bin: Jeffries (18) - holding down.
GIANTS: 34 Marcus St Hilaire; 2 Hefin O'Hare; 3 James Evans; 11 Chris Nero; 28 Lee Greenwood; 6 Chris Thorman (C); 7 Paul March; 27 Wayne McDonald; 9 Brad Drew; 10 Jim Gannon; 18 Eorl Crabtree; 17 Paul Smith; 13 Stanley Gene. Subs (all used): 16 Iain Morrison; 19 Jon Grayshon; 20 Paul White; 24 Bolouagi Fagborun.
Tries: Nero (20), Thorman (44), March (47, 68), St Hilaire (55), Grayshon (72), Smith (75);
Goals: Thorman 8/10.
Sin bin: Crabtree (11) - holding down.
Rugby Leaguer & League Express Men of the Match: *Wildcats:* Jamie Field; *Giants:* Chris Thorman.
Penalty count: 9-9; **Half-time:** 2-10; **Referee:** Richard Silverwood (Dewsbury); **Attendance:** 4,476.

HULL FC 16 LONDON BRONCOS 17

HULL: 1 Shaun Briscoe; 14 Motu Tony; 30 Richard Whiting; 3 Kirk Yeaman; 5 Gareth Raynor; 6 Richard Horne; 21 Danny Brough; 8 Ewan Dowes; 9 Richard Swain (C); 20 Garreth Carvell; 11 Shayne McMenemy; 24 Graeme Horne; 13 Paul Cooke. Subs (all used): 10 Paul King; 12 Stephen Kearney; 15 Jamie Thackray; 16 Tom Saxton.
Tries: Dowes (3), Cooke (13), McMenemy (47);
Goals: Cooke 2/5.
BRONCOS: 25 Zebastian Luisi; 2 Jon Wells; 24 Tyrone Smith; 1 Paul Sykes; 3 Nick Bradley-Qalilawa; 6 Mark McLinden (C); 21 Luke Dorn; 8 Francis Stephenson; 19 David Highton; 10 Steve Trindall; 11 Solomon Haumono; 12 Lee Hopkins; 16 Joe Mbu. Subs (all used): 13 Rob Purdham; 14 Danny Williams; 17 Mark Tookey; 30 Feleti Mateo.
Tries: Smith (18), Sykes (39), Dorn (58);
Goals: Sykes 2/3; **Field goal:** Sykes.
Rugby Leaguer & League Express Men of the Match: *Hull:* Jamie Thackray; *Broncos:* Paul Sykes.
Penalty count: 8-8; **Half-time:** 10-10; **Referee:** Karl Kirkpatrick (Warrington); **Attendance:** 8,109.

ROUND 24

Friday 12th August 2005

HUDDERSFIELD GIANTS 38 WARRINGTON WOLVES 22

GIANTS: 1 Paul Reilly; 2 Hefin O'Hare; 3 James Evans; 11 Chris Nero; 28 Lee Greenwood; 6 Chris Thorman (C); 7 Paul March; 27 Wayne McDonald; 9 Brad Drew; 10 Jim Gannon; 18 Eorl Crabtree; 17 Paul Smith; 13 Stanley Gene. Subs (all used): 14 Stuart Jones; 19 Jon Grayshon; 20 Paul White; 21 Paul Jackson.
Tries: Reilly (1), Drew (3), Crabtree (12, 26), Nero (30, 67), Gannon (47); **Goals:** Thorman 5/7.
WOLVES: 1 Brent Grose; 2 Henry Fa'afili; 3 Martin Gleeson; 4 Toa Kohe-Love; 28 Chris Riley (D); 25 Chris Bridge; 7 Nathan Wood (C); 8 Chris Leikvoll; 9 Jon Clarke; 10 Mark Hilton; 11 Logan Swann; 12 Mike Wainwright; 15 Ben Westwood. Subs (all used): 14 Mark Gleeson; 13 Paul Noone; 16 Paul Wood; 17 Danny Lima.
Tries: Martin Gleeson (21), Swann (54), N Wood (59), Bridge (76); **Goals:** Bridge 3/4.
Rugby Leaguer & League Express Men of the Match: *Giants:* Brad Drew; *Wolves:* Chris Bridge.
Penalty count: 3-3; **Half-time:** 26-6;
Referee: Ashley Klein (Keighley); **Attendance:** 4,077.

ST HELENS 60 WAKEFIELD TRINITY WILDCATS 4

SAINTS: 1 Paul Wellens; 5 Darren Albert; 3 Jamie Lyon; 4 Willie Talau; 2 Ade Gardner; 6 Jason Hooper; 7 Sean Long (C); 8 Nick Fozzard; 9 Keiron Cunningham; 17 Paul Anderson; 15 Mike Bennett; 12 Jon Wilkin; 27 Vinnie Anderson. Subs (all used): 21 James Roby; 19 James Graham; 24 Maurie Fa'asavalu; 11 Lee Gilmour.
Tries: P Anderson (13), Albert (21, 66, 73), Long (35), Wellens (42), Lyon (45, 63), Roby (77), Graham (80);
Goals: Long 10/10.
WILDCATS: 1 Colum Halpenny; 2 Michael Wainwright; 4 Sid Domic (C); 29 Kevin Henderson (D); 5 Semi Tadulala; 7 Ben Jeffries; 14 Sam Obst; 8 Darrell Griffin; 9 David March; 10 Michael Korkidas; 11 David Solomona; 17 Duncan MacGillivray; 12 Jamie Field. Subs (all used): 18 Olivier Elima; 27 Chris Feather; 15 David Wrench; 13 Rob Spicer.
Try: Wainwright (26); **Goals:** March 0/2.
Rugby Leaguer & League Express Men of the Match: *Saints:* Sean Long; *Wildcats:* David Solomona.
Penalty count: 8-2; **Half-time:** 18-4;
Referee: Glen Black (New Zealand); **Attendance:** 8,153.

Saturday 13th August 2005

LEEDS RHINOS 44 LONDON BRONCOS 24

RHINOS: 1 Richard Mathers; 2 Mark Calderwood; 3 Chev Walker; 4 Keith Senior; 5 Marcus Bai; 6 Danny McGuire; 14 Andrew Dunemann; 8 Ryan Bailey; 9 Matt Diskin; 10 Barrie McDermott; 20 Gareth Ellis; 12 Chris McKenna; 13 Kevin Sinfield (C). Subs (all used): 7 Rob Burrow; 11 Ali Lauitiiti; 22 Nick Scruton; 23 Lee Smith.
Tries: Bai (6), Calderwood (20), McKenna (28), Senior (38, 46), McGuire (42, 63, 73, 75);
Goals: Sinfield 3/5, Burrow 1/3, McGuire 0/1.
BRONCOS: 2 Jon Wells; 5 John Kirkpatrick; 24 Tyrone Smith; 1 Paul Sykes; 3 Nick Bradley-Qalilawa; 6 Mark McLinden (C); 21 Luke Dorn; 10 Steve Trindall; 12 Lee Hopkins; 18 Anthony Armour; 11 Solomon Haumono; 30 Feleti Mateo; 16 Joe Mbu. Subs (all used): 14 Danny Williams; 8 Francis Stephenson; 17 Mark Tookey; 19 David Highton.
Tries: Wells (14), Dorn (17), Sykes (50, 78);
Goals: Sykes 4/4.
Rugby Leaguer & League Express Men of the Match: *Rhinos:* Danny McGuire; *Broncos:* Luke Dorn.
Penalty count: 5-4; **Half-time:** 16-12; **Referee:** Richard Silverwood (Dewsbury); **Attendance:** 13,318.

Sunday 14th August 2005

BRADFORD BULLS 58 SALFORD CITY REDS 12

BULLS: 6 Michael Withers; 3 Leon Pryce; 13 Ben Harris; 4 Shontayne Hape; 5 Lesley Vainikolo; 18 Iestyn Harris; 7 Paul Deacon; 12 Jamie Peacock (C); 9 Ian Henderson; 29 Stuart Fielden; 16 Paul Johnson; 10 Brad Meyers; 11 Lee Radford. Subs (all used): 8 Joe Vagana; 1 Robbie Paul; 14 Andy Lynch; 27 Rob Parker.
Tries: Hape (8, 77), Peacock (18), I Harris (27, 48), L Pryce (38), Lynch (51), Johnson (53), Deacon (64), Vainikolo (73); **Goals:** Deacon 7/8, I Harris 2/2.
CITY REDS: 2 David Hodgson; 28 Andy Smith; 1 Cliff Beverley; 3 Stuart Littler; 5 Anthony Stewart; 25 Tim Hartley; 7 Luke Robinson; 10 Sean Rutgerson; 9 Malcolm Alker (C); 27 Mitchell Stringer; 12 Ian Sibbit; 23 Andrew Brocklehurst; 13 Chris Charles. Subs (all used): 16 Nathan McAvoy; 17 Gareth Haggerty; 8 Andy Coley; 15 Karl Fitzpatrick.
Tries: Smith (22), Alker (61); **Goals:** Charles 2/2.
Rugby Leaguer & League Express Men of the Match: *Bulls:* Iestyn Harris; *City Reds:* Malcolm Alker.
Penalty count: 6-4; **Half-time:** 22-6; **Referee:** Ronnie Laughton (Barnsley); **Attendance:** 10,113.

WIDNES VIKINGS 24 WIGAN WARRIORS 48

VIKINGS: 35 Brad Watts; 4 Adam Hughes; 1 Gary Connolly; 21 Jon Whittle; 28 Gray Viane; 7 Stephen Myler; 36 Keiran Kerr; 8 Terry O'Connor (C); 20 Mark Smith; 10 Julian O'Neill; 11 Mick Cassidy; 25 Stephen Nash; 13 Simon Finnigan. Subs (all used): 33 Jules O'Neill; 14 Gary Hulse; 17 David Mills; 31 Paul Alcock.
Tries: Kerr (7), Myler (16), Hughes (31), Watts (75);
Goals: Myler 4/4.
WARRIORS: 2 Brett Dallas; 5 Brian Carney; 14 Kevin Brown; 33 Darrell Goulding (D); 3 Martin Aspinwall; 25 James Coyle; 7 Dennis Moran; 8 Jerry Seuseu; 9 Terry Newton (C); 27 Bryn Hargreaves; 19 Stephen Wild; 29 Joel Tomkins; 12 Danny Tickle. Subs (all used): 20 Harrison Hansen; 16 Danny Sculthorpe; 22 David Allen; 24 Bob Beswick.
Tries: Brown (20), Sculthorpe (23), Wild (26), Allen (29), Coyle (46), Newton (56), Hansen (59), Beswick (62), Moran (65); **Goals:** Tickle 6/10.
Sin bin: Newton (6) – late tackle on Myler.
Rugby Leaguer & League Express Men of the Match: *Vikings:* Mark Smith; *Warriors:* Dennis Moran.
Penalty count: 3-8; **Half-time:** 18-24;
Referee: Ian Smith (Oldham); **Attendance:** 6,384.

HULL FC 76 LEIGH CENTURIONS 20

HULL: 1 Shaun Briscoe; 14 Motu Tony; 22 Kirk Dixon; 3 Kirk Yeaman; 5 Gareth Raynor; 33 Tommy Lee (D); 21 Danny Brough; 10 Paul King; 9 Richard Swain (C); 20 Garreth Carvell; 11 Shayne McMenemy; 12 Stephen Kearney; 30 Richard Whiting. Subs (all used): 2 Nathan Blacklock; 8 Ewan Dowes; 15 Jamie Thackray; 16 Tom Saxton.
Tries: Raynor (2, 71), Carvell (6, 13), Briscoe (10, 28), Brough (14), Whiting (18), Thackray (22), Dixon (45), Dowes (51), Yeaman (54, 64); **Goals:** Brough 12/13.
CENTURIONS: 26 Nick Owen; 14 Steve Maden; 1 Ben Cooper; 8 Rob Jackson; 19 Rob Smyth; 24 John Wilshere; 10 Jason Kent; 4 Darren Fleary (C); 32 Robbie Mears; 31 Warren Stevens; 20 Craig Stapleton; 12 Oliver Wilkes; 13 Mark Leafa. Subs (all used): 5 Mick Govin; 18 Paul Rowley; 21 Matt Sturm; 33 Liam Coleman.

Tries: Jackson (26), Govin (48), Stapleton (78), Rowley (79); **Goals:** Owen 2/3, Wilshere 0/1.
Sin bin: Jackson (70) - punching; Maden (76) - obstruction.
Rugby Leaguer & League Express Men of the Match: *Hull:* Danny Brough; *Centurions:* John Wilshere.
Penalty count: 8-3; **Half-time:** 48-4;
Referee: Steve Ganson (St Helens); **Attendance:** 6,576.

ROUND 25

Friday 19th August 2005

LEEDS RHINOS 10 BRADFORD BULLS 42

RHINOS: 1 Richard Mathers; 23 Lee Smith; 3 Chev Walker; 4 Keith Senior; 5 Marcus Bai; 14 Andrew Dunemann; 6 Danny McGuire; 8 Ryan Bailey; 9 Matt Diskin; 15 Danny Ward; 20 Gareth Ellis; 12 Chris McKenna; 13 Kevin Sinfield (C). Subs (all used): 18 Jamie Jones-Buchanan; 10 Barrie McDermott; 7 Rob Burrow; 11 Ali Lauitiiti.
Tries: Smith (5), Sinfield (38); **Goals:** Sinfield 1/2.
BULLS: 6 Michael Withers; 3 Leon Pryce; 13 Ben Harris; 4 Shontayne Hape; 5 Lesley Vainikolo; 18 Iestyn Harris; 7 Paul Deacon; 12 Jamie Peacock (C); 9 Ian Henderson; 29 Stuart Fielden; 10 Brad Meyers; 16 Paul Johnson; 11 Lee Radford. Subs (all used): 19 Jamie Langley; 8 Joe Vagana; 14 Andy Lynch; 1 Robbie Paul.
Tries: Hape (26, 56, 73), Lynch (32), Langley (46), Deacon (53), Paul (58), I Harris (63); **Goals:** Deacon 5/8.
Rugby Leaguer & League Express Men of the Match: *Rhinos:* Richard Mathers; *Bulls:* Shontayne Hape.
Penalty count: 8-7; **Half time:** 10-12;
Referee: Ashley Klein (Keighley); **Attendance:** 20,220.

SALFORD CITY REDS 37 WAKEFIELD TRINITY WILDCATS 0

CITY REDS: 15 Karl Fitzpatrick; 4 Junior Langi; 5 Anthony Stewart; 3 Stuart Littler; 2 David Hodgson; 1 Cliff Beverley; 7 Luke Robinson; 8 Andy Coley; 9 Malcolm Alker (C); 14 Paul Highton; 12 Ian Sibbit; 23 Andrew Brocklehurst; 13 Chris Charles. Subs (all used): 21 John Clough; 17 Gareth Haggerty; 22 Simon Baldwin; 16 Nathan McAvoy.
Tries: Coley (15), Robinson (32), Stewart (43, 52, 61), Fitzpatrick (77); **Goals:** Charles 5/5, Robinson 1/1;
Field goal: Robinson.
WILDCATS: 1 Colum Halpenny; 2 Michael Wainwright; 4 Sid Domic (C); 29 Kevin Henderson; 5 Semi Tadulala; 7 Ben Jeffries; 14 Sam Obst; 8 Darrell Griffin; 9 David March; 10 Michael Korkidas; 17 Duncan MacGillivray; 11 David Solomona; 12 Jamie Field. Subs (all used): 18 Olivier Elima; 13 Rob Spicer; 15 David Wrench; 27 Chris Feather.
Rugby Leaguer & League Express Men of the Match: *City Reds:* Ian Sibbit; *Wildcats:* David Solomona.
Penalty count: 6-7; **Half-time:** 12-0;
Referee: Ronnie Laughton (Barnsley); **Attendance:** 3,005.

Saturday 20th August 2005

ST HELENS 50 LONDON BRONCOS 4

SAINTS: 1 Paul Wellens; 5 Darren Albert; 3 Jamie Lyon; 4 Willie Talau; 2 Ade Gardner; 6 Jason Hooper; 7 Sean Long (C); 8 Nick Fozzard; 9 Keiron Cunningham; 17 Paul Anderson; 11 Lee Gilmour; 12 Jon Wilkin; 27 Vinnie Anderson. Subs (all used): 10 Mark Edmondson; 24 Maurie Fa'asavalu; 21 James Roby; 19 James Graham.
Tries: Albert (6, 61), Hooper (13), Long (37), Gilmour (43), P Anderson (47), Wilkin (52), Cunningham (68), Wellens (77); **Goals:** Long 6/8, Lyon 1/1.
BRONCOS: 25 Zebastian Luisi; 3 Nick Bradley-Qalilawa; 24 Tyrone Smith; 1 Paul Sykes; 2 Jon Wells; 6 Mark McLinden (C); 21 Luke Dorn; 17 Mark Tookey; 12 Lee Hopkins; 18 Anthony Armour; 11 Solomon Haumono; 30 Feleti Mateo; 16 Joe Mbu. Subs (all used): 14 Danny Williams; 20 Filimone Lolohea; 26 Carl Ablett (D); 8 Francis Stephenson.
Try: Bradley-Qalilawa (55); **Goals:** Sykes 0/1.
Rugby Leaguer & League Express Men of the Match: *Saints:* Jamie Lyon; *Broncos:* Nick Bradley-Qalilawa.
Penalty count: 6-4; **Half-time:** 16-0;
Referee: Glen Black (New Zealand); **Attendance:** 7,604.

Sunday 21st August 2005

HUDDERSFIELD GIANTS 68 LEIGH CENTURIONS 16

GIANTS: 34 Marcus St Hilaire; 2 Hefin O'Hare; 11 Chris Nero; 4 Michael De Vere; 28 Lee Greenwood; 6 Chris Thorman (C); 7 Paul March; 27 Wayne McDonald; 9 Brad Drew; 21 Paul Jackson; 18 Eorl Crabtree; 17 Paul Smith; 13 Stanley Gene. Subs (all used): 14 Stuart Jones; 16 Iain Morrison; 19 Jon Grayshon; 20 Paul White.
Tries: Thorman (5, 19, 56, 68), O'Hare (9), March (13, 37), Nero (26, 34, 77), Greenwood (51), White (65); **Goals:** Thorman 10/12.
CENTURIONS: 24 John Wilshere; 14 Steve Maden; 1 Ben Cooper; 8 Rob Jackson; 26 Nick Owen; 28 Jason Duffy; 37 Carl Forber (D); 4 Darren Fleary (C); 18 Paul Rowley; 21 Matt Sturm; 20 Craig Stapleton; 13 Mark Leafa; 10 Jason Kent. Subs: 15 Richard Marshall (not used); 31 Warren Stevens; 32 Robbie Mears; 33 Liam Coleman.
Tries: Stapleton (29), Stevens (41), Jackson (74);
Goals: Owen 2/3.
Rugby Leaguer & League Express Men of the Match: *Giants:* Chris Thorman; *Centurions:* Paul Rowley.
Penalty count: 7-6; **Half-time:** 40-4;
Referee: Ian Smith (Oldham); **Attendance:** 3,902.

WIDNES VIKINGS 16 WARRINGTON WOLVES 60

VIKINGS: 33 Jules O'Neill; 35 Brad Watts; 1 Gary Connolly; 4 Adam Hughes; 28 Gray Viane; 7 Stephen Myler; 36 Keiran Kerr; 10 Julian O'Neill; 20 Mark Smith (C); 25 Stephen Nash; 11 Mick Cassidy; 16 Daniel Frame; 13 Simon Finnigan. Subs (all used): 5 Andrew Emelio; 15 Matt Whitaker; 17 David Mills; 31 Paul Alcock.
Tries: Hughes (11), Kerr (71), Finnigan (76);
Goals: Myler 2/3.
Sin bin: Finnigan (34) - late tackle on Briers.
On report: Finnigan (34) - late tackle on Briers.
WOLVES: 1 Brent Grose; 2 Henry Fa'afili; 3 Martin Gleeson; 4 Toa Kohe-Love; 25 Chris Bridge; 6 Lee Briers (C); 7 Nathan Wood; 8 Chris Leikvoll; 14 Mark Gleeson; 16 Paul Wood; 11 Logan Swann; 15 Ben Westwood; 9 Jon Clarke. Subs (all used): 28 Chris Riley; 23 Andy Bracek; 10 Mark Hilton; 17 Danny Lima.
Tries: Fa'afili (2, 48), Westwood (20), Lima (25), Mark Gleeson (35), Kohe-Love (40, 67), Grose (43), Martin Gleeson (53), P Wood (57), Riley (62); **Goals:** Bridge 8/11.
Rugby Leaguer & League Express Men of the Match: *Vikings:* Mark Smith; *Wolves:* Mark Gleeson.
Penalty count: 7-9; **Half-time:** 4-26; **Referee:** Richard Silverwood (Dewsbury); **Attendance:** 7,878.

HULL FC 24 WIGAN WARRIORS 28

HULL: 1 Shaun Briscoe; 2 Nathan Blacklock; 14 Motu Tony; 24 Graeme Horne; 5 Gareth Raynor; 33 Tommy Lee; 21 Danny Brough; 8 Ewan Dowes; 9 Richard Swain (C); 15 Jamie Thackray; 11 Shayne McMenemy; 12 Stephen Kearney; 30 Richard Whiting. Subs (all used): 16 Tom Saxton; 17 Chris Chester; 18 Liam Higgins; 23 Paul McNicholas.
Tries: Blacklock (62), G Horne (65), Saxton (66), Raynor (70); **Goals:** Brough 4/5.
WARRIORS: 2 Brett Dallas; 5 Brian Carney; 14 Kevin Brown; 4 David Vaealiki; 3 Martin Aspinwall; 6 Danny Orr; 7 Dennis Moran; 8 Jerry Seuseu; 9 Terry Newton (C); 27 Bryn Hargreaves; 19 Stephen Wild; 29 Joel Tomkins; 12 Danny Tickle. Subs (all used): 20 Harrison Hansen; 16 Danny Sculthorpe; 22 David Allen; 25 James Coyle.
Tries: Wild (16), Newton (24), Orr (32), Brown (51), Moran (57); **Goals:** Tickle 4/6.
Sin bin: Wild (73) – holding down.
Rugby Leaguer & League Express Men of the Match: *Hull:* Danny Brough; *Warriors:* Danny Orr.
Penalty count: 5-7; **Half-time:** 2-16; **Referee:** Karl Kirkpatrick (Warrington); **Attendance:** 9,935.

ROUND 26

Friday 2nd September 2005

BRADFORD BULLS 49 HULL FC 6

BULLS: 6 Michael Withers; 3 Leon Pryce; 13 Ben Harris; 4 Shontayne Hape; 5 Lesley Vainikolo; 18 Iestyn Harris; 7 Paul Deacon; 12 Jamie Peacock (C); 9 Ian Henderson; 29 Stuart Fielden; 16 Paul Johnson; 10 Brad Meyers; 11 Lee Radford. Subs (all used): 8 Joe Vagana; 1 Robbie Paul; 14 Andy Lynch; 19 Jamie Langley.
Tries: Vainikolo (1, 6, 38, 63, 65, 80), Hape (49), Fielden (52), Vagana (72), Peacock (76);
Goals: Deacon 4/10; **Field goal:** Deacon.
HULL: 2 Nathan Blacklock; 14 Motu Tony; 30 Richard Whiting; 3 Kirk Yeaman; 5 Gareth Raynor; 13 Paul Cooke; 21 Danny Brough; 8 Ewan Dowes; 9 Richard Swain (C); 15 Jamie Thackray; 11 Shayne McMenemy; 12 Stephen Kearney; 17 Chris Chester. Subs (all used): 10 Paul King; 16 Tom Saxton; 18 Liam Higgins; 24 Graeme Horne.
Try: Raynor (27); **Goals:** Brough 1/1.
On report: Yeaman (20) - alleged spear tackle on Fielden.
Rugby Leaguer & League Express Men of the Match: *Bulls:* Lesley Vainikolo; *Hull:* Jamie Thackray.
Penalty count: 6-6; **Half-time:** 17-6;
Referee: Ashley Klein (Keighley); **Attendance:** 13,326.

WIGAN WARRIORS 24 LEEDS RHINOS 22

WARRIORS: 2 Brett Dallas; 5 Brian Carney; 14 Kevin Brown; 4 David Vaealiki; 3 Martin Aspinwall; 6 Danny Orr; 7 Dennis Moran; 27 Bryn Hargreaves; 9 Terry Newton (C); 10 Jerome Guisset; 19 Stephen Wild; 29 Joel Tomkins; 12 Danny Tickle. Subs (all used): 16 Danny Sculthorpe; 20 Harrison Hansen; 22 David Allen; 24 Bob Beswick.
Tries: Moran (12, 36), Orr (20), Hansen (77);
Goals: Tickle 3/3, Orr 1/1.
RHINOS: 23 Lee Smith; 2 Mark Calderwood; 3 Chev Walker; 20 Gareth Ellis; 5 Marcus Bai; 13 Kevin Sinfield (C); 7 Rob Burrow; 8 Ryan Bailey; 9 Matt Diskin; 15 Danny Ward; 11 Ali Lauitiiti; 18 Jamie Jones-Buchanan; 14 Andrew Dunemann. Subs (all used): 6 Danny McGuire; 16 Willie Poching; 22 Nick Scruton; 10 Barrie McDermott.
Tries: Smith (15, 59), Walker (28), Dunemann (30);
Goals: Sinfield 3/4.
Rugby Leaguer & League Express Men of the Match: *Warriors:* Danny Orr; *Rhinos:* Kevin Sinfield.
Penalty count: 10-8; **Half-time:** 18-16; **Referee:** Ronnie Laughton (Barnsley); **Attendance:** 14,158.

Saturday 3rd September 2005

LONDON BRONCOS 16 HUDDERSFIELD GIANTS 12

BRONCOS: 25 Zebastian Luisi; 2 Jon Wells; 24 Tyrone Smith; 1 Paul Sykes; 3 Nick Bradley-Qalilawa; 12 Lee Hopkins (C); 21 Luke Dorn; 10 Steve Trindall; 19 David Highton; 18 Anthony Armour; 11 Solomon Haumono; 26 Carl Ablett; 16 Joe Mbu. Subs (all used): 17 Mark Tookey; 20 Filimone Lolohea; 30 Feleti Mateo; 14 Danny Williams.
Tries: Bradley-Qalilawa (6), Luisi (35), Wells (58);
Goals: Sykes 2/3.
GIANTS: 1 Paul Reilly; 2 Hefin O'Hare; 3 James Evans; 4 Michael De Vere; 34 Marcus St Hilaire; 6 Chris Thorman (C); 7 Paul March; 27 Wayne McDonald; 9 Brad Drew; 18 Eorl Crabtree; 11 Chris Nero; 14 Stuart Jones; 13 Stanley Gene. Subs (all used): 10 Jim Gannon; 20 Paul White; 19 Jon Grayshon; 21 Paul Jackson.
Try: Thorman (51); **Goals:** Thorman 4/4.
Rugby Leaguer & League Express Men of the Match: *Broncos:* Solomon Haumono; *Giants:* Chris Thorman.
Penalty count: 10-10; **Half-time:** 10-6; **Referee:** Richard Silverwood (Dewsbury); **Attendance:** 2,877.

Sunday 4th September 2005

LEIGH CENTURIONS 4 ST HELENS 78

CENTURIONS: 24 John Wilshere; 26 Nick Owen; 8 Rob Jackson; 1 Ben Cooper; 14 Steve Maden; 37 Carl Forber; 2 John Duffy; 4 Darren Fleary (C); 32 Robbie Mears; 15 Richard Marshall; 13 Mark Leafa; 20 Craig Stapleton; 33 Liam Coleman. Subs (all used): 21 Matt Sturm; 31 Warren Stevens; 30 Keiron Maddocks; 36 Chris Hill (D).
Try: Cooper (73); **Goals:** Owen 0/1.
SAINTS: 1 Paul Wellens; 5 Darren Albert; 3 Jamie Lyon; 4 Willie Talau; 2 Ade Gardner; 6 Jason Hooper; 7 Sean Long (C); 8 Nick Fozzard; 9 Keiron Cunningham; 17 Paul Anderson; 11 Lee Gilmour; 15 Mike Bennett; 21 James Roby. Subs (all used): 20 Ian Hardman; 14 Mick Higham; 19 James Graham; 24 Maurie Fa'asavalu.
Tries: Bennett (2), Long (4, 19), Wellens (11), Albert (29), Higham (34), Roby (41), P Anderson (45, 76), Gardner (49, 65), Cunningham (56), Graham (59), Fa'asavalu (69); **Goals:** Long 6/9, Lyon 2/2, Hooper 3/3.
Rugby Leaguer & League Express Men of the Match: *Centurions:* John Duffy; *Saints:* Sean Long.
Penalty count: 4-7; **Half-time:** 0-32; **Referee:** Karl Kirkpatrick (Warrington); **Attendance:** 5,534.

WARRINGTON WOLVES 32 SALFORD CITY REDS 22

WOLVES: 1 Brent Grose; 2 Henry Fa'afili; 3 Martin Gleeson; 4 Toa Kohe-Love; 25 Chris Bridge; 6 Lee Briers (C); 7 Nathan Wood; 8 Chris Leikvoll; 14 Mark Gleeson; 16 Paul Wood; 11 Logan Swann; 15 Ben Westwood; 9 Jon Clarke. Subs (all used): 13 Paul Noone; 28 Chris Riley; 17 Danny Lima; 10 Mark Hilton.
Tries: Westwood (23), N Wood (33), Martin Gleeson (48), Bridge (62), Briers (74), Leikvoll (80); **Goals:** Bridge 4/5, Briers 0/1.
CITY REDS: 15 Karl Fitzpatrick; 4 Junior Langi; 5 Anthony Stewart; 3 Stuart Littler; 2 David Hodgson; 1 Cliff Beverley; 7 Luke Robinson; 8 Andy Coley; 9 Malcolm Alker (C); 14 Paul Highton; 23 Andrew Brocklehurst; 12 Ian Sibbit; 13 Chris Charles. Subs (all used): 21 John Clough; 22 Simon Baldwin; 17 Gareth Haggerty; 16 Nathan McAvoy.
Tries: Stewart (9), Sibbit (17), Littler (28), Fitzpatrick (78); **Goals:** Charles 3/4.
Rugby Leaguer & League Express Men of the Match: *Wolves:* Nathan Wood; *City Reds:* Karl Fitzpatrick.
Penalty count: 4-2; **Half-time:** 12-16;
Referee: Ian Smith (Oldham); **Attendance:** 9,619.

WAKEFIELD TRINITY WILDCATS 46 WIDNES VIKINGS 6

WILDCATS: 1 Colum Halpenny; 31 Austin Buchanan (D); 4 Sid Domic (C); 13 Rob Spicer; 5 Semi Tadulala; 7 Ben Jeffries; 14 Sam Obst; 18 Olivier Elima; 9 David March; 10 Michael Korkidas; 11 David Solomona; 29 Kevin Henderson; 12 Jamie Field. Subs (all used): 2 Michael Wainwright; 8 Darrell Griffin; 15 David Wrench; 27 Chris Feather.
Tries: Obst (4), Elima (9, 38), J Field (12), Domic (18, 25), Henderson (54), Griffin (63); **Goals:** March 7/8.
VIKINGS: 35 Brad Watts; 5 Andrew Emelio; 1 Gary Connolly; 4 Adam Hughes; 28 Gray Viane; 7 Stephen Myler; 36 Keiran Kerr; 25 Stephen Nash; 20 Mark Smith (C); 10 Julian O'Neill; 11 Mick Cassidy; 16 Daniel Frame; 33 Jules O'Neill. Subs (all used): 13 Simon Finnigan; 15 Matt Whitaker; 24 Tim Holmes; 17 David Mills.
Try: Myler (21); **Goals:** Myler 1/1.
Rugby Leaguer & League Express Men of the Match: *Wildcats:* Sam Obst; *Vikings:* Mark Smith.
Penalty count: 7-6; **Half-time:** 34-6;
Referee: Julian King (St Helens); **Attendance:** 3,234.

ROUND 27

Friday 9th September 2005

SALFORD CITY REDS 26 LONDON BRONCOS 18

CITY REDS: 15 Karl Fitzpatrick; 4 Junior Langi; 5 Anthony Stewart; 3 Stuart Littler; 2 David Hodgson; 1 Cliff Beverley; 7 Luke Robinson; 8 Andy Coley; 9 Malcolm Alker (C); 14 Paul Highton; 12 Ian Sibbit; 23 Andrew Brocklehurst; 13 Chris Charles. Subs (all used): 21 John Clough; 17 Gareth Haggerty; 22 Simon Baldwin; 10 Sean Rutgerson.
Tries: Stewart (22), Langi (45), Fitzpatrick (51), Littler (63), Haggerty (73); **Goals:** Charles 3/5.
BRONCOS: 25 Zebastian Luisi; 2 Jon Wells; 24 Tyrone Smith; 1 Paul Sykes; 3 Nick Bradley-Qalilawa; 12 Lee Hopkins (C); 21 Luke Dorn; 18 Anthony Armour; 19 David Highton; 17 Mark Tookey; 11 Solomon Haumono; 27 Karl Temata (D); 16 Joe Mbu. Subs (all used): 20 Filimone Lolohea; 30 Feleti Mateo; 8 Francis Stephenson; 26 Carl Ablett.
Tries: Sykes (55), Haumono (74), Wells (80);
Goals: Sykes 3/4.

Sin bin: Mateo (40) - dissent.
Rugby Leaguer & League Express Men of the Match: *City Reds:* Karl Fitzpatrick; *Broncos:* Paul Sykes.
Penalty count: 4-6; **Half-time:** 4-2;
Referee: Julian King (St Helens); **Attendance:** 2,683.

WIGAN WARRIORS 12 ST HELENS 38

WARRIORS: 2 Brett Dallas; 5 Brian Carney; 14 Kevin Brown; 4 David Vaealiki; 3 Martin Aspinwall; 6 Danny Orr; 7 Dennis Moran; 22 David Allen; 9 Terry Newton (C); 10 Jerome Guisset; 19 Stephen Wild; 29 Joel Tomkins; 12 Danny Tickle. Subs (all used): 20 Harrison Hansen; 16 Danny Sculthorpe; 24 Bob Beswick; 34 Lee Jewitt (D).
Tries: Vaealiki (11), Tomkins (38); **Goals:** Tickle 2/2.
On report: Newton (22) - swinging arm on Gilmour.
SAINTS: 1 Paul Wellens; 5 Darren Albert; 3 Jamie Lyon; 4 Willie Talau; 2 Ade Gardner; 6 Jason Hooper; 7 Sean Long (C); 8 Nick Fozzard; 9 Keiron Cunningham; 17 Paul Anderson; 11 Lee Gilmour; 15 Mike Bennett; 21 James Roby. Subs (all used): 14 Mick Higham; 19 James Graham; 24 Maurie Fa'asavalu; 12 Jon Wilkin.
Tries: Cunningham (5, 35), Wellens (18), Gardner (30), Wilkin (53), Fa'asavalu (68);
Goals: Long 3/4, Hooper 1/1, Lyon 3/3.
Sin bin: Lyon (28) - holding down; Wilkin (57) - fighting.
Rugby Leaguer & League Express Men of the Match: *Warriors:* Joel Tomkins; *Saints:* Keiron Cunningham.
Penalty count: 6-9; **Half-time:** 12-24;
Referee: Ian Smith (Oldham); **Attendance:** 20,274.

Saturday 10th September 2005

WARRINGTON WOLVES 33 LEEDS RHINOS 16

WOLVES: 1 Brent Grose; 2 Henry Fa'afili; 3 Martin Gleeson; 4 Toa Kohe-Love; 25 Chris Bridge; 6 Lee Briers; 31 Andrew Johns (D); 8 Chris Leikvoll; 7 Nathan Wood (C); 16 Paul Wood; 11 Logan Swann; 13 Paul Noone; 9 Jon Clarke. Subs: 28 Chris Riley (not used); 23 Andy Bracek; 14 Mark Gleeson; 17 Danny Lima.
Tries: Fa'afili (1), Martin Gleeson (26), Grose (34), Swann (49), N Wood (79);
Goals: Johns 6/7; **Field goal:** Johns.
RHINOS: 1 Richard Mathers; 2 Mark Calderwood; 3 Chev Walker; 23 Lee Smith; 5 Marcus Bai; 13 Kevin Sinfield (C); 7 Rob Burrow; 18 Jamie Jones-Buchanan; 14 Andrew Dunemann; 15 Danny Ward; 11 Ali Lauitiiti; 16 Willie Poching; 20 Gareth Ellis. Subs (all used): 6 Danny McGuire; 9 Matt Diskin; 22 Nick Scruton; 10 Barrie McDermott.
Tries: Mathers (9), Diskin (40), Bai (45);
Goals: Sinfield 2/3.
Rugby Leaguer & League Express Men of the Match: *Wolves:* Andrew Johns; *Rhinos:* Richard Mathers.
Penalty count: 9-5; **Half-time:** 18-12;
Referee: Ashley Klein (Keighley); **Attendance:** 13,024.

Sunday 11th September 2005

BRADFORD BULLS 52 HUDDERSFIELD GIANTS 34

BULLS: 6 Michael Withers; 3 Leon Pryce; 13 Ben Harris; 4 Shontayne Hape; 5 Lesley Vainikolo; 18 Iestyn Harris; 7 Paul Deacon; 12 Jamie Peacock (C); 9 Ian Henderson; 29 Stuart Fielden; 16 Paul Johnson; 10 Brad Meyers; 11 Lee Radford. Subs (all used): 1 Robbie Paul; 8 Joe Vagana; 14 Andy Lynch; 24 Adrian Morley (D).
Tries: Henderson (23), Johnson (26, 63), Deacon (33), Vainikolo (67, 73), Fielden (70), Meyers (77), Radford (80); **Goals:** Deacon 8/9.
GIANTS: 34 Marcus St Hilaire; 2 Hefin O'Hare; 3 James Evans; 4 Michael De Vere; 28 Lee Greenwood; 6 Chris Thorman (C); 13 Stanley Gene; 10 Jim Gannon; 9 Brad Drew; 21 Paul Jackson; 11 Chris Nero; 14 Stuart Jones; 18 Eorl Crabtree. Subs (all used): 7 Paul March; 17 Paul Smith; 19 Jon Grayshon; 27 Wayne McDonald.
Tries: St Hilaire (8), Evans (20), Gene (36), March (38), Crabtree (56), Greenwood (60); **Goals:** Thorman 5/6.
Rugby Leaguer & League Express Men of the Match: *Bulls:* Paul Deacon; *Giants:* Stanley Gene.
Penalty count: 5-3; **Half-time:** 18-24; **Referee:** Karl Kirkpatrick (Warrington); **Attendance:** 13,207.

WIDNES VIKINGS 36 LEIGH CENTURIONS 20

VIKINGS: 35 Brad Watts; 23 Paul Ballard; 1 Gary Connolly; 4 Adam Hughes; 28 Gray Viane; 7 Stephen Myler; 36 Keiran Kerr; 8 Terry O'Connor (C); 20 Mark Smith; 10 Julian O'Neill; 13 Simon Finnigan; 16 Daniel Frame; 33 Jules O'Neill. Subs (all used): 25 Stephen Nash; 15 Matt Whitaker; 17 David Mills; 24 Tim Holmes.
Tries: Ballard (14, 56), Connolly (23), Jules O'Neill (34), Watts (58), Finnigan (63); **Goals:** Myler 6/6.
Sin bin: Frame (74) - fighting.
CENTURIONS: 24 John Wilshere; 26 Nick Owen; 8 Rob Jackson; 1 Ben Cooper; 14 Steve Maden; 37 Carl Forber; 2 John Duffy; 4 Darren Fleary (C); 18 Paul Rowley; 15 Richard Marshall; 12 Oliver Wilkes; 20 Craig Stapleton; 13 Mark Leafa. Subs (all used): 21 Matt Sturm; 31 Warren Stevens; 30 Keiron Maddocks; 33 Liam Coleman.
Tries: Owen (3), John Duffy (31), Jackson (42), Forber (51); **Goals:** Owen 2/4.
Sin bin: Rowley (74) - fighting.
Rugby Leaguer & League Express Men of the Match: *Vikings:* Stephen Myler; *Centurions:* Mark Leafa.
Penalty count: 10-2; **Half-time:** 18-10;
Referee: Julian King (St Helens); **Attendance:** 5,293.

WAKEFIELD TRINITY WILDCATS 30 HULL FC 32

WILDCATS: 1 Colum Halpenny; 2 Michael Wainwright; 4 Sid Domic (C); 13 Rob Spicer; 31 Austin Buchanan; 7 Ben Jeffries; 14 Sam Obst; 18 Olivier Elima; 9 David March; 10 Michael Korkidas; 11 David Solomona; 29 Kevin Henderson; 12 Jamie Field. Subs (all used): 8 Darrell Griffin; 15 David Wrench; 21 Mark Field; 27 Chris Feather.
Tries: Wainwright (4), Jeffries (18), Domic (23), Elima (48), Buchanan (65); **Goals:** March 5/7.
HULL: 14 Motu Tony; 2 Nathan Blacklock; 30 Richard Whiting; 19 Sione Faumuina (D); 5 Gareth Raynor; 13 Paul Cooke; 21 Danny Brough; 20 Garreth Carvell; 9 Richard Swain (C); 15 Jamie Thackray; 17 Chris Chester; 12 Stephen Kearney; 11 Shayne McMenemy. Subs (all used): 8 Ewan Dowes; 10 Paul King; 22 Kirk Dixon; 23 Paul McNicholas.
Tries: Carvell (9), Swain (12), Raynor (28), Chester (44), Cooke (62), Faumuina (79); **Goals:** Brough 4/6.
Rugby Leaguer & League Express Men of the Match: *Wildcats:* David Solomona; *Hull:* Paul Cooke.
Penalty count: 7-9; **Half-time:** 20-16;
Referee: Phil Bentham (Warrington); **Attendance:** 5,721.

St Helens celebrate winning the League Leaders Shield

ROUND 28

Friday 16th September 2005

HULL FC 16 WARRINGTON WOLVES 30

HULL: 16 Tom Saxton; 2 Nathan Blacklock; 19 Sione Faumuina; 5 Gareth Raynor; 26 Richie Barnett; 30 Richard Whiting; 21 Danny Brough; 20 Garreth Carvell; 9 Richard Swain (C); 8 Ewan Dowes; 11 Shayne McMenemy; 12 Stephen Kearney; 13 Paul Cooke. Subs (all used): 15 Jamie Thackray; 10 Paul King; 17 Chris Chester; 24 Graeme Horne.
Tries: Kearney (34), Blacklock (54, 79);
Goals: Cooke 2/3.
WOLVES: 1 Brent Grose; 2 Henry Fa'afili; 3 Martin Gleeson; 4 Toa Kohe-Love; 25 Chris Bridge; 6 Lee Briers (C); 31 Andrew Johns; 8 Chris Leikvoll; 7 Nathan Wood; 16 Paul Wood; 11 Logan Swann; 13 Paul Noone; 9 Jon Clarke. Subs (all used): 10 Mark Hilton; 23 Andy Bracek; 14 Mark Gleeson; 17 Danny Lima.
Tries: Swann (5, 11), Grose (19), Kohe-Love (68, 74);
Goals: Johns 5/6.
Sin bin: Bridge (54) - holding down.
Rugby Leaguer & League Express Men of the Match: *Hull:* Tom Saxton; *Wolves:* Brent Grose.
Penalty count: 6-4; **Half-time:** 6-16;
Referee: Steve Ganson (St Helens); **Attendance:** 15,763.

LEEDS RHINOS 34 WAKEFIELD TRINITY WILDCATS 26

RHINOS: 1 Richard Mathers; 2 Mark Calderwood; 3 Chev Walker; 12 Chris McKenna; 5 Marcus Bai; 6 Danny McGuire; 7 Rob Burrow; 8 Ryan Bailey; 14 Andrew Dunemann; 15 Danny Ward; 20 Gareth Ellis; 16 Willie Poching; 13 Kevin Sinfield (C). Subs (all used): 18 Jamie Jones-Buchanan; 10 Barrie McDermott; 9 Matt Diskin; 27 Francis Cummins.
Tries: Walker (8), McKenna (18), Poching (52, 63), Calderwood (60, 78); **Goals:** Sinfield 5/7.
Sin bin: Mathers (58) – retaliation.
WILDCATS: 1 Colum Halpenny; 2 Michael Wainwright; 4 Sid Domic (C); 13 Rob Spicer; 31 Austin Buchanan; 7 Ben Jeffries; 14 Sam Obst; 27 Chris Feather; 9 David March; 18 Olivier Elima; 11 David Solomona; 29 Kevin Henderson; 22 Mark Applegarth. Subs (all used): 8 Darrell Griffin; 10 Michael Korkidas; 12 Jamie Field; 23 Liam Campbell (D).
Tries: Spicer (15), Jeffries (28), Buchanan (66), Domic (75), Obst (77); **Goals:** March 1/3, Griffin 2/2.
Sin bin: Henderson (58) – foul play.
Rugby Leaguer & League Express Men of the Match: *Rhinos:* Kevin Sinfield; *Wildcats:* David Solomona.
Penalty count: 8-7; **Half-time:** 10-10;
Referee: Julian King (St Helens); **Attendance:** 17,619.

LEIGH CENTURIONS 14 SALFORD CITY REDS 20

CENTURIONS: 24 John Wilshere; 14 Steve Maden; 8 Rob Jackson; 1 Ben Cooper; 26 Nick Owen; 37 Carl Forber; 2 John Duffy; 4 Darren Fleary (C); 18 Paul Rowley; 21 Matt Sturm; 20 Craig Stapleton; 13 Mark Leafa; 10 Jason Kent. Subs (all used): 12 Oliver Wilkes; 15 Richard Marshall; 31 Warren Stevens; 28 Jason Duffy.
Tries: Rowley (22), John Duffy (35), Maden (59);
Goals: Owen 1/4.
On report: Leafa (50) - late tackle.
CITY REDS: 15 Karl Fitzpatrick; 4 Junior Langi; 5 Anthony Stewart; 3 Stuart Littler; 2 David Hodgson; 1 Cliff Beverley; 7 Luke Robinson; 8 Andy Coley; 9 Malcolm Alker (C); 14 Paul Highton; 23 Andrew Brocklehurst; 11 Mark Shipway; 13 Chris Charles. Subs (all used): 16 Nathan McAvoy; 22 Simon Baldwin; 17 Gareth Haggerty; 10 Sean Rutgerson.
Tries: Hodgson (11, 30), Littler (50), Stewart (67);
Goals: Charles 2/5.
Rugby Leaguer & League Express Men of the Match: *Centurions:* John Duffy; *City Reds:* Luke Robinson.
Penalty count: 11-11; **Half-time:** 10-10; **Referee:** Richard Silverwood (Dewsbury); **Attendance:** 3,519.

Saturday 17th September 2005

ST HELENS 18 BRADFORD BULLS 32

SAINTS: 1 Paul Wellens (C); 20 Ian Hardman; 3 Jamie Lyon; 4 Willie Talau; 2 Ade Gardner; 6 Jason Hooper; 21 James Roby; 8 Nick Fozzard; 14 Mick Higham; 17 Paul Anderson; 19 James Graham; 15 Mike Bennett; 12 Jon Wilkin. Subs (all used): 9 Keiron Cunningham; 16 Keith Mason; 24 Maurie Fa'asavalu; 27 Vinnie Anderson.
Tries: Talau (31, 62), Wellens (51); **Goals:** Lyon 3/4.
BULLS: 3 Leon Pryce; 16 Paul Johnson; 13 Ben Harris; 4 Shontayne Hape; 5 Lesley Vainikolo; 18 Iestyn Harris; 7 Paul Deacon; 29 Stuart Fielden; 9 Ian Henderson; 24 Adrian Morley; 10 Brad Meyers; 12 Jamie Peacock (C); 11 Lee Radford. Subs (all used): 1 Robbie Paul; 8 Joe Vagana; 14 Andy Lynch; 19 Jamie Langley.
Tries: Vainikolo (18, 69), Johnson (67, 73), L Pryce (78), B Harris (79); **Goals:** Deacon 4/7.
Rugby Leaguer & League Express Men of the Match: *Saints:* Mike Bennett; *Bulls:* Paul Johnson.
Penalty count: 11-9; **Half-time:** 6-8;
Referee: Ashley Klein (Keighley); **Attendance:** 11,064.

Sunday 18th September 2005

HUDDERSFIELD GIANTS 22 WIGAN WARRIORS 36

GIANTS: 1 Paul Reilly; 2 Hefin O'Hare; 3 James Evans; 4 Michael De Vere; 28 Lee Greenwood; 6 Chris Thorman (C); 13 Stanley Gene; 18 Eorl Crabtree; 9 Brad Drew; 27 Wayne McDonald; 11 Chris Nero; 17 Paul Smith; 14 Stuart Jones. Subs (all used): 7 Paul March; 19 Jon Grayshon; 20 Paul White; 21 Paul Jackson.
Tries: Smith (23), Evans (43), White (71), Thorman (77); **Goals:** Thorman 3/4.
WARRIORS: 2 Brett Dallas; 5 Brian Carney; 14 Kevin Brown; 30 Sean Gleeson; 31 Chris Ashton (D); 6 Danny Orr; 7 Dennis Moran (C); 10 Jerome Guisset; 24 Bob Beswick; 12 Danny Tickle; 19 Stephen Wild; 29 Joel Tomkins; 20 Harrison Hansen. Subs (all used): 18 Wayne Godwin; 22 David Allen; 16 Danny Sculthorpe; 34 Lee Jewitt.
Tries: Moran (19), Ashton (36, 80), Orr (38), Brown (53), Sculthorpe (64), Carney (66);
Goals: Tickle 3/6, Carney 1/1.
Rugby Leaguer & League Express Men of the Match: *Giants:* Chris Nero; *Warriors:* Dennis Moran.
Penalty count: 6-4; **Half-time:** 4-18;
Referee: Karl Kirkpatrick (Warrington); **Attendance:** 5,917.

LONDON BRONCOS 68 WIDNES VIKINGS 10

BRONCOS: 6 Mark McLinden (C); 2 Jon Wells; 24 Tyrone Smith; 1 Paul Sykes; 3 Nick Bradley-Qalilawa; 30 Feleti Mateo; 21 Luke Dorn; 8 Francis Stephenson; 19 David Highton; 17 Mark Tookey; 11 Solomon Haumono; 12 Lee Hopkins; 26 Carl Ablett. Subs (all used): 13 Rob Purdham; 16 Joe Mbu; 25 Zebastian Luisi; 27 Karl Temata.
Tries: Smith (8), McLinden (12), Tookey (16), Dorn (20, 32, 45, 68), Luisi (37, 70), Mateo (40), Wells (42), Temata (47); **Goals:** Sykes 10/12.
VIKINGS: 19 Steve Rowlands; 23 Paul Ballard; 1 Gary Connolly; 4 Adam Hughes; 28 Gray Viane; 35 Brad Watts; 36 Keiran Kerr; 8 Terry O'Connor (C); 27 Paul Crook; 25 Stephen Nash; 16 Daniel Frame; 13 Simon Finnigan; 33 Jules O'Neill. Subs (all used): 5 Andrew Emelio; 31 Paul Alcock; 34 Bruce Johnson; 37 Darren Woods (D).
Tries: Alcock (59), Watts (76); **Goals:** Jules O'Neill 1/2.
Rugby Leaguer & League Express Men of the Match: *Broncos:* Luke Dorn; *Vikings:* Brad Watts.
Penalty count: 10-3; **Half-time:** 38-0;
Referee: Phil Bentham (Warrington); **Attendance:** 3,885

Warrington's Andrew Johns scores against Hull in the play-offs, despite the attentions of Paul Cooke and Richard Swain

PLAY-OFFS

Friday 23rd September 2005

ELIMINATION PLAY-OFF

BRADFORD BULLS 44 LONDON BRONCOS 22

BULLS: 3 Leon Pryce; 16 Paul Johnson; 13 Ben Harris; 4 Shontayne Hape; 5 Lesley Vainikolo; 18 Iestyn Harris; 1 Robbie Paul; 24 Adrian Morley; 9 Ian Henderson; 29 Stuart Fielden; 12 Jamie Peacock (C); 10 Brad Meyers; 11 Lee Radford. Subs (all used): 8 Joe Vagana; 14 Andy Lynch; 22 Karl Pryce; 19 Jamie Langley.
Tries: I Harris (25, 59), Vainikolo (31, 56), Peacock (43), Hape (49), Henderson (51), K Pryce (70);
Goals: I Harris 5/7, K Pryce 1/1.
On report: L Pryce (57) - high tackle.
BRONCOS: 25 Zebastian Luisi; 2 Jon Wells; 24 Tyrone Smith; 1 Paul Sykes; 3 Nick Bradley-Qalilawa; 30 Feleti Mateo; 21 Luke Dorn; 10 Steve Trindall; 19 David Highton; 17 Mark Tookey; 11 Solomon Haumono; 12 Lee Hopkins (C); 26 Carl Ablett. Subs (all used): 13 Rob Purdham; 16 Joe Mbu; 14 Danny Williams; 27 Karl Temata.
Tries: Wells (13), Haumono (62, 76), Luisi (65);
Goals: Sykes 3/4.
Rugby Leaguer & League Express Men of the Match: *Bulls:* Iestyn Harris; *Broncos:* Solomon Haumono.
Penalty count: 7-6; **Half-time:** 10-6;
Referee: Karl Kirkpatrick (Warrington); **Attendance:** 9,167.

Saturday 24th September 2005

ELIMINATION PLAY-OFF

WARRINGTON WOLVES 6 HULL FC 40

WOLVES: 1 Brent Grose; 2 Henry Fa'afili; 3 Martin Gleeson; 4 Toa Kohe-Love; 25 Chris Bridge; 6 Lee Briers (C); 31 Andrew Johns; 8 Chris Leikvoll; 7 Nathan Wood; 16 Paul Wood; 11 Logan Swann; 13 Paul Noone; 9 Jon Clarke. Subs (all used): 14 Mark Gleeson; 15 Ben Westwood; 10 Mark Hilton; 17 Danny Lima.
Try: Johns (62); **Goals:** Johns 1/1.
HULL: 16 Tom Saxton; 2 Nathan Blacklock; 3 Kirk Yeaman; 30 Richard Whiting; 5 Gareth Raynor; 6 Richard Horne; 21 Danny Brough; 8 Ewan Dowes; 9 Richard Swain (C); 20 Garreth Carvell; 11 Shayne McMenemy; 12 Stephen Kearney; 13 Paul Cooke. Subs (all used): 14 Motu Tony; 10 Paul King; 15 Jamie Thackray; 17 Chris Chester.
Tries: Blacklock (18, 32, 39), Chester (69), Yeaman (74), Whiting (77), Raynor (80); **Goals:** Brough 6/8.
Sin bin: R Horne (55) - interference.
Rugby Leaguer & League Express Men of the Match: *Wolves:* Brent Grose; *Hull:* Kirk Yeaman.
Penalty count: 7-2; **Half-time:** 0-18;
Referee: Ashley Klein (Keighley); **Attendance:** 12,243.

Friday 30th September 2005

QUALIFYING SEMI-FINAL

ST HELENS 16 LEEDS RHINOS 19

SAINTS: 1 Paul Wellens; 20 Ian Hardman; 3 Jamie Lyon; 4 Willie Talau; 2 Ade Gardner; 6 Jason Hooper; 21 James Roby; 8 Nick Fozzard; 9 Keiron Cunningham (C); 17 Paul Anderson; 15 Mike Bennett; 11 Lee Gilmour; 12 Jon Wilkin. Subs (all used): 14 Mick Higham; 24 Maurie Fa'asavalu; 27 Vinnie Anderson; 19 James Graham.
Tries: Lyon (69, 74), Hardman (71); **Goals:** Lyon 2/3.
RHINOS: 1 Richard Mathers; 2 Mark Calderwood; 3 Chev Walker; 12 Chris McKenna; 5 Marcus Bai; 6 Danny McGuire; 7 Rob Burrow; 8 Ryan Bailey; 14 Andrew Dunemann; 15 Danny Ward; 20 Gareth Ellis; 16 Willie Poching; 13 Kevin Sinfield (C). Subs (all used): 11 Ali Lauitiiti; 9 Matt Diskin; 18 Jamie Jones-Buchanan; 10 Barrie McDermott.
Tries: McGuire (13), Ward (33), Lauitiiti (51);
Goals: Sinfield 3/3; **Field goal:** Sinfield.
On report:
Bailey (24) - alleged dangerous throw on Graham.
Rugby Leaguer & League Express Men of the Match: *Saints:* Jamie Lyon; *Rhinos:* Kevin Sinfield.
Penalty count: 7-5; **Half-time:** 0-12;
Referee: Ashley Klein (Keighley); **Attendance:** 13,209.

Saturday 1st October 2005

ELIMINATION SEMI-FINAL

BRADFORD BULLS 71 HULL FC 0

BULLS: 6 Michael Withers; 3 Leon Pryce; 13 Ben Harris; 4 Shontayne Hape; 5 Lesley Vainikolo; 18 Iestyn Harris; 7 Paul Deacon; 12 Jamie Peacock (C); 9 Ian Henderson; 29 Stuart Fielden; 16 Paul Johnson; 10 Brad Meyers; 11 Lee Radford. Subs (all used): 8 Joe Vagana; 24 Adrian Morley; 1 Robbie Paul; 19 Jamie Langley.
Tries: Henderson (4, 30), Peacock (14), Withers (17), Vainikolo (21, 39, 41, 51), Johnson (37), Hape (44), I Harris (64), Fielden (76);
Goals: Deacon 10/11, Paul 1/1; **Field goal:** I Harris.
On report: Meyers (67) – alleged spear tackle.
HULL: 16 Tom Saxton; 2 Nathan Blacklock; 3 Kirk Yeaman; 30 Richard Whiting; 5 Gareth Raynor; 19 Sione Faumuina; 6 Richard Horne; 20 Garreth Carvell; 9 Richard Swain (C); 8 Ewan Dowes; 11 Shayne McMenemy; 12 Stephen Kearney; 13 Paul Cooke. Subs (all used): 14 Motu Tony; 15 Jamie Thackray; 10 Paul King; 17 Chris Chester.
Dismissal: Kearney (7) – high tackle on Fielden.
Rugby Leaguer & League Express Men of the Match: *Bulls:* Ian Henderson; *Hull:* Richard Horne.
Penalty count: 7-4; **Half-time:** 41-0;
Referee: Steve Ganson (St Helens); **Attendance:** 13,148.

Friday 7th October 2005

FINAL ELIMINATOR

ST HELENS 18 BRADFORD BULLS 23

SAINTS: 1 Paul Wellens; 2 Ade Gardner; 3 Jamie Lyon; 4 Willie Talau; 20 Ian Hardman; 12 Jon Wilkin; 26 Scott Moore; 8 Nick Fozzard; 9 Keiron Cunningham (C); 17 Paul Anderson; 11 Lee Gilmour; 15 Mike Bennett; 27 Vinnie Anderson. Subs (all used): 14 Mick Higham; 21 James Roby; 24 Maurie Fa'asavalu; 19 James Graham.
Tries: Wilkin (19, 28, 50); **Goals:** Lyon 3/4.
BULLS: 6 Michael Withers; 3 Leon Pryce; 13 Ben Harris; 4 Shontayne Hape; 5 Lesley Vainikolo; 18 Iestyn Harris; 7 Paul Deacon; 12 Jamie Peacock (C); 9 Ian Henderson; 29 Stuart Fielden; 16 Paul Johnson; 10 Brad Meyers; 11 Lee Radford. Subs (all used): 1 Robbie Paul; 19 Jamie Langley; 24 Adrian Morley; 8 Joe Vagana.
Tries: Hape (3, 77), Johnson (13), Langley (43);
Goals: Deacon 3/5; **Field goal:** Deacon.
Rugby Leaguer & League Express Men of the Match: *Saints:* Jon Wilkin; *Bulls:* Shontayne Hape.
Penalty count: 6-6; **Half-time:** 14-12; **Referee:** Karl Kirkpatrick (Warrington); **Attendance:** 11,604.

Saturday 15th October 2005

GRAND FINAL

BRADFORD BULLS 15 LEEDS RHINOS 6

BULLS: 6 Michael Withers; 3 Leon Pryce; 13 Ben Harris; 4 Shontayne Hape; 5 Lesley Vainikolo; 18 Iestyn Harris; 7 Paul Deacon; 12 Jamie Peacock (C); 9 Ian Henderson; 29 Stuart Fielden; 16 Paul Johnson; 10 Brad Meyers; 11 Lee Radford. Subs (all used): Johnson (5); 19 Jamie Langley for Peacock (24); 8 Joe Vagana for Fielden (24); Johnson for Radford (24); 1 Robbie Paul for Henderson (31); Peacock for Vagana (45); Fielden for Morley (49); Henderson for Paul (54); Radford for Meyers (60); Morley for Peacock (62); Meyers for Langley (73); Peacock for Johnson (74).
Tries: L Pryce (29), Vainikolo (53); **Goals:** Deacon 3/5;
Field goal: I Harris.
RHINOS: 1 Richard Mathers; 2 Mark Calderwood; 3 Chev Walker; 12 Chris McKenna; 5 Marcus Bai; 6 Danny McGuire; 7 Rob Burrow; 8 Ryan Bailey; 14 Andrew Dunemann; 15 Danny Ward; 20 Gareth Ellis; 16 Willie Poching; 13 Kevin Sinfield (C). Subs (all used): 10 Barrie McDermott for Ward (17); 11 Ali Lauitiiti for Poching (21); 18 Jamie Jones-Buchanan for Bailey (31); Ward for McDermott (34); 9 Matt Diskin for Ellis (48); Poching for Lauitiiti (48); McDermott for Ward (54); Ellis for Poching (54); Lauitiiti for McDermott (61); Poching for Dunemann (65); Ward for Jones-Buchanan (68); Dunemann for Ellis (71).
Try: McGuire (22); **Goals:** Sinfield 1/2.
Rugby Leaguer & League Express Men of the Match: *Bulls:* Leon Pryce; *Rhinos:* Danny McGuire.
Penalty count: 6-8; **Half-time:** 8-6;
Referee: Ashley Klein (Keighley);
Attendance: 65,537 (at Old Trafford, Manchester).

Bradford's Lee Radford takes on Leeds' Kevin Sinfield during the Super League Grand Final

SUPER LEAGUE X
Opta Index Analysis

SUPER LEAGUE X TOP PERFORMERS *(BY CATEGORY)*

TACKLES

Malcolm Alker	Salford	938
Chris Charles	Salford	833
Danny Tickle	Wigan	696
Jon Clarke	Warrington	675
David March	Wakefield	667
Shayne McMenemy	Hull	665
Jamie Peacock	Bradford	659
Lee Hopkins	London	636
Mick Cassidy	Widnes	634
Harrison Hansen	Wigan	616

TACKLES MADE *(% Success)*

Chris Charles	Salford	98.00%
Paul Wood	Warrington	97.93%
Vinnie Anderson	St Helens	97.45%
Mike Bennett	St Helens	97.44%
Rob Parker	Bradford	97.36%
Andy Coley	Salford	97.10%
Sean Rutgerson	Salford	96.98%
Malcolm Alker	Salford	96.90%
Paul Noone	Warrington	96.77%
James Graham	St Helens	96.71%

OFFLOADS

Jamie Peacock	Bradford	83
Ali Lauitiiti	Leeds	81
Kevin Sinfield	Leeds	77
David Solomona	Wakefield	69
Mark Leafa	Leigh	64
Stuart Fielden	Bradford	60
Lee Hopkins	London	56
Gareth Ellis	Leeds	55
Julian O'Neill	Widnes	55
Jamie Thackray	Hull	53

CLEAN BREAKS

Keith Senior	Leeds	38
Martin Gleeson	Warrington	30
Mark Calderwood	Leeds	30
Luke Dorn	London	28
Chev Walker	Leeds	26
Darren Albert	St Helens	26
Chris Nero	Huddersfield	24
Richard Mathers	Leeds	24
Marcus Bai	Leeds	23
Lesley Vainikolo	Bradford	23

TRY ASSISTS

Iestyn Harris	Bradford	31
Paul Cooke	Hull	30
Kevin Sinfield	Leeds	29
Lee Briers	Warrington	26
Dennis Moran	Wigan	26
Jamie Lyon	St Helens	26
Ben Jeffries	Wakefield	23
Leon Pryce	Bradford	21
Luke Dorn	London	20
Sean Long	St Helens	19

MARKER TACKLES

Malcolm Alker	Salford	107
Lee Radford	Bradford	104
Jamie Peacock	Bradford	93
Shayne McMenemy	Hull	89
Danny Tickle	Wigan	83
David March	Wakefield	83
Andrew Dunemann	Leeds	81
Chev Walker	Leeds	81
Kevin Sinfield	Leeds	79
Ben Westwood	Warrington	78

METRES

Terry O'Connor	Widnes	4250
Jamie Thackray	Hull	3935
Jamie Peacock	Bradford	3677
Brent Grose	Warrington	3461
Stuart Fielden	Bradford	3448
Danny Lima	Warrington	3435
Marcus Bai	Leeds	3384
Richard Mathers	Leeds	3327
Malcolm Alker	Salford	3235
Nick Fozzard	St Helens	3170

CARRIES

Paul Wellens	St Helens	494
Terry O'Connor	Widnes	487
Jamie Peacock	Bradford	484
Jamie Thackray	Hull	450
Brent Grose	Warrington	436
Stuart Fielden	Bradford	435
Kevin Sinfield	Leeds	431
Ewan Dowes	Hull	425
Richard Mathers	Leeds	423
John Wilshere	Leigh	422

Chris Charles

AVERAGE GAIN PER CARRY *(Metres)*

Karl Pryce	Bradford	11.10
Paul White	Huddersfield	10.06
Chris Nero	Huddersfield	9.76
Luke Dorn	London	9.74
Mark Calderwood	Leeds	9.55
Keith Senior	Leeds	9.30
Darren Albert	St Helens	9.15
Jamie Lyon	St Helens	9.11
Lesley Vainikolo	Bradford	9.02
Joe Vagana	Bradford	8.99

TACKLE BUSTS

Keith Senior	Leeds	94
Jamie Thackray	Hull	91
Martin Gleeson	Warrington	65
Brent Grose	Warrington	65
Stanley Gene	Huddersfield	64
Lee Hopkins	London	64
Iestyn Harris	Bradford	63
Richard Mathers	Leeds	62
Mark McLinden	London	61
Lesley Vainikolo	Bradford	61

40/20s

Paul Deacon	Bradford	3
Sean Long	St Helens	3
Stephen Myler	Widnes	3
Richard Horne	Hull	3
Lee Briers	Warrington	2
Ben Jeffries	Wakefield	2
Luke Robinson	Salford	2
Chris Thorman	Huddersfield	2
Paul Sculthorpe	St Helens	1

2005's top try scorer Mark Calderwood touches down for Leeds. The Rhinos scored more tries than any other team in Super League X.

SUPER LEAGUE X AVERAGES PER MATCH

TACKLES
Salford City Reds	260
Warrington Wolves	246
Wigan Warriors	245
Hull FC	243
St Helens	239
Leeds Rhinos	237
Huddersfield Giants	230
Bradford Bulls	228
London Broncos	227
Wakefield T Wildcats	226
Widnes Vikings	222
Leigh Centurions	204

OFFLOADS
Leeds Rhinos	20
Bradford Bulls	18
St Helens	16
Wigan Warriors	14
Hull FC	14
London Broncos	14
Widnes Vikings	13
Huddersfield Giants	11
Warrington Wolves	11
Leigh Centurions	11
Salford City Reds	11
Wakefield T Wildcats	11

METRES
Leeds Rhinos	1517
Bradford Bulls	1432
St Helens	1426
Warrington Wolves	1342
Huddersfield Giants	1327
Wigan Warriors	1303
Hull FC	1284
Salford City Reds	1236
Wakefield T Wildcats	1236
London Broncos	1226
Widnes Vikings	1113
Leigh Centurions	975

ERRORS
Leeds Rhinos	13
St Helens	12
London Broncos	11
Wakefield T Wildcats	10
Wigan Warriors	10
Bradford Bulls	9
Widnes Vikings	9
Warrington Wolves	9
Huddersfield Giants	9
Salford City Reds	9
Hull FC	8
Leigh Centurions	8

MISSED TACKLES
Wakefield T Wildcats	26
London Broncos	21
Widnes Vikings	20
Hull FC	20
Huddersfield Giants	19
Bradford Bulls	19
Wigan Warriors	19
Leigh Centurions	19
Leeds Rhinos	18
Warrington Wolves	18
Salford City Reds	14
St Helens	13

CLEAN BREAKS
Leeds Rhinos	11
Bradford Bulls	9
St Helens	8
Warrington Wolves	7
Wakefield T Wildcats	7
Huddersfield Giants	7
Hull FC	6
London Broncos	6
Wigan Warriors	6
Salford City Reds	5
Widnes Vikings	5
Leigh Centurions	3

CARRIES
Leeds Rhinos	203
St Helens	192
Warrington Wolves	186
Bradford Bulls	185
Wigan Warriors	184
Huddersfield Giants	177
Hull FC	176
Salford City Reds	171
Wakefield T Wildcats	163
London Broncos	162
Widnes Vikings	162
Leigh Centurions	147

KICKS IN GENERAL PLAY
Salford City Reds	19
Hull FC	19
Warrington Wolves	19
Huddersfield Giants	19
Wigan Warriors	17
St Helens	17
Widnes Vikings	16
Bradford Bulls	16
Leigh Centurions	15
Wakefield T Wildcats	15
London Broncos	15
Leeds Rhinos	14

SUPER LEAGUE X TRIES SCORED/CONCEDED

TOTAL TRIES SCORED
Leeds Rhinos	213
Bradford Bulls	210
St Helens	187
London Broncos	145
Warrington Wolves	145
Hull FC	138
Huddersfield Giants	123
Wakefield T Wildcats	122
Wigan Warriors	119
Widnes Vikings	105
Salford City Reds	99
Leigh Centurions	77

TOTAL TRIES CONCEDED
Leigh Centurions	214
Widnes Vikings	187
Wakefield T Wildcats	173
London Broncos	140
Huddersfield Giants	139
Hull FC	131
Warrington Wolves	130
Salford City Reds	129
Wigan Warriors	128
Bradford Bulls	127
St Helens	101
Leeds Rhinos	93

TRIES SCORED (KICKS)
Wigan Warriors	26
Leeds Rhinos	25
Hull FC	23
Bradford Bulls	22
London Broncos	22
St Helens	22
Huddersfield Giants	19
Wakefield T Wildcats	19
Warrington Wolves	17
Widnes Vikings	17
Leigh Centurions	14
Salford City Reds	12

TRIES CONCEDED (KICKS)
Widnes Vikings	29
Hull FC	26
St Helens	23
London Broncos	22
Salford City Reds	21
Wigan Warriors	18
Warrington Wolves	18
Bradford Bulls	17
Huddersfield Giants	17
Wakefield T Wildcats	17
Leigh Centurions	16
Leeds Rhinos	14

SUPER LEAGUE X TRIES SCORED/CONCEDED

TRIES SCORED FROM OWN HALF
St Helens 52
Leeds Rhinos 46
Huddersfield Giants 33
Bradford Bulls 30
London Broncos..............26
Warrington Wolves...........21
Wakefield T Wildcats 20
Hull FC 17
Wigan Warriors 15
Salford City Reds 14
Widnes Vikings 13
Leigh Centurions 12

TRIES CONCEDED FROM OVER 50M
Leigh Centurions 61
Widnes Vikings 30
Bradford Bulls 29
Wakefield T Wildcats 28
Huddersfield Giants 27
Hull FC 24
London Broncos..............23
Salford City Reds 22
Warrington Wolves...........21
Wigan Warriors 14
St Helens 11
Leeds Rhinos 9

TRIES SCORED FROM UNDER 10M
Bradford Bulls 106
Leeds Rhinos 76
St Helens 66
Hull FC 63
Widnes Vikings 58
London Broncos..............55
Warrington Wolves...........54
Wigan Warriors 53
Wakefield T Wildcats 49
Huddersfield Giants 39
Salford City Reds 39
Leigh Centurions 35

TRIES CONCEDED FROM UNDER 10M
Wakefield T Wildcats 77
Widnes Vikings 73
Leigh Centurions 67
Wigan Warriors 61
London Broncos..............60
Huddersfield Giants 57
Hull FC 56
Salford City Reds 55
Warrington Wolves...........51
St Helens 50
Bradford Bulls 48
Leeds Rhinos 46

SUPER LEAGUE X PENALTIES

TOTAL PENALTIES AWARDED
Widnes Vikings 222
Bradford Bulls 218
Wakefield T Wildcats 218
Wigan Warriors 214
Huddersfield Giants 205
London Broncos.............204
St Helens 204
Hull FC 202
Salford City Reds 193
Leeds Rhinos 191
Warrington Wolves.........189
Leigh Centurions 178

TOTAL PENALTIES CONCEDED
Leigh Centurions 244
Hull FC 233
London Broncos.............223
St Helens 203
Salford City Reds 199
Widnes Vikings 197
Huddersfield Giants 194
Bradford Bulls 193
Wigan Warriors 193
Wakefield T Wildcats 191
Leeds Rhinos 190
Warrington Wolves.........178

FOUL PLAY - AWARDED
London Broncos..............61
Huddersfield Giants 59
Hull FC 58
Warrington Wolves...........53
Bradford Bulls 52
Wigan Warriors 50
Salford City Reds 50
Wakefield T Wildcats 48
St Helens 44
Widnes Vikings 42
Leeds Rhinos 36
Leigh Centurions 32

FOUL PLAY - CONCEDED
Leigh Centurions 79
Wigan Warriors 62
Widnes Vikings 59
Hull FC 58
Leeds Rhinos 57
Warrington Wolves...........46
Wakefield T Wildcats 44
St Helens 41
London Broncos..............37
Huddersfield Giants 36
Salford City Reds 34
Bradford Bulls 32

OFFSIDE - AWARDED
Wigan Warriors 37
Warrington Wolves...........35
Wakefield T Wildcats 33
St Helens 30
Leeds Rhinos 30
Widnes Vikings 29
Salford City Reds 28
Bradford Bulls 27
London Broncos..............26
Hull FC 25
Huddersfield Giants 24
Leigh Centurions 22

OFFSIDE - CONCEDED
London Broncos..............40
St Helens 35
Wakefield T Wildcats 34
Hull FC 33
Huddersfield Giants 33
Leigh Centurions 30
Widnes Vikings 26
Bradford Bulls 26
Leeds Rhinos 25
Salford City Reds 23
Warrington Wolves...........22
Wigan Warriors 19

INTERFERENCE - AWARDED
Wakefield T Wildcats 77
St Helens 71
Wigan Warriors 70
Leeds Rhinos 68
Leigh Centurions 68
Widnes Vikings 66
Hull FC 66
Salford City Reds 61
Bradford Bulls 61
Huddersfield Giants 58
Warrington Wolves...........56
London Broncos..............54

INTERFERENCE - CONCEDED
London Broncos..............83
Hull FC 80
Salford City Reds 79
Leigh Centurions 78
Bradford Bulls 67
Wakefield T Wildcats 63
St Helens 62
Huddersfield Giants 62
Widnes Vikings 54
Wigan Warriors 54
Leeds Rhinos 47
Warrington Wolves...........47

OBSTRUCTION - AWARDED
Warrington Wolves...........12
Widnes Vikings 10
Wigan Warriors 7
Leigh Centurions 7
Wakefield T Wildcats 6
Salford City Reds 6
Huddersfield Giants 6
Hull FC 5
London Broncos..............5
Bradford Bulls 3
St Helens 2
Leeds Rhinos 2

OBSTRUCTION - CONCEDED
Bradford Bulls 12
Leigh Centurions 10
Leeds Rhinos 9
St Helens 6
Huddersfield Giants 6
London Broncos..............5
Salford City Reds 5
Widnes Vikings 5
Wakefield T Wildcats 3
Hull FC 3
Wigan Warriors 3
Warrington Wolves............3

BALL STEALING - AWARDED
Bradford Bulls 28
Leeds Rhinos 25
Widnes Vikings 21
Wigan Warriors 21
Huddersfield Giants 21
Hull FC 17
Wakefield T Wildcats 16
London Broncos..............14
St Helens 14
Warrington Wolves...........11
Leigh Centurions 7
Salford City Reds 3

BALL STEALING - CONCEDED
Warrington Wolves...........27
Hull FC 22
St Helens 21
Wigan Warriors 18
Widnes Vikings 17
Leigh Centurions 16
Salford City Reds 15
Bradford Bulls 14
Leeds Rhinos 14
Huddersfield Giants 13
Wakefield T Wildcats 12
London Broncos...............9

OFFSIDE MARKERS - AWARDED
Leigh Centurions 20
Bradford Bulls 19
St Helens 19
Huddersfield Giants 15
Salford City Reds 14
Hull FC 13
London Broncos..............13
Wigan Warriors 12
Wakefield T Wildcats 12
Widnes Vikings 11
Leeds Rhinos 6
Warrington Wolves............4

OFFSIDE MARKERS - CONCEDED
Salford City Reds 20
London Broncos..............17
St Helens 15
Leeds Rhinos 15
Huddersfield Giants 15
Wigan Warriors 14
Bradford Bulls 12
Wakefield T Wildcats 12
Leigh Centurions 11
Hull FC 10
Warrington Wolves............9
Widnes Vikings 8

NOT PLAYING BALL CORRECTLY - AWARDED
Leigh Centurions 7
Widnes Vikings 7
St Helens 6
Huddersfield Giants 6
Salford City Reds 6
Warrington Wolves............6
London Broncos..............5
Wigan Warriors 5
Wakefield T Wildcats 5
Leeds Rhinos 4
Bradford Bulls 3
Hull FC 2

NOT PLAYING BALL CORRECTLY - CONCEDED
Widnes Vikings 9
Huddersfield Giants 8
Salford City Reds 7
St Helens 6
Bradford Bulls 6
Wakefield T Wildcats 5
Leigh Centurions 5
Wigan Warriors 4
Hull FC 4
Leeds Rhinos 3
Warrington Wolves............3
London Broncos..............2

DISSENT - AWARDED
London Broncos...............8
Salford City Reds 7
Bradford Bulls 6
Leigh Centurions 5
Leeds Rhinos 5
Hull FC 5
Widnes Vikings 4
St Helens 4
Huddersfield Giants 4
Wakefield T Wildcats 4
Warrington Wolves............3
Wigan Warriors 3

DISSENT - CONCEDED
Bradford Bulls 9
Hull FC 8
Huddersfield Giants 6
Salford City Reds 6
Wakefield T Wildcats 4
Leigh Centurions 4
Wigan Warriors 4
Warrington Wolves............4
London Broncos..............4
Widnes Vikings 3
St Helens 3
Leeds Rhinos 3

BRADFORD BULLS

Stuart Fielden

Jamie Peacock

TACKLES
Jamie Peacock	659
Stuart Fielden	610
Lee Radford	588
Paul Deacon	438
Andy Lynch	430

OFFLOADS
Jamie Peacock	83
Stuart Fielden	60
Andy Lynch	48
Leon Pryce	40
Iestyn Harris	40

CLEAN BREAKS
Lesley Vainikolo	23
Iestyn Harris	21
Paul Deacon	21
Stuart Reardon	21
Leon Pryce	18

TRY ASSISTS
Iestyn Harris	31
Leon Pryce	21
Paul Deacon	19
Robbie Paul	16
Karl Pratt	6

METRES
Jamie Peacock	3677
Stuart Fielden	3448
Leon Pryce	2464
Joe Vagana	2398
Iestyn Harris	2304

TACKLE BUSTS
Iestyn Harris	63
Stuart Fielden	61
Lesley Vainikolo	61
Leon Pryce	58
Stuart Reardon	54

MARKER TACKLES
Lee Radford	104
Jamie Peacock	93
Rob Parker	78
Stuart Fielden	76
Brad Meyers	67

CARRIES
Jamie Peacock	484
Stuart Fielden	435
Iestyn Harris	381
Andy Lynch	318
Leon Pryce	282

AVERAGE OPTA INDEX
Jamie Peacock	742.39
Stuart Fielden	712.68
Iestyn Harris	687.11
Leon Pryce	548.57
Lesley Vainikolo	473.82

HUDDERSFIELD GIANTS

Chris Nero

Chris Thorman

TACKLES
Paul Smith	549
Brad Drew	524
Eorl Crabtree	501
Jim Gannon	483
Chris Nero	472

OFFLOADS
Eorl Crabtree	37
Jim Gannon	33
Wayne McDonald	29
Chris Thorman	27
Stanley Gene	26

CLEAN BREAKS
Chris Nero	24
Stanley Gene	22
Brad Drew	16
Chris Thorman	16
James Evans	13

TRY ASSISTS
Chris Thorman	18
Stanley Gene	12
Paul March	8
Brad Drew	7
Chris Nero	7

METRES
Jim Gannon	3025
Eorl Crabtree	2920
Chris Nero	2548
Stanley Gene	2377
Paul Jackson	2348

TACKLE BUSTS
Stanley Gene	64
Chris Nero	53
Eorl Crabtree	49
Marcus St Hilaire	46
Chris Thorman	40

MARKER TACKLES
Paul Smith	61
Paul March	58
Brad Drew	57
Chris Nero	53
Eorl Crabtree	49

CARRIES
Jim Gannon	406
Eorl Crabtree	396
Stanley Gene	350
Chris Thorman	314
Paul Jackson	294

AVERAGE OPTA INDEX
Chris Thorman	606.00
Chris Nero	545.61
Eorl Crabtree	545.29
Brad Drew	510.89
Stanley Gene	499.82

HULL FC

HULL F.C.

Jamie
Thackray

TACKLES
Shayne McMenemy	665
Ewan Dowes	544
Richard Swain	499
Danny Brough	477
Paul Cooke	476

OFFLOADS
Jamie Thackray	53
Shayne McMenemy	41
Tom Saxton	29
Paul Cooke	29
Stephen Kearney	26

CLEAN BREAKS
Kirk Yeaman	23
Richard Horne	18
Nathan Blacklock	15
Gareth Raynor	12
Shaun Briscoe	12

TRY ASSISTS
Paul Cooke	30
Richard Horne	14
Danny Brough	7
Kirk Yeaman	6
Chris Chester	5

METRES
Jamie Thackray	3935
Ewan Dowes	3130
Stephen Kearney	2181
Shaun Briscoe	2174
Shayne McMenemy	2110

TACKLE BUSTS
Jamie Thackray	91
Gareth Raynor	46
Kirk Yeaman	38
Richard Horne	34
Shaun Briscoe	27

MARKER TACKLES
Shayne McMenemy	89
Danny Brough	68
Richard Swain	65
Richard Horne	62
Paul Cooke	58

CARRIES
Jamie Thackray	450
Ewan Dowes	425
Shayne McMenemy	319
Stephen Kearney	304
Shaun Briscoe	300

AVERAGE OPTA INDEX
Jamie Thackray	595.82
Shayne McMenemy	537.71
Ewan Dowes	502.96
Paul Cooke	484.00
Richard Horne	471.68

Shayne
McMenemy

LEEDS RHINOS

Kevin
Sinfield

TACKLES
Andrew Dunemann	602
Kevin Sinfield	530
Gareth Ellis	526
Jamie Jones-Buchanan	495
Ryan Bailey	434

OFFLOADS
Ali Lauitiiti	81
Kevin Sinfield	77
Gareth Ellis	55
Keith Senior	44
Barrie McDermott	39

CLEAN BREAKS
Keith Senior	38
Mark Calderwood	30
Chev Walker	26
Richard Mathers	24
Marcus Bai	23

TRY ASSISTS
Kevin Sinfield	29
Ali Lauitiiti	17
Andrew Dunemann	14
Danny McGuire	13
Keith Senior	13

METRES
Marcus Bai	3384
Richard Mathers	3327
Kevin Sinfield	2752
Ali Lauitiiti	2752
Chev Walker	2560

TACKLE BUSTS
Keith Senior	94
Richard Mathers	62
Gareth Ellis	58
Chev Walker	54
Mark Calderwood	53

MARKER TACKLES
Andrew Dunemann	81
Chev Walker	81
Kevin Sinfield	79
Jamie Jones-Buchanan	77
Gareth Ellis	73

CARRIES
Kevin Sinfield	431
Richard Mathers	423
Andrew Dunemann	403
Marcus Bai	388
Gareth Ellis	349

AVERAGE OPTA INDEX
Kevin Sinfield	745.57
Keith Senior	678.82
Richard Mathers	662.00
Mark Calderwood	591.93
Ali Lauitiiti	584.00

Keith
Senior

LEIGH CENTURIONS

Craig Stapleton

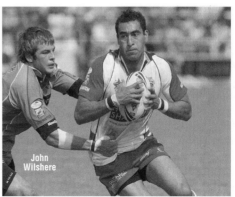

John Wilshere

TACKLES
Craig Stapleton 493
Mark Leafa......................433
Matt Sturm 408
Darren Fleary 383
Paul Rowley...................347

OFFLOADS
Mark Leafa.......................64
John Wilshere 48
Craig Stapleton 22
Matt Sturm 21
Darren Fleary 18

CLEAN BREAKS
John Wilshere 13
Ben Cooper 7
Phil Jones 6
Steve Maden 5
John Duffy.........................5

TRY ASSISTS
John Duffy.......................15
John Wilshere 11
Mark Leafa.........................5
Ben Cooper 4
Paul Rowley.......................3

METRES
John Wilshere 2944
Craig Stapleton 2274
Matt Sturm 2257
Mark Leafa...................2072
Darren Fleary 1547

TACKLE BUSTS
John Wilshere 56
John Duffy.......................23
Mark Leafa.......................17
Craig Stapleton 16
Matt Sturm 15

MARKER TACKLES
Craig Stapleton 57
Paul Rowley.....................55
John Duffy.......................43
Richard Marshall 39
Mark Leafa.......................38

CARRIES
John Wilshere 422
Matt Sturm 347
Mark Leafa.....................321
Craig Stapleton 310
Darren Fleary 220

AVERAGE OPTA INDEX
John Wilshere............500.25
Craig Stapleton 403.14
Mark Leafa..................394.71
Matt Sturm 361.46
John Duffy 347.18

LONDON BRONCOS

Mark McLinden

Lee Hopkins

TACKLES
Lee Hopkins....................636
Solomon Haumono 414
Joe Mbu 404
Rob Purdham 403
Steve Trindall 398

OFFLOADS
Lee Hopkins.....................56
Solomon Haumono 39
Feleti Mateo 30
Nick Bradley-Qalilawa 27
Paul Sykes.......................24

CLEAN BREAKS
Luke Dorn 28
Paul Sykes.......................22
Mark McLinden 20
Lee Hopkins.....................17
Tyrone Smith 14

TRY ASSISTS
Luke Dorn 20
Mark McLinden 19
Thomas Leuluai 16
Lee Hopkins.......................9
Paul Sykes.........................8

METRES
Lee Hopkins..................2811
Mark McLinden 2760
Solomon Haumono 2686
Paul Sykes...................2305
Nick Bradley-Qalilawa ..2199

TACKLE BUSTS
Lee Hopkins.....................64
Mark McLinden 61
Luke Dorn 43
Paul Sykes.......................43
Thomas Leuluai 37

MARKER TACKLES
Lee Hopkins.....................69
Joe Mbu 59
Steve Trindall 55
Rob Purdham 48
Mark McLinden 46

CARRIES
Lee Hopkins...................359
Mark McLinden 355
Solomon Haumono 328
Nick Bradley-Qalilawa 287
Paul Sykes.....................262

AVERAGE OPTA INDEX
Lee Hopkins 668.86
Mark McLinden.........592.43
Luke Dorn 550.07
Solomon Haumono....445.89
Paul Sykes 429.43

249

SALFORD CITY REDS

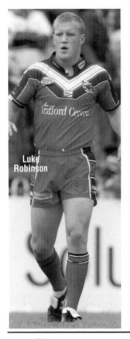

Luke Robinson

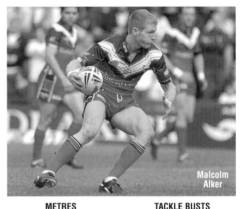

Malcolm Alker

TACKLES
Malcolm Alker	938
Chris Charles	833
Stuart Littler	512
Cliff Beverley	503
Andy Coley	502

OFFLOADS
Gareth Haggerty	39
Chris Charles	37
Stuart Littler	25
Andy Coley	24
Cliff Beverley	20

CLEAN BREAKS
Malcolm Alker	17
Stuart Littler	15
David Hodgson	14
Luke Robinson	14
Karl Fitzpatrick	12

TRY ASSISTS
Luke Robinson	18
Cliff Beverley	11
Malcolm Alker	7
Chris Charles	6
Andy Coley	5

METRES
Malcolm Alker	3235
David Hodgson	3027
Andy Coley	2385
Stuart Littler	2127
Sean Rutgerson	2071

TACKLE BUSTS
David Hodgson	58
Luke Robinson	40
Stuart Littler	39
Junior Langi	35
Gareth Haggerty	34

MARKER TACKLES
Malcolm Alker	107
Chris Charles	78
Cliff Beverley	61
Luke Robinson	53
Stuart Littler	47

CARRIES
David Hodgson	377
Malcolm Alker	374
Sean Rutgerson	312
Andy Coley	309
Stuart Littler	281

AVERAGE OPTA INDEX
Malcolm Alker	757.32
Luke Robinson	538.82
Chris Charles	507.75
David Hodgson	504.43
Stuart Littler	481.04

ST HELENS

Keiron Cunningham

Paul Wellens

TACKLES
Keiron Cunningham	557
Jon Wilkin	505
Nick Fozzard	492
Lee Gilmour	461
Mike Bennett	451

OFFLOADS
Keiron Cunningham	53
Nick Fozzard	42
Jamie Lyon	39
Maurie Fa'asavalu	29
Lee Gilmour	26

CLEAN BREAKS
Darren Albert	26
Jamie Lyon	23
Sean Long	20
Paul Wellens	18
Lee Gilmour	17

TRY ASSISTS
Jamie Lyon	26
Sean Long	19
Keiron Cunningham	18
Paul Wellens	11
Willie Talau	9

METRES
Nick Fozzard	3170
Paul Wellens	3080
Ade Gardner	2943
Paul Anderson	2905
Keiron Cunningham	2558

TACKLE BUSTS
Keiron Cunningham	56
Paul Wellens	54
Darren Albert	44
Jamie Lyon	39
Ade Gardner	37

MARKER TACKLES
Keiron Cunningham	68
Lee Gilmour	56
Jamie Lyon	54
Jon Wilkin	52
Nick Fozzard	50

CARRIES
Paul Wellens	494
Nick Fozzard	415
Keiron Cunningham	406
Ade Gardner	357
Paul Anderson	348

AVERAGE OPTA INDEX
Paul Wellens	649.25
Keiron Cunningham	639.25
Jamie Lyon	638.64
Darren Albert	532.75
Nick Fozzard	514.54

WAKEFIELD T WILDCATS

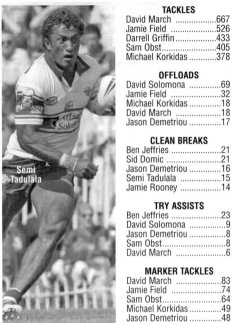

Semi Tadulala

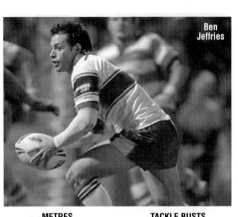

Ben Jeffries

TACKLES
David March 667
Jamie Field 526
Darrell Griffin..................433
Sam Obst....................405
Michael Korkidas 378

OFFLOADS
David Solomona 69
Jamie Field 32
Michael Korkidas.............18
David March 18
Jason Demetriou 17

CLEAN BREAKS
Ben Jeffries 21
Sid Domic 21
Jason Demetriou 16
Semi Tadulala 15
Jamie Rooney 14

TRY ASSISTS
Ben Jeffries 23
David Solomona 9
Jason Demetriou 8
Sam Obst..........................8
David March 6

MARKER TACKLES
David March 83
Jamie Field 74
Sam Obst..........................64
Michael Korkidas 49
Jason Demetriou 48

METRES
Semi Tadulala 2594
Darrell Griffin...............2527
Michael Korkidas 2477
Sid Domic 2304
David Solomona 2274

TACKLE BUSTS
Ben Jeffries 37
Sid Domic 36
David Solomona 35
Jason Demetriou 32
Semi Tadulala 31

CARRIES
Darrell Griffin..................308
Semi Tadulala 308
David Solomona 300
Ben Jeffries 299
Sid Domic 284

AVERAGE OPTA INDEX
Ben Jeffries..............575.32
Semi Tadulala 423.50
David March 405.11
Darrell Griffin..............386.61
Sid Domic.................379.93

WARRINGTON WOLVES

Martin Gleeson

Brent Grose

TACKLES
Jon Clarke 675
Mark Gleeson 606
Ben Westwood..............573
Logan Swann.................570
Mike Wainwright 542

OFFLOADS
Martin Gleeson 42
Nathan Wood..................39
Danny Lima 30
Brent Grose 27
Ben Westwood.................22

CLEAN BREAKS
Martin Gleeson 30
Brent Grose 22
Henry Fa'afili 20
Nathan Wood..................19
Lee Briers 17

TRY ASSISTS
Lee Briers 26
Martin Gleeson 11
Chris Bridge......................9
Nathan Wood....................8
Brent Grose 6

METRES
Brent Grose 3461
Danny Lima 3435
Paul Wood....................2498
Henry Fa'afili 2460
Martin Gleeson 2354

TACKLE BUSTS
Brent Grose 65
Martin Gleeson 65
Nathan Wood..................42
Ben Westwood.................39
Chris Bridge......................34

MARKER TACKLES
Ben Westwood..................78
Jon Clarke 68
Logan Swann...................67
Mike Wainwright 65
Mark Gleeson 65

CARRIES
Brent Grose 436
Danny Lima 415
Martin Gleeson 347
Paul Wood......................327
Henry Fa'afili 321

AVERAGE OPTA INDEX
Brent Grose 680.29
Martin Gleeson 633.11
Danny Lima 525.18
Ben Westwood 511.71
Henry Fa'afili..............496.43

251

WIDNES VIKINGS

Mick Cassidy

Terry O'Connor

TACKLES
Mick Cassidy 634
Mark Smith 537
Daniel Frame 531
Terry O'Connor 436
Simon Finnigan 435

OFFLOADS
Julian O'Neill 55
John Stankevitch 40
Daniel Frame 31
Simon Finnigan 29
Mick Cassidy 29

CLEAN BREAKS
Aaron Moule 12
Daniel Frame 10
Gray Viane 10
Shane Millard 9
Owen Craigie 9

TRY ASSISTS
Owen Craigie 13
Mark Smith 9
Simon Finnigan 7
Sala Fa'alogo 7
Gary Hulse 5

METRES
Terry O'Connor 4250
Julian O'Neill 2004
Daniel Frame 1859
Matt Whitaker 1803
Mick Cassidy 1764

TACKLE BUSTS
Shane Millard 31
Gray Viane 28
Aaron Moule 24
Daniel Frame 17
Gary Hulse....................17

MARKER TACKLES
Mick Cassidy 76
Mark Smith 75
Daniel Frame 68
John Stankevitch 48
Shane Millard 48

CARRIES
Terry O'Connor 487
Daniel Frame 292
Mick Cassidy 280
Julian O'Neill 263
Simon Finnigan 262

AVERAGE OPTA INDEX
Terry O'Connor 532.04
Mick Cassidy 376.07
Julian O'Neill 366.89
Simon Finnigan..........365.11
Shane Millard 356.64

WIGAN WARRIORS

Danny Tickle

Dennis Moran

TACKLES
Danny Tickle 696
Harrison Hansen 616
Stephen Wild 565
Terry Newton 494
Jerome Guisset 429

OFFLOADS
Terry Newton 42
Danny Sculthorpe 41
David Vaealiki 35
Danny Orr 24
Jerome Guisset 23

CLEAN BREAKS
Dennis Moran 18
Stephen Wild 16
Kevin Brown 15
Brett Dallas 12
Danny Tickle 12

TRY ASSISTS
Dennis Moran 26
Terry Newton 12
Danny Orr 9
David Vaealiki 8
Kevin Brown 7

METRES
Brett Dallas 3043
Danny Tickle 2541
Jerry Seuseu 2368
Martin Aspinwall 2199
Stephen Wild 2107

TACKLE BUSTS
Jerome Guisset 42
Brett Dallas 38
David Vaealiki 38
Martin Aspinwall 37
Kevin Brown 37

MARKER TACKLES
Danny Tickle 83
Harrison Hansen 74
Stephen Wild 73
Terry Newton 69
Wayne Godwin................54

CARRIES
Danny Tickle 370
Brett Dallas 356
Terry Newton 343
Jerry Seuseu 331
Martin Aspinwall 300

AVERAGE OPTA INDEX
Dennis Moran 572.07
Danny Tickle..............528.86
Terry Newton 499.39
Stephen Wild 481.82
Brett Dallas................449.71

NATIONAL LEAGUE 2005
Club by Club

BARROW RAIDERS

DATE	FIXTURE	RESULT	SCORERS	LGE	ATT
13/2/05	Gateshead (h) (NLC)	L28-35	t:Archer,Mulcahy,Wilcock,Knox,Zitter g:Holt(4)	3rd(NLC-G1)	778
20/2/05	Whitehaven (a) (NLC)	L44-0		4th(NLC-G1)	1,606
27/2/05	Workington (a) (NLC)	L28-18	t:Roach,Zitter,Atkinson,Hersnip g:Atkinson	4th(NLC-G1)	1,097
6/3/05	Workington (h) (NLC)	L12-54	t:J Osborn,Roach,A Fisher	4th(NLC-G1)	844
13/3/05	East Hull (h) (CCR3)	W42-22	t:Mulcahy,A Fisher,J Osborn,Zitter(2),Nixon,Knox,Roach g:Holt(5)	N/A	564
20/3/05	Whitehaven (h) (NLC)	L2-42	g:Holt	4th(NLC-G1)	877
24/3/05	Gateshead (a) (NLC)	W20-29	t:Zitter(2),Atkinson,A Fisher,Mulcahy g:Holt(4) fg:Holt	4th(NLC-G1)	268
28/3/05	Whitehaven (h)	L11-24	t:Whitehead g:Holt(3) fg:Holt	9th	1,112
3/4/05	Sheffield (h) (CCR4)	W33-26	t:Whitehead,Mulcahy(2),A Fisher,Clark g:Holt(5) fg:Holt(3)	N/A	893
10/4/05	Batley (a)	L50-30	t:Roach,Whitehead,Holt(2),D Fisher g:Holt(5)	9th	588
17/4/05	Rochdale (h)	W24-20	t:J Osborn,Holt,Horton g:Holt(6)	8th	814
24/4/05	Castleford (h)	L22-36	t:Nixon,Whitehead,Muff,Marshall g:Holt(3)	9th	1,816
8/5/05	Widnes (h) (CCR5)	L8-50	t:Nixon,Whitehead	N/A	2,599
15/5/05	Halifax (a)	L48-26	t:Zitter,Nixon,Raftrey,J Osborn g:Holt(5)	9th	1,446
22/5/05	Featherstone (h)	L16-38	t:Zitter,Mulcahy g:Holt(3),J Osborn	9th	1,008
5/6/05	Doncaster (a)	L42-12	t:Horton,Whitehead g:Holt(2)	10th	686
12/6/05	Oldham (h)	L22-40	t:Colley,Zitter,Wood,J Osborn g:Holt(3)	10th	1,073
26/6/05	Hull KR (a)	L48-10	t:Zitter g:Holt(3)	10th	1,921
3/7/05	Whitehaven (a)	L56-6	t:Clark g:J Osborn	10th	1,455
10/7/05	Batley (h)	L18-40	t:Dancer,Clark,Tandy g:Holt(3)	10th	743
24/7/05	Rochdale (a)	L36-22	t:Finch,Clark,G Osborn,Nixon g:Holt(3)	10th	732
31/7/05	Castleford (a)	L76-12	t:Tandy,J Osborn g:Holt(2)	10th	4,066
7/8/05	Halifax (h)	L12-76	t:J Osborn,Nixon,Irabor	10th	729
14/8/05	Doncaster (h)	L16-34	t:Zitter(3) g:Beech,J Osborn	10th	506
21/8/05	Featherstone (a)	L74-22	t:Marshall,Irabor,J Osborn(2) g:Holt(3)	10th	1,171
4/9/05	Oldham (a)	L52-12	t:Finch,Roach g:J Osborn(2)	10th	1,059
11/9/05	Hull KR (h)	L10-42	t:Zitter,Marshall g:J Osborn	10th	584

		APP		TRIES		GOALS		FG		PTS	
	D.O.B.	ALL	NL1	ALL	NL1	ALL	NL1	ALL	NL1	ALL	NL1
Chris Archer	18/9/83	5(10)	2(8)	1	0	0	0	0	0	4	0
Phil Atkinson	25/9/74	20	11	2	0	1	0	0	0	10	0
Nick Beech	22/1/85	5(1)	4	0	0	1	1	0	0	2	2
Jamie Butler	29/8/80	1(10)	1(10)	0	0	0	0	0	0	0	0
Ryan Campbell	23/9/81	1(2)	1(2)	0	0	0	0	0	0	0	0
Dave Clark	6/4/71	19	13	4	3	0	0	0	0	16	12
Richard Colley	9/1/84	19(3)	15(1)	1	1	0	0	0	0	4	4
Stuart Dancer	9/10/74	15(5)	11(3)	1	1	0	0	0	0	4	4
James Finch	9/7/83	9(1)	9(1)	2	2	0	0	0	0	8	8
Andy Fisher	17/11/67	11(2)	5	4	0	0	0	0	0	16	0
Darren Fisher	13/4/83	3(7)	2(3)	1	0	0	0	0	0	4	0
Keiron Hersnip	30/9/84	2(1)	0	1	0	0	0	0	0	4	0
Darren Holt	21/9/76	22(1)	13(1)	3	3	63	44	5	1	143	101
Anthony Horton	11/9/79	7(3)	7(2)	2	2	0	0	0	0	8	8
Shane Irabor	14/1/82	11(2)	11(2)	2	2	0	0	0	0	8	8
Matt Jefferson	10/3/84	(1)	(1)	0	0	0	0	0	0	0	0
Paul Jones	1/2/79	6(1)	0	0	0	0	0	0	0	0	0
Simon Knox	14/10/72	2(1)	(1)	2	0	0	0	0	0	8	0
Jamie Marshall	17/7/78	13(1)	13(1)	3	3	0	0	0	0	12	12
Alex Muff	17/8/82	6(5)	2(2)	1	1	0	0	0	0	4	4
Adrian Mulcahy	19/10/85	7(5)	2(1)	6	1	0	0	0	0	24	4
James Nixon	10/8/85	22	15	6	4	0	0	0	0	24	16
Glenn Osborn	17/8/83	12(7)	6(5)	1	1	0	0	0	0	4	4
Joel Osborn	22/12/81	23(2)	15(2)	9	7	6	6	0	0	48	40
Adam Pate	19/8/83	4(1)	4	0	0	0	0	0	0	0	0
Barry Pugh	17/10/84	1	0	0	0	0	0	0	0	0	0
Paul Raftrey	26/1/78	2(11)	2(11)	1	1	0	0	0	0	4	4
Jason Roach	2/5/71	16(7)	8(7)	5	2	0	0	0	0	20	8
Chris Roe	13/7/84	(3)	0	0	0	0	0	0	0	0	0
Ryan Tandy	20/9/81	7	7	2	2	0	0	0	0	8	8
Mike Whitehead	25/8/78	26	18	6	4	0	0	0	0	24	16
Paul Wilcock	9/12/79	15(8)	8(6)	1	0	0	0	0	0	4	0
Jon Williamson	30/10/86	4(6)	3(3)	0	0	0	0	0	0	0	0
Ryan Wood	11/8/80	10	10	1	1	0	0	0	0	4	4
Freddie Zitter	28/10/79	25	16	14	8	0	0	0	0	56	32

Freddie Zitter

LEAGUE RECORD
P18-W1-D0-L17
(10th, NL1)
F303, A832, Diff-529
2 points.

CHALLENGE CUP
Round Five

NATIONAL LEAGUE CUP
4th, Group 1

ATTENDANCES
Best - v Widnes (CC - 2,599)
Worst - v Doncaster (NL1 - 506)
Total (NL1 & NLC only) - 10,884
Average (NL1 & NLC only) - 907
(Down by 18 on 2004, NL2)

BATLEY BULLDOGS

DATE	FIXTURE	RESULT	SCORERS	LGE	ATT
13/2/05	Doncaster (h) (NLC)	W28-22	t:Flynn,Roden(2),McLoughlin g:Eaton(6)	2nd(NLC-G5)	788
20/2/05	Dewsbury (a) (NLC)	L32-22	t:Lythe,Roden,Royston,Toohey g:Eaton(3)	3rd(NLC-G5)	1,311
27/2/05	Sheffield (h) (NLC)	W28-16	t:Lingard,Royston,Morgan,Stokes,Horsley g:Eaton(4)	2nd(NLC-G5)	492
4/3/05	Sheffield (a) (NLC)	W6-34	t:Lingard(3),Eaton,O'Regan g:Eaton(7)	2nd(NLC-G5)	875
13/3/05	St Gaudens (h) (CCR3)	W40-14	t:Royston,O'Regan(3),Roden,Richardson,Marsh g:Eaton(6)	N/A	569
20/3/05	Doncaster (a) (NLC)	L54-0		2nd(NLC-G5)	804
25/3/05	Dewsbury (h) (NLC)	W12-10	t:Roden,Eaton g:Eaton(2)	2nd(NLC-G5)	1,234
29/3/05	Rochdale (a)	L26-25	t:Flynn,Stokes(2),Royston g:Eaton(4) fg:Eaton	7th	646
3/4/05	Leigh (h) (CCR4)	L8-25	t:Flynn(2)	N/A	1,661
10/4/05	Barrow (h)	W50-30	t:Morgan(2),Lingard(2),Harrison,Flynn,Robinson(2),Marsh g:Eaton(7)	4th	588
17/4/05	Halifax (a)	L38-16	t:Royston,Spears,Harrison g:Eaton(2)	4th	1,715
24/4/05	Featherstone (h)	L10-18	t:Flynn,Stokes g:Eaton	6th	947
1/5/05	Swinton (a) (NLCQPO)	L40-24	t:Lingard,Toohey,Sibson(2) g:Eaton(4)	N/A	689
15/5/05	Doncaster (a)	L35-28	t:Eaton,Sibson,Marsh,Morgan,Robinson g:Eaton(4)	8th	653
22/5/05	Oldham (h)	W25-18	t:Pennington,Morgan,Toohey,Marsh g:Eaton(4) fg:Roden	7th	792
5/6/05	Hull KR (a)	L15-6	t:Toohey g:Eaton	8th	2,084
12/6/05	Whitehaven (h)	L8-18	t:Stokes g:Eaton(2)	9th	653
26/6/05	Castleford (a)	L60-12	t:Lister,Lingard g:Eaton(2)	9th	4,487
3/7/05	Rochdale (h)	L28-40	t:McLoughlin,Lingard,Lister,Robinson,Shillabeer g:Eaton(4)	9th	587
10/7/05	Barrow (a)	W18-40	t:Robinson(2),Lythe,Flynn,Sibson,Lingard(2) g:Eaton(6)	8th	743
24/7/05	Halifax (a)	L26-34	t:Robinson(2),Marsh,Lingard,Sibson g:Eaton(3)	8th	1,277
31/7/05	Featherstone (a)	W24-50	t:Stokes(4),McLoughlin,Roden,Lythe,Lingard g:Eaton(9)	8th	1,486
7/8/05	Doncaster (h)	L10-20	t:Richardson,Stokes g:Eaton	8th	718
14/8/05	Hull KR (a)	L25-40	t:Lythe,Lingard,Royston(2) g:Robinson(4) fg:Roden	8th	1,214
21/8/05	Oldham (a)	W32-34	t:Richardson,Lythe,Royston,Gallagher(3) g:Eaton(4),Robinson	8th	1,187
4/9/05	Whitehaven (a)	L54-12	t:Lingard,Jones g:Eaton(2)	8th	1,903
11/9/05	Castleford (h)	L12-54	t:Sibson,Jones g:Eaton(2)	8th	2,230
25/9/05	Dewsbury (h) (NL1QS-QSF)	W40-20	t:Eaton,Lingard,Robinson,Roden(2),Stokes,Sibson g:Eaton(6)	N/A	1,961
9/10/05	Dewsbury (NL1QS-F) ●	W28-26	t:Marsh,Sibson,Jones,Eaton,Gallagher g:Eaton(4)	N/A	N/A

● Played at Halton Stadium, Widnes

		APP		TRIES		GOALS		FG		PTS	
	D.O.B.	ALL	NL1	ALL	NL1	ALL	NL1	ALL	NL1	ALL	NL1
Steve Beard	21/6/79	2(1)	0	0	0	0	0	0	0	0	0
Joe Berry	7/5/74	18(2)	12(2)	0	0	0	0	0	0	0	0
Will Cartledge	11/9/79	1(16)	(10)	0	0	0	0	0	0	0	0
Barry Eaton	30/9/73	29	20	5	3	100	68	1	1	221	149
Adrian Flynn	9/9/74	16	9	7	4	0	0	0	0	28	16
John Gallagher	25/9/85	3(2)	3(2)	4	4	0	0	0	0	16	16
Paul Harrison	24/9/70	2(12)	2(8)	2	2	0	0	0	0	8	8
Ryan Horsley	21/8/78	2(4)	1	1	0	0	0	0	0	4	0
Stephen Jones	9/1/83	5	5	3	3	0	0	0	0	12	12
Craig Lingard	11/12/77	21(4)	14(4)	16	11	0	0	0	0	64	44
Aiden Lister	8/1/85	5(1)	4(1)	2	2	0	0	0	0	8	8
Kris Lythe	29/3/83	19(6)	13(4)	5	4	0	0	0	0	20	16
Iain Marsh	6/10/80	26	18	6	5	0	0	0	0	24	20
Wayne McHugh	1/2/80	4	4	0	0	0	0	0	0	0	0
Martin McLoughlin	2/8/80	12(4)	10(4)	3	2	0	0	0	0	12	8
Dane Morgan	30/1/79	28	19	5	4	0	0	0	0	20	16
Alex Muff	17/8/82	3	3	0	0	0	0	0	0	0	0
Gary O'Regan	5/6/84	3	0	4	0	0	0	0	0	16	0
Matt Pennington	24/2/76	2(1)	2(1)	1	1	0	0	0	0	4	4
Sean Richardson	20/8/73	21(6)	14(4)	3	2	0	0	0	0	12	8
Darren Robinson	28/5/79	15(4)	15(3)	9	9	5	5	0	0	46	46
Neil Roden	9/4/80	25(1)	17(1)	8	3	0	0	2	2	34	14
David Rourke	12/3/81	15(6)	10(6)	0	0	0	0	0	0	0	0
Shad Royston	29/11/82	21(2)	13(2)	8	5	0	0	0	0	32	20
Gary Shillabeer	23/11/79	3(17)	3(10)	1	1	0	0	0	0	4	4
Mark Sibson	20/10/76	17(6)	15(4)	8	6	0	0	0	0	32	24
Tim Spears	27/7/84	5(21)	5(14)	1	1	0	0	0	0	4	4
Jamie Stokes	13/8/79	26	19	11	10	0	0	0	0	44	40
Mark Toohey	16/6/82	16	7	4	2	0	0	0	0	16	8
Craig Wright	8/9/71	12	3	0	0	0	0	0	0	0	0

Dane Morgan

LEAGUE RECORD
P18-W5-D0-L13
(8th, NL1)
(Winners, NL1 Qualifying Series)
F417, A574, Diff-157
10 points.

CHALLENGE CUP
Round Four

NATIONAL LEAGUE CUP
Qualifying Play-Off/2nd, Group 5

ATTENDANCES
Best - v Castleford (NL1 - 2,230)
Worst - v Sheffield (NLC - 492)
Total (NL1, NL1QS & NLC only) - 13,481
Average (NL1, NL1QS
& NLC only) - 1,037
(Up by 123 on 2004)

CASTLEFORD TIGERS

DATE	FIXTURE	RESULT	SCORERS	LGE	ATT
13/2/05	York (h) (NLC)	W52-2	t:Hepworth(2),A Smith,A Kain(2),Shenton,Pryce,Bird,Huby(2) g:Huby(4),Handforth(2)	1st(NLC-G4)	5,768
20/2/05	Featherstone (a) (NLC)	W10-22	t:Shenton,A Kain,Haughey,Platt g:Handforth(2),Huby	1st(NLC-G4)	6,353
27/2/05	Hunslet (h) (NLC)	W70-0	t:Shenton(2),Huby(2),Reid,James,F Watene,Haughey,Hepworth(3),Platt, Handforth g:Huby(8),Handforth	1st(NLC-G4)	4,483
6/3/05	Hunslet (a) (NLC)	W6-34	t:A Kain,James,Pryce(2),Shenton,Henderson,Reid g:Huby(3)	1st(NLC-G4)	1,432
13/3/05	Hull Dockers (h) (CCR3)	W72-10	t:A Kain(2),Reid(3),James,Hepworth(3),Pryce,F Watene,A Watene,Shenton g:Handforth(10)	N/A	3,331
20/3/05	York (a) (NLC)	W16-24	t:Haughey(2),Shenton,Henderson,A Kain g:Handforth(2),A Kain	1st(NLC-G4)	2,340
25/3/05	Featherstone (h) (NLC)	W35-16	t:Pryce(3),S Kain,Robinson,Shenton g:A Kain(5) fg:A Kain	1st(NLC-G4)	7,338
28/3/05	Doncaster (a)	W10-29	t:Reid,Haughey,Shenton,James,Robinson g:A Kain(4) fg:A Kain	1st	3,371
3/4/05	Halifax (a) (CCR4)	L23-14	t:Shenton(2) g:Davis(3)	N/A	3,925
10/4/05	Rochdale (h)	W36-22	t:James,Haughey,Platt,Pryce(2),Hepworth,Shenton(2) g:Davis(2)	2nd	4,776
17/4/05	Oldham (a)	W20-32	t:Davis(2),Pryce(2),Shenton,A Kain g:A Kain(4)	2nd	2,054
24/4/05	Barrow (a)	W22-36	t:Reid,Haughey(2),A Watene,Pryce(2),Davis g:A Kain(4)	2nd	1,816
15/5/05	Hull KR (h)	W32-26	t:Bird,Davis(2),A Kain,Huby,A Watene g:A Kain,Huby(3)	2nd	8,078
22/5/05	Halifax (a)	W16-48	t:Bird,Henderson,Shenton(2),Haughey,Pryce(2),Hepworth,Huby g:Huby(5),A Kain	2nd	3,259
29/5/05	Featherstone (a) (NLCQF)	W14-38	t:Platt(4),Davis,Bird g:Huby(3),Handforth(4)	N/A	3,418
5/6/05	Whitehaven (h)	W42-24	t:Pryce(2),Crouch,Platt,Hepworth(2),Bird,Haughey g:Handforth,Fletcher(2),Huby(2)	1st	7,323
12/6/05	Featherstone (a)	W34-38	t:Handforth,Henderson,Huby,Pryce,James,Shenton g:Huby(6),Fletcher	1st	3,334
19/6/05	Whitehaven (h) (NLCSF)	W42-14	t:Haughey,Handforth,Crouch,Bird,Platt,F Watene,A Kain g:Fletcher,Huby(5),Davis	N/A	5,019
26/6/05	Batley (h)	W60-12	t:Davis,Henderson,F Watene,Bird(2),Shenton(2),Reid,Crouch,Platt,Boyle g:Huby(5),Davis,A Kain,Boyle	1st	4,487
3/7/05	Doncaster (h)	W40-16	t:Shenton,Bailey,Platt(3),F Watene,Handforth g:Huby(3),A Kain(3)	1st	5,005
10/7/05	Rochdale (a)	L17-16	t:Haughey,Reid,Davis g:Huby(2)	1st	1,728
17/7/05	Hull KR (NLCF) ●	L16-18	t:Platt,Hepworth g:Huby(4)	N/A	9,400
24/7/05	Oldham (a)	W32-20	t:Huby(2),A Kain,Bird,Pryce(2) g:Huby(3),Fletcher	1st	4,600
31/7/05	Barrow (h)	W76-12	t:James,Crouch,Eagar,Pryce(3),A Watene,Shenton(2),Platt,Huby(3),Davis g:Huby(9),Fletcher	1st	4,066
7/8/05	Hull KR (a)	L46-18	t:James,Pryce,A Kain g:Huby(2),A Kain	2nd	5,023
14/8/05	Whitehaven (a)	L19-16	t:Pryce(2),A Kain g:Huby(2)	2nd	4,437
21/8/05	Halifax (a)	W38-34	t:Henderson(2),Bird,Pryce,Fletcher,Blanch g:A Kain(6),Fletcher	2nd	4,941
4/9/05	Featherstone (h)	W40-6	t:Shenton,Haughey(2),Blanch,Crouch,Pryce,Bird g:Huby(3),A Kain(3)	2nd	5,943
11/9/05	Batley (a)	W12-54	t:Haughey(3),A Watene(2),Pryce,A Kain,James,Hepworth,Davis g:Huby(5),Fletcher(2)	2nd	2,230
25/9/05	Whitehaven (a) (QSF)	L32-22	t:Pryce,Bird,Eagar g:Huby(5)	N/A	6,154
2/10/05	Halifax (h) (FE)	W15-12	t:Platt,Blanch g:Fletcher(2),Crouch fg:Handforth	N/A	6,197
9/10/05	Whitehaven (GF) ●●	W36-8	t:Huby,Crouch,Blanch,Davis(2),Haughey g:Fletcher(2),Huby(3),Hepworth	N/A	13,300

● Played at Bloomfield Road, Blackpool
●● Played at Halton Stadium, Widnes

		APP		TRIES		GOALS		FG		PTS	
	D.O.B.	ALL	NL1	ALL	NL1	ALL	NL1	ALL	NL1	ALL	NL1
Andy Bailey	15/10/82	7(5)	6(4)	1	1	0	0	0	0	4	4
Deon Bird	27/1/76	20(2)	17	12	9	0	0	0	0	48	36
Damien Blanch	24/5/83	4(2)	4(2)	4	4	0	0	0	0	16	16
Ryan Boyle	17/10/87	(1)	(1)	1	1	1	1	0	0	6	6
Dominic Brambani	10/5/85	1(3)	(1)	0	0	0	0	0	0	0	0
Leigh Cooke	26/2/86	1(7)	(1)	0	0	0	0	0	0	0	0
Steve Crouch	24/12/77	28(1)	20(1)	6	5	1	1	0	0	26	22
Brad Davis	13/3/68	22(1)	18(1)	12	11	7	3	0	0	62	50
Michael Eagar	15/8/73	8	8	2	2	0	0	0	0	8	8
Anthony England	19/10/86	(2)	0	0	0	0	0	0	0	0	0
Richard Fletcher	17/5/81	10(5)	8(4)	1	1	13	12	0	0	30	28
Lance Hamilton	2/9/79	1(1)	0	0	0	0	0	0	0	0	0
Paul Handforth	6/10/81	15(7)	5(6)	4	2	21	1	1	1	59	11
Tom Haughey	30/1/82	26(4)	17(3)	18	13	0	0	0	0	72	52
Andrew Henderson	17/6/79	31	21	7	5	0	0	0	0	28	20
Jon Hepworth	25/12/82	25(1)	15(1)	14	5	1	1	0	0	58	22
Craig Huby	21/5/86	17(8)	12(6)	13	9	86	58	0	0	224	152
Jordan James	24/5/80	8(14)	4(11)	9	6	0	0	0	0	36	24
Andy Kain	1/9/85	20(6)	13(3)	14	6	34	28	2	1	126	81
Stuart Kain	18/9/85	4(1)	1(1)	1	0	0	0	0	0	4	0
Michael Knowles	2/5/87	(3)	(1)	0	0	0	0	0	0	0	0
Shaun Lunt	15/4/86	1(3)	(2)	0	0	0	0	0	0	0	0
Dominic Maloney	12/3/87	(2)	(2)	0	0	0	0	0	0	0	0
Jason Mossop	12/9/85	(1)	(1)	0	0	0	0	0	0	0	0
Michael Platt	23/3/84	28	20	16	8	0	0	0	0	64	32
Waine Pryce	3/10/81	28	18	30	23	0	0	0	0	120	92
Damien Reid	14/3/84	15(1)	7(1)	9	4	0	0	0	0	36	16
Tim Robinson	10/10/84	2(2)	1(1)	2	1	0	0	0	0	8	4
Alex Rowe	11/3/85	1(3)	(2)	0	0	0	0	0	0	0	0
Dean Sampson	27/6/67	(1)	0	0	0	0	0	0	0	0	0
Michael Shenton	22/7/86	29	18	23	13	0	0	0	0	92	52
Aaron Smith	10/9/82	23	15	1	0	0	0	0	0	4	0
Byron Smith	5/3/84	8(17)	4(12)	0	0	0	0	0	0	0	0
Adrian Vowles	30/5/71	(3)	(3)	0	0	0	0	0	0	0	0
Adam Watene	7/10/77	25(2)	17	6	5	0	0	0	0	24	20
Frank Watene	15/2/77	8(17)	4(12)	5	2	0	0	0	0	20	8
Rob Worrincy	9/7/85	(1)	0	0	0	0	0	0	0	0	0

Waine Pryce

LEAGUE RECORD
P18-W15-D0-L3
(2nd, NL1/Grand Final Winners, Champions)
F683, A368, Diff+315
30 points.

CHALLENGE CUP
Round Four

NATIONAL LEAGUE CUP
Runners-Up/1st, Group 4

ATTENDANCES
Best - v Hull KR (NL1 - 8,078)
Worst - v Hull Dockers (CC - 3,331)
Total (NL1, inc play-offs,
& NLC, inc SF, only) - 78,024
Average (NL1, inc play-offs,
& NLC, inc SF, only) - 5,573
(Down by 1,462 on 2004, SL)

DONCASTER DRAGONS

DATE	FIXTURE	RESULT	SCORERS	LGE	ATT
13/2/05	Batley (a) (NLC)	L28-22	t:Handford,Wood,Holroyd,Hay g:Holroyd(3)	3rd(NLC-G5)	788
18/2/05	Sheffield (h) (NLC)	W58-20	t:Horne,Ostler,Cook,Moana,Langley,Crooks,Miles,Tawhai,Holroyd,Wood g:Holroyd(9)	1st(NLC-G5)	727
27/2/05	Dewsbury (a) (NLC)	W27-32	t:Cardoza,Cook,Miles(2),Holroyd,Langley g:Holroyd(4)	1st(NLC-G5)	1,097
6/3/05	Dewsbury (h) (NLC)	W40-10	t:Farrell,Langley,W Green,P Green(2),Handford,Holroyd,Cockayne g:Holroyd(4)	1st(NLC-G5)	710
13/3/05	Stanningley (h) (CCR3)	W54-6	t:W Green(3),Wood(2),Handford,Farrell,Cockayne,Netherton,Andrews g:Holroyd(6),Cockayne	N/A	839
20/3/05	Batley (h) (NLC)	W54-0	t:Hay(2),Holroyd,Cardoza(2),Colton,Netherton,Wood,Miles g:Holroyd(9)	1st(NLC-G5)	804
25/3/05	Sheffield (a) (NLC) ●	W20-38	t:Cockayne(3),Langley,Colton(2),Netherton,Andrews g:Cockayne,W Green(2)	1st(NLC-G5)	1,003
28/3/05	Castleford (h)	L10-29	t:Miles,Holroyd g:Holroyd	10th	3,371
3/4/05	Workington (h) (CCR4)	W54-18	t:Langley,Farrell,W Green,Colton(2),P Green(2),Wood,Cardoza,Moana g:W Green(7)	N/A	770
10/4/05	Oldham (a)	W22-44	t:Hay,Wood(2),Harland,Moana,Miles,Cook g:W Green(7),Miles	5th	1,266
17/4/05	Hull KR (h)	L20-36	t:P Green,Lawton,Handford,Cook g:Wood(2)	5th	1,620
24/4/05	Whitehaven (a)	L20-6	t:Cockayne g:Holroyd	8th	1,945
7/5/05	Toulouse (a) (CCR5)	L32-18	t:Cockayne,Tawhai,Colton g:Holroyd(3)	N/A	1,200
15/5/05	Batley (h)	W35-28	t:Moana,Holroyd,Cockayne(3),Colton g:Holroyd(5) fg:Cook	6th	653
22/5/05	Rochdale (a)	W24-34	t:Harland,Miles,Cockayne,Farrell(2),Lawton g:Holroyd(5)	5th	806
29/5/05	Halifax (h) (NLCQF)	W54-38	t:Colton,Lawton(2),Cockayne,Harland,Handford(2),Tawhai,W Green g:Holroyd(3),W Green(6)	N/A	1,008
5/6/05	Barrow (h)	W42-12	t:Golden,Lawton,Farrell,Cook(2),Harland,Colton g:Holroyd(7)	4th	686
12/6/05	Halifax (a)	L36-16	t:Moana(2),Golden g:Holroyd(2)	5th	1,737
19/6/05	Hull KR (a) (NLCSF)	L34-26	t:Moana,Cockayne,Golden,Colton(2) g:Holroyd(3)	N/A	2,474
26/6/05	Featherstone (h)	W32-24	t:D Mills,Cook,Handford,Wood,Farrell,Leaf g:Cockayne(3),Miles	5th	973
3/7/05	Castleford (a)	L40-16	t:Colton,Lawton(2) g:Cockayne,Miles	5th	5,005
10/7/05	Oldham (h)	W34-26	t:Miles(2),Holroyd,Farrell(2),Moana g:Holroyd(5)	5th	896
24/7/05	Hull KR (a)	L28-18	t:Hay,D Mills,P Green g:Holroyd(3)	5th	3,011
31/7/05	Whitehaven (h)	L20-30	t:Farrell,Moana,Poucher,Miles g:Holroyd(2)	6th	690
7/8/05	Batley (a)	W10-20	t:Cockayne,Lawton,Farrell g:Holroyd(4)	6th	718
14/8/05	Barrow (a)	W16-34	t:Langley,Moana(2),Miles,Lawton,Holroyd g:Holroyd(5)	5th	506
21/8/05	Rochdale (h)	L30-45	t:Cockayne(3),Fa'alogo,Cook g:Holroyd(5)	6th	630
4/9/05	Halifax (h)	W28-22	t:Hulse,Farrell,Colton(2),Cook g:Holroyd(4)	6th	1,024
11/9/05	Featherstone (h)	W22-46	t:Moana(2),Hulse,Harland,Colton,Holroyd,Lawton g:Holroyd(9)	5th	1,495
18/9/05	Halifax (a) (EPO)	L64-10	t:Cook,Langley g:Holroyd	N/A	1,863

● Played at Clifton Lane, Rotherham

		APP		TRIES		GOALS		FG		PTS	
	D.O.B.	ALL	NL1	ALL	NL1	ALL	NL1	ALL	NL1	ALL	NL1
Dean Andrews	1/7/79	2(9)	1(5)	2	0	0	0	0	0	8	0
Tom Buckenham	15/8/84	(2)	(1)	0	0	0	0	0	0	0	0
Dale Cardoza	13/9/79	9(1)	3	4	0	0	0	0	0	16	0
Ben Cockayne	20/7/83	15(7)	11(5)	17	9	6	4	0	0	80	44
Dean Colton	18/2/83	19(1)	14	15	6	0	0	0	0	60	24
Craig Cook	26/5/83	23	14	10	8	0	0	1	1	41	33
Stuart Crooks	23/10/84	(3)	1	1	0	0	0	0	0	4	0
Sala Fa'alogo	20/9/77	4	4	1	1	0	0	0	0	4	4
Craig Farrell	8/10/81	29	19	12	9	0	0	0	0	48	36
Andy Fisher	17/11/67	1	1	0	0	0	0	0	0	0	0
Marvin Golden	21/12/76	7	6	3	2	0	0	0	0	12	8
Peter Green	2/12/81	19(1)	10	6	2	0	0	0	0	24	8
Wayne Green	1/1/83	6(4)	2(2)	6	0	22	7	0	0	68	14
Gareth Handford	22/4/80	25(5)	15(4)	7	2	0	0	0	0	28	8
Lee Harland	4/9/74	19(5)	13(4)	5	4	0	0	0	0	20	16
Andy Hay	5/11/73	19	13	5	2	0	0	0	0	20	8
Graham Holroyd	25/10/75	24	15	10	5	103	59	0	0	246	138
Craig Horne	20/5/78	4	1	1	0	0	0	0	0	4	0
Gary Hulse	20/1/81	4	4	2	2	0	0	0	0	8	8
Jonathan Jones	9/4/84	1(1)	0	0	0	0	0	0	0	0	0
Chris Langley	11/10/80	11(4)	4(4)	7	2	0	0	0	0	28	8
Craig Lawton	17/2/81	18(11)	14(5)	10	8	0	0	0	0	40	32
Shaun Leaf	10/2/84	7(4)	5(3)	1	1	0	0	0	0	4	4
Craig Miles	8/7/81	26(2)	15(2)	11	7	3	3	0	0	50	34
Danny Mills	10/8/82	8(1)	7(1)	2	2	0	0	0	0	8	8
Karl Mills	7/2/84	1(10)	1(8)	0	0	0	0	0	0	0	0
Martin Moana	13/8/73	26(1)	16(1)	13	10	0	0	0	0	52	40
Kirk Netherton	10/5/85	1(7)	(4)	3	0	0	0	0	0	12	0
Dean O'Loughlin	25/9/82	10(18)	6(12)	0	0	0	0	0	0	0	0
Martin Ostler	21/6/80	16(13)	10(9)	1	0	0	0	0	0	4	0
Craig Poucher	12/9/80	5(1)	5(1)	1	1	0	0	0	0	4	4
Latham Tawhai	23/8/71	20(1)	11(1)	3	0	0	0	0	0	12	0
Aaron Wood	5/2/79	11(8)	7(4)	9	3	2	2	0	0	40	16

Craig Lawton

LEAGUE RECORD
P18-W10-D0-L8
(5th, NL1/Elimination Play-Off)
F485, A470, Diff+15
20 points.

CHALLENGE CUP
Round Five

NATIONAL LEAGUE CUP
Semi Finalists/1st, Group 5

ATTENDANCES
Best - v Castleford (NL1 - 3,371)
Worst - v Rochdale (NL1 - 630)
Total (NL1 & NLC, inc QF, only) - 13,792
Average (NL1 & NLC, inc QF, only) - 1,061
(Up by 187 on 2004)

FEATHERSTONE ROVERS

DATE	FIXTURE	RESULT	SCORERS	LGE	ATT
13/2/05	Hunslet (a) (NLC)	W12-28	t:Weeden(2),McNally(2),Wray g:Weeden(4)	2nd(NLC-G4)	1,102
20/2/05	Castleford (h) (NLC)	L10-22	t:Weeden g:Weeden(3)	2nd(NLC-G4)	6,353
27/2/05	York (h) (NLC)	W21-20	t:Powell,Dooler,Jarrett g:Weeden(4) fg:Weeden	2nd(NLC-G4)	1,463
6/3/05	York (a) (NLC)	D20-20	t:Presley,C Hughes,Wray,Powell g:Weeden(2)	2nd(NLC-G4)	1,463
13/3/05	Thornhill (h) (CCR3)	W48-10	t:Wray(4),Powell,Sykes,McNally,Newlove,Moss g:Weeden(6)	N/A	774
20/3/05	Hunslet (h) (NLC)	W28-18	t:Jarrett,Moss,Tonks,Newlove,Maun(2) g:Weeden(2)	2nd(NLC-G4)	1,150
25/3/05	Castleford (a) (NLC)	L35-16	t:Newlove,Lowe,McNally,C Hughes	2nd(NLC-G4)	7,338
28/3/05	Oldham (h)	D20-20	t:Wray,Maun,McNally,Ripley g:Weeden(2)	6th	1,463
3/4/05	Bradford (h) (CCR4)	L14-80	t:Newlove(2),Tonks g:Ripley	N/A	3,355
10/4/05	Hull KR (a)	L44-30	t:Newlove,Southwell,Weeden(2),Ripley g:Finn(5)	7th	2,510
17/4/05	Whitehaven (h)	L20-40	t:Maun(2),Dooler,Weeden g:Finn(2)	9th	1,269
24/4/05	Batley (a)	W10-18	t:Maun,Finn,Lowe g:Finn(3)	5th	947
1/5/05	Workington (h) (NLCQPO)	W44-20	t:Finn,Powell,Newlove(2),Lowe(2),C Hughes g:Finn(8)	N/A	836
15/5/05	Rochdale (h)	D30-30	t:Kirmond(2),Powell,Finn(2) g:Finn(5)	7th	1,250
22/5/05	Barrow (a)	W16-38	t:Maun,C Hughes(2),Newlove,Powell,McNally,Weeden g:Finn(5)	4th	1,008
29/5/05	Castleford (h) (NLCQF)	L14-38	t:Georgiadis,Newlove g:Finn(3)	N/A	3,418
5/6/05	Halifax (h)	L28-38	t:Powell,Georgiadis,Hayes,Kirmond,Dooler g:Finn(4)	5th	1,461
12/6/05	Castleford (h)	L34-38	t:Finn,Dooler,C Hughes,Weeden,Finn g:Finn(7)	6th	3,334
26/6/05	Doncaster (a)	L32-24	t:Finn(2),C Hughes,Batty g:Finn(4)	6th	973
3/7/05	Oldham (a) ●	L38-20	t:Georgiadis,Southwell,Moss g:Finn(4)	8th	948
10/7/05	Hull KR (h)	L10-78	t:C Hughes,Maun g:Finn	9th	1,873
24/7/05	Whitehaven (a)	L50-16	t:Maun,Newlove,Lowe g:Finn(2)	9th	1,458
31/7/05	Batley (h)	L24-50	t:Powell,Georgiadis,Maun,Newlove g:Finn(4)	9th	1,486
7/8/05	Rochdale (a)	L30-18	t:Batty,Powell g:Finn(5)	9th	663
14/8/05	Halifax (a)	L26-22	t:Dickens,Kirmond,Batty g:Finn(5)	9th	1,629
21/8/05	Barrow (h)	W74-22	t:Dickens(2),Dooler(3),Ford,Evans,Powell(2),Newlove,P Hughes,Batty,Brambani g:Finn(11)	9th	1,171
4/9/05	Castleford (a)	L40-6	t:Moss g:Finn	9th	5,943
11/9/05	Doncaster (h)	L22-46	t:Batty(2),Newlove,Kay,Tonks g:Finn	9th	1,495

● Played at Park Lane, Sedgley Park

		APP		TRIES		GOALS		FG		PTS	
	D.O.B.	ALL	NL1	ALL	NL1	ALL	NL1	ALL	NL1	ALL	NL1
Nathan Batty	20/5/82	19	15	6	6	0	0	0	0	24	24
Richard Blakeway	22/7/83	2		0	0	0	0	0	0	0	0
Dominic Brambani	10/5/85	6(1)	6(1)	1	1	0	0	0	0	4	4
Jim Carlton	26/4/80	1(16)	(7)	0	0	0	0	0	0	0	0
Steve Coulson	5/4/86	(1)	0	0	0	0	0	0	0	0	0
Stuart Dickens	23/3/82	4	4	3	3	0	0	0	0	12	12
Steve Dooler	31/12/77	21(3)	17(1)	7	6	0	0	0	0	28	24
Danny Evans	15/10/74	6(13)	4(9)	1	1	0	0	0	0	4	4
Liam Finn	2/11/83	19	17	8	7	80	69	0	0	192	166
James Ford	29/9/82	6(3)	6	1	1	0	0	0	0	4	4
John Fowler	18/7/85	(1)	0	0	0	0	0	0	0	0	0
Andrew Georgiadis	8/2/84	3(6)	2(6)	4	3	0	0	0	0	16	12
Adam Hayes	30/11/81	25	17	1	1	0	0	0	0	4	4
James Houston	28/12/82	16(7)	10(6)	0	0	0	0	0	0	0	0
Carl Hughes	30/11/82	20(2)	11(1)	8	5	0	0	0	0	32	20
Paul Hughes	28/12/84	1(3)	1(3)	1	1	0	0	0	0	4	4
Andy Jarrett	26/4/83	2(1)	0	2		0	0	0	0	8	0
Stephen Jones	9/1/83	2(2)	2(1)	0	0	0	0	0	0	0	0
Andy Kay	1/6/86	5(2)	1(2)	1	1	0	0	0	0	4	4
Danny Kirmond	11/11/85	11(3)	9(3)	4	4	0	0	0	0	16	16
Neil Lowe	20/12/78	14(8)	10(6)	5	2	0	0	0	0	20	8
Danny Maun	5/1/81	20(1)	11(1)	10	8	0	0	0	0	40	32
Andy McNally	9/1/82	6(4)	1(2)	6	2	0	0	0	0	24	8
Craig Moss	4/8/84	17(6)	12(3)	4	2	0	0	0	0	16	8
Richard Newlove	18/7/78	25(1)	15(1)	14	6	0	0	0	0	56	24
Greg Nicholson	24/9/85	7(10)	6(7)	0	0	0	0	0	0	0	0
Bryn Powell	5/9/79	26(1)	17	11	7	0	0	0	0	44	28
Jon Presley	8/7/84	4	0	1	0	0	0	0	0	4	0
Dean Ripley	13/9/83	7(1)	4	2	2	1	0	0	0	10	8
Jason Southwell	14/7/85	4(3)	3(3)	2	2	0	0	0	0	8	8
Danny Stanley	15/8/86	(1)	(1)	0	0	0	0	0	0	0	0
Wayne Sutcliffe	6/5/83	(1)	(1)	0	0	0	0	0	0	0	0
Nathan Sykes	8/9/74	18(2)	9(2)	1	0	0	0	0	0	4	0
Ian Tonks	13/2/76	14(6)	9(3)	3	1	0	0	0	0	12	4
Josh Weeden	10/11/83	21	11	8	5	23	2	1	0	79	24
Scott Wheeldon	23/2/86	1(2)	1(2)	0	0	0	0	0	0	0	0
Matthew Wray	15/5/84	11	3	7	1	0	0	0	0	28	4

Bryn Powell

LEAGUE RECORD
P18-W3-D2-L13
(9th, NL1)
F454, A648, Diff-194
8 points.

CHALLENGE CUP
Round Four

NATIONAL LEAGUE CUP
Quarter Finalists/2nd, Group 4

ATTENDANCES
Best - v Castleford (NLC - 6,353)
Worst - v Thornhill (CC - 774)
Total (NL1 & NLC,
inc QPO and QF, only) - 28,019
Average (NL1 & NLC,
inc QPO and QF, only) - 2,001
(Up by 582 on 2004)

HALIFAX

DATE	FIXTURE	RESULT	SCORERS	LGE	ATT
13/2/05	London Skolars (a) (NLC)	W0-40	t:Haley(2),R Sheriffe(3),Black,Weisner g:Jones(6)	1st(NLC-G3)	543
20/2/05	London Skolars (h) (NLC)	W60-12	t:Spink,Bunyan(2),Haley,R Sheriffe,Blackwood,Fisher,Weisner,Black(2), Greenwood g:Jones(5),Corcoran(3)	1st(NLC-G3)	1,329
27/2/05	Hull KR (a) (NLC)	L21-14	t:Gibson,Larder g:Lawford(3)	2nd(NLC-G3)	2,227
6/3/05	Keighley (h) (NLC)	W42-12	t:Larder,Lawford,Weisner,R Sheriffe(2),Haley,Gibson(2),Corcoran g:Lawford(2),Corcoran	2nd(NLC-G3)	1,526
11/3/05	Castleford Lock Lane (a) (CCR3) ●	W0-76	t:Jones,Lawford,Blackwood(3),O'Brien,Haley(2),R Sheriffe(3),Gibson,Weisner, J Sheriffe g:Jones(8),Corcoran(2)	N/A	747
20/3/05	Hull KR (h) (NLC)	W34-26	t:Blackwood,Spink,Haley,Gibson,R Sheriffe(2) g:Lawford(4),Bloem	1st(NLC-G3)	2,095
25/3/05	Keighley (a) (NLC)	W24-50	t:Weisner,Birchall,Haley(2),Gibson,Spink,Black(2),Tuilagi g:Bloem(7)	1st(NLC-G3)	1,404
28/3/05	Hull KR (h)	L10-11	t:Haley g:Bloem(3)	8th	2,474
3/4/05	Castleford (h) (CCR4)	W23-14	t:Weisner,Fisher,Bunyan,Black g:Bloem(3) fg:Weisner	N/A	3,925
10/4/05	Whitehaven (a)	L54-18	t:Fisher,Corcoran,Blackwood g:Bloem(3)	10th	2,159
17/4/05	Batley (h)	W38-16	t:Haley(2),Larder(2),Fisher,Blackwood,Hadcroft,Bunyan g:Bloem(3)	6th	1,715
24/4/05	Rochdale (a)	L22-19	t:Gibson,Haley,Hadcroft g:Jones(3) fg:Jones	7th	1,201
8/5/05	Leigh (a) (CCR5)	L40-20	t:Bunyan,Haley,Fisher,Spink g:Jones(2)	N/A	3,255
15/5/05	Barrow (h)	W48-26	t:Fisher(2),Weisner(2),Corcoran,Jones,Spink,Bloem,R Sheriffe g:Bloem(6)	5th	1,446
22/5/05	Castleford (h)	L16-48	t:Ball,R Sheriffe(2) g:Weisner(2)	8th	3,259
29/5/05	Doncaster (a) (NLCQF)	L54-38	t:Gibson(3),Larder,Fisher,Haley,Spink g:Bloem(5)	N/A	1,008
5/6/05	Featherstone (a)	W28-38	t:Haley,Weisner,Black,Morley,R Sheriffe,Fisher g:Bloem(7)	6th	1,461
12/6/05	Doncaster (h)	W36-16	t:Fisher,Larder,Black,Haley(2),R Sheriffe g:Booth(2),Bloem(4)	4th	1,737
24/6/05	Oldham (a) ●●	W14-28	t:McDonald,Gibson,Haley,Black,Blackwood g:Booth(4)	4th	1,227
3/7/05	Hull KR (a)	L38-30	t:Weisner(2),Fisher,Gibson,R Sheriffe g:Weisner(5)	4th	2,565
10/7/05	Whitehaven (h)	W60-18	t:Black(3),Weisner(2),Blackwood(2),Spink,Morley,R Sheriffe,Fisher g:Weisner(8)	4th	1,550
24/7/05	Batley (a)	W26-34	t:Hadcroft,Black(3),R Sheriffe(2),Gibson g:Weisner(2),Bloem	4th	1,277
31/7/05	Rochdale (h)	L25-30	t:McDonald,Larder,Weisner,R Sheriffe g:Weisner(4) fg:Weisner	4th	1,594
7/8/05	Barrow (a)	W12-76	t:Spink,Ball(2),R Sheriffe(2),Black(2),Fisher(3),Weisner,Hadcroft,Larder g:Bloem(11),Corcoran	4th	729
14/8/05	Featherstone (h)	W26-22	t:Corcoran,Weisner,Haley(2),Morley g:Weisner,Corcoran,Bloem	4th	1,629
21/8/05	Castleford (a)	L38-34	t:Spink,Blackwood,Black(2),Weisner,Reid g:Corcoran(2),Bloem(2),Weisner	4th	4,941
4/9/05	Doncaster (a)	L28-22	t:Black(3) g:Weisner(2),Bloem(3)	5th	1,024
11/9/05	Oldham (h)	W46-20	t:Haley,R Sheriffe(2),Weisner,Reid,Black,Boults,McDonald,Hobson g:Haley,Bloem(4)	4th	1,504
18/9/05	Doncaster (h) (EPO)	W64-10	t:Weisner,Gibson(2),R Sheriffe(2),Black(3),Kirk(2),Blackwood g:Weisner(8),Bloem(2)	N/A	1,863
25/9/05	Hull KR (a) (ESF)	W22-36	t:Hobson,Fisher(2),Blackwood,Weisner,Larder g:Weisner(5),Bloem	N/A	3,400
2/10/05	Castleford (a) (FE)	L15-12	t:R Sheriffe,Kirk g:Weisner,Bloem	N/A	6,197

● Played at The Shay
●● Played at Park Lane, Sedgley Park

	D.O.B.	APP ALL	APP NL1	TRIES ALL	TRIES NL1	GOALS ALL	GOALS NL1	FG ALL	FG NL1	PTS ALL	PTS NL1
Brad Attwood	24/11/84	(1)	0	0	0	0	0	0	0	0	0
Damian Ball	14/7/75	15(2)	15(1)	3	3	0	0	0	0	12	12
Chris Birchall	25/3/81	7(3)	2(1)	1	0	0	0	0	0	4	0
Ben Black	29/4/81	18(5)	12(4)	26	20	0	0	0	0	104	80
Anthony Blackwood	13/9/82	22(3)	16(1)	13	8	0	0	0	0	52	32
Jamie Bloem	26/5/71	11(13)	7(12)	1	1	68	52	0	0	140	108
Steve Booth	18/9/76	2(1)	2(1)	0	0	6	6	0	0	12	12
Andy Boothroyd	7/1/85	1(1)	0	0	0	0	0	0	0	0	0
Jason Boults	7/9/83	26(4)	18(3)	1	1	0	0	0	0	4	4
James Bunyan	2/11/77	13(1)	5(1)	5	1	0	0	0	0	20	4
Wayne Corcoran	10/7/85	11(6)	8(2)	4	3	10	4	0	0	36	20
Ben Fisher	4/2/81	29(2)	21	17	13	0	0	0	0	68	52
Damian Gibson	14/5/75	30	20	15	6	0	0	0	0	60	24
Gareth Greenwood	14/11/83	(5)	(1)	1	0	0	0	0	0	4	0
Alan Hadcroft	31/3/77	14(3)	9(3)	4	4	0	0	0	0	16	16
James Haley	2/7/85	31	21	22	11	1	1	0	0	90	46
Andy Hobson	26/12/78	9(7)	7(6)	2	2	0	0	0	0	8	8
Danny Jones	6/3/86	8	3	2	1	24	3	1	1	57	11
Andy Kirk	2/8/82	6	4	3	3	0	0	0	0	12	12
David Larder	5/6/76	28(1)	19	9	6	0	0	0	0	36	24
Scott Law	19/2/85	(8)	(7)	0	0	0	0	0	0	0	0
Dean Lawford	9/5/77	17	11	2	0	9	0	0	0	26	0
Ryan McDonald	24/2/78	3(22)	2(19)	3	3	0	0	0	0	12	12
Chris Morley	22/9/73	16(4)	13(3)	3	3	0	0	0	0	12	12
Todd O'Brien	5/10/84	1	0	1	0	0	0	0	0	4	0
Damien Reid	14/3/84	1(3)	1(3)	2	2	0	0	0	0	8	8
Jode Sheriffe	4/7/86	1(7)	(2)	1	0	0	0	0	0	4	0
Rikki Sheriffe	5/5/84	28	19	28	17	0	0	0	0	112	68
Luke Simeunovich	28/9/85	(1)	(1)	0	0	0	0	0	0	0	0
Jon Simpson	16/7/83	(9)	(4)	0	0	0	0	0	0	0	0
Andy Spink	12/1/79	21(6)	12(6)	9	4	0	0	0	0	36	16
Fereti Tuilagi	9/6/71	3(6)	3(3)	1	0	0	0	0	0	4	0
Pat Weisner	17/3/82	31	21	20	14	39	39	2	1	160	135

Pat Weisner

LEAGUE RECORD
P18-W10-D0-L8
(4th, NL1/Final Eliminator)
F604, A467, Diff+137
20 points.

CHALLENGE CUP
Round Five

NATIONAL LEAGUE CUP
Quarter Finalists/1st, Group 3

ATTENDANCES
Best - v Castleford (CC - 3,925)
Worst - v London Skolars (NLC - 1,329)
Total (NL1, inc play-offs, & NLC only) - 23,72?
Average (NL1, inc play-offs, & NLC only) - 1,825
(Down by 128 on 2004)

HULL KINGSTON ROVERS

DATE	FIXTURE	RESULT	SCORERS	LGE	ATT
13/2/05	Keighley (a) (NLC)	W26-27	t:Webster(2),Ellis,Mansson,Raleigh g:Poucher(3) fg:Mansson	2nd(NLC-G3)	1,008
20/2/05	Keighley (h) (NLC)	W36-6	t:Webster(3),Aizue,Parker,Raleigh,Epati g:Poucher(4)	2nd(NLC-G3)	2,141
27/2/05	Halifax (h) (NLC)	W21-14	t:Hasty,Ellis,Aizue g:Poucher(4) fg:Mansson	1st(NLC-G3)	2,227
6/3/05	London Skolars (a) (NLC)	W4-56	t:Parker,Steel(5),Ford,Wildbore,Mansson,Aizue,Garmston g:Wildbore(4),Poucher(2)	1st(NLC-G3)	450
13/3/05	Siddal (a) (CCR3) ●	W6-50	t:Mansson,Epati(3),Bovill,Steel(2),Aizue,Parker g:Wildbore(7)	N/A	1,705
20/3/05	Halifax (a) (NLC)	L34-26	t:Mansson,Epati,Holdstock,Poucher g:Poucher(5)	2nd(NLC-G3)	2,095
25/3/05	London Skolars (h) (NLC)	W78-20	t:Raleigh(3),Bovill,Hasty(2),Ford,Wildbore,Barker(3),Webster,Epati,Blanchard g:Wildbore(11)	2nd(NLC-G3)	2,009
28/3/05	Halifax (a)	W10-11	t:Ellis,Webster g:Wildbore fg:Webster	4th	2,474
3/4/05	Union Treiziste Catalane (a) (CCR4)	L32-18	t:Epati(2),Smith g:Wildbore(3)	N/A	3,000
10/4/05	Featherstone (h)	W44-30	t:Ford(3),Tangata-Toa,Epati,Mansson,Parker,Blanchard g:Webster(5),Steel	3rd	2,510
17/4/05	Doncaster (a)	W20-36	t:Raleigh,Webster,Mansson,Steel,Ellis,Walker,Parker g:Webster(2),Steel(2)	3rd	1,620
24/4/05	Oldham (h)	W32-19	t:Raleigh(2),Walker,Parker,Ellis,Mansson g:Steel(4)	3rd	2,474
1/5/05	Bradford-Dudley Hill (h) (NLCQPO)	W64-14	t:Hasty(2),Parker,Ford,Rivett,Blanchard(2),Pickering,Aizue,Wildbore,Steel g:Wildbore(9),Steel	N/A	1,133
15/5/05	Castleford (a)	L32-26	t:Mansson,Raleigh,Epati(3) g:Steel(3)	3rd	8,078
22/5/05	Whitehaven (a)	L51-0		3rd	2,604
29/5/05	Swinton (h) (NLCQF)	W62-0	t:Hasty(3),Aizue,Raleigh,Smith,Mansson,Morton,Blanchard,Ellis,Rivett g:Morton(9)	N/A	1,506
5/6/05	Batley (h)	W15-6	t:Ellis,Mansson,Blanchard g:Morton fg:Hasty	3rd	2,084
12/6/05	Rochdale (h)	W45-12	t:Webster,Ford,Smith,Hasty,McClarron,Rivett g:Morton(10) fg:Webster	3rd	2,121
19/6/05	Doncaster (h) (NLCSF)	W34-26	t:Bovill,Parker,Mansson,Ford,Epati,Morton g:Morton(5)	N/A	2,474
26/6/05	Barrow (h)	W48-10	t:Smith,Hasty,Mansson,Webster,Holdstock,Steel(2),Barker g:Morton(8)	3rd	1,921
3/7/05	Halifax (h)	W38-30	t:Rivett,Raleigh(2),Ford,Holdstock,Parker g:Morton(7)	3rd	2,565
10/7/05	Featherstone (a)	W10-78	t:Steel,Ellis,Aizue(2),Netherton,Raleigh,Parker(2),Tangata-Toa(2),Ford,Rivett,Garmston,Webster g:Morton(11)	3rd	1,873
17/7/05	Castleford (NLCF) ●●	W16-18	t:Raleigh,Ford g:Morton(5)	N/A	9,400
24/7/05	Doncaster (h)	W28-18	t:Steel,Walker,Ellis,Ford(2) g:Steel(4)	3rd	3,011
31/7/05	Oldham (a)	L40-20	t:Raleigh(2),Morton g:Morton(4)	3rd	1,414
7/8/05	Castleford (h)	W46-18	t:Ford,Rivett,Mansson,Barker,Ellis,Webster,Blanchard,Holdstock g:Morton(7)	3rd	5,023
14/8/05	Batley (a)	W25-40	t:Mansson,Gallagher,Epati(2),Webster(2),Ford g:Morton(6)	3rd	1,214
21/8/05	Whitehaven (h)	L14-18	t:Ford,Gallagher g:Morton(3)	3rd	3,508
4/9/05	Rochdale (a)	L30-26	t:Morton,Webster(2),Rivett,Ford g:Morton(3)	3rd	1,173
11/9/05	Barrow (a)	W10-42	t:Hasty(2),Walker,Tangata-Toa(2),Pickering(2) g:Wildbore(5),Couturier(2)	3rd	584
18/9/05	Rochdale (h) (EPO)	W45-4	t:Ford(2),Gallagher,Raleigh,Smith,Parker,Aizue g:Morton(8) fg:Webster	N/A	2,420
25/9/05	Halifax (h) (ESF)	L22-36	t:Morton,Ford(2),Epati g:Morton(3)	N/A	3,400

● Played at Craven Park
●● Played at Bloomfield Road, Blackpool

	D.O.B.	APP		TRIES		GOALS		FG		PTS	
		ALL	NL1	ALL	NL1	ALL	NL1	ALL	NL1	ALL	NL1
Makali Aizue	30/12/77	12(18)	9(9)	9	3	0	0	0	0	36	12
Dean Andrews	1/6/79	1(2)	1(2)	0	0	0	0	0	0	0	0
Dwayne Barker	21/9/83	20(3)	14	5	2	0	0	0	0	20	8
Mark Blanchard	11/7/82	4(12)	1(10)	7	3	0	0	0	0	28	12
Jamie Bovill	21/3/83	6(19)	3(11)	3	0	0	0	0	0	12	0
Damien Couturier	9/7/81	2(1)	2(1)	0	0	2	2	0	0	4	4
Andy Ellis	15/12/84	21(6)	12(5)	10	7	0	0	0	0	40	28
Kane Epati	13/8/81	26(4)	16(3)	16	7	0	0	0	0	64	28
Paul Fletcher	17/3/70	(5)	(4)	0	0	0	0	0	0	0	0
Byron Ford	21/8/81	28	18	21	16	0	0	0	0	84	64
Tommy Gallagher	10/9/83	4(1)	4(1)	3	3	0	0	0	0	12	12
James Garmston	6/8/86	10(8)	7(5)	2	1	0	0	0	0	8	4
Neil Harmon	9/1/69	9(3)	9(3)	0	0	0	0	0	0	0	0
Phil Hasty	28/5/80	13(8)	5(5)	12	4	0	0	1	1	49	17
Dale Holdstock	2/8/79	19(1)	10(1)	4	3	0	0	0	0	16	12
Paul Mansson	13/3/72	30	19	14	8	0	0	2	0	58	32
Misili Manu	4/3/80	2	2	0	0	0	0	0	0	0	0
Alasdair McClarron	19/6/73	4	2	1	1	0	0	0	0	4	4
Gareth Morton	21/10/82	15(1)	12(1)	5	3	90	71	0	0	200	154
Jason Netherton	5/10/82	12(2)	8(1)	1	1	0	0	0	0	4	4
Paul Parker	13/2/79	18(3)	8(2)	12	7	0	0	0	0	48	28
Paul Pickering	16/12/82	11(7)	8(5)	3	2	0	0	0	0	12	8
Craig Poucher	12/9/80	5(3)	1(1)	1	0	18	0	0	0	40	0
Olivier Pramil	7/6/79	(1)	(1)	0	0	0	0	0	0	0	0
Andy Raleigh	17/3/81	28(1)	18(1)	17	10	0	0	0	0	68	40
Leroy Rivett	17/12/76	16	13	7	5	0	0	0	0	28	20
Michael Smith	10/5/76	11(3)	8(3)	5	3	0	0	0	0	20	12
Jon Steel	14/3/80	23(1)	14	13	5	15	14	0	0	82	48
David Tangata-Toa	15/7/81	25(2)	16(1)	5	5	0	0	0	0	20	20
Jimmy Walker	22/11/73	4(11)	3(6)	4	4	0	0	0	0	16	16
James Webster	11/7/79	26(1)	18	16	10	7	7	3	3	81	57
Loz Wildbore	23/9/84	11(1)	5	3	0	40	6	0	0	92	12

Andy Raleigh

LEAGUE RECORD
P18-W13-D0-L5
(3rd, NL1/Elimination Semi Finalists)
F589, A389, Diff+200
26 points.

CHALLENGE CUP
Round Four

NATIONAL LEAGUE CUP
Winners/2nd, Group 3

ATTENDANCES
Best - v Castleford (NL1 - 5,023)
Worst - v Bradford-Dudley Hill
(NLCQPO - 1,133)
Total (NL1, inc play-offs,
& NLC, inc QPO, QF & SF, only) - 42,527
Average (NL1, inc play-offs,
& NLC, inc QPO, QF & SF, only) - 2,502
(Up by 316 on 2004)

OLDHAM

DATE	FIXTURE	RESULT	SCORERS	LGE	ATT
13/2/05	Blackpool (h) (NLC)	W22-20	t:Elswood,Glassie,Munro,Cowell,Dodd g:Turner	2nd(NLC-G2)	1,337
27/2/05	Swinton (a) (NLC)	L46-14	t:Johnson,Munro,Wilson g:Svabic	3rd(NLC-G2)	1,101
6/3/05	Swinton (h) (NLC)	L30-37	t:Barber,Mataora,Roberts,Wilkinson,Dodd g:Turner(5)	3rd(NLC-G2)	1,116
11/3/05	Sharlston (a) (CCR3) ●	W14-46	t:Roberts,Haughton(4),Elswood,Barber,Gorey,Dodd,Cowell g:Turner,Svabic(2)	N/A	852
16/3/05	Rochdale (a) (NLC)	L68-26	t:Dodd(3),Haughton g:Turner(5)	3rd(NLC-G2)	1,161
20/3/05	Blackpool (a) (NLC) ●●	W16-35	t:Wilkinson,Svabic,Goddard(2),Turner,Norman g:Turner(5) fg:Svabic	3rd(NLC-G2)	250
25/3/05	Rochdale (h) (NLC)	L10-54	t:Johnson,Wilkinson g:Turner	3rd(NLC-G2)	1,544
28/3/05	Featherstone (a)	D20-20	t:Gorey,Cowell,Turner g:Turner(4)	5th	1,463
3/4/05	York (h) (CCR4)	L28-32	t:Haughton,Dodd(3),Johnson g:Turner(4)	N/A	1,282
10/4/05	Doncaster (h)	L22-44	t:Goddard,Turner,Dodd,Gorey g:Turner(3)	8th	1,266
17/4/05	Castleford (h)	L20-32	t:Johnson,Wilson,Dodd g:Turner(3),Barber	10th	2,054
24/4/05	Hull KR (a)	L32-19	t:Dodd,Svabic,Johnson g:Svabic(3) fg:Svabic	10th	2,474
15/5/05	Whitehaven (h)	L6-60	t:Svabic g:Turner	10th	1,284
22/5/05	Batley (a)	L25-18	t:Johnson,Glassie,Munro g:Turner(3)	10th	792
5/6/05	Rochdale (h) ●●●	W25-24	t:Wilkinson,C Hough,Dodd g:Turner(6) fg:Turner	9th	827
12/6/05	Barrow (a)	W22-40	t:Johnson(2),Turner,Svabic,Wilkinson,Munro,Wilson g:Turner(6)	8th	1,073
24/6/05	Halifax (h) ●●●	L14-28	t:Turner,Mills g:Turner(3)	8th	1,227
3/7/05	Featherstone (h) ●●●	W38-20	t:Svabic,Turner,Goddard,Glassie,Mataora,Cowell g:Turner(7)	7th	948
10/7/05	Doncaster (a)	L34-26	t:Dodd,Goddard,Glassie,Svabic,Johnson g:Turner(3)	7th	896
24/7/05	Castleford (a)	L32-20	t:C Hough,Barber,Goddard,Johnson g:Turner(2)	7th	4,600
31/7/05	Hull KR (h)	W40-20	t:Barber(2),C Hough,Munro(3),Turner g:Turner(6)	7th	1,414
7/8/05	Whitehaven (a)	L36-16	t:Mataora,J Hough,Dodd g:Turner(2)	7th	1,669
14/8/05	Rochdale (a)	W24-27	t:Munro,Johnson,Goddard g:Turner(7) fg:C Hough	7th	1,426
21/8/05	Batley (h)	L32-34	t:Svabic,Johnson,Barber,Turner,Haughton g:Turner(6)	7th	1,187
4/9/05	Barrow (h)	W52-12	t:Munro(3),Norman,Dodd,Glassie,Svabic,Hodson,Barber(2) g:Svabic(4),C Hough(2)	7th	1,059
11/9/05	Halifax (a)	L46-20	t:Dodd,Munro,Glassie,Svabic g:C Hough(2)	7th	1,504

● Played at Lionheart Stadium, Featherstone
●● Played at Lightfoot Green, Preston
●●● Played at Park Lane, Sedgley Park

	D.O.B.	APP ALL	APP NL1	TRIES ALL	TRIES NL1	GOALS ALL	GOALS NL1	FG ALL	FG NL1	PTS ALL	PTS NL1
Gareth Barber	15/12/80	17(5)	11(5)	8	6	1	1	0	0	34	26
Ricky Bibey	22/9/81	21	15	0	0	0	0	0	0	0	0
Keith Brennan	31/10/73	1(1)	1	0	0	0	0	0	0	0	0
Will Cowell	31/12/79	8(2)	2(2)	4	2	0	0	0	0	16	8
Gavin Dodd	28/2/81	25(1)	18	17	8	0	0	0	0	68	32
Martin Elswood	18/10/83	5(8)	1(7)	2	0	0	0	0	0	8	0
Craig Farrimond	20/11/82	(4)	0	0	0	0	0	0	0	0	0
Tere Glassie	1/12/77	20(3)	16(1)	6	5	0	0	0	0	24	20
Jon Goddard	21/6/82	19	15	7	5	0	0	0	0	28	20
Andy Gorey	31/10/85	2(5)	2(4)	3	2	0	0	0	0	12	8
Simon Haughton	10/11/75	11(3)	4(3)	7	1	0	0	0	0	28	4
Ian Hodson	23/10/81	13(2)	13(2)	1	1	0	0	0	0	4	4
Chris Hough	30/8/81	11(2)	11(2)	3	3	4	4	1	1	21	21
John Hough	14/4/76	11(9)	7(6)	1	1	0	0	0	0	4	4
Nick Johnson	16/4/83	25	17	12	9	0	0	0	0	48	36
James Kirkland	17/7/85	6(8)	6(4)	0	0	0	0	0	0	0	0
Carlos Mataora	20/3/82	13(11)	8(9)	3	2	0	0	0	0	12	8
Rob Mills	17/8/79	8	8	1	1	0	0	0	0	4	4
Damian Munro	6/10/76	17	13	12	10	0	0	0	0	48	40
Danny Nanyn	8/10/84	5(5)	1(2)	0	0	0	0	0	0	0	0
Paul Norman	25/3/74	9(5)	4(3)	2	1	0	0	0	0	8	4
Mark Roberts	9/11/82	10(3)	5(2)	2	0	0	0	0	0	8	0
Andy Sands	29/3/79	1(1)	1(1)	0	0	0	0	0	0	0	0
Adam Sharples	19/4/85	1(8)	1(8)	0	0	0	0	0	0	0	0
Simon Svabic	18/1/80	20(3)	12(3)	9	8	10	7	2	1	58	47
David Tootill	22/5/86	(2)	(2)	0	0	0	0	0	0	0	0
Marty Turner	7/5/81	23	15	8	7	84	62	1	1	201	153
Alex Wilkinson	9/10/82	22	15	5	2	0	0	0	0	20	8
Dana Wilson	22/5/83	14(8)	12(3)	3	2	0	0	0	0	12	8

Marty Turner

LEAGUE RECORD
P18-W6-D1-L11
(7th, NL1)
F455, A545, Diff-90
13 points.

CHALLENGE CUP
Round Four

NATIONAL LEAGUE CUP
3rd, Group 2

ATTENDANCES
Best - v Castleford (NL1 - 2,054)
Worst - v Rochdale (NL1 - 827)
Total (NL1 & NLC only) - 15,263
Average (NL1 & NLC only) - 1,272
(Down by 80 on 2004)

ROCHDALE HORNETS

DATE	FIXTURE	RESULT	SCORERS	LGE	ATT
13/2/05	Swinton (a) (NLC)	L20-14	t:Cantillon,Campbell g:Birdseye(3)	4th(NLC-G2)	685
27/2/05	Blackpool (a) (NLC) ●	W26-36	t:McCully,Braddish(3),Varkulis,Alstead,Cantillon g:Braddish(4)	2nd(NLC-G2)	220
6/3/05	Blackpool (h) (NLC)	W62-16	t:Cunliffe,Cantillon(2),Doran(2),Alstead,Braddish,Butterworth,McConnell, Saywell,Gorski g:Braddish(9)	2nd(NLC-G2)	731
13/3/05	Illingworth (h) (CCR3)	W120-4	t:Braddish,Doran(2),Giles(2),McConnell(3),Cantillon(3),Birdseye(2),Gorski(2), Owen(2),Saywell,McCully,Bowker,Ball g:Birdseye(18)	N/A	654
16/3/05	Oldham (h) (NLC)	W68-26	t:Braddish(2),Cunliffe(2),Gorski(2),Campbell,Owen,Giles,Cantillon,Doran, McCully,McConnell g:McCully(8)	2nd(NLC-G2)	1,161
20/3/05	Swinton (h) (NLC)	W54-20	t:McCully(2),Gorski(2),Braddish(3),Campbell,Bowker g:McCully(9)	1st(NLC-G2)	967
25/3/05	Oldham (a) (NLC)	W10-54	t:Saywell(4),Campbell(2),McConnell,Gorski,Doran,Cunliffe g:McCully,Birdseye(6)	1st(NLC-G2)	1,544
29/3/05	Batley (h)	W26-25	t:Bowker(2),McConnell,Varkulis g:McCully(5)	3rd	646
3/4/05	Salford (h) (CCR4)	L24-30	t:McCully,Bowker(2),Saywell g:McCully(4)	N/A	1,971
10/4/05	Castleford (a)	L36-22	t:Bowker,Saywell,Farrell,McCully g:McCully(3)	6th	4,776
17/4/05	Barrow (a)	L24-20	t:Saywell,Birdseye,Giles,Bowker g:Birdseye(2)	7th	814
24/4/05	Halifax (h)	W22-19	t:Giles,Goulding,Saywell,Bowker g:McCully(3)	4th	1,201
15/5/05	Featherstone (a)	D30-30	t:Owen,Gorski,Saywell(2),Ball,Varkulis(2) g:McCully	4th	1,250
22/5/05	Doncaster (a)	L24-34	t:Price,Alstead,Campbell,Butterworth g:McCully(4)	6th	806
29/5/05	Whitehaven (a) (NLCQF)	L28-22	t:Cantillon(2),Alstead(2) g:McCully(3)	N/A	1,748
5/6/05	Oldham (a) ●●	L25-24	t:Campbell(2),Varkulis,Butterworth,Giles g:Goulding(2)	7th	827
12/6/05	Hull KR (h)	L45-12	t:Price,Butterworth g:McCully(2)	7th	2,121
26/6/05	Whitehaven (a)	L32-16	t:Varkulis,Gorski,Bowker g:Goulding(2)	7th	1,661
3/7/05	Batley (a)	W28-40	t:Alstead(2),Varkulis(2),Butterworth,McCully,Goulding g:Goulding(5),McCully	6th	587
10/7/05	Castleford (h)	W17-16	t:Campbell,Butterworth g:Goulding(4) fg:Goulding	6th	1,728
24/7/05	Barrow (h)	W36-22	t:McCully(2),McConnell(2),Campbell,Butterworth,Durbin g:Goulding(2),McCully(2)	6th	732
31/7/05	Halifax (a)	W25-30	t:Campbell(3),McCully,Alstead g:McCully(5)	5th	1,594
7/8/05	Featherstone (h)	W30-18	t:Varkulis(2),Alstead(3),Gorski g:McCully(3)	5th	663
14/8/05	Oldham (h)	L24-27	t:Butterworth(2),Alstead,McCully g:McCully(4)	6th	1,426
21/8/05	Doncaster (a)	W30-45	t:Varkulis,McCully,McConnell,Royle,Cantillon,Alstead(2),Campbell g:McCully(6) fg:McConnell	5th	630
4/9/05	Hull KR (h)	W30-26	t:Gorski,Varkulis,Cantillon,Price,Royle g:McCully(5)	4th	1,173
11/9/05	Whitehaven (h)	L20-44	t:Varkulis,Alstead,Cunliffe g:McCully(2),McConnell(2)	6th	1,770
18/9/05	Hull KR (a) (EPO)	L45-4	t:Gorski	N/A	2,420

● Played at Lightfoot Green, Preston
●● Played at Park Lane, Sedgley Park

		APP		TRIES		GOALS		FG		PTS	
	D.O.B.	ALL	NL1	ALL	NL1	ALL	NL1	ALL	NL1	ALL	NL1
David Alstead	18/2/82	15(4)	11(3)	15	11	0	0	0	0	60	44
Paul Anderson	2/4/77	2(7)	1(6)	0	0	0	0	0	0	0	0
Rob Ball	22/3/76	9(13)	8(9)	2	1	0	0	0	0	8	4
Lee Birdseye	5/8/79	6(1)	1(1)	3	1	29	2	0	0	70	8
Radney Bowker	5/2/79	22(2)	18	10	6	0	0	0	0	40	24
John Braddish	25/1/81	12(1)	5(1)	10	0	13	0	0	0	66	0
Sam Butterworth	12/2/78	6(14)	4(11)	9	8	0	0	0	0	36	32
Chris Campbell	2/12/80	22	14	14	9	0	0	0	0	56	36
Phil Cantillon	2/6/76	7(12)	4(6)	12	2	0	0	0	0	48	8
Dave Cunliffe	15/1/80	10(12)	6(10)	5	1	0	0	0	0	20	4
Lee Doran	23/3/81	28	19	6	0	0	0	0	0	24	0
Jamie Durbin	7/9/84	2(1)	2(1)	1	1	0	0	0	0	4	4
Phil Farrell	14/2/80	19(2)	15(1)	1	1	0	0	0	0	4	4
Chris Giles	26/12/81	27	18	6	3	0	0	0	0	24	12
Andy Gorski	31/3/81	28	19	13	5	0	0	0	0	52	20
Tommy Goulden	30/6/81	(4)	(4)	0	0	0	0	0	0	0	0
Bobbie Goulding	4/2/72	6(1)	6(1)	2	2	15	15	1	1	39	39
Lee Hansen	23/7/82	2(5)	(1)	0	0	0	0	0	0	0	0
John Hill	7/10/81	7(5)	7(5)	0	0	0	0	0	0	0	0
Tommy Hodgkinson	15/4/70	9(3)	4(1)	0	0	0	0	0	0	0	0
Andy Leathem	30/3/77	1	0	0	0	0	0	0	0	0	0
Dave McConnell	25/3/81	22(3)	16(1)	10	4	2	2	1	1	45	21
Mark McCully	24/10/79	26	17	13	7	71	46	0	0	194	120
Dave Newton	22/12/81	3(10)	(6)	0	0	0	0	0	0	0	0
Paul Owen	15/8/78	10(1)	7(1)	4	1	0	0	0	0	16	4
Gareth Price	28/6/80	23(1)	17	3	3	0	0	0	0	12	12
Kris Ratcliffe	28/5/81	1(4)	(3)	0	0	0	0	0	0	0	0
Nicky Royle	25/9/83	3	3	2	2	0	0	0	0	8	8
Andy Saywell	1/1/79	14(1)	9(1)	12	5	0	0	0	0	48	20
Darren Shaw	5/10/71	(1)	0	0	0	0	0	0	0	0	0
Richard Varkulis	21/5/82	22(4)	16(3)	13	12	0	0	0	0	52	48

Mark McCully

LEAGUE RECORD
P18-W9-D1-L8
(6th, NL1/Elimination Play-Off)
F468, A506, Diff-38
19 points.

CHALLENGE CUP
Round Four

NATIONAL LEAGUE CUP
Quarter Finalists/1st, Group 2

ATTENDANCES
Best - v Salford (CC - 1,971)
Worst - v Batley (NL1 - 646)
Total (NL1 & NLC only) - 13,004
Average (NL1 & NLC only) - 1,084
(Up by 74 on 2004)

WHITEHAVEN

DATE	FIXTURE	RESULT	SCORERS	LGE	ATT
13/2/05	Workington (a) (NLC)	L28-8	t:Wood,Wilson	4th(NLC-G1)	3,012
20/2/05	Barrow (h) (NLC)	W44-0	t:Eilbeck,Sice(3),Fatialofa,Seeds,Lebbon,Broadbent g:Penny(5),Sice	1st(NLC-G1)	1,606
27/2/05	Gateshead (h) (NLC)	W42-12	t:Calvert,Joe(2),Seeds,Lebbon(2),Hill,Davidson g:Penny(5)	1st(NLC-G1)	1,421
13/3/05	Oldham St Annes (a) (CCR3) ●	W30-62	t:Fatialofa,Broadbent(2),Calvert(3),Penny(2),Lester,O'Neil,Wilson g:Penny(7),Kirkbride(2)	N/A	968
20/3/05	Barrow (a) (NLC)	W2-42	t:Penny(2),Wood,Nanyn,Sice(2),Broadbent(2) g:Nanyn(5)	2nd(NLC-G1)	877
25/3/05	Workington (h) (NLC)	W58-10	t:Nanyn(3),Calvert(3),Penny(2),Broadbent,Sice(2),Wilson g:Nanyn(5)	1st(NLC-G1)	3,439
28/3/05	Barrow (a)	W11-24	t:Walsh,Sice,Fatialofa,Nanyn(2) g:Nanyn,Kirkbride	2nd	1,112
3/4/05	Wigan (a) (CCR4)	L42-4	t:Joe	N/A	6,974
6/4/05	Gateshead (a) (NLC)	W4-44	t:Seeds(2),Lebbon,Marshall,Eilbeck(2),Rudd,Kirkbride g:Kirkbride(6)	1st(NLC-G1)	266
10/4/05	Halifax (h)	W54-18	t:Chambers(2),Calvert(2),Nanyn,Joe,Penny,Sice(2) g:Nanyn(9)	1st	2,159
17/4/05	Featherstone (a)	W20-40	t:Joe(2),Kirkbride,Calvert,Chambers,Purdham,Broadbent g:Nanyn(6)	1st	1,269
24/4/05	Doncaster (h)	W20-6	t:Summers,Wilson,Calvert,Rudd g:Nanyn(2)	1st	1,945
15/5/05	Oldham (a)	W6-60	t:Calvert(2),Broadbent,Seeds,Nanyn(2),Penny,Lester,Sice,Hill,Kirkbride g:Nanyn(5),Kirkbride(3)	1st	1,284
22/5/05	Hull KR (h)	W51-0	t:Seeds(2),Hill(3),Fatialofa,Broadbent,Sice,Joe g:Nanyn(7) fg:Penny	1st	2,604
29/5/05	Rochdale (h) (NLCQF)	W28-22	t:Joe,Calvert,Broadbent,Lester g:Nanyn(6)	N/A	1,748
5/6/05	Castleford (a)	L42-24	t:Wilson,Fatialofa,Sice,Lester g:Nanyn(4)	2nd	7,323
12/6/05	Batley (a)	W8-18	t:Nanyn(3),Seeds g:Nanyn	2nd	653
19/6/05	Castleford (a) (NLCSF)	L42-14	t:Fatialofa,Nanyn,Calvert g:Nanyn	N/A	5,019
26/6/05	Rochdale (h)	W32-16	t:Calvert(2),Seeds,Nanyn(2),Penny g:Nanyn(2),Kirkbride(2)	2nd	1,661
3/7/05	Barrow (h)	W56-6	t:Nanyn(3),Seeds(3),Joe,Eilbeck,Summers,Penny g:Nanyn(8)	2nd	1,455
10/7/05	Halifax (a)	L60-18	t:Nanyn,Sice,Hill g:Nanyn(3)	2nd	1,550
24/7/05	Featherstone (h)	W50-16	t:Calvert(2),Sice(2),Seeds,Joe,Davidson,Kirkbride,Broadbent g:Nanyn(7)	2nd	1,458
31/7/05	Doncaster (a)	W20-30	t:Hill,Calvert,Penny(3) g:O'Neil(5)	2nd	690
7/8/05	Oldham (h)	W36-16	t:Sice(2),Calvert,Broadbent,Lester,O'Neil,Rudd g:O'Neil(4)	1st	1,669
14/8/05	Castleford (h)	W19-16	t:Sice,Penny,Seeds g:Nanyn(3) fg:Rudd	1st	4,437
21/8/05	Hull KR (a)	W14-18	t:Nanyn(2),Jackson g:Nanyn(3)	1st	3,508
4/9/05	Batley (h)	W54-12	t:Penny,Seeds,Nanyn(3),Sice(2),Hill,Joe,Rudd g:Nanyn(7)	1st	1,903
11/9/05	Rochdale (a)	W20-44	t:Penny(3),Sice,Nanyn(2),Calvert,Fatialofa g:Nanyn(6)	1st	1,770
25/9/05	Castleford (h) (QSF)	W32-22	t:Sice(2),Chambers,Calvert,Nanyn(2) g:Nanyn(4)	N/A	6,154
9/10/05	Castleford (GF) ●●	L36-8	t:Nanyn,Calvert	N/A	13,300

● Played at Recreation Ground
●● Played at Halton Stadium, Widnes

		APP		TRIES		GOALS		FG		PTS	
	D.O.B.	ALL	NL1	ALL	NL1	ALL	NL1	ALL	NL1	ALL	NL1
Neil Baynes	14/9/77	7(2)	5(2)	0	0	0	0	0	0	0	0
Gary Broadbent	31/10/76	27	18	12	5	0	0	0	0	48	20
Craig Calvert	10/2/84	26	18	24	15	0	0	0	0	96	60
Ryan Campbell	23/9/81	2	0	0	0	0	0	0	0	0	0
Craig Chambers	25/4/73	4(6)	2(5)	4	4	0	0	0	0	16	16
Mark Cox	22/1/78	2(6)	1(4)	0	0	0	0	0	0	0	0
Tony Cunningham	4/7/74	(2)		0	0	0	0	0	0	0	0
Paul Davidson	1/8/69	1(16)	(9)	2	1	0	0	0	0	8	4
Mark Deans	11/5/82	(1)	0	0	0	0	0	0	0	0	0
Derry Eilbeck	1/6/84	4	1	4	1	0	0	0	0	16	4
David Fatialofa	11/6/74	28	19	7	4	0	0	0	0	28	16
Howard Hill	16/1/75	22(3)	16(2)	7	7	0	0	0	0	32	28
Marc Jackson	21/8/79	1(8)	(7)	1	1	0	0	0	0	4	4
Leroy Joe	31/12/74	28(1)	20	11	7	0	0	0	0	44	28
Steve Kirkbride	10/1/81	5(13)	3(8)	4	3	14	6	0	0	44	24
John Lebbon	30/12/84	8	3	4	0	0	0	0	0	16	0
Aaron Lester	16/5/73	27	20	5	3	0	0	0	0	20	12
Jamie Marshall	17/7/78	2	0	1	0	0	0	0	0	4	0
Graeme Mattinson	24/4/85	(1)	(1)	0	0	0	0	0	0	0	0
Brett McDermott	10/9/78	19(3)	12(3)	0	0	0	0	0	0	0	0
Chris McKinney	12/11/76	2(6)	(4)	0	0	0	0	0	0	0	0
Spencer Miller	27/2/80	13(3)	9(2)	0	0	0	0	0	0	0	0
Iain Morrison	6/5/83	2(1)	2(1)	0	0	0	0	0	0	0	0
Graeme Morton	15/1/73	1(3)	(2)	0	0	0	0	0	0	0	0
Mick Nanyn	3/6/82	23(1)	18	29	24	95	78	0	0	306	252
Paul O'Neil	23/11/79	6	3	2	1	9	9	0	0	26	22
Joel Penny	22/1/80	26(1)	17(1)	18	12	17	0	1	1	107	49
Garry Purdham	20/10/78	(4)	(2)	1	1	0	0	0	0	4	4
Carl Rudd	10/10/82	20(6)	14(5)	4	3	0	0	1	1	17	13
Jamie Seaton	8/2/81	(2)	0	0	0	0	0	0	0	0	0
David Seeds	23/6/74	21	16	15	11	0	0	0	0	60	44
Carl Sice	13/4/80	13(16)	9(10)	24	17	1	0	0	0	98	68
Aaron Summers	11/8/81	12(12)	8(10)	2	2	0	0	0	0	8	8
Ryan Tandy	20/9/81	5(2)	5(2)	0	0	0	0	0	0	0	0
Craig Walsh	19/9/78	3	1	1	1	0	0	0	0	4	4
Wesley Wilson	30/5/77	27	20	5	2	0	0	0	0	20	8
Steven Wood	28/1/77	3	0	2	0	0	0	0	0	8	0

Mick Nanyn

LEAGUE RECORD
P18-W16-D0-L2
(1st, NL1/Grand Final Runners-Up)
F648, A307, Diff+341
32 points.

CHALLENGE CUP
Round Four

NATIONAL LEAGUE CUP
Semi Finalists/1st, Group 1

ATTENDANCES
Best - v Castleford (QSF - 6,154)
Worst - v Gateshead (NLC - 1,421)
Total (NL1, inc play-offs,
& NLC, inc QF, only) - 33,659
Average (NL1, inc play-offs,
& NLC, inc QF, only) - 2,404
(Up by 641 on 2004)

BLACKPOOL PANTHERS

DATE	FIXTURE	RESULT	SCORERS	LGE	ATT
13/2/05	Oldham (a) (NLC)	L22-20	t:Bretherton,Godbee(2),G Smith g:Bretherton(2)	3rd(NLC-G2)	1,337
18/2/05	Swinton (h) (NLC)	L24-34	t:Andrews,G Smith,Barton,Johnstone g:Johnstone(4)	4th(NLC-G2)	512
27/2/05	Rochdale (h) (NLC) ●	L26-36	t:Andrews,Bretherton,Arnold,Johnstone(2) g:Johnstone(3)	4th(NLC-G2)	220
6/3/05	Rochdale (a) (NLC)	L62-16	t:Parry,Redford,Gambles g:Johnstone(2)	4th(NLC-G2)	731
13/3/05	Toulouse (h) (CCR3)	L18-58	t:Andrews,Hill,Godbee g:Johnstone(3)	N/A	410
20/3/05	Oldham (h) (NLC) ●	L16-35	t:Godbee,Andrews g:McGovern(4)	4th(NLC-G2)	250
25/3/05	Swinton (a) (NLC)	D14-14	t:Gambles,Rourke,Stenhouse g:Johnstone	4th(NLC-G2)	541
28/3/05	Keighley (h) ●	L12-26	t:Godbee(2) g:Ramsdale(2)	7th	290
8/4/05	Sheffield (a)	W6-14	t:Godbee,Barton g:Bretherton(3)	7th	727
17/4/05	London Skolars (h)	L16-23	t:Johnstone(2),Rourke g:Johnstone(2)	7th	797
23/4/05	Gateshead (a)	L29-20	t:Bretherton,Godbee g:Johnstone(4)	7th	253
15/5/05	Swinton (a)	L84-12	t:Godbee(2) g:Johnstone(2)	10th	588
22/5/05	Workington (h)	L26-38	t:Godbee(3),Bretherton g:Ramsdale(2),McGovern(3)	10th	350
4/6/05	York (a)	L60-10	t:Ramsdale,Andrews g:Ramsdale	10th	1,981
12/6/05	Hunslet (a)	L23-22	t:Martin,Redford,Ramsdale,Andrews g:Johnstone(3)	10th	350
26/6/05	Dewsbury (a)	L32-8	t:Redford g:Johnstone(2)	10th	845
3/7/05	Sheffield (h)	L26-44	t:Andrews,Gambles,Roden,Kilgannon,Swann g:Johnstone(3)	10th	410
10/7/05	Keighley (a)	L28-20	t:Martin,Ramsdale,G Smith,Redford g:Johnstone(2)	10th	1,142
24/7/05	Swinton (h)	L26-51	t:McGovern,Ratcliffe,Johnstone,Kilgannon g:Johnstone(5)	10th	428
31/7/05	Gateshead (h)	W41-20	t:McGovern(2),G Smith,Grundy(2),Johnstone(2) g:Johnstone(6) fg:McGovern	10th	295
7/8/05	York (a)	L22-54	t:Ormesher,Martin,Gambles,Swann g:Johnstone(3)	10th	635
14/8/05	Hunslet (h)	L12-36	t:Gambles,Johnstone g:Johnstone(2)	9th	358
21/8/05	Workington (a)	L24-23	t:McGovern,Ormesher,Bretherton g:Johnstone(5) fg:McGovern	9th	767
4/9/05	Dewsbury (h)	L26-39	t:Tipeny,Bretherton(2),Martin,Johnstone g:Johnstone(3)	9th	540
10/9/05	London Skolars (a)	W6-20	t:Bretherton,Redford,Kilgannon g:Johnstone(4)	9th	240

● Played at Lightfoot Green, Preston

	D.O.B.	APP		TRIES		GOALS		FG		PTS	
		ALL	NL2	ALL	NL2	ALL	NL2	ALL	NL2	ALL	NL2
Eric Andrews	11/2/82	19(1)	13(1)	7	3	0	0	0	0	28	12
Danny Arnold	15/4/77	7(1)	2(1)	1	0	0	0	0	0	4	0
Dean Balmer	3/1/82	5(1)	5(1)	0	0	0	0	0	0	0	0
Danny Barton	7/9/83	6(2)	2	2	1	0	0	0	0	8	4
Liam Bretherton	20/6/79	15	10	8	6	5	3	0	0	42	30
Mike Callan	8/8/83	3(3)	2(1)	0	0	0	0	0	0	0	0
John Chamberlain	1/5/82	8	7	0	0	0	0	0	0	0	0
Martin Gambles	8/3/80	18(5)	16(1)	5	3	0	0	0	0	20	12
Glen Godbee	1/6/76	10	7	14	10	0	0	0	0	56	40
Tommy Grundy	19/11/77	11	10	2	2	0	0	0	0	8	8
John Hill	7/10/81	7(1)	3	1	0	0	0	0	0	4	0
Chris Hough	30/8/81	4(2)	0	0	0	0	0	0	0	0	0
Jake Johnstone	6/12/77	21	16	10	7	59	46	0	0	158	120
Gareth Jones	14/10/82	2(12)	2(7)	0	0	0	0	0	0	0	0
Eddie Kilgannon	4/12/77	18	16	3	3	0	0	0	0	12	12
Matt Leigh	24/2/78	5(2)	2	0	0	0	0	0	0	0	0
James Lomax	20/10/81	1(6)	(6)	0	0	0	0	0	0	0	0
Gus Martin	13/2/79	16(3)	14(2)	4	4	0	0	0	0	16	16
Liam McGovern	6/10/84	19(4)	12(4)	4	4	7	3	2	2	32	24
Steve Molloy	11/3/69	2(3)	0	0	0	0	0	0	0	0	0
Steve Ormesher	5/4/78	12(4)	10(4)	2	2	0	0	0	0	8	8
Ian Parry	2/4/81	5(4)	(3)	1	0	0	0	0	0	4	0
Richard Rafferty	12/8/84	(1)	(1)	0	0	0	0	0	0	0	0
Chris Ramsdale	25/4/82	10(8)	8(6)	3	3	5	5	0	0	22	22
Kris Ratcliffe	28/5/81	5(2)	5(2)	1	1	0	0	0	0	4	4
Mick Redford	24/6/81	14(1)	9(1)	5	4	0	0	0	0	20	16
Martin Roden	26/12/79	16(4)	13(4)	1	1	0	0	0	0	4	4
Gary Rourke	9/5/83	7(1)	4	2	1	0	0	0	0	8	4
Dave Rowland	18/9/82	4(5)	3(5)	0	0	0	0	0	0	0	0
Lee Rowley	3/2/83	4(10)	3(10)	0	0	0	0	0	0	0	0
Chris Smith	8/1/83	3	3	0	0	0	0	0	0	0	0
Gary Smith	11/1/81	24	18	4	2	0	0	0	0	16	8
Jamie Stenhouse	9/10/80	1(2)	1(1)	1	0	0	0	0	0	4	0
Willie Swann	25/2/74	13(1)	9(1)	2	2	0	0	0	0	8	8
Craig Tipeny	13/9/85	6(5)	6(4)	1	1	0	0	0	0	4	4
Michael Watts	23/9/76	3(1)	2(1)	0	0	0	0	0	0	0	0
Sion Williams	3/4/81	1(4)	1(4)	0	0	0	0	0	0	0	0

Jake Johnstone

LEAGUE RECORD
P18-W3-D0-L15
(9th, NL2)
F356, A623, Diff-267
6 points.

CHALLENGE CUP
Round Three

NATIONAL LEAGUE CUP
4th, Group 2

ATTENDANCES
Best - v London Skolars (NL2 - 797)
Worst - v Rochdale (NLC - 220)
Total (NL2 & NLC only) - 5,080
Average (NL2 & NLC only) - 423

DEWSBURY RAMS

DATE	FIXTURE	RESULT	SCORERS	LGE	ATT
11/2/05	Sheffield (a) (NLC)	L23-16	t:Henderson,Tillotson(2) g:Maloney(2)	4th(NLC-G5)	959
20/2/05	Batley (h) (NLC)	W32-22	t:Crouthers,Bretherton,J Walker,McHugh,Maloney,Preece g:Chapman(2),Maloney(2)	2nd(NLC-G5)	1,311
27/2/05	Doncaster (h) (NLC)	L27-32	t:McHugh(3),Fairbank,Maloney g:Maloney(3) fg:Mycoe	3rd(NLC-G5)	1,097
6/3/05	Doncaster (a) (NLC)	L40-10	t:Fairbank g:Maloney(3)	3rd(NLC-G5)	710
12/3/05	Wath Brow (a) (CCR3) ●	L32-30	t:McHugh,Maloney,Preece,Hicks,Crouthers g:Maloney(5)	N/A	741
20/3/05	Sheffield (h) (NLC)	W40-8	t:McHugh,Chapman(3),Maloney,Jowitt,Bretherton g:Maloney(6)	3rd(NLC-G5)	862
25/3/05	Batley (a) (NLC)	L12-10	t:Preece g:Maloney(3)	3rd(NLC-G5)	1,234
28/3/05	Hunslet (h)	W34-8	t:Jowitt,Crouthers,Chapman,Williamson(2) g:Maloney(7)	2nd	1,077
10/4/05	Gateshead (a)	W18-24	t:Williamson(2),McHugh,Rudder g:Maloney(4)	2nd	403
17/4/05	Swinton (h)	W48-10	t:Crouthers,Jowitt,McHugh,Chapman,Rudder,M Walker,Rogers,Williamson g:Maloney(8)	1st	1,112
24/4/05	York (a)	L74-12	t:Rogers(2) g:Maloney(2)	3rd	2,056
15/5/05	Workington (h)	W38-10	t:Bretherton(2),Maloney,Hall,Woodcock,Sheridan,Chapman g:Maloney(5)	3rd	970
21/5/05	London Skolars (a)	W18-22	t:Rogers,Crouthers,Chapman,Sheridan g:Maloney(3)	3rd	354
5/6/05	Sheffield (h)	L24-31	t:Thewliss,Preece,Maloney,Sheridan g:Maloney(4)	3rd	988
12/6/05	Keighley (h)	W14-28	t:Crouthers,Rogers(2),Sheridan,Hall g:Maloney(4)	2nd	972
26/6/05	Blackpool (h)	W32-8	t:Rogers(2),Hall,Chapman,Maloney g:Maloney(6)	2nd	845
3/7/05	Gateshead (h)	W55-6	t:Bretherton(2),Rogers,J Walker,Corcoran,Chapman,Maloney(2),Preece g:Maloney(9) fg:Maloney	2nd	1,003
10/7/05	Hunslet (a)	W14-40	t:Rogers(3),Hall,Mycoe,Preece,Fairbank g:Chapman(6)	2nd	862
24/7/05	Workington (a)	D15-15	t:Sheridan,Hicks g:Mycoe(2),J Walker fg:Corcoran	2nd	969
31/7/05	York (h)	L15-23	t:Bretherton,Hall,Crouthers g:J Walker fg:Corcoran	2nd	1,884
5/8/05	Sheffield (a)	L27-12	t:Rudder,Thewliss g:Fairbank(2)	2nd	884
14/8/05	Keighley (h)	W32-22	t:Thewliss,Rogers,McHugh(2),Hall,Chapman g:Mycoe(3),Chapman	2nd	768
21/8/05	London Skolars (h)	W34-8	t:Chapman,Rogers,Tillotson(2),Stubley,McHugh g:Maloney(4),Mycoe	2nd	682
4/9/05	Blackpool (a)	W26-39	t:Tillotson,Mycoe,McHugh(2),Rogers,Chapman,Sheridan,Maloney g:Maloney(3) fg:Chapman	2nd	540
11/9/05	Swinton (a)	W18-22	t:Rogers,Chapman(2),Lockwood g:Maloney,Mycoe(2)	2nd	618
25/9/05	Batley (a) (NL1QS-QSF)	L40-20	t:Rogers(2),McHugh,Maloney g:Maloney(2)	N/A	1,961
2/10/05	Workington (h) (NL1QS-FE)	W26-18	t:Preece,Rogers(2),Chapman,Crouthers g:Maloney(3)	N/A	1,452
9/10/05	Batley (NL1QS-F) ●●	L28-26	t:Rogers,Sheridan,Hall,Crouthers g:Maloney(5)	N/A	N/A

● Played at Recreation Ground, Whitehaven
●● Played at Halton Stadium, Widnes

		APP		TRIES		GOALS		FG		PTS	
	D.O.B.	ALL	NL2	ALL	NL2	ALL	NL2	ALL	NL2	ALL	NL2
Alex Bretherton	5/12/82	23(1)	16(1)	7	5	0	0	0	0	28	20
Andy Burland	5/11/77	(2)	(2)	0	0	0	0	0	0	0	0
Richard Chapman	5/9/75	24(2)	18(1)	15	12	9	7	1	1	79	63
Ged Corcoran	28/3/83	13	13	1	1	0	0	2	2	6	6
Kevin Crouthers	3/1/76	26	19	9	7	0	0	0	0	36	28
Oliver Fairbank	19/3/81	12	5	3	1	2	2	0	0	16	8
Chris Hall	12/12/82	16	16	7	7	0	0	0	0	28	28
Mark Hawksley	23/2/73	2(8)	2(2)	0	0	0	0	0	0	0	0
Anthony Henderson	9/12/82	1(5)	(4)	1	0	0	0	0	0	4	0
Paul Hicks	22/6/77	23(2)	16(2)	2	1	0	0	0	0	8	4
Warren Jowitt	9/9/74	21(1)	15(1)	3	2	0	0	0	0	12	8
Rob Kelly	1/3/86	3(3)	3(3)	0	0	0	0	0	0	0	0
Jonlee Lockwood	18/3/78	7(12)	2(11)	1	1	0	0	0	0	4	4
Francis Maloney	26/5/73	24	17	11	7	94	70	1	1	233	169
Wayne McHugh	1/2/80	17(1)	10(1)	14	8	0	0	0	0	56	32
Liam Morley	13/3/85	1(1)	1(1)	0	0	0	0	0	0	0	0
David Mycoe	1/5/72	6(20)	6(14)	2	2	8	8	1	0	25	24
Ian Preece	13/6/85	27	20	7	4	0	0	0	0	28	16
Darren Rogers	6/5/74	26	21	21	21	0	0	0	0	84	84
Kurt Rudder	29/1/80	18(1)	17(1)	3	3	0	0	0	0	12	12
Paul Seal	21/4/78	3(6)	3(6)	0	0	0	0	0	0	0	0
Ryan Sheridan	24/5/75	22(5)	15(5)	7	7	0	0	0	0	28	28
Mark Stubley	27/6/82	1(7)	(2)	1	1	0	0	0	0	4	4
Anthony Thewliss	22/6/85	4(7)	2(5)	3	3	0	0	0	0	12	12
Richard Tillotson	26/5/84	10	5	5	3	0	0	0	0	20	12
James Walker	15/4/77	5(19)	3(14)	2	1	2	2	0	0	12	8
Matt Walker	23/11/78	15(3)	15(3)	1	1	0	0	0	0	4	4
Leon Williamson	22/8/74	10	10	5	5	0	0	0	0	20	20
Scott Woodcock	15/11/83	(4)	(4)	1	1	0	0	0	0	4	4
Chris Woolford	4/1/84	4(2)	3(1)	0	0	0	0	0	0	0	0

Darren Rogers

LEAGUE RECORD
P18-W13-D1-L4
(2nd, NL2)
(Runners-Up, NL1 Qualifying Series)
F526, A350, Diff+176
27 points.

CHALLENGE CUP
Round Three

NATIONAL LEAGUE CUP
3rd, Group 5

ATTENDANCES
Best - v York (NL2 - 1,884)
Worst - v London Skolars (NL2 - 682)
Total (NL2, NL1QS & NLC only) - 14,051
Average (NL2, NL1QS
& NLC only) - 1,081
(Up by 272 on 2004)

GATESHEAD THUNDER

DATE	FIXTURE	RESULT	SCORERS	LGE	ATT
13/2/05	Barrow (a) (NLC)	W28-35	t:Peers,Tomes,Hobbs,Bradley,Barnes g:Birch(7) fg:Hobbs	2nd(NLC-G1)	778
27/2/05	Whitehaven (a) (NLC)	L42-12	t:Peers,Firth g:Birch(2)	3rd(NLC-G1)	1,421
13/3/05	Union Treiziste Catalane (h) (CCR3)	L6-56	t:Peers g:Birch	N/A	296
16/3/05	Workington (h) (NLC)	W30-20	t:Elms,Neighbour,Carleton,Firth,Stephenson g:Birch(5)	3rd(NLC-G1)	303
20/3/05	Workington (a) (NLC)	L44-14	t:Bradley,Birch g:Birch(3)	3rd(NLC-G1)	888
24/3/05	Barrow (h) (NLC)	L20-29	t:Liddell,Bradley,Peers,Arizmendez g:Birch(2)	3rd(NLC-G1)	268
28/3/05	Workington (a)	L36-30	t:Arizmendez,Elms,Birch,Tomes g:Birch(7)	6th	852
6/4/05	Whitehaven (h) (NLC)	L4-44	t:Neighbour	3rd(NLC-G1)	266
10/4/05	Dewsbury (h)	L18-24	t:Neighbour,Line,Arizmendez g:Birch(3)	9th	403
17/4/05	Hunslet (h)	L0-50		10th	288
23/4/05	Blackpool (h)	W29-20	t:Birch,Day(2),Firth,Stringer g:Birch(4) fg:Birch	9th	253
15/5/05	York (h) ●	L16-24	t:I Brown,Collins,J Brown g:Birch(2)	7th	705
20/5/05	Sheffield (a)	L30-18	t:Cakacaka,Hobbs,Garside g:Birch(3)	8th	664
12/6/05	Swinton (a)	W32-57	t:Liddell(3),Firth(2),Birch(2),Barnes(2),Peers g:Birch(8) fg:Birch	8th	553
18/6/05	Keighley (h)	W15-14	t:Hobbs,Barnes g:Birch(3) fg:Birch	8th	357
26/6/05	London Skolars (h)	W52-18	t:Liddell,Birch,Hobbs,I Brown,Neighbour,Firth,St Bernard,Line,Rutherford,Peers g:Birch(6)	6th	371
3/7/05	Dewsbury (a)	L55-6	t:I Brown g:Neighbour	7th	1,003
10/7/05	Workington (h)	W30-20	t:Birch,Rowe,Stringer,Thorman,Line g:Birch(5)	7th	432
24/7/05	York (a)	L37-36	t:Burley,Firth,Rowe,Liddell,Birch,Cakacaka g:Birch(6)	7th	1,586
31/7/05	Blackpool (a)	L41-20	t:Neighbour,Liddell,Firth,Birch g:Birch(2)	7th	295
7/8/05	Keighley (a)	D20-20	t:Birch(2),Peers,Liddell g:Birch(2)	7th	545
14/8/05	Swinton (h)	W58-10	t:Lewis,Hobbs(3),Peers,Neighbour(2),Liddell(2),Pierce g:Birch(9)	7th	319
21/8/05	Sheffield (h)	W41-18	t:Birch,Collins(2),Rowe,Liddell,Neighbour,Line g:Birch(6) fg:Birch	6th	371
3/9/05	London Skolars (a)	W24-54	t:Pierce,Collins(2),Liddell(3),Hobbs,Lewis,I Brown g:Birch(9)	6th	330
11/9/05	Hunslet (a)	L26-16	t:I Brown,Thorman,Lewis g:Birch(2)	6th	491
18/9/05	Workington (a) (NL1QS-EPO)	L47-12	t:Lewis,Burley g:Neighbour(2)	N/A	949

● Played at Kingston Park, Newcastle

		APP		TRIES		GOALS		FG		PTS	
	D.O.B.	ALL	NL2	ALL	NL2	ALL	NL2	ALL	NL2	ALL	NL2
Nigel Arizmendez	4/4/74	6(3)	3(1)	3	2	0	0	0	0	12	8
Ian Ball	15/3/84	2(1)	1	0	0	0	0	0	0	0	0
Joel Barnes	28/9/83	4(1)	2(1)	4	3	0	0	0	0	16	12
Chris Birch	23/1/84	23	17	12	11	97	77	4	4	246	202
Steven Bradley	27/7/81	18(1)	12(1)	3	0	0	0	0	0	12	0
Ian Brown	27/1/74	15(1)	12	5	5	0	0	0	0	20	20
Joe Brown	24/4/87	7(3)	5(3)	1	1	0	0	0	0	4	4
Joe Burley	7/1/82	22	18	2	2	0	0	0	0	8	8
Tabua Cakacaka	8/3/77	22	16	2	2	0	0	0	0	8	8
Phil Carleton	2/5/84	7(1)	2(1)	1	0	0	0	0	0	4	0
Ryan Clark	8/9/85	1	1	0	0	0	0	0	0	0	0
Scott Collins	9/5/79	14(1)	13(1)	5	5	0	0	0	0	20	20
Leroy Day	28/3/78	4(1)	4(1)	2	2	0	0	0	0	8	8
Paul Dodsworth	24/1/80	(4)	(2)	0	0	0	0	0	0	0	0
Tony Doherty	3/8/83	4(8)	4(5)	0	0	0	0	0	0	0	0
Steve Elms	11/8/87	3(2)	(2)	2	1	0	0	0	0	8	4
Brandon Fall	6/11/79	(2)	0	0	0	0	0	0	0	0	0
Craig Firth	4/11/82	17(2)	14	8	6	0	0	0	0	32	24
Liam Garside	9/10/82	7(6)	4(3)	1	1	0	0	0	0	4	4
James Hauxwell	28/9/84	1	0	0	0	0	0	0	0	0	0
Mike Hobbs	6/11/78	13(1)	11(1)	8	7	0	0	1	0	33	28
Scott Kelly	2/3/79	1	1	0	0	0	0	0	0	0	0
Aaron Lewis	17/1/85	6	6	4	4	0	0	0	0	16	16
Wade Liddell	1/6/79	18	14	14	13	0	0	0	0	56	52
Rob Line	13/10/82	14(11)	12(7)	4	4	0	0	0	0	16	16
Damian Martinez	13/8/78	3(8)	(6)	0	0	0	0	0	0	0	0
Kevin Neighbour	10/7/83	25	19	8	6	3	3	0	0	38	30
Robin Peers	18/1/82	23(1)	18	8	4	0	0	0	0	32	16
Andrew Pierce	14/1/74	13(1)	13(1)	2	2	0	0	0	0	8	8
Phil Pitt	2/11/78	1(1)	0	0	0	0	0	0	0	0	0
Alex Rowe	11/3/85	3(6)	3(6)	3	3	0	0	0	0	12	12
Steve Rutherford	24/8/81	9(7)	3(7)	1	1	0	0	0	0	4	4
Selwyn St Bernard	30/7/77	7(17)	3(14)	1	1	0	0	0	0	4	4
Graham Stephenson	10/5/84	9(7)	6(6)	1	0	0	0	0	0	4	0
Luke Stringer	23/2/84	4	4	2	2	0	0	0	0	8	8
Neil Thorman	4/6/84	2(7)	2(7)	2	2	0	0	0	0	8	8
John Tomes	4/12/78	10	4	2	1	0	0	0	0	8	4

Chris Birch

LEAGUE RECORD
P18-W8-D1-L9
(6th, NL2)
(Elimination Play-Off,
NL1 Qualifying Series)
F516, A508, Diff+8
17 points.

CHALLENGE CUP
Round Three

NATIONAL LEAGUE CUP
3rd, Group 1

ATTENDANCES
Best - v York (NL2 - 705)
Worst - v Blackpool (NL2 - 253)
Total (NL2 & NLC only) - 4,336
Average (NL2 & NLC only) - 361
(Up by 58 on 2004)

HUNSLET HAWKS

DATE	FIXTURE	RESULT	SCORERS	LGE	ATT
13/2/05	Featherstone (h) (NLC)	L12-28	t:Bastow,G Freeman g:Wray(2)	3rd(NLC-G4)	1,102
20/2/05	York (a) (NLC)	L34-6	t:G Freeman g:Wray	4th(NLC-G4)	1,320
27/2/05	Castleford (a) (NLC)	L70-0		4th(NLC-G4)	4,483
6/3/05	Castleford (h) (NLC)	L6-34	t:Morton g:Dyson	4th(NLC-G4)	1,432
13/3/05	Haydock (a) (CCR3) ●	W4-46	t:G Rayner,Mears,Cook,Moxon(2),Morton(2),Dyson,Staveley g:Dyson(5)	N/A	971
20/3/05	Featherstone (a) (NLC)	L28-18	t:A Shickell,North,Moxon g:Dyson(3)	4th(NLC-G4)	1,150
25/3/05	York (h) (NLC)	W18-12	t:Wray(2),North g:Dyson(3)	4th(NLC-G4)	657
28/3/05	Dewsbury (a)	L34-8	t:Cass,Naylor	9th	1,077
3/4/05	London (h) (CCR4)	L4-70	t:Cass	N/A	450
10/4/05	London Skolars (h)	W32-8	t:A Shickell,Dyson,A Gibbons,Cass(3) g:Dyson(4)	5th	335
17/4/05	Gateshead (a)	W0-50	t:D Gibbons,A Gibbons(2),Dyson(2),North,G Rayner(2),Wray,A Shickell g:Dyson(5)	2nd	288
24/4/05	Workington (a)	L44-24	t:D Gibbons,Wray,A Gibbons,G Rayner(2) g:Dyson(2)	5th	764
15/5/05	Sheffield (h)	W30-12	t:Watson(3),A Shickell,North,D Gibbons g:Wray(3)	4th	383
22/5/05	York (a)	L17-16	t:G Rayner,Wray g:Dyson(4)	5th	3,224
5/6/05	Swinton (h)	W30-20	t:G Rayner(3),Cook,Morton g:Wray(5)	5th	529
12/6/05	Blackpool (h)	W23-22	t:A Gibbons,Cook(2),G Rayner g:Wray(3) fg:D Gibbons	4th	350
26/6/05	Keighley (h)	W37-28	t:Watson,G Rayner(2),D Gibbons,Moxon g:Wray(2),Naylor(6) fg:Moxon	4th	445
3/7/05	London Skolars (a)	W4-22	t:Staveley(2),G Rayner,Cass g:Wray(3)	3rd	364
10/7/05	Dewsbury (h)	L14-40	t:Moxon,Redfearn,Brent g:Wray	3rd	862
22/7/05	Sheffield (a)	W24-34	t:Williamson,A Gibbons,Redfearn(2),North,M Shickell g:Wray(5)	3rd	846
31/7/05	Workington (h)	L25-26	t:Cass,G Rayner,Redfearn,A Gibbons g:Naylor(4) fg:Bastow	5th	340
7/8/05	Swinton (a)	L34-20	t:Bastow,Pryce,Brent g:Wray(4)	5th	512
14/8/05	Blackpool (a)	W12-36	t:Cummins,Naylor,Wray,Morton,Cass,A Shickell g:Wray(6)	5th	358
21/8/05	York (h)	L22-24	t:W Freeman,Naylor,Cook,North g:Wray(3)	5th	1,200
4/9/05	Keighley (a)	W20-27	t:G Rayner,A Gibbons(2),Brent g:Wray(4),Naylor fg:G Rayner	5th	749
11/9/05	Gateshead (h)	W26-16	t:A Shickell,A Gibbons,G Rayner,Coyle g:Wray(5)	5th	491
18/9/05	Swinton (a) (NL1QS-EPO)	L40-28	t:A Shickell,Williamson(3),A Gibbons g:Wray(4)	N/A	581

● Played at Knowsley Road, St Helens

		APP		TRIES		GOALS		FG		PTS	
	D.O.B.	ALL	NL2	ALL	NL2	ALL	NL2	ALL	NL2	ALL	NL2
Andy Bastow	25/5/78	7(9)	5(8)	2	1	0	0	1	1	9	5
Andy Brent	1/5/76	11	11	3	3	0	0	0	0	12	12
Matt Carbutt	3/10/85	5(11)	2(7)	0	0	0	0	0	0	0	0
Mark Cass	17/11/71	10(14)	6(11)	8	7	0	0	0	0	32	28
Craig Cawthray	19/2/85	2	1	0	0	0	0	0	0	0	0
Danny Cook	14/10/81	1(17)	1(13)	5	4	0	0	0	0	20	16
Mick Coyle	5/3/71	12(1)	12(1)	1	1	0	0	0	0	4	4
Paul Cummins	21/5/81	25(1)	17(1)	1	1	0	0	0	0	4	4
Jeremy Dyson	15/2/72	9	4	4	3	27	15	0	0	70	42
Chris Fletcher	21/6/83	1	0	0	0	0	0	0	0	0	0
Glen Freeman	9/4/72	2(5)	(2)	2	0	0	0	0	0	8	0
Wayne Freeman	30/4/74	26	19	1	1	0	0	0	0	4	4
Liam Garside	9/10/82	(3)	(3)	0	0	0	0	0	0	0	0
Anthony Gibbons	18/1/76	23	15	11	11	0	0	0	0	44	44
David Gibbons	18/1/76	20	16	4	4	0	0	1	1	17	17
Michael Gibbons	12/5/81	(1)	0	0	0	0	0	0	0	0	0
Amraz Hamid	2/6/84	1	0	0	0	0	0	0	0	0	0
Joe Hawley	11/2/85	7(4)	1(3)	0	0	0	0	0	0	0	0
Jason Hunter	4/6/85	2	0	0	0	0	0	0	0	0	0
Shaun Ibbetson	13/4/85	2(1)	0	0	0	0	0	0	0	0	0
Gary McLelland	30/12/84	2	0	0	0	0	0	0	0	0	0
Neil Mears	9/1/79	6(1)	2	1	0	0	0	0	0	4	0
Steve Morton	10/5/69	9(2)	5(1)	5	2	0	0	0	0	20	8
Mark Moxon	22/8/80	22	14	5	2	0	0	1	1	21	9
Gareth Naylor	18/12/80	13(5)	12(4)	3	3	11	11	0	0	34	34
David Norcross	24/3/83	(2)	0	0	0	0	0	0	0	0	0
Chris North	6/1/76	10(3)	7(1)	6	4	0	0	0	0	24	16
Steve Pryce	12/5/69	3(5)	1(4)	1	1	0	0	0	0	4	4
George Rayner	19/9/80	26	19	16	15	0	0	1	1	65	61
Luke Rayner	8/11/87	(1)	(1)	0	0	0	0	0	0	0	0
Chris Redfearn	4/12/80	22(2)	18	4	4	0	0	0	0	16	16
Andy Shickell	9/5/81	17(3)	17(1)	7	6	0	0	0	0	28	24
Marc Shickell	2/5/75	4(11)	4(9)	1	1	0	0	0	0	4	4
Nick Staveley	24/6/82	15(1)	9(1)	3	2	0	0	0	0	12	8
Danny Thomas	21/12/83	2	0	0	0	0	0	0	0	0	0
Calvin Watson	13/5/85	6	6	4	4	0	0	0	0	16	16
Lee Williamson	21/9/80	6(4)	6(4)	4	4	0	0	0	0	16	16
Jamaine Wray	15/3/84	22(1)	17(1)	6	4	51	48	0	0	126	112

Jamaine Wray

LEAGUE RECORD
P18-W11-D0-L7
(5th, NL2)
(Elimination Play-Off,
NL1 Qualifying Series)
F476, A385, Diff+91
22 points.

CHALLENGE CUP
Round Four

NATIONAL LEAGUE CUP
4th, Group 4

ATTENDANCES
Best - v Castleford (NLC - 1,432)
Worst - v London Skolars (NL2 - 335)
Total (NL2 & NLC only) - 8,126
Average (NL2 & NLC only) - 677
(Up by 133 on 2004)

KEIGHLEY COUGARS

DATE	FIXTURE	RESULT	SCORERS	LGE	ATT
13/2/05	Hull KR (h) (NLC)	L26-27	t:Steel,Harvey,D Foster,Mitchell g:Mitchell(5)	3rd(NLC-G3)	1,008
20/2/05	Hull KR (a) (NLC)	L36-6	t:M Foster g:Mitchell	3rd(NLC-G3)	2,141
27/2/05	London Skolars (h) (NLC)	W38-10	t:Robinson(3),M Foster,Bramald(3) g:Mitchell(3),Ashton(2)	3rd(NLC-G3)	707
6/3/05	Halifax (a) (NLC)	L42-12	t:Rushforth,Wainhouse g:Mitchell,Ashton	3rd(NLC-G3)	1,526
13/3/05	Strela Kazan (h) (CCR3)	W62-14	t:Bramald(4),Robinson,Firth(2),Stephenson,Taylor(2),Wainhouse g:Ashton(8),Mitchell	N/A	1,176
19/3/05	London Skolars (a) (NLC)	W16-41	t:M Foster(2),D Foster,Bramald,Mervill,Ashton(2) g:Ashton(6) fg:Ashton	3rd(NLC-G3)	353
25/3/05	Halifax (h) (NLC)	L24-50	t:Steel(2),Gardner,Bramald g:Ashton(4)	3rd(NLC-G3)	1,404
28/3/05	Blackpool (a) ●	W12-26	t:Ashton,M Foster,Gardner,Bramald g:Ashton(5)	4th	290
2/4/05	Pia (a) (CCR4)	L53-26	t:Bramald,Robinson(2),Gardner,Mitchell g:Ashton(2),Mitchell	N/A	300
10/4/05	York (h)	L31-42	t:Rushforth,Steel,Firth,Bramald,M Foster g:Ashton(5) fg:Ashton	4th	1,307
17/4/05	Workington (a)	L30-24	t:Bramald(3),Ashton g:Ashton(4)	6th	669
22/4/05	Sheffield (a)	W4-28	t:D Foster,Steel,Ashton,Murgatroyd g:Ashton(5),Mitchell	6th	804
15/5/05	London Skolars (h)	W28-16	t:M Foster,Harvey,Smith(2),Ashton,Bramald g:Ashton(2)	5th	726
22/5/05	Swinton (h)	L12-30	t:M Foster(2),Steel	6th	967
12/6/05	Dewsbury (h)	L14-28	t:Bramald,M Foster g:Mitchell(3)	7th	972
18/6/05	Gateshead (a)	L15-14	t:Bramald,M Foster g:Mitchell(3)	7th	357
26/6/05	Hunslet (h)	L37-28	t:D Foster,Firth,Harvey,Stephenson g:Ashton(4),Mitchell(2)	8th	445
3/7/05	York (a)	L44-16	t:Wainhouse,Williams,Jackson g:Mitchell,Ashton	8th	1,756
10/7/05	Blackpool (h)	W28-20	t:Rushforth,Harvey,Bramald,Greenwood(2) g:Mitchell(2),Ashton(2)	8th	1,142
23/7/05	London Skolars (a)	L15-12	t:Steel,M Foster g:Mitchell,Ashton	8th	412
31/7/05	Sheffield (a)	L20-33	t:Harvey,Robinson,Murgatroyd,Steel g:Mitchell(2)	8th	609
7/8/05	Gateshead (h)	D20-20	t:D Foster,Gardner,Ashton g:Mitchell(4)	8th	545
14/8/05	Dewsbury (a)	L32-22	t:Mervill,Robinson,Williams,Steel g:Mitchell,Ashton(2)	8th	768
21/8/05	Swinton (a)	L46-0		8th	466
4/9/05	Hunslet (h)	L20-27	t:Jackson,M Foster,Stephenson,Bramald g:Bramald(2)	8th	749
11/9/05	Workington (h)	L16-20	t:Steel,D Foster g:Ashton(4)	8th	778

● Played at Lightfoot Green, Preston

		APP		TRIES		GOALS		FG		PTS	
	D.O.B.	ALL	NL2	ALL	NL2	ALL	NL2	ALL	NL2	ALL	NL2
Paul Ashton	17/6/79	15(7)	11(5)	7	5	58	35	2	1	146	91
Chris Beever	18/2/81	2(2)	1(1)	0	0	0	0	0	0	0	0
Matt Bramald	6/2/73	26	18	20	10	2	2	0	0	84	44
Stuart Calvert	14/12/79	8(2)	8(2)	0	0	0	0	0	0	0	0
Jason Clegg	24/3/71	1(14)	1(7)	0	0	0	0	0	0	0	0
Danny Ekis	17/1/82	(6)	(6)	0	0	0	0	0	0	0	0
Matt Firth	19/2/81	23	15	4	2	0	0	0	0	16	8
David Foster	8/4/81	24	16	6	4	0	0	0	0	24	16
Matt Foster	10/6/76	23(1)	15(1)	13	9	0	0	0	0	52	36
Sam Gardner	28/8/77	16	13	4	2	0	0	0	0	16	8
Gareth Greenwood	14/1/83	6(6)	6(6)	2	2	0	0	0	0	8	8
Daniel Harvey	23/3/82	18(4)	10(4)	5	4	0	0	0	0	20	16
Andrew Jackson	14/11/83	7	5	2	2	0	0	0	0	8	8
Richard Mervill	24/6/81	4(17)	2(12)	2	1	0	0	0	0	8	4
Adam Mitchell	7/8/81	14(10)	9(7)	2	0	32	20	0	0	72	40
Danny Murgatroyd	23/10/80	19(6)	13(5)	2	2	0	0	0	0	8	8
Chris Parker	9/9/78	4(3)	1(1)	0	0	0	0	0	0	0	0
Andy Robinson	15/11/78	18(4)	12(2)	8	2	0	0	0	0	32	8
Jordan Ross	25/10/84	6(2)	2(1)	0	0	0	0	0	0	0	0
James Rushforth	9/2/77	13(5)	9(3)	3	2	0	0	0	0	12	8
Karl Smith	28/5/77	7(3)	7(1)	2	2	0	0	0	0	8	8
Matthew Steel	5/10/84	24(1)	17	10	7	0	0	0	0	40	28
Phil Stephenson	17/6/72	25(1)	17(1)	3	2	0	0	0	0	12	8
Lewis Taylor	5/2/85	6(8)	4(5)	2	0	0	0	0	0	8	0
Jonny Wainhouse	12/1/84	23	16	3	1	0	0	0	0	12	4
Daley Williams	15/5/86	6(1)	6(1)	2	2	0	0	0	0	8	8

Matt Bramald

LEAGUE RECORD
P18-W4-D1-L13
(8th, NL2)
F359, A471, Diff-112
9 points.

CHALLENGE CUP
Round Four

NATIONAL LEAGUE CUP
3rd, Group 3

ATTENDANCES
Best - v Halifax (NLC - 1,404)
Worst - v Gateshead (NL2 - 545)
Total (NL2 & NLC only) - 10,914
Average (NL2 & NLC only) - 910
(Down by 274 on 2004, NL1)

LONDON SKOLARS

DATE	FIXTURE	RESULT	SCORERS	LGE	ATT
13/2/05	Halifax (h) (NLC)	L0-40		4th(NLC-G3)	543
20/2/05	Halifax (a) (NLC)	L60-12	t:T Gee,Parillon g:T Gee(2)	4th(NLC-G3)	1,329
27/2/05	Keighley (a) (NLC)	L38-10	t:K Pittman,Tozer g:T Gee	4th(NLC-G3)	707
6/3/05	Hull KR (h) (NLC)	L4-56	t:Barker	4th(NLC-G3)	450
13/3/05	Pia (h) (CCR3)	L14-58	t:Tozer,Blaker,K Pittman g:T Gee	N/A	209
19/3/05	Keighley (h) (NLC)	L16-41	t:Aggrey,Honor,Tozer g:T Gee(2)	4th(NLC-G3)	353
25/3/05	Hull KR (a) (NLC)	L78-20	t:Aggrey,Jonker,Blaker g:T Gee(2),K Pittman(2)	4th(NLC-G3)	2,009
28/3/05	Sheffield (h)	L26-56	t:T Gee(2),Tozer,M Pittman(2) g:T Gee(3)	10th	200
10/4/05	Hunslet (a)	L32-8	t:Honor g:T Gee(2)	10th	335
17/4/05	Blackpool (a)	W16-23	t:Blaker,K Pittman,Tozer,S Singleton g:T Gee(3) fg:Joyce	9th	797
24/4/05	Swinton (h)	L8-38	t:M Pitman g:T Gee(2)	10th	543
15/5/05	Keighley (a)	L28-16	t:Simms,Honor,Jonker g:T Gee(2)	9th	726
21/5/05	Dewsbury (h)	L18-22	t:Meischke,Price(2) g:T Gee(3)	9th	354
5/6/05	Workington (a)	L40-24	t:T Gee,Jonker(2),K Pittman g:T Gee(4)	9th	712
12/6/05	York (h)	L14-32	t:Wheele,Meischke,Jonker g:T Gee	9th	1,018
26/6/05	Gateshead (a)	L52-18	t:T Gee,Aggrey,Wheele g:T Gee(3)	9th	371
3/7/05	Hunslet (a)	L4-22	t:Aggrey	9th	364
23/7/05	Keighley (h)	W15-12	t:Aggrey,Castle,Aderiye g:T Gee fg:Joyce	9th	412
31/7/05	Swinton (a)	L44-12	t:Aggrey,Jonker g:T Gee(2)	9th	401
7/8/05	Workington (h)	L4-28	t:T Gee	9th	372
14/8/05	York (a)	L60-12	t:Meischke(2) g:Elms(2)	10th	1,610
21/8/05	Dewsbury (a)	L34-8	t:Thompson,Coleman	10th	682
29/8/05	Sheffield (a)	L30-18	t:M Pitman,Castle,Parillon g:K Pittman(3)	10th	764
3/9/05	Gateshead (h)	L24-54	t:Tozer(2),Aderiye(2) g:T Gee(4)	10th	330
10/9/05	Blackpool (h)	L6-20	t:Tozer g:T Gee	10th	240

		APP		TRIES		GOALS		FG		PTS	
	D.O.B.	ALL	NL2	ALL	NL2	ALL	NL2	ALL	NL2	ALL	NL2
Ade Aderiye	26/2/85	9(10)	7(9)	3	3	0	0	0	0	12	12
Austin Aggrey	12/5/79	14	8	6	4	0	0	0	0	24	16
Alan Barker	10/12/78	7(4)	5(2)	1	0	0	0	0	0	4	0
Keir Bell	14/6/85	(1)	0	0	0	0	0	0	0	0	0
Brett Blaker	1/11/81	19(1)	13(1)	3	1	0	0	0	0	12	4
Dave Brown	17/10/81	1(2)	(1)	0	0	0	0	0	0	0	0
Dean Callis	24/11/82	1	0	0	0	0	0	0	0	0	0
Mike Castle	21/5/85	6(6)	3(5)	2	2	0	0	0	0	8	8
Jermaine Coleman	17/6/82	12(1)	9(1)	1	1	0	0	0	0	4	4
Oran D'Arcy	12/3/82	4	0	0	0	0	0	0	0	0	0
Mario Du Toit	27/10/81	1(3)	1(3)	0	0	0	0	0	0	0	0
Steve Elms	11/8/87	1	1	0	0	2	2	0	0	4	4
Nathan Gee	20/5/77	6(9)	6(7)	0	0	0	0	0	0	0	0
Tim Gee	5/10/78	21	18	6	5	39	31	0	0	102	82
Andrew Gourlay	22/6/82	7(1)	1(1)	0	0	0	0	0	0	0	0
Toby Hall	6/11/77	17(1)	11	0	0	0	0	0	0	0	0
Gareth Honor	1/10/81	15(5)	9(4)	3	2	0	0	0	0	12	8
Rubert Jonker	7/1/79	18(1)	16	6	5	0	0	0	0	24	20
Ben Joyce	13/2/80	13(5)	12(4)	0	0	0	0	2	2	2	2
Iain Lane	12/12/85	5(4)	5(4)	0	0	0	0	0	0	0	0
Nathan Meischke	7/5/84	12(4)	9(1)	4	4	0	0	0	0	16	16
Troy O'Shea	9/8/82	1	0	0	0	0	0	0	0	0	0
Wayne Parillon	27/11/80	3(11)	(9)	2	1	0	0	0	0	8	4
Matt Pitman	7/12/83	13(5)	11(1)	4	4	0	0	0	0	16	16
Kurt Pittman	11/10/77	20(4)	13(4)	4	2	5	3	0	0	26	14
Joe Price	7/10/85	24	18	2	2	0	0	0	0	8	8
Matt Ryan	11/8/86	(6)	(4)	0	0	0	0	0	0	0	0
Lee Sanderson	16/12/81	1	1	0	0	0	0	0	0	0	0
Corey Simms	18/2/80	14	14	1	1	0	0	0	0	4	4
Richard Singleton	12/5/78	1	0	0	0	0	0	0	0	0	0
Stuart Singleton	17/3/76	9	3	1	1	0	0	0	0	4	4
Alex Smits	5/8/74	15(4)	14(2)	0	0	0	0	0	0	0	0
James Sullivan	2/2/82	6(7)	6(4)	0	0	0	0	0	0	0	0
Tane Taitoko	21/11/78	(1)	(1)	0	0	0	0	0	0	0	0
James Thompson	21/9/87	1(1)	1(1)	1	1	0	0	0	0	4	4
Ashley Tozer	19/8/78	14(2)	8(2)	8	5	0	0	0	0	32	20
Brett Westwood	16/6/80	2	2	0	0	0	0	0	0	0	0
Ryan Wheele	6/7/79	12	12	2	2	0	0	0	0	8	8
Tim Williams	12/10/72	(1)	(1)	0	0	0	0	0	0	0	0

Gareth Honor

LEAGUE RECORD
P18-W2-D0-L16
(10th, NL2)
F258, A620, Diff-362
4 points.

CHALLENGE CUP
Round Three

NATIONAL LEAGUE CUP
4th, Group 3

ATTENDANCES
Best - v York (NL2 - 1,018)
Worst - v Sheffield (NL2 - 200)
Total (NL2 & NLC only) - 5,179
Average (NL2 & NLC only) - 432
(Up by 25 on 2004)

SHEFFIELD EAGLES

DATE	FIXTURE	RESULT	SCORERS	LGE	ATT
11/2/05	Dewsbury (h) (NLC)	W23-16	t:R Dickinson,Veamatahau,Crawford g:Crawford(2),G Brown(3) fg:G Brown	1st(NLC-G5)	959
18/2/05	Doncaster (a) (NLC)	L58-20	t:De Chenu,Mills,Veamatahau,Breakingbury g:G Brown(2)	4th(NLC-G5)	727
27/2/05	Batley (a) (NLC)	L28-16	t:Crawford,Hurst(2) g:G Brown(2)	4th(NLC-G5)	492
4/3/05	Batley (h) (NLC)	L6-34	t:G Brown g:G Brown	4th(NLC-G5)	875
13/3/05	Waterhead (a) (CCR3) ●	W16-22	t:Breakingbury,Crawford,R Dickinson,De Chenu,C Brown g:G Brown	N/A	390
20/3/05	Dewsbury (a) (NLC)	L40-8	t:Crawford g:G Brown(2)	4th(NLC-G5)	862
25/3/05	Doncaster (h) (NLC) ●●	L20-38	t:Veamatahau,Chapman,Mills,Pitt g:Pearson(2)	4th(NLC-G5)	1,003
28/3/05	London Skolars (a)	W26-56	t:C Brown,Crawford(2),De Chenu(2),James,Turnbull,S Dickinson,Mills,Veamatahau g:G Brown(8)	1st	200
3/4/05	Barrow (a) (CCR4)	L33-26	t:Turnbull,Crawford,James,Morton,S Dickinson g:G Brown(2),Stott	N/A	893
8/4/05	Blackpool (h)	L6-14	t:Turnbull g:G Brown	3rd	727
17/4/05	York (a)	L60-10	t:Turnbull,Hurst g:Stott	8th	1,596
22/4/05	Keighley (h)	L4-28	t:Worrincy	8th	804
15/5/05	Hunslet (a)	L30-12	t:C Brown,Presley g:Crawford(2)	8th	383
20/5/05	Gateshead (h)	W30-18	t:De Chenu(2),Presley,Brentley,Crawford g:Crawford(5)	7th	664
5/6/05	Dewsbury (a)	W24-31	t:Lynch,Ford(2),Crawford,Sovatabua g:Crawford(4),G Brown fg:G Brown	7th	988
11/6/05	Workington (h) ●●●	W31-28	t:S Dickinson,Crawford(2),Sovatabua,Ford g:Crawford(5) fg:G Brown	6th	650
26/6/05	Swinton (a)	L42-24	t:A Dickinson,James,De Chenu,Tillyer g:Crawford(3),G Brown	7th	425
3/7/05	Blackpool (a)	W26-44	t:A Dickinson,Crawford(2),James(2),De Chenu(2),Ford g:Crawford(6)	6th	410
22/7/05	Hunslet (h)	L24-34	t:Brentley,Hurst(2),James,Sovatabua g:Crawford(2)	6th	846
31/7/05	Keighley (a)	W20-33	t:Presley(2),Morton,A Dickinson(2),Turnbull g:Crawford(4) fg:Crawford	6th	609
5/8/05	Dewsbury (h)	W27-12	t:G Brown,Crawford(2),A Dickinson(2) g:Crawford(2),G Brown fg:G Brown	6th	884
14/8/05	Workington (a)	L34-10	t:Presley,De Chenu g:Crawford	6th	866
21/8/05	Gateshead (a)	L41-18	t:Tillyer,Mills,Molyneux,Hurst g:G Brown	7th	371
29/8/05	London Skolars (h)	W30-18	t:Hurst(2),Brentley(2),Presley,Mills g:Crawford(2),James	6th	764
2/9/05	Swinton (a)	L14-38	t:De Chenu(2),Presley g:Crawford	7th	806
9/9/05	York (h)	L10-36	t:A Dickinson,Worrincy g:G Brown	7th	1,154

● Played at Castleton Gabriels AFC, Rochdale
●● Played at Clifton Lane, Rotherham
●●● Played at Woodbourn Athletic Stadium, Sheffield

		APP		TRIES		GOALS		FG		PTS	
	D.O.B.	ALL	NL2	ALL	NL2	ALL	NL2	ALL	NL2	ALL	NL2
Jon Breakingbury	5/10/82	2(3)	1	2	0	0	0	0	0	8	0
Liam Brentley	27/6/85	20(2)	16(1)	4	4	0	0	0	0	16	16
Craig Brown	2/12/80	22	16	3	2	0	0	0	0	12	8
Gavin Brown	18/9/77	20(1)	13(1)	2	1	27	14	4	3	66	35
Tom Buckenham	15/8/84	6(2)	6(2)	0	0	0	0	0	0	0	0
Jaymes Chapman	17/12/83	2(3)	1(1)	1	0	0	0	0	0	4	0
Kieron Collins	20/10/82	2	0	0	0	0	0	0	0	0	0
Scott Collins	9/5/79	2	0	0	0	0	0	0	0	0	0
John Crawford	12/8/85	24(1)	17(1)	15	10	39	37	1	1	139	115
Carl De Chenu	18/6/82	21	16	12	10	0	0	0	0	48	40
Alex Dickinson	27/11/84	19	12	7	7	0	0	0	0	28	28
Ryan Dickinson	9/6/86	5(5)	1(3)	2	0	0	0	0	0	8	0
Sean Dickinson	17/8/83	7(11)	6(7)	3	2	0	0	0	0	12	8
James Ford	29/9/82	4	4	4	4	0	0	0	0	16	16
Jack Howieson	28/7/81	13	11	0	0	0	0	0	0	0	0
Greg Hurst	22/6/80	7(13)	4(11)	8	6	0	0	0	0	32	24
Aled James	17/2/82	18(1)	14	6	5	1	1	0	0	26	22
Damien Lynch	22/9/76	12(3)	8(3)	1	1	0	0	0	0	4	4
Danny Mills	10/8/82	14	7	5	3	0	0	0	0	20	12
Chris Molyneux	5/5/80	15(1)	11(1)	1	1	0	0	0	0	4	4
Peter Moore	25/3/83	1(2)	0	0	0	0	0	0	0	0	0
Simon Morton	4/10/82	6(13)	3(8)	2	1	0	0	0	0	8	4
Rob North	19/11/77	1(3)	0	0	0	0	0	0	0	0	0
Jimmy Pearson	25/7/78	3(8)	3(6)	0	0	2	0	0	0	4	0
Joseph Pitt	29/6/80	2(2)	(2)	1	0	0	0	0	0	4	0
Jon Presley	8/7/84	14	14	7	7	0	0	0	0	28	28
Andy Rice	9/6/80	10(7)	4(7)	0	0	0	0	0	0	0	0
Waisale Sovatabua	26/6/73	6(1)	6(1)	3	3	0	0	0	0	12	12
Gareth Stanley	20/5/81	4	2	0	0	0	0	0	0	0	0
Lynton Stott	9/5/71	11(3)	10(3)	0	0	2	1	0	0	4	2
Mitchell Stringer	1/11/83	(1)	0	0	0	0	0	0	0	0	0
Simon Tillyer	9/5/80	6(14)	(13)	2	2	0	0	0	0	8	8
Nick Turnbull	22/11/82	20(3)	16	5	4	0	0	0	0	20	16
Adrian Veamatahau	13/9/80	10	3	4	1	0	0	0	0	16	4
Rob Worrincy	9/7/85	9(1)	9(1)	2	2	0	0	0	0	8	8

Chris Molyneux

LEAGUE RECORD
P18-W8-D0-L10
(7th, NL2)
F414, A529, Diff-115
16 points.

CHALLENGE CUP
Round Four

NATIONAL LEAGUE CUP
4th, Group 5

ATTENDANCES
Best - v York (NL2 - 1,154)
Worst - v Workington (NL2 - 650)
Total (NL2 & NLC only) - 10,136
Average (NL2 & NLC only) - 845
(Down by 57 on 2004)

SWINTON LIONS

DATE	FIXTURE	RESULT	SCORERS	LGE	ATT
13/2/05	Rochdale (h) (NLC)	W20-14	t:Maye,Marsh(2),English g:Marsh(2)	1st(NLC-G2)	685
18/2/05	Blackpool (a) (NLC)	W24-34	t:Joseph,Maye(2),Billy(2),Oldham g:Marsh(5)	1st(NLC-G2)	512
27/2/05	Oldham (h) (NLC)	W46-14	t:Marsh,Heaton,English(3),Sinfield,Rogers,Watson g:Marsh(7)	1st(NLC-G2)	1,101
6/3/05	Oldham (a) (NLC)	W30-37	t:English(2),Billy,Heaton,Patterson,Sinfield,Joseph g:Marsh,Watson(3) fg:Marsh	1st(NLC-G2)	1,116
13/3/05	Locomotiv Moscow (h) (CCR3)	W70-10	t:Maye(4),Marsh,Joseph,Russell,Patterson(2),Billy(2),Oldham,Watson g:Marsh(9)	N/A	544
20/3/05	Rochdale (a) (NLC)	L54-20	t:Patterson,Irwin(2),Patel,Maye	2nd(NLC-G2)	967
25/3/05	Blackpool (h) (NLC)	D14-14	t:Irwin,Coates,Maye g:Marsh	2nd(NLC-G2)	541
28/3/05	York (a)	W18-34	t:Marsh,English,Patterson,Gardner,Coates,Maye g:Marsh(5)	3rd	1,890
3/4/05	Widnes (a) (CCR4)	L32-18	t:Billy(2),Joseph g:Marsh(3)	N/A	2,263
10/4/05	Workington (h)	W56-18	t:English(3),Joseph,Southern,Coates(2),Patterson(2),Billy g:Marsh(8)	1st	602
17/4/05	Dewsbury (a)	L48-10	t:Heaton(2) g:Marsh	4th	1,112
24/4/05	London Skolars (a)	W8-38	t:Marsh(2),Billy(3),English,Patterson,Russell g:Marsh(3)	2nd	543
1/5/05	Batley (h) (NLCQPO)	W40-24	t:Patterson(3),English,Billy,Maye(2),Smith(2)	N/A	689
15/5/05	Blackpool (h)	W84-12	t:English(2),Patterson(3),Billy(2),Marsh(2),Coates,Oldham(2),Southern,Parry, Rogers,Ayres g:Marsh(9),Joseph	1st	588
22/5/05	Keighley (a)	W12-30	t:Coates(2),Marsh,Irwin,English g:Marsh(5)	1st	967
29/5/05	Hull KR (a) (NLCQF)	L62-0		N/A	1,506
5/6/05	Hunslet (a)	L30-20	t:Billy,Irwin,English,Patterson g:Coates(2)	2nd	529
12/6/05	Gateshead (h)	L32-57	t:Billy,Heaton,Leigh,Joseph,Patterson,Coates,Irwin g:Coates,Ayres	3rd	553
26/6/05	Sheffield (h)	W42-24	t:Patterson(2),English,Watson(2),Oldham,Sinfield g:Marsh(7)	3rd	425
3/7/05	Workington (a)	L23-20	t:Marsh,Joseph,Maye,English g:Marsh(2)	5th	995
10/7/05	York (h)	L16-32	t:Maye,Marsh,English g:Marsh(2)	5th	802
24/7/05	Blackpool (a)	W26-51	t:Billy(3),Joseph,Maye,Parry,English(2),Marsh g:Marsh(7) fg:Marsh	5th	428
31/7/05	London Skolars (h)	W44-12	t:Maye,Billy(2),English,Heaton(2),Smith,Patel g:Marsh(6)	4th	401
7/8/05	Hunslet (h)	W34-20	t:Patterson,English(2),Billy,Oldham,Marsh,Maye g:Marsh(3)	4th	512
14/8/05	Gateshead (a)	L58-10	t:Farrimond,Billy g:Marsh	4th	319
21/8/05	Keighley (h)	W46-0	t:Joseph(2),Oldham,Marsh(2),English,Heaton(2) g:Marsh(7)	4th	466
2/9/05	Sheffield (a)	W14-38	t:Billy(2),Joseph,Llewellyn,Parry,Marsh,Patterson g:Marsh(5)	4th	806
11/9/05	Dewsbury (h)	L18-22	t:Marsh(2),Parry g:Marsh(3)	4th	618
18/9/05	Hunslet (h) (NL1QS-EPO)	W40-28	t:Maye,Parry,Marsh,Heaton,Crabtree,Patterson,English g:Marsh(6)	N/A	581
25/9/05	Workington (a) (NL1QS-ESF)	L17-16	t:Billy,Llewellyn g:Marsh(4)	N/A	1,263

			APP		TRIES		GOALS		FG		PTS	
	D.O.B.		ALL	NL2	ALL	NL2	ALL	NL2	ALL	NL2	ALL	NL2
Phil Anderton	19/1/84		2	2	0	0	0	0	0	0	0	0
Warren Ayres	11/12/78		3(15)	1(9)	1	1	1	1	0	0	6	6
Danny Barton	7/9/83		5(6)	4(5)	0	0	0	0	0	0	0	0
Marlon Billy	22/11/73		27	18	26	18	0	0	0	0	104	72
Mick Coates	8/3/80		26(1)	18(1)	8	7	3	3	0	0	38	34
Andy Crabtree	7/12/82		5(7)	4(2)	1	1	0	0	0	0	4	4
Ben Cramant	17/6/78		1(2)	0	0	0	0	0	0	0	0	0
Wayne English	8/3/80		27	18	25	19	0	0	0	0	100	76
Craig Farrimond	20/11/82		1(5)	1(5)	1	1	0	0	0	0	4	4
Lee Gardner	24/8/82		1(4)	(1)	1	1	0	0	0	0	4	0
Neil Hayden	25/11/82		(1)	0	0	0	0	0	0	0	0	0
Danny Heaton	19/4/81		27(1)	18(1)	12	8	0	0	0	0	48	32
Ian Hodson	23/10/81		2(2)	0	0	0	0	0	0	0	0	0
Chris Irwin	11/3/82		10(1)	6	6	3	0	0	0	0	24	12
Phil Joseph	10/1/85		29	20	11	7	1	1	0	0	46	30
Matt Leigh	24/2/78		4(3)	4(3)	1	1	0	0	0	0	4	4
Dave Llewellyn	3/12/82		3	3	2	2	0	0	0	0	8	8
Lee Marsh	5/3/83		27	18	20	16	114	84	2	1	310	233
Chris Maye	28/2/84		24	16	17	7	0	0	0	0	68	28
Alex Muff	17/8/82		1(1)	1(1)	0	0	0	0	0	0	0	0
Stuart Oldham	8/3/83		22(1)	15	7	5	0	0	0	0	28	20
Ian Parry	2/4/81		4(11)	4(10)	5	5	0	0	0	0	20	20
Safraz Patel	20/10/76		(5)	(4)	2	1	0	0	0	0	8	4
Lee Patterson	20/7/82		30	20	21	14	0	0	0	0	84	56
Wes Rogers	3/11/77		25(1)	16(1)	2	1	0	0	0	0	8	4
Rob Russell	12/3/79		12(11)	8(7)	2	1	0	0	0	0	8	4
Ian Sinfield	7/4/77		20(6)	12(6)	4	1	0	0	0	0	16	4
Kris Smith	20/8/78		5(7)	5(6)	1	1	2	0	0	0	8	4
Paul Southern	18/3/76		16(2)	9(2)	2	2	0	0	0	0	8	8
Darren Speakman	24/3/74		1(2)	0	0	0	0	0	0	0	0	0
Hugh Thorpe	19/12/78		2	1	0	0	0	0	0	0	0	0
Ian Watson	27/10/76		22(2)	13(2)	4	2	3	0	0	0	22	8
Rob Whittaker	13/5/79		6(22)	5(13)	0	0	0	0	0	0	0	0

Lee Marsh

LEAGUE RECORD
P18-W11-D0-L7
(4th, NL2)
(Elimination Semi Finalists,
NL1 Qualifying Series)
F623, A434, Diff+189
22 points.

CHALLENGE CUP
Round Four

NATIONAL LEAGUE CUP
Quarter Finalists/2nd, Group 2

ATTENDANCES
Best - v Oldham (NLC - 1,101)
Worst - v London Skolars (NL2 - 401)
Total (NL2, NL1QS
& NLC, inc QPO, only) - 8,564
Average (NL2, NL1QS
& NLC, inc QPO, only) - 612
(Up by 32 on 2004)

WORKINGTON TOWN

DATE	FIXTURE	RESULT	SCORERS	LGE	ATT
13/2/05	Whitehaven (h) (NLC)	W28-8	t:Wright,Limmer,Roper,Johnson g:Smith(6)	1st(NLC-G1)	3,012
27/2/05	Barrow (h) (NLC)	W28-18	t:Hetherington,Frazer,Sione,Tuimaualuga g:Hetherington(6)	2nd(NLC-G1)	1,097
6/3/05	Barrow (a) (NLC)	W12-54	t:Sione(2),Fearon,Frazer(2),Limmer(2),Hetherington,Woodcock,Tunstall g:Bragg(2),Sione,Hetherington(2),Roper(2)	1st(NLC-G1)	844
13/3/05	Wigan St Judes (h) (CCR3)	W44-20	t:Roper,McGuiness(2),Limmer,Kiddie(2),Tuimaualuga,Johnson g:Smith(6)	N/A	899
16/3/05	Gateshead (a) (NLC)	L30-20	t:Bragg,Woodcock,Armstrong,Roper g:Hetherington(2)	1st(NLC-G1)	303
20/3/05	Gateshead (h) (NLC)	W44-14	t:Frazer(2),Woodcock(2),Kiddie(2),Johnson,Beaumont g:Smith(3),Roper(3)	1st(NLC-G1)	888
25/3/05	Whitehaven (a) (NLC)	L58-10	t:Bragg g:Hetherington(2),Bragg	2nd(NLC-G1)	3,439
28/3/05	Gateshead (h)	W36-30	t:Robinson,Sione,Roper,Kiddie,Woodcock,Wilson g:Smith(6)	5th	852
3/4/05	Doncaster (a) (CCR4)	L54-18	t:Lavulavu,Manihera,Limmer g:Manihera(3)	N/A	770
10/4/05	Swinton (a)	L56-18	t:Limmer,Kiddie,Manihera g:Manihera(3)	8th	602
17/4/05	Keighley (h)	W30-24	t:Manihera(2),Chilton,Beaumont,Lavulavu g:Manihera(5)	5th	669
24/4/05	Hunslet (h)	W44-24	t:Woodcock(2),Limmer,Chilton(2),Sione,Frazer,Kiddie g:Manihera(6)	4th	764
1/5/05	Featherstone (a) (NLCQPO)	L44-20	t:Limmer(2),Lavulavu,Sione g:Hetherington(2)	N/A	836
15/5/05	Dewsbury (a)	L38-10	t:Sione,Manihera g:Manihera	6th	970
22/5/05	Blackpool (a)	W26-38	t:Woodcock,Limmer,Sione(2),Manihera(2),Wilson g:Manihera(4),Smith	4th	350
5/6/05	London Skolars (h)	W40-24	t:Limmer(2),Woodcock,Roper,Lavulavu,Sione,Tinnion g:Roper(6)	4th	712
11/6/05	Sheffield (a) ●	L31-28	t:Frazer,Woodcock,Limmer(2),Manihera g:Roper(4)	5th	650
26/6/05	York (h)	W44-28	t:Miller,Sione(3),Chilton,Wilson,Tinnion g:Manihera(8)	5th	1,139
3/7/05	Swinton (h)	W23-20	t:Sione(2),Kiddie g:Manihera(5) fg:Kiddie	4th	995
10/7/05	Gateshead (a)	L30-29	t:Tuimaualuga,Campbell,Limmer(3) g:Manihera(4) fg:Purdham	4th	432
24/7/05	Dewsbury (h)	D15-15	t:Kiddie,Roper g:Manihera(3) fg:Kiddie	4th	969
31/7/05	Hunslet (a)	W25-26	t:Limmer,Sione,Frazer(2),Smith g:Manihera(3)	3rd	340
7/8/05	London Skolars (a)	W4-28	t:Roper,Woodcock(2),Limmer,Purdham g:Manihera(4)	3rd	372
14/8/05	Sheffield (h)	W34-10	t:Limmer(3),Manihera,Sione,Woodcock g:Roper(5)	3rd	866
21/8/05	Blackpool (h)	W24-23	t:Roper,Manihera,Limmer,Campbell g:Roper(4)	3rd	767
4/9/05	York (a)	W18-20	t:Kiddie,Smith,Sione(2) g:Smith(2)	3rd	2,177
11/9/05	Keighley (a)	W16-20	t:Sione(2),Limmer,Tuimaualuga g:Smith(2)	3rd	778
18/9/05	Gateshead (h) (NL1QS-EPO)	W47-12	t:Sione,Manihera,Wilson,Frazer(3),Lavulavu,Smith,Robinson g:Roper(5) fg:Roper	N/A	949
25/9/05	Swinton (h) (NL1QS-ESF)	W17-16	t:Wilson,Sione,Manihera g:Roper(2) fg:Kiddie	N/A	1,263
2/10/05	Dewsbury (a) (NL1QS-FE)	L26-18	t:Limmer,Purdham g:Roper(4),Smith	N/A	1,452

● Played at Woodbourn Athletic Stadium, Sheffield

APP TRIES GOALS FG PTS

	D.O.B.	ALL	NL2	ALL	NL2	ALL	NL2	ALL	NL2	ALL	NL2
Tom Armstrong	29/10/81	1(5)	(4)	1	0	0	0	0	0	4	0
Jamie Beaumont	22/1/75	7(18)	3(15)	2	1	0	0	0	0	8	4
Dean Bragg	14/1/82	4(4)	1	2	0	3	0	0	0	14	0
Dean Burgess	11/10/84	7(2)	2	0	0	0	0	0	0	0	0
Lee Burns	10/8/86	2(2)	2(1)	0	0	0	0	0	0	0	0
Ryan Campbell	23/9/81	5(3)	5(3)	2	2	0	0	0	0	8	8
Malcolm Caton	24/11/82	1(8)	(5)	0	0	0	0	0	0	0	0
Scott Chilton	26/10/80	13(1)	8(1)	4	4	0	0	0	0	16	16
Mark Cox	22/1/78	9	9	0	0	0	0	0	0	0	0
Stephen Dawes	14/1/85	1(1)	0	0	0	0	0	0	0	0	0
Gareth Dean	31/3/81	2	2	0	0	0	0	0	0	0	0
Andrew Fearon	21/9/74	5	2	1	0	0	0	0	0	4	0
Neil Frazer	7/3/76	25	17	12	7	0	0	0	0	48	28
Kevin Hetherington	7/6/76	7	2	2	0	14	0	0	0	36	0
Matthew Johnson	18/3/82	8(4)	2(3)	3	0	0	0	0	0	12	0
Lee Kiddie	2/1/75	27(1)	21	10	6	0	0	3	3	43	27
Taani Lavulavu	22/3/76	9(18)	7(11)	5	3	0	0	0	0	20	12
Jonny Limmer	8/5/79	29	21	25	18	0	0	0	0	100	72
Tane Manihera	6/8/74	18(2)	17(2)	12	11	49	46	0	0	146	136
Allan McGuiness	30/6/82	1(15)	1(12)	2	0	0	0	0	0	8	0
Dexter Miller	3/6/82	6(5)	6(5)	1	1	0	0	0	0	4	4
Garry Purdham	20/10/78	11	11	2	2	0	0	1	1	9	9
James Robinson	4/3/79	11(9)	5(9)	2	2	0	0	0	0	8	8
Jon Roper	5/5/76	24	16	8	5	35	30	1	1	103	81
Wendell Saayman	24/10/74	(1)	(1)	0	0	0	0	0	0	0	0
Lusi Sione	26/12/74	25	18	23	19	1	0	0	0	94	76
Gareth Skillen	10/10/82	(1)	(1)	0	0	0	0	0	0	0	0
Brett Smith	17/10/77	11(4)	6(3)	3	3	27	12	0	0	66	36
Lee Tinnion	16/11/82	4(1)	4(1)	2	2	0	0	0	0	8	8
John Tuimaualuga	29/10/77	27(1)	20	4	2	0	0	0	0	16	8
Matthew Tunstall	7/9/77	7(3)	5(1)	1	0	0	0	0	0	4	0
Dean Vaughan	9/2/78	21(4)	16(1)	0	0	0	0	0	0	0	0
Martyn Wilson	22/10/82	27(2)	21	5	5	0	0	0	0	20	20
Matthew Woodcock	26/10/77	28	21	13	9	0	0	0	0	52	36
Ricky Wright	15/3/77	7(3)	2(3)	1	0	0	0	0	0	4	0

Lusi Sione

LEAGUE RECORD
P18-W13-D1-L4
(3rd, NL2)
(Final Eliminator, NL1 Qualifying Series)
F507, A442, Diff+65
27 points.

CHALLENGE CUP
Round Four

NATIONAL LEAGUE CUP
Qualifying Play-Off/2nd, Group 1

ATTENDANCES
Best - v Whitehaven (NLC - 3,012)
Worst - v Keighley (NL2 - 669)
Total (NL2, NL1QS & NLC only) - 14,942
Average (NL2, NL1QS & NLC only) - 1,067
(Up by 205 on 2004)

YORK CITY KNIGHTS

DATE	FIXTURE	RESULT	SCORERS	LGE	ATT
13/2/05	Castleford (a) (NLC)	L52-2	g:P Thorman	4th(NLC-G4)	5,768
20/2/05	Hunslet (h) (NLC)	W34-6	t:Law(2),Potter,Smith(2) g:Ross(7)	3rd(NLC-G4)	1,320
27/2/05	Featherstone (a) (NLC)	L21-20	t:Levy,Potter,Sozi g:Ross(4)	3rd(NLC-G4)	1,460
6/3/05	Featherstone (h) (NLC)	D20-20	t:Levy,Law,Callaghan,Fox g:Ross(2)	3rd(NLC-G4)	1,463
13/3/05	Elland (a) (CCR3) ●	W12-50	t:Fox(2),Smith,Watson,Rhodes,P Thorman,Callaghan,Elston,N Thorman g:Ross(7)	N/A	930
20/3/05	Castleford (h) (NLC)	L16-24	t:Watson,Lingard g:P Thorman(4)	3rd(NLC-G4)	2,340
25/3/05	Hunslet (a) (NLC)	L18-12	t:Blaymire,Ramsden g:Ross,Cain	3rd(NLC-G4)	657
28/3/05	Swinton (h)	L18-34	t:Law(2),Cain g:P Thorman(3)	8th	1,890
3/4/05	Oldham (a) (CCR4)	W28-32	t:Potter(2),Liddell,Fox,Friend,Ward g:Liddell(4)	N/A	1,282
10/4/05	Keighley (a)	W31-42	t:Sullivan,Cain,Law,Potter(2),Fairfield,Fox(2) g:Liddell(5)	6th	1,307
17/4/05	Sheffield (h)	W60-10	t:Potter,Fox(4),Levy(2),Liddell,Smith,Elston,Friend g:P Thorman(8)	3rd	1,596
24/4/05	Dewsbury (h)	W74-12	t:Potter(3),Fox(2),Jackson,Kirke(2),Sozi(2),Law,Rhodes,Blaymire g:Liddell(11)	1st	2,056
6/5/05	St Helens (a) (CCR5)	L62-0		N/A	6,640
15/5/05	Gateshead (a) ●●	W16-24	t:Kirke,Callaghan,Sozi,Fox g:P Thorman(4)	1st	705
22/5/05	Hunslet (h)	W17-16	t:Lingard,Rhodes,Blaymire g:P Thorman(2) fg:Levy	2nd	3,224
4/6/05	Blackpool (h)	W60-10	t:Jackson,Lingard(2),Potter,Ramsden(2),Law,Levy,Elston,Fox(2),Sullivan g:P Thorman(6)	1st	1,981
12/6/05	London Skolars (a)	W14-32	t:Fox(2),Sullivan,Bates,Lingard,Blaymire g:P Thorman(3),Lingard	1st	1,018
26/6/05	Workington (a)	L44-28	t:Levy,Blaymire,Fox,Rhodes,Sozi g:P Thorman(4)	1st	1,139
3/7/05	Keighley (h)	W44-16	t:Fox,Levy,Sozi,Liddell(2),Bates,Ross,Kirke g:P Thorman(5),Liddell	1st	1,756
10/7/05	Swinton (a)	W16-32	t:Blaymire(2),Elston,Fox,Ross g:P Thorman(6)	1st	802
24/7/05	Gateshead (h)	W37-36	t:Levy,Ross,Elston,Helme,Law,Blaymire g:P Thorman(6) fg:P Thorman	1st	1,586
31/7/05	Dewsbury (a)	W15-23	t:Elston,Law,Fox,Callaghan g:P Thorman,Ross(2) fg:Levy	1st	1,884
7/8/05	Blackpool (a)	W22-54	t:Law,Levy,Jackson,Ross,Potter,Elston(2),Smith,Sullivan,Blaymire g:P Thorman(7)	1st	635
14/8/05	London Skolars (h)	W60-12	t:Buchanan(2),Fox(4),Lingard,Potter(3),Ross,Elston g:P Thorman(4),Ross(2)	1st	1,610
21/8/05	Hunslet (a)	W22-24	t:Potter(2),Law,Blaymire g:P Thorman(2),Patterson(2)	1st	1,200
4/9/05	Workington (h)	L18-20	t:Smith,Levy(2) g:P Thorman(3)	1st	2,177
9/9/05	Sheffield (a)	W10-36	t:Sozi,Rhodes,Law(2),Lingard,Smith,Ross g:Liddell,Ross,Levy,Jackson	1st	1,154

● Played at Huntington Stadium
●● Played at Kingston Park, Newcastle

		APP		TRIES		GOALS		FG		PTS	
	D.O.B.	ALL	NL2	ALL	NL2	ALL	NL2	ALL	NL2	ALL	NL2
David Bates	23/10/80	3(5)	3(4)	2	2	0	0	0	0	8	8
Matt Blaymire	10/6/82	22	15	10	9	0	0	0	0	40	36
Austin Buchanan	22/5/84	3(1)	2(1)	2	2	0	0	0	0	8	8
Tom Buckenham	15/8/84	3(6)	(2)	0	0	0	0	0	0	0	0
Mark Cain	3/5/76	1(6)	(2)	2	2	1	0	0	0	10	8
Darren Callaghan	6/8/76	15(9)	6(9)	4	2	0	0	0	0	16	8
Jimmy Elston	8/12/79	8(17)	3(14)	9	8	0	0	0	0	36	32
Paul Fairfield	1/6/83	2	2	1	1	0	0	0	0	4	4
Craig Forsyth	24/10/70	6(5)	6(3)	0	0	0	0	0	0	0	0
Peter Fox	5/11/83	26	17	25	21	0	0	0	0	100	84
Simon Friend	6/5/77	4(1)	2(1)	2	1	0	0	0	0	8	4
Joe Helme	1/4/84	3(3)	3(3)	1	1	0	0	0	0	4	4
Shaun Ibbetson	13/4/85	(1)	(1)	0	0	0	0	0	0	0	0
Lee Jackson	12/3/69	15(6)	12(2)	3	3	1	1	0	0	14	14
Ian Kirke	26/12/80	21	14	4	4	0	0	0	0	16	16
Neil Law	23/10/74	23	16	11	11	0	0	0	0	56	44
Chris Levy	31/10/77	19	13	11	9	1	1	2	2	48	40
Jon Liddell	25/8/82	13(4)	7(4)	4	3	22	18	0	0	60	48
Lee Lingard	21/10/83	7	6	7	6	1	1	0	0	30	26
Craig McDowell	5/11/81	(2)	0	0	0	0	0	0	0	0	0
Lee Patterson	5/7/81	21(1)	15(1)	0	0	2	2	0	0	4	4
Dan Potter	8/11/78	22	17	17	13	0	0	0	0	68	52
Mick Ramsden	13/11/71	6(3)	5(2)	3	2	0	0	0	0	12	8
Scott Rhodes	21/6/80	13(4)	9(2)	5	4	0	0	0	0	20	16
Chris Ross	23/8/78	15	9	6	6	26	5	0	0	76	34
John Smith	14/8/80	22(2)	15(1)	7	4	0	0	0	0	28	16
Yusuf Sozi	20/12/81	5(20)	3(13)	7	6	0	0	0	0	28	24
Adam Sullivan	14/11/82	22(3)	14(3)	4	4	0	0	0	0	16	16
Neil Thorman	4/6/84	2(3)	(1)	1	0	0	0	0	0	4	0
Paul Thorman	28/9/82	19	15	1	0	69	64	1	1	143	129
James Ward	22/1/78	6(5)	4(3)	1	0	0	0	0	0	4	0
Calvin Watson	13/5/85	4(1)	1	2	0	0	0	0	0	8	0

Peter Fox

LEAGUE RECORD
P18-W15-D0-L3
(1st, NL2/Champions)
F683, A356, Diff+327
30 points.

CHALLENGE CUP
Round Five

NATIONAL LEAGUE CUP
3rd, Group 4

ATTENDANCES
Best - v Hunslet (NL2 - 3,224)
Worst - v Hunslet (NLC - 1,320)
Total (NL2 & NLC only) - 22,999
Average (NL2 & NLC only) - 1,917
(Up by 338 on 2004)

NATIONAL LEAGUE ONE 2005
Round by Round

WEEK 1

Monday 28th March 2005

BARROW RAIDERS 11 WHITEHAVEN 24

RAIDERS: 1 Joel Osborn; 2 Jason Roach; 3 Adrian Mulcahy; 4 Freddie Zitter; 5 James Nixon; 6 Richard Colley; 7 Darren Holt; 8 Andy Fisher; 9 Dave Clark; 10 Paul Wilcock; 11 Mike Whitehead; 12 Glenn Osborn; 13 Phil Atkinson. Subs (all used): 14 Jon Williamson; 15 Anthony Horton; 16 Darren Fisher; 17 Jamie Butler.
Try: Whitehead (32); **Goals:** Holt 3/3; **Field goal:** Holt.
WHITEHAVEN: 1 Gary Broadbent; 2 Craig Calvert; 3 Craig Walsh; 4 Wesley Wilson; 5 John Lebbon; 6 Leroy Joe; 7 Joel Penny; 8 Neil Baynes; 9 Aaron Lester; 10 David Fatialofa; 11 Brett McDermott; 12 Mick Nanyn; 13 Carl Rudd. Subs (all used): 14 Steve Kirkbride; 15 Paul Davidson; 16 Carl Sice; 17 Aaron Summers.
Tries: Walsh (15), Sice (36), Fatialofa (71), Nanyn (75, 79); **Goals:** Nanyn 1/3, Kirkbride 1/2.
Rugby Leaguer & League Express Men of the Match: *Raiders:* Dave Clark; *Whitehaven:* Joel Penny.
Penalty count: 4-8; **Half-time:** 10-10;
Referee: Ben Thaler (Wakefield); **Attendance:** 1,112.

HALIFAX 10 HULL KINGSTON ROVERS 11

HALIFAX: 1 Damian Gibson; 2 James Haley; 3 Jamie Bloem; 4 Andy Spink; 5 Rikki Sheriffe; 6 Dean Lawford; 7 Ben Black; 8 Chris Birchall; 9 Ben Fisher; 10 Jason Boults; 11 David Larder; 12 Wayne Corcoran; 13 Pat Weisner. Subs (all used): 14 Gareth Greenwood; 15 Jode Sheriffe; 16 Ryan McDonald; 17 Fereti Tuilagi.
Try: Haley (74); **Goals:** Bloem 3/3.
ROVERS: 1 Loz Wildbore; 2 Jon Steel; 3 Paul Mansson; 4 Kane Epati; 5 Byron Ford; 6 James Webster; 7 Phil Hasty; 8 Neil Harmon; 9 Paul Pickering; 10 Jamie Bovill; 11 Dale Holdstock; 12 Andy Raleigh; 13 Dwayne Barker. Subs (all used): 14 Mark Blanchard; 15 Andy Ellis; 16 Paul Fletcher; 17 Makali Aizue.
Tries: Ellis (31), Webster (67); **Goals:** Wildbore 1/2;
Field goal: Webster.
Rugby Leaguer & League Express Men of the Match: *Halifax:* Ben Black; *Rovers:* Andy Raleigh.
Penalty count: 11-5; **Half-time:** 4-6;
Referee: Mike Dawber (Wigan); **Attendance:** 2,474.

DONCASTER DRAGONS 10 CASTLEFORD TIGERS 29

DRAGONS: 1 Craig Horne; 2 Dean Colton; 3 Craig Farrell; 4 Dale Cardoza; 5 Craig Miles; 6 Graham Holroyd; 7 Latham Tawhai; 8 Gareth Handford; 9 Craig Cook; 10 Martin Ostler; 11 Andy Hay; 12 Peter Green; 13 Martin Moana. Subs (all used): 14 Ben Cockayne; 15 Craig Lawton; 16 Dean O'Loughlin; 17 Lee Harland.
Tries: Miles (2), Holroyd (26); **Goals:** Holroyd 1/2.
TIGERS: 1 Michael Platt; 2 Tim Robinson; 3 Damien Reid; 4 Jon Hepworth; 5 Michael Shenton; 6 Andy Kain; 7 Paul Handforth; 8 Adam Watene; 9 Andrew Henderson; 10 Frank Watene; 11 Tom Haughey; 12 Steve Crouch; 13 Aaron Smith. Subs (all used): 14 Shaun Lunt; 15 Jordan James; 16 Byron Smith; 17 Alex Rowe.
Tries: Reid (20), Haughey (30), Shenton (63), James (73), Robinson (77);
Goals: A Kain 4/6; **Field goal:** A Kain.
Rugby Leaguer & League Express Men of the Match: *Dragons:* Andy Hay; *Tigers:* Andy Kain.
Penalty count: 7-10; **Half-time:** 10-12;
Referee: Julian King (St Helens); **Attendance:** 3,371.

FEATHERSTONE ROVERS 20 OLDHAM 20

ROVERS: 1 Andy McNally; 2 Nathan Batty; 3 Danny Maun; 4 Richard Newlove; 5 Matthew Wray; 6 Josh Weeden; 7 Dean Ripley; 8 Ian Tonks; 9 Carl Hughes; 10 Nathan Sykes; 11 James Houston; 12 Neil Lowe; 13 Adam Hayes. Subs (all used): 14 Craig Moss; 15 Greg Nicholson; 16 Steve Dooler; 17 Jim Carlton.
Tries: Wray (10), Maun (17), McNally (55), Ripley (62);
Goals: Weeden 2/5.
OLDHAM: 1 Jon Goddard; 2 Gavin Dodd; 3 Will Cowell; 4 Alex Wilkinson; 5 Nick Johnson; 6 Marty Turner; 7 Carlos Mataora; 8 Ricky Bibey; 9 John Hough; 10 Dana Wilson; 11 Simon Haughton; 12 Tere Glassie; 13 Keith Brennan. Subs (three only): 14 Andy Gorey; 15 Mark Roberts (not used); 16 James Kirkland.
Tries: Gorey (29), Cowell (33), Turner (36);
Goals: Turner 4/4.
Rugby Leaguer & League Express Men of the Match: *Rovers:* Nathan Sykes; *Oldham:* Marty Turner.
Penalty count: 5-10; **Half-time:** 8-18;
Referee: Colin Morris (Huddersfield); **Attendance:** 1,463.

Tuesday 29th March 2005

ROCHDALE HORNETS 26 BATLEY BULLDOGS 25

HORNETS: 1 Paul Owen; 2 Chris Campbell; 3 Mark McCully; 4 Richard Varkulis; 5 Chris Giles; 6 Radney Bowker; 7 John Braddish; 8 Tommy Hodgkinson; 9 Dave McConnell; 10 Dave Cuniffe; 11 Andy Gorski; 12 Lee Doran; 13 Phil Farrell. Subs (all used): 14 Sam Butterworth; 15 Rob Ball; 16 Phil Cantillon; 17 Dave Newton.
Tries: Bowker (20, 32), McConnell (48), Varkulis (75);
Goals: McCully 5/6.
BULLDOGS: 1 Craig Lingard; 2 Jamie Stokes; 3 Iain Marsh; 4 Shad Royston; 5 Adrian Flynn; 6 Mark Toohey; 7 Barry Eaton; 8 Craig Wright; 9 Kris Lythe; 10 Joe Berry; 11 Sean Richardson; 12 Dane Morgan; 13 Ryan Horsley. Subs (all used): 14 Mark Sibson; 15 Darren Robinson; 16 Paul Harrison; 17 Gary Shillabeer.
Tries: Flynn (23), Stokes (41, 59), Royston (79);
Goals: Eaton 4/6; **Field goal:** Eaton.
Rugby Leaguer & League Express Men of the Match: *Hornets:* Radney Bowker; *Bulldogs:* Mark Toohey.
Penalty count: 8-8; **Half-time:** 16-8;
Referee: Gareth Hewer (Whitehaven); **Attendance:** 646.

WEEK 2

Sunday 10th April 2005

BATLEY BULLDOGS 50 BARROW RAIDERS 30

BULLDOGS: 1 Craig Lingard; 2 Jamie Stokes; 3 Iain Marsh; 4 Shad Royston; 5 Adrian Flynn; 6 Neil Roden; 7 Barry Eaton; 8 David Rourke; 9 Kris Lythe; 10 Joe Berry; 11 Sean Richardson; 12 Dane Morgan; 13 Mark Toohey. Subs (all used): 14 Mark Sibson; 15 Tim Spears; 16 Darren Robinson; 17 Paul Harrison.
Tries: Morgan (2, 22), Lingard (7, 47), Harrison (31), Flynn (40), Robinson (55, 66), Marsh (72);
Goals: Eaton 7/9.
RAIDERS: 1 Joel Osborn; 2 Jason Roach; 3 Adrian Mulcahy; 4 Freddie Zitter; 5 James Nixon; 6 Richard Colley; 7 Darren Holt; 8 Andy Fisher; 9 Dave Clark; 10 Paul Wilcock; 11 Mike Whitehead; 12 Glenn Osborn; 13 Phil Atkinson. Subs (all used): 14 Alex Muff; 15 Chris Archer; 16 Anthony Horton; 17 Darren Fisher.
Tries: Roach (14), Whitehead (36), Holt (45, 61), D Fisher (53); **Goals:** Holt 5/5.
Rugby Leaguer & League Express Men of the Match: *Bulldogs:* Neil Roden; *Raiders:* Darren Holt.
Penalty count: 6-2; **Half-time:** 28-12;
Referee: Colin Morris (Huddersfield); **Attendance:** 588.

HULL KINGSTON ROVERS 44 FEATHERSTONE ROVERS 30

ROBINS: 1 Phil Hasty; 2 Jon Steel; 3 Kane Epati; 4 Paul Parker; 5 Byron Ford; 6 Paul Mansson; 7 James Webster; 8 Jamie Bovill; 9 Paul Pickering; 10 David Tangata-Toa; 11 Michael Smith; 12 Andy Raleigh; 13 Dwayne Barker. Subs (all used): 14 James Walker; 15 Mark Blanchard; 16 Paul Fletcher; 17 Makali Aizue.
Tries: Ford (4, 32, 38), Tangata-Toa (7), Epati (15), Mansson (39), Parker (63), Blanchard (70);
Goals: Webster 5/8, Steel 1/1.
ROVERS: 1 Nathan Batty; 2 Bryn Powell; 3 Stephen Jones; 4 Richard Newlove; 5 Matthew Wray; 6 Josh Weeden; 7 Liam Finn; 8 James Houston; 9 Andy Kay; 10 Danny Evans; 11 Steve Dooler; 12 Adam Hayes; 13 Dean Ripley. Subs (all used): 14 Craig Moss; 15 Greg Nicholson; 16 Jason Southwell; 17 Neil Lowe.
Tries: Newlove (48), Southwell (50), Weeden (57, 79), Ripley (73); **Goals:** Finn 5/5.
Rugby Leaguer & League Express Men of the Match: *Robins:* Byron Ford; *Rovers:* Josh Weeden.
Penalty count: 7-6; **Half-time:** 34-0;
Referee: Mike Dawber (Wigan); **Attendance:** 2,510.

OLDHAM 22 DONCASTER DRAGONS 44

OLDHAM: 1 Jon Goddard; 2 Gavin Dodd; 3 Will Cowell; 4 Alex Wilkinson; 5 Damian Munro; 6 Simon Svabic; 7 Marty Turner; 8 Dana Wilson; 9 Gareth Barber; 10 Danny Nanyn; 11 Simon Haughton; 12 Tere Glassie; 13 Ian Hodson. Subs (all used): 14 James Kirkland; 15 Andy Gorey; 16 Carlos Mataora; 17 John Hough.
Tries: Goddard (4), Turner (15), Dodd (26), Gorey (47);
Goals: Turner 3/4.
Sin bin: Glassie (57) – fighting.
DRAGONS: 1 Aaron Wood; 2 Wayne Green; 3 Craig Farrell; 4 Dale Cardoza; 5 Craig Miles; 6 Martin Moana; 7 Latham Tawhai; 8 Gareth Handford; 9 Craig Cook; 10 Dean O'Loughlin; 11 Craig Lawton; 12 Peter Green; 13 Andy Hay. Subs (all used): 14 Shaun Leaf; 15 Martin Ostler; 16 Kirk Netherton; 17 Lee Harland.
Tries: Hay (8), Wood (26, 65), Harland (35), Moana (61), Miles (69), Cook (75);
Goals: W Green 7/8, Wood 0/1, Miles 1/1.
Sin bin: Hay (57) - fighting.
Rugby Leaguer & League Express Men of the Match: *Oldham:* Marty Turner; *Dragons:* Martin Moana.
Penalty count: 10-8; **Half-time:** 18-18;
Referee: Julian King (St Helens); **Attendance:** 1,266.

WHITEHAVEN 54 HALIFAX 18

WHITEHAVEN: 1 Gary Broadbent; 2 Craig Calvert; 3 David Seeds; 4 Mick Nanyn; 5 Wesley Wilson; 6 Leroy Joe; 7 Joel Penny; 8 Neil Baynes; 9 Aaron Lester; 10 David Fatialofa; 11 Brett McDermott; 12 Craig Chambers; 13 Carl Rudd. Subs (all used): 14 Steve Kirkbride; 15 Aaron Summers; 16 Carl Sice; 17 Mark Cox.
Tries: Chambers (3, 36), Calvert (19, 76), Nanyn (32), Joe (43), Penny (49), Sice (70, 79); **Goals:** Nanyn 9/11.
HALIFAX: 1 Damian Gibson; 2 James Haley; 3 James Bunyan; 4 Anthony Blackwood; 5 Alan Hadcroft; 6 Wayne Corcoran; 7 Dean Lawford; 8 Chris Morley; 9 Ben Fisher; 10 Chris Birchall; 11 David Larder; 12 Jamie Bloem; 13 Pat Weisner. Subs (all used): 14 Jon Simpson; 15 Jode Sheriffe; 16 Ryan McDonald; 17 Jason Boults.
Tries: Fisher (9), Corcoran (56), Blackwood (65);
Goals: Bloem 3/3.
Dismissal: Bunyan (15) - off the ball challenge.
Sin bin: McDonald (77) - high tackle.
Rugby Leaguer & League Express Men of the Match: *Whitehaven:* Carl Rudd; *Halifax:* Wayne Corcoran.
Penalty count: 8-10; **Half-time:** 26-6;
Referee: Ben Thaler (Wakefield); **Attendance:** 2,159.

CASTLEFORD TIGERS 36 ROCHDALE HORNETS 22

TIGERS: 1 Michael Platt; 2 Waine Pryce; 3 Damien Reid; 4 Jon Hepworth; 5 Michael Shenton; 6 Brad Davis; 7 Andrew Henderson; 8 Adam Watene; 9 Aaron Smith; 10 Byron Smith; 11 Tom Haughey; 12 Jordan James; 13 Steve Crouch. Subs (all used): 14 Dominic Brambani; 15 Craig Huby; 16 Leigh Cooke; 17 Shaun Lunt.
Tries: James (5), Haughey (14), Platt (27), Pryce (38, 67), Hepworth (50), Shenton (61, 77);
Goals: Davis 2/7, Hepworth 0/1, Brambani 0/1.
HORNETS: 1 Chris Giles; 2 Andy Saywell; 3 Mark McCully; 4 Richard Varkulis; 5 Chris Campbell; 6 Radney Bowker; 7 Bobbie Goulding; 8 Tommy Hodgkinson; 9 Dave McConnell; 10 Gareth Price; 11 Andy Gorski; 12 Lee Doran; 13 Phil Farrell. Subs (all used): 14 Lee Birdseye; 15 Dave Newton; 16 Dave Cunliffe; 17 Lee Hansen.
Tries: Bowker (8), Saywell (41), Farrell (70), McCully (72); **Goals:** McCully 3/4.
Dismissal: Cunliffe (76) - punching.
Sin bin: Goulding (66) - dissent.
Rugby Leaguer & League Express Men of the Match: *Tigers:* Brad Davis; *Hornets:* Mark McCully.
Penalty count: 12-9; **Half-time:** 18-4;
Referee: Gareth Hewer (Whitehaven); **Attendance:** 4,776.

WEEK 3

Sunday 17th April 2005

BARROW RAIDERS 24 ROCHDALE HORNETS 20

RAIDERS: 1 Joel Osborn; 2 Jamie Marshall; 3 Jason Roach; 4 Alex Muff; 5 James Nixon; 6 Richard Colley; 7 Darren Holt; 8 Andy Fisher; 9 Dave Clark; 10 Darren Fisher; 11 Mike Whitehead; 12 Anthony Horton; 13 Phil Atkinson. Subs (all used): 14 Glenn Osborn; 15 Stuart Dancer; 16 Chris Archer; 17 Paul Wilcock.
Tries: J Osborn (6), Holt (51), Horton (79);
Goals: Holt 6/6.
HORNETS: 1 Chris Giles; 2 Andy Saywell; 3 Paul Anderson; 4 Richard Varkulis; 5 Chris Campbell; 6 Radney Bowker; 7 Lee Birdseye; 8 Dave Cunliffe; 9 Dave McConnell; 10 Gareth Price; 11 Andy Gorski; 12 Lee Doran; 13 Phil Farrell. Subs (all used): 14 Sam Butterworth; 15 Rob Ball; 16 Phil Cantillon; 17 Dave Newton.
Tries: Saywell (3), Birdseye (39), Giles (69), Bowker (74); **Goals:** Birdseye 2/3, Butterworth 0/1.
Rugby Leaguer & League Express Men of the Match: *Raiders:* Darren Holt; *Hornets:* Gareth Price.
Penalty count: 8-6; **Half-time:** 8-10;
Referee: Ben Thaler (Wakefield); **Attendance:** 814.

DONCASTER DRAGONS 20 HULL KINGSTON ROVERS 36

DRAGONS: 1 Aaron Wood; 2 Dean Colton; 3 Craig Farrell; 4 Dale Cardoza; 5 Craig Miles; 6 Martin Moana; 7 Shaun Leaf; 8 Gareth Handford; 9 Craig Cook; 10 Martin Ostler; 11 Andy Hay; 12 Lee Harland; 13 Peter Green. Subs (all used): 14 Kirk Netherton; 15 Dean O'Loughlin; 16 Dean Andrews; 17 Craig Lawton.
Tries: P Green (21), Lawton (31), Handford (52), Cook (56); **Goals:** Wood 2/4.
ROVERS: 1 Byron Ford; 2 Jon Steel; 3 Paul Parker; 4 Kane Epati; 5 Phil Hasty; 6 Paul Mansson; 7 James Webster; 8 Neil Harmon; 9 Paul Pickering; 10 Makali Aizue; 11 Andy Raleigh; 12 Michael Smith; 13 Dwayne Barker. Subs (all used): 14 Andy Ellis; 15 Jimmy Walker; 16 Jamie Bovill; 17 David Tangata-Toa.
Tries: Raleigh (1), Webster (4), Mansson (34), Steel (39), Ellis (40), Walker (64), Parker (79);
Goals: Webster 2/5, Steel 2/3.
Rugby Leaguer & League Express Men of the Match: *Dragons:* Aaron Wood; *Rovers:* Jon Steel.
Penalty count: 9-6; **Half-time:** 8-26; **Referee:** Karl Kirkpatrick (Warrington); **Attendance:** 1,620.

FEATHERSTONE ROVERS 20 WHITEHAVEN 40

ROVERS: 1 Nathan Batty; 2 Stephen Jones; 3 Danny Maun; 4 Richard Newlove; 5 Bryn Powell; 6 Josh Weeden; 7 Liam Finn; 8 Jason Southwell; 9 Carl Hughes; 10 Nathan Sykes; 11 Steve Dooler; 12 Adam Hayes; 13 Dean Ripley. Subs (all used): 14 Craig Moss; 15 Danny Evans; 16 Ian Tonks; 17 Neil Lowe.
Tries: Maun (6, 76), Dooler (8), Weeden (24);
Goals: Finn 2/4.
WHITEHAVEN: 1 Gary Broadbent; 2 Craig Calvert; 3 David Seeds; 4 Mick Nanyn; 5 Wesley Wilson; 6 Leroy Joe; 7 Steve Kirkbride; 8 Neil Baynes; 9 Aaron Lester; 10 David Fatialofa; 11 Brett McDermott; 12 Craig Chambers; 13 Carl Rudd. Subs (all used): 14 Howard Hill; 15 Aaron Summers; 16 Garry Purdham; 17 Mark Cox.
Tries: Joe (2, 20), Kirkbride (15), Calvert (29), Chambers (63), Purdham (70), Broadbent (72);
Goals: Nanyn 6/8.
Rugby Leaguer & League Express Men of the Match: *Rovers:* Steve Dooler; *Whitehaven:* Leroy Joe.
Penalty count: 13-11; **Half-time:** 14-22;
Referee: Julian King (St Helens); **Attendance:** 1,269.

HALIFAX 38 BATLEY BULLDOGS 16

HALIFAX: 1 Damian Gibson; 2 James Haley; 3 James Bunyan; 4 Anthony Blackwood; 5 Alan Hadcroft; 6 Wayne Corcoran; 7 Danny Jones; 8 Chris Morley; 9 Ben Fisher; 10 Jason Boults; 11 David Larder; 12 Jamie Bloem; 13 Pat Weisner. Subs (all used): 14 Andy Spink; 15 Jon Simpson; 16 Ryan McDonald; 17 Fereti Tuilagi.
Tries: Haley (3, 73), Larder (14, 80), Fisher (20), Blackwood (36), Hadcroft (39), Bunyan (46);

Goals: Bloem 3/4, Corcoran 0/2, Weisner 0/2.
Sin bin: Morley (78) - fighting.
On report: Corcoran (28) - late tackle.
BULLDOGS: 1 Mark Sibson; 2 Jamie Stokes; 3 Iain Marsh; 4 Shad Royston; 5 Adrian Flynn; 6 Neil Roden; 7 Barry Eaton; 8 Craig Wright; 9 Kris Lythe; 10 Joe Berry; 11 Sean Richardson; 12 Paul Harrison; 13 Mark Toohey. Subs (all used): 14 Craig Lingard; 15 David Rourke; 16 Darren Robinson; 17 Tim Spears.
Tries: Royston (23), Spears (51), Harrison (54);
Goals: Eaton 2/3.
Sin bin: Stokes (34) - deliberate offside; Wright (78) - fighting.
Rugby Leaguer & League Express Men of the Match: *Halifax:* James Haley; *Bulldogs:* Tim Spears.
Penalty count: 8-10; **Half-time:** 24-6;
Referee: Gareth Hewer (Whitehaven); **Attendance:** 1,715.

OLDHAM 20 CASTLEFORD TIGERS 32

OLDHAM: 1 Gavin Dodd; 2 Andy Gorey; 3 Damian Munro; 4 Jon Goddard; 5 Nick Johnson; 6 Marty Turner; 7 Carlos Mataora; 8 Ricky Bibey; 9 Gareth Barber; 10 Dana Wilson; 11 Simon Haughton; 12 Mark Roberts; 13 John Hough. Subs (all used): 14 James Kirkland; 15 Simon Svabic; 16 Ian Hodson; 17 David Tootill.
Tries: Johnson (1), Wilson (22), Dodd (56);
Goals: Turner 3/4, Barber 1/1.
TIGERS: 1 Michael Platt; 2 Waine Pryce; 3 Damien Reid; 4 Jon Hepworth; 5 Michael Shenton; 6 Andy Kain; 7 Brad Davis; 8 Adam Watene; 9 Andrew Henderson; 10 Byron Smith; 11 Tom Haughey; 12 Steve Crouch; 13 Aaron Smith. Subs (all used): 14 Tim Robinson; 15 Jordan James; 16 Alex Rowe; 17 Craig Huby.
Tries: Davis (10, 20), Pryce (26, 75), Shenton (37), A Kain (47); **Goals:** A Kain 4/6.
Rugby Leaguer & League Express Men of the Match: *Oldham:* Gareth Barber; *Tigers:* Brad Davis.
Penalty count: 6-5; **Half-time:** 14-22;
Referee: Mike Dawber (Wigan); **Attendance:** 2,054.

WEEK 4

Sunday 24th April 2005

BARROW RAIDERS 22 CASTLEFORD TIGERS 36

RAIDERS: 1 Freddie Zitter; 2 Jamie Marshall; 3 Jason Roach; 4 Alex Muff; 5 James Nixon; 6 Richard Colley; 7 Darren Holt; 8 Andy Fisher; 9 Dave Clark; 10 Darren Fisher; 11 Mike Whitehead; 12 Anthony Horton; 13 Phil Atkinson. Subs (all used): 14 Chris Archer; 15 Stuart Dancer; 16 Joel Osborn; 17 Paul Wilcock.
Tries: Nixon (22), Whitehead (34), Muff (52), Marshall (55); **Goals:** Holt 3/4.
Sin bin: Muff (24) - holding down; Holt (76) - fighting.
TIGERS: 1 Michael Platt; 2 Waine Pryce; 3 Damien Reid; 4 Jon Hepworth; 5 Michael Shenton; 6 Andy Kain; 7 Brad Davis; 8 Adam Watene; 9 Andrew Henderson; 10 Byron Smith; 11 Tom Haughey; 12 Steve Crouch; 13 Aaron Smith. Subs: 14 Stuart Kain (not used); 15 Jordan James; 16 Michael Knowles; 17 Craig Huby.
Tries: Reid (9), Haughey (16, 27), A Watene (61), Pryce (66, 70), Davis (79); **Goals:** A Kain 4/7.
Sin bin: Hepworth (76) - fighting.
Rugby Leaguer & League Express Men of the Match: *Raiders:* Mike Whitehead; *Tigers:* Brad Davis.
Penalty count: 10-7; **Half-time:** 12-16;
Referee: Peter Taberner (Wigan); **Attendance:** 1,816.

BATLEY BULLDOGS 10 FEATHERSTONE ROVERS 18

BULLDOGS: 1 Mark Sibson; 2 Jamie Stokes; 3 Darren Robinson; 4 Shad Royston; 5 Adrian Flynn; 6 Neil Roden; 7 Barry Eaton; 8 Craig Wright; 9 Kris Lythe; 10 Joe Berry; 11 Sean Richardson; 12 Dane Morgan; 13 Paul Harrison. Subs (all used): 14 Craig Lingard; 15 Will Cartledge; 16 Tim Spears; 17 David Rourke.
Tries: Flynn (49), Stokes (52); **Goals:** Eaton 1/3.
Sin bin: Robinson (79) - striking.
ROVERS: 1 Nathan Batty; 2 Danny Kirmond; 3 Danny Maun; 4 Richard Newlove; 5 Bryn Powell; 6 Josh Weeden; 7 Liam Finn; 8 Jason Southwell; 9 Carl Hughes; 10 Nathan Sykes; 11 Steve Dooler; 12 Adam Hayes; 13 Dean Ripley. Subs (all used): 14 Stephen Jones; 15 James Houston; 16 Ian Tonks; 17 Neil Lowe.
Tries: Maun (8), Finn (27), Lowe (64); **Goals:** Finn 3/6.
Rugby Leaguer & League Express Men of the Match: *Bulldogs:* Shad Royston; *Rovers:* Carl Hughes.
Penalty count: 7-9; **Half-time:** 2-10;
Referee: Ben Thaler (Wakefield); **Attendance:** 947.

HULL KINGSTON ROVERS 32 OLDHAM 19

ROVERS: 1 Byron Ford; 2 Jon Steel; 3 Paul Parker; 4 Kane Epati; 5 Leroy Rivett; 6 Paul Mansson; 7 James Webster; 8 David Tangata-Toa; 9 Paul Pickering; 10 Jamie Bovill; 11 Andy Raleigh; 12 Michael Smith; 13 Jimmy Walker. Subs (all used): 14 Andy Ellis; 15 James Garmston; 16 Paul Fletcher; 17 Makali Aizue.
Tries: Raleigh (25, 52), Walker (41), Parker (54), Ellis (58), Mansson (73); **Goals:** Steel 4/6.
Dismissal: Epati (34) - use of the elbow.
Sin bin: Smith (34) - dissent.
OLDHAM: 1 Gavin Dodd; 2 Rob Mills; 3 Damian Munro; 4 Jon Goddard; 5 Nick Johnson; 6 Simon Svabic; 7 Carlos Mataora; 8 Ricky Bibey; 9 Gareth Barber; 10 Dana Wilson; 11 Ian Hodson; 12 Mark Roberts; 13 John Hough. Subs (all used): 14 James Kirkland; 15 David Tootill; 16 Chris Hough; 17 Tere Glassie.
Tries: Dodd (39), Svabic (70), Johnson (78);
Goals: Svabic 3/4; **Field goal:** Svabic.
Sin bin: Munro (45) - interference.
Rugby Leaguer & League Express Men of the Match: *Rovers:* James Webster; *Oldham:* Ricky Bibey.
Penalty count: 11-7; **Half-time:** 6-9;
Referee: Gareth Hewer (Whitehaven); **Attendance:** 2,474.

ROCHDALE HORNETS 22 HALIFAX 19

HORNETS: 1 Paul Owen; 2 Andy Saywell; 3 Mark McCully; 4 Richard Varkulis; 5 Chris Giles; 6 Radney Bowker; 7 John Braddish; 8 Rob Ball; 9 Phil Cantillon; 10 Gareth Price; 11 Phil Farrell; 12 Lee Doran; 13 Andy Gorski. Subs (all used): 14 Bobbie Goulding; 15 Dave Newton; 16 David Alstead; 17 John Hill.
Tries: Giles (5), Goulding (58), Saywell (65), Bowker (80); **Goals:** McCully 3/5.
Sin bin: Giles (63) – holding down.
HALIFAX: 1 Damian Gibson; 2 James Haley; 3 James Bunyan; 4 Anthony Blackwood; 5 Rikki Sheriffe; 6 Wayne Corcoran; 7 Danny Jones; 8 Chris Morley; 9 Ben Fisher; 10 Jason Boults; 11 David Larder; 12 Andy Spink; 13 Pat Weisner. Subs (all used): 14 Alan Hadcroft; 15 Jamie Bloem; 16 Ryan McDonald; 17 Jon Simpson.
Tries: Gibson (11), Haley (18), Hadcroft (36);
Goals: Jones 3/5; **Field goal:** Jones.
Sin bin: McDonald (42) – dissent.
Rugby Leaguer & League Express Men of the Match: *Hornets:* John Hill; *Halifax:* Danny Jones.
Penalty count: 6-4; **Half-time:** 6-16;
Referee: Steve Ganson (St Helens); **Attendance:** 1,201.

WHITEHAVEN 20 DONCASTER DRAGONS 6

WHITEHAVEN: 1 Gary Broadbent; 2 Craig Calvert; 3 David Seeds; 4 Mick Nanyn; 5 Wesley Wilson; 6 Leroy Joe; 7 Steve Kirkbride; 8 Aaron Summers; 9 Aaron Lester; 10 David Fatialofa; 11 Brett McDermott; 12 Howard Hill; 13 Carl Rudd. Subs (all used): 14 Garry Purdham; 15 Chris McKinney; 16 Mark Cox; 17 Carl Sice.
Tries: Summers (20), Wilson (34), Calvert (46), Rudd (68); **Goals:** Nanyn 2/4.
Sin bin: Summers (20) - ungentlemanly conduct.
DRAGONS: 1 Shaun Leaf; 2 Dean Colton; 3 Craig Farrell; 4 Martin Moana; 5 Aaron Wood; 6 Graham Holroyd; 7 Latham Tawhai; 8 Gareth Handford; 9 Craig Cook; 10 Craig Lawton; 11 Andy Hay; 12 Lee Harland; 13 Peter Green. Subs (all used): 14 Ben Cockayne; 15 Dean O'Loughlin; 16 Dean Andrews; 17 Martin Ostler.
Try: Cockayne (72); **Goals:** Holroyd 1/1.
Rugby Leaguer & League Express Men of the Match: *Whitehaven:* Aaron Summers; *Dragons:* Lee Harland.
Penalty count: 7-7; **Half time:** 10-0;
Referee: Colin Morris (Huddersfield); **Attendance:** 1,945.

WEEK 5

Sunday 15th May 2005

DONCASTER DRAGONS 35 BATLEY BULLDOGS 28

DRAGONS: 1 Ben Cockayne; 2 Dean Colton; 3 Craig Farrell; 4 Shaun Leaf; 5 Craig Miles; 6 Graham Holroyd; 7 Latham Tawhai; 8 Dean O'Loughlin; 9 Craig Cook; 10 Martin Ostler; 11 Dean Andrews; 12 Peter Green; 13 Craig Lawton. Subs (all used): 14 Gareth Handford; 15 Kirk Netherton; 16 Martin Moana; 17 Lee Harland.
Tries: Moana (22), Holroyd (25), Cockayne (29, 55, 58), Colton (31); **Goals:** Holroyd 5/7; **Field goal:** Cook.
BULLDOGS: 1 Craig Lingard; 2 Mark Sibson; 3 Iain Marsh; 4 Shad Royston; 5 Adrian Flynn; 6 Neil Roden; 7 Barry Eaton; 8 Dane Morgan; 9 Darren Robinson; 10 Joe Berry; 11 Sean Richardson; 12 Gary Shillabeer; 13 Mark Toohey. Subs (all used): 14 Matt Pennington; 15 Paul Harrison; 16 Tim Spears; 17 Will Cartledge.
Tries: Eaton (1), Sibson (46), Marsh (50), Morgan (64), Robinson (70); **Goals:** Eaton 4/5.
Rugby Leaguer & League Express Men of the Match: *Dragons:* Ben Cockayne; *Bulldogs:* Iain Marsh.
Penalty count: 3-1; **Half-time:** 20-6;
Referee: Colin Morris (Huddersfield); **Attendance:** 653.

FEATHERSTONE ROVERS 30 ROCHDALE HORNETS 30

ROVERS: 1 Nathan Batty; 2 Danny Kirmond; 3 Danny Maun; 4 Richard Newlove; 5 Bryn Powell; 6 Josh Weeden; 7 Liam Finn; 8 Ian Tonks; 9 Carl Hughes; 10 Nathan Sykes; 11 Steve Dooler; 12 Neil Lowe; 13 Adam Hayes. Subs (all used): 14 Andy McNally; 15 Danny Evans; 16 James Houston; 17 Jim Carlton.
Tries: Kirmond (2, 74), Powell (41), Finn (46, 49);
Goals: Finn 5/6.
HORNETS: 1 Paul Owen; 2 Andy Saywell; 3 Mark McCully; 4 David Alstead; 5 Chris Giles; 6 Radney Bowker; 7 John Braddish; 8 Rob Ball; 9 Dave McConnell; 10 Gareth Price; 11 Richard Varkulis; 12 Lee Doran; 13 Andy Gorski. Subs (all used): 14 Sam Butterworth; 15 Dave Cunliffe; 16 Paul Anderson; 17 John Hill.
Tries: Owen (13), Gorski (16), Saywell (36, 61), Ball (57), Varkulis (73, 77); **Goals:** McCully 1/8.
Dismissal: Hill (38) - striking.
Rugby Leaguer & League Express Men of the Match: *Rovers:* Liam Finn; *Hornets:* Lee Doran.
Penalty count: 9-6; **Half-time:** 6-12;
Referee: Ben Thaler (Wakefield); **Attendance:** 1,250.

HALIFAX 48 BARROW RAIDERS 26

HALIFAX: 1 Jamie Bloem; 2 James Haley; 3 James Bunyan; 4 Alan Hadcroft; 5 Rikki Sheriffe; 6 Wayne Corcoran; 7 Danny Jones; 8 Chris Morley; 9 Ben Fisher; 10 Ryan McDonald; 11 David Larder; 12 Andy Spink; 13 Pat Weisner. Subs (all used): 14 Steve Booth; 15 Damian Ball; 16 Andy Hobson; 17 Jason Boults.
Tries: Fisher (5, 23), Weisner (29, 62), Corcoran (36), Jones (43), Spink (50), Bloem (59), R Sheriffe (66);
Goals: Bloem 6/9.
RAIDERS: 1 Joel Osborn; 2 Jamie Marshall; 3 Shane Irabor; 4 Freddie Zitter; 5 James Nixon; 6 Richard Colley; 7 Darren Holt; 8 Jamie Butler; 9 Dave Clark; 10 Stuart Dancer; 11 Anthony Horton; 12 Glenn Osborn; 13 Mike Whitehead. Subs (all used): 14 Chris Archer; 15 Jon Williamson; 16 Ryan Campbell; 17 Paul Raftrey.
Tries: Zitter (9), Nixon (39), Raftrey (68), J Osborn (78);
Goals: Holt 5/5.
Rugby Leaguer & League Express Men of the Match: *Halifax:* Ben Fisher; *Raiders:* Darren Holt.
Penalty count: 9-6; **Half-time:** 22-14;
Referee: Mike Dawber (Wigan), replaced by Matthew Kidd (Castleford) (40); **Attendance:** 1,446.

OLDHAM 6 WHITEHAVEN 60

OLDHAM: 1 Gavin Dodd; 2 Rob Mills; 3 Alex Wilkinson; 4 Jon Goddard; 5 Nick Johnson; 6 Marty Turner; 7 Carlos Mataora; 8 Ricky Bibey; 9 Gareth Barber; 10 Dana Wilson; 11 Mark Roberts; 12 Tere Glassie; 13 John Hough. Subs (all used): 14 Chris Hough; 15 Simon Haughton; 16 Simon Svabic; 17 Adam Sharples.
Try: Svabic (31); **Goals:** Turner 1/1.
WHITEHAVEN: 1 Gary Broadbent; 2 Craig Calvert; 3 David Seeds; 4 Mick Nanyn; 5 Wesley Wilson; 6 Leroy Joe; 7 Joel Penny; 8 Neil Baynes; 9 Aaron Lester; 10 David Fatialofa; 11 Brett McDermott; 12 Howard Hill; 13 Carl Rudd. Subs (all used): 14 Steve Kirkbride; 15 Aaron Summers; 16 Carl Sice; 17 Chris McKinney.
Tries: Calvert (4, 23), Broadbent (12), Seeds (19), Nanyn (42, 62), Penny (48), Lester (57), Sice (71), Hill (73), Kirkbride (75); **Goals:** Nanyn 5/8, Kirkbride 3/3.
Rugby Leaguer & League Express Men of the Match: *Oldham:* Gavin Dodd; *Whitehaven:* Joel Penny.
Penalty count: 8-3; **Half-time:** 6-22;
Referee: Peter Taberner (Wigan); **Attendance:** 1,284.

CASTLEFORD TIGERS 32 HULL KINGSTON ROVERS 26

TIGERS: 1 Jon Hepworth; 2 Waine Pryce; 3 Damien Reid; 4 Deon Bird; 5 Michael Shenton; 6 Andy Kain; 9 Andrew Henderson; 8 Adam Watene; 13 Aaron Smith; 10 Byron Smith; 11 Tom Haughey; 12 Steve Crouch; 14 Richard Fletcher. Subs (all used): 7 Brad Davis; 15 Craig Huby; 16 Jordan James; 17 Paul Handforth.
Tries: Bird (14), Davis (19, 36), A Kain (32), Huby (53), A Watene (61); **Goals:** A Kain 1/3, Huby 3/3.
ROVERS: 1 Leroy Rivett; 2 Jon Steel; 3 Paul Parker; 4 Kane Epati; 5 Byron Ford; 6 Paul Mansson; 7 James Webster; 8 Neil Harmon; 9 Paul Pickering; 10 David Tangata-Toa; 11 Andy Raleigh; 12 Michael Smith; 13 Mark Blanchard. Subs (all used): 14 Andy Ellis; 15 James Garmston; 16 Jamie Bovill; 17 Makali Aizue.
Tries: Mansson (4), Raleigh (26), Epati (40, 58, 72);
Goals: Steel 3/5.
Rugby Leaguer & League Express Men of the Match: *Tigers:* Adam Watene; *Rovers:* Kane Epati.
Penalty count: 9-7; **Half-time:** 20-16;
Referee: Julian King (St Helens); **Attendance:** 8,078.

WEEK 6

Sunday 22nd May 2005

BARROW RAIDERS 16 FEATHERSTONE ROVERS 38

RAIDERS: 1 Joel Osborn; 2 Jamie Marshall; 3 Shane Irabor; 4 Freddie Zitter; 5 Jason Roach; 6 Jon Williamson; 7 Darren Holt; 8 Paul Raftrey; 9 Dave Clark; 10 Paul Wilcock; 11 Mike Whitehead; 12 Ryan Campbell; 13 Richard Colley. Subs (all used): 14 Jamie Butler; 15 Darren Fisher; 16 Chris Archer; 17 Adrian Mulcahy.
Tries: Zitter (27), Mulcahy (76);
Goals: Holt 3/3, J Osborn 1/1.
ROVERS: 1 Nathan Batty; 2 Danny Kirmond; 3 Danny Maun; 4 Richard Newlove; 5 Bryn Powell; 6 Josh Weeden; 7 Liam Finn; 8 Ian Tonks; 9 Carl Hughes; 10 Nathan Sykes; 11 Steve Dooler; 12 Neil Lowe; 13 Adam Hayes. Subs (all used): 14 Andy McNally; 15 Andrew Georgiadis; 16 Danny Evans; 17 Jim Carlton.
Tries: Maun (7), C Hughes (21, 51), Newlove (46), Powell (57), McNally (70), Weeden (74); **Goals:** Finn 5/7.
Rugby Leaguer & League Express Men of the Match: *Raiders:* Freddie Zitter; *Rovers:* Andrew Georgiadis.
Penalty count: 6-4; **Half-time:** 10-10;
Referee: Peter Taberner (Wigan); **Attendance:** 1,008.

BATLEY BULLDOGS 25 OLDHAM 18

BULLDOGS: 1 Mark Sibson; 2 Jamie Stokes; 3 Matt Pennington; 4 Shad Royston; 5 Adrian Flynn; 6 Neil Roden; 7 Barry Eaton; 8 Dane Morgan; 9 Darren Robinson; 10 Joe Berry; 11 Iain Marsh; 12 David Rourke; 13 Mark Toohey. Subs (all used): 14 Kris Lythe; 15 Paul Harrison; 16 Tim Spears; 17 Sean Richardson.
Tries: Pennington (20), Morgan (22), Toohey (25), Marsh (52); **Goals:** Eaton 4/6; **Field goal:** Roden.
OLDHAM: 1 Gavin Dodd; 2 Rob Mills; 3 Damian Munro; 4 Alex Wilkinson; 5 Nick Johnson; 6 Simon Svabic; 7 Marty Turner; 8 Ricky Bibey; 9 James Kirkland; 10 Andy Sands; 11 Mark Roberts; 12 Tere Glassie; 13 Carlos Mataora. Subs (all used): 14 John Hough; 15 Adam Sharples; 16 Dana Wilson; 17 Gareth Barber.
Tries: Johnson (35), Glassie (45), Munro (64);
Goals: Turner 3/3.
Rugby Leaguer & League Express Men of the Match: *Bulldogs:* Neil Roden; *Oldham:* Ricky Bibey.
Penalty count: 11-7; **Half-time:** 18-6;
Referee: Phil Bentham (Warrington); **Attendance:** 792.

HALIFAX 16 CASTLEFORD TIGERS 48

HALIFAX: 1 Damian Gibson; 2 James Haley; 3 James Bunyan; 4 Anthony Blackwood; 5 Rikki Sheriffe; 6 Wayne Corcoran; 7 Pat Weisner; 8 Andy Hobson; 9 Ben Fisher; 10 Jason Boults; 11 David Larder; 12 Andy Spink; 13 Damian Ball. Subs (all used): 14 Jamie Bloem; 15 Chris Morley; 16 Ryan McDonald; 17 Fereti Tuilagi.
Tries: Ball (29), R Sheriffe (43, 58);
Goals: Weisner 2/3, Bloem 0/1.
TIGERS: 1 Michael Platt; 2 Waine Pryce; 3 Deon Bird; 4 Jon Hepworth; 5 Michael Shenton; 6 Andy Kain; 7 Brad Davis; 8 Adam Watene; 9 Andrew Henderson; 10 Richard Fletcher; 11 Tom Haughey; 12 Craig Huby; 13 Steve Crouch. Subs (all used): 14 Andy Bailey; 15 Byron Smith; 16 Paul Handforth; 17 Jordan James.
Tries: Bird (2), Henderson (10), Shenton (13, 26), Haughey (22), Pryce (35, 50), Hepworth (39), Huby (77); **Goals:** Huby 5/7, A Kain 1/3.
Sin bin: Haughey (69) - professional foul.
Rugby Leaguer & League Express Men of the Match: *Halifax:* Ben Fisher; *Tigers:* Brad Davis.
Penalty count: 2-3; **Half-time:** 6-38; **Referee:** Colin Morris (Huddersfield); **Attendance:** 3,259.

ROCHDALE HORNETS 24 DONCASTER DRAGONS 34

HORNETS: 1 Chris Giles; 2 Andy Saywell; 3 Mark McCully; 4 David Alstead; 5 Chris Campbell; 6 Radney Bowker; 7 John Braddish; 8 Rob Ball; 9 Dave McConnell; 10 Gareth Price; 11 Richard Varkulis; 12 Lee Doran; 13 Andy Gorski. Subs (all used): 14 Sam Butterworth; 15 Tommy Hodgkinson; 16 Dave Cunliffe; 17 John Hill.
Tries: Price (55), Alstead (59), Campbell (62), Butterworth (71); **Goals:** McCully 4/5.
DRAGONS: 1 Ben Cockayne; 2 Dean Colton; 3 Marvin Golden; 4 Craig Farrell; 5 Craig Miles; 6 Graham Holroyd; 7 Latham Tawhai; 8 Gareth Handford; 9 Craig Cook; 10 Lee Harland; 11 Craig Lawton; 12 Peter Green; 13 Martin Moana. Subs (all used): 14 Danny Mills; 15 Tom Buckenham; 16 Martin Ostler; 17 Dean Andrews.
Tries: Harland (10), Miles (12), Cockayne (26), Farrell (34, 69), Lawton (47); **Goals:** Holroyd 5/7.
Rugby Leaguer & League Express Men of the Match: *Hornets:* Andy Gorski; *Dragons:* Graham Holroyd.
Penalty count: 12-9; **Half-time:** 2-20;
Referee: Julian King (St Helens); **Attendance:** 806.

WHITEHAVEN 51 HULL KINGSTON ROVERS 0

WHITEHAVEN: 1 Gary Broadbent; 2 Craig Calvert; 3 David Seeds; 4 Mick Nanyn; 5 Wesley Wilson; 6 Leroy Joe; 7 Joel Penny; 8 Neil Baynes; 9 Aaron Lester; 10 David Fatialofa; 11 Brett McDermott; 12 Howard Hill; 13 Carl Rudd. Subs (all used): 14 Steve Kirkbride; 15 Aaron Summers; 16 Carl Sice; 17 Spencer Miller.
Tries: Seeds (3, 69), Hill (26, 34, 53), Fatialofa (38), Broadbent (56), Sice (61), Joe (73);
Goals: Nanyn 7/10; **Field goal:** Penny.
ROVERS: 1 Leroy Rivett; 2 Jon Steel; 3 Paul Parker; 4 Kane Epati; 5 Byron Ford; 6 Paul Mansson; 7 James Webster; 8 Makali Aizue; 9 Paul Pickering; 10 David Tangata-Toa; 11 Andy Raleigh; 12 Michael Smith; 13 Dwayne Barker. Subs (all used): 14 Mark Blanchard; 15 Craig Poucher; 16 Gareth Morton; 17 Andy Ellis.
Rugby Leaguer & League Express Men of the Match: *Whitehaven:* Leroy Joe; *Rovers:* Makali Aizue.
Penalty count: 17-5; **Half time:** 22-0;
Referee: Ben Thaler (Wakefield); **Attendance:** 2,604.

WEEK 7

Sunday 5th June 2005

DONCASTER DRAGONS 42 BARROW RAIDERS 12

DRAGONS: 1 Ben Cockayne; 2 Dean Colton; 3 Marvin Golden; 4 Craig Farrell; 5 Wayne Green; 6 Graham Holroyd; 7 Latham Tawhai; 8 Gareth Handford; 9 Craig Cook; 10 Martin Ostler; 11 Lee Harland; 12 Craig Lawton; 13 Martin Moana. Subs (all used): 14 Aaron Wood; 15 Dean O'Loughlin; 16 Karl Mills; 17 Craig Miles.
Tries: Golden (12), Lawton (19), Farrell (29), Cook (45, 72), Harland (49), Colton (56); **Goals:** Holroyd 7/7.
RAIDERS: 1 Joel Osborn; 2 Jamie Marshall; 3 Shane Irabor; 4 Freddie Zitter; 5 Jason Roach; 6 Richard Colley; 7 Darren Holt; 8 Paul Wilcock; 9 Dave Clark; 10 Ryan Tandy; 11 Anthony Horton; 12 Ryan Wood; 13 Mike Whitehead. Subs (all used): 14 Paul Raftrey; 15 Ryan Campbell; 16 Chris Archer; 17 Alex Muff.
Tries: Horton (10), Whitehead (40); **Goals:** Holt 2/4.
Rugby Leaguer & League Express Men of the Match: *Dragons:* Martin Ostler; *Raiders:* Ryan Tandy.
Penalty count: 15-8; **Half-time:** 18-12;
Referee: Jamie Leahy (Dewsbury); **Attendance:** 686.

FEATHERSTONE ROVERS 28 HALIFAX 38

ROVERS: 1 Craig Moss; 2 Danny Kirmond; 3 Nathan Batty; 4 Richard Newlove; 5 Bryn Powell; 6 Josh Weeden; 7 Liam Finn; 8 Danny Evans; 9 Carl Hughes; 10 Nathan Sykes; 11 Steve Dooler; 12 Neil Lowe; 13 Adam Hayes. Subs (all used): 14 Andrew Georgiadis; 15 James Houston; 16 Greg Nicholson; 17 Jim Carlton.
Tries: Powell (13), Georgiadis (42), Hayes (33), Kirmond (47), Dooler (70); **Goals:** Finn 4/5.
HALIFAX: 1 Damian Gibson; 2 James Haley; 3 Alan Hadcroft; 4 Jamie Bloem; 5 Rikki Sheriffe; 6 Pat Weisner; 7 Dean Lawford; 8 Chris Morley; 9 Ben Fisher; 10 Jason Boults; 11 Fereti Tuilagi; 12 Andy Spink; 13 Damian Ball. Subs (all used): 14 Jon Simpson; 15 Ben Black; 16 Ryan McDonald; 17 James Bunyan.
Tries: Haley (8), Weisner (50), Black (56), Morley (65), R Sheriffe (76), Fisher (79); **Goals:** Bloem 7/7.
Rugby Leaguer & League Express Men of the Match: *Rovers:* Liam Finn; *Halifax:* Dean Lawford.
Penalty count: 7-10; **Half-time:** 12-8; **Referee:** Gareth Hewer (Whitehaven); **Attendance:** 1,461.

HULL KINGSTON ROVERS 15 BATLEY BULLDOGS 6

ROVERS: 1 Leroy Rivett; 2 Alasdair McClarron; 3 Craig Poucher; 4 Paul Mansson; 5 Byron Ford; 6 James Webster; 7 Phil Hasty; 8 Makali Aizue; 9 Andy Ellis; 10 David Tangata-Toa; 11 Andy Raleigh; 12 Jason Netherton; 13 Gareth Morton. Subs (all used): 14 Mark Blanchard; 15 Jamie Bovill; 16 Paul Fletcher; 17 Neil Harmon.
Tries: Ellis (43), Mansson (55), Blanchard (70);
Goals: Morton 1/3; **Field goal:** Hasty.
BULLDOGS: 1 Mark Sibson; 2 Jamie Stokes; 3 Matt Pennington; 4 Shad Royston; 5 Adrian Flynn; 6 Neil Roden; 7 Barry Eaton; 8 Dane Morgan; 9 Darren Robinson; 10 Joe Berry; 11 Iain Marsh; 12 David Rourke; 13 Mark Toohey. Subs (all used): 14 Tim Spears; 15 Paul Harrison; 16 Kris Lythe; 17 Martin McLoughlin.
Try: Toohey (15); **Goals:** Eaton 1/2.
Rugby Leaguer & League Express Men of the Match: *Rovers:* Andy Ellis; *Bulldogs:* Neil Roden.
Penalty count: 8-6; **Half-time:** 0-4;
Referee: Peter Taberner (Wigan); **Attendance:** 2,084.

OLDHAM 25 ROCHDALE HORNETS 24

OLDHAM: 1 Gavin Dodd; 2 Damian Munro; 3 Alex Wilkinson; 4 Jon Goddard; 5 Nick Johnson; 6 Marty Turner; 7 Chris Hough; 8 Ricky Bibey; 9 James Kirkland; 10 Dana Wilson; 11 Ian Hodson; 12 Tere Glassie; 13 Simon Svabic. Subs (all used): 14 John Hough; 15 Carlos Mataora; 16 Andy Sands; 17 Adam Sharples.
Tries: Wilkinson (32), C Hough (37), Dodd (42);
Goals: Turner 6/6; **Field goal:** Turner.
HORNETS: 1 Chris Giles; 2 Andy Saywell; 3 Mark McCully; 4 David Alstead; 5 Chris Campbell; 6 Radney Bowker; 7 Bobbie Goulding; 8 Tommy Hodgkinson; 9 Phil Cantillon; 10 Gareth Price; 11 Richard Varkulis; 12 Lee Doran; 13 Andy Gorski. Subs (all used): 14 Sam Butterworth; 15 Dave Newton; 16 John Braddish; 17 Rob Ball.
Try: Campbell (11, 72), Varkulis (51), Butterworth (69), Giles (78); **Goals:** McCully 0/2, Goulding 2/3.
Rugby Leaguer & League Express Men of the Match: *Oldham:* Marty Turner; *Hornets:* Gareth Price.
Penalty count: 10-10; **Half-time:** 16-4;
Referee: Steve Nicholson (Whitehaven);
Attendance: 827 *(at Park Lane, Sedgley Park).*

CASTLEFORD TIGERS 42 WHITEHAVEN 24

TIGERS: 1 Michael Platt; 2 Waine Pryce; 3 Deon Bird; 4 Jon Hepworth; 5 Michael Shenton; 6 Paul Handforth; 7 Brad Davis; 8 Adam Watene; 9 Andrew Henderson; 10 Richard Fletcher; 11 Tom Haughey; 12 Steve Crouch; 13 Aaron Smith. Subs (all used): 14 Craig Huby; 15 Byron Smith; 16 Andy Bailey; 17 Frank Watene.
Tries: Pryce (4, 19), Crouch (15), Platt (24), Hepworth (28, 30), Bird (37), Haughey (48);
Goals: Handforth 1/3, Fletcher 2/3, Huby 2/2.
WHITEHAVEN: 1 Gary Broadbent; 2 Craig Calvert; 3 Wesley Wilson; 4 Mick Nanyn; 5 John Lebbon; 6 Leroy Joe; 7 Joel Penny; 8 Mark Cox; 9 Aaron Lester; 10 David Fatialofa; 11 Brett McDermott; 12 Howard Hill; 13 Carl Rudd. Subs (all used): 14 Steve Kirkbride; 15 Paul Davidson; 16 Carl Sice; 17 Graeme Morton.
Tries: Wilson (7), Fatialofa (26), Sice (57), Lester (74);
Goals: Nanyn 4/4.
Sin bin: Davidson (26) – high tackle.
Rugby Leaguer & League Express Men of the Match: *Tigers:* Andrew Henderson; *Whitehaven:* David Fatialofa.
Penalty count: 11-9; **Half-time:** 36-12;
Referee: Phil Bentham (Warrington); **Attendance:** 7,323.

WEEK 8

Sunday 12th June 2005

BARROW RAIDERS 22 OLDHAM 40

RAIDERS: 1 Nick Beech; 2 Jamie Marshall; 3 Shane Irabor; 4 Freddie Zitter; 5 James Nixon; 6 Joel Osborn; 7 Darren Holt; 8 Andy Fisher; 9 Richard Colley; 10 Ryan Tandy; 11 Anthony Horton; 12 Ryan Wood; 13 Mike Whitehead. Subs (all used): 14 James Finch; 15 Stuart Dancer; 16 Jamie Butler; 17 Matt Jefferson.
Tries: Colley (36), Zitter (39), Wood (58), J Osborn (70);
Goals: Holt 3/4.
OLDHAM: 1 Gavin Dodd; 2 Damian Munro; 3 Alex Wilkinson; 4 Jon Goddard; 5 Nick Johnson; 6 Marty Turner; 7 Chris Hough; 8 Ricky Bibey; 9 James Kirkland; 10 Dana Wilson; 11 Ian Hodson; 12 Tere Glassie; 13 Simon Svabic. Subs (all used): 14 Carlos Mataora; 15 Mark Roberts; 16 Adam Sharples; 17 Gareth Barber.
Tries: Johnson (5, 22), Turner (14), Svabic (19), Wilkinson (25), Munro (43), Wilson (65);
Goals: Turner 6/7.
Rugby Leaguer & League Express Men of the Match: *Raiders:* Darren Holt; *Oldham:* Marty Turner.
Penalty count: 4-2; **Half-time:** 12-28;
Referee: Peter Taberner (Wigan); **Attendance:** 1,073.

BATLEY BULLDOGS 8 WHITEHAVEN 18

BULLDOGS: 1 Mark Sibson; 2 Jamie Stokes; 3 Shad Royston; 4 Alex Muff; 5 Aiden Lister; 6 Neil Roden; 7 Barry Eaton; 8 Dane Morgan; 9 Joe Berry; 10 Martin McLoughlin; 11 Sean Richardson; 12 Gary Shillabeer; 13 Iain Marsh. Subs (all used): 14 Craig Lingard; 15 Paul Harrison; 16 Tim Spears; 17 Will Cartledge.
Try: Stokes (20); **Goals:** Eaton 2/4.
WHITEHAVEN: 1 Wesley Wilson; 2 Paul O'Neil; 3 David Seeds; 4 Mick Nanyn; 5 John Lebbon; 6 Leroy Joe; 7 Joel Penny; 8 Aaron Summers; 9 Aaron Lester; 10 David Fatialofa; 11 Brett McDermott; 12 Howard Hill; 13 Carl Rudd. Subs (all used): 14 Graeme Morton; 15 Paul Davidson; 16 Carl Sice; 17 Mark Cox.
Tries: Nanyn (13, 40, 48), Seeds (57); **Goals:** Nanyn 1/6.
Rugby Leaguer & League Express Men of the Match: *Bulldogs:* Dane Morgan; *Whitehaven:* Mick Nanyn.
Penalty count: 11-9; **Half-time:** 8-8;
Referee: Jamie Leahy (Dewsbury); **Attendance:** 653.

FEATHERSTONE ROVERS 34 CASTLEFORD TIGERS 38

ROVERS: 1 Craig Moss; 2 Danny Kirmond; 3 Nathan Batty; 4 Richard Newlove; 5 Bryn Powell; 6 Josh Weeden; 7 Liam Finn; 8 Ian Tonks; 9 Carl Hughes; 10 James Houston; 11 Adam Hayes; 12 Neil Lowe; 13 Steve Dooler. Subs (all used): 14 Andrew Georgiadis; 15 Danny Evans; 16 Greg Nicholson; 17 Jim Carlton.
Tries: Finn (8), Dooler (20), C Hughes (26), Weeden (35), Finn (53); **Goals:** Finn 7/7.
TIGERS: 1 Michael Platt; 2 Waine Pryce; 3 Deon Bird; 4 Jon Hepworth; 5 Michael Shenton; 6 Paul Handforth; 7 Brad Davis; 8 Andy Bailey; 9 Andrew Henderson; 10 Richard Fletcher; 11 Craig Huby; 12 Jordan James; 13 Aaron Smith. Subs (all used): 14 Tom Haughey; 15 Steve Crouch; 16 Byron Smith; 17 Frank Watene.
Tries: Handforth (2), Henderson (29), Huby (47), Pryce (57), James (68), Shenton (75);
Goals: Huby 6/7, Fletcher 1/1.
Rugby Leaguer & League Express Men of the Match: *Rovers:* Liam Finn; *Tigers:* Aaron Smith.
Penalty count: 8-10; **Half-time:** 26-14;
Referee: Ben Thaler (Wakefield); **Attendance:** 3,334.

HALIFAX 36 DONCASTER DRAGONS 16

HALIFAX: 1 Steve Booth; 2 James Haley; 3 Damian Gibson; 4 Anthony Blackwood; 5 Rikki Sheriffe; 6 Pat Weisner; 7 Dean Lawford; 8 Chris Morley; 9 Ben Fisher; 10 Jason Boults; 11 David Larder; 17 Fereti Tuilagi; 13 Damian Ball. Subs (all used): 14 Ben Black; 15 Jamie Bloem; 16 Ryan McDonald; 12 Scott Law.
Tries: Fisher (24), Larder (34), Black (39), Haley (46, 67), R Sheriffe (63); **Goals:** Booth 2/2, Bloem 4/6.
DRAGONS: 1 Ben Cockayne; 2 Karl Mills; 3 Marvin Golden; 4 Craig Farrell; 5 Craig Miles; 6 Martin Moana; 7 Graham Holroyd; 8 Gareth Handford; 9 Craig Cook; 10 Martin Ostler; 11 Lee Harland; 12 Craig Lawton; 13 Aaron Wood. Subs (all used): 14 Shaun Leaf; 15 Karl Mills; 16 Dean O'Loughlin; 17 Kirk Netherton.
Tries: Moana (14, 56), Golden (73); **Goals:** Holroyd 2/3.
On report: Golden (21) - alleged biting.
Rugby Leaguer & League Express Men of the Match: *Halifax:* Ryan McDonald; *Dragons:* Karl Mills.
Penalty count: 11-7; **Half-time:** 16-6;
Referee: Phil Bentham (Warrington); **Attendance:** 1,737.

HULL KINGSTON ROVERS 45 ROCHDALE HORNETS 12

ROVERS: 1 Leroy Rivett; 2 Alasdair McClarron; 3 Paul Parker; 4 Gareth Morton; 5 Byron Ford; 6 Paul Mansson; 7 James Webster; 8 Jason Netherton; 9 Andy Ellis; 10 David Tangata-Toa; 11 Andy Raleigh; 12 Michael Smith; 13 Dale Holdstock. Subs (all used): 14 Phil Hasty; 15 Kane Epati; 16 Jamie Bovill; 17 Makali Aizue.
Tries: Webster (5), Ford (15), Smith (24), Hasty (43), McClarron (65), Rivett (69); **Goals:** Morton 10/11;
Field goal: Webster.
HORNETS: 1 Chris Giles; 2 Sam Butterworth; 3 Mark McCully; 4 Richard Varkulis; 5 Chris Campbell; 6 Radney Bowker; 7 John Braddish; 8 Tommy Hodgkinson; 9 Phil Cantillon; 10 Gareth Price; 11 Andy Gorski; 12 Lee Doran; 13 Dave McConnell. Subs (all used): 14 Phil Farrell; 15 Rob Ball; 16 Dave Newton; 17 John Hill.
Tries: Price (2), Butterworth (10); **Goals:** McCully 2/2.
Rugby Leaguer & League Express Men of the Match: *Rovers:* Michael Smith; *Hornets:* Mark McCully.
Penalty count: 13-13; **Half-time:** 24-12;
Referee: Gareth Hewer (Whitehaven); **Attendance:** 2,121.

WEEK 9

Friday 24th June 2005

OLDHAM 14 HALIFAX 28

OLDHAM: 1 Gavin Dodd; 2 Rob Mills; 3 Alex Wilkinson; 4 Jon Goddard; 5 Nick Johnson; 6 Simon Svabic; 7 Marty Turner; 8 Ricky Bibey; 9 Gareth Barber; 10 Dana Wilson; 11 Ian Hodson; 12 Tere Glassie; 13 Carlos Mataora. Subs (all used): 14 Adam Sharples; 15 Mark Roberts; 16 Martin Elswood; 17 Andy Gorey.
Tries: Turner (4), Mills (60); **Goals:** Turner 3/4.
HALIFAX: 1 Steve Booth; 2 James Haley; 3 Damian Gibson; 4 Anthony Blackwood; 5 Rikki Sheriffe; 6 Pat Weisner; 7 Dean Lawford; 8 Chris Morley; 9 Ben Fisher; 10 Jason Boults; 11 Jamie Bloem; 12 Fereti Tuilagi; 13 Damian Ball. Subs (all used): 14 Ben Black; 15 Alan Hadcroft; 16 Ryan McDonald; 17 Scott Law.
Tries: McDonald (43), Gibson (50), Haley (57), Black (71), Blackwood (74); **Goals:** Booth 4/8, Bloem 0/1.
Rugby Leaguer & League Express Men of the Match: *Oldham:* Alex Wilkinson; *Halifax:* Ben Black.
Penalty count: 10-9; **Half-time:** 8-4;
Referee: Ben Thaler (Wakefield);
Attendance: 1,227 *(at Park Lane, Sedgley Park).*

National League One 2005 - Round by Round

WEEK 10

Sunday 26th June 2005

DONCASTER DRAGONS 32 FEATHERSTONE ROVERS 24

DRAGONS: 1 Craig Miles; 2 Danny Mills; 3 Marvin Golden; 4 Craig Farrell; 5 Dean Colton; 6 Ben Cockayne; 7 Latham Tawhai; 8 Dean O'Loughlin; 9 Craig Cook; 10 Karl Mills; 11 Lee Harland; 12 Craig Lawton; 13 Shaun Leaf. Subs (all used): 14 Gareth Handford; 15 Martin Ostler; 16 Aaron Wood; 17 Dean Andrews.
Tries: D Mills (7), Cook (31), Handford (40), Wood (55), Farrell (66), Leaf (72); **Goals:** Cockayne 3/5, Miles 1/1.
Sin bin: Miles (21) – deliberate offside.
ROVERS: 1 Craig Moss; 2 Danny Kirmond; 3 Nathan Batty; 4 Richard Newlove; 5 Bryn Powell; 6 Josh Weeden; 7 Liam Finn; 8 Ian Tonks; 9 Carl Hughes; 10 Nathan Sykes; 11 Adam Hayes; 12 James Houston; 13 Steve Dooler. Subs (all used): 14 Andrew Georgiadis; 15 Danny Maun; 16 Jason Southwell; 17 Jim Carlton.
Tries: Finn (10, 45), C Hughes (11), Batty (50);
Goals: Finn 4/5.
Rugby Leaguer & League Express Men of the Match:
Dragons: Lee Harland; *Rovers:* Liam Finn.
Penalty count: 7-10; **Half-time:** 18-12;
Referee: Peter Taberner (Wigan); **Attendance:** 973.

HULL KINGSTON ROVERS 48 BARROW RAIDERS 10

ROVERS: 1 Loz Wildbore; 2 Jon Steel; 3 Dwayne Barker; 4 Gareth Morton; 5 Kane Epati; 6 Paul Mansson; 7 James Webster; 8 James Garmston; 9 Paul Pickering; 10 David Tangata-Toa; 11 Jason Netherton; 12 Michael Smith; 13 Dale Holdstock. Subs (all used): 14 Phil Hasty; 15 Jimmy Walker; 16 Andy Raleigh; 17 Jamie Bovill.
Tries: Smith (2), Hasty (19), Mansson (28), Webster (51), Holdstock (54), Steel (64, 69), Barker (73);
Goals: Morton 8/9.
RAIDERS: 1 Joel Osborn; 2 Freddie Zitter; 3 Shane Irabor; 4 James Finch; 5 James Nixon; 6 Phil Atkinson; 7 Darren Holt; 8 Stuart Dancer; 9 Dave Clark; 10 Ryan Tandy; 11 Mike Whitehead; 12 Ryan Wood; 13 Richard Colley. Subs (all used): 14 Jason Roach; 15 Glenn Osborn; 16 Paul Wilcock; 17 Paul Raftrey.
Try: Zitter (35); **Goals:** Holt 3/3.
Rugby Leaguer & League Express Men of the Match:
Rovers: James Webster; *Raiders:* Ryan Tandy.
Penalty count: 11-9; **Half-time:** 16-8;
Referee: Phil Bentham (Warrington); **Attendance:** 1,921.

WHITEHAVEN 32 ROCHDALE HORNETS 16

WHITEHAVEN: 1 Gary Broadbent; 2 Craig Calvert; 3 David Seeds; 4 Mick Nanyn; 5 Wesley Wilson; 6 Leroy Joe; 7 Steve Kirkbride; 8 Aaron Summers; 9 Aaron Lester; 10 David Fatialofa; 11 Brett McDermott; 12 Howard Hill; 13 Carl Rudd. Subs (all used): 14 Joel Penny; 15 Iain Morrison; 16 Carl Sice; 17 Paul Davidson.
Tries: Calvert (7, 9), Seeds (25), Nanyn (35, 44), Penny (66); **Goals:** Nanyn 2/4, Kirkbride 2/2.
HORNETS: 1 Chris Giles; 2 David Alstead; 3 Mark McCully; 4 Richard Varkulis; 5 Chris Campbell; 6 Radney Bowker; 7 Bobbie Goulding; 8 Rob Ball; 9 Phil Cantillon; 10 Gareth Price; 11 Andy Gorski; 12 Lee Doran; 13 Phil Farrell. Subs (all used): 14 Sam Butterworth; 15 Dave Cunliffe; 16 Dave McConnell; 17 John Hill.
Tries: Varkulis (15), Gorski (29), Bowker (53);
Goals: Goulding 2/2, McCully 0/1.
Rugby Leaguer & League Express Men of the Match:
Whitehaven: Gary Broadbent; *Hornets:* Radney Bowker.
Penalty count: 4-2; **Half-time:** 20-12; **Referee:** Colin Morris (Huddersfield); **Attendance:** 1,661.

CASTLEFORD TIGERS 60 BATLEY BULLDOGS 12

TIGERS: 1 Michael Platt; 2 Damien Reid; 3 Deon Bird; 4 Jon Hepworth; 5 Michael Shenton; 6 Andy Kain; 7 Brad Davis; 17 Frank Watene; 9 Andrew Henderson; 10 Craig Huby; 11 Tom Haughey; 12 Steve Crouch; 13 Aaron Smith. Subs (all used): 14 Andy Bailey; 15 Jordan James; 16 Ryan Boyle; 8 Byron Smith.
Tries: Davis (8), Henderson (13), F Watene (22), Bird (32, 50), Shenton (55, 63), Reid (60), Crouch (72), Platt (74), Boyle (79);
Goals: Huby 5/6, Davis 1/2, A Kain 1/2, Boyle 1/1.
BULLDOGS: 1 Mark Sibson; 2 Jamie Stokes; 3 Shad Royston; 4 Alex Muff; 5 Aiden Lister; 6 Mark Toohey; 7 Barry Eaton; 8 Dane Morgan; 9 Neil Roden; 10 Joe Berry; 11 Sean Richardson; 12 Gary Shillabeer; 13 Iain Marsh. Subs (all used): 14 Craig Lingard; 15 Tim Spears; 16 David Rourke; 17 Martin McLoughlin.
Tries: Lister (3), Lingard (45); **Goals:** Eaton 2/2.
Dismissal: Richardson (35) – late challenge on Davis.
Sin bin: Eaton (31) – interference.
Rugby Leaguer & League Express Men of the Match:
Tigers: Brad Davis; *Bulldogs:* Dane Morgan.
Penalty count: 13-5; **Half-time:** 24-6;
Referee: Julian King (St Helens); **Attendance:** 4,487.

WEEK 11

Sunday 3rd July 2005

BATLEY BULLDOGS 28 ROCHDALE HORNETS 40

BULLDOGS: 1 Craig Lingard; 2 Jamie Stokes; 3 Shad Royston; 4 Alex Muff; 5 Aiden Lister; 6 Neil Roden; 7 Barry Eaton; 8 Dane Morgan; 9 Darren Robinson; 10 Tim Spears; 11 David Rourke; 12 Martin McLoughlin; 13 Iain Marsh. Subs (all used): 14 Kris Lythe; 15 Paul Harrison; 16 Will Cartledge; 17 Gary Shillabeer.
Tries: McLoughlin (35), Lingard (39), Lister (57), Robinson (63), Shillabeer (69); **Goals:** Eaton 4/6.
HORNETS: 1 Chris Giles; 2 David Alstead; 3 Mark McCully; 4 Andy Gorski; 5 Chris Campbell; 6 Radney Bowker; 7 Bobbie Goulding; 8 John Hill; 9 Dave McConnell; 10 Gareth Price; 11 Richard Varkulis; 12 Lee Doran; 13 Phil Farrell. Subs (all used): 14 Sam Butterworth; 15 Paul Anderson; 16 Dave Cunliffe; 17 Rob Ball.
Tries: Alstead (19, 30), Varkulis (23, 80), Butterworth (45), McCully (61), Goulding (78);
Goals: Goulding 5/7, McCully 1/1.
Rugby Leaguer & League Express Men of the Match:
Bulldogs: Craig Lingard; *Hornets:* Dave McConnell.
Penalty count: 12-5; **Half-time:** 14-18;
Referee: Gareth Hewer (Whitehaven); **Attendance:** 587.

HULL KINGSTON ROVERS 38 HALIFAX 30

ROVERS: 1 Leroy Rivett; 2 Jon Steel; 3 Paul Parker; 4 Gareth Morton; 5 Byron Ford; 6 Paul Mansson; 7 James Webster; 8 James Garmston; 9 Andy Ellis; 10 David Tangata-Toa; 11 Andy Raleigh; 12 Jason Netherton; 13 Dale Holdstock. Subs (all used): 14 Phil Hasty; 15 Kane Epati; 16 Jamie Bovill; 17 Makali Aizue.
Tries: Rivett (4), Raleigh (8, 14), Ford (28), Holdstock (35), Parker (55); **Goals:** Morton 7/7.
HALIFAX: 1 Damian Gibson; 2 James Haley; 3 Damian Ball; 4 Anthony Blackwood; 5 Rikki Sheriffe; 6 Dean Lawford; 7 Ben Black; 8 Chris Morley; 9 Ben Fisher; 10 Jason Boults; 11 David Larder; 12 Andy Spink; 13 Pat Weisner. Subs (all used): 14 Alan Hadcroft; 15 Scott Law; 16 Ryan McDonald; 17 Luke Simeunovich.
Tries: Weisner (18, 38), Fisher (51), Gibson (74), R Sheriffe (77); **Goals:** Weisner 5/5.
Rugby Leaguer & League Express Men of the Match:
Rovers: Leroy Rivett; *Halifax:* Pat Weisner.
Penalty count: 3-4; **Half-time:** 30-12;
Referee: Colin Morris (Huddersfield); **Attendance:** 2,565.

OLDHAM 38 FEATHERSTONE ROVERS 20

OLDHAM: 1 Gavin Dodd; 2 Rob Mills; 3 Alex Wilkinson; 4 Jon Goddard; 5 Nick Johnson; 6 Marty Turner; 7 Chris Hough; 8 Adam Sharples; 9 Gareth Barber; 10 Dana Wilson; 11 Ian Hodson; 12 Tere Glassie; 13 Simon Svabic. Subs (all used): 14 Andy Gorey; 15 Carlos Mataora; 16 Martin Elswood; 17 Will Cowell.
Tries: Svabic (2), Turner (16), Goddard (36), Glassie (51), Mataora (64), Cowell (70); **Goals:** Turner 7/7.
ROVERS: 1 Nathan Batty; 2 Craig Moss; 3 Danny Maun; 4 Richard Newlove; 5 Bryn Powell; 6 Josh Weeden; 7 Liam Finn; 8 Ian Tonks; 9 Carl Hughes; 10 Nathan Sykes; 11 Greg Nicholson; 12 Neil Lowe; 13 Steve Dooler. Subs (all used): 14 Andrew Georgiadis; 15 James Houston; 16 Jason Southwell; 17 Jim Carlton.
Tries: Georgiadis (32), Southwell (66), Moss (74);
Goals: Finn 4/4.
Rugby Leaguer & League Express Men of the Match:
Oldham: Marty Turner; *Rovers:* Ian Tonks.
Penalty count: 5-6; **Half-time:** 20-8;
Referee: Julian King (St Helens);
Attendance: 948 *(at Park Lane, Sedgley Park).*

WHITEHAVEN 56 BARROW RAIDERS 6

WHITEHAVEN: 1 Wesley Wilson; 2 Craig Calvert; 3 David Seeds; 4 Mick Nanyn; 5 Derry Eilbeck; 6 Leroy Joe; 7 Joel Penny; 8 Aaron Summers; 9 Aaron Lester; 10 Howard Hill; 11 Brett McDermott; 12 Iain Morrison; 13 Carl Rudd. Subs (all used): 14 Steve Kirkbride; 15 Paul Davidson; 16 Carl Sice; 17 Chris McKinney.
Tries: Nanyn (10, 25, 71), Seeds (18, 29, 61), Joe (39), Eilbeck (48), Summers (57), Penny (74);
Goals: Nanyn 8/10.
RAIDERS: 1 Joel Osborn; 2 Freddie Zitter; 3 Shane Irabor; 4 James Finch; 5 James Nixon; 6 Phil Atkinson; 7 Jamie Marshall; 8 Stuart Dancer; 9 Dave Clark; 10 Ryan Tandy; 11 Mike Whitehead; 12 Glenn Osborn; 13 Richard Colley. Subs (all used): 14 Jason Roach; 15 Paul Raftrey; 16 Chris Archer; 17 Paul Wilcock.
Try: Clark (33); **Goals:** J Osborn 1/1.
Rugby Leaguer & League Express Men of the Match:
Whitehaven: Iain Morrison; *Raiders:* Ryan Tandy.
Penalty count: 10-4; **Half-time:** 26-6;
Referee: Mike Dawber (Wigan); **Attendance:** 1,455.

CASTLEFORD TIGERS 40 DONCASTER DRAGONS 16

TIGERS: 1 Michael Platt; 2 Stuart Kain; 3 Deon Bird; 4 Tom Haughey; 5 Michael Shenton; 6 Andy Kain; 7 Paul Handforth; 8 Adam Watene; 9 Andrew Henderson; 10 Andy Bailey; 11 Craig Huby; 12 Steve Crouch; 13 Aaron Smith. Subs (all used): 14 Jordan James; 15 Byron Smith; 16 Damien Reid; 17 Frank Watene.
Tries: Shenton (15), Bailey (18), Platt (20, 58, 72), F Watene (43), Handforth (50);
Goals: Huby 3/4, A Kain 3/4.
Sin bin: A Watene (9) – fighting.
DRAGONS: 1 Craig Miles; 2 Danny Mills; 3 Aaron Wood; 4 Craig Farrell; 5 Dean Colton; 6 Ben Cockayne; 7 Latham Tawhai; 8 Gareth Handford; 9 Craig Cook; 10 Andy Fisher; 11 Martin Ostler; 12 Craig Lawton; 13 Shaun Leaf. Subs (all used): 14 Wayne Green; 15 Dean O'Loughlin; 16 Karl Mills; 17 Dean Andrews.
Tries: Colton (33), Lawton (53, 62);
Goals: Cockayne 1/4, Miles 1/1.
Sin bin: Handford (9) – fighting, (68) - dissent.
Rugby Leaguer & League Express Men of the Match:
Tigers: Andrew Henderson; *Dragons:* Aaron Wood.
Penalty count: 17-10; **Half-time:** 18-6;
Referee: Phil Bentham (Warrington); **Attendance:** 5,005.

WEEK 12

Sunday 10th July 2005

BARROW RAIDERS 18 BATLEY BULLDOGS 40

RAIDERS: 1 Adam Pate; 2 Jamie Marshall; 3 Jason Roach; 4 Freddie Zitter; 5 Nick Beech; 6 Joel Osborn; 7 Darren Holt; 8 Stuart Dancer; 9 Dave Clark; 10 Ryan Tandy; 11 Mike Whitehead; 12 Ryan Wood; 13 Phil Atkinson. Subs (all used): 14 Jamie Butler; 15 Paul Raftrey; 16 Chris Archer; 17 Richard Colley.
Tries: Dancer (10), Clark (13), Tandy (24);
Goals: Holt 3/4.
BULLDOGS: 1 Craig Lingard; 2 Adrian Flynn; 3 Wayne McHugh; 4 Shad Royston; 5 Jamie Stokes; 6 Neil Roden; 7 Barry Eaton; 8 Dane Morgan; 9 Kris Lythe; 10 Tim Spears; 11 Martin McLoughlin; 12 Iain Marsh; 13 Darren Robinson. Subs (all used): 14 Mark Sibson; 15 Sean Richardson; 16 Will Cartledge; 17 Gary Shillabeer.
Tries: Robinson (1, 41), Lythe (17), Flynn (31), Sibson (54), Lingard (67, 71); **Goals:** Eaton 6/8.
Rugby Leaguer & League Express Men of the Match:
Raiders: Ryan Tandy; *Bulldogs:* Neil Roden.
Penalty count: 7-6; **Half-time:** 18-18;
Referee: Ben Thaler (Wakefield); **Attendance:** 743.

DONCASTER DRAGONS 34 OLDHAM 26

DRAGONS: 1 Craig Miles; 2 Craig Farrell; 3 Marvin Golden; 4 Aaron Wood; 5 Dean Colton; 6 Graham Holroyd; 7 Latham Tawhai; 8 Gareth Handford; 9 Peter Green; 10 Martin Ostler; 11 Andy Hay; 12 Craig Lawton; 13 Martin Moana. Subs (all used): 14 Dean O'Loughlin; 15 Karl Mills; 16 Shaun Leaf; 17 Ben Cockayne.
Tries: Miles (2, 7), Holroyd (20), Farrell (34, 66), Moana (47); **Goals:** Holroyd 5/7.
Sin bin: Cockayne (80) - fighting.
OLDHAM: 1 Gavin Dodd; 2 Rob Mills; 3 Alex Wilkinson; 4 Jon Goddard; 5 Nick Johnson; 6 Marty Turner; 7 Chris Hough; 8 Ricky Bibey; 9 Gareth Barber; 10 Dana Wilson; 11 Ian Hodson; 12 Tere Glassie; 13 Simon Svabic. Subs (all used): 14 Carlos Mataora; 15 Adam Sharples; 16 Martin Elswood; 17 Will Cowell.
Tries: Dodd (11), Goddard (40), Glassie (55), Svabic (71), Johnson (78); **Goals:** Turner 3/5.
Sin bin: Turner (80) - fighting.
Rugby Leaguer & League Express Men of the Match:
Dragons: Graham Holroyd; *Oldham:* Marty Turner.
Penalty count: 5-8; **Half-time:** 22-12;
Referee: Peter Taberner (Wigan); **Attendance:** 896.

FEATHERSTONE ROVERS 10
HULL KINGSTON ROVERS 78

ROVERS: 1 Craig Moss; 2 James Ford; 3 Danny Maun; 4 Danny Kirmond; 5 Bryn Powell; 6 Josh Weeden; 7 Liam Finn; 8 Jason Southwell; 9 Carl Hughes; 10 James Houston; 11 Adam Hayes; 12 Neil Lowe; 13 Steve Dooler. Subs (all used): 14 Andrew Georgiadis; 15 Danny Evans; 16 Greg Nicholson; 17 Danny Stanley.
Tries: C Hughes (20), Maun (71);
Goals: Finn 1/2, Hughes 0/1.
ROBINS: 1 Leroy Rivett; 2 Jon Steel; 3 Paul Parker; 4 Gareth Morton; 5 Byron Ford; 6 Paul Mansson; 7 James Webster; 8 James Garmston; 9 Andy Ellis; 10 David Tangata-Toa; 11 Andy Raleigh; 12 Jason Netherton; 13 Dale Holdstock. Subs (all used): 14 Phil Hasty; 15 Kane Epati; 16 Jamie Bovill; 17 Makali Aizue.
Tries: Steel (2), Ellis (25), Aizue (33, 35), Netherton (37), Raleigh (39), Parker (42, 78), Tangata-Toa (47, 49), Ford (51), Rivett (58), Garmston (63), Webster (76);
Goals: Morton 11/14.
Rugby Leaguer & League Express Men of the Match:
Rovers: Danny Maun; *Robins:* Makali Aizue.
Penalty count: 4-8; **Half-time:** 6-32;
Referee: Phil Bentham (Warrington); **Attendance:** 1,873.

HALIFAX 60 WHITEHAVEN 18

HALIFAX: 1 Damian Gibson; 2 Alan Hadcroft; 3 James Haley; 4 Anthony Blackwood; 5 Rikki Sheriffe; 6 Pat Weisner; 7 Dean Lawford; 8 Chris Morley; 9 Ben Fisher; 10 Jason Boults; 11 David Larder; 12 Andy Spink; 13 Damian Ball. Subs (all used): 14 Ben Black; 15 Ryan McDonald; 16 Andy Hobson; 17 Scott Law.
Tries: Black (10, 31, 60), Weisner (13, 28), Blackwood (39, 40), Spink (41), Morley (43), R Sheriffe (70), Fisher (79); **Goals:** Weisner 8/11.
WHITEHAVEN: 1 Gary Broadbent; 2 Craig Calvert; 3 David Seeds; 4 Mick Nanyn; 5 Wesley Wilson; 6 Leroy Joe; 7 Joel Penny; 8 Howard Hill; 9 Aaron Lester; 10 David Fatialofa; 11 Iain Morrison; 12 Brett McDermott; 13 Carl Rudd. Subs (all used): 14 Spencer Miller; 15 Paul Davidson; 16 Carl Sice; 17 Chris McKinney.
Tries: Nanyn (53), Sice (61), Hill (65); **Goals:** Nanyn 3/3.
Sin bin: Davidson (79) - swinging arm.
Rugby Leaguer & League Express Men of the Match:
Halifax: Pat Weisner; *Whitehaven:* Joel Penny.
Penalty count: 7-9; **Half-time:** 34-0;
Referee: Julian King (St Helens); **Attendance:** 1,550.

ROCHDALE HORNETS 17 CASTLEFORD TIGERS 16

HORNETS: 1 Chris Giles; 2 Andy Saywell; 3 Mark McCully; 4 Andy Gorski; 5 Chris Campbell; 6 Radney Bowker; 7 Bobbie Goulding; 8 John Hill; 9 Dave McConnell; 10 Gareth Price; 11 Richard Varkulis; 12 Lee Doran; 13 Phil Farrell. Subs (all used): 14 Sam Butterworth; 15 Paul Anderson; 16 Dave Cunliffe; 17 Rob Ball.
Tries: Campbell (5), Butterworth (51);
Goals: Goulding 4/4; **Field goal:** Goulding.
Sin bin: Goulding (54) - fighting.

TIGERS: 1 Michael Platt; 2 Waine Pryce; 3 Deon Bird; 4 Damien Reid; 5 Michael Shenton; 6 Andy Kain; 7 Brad Davis; 8 Craig Huby; 9 Andrew Henderson; 10 Andy Bailey; 11 Tom Haughey; 12 Steve Crouch; 13 Aaron Smith. Subs (all used): 14 Paul Handforth; 15 Byron Smith; 16 Dominic Maloney; 17 Frank Watene.
Tries: Haughey (10), Reid (18), Davis (45);
Goals: Huby 2/3, A Kain 0/1
Sin bin: F Watene (34) - retaliation; Bird (54) - fighting.
Rugby Leaguer & League Express Men of the Match:
Hornets: Bobbie Goulding; *Tigers:* Steve Crouch.
Penalty count: 8-8; **Half-time:** 11-10;
Referee: Mike Dawber (Wigan); **Attendance:** 1,728.

WEEK 13

Sunday 24th July 2005

BATLEY BULLDOGS 26 HALIFAX 34

BULLDOGS: 1 Craig Lingard; 2 Jamie Stokes; 3 Wayne McHugh; 4 Iain Marsh; 5 Adrian Flynn; 6 Neil Roden; 7 Barry Eaton; 8 Dane Morgan; 9 Kris Lythe; 10 Joe Berry; 11 Martin McLoughlin; 12 Sean Richardson; 13 Darren Robinson. Subs (all used): 14 Mark Sibson; 15 Tim Spears; 16 Will Cartledge; 17 David Rourke.
Tries: Robinson (1, 25), Marsh (15), Lingard (49), Sibson (55); **Goals:** Eaton 3/5.
HALIFAX: 1 Damian Gibson; 2 Alan Hadcroft; 3 James Haley; 4 Anthony Blackwood; 5 Rikki Sheriffe; 6 Pat Weisner; 7 Ben Black; 8 Chris Morley; 9 Ben Fisher; 10 Jason Boults; 11 David Larder; 12 Andy Spink; 13 Damian Ball. Subs (all used): 14 Ryan McDonald; 15 Jamie Bloem; 16 Andy Hobson; 17 Scott Law.
Tries: Hadcroft (7), Black (10, 45, 79), R Sheriffe (34, 72), Gibson (66); **Goals:** Weisner 2/6, Bloem 1/1.
Rugby Leaguer & League Express Men of the Match:
Bulldogs: Darren Robinson; *Halifax:* Damian Ball.
Penalty count: 5-2; **Half-time:** 14-14;
Referee: Colin Morris (Huddersfield); **Attendance:** 1,277.

HULL KINGSTON ROVERS 28 DONCASTER DRAGONS 18

ROVERS: 1 Leroy Rivett; 2 Jon Steel; 3 Kane Epati; 4 Misili Manu; 5 Byron Ford; 6 Paul Mansson; 7 James Webster; 8 James Garmston; 9 Andy Ellis; 10 David Tangata-Toa; 11 Andy Raleigh; 12 Dwayne Barker; 13 Jimmy Walker. Subs (all used): 14 Paul Pickering; 15 Mark Blanchard; 16 Jamie Bovill; 17 Makali Aizue.
Tries: Steel (5), Walker (9), Ellis (15), Ford (45, 72);
Goals: Steel 4/6.
DRAGONS: 1 Craig Miles; 2 Danny Mills; 3 Marvin Golden; 4 Craig Farrell; 5 Dean Colton; 6 Graham Holroyd; 7 Latham Tawhai; 8 Dean O'Loughlin; 9 Peter Green; 10 Martin Ostler; 11 Andy Hay; 12 Lee Harland; 13 Martin Moana. Subs (all used): 14 Gareth Handford; 15 Chris Langley; 16 Craig Lawton; 17 Ben Cockayne.
Tries: Hay (20), D Mills (37), P Green (54);
Goals: Holroyd 3/3.
Rugby Leaguer & League Express Men of the Match:
Rovers: James Webster; *Dragons:* Graham Holroyd.
Penalty count: 8-8; **Half-time:** 18-12;
Referee: Phil Bentham (Warrington); **Attendance:** 3,011.

ROCHDALE HORNETS 36 BARROW RAIDERS 22

HORNETS: 1 Chris Giles; 2 Andy Saywell; 3 Mark McCully; 4 Andy Gorski; 5 Chris Campbell; 6 Sam Butterworth; 7 Bobbie Goulding; 8 John Hill; 9 Dave McConnell; 10 Gareth Price; 11 Richard Varkulis; 12 Lee Doran; 13 Phil Farrell. Subs (all used): 14 Jamie Durbin; 15 Dave Cunliffe; 16 David Alstead; 17 Rob Ball.
Tries: McCully (5, 59), McConnell (7, 43), Campbell (20), Butterworth (25), Durbin (63);
Goals: Goulding 2/4, McCully 2/3.
RAIDERS: 1 Adam Pate; 2 Jason Roach; 3 James Finch; 4 Freddie Zitter; 5 James Nixon; 6 Richard Colley; 7 Darren Holt; 8 Stuart Dancer; 9 Dave Clark; 10 Ryan Tandy; 11 Mike Whitehead; 12 Ryan Wood; 13 Phil Atkinson. Subs (all used): 14 Paul Raftrey; 15 Glenn Osborn; 16 Jamie Butler; 17 Shane Irabor.
Tries: Finch (2), Clark (12), G Osborn (33), Nixon (37);
Goals: Holt 3/4.
Rugby Leaguer & League Express Men of the Match:
Hornets: Dave McConnell; *Raiders:* Ryan Tandy.
Penalty count: 8-5; **Half-time:** 20-22;
Referee: Julian King (St Helens); **Attendance:** 732.

WHITEHAVEN 50 FEATHERSTONE ROVERS 16

WHITEHAVEN: 1 Gary Broadbent; 2 Craig Calvert; 3 David Seeds; 4 Mick Nanyn; 5 Wesley Wilson; 6 Leroy Joe; 7 Joel Penny; 8 Aaron Summers; 9 Carl Sice; 10 David Fatialofa; 11 Brett McDermott; 12 Spencer Miller; 13 Aaron Lester. Subs (all used): 14 Steve Kirkbride; 15 Paul Davidson; 16 Marc Jackson; 17 Howard Hill.
Tries: Calvert (2, 21), Sice (15, 80), Seeds (16), Joe (24), Davidson (31), Kirkbride (73), Broadbent (78);
Goals: Nanyn 7/9.
ROVERS: 1 Craig Moss; 2 Danny Kirmond; 3 Danny Maun; 4 Richard Newlove; 5 Bryn Powell; 6 Andrew Georgiadis; 7 Liam Finn; 8 James Houston; 9 Carl Hughes; 10 Danny Evans; 11 Adam Hayes; 12 Neil Lowe; 13 Steve Dooler. Subs (all used): 14 Dominic Brambani; 15 Scott Wheeldon; 16 Greg Nicholson; 17 Nathan Sykes.
Tries: Maun (39), Newlove (51), Lowe (58);
Goals: Finn 2/4.
Rugby Leaguer & League Express Men of the Match:
Whitehaven: Carl Sice; *Rovers:* Andrew Georgiadis.
Penalty count: 11-8; **Half-time:** 32-6;
Referee: Mike Dawber (Wigan); **Attendance:** 1,458.

CASTLEFORD TIGERS 32 OLDHAM 20

TIGERS: 1 Michael Platt; 2 Waine Pryce; 3 Deon Bird; 4 Michael Eagar; 5 Michael Shenton; 6 Andy Kain; 7 Brad Davis; 8 Adam Watene; 9 Andrew Henderson; 10 Andy Bailey; 11 Craig Huby; 12 Jordan James; 13 Steve Crouch. Subs (all used): 14 Tom Haughey; 15 Stuart Kain; 16 Dominic Maloney; 17 Richard Fletcher.
Tries: Huby (9, 16), A Kain (35), Bird (41), Pryce (51, 62); **Goals:** Huby 3/3, Fletcher 1/3.
OLDHAM: 1 Gavin Dodd; 2 Damian Munro; 3 Alex Wilkinson; 4 Jon Goddard; 5 Nick Johnson; 6 Marty Turner; 7 Chris Hough; 8 Ricky Bibey; 9 James Kirkland; 10 Tere Glassie; 11 Ian Hodson; 12 Mark Roberts; 13 Simon Svabic. Subs (all used): 14 Gareth Barber; 15 Dana Wilson; 16 Paul Norman; 17 John Hough.
Tries: C Hough (3), Barber (30), Goddard (39), Johnson (45); **Goals:** Turner 2/4.
Rugby Leaguer & League Express Men of the Match:
Tigers: Andy Kain; *Oldham:* Gareth Barber.
Penalty count: 16-4; **Half-time:** 18-16;
Referee: Thierry Alibert (France); **Attendance:** 4,600.

WEEK 14

Sunday 31st July 2005

DONCASTER DRAGONS 20 WHITEHAVEN 30

DRAGONS: 1 Ben Cockayne; 2 Danny Mills; 3 Chris Langley; 4 Craig Farrell; 5 Dean Colton; 6 Graham Holroyd; 7 Latham Tawhai; 8 Gareth Handford; 9 Peter Green; 10 Craig Lawton; 11 Andy Hay; 12 Lee Harland; 13 Martin Moana. Subs (all used): 14 Craig Poucher; 15 Martin Ostler; 16 Dean O'Loughlin; 17 Craig Miles.
Tries: Farrell (7), Moana (46), Poucher (63), Miles (75);
Goals: Holroyd 2/4.
WHITEHAVEN: 1 Gary Broadbent; 2 Craig Calvert; 3 Carl Rudd; 4 Wesley Wilson; 5 Paul O'Neil; 6 Leroy Joe; 7 Joel Penny; 8 Aaron Summers; 9 Carl Sice; 10 David Fatialofa; 11 Spencer Miller; 12 Howard Hill; 13 Aaron Lester. Subs (all used): 14 Steve Kirkbride; 15 Paul Davidson; 16 Marc Jackson; 17 Neil Baynes.
Tries: Hill (12), Calvert (31), Penny (50, 58, 67);
Goals: O'Neil 5/6.
Rugby Leaguer & League Express Men of the Match:
Dragons: Peter Green; *Whitehaven:* Joel Penny.
Penalty count: 7-8; **Half-time:** 4-12;
Referee: Julian King (St Helens); **Attendance:** 690.

HALIFAX 25 ROCHDALE HORNETS 30

HALIFAX: 1 Damian Gibson; 2 Alan Hadcroft; 3 James Haley; 4 Anthony Blackwood; 5 Rikki Sheriffe; 6 Pat Weisner; 7 Ben Black; 8 Andy Hobson; 9 Ben Fisher; 10 Jason Boults; 11 David Larder; 12 Andy Spink; 13 Damian Ball. Subs (all used): 14 Jamie Bloem; 15 Scott Law; 16 Ryan McDonald; 17 Chris Morley.
Tries: McDonald (29), Larder (33), Weisner (38), R Sheriffe (73); **Goals:** Weisner 4/6; **Field goal:** Weisner.
HORNETS: 1 Chris Giles; 2 David Alstead; 3 Mark McCully; 4 Andy Gorski; 5 Chris Campbell; 6 Radney Bowker; 7 Jamie Durbin; 8 John Hill; 9 Dave McConnell; 10 Gareth Price; 11 Richard Varkulis; 12 Lee Doran; 13 Phil Farrell. Subs (all used): 14 Sam Butterworth; 15 Kris Ratcliffe; 16 Dave Cunliffe; 17 Rob Ball.
Tries: Campbell (12, 50, 63), McCully (55), Alstead (80);
Goals: McCully 5/7.
Sin bin: Doran (28) - holding down.
Rugby Leaguer & League Express Men of the Match:
Halifax: Damian Ball; *Hornets:* Radney Bowker.
Penalty count: 7-9; **Half-time:** 19-8;
Referee: Steve Ganson (St Helens); **Attendance:** 1,594.

OLDHAM 40 HULL KINGSTON ROVERS 20

OLDHAM: 1 Gavin Dodd; 2 Damian Munro; 3 Alex Wilkinson; 4 Jon Goddard; 5 Nick Johnson; 6 Marty Turner; 7 Chris Hough; 8 Ricky Bibey; 9 Gareth Barber; 10 Dana Wilson; 11 Ian Hodson; 12 Tere Glassie; 13 John Hough. Subs: 14 Carlos Mataora; 15 Martin Elswood; 16 Paul Norman; 17 Adam Sharples (not used).
Tries: Barber (2, 7), C Hough (25), Munro (44, 57, 78), Turner (73); **Goals:** Turner 6/10.
ROVERS: 1 Leroy Rivett; 2 Jon Steel; 3 Kane Epati; 4 Misili Manu; 5 Byron Ford; 6 Dwayne Barker; 7 Paul Mansson; 8 James Garmston; 9 Andy Ellis; 10 David Tangata-Toa; 11 Andy Raleigh; 12 Dale Holdstock; 13 Gareth Morton. Subs (all used): 14 Paul Pickering; 15 Jimmy Walker; 16 Jamie Bovill; 17 Makali Aizue.
Tries: Raleigh (12, 20), Morton (50); **Goals:** Morton 4/4.
Rugby Leaguer & League Express Men of the Match:
Oldham: Damian Munro; *Rovers:* David Tangata-Toa.
Penalty count: 9-9; **Half-time:** 20-14;
Referee: Ben Thaler (Wakefield); **Attendance:** 1,414.

CASTLEFORD TIGERS 76 BARROW RAIDERS 12

TIGERS: 1 Michael Platt; 2 Waine Pryce; 3 Deon Bird; 4 Michael Eagar; 5 Michael Shenton; 6 Andy Kain; 7 Brad Davis; 8 Adam Watene; 9 Andrew Henderson; 10 Richard Fletcher; 11 Craig Huby; 12 Jordan James; 13 Steve Crouch. Subs (all used): 14 Tom Haughey; 15 Paul Handforth; 16 Andy Bailey; 17 Frank Watene.
Tries: James (3), Crouch (5), Eagar (15), Pryce (23, 53, 66), A Watene (27), Shenton (30, 77), Platt (32), Huby (35, 43, 61), Davis (59); **Goals:** Huby 9/12, Fletcher 1/2.
RAIDERS: 1 Adam Pate; 2 Jamie Marshall; 3 James Finch; 4 Freddie Zitter; 5 James Nixon; 6 Richard Colley; 7 Darren Holt; 8 Stuart Dancer; 9 Dave Clark; 10 Ryan Tandy; 11 Mike Whitehead; 12 Glenn Osborn; 13 Phil Atkinson. Subs (all used): 14 Shane Irabor; 15 Joel Osborn; 16 Paul Wilcock; 17 Paul Raftrey.
Tries: Tandy (71), J Osborn (79); **Goals:** Holt 2/2.
Rugby Leaguer & League Express Men of the Match:
Tigers: Craig Huby; *Raiders:* Shane Irabor.
Penalty count: 13-8; **Half-time:** 44-0; **Referee:** Karl Kirkpatrick (Warrington); **Attendance:** 4,066.

FEATHERSTONE ROVERS 24 BATLEY BULLDOGS 50

ROVERS: 1 Craig Moss; 2 Matthew Wray; 3 Danny Maun; 4 Richard Newlove; 5 Bryn Powell; 6 Dominic Brambani; 7 Liam Finn; 8 Ian Tonks; 9 Andrew Georgiadis; 10 Nathan Sykes; 11 Adam Hayes; 12 Neil Lowe; 13 Steve Dooler. Subs (all used): 14 Danny Kirmond; 15 Greg Nicholson; 16 James Houston; 17 Scott Wheeldon.
Tries: Powell (7), Georgiadis (23), Maun (54), Newlove (78); **Goals:** Finn 4/5.
BULLDOGS: 1 Craig Lingard; 2 Jamie Stokes; 3 Iain Marsh; 4 Wayne McHugh; 5 Mark Sibson; 6 Neil Roden; 7 Barry Eaton; 8 Dane Morgan; 9 Kris Lythe; 10 David Rourke; 11 Sean Richardson; 12 Martin McLoughlin; 13 Darren Robinson. Subs (all used): 14 Will Cartledge; 15 Tim Spears; 16 Shad Royston; 17 Gary Shillabeer.
Tries: Stokes (14, 62, 66, 73), McLoughlin (18), Roden (27), Lythe (32), Lingard (69); **Goals:** Eaton 9/10.
Rugby Leaguer & League Express Men of the Match:
Rovers: Ian Tonks; *Bulldogs:* Neil Roden.
Penalty count: 10-8; **Half-time:** 14-24;
Referee: Phil Bentham (Warrington); **Attendance:** 1,486.

WEEK 15

Sunday 7th August 2005

BARROW RAIDERS 12 HALIFAX 76

RAIDERS: 1 Adam Pate; 2 Nick Beech; 3 James Finch; 4 Shane Irabor; 5 James Nixon; 6 Joel Osborn; 7 Richard Colley; 8 Stuart Dancer; 9 Dave Clark; 10 Paul Raftrey; 11 Glenn Osborn; 12 Ryan Wood; 13 Mike Whitehead. Subs (all used): 14 Jamie Butler; 15 Paul Wilcock; 16 Jamie Marshall; 17 Jason Roach.
Tries: J Osborn (7), Nixon (46), Irabor (65);
Goals: Beech 0/3.
HALIFAX: 1 Damian Gibson; 2 Alan Hadcroft; 3 James Haley; 4 Jamie Bloem; 5 Rikki Sheriffe; 6 Pat Weisner; 7 Ben Black; 8 Chris Morley; 9 Ben Fisher; 10 Jason Boults; 11 David Larder; 12 Andy Spink; 13 Damian Ball. Subs (all used): 14 Wayne Corcoran; 15 Anthony Blackwood; 16 Andy Hobson; 17 Ryan McDonald.
Tries: Spink (3), Ball (13, 23), R Sheriffe (17, 74), Black (28, 57), Fisher (30, 65, 79), Weisner (38), Hadcroft (42), Larder (44); **Goals:** Bloem 11/12, Corcoran 1/1.
Rugby Leaguer & League Express Men of the Match:
Raiders: Joel Osborn; *Halifax:* Ben Black.
Penalty count: 3-3; **Half-time:** 4-40;
Referee: Julian King (St Helens); **Attendance:** 729.

BATLEY BULLDOGS 10 DONCASTER DRAGONS 20

BULLDOGS: 1 Craig Lingard; 2 Jamie Stokes; 3 Iain Marsh; 4 Wayne McHugh; 5 Mark Sibson; 6 Neil Roden; 7 Barry Eaton; 8 Dane Morgan; 9 Kris Lythe; 10 David Rourke; 11 Sean Richardson; 12 Martin McLoughlin; 13 Darren Robinson. Subs (all used): 14 Shad Royston; 15 Tim Spears; 16 Will Cartledge; 17 Gary Shillabeer.
Tries: Richardson (15), Stokes (33); **Goals:** Eaton 1/3.
DRAGONS: 1 Ben Cockayne; 2 Danny Mills; 3 Chris Langley; 4 Craig Poucher; 5 Craig Miles; 6 Graham Holroyd; 7 Martin Moana; 8 Gareth Handford; 9 Peter Green; 10 Martin Ostler; 11 Andy Hay; 12 Craig Farrell; 13 Craig Lawton. Subs (all used): 14 Lee Harland; 15 Dean O'Loughlin; 16 Karl Mills; 17 Aaron Wood.
Tries: Cockayne (5), Lawton (40), Farrell (48);
Goals: Holroyd 4/6.
Sin bin: Farrell (26) - ball stealing.
Rugby Leaguer & League Express Men of the Match:
Bulldogs: Shad Royston; *Dragons:* Gareth Handford.
Penalty count: 11-9; **Half-time:** 10-12;
Referee: Mike Dawber (Wigan); **Attendance:** 718.

HULL KINGSTON ROVERS 46 CASTLEFORD TIGERS 18

ROVERS: 1 Leroy Rivett; 2 Jon Steel; 3 Kane Epati; 4 Gareth Morton; 5 Byron Ford; 6 Paul Mansson; 7 James Webster; 8 Makali Aizue; 9 Andy Ellis; 10 David Tangata-Toa; 11 Andy Raleigh; 12 Dwayne Barker; 13 Dale Holdstock. Subs (all used): 14 Paul Pickering; 15 Jimmy Walker; 16 Mark Blanchard; 17 Olivier Pramil.
Tries: Ford (7), Rivett (15), Mansson (18), Barker (45), Ellis (55), Webster (70), Blanchard (72), Holdstock (78);
Goals: Morton 7/9.
TIGERS: 1 Michael Platt; 2 Waine Pryce; 3 Deon Bird; 4 Paul Handforth; 5 Michael Shenton; 6 Andy Kain; 7 Brad Davis; 8 Adam Watene; 9 Andrew Henderson; 10 Andy Bailey; 11 Craig Huby; 12 Richard Fletcher; 13 Steve Crouch. Subs (all used): 14 Jason Mossop; 15 Jordan James; 16 Byron Smith; 17 Frank Watene.
Tries: James (28), Pryce (50), A Kain (64);
Goals: Huby 2/2, A Kain 1/1.
Rugby Leaguer & League Express Men of the Match:
Rovers: Andy Ellis; *Tigers:* Brad Davis.
Penalty count: 12-14; **Half-time:** 18-6;
Referee: Ashley Klein (Keighley); **Attendance:** 5,023.

ROCHDALE HORNETS 30 FEATHERSTONE ROVERS 18

HORNETS: 1 Chris Giles; 2 David Alstead; 3 Mark McCully; 4 Andy Gorski; 5 Chris Campbell; 6 Radney Bowker; 7 Jamie Durbin; 8 John Hill; 9 Dave McConnell; 10 Rob Ball; 11 Richard Varkulis; 12 Lee Doran; 13 Phil Farrell. Subs (all used): 14 Sam Butterworth; 15 Kris Ratcliffe; 16 Dave Cunliffe; 17 Paul Anderson.

National League One 2005 - Round by Round

Tries: Varkulis (7, 12), Alstead (22, 59, 79), Gorski (46); **Goals:** McCully 3/6.
Sin bin: Giles (21) - interference.
ROVERS: 1 Craig Moss; 2 James Ford; 3 Nathan Batty; 4 Richard Newlove; 5 Bryn Powell; 6 Dominic Brambani; 7 Liam Finn; 8 Ian Tonks; 9 Danny Evans; 10 Scott Wheeldon; 11 Steve Dooler; 12 Adam Hayes; 13 Greg Nicholson. Subs (all used): 14 Danny Kirmond; 15 Nathan Sykes; 16 Neil Lowe; 17 James Houston.
Tries: Batty (29), Powell (70); **Goals:** Finn 5/6.
Sin bin: Tonks (28) - foul play; Evans (60) - dissent.
Rugby Leaguer & League Express Men of the Match: *Hornets:* Richard Varkulis; *Rovers:* Dominic Brambani.
Penalty count: 7-7; **Half-time:** 16-12;
Referee: Colin Morris (Huddersfield); **Attendance:** 663.

WHITEHAVEN 36 OLDHAM 16

WHITEHAVEN: 1 Gary Broadbent; 2 Craig Calvert; 3 Carl Rudd; 4 Wesley Wilson; 5 Paul O'Neil; 6 Leroy Joe; 7 Joel Penny; 8 Aaron Summers; 9 Carl Sice; 10 David Fatialofa; 11 Spencer Miller; 12 Howard Hill; 13 Aaron Lester. Subs (all used): 14 Graeme Mattinson; 15 Paul Davidson; 16 Marc Jackson; 17 Ryan Tandy.
Tries: Sice (3, 57), Calvert (7), Broadbent (10), Lester (20), O'Neil (35), Rudd (63); **Goals:** O'Neil 4/7.
OLDHAM: 1 Gavin Dodd; 2 Damian Munro; 3 Alex Wilkinson; 4 Jon Goddard; 5 Nick Johnson; 6 Marty Turner; 7 Chris Hough; 8 Ricky Bibey; 9 Gareth Barber; 10 Dana Wilson; 11 Ian Hodson; 12 Tere Glassie; 13 John Hough. Subs (all used): 14 Carlos Mataora; 15 Martin Elswood; 16 Adam Sharples; 17 Paul Norman.
Tries: Mataora (39), J Hough (55), Dodd (79);
Goals: Turner 2/3.
Rugby Leaguer & League Express Men of the Match: *Whitehaven:* Carl Sice; *Oldham:* Dana Wilson.
Penalty count: 9-5; **Half-time:** 26-6;
Referee: Phil Bentham (Warrington); **Attendance:** 1,669.

WEEK 16

Sunday 14th August 2005

BARROW RAIDERS 16 DONCASTER DRAGONS 34

RAIDERS: 1 Freddie Zitter; 2 Nick Beech; 3 James Finch; 4 Shane Irabor; 5 James Nixon; 6 Joel Osborn; 7 Jamie Marshall; 8 Stuart Dancer; 9 Jon Williamson; 10 Paul Wilcock; 11 Mike Whitehead; 12 Ryan Wood; 13 Phil Atkinson. Subs (all used): 14 Jamie Butler; 15 Paul Raftrey; 16 Glenn Osborn; 17 Jason Roach.
Tries: Zitter (15, 17, 75); **Goals:** Beech 1/2, J Osborn 1/1.
DRAGONS: 1 Ben Cockayne; 2 Danny Mills; 3 Chris Langley; 4 Craig Poucher; 5 Craig Miles; 6 Graham Holroyd; 7 Martin Moana; 8 Gareth Handford; 9 Aaron Wood; 10 Lee Harland; 11 Andy Hay; 12 Craig Farrell; 13 Craig Lawton. Subs (all used): 14 Dean O'Loughlin; 15 Karl Mills; 16 Martin Ostler; 17 Wayne Green.
Tries: Langley (7), Moana (26, 61), Miles (31), Lawton (39), Holroyd (69); **Goals:** Holroyd 5/6.
Rugby Leaguer & League Express Men of the Match: *Raiders:* Freddie Zitter; *Dragons:* Graham Holroyd.
Penalty count: 10-6; **Half-time:** 10-24;
Referee: Peter Taberner (Wigan); **Attendance:** 506.

BATLEY BULLDOGS 25 HULL KINGSTON ROVERS 40

BULLDOGS: 1 Craig Lingard; 2 Jamie Stokes; 3 Shad Royston; 4 Aiden Lister; 5 Mark Sibson; 6 Neil Roden; 7 Barry Eaton; 8 Dane Morgan; 9 Kris Lythe; 10 David Rourke; 11 Sean Richardson; 12 Martin McLoughlin; 13 Darren Robinson. Subs (all used): 14 Tim Spears; 15 Paul Harrison; 16 Will Cartledge; 17 Gary Shillabeer.
Tries: Lythe (40), Lingard (41), Royston (43, 79);
Goals: Robinson 4/6; **Field goal:** Roden.
ROVERS: 1 Loz Wildbore; 2 Jon Steel; 3 Kane Epati; 4 Gareth Morton; 5 Byron Ford; 6 Paul Mansson; 7 James Webster; 8 Makali Aizue; 9 Andy Ellis; 10 David Tangata-Toa; 11 Andy Raleigh; 12 Dwayne Barker; 13 Dale Holdstock. Subs (all used): 14 Paul Pickering; 15 Mark Blanchard; 16 Dean Andrews; 17 Tommy Gallagher.
Tries: Mansson (16), Gallagher (55), Epati (63, 76), Webster (65, 72), Ford (69); **Goals:** Morton 6/7.
Rugby Leaguer & League Express Men of the Match: *Bulldogs:* Darren Robinson; *Rovers:* James Webster.
Penalty count: 7-6; **Half-time:** 8-6;
Referee: Phil Bentham (Warrington); **Attendance:** 1,214.

HALIFAX 26 FEATHERSTONE ROVERS 22

HALIFAX: 1 Damian Gibson; 2 James Haley; 3 Alan Hadcroft; 4 Anthony Blackwood; 5 Rikki Sheriffe; 6 Wayne Corcoran; 7 Ben Black; 8 Chris Morley; 9 Ben Fisher; 10 Jason Boults; 11 David Larder; 12 Damian Ball; 13 Pat Weisner. Subs (all used): 14 Jamie Bloem; 15 Ryan McDonald; 16 Andy Hobson; 17 Andy Spink.
Tries: Corcoran (20), Weisner (23), Haley (45, 66), Morley (77); **Goals:** Weisner 1/2, Corcoran 1/1, Bloem 1/2.
Sin bin: Blackwood (42) - persistent offside.
On report: Hobson (37) - fighting.
ROVERS: 1 Craig Moss; 2 James Ford; 3 Nathan Batty; 4 Danny Maun; 5 Bryn Powell; 6 Dominic Brambani; 7 Liam Finn; 8 Stuart Dickens; 9 Greg Nicholson; 10 James Houston; 11 Adam Hayes; 12 Neil Lowe; 13 Steve Dooler. Subs (all used): 14 Danny Kirmond; 15 Danny Evans; 16 Paul Hughes; 17 Wayne Sutcliffe.
Tries: Dickens (6), Kirmond (49), Batty (57);
Goals: Finn 5/9.
Rugby Leaguer & League Express Men of the Match: *Halifax:* Damian Gibson; *Rovers:* Stuart Dickens.
Penalty count: 8-11; **Half-time:** 10-10;
Referee: Mike Dawber (Wigan); **Attendance:** 1,629.

ROCHDALE HORNETS 24 OLDHAM 27

HORNETS: 1 Chris Giles; 2 David Alstead; 3 Mark McCully; 4 Andy Gorski; 5 Chris Campbell; 6 Radney Bowker; 7 Sam Butterworth; 8 John Hill; 9 Dave McConnell; 10 Gareth Price; 11 Richard Varkulis; 12 Lee Doran; 13 Phil Farrell. Subs (all used): 14 Paul Owen; 15 Dave Cunliffe; 16 Paul Anderson; 17 Tommy Goulden.
Tries: Butterworth (8, 15), Alstead (53), McCully (65);
Goals: McCully 4/5.
On report: Doran (36) - alleged spear tackle.
OLDHAM: 1 Gavin Dodd; 2 Damian Munro; 3 Alex Wilkinson; 4 Jon Goddard; 5 Nick Johnson; 6 Marty Turner; 7 Chris Hough; 8 Ricky Bibey; 9 Gareth Barber; 10 Paul Norman; 11 Ian Hodson; 12 Tere Glassie; 13 John Hough. Subs (all used): 14 Carlos Mataora; 15 Martin Elswood; 16 Simon Svabic; 17 Dana Wilson.
Tries: Munro (3), Johnson (22), Goddard (43);
Goals: Turner 7/8; **Field goal:** C Hough.
Rugby Leaguer & League Express Men of the Match: *Hornets:* Dave McConnell; *Oldham:* Marty Turner.
Penalty count: 8-9; **Half-time:** 10-17;
Referee: Julian King (St Helens); **Attendance:** 1,426.

WHITEHAVEN 19 CASTLEFORD TIGERS 16

WHITEHAVEN: 1 Gary Broadbent; 2 Craig Calvert; 3 David Seeds; 4 Mick Nanyn; 5 Wesley Wilson; 6 Leroy Joe; 7 Joel Penny; 8 Aaron Summers; 9 Carl Sice; 10 David Fatialofa; 11 Spencer Miller; 12 Howard Hill; 13 Aaron Lester. Subs (all used): 14 Brett McDermott; 15 Carl Rudd; 16 Marc Jackson; 17 Ryan Tandy.
Tries: Sice (4), Penny (31), Seeds (34);
Goals: Nanyn 3/4; **Field goal:** Rudd.
TIGERS: 1 Michael Platt; 2 Waine Pryce; 3 Deon Bird; 4 Michael Eagar; 5 Michael Shenton; 6 Andy Kain; 7 Brad Davis; 8 Adam Watene; 9 Andrew Henderson; 10 Andy Bailey; 11 Craig Huby; 12 Tom Haughey; 13 Steve Crouch. Subs (all used): 14 Jon Hepworth; 15 Jordan James; 16 Byron Smith; 17 Frank Watene.
Tries: Pryce (48, 79), A Kain (58); **Goals:** Huby 2/3.
Rugby Leaguer & League Express Men of the Match: *Whitehaven:* Ryan Tandy; *Tigers:* Andy Kain.
Penalty count: 8-8; **Half-time:** 18-0; **Referee:** Karl Kirkpatrick (Warrington); **Attendance:** 4,437.

WEEK 17

Sunday 21st August 2005

DONCASTER DRAGONS 30 ROCHDALE HORNETS 45

DRAGONS: 1 Ben Cockayne; 2 Craig Farrell; 3 Chris Langley; 4 Sala Fa'alogo; 5 Craig Miles; 6 Graham Holroyd; 7 Gary Hulse; 8 Gareth Handford; 9 Craig Cook; 10 Lee Harland; 11 Andy Hay; 12 Craig Lawton; 13 Martin Moana. Subs (all used): 14 Aaron Wood; 15 Martin Ostler; 16 Dean O'Loughlin; 17 Karl Mills.
Tries: Cockayne (9, 11, 28), Fa'alogo (63), Cook (67);
Goals: Holroyd 5/6.
HORNETS: 1 Paul Owen; 2 Nicky Royle; 3 Mark McCully; 4 Sam Butterworth; 5 Chris Campbell; 6 Radney Bowker; 7 Dave McConnell; 8 John Hill; 9 Phil Farrell; 10 Gareth Price; 11 Dave Cunliffe; 12 Lee Doran; 13 Andy Gorski. Subs (all used): 14 David Alstead; 15 Richard Varkulis; 16 Phil Cantillon; 17 Rob Ball.
Tries: Varkulis (34), McCully (37), McConnell (42), Royle (48), Cantillon (53), Alstead (61, 70), Campbell (77); **Goals:** McCully 6/9; **Field goal:** McConnell.
Sin bin: Cantillon (74) - persistent offside.
Rugby Leaguer & League Express Men of the Match: *Dragons:* Ben Cockayne; *Hornets:* Phil Cantillon.
Penalty count: 10-8; **Half-time:** 20-11;
Referee: Mike Dawber (Wigan); **Attendance:** 630.

FEATHERSTONE ROVERS 74 BARROW RAIDERS 22

ROVERS: 1 Craig Moss; 2 James Ford; 3 Nathan Batty; 4 Danny Maun; 5 Bryn Powell; 6 Dominic Brambani; 7 Liam Finn; 8 Stuart Dickens; 9 Greg Nicholson; 10 James Houston; 11 Adam Hayes; 12 Danny Kirmond; 13 Steve Dooler. Subs (all used): 14 Paul Hughes; 15 Danny Evans; 16 Neil Lowe; 17 Richard Newlove.
Tries: Dickens (9, 57), Dooler (13, 46, 74), Ford (20), Evans (27), Powell (33, 79), Newlove (51), P Hughes (54), Batty (60), Brambani (63); **Goals:** Finn 11/13.
RAIDERS: 1 Freddie Zitter; 2 Jamie Marshall; 3 Shane Irabor; 4 James Finch; 5 James Nixon; 6 Joel Osborn; 7 Darren Holt; 8 Stuart Dancer; 9 Jon Williamson; 10 Paul Wilcock; 11 Mike Whitehead; 12 Ryan Wood; 13 Phil Atkinson. Subs (all used): 14 Jason Roach; 15 Paul Raftrey; 16 Glenn Osborn; 17 Jamie Butler.
Tries: Marshall (2), Irabor (6), J Osborn (38, 70);
Goals: Holt 3/4.
Rugby Leaguer & League Express Men of the Match: *Rovers:* Stuart Dickens; *Raiders:* Joel Osborn.
Penalty count: 8-4; **Half-time:** 28-16;
Referee: Julian King (St Helens); **Attendance:** 1,171.

HULL KINGSTON ROVERS 14 WHITEHAVEN 18

ROVERS: 1 Loz Wildbore; 2 Kane Epati; 3 Damien Couturier; 4 Gareth Morton; 5 Byron Ford; 6 Paul Mansson; 7 James Webster; 8 Makali Aizue; 9 Andy Ellis; 10 Tommy Gallagher; 11 Andy Raleigh; 12 Dwayne Barker; 13 Dale Holdstock. Subs (all used): 14 Jimmy Walker; 15 Mark Blanchard; 16 Dean Andrews; 17 James Garmston.
Tries: Ford (11), Gallagher (47); **Goals:** Morton 3/4.
WHITEHAVEN: 1 Gary Broadbent; 2 Carl Rudd; 3 David Seeds; 4 Mick Nanyn; 5 Wesley Wilson; 6 Leroy Joe; 7 Joel Penny; 8 Ryan Tandy; 9 Carl Sice; 10 David Fatialofa; 11 Spencer Miller; 12 Howard Hill; 13 Aaron Lester. Subs (all used): 14 Brett McDermott; 15 Aaron Summers; 16 Craig Chambers; 17 Marc Jackson.
Tries: Nanyn (52, 72), Jackson (79); **Goals:** Nanyn 3/3.
Rugby Leaguer & League Express Men of the Match: *Rovers:* James Webster; *Whitehaven:* Mick Nanyn.
Penalty count: 7-5; **Half-time:** 8-0;
Referee: Steve Ganson (St Helens); **Attendance:** 3,508.

OLDHAM 32 BATLEY BULLDOGS 34

OLDHAM: 1 Gavin Dodd; 2 Damian Munro; 3 Alex Wilkinson; 4 Jon Goddard; 5 Nick Johnson; 6 Marty Turner; 7 Chris Hough; 8 Ricky Bibey; 9 Gareth Barber; 10 Paul Norman; 11 Ian Hodson; 12 Tere Glassie; 13 Simon Svabic. Subs (all used): 14 Carlos Mataora; 15 John Hough; 16 Simon Haughton; 17 Adam Sharples.
Tries: Svabic (7), Johnson (10), Barber (20), Turner (22), Haughton (26); **Goals:** Turner 6/7.
Sin bin: Glassie (62) - dissent.
BULLDOGS: 1 Craig Lingard; 2 Jamie Stokes; 3 Shad Royston; 4 Stephen Jones; 5 Mark Sibson; 6 Neil Roden; 7 Barry Eaton; 8 Dane Morgan; 9 Kris Lythe; 10 David Rourke; 11 Martin McLoughlin; 12 Iain Marsh; 13 Darren Robinson. Subs (all used): 14 Will Cartledge; 15 Tim Spears; 16 John Gallagher; 17 Sean Richardson.
Tries: Richardson (31), Lythe (38), Royston (40), Gallagher (43, 51, 75); **Goals:** Eaton 4/6, Robinson 1/1.
Rugby Leaguer & League Express Men of the Match: *Oldham:* Jon Goddard; *Bulldogs:* Barry Eaton.
Penalty count: 8-10; **Half-time:** 28-16;
Referee: Peter Taberner (Wigan); **Attendance:** 1,187.

CASTLEFORD TIGERS 38 HALIFAX 34

TIGERS: 1 Michael Platt; 2 Waine Pryce; 3 Michael Eagar; 4 Jon Hepworth; 5 Michael Shenton; 6 Andy Kain; 7 Brad Davis; 8 Adam Watene; 9 Andrew Henderson; 10 Frank Watene; 11 Tom Haughey; 12 Steve Crouch; 13 Deon Bird. Subs (all used): 14 Damien Blanch; 15 Jordan James; 16 Richard Fletcher; 17 Byron Smith.
Tries: Henderson (12, 57), Bird (33), Pryce (37), Fletcher (47), Blanch (72);
Goals: A Kain 6/6, Fletcher 1/1, Davis 0/1.
HALIFAX: 1 Damian Gibson; 2 James Haley; 3 Andy Kirk; 4 Anthony Blackwood; 5 Rikki Sheriffe; 6 Wayne Corcoran; 7 Ben Black; 8 Andy Hobson; 9 Ben Fisher; 10 Jason Boults; 11 David Larder; 12 Andy Spink; 13 Pat Weisner. Subs (all used): 14 Jamie Bloem; 15 Ryan McDonald; 16 Scott Law; 17 Damien Reid.
Tries: Spink (2), Blackwood (43), Black (49, 79), Weisner (53), Reid (67);
Goals: Corcoran 2/2, Bloem 2/3, Weisner 1/1.
Rugby Leaguer & League Express Men of the Match: *Tigers:* Andrew Henderson; *Halifax:* Ben Black.
Penalty count: 10-6; **Half-time:** 22-6;
Referee: Phil Bentham (Warrington); **Attendance:** 4,941.

WEEK 18

Sunday 4th September 2005

DONCASTER DRAGONS 28 HALIFAX 22

DRAGONS: 1 Craig Poucher; 2 Dean Colton; 3 Craig Farrell; 4 Sala Fa'alogo; 5 Craig Miles; 6 Graham Holroyd; 7 Gary Hulse; 8 Martin Ostler; 9 Craig Cook; 10 Craig Lawton; 11 Andy Hay; 12 Lee Harland; 13 Martin Moana. Subs (all used): 14 Gareth Handford; 15 Chris Langley; 16 Karl Mills; 17 Dean O'Loughlin.
Tries: Hulse (9), Farrell (40), Colton (52, 61), Cook (71);
Goals: Holroyd 4/7.
Sin bin: O'Loughlin (34) - fighting;
Hay (77) - deliberate offside.
HALIFAX: 1 Damian Gibson; 2 James Haley; 3 Andy Kirk; 4 Anthony Blackwood; 5 Rikki Sheriffe; 6 Pat Weisner; 7 Ben Black; 8 Andy Hobson; 9 Ben Fisher; 10 Jason Boults; 11 David Larder; 12 Andy Spink; 13 Damian Ball. Subs (all used): 14 Wayne Corcoran; 15 Damien Reid; 16 Ryan McDonald; 17 Jamie Bloem.
Tries: Black (31, 38, 56); **Goals:** Weisner 2/2, Bloem 3/3.
Sin bin: Fisher (30) - holding down;
McDonald (34) - fighting.
Rugby Leaguer & League Express Men of the Match: *Dragons:* Craig Farrell; *Halifax:* Ben Black.
Penalty count: 12-5; **Half-time:** 10-16;
Referee: Thierry Alibert (France); **Attendance:** 1,024.

OLDHAM 52 BARROW RAIDERS 12

OLDHAM: 1 Gavin Dodd; 2 Andy Gorey; 3 Damian Munro; 4 Rob Mills; 5 Nick Johnson; 6 Carlos Mataora; 7 Chris Hough; 8 Ricky Bibey; 9 James Kirkland; 10 Paul Norman; 11 Simon Haughton; 12 Tere Glassie; 13 Simon Svabic. Subs (all used): 14 Gareth Barber; 15 Martin Elswood; 16 Ian Hodson; 17 Danny Nanyn.
Tries: Munro (2, 20, 36), Norman (10), Dodd (25), Glassie (43), Svabic (47), Hodson (50), Barber (52, 57);
Goals: Svabic 4/8, C Hough 2/2.
RAIDERS: 1 Freddie Zitter; 2 Jamie Marshall; 3 James Finch; 4 Shane Irabor; 5 James Nixon; 6 Joel Osborn; 7 Richard Colley; 8 Stuart Dancer; 9 Chris Archer; 10 Paul Wilcock; 11 Anthony Horton; 12 Ryan Wood; 13 Mike Whitehead. Subs (all used): 14 Jason Roach; 15 Darren Holt; 16 Jamie Butler; 17 Paul Raftrey.
Tries: Finch (33), Roach (67); **Goals:** J Osborn 2/2.
Rugby Leaguer & League Express Men of the Match: *Oldham:* Damian Munro; *Raiders:* Joel Osborn.
Penalty count: 5-8; **Half-time:** 26-6;
Referee: Peter Taberner (Wigan); **Attendance:** 1,059.

ROCHDALE HORNETS 30 HULL KINGSTON ROVERS 26

HORNETS: 1 Paul Owen; 2 Nicky Royle; 3 Mark McCully;

Whitehaven celebrate finishing top of National League One with their supporters, after defeating Rochdale

4 David Alstead; 5 Chris Giles; 6 Radney Bowker; 7 Dave McConnell; 8 Rob Ball; 9 Phil Farrell; 10 Gareth Price; 11 Dave Cunliffe; 12 Lee Doran; 13 Andy Gorski. Subs (all used): 14 Phil Cantillon; 15 Richard Varkulis; 16 Andy Saywell; 17 Tommy Goulden.
Tries: Gorski (4), Varkulis (34), Cantillon (57), Price (58), Royle (67); **Goals:** McCully 5/7.
ROVERS: 1 Leroy Rivett; 2 Kane Epati; 4 Gareth Morton; 3 Damien Couturier; 5 Byron Ford; 6 Paul Mansson; 7 James Webster; 8 Makali Aizue; 9 Paul Pickering; 10 James Garmston; 11 Andy Raleigh; 12 Dwayne Barker; 13 Tommy Gallagher. Subs (all used): 14 Phil Hasty; 15 Dale Holdstock; 16 Michael Smith; 17 Jason Netherton.
Tries: Morton (16), Webster (24, 75), Rivett (37), Ford (77); **Goals:** Morton 3/5.
Rugby Leaguer & League Express Men of the Match:
Hornets: Nicky Royle; *Rovers:* Leroy Rivett.
Penalty count: 9-7; **Half-time:** 12-16;
Referee: Phil Bentham (Warrington); **Attendance:** 1,173.

WHITEHAVEN 54 BATLEY BULLDOGS 12

WHITEHAVEN: 1 Gary Broadbent; 2 Craig Calvert; 3 David Seeds; 4 Mick Nanyn; 5 Wesley Wilson; 6 Leroy Joe; 7 Joel Penny; 8 Ryan Tandy; 9 Carl Sice; 10 David Fatialofa; 11 Spencer Miller; 12 Howard Hill; 13 Aaron Lester. Subs (all used): 14 Craig Chambers; 15 Aaron Summers; 16 Carl Rudd; 17 Brett McDermott.
Tries: Penny (3), Seeds (8), Nanyn (15, 35, 74), Sice (27, 39), Hill (32), Joe (60), Rudd (71);
Goals: Nanyn 7/10.
BULLDOGS: 1 Craig Lingard; 2 Jamie Stokes; 3 Stephen Jones; 4 Iain Marsh; 5 Mark Sibson; 6 Neil Roden; 7 Barry Eaton; 8 Dane Morgan; 9 Kris Lythe; 10 David Rourke; 11 Sean Richardson; 12 Martin McLoughlin; 13 Darren Robinson. Subs (all used): 14 John Gallagher; 15 Gary Shillabeer; 16 Tim Spears; 17 Joe Berry.
Tries: Lingard (5), Jones (65); **Goals:** Eaton 2/2.
Sin bin: Jones (20) - high tackle on Tandy.
Rugby Leaguer & League Express Men of the Match:
Whitehaven: Joel Penny; *Bulldogs:* Sean Richardson.
Penalty count: 8-3; **Half-time:** 38-6;
Referee: Ben Thaler (Wakefield); **Attendance:** 1,903.

CASTLEFORD TIGERS 40 FEATHERSTONE ROVERS 6

TIGERS: 1 Michael Platt; 2 Waine Pryce; 3 Michael Eagar; 4 Jon Hepworth; 5 Michael Shenton; 6 Brad Davis; 7 Andrew Henderson; 8 Adam Watene; 9 Aaron Smith; 10 Craig Huby; 11 Tom Haughey; 12 Steve Crouch; 13 Deon Bird. Subs (all used): 14 Damien Blanch; 15 Andy Kain; 16 Byron Smith; 17 Frank Watene.
Tries: Shenton (8), Haughey (18, 64), Blanch (45), Crouch (49), Pryce (59), Bird (68);
Goals: Huby 3/4, 8. Half 3/4.
ROVERS: 1 Craig Moss; 2 James Ford; 3 Nathan Batty; 4 Richard Newlove; 5 Bryn Powell; 6 Dominic Brambani; 7 Liam Finn; 8 Ian Tonks; 9 Greg Nicholson; 10 Stuart Dickens; 11 James Houston; 12 Steve Dooler. Subs (all used): 14 Paul Hughes; 15 Danny Evans; 16 Neil Lowe; 17 Andy Kay.
Try: Moss (53); **Goals:** Finn 1/2.
Sin bin: Evans (35) – holding down.
Rugby Leaguer & League Express Men of the Match:

Tigers: Michael Shenton; *Rovers:* Greg Nicholson.
Penalty count: 12-5; **Half-time:** 14-2;
Referee: Mike Dawber (Wigan); **Attendance:** 5,943.

WEEK 19

Sunday 11th September 2005

BARROW RAIDERS 10 HULL KINGSTON ROVERS 42

RAIDERS: 1 Freddie Zitter; 2 Jamie Marshall; 3 James Finch; 4 Shane Irabor; 5 James Nixon; 6 Joel Osborn; 7 Richard Colley; 8 Stuart Dancer; 9 Chris Archer; 10 Paul Wilcock; 11 Ryan Wood; 12 Anthony Horton; 13 Mike Whitehead. Subs (all used): 14 Paul Raftrey; 15 Jason Roach; 16 Jamie Butler; 17 Jon Williamson.
Tries: Zitter (7), Marshall (36); **Goals:** J Osborn 1/2.
ROVERS: 1 Loz Wildbore; 2 Jon Steel; 3 Jimmy Walker; 4 Dean Andrews; 5 Kane Epati; 6 Dwayne Barker; 7 Phil Hasty; 8 James Garmston; 9 Andy Ellis; 10 David Tangata-Toa; 11 Jason Netherton; 12 Michael Smith; 13 Damien Couturier; 16 Mark Blanchard; 17 Jamie Bovill.
Tries: Hasty (15, 45), Walker (32), Tangata-Toa (46, 73), Pickering (51, 73); **Goals:** Wildbore 5/5, Couturier 2/2.
Rugby Leaguer & League Express Men of the Match:
Raiders: Joel Osborn; *Rovers:* David Tangata-Toa.
Penalty count: 3-7; **Half-time:** 10-12;
Referee: Thierry Alibert (France); **Attendance:** 584.

BATLEY BULLDOGS 12 CASTLEFORD TIGERS 54

BULLDOGS: 1 Craig Lingard; 2 Jamie Stokes; 3 Iain Marsh; 4 Stephen Jones; 5 Mark Sibson; 6 John Gallagher; 7 Barry Eaton; 8 Dane Morgan; 9 Neil Roden; 10 David Rourke; 11 Tom Haughey; 12 Martin McLoughlin; 13 Darren Robinson. Subs (all used): 14 Kris Lythe; 15 Gary Shillabeer; 16 Joe Berry; 17 Sean Richardson.
Tries: Sibson (15), Jones (74); **Goals:** Eaton 2/2.
Sin bin: Gallagher (71) - holding down.
TIGERS: 1 Michael Platt; 2 Waine Pryce; 3 Michael Eagar; 4 Jon Hepworth; 5 Damien Blanch; 6 Brad Davis; 7 Andrew Henderson; 8 Adam Watene; 9 Aaron Smith; 10 Craig Huby; 11 Tom Haughey; 12 Steve Crouch; 13 Deon Bird. Subs (all used): 14 Andy Kain; 15 Jordan James; 16 Richard Fletcher; 17 Frank Watene.
Tries: Haughey (11, 30, 62), A Watene (18, 25), Pryce (22), A Kain (52), James (60), Hepworth (78), Davis (80); **Goals:** Huby 5/8, Fletcher 2/2.
Rugby Leaguer & League Express Men of the Match:
Bulldogs: Tim Spears; *Tigers:* Andrew Henderson.
Penalty count: 8-11; **Half-time:** 6-28;
Referee: Peter Taberner (Wigan); **Attendance:** 2,230.

FEATHERSTONE ROVERS 22 DONCASTER DRAGONS 46

ROVERS: 1 Craig Moss; 2 James Ford; 3 Nathan Batty; 4 Richard Newlove; 5 Bryn Powell; 6 Dominic Brambani; 7 Liam Finn; 8 Stuart Dickens; 9 Paul Hughes; 10 James Houston; 11 Steve Dooler; 12 Adam Hayes; 13 Greg Nicholson. Subs (all used): 14 Andy Kay; 15 Danny Evans; 16 Ian Tonks; 17 Carl Hughes.

Tries: Batty (11, 30), Newlove (14), Kay (55), Tonks (78); **Goals:** Finn 1/5.
DRAGONS: 1 Craig Poucher; 2 Dean Colton; 3 Craig Farrell; 4 Sala Fa'alogo; 5 Craig Miles; 6 Graham Holroyd; 7 Gary Hulse; 8 Gareth Handford; 9 Craig Cook; 10 Dean O'Loughlin; 11 Andy Hay; 12 Lee Harland; 13 Martin Moana. Subs (all used): 14 Craig Lawton; 15 Martin Ostler; 16 Chris Langley; 17 Ben Cockayne.
Tries: Moana (3, 18), Hulse (5), Harland (8), Colton (27), Holroyd (73), Lawton (75); **Goals:** Holroyd 9/9.
Rugby Leaguer & League Express Men of the Match:
Rovers: Nathan Batty; *Dragons:* Lee Harland.
Penalty count: 14-6; **Half-time:** 12-32;
Referee: Ronnie Laughton (Barnsley); **Attendance:** 1,495.

HALIFAX 46 OLDHAM 20

HALIFAX: 1 Damian Gibson; 2 James Haley; 3 Andy Kirk; 4 Damien Reid; 5 Rikki Sheriffe; 6 Dean Lawford; 7 Ben Black; 8 Chris Morley; 9 Ben Fisher; 10 Ryan McDonald; 11 David Larder; 12 Damian Ball; 13 Pat Weisner. Subs (all used): 14 Jamie Bloem; 15 Andy Spink; 16 Andy Hobson; 17 Jason Boults.
Tries: Haley (7), R Sheriffe (15, 31), Weisner (19), Reid (29), Black (41), Boults (48), McDonald (62), Hobson (79); **Goals:** Haley 1/2, Bloem 4/4.
OLDHAM: 1 Gavin Dodd; 2 Damian Munro; 3 Rob Mills; 4 Alex Wilkinson; 5 Nick Johnson; 6 Simon Svabic; 7 Chris Hough; 8 Tere Glassie; 9 James Kirkland; 10 Paul Norman; 11 Ian Hodson; 12 Martin Elswood; 13 Carlos Mataora. Subs (all used): 14 Gareth Barber; 15 Danny Nanyn; 16 Simon Haughton; 17 John Hough.
Tries: Dodd (24), Munro (37), Glassie (56), Svabic (70); **Goals:** C Hough 2/5.
Sin bin: Dodd (62) - dissent.
Rugby Leaguer & League Express Men of the Match:
Halifax: Damian Ball; *Oldham:* Chris Hough.
Penalty count: 6-11; **Half-time:** 22-10;
Referee: Mike Dawber (Wigan); **Attendance:** 1,504.

ROCHDALE HORNETS 20 WHITEHAVEN 44

HORNETS: 1 Paul Owen; 2 Nicky Royle; 3 Mark McCully; 4 David Alstead; 5 Chris Giles; 6 Radney Bowker; 7 Dave McConnell; 8 Rob Ball; 9 Phil Farrell; 10 Gareth Price; 11 Dave Cunliffe; 12 Lee Doran; 13 Andy Gorski. Subs (all used): 14 Phil Cantillon; 15 Richard Varkulis; 16 Paul Anderson; 17 Tommy Goulden.
Tries: Varkulis (32), Alstead (49), Cunliffe (75);
Goals: McCully 2/2, McConnell 2/2.
Sin bin: Alstead (61) - fighting.
WHITEHAVEN: 1 Gary Broadbent; 2 Craig Calvert; 3 David Seeds; 4 Mick Nanyn; 5 Wesley Wilson; 6 Leroy Joe; 7 Joel Penny; 8 Ryan Tandy; 9 Carl Sice; 10 David Fatialofa; 11 Spencer Miller; 12 Howard Hill; 13 Aaron Lester. Subs (all used): 14 Carl Rudd; 15 Aaron Summers; 16 Craig Chambers; 17 Carl Sice.
Tries: Penny (9, 17, 72), Sice (13), Nanyn (26, 40), Calvert (37), Fatialofa (69); **Goals:** Nanyn 6/9.
Sin bin: Wilson (61) - fighting.
Rugby Leaguer & League Express Men of the Match:
Hornets: Dave Cunliffe; *Whitehaven:* Joel Penny.
Penalty count: 10-12; **Half-time:** 8-30; **Referee:** Richard Silverwood (Dewsbury); **Attendance:** 1,770.

Anthony Blackwood halted by Tommy Gallagher and Andy Raleigh during Halifax's play-off win over Hull Kingston Rovers

PLAY-OFFS

Sunday 18th September 2005

ELIMINATION PLAY-OFFS

HULL KINGSTON ROVERS 45 ROCHDALE HORNETS 4

ROVERS: 1 Leroy Rivett; 2 Kane Epati; 3 Paul Mansson; 4 Gareth Morton; 5 Byron Ford; 6 Dwayne Barker; 7 James Webster; 8 Makali Aizue; 9 Andy Ellis; 10 David Tangata-Toa; 11 Andy Raleigh; 12 Jason Netherton; 13 Tommy Gallagher. Subs (all used): 14 Michael Smith; 15 Paul Parker; 16 James Garmston; 17 Jamie Bovill. **Tries:** Ford (8, 16), Gallagher (20), Raleigh (45), Smith (53), Parker (72), Aizue (77); **Goals:** Morton 8/10; **Field goal:** Webster.
HORNETS: 1 Chris Giles; 2 Andy Saywell; 3 David Alstead; 4 Richard Varkulis; 5 Paul Owen; 6 Radney Bowker; 7 Dave McConnell; 8 Rob Ball; 9 Phil Farrell; 10 Gareth Price; 11 Dave Cunliffe; 12 Lee Doran; 13 Andy Gorski. Subs (all used): 14 Sam Butterworth; 15 Kris Ratcliffe; 16 Phil Cantillon; 17 Tommy Goulden. **Try:** Gorski (30); **Goals:** McConnell 0/1.
Dismissal: Ball (76) - dissent.
Rugby Leaguer & League Express Men of the Match: *Rovers:* James Webster; *Hornets:* Andy Gorski.
Penalty count: 8-6; **Half-time:** 23-4;
Referee: Ben Thaler (Wakefield); **Attendance:** 2,420.

HALIFAX 64 DONCASTER DRAGONS 10

HALIFAX: 1 Damian Gibson; 2 James Haley; 3 Andy Kirk; 4 Anthony Blackwood; 5 Rikki Sheriffe; 6 Dean Lawford; 7 Ben Black; 8 Andy Hobson; 9 Ben Fisher; 10 Jason Boults; 11 David Larder; 12 Damian Ball; 13 Pat Weisner. Subs (all used): 14 Jamie Bloem; 15 Andy Spink; 16 Ryan McDonald; 17 Damien Reid.
Tries: Weisner (4), Gibson (14, 72), R Sheriffe (19, 79), Black (21, 38, 64), Kirk (33, 44), Blackwood (55); **Goals:** Weisner 8/11, Bloem 2/3.
DRAGONS: 1 Ben Cockayne; 2 Dean Colton; 3 Sala Fa'alogo; 4 Craig Farrell; 5 Craig Poucher; 6 Graham Holroyd; 7 Gary Hulse; 8 Gareth Handford; 9 Craig Cook; 10 Dean O'Loughlin; 11 Andy Hay; 12 Lee Harland; 13 Martin Moana. Subs (all used): 14 Chris Langley; 15 Martin Ostler; 16 Craig Lawton; 17 Latham Tawhai.
Tries: Cook (25), Langley (47); **Goals:** Holroyd 1/2.
Dismissal: Ostler (31) - spear tackle on McDonald.
Rugby Leaguer & League Express Men of the Match: *Halifax:* Ben Fisher; *Dragons:* Ben Cockayne.
Penalty count: 7-10; **Half-time:** 36-4;
Referee: Ian Smith (Oldham); **Attendance:** 1,863.

Sunday 25th September 2005

QUALIFYING SEMI-FINAL

WHITEHAVEN 32 CASTLEFORD TIGERS 22

WHITEHAVEN: 1 Gary Broadbent; 2 Craig Calvert; 3 David Seeds; 4 Mick Nanyn; 5 Wesley Wilson; 6 Leroy Joe; 7 Joel Penny; 8 Ryan Tandy; 9 Carl Sice; 10 David Lester. Subs (all used): 14 Carl Rudd; 15 Aaron Summers; 16 Craig Chambers; 17 Marc Jackson.
Tries: Sice (30, 41), Chambers (62), Calvert (66), Nanyn (74, 78); **Goals:** Nanyn 4/6.
TIGERS: 1 Michael Platt; 2 Waine Pryce; 3 Michael Eagar; 4 Jon Hepworth; 5 Damien Blanch; 6 Brad Davis; 7 Andrew Henderson; 8 Adam Watene; 9 Aaron Smith; 10 Craig Huby; 11 Tom Haughey; 12 Steve Crouch; 13 Deon Bird. Subs (all used): 14 Andy Kain; 15 Adrian Vowles; 16 Richard Fletcher; 17 Frank Watene.
Tries: Pryce (3), Bird (10), Eagar (17); **Goals:** Huby 5/6.
Rugby Leaguer & League Express Men of the Match: *Whitehaven:* Carl Sice; *Tigers:* Brad Davis.
Penalty count: 9-7; **Half-time:** 6-18;
Referee: Steve Ganson (St Helens); **Attendance:** 6,154.

ELIMINATION SEMI-FINAL

HULL KINGSTON ROVERS 22 HALIFAX 36

ROVERS: 1 Leroy Rivett; 2 Kane Epati; 3 Paul Mansson; 4 Gareth Morton; 5 Byron Ford; 6 Dwayne Barker; 7 James Webster; 8 Makali Aizue; 9 Andy Ellis; 10 David Tangata-Toa; 11 Andy Raleigh; 12 Jason Netherton; 13 Tommy Gallagher. Subs (all used): 14 Michael Smith; 15 Paul Parker; 16 Mark Blanchard; 17 James Garmston.
Tries: Morton (42), Ford (49, 62), Epati (71); **Goals:** Morton 3/4.
HALIFAX: 1 Damian Gibson; 2 James Haley; 3 Andy Kirk; 4 Anthony Blackwood; 5 Rikki Sheriffe; 6 Dean Lawford; 7 Ben Black; 8 Andy Hobson; 9 Ben Fisher; 10 Jason Boults; 11 David Larder; 12 Damian Ball; 13 Pat Weisner. Subs (all used): 14 Jamie Bloem; 15 Andy Spink; 16 Ryan McDonald; 17 Chris Morley.
Tries: Hobson (14), Fisher (27, 39), Blackwood (52), Weisner (69), Larder (79); **Goals:** Weisner 5/7, Bloem 1/1.
Rugby Leaguer & League Express Men of the Match: *Rovers:* Makali Aizue; *Halifax:* Pat Weisner.
Penalty count: 10-8; **Half-time:** 0-20;
Referee: Julian King (St Helens); **Attendance:** 3,400.

Sunday 2nd October 2005

FINAL ELIMINATOR

CASTLEFORD TIGERS 15 HALIFAX 12

TIGERS: 1 Michael Platt; 2 Waine Pryce; 3 Michael Eagar; 4 Jon Hepworth; 5 Damien Blanch; 6 Brad Davis; 7 Andrew Henderson; 8 Adam Watene; 9 Aaron Smith; 10 Richard Fletcher; 11 Tom Haughey; 12 Steve Crouch; 13 Deon Bird. Subs (all used): 14 Paul Handforth; 15 Byron Smith; 16 Adrian Vowles; 17 Frank Watene.
Tries: Platt (30), Blanch (56); **Goals:** Fletcher 2/3, Crouch 1/1; **Field goal:** Handforth.
HALIFAX: 1 Damian Gibson; 2 James Haley; 3 Andy Kirk; 4 Anthony Blackwood; 5 Rikki Sheriffe; 6 Dean Lawford; 7 Ben Black; 8 Andy Hobson; 9 Ben Fisher; 10 Jason Boults; 11 David Larder; 12 Damian Ball; 13 Pat Weisner. Subs (all used): 14 Jamie Bloem; 15 Andy Spink; 16 Ryan McDonald; 17 Chris Birchall.
Tries: R Sheriffe (67), Kirk (73); **Goals:** Weisner 1/1, Bloem 1/2.
Rugby Leaguer & League Express Men of the Match: *Tigers:* Michael Platt; *Halifax:* Andy Kirk.
Penalty count: 12-7; **Half-time:** 10-2; **Referee:** Karl Kirkpatrick (Warrington); **Attendance:** 6,197.

Sunday 9th October 2005

GRAND FINAL

CASTLEFORD TIGERS 36 WHITEHAVEN 8

TIGERS: 1 Michael Platt; 2 Waine Pryce; 3 Michael Shenton; 4 Jon Hepworth; 5 Damien Blanch; 6 Brad Davis; 7 Andrew Henderson; 8 Adam Watene; 9 Aaron Smith; 10 Richard Fletcher; 11 Tom Haughey; 12 Steve Crouch; 13 Deon Bird. Subs (all used): 14 Paul Handforth; 15 Craig Huby; 16 Adrian Vowles; 17 Frank Watene.
Tries: Huby (22), Crouch (24), Blanch (26), Davis (33, 45), Haughey (52); **Goals:** Fletcher 2/3, Huby 3/4, Hepworth 1/1.
WHITEHAVEN: 1 Gary Broadbent; 2 Craig Calvert; 3 David Seeds; 4 Mick Nanyn; 5 Wesley Wilson; 6 Leroy Joe; 7 Joel Penny; 8 Ryan Tandy; 9 Carl Sice; 10 David Fatialofa; 11 Spencer Miller; 12 Howard Hill; 13 Aaron Summers; 16 Craig Chambers; 17 Marc Jackson.
Tries: Nanyn (56), Calvert (78); **Goals:** Nanyn 0/2.
Sin bin: Joe (16) - late tackle on Davis.
On report: Joe (16) - late tackle on Davis; Sice (40) - alleged biting.
Rugby Leaguer & League Express Men of the Match: *Tigers:* Brad Davis; *Whitehaven:* Wesley Wilson.
Penalty count: 4-9; **Half-time:** 26-0;
Referee: Steve Ganson (St Helens);
Attendance: 13,300 *(at Halton Stadium, Widnes).*

Whitehaven's Carl Sice gets to grips with Castleford's Adam Watene during the National League One Grand Final

NATIONAL LEAGUE TWO 2005
Round by Round

WEEK 1

Monday 28th March 2005

BLACKPOOL PANTHERS 12 KEIGHLEY COUGARS 26

PANTHERS: 1 Danny Arnold; 2 Gary Rourke; 3 Tommy Grundy; 4 Eddie Kilgannon; 5 Eric Andrews; 6 Glen Godbee; 7 Liam McGovern; 8 Mike Callan; 9 Chris Ramsdale; 10 John Hill; 11 Matt Leigh; 12 Gary Smith; 13 Danny Barton. Subs (all used): 14 Jamie Stenhouse; 15 Ian Parry; 16 Michael Watts; 17 Mick Redford.
Tries: Godbee (36, 54); **Goals:** Ramsdale 2/2.
Sin bin: Stenhouse (68) - striking.
COUGARS: 1 Matt Bramald; 2 Sam Gardner; 3 David Foster; 4 Matt Foster; 5 Andy Robinson; 6 Paul Ashton; 7 Matt Firth; 8 Phil Stephenson; 9 Jonny Wainhouse; 10 Danny Murgatroyd; 11 Jordan Ross; 12 Matthew Steel; 13 Daniel Harvey. Subs (all used): 14 Adam Mitchell; 15 Chris Parker; 16 Richard Mervill; 17 Jason Clegg.
Tries: Ashton (17), M Foster (45), Gardner (58), Bramald (75); **Goals:** Ashton 5/7.
Rugby Leaguer & League Express Men of the Match: *Panthers:* Glen Godbee; *Cougars:* Matt Firth.
Penalty count: 7-7; **Half-time:** 6-12;
Referee: Jamie Leahy (Dewsbury);
Attendance: 290 *(at Lightfoot Green, Preston).*

DEWSBURY RAMS 34 HUNSLET HAWKS 8

RAMS: 1 Ian Preece; 2 Leon Williamson; 3 Wayne McHugh; 4 Kevin Crouthers; 5 Darren Rogers; 6 Francis Maloney; 7 Ryan Sheridan; 8 Paul Hicks; 9 Richard Chapman; 10 Jonlee Lockwood; 11 Anthony Thewliss; 12 Warren Jowitt; 13 Kurt Rudder. Subs (all used): 14 David Mycoe; 15 Anthony Henderson; 16 James Walker; 17 Mark Hawksley.
Tries: Jowitt (6), Crouthers (18), Chapman (25), Williamson (32, 79); **Goals:** Maloney 7/7.
HAWKS: 1 George Rayner; 2 Steve Morton; 3 Anthony Gibbons; 4 Chris Redfearn; 5 Paul Cummins; 6 Mark Cass; 7 Mark Moxon; 8 Marc Shickell; 9 Joe Hawley; 10 Matt Carbutt; 11 Wayne Freeman; 12 Craig Cawthray; 13 David Gibbons. Subs (all used): 14 Gareth Naylor; 15 Jamaine Wray; 16 Andy Shickell; 17 Glen Freeman.
Tries: Cass (44), Naylor (71); **Goals:** Wray 0/2.
Rugby Leaguer & League Express Men of the Match: *Rams:* Warren Jowitt; *Hawks:* Wayne Freeman.
Penalty count: 7-5; **Half-time:** 24-0;
Referee: Peter Taberner (Wigan); **Attendance:** 1,077.

LONDON SKOLARS 26 SHEFFIELD EAGLES 56

SKOLARS: 1 Ashley Tozer; 2 Austin Aggrey; 3 Joe Price; 4 Ben Joyce; 5 Ade Aderiye; 6 Tim Gee; 7 Gareth Honor; 8 Alex Smits; 9 Kurt Pittman; 10 Toby Hall; 11 Rubert Jonker; 12 Matt Pitman; 13 Brett Blaker. Subs (all used): 14 Dave Brown; 15 James Sullivan; 16 Matt Ryan; 17 Andrew Gourlay.
Tries: T Gee (1, 36), Tozer (47), M Pitman (61, 71); **Goals:** T Gee 3/5.
EAGLES: 1 John Crawford; 2 Danny Mills; 3 Lynton Stott; 4 Adrian Veamatahau; 5 Carl De Chenu; 6 Aled James; 7 Gavin Brown; 8 Damien Lynch; 9 Liam Brentley; 10 Chris Molyneux; 11 Andy Rice; 12 Craig Brown; 13 Nick Turnbull. Subs (all used): 14 Greg Hurst; 15 Jimmy Pearson; 16 Sean Dickinson; 17 Simon Morton.
Tries: C Brown (11), Crawford (20, 77), De Chenu (21, 57), James (36), Turnbull (50), S Dickinson (51), Mills (66), Veamatahau (76); **Goals:** G Brown 8/10.
Rugby Leaguer & League Express Men of the Match: *Skolars:* Tim Gee; *Eagles:* Nick Turnbull.
Penalty count: 9-4; **Half-time:** 12-18;
Referee: Paul Carr (Castleford); **Attendance:** 200.

WORKINGTON TOWN 36 GATESHEAD THUNDER 30

TOWN: 1 Lusi Sione; 2 Matthew Woodcock; 3 Neil Frazer; 4 Jon Roper; 5 Martyn Wilson; 6 James Robinson; 7 Lee Kiddie; 8 Dean Burgess; 9 Jonny Limmer; 10 Dean Bragg; 11 John Tuimaualuga; 12 Dean Vaughan; 13 Brett Smith. Subs (all used): 14 Tane Manihera; 15 Jamie Beaumont; 16 Taani Lavulavu; 17 Malcolm Caton.
Tries: Robinson (18), Sione (27), Roper (35), Kiddie (52), Woodcock (62), Wilson (76); **Goals:** Smith 6/8.
Sin bin: Kiddie (57) - dissent.
THUNDER: 1 Kevin Neighbour; 2 Graham Stephenson; 3 Ian Ball; 4 Nigel Arizmendez; 5 Robin Peers; 6 Phil Carleton; 7 Chris Birch; 8 Rob Line; 9 John Tomes; 10 Selwyn St Bernard; 11 Tony Doherty; 12 Liam Garside; 13 Joe Burley. Subs (all used): 14 Steve Elms; 15 Joe Brown; 16 Damian Martinez; 17 Paul Dodsworth.
Tries: Arizmendez (43), Elms (56), Birch (64), Tomes (66); **Goals:** Birch 7/7.
Sin bin: Arizmendez (61) – persistent interference.
Rugby Leaguer & League Express Men of the Match: *Town:* Brett Smith; *Thunder:* Chris Birch.
Penalty count: 9-10; **Half-time:** 20–2;
Referee: Phil Bentham (Warrington); **Attendance:** 852.

YORK CITY KNIGHTS 18 SWINTON LIONS 34

CITY KNIGHTS: 1 Matt Blaymire; 2 Neil Law; 3 Dan Potter; 4 Ian Kirke; 5 Calvin Watson; 6 Scott Rhodes; 7 Paul Thorman; 8 John Smith; 9 Jimmy Elston; 10 Adam Sullivan; 11 Darren Callaghan; 12 Simon Friend; 13 Jon Liddell. Subs (all used): 14 Lee Jackson; 15 Lee Patterson; 16 Mark Cain; 17 Tom Buckenham.
Tries: Law (30, 70), Cain (45); **Goals:** P Thorman 3/3.
LIONS: 1 Wayne English; 2 Stuart Oldham; 3 Lee Patterson; 4 Chris Maye; 5 Marlon Billy; 6 Mick Coates; 7 Ian Watson; 8 Paul Southern; 9 Phil Joseph; 10 Wes Rogers; 11 Danny Heaton; 12 Ian Sinfield; 13 Lee Marsh. Subs (all used): 14 Warren Ayres; 15 Rob Russell; 16 Lee Gardner; 17 Rob Whittaker.
Tries: Marsh (15), English (20), Patterson (24), Gardner (58), Coates (65), Maye (77); **Goals:** Marsh 5/6.
Rugby Leaguer & League Express Men of the Match: *City Knights:* Ian Kirke; *Lions:* Lee Marsh.
Penalty count: 5-4; **Half-time:** 6-18;
Referee: Craig Halloran (Dewsbury); **Attendance:** 1,890.

WEEK 2

Friday 8th April 2005

SHEFFIELD EAGLES 6 BLACKPOOL PANTHERS 14

EAGLES: 1 Lynton Stott; 2 Danny Mills; 3 Alex Dickinson; 4 Adrian Veamatahau; 5 Carl De Chenu; 6 John Crawford; 7 Gavin Brown; 8 Jack Howieson; 9 Gareth Stanley; 10 Chris Molyneux; 11 Nick Turnbull; 12 Craig Brown; 13 Aled James. Subs (all used): 14 Greg Hurst; 15 Liam Brentley; 16 Sean Dickinson; 17 Damien Lynch.
Try: Turnbull (13); **Goals:** G Brown 1/1.
PANTHERS: 1 Michael Watts; 2 Danny Arnold; 3 Glen Godbee; 4 Eddie Kilgannon; 5 Gary Rourke; 6 Liam Bretherton; 7 Martin Gambles; 8 Gus Martin; 9 Martin Roden; 10 John Hill; 11 John Chamberlain; 12 Gary Smith; 13 Danny Barton. Subs (all used): 14 Chris Ramsdale; 15 Ian Parry; 16 Steve Ormesher; 17 Gareth Jones.
Tries: Godbee (31), Barton (48); **Goals:** Bretherton 3/3.
Rugby Leaguer & League Express Men of the Match: *Eagles:* Nick Turnbull; *Panthers:* Martin Gambles.
Penalty count: 11-12; **Half-time:** 6-8;
Referee: Paul Carr (Castleford); **Attendance:** 727.

WEEK 3

Sunday 10th April 2005

GATESHEAD THUNDER 18 DEWSBURY RAMS 24

THUNDER: 1 Kevin Neighbour; 2 Graham Stephenson; 3 Craig Firth; 4 Nigel Arizmendez; 5 Robin Peers; 6 Phil Carleton; 7 Chris Birch; 8 Rob Line; 9 John Tomes; 10 Selwyn St Bernard; 11 Tabua Cakacaka; 12 Steven Bradley; 13 Joe Burley. Subs (all used): 14 Paul Dodsworth; 15 Scott Collins; 16 Damian Martinez; 17 Liam Garside.
Tries: Neighbour (6), Line (56), Arizmendez (62); **Goals:** Birch 3/5.
RAMS: 1 Ian Preece; 2 Leon Williamson; 3 Wayne McHugh; 4 Kevin Crouthers; 5 Darren Rogers; 6 Francis Maloney; 7 Ryan Sheridan; 8 Paul Hicks; 9 Richard Chapman; 10 Jonlee Lockwood; 11 Anthony Thewliss; 12 Warren Jowitt; 13 Kurt Rudder. Subs (all used): 14 David Mycoe; 15 Anthony Henderson; 16 James Walker; 17 Mark Hawksley.
Tries: Williamson (16, 38), McHugh (27), Rudder (47); **Goals:** Maloney 4/6.
Rugby Leaguer & League Express Men of the Match: *Thunder:* John Tomes; *Rams:* Francis Maloney.
Penalty count: 11-8; **Half-time:** 8-16;
Referee: Robert Hicks (Oldham); **Attendance:** 403.

KEIGHLEY COUGARS 31 YORK CITY KNIGHTS 42

COUGARS: 1 Matt Bramald; 2 Karl Smith; 3 David Foster; 4 Matt Foster; 5 Andy Robinson; 6 Paul Ashton; 7 Matt Firth; 8 Phil Stephenson; 9 Adam Mitchell; 10 Danny Murgatroyd; 11 Chris Parker; 12 James Rushforth; 13 Matthew Steel. Subs (all used): 14 Chris Beever; 15 Lewis Taylor; 16 Richard Mervill; 17 Jason Clegg.
Tries: Rushforth (4), Steel (18), Firth (33), Bramald (35), M Foster (42); **Goals:** Ashton 5/6; **Field goal:** Ashton.
Dismissal: Bramald (58) - high tackle.
Sin bin: Murgatroyd (46) - fighting.
CITY KNIGHTS: 1 Jon Liddell; 2 Paul Fairfield; 3 Dan Potter; 4 Neil Law; 5 Peter Fox; 6 Lee Patterson; 7 Scott Rhodes; 8 John Smith; 9 Lee Jackson; 10 Adam Sullivan; 11 James Ward; 12 Darren Callaghan; 13 Ian Kirke. Subs (all used): 14 Jimmy Elston; 15 Mark Cain; 16 Yusuf Sozi; 17 Tom Buckenham.
Tries: Sullivan (6), Cain (30), Law (62), Potter (65, 76), Fairfield (74), Fox (78, 79); **Goals:** Liddell 5/8.
Sin bin: Potter (25) - obstruction; Elston (46) - fighting.
Rugby Leaguer & League Express Men of the Match: *Cougars:* Phil Stephenson; *City Knights:* Adam Sullivan.
Penalty count: 7-8; **Half-time:** 27-12;
Referee: Phil Bentham (Warrington); **Attendance:** 1,307.

SWINTON LIONS 56 WORKINGTON TOWN 18

LIONS: 1 Wayne English; 2 Chris Irwin; 3 Lee Patterson; 4 Chris Maye; 5 Marlon Billy; 6 Mick Coates; 7 Ian Watson; 8 Paul Southern; 9 Phil Joseph; 10 Wes Rogers; 11 Danny Heaton; 12 Rob Russell; 13 Lee Marsh. Subs (all used): 14 Warren Ayres; 15 Kris Smith; 16 Ian Sinfield; 17 Rob Whittaker.
Tries: English (5, 45, 57), Joseph (13), Southern (22), Coates (30, 35), Patterson (51, 61), Billy (72);
Goals: Marsh 8/11.
TOWN: 1 Scott Chilton; 2 Matthew Woodcock; 3 Neil Frazer; 4 Kevin Hetherington; 5 Martyn Wilson; 6 Lee Kiddie; 7 Tane Manihera; 8 Jamie Beaumont; 9 Lee Burns; 10 Dean Burgess; 11 John Tuimaualuga; 12 Jonny Limmer; 13 James Robinson. Subs (all used): 14 Matthew Johnson; 15 Taani Lavulavu; 16 Tom Armstrong; 17 Malcolm Caton.
Tries: Limmer (18), Kiddie (55), Manihera (64);
Goals: Manihera 3/3.
Sin bin: Lavulavu (71) - dissent.
Rugby Leaguer & League Express Men of the Match: *Lions:* Lee Patterson; *Town:* Lee Burns.
Penalty count: 11-7; **Half-time:** 32-6;
Referee: Jamie Leahy (Dewsbury); **Attendance:** 602.

HUNSLET HAWKS 32 LONDON SKOLARS 8

HAWKS: 1 George Rayner; 2 Jeremy Dyson; 3 Anthony Gibbons; 4 Paul Cummins; 5 Chris North; 6 David Gibbons; 7 Mark Moxon; 8 Matt Carbutt; 9 Jamaine Wray; 10 Neil Mears; 11 Wayne Freeman; 12 Andy Shickell; 13 Gareth Naylor. Subs (all used): 14 Mark Cass; 15 Glen Freeman; 16 Marc Shickell; 17 Danny Cook.
Tries: A Shickell (21), Dyson (55), A Gibbons (59), Cass (66, 68, 70); **Goals:** Dyson 4/8.
SKOLARS: 1 Brett Westwood; 2 Ryan Wheele; 3 Joe Price; 4 Stuart Singleton; 5 Ashley Tozer; 6 Tim Gee; 7 Gareth Honor; 8 Rubert Jonker; 9 Kurt Pittman; 10 Toby Hall; 11 Andrew Gourlay; 12 Matt Pitman; 13 Brett Blaker. Subs (all used): 14 James Sullivan; 15 Wayne Parillon; 16 Ben Joyce; 17 Alex Smits.
Try: Honor (48); **Goals:** T Gee 2/2.
Rugby Leaguer & League Express Men of the Match: *Hawks:* Mark Cass; *Skolars:* Gareth Honor.
Penalty count: 5-6; **Half-time:** 6-2;
Referee: Craig Halloran (Dewsbury); **Attendance:** 335.

WEEK 4

Sunday 17th April 2005

BLACKPOOL PANTHERS 16 LONDON SKOLARS 23

PANTHERS: 1 Michael Watts; 2 Jake Johnstone; 3 Glen Godbee; 4 Jamie Stenhouse; 5 Gary Rourke; 6 Liam Bretherton; 7 Martin Gambles; 8 Gus Martin; 9 Martin Roden; 10 John Hill; 11 Mike Callan; 12 Matt Leigh; 13 Gary Smith. Subs (all used): 14 Danny Arnold; 15 Gareth Jones; 16 Steve Ormesher; 17 Ian Parry.
Tries: Johnstone (26, 38), Rourke (53);
Goals: Johnstone 2/4.
SKOLARS: 1 Brett Westwood; 2 Ryan Wheele; 3 Joe Price; 4 Stuart Singleton; 5 Ashley Tozer; 6 Tim Gee; 7 Gareth Honor; 8 Toby Hall; 9 Kurt Pittman; 10 Alex Smits; 11 Rubert Jonker; 12 Matt Pitman; 13 Brett Blaker. Subs (all used): 14 Matt Ryan; 15 Wayne Parillon; 16 Alan Barker; 17 Ben Joyce.
Tries: Blaker (5), K Pittman (10), Tozer (57), S Singleton (61); **Goals:** T Gee 3/4; **Field goal:** Joyce.
Rugby Leaguer & League Express Men of the Match: *Panthers:* Jake Johnstone; *Skolars:* Brett Blaker.
Penalty count: 6-7; **Half-time:** 12-10;
Referee: Robert Hicks (Oldham); **Attendance:** 797.

DEWSBURY RAMS 48 SWINTON LIONS 10

RAMS: 1 Darren Rogers; 2 Leon Williamson; 3 Wayne McHugh; 4 Kevin Crouthers; 5 Ian Preece; 6 Francis Maloney; 7 Ryan Sheridan; 8 Paul Hicks; 9 Richard Chapman; 10 Mark Hawksley; 11 Alex Bretherton; 12 Warren Jowitt; 13 Kurt Rudder. Subs (all used): 14 David Mycoe; 15 Anthony Henderson; 16 James Walker; 17 Matt Walker.
Tries: Crouthers (6), Jowitt (12), McHugh (16), Chapman (46), Rudder (65), M Walker (67), Rogers (70), Williamson (78); **Goals:** Maloney 8/10.
LIONS: 1 Wayne English; 2 Stuart Oldham; 3 Lee Patterson; 4 Chris Maye; 5 Marlon Billy; 6 Mick Coates; 7 Ian Watson; 8 Paul Southern; 9 Phil Joseph; 10 Wes Rogers; 11 Danny Heaton; 12 Rob Russell; 13 Lee Marsh. Subs (all used): 14 Warren Ayres; 15 Kris Smith; 16 Ian Sinfield; 17 Rob Whittaker.
Tries: Heaton (21, 73); **Goals:** Marsh 1/2.
Rugby Leaguer & League Express Men of the Match: *Rams:* Francis Maloney; *Lions:* Danny Heaton.
Penalty count: 7-8; **Half-time:** 20-4;
Referee: Phil Bentham (Warrington); **Attendance:** 1,112.

GATESHEAD THUNDER 0 HUNSLET HAWKS 50

THUNDER: 1 Kevin Neighbour; 2 Graham Stephenson; 3 Nigel Arizmendez; 4 Craig Firth; 5 Robin Peers; 6 Scott Kelly; 7 Chris Birch; 8 Rob Line; 9 John Tomes; 10 Selwyn St Bernard; 11 Tabua Cakacaka; 12 Steven Bradley; 13 Joe Burley. Subs (all used): 14 Steve Elms; 15 Leroy Day; 16 Damian Martinez; 17 Liam Garside.
Goals: Birch 0/1.
HAWKS: 1 George Rayner; 2 Jeremy Dyson; 3 Anthony Gibbons; 4 Paul Cummins; 5 Chris North; 6 David Gibbons; 7 Mark Moxon; 8 Marc Shickell; 9 Jamaine Wray; 10 Neil Mears; 11 Wayne Freeman; 12 Andy Shickell; 13 Chris Redfearn. Subs (all used): 14 Matt Carbutt; 15 Danny Cook; 16 Mick Coyle; 17 Mark Cass.
Tries: D Gibbons (7), A Gibbons (13, 51), Dyson (16, 70), North (20), G Rayner (27, 67), Wray (45), A Shickell (75); **Goals:** Dyson 5/10.
Rugby Leaguer & League Express Men of the Match: *Thunder:* Leroy Day; *Hawks:* David Gibbons.
Penalty count: 8-13; **Half-time:** 0-22;
Referee: Paul Carr (Castleford); **Attendance:** 288.

WORKINGTON TOWN 30 KEIGHLEY COUGARS 24

TOWN: 1 Scott Chilton; 2 Matthew Woodcock; 3 Neil Frazer; 4 Kevin Hetherington; 5 Martyn Wilson; 6 Lee Kiddie; 7 Tane Manihera; 8 Taani Lavulavu; 9 Lee Burns; 10 John Tuimaualuga; 11 James Robinson; 12 Brett Smith; 13 Jonny Limmer. Subs: 14 Matthew Johnson; 15 Jamie Beaumont; 16 Andrew Fearon (not used); 17 Malcolm Caton.
Tries: Manihera (18, 25), Chilton (57), Beaumont (60), Lavulavu (74); **Goals:** Manihera 5/5.
COUGARS: 1 Matt Bramald; 2 Karl Smith; 3 Chris Beever;

4 Matt Foster; 5 Andy Robinson; 6 Paul Ashton; 7 Matt Firth; 8 Phil Stephenson; 9 Jonny Wainhouse; 10 Lewis Taylor; 11 David Foster; 12 James Rushforth; 13 Matthew Steel. Subs (all used): 14 Adam Mitchell; 15 Stuart Calvert; 16 Danny Murgatroyd; 17 Richard Mervill.
Tries: Bramald (8, 31, 51), Ashton (47);
Goals: Ashton 4/5.
Rugby Leaguer & League Express Men of the Match: *Town:* Tane Manihera; *Cougars:* Paul Ashton.
Penalty count: 7-7; **Half-time:** 12-12;
Referee: Peter Taberner (Wigan); **Attendance:** 669.

YORK CITY KNIGHTS 60 SHEFFIELD EAGLES 10

CITY KNIGHTS: 1 Jon Liddell; 2 Paul Fairfield; 3 Dan Potter; 4 Neil Law; 5 Peter Fox; 6 Paul Thorman; 7 Chris Levy; 8 John Smith; 9 Lee Jackson; 10 Adam Sullivan; 11 James Ward; 12 Ian Kirke; 13 Lee Patterson. Subs (all used): 14 Jimmy Elston; 15 Darren Callaghan; 16 Simon Friend; 17 Yusuf Sozi.
Tries: Potter (5), Fox (17, 24, 35, 45), Levy (31, 55), Liddell (49), Smith (52), Elston (59), Friend (62);
Goals: P Thorman 8/12.
EAGLES: 1 Lynton Stott; 2 Danny Mills; 3 Alex Dickinson; 4 Adrian Veamatahau; 5 Carl De Chenu; 6 Jimmy Pearson; 7 John Crawford; 8 Jack Howieson; 9 Gareth Stanley; 10 Damien Lynch; 11 Nick Turnbull; 12 Andy Rice; 13 Aled James. Subs (all used): 14 Greg Hurst; 15 Sean Dickinson; 16 Joseph Pitt; 17 Jaymes Chapman.
Tries: Turnbull (11), Hurst (74);
Goals: Stott 1/1, Crawford 0/1.
Rugby Leaguer & League Express Men of the Match: *City Knights:* Jimmy Elston; *Eagles:* Damien Lynch.
Penalty count: 10-3; **Half-time:** 28-6;
Referee: Jamie Leahy (Dewsbury); **Attendance:** 1,596.

Friday 22nd April 2005

SHEFFIELD EAGLES 4 KEIGHLEY COUGARS 28

EAGLES: 1 John Crawford; 2 Rob Worrincy; 3 Lynton Stott; 4 Nick Turnbull; 5 Carl De Chenu; 6 Aled James; 7 Ryan Dickinson; 8 Jack Howieson; 9 Liam Brentley; 10 Damien Lynch; 11 Andy Rice; 12 Jaymes Chapman; 13 Sean Dickinson. Subs (all used): 14 Jimmy Pearson; 15 Joseph Pitt; 16 Simon Morton; 17 Simon Tillyer.
Try: Worrincy (35); **Goals:** James 0/1.
COUGARS: 1 Matt Bramald; 2 Karl Smith; 3 David Foster; 4 Matt Foster; 5 Andy Robinson; 6 Paul Ashton; 7 Matt Firth; 8 Phil Stephenson; 9 Jonny Wainhouse; 10 Lewis Taylor; 11 Stuart Calvert; 12 James Rushforth; 13 Matthew Steel. Subs (all used): 14 Adam Mitchell; 15 Daniel Harvey; 16 Danny Murgatroyd; 17 Richard Mervill.
Tries: D Foster (5), Steel (13), Ashton (58), Murgatroyd (79); **Goals:** Ashton 5/6, Mitchell 1/1.
Rugby Leaguer & League Express Men of the Match: *Eagles:* Liam Brentley; *Cougars:* Paul Ashton.
Penalty count: 8-13; **Half-time:** 4-14;
Referee: Phil Bentham (Warrington); **Attendance:** 804.

Saturday 23rd April 2005

GATESHEAD THUNDER 29 BLACKPOOL PANTHERS 20

THUNDER: 1 Kevin Neighbour; 2 Joe Brown; 3 Tony Doherty; 4 Craig Firth; 5 Robin Peers; 6 Luke Stringer; 7 Chris Birch; 8 Tabua Cakacaka; 9 John Tomes; 10 Leroy Day; 11 Liam Garside; 12 Steven Bradley; 13 Joe Burley. Subs (all used): 14 Graham Stephenson; 15 Steve Rutherford; 16 Selwyn St Bernard; 17 Rob Line.
Tries: Birch (16), Day (21, 60), Firth (34), Stringer (47);
Goals: Birch 4/7; **Field goal:** Birch.
Dismissal: Tomes (72) - fighting.
PANTHERS: 1 Liam Bretherton; 2 Jake Johnstone; 3 Glen Godbee; 4 Eddie Kilgannon; 5 Gary Rourke; 6 Liam McGovern; 7 Martin Gambles; 8 Gus Martin; 9 Martin Roden; 10 Gareth Jones; 11 Mick Redford; 12 John Chamberlain; 13 Gary Smith. Subs (all used): 14 Dave Rowland; 15 Lee Rowley; 16 Mike Callan; 17 Craig Tipeny.
Tries: Bretherton (4), Godbee (12, 29);
Goals: Johnstone 4/4.
Rugby Leaguer & League Express Men of the Match: *Thunder:* Leroy Day; *Panthers:* Jake Johnstone.
Penalty count: 11-10; **Half-time:** 16-20;
Referee: Jamie Leahy (Dewsbury); **Attendance:** 253.

WEEK 5

Sunday 24th April 2005

LONDON SKOLARS 8 SWINTON LIONS 38

SKOLARS: 1 Tim Gee; 2 Ryan Wheele; 3 Joe Price; 4 Stuart Singleton; 5 Ashley Tozer; 6 Ben Joyce; 7 Gareth Honor; 8 Toby Hall; 9 Kurt Pittman; 10 Alan Barker; 11 Rubert Jonker; 12 Matt Pitman; 13 Brett Blaker. Subs (all used): 14 Matt Ryan; 15 Wayne Parillon; 16 Nathan Gee; 17 Ade Aderiye.
Tries: M Pitman (51); **Goals:** T Gee 2/2.
Sin bin: Honor (66) - dissent.
LIONS: 1 Wayne English; 2 Stuart Oldham; 3 Lee Patterson; 4 Rob Russell; 5 Marlon Billy; 6 Mick Coates; 7 Ian Watson; 8 Paul Southern; 9 Phil Joseph; 10 Wes Rogers; 11 Danny Heaton; 12 Ian Sinfield; 13 Lee Marsh. Subs (all used): 14 Warren Ayres; 15 Andy Crabtree; 16 Kris Smith; 17 Rob Whittaker.
Tries: Marsh (7, 66), Billy (12, 58, 73), English (13), Patterson (37), Russell (62); **Goals:** Marsh 3/8.
Rugby Leaguer & League Express Men of the Match: *Skolars:* Matt Pitman; *Lions:* Marlon Billy.
Penalty count: 12-10; **Half-time:** 2-20;
Referee: Paul Carr (Castleford); **Attendance:** 543.

WORKINGTON TOWN 44 HUNSLET HAWKS 24

TOWN: 1 Lusi Sione; 2 Matthew Woodcock; 3 Neil Frazer; 4 Scott Chilton; 5 Martyn Wilson; 6 Lee Kiddie; 7 Tane Manihera; 8 Taani Lavulavu; 9 Jonny Limmer; 10 John Tuimaualuga; 11 James Robinson; 12 Jon Roper; 13 Brett Smith. Subs: 14 Kevin Hetherington (not used); 15 Jamie Beaumont; 16 Dean Vaughan; 17 Malcolm Caton.
Tries: Woodcock (8, 30), Limmer (21), Chilton (27, 35), Sione (52), Frazer (68), Kiddie (78); **Goals:** Manihera 6/8.
HAWKS: 1 George Rayner; 2 Jeremy Dyson; 3 Anthony Gibbons; 4 Paul Cummins; 5 Chris North; 6 David Gibbons; 7 Mark Moxon; 8 Marc Shickell; 9 Jamaine Wray; 10 Danny Cook; 11 Wayne Freeman; 12 Andy Shickell; 13 Chris Redfearn. Subs (all used): 14 Mark Cass; 15 Joe Hawley; 16 Matt Carbutt; 17 Gareth Naylor.
Tries: D Gibbons (5), Wray (15), A Gibbons (58), G Rayner (61, 72); **Goals:** Dyson 2/6.
Rugby Leaguer & League Express Men of the Match: *Town:* Tane Manihera; *Hawks:* George Rayner.
Penalty count: 8-4; **Half-time:** 28-10;
Referee: Robert Hicks (Oldham); **Attendance:** 764.

YORK CITY KNIGHTS 74 DEWSBURY RAMS 12

CITY KNIGHTS: 1 Jon Liddell; 2 Matt Blaymire; 3 Dan Potter; 4 Neil Law; 5 Peter Fox; 6 Scott Rhodes; 7 Chris Levy; 8 John Smith; 9 Lee Jackson; 10 Adam Sullivan; 11 Simon Friend; 12 Ian Kirke; 13 Lee Patterson. Subs (all used): 14 Jimmy Elston; 15 Darren Callaghan; 16 Mick Ramsden; 17 Yusuf Sozi.
Tries: Potter (7, 21, 73), Fox (16, 66), Jackson (19), Kirke (26, 61), Sozi (32, 48), Law (52), Rhodes (69), Blaymire (79); **Goals:** Liddell 11/14.
Sin bin: Friend (70) - fighting.
RAMS: 1 Darren Rogers; 2 Leon Williamson; 3 Wayne McHugh; 4 Kevin Crouthers; 5 Ian Preece; 6 Francis Maloney; 7 Ryan Sheridan; 8 Matt Walker; 9 Richard Chapman; 10 Mark Hawksley; 11 Alex Bretherton; 12 Warren Jowitt; 13 Kurt Rudder. Subs (all used): 14 David Mycoe; 15 Anthony Henderson; 16 James Walker; 17 Scott Woodcock.
Tries: Rogers (38, 56); **Goals:** Maloney 2/2.
Sin bin: Mycoe (68) - holding down;
Jowitt (70) - fighting.
Rugby Leaguer & League Express Men of the Match: *City Knights:* Ian Kirke; *Rams:* Francis Maloney.
Penalty count: 13-7; **Half-time:** 38-6;
Referee: Ronnie Laughton (Barnsley); **Attendance:** 2,056.

WEEK 6

Sunday 15th May 2005

DEWSBURY RAMS 38 WORKINGTON TOWN 10

RAMS: 1 Darren Rogers; 2 Leon Williamson; 3 Chris Hall; 4 Kevin Crouthers; 5 Ian Preece; 6 Francis Maloney; 7 Ryan Sheridan; 8 James Walker; 9 Richard Chapman; 10 Matt Walker; 11 Alex Bretherton; 12 Paul Seal; 13 Kurt Rudder. Subs (all used): 14 David Mycoe; 15 Warren Jowitt; 16 Scott Woodcock; 17 Andy Burland.
Tries: Bretherton (20, 28), Maloney (29), Hall (49), Woodcock (57), Sheridan (60), Chapman (71);
Goals: Maloney 5/9.
TOWN: 1 Lusi Sione; 2 Matthew Woodcock; 3 Scott Chilton; 4 Jon Roper; 5 Matthew Johnson; 6 Lee Kiddie; 7 Tane Manihera; 8 Taani Lavulava; 9 Jonny Limmer; 10 John Tuimaualuga; 11 Dean Vaughan; 12 Ricky Wright; 13 Martyn Wilson. Subs (all used): 14 Lee Burns; 15 Jamie Beaumont; 16 James Robinson; 17 Malcolm Caton.
Tries: Sione (2), Manihera (63); **Goals:** Manihera 1/2.
Sin bin: Sione (19) - professional foul.
Rugby Leaguer & League Express Men of the Match: *Rams:* Alex Bretherton; *Town:* Tane Manihera.
Penalty count: 15-9; **Half-time:** 16-4;
Referee: Paul Carr (Castleford); **Attendance:** 970.

GATESHEAD THUNDER 16 YORK CITY KNIGHTS 24

THUNDER: 1 Kevin Neighbour; 2 Robin Peers; 3 Ian Brown; 4 Craig Firth; 5 Joe Brown; 6 Luke Stringer; 7 Chris Birch; 8 Tabua Cakacaka; 9 Scott Collins; 10 Leroy Day; 11 Liam Garside; 12 Steven Bradley; 13 Joe Burley. Subs (all used): 14 Phil Carleton; 15 Steve Rutherford; 16 Selwyn St Bernard; 17 Rob Line.
Tries: I Brown (17), Collins (36), J Brown (46);
Goals: Birch 2/6.
CITY KNIGHTS: 1 Matt Blaymire; 2 Lee Lingard; 3 Dan Potter; 4 Neil Law; 5 Peter Fox; 6 Chris Ross; 7 Paul Thorman; 8 David Bates; 9 Jimmy Elston; 10 Adam Sullivan; 11 Darren Callaghan; 12 Ian Kirke; 13 Lee Patterson. Subs (all used): 14 Neil Thorman; 15 James Ward; 16 John Smith; 17 Yusuf Sozi.
Tries: Kirke (7), Callaghan (13), Sozi (30), Fox (63);
Goals: P Thorman 4/5.
Rugby Leaguer & League Express Men of the Match: *Thunder:* Scott Collins; *City Knights:* Adam Sullivan.
Penalty count: 6-6; **Half-time:** 10-16;
Referee: Robert Hicks (Oldham);
Attendance: 705 *(at Kingston Park, Newcastle).*

KEIGHLEY COUGARS 28 LONDON SKOLARS 16

COUGARS: 1 Matt Bramald; 2 Karl Smith; 3 David Foster; 4 Matt Foster; 5 Andy Robinson; 6 Paul Ashton; 7 Matt Firth; 8 Phil Stephenson; 9 Jonny Wainhouse; 10 Jason Clegg; 11 Daniel Harvey; 12 James Rushforth; 13 Matthew Steel. Subs (all used): 14 Adam Mitchell; 15 Stuart Calvert; 16 Danny Murgatroyd; 17 Richard Mervill.
Tries: M Foster (5), Harvey (10), Smith (14, 58), Ashton (48), Bramald (68); **Goals:** Ashton 2/5, Mitchell 0/1.
Sin bin: Ashton (65) - dissent.
SKOLARS: 1 Tim Gee; 2 Ryan Wheele; 3 Joe Price; 4 Ben Joyce; 5 Corey Simms; 6 Jermaine Coleman; 7 Gareth Honor; 8 Toby Hall; 9 James Sullivan; 10 Alex Smits; 11 Rubert Jonker; 12 Alan Barker; 13 Brett Blaker. Subs (all used): 14 Nathan Meischke; 15 Wayne Parillon; 16 Ade Aderiye; 17 Nathan Gee.
Tries: Simms (45), Honor (66), Jonker (76);
Goals: T Gee 2/3.
Rugby Leaguer & League Express Men of the Match: *Cougars:* Phil Stephenson; *Skolars:* Rubert Jonker.
Penalty count: 10-9; **Half-time:** 14-0;
Referee: Steve Nicholson (Whitehaven); **Attendance:** 726.

SWINTON LIONS 84 BLACKPOOL PANTHERS 12

LIONS: 1 Wayne English; 2 Stuart Oldham; 3 Lee Patterson; 4 Chris Maye; 5 Marlon Billy; 6 Mick Coates; 7 Ian Watson; 8 Paul Southern; 9 Phil Joseph; 10 Wes Rogers; 11 Danny Barton; 12 Ian Sinfield; 13 Lee Marsh. Subs (all used): 14 Warren Ayres; 15 Rob Russell; 16 Danny Heaton; 17 Ian Parry.
Tries: English (2, 56), Patterson (5, 35, 64), Billy (7, 39), Marsh (13, 61), Coates (15), Oldham (20, 53), Southern (25), Parry (49), Rogers (75), Ayres (78);
Goals: Marsh 9/15, Joseph 1/1.
PANTHERS: 1 Liam Bretherton; 2 Jake Johnstone; 3 Glen Godbee; 4 Eddie Kilgannon; 5 Eric Andrews; 6 Liam McGovern; 7 Martin Gambles; 8 Gus Martin; 9 Martin Roden; 10 Gareth Jones; 11 John Chamberlain; 12 Mick Redford; 13 Gary Smith. Subs (all used): 14 Chris Ramsdale; 15 James Lomax; 16 Steve Ormesher; 17 Craig Tipeny.
Tries: Godbee (68, 72); **Goals:** Johnstone 2/2.
Rugby Leaguer & League Express Men of the Match: *Lions:* Lee Marsh; *Panthers:* Martin Gambles.
Penalty count: 6-3; **Half-time:** 48-0;
Referee: Phil Bentham (Warrington); **Attendance:** 588.

HUNSLET HAWKS 30 SHEFFIELD EAGLES 12

HAWKS: 1 George Rayner; 2 Calvin Watson; 3 Anthony Gibbons; 4 Paul Cummins; 5 Chris North; 6 David Gibbons; 7 Mark Moxon; 8 Marc Shickell; 9 Jamaine Wray; 10 Mick Coyle; 11 Wayne Freeman; 12 Andy Shickell; 13 Chris Redfearn. Subs (all used): 14 Mark Cass; 15 Nick Staveley; 16 Danny Cook; 17 Andy Bastow.
Tries: Watson (7, 42, 70), A Shickell (20), North (37), D Gibbons (40); **Goals:** Wray 3/6, Bastow 0/2.
EAGLES: 1 John Crawford; 2 Rob Worrincy; 3 Lynton Stott; 4 John Breakingbury; 5 Carl De Chenu; 6 Aled James; 7 Jon Presley; 8 Jack Howieson; 9 Liam Brentley; 10 Damien Lynch; 11 Nick Turnbull; 12 Craig Brown; 13 Waisale Sovatabua. Subs (all used): 14 Jimmy Pearson; 15 Sean Dickinson; 16 Andy Rice; 17 Simon Morton.
Tries: C Brown (9), Presley (10); **Goals:** Crawford 2/2.
Rugby Leaguer & League Express Men of the Match: *Hawks:* Calvin Watson; *Eagles:* Jon Presley.
Penalty count: 14-9; **Half-time:** 22-12;
Referee: Jamie Leahy (Dewsbury); **Attendance:** 383.

Friday 20th May 2005

SHEFFIELD EAGLES 30 GATESHEAD THUNDER 18

EAGLES: 1 John Crawford; 5 Carl De Chenu; 4 Lynton Stott; 3 Waisale Sovatabua; 2 Rob Worrincy; 6 Gavin Brown; 7 Jon Presley; 8 Jack Howieson; 9 Liam Brentley; 10 Chris Molyneux; 11 Nick Turnbull; 12 Craig Brown; 13 Aled James. Subs (all used): 14 Greg Hurst; 15 Simon Tillyer; 16 Sean Dickinson; 17 Damien Lynch.
Tries: De Chenu (29, 31), Presley (34), Brentley (46), Crawford (55); **Goals:** Crawford 5/6.
Sin bin: Tillyer (52) - high tackle;
De Chenu (70) - fighting.
THUNDER: 1 Kevin Neighbour; 5 Joe Brown; 4 Craig Firth; 3 Wade Liddell; 2 Robin Peers; 6 Luke Stringer; 7 Chris Birch; 8 Rob Line; 9 Scott Collins; 10 Leroy Day; 11 Liam Garside; 12 Tabua Cakacaka; 13 Joe Burley. Subs (all used): 14 Mike Hobbs; 15 Joel Barnes; 16 Andrew Pierce; 17 Selwyn St Bernard.
Tries: Cakacaka (20), Hobbs (62), Garside (80);
Goals: Birch 3/5.
Sin bin: Collins (70) - fighting.
On report: Line (60) - spear tackle on James.
Rugby Leaguer & League Express Men of the Match: *Eagles:* Jon Presley; *Thunder:* Chris Birch.
Penalty count: 12-7; **Half-time:** 18-8;
Referee: Craig Halloran (Dewsbury); **Attendance:** 664.

Saturday 21st May 2005

LONDON SKOLARS 18 DEWSBURY RAMS 22

SKOLARS: 1 Tim Gee; 2 Ryan Wheele; 3 Joe Price; 4 Ben Joyce; 5 Corey Simms; 6 Jermaine Coleman; 7 Nathan Meischke; 8 Toby Hall; 9 Gareth Honor; 10 Alex Smits; 11 Rubert Jonker; 12 Alan Barker; 13 Brett Blaker. Subs (all used): 14 James Sullivan; 15 Wayne Parillon; 16 Kurt Pittman; 17 Ade Aderiye.
Tries: Meischke (39), Price (52, 56); **Goals:** T Gee 3/4.
RAMS: 1 Darren Rogers; 2 Leon Williamson; 3 Chris Hall; 4 Kevin Crouthers; 5 Ian Preece; 6 Francis Maloney; 7 Ryan Sheridan; 8 James Walker; 9 Richard Chapman; 10 Matt Walker; 11 Alex Bretherton; 12 Warren Jowitt; 13 Kurt Rudder. Subs (all used): 14 David Mycoe; 15 Paul Seal; 16 Scott Woodcock; 17 Andy Burland.
Tries: Rogers (7), Crouthers (23), Chapman (26), Sheridan (46); **Goals:** Maloney 3/4.
Rugby Leaguer & League Express Men of the Match: *Skolars:* Joe Price; *Rams:* James Walker.
Penalty count: 8-8; **Half-time:** 8-16;
Referee: Gareth Hewer (Whitehaven); **Attendance:** 354.

WEEK 7

Sunday 22nd May 2005

BLACKPOOL PANTHERS 26 WORKINGTON TOWN 38

PANTHERS: 1 Glen Godbee; 2 Jake Johnstone; 3 Steve Ormesher; 4 Liam Bretherton; 5 Eddie Kilgannon; 6 Chris Ramsdale; 7 Martin Gambles; 8 Lee Rowley; 9 Dave Rowland; 10 Mick Redford; 11 Kris Ratcliffe; 12 Gary Smith; 13 John Chamberlain. Subs (all used): 14 Martin Roden; 15 Gareth Jones; 16 Liam McGovern; 17 Gus Martin.
Tries: Godbee (19, 34, 43), Bretherton (34);
Goals: Ramsdale 2/2, McGovern 3/3.
TOWN: 1 Lusi Sione; 2 Matthew Woodcock; 3 Neil Frazer; 4 Martyn Wilson; 5 Andrew Fearon; 6 Lee Kiddie; 7 Tane Manihera; 8 Taani Lavulavu; 9 Jonny Limmer; 10 John Tuimaualuga; 11 Dean Vaughan; 12 Jon Roper; 13 Brett Smith. Subs (all used): 14 Gareth Skillen; 15 Jamie Beaumont; 16 Wendell Saayman; 17 Tom Armstrong.
Tries: Woodcock (3), Limmer (7), Sione (14, 76), Manihera (37, 56), Wilson (80);
Goals: Manihera 4/6, Smith 1/1.
Rugby Leaguer & League Express Men of the Match: *Panthers:* Glen Godbee; *Town:* Tane Manihera.
Penalty count: 7-5; **Half-time:** 12-22;
Referee: Jamie Leahy (Dewsbury); **Attendance:** 350.

KEIGHLEY COUGARS 12 SWINTON LIONS 30

COUGARS: 1 Matt Bramald; 2 Karl Smith; 3 David Foster; 4 Matt Foster; 5 Andy Robinson; 6 Paul Ashton; 7 Matt Firth; 8 Phil Stephenson; 9 Jonny Wainhouse; 10 Lewis Taylor; 11 Stuart Calvert; 12 Daniel Harvey; 13 Matthew Steel. Subs (all used): 14 Adam Mitchell; 15 Danny Murgatroyd; 16 Richard Mervill; 17 Jason Clegg.
Tries: M Foster (5, 56), Steel (21);
Goals: Ashton 0/2, Mitchell 0/1.
LIONS: 1 Wayne English; 2 Chris Irwin; 3 Lee Patterson; 4 Chris Maye; 5 Marlon Billy; 6 Mick Coates; 7 Ian Watson; 8 Paul Southern; 9 Phil Joseph; 10 Wes Rogers; 11 Danny Heaton; 12 Ian Sinfield; 13 Lee Marsh. Subs (all used): 14 Warren Ayres; 15 Rob Russell; 16 Kris Smith; 17 Rob Whittaker.
Tries: Coates (2, 14), Marsh (34), Irwin (38), English (75); **Goals:** Marsh 5/5.
Rugby Leaguer & League Express Men of the Match: *Cougars:* Phil Stephenson; *Lions:* Lee Marsh.
Penalty count: 10-6; **Half-time:** 8-24;
Referee: Robert Hicks (Oldham); **Attendance:** 967.

YORK CITY KNIGHTS 17 HUNSLET HAWKS 16

CITY KNIGHTS: 1 Matt Blaymire; 2 Lee Lingard; 3 Dan Potter; 4 Neil Law; 5 Peter Fox; 6 Chris Levy; 7 Paul Thorman; 8 Adam Sullivan; 9 Jimmy Elston; 10 David Bates; 11 Darren Callaghan; 12 Ian Kirke; 13 Lee Patterson. Subs (all used): 14 Scott Rhodes; 15 Lee Jackson; 16 James Ward; 17 Yusuf Sozi.
Tries: Lingard (29), Rhodes (43), Blaymire (61);
Goals: P Thorman 2/2, Lingard 0/1; **Field goal:** Levy.
HAWKS: 1 George Rayner; 2 Calvin Watson; 3 Anthony Gibbons; 4 Paul Cummins; 5 Jeremy Dyson; 6 David Gibbons; 7 Mark Moxon; 8 Nick Staveley; 9 Jamaine Wray; 10 Mick Coyle; 11 Wayne Freeman; 12 Andy Shickell; 13 Chris Redfearn. Subs (all used): 14 Andy Bastow; 15 Danny Cook; 16 Lee Williamson; 17 Gareth Naylor.
Tries: G Rayner (14), Wray (22); **Goals:** Dyson 4/5.
Rugby Leaguer & League Express Men of the Match: *City Knights:* Matt Blaymire; *Hawks:* Jamaine Wray.
Penalty count: 9-8; **Half-time:** 6-16; **Referee:** Steve Nicholson (Whitehaven); **Attendance:** 3,224.

WEEK 8

Saturday 4th June 2005

YORK CITY KNIGHTS 60 BLACKPOOL PANTHERS 10

CITY KNIGHTS: 1 Matt Blaymire; 2 Lee Lingard; 3 Dan Potter; 4 Neil Law; 5 Peter Fox; 6 Chris Levy; 7 Paul Thorman; 8 John Smith; 9 Lee Jackson; 10 Adam Sullivan; 11 Mick Ramsden; 12 Ian Kirke; 13 Lee Patterson. Subs (all used): 14 Jimmy Elston; 15 Shaun Ibbetson; 16 David Bates; 17 Yusuf Sozi.
Tries: Jackson (8), Lingard (13, 32), Potter (17), Ramsden (25, 38), Law (43), Levy (56), Elston (58), Fox (63, 72), Sullivan (75); **Goals:** P Thorman 6/12.
PANTHERS: 1 Glen Godbee; 2 Jake Johnstone; 3 Liam Bretherton; 4 Tommy Grundy; 5 Eddie Kilgannon; 6 Chris Ramsdale; 7 Martin Gambles; 8 Steve Ormesher; 9 Martin Roden; 10 Lee Rowley; 11 Gary Smith; 12 John Chamberlain; 13 Willie Swann. Subs (all used): 14 Liam McGovern; 15 Gareth Jones; 16 Kris Ratcliffe; 17 Eric Andrews.
Tries: Ramsdale (21), Andrews (48); **Goals:** Ramsdale 1/2.
On report: Godbee (63) - swinging arm.
Rugby Leaguer & League Express Men of the Match: *City Knights:* Chris Levy; *Panthers:* Chris Ramsdale.
Penalty count: 7-10; **Half-time:** 30-6;
Referee: Paul Carr (Castleford); **Attendance:** 1,981.

WEEK 9

Sunday 5th June 2005

DEWSBURY RAMS 24 SHEFFIELD EAGLES 31

RAMS: 1 Darren Rogers; 2 Leon Williamson; 3 Chris Hall; 4 Kevin Crouthers; 5 Ian Preece; 6 Francis Maloney; 7 Ryan Sheridan; 8 James Walker; 9 Richard Chapman; 10 Warren Jowitt; 11 Alex Bretherton; 12 Paul Seal; 13 Kurt Rudder. Subs (all used): 14 David Mycoe; 15 Rob Kelly; 16 Anthony Thewliss; 17 Paul Hicks.
Tries: Thewliss (34), Preece (55), Maloney (57), Sheridan (62); **Goals:** Maloney 4/5.
Sin bin: Jowitt (52) - fighting.
EAGLES: 1 John Crawford; 5 James Ford; 4 Alex Dickinson; 3 Waisale Sovatabua; 2 Rob Worrincy; 6 Gavin Brown; 7 Jon Presley; 8 Jack Howieson; 9 Liam Brentley; 10 Damien Lynch; 11 Chris Molyneux; 12 Craig Brown; 13 Aled James. Subs (all used): 14 Greg Hurst; 15 Simon Tillyer; 16 Sean Dickinson; 17 Simon Morton.
Tries: Lynch (13), Ford (23, 27), Crawford (42), Sovatabua (70); **Goals:** Crawford 4/5, G Brown 1/1;
Field goal: G Brown.
Sin bin: Molyneux (52) - fighting.
Rugby Leaguer & League Express Men of the Match: *Rams:* James Walker; *Eagles:* John Crawford.
Penalty count: 8-9; **Half-time:** 6-18;
Referee: Colin Morris (Huddersfield); **Attendance:** 988.

WORKINGTON TOWN 40 LONDON SKOLARS 24

TOWN: 1 Lusi Sione; 2 Matthew Woodcock; 3 Neil Frazer; 4 Martyn Wilson; 5 Lee Tinnion; 6 Lee Kiddie; 7 Andrew Fearon; 8 Jamie Beaumont; 9 Jonny Limmer; 10 John Tuimaualuga; 11 Dean Vaughan; 12 Dexter Miller; 13 Jon Roper. Subs (all used): 14 James Robinson; 15 Ricky Wright; 16 Taani Lavulavu; 17 Tane Manihera.
Tries: Limmer (5, 77), Woodcock (8), Roper (12), Lavulavu (35), Sione (44), Tinnion (65); **Goals:** Roper 6/7.
SKOLARS: 1 Tim Gee; 2 Ryan Wheele; 3 Joe Price; 4 Ben Joyce; 5 Corey Simms; 6 Jermaine Coleman; 7 Nathan Meischke; 8 Toby Hall; 9 Gareth Honor; 10 Alan Barker; 11 Rubert Jonker; 12 Matt Pitman; 13 Brett Blaker. Subs (all used): 14 Kurt Pittman; 15 Nathan Gee; 16 Iain Lane; 17 Ade Aderiye.
Tries: T Gee (10), Jonker (26, 58), K Pittman (68);
Goals: T Gee 4/5.
Sin bin: Wheele (49) - holding down.
Rugby Leaguer & League Express Men of the Match: *Town:* Dean Vaughan; *Skolars:* Brett Blaker.
Penalty count: 7-8; **Half-time:** 24-14;
Referee: Craig Halloran (Dewsbury); **Attendance:** 712.

HUNSLET HAWKS 30 SWINTON LIONS 20

HAWKS: 1 George Rayner; 2 Steve Morton; 3 Anthony Gibbons; 4 Chris Redfearn; 5 Paul Cummins; 6 David Gibbons; 7 Mark Moxon; 8 Nick Staveley; 9 Jamaine Wray; 10 Mick Coyle; 11 Wayne Freeman; 12 Gareth Naylor; 13 Andy Bastow. Subs (all used): 14 Danny Cook; 15 Matt Carbutt; 16 Joe Hawley; 17 Mark Cass.
Tries: G Rayner (20, 68, 76), Cook (58), Morton (66);
Goals: Wray 5/7.
LIONS: 1 Wayne English; 2 Chris Irwin; 3 Lee Patterson; 4 Chris Maye; 5 Marlon Billy; 6 Mick Coates; 7 Ian Watson; 8 Paul Southern; 9 Phil Joseph; 10 Wes Rogers; 11 Danny Heaton; 12 Ian Sinfield; 13 Danny Barton. Subs (all used): 14 Warren Ayres; 15 Rob Russell; 16 Ian Parry; 17 Rob Whittaker.
Tries: Billy (15), Irwin (30), English (44), Patterson (78);
Goals: Coates 2/4.
Rugby Leaguer & League Express Men of the Match: *Hawks:* George Rayner; *Lions:* Chris Irwin.
Penalty count: 9-7; **Half-time:** 10-10;
Referee: Robert Hicks (Oldham); **Attendance:** 529.

Saturday 11th June 2005

SHEFFIELD EAGLES 31 WORKINGTON TOWN 28

EAGLES: 1 John Crawford; 2 Rob Worrincy; 3 Waisale Sovatabua; 4 Alex Dickinson; 5 James Ford; 6 Gavin Brown; 7 Jon Presley; 8 Jack Howieson; 9 Liam Brentley; 10 Damien Lynch; 11 Nick Turnbull; 12 Craig Brown; 13 Sean Dickinson. Subs (all used): 14 Greg Hurst; 15 Simon Tillyer; 16 Lynton Stott; 17 Simon Morton.
Tries: S Dickinson (9), Crawford (14, 62), Sovatabua (56), Ford (73); **Goals:** Crawford 5/5;
Field goal: G Brown.
TOWN: 1 Martyn Wilson; 2 Matthew Woodcock; 3 Neil Frazer; 4 Matthew Johnson; 5 Scott Chilton; 6 Lee Kiddie; 7 Tane Manihera; 8 Jamie Beaumont; 9 Jonny Limmer; 10 John Tuimaualuga; 11 Dean Vaughan; 12 Dexter Miller; 13 Jon Roper. Subs (all used): 14 James Robinson; 15 Allan McGuiness; 16 Taani Lavulavu; 17 Tom Armstrong.
Tries: Frazer (3), Woodcock (18), Limmer (33, 78), Manihera (42); **Goals:** Roper 4/6.
Rugby Leaguer & League Express Men of the Match: *Eagles:* Liam Brentley; *Town:* Jonny Limmer.
Penalty count: 5-10; **Half-time:** 12-18;
Referee: Paul Carr (Castleford); **Attendance:** 650
(at Woodbourn Athletic Stadium, Sheffield).

WEEK 10

Sunday 12th June 2005

KEIGHLEY COUGARS 14 DEWSBURY RAMS 28

COUGARS: 1 Matt Bramald; 2 Sam Gardner; 3 David Foster; 4 Matt Foster; 5 Andy Robinson; 6 Adam Mitchell; 7 Matt Firth; 8 Phil Stephenson; 9 Jonny Wainhouse; 10 Danny Murgatroyd; 11 Stuart Calvert; 12 Matthew Steel; 13 Daniel Harvey. Subs: 14 Gareth Greenwood; 15 Karl Smith (not used); 16 Jordan Ross; 17 Richard Mervill.
Tries: Bramald (45), M Foster (54); **Goals:** Mitchell 3/3.
On report: Stephenson (15) – high tackle on Corcoran.
RAMS: 1 Ian Preece; 2 Darren Rogers; 3 Chris Hall; 4 Kevin Crouthers; 5 Leon Williamson; 6 Francis Maloney; 7 Ryan Sheridan; 8 Paul Hicks; 9 Richard Chapman; 10 Warren Jowitt; 11 Alex Bretherton; 12 Ged Corcoran; 13 Kurt Rudder. Subs (all used): 14 David Mycoe; 15 Paul Seal; 16 James Walker; 17 Matt Walker.
Tries: Crouthers (10), Rogers (21, 74), Sheridan (40), Hall (70); **Goals:** Maloney 4/6.
Rugby Leaguer & League Express Men of the Match: *Cougars:* Phil Stephenson; *Rams:* Ryan Sheridan.
Penalty count: 8-6; **Half-time:** 2-16;
Referee: Colin Morris (Huddersfield); **Attendance:** 972.

LONDON SKOLARS 14 YORK CITY KNIGHTS 32

SKOLARS: 1 Tim Gee; 2 Ryan Wheele; 3 Joe Price; 4 Ben Joyce; 5 Corey Simms; 6 Jermaine Coleman; 7 Nathan Meischke; 8 Toby Hall; 9 Gareth Honor; 10 Alan Barker; 11 Rubert Jonker; 12 Iain Lane; 13 Brett Blaker. Subs (all used): 14 Kurt Pittman; 15 Alex Smits; 16 Ade Aderiye; 17 Nathan Gee.
Tries: Wheele (17), Meischke (38), Jonker (71);
Goals: T Gee 1/3.
CITY KNIGHTS: 1 Matt Blaymire; 2 Lee Lingard; 3 Dan Potter; 4 Neil Law; 5 Peter Fox; 6 Chris Levy; 7 Paul Thorman; 8 John Smith; 9 Lee Jackson; 10 Adam Sullivan; 11 Mick Ramsden; 12 Ian Kirke; 13 Lee Patterson. Subs (all used): 14 Jimmy Elston; 15 Darren Callaghan; 16 David Bates; 17 Yusuf Sozi.
Tries: Fox (7, 9), Sullivan (27), Bates (35), Lingard (48), Blaymire (66); **Goals:** P Thorman 3/5, Lingard 1/1.
Rugby Leaguer & League Express Men of the Match: *Skolars:* Nathan Meischke; *City Knights:* Peter Fox.
Penalty count: 7-8; **Half-time:** 10-22;
Referee: Robert Hicks (Oldham); **Attendance:** 1,018.

SWINTON LIONS 32 GATESHEAD THUNDER 57

LIONS: 1 Lee Patterson; 2 Chris Irwin; 3 Rob Russell; 4 Chris Maye; 5 Marlon Billy; 6 Mick Coates; 7 Ian Watson; 8 Paul Southern; 9 Andy Crabtree; 10 Ian Parry; 11 Danny Heaton; 12 Danny Barton; 13 Phil Joseph. Subs (all used): 14 Warren Ayres; 15 Ian Sinfield; 16 Matt Leigh; 17 Wes Rogers.
Tries: Billy (6), Heaton (22), Leigh (24), Joseph (32), Patterson (48), Coates (51), Irwin (66);
Goals: Coates 1/4, Ayres 1/3.
THUNDER: 1 Wade Liddell; 2 Kevin Neighbour; 3 Joel Barnes; 4 Craig Firth; 5 Robin Peers; 6 Mike Hobbs; 7 Chris Birch; 8 Andrew Pierce; 9 Scott Collins; 10 Leroy Day; 11 Tabua Cakacaka; 12 Steven Bradley; 13 Joe Burley. Subs (all used): 14 Steve Rutherford; 15 Tony Doherty; 16 Selwyn St Bernard; 17 Rob Line.
Tries: Liddell (3, 35, 58), Firth (13, 53), Birch (18, 71), Barnes (38, 78), Peers (80); **Goals:** Birch 8/10;
Field goal: Birch.
Sin bin: Liddell (22) - holding down.
Rugby Leaguer & League Express Men of the Match: *Lions:* Marlon Billy; *Thunder:* Chris Birch.
Penalty count: 6-9; **Half-time:** 18-28;
Referee: Craig Halloran (Dewsbury); **Attendance:** 553.

HUNSLET HAWKS 23 BLACKPOOL PANTHERS 22

HAWKS: 1 George Rayner; 2 Steve Morton; 3 Anthony Gibbons; 4 Chris Redfearn; 5 Paul Cummins; 6 David Gibbons; 7 Mark Cass; 8 Nick Staveley; 9 Jermaine Wray; 10 Andy Shickell; 11 Wayne Freeman; 12 Gareth Naylor; 13 Andy Bastow. Subs (all used): 14 Danny Cook; 15 Marc Shickell; 16 Steve Pryce; 17 Joe Hawley.
Tries: A Gibbons (7), Cook (30, 49), G Rayner (43);
Goals: Wray 3/6; **Field goal:** D Gibbons.
PANTHERS: 1 Eddie Kilgannon; 2 Jake Johnstone; 3 Craig Tipeny; 4 Tommy Grundy; 5 Eric Andrews; 6 Chris Ramsdale; 7 Martin Gambles; 8 Steve Ormesher; 9 Martin Roden; 10 Mick Redford; 11 Gary Smith; 12 John Chamberlain; 13 Kris Ratcliffe. Subs (all used): 14 Liam McGovern; 15 Gus Martin; 16 Gareth Jones; 17 Lee Rowley.
Tries: Martin (20), Redford (56), Ramsdale (63), Andrews (74); **Goals:** Johnstone 3/4.
Rugby Leaguer & League Express Men of the Match: *Hawks:* David Gibbons; *Panthers:* Eddie Kilgannon.
Penalty count: 8-9; **Half-time:** 10-6;
Referee: Ashley Klein (Keighley); **Attendance:** 350.

Saturday 18th June 2005

GATESHEAD THUNDER 15 KEIGHLEY COUGARS 14

THUNDER: 1 Wade Liddell; 2 Kevin Neighbour; 3 Joel Barnes; 4 Craig Firth; 5 Robin Peers; 6 Mike Hobbs; 7 Chris Birch; 8 Andrew Pierce; 9 Scott Collins; 10 Rob Line; 11 Tabua Cakacaka; 12 Steven Bradley; 13 Steve Rutherford. Subs (all used): 14 Graham Stephenson; 15 Tony Doherty; 16 Damian Martinez; 17 Selwyn St Bernard.
Tries: Hobbs (2), Barnes (17); **Goals:** Birch 3/4;
Field goal: Birch.
COUGARS: 1 Sam Gardner; 2 Karl Smith; 3 David Foster; 4 Matt Foster; 5 Andy Robinson; 6 Matt Bramald; 7 Matt Firth; 8 Phil Stephenson; 9 Jonny Wainhouse; 10 Danny Murgatroyd; 11 Stuart Calvert; 12 Matthew Steel; 13 Daniel Harvey. Subs (all used): 14 Gareth Greenwood; 15 Adam Mitchell; 16 James Rushforth; 17 Richard Mervill.
Tries: Bramald (52), M Foster (71); **Goals:** Mitchell 3/3.
Rugby Leaguer & League Express Men of the Match: *Thunder:* Mike Hobbs; *Cougars:* Danny Murgatroyd.
Penalty count: 7-9; **Half-time:** 12-0;
Referee: Mike Dawber (Wigan); **Attendance:** 357.

WEEK 11

Sunday 26th June 2005

DEWSBURY RAMS 32 BLACKPOOL PANTHERS 8

RAMS: 1 Ian Preece; 2 Darren Rogers; 3 Chris Hall; 4 Kevin Crouthers; 5 Leon Williamson; 6 Francis Maloney; 7 Ryan Sheridan; 8 Paul Hicks; 9 Richard Chapman; 10 Warren Jowitt; 11 Alex Bretherton; 12 Ged Corcoran; 13 Kurt Rudder. Subs (all used): 14 David Mycoe; 15 Paul Seal; 16 James Walker; 17 Matt Walker.
Tries: Rogers (8, 63), Hall (33), Chapman (70), Maloney (80); **Goals:** Maloney 6/7.
Sin bin: Corcoran (48) – fighting.
PANTHERS: 1 Eddie Kilgannon; 2 Jake Johnstone; 3 Tommy Grundy; 4 Craig Tipeny; 5 Eric Andrews; 6 Chris Ramsdale; 7 Liam Bretherton; 8 Gus Martin; 9 Martin Roden; 10 Steve Ormesher; 11 Mick Redford; 12 Gary Smith; 13 Willie Swann. Subs (all used): 14 Martin Gambles; 15 Gareth Jones; 16 Liam McGovern; 17 Kris Ratcliffe.
Try: Redford (53); **Goals:** Johnstone 2/2.
Sin bin: Smith (48) – fighting.
Rugby Leaguer & League Express Men of the Match: *Rams:* Francis Maloney; *Panthers:* Martin Roden.
Penalty count: 13-7; **Half-time:** 12-2;
Referee: Dave Merrick (Castleford); **Attendance:** 845.

GATESHEAD THUNDER 52 LONDON SKOLARS 18

THUNDER: 1 Wade Liddell; 2 Kevin Neighbour; 3 Ian Brown; 4 Craig Firth; 5 Robin Peers; 6 Mike Hobbs; 7 Chris Birch; 8 Andrew Pierce; 9 Scott Collins; 10 Rob Line; 11 Tabua Cakacaka; 12 Tony Doherty; 13 Joe Burley. Subs (all used): 14 Damian Martinez; 15 Selwyn St Bernard; 16 Liam Garside; 17 Steve Rutherford.
Tries: Liddell (7), Birch (11), Hobbs (26), I Brown (29), Neighbour (33), Firth (50), St Bernard (52), Line (63), Rutherford (72), Peers (75); **Goals:** Birch 6/10.
SKOLARS: 1 Tim Gee; 2 Ryan Wheele; 3 Joe Price; 4 Austin Aggrey; 5 Corey Simms; 6 Jermaine Coleman; 7 Nathan Meischke; 8 Toby Hall; 9 Gareth Honor; 10 Alex Smits; 11 Rubert Jonker; 12 Ben Joyce; 13 Brett Blaker. Subs (all used): 14 Kurt Pittman; 15 Ade Aderiye; 16 Nathan Gee; 17 Iain Iane.
Tries: T Gee (17), Aggrey (43), Wheele (66);
Goals: T Gee 3/4.
Dismissal: Honor (61) - dissent.
Sin bin: Blaker (51) - dissent.
Rugby Leaguer & League Express Men of the Match: *Thunder:* Wade Liddell; *Skolars:* Tim Gee.
Penalty count: 11-6; **Half-time:** 26-8;
Referee: Gareth Hewer (Whitehaven); **Attendance:** 371.

SWINTON LIONS 42 SHEFFIELD EAGLES 24

LIONS: 1 Wayne English; 2 Stuart Oldham; 3 Lee Patterson; 4 Chris Maye; 5 Marlon Billy; 6 Mick Coates; 7 Ian Watson; 8 Paul Southern; 9 Phil Joseph; 10 Danny Heaton; 11 Matt Leigh; 12 Ian Sinfield; 13 Lee Marsh. Subs (all used): 14 Rob Russell; 15 Danny Barton; 16 Ian Parry; 17 Rob Whittaker.
Tries: Patterson (14, 43), English (24), Watson (35, 65), Oldham (55), Sinfield (70); **Goals:** Marsh 7/9.
EAGLES: 1 John Crawford; 2 James Ford; 3 Waisale Sovatabua; 4 Alex Dickinson; 5 Carl De Chenu; 6 Gavin Brown; 7 Jon Presley; 8 Jack Howieson; 9 Liam Brentley; 10 Damien Lynch; 11 Craig Brown; 12 Nick Turnbull; 13 Aled James. Subs (all used): 14 Lynton Stott; 15 Sean Dickinson; 16 Simon Tillyer; 17 Simon Morton.
Tries: A Dickinson (1), James (16), De Chenu (45), Tillyer (76); **Goals:** Crawford 3/3, G Brown 1/1.
Sin bin: Sovatabua (60) - dissent.
Rugby Leaguer & League Express Men of the Match: *Lions:* Danny Heaton; *Eagles:* Carl De Chenu.
Penalty count: 3-8; **Half-time:** 20-12;
Referee: Mike Dawber (Wigan); **Attendance:** 425.

WORKINGTON TOWN 44 YORK CITY KNIGHTS 28

TOWN: 1 Lusi Sione; 2 Matthew Woodcock; 3 Scott Chilton; 4 Dexter Miller; 5 Martyn Wilson; 6 Lee Kiddie; 7 Tane Manihera; 8 Taani Lavulavu; 9 Jonny Limmer; 10 John Tuimaualuga; 11 Dean Vaughan; 12 Garry Purdham; 13 Jon Roper. Subs (all used): 14 Lee Tinnion; 15 Allan McGuiness; 16 Jamie Beaumont; 17 Ricky Wright.
Tries: Miller (7), Sione (11, 39, 56), Chilton (14), Wilson (45), Tinnion (71); **Goals:** Manihera 8/9.
On report: McGuiness (63) - leading with the elbow.
CITY KNIGHTS: 1 Jon Liddell; 2 Matt Blaymire; 3 Dan Potter; 4 Neil Law; 5 Peter Fox; 6 Chris Levy; 7 Paul Thorman; 8 John Smith; 9 Lee Jackson; 10 Adam Sullivan; 11 Mick Ramsden; 12 Ian Kirke; 13 Lee Patterson. Subs (all used): 14 Scott Rhodes; 15 Darren Callaghan; 16 David Bates; 17 Yusuf Sozi.
Tries: Levy (32), Blaymire (37), Fox (41), Rhodes (51), Sozi (74); **Goals:** P Thorman 4/6.
Rugby Leaguer & League Express Men of the Match: *Town:* Lusi Sione; *City Knights:* Dan Potter.
Penalty count: 6-16; **Half-time:** 24-12;
Referee: Jamie Leahy (Dewsbury); **Attendance:** 1,139.

HUNSLET HAWKS 37 KEIGHLEY COUGARS 28

HAWKS: 1 George Rayner; 2 Calvin Watson; 3 Gareth Naylor; 4 Paul Cummins; 5 Andy Brent; 6 David Gibbons; 7 Mark Moxon; 8 Nick Staveley; 9 Jamaine Wray; 10 Mick Coyle; 11 Wayne Freeman; 12 Andy Shickell; 13 Chris Redfearn. Subs (all used): 14 Mark Cass; 15 Danny Cook; 16 Lee Williamson; 17 Marc Shickell.
Tries: Watson (4), G Rayner (42, 71), D Gibbons (50), Moxon (79);
Goals: Wray 2/2, Naylor 6/7; **Field goal:** Moxon.
COUGARS: 1 Matt Bramald; 2 Sam Gardner; 3 David Foster; 4 Matt Foster; 5 Andrew Jackson; 6 Paul Ashton; 7 Matt Firth; 8 Phil Stephenson; 9 Gareth Greenwood; 10 Danny Murgatroyd; 11 Stuart Calvert; 12 Matthew Steel; 13 Daniel Harvey. Subs (all used): 14 Adam Mitchell; 15 James Rushforth; 16 Danny Ekis; 17 Jason Clegg.
Tries: D Foster (35), Firth (37), Harvey (48), Stephenson (75); **Goals:** Ashton 4/4, Mitchell 2/2.
Rugby Leaguer & League Express Men of the Match: *Hawks:* David Gibbons; *Cougars:* Danny Murgatroyd.
Penalty count: 9-6; **Half-time:** 10-14;
Referee: Craig Halloran (Dewsbury); **Attendance:** 445.

WEEK 12

Sunday 3rd July 2005

BLACKPOOL PANTHERS 26 SHEFFIELD EAGLES 44

PANTHERS: 1 Eddie Kilgannon; 2 Jake Johnstone; 3 Tommy Grundy; 4 Sion Williams; 5 Eric Andrews; 6 Liam McGovern; 7 Martin Gambles; 8 Gus Martin; 9 Martin Roden; 10 Steve Ormesher; 11 Mick Redford; 12 Gary Smith; 13 Kris Ratcliffe. Subs (all used): 14 Willie Swann; 15 Gareth Jones; 16 Dave Rowland; 17 Lee Rowley.
Tries: Andrews (17), Gambles (25), Roden (32), Kilgannon (41), Swann (47); **Goals:** Johnstone 3/6.
EAGLES: 1 John Crawford; 2 Rob Worrincy; 3 James Ford; 4 Alex Dickinson; 5 Carl De Chenu; 6 Gavin Brown; 7 Jon Presley; 8 Jack Howieson; 9 Liam Brentley; 10 Craig Brown; 11 Nick Turnbull; 12 Waisale Sovatabua; 13 Aled James. Subs (all used): 14 Lynton Stott; 15 Simon Tillyer; 16 Greg Hurst; 17 Tom Buckenham.
Tries: A Dickinson (1), Crawford (8, 70), James (20, 50), De Chenu (28, 79), Ford (55); **Goals:** Crawford 6/9.
Sin bin: Sovatabua (15) - tripping.
Rugby Leaguer & League Express Men of the Match: *Panthers:* Gary Smith; *Eagles:* Jack Howieson.
Penalty count: 11-4; **Half-time:** 16-24;
Referee: Jamie Leahy (Dewsbury); **Attendance:** 410.

DEWSBURY RAMS 55 GATESHEAD THUNDER 6

RAMS: 1 Ian Preece; 2 Darren Rogers; 3 Chris Hall; 4 Kevin Crouthers; 5 Leon Williamson; 6 Francis Maloney; 7 Ryan Sheridan; 8 Paul Hicks; 9 Richard Chapman; 10 Matt Walker; 11 Warren Jowitt; 12 Ged Corcoran; 13 Alex Bretherton. Subs (all used): 14 David Mycoe; 15 Paul Seal; 16 James Walker; 17 Jonlee Lockwood.
Tries: Bretherton (3, 75), Rogers (19), J Walker (34), Corcoran (37), Chapman (55), Maloney (63, 71), Preece (66); **Goals:** Maloney 9/10; **Field goal:** Maloney.
THUNDER: 1 Wade Liddell; 2 Joe Brown; 3 Kevin Neighbour; 4 Craig Firth; 5 Robin Peers; 6 Mike Hobbs; 7 Joe Burley; 8 Andrew Pierce; 9 Ryan Clark; 10 Rob Line; 11 Tony Doherty; 12 Ian Brown; 13 Steve Rutherford. Subs (all used): 14 Graham Stephenson; 15 Nigel Arizmendez; 16 Damian Martinez; 17 Alex Rowe.
Try: I Brown (45); **Goals:** Neighbour 1/1.
Rugby Leaguer & League Express Men of the Match: *Rams:* Francis Maloney; *Thunder:* Ian Brown.
Penalty count: 9-7; **Half-time:** 24-0; **Referee:** Steve Nicholson (Whitehaven); **Attendance:** 1,003.

LONDON SKOLARS 4 HUNSLET HAWKS 22

SKOLARS: 1 Tim Gee; 2 Austin Aggrey; 3 Joe Price; 4 Ryan Wheele; 5 Corey Simms; 6 Brett Blaker; 7 Jermaine Coleman; 8 Toby Hall; 9 Kurt Pittman; 10 Alex Smits; 11 Rubert Jonker; 12 Matt Pitman; 13 Ben Joyce. Subs (all used): 14 Gareth Honor; 15 Nathan Gee; 16 Tane Taitoko; 17 Ade Aderiye.
Try: Aggrey (59); **Goals:** T Gee 0/1.
HAWKS: 1 George Rayner; 2 Calvin Watson; 3 Gareth Naylor; 4 Paul Cummins; 5 Andy Brent; 6 David Gibbons; 7 Mark Moxon; 8 Nick Staveley; 9 Jamaine Wray; 10 Mick Coyle; 11 Wayne Freeman; 12 Andy Shickell; 13 Chris Redfearn. Subs (all used): 14 Mark Cass; 15 Danny Cook; 16 Marc Shickell; 17 Lee Williamson.
Tries: Staveley (5, 78), G Rayner (42), Cass (72);
Goals: Wray 3/5.
Rugby Leaguer & League Express Men of the Match: *Skolars:* Corey Simms; *Hawks:* Nick Staveley.
Penalty count: 9-8; **Half-time:** 0-6;
Referee: Dave Merrick (Castleford); **Attendance:** 364.

WORKINGTON TOWN 23 SWINTON LIONS 20

TOWN: 1 Lusi Sione; 2 Matthew Woodcock; 3 Scott Chilton; 4 Martyn Wilson; 5 Lee Tinnion; 6 Lee Kiddie; 7 Tane Manihera; 8 Taani Lavulavu; 9 Jonny Limmer; 10 Allan McGuiness; 11 Dean Vaughan; 12 Garry Purdham; 13 Ryan Campbell. Subs (all used): 14 James Robinson; 15 Matthew Johnson; 16 Dexter Miller; 17 Ricky Wright.
Tries: Sione (15, 43), Kiddie (69); **Goals:** Manihera 5/7;
Field goal: Kiddie.
On report: McGuiness (26) - late tackle.
LIONS: 1 Wayne English; 2 Stuart Oldham; 3 Lee Patterson; 4 Chris Maye; 5 Chris Irwin; 6 Mick Coates; 7 Ian Watson; 8 Danny Heaton; 9 Phil Joseph; 10 Wes Rogers; 11 Matt Leigh; 12 Ian Sinfield; 13 Lee Marsh. Subs: 14 Hugh Thorpe (not used); 15 Danny Barton; 16 Ian Parry; 17 Rob Whittaker.
Tries: Marsh (26), Joseph (34), Maye (47), English (73);
Goals: Marsh 2/5.
Rugby Leaguer & League Express Men of the Match: *Town:* Lusi Sione; *Lions:* Lee Marsh.
Penalty count: 11-2; **Half-time:** 10-12;
Referee: Peter Taberner (Wigan); **Attendance:** 995.

YORK CITY KNIGHTS 44 KEIGHLEY COUGARS 16

CITY KNIGHTS: 1 Matt Blaymire; 2 Chris Ross; 3 Dan Potter; 4 Neil Law; 5 Peter Fox; 6 Scott Rhodes; 7 Paul Thorman; 8 Yusuf Sozi; 9 Chris Levy; 10 David Bates; 11 James Ward; 12 Ian Kirke; 13 Lee Patterson. Subs (all used): 14 Jimmy Elston; 15 Jon Liddell; 16 Adam Sullivan; 17 Craig Forsyth.
Tries: Fox (2), Levy (23), Sozi (46), Liddell (49, 61), Bates (54), Ross (59), Kirke (73);
Goals: P Thorman 5/5, Liddell 1/3.
COUGARS: 1 Matt Bramald; 2 Sam Gardner; 3 David Foster; 4 Daley Williams; 5 Andrew Jackson; 6 Adam Mitchell; 7 Matt Firth; 8 Phil Stephenson; 9 Jonny Wainhouse; 10 Danny Murgatroyd; 11 Matthew Steel; 12 Daniel Harvey; 13 Gareth Greenwood. Subs (all used): 14 Paul Ashton; 15 Andy Robinson; 16 Danny Ekis; 17 Jason Clegg.
Tries: Wainhouse (13), Williams (39), Jackson (80);
Goals: Mitchell 1/1, Ashton 1/2.
Rugby Leaguer & League Express Men of the Match: *City Knights:* Yusuf Sozi; *Cougars:* Danny Murgatroyd.
Penalty count: 8-3; **Half-time:** 12-10;
Referee: Thierry Alibert (France); **Attendance:** 1,756.

WEEK 13

Sunday 10th July 2005

GATESHEAD THUNDER 30 WORKINGTON TOWN 29

THUNDER: 1 Wade Liddell; 2 Kevin Neighbour; 3 Ian Brown; 4 Craig Firth; 5 Robin Peers; 6 Luke Stringer; 7 Chris Birch; 8 Andrew Pierce; 9 Steve Rutherford; 10 Alex Rowe; 11 Tabua Cakacaka; 12 Steven Bradley; 13 Joe Burley. Subs (all used): 14 Neil Thorman; 15 Graham Stephenson; 16 Selwyn St Bernard; 17 Rob Line.
Tries: Birch (3), Rowe (10), Stringer (18), Thorman (34), Line (77); **Goals:** Birch 5/6.
TOWN: 1 Lusi Sione; 2 Matthew Woodcock; 3 Neil Frazer; 4 Martyn Wilson; 5 Lee Tinnion; 6 Lee Kiddie; 7 Tane Manihera; 8 Taani Lavulavu; 9 Jonny Limmer; 10 John Tuimaualuga; 11 Dean Vaughan; 12 Garry Purdham; 13 Ryan Campbell. Subs (all used): 14 Scott Chilton; 15 Dexter Miller; 16 James Robinson; 17 Allan McGuiness.
Tries: Tuimaualuga (23), Campbell (29), Limmer (44, 58, 65); **Goals:** Manihera 4/5; **Field goal:** Purdham.
Rugby Leaguer & League Express Men of the Match: *Thunder:* Chris Birch; *Town:* Jonny Limmer.
Penalty count: 10-12; **Half-time:** 22-12;
Referee: Jamie Leahy (Dewsbury); **Attendance:** 432.

KEIGHLEY COUGARS 28 BLACKPOOL PANTHERS 20

COUGARS: 1 Matt Bramald; 2 Sam Gardner; 3 David Foster; 4 Daley Williams; 5 Andrew Jackson; 6 Adam Mitchell; 7 Matt Firth; 8 Phil Stephenson; 9 Jonny Wainhouse; 10 Danny Murgatroyd; 11 James Rushforth; 12 Matthew Steel; 13 Daniel Harvey. Subs (all used): 14 Paul Ashton; 15 Gareth Greenwood; 16 Lewis Taylor; 17 Danny Ekis.
Tries: Rushforth (16), Harvey (43), Bramald (48), Greenwood (65, 74); **Goals:** Mitchell 2/4, Ashton 2/3.
PANTHERS: 1 Chris Ramsdale; 2 Jake Johnstone; 3 Tommy Grundy; 4 Mick Redford; 5 Eric Andrews; 6 Liam McGovern; 7 Martin Gambles; 8 Gus Martin; 9 Dave Rowland; 10 Steve Ormesher; 11 Kris Ratcliffe; 12 Gary Smith; 13 Willie Swann. Subs (all used): 14 Martin Roden; 15 Dean Balmer; 16 Sion Williams; 17 Lee Rowley.
Tries: Martin (4), Ramsdale (35), G Smith (38), Redford (53); **Goals:** Johnstone 2/4.
Rugby Leaguer & League Express Men of the Match: *Cougars:* Gareth Greenwood; *Panthers:* Gary Smith.
Penalty count: 9-12; **Half-time:** 8-16;
Referee: Gareth Hewer (Whitehaven); **Attendance:** 1,142.

SWINTON LIONS 16 YORK CITY KNIGHTS 32

LIONS: 1 Wayne English; 2 Stuart Oldham; 3 Lee Patterson; 4 Chris Maye; 5 Chris Irwin; 6 Mick Coates; 7 Phil Anderton; 8 Danny Heaton; 9 Phil Joseph; 10 Wes Rogers; 11 Matt Leigh; 12 Ian Sinfield; 13 Lee Marsh. Subs (all used): 14 Warren Ayres; 15 Rob Russell; 16 Paul Southern; 17 Rob Whittaker.
Tries: Maye (4), Marsh (24), English (52);
Goals: Marsh 2/3.
CITY KNIGHTS: 1 Matt Blaymire; 2 Chris Ross; 3 Dan Potter; 4 Darren Callaghan; 5 Peter Fox; 6 Scott Rhodes; 7 Paul Thorman; 8 Adam Sullivan; 9 Chris Levy; 10 Yusuf Sozi; 11 John Smith; 12 Ian Kirke; 13 Lee Patterson. Subs (all used): 14 Jimmy Elston; 15 Jon Liddell; 16 David Bates; 17 Craig Forsyth.
Tries: Blaymire (9, 39), Elston (46), Fox (56), Ross (75);
Goals: P Thorman 6/7.
Rugby Leaguer & League Express Men of the Match: *Lions:* Wayne English; *City Knights:* Jimmy Elston.
Penalty count: 2-9; **Half-time:** 10-12;
Referee: Colin Morris (Huddersfield); **Attendance:** 802.

HUNSLET HAWKS 14 DEWSBURY RAMS 40

HAWKS: 1 George Rayner; 2 Calvin Watson; 3 Gareth Naylor; 4 Paul Cummins; 5 Andy Brent; 6 David Gibbons; 7 Mark Moxon; 8 Nick Staveley; 9 Jamaine Wray; 10 Mick Coyle; 11 Wayne Freeman; 12 Andy Shickell; 13 Chris Redfearn. Subs (all used): 14 Mark Cass; 15 Lee Williamson; 16 Marc Shickell; 17 Andy Bastow.
Tries: Moxon (55), Redfearn (63), Brent (78);
Goals: Wray 1/3.
RAMS: 1 Ian Preece; 2 Darren Rogers; 3 Chris Hall; 4 Kevin Crouthers; 5 Oliver Fairbank; 6 Francis Maloney; 7 Ryan Sheridan; 8 Paul Hicks; 9 Richard Chapman; 10 Matt Walker; 11 Warren Jowitt; 12 Ged Corcoran; 13 Alex Bretherton. Subs (all used): 14 David Mycoe; 15 Kurt Rudder; 16 James Walker; 17 Jonlee Lockwood.

Tries: Rogers (6, 18, 26), Hall (9), Mycoe (45), Preece (71), Fairbank (79); **Goals:** Chapman 6/8.
Rugby Leaguer & League Express Men of the Match: *Hawks:* Wayne Freeman; *Rams:* Darren Rogers.
Penalty count: 16-8; **Half-time:** 0-24; **Referee:** Jean Pierre Boulagnon (France); **Attendance:** 862.

WEEK 14

Friday 22nd July 2005

SHEFFIELD EAGLES 24 HUNSLET HAWKS 34

EAGLES: 1 John Crawford; 2 Greg Hurst; 3 Alex Dickinson; 4 Lynton Stott; 5 Carl De Chenu; 6 Gavin Brown; 7 Jon Presley; 8 Jack Howieson; 9 Liam Brentley; 10 Damien Lynch; 11 Craig Brown; 12 Nick Turnbull; 13 Aled James. Subs (all used): 14 Simon Tillyer; 15 Andy Rice; 16 Waisale Sovatabua; 17 Chris Molyneux.
Tries: Brentley (6), Hurst (14, 65), James (27), Sovatabua (47); **Goals:** Crawford 2/5.
HAWKS: 1 George Rayner; 2 Calvin Watson; 3 Anthony Gibbons; 4 Chris North; 5 Andy Brent; 6 Andy Bastow; 7 Mark Moxon; 8 Nick Staveley; 9 Jamaine Wray; 10 Lee Williamson; 11 Wayne Freeman; 12 Andy Shickell; 13 Chris Redfearn. Subs (all used): 14 Mark Cass; 15 Marc Shickell; 16 Danny Cook; 17 Matt Carbutt.
Tries: Williamson (10), A Gibbons (20), Redfearn (32, 55), North (38), M Shickell (79); **Goals:** Wray 5/7.
Rugby Leaguer & League Express Men of the Match: *Eagles:* Lynton Stott; *Hawks:* Jamaine Wray.
Penalty count: 8-10; **Half-time:** 16-22;
Referee: Ben Thaler (Wakefield); **Attendance:** 846.

Saturday 23rd July 2005

LONDON SKOLARS 15 KEIGHLEY COUGARS 12

SKOLARS: 1 Tim Gee; 2 Austin Aggrey; 3 Joe Price; 4 Ryan Wheele; 5 Corey Simms; 6 Brett Blaker; 7 Lee Sanderson; 8 Toby Hall; 9 Kurt Pittman; 10 Alex Smits; 11 Rubert Jonker; 12 Iain Lane; 13 Ben Joyce. Subs (all used): 14 Ashley Tozer; 15 Mike Castle; 16 Nathan Gee; 17 Ade Aderiye.
Tries: Aggrey (46), Castle (66), Aderiye (69);
Goals: T Gee 1/3; **Field goal:** Joyce.
COUGARS: 1 Matt Bramald; 2 Sam Gardner; 3 Daley Williams; 4 Matt Foster; 5 Andrew Jackson; 6 Adam Mitchell; 7 Matt Firth; 8 Phil Stephenson; 9 Jonny Wainhouse; 10 Danny Murgatroyd; 11 David Foster; 12 James Rushforth; 13 Matthew Steel. Subs (all used): 14 Paul Ashton; 15 Gareth Greenwood; 16 Daniel Harvey; 17 Danny Ekis.
Tries: Steel (19), M Foster (79);
Goals: Mitchell 1/1, Ashton 1/2.
Rugby Leaguer & League Express Men of the Match: *Skolars:* Austin Aggrey; *Cougars:* James Rushforth.
Penalty count: 6-8; **Half-time:** 0-6;
Referee: Jamie Leahy (Dewsbury); **Attendance:** 412.

WEEK 15

Sunday 24th July 2005

BLACKPOOL PANTHERS 26 SWINTON LIONS 51

PANTHERS: 1 Eddie Kilgannon; 2 Jake Johnstone; 3 Chris Ramsdale; 4 Chris Smith; 5 Eric Andrews; 6 Liam McGovern; 7 Martin Gambles; 8 Gus Martin; 9 Martin Roden; 10 Dean Balmer; 11 Kris Ratcliffe; 12 Gary Smith; 13 John Chamberlain. Subs (all used): 14 James Lomax; 15 Steve Ormesher; 16 Dave Rowland; 17 Lee Rowley.
Tries: McGovern (10), Ratcliffe (16), Johnstone (34), Kilgannon (57); **Goals:** Johnstone 5/5.
LIONS: 1 Wayne English; 2 Stuart Oldham; 3 Lee Patterson; 4 Chris Maye; 5 Marlon Billy; 6 Lee Marsh; 7 Mick Coates; 8 Danny Heaton; 9 Phil Joseph; 10 Wes Rogers; 11 Matt Leigh; 12 Ian Sinfield; 13 Kris Smith. Subs (all used): 14 Safraz Patel; 15 Danny Barton; 16 Ian Parry; 17 Rob Whittaker.
Tries: Billy (7, 44, 66), Joseph (26), Maye (52), Parry (63), English (70, 79), Marsh (78);
Goals: Marsh 7/9; **Field goal:** Marsh.
Rugby Leaguer & League Express Men of the Match: *Panthers:* Jake Johnstone; *Lions:* Marlon Billy.
Penalty count: 6-8; **Half-time:** 18-13;
Referee: Dave Merrick (Castleford); **Attendance:** 428.

WORKINGTON TOWN 15 DEWSBURY RAMS 15

TOWN: 1 Lusi Sione; 2 Matthew Woodcock; 3 Martyn Wilson; 4 Dexter Miller; 5 Lee Tinnion; 6 Lee Kiddie; 7 Tane Manihera; 8 Mark Cox; 9 Jonny Limmer; 10 John Tuimaualuga; 11 Dean Vaughan; 12 Garry Purdham; 13 Jon Roper. Subs (all used): 14 Jamie Beaumont; 15 Allan McGuiness; 16 Tom Armstrong; 17 Ryan Campbell.
Tries: Kiddie (31), Roper (43); **Goals:** Manihera 3/3;
Field goal: Kiddie.
RAMS: 1 Ian Preece; 2 Darren Rogers; 3 Chris Hall; 4 Kevin Crouthers; 5 Oliver Fairbank; 6 Kurt Rudder; 7 Ryan Sheridan; 8 Paul Hicks; 9 Richard Chapman; 10 Matt Walker; 11 Warren Jowitt; 12 Ged Corcoran; 13 Alex Bretherton. Subs (all used): 14 David Mycoe; 15 Rob Kelly; 16 James Walker; 17 Jonlee Lockwood.
Tries: Sheridan (16), Hicks (59); **Goals:** Mycoe 2/2, Rudder 0/1, J Walker 1/1; **Field goal:** Corcoran.
Rugby Leaguer & League Express Men of the Match: *Town:* John Tuimaualuga; *Rams:* Warren Jowitt.
Penalty count: 8-9; **Half-time:** 6-8;
Referee: Ian Smith (Oldham); **Attendance:** 969.

YORK CITY KNIGHTS 37 GATESHEAD THUNDER 36

CITY KNIGHTS: 1 Matt Blaymire; 2 Chris Ross; 3 Dan Potter; 4 Neil Law; 5 Peter Fox; 6 Scott Rhodes; 7 Paul Thorman; 8 Yusuf Sozi; 9 Chris Levy; 10 Adam Sullivan; 11 John Smith; 12 Darren Callaghan; 13 Lee Patterson. Subs (all used): 14 Jimmy Elston; 15 Jon Liddell; 16 Joe Helme; 17 Craig Forsyth.
Tries: Levy (3), Ross (21), Elston (32), Helme (37), Law (43), Blaymire (48); **Goals:** P Thorman 6/7;
Field goal: P Thorman.
THUNDER: 1 Wade Liddell; 2 Kevin Neighbour; 3 Ian Brown; 4 Craig Firth; 5 Robin Peers; 6 Mike Hobbs; 7 Chris Birch; 8 Andrew Pierce; 9 Scott Collins; 10 Alex Rowe; 11 Tabua Cakacaka; 12 Steven Bradley; 13 Joe Burley. Subs (all used): 14 Neil Thorman; 15 Tony Doherty; 16 Selwyn St Bernard; 17 Rob Line.
Tries: Burley (7), Firth (11), Rowe (51), Liddell (60), Birch (63), Cakacaka (74); **Goals:** Birch 6/7.
Sin bin: Liddell (39) - holding down.
Rugby Leaguer & League Express Men of the Match: *City Knights:* Lee Patterson; *Thunder:* Chris Birch.
Penalty count: 9-6; **Half-time:** 26-12;
Referee: Gareth Hewer (Whitehaven); **Attendance:** 1,586.

WEEK 16

Sunday 31st July 2005

DEWSBURY RAMS 15 YORK CITY KNIGHTS 23

RAMS: 1 Ian Preece; 2 Darren Rogers; 3 Chris Hall; 4 Kevin Crouthers; 5 Oliver Fairbank; 6 Alex Bretherton; 7 Ryan Sheridan; 8 Paul Hicks; 9 Chris Woolford; 10 Matt Walker; 11 Warren Jowitt; 12 Ged Corcoran; 13 Kurt Rudder. Subs (all used): 14 Liam Morley; 15 Rob Kelly; 16 James Walker; 17 Jonlee Lockwood.
Tries: Bretherton (2), Hall (16), Crouthers (37);
Goals: J Walker 1/1, Corcoran 0/2; **Field goal:** Corcoran.
CITY KNIGHTS: 1 Matt Blaymire; 2 Chris Ross; 3 Dan Potter; 4 Neil Law; 5 Peter Fox; 6 Chris Levy; 7 Paul Thorman; 8 Craig Forsyth; 9 Lee Jackson; 10 Adam Sullivan; 11 John Smith; 12 Ian Kirke; 13 Lee Patterson. Subs (all used): 14 Jimmy Elston; 15 Darren Callaghan; 16 Joe Helme; 17 Yusuf Sozi.
Tries: Elston (45), Law (63), Fox (68), Callaghan (79);
Goals: P Thorman 1/3, Ross 2/2; **Field goal:** Levy.
Rugby Leaguer & League Express Men of the Match: *Rams:* Ryan Sheridan; *City Knights:* Matt Blaymire.
Penalty count: 6-13; **Half-time:** 14-0;
Referee: Mike Dawber (Wigan); **Attendance:** 1,884.

KEIGHLEY COUGARS 20 SHEFFIELD EAGLES 33

COUGARS: 1 Matt Bramald; 2 Sam Gardner; 3 David Foster; 4 Matt Foster; 5 Andy Robinson; 6 Adam Mitchell; 7 Matt Firth; 8 Phil Stephenson; 9 Jonny Wainhouse; 10 Danny Murgatroyd; 11 James Rushforth; 12 Matthew Steel; 13 Daniel Harvey. Subs (all used): 14 Paul Ashton; 15 Gareth Greenwood; 16 Lewis Taylor; 17 Richard Mervill.
Tries: Harvey (14), Robinson (22), Murgatroyd (45), Steel (56); **Goals:** Mitchell 2/4.
EAGLES: 1 John Crawford; 5 Carl De Chenu; 4 Alex Dickinson; 3 Nick Turnbull; 2 Greg Hurst; 6 Gavin Brown; 7 Jon Presley; 8 Jack Howieson; 9 Liam Brentley; 10 Chris Molyneux; 11 Andy Rice; 12 Craig Brown; 13 Aled James. Subs (all used): 14 Simon Tillyer; 15 Simon Morton; 16 Jimmy Pearson; 17 Tom Buckenham.
Tries: Presley (6, 40), Morton (39), A Dickinson (48, 68), Turnbull (80); **Goals:** Crawford 4/6; **Field goal:** Crawford.
Rugby Leaguer & League Express Men of the Match: *Cougars:* Danny Murgatroyd; *Eagles:* Jon Presley.
Penalty count: 5-1; **Half-time:** 10-18;
Referee: Colin Morris (Huddersfield); **Attendance:** 609.

SWINTON LIONS 44 LONDON SKOLARS 12

LIONS: 1 Wayne English; 2 Stuart Oldham; 3 Lee Patterson; 4 Chris Maye; 5 Marlon Billy; 6 Lee Marsh; 7 Mick Coates; 8 Ian Parry; 9 Phil Joseph; 10 Wes Rogers; 11 Danny Heaton; 12 Rob Russell; 13 Kris Smith. Subs (all used): 14 Safraz Patel; 15 Danny Barton; 16 Paul Southern; 17 Rob Whittaker.
Tries: Maye (15), Billy (20, 36), English (32), Heaton (40, 80), Smith (52), Patel (78); **Goals:** Marsh 6/9.
Sin bin: Russell (49) - dissent.
SKOLARS: 1 Tim Gee; 2 Austin Aggrey; 3 Joe Price; 4 Ryan Wheele; 5 Corey Simms; 6 Brett Blaker; 7 Kurt Pittman; 8 Nathan Gee; 9 Mike Castle; 10 Alex Smits; 11 Rubert Jonker; 12 Ade Aderiye; 13 Ben Joyce. Subs (all used): 14 Iain Lane; 15 Ashley Tozer; 16 Jermaine Coleman; 17 Matt Pitman.
Tries: Aggrey (7), Jonker (45); **Goals:** T Gee 2/2.
Rugby Leaguer & League Express Men of the Match: *Lions:* Lee Marsh; *Skolars:* Austin Aggrey.
Penalty count: 11-14; **Half-time:** 28-6;
Referee: Gareth Hewer (Whitehaven); **Attendance:** 401.

HUNSLET HAWKS 25 WORKINGTON TOWN 26

HAWKS: 1 George Rayner; 2 Steve Morton; 3 Anthony Gibbons; 4 Paul Cummins; 5 Andy Brent; 6 Andy Bastow; 7 Chris Redfearn; 8 Mick Coyle; 9 Mark Cass; 10 Lee Williamson; 11 Wayne Freeman; 12 Andy Shickell; 13 Gareth Naylor. Subs (all used): 14 Marc Shickell; 15 Matt Carbutt; 16 Liam Garside; 17 Chris North.
Tries: Cass (15), G Rayner (23), Redfearn (27), A Gibbons (77); **Goals:** Naylor 4/5; **Field goal:** Bastow.
TOWN: 1 Lusi Sione; 2 Matthew Woodcock; 3 Neil Frazer; 4 Jon Roper; 5 Martyn Wilson; 6 Lee Kiddie; 7 Tane Manihera; 8 Mark Cox; 9 Jonny Limmer; 10 John Tuimaualuga; 11 Dean Vaughan; 12 James Robinson; 13 Ryan Campbell. Subs (all used): 14 Brett Smith; 15 Allan McGuiness; 16 Jamie Beaumont; 17 Dexter Miller.
Tries: Limmer (6), Sione (34), Frazer (38, 40), Smith (60); **Goals:** Manihera 3/5.
Rugby Leaguer & League Express Men of the Match: *Hawks:* Gareth Naylor; *Town:* Lusi Sione.
Penalty count: 10-4; **Half-time:** 19-20;
Referee: Peter Taberner (Wigan); **Attendance:** 340.

BLACKPOOL PANTHERS 41 GATESHEAD THUNDER 20

PANTHERS: 1 Eddie Kilgannon; 2 Jake Johnstone; 3 Tommy Grundy; 4 Chris Smith; 5 Eric Andrews; 6 Liam McGovern; 7 Martin Gambles; 8 Gus Martin; 9 Chris Ramsdale; 10 Dean Balmer; 11 Steve Ormesher; 12 Gary Smith; 13 Willie Swann. Subs (all used): 14 Martin Roden; 15 Lee Rowley; 16 Richard Rafferty; 17 Craig Tipeny.
Tries: McGovern (8, 65), G Smith (13), Grundy (27, 46), Johnstone (33, 62); **Goals:** Johnstone 6/10;
Field goal: McGovern.
THUNDER: 1 Wade Liddell; 2 Kevin Neighbour; 3 Ian Brown; 4 Craig Firth; 5 Robin Peers; 6 Mike Hobbs; 7 Chris Birch; 8 Andrew Pierce; 9 Scott Collins; 10 Alex Rowe; 11 Tabua Cakacaka; 12 Steven Bradley; 13 Joe Burley. Subs (all used): 14 Neil Thorman; 15 Joe Brown; 16 Selwyn St Bernard; 17 Rob Line.
Tries: Neighbour (21), Liddell (42), Firth (58), Birch (73); **Goals:** Birch 2/4.
Rugby Leaguer & League Express Men of the Match: *Panthers:* Jake Johnstone; *Thunder:* Craig Firth.
Penalty count: 6-8; **Half-time:** 22-4;
Referee: Jamie Leahy (Dewsbury); **Attendance:** 295.

Friday 5th August 2005

SHEFFIELD EAGLES 27 DEWSBURY RAMS 12

EAGLES: 1 John Crawford; 2 Rob Worrincy; 3 Alex Dickinson; 4 Lynton Stott; 5 Carl De Chenu; 6 Gavin Brown; 7 Jon Presley; 8 Tom Buckenham; 9 Liam Brentley; 10 Chris Molyneux; 11 Nick Turnbull; 12 Craig Brown; 13 Sean Dickinson. Subs (all used): 14 Greg Hurst; 15 Andy Rice; 16 Jimmy Pearson; 17 Simon Tillyer.
Tries: G Brown (20), Crawford (27, 36), A Dickinson (51, 64); **Goals:** Crawford 2/5, G Brown 1/1;
Field goal: G Brown.
Sin bin: Brentley (73) - holding down.
RAMS: 1 Ian Preece; 2 Darren Rogers; 3 Chris Hall; 4 Kevin Crouthers; 5 Oliver Fairbank; 6 Kurt Rudder; 7 Ryan Sheridan; 8 Paul Hicks; 9 Chris Woolford; 10 Matt Walker; 11 Alex Bretherton; 12 Ged Corcoran; 13 Rob Kelly. Subs (all used): 14 David Mycoe; 15 Mark Stubley; 16 Anthony Thewliss; 17 Scott Woodcock.
Tries: Rudder (42), Thewliss (67); **Goals:** Fairbank 2/3.
Sin bin: Hall (60) - punching.
Rugby Leaguer & League Express Men of the Match: *Eagles:* Sean Dickinson; *Rams:* Kurt Rudder.
Penalty count: 13-12; **Half-time:** 17-0;
Referee: Gareth Hewer (Whitehaven); **Attendance:** 884.

WEEK 17

Sunday 7th August 2005

BLACKPOOL PANTHERS 22 YORK CITY KNIGHTS 54

PANTHERS: 1 Eddie Kilgannon; 2 Jake Johnstone; 3 Tommy Grundy; 4 Craig Tipeny; 5 Eric Andrews; 6 Liam McGovern; 7 Martin Gambles; 8 Gus Martin; 9 Martin Roden; 10 Dean Balmer; 11 Gary Smith; 12 Steve Ormesher; 13 Willie Swann. Subs (all used): 14 Dave Rowland; 15 Lee Rowley; 16 James Lomax; 17 Sion Williams.
Tries: Ormesher (5), Martin (40), Gambles (48), Swann (65); **Goals:** Johnstone 3/4.
CITY KNIGHTS: 1 Matt Blaymire; 2 Chris Ross; 3 Dan Potter; 4 Neil Law; 5 Peter Fox; 6 Chris Levy; 7 Paul Thorman; 8 Craig Forsyth; 9 Lee Jackson; 10 Adam Sullivan; 11 John Smith; 12 Ian Kirke; 13 Lee Patterson. Subs (all used): 14 Jimmy Elston; 15 Austin Buchanan; 16 Darren Callaghan; 17 James Ward.
Tries: Law (20), Levy (25), Jackson (28), Ross (30), Potter (35), Elston (45, 75), Smith (60), Sullivan (72), Blaymire (80); **Goals:** P Thorman 7/10.
Rugby Leaguer & League Express Men of the Match: *Panthers:* Gus Martin; *City Knights:* John Smith.
Penalty count: 9-9; **Half-time:** 12-28;
Referee: Robert Hicks (Oldham); **Attendance:** 635.

KEIGHLEY COUGARS 20 GATESHEAD THUNDER 20

COUGARS: 1 Matt Bramald; 2 Sam Gardner; 3 David Foster; 4 Matt Foster; 5 Andy Robinson; 6 Adam Mitchell; 7 Paul Ashton; 8 Phil Stephenson; 9 Jonny Wainhouse; 10 Danny Murgatroyd; 11 James Rushforth; 12 Stuart Calvert; 13 Matthew Steel. Subs (all used): 14 Karl Smith; 15 Gareth Greenwood; 16 Lewis Taylor; 17 Richard Mervill.
Tries: D Foster (14), Gardner (30), Ashton (36);
Goals: Mitchell 4/7.
THUNDER: 1 Wade Liddell; 2 Kevin Neighbour; 3 Aaron Lewis; 4 Craig Firth; 5 Robin Peers; 6 Neil Thorman; 7 Chris Birch; 8 Andrew Pierce; 9 Scott Collins; 10 Tabua Cakacaka; 11 Ian Brown; 12 Steven Bradley; 13 Joe Burley. Subs (all used): 14 Joe Brown; 15 Tony Doherty; 16 Selwyn St Bernard; 17 Rob Line.
Tries: Birch (7, 50), Peers (21), Liddell (62);
Goals: Birch 2/5.
Rugby Leaguer & League Express Men of the Match: *Cougars:* Sam Gardner; *Thunder:* Chris Birch.
Penalty count: 7-6; **Half-time:** 16-8;
Referee: Peter Taberner (Wigan); **Attendance:** 545.

LONDON SKOLARS 4 WORKINGTON TOWN 28

SKOLARS: 1 Tim Gee; 2 Ashley Tozer; 3 Joe Price; 4 Ryan Wheele; 5 Corey Simms; 6 Jermaine Coleman; 7 Kurt Pittman; 8 Nathan Gee; 9 Mike Castle; 10 Alex Smits; 11 Rubert Jonker; 12 Ade Aderiye; 13 Ben Joyce. Subs (all used): 14 Gareth Honor; 15 Iain Lane; 16 James Sullivan; 17 Alan Barker.
Try: T Gee (37); **Goals:** T Gee 0/1.
TOWN: 1 Lusi Sione; 2 Matthew Woodcock; 3 Neil Frazer; 4 Scott Chilton; 5 Martyn Wilson; 6 Lee Kiddie; 7 Tane Manihera; 8 Mark Cox; 9 Jonny Limmer; 10 John Tuimaualuga; 11 Dean Vaughan; 12 Garry Purdham; 13 Jon Roper. Subs (all used): 14 James Robinson; 15 Allan McGuiness; 16 Jamie Beaumont; 17 Ryan Campbell.
Tries: Roper (13), Woodcock (26, 39), Limmer (55), Purdham (72); **Goals:** Manihera 4/5.
Rugby Leaguer & League Express Men of the Match: *Skolars:* Gareth Honor; *Town:* Jon Roper.
Penalty count: 8-7; **Half-time:** 4-18;
Referee: Paul Carr (Castleford); **Attendance:** 372.

SWINTON LIONS 34 HUNSLET HAWKS 20

LIONS: 1 Wayne English; 2 Stuart Oldham; 3 Lee Patterson; 4 Chris Maye; 5 Marlon Billy; 6 Lee Marsh; 7 Mick Coates; 8 Ian Parry; 9 Phil Joseph; 10 Wes Rogers; 11 Danny Heaton; 12 Ian Sinfield; 13 Kris Smith. Subs (all used): 14 Safraz Patel; 15 Danny Barton; 16 Matt Leigh; 17 Rob Whittaker.
Tries: Patterson (19), English (21, 69), Billy (25), Oldham (41), Marsh (46), Maye (65); **Goals:** Marsh 3/9.
Dismissal: Billy (52) - fighting.
HAWKS: 1 George Rayner; 2 Steve Morton; 3 Anthony Gibbons; 4 Paul Cummins; 5 Andy Brent; 6 Andy Bastow; 7 Mark Cass; 8 Lee Williamson; 9 Jamaine Wray; 10 Mick Coyle; 11 Wayne Freeman; 12 Andy Shickell; 13 Chris Redfearn. Subs (all used): 14 Gareth Naylor; 15 Marc Shickell; 16 Matt Carbutt; 17 Steve Pryce.
Tries: Bastow (14), Pryce (40), Brent (76);
Goals: Wray 4/4.
Sin bin: A Gibbons (6) - dissent.
Rugby Leaguer & League Express Men of the Match: *Lions:* Phil Joseph; *Hawks:* Jamaine Wray.
Penalty count: 8-9; **Half-time:** 12-14;
Referee: Jamie Leahy (Dewsbury); **Attendance:** 512.

WEEK 18

Sunday 14th August 2005

BLACKPOOL PANTHERS 12 HUNSLET HAWKS 36

PANTHERS: 1 Eddie Kilgannon; 2 Jake Johnstone; 3 Tommy Grundy; 4 Chris Smith; 5 Eric Andrews; 6 Liam McGovern; 7 Martin Gambles; 8 Gus Martin; 9 Martin Roden; 10 Dean Balmer; 11 Craig Tipeny; 12 Gary Smith; 13 Willie Swann. Subs (all used): 14 Dave Rowland; 15 Lee Rowley; 16 Chris Ramsdale; 17 James Lomax.
Tries: Gambles (31), Johnstone (70);
Goals: Johnstone 2/4.
HAWKS: 1 George Rayner; 2 Chris North; 3 Gareth Naylor; 4 Paul Cummins; 5 Andy Brent; 6 David Gibbons; 7 Mark Cass; 8 Nick Staveley; 9 Jamaine Wray; 10 Mick Coyle; 11 Wayne Freeman; 12 Andy Shickell; 13 Chris Redfearn. Subs (all used): 14 Danny Cook; 15 Steve Pryce; 16 Andy Bastow; 17 Steve Morton.
Tries: Cummins (7), Naylor (23), Wray (38), Morton (65), Cass (77), A Shickell (79); **Goals:** Wray 6/7.
Rugby Leaguer & League Express Men of the Match: *Panthers:* Martin Gambles; *Hawks:* Jamaine Wray.
Penalty count: 9-6; **Half-time:** 6-16;
Referee: Paul Carr (Castleford); **Attendance:** 358.

DEWSBURY RAMS 32 KEIGHLEY COUGARS 22

RAMS: 1 Ian Preece; 2 Darren Rogers; 3 Chris Hall; 4 Wayne McHugh; 5 Oliver Fairbank; 6 Liam Morley; 7 David Mycoe; 8 Paul Hicks; 9 Chris Woolford; 10 Matt Walker; 11 Kevin Crouthers; 12 Rob Kelly; 13 Alex Bretherton. Subs (all used): 14 Ryan Sheridan; 15 Richard Chapman; 16 Anthony Thewliss; 17 Jonlee Lockwood.
Tries: Thewliss (19), Rogers (33), McHugh (44, 56), Hall (60), Chapman (65); **Goals:** Mycoe 3/6, Chapman 1/1.
Sin bin: Chapman (78) - dissent.
COUGARS: 1 Matt Bramald; 2 Sam Gardner; 3 Daley Williams; 4 Matt Foster; 5 Andy Robinson; 6 Adam Mitchell; 7 Paul Ashton; 8 Phil Stephenson; 9 Jonny Wainhouse; 10 Richard Mervill; 11 Stuart Calvert; 12 Matthew Steel; 13 Gareth Greenwood. Subs (all used): 14 James Rushforth; 15 Daniel Harvey; 16 Danny Murgatroyd; 17 Jason Clegg.
Tries: Mervill (4), Robinson (48), Williams (68), Steel (78); **Goals:** Mitchell 1/3, Ashton 2/2.
Rugby Leaguer & League Express Men of the Match: *Rams:* Richard Chapman; *Cougars:* Phil Stephenson.
Penalty count: 11-7; **Half-time:** 14-6;
Referee: Colin Morris (Huddersfield); **Attendance:** 768.

GATESHEAD THUNDER 58 SWINTON LIONS 10

THUNDER: 1 Wade Liddell; 2 Kevin Neighbour; 3 Aaron Lewis; 4 Craig Firth; 5 Robin Peers; 6 Mike Hobbs; 7 Chris Birch; 8 Andrew Pierce; 9 Scott Collins; 10 Rob Line; 11 Ian Brown; 12 Steven Bradley; 13 Joe Burley. Subs (all used): 14 Neil Thorman; 15 Graham Stephenson; 16 Alex Rowe; 17 Selwyn St Bernard.
Tries: Lewis (19), Hobbs (23, 31, 59), Peers (35), Neighbour (38, 56), Liddell (41, 73), Pierce (68);
Goals: Birch 9/11.
LIONS: 1 Lee Patterson; 2 Hugh Thorpe; 3 Alex Muff; 4 Chris Maye; 5 Marlon Billy; 6 Mick Coates; 7 Phil Anderton; 8 Ian Parry; 9 Phil Joseph; 10 Ian Sinfield; 11 Kris Smith; 12 Danny Barton; 13 Lee Marsh. Subs (all used): 14 Safraz Patel; 15 Craig Farrimond; 16 Matt Leigh; 17 Rob Whittaker.
Tries: Farrimond (16), Billy (50); **Goals:** Marsh 1/2.
Rugby Leaguer & League Express Men of the Match: *Thunder:* Wade Liddell; *Lions:* Phil Joseph.
Penalty count: 9-10; **Half-time:** 28-6;
Referee: Gareth Hewer (Whitehaven); **Attendance:** 319.

WORKINGTON TOWN 34 SHEFFIELD EAGLES 10

TOWN: 1 Lusi Sione; 2 Matthew Woodcock; 3 Neil Frazer; 4 Jon Roper; 5 Martyn Wilson; 6 Lee Kiddie; 7 Tane Manihera; 8 Mark Cox; 9 Jonny Limmer; 10 John Tuimaualuga; 11 Dean Vaughan; 12 Ryan Campbell; 13 Gareth Dean. Subs (all used): 14 James Robinson; 15 Allan McGuiness; 16 Jamie Beaumont; 17 Taani Lavulavu.
Tries: Limmer (7, 37, 69), Manihera (15), Sione (28), Woodcock (58); **Goals:** Roper 5/6.
EAGLES: 1 John Crawford; 2 Greg Hurst; 3 Alex Dickinson; 4 Lynton Stott; 5 Carl De Chenu; 6 Gavin Brown; 7 Jon Presley; 8 Tom Buckenham; 9 Liam Brentley; 10 Chris Molyneux; 11 Nick Turnbull; 12 Craig Brown; 13 Sean Dickinson. Subs (all used): 14 Jimmy Pearson; 15 Andy Rice; 16 Simon Tillyer; 17 Damien Lynch.
Tries: Presley (10), De Chenu (73); **Goals:** Crawford 1/2.
Sin bin: Lynch (56) - holding down.
On report: Turnbull (58) - high tackle.
Rugby Leaguer & League Express Men of the Match: *Town:* Jonny Limmer; *Eagles:* Liam Brentley.
Penalty count: 13-7; **Half-time:** 24-6;
Referee: Jamie Leahy (Dewsbury); **Attendance:** 866.

YORK CITY KNIGHTS 60 LONDON SKOLARS 12

CITY KNIGHTS: 1 Lee Lingard; 2 Austin Buchanan; 3 Dan Potter; 4 Chris Ross; 5 Peter Fox; 6 Scott Rhodes; 7 Paul Thorman; 8 Craig Forsyth; 9 Lee Jackson; 10 Adam Sullivan; 11 John Smith; 12 James Ward; 13 Jon Liddell. Subs (all used): 14 Jimmy Elston; 15 Mick Ramsden; 16 Joe Helme; 17 Yusuf Sozi.
Tries: Buchanan (1, 31), Fox (23, 36, 42, 53), Lingard (48), Potter (61, 66, 80), Ross (72), Elston (78);
Goals: P Thorman 4/9, Ross 2/3.
SKOLARS: 1 Steve Elms; 2 James Thompson; 3 Joe Price; 4 Ashley Tozer; 5 Corey Simms; 6 Nathan Meischke; 7 Kurt Pittman; 8 Nathan Gee; 9 James Sullivan; 10 Alex Smits; 11 Ade Aderiye; 12 Matt Pitman; 13 Iain Lane. Subs (all used): 14 Mario Du Toit; 15 Mike Castle; 16 Matt Ryan; 17 Tim Williams.
Tries: Meischke (9, 18); **Goals:** Elms 2/3.
Sin bin: K Pittman (22) - holding down.
Rugby Leaguer & League Express Men of the Match: *City Knights:* Peter Fox; *Skolars:* Kurt Pittman.
Penalty count: 8-8; **Half-time:** 20-12;
Referee: Robert Hicks (Oldham); **Attendance:** 1,610.

WEEK 19

Sunday 21st August 2005

DEWSBURY RAMS 34 LONDON SKOLARS 8

RAMS: 1 Chris Hall; 2 Darren Rogers; 3 Wayne McHugh; 4 Kevin Crouthers; 5 Richard Tillotson; 6 Francis Maloney; 7 Ryan Sheridan; 8 Paul Hicks; 9 Richard Chapman; 10 Matt Walker; 11 Rob Kelly; 12 Ged Corcoran; 13 Alex Bretherton. Subs (all used): 14 David Mycoe; 15 Anthony Thewliss; 16 Mark Stubley; 17 Jonlee Lockwood.
Tries: Chapman (4), Rogers (17), Tillotson (29, 45), Stubley (55), McHugh (76);
Goals: Maloney 4/5, Mycoe 1/1.
On report: M Walker (55) - foul play.
SKOLARS: 1 Jermaine Coleman; 2 Austin Aggrey; 3 Joe Price; 4 Ade Aderiye; 5 Corey Simms; 6 Nathan Meischke; 7 Kurt Pittman; 8 Nathan Gee; 9 James Sullivan; 10 Alex Smits; 11 Rubert Jonker; 12 Matt Pitman; 13 Iain Lane. Subs (all used): 14 Mario Du Toit; 15 Mike Castle; 16 Wayne Parillon; 17 James Thompson.
Tries: Thompson (48), Coleman (70);
Goals: K Pittman 0/2.
Rugby Leaguer & League Express Men of the Match: *Rams:* Ryan Sheridan; *Skolars:* Kurt Pittman.
Penalty count: 8-4; **Half-time:** 16-0;
Referee: Paul Carr (Castleford); **Attendance:** 682.

GATESHEAD THUNDER 41 SHEFFIELD EAGLES 18

THUNDER: 1 Wade Liddell; 2 Graham Stephenson; 3 Kevin Neighbour; 4 Aaron Lewis; 5 Robin Peers; 6 Mike Hobbs; 7 Chris Birch; 8 Andrew Pierce; 9 Scott Collins; 10 Rob Line; 11 Ian Brown; 12 Tabua Cakacaka; 13 Joe Burley. Subs (all used): 14 Neil Thorman; 15 Tony Doherty; 16 Selwyn St Bernard; 17 Alex Rowe.
Tries: Birch (4), Collins (13, 61), Rowe (41), Liddell (44), Neighbour (48), Line (71); **Goals:** Birch 6/8;
Field goal: Birch.
Dismissal: Hobbs (79) - fighting.
Sin bin: Liddell (32) - interference.
On report: Brawl (79).
EAGLES: 1 John Crawford; 2 Danny Mills; 3 Alex Dickinson; 4 Lynton Stott; 5 Carl De Chenu; 6 Gavin Brown; 7 Jon Presley; 8 Tom Buckenham; 9 Liam Brentley; 10 Chris Molyneux; 11 Sean Dickinson; 12 Craig Brown; 13 Aled James. Subs (all used): 14 Ryan Dickinson; 15 Simon Morton; 16 Greg Hurst; 17 Simon Tillyer.
Tries: Tillyer (27), Mills (33), Molyneux (52), Hurst (68);
Goals: G Brown 1/2, Crawford 0/2.
Dismissal: Stott (79) - fighting.
Sin bin: Tillyer (58) - punching.
On report: Brawl (79).
Rugby Leaguer & League Express Men of the Match: *Thunder:* Kevin Neighbour; *Eagles:* Chris Molyneux.
Penalty count: 6-8; **Half-time:** 12-8;
Referee: Colin Morris (Huddersfield); **Attendance:** 371.

SWINTON LIONS 46 KEIGHLEY COUGARS 0

LIONS: 1 Wayne English; 2 Stuart Oldham; 3 Lee Patterson; 4 Chris Maye; 5 Marlon Billy; 6 Lee Marsh; 7 Warren Ayres; 8 Rob Whittaker; 9 Andy Crabtree; 10 Wes Rogers; 11 Danny Heaton; 12 Ian Sinfield; 13 Phil Joseph. Subs (all used): 14 Ian Watson; 15 Rob Russell; 16 Craig Farrimond; 17 Ian Parry.
Tries: Joseph (20, 32), Oldham (25), Marsh (43, 78), English (53), Heaton (62, 70); **Goals:** Marsh 7/9.
Sin bin: Heaton (49) - fighting.
COUGARS: 1 Matt Bramald; 2 Sam Gardner; 3 Daley Williams; 4 Matt Foster; 5 Karl Smith; 6 Gareth Greenwood; 7 Adam Mitchell; 8 Richard Mervill; 9 Jonny Wainhouse; 10 Danny Murgatroyd; 11 Stuart Calvert; 12 James Rushforth; 13 Matthew Steel. Subs (all used): 14 Paul Ashton; 15 Andy Robinson; 16 Phil Stephenson; 17 Lewis Taylor.
Sin bin: Mervill (49) - fighting;
Smith (58) - holding down.
Rugby Leaguer & League Express Men of the Match: *Lions:* Phil Joseph; *Cougars:* Danny Murgatroyd.
Penalty count: 13-8; **Half-time:** 18-0;
Referee: Jamie Leahy (Dewsbury); **Attendance:** 466.

WORKINGTON TOWN 24 BLACKPOOL PANTHERS 23

TOWN: 1 Lusi Sione; 2 Matthew Woodcock; 3 Neil Frazer; 4 Jon Roper; 5 Martyn Wilson; 6 Lee Kiddie; 7 Tane Manihera; 8 Mark Cox; 9 Jonny Limmer; 10 John Tuimaualuga; 11 Gareth Dean; 12 Garry Purdham; 13 Matthew Tunstall. Subs (all used): 14 Ryan Campbell; 15 Allan McGuiness; 16 Jamie Beaumont; 17 Taani Lavulavu.
Tries: Roper (16), Manihera (66), Limmer (74), Campbell (76); **Goals:** Roper 4/4.
PANTHERS: 1 Eddie Kilgannon; 2 Jake Johnstone; 3 Liam Bretherton; 4 Tommy Grundy; 5 Eric Andrews; 6 Liam McGovern; 7 Martin Gambles; 8 Gus Martin; 9 Martin Roden; 10 Dean Balmer; 11 Steve Ormesher; 12 Gary Smith; 13 Willie Swann. Subs: 14 Dave Rowland (not used); 15 Lee Rowley; 16 Chris Ramsdale; 17 Craig Tipeny.
Tries: McGovern (3), Ormesher (24), Bretherton (53);
Goals: Johnstone 5/5; **Field goal:** McGovern.
Sin bin: Ramsdale (73) - foul play.
Rugby Leaguer & League Express Men of the Match: *Town:* Jonny Limmer; *Panthers:* Liam McGovern.
Penalty count: 14-8; **Half-time:** 6-15;
Referee: Robert Hicks (Oldham); **Attendance:** 767.

HUNSLET HAWKS 22 YORK CITY KNIGHTS 24

HAWKS: 1 George Rayner; 2 Chris North; 3 Anthony Gibbons; 4 Gareth Naylor; 5 Andy Brent; 6 David Gibbons; 7 Mark Moxon; 8 Nick Staveley; 9 Jamaine Wray; 10 Steve Pryce; 11 Wayne Freeman; 12 Andy Shickell; 13 Chris Redfearn. Subs (all used): 14 Mark Cass; 15 Andy Bastow; 16 Danny Cook; 17 Paul Cummins.
Tries: W Freeman (3), Naylor (6), Cook (20), North (35);
Goals: Wray 3/4, Naylor 0/1.
Sin bin: A Shickell (37) - high tackle;
A Gibbons (42) - interference.
CITY KNIGHTS: 1 Matt Blaymire; 2 Austin Buchanan; 3 Dan Potter; 4 Neil Law; 5 Peter Fox; 6 Scott Rhodes; 7 Paul Thorman; 8 Craig Forsyth; 9 Lee Jackson; 10 Joe Helme; 11 John Smith; 12 Ian Kirke; 13 Lee Patterson. Subs (all used): 14 Jimmy Elston; 15 Jon Liddell; 16 Darren Callaghan; 17 Yusuf Sozi.
Tries: Potter (38, 60), Law (44), Blaymire (50);
Goals: P Thorman 2/3, Patterson 2/2.
Rugby Leaguer & League Express Men of the Match: *Hawks:* Jamaine Wray; *City Knights:* Dan Potter.
Penalty count: 10-14; **Half-time:** 22-6;
Referee: Gareth Hewer (Whitehaven); **Attendance:** 1,200.

WEEK 20

Monday 29th August 2005

SHEFFIELD EAGLES 30 LONDON SKOLARS 18

EAGLES: 1 Greg Hurst; 2 Danny Mills; 3 Jimmy Pearson; 4 Nick Turnbull; 5 Carl De Chenu; 6 John Crawford; 7 Jon Presley; 8 Tom Buckenham; 9 Liam Brentley; 10 Simon Morton; 11 Chris Molyneux; 12 Craig Brown; 13 Aled James. Subs (all used): 14 Ryan Dickinson; 15 Andy Rice; 16 Rob Worrincy; 17 Simon Tillyer.
Tries: Hurst (4, 19), Brentley (35, 56), Presley (64), Mills (78); **Goals:** Crawford 2/3, James 1/3.
SKOLARS: 1 Jermaine Coleman; 2 Austin Aggrey; 3 Joe Price; 4 Ade Aderiye; 5 Corey Simms; 6 Nathan Meischke; 7 Kurt Pittman; 8 Alex Smits; 9 James Sullivan; 10 Nathan Gee; 11 Rubert Jonker; 12 Matt Pitman; 13 Iain Lane. Subs (all used): 14 Mario Du Toit; 15 Ben Joyce; 16 Wayne Parillon; 17 Mike Castle.
Tries: M Pitman (43), Castle (76), Parillon (80);
Goals: K Pittman 3/3.
Rugby Leaguer & League Express Men of the Match: *Eagles:* Liam Brentley; *Skolars:* Kurt Pittman.
Penalty count: 7-7; **Half-time:** 16-0;
Referee: Gareth Hewer (Whitehaven); **Attendance:** 764.

Friday 2nd September 2005

SHEFFIELD EAGLES 14 SWINTON LIONS 38

EAGLES: 1 Rob Worrincy; 2 Danny Mills; 3 Jimmy Pearson; 4 Nick Turnbull; 5 Carl De Chenu; 6 John

York celebrate winning the National League Two title after a thrilling win at Hunslet

Crawford; 7 Jon Presley; 8 Tom Buckenham; 9 Liam Brentley; 10 Simon Morton; 11 Chris Molyneux; 12 Craig Brown; 13 Aled James. Subs (all used): 14 Gavin Brown; 15 Andy Rice; 16 Greg Hurst; 17 Simon Tillyer.
Tries: De Chenu (3, 60), Presley (5);
Goals: Crawford 1/2, G Brown 0/1.
LIONS: 1 Wayne English; 2 Stuart Oldham; 3 Lee Patterson; 4 Dave Llewellyn; 5 Marlon Billy; 6 Lee Marsh; 7 Mick Coates; 8 Rob Whittaker; 9 Andy Crabtree; 10 Danny Heaton; 11 Craig Farrimond; 12 Rob Russell; 13 Phil Joseph. Subs (all used): 14 Ian Watson; 15 Alex Muff; 16 Kris Smith; 17 Ian Parry.
Tries: Billy (18, 48), Joseph (24), Llewellyn (34), Parry (57), Marsh (68), Patterson (76); **Goals:** Marsh 5/7.
Rugby Leaguer & League Express Men of the Match:
Eagles: Liam Brentley; *Lions:* Lee Marsh.
Penalty count: 7-9; **Half-time:** 10-16;
Referee: Jamie Leahy (Dewsbury); **Attendance:** 806.

Saturday 3rd September 2005

LONDON SKOLARS 24 GATESHEAD THUNDER 54

SKOLARS: 1 Ashley Tozer; 2 Austin Aggrey; 3 Joe Price; 4 Tim Gee; 5 Corey Simms; 6 Nathan Meischke; 7 Kurt Pittman; 8 Nathan Gee; 9 James Sullivan; 10 Alex Smits; 11 Mike Castle; 12 Matt Pitman; 13 Ben Joyce. Subs (all used): 14 Gareth Honor; 15 Brett Blaker; 16 Ade Aderiye; 17 Wayne Parillon.
Tries: Tozer (13, 35), Aderiye (47, 62); **Goals:** T Gee 4/5.
THUNDER: 1 Wade Liddell; 2 Graham Stephenson; 3 Kevin Neighbour; 4 Aaron Lewis; 5 Joe Brown; 6 Mike Hobbs; 7 Chris Birch; 8 Andrew Pierce; 9 Scott Collins; 10 Rob Line; 11 Ian Brown; 12 Tabua Cakacaka; 13 Joe Burley. Subs (all used): 14 Neil Thorman; 15 Steve Rutherford; 16 Selwyn St Bernard; 17 Alex Rowe.
Tries: Pierce (3), Collins (9, 77), Liddell (22, 37, 67), Hobbs (25), Lewis (29), I Brown (54); **Goals:** Birch 9/9.
Dismissal: Birch (78) - swinging arm.
Rugby Leaguer & League Express Men of the Match:
Skolars: Ade Aderiye; *Thunder:* Ian Brown.
Penalty count: 8-6; **Half-time:** 12-36;
Referee: Paul Carr (Castleford); **Attendance:** 330.

WEEK 21

Sunday 4th September 2005

BLACKPOOL PANTHERS 26 DEWSBURY RAMS 39

PANTHERS: 1 Liam Bretherton; 2 Jake Johnstone; 3 Craig Tipeny; 4 Eddie Kilgannon; 5 Eric Andrews; 6 Liam McGovern; 7 Martin Gambles; 8 Gus Martin; 9 Dave Rowland; 10 Lee Rowley; 11 Mick Redford; 12 Gary Smith; 13 Willie Swann. Subs (all used): 14 Martin Roden; 15 James Lomax; 16 Chris Ramsdale; 17 Sion Williams.
Tries: Tipeny (2), Bretherton (36, 66), Martin (64), Johnstone (73); **Goals:** Johnstone 3/5.

Sin bin: Redford (80) - fighting.
RAMS: 1 Ian Preece; 2 Darren Rogers; 3 Chris Hall; 4 Wayne McHugh; 5 Richard Tillotson; 6 Francis Maloney; 7 David Mycoe; 8 Paul Hicks; 9 Richard Chapman; 10 Matt Walker; 11 Alex Bretherton; 12 Ged Corcoran; 13 Kurt Rudder. Subs (all used): 14 Ryan Sheridan; 15 Anthony Thewliss; 16 James Walker; 17 Jonlee Lockwood.
Tries: Tillotson (8), Mycoe (18), McHugh (21, 26), Rogers (43), Chapman (47), Sheridan (54),
Maloney (77); **Goals:** Maloney 3/8; **Field goal:** Chapman.
Sin bin: Corcoran (80) - fighting.
Rugby Leaguer & League Express Men of the Match:
Panthers: Liam Bretherton; *Rams:* Darren Rogers.
Penalty count: 7-5; **Half-time:** 10-21;
Referee: Dave Merrick (Castleford); **Attendance:** 540.

KEIGHLEY COUGARS 20 HUNSLET HAWKS 27

COUGARS: 1 Matt Bramald; 2 Sam Gardner; 3 David Foster; 4 Daley Williams; 5 Andrew Jackson; 6 Paul Ashton; 7 Matt Firth; 8 Phil Stephenson; 9 Jonny Wainhouse; 10 Danny Murgatroyd; 11 Jordan Ross; 12 Lewis Taylor; 13 Gareth Greenwood. Subs (all used): 14 Matt Foster; 15 Daniel Harvey; 16 Danny Ekis; 17 Richard Mervill.
Tries: Jackson (42), M Foster (58), Stephenson (73), Bramald (79); **Goals:** Bramald 2/4.
Sin bin: M Foster (37) - dissent.
HAWKS: 1 George Rayner; 2 Paul Cummins; 3 Anthony Gibbons; 4 Gareth Naylor; 5 Andy Brent; 6 David Gibbons; 7 Mark Moxon; 8 Mick Coyle; 9 Jamaine Wray; 10 Lee Williamson; 11 Wayne Freeman; 12 Andy Shickell; 13 Chris Redfearn. Subs (all used): 14 Andy Bastow; 15 Danny Cook; 16 Matt Carbutt; 17 Liam Garside.
Tries: G Rayner (5), A Gibbons (29, 53), Brent (68);
Goals: Wray 4/4, Naylor 1/1; **Field goal:** G Rayner.
Sin bin: D Gibbons (34) - obstruction.
Rugby Leaguer & League Express Men of the Match:
Cougars: Phil Stephenson; *Hawks:* Jamaine Wray.
Penalty count: 16-12; **Half time:** 0-12;
Referee: Gareth Hewer (Whitehaven); **Attendance:** 749.

YORK CITY KNIGHTS 18 WORKINGTON TOWN 20

CITY KNIGHTS: 1 Matt Blaymire; 2 Chris Ross; 3 Dan Potter; 4 Neil Law; 5 Peter Fox; 6 Chris Levy; 7 Paul Thorman; 8 Craig Forsyth; 9 Lee Jackson; 10 Joe Helme; 11 Mick Ramsden; 12 John Smith; 13 Lee Patterson. Subs (all used): 14 Jimmy Elston; 15 Darren Callaghan; 16 Adam Sullivan; 17 Yusuf Sozi.
Tries: Smith (27), Levy (39, 55); **Goals:** P Thorman 3/4.
Sin bin: Helme (66) - interference.
TOWN: 1 Lusi Sione; 2 Matthew Woodcock; 3 Neil Frazer; 4 Jon Roper; 5 Martyn Wilson; 6 Lee Kiddie; 7 Tane Manihera; 8 Mark Cox; 9 Jonny Limmer; 10 Dean Vaughan; 11 Matthew Tunstall; 12 John Tuimaualuga; 13 Garry Purdham. Subs (all used): 14 James Robinson; 15 Allan McGuiness; 16 Brett Smith; 17 Taani Lavulavu.
Tries: Kiddie (23), Smith (64), Sione (67, 75);

Goals: Smith 2/3, Sione 0/1.
Rugby Leaguer & League Express Men of the Match:
City Knights: Chris Levy; *Town:* Jonny Limmer.
Penalty count: 5-7; **Half-time:** 12-4;
Referee: Colin Morris (Huddersfield); **Attendance:** 2,177.

Friday 9th September 2005

SHEFFIELD EAGLES 10 YORK CITY KNIGHTS 36

EAGLES: 1 Rob Worrincy; 2 Danny Mills; 3 Alex Dickinson; 4 Nick Turnbull; 5 Carl De Chenu; 6 Gavin Brown; 7 Jon Presley; 8 Tom Buckenham; 9 Liam Brentley; 10 Simon Morton; 11 Chris Molyneux; 12 Craig Brown; 13 Sean Dickinson. Subs (all used): 14 John Crawford; 15 Greg Hurst; 16 Ryan Dickinson; 17 Andy Rice.
Tries: A Dickinson (3), Worrincy (11); **Goals:** G Brown 1/2.
Sin bin: Brentley (70) - holding down.
CITY KNIGHTS: 1 Matt Blaymire; 2 Lee Lingard; 3 Chris Ross; 4 Neil Law; 5 Peter Fox; 6 Scott Rhodes; 7 Chris Levy; 8 Craig Forsyth; 9 Lee Jackson; 10 Joe Helme; 11 Mick Ramsden; 12 John Smith; 13 Jon Liddell. Subs (all used): 14 Jimmy Elston; 15 Darren Callaghan; 16 Adam Sullivan; 17 Yusuf Sozi.
Tries: Sozi (20), Rhodes (23), Law (33, 54), Lingard (43), Smith (71), Ross (74);
Goals: Liddell 1/4, Ross 1/1, Levy 1/1, Jackson 1/1.
Rugby Leaguer & League Express Men of the Match:
Eagles: Rob Worrincy; *City Knights:* Yusuf Sozi.
Penalty count: 7-9; **Half-time:** 10-14;
Referee: Gareth Hewer (Whitehaven); **Attendance:** 1,154.

Saturday 10th September 2005

LONDON SKOLARS 6 BLACKPOOL PANTHERS 20

SKOLARS: 1 Ashley Tozer; 2 Mario Du Toit; 3 Joe Price; 4 Tim Gee; 5 Corey Simms; 6 Nathan Meischke; 7 Kurt Pittman; 8 Alex Smits; 9 James Sullivan; 10 Rubert Jonker; 11 Ade Aderiye; 12 Matt Pitman; 13 Brett Blaker. Subs (all used): 14 Gareth Honor; 15 Ben Joyce; 16 Wayne Parillon; 17 Mike Castle.
Try: Tozer (19); **Goals:** T Gee 1/1.
Sin bin: K Pittman (19) - dissent.
PANTHERS: 1 Liam Bretherton; 2 Jake Johnstone; 3 Craig Tipeny; 4 Eddie Kilgannon; 5 Eric Andrews; 6 Liam McGovern; 7 Martin Gambles; 8 Gus Martin; 9 Martin Roden; 10 Mick Redford; 11 Steve Ormesher; 12 Gary Smith; 13 Willie Swann. Subs (all used): 14 Chris Ramsdale; 15 Sion Williams; 16 James Lomax; 17 Lee Rowley.
Tries: Bretherton (4), Redford (21), Kilgannon (39);
Goals: Johnstone 4/5.
Sin bin: Martin (21) - fighting.
Rugby Leaguer & League Express Men of the Match:
Skolars: Ashley Tozer; *Panthers:* Mick Redford.
Penalty count: 7-15; **Half-time:** 6-18;
Referee: Craig Halloran (Dewsbury); **Attendance:** 240.

WEEK 22

Sunday 11th September 2005

KEIGHLEY COUGARS 16 WORKINGTON TOWN 20

COUGARS: 1 Matt Bramald; 2 Sam Gardner; 3 David Foster; 4 Matt Foster; 5 Andy Robinson; 6 Paul Ashton; 7 Matt Firth; 8 Phil Stephenson; 9 Jonny Wainhouse; 10 Danny Murgatroyd; 11 Matthew Steel; 12 Daniel Harvey; 13 Gareth Greenwood. Subs (all used): 14 Daley Williams; 15 Danny Ekis; 16 Richard Mervill; 17 Jason Clegg. **Tries:** Steel (5), D Foster (20); **Goals:** Ashton 4/5. **Sin bin:** Bramald (68) - dissent. **On report:** Ekis (70) - high tackle on Woodcock. **TOWN:** 1 Lusi Sione; 2 Matthew Woodcock; 3 Neil Frazer; 4 Ryan Campbell; 5 Martyn Wilson; 6 Lee Kiddie; 7 Brett Smith; 8 Mark Cox; 9 Jonny Limmer; 10 Ricky Wright; 11 Matthew Tunstall; 12 John Tuimaualuga; 13 Garry Purdham. Subs (all used): 14 Dexter Miller; 15 Taani Lavulavu; 16 Jamie Beaumont; 17 Allan McGuiness. **Tries:** Sione (2, 28), Limmer (38), Tuimaualuga (50); **Goals:** Smith 2/4. **Sin bin:** Lavulavu (74) - interference. **Rugby Leaguer & League Express Men of the Match:** *Cougars:* Paul Ashton; *Town:* Lusi Sione. **Penalty count:** 13-15; **Half-time:** 12-16; **Referee:** Dave Merrick (Castleford); **Attendance:** 778.

SWINTON LIONS 18 DEWSBURY RAMS 22

LIONS: 1 Wayne English; 2 Stuart Oldham; 3 Lee Patterson; 4 Dave Llewellyn; 5 Marlon Billy; 6 Lee Marsh; 7 Ian Watson; 8 Rob Whittaker; 9 Andy Crabtree; 10 Wes Rogers; 11 Danny Heaton; 12 Kris Smith; 13 Phil Joseph. Subs (all used): 14 Mick Coates; 15 Craig Farrimond; 16 Ian Sinfield; 17 Ian Parry. **Tries:** Marsh (39, 44), Parry (66); **Goals:** Marsh 3/4. **RAMS:** 1 Ian Preece; 2 Darren Rogers; 3 Chris Hall; 4 Wayne McHugh; 5 Richard Tillotson; 6 Francis Maloney; 7 David Mycoe; 8 Paul Hicks; 9 Richard Chapman; 10 Matt Walker; 11 Alex Bretherton; 12 Ged Corcoran; 13 Kurt Rudder. Subs (all used): 14 Ryan Sheridan; 15 Paul Seal; 16 James Walker; 17 Jonlee Lockwood. **Tries:** Rogers (31), Chapman (52, 58), Lockwood (62); **Goals:** Maloney 1/2, Mycoe 2/2. **Sin bin:** Chapman (27) - dissent. **On report:** Corcoran (14) - alleged use of the elbow. **Rugby Leaguer & League Express Men of the Match:** *Lions:* Lee Marsh; *Rams:* Richard Chapman. **Penalty count:** 5-7; **Half-time:** 6-4; **Referee:** Colin Morris (Huddersfield); **Attendance:** 618.

HUNSLET HAWKS 26 GATESHEAD THUNDER 16

HAWKS: 1 George Rayner; 2 Paul Cummins; 3 Anthony Gibbons; 4 Gareth Naylor; 5 Andy Brent; 6 David Gibbons; 7 Mark Cass; 8 Mick Coyle; 9 Jamaine Wray; 10 Lee Williamson; 11 Wayne Freeman; 12 Andy Shickell; 13 Chris Redfearn. Subs (all used): 14 Andy Bastow; 15 Liam Garside; 16 Luke Rayner; 17 Steve Pryce. **Tries:** A Shickell (24), A Gibbons (56), G Rayner (65), Coyle (68); **Goals:** Wray 5/5. **Sin bin:** A Gibbons (35) - fighting. **THUNDER:** 1 Wade Liddell; 2 Graham Stephenson; 3 Kevin Neighbour; 4 Aaron Lewis; 5 Robin Peers; 6 Mike Hobbs; 7 Chris Birch; 8 Andrew Pierce; 9 Scott Collins; 10 Rob Line; 11 Ian Brown; 12 Tabua Cakacaka; 13 Joe Burley. Subs (all used): 14 Neil Thorman; 15 Steve Rutherford; 16 Steven Bradley; 17 Alex Rowe. **Tries:** I Brown (24), Thorman (77), Lewis (79); **Goals:** Birch 2/3. **Sin bin:** Lewis (35) - fighting. **Rugby Leaguer & League Express Men of the Match:** *Hawks:* Jamaine Wray; *Thunder:* Neil Thorman. **Penalty count:** 7-6; **Half-time:** 8-6; **Referee:** Jamie Leahy (Dewsbury); **Attendance:** 491.

NATIONAL LEAGUE ONE QUALIFYING SERIES

Sunday 18th September 2005

ELIMINATION PLAY-OFFS

WORKINGTON TOWN 47 GATESHEAD THUNDER 12

TOWN: 1 Lusi Sione; 2 Matthew Woodcock; 3 Neil Frazer; 4 Dexter Miller; 5 Martyn Wilson; 6 Lee Kiddie; 7 Tane Manihera; 8 Dean Vaughan; 9 Jonny Limmer; 10 John Tuimaualuga; 11 Matthew Tunstall; 12 Garry Purdham; 13 Jon Roper. Subs (all used): 14 Taani Lavulavu; 15 Brett Smith; 16 Jamie Beaumont; 17 Taani Lavulavu. **Tries:** Sione (26), Manihera (30), Wilson (40), Frazer (48, 66, 73), Lavulavu (69), Smith (76), Robinson (78); **Goals:** Roper 5/9; **Field goal:** Roper. **On report:** Alleged biting incident (57). **THUNDER:** 1 Wade Liddell; 2 Kevin Neighbour; 3 Ian Brown; 4 Aaron Lewis; 5 Robin Peers; 6 Mike Hobbs; 7 Neil Thorman; 8 Andrew Pierce; 9 Scott Collins; 10 Rob Line; 11 Tabua Cakacaka; 12 Steven Bradley; 13 Joe Burley. Subs (all used): 14 Graham Stephenson; 15 Steve Rutherford; 16 Selwyn St Bernard; 17 Alex Rowe. **Tries:** Lewis (19), Burley (34); **Goals:** Neighbour 2/3. **Sin bin:** Cakacaka (18) - foul play; Liddell (48) - interference. **On report:** Alleged biting incident (57); Collins (64) - late tackle. **Rugby Leaguer & League Express Men of the Match:** *Town:* Lusi Sione; *Thunder:* Tabua Cakacaka. **Penalty count:** 12-7; **Half-time:** 16-12; **Referee:** Mike Dawber (Wigan); **Attendance:** 949.

Workington's Lusi Sione soars high to score against Swinton in the play-offs

SWINTON LIONS 40 HUNSLET HAWKS 28

LIONS: 1 Wayne English; 2 Stuart Oldham; 3 Lee Patterson; 4 Chris Maye; 5 Marlon Billy; 6 Mick Coates; 7 Ian Watson; 8 Rob Whittaker; 9 Phil Joseph; 10 Wes Rogers; 11 Danny Heaton; 12 Rob Russell; 13 Lee Marsh. Subs (all used): 14 Andy Crabtree; 16 Ian Sinfield; 17 Ian Parry. **Tries:** Maye (6), Parry (29), Marsh (42), Heaton (50), Crabtree (52), Patterson (57), English (71); **Goals:** Marsh 6/8. **Dismissal:** Crabtree (64) - late tackle on Moxon. **HAWKS:** 1 George Rayner; 2 Paul Cummins; 3 Anthony Gibbons; 4 Gareth Naylor; 5 David Gibbons; 7 Mark Moxon; 8 Mick Coyle; 9 Jamaine Wray; 10 Lee Williamson; 11 Wayne Freeman; 12 Andy Shickell; 13 Chris Redfearn. Subs (all used): 14 Mark Cass; 15 Marc Shickell; 16 Andy Bastow; 17 Danny Cook. **Tries:** A Shickell (3), Williamson (17, 61, 66), A Gibbons (75); **Goals:** Wray 4/5. **Rugby Leaguer & League Express Men of the Match:** *Lions:* Danny Heaton; *Hawks:* Lee Williamson. **Penalty count:** 14-10; **Half-time:** 10-12; **Referee:** Ronnie Laughton (Barnsley); **Attendance:** 581.

Sunday 25th September 2005

QUALIFYING SEMI-FINAL

BATLEY BULLDOGS 40 DEWSBURY RAMS 20

BULLDOGS: 1 Craig Lingard; 2 Jamie Stokes; 3 Iain Marsh; 4 Stephen Jones; 5 Mark Sibson; 6 John Gallagher; 7 Barry Eaton; 8 Dane Morgan; 9 Kris Lythe; 10 Joe Berry; 11 Sean Richardson; 12 Tim Spears; 13 Darren Robinson. Subs (all used): 14 Neil Roden; 15 David Rourke; 16 Gary Shillabeer; 17 Martin McLoughlin. **Tries:** Eaton (9), Lingard (17), Robinson (22), Roden (25, 28), Stokes (55), Sibson (78); **Goals:** Eaton 6/7. **Sin bin:** Marsh (67) - fighting. **RAMS:** 1 Ian Preece; 2 Darren Rogers; 3 Chris Hall; 4 Kevin Crouthers; 5 Wayne McHugh; 6 Francis Maloney; 7 David Mycoe; 8 Matt Walker; 9 Richard Chapman; 10 Warren Jowitt; 11 Paul Seal; 12 Ged Corcoran; 13 Kurt Rudder. Subs (all used): 14 Ryan Sheridan; 15 Alex Bretherton; 16 Paul Hicks; 17 Jonlee Lockwood. **Tries:** Rogers (13, 68), McHugh (59), Maloney (64); **Goals:** Maloney 2/4. **Sin bin:** Lockwood (67) - fighting. **Rugby Leaguer & League Express Men of the Match:** *Bulldogs:* John Gallagher; *Rams:* Ryan Sheridan. **Penalty count:** 10-10; **Half-time:** 30-4; **Referee:** Phil Bentham (Warrington); **Attendance:** 1,961.

ELIMINATION SEMI-FINAL

WORKINGTON TOWN 17 SWINTON LIONS 16

TOWN: 1 Lusi Sione; 2 Matthew Woodcock; 3 Neil Frazer; 4 Dexter Miller; 5 Martyn Wilson; 6 Lee Kiddie; 7 Tane Manihera; 8 Mark Cox; 9 Jonny Limmer; 10 John Tuimaualuga; 11 Matthew Tunstall; 12 Garry Purdham; 13 Jon Roper. Subs (all used): 14 Jamie Beaumont; 15 Matthew Tunstall; 16 Allan McGuiness; 17 Taani Lavulavu. **Tries:** Wilson (13), Sione (22), Manihera (50); **Goals:** Roper 2/4; **Field goal:** Kiddie. **LIONS:** 1 Wayne English; 2 Stuart Oldham; 3 Lee Patterson; 4 Dave Llewellyn; 5 Marlon Billy; 6 Mick Coates; 7 Ian Watson; 8 Rob Whittaker; 9 Phil Joseph; 10 Wes Rogers; 11 Danny Heaton; 12 Rob Russell; 13 Lee Marsh. Subs (all used): 14 Ian Sinfield; 15 Kris Smith; 16 Ian Parry; 17 Craig Farrimond. **Tries:** Billy (2), Llewellyn (60); **Goals:** Marsh 4/4. **Rugby Leaguer & League Express Men of the Match:** *Town:* Dean Vaughan; *Lions:* Ian Parry. **Penalty count:** 12-7; **Half-time:** 7-8; **Referee:** Ben Thaler (Wakefield); **Attendance:** 1,263.

Sunday 2nd October 2005

FINAL ELIMINATOR

DEWSBURY RAMS 26 WORKINGTON TOWN 18

RAMS: 1 Ian Preece; 2 Darren Rogers; 3 Wayne McHugh; 4 Kevin Crouthers; 5 Richard Tillotson; 6 Francis Maloney; 7 David Mycoe; 8 Paul Hicks; 9 Richard Chapman; 10 Matt Walker; 11 Warren Jowitt; 12 Ged Corcoran; 13 Kurt Rudder. Subs (all used): 14 Chris Woolford; 15 Paul Seal; 16 James Walker; 17 Jonlee Lockwood. **Tries:** Preece (6), Rogers (20, 56), Chapman (30), Crouthers (49); **Goals:** Maloney 3/5. **TOWN:** 1 Lusi Sione; 2 Matthew Woodcock; 3 Neil Frazer; 4 Jon Roper; 5 Martyn Wilson; 6 Lee Kiddie; 7 Brett Smith; 8 Mark Cox; 9 Jonny Limmer; 10 John Tuimaualuga; 11 Dean Vaughan; 12 Matthew Tunstall; 13 Garry Purdham. Subs (all used): 14 Dexter Miller; 15 Jamie Beaumont; 16 Allan McGuiness; 17 Taani Lavulavu. **Tries:** Limmer (23), Purdham (74); **Goals:** Roper 4/5, Smith 1/1. **Rugby Leaguer & League Express Men of the Match:** *Rams:* Ian Preece; *Town:* Lusi Sione. **Penalty count:** 6-5; **Half-time:** 16-10; **Referee:** Julian King (St Helens); **Attendance:** 1,452.

Sunday 9th October 2005

FINAL

BATLEY BULLDOGS 28 DEWSBURY RAMS 26

BULLDOGS: 1 Craig Lingard; 2 Jamie Stokes; 3 Iain Marsh; 4 Stephen Jones; 5 Mark Sibson; 6 John Gallagher; 7 Barry Eaton; 8 Dane Morgan; 9 Kris Lythe; 10 Joe Berry; 11 Sean Richardson; 12 Tim Spears; 13 Darren Robinson. Subs (all used): 14 Aiden Lister; 15 David Rourke; 16 Gary Shillabeer; 17 Martin McLoughlin. **Tries:** Marsh (5), Sibson (15), Jones (26), Eaton (38), Gallagher (66); **Goals:** Eaton 4/5. **Sin bin:** Robinson (38) - striking. **RAMS:** 1 Ian Preece; 2 Darren Rogers; 3 Chris Hall; 4 Kevin Crouthers; 5 Richard Tillotson; 6 Francis Maloney; 7 David Mycoe; 8 Paul Hicks; 9 Richard Chapman; 10 Kurt Rudder. Subs (all used): 14 Ryan Sheridan; 15 Wayne McHugh; 16 James Walker; 17 Jonlee Lockwood. **Tries:** Rogers (17), Sheridan (21), Hall (31), Crouthers (53); **Goals:** Maloney 5/5. **Sin bin:** Lythe (47) - retaliation. **Rugby Leaguer & League Express Men of the Match:** *Bulldogs:* John Gallagher; *Rams:* Francis Maloney. **Penalty count:** 3-3; **Half-time:** 22-18; **Referee:** Ben Thaler (Wakefield). *(at Halton Stadium, Widnes).*

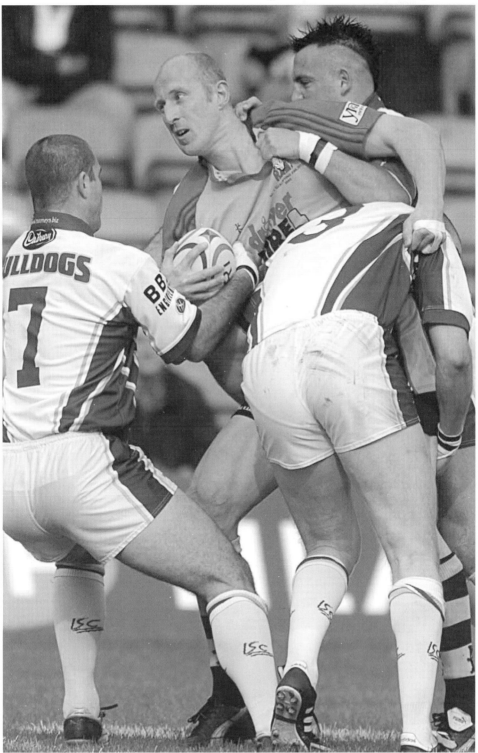

Batley trio Barry Eaton, Iain Marsh and Darren Robinson halt Dewsbury's Darren Rogers during the NL1 Qualifying Final

NATIONAL LEAGUE CUP 2005
Round by Round

National League Cup 2005 - Round by Round

WEEK 1

Friday 11th February 2005

GROUP 5

SHEFFIELD EAGLES 23 DEWSBURY RAMS 16

EAGLES: 1 John Crawford; 2 Danny Mills; 3 Alex Dickinson; 4 Adrian Veamatahau; 5 Carl De Chenu; 6 Ryan Dickinson; 7 Gavin Brown; 8 Jack Howieson; 9 Scott Collins; 10 Chris Molyneux; 11 Andy Rice; 12 Craig Brown; 13 Simon Tillyer. Subs (all used): 14 Greg Hurst; 15 Simon Morton; 16 Liam Brentley; 17 Nick Turnbull.
Tries: R Dickinson (19), Veamatahau (23), Crawford (49); **Goals:** Crawford 2/2, G Brown 3/4;
Field goal: G Brown.
RAMS: 1 Ian Preece; 2 Richard Tillotson; 3 Wayne McHugh; 4 Kevin Crouthers; 5 Oliver Fairbank; 6 Francis Maloney; 7 Ryan Sheridan; 8 Paul Hicks; 9 Richard Chapman; 10 Jonlee Lockwood; 11 Anthony Henderson; 12 Mark Stubley; 13 Alex Bretherton. Subs (all used): 14 Chris Woolford; 15 David Mycoe; 16 Mark Hawksley; 17 James Walker.
Tries: Henderson (30), Tillotson (62, 67);
Goals: Maloney 2/4.
Rugby Leaguer & League Express Men of the Match:
Eagles: Ryan Dickinson; *Rams:* Francis Maloney.
Penalty count: 8-12; **Half-time:** 14-6;
Referee: Julian King (St Helens); **Attendance:** 959.

Saturday 12th February 2005

GROUP 6

HEMEL HEMPSTEAD STAGS 14
BRAMLEY BUFFALOES 6

Sunday 13th February 2005

GROUP 1

BARROW RAIDERS 28 GATESHEAD THUNDER 35

RAIDERS: 1 Joel Osborn; 2 Jason Roach; 3 Alex Muff; 4 Freddie Zitter; 5 Paul Jones; 6 Phil Atkinson; 7 Darren Holt; 8 Stuart Dancer; 9 Chris Archer; 10 Paul Wilcock; 11 Glenn Osborn; 12 Kieron Hersnip; 13 Barry Pugh. Subs (all used): 14 Adrian Mulcahy; 15 Andy Fisher; 16 Darren Fisher; 17 Simon Knox.
Tries: Archer (27), Mulcahy (32), Wilcock (57), Knox (68), Zitter (76); **Goals:** Holt 4/5.
THUNDER: 1 Kevin Neighbour; 2 Nigel Arizmendez; 3 Joel Barnes; 4 Wade Liddell; 5 Robin Peers; 6 Mike Hobbs; 7 Chris Birch; 8 Tabua Cakacaka; 9 John Tomes; 10 Selwyn St Bernard; 11 Joe Burley; 12 Steven Bradley; 13 Steve Rutherford. Subs (all used): 14 Graham Stephenson; 15 Damien Martinez; 16 Ian Ball; 17 Tony Doherty.
Tries: Peers (8), Tomes (19), Hobbs (25), Bradley (34), Barnes (38); **Goals:** Birch 7/8; **Field goal:** Hobbs.
Rugby Leaguer & League Express Men of the Match:
Raiders: Chris Archer; *Thunder:* John Tomes.
Penalty count: 4-8; **Half-time:** 12-30;
Referee: Phil Bentham (Warrington); **Attendance:** 778.

WORKINGTON TOWN 28 WHITEHAVEN 8

TOWN: 1 Martyn Wilson; 2 Matthew Johnson; 3 Neil Frazer; 4 Jon Roper; 5 Stephen Dawes; 6 Lusi Sione; 7 Lee Kiddie; 8 Matthew Tunstall; 9 Jonny Limmer; 10 Dean Burgess; 11 John Tuimaualuga; 12 Ricky Wright; 13 Brett Smith. Subs (all used): 14 Jamie Beaumont; 15 Allan McGuiness; 16 Taani Lavulavu; 17 Dean Vaughan.
Tries: Wright (23), Limmer (29), Roper (32), Johnson (60); **Goals:** Smith 6/7, Sione 0/1.
WHITEHAVEN: 1 Gary Broadbent; 2 Craig Calvert; 3 David Seeds; 4 Wesley Wilson; 5 Steven Wood; 6 Joel Penny; 7 Steve Kirkbride; 8 Paul Davidson; 9 Aaron Lester; 10 David Fatialofa; 11 Brett McDermott; 12 Howard Hill; 13 Craig Walsh. Subs (all used): 14 Leroy Joe; 15 Chris McKinney; 16 Carl Sice; 17 Mark Cox.
Tries: Wood (6), Wilson (44); **Goals:** Kirkbride 0/2.
Rugby Leaguer & League Express Men of the Match:
Town: John Tuimaualuga; *Whitehaven:* Brett McDermott.
Penalty count: 14-9; **Half-time:** 20-4;
Referee: Mike Dawber (Wigan); **Attendance:** 3,012.

GROUP 2

OLDHAM 22 BLACKPOOL PANTHERS 20

OLDHAM: 1 Jon Goddard; 2 Will Cowell; 3 Damian Munro; 4 Alex Wilkinson; 5 Nick Johnson; 6 Simon Svabic; 7 Marty Turner; 8 Paul Norman; 9 Gareth Barber; 10 Danny Nanyn; 11 Ricky Bibey; 12 Tere Glassie; 13 Carlos Mataora. Subs: 14 Craig Farrimond; 15 Gavin Dodd; 16 Martin Elswood; 17 James Kirkland (not used).
Tries: Elswood (30), Glassie (45), Munro (59), Cowell (65), Dodd (70); **Goals:** Turner 1/5.
PANTHERS: 1 Liam Bretherton; 2 Danny Arnold; 3 Mick Redford; 4 Glen Godbee; 5 Eric Andrews; 6 Liam McGovern; 7 Martin Gambles; 8 Steve Molloy; 9 Martin Roden; 10 Ian Parry; 11 Matt Leigh; 12 John Hill; 13 Gary Smith. Subs (all used): 14 Chris Hough; 15 Gus Martin; 16 Danny Barton; 17 Mike Callan.
Tries: Bretherton (4), Godbee (15, 25), G Smith (36);
Goals: Bretherton 2/3, McGovern 0/2.
Rugby Leaguer & League Express Men of the Match:
Oldham: Gavin Dodd; *Panthers:* Martin Gambles.
Penalty count: 7-8; **Half-time:** 4-20; **Referee:** Gareth Hewer (Whitehaven); **Attendance:** 1,337.

SWINTON LIONS 20 ROCHDALE HORNETS 14

LIONS: 1 Wayne English; 2 Stuart Oldham; 3 Lee Patterson; 4 Chris Maye; 5 Marlon Billy; 6 Mick Coates; 7 Ian Watson; 8 Paul Southern; 9 Phil Joseph; 10 Wes Rogers; 11 Danny Heaton; 12 Ian Sinfield; 13 Lee Marsh. Subs (all used): 14 Warren Ayres; 15 Rob Russell; 16 Darren Speakman; 17 Rob Whittaker.
Tries: Maye (24), Marsh (56, 77), English (61);
Goals: Marsh 2/4.
Sin bin: Watson (22) - dissent; Maye (39) - dissent; Heaton (70) - dissent.
HORNETS: 1 David Alstead; 2 Chris Giles; 3 Mark McCully; 4 Richard Varkulis; 5 Chris Campbell; 6 Lee Birdseye; 7 John Braddish; 8 Andy Leathem; 9 Dave McConnell; 10 Gareth Price; 11 Andy Gorski; 12 Lee Doran; 13 Phil Farrell. Subs (all used): 14 Sam Butterworth; 15 Tommy Hodgkinson; 16 Phil Cantillon; 17 Dave Newton.
Tries: Cantillon (35), Campbell (74); **Goals:** Birdseye 3/3.
Rugby Leaguer & League Express Men of the Match:
Lions: Lee Marsh; *Hornets:* Andy Gorski.
Penalty count: 14-14; **Half-time:** 6-8; **Referee:** Steve Nicholson (Whitehaven); **Attendance:** 685.

GROUP 3

KEIGHLEY COUGARS 26 HULL KINGSTON ROVERS 27

COUGARS: 1 James Rushforth; 2 Matt Bramald; 3 David Foster; 4 Matt Foster; 5 Andy Robinson; 6 Adam Mitchell; 7 Matt Firth; 8 Phil Stephenson; 9 Jonny Wainhouse; 10 Richard Mervill; 11 Chris Parker; 12 Matthew Steel; 13 Daniel Harvey. Subs (all used): 14 Karl Smith; 15 Jordan Ross; 16 Lewis Taylor; 17 Jason Clegg.
Tries: Steel (16), Harvey (27), D Foster (54), Mitchell (69); **Goals:** Mitchell 5/8.
ROVERS: 1 Phil Hasty; 2 Jon Steel; 3 Craig Poucher; 4 Paul Parker; 5 Kane Epati; 6 Paul Mansson; 7 James Webster; 8 Neil Harmon; 9 Andy Ellis; 10 David Tangata-Toa; 11 Andy Raleigh; 12 Jason Netherton; 13 Dwayne Barker. Subs (all used): 14 Paul Pickering; 15 Jimmy Walker; 16 Jamie Bovill; 17 Makali Aizue.
Tries: Webster (7, 22), Ellis (43), Mansson (45), Raleigh (64); **Goals:** Poucher 3/5; **Field goal:** Mansson.
Sin bin: Parker (41) - interference.
Rugby Leaguer & League Express Men of the Match:
Cougars: Adam Mitchell; *Rovers:* James Webster.
Penalty count: 7-12; **Half-time:** 14-10;
Referee: Peter Taberner (Wigan); **Attendance:** 1,008.

LONDON SKOLARS 0 HALIFAX 40

SKOLARS: 1 Dean Callis; 2 Austin Aggrey; 3 Stuart Singleton; 4 Tim Gee; 5 Ashley Tozer; 6 Jermaine Coleman; 7 Gareth Honor; 8 Rubert Jonker; 9 Kurt Pittman; 10 Toby Hall; 11 Andrew Gourlay; 12 Richard Singleton; 13 Troy O'Shea. Subs (all used): 14 Wayne Parillon; 15 Nathan Meischke; 16 Nathan Gee; 17 Mike Castle.
HALIFAX: 1 Damian Gibson; 2 James Haley; 3 James Bunyan; 4 Alan Hadcroft; 5 Rikki Sheriffe; 6 Danny Jones; 7 Ben Black; 8 Andy Hobson; 9 Ben Fisher; 10 Jason Boults; 11 David Larder; 12 Andy Spink; 13 Pat Weisner. Subs (all used): 14 Anthony Blackwood; 15 Gareth Greenwood; 16 Chris Birchall; 17 Jon Simpson.
Tries: Haley (5, 61), R Sheriffe (11, 42, 70), Black (20), Weisner (25); **Goals:** Jones 6/7.
Rugby Leaguer & League Express Men of the Match:
Skolars: Wayne Parillon; *Halifax:* Rikki Sheriffe.
Penalty count: 6-13; **Half-time:** 0-22;
Referee: Jamie Leahy (Dewsbury); **Attendance:** 543.

GROUP 4

CASTLEFORD TIGERS 52 YORK CITY KNIGHTS 2

TIGERS: 1 Michael Platt; 2 Waine Pryce; 3 Damien Reid; 4 Jon Hepworth; 5 Michael Shenton; 6 Andy Kain; 7 Paul Handforth; 8 Adam Watene; 9 Andrew Henderson; 10 Craig Huby; 11 Tom Haughey; 12 Steve Crouch; 13 Aaron Smith. Subs (all used): 14 Deon Bird; 15 Leigh Cooke; 16 Byron Smith; 17 Frank Watene.
Tries: Hepworth (5, 47), A Smith (23), A Kain (42, 70), Shenton (52), Pryce (57), Bird (60), Huby (66, 76);
Goals: Huby 4/5, Handforth 2/6.
CITY KNIGHTS: 1 Matt Blaymire; 2 Peter Fox; 3 Dan Potter; 4 Chris Ross; 5 Austin Buchanan; 6 Paul Thorman; 7 Chris Levy; 8 Yusuf Sozi; 9 Lee Jackson; 10 Adam Sullivan; 11 Ian Kirke; 12 Darren Callaghan; 13 Lee Patterson. Subs (all used): 14 Jimmy Elston; 15 Mark Cain; 16 John Smith; 17 Tom Buckenham.
Goals: P Thorman 1/1.
Rugby Leaguer & League Express Men of the Match:
Tigers: Paul Handforth; *City Knights:* John Smith.
Penalty count: 5-8; **Half-time:** 12-2;
Referee: Ben Thaler (Wakefield); **Attendance:** 5,768.

HUNSLET HAWKS 12 FEATHERSTONE ROVERS 28

HAWKS: 1 George Rayner; 2 Jason Hunter; 3 Anthony Gibbons; 4 Paul Cummins; 5 Steve Morton; 6 Danny Thomas; 7 Mark Moxon; 8 Matt Carbutt; 9 Joe Hawley; 10 Glen Freeman; 11 Wayne Freeman; 12 Shaun Ibbetson; 13 Jamaine Wray. Subs (all used): 14 Mark Cass; 15 Andy Bastow; 16 Chris Redfearn; 17 Steve Pryce.
Tries: Bastow (36), G Freeman (67);
Goals: Thomas 0/1, Wray 2/3.
ROVERS: 1 Andy McNally; 2 Bryn Powell; 3 Danny Maun; 4 Richard Newlove; 5 Matthew Wray; 6 Josh Weeden; 7 Jon Presley; 8 Ian Tonks; 9 Carl Hughes; 10 Nathan Sykes; 11 Steve Dooler; 12 Adam Hayes; 13 Richard Blakeway. Subs (all used): 14 Dean Ripley; 15 Neil Lowe; 16 Jim Carlton; 17 Craig Moss.
Tries: Weeden (18, 55), McNally (20, 79), Wray (70);
Goals: Weeden 4/6.
Rugby Leaguer & League Express Men of the Match:
Hawks: Jamaine Wray; *Rovers:* Josh Weeden.
Penalty count: 7-8; **Half-time:** 6-14; **Referee:** Colin Morris (Huddersfield); **Attendance:** 1,102.

GROUP 5

BATLEY BULLDOGS 28 DONCASTER DRAGONS 22

BULLDOGS: 1 Mark Sibson; 2 Jamie Stokes; 3 Iain Marsh; 4 Shad Royston; 5 Adrian Flynn; 6 Neil Roden; 7 Barry Eaton; 8 Craig Wright; 9 Kris Lythe; 10 David Rourke; 11 Martin McLoughlin; 12 Dane Morgan; 13 Mark Toohey. Subs (all used): 14 Tim Spears; 15 Gary Shillabeer; 16 Will Cartledge; 17 Sean Richardson.
Tries: Flynn (12), Roden (19, 22), McLoughlin (53);
Goals: Eaton 6/8.
DRAGONS: 1 Craig Horne; 2 Craig Farrell; 3 Chris Langley; 4 Dale Cardoza; 5 Craig Miles; 6 Graham Holroyd; 7 Aaron Wood; 8 Gareth Handford; 9 Peter Green; 10 Martin Ostler; 11 Lee Harland; 12 Andy Hay; 13 Martin Moana. Subs (all used): 14 Wayne Green; 15 Craig Lawton; 16 Dean O'Loughlin; 17 Stuart Crooks.
Tries: Handford (3), Wood (37), Holroyd (70), Hay (75);
Goals: Holroyd 3/4.
Rugby Leaguer & League Express Men of the Match:
Bulldogs: Neil Roden; *Dragons:* Peter Green.
Penalty count: 9-9; **Half-time:** 16-12;
Referee: Russell Smith (Castleford); **Attendance:** 788.

Friday 18th February 2005

GROUP 2

BLACKPOOL PANTHERS 24 SWINTON LIONS 34

PANTHERS: 1 Liam Bretherton; 2 Steve Ormesher; 3 Mick Redford; 4 Jake Johnstone; 5 Eric Andrews; 6 Chris Hough; 7 Liam McGovern; 8 Ian Parry; 9 Martin Roden; 10 John Hill; 11 Matt Leigh; 12 Gary Smith; 13 Danny Barton. Subs (all used): 14 Martin Gambles; 15 Chris Ramsdale; 16 Gareth Jones; 17 Steve Molloy.
Tries: Andrews (2), G Smith (64), Barton (70), Johnstone (80); **Goals:** Johnstone 4/5.
LIONS: 1 Wayne English; 2 Stuart Oldham; 3 Lee Patterson; 4 Chris Maye; 5 Marlon Billy; 6 Mick Coates; 7 Ian Watson; 8 Paul Southern; 9 Phil Joseph; 10 Wes Rogers; 11 Danny Heaton; 12 Ian Sinfield; 13 Lee Marsh. Subs (all used): 14 Warren Ayres; 15 Ben Cramant; 16 Rob Russell; 17 Rob Whittaker.
Tries: Joseph (22), Maye (24, 55), Billy (37, 50), Oldham (60); **Goals:** Marsh 5/7.
Sin bin: Marsh (69) - interference.
Rugby Leaguer & League Express Men of the Match:
Panthers: Gary Smith; *Lions:* Danny Heaton.
Penalty count: 10-8; **Half-time:** 8-16; **Referee:** Steve Nicholson (Whitehaven); **Attendance:** 512.

GROUP 5

DONCASTER DRAGONS 58 SHEFFIELD EAGLES 20

DRAGONS: 1 Craig Horne; 2 Craig Farrell; 3 Chris Langley; 4 Dale Cardoza; 5 Craig Miles; 6 Graham Holroyd; 7 Latham Tawhai; 8 Gareth Handford; 9 Craig Cook; 10 Andy Hay; 11 Lee Harland; 12 Peter Green; 13 Martin Moana. Subs (all used): 14 Aaron Wood; 15 Martin Ostler; 16 Stuart Crooks; 17 Craig Lawton.
Tries: Horne (7), Ostler (40), Cook (43), Moana (45), Langley (48), Crooks (51), Miles (62), Tawhai (66), Holroyd (70), Wood (73); **Goals:** Holroyd 9/10.
EAGLES: 1 John Crawford; 2 Danny Mills; 3 Alex Dickinson; 4 Adrian Veamatahau; 5 Carl De Chenu; 6 Ryan Dickinson; 7 Gavin Brown; 8 Chris Molyneux; 9 Scott Collins; 10 Simon Morton; 11 Andy Rice; 12 Craig Brown; 13 Simon Tillyer. Subs (all used): 14 Aled James; 15 Sean Dickinson; 16 Jon Breakingbury; 17 Nick Turnbull.
Tries: De Chenu (19), Mills (32), Veamatahau (55), Breakingbury (77); **Goals:** G Brown 2/4.
Rugby Leaguer & League Express Men of the Match:
Dragons: Craig Cook; *Eagles:* Gavin Brown.
Penalty count: 8-9; **Half-time:** 12-12;
Referee: Russell Smith (Castleford); **Attendance:** 727.

Saturday 19th February 2005

GROUP 6

BRADFORD-DUDLEY HILL DEMONS 39
WARRINGTON WIZARDS 12

WEEK 2

Sunday 20th February 2005

GROUP 1

WHITEHAVEN 44 BARROW RAIDERS 0

WHITEHAVEN: 1 Gary Broadbent; 2 Craig Calvert; 3 Derry Eilbeck; 4 David Seeds; 5 John Lebbon; 6 Leroy Joe; 7 Joel Penny; 8 Chris McKinney; 9 Carl Sice; 10 David Fatialofa; 11 Brett McDermott; 12 Spencer Miller; 13 Craig Walsh. Subs (all used): 14 Howard Hill; 15 Paul Davidson; 16 Jamie Seaton; 17 Tony Cunningham.
Tries: Eilbeck (4), Sice (22, 26, 75), Fatialofa (35), Seeds (41), Lebbon (54), Broadbent (67);
Goals: Penny 5/6, Sice 1/2.
Sin bin: McDermott (16) - fighting; Joe (28) - fighting, (74) - high tackle.
RAIDERS: 1 Freddie Zitter; 2 Jason Roach; 3 Paul Jones;

4 Alex Muff; 5 James Nixon; 6 Adrian Mulcahy; 7 Darren Holt; 8 Andy Fisher; 9 Chris Archer; 10 Paul Wilcock; 11 Simon Knox; 12 Mike Whitehead; 13 Phil Atkinson. Subs (all used): 14 Kieron Hersnip; 15 Chris Roe; 16 Stuart Dancer; 17 Glenn Osborn.
Sin bin: Knox (16) - fighting; Jones (28) - fighting, (54) - holding down; Wilcock (53) - holding down, (65) - high tackle.
Rugby Leaguer & League Express Men of the Match: *Whitehaven:* David Fatialofa; *Raiders:* Freddie Zitter.
Penalty count: 15-12; **Half-time:** 22-0;
Referee: Ben Thaler (Wakefield); **Attendance:** 1,606.

GROUP 3

HALIFAX 60 LONDON SKOLARS 12

HALIFAX: 1 Damian Gibson; 2 James Haley; 3 James Bunyan; 4 Alan Hadcroft; 5 Rikki Sheriffe; 6 Danny Jones; 7 Ben Black; 8 Chris Morley; 9 Ben Fisher; 10 Jason Boults; 11 David Larder; 12 Andy Spink; 13 Pat Weisner. Subs (all used): 14 Wayne Corcoran; 15 Gareth Greenwood; 16 Jode Sheriffe; 17 Anthony Blackwood.
Tries: Spink (20), Bunyan (24, 48), Haley (29), R Sheriffe (32), Blackwood (39), Fisher (43), Weisner (51), Black (53, 71), Greenwood (59);
Goals: Jones 5/8, Corcoran 3/3.
SKOLARS: 1 Jermaine Coleman; 2 Joe Price; 3 Brett Blaker; 4 Ade Aderiye; 5 Ashley Tozer; 6 Tim Gee; 7 Gareth Honor; 8 Wayne Parillon; 9 Kurt Pittman; 10 Toby Hall; 11 Andrew Gourlay; 12 Mike Castle; 13 Stuart Singleton. Subs (all used): 14 Matt Pitman; 15 Nathan Meischke; 16 Alan Baker; 17 Dave Brown.
Tries: T Gee (11), Parillon (67); **Goals:** T Gee 2/2.
Sin bin: M Pitman (31) - persistent interference.
Rugby Leaguer & League Express Men of the Match: *Halifax:* Ben Black; *Skolars:* Wayne Parillon.
Penalty count: 7-3; **Half-time:** 24-6;
Referee: Phil Bentham (Warrington); **Attendance:** 1,329.

HULL KINGSTON ROVERS 36 KEIGHLEY COUGARS 6

ROVERS: 1 Craig Poucher; 2 Jon Steel; 3 Paul Mansson; 4 Paul Parker; 5 Byron Ford; 6 James Webster; 7 Phil Hasty; 8 Neil Harmon; 9 Andy Ellis; 10 David Tangata-Toa; 11 Dale Holdstock; 12 Andy Raleigh; 13 Dwayne Barker. Subs (all used): 14 Kane Epati; 15 James Garmston; 16 Jamie Bovill; 17 Makali Aizue.
Tries: Webster (3, 10, 27), Aizue (33), Parker (55), Raleigh (62), Epati (69); **Goals:** Poucher 4/8.
COUGARS: 1 James Rushforth; 2 Matt Bramald; 3 David Foster; 4 Matt Foster; 5 Andy Robinson; 6 Adam Mitchell; 7 Matt Firth; 8 Phil Stephenson; 9 Jonny Wainhouse; 10 Richard Mervill; 11 Chris Parker; 12 Jordan Ross; 13 Daniel Harvey. Subs (all used): 14 Karl Smith; 15 Matthew Steel; 16 Danny Murgatroyd; 17 Jason Clegg.
Try: M Foster (19); **Goals:** Mitchell 1/1.
Rugby Leaguer & League Express Men of the Match: *Rovers:* James Webster; *Cougars:* Matt Firth.
Penalty count: 8-6; **Half-time:** 24-6; **Referee:** Gareth Hewer (Whitehaven); **Attendance:** 2,141.

GROUP 4

FEATHERSTONE ROVERS 10 CASTLEFORD TIGERS 22

ROVERS: 1 Andy McNally; 2 Bryn Powell; 3 Danny Maun; 4 Richard Newlove; 5 Matthew Wray; 6 Josh Weeden; 7 Dean Ripley; 8 Ian Tonks; 9 Carl Hughes; 10 Nathan Sykes; 11 Steve Dooler; 12 Adam Hayes; 13 Richard Blakeway. Subs (all used): 14 Craig Moss; 15 Neil Lowe; 16 Danny Evans; 17 Jim Carlton.
Try: Weeden (36); **Goals:** Weeden 3/4.
Sin bin: Evans (40) - fighting.
On report: Evans (40) - fighting.
TIGERS: 1 Michael Platt; 2 Waine Pryce; 3 Damien Reid; 4 Jon Hepworth; 5 Michael Shenton; 6 Andy Kain; 7 Paul Handforth; 17 Frank Watene; 9 Andrew Henderson; 10 Byron Smith; 11 Tom Haughey; 12 Steve Crouch; 13 Aaron Smith. Subs (all used): 8 Adam Watene; 14 Deon Bird; 15 Leigh Cooke; 16 Craig Huby.
Tries: Shenton (37), A Kain (45), Haughey (51), Platt (57); **Goals:** Handforth 2/6, Huby 1/2.
Sin bin: Smith (40) - fighting.
On report: Smith (40) - fighting
Rugby Leaguer & League Express Men of the Match: *Rovers:* Richard Blakeway; *Tigers:* Paul Handforth.
Penalty count: 10-15; **Half-time:** 8-8;
Referee: Julian King (St Helens); **Attendance:** 6,353.

YORK CITY KNIGHTS 34 HUNSLET HAWKS 6

CITY KNIGHTS: 1 Matt Blaymire; 2 Peter Fox; 3 Dan Potter; 4 Neil Law; 5 Chris Ross; 6 Lee Patterson; 7 Chris Levy; 8 John Smith; 9 Jimmy Elston; 10 Adam Sullivan; 11 Darren Callaghan; 12 Ian Kirke; 13 Jon Liddell. Subs (all used): 14 Lee Jackson; 15 Neil Thorman; 16 Yusuf Sozi; 17 Tom Buckenham.
Tries: Law (22, 69), Potter (31), Smith (52, 66);
Goals: Ross 7/8.
HAWKS: 1 George Rayner; 2 Jason Hunter; 3 Anthony Gibbons; 4 Chris Redfearn; 5 Steve Morton; 6 Danny Thomas; 7 Mark Moxon; 8 Nick Staveley; 9 Joe Hawley; 10 Glen Freeman; 11 Wayne Freeman; 12 Paul Cummins; 13 Jamaine Wray. Subs (all used): 14 Mark Cass; 15 Neil Mears; 16 Matt Carbutt; 17 Michael Gibbons.
Try: G Freeman (15); **Goals:** Wray 1/2.
Rugby Leaguer & League Express Men of the Match: *City Knights:* John Smith; *Hawks:* Nick Staveley.
Penalty count: 13-11; **Half-time:** 14-6;
Referee: Jamie Leahy (Dewsbury); **Attendance:** 1,320.

GROUP 5

DEWSBURY RAMS 32 BATLEY BULLDOGS 22

RAMS: 1 Ian Preece; 2 Oliver Fairbank; 3 Kurt Rudder; 4 Wayne McHugh; 5 Richard Tillotson; 6 Francis Maloney; 7 Ryan Sheridan; 8 Paul Hicks; 9 Richard Chapman; 10 Jonlee Lockwood; 11 Kevin Crouthers; 12 Warren Jowitt; 13 Alex Bretherton. Subs (all used): 14 David Mycoe; 15 Mark Stubley; 16 James Walker; 17 Mark Hawksley.
Tries: Crouthers (26), Bretherton (39), J Walker (48), McHugh (56), Maloney (60), Preece (75);
Goals: Chapman 2/4, Maloney 2/2.
Sin bin: Bretherton (17) - holding down; Maloney (30) - dissent; J Walker (53) - retaliation.
On report: Bretherton (1) - fighting.
BULLDOGS: 1 Steve Beard; 2 Jamie Stokes; 3 Iain Marsh; 4 Shad Royston; 5 Adrian Flynn; 6 Neil Roden; 7 Barry Eaton; 8 Craig Wright; 9 Kris Lythe; 10 Joe Berry; 11 Martin McLoughlin; 12 Dane Morgan; 13 Mark Toohey. Subs (all used): 14 Ryan Horsley; 15 Tim Spears; 16 Will Cartledge; 17 Sean Richardson.
Tries: Lythe (9), Roden (31), Royston (64), Toohey (67);
Goals: Eaton 3/5.
Sin bin: Wright (53) - punching.
On report: Roden (1) - fighting.
Rugby Leaguer & League Express Men of the Match: *Rams:* Ryan Sheridan; *Bulldogs:* Craig Wright.
Penalty count: 10-7; **Half-time:** 12-10;
Referee: Mike Dawber (Wigan); **Attendance:** 1,311.

WEEK 3

Sunday 27th February 2005

GROUP 6

BRAMLEY BUFFALOES 16 WARRINGTON WIZARDS 18

GROUP 1

WHITEHAVEN 42 GATESHEAD THUNDER 12

WHITEHAVEN: 1 Gary Broadbent; 2 Craig Calvert; 3 David Seeds; 4 Derry Eilbeck; 5 John Lebbon; 6 Leroy Joe; 7 Joel Penny; 8 Aaron Summers; 9 Carl Sice; 10 David Fatialofa; 11 Howard Hill; 12 Spencer Miller; 13 Aaron Lester. Subs (all used): 14 Jamie Seaton; 15 Paul Davidson; 16 Carl Rudd; 17 Tony Cunningham.
Tries: Calvert (2), Joe (9, 17), Seeds (36), Lebbon (42, 67), Hill (49), Davidson (73); **Goals:** Penny 5/8.
THUNDER: 1 Kevin Neighbour; 2 Graham Stephenson; 3 Joel Barnes; 4 Wade Liddell; 5 Robin Peers; 6 Mike Hobbs; 7 Chris Birch; 8 Selwyn St Bernard; 9 John Tomes; 10 Tabua Cakacaka; 11 Joe Burley; 12 Steven Bradley; 13 Steve Rutherford. Subs (all used): 14 Rob Line; 15 Ian Brown; 16 Craig Firth; 17 Liam Garside.
Tries: Peers (30), Firth (63); **Goals:** Birch 2/3.
Sin bin: Liddell (61) - holding down.
Rugby Leaguer & League Express Men of the Match: *Whitehaven:* Leroy Joe; *Thunder:* Chris Birch.
Penalty count: 12-11; **Half-time:** 20-6;
Referee: Paul Carr (Castleford); **Attendance:** 1,421.

WORKINGTON TOWN 28 BARROW RAIDERS 18

TOWN: 1 Lusi Sione; 2 Matthew Woodcock; 3 Neil Frazer; 4 Jon Roper; 5 Scott Chilton; 6 James Robinson; 7 Lee Kiddie; 8 Matthew Tunstall; 9 Jonny Limmer; 10 Dean Burgess; 11 Ricky Wright; 12 John Tuimaualuga; 13 Kevin Hetherington. Subs (all used): 14 Stephen Dawes; 15 Taani Lavulavu; 16 Dean Vaughan; 17 Dean Bragg.
Tries: Hetherington (12), Frazer (22), Sione (25), Tuimaualuga (52); **Goals:** Hetherington 6/6.
Sin bin: Hetherington (36) – interference.
RAIDERS: 1 Joel Osborn; 2 Jason Roach; 3 Paul Jones; 4 Freddie Zitter; 5 James Nixon; 6 Jon Williamson; 7 Darren Holt; 8 Stuart Dancer; 9 Chris Archer; 10 Paul Wilcock; 11 Mike Whitehead; 12 Kieron Hersnip; 13 Phil Atkinson. Subs (all used): 14 Alex Muff; 15 Chris Roe; 16 Andy Fisher; 17 Adrian Mulcahy.
Tries: Roach (27), Zitter (39), Atkinson (58), Hersnip (77); **Goals:** Atkinson 1/2, Holt 0/4.
Sin bin: Holt (34) – interference.
Rugby Leaguer & League Express Men of the Match: *Town:* Kevin Hetherington; *Raiders:* Andy Fisher.
Penalty count: 14-13; **Half-time:** 22-10;
Referee: Peter Taberner (Wigan); **Attendance:** 1,097.

GROUP 2

BLACKPOOL PANTHERS 26 ROCHDALE HORNETS 36

PANTHERS: 1 Michael Watts; 2 Danny Arnold; 3 Liam Bretherton; 4 Jake Johnstone; 5 Eric Andrews; 6 Willie Swann; 7 Chris Hough; 8 Ian Parry; 9 Liam McGovern; 10 Gus Martin; 11 Mick Redford; 12 Gary Smith; 13 Danny Barton. Subs (all used): 14 Chris Ramsdale; 15 Mike Callan; 16 Gary Rourke; 17 Gareth Jones.
Tries: Andrews (26), Bretherton (40), Arnold (43), Johnstone (59, 70); **Goals:** Johnstone 3/5.
Dismissal: Callan (49) - fighting.
HORNETS: 1 David Alstead; 2 Chris Giles; 3 Mark McCully; 4 Richard Varkulis; 5 Chris Campbell; 6 Sam Butterworth; 7 John Braddish; 8 Lee Hansen; 9 Phil Cantillon; 10 Gareth Price; 11 Andy Gorski; 12 Lee Doran; 13 Phil Farrell. Subs (all used): 14 Dave McConnell; 15 Rob Ball; 16 Dave Cunliffe; 17 Dave Newton.
Tries: McCully (13), Braddish (16, 63, 74), Varkulis (33), Alstead (36), Cantillon (55); **Goals:** Braddish 4/7.
Dismissal: Doran (49) - fighting.
Sin bin: Alstead (65) - dissent.
Rugby Leaguer & League Express Men of the Match: *Panthers:* Liam McGovern; *Hornets:* John Braddish.
Penalty count: 7-2; **Half-time:** 10-22;
Referee: Colin Morris (Huddersfield);
Attendance: 220 *(at Lightfoot Green, Preston).*

SWINTON LIONS 46 OLDHAM 14

LIONS: 1 Wayne English; 2 Stuart Oldham; 3 Lee Patterson; 4 Rob Russell; 5 Marlon Billy; 6 Mick Coates; 7 Ian Watson; 8 Paul Southern; 9 Phil Joseph; 10 Wes Rogers; 11 Danny Heaton; 12 Ian Sinfield; 13 Lee Marsh. Subs (all used): 14 Warren Ayres; 15 Ben Cramant; 16 Ian Hodson; 17 Rob Whittaker.
Tries: Marsh (13), Heaton (15), English (21, 65, 75), Sinfield (34), Rogers (57), Watson (72); **Goals:** Marsh 7/9.
OLDHAM: 1 Gavin Dodd; 2 Damian Munro; 3 Simon Haughton; 4 Alex Wilkinson; 5 Nick Johnson; 6 Simon Svabic; 7 Marty Turner; 8 Ricky Bibey; 9 Gareth Barber; 10 Danny Nanyn; 11 Martin Elswood; 12 Tere Glassie; 13 Carlos Mataora. Subs (all used): 14 John Hough; 15 Dana Wilson; 16 Paul Norman; 17 Craig Farrimond.
Tries: Johnson (3), Munro (10), Wilson (39);
Goals: Turner 0/2, Svabic 1/1.
Rugby Leaguer & League Express Men of the Match: *Lions:* Phil Joseph; *Oldham:* Simon Svabic.
Penalty count: 8-6; **Half-time:** 22-14;
Referee: Mike Dawber (Wigan); **Attendance:** 1,101.

GROUP 3

HULL KINGSTON ROVERS 21 HALIFAX 14

ROVERS: 1 Craig Poucher; 2 Jon Steel; 3 Paul Parker; 4 Paul Mansson; 5 Byron Ford; 6 James Webster; 7 Phil Hasty; 8 Neil Harmon; 9 Andy Ellis; 10 David Tangata-Toa; 11 Dale Holdstock; 12 Andy Raleigh; 13 Dwayne Barker. Subs (all used): 14 Jimmy Walker; 15 James Garmston; 16 Jamie Bovill; 17 Makali Aizue.
Tries: Hasty (13), Ellis (39), Aizue (43);
Goals: Poucher 4/4; **Field goal:** Mansson.
HALIFAX: 1 Damian Gibson; 2 James Haley; 3 James Bunyan; 4 Alan Hadcroft; 5 Rikki Sheriffe; 6 Anthony Blackwood; 7 Dean Lawford; 8 Chris Birchall; 9 Ben Fisher; 10 Jason Boults; 11 David Larder; 12 Andy Spink; 13 Pat Weisner. Subs (all used): 14 Ben Black; 15 Jode Sheriffe; 16 Jon Simpson; 17 Scott Law.
Tries: Gibson (9), Larder (52); **Goals:** Lawford 3/3.
Rugby Leaguer & League Express Men of the Match: *Rovers:* Craig Poucher; *Halifax:* Pat Weisner.
Penalty count: 7-7; **Half-time:** 14-8; **Referee:** Steve Nicholson (Whitehaven); **Attendance:** 2,227.

KEIGHLEY COUGARS 38 LONDON SKOLARS 10

COUGARS: 1 James Rushforth; 2 Matt Bramald; 3 David Foster; 4 Matt Foster; 5 Andy Robinson; 6 Adam Mitchell; 7 Matt Firth; 8 Phil Stephenson; 9 Jonny Wainhouse; 10 Danny Murgatroyd; 11 Jordan Ross; 12 Matthew Steel; 13 Daniel Harvey. Subs (all used): 14 Paul Ashton; 15 Chris Parker; 16 Richard Mervill; 17 Jason Clegg.
Tries: Robinson (10, 14, 68), M Foster (25), Bramald (44, 64, 72); **Goals:** Mitchell 3/4, Ashton 2/4.
Sin bin: Wainhouse (58) - fighting.
SKOLARS: 1 Jermaine Coleman; 2 Joe Price; 3 Austin Aggrey; 4 Brett Blaker; 5 Ashley Tozer; 6 Tim Gee; 7 Gareth Honor; 8 Wayne Parillon; 9 Kurt Pittman; 10 Toby Hall; 11 Andrew Gourlay; 12 Mike Castle; 13 Stuart Singleton. Subs (all used): 14 Nathan Meischke; 15 Rubert Jonker; 16 Matt Pitman; 17 Alan Barker.
Tries: K Pittman (28), Tozer (74); **Goals:** T Gee 1/2.
Sin bin: Singleton (55) - professional foul; Jonker (58) - fighting.
Rugby Leaguer & League Express Men of the Match: *Cougars:* Matt Foster; *Skolars:* Rubert Jonker.
Penalty count: 10-10; **Half-time:** 18-6;
Referee: Robert Hicks (Oldham); **Attendance:** 707.

GROUP 4

FEATHERSTONE ROVERS 21 YORK CITY KNIGHTS 20

ROVERS: 1 Craig Moss; 2 Bryn Powell; 3 Danny Maun; 4 Richard Newlove; 5 Matthew Wray; 6 Josh Weeden; 7 Jon Presley; 8 Ian Tonks; 9 Carl Hughes; 10 Nathan Sykes; 11 Steve Dooler; 12 James Houston; 13 Adam Hayes. Subs (all used): 14 James Ford; 15 Andy Jarrett; 16 Danny Evans; 17 Jim Carlton.
Tries: Powell (5), Dooler (10), Jarrett (43);
Goals: Weeden 4/6; **Field goal:** Weeden.
CITY KNIGHTS: 1 Matt Blaymire; 2 Peter Fox; 3 Dan Potter; 4 Neil Law; 5 Chris Ross; 6 Lee Patterson; 7 Chris Levy; 8 John Smith; 9 Jimmy Elston; 10 Adam Sullivan; 11 Darren Callaghan; 12 Ian Kirke; 13 Jon Liddell. Subs (all used): 14 Lee Jackson; 15 Calvin Watson; 16 Yusuf Sozi; 17 Tom Buckenham.
Tries: Levy (14), Potter (21), Sozi (52); **Goals:** Ross 4/4.
Rugby Leaguer & League Express Men of the Match: *Rovers:* Josh Weeden; *City Knights:* Chris Levy.
Penalty count: 8-5; **Half-time:** 14-12;
Referee: Ben Thaler (Wakefield); **Attendance:** 1,460.

CASTLEFORD TIGERS 70 HUNSLET HAWKS 0

TIGERS: 1 Michael Platt; 2 Waine Pryce; 3 Damien Reid; 4 Jon Hepworth; 5 Michael Shenton; 6 Andy Kain; 7 Paul Handforth; 8 Byron Smith; 9 Andrew Henderson; 10 Craig Huby; 11 Tom Haughey; 12 Jordan James; 13 Aaron Smith. Subs (all used): 14 Dominic Brambani; 15 Leigh Cooke; 16 Adam Watene; 17 Frank Watene.
Tries: Shenton (4, 14), Huby (11, 67), Reid (16), James (22), F Watene (25), Haughey (32), Hepworth (46, 53, 69), Platt (56), Handforth (62);
Goals: Huby 8/11, Handforth 1/2.
Sin bin: James (71) - fighting.
HAWKS: 1 George Rayner; 2 Amraz Hamid; 3 Anthony Gibbons; 4 Paul Cummins; 5 Gary McClelland; 6 David

Gibbons; 7 Mark Moxon; 8 Nick Staveley; 9 Joe Hawley; 10 Steve Pryce; 11 Wayne Freeman; 12 Neil Mears; 13 Jamaine Wray. Subs (all used): 14 Mark Cass; 15 Glen Freeman; 16 Matt Carbutt; 17 Chris Redfearn.
Sin bin: D Gibbons (19) - dissent, Wray (71) - fighting.
Rugby Leaguer & League Express Men of the Match: *Tigers:* Craig Huby; *Hawks:* Joe Hawley.
Penalty count: 15-7; **Half-time:** 38-0;
Referee: Phil Bentham (Warrington); **Attendance:** 4,483.

GROUP 5

BATLEY BULLDOGS 28 SHEFFIELD EAGLES 16

BULLDOGS: 1 Craig Lingard; 2 Jamie Stokes; 3 Iain Marsh; 4 Shad Royston; 5 Adrian Flynn; 6 Neil Roden; 7 Barry Eaton; 8 Craig Wright; 9 Kris Lythe; 10 David Rourke; 11 Sean Richardson; 12 Dane Morgan; 13 Mark Toohey. Subs (all used): 14 Steve Beard; 15 Paul Harrison; 16 Tim Spears; 17 Ryan Horsley.
Tries: Lingard (9), Royston (11), Morgan (16), Stokes (40), Horsley (60); **Goals:** Eaton 4/6.
EAGLES: 1 John Crawford; 2 Danny Mills; 3 Alex Dickinson; 4 Adrian Veamatahau; 5 Greg Hurst; 6 Aled James; 7 Gavin Brown; 8 Jack Howieson; 9 Liam Brentley; 10 Craig Brown; 11 Andy Rice; 12 Nick Turnbull; 13 Simon Tillyer. Subs (all used): 14 Peter Moore; 15 Simon Morton; 16 Jon Breakingbury; 17 Jaymes Chapman.
Tries: Crawford (34), Hurst (42, 63); **Goals:** G Brown 2/3.
Rugby Leaguer & League Express Men of the Match: *Bulldogs:* Neil Roden; *Eagles:* Simon Tillyer.
Penalty count: 12-9; **Half-time:** 20-6;
Referee: Julian King (St Helens); **Attendance:** 492.

DEWSBURY RAMS 27 DONCASTER DRAGONS 32

RAMS: 1 Ian Preece; 2 Oliver Fairbank; 3 Wayne McHugh; 4 Darren Rogers; 5 Richard Tillotson; 6 Francis Maloney; 7 Ryan Sheridan; 8 Paul Hicks; 9 Richard Chapman; 10 Jonlee Lockwood; 11 Kevin Crouthers; 12 Warren Jowitt; 13 Alex Bretherton. Subs (all used): 14 David Mycoe; 15 Mark Stubley; 16 James Walker; 17 Mark Hawksley.
Tries: McHugh (10, 40, 58), Fairbank (22), Maloney (43); **Goals:** Maloney 3/5; **Field goal:** Mycoe.
On report: Tackle (39) involving Bretherton and Green.
DRAGONS: 1 Aaron Wood; 2 Craig Farrell; 3 Chris Langley; 4 Dale Cardoza; 5 Craig Miles; 6 Graham Holroyd; 7 Latham Tawhai; 8 Gareth Handford; 9 Craig Cook; 10 Martin Ostler; 11 Andy Hay; 12 Peter Green; 13 Martin Moana. Subs (all used): 14 Kirk Netherton; 15 Stuart Crooks; 16 Dean O'Loughlin; 17 Craig Lawton.
Tries: Cardoza (27), Cook (49), Miles (54, 73), Holroyd (64), Langley (77); **Goals:** Holroyd 4/8.
On report: Tackle (39) involving Bretherton and Green.
Rugby Leaguer & League Express Men of the Match: *Rams:* Ryan Sheridan; *Dragons:* Craig Cook.
Penalty count: 10-12; **Half-time:** 16-8; **Referee:** Gareth Hewer (Whitehaven); **Attendance:** 1,097.

Friday 4th March 2005

GROUP 5

SHEFFIELD EAGLES 6 BATLEY BULLDOGS 34

EAGLES: 1 John Crawford; 2 Danny Mills; 3 Alex Dickinson; 4 Adrian Veamatahau; 5 Greg Hurst; 6 Aled James; 7 Gavin Brown; 8 Rob North; 9 Liam Brentley; 10 Craig Brown; 11 Andy Rice; 12 Nick Turnbull; 13 Simon Tillyer. Subs (all used): 14 Ryan Dickinson; 15 Jaymes Chapman; 16 Simon Morton; 17 Mitchell Stringer.
Try: G Brown (62); **Goals:** G Brown 1/1.
Sin bin: Veamatahau (19) - holding down; Chapman (45) - fighting.
BULLDOGS: 1 Craig Lingard; 2 Jamie Stokes; 3 Iain Marsh; 4 Shad Royston; 5 Gary O'Regan; 6 Neil Roden; 7 Barry Eaton; 8 Craig Wright; 9 Joe Berry; 10 David Rourke; 11 Sean Richardson; 12 Dane Morgan; 13 Mark Toohey. Subs (all used): 14 Ryan Horsley; 15 Will Cartledge; 16 Tim Spears; 17 Gary Shillabeer.
Tries: Lingard (6, 52, 75), Eaton (26), O'Regan (33); **Goals:** Eaton 7/7.
Rugby Leaguer & League Express Men of the Match: *Eagles:* Mitchell Stringer; *Bulldogs:* Barry Eaton.
Penalty count: 9-9; **Half-time:** 0-22;
Referee: Peter Taberner (Wigan); **Attendance:** 875.

Saturday 5th March 2005

GROUP 6

WARRINGTON WIZARDS 20
HEMEL HEMPSTEAD STAGS 20

WEEK 4

Sunday 6th March 2005

GROUP 1

BARROW RAIDERS 12 WORKINGTON TOWN 54

RAIDERS: 1 Joel Osborn; 2 Jason Roach; 3 Paul Jones; 4 Alex Muff; 5 Freddie Zitter; 6 Adrian Mulcahy; 7 Darren Holt; 8 Andy Fisher; 9 Dave Clark; 10 Stuart Dancer; 11 Glenn Osborn; 12 Mike Whitehead; 13 Phil Atkinson. Subs (all used): 14 Chris Roe; 15 Chris Archer; 16 Paul Wilcock; 17 Richard Colley.
Tries: J Osborn (2), Roach (47), A Fisher (78); **Goals:** Holt 0/4.
TOWN: 1 Lusi Sione; 2 Matthew Johnson; 3 Neil Frazer; 4 Jon Roper; 5 Matthew Woodcock; 6 Andrew Fearon; 7 Martyn Wilson; 8 Dean Vaughan; 9 Jonny Limmer; 10 Dean Bragg; 11 John Tuimaualuga; 12 Jamie Beaumont; 13 Kevin Hetherington. Subs (all used): 14 Matthew Tunstall; 15 Taani Lavulavu; 16 Allan McGuiness; 17 Malcolm Caton.
Tries: Sione (25, 44), Fearon (33), Frazer (36, 68), Limmer (38, 75), Hetherington (57), Woodcock (67), Tunstall (80); **Goals:** Bragg 2/4, Sione 1/2, Hetherington 2/2, Roper 2/2.
Sin bin: Fearon (17) - holding down.
Rugby Leaguer & League Express Men of the Match: *Raiders:* Freddie Zitter; *Town:* Lusi Sione.
Penalty count: 8-7; **Half-time:** 4-20;
Referee: Mike Dawber (Wigan); **Attendance:** 844.

GROUP 6

BRAMLEY BUFFALOES 8
BRADFORD-DUDLEY HILL DEMONS 56

GROUP 2

OLDHAM 30 SWINTON LIONS 37

OLDHAM: 1 Gavin Dodd; 2 Will Cowell; 3 Damian Munro; 4 Alex Wilkinson; 5 Nick Johnson; 6 Carlos Mataora; 7 Marty Turner; 8 Paul Norman; 9 Gareth Barber; 10 Danny Nanyn; 11 Simon Haughton; 12 Tere Glassie; 13 Simon Svabic. Subs (all used): 14 John Hough; 15 Dana Wilson; 16 Mark Roberts; 17 Craig Farrimond.
Tries: Barber (13), Mataora (48), Roberts (54), Wilkinson (65), Dodd (71); **Goals:** Turner 5/8.
Sin bin: Munro (33) - dissent.
LIONS: 1 Wayne English; 2 Chris Irwin; 3 Lee Patterson; 4 Hugh Thorpe; 5 Marlon Billy; 6 Lee Marsh; 7 Ian Watson; 8 Paul Southern; 9 Phil Joseph; 10 Wes Rogers; 11 Danny Heaton; 12 Ian Sinfield; 13 Ian Hodson. Subs (all used): 14 Warren Ayres; 15 Rob Russell; 16 Andy Crabtree; 17 Rob Whittaker.
Tries: English (33, 41), Billy (36), Heaton (43), Patterson (56), Sinfield (60), Joseph (79); **Goals:** Marsh 1/2, Watson 3/5; **Field goal:** Marsh.
Rugby Leaguer & League Express Men of the Match: *Oldham:* Simon Svabic; *Lions:* Phil Joseph.
Penalty count: 8-6; **Half-time:** 10-11; **Referee:** Colin Morris (Huddersfield); **Attendance:** 1,116.

ROCHDALE HORNETS 62 BLACKPOOL PANTHERS 16

HORNETS: 1 Chris Giles; 2 Andy Saywell; 3 Mark McCully; 4 David Alstead; 5 Chris Campbell; 6 Sam Butterworth; 7 John Braddish; 8 Dave Newton; 9 Phil Cantillon; 10 Gareth Price; 11 Dave Cunliffe; 12 Lee Doran; 13 Andy Gorski. Subs (all used): 14 Dave McConnell; 15 Rob Ball; 16 Kris Ratcliffe; 17 Lee Hansen.
Tries: Cunliffe (4), Cantillon (14, 17), Doran (23, 40), Alstead (25), Braddish (44), Butterworth (60), McConnell (64), Saywell (70), Gorski (75);
Goals: Braddish 9/11.
Sin bin: Price (53) - fighting.
PANTHERS: 1 Liam Bretherton; 2 Danny Arnold; 3 Gary Rourke; 4 Jake Johnstone; 5 Eric Andrews; 6 Chris Hough; 7 Willie Swann; 8 Ian Parry; 9 Liam McGovern; 10 John Hill; 11 Mick Redford; 12 Gary Smith; 13 Danny Barton. Subs (all used): 14 Martin Gambles; 15 Matt Leigh; 16 Gareth Jones; 17 Steve Molloy.
Tries: Parry (12), Redford (32), Gambles (54);
Goals: Johnstone 2/3.
Sin bin: Hill (53) - fighting.
Rugby Leaguer & League Express Men of the Match: *Hornets:* Sam Butterworth; *Panthers:* Gary Smith.
Penalty count: 10-9; **Half-time:** 34-10;
Referee: Jamie Leahy (Dewsbury); **Attendance:** 731.

GROUP 3

HALIFAX 42 KEIGHLEY COUGARS 12

HALIFAX: 1 Damian Gibson; 2 James Haley; 3 Jamie Bloem; 4 Alan Hadcroft; 5 Rikki Sheriffe; 6 Danny Jones; 7 Dean Lawford; 8 Chris Birchall; 9 Ben Fisher; 10 Jason Boults; 11 David Larder; 12 Andy Spink; 13 Pat Weisner. Subs (all used): 14 Wayne Corcoran; 15 Gareth Greenwood; 16 Jon Simpson; 17 Jode Sheriffe.
Tries: Larder (8), Lawford (12), Weisner (16), R Sheriffe (31, 51), Haley (39), Gibson (60, 76), Corcoran (79);
Goals: Lawford 2/4, Weisner 0/2, Corcoran 1/3.
COUGARS: 1 James Rushforth; 2 Matt Bramald; 3 David Foster; 4 Matt Foster; 5 Andy Robinson; 6 Adam Mitchell; 7 Matt Firth; 8 Phil Stephenson; 9 Jonny Wainhouse; 10 Danny Murgatroyd; 11 Jordan Ross; 12 Matthew Steel; 13 Daniel Harvey. Subs (all used): 14 Paul Ashton; 15 Lewis Taylor; 16 Richard Mervill; 17 Jason Clegg.
Tries: Rushforth (25), Wainhouse (70);
Goals: Mitchell 1/1, Ashton 1/1.
Sin bin: Bramald (68) - holding down; Wainhouse (70) - fighting.
Rugby Leaguer & League Express Men of the Match: *Halifax:* Dean Lawford; *Cougars:* Daniel Harvey.
Penalty count: 11-11; **Half-time:** 24-6; **Referee:** Gareth Hewer (Whitehaven); **Attendance:** 1,526.

LONDON SKOLARS 4 HULL KINGSTON ROVERS 56

SKOLARS: 1 Nathan Meischke; 2 Oran D'Arcy; 3 Austin Aggrey; 4 Brett Blaker; 5 Ashley Tozer; 6 Joe Price; 7 Gareth Honor; 8 Alan Barker; 9 Kurt Pittman; 10 Toby Hall; 11 Mike Castle; 12 Andrew Gourlay; 13 Stuart Singleton. Subs (all used): 14 Ade Aderiye; 15 Alex Smits; 16 Mat Pitman; 17 James Sullivan.
Try: Barker (24); **Goals:** Blaker 0/1.
ROVERS: 1 Loz Wildbore; 2 Jon Steel; 3 Paul Parker; 4 Kane Epati; 5 Byron Ford; 6 Paul Mansson; 7 Phil Hasty; 8 Jamie Bovill; 9 Paul Pickering; 10 Makali Aizue; 11 Andy Raleigh; 12 Jason Netherton; 13 Mark Blanchard. Subs (all used): 14 Jimmy Walker; 15 James Garmston; 16 Craig Poucher; 17 Neil Harmon.
Tries: Parker (2), Steel (6, 17, 30, 58, 78), Ford (10), Wildbore (18), Mansson (51), Aizue (68), Garmston (75); **Goals:** Wildbore 4/9, Poucher 2/2.
Rugby Leaguer & League Express Men of the Match: *Skolars:* Alan Barker; *Rovers:* Jon Steel.
Penalty count: 4-5; **Half-time:** 4-30;
Referee: Craig Halloran (Dewsbury); **Attendance:** 450.

GROUP 4

YORK CITY KNIGHTS 20 FEATHERSTONE ROVERS 20

CITY KNIGHTS: 1 Matt Blaymire; 2 Peter Fox; 3 Darren Callaghan; 4 Neil Law; 5 Chris Ross; 6 Paul Thorman; 7 Chris Levy; 8 Tom Buckenham; 9 Jimmy Elston; 10 Adam Sullivan; 11 John Smith; 12 Ian Kirke; 13 Jon Liddell. Subs (all used): 14 Scott Rhodes; 15 Mark Cain; 16 James Ward; 17 Yusuf Sozi.
Tries: Levy (30), Law (69), Callaghan (72), Fox (74);
Goals: Ross 2/4.
ROVERS: 1 Craig Moss; 2 Bryn Powell; 3 Danny Maun; 4 Richard Newlove; 5 Matthew Wray; 6 Josh Weeden; 7 Jon Presley; 8 Jim Carlton; 9 Andy Kay; 10 Danny Evans; 11 James Houston; 12 Adam Hayes; 13 Carl Hughes. Subs: 14 James Ford (not used); 15 John Fowler; 16 Greg Nicholson; 17 Steve Coulson.
Tries: Presley (18), C Hughes (36), Wray (57), Powell (64); **Goals:** Weeden 2/5.
Rugby Leaguer & League Express Men of the Match: *City Knights:* Scott Rhodes; *Rovers:* Josh Weeden.
Penalty count: 8-8; **Half-time:** 6-12; **Referee:** Steve Nicholson (Whitehaven); **Attendance:** 1,463

HUNSLET HAWKS 6 CASTLEFORD TIGERS 34

HAWKS: 1 George Rayner; 2 Jeremy Dyson; 3 Anthony Gibbons; 4 Chris Redfearn; 5 Steve Morton; 6 Mark Cass; 7 Mark Moxon; 8 Nick Staveley; 9 Joe Hawley; 10 Steve Pryce; 11 Chris Fletcher; 12 Paul Cummins; 13 David Gibbons. Subs (all used): 14 Matt Carbutt; 15 Chris North; 16 David Norcross; 17 Danny Cook.
Try: Morton (37); **Goals:** Dyson 1/1.
TIGERS. 1 Michael Platt; 2 Waine Pryce; 3 Damien Reid; 4 Jon Hepworth; 5 Michael Shenton; 6 Andy Kain; 7 Paul Handforth; 8 Adam Watene; 9 Andrew Henderson; 10 Frank Watene; 11 Jordan James; 12 Craig Huby; 13 Tom Haughey. Subs (all used): 14 Leigh Cooke; 15 Anthony England; 16 Michael Knowles; 17 Tim Robinson.
Tries: A Kain (1), James (17), Pryce (22, 74), Shenton (44), Henderson (55), Reid (58); **Goals:** Huby 3/7.
Rugby Leaguer & League Express Men of the Match: *Hawks:* Nick Staveley; *Tigers:* Frank Watene.
Penalty count: 5-9; **Half-time:** 6-14;
Referee: Ben Thaler (Wakefield); **Attendance:** 1,432.

GROUP 5

DONCASTER DRAGONS 40 DEWSBURY RAMS 10

DRAGONS: 1 Wayne Green; 2 Craig Farrell; 3 Chris Langley; 4 Dale Cardoza; 5 Craig Miles; 6 Graham Holroyd; 7 Latham Tawhai; 8 Gareth Handford; 9 Craig Cook; 10 Martin Ostler; 11 Andy Hay; 12 Peter Green; 13 Martin Moana. Subs (all used): 14 Craig Lawton; 15 Dean O'Loughlin; 16 Ben Cockayne; 17 Dean Andrews.
Tries: Farrell (5), Langley (16), W Green (19), P Green (42, 46), Handford (55), Holroyd (73), Cockayne (76);
Goals: Holroyd 4/8.
RAMS: 1 Ian Preece; 2 Oliver Fairbank; 3 Wayne McHugh; 4 Darren Rogers; 5 Richard Tillotson; 6 Francis Maloney; 7 Ryan Sheridan; 8 James Walker; 9 Richard Chapman; 10 Paul Hicks; 11 Kevin Crouthers; 12 Warren Jowitt; 13 Alex Bretherton. Subs (all used): 14 David Mycoe; 15 Mark Stubley; 16 Anthony Henderson; 17 Anthony Thewliss.
Try: Fairbank (23); **Goals:** Maloney 3/3.
Sin bin: Thewliss (45) - late challenge.
Rugby Leaguer & League Express Men of the Match: *Dragons:* Peter Green; *Rams:* Francis Maloney.
Penalty count: 11-12; **Half-time:** 14-10;
Referee: Julian King (St Helens); **Attendance:** 710.

Saturday 12th March 2005

GROUP 6

HEMEL HEMPSTEAD STAGS 16
BRADFORD-DUDLEY HILL DEMONS 52

WEEK 5

Sunday 13th March 2005

GROUP 6

WARRINGTON WIZARDS 24 BRAMLEY BUFFALOES 24

Wednesday 16th March 2005

GROUP 1

GATESHEAD THUNDER 30 WORKINGTON TOWN 20

THUNDER: 1 Kevin Neighbour; 2 Steve Elms; 3 Ian Brown; 4 Craig Firth; 5 Graham Stephenson; 6 Phil Carleton; 7 Chris Birch; 8 Damian Martinez; 9 John Tomes; 10 Rob Line; 11 Tabua Cakacaka; 12 Steven Bradley; 13 Steve Rutherford. Subs (all used): 14 Liam

Garside; 15 Brandon Fall; 16 Nigel Arizmendez; 17 Selwyn St Bernard.
Tries: Elms (12), Neighbour (19), Carleton (56), Firth (61), Stephenson (68); **Goals:** Birch 5/8.
TOWN: 1 Luisi Sione; 2 Matthew Woodcock; 3 Scott Chilton; 4 Jon Roper; 5 Tom Armstrong; 6 Andrew Fearon; 7 Martyn Wilson; 8 Malcolm Caton; 9 Jonny Limmer; 10 Dean Bragg; 11 Jamie Beaumont; 12 Dean Vaughan; 13 Kevin Hetherington. Subs (all used): 14 Lee Kiddie; 15 Taani Lavulavu; 16 Dean Burgess; 17 John Tuimaualuga.
Tries: Bragg (3), Woodcock (7), Armstrong (22), Roper (72); **Goals:** Hetherington 2/4.
Rugby Leaguer & League Express Men of the Match: *Thunder:* Chris Birch; *Town:* Taani Lavulavu.
Penalty count: 10-9; **Half-time:** 14-16;
Referee: Robert Hicks (Oldham); **Attendance:** 303.

GROUP 2

ROCHDALE HORNETS 68 OLDHAM 26

HORNETS: 1 Paul Owen; 2 Chris Campbell; 3 Mark McCully; 4 Richard Varkulis; 5 Chris Giles; 6 John Braddish; 7 Lee Birdseye; 8 Tommy Hodgkinson; 9 Dave McConnell; 10 Gareth Price; 11 Dave Cunliffe; 12 Lee Doran; 13 Andy Gorski. Subs (all used): 14 Phil Cantillon; 15 Dave Newton; 16 Radney Bowker; 17 Lee Hansen.
Tries: Braddish (11, 37), Cunliffe (19, 25), Gorski (21, 50), Campbell (30), Owen (35), Giles (57), Cantillon (67), Doran (70), McCully (76), McConnell (79);
Goals: Birdseye 0/3, Braddish 0/2, McCully 8/9.
OLDHAM: 1 Gavin Dodd; 2 Carlos Mataora; 3 Will Cowell; 4 Alex Wilkinson; 5 Nick Johnson; 6 Simon Svabic; 7 Marty Turner; 8 Paul Norman; 9 Gareth Barber; 10 Ricky Bibey; 11 Simon Haughton; 12 Martin Elswood; 13 Mark Roberts. Subs (all used): 14 Danny Nanyn; 15 Dana Wilson; 16 John Hough; 17 James Kirkland.
Tries: Dodd (3, 48, 64), Haughton (7); **Goals:** Turner 5/5.
Rugby Leaguer & League Express Men of the Match: *Hornets:* Andy Gorski; *Oldham:* Simon Haughton.
Penalty count: 13-7; **Half-time:** 32-14;
Referee: Peter Taberner (Wigan); **Attendance:** 1,161.

Saturday 19th March 2005

GROUP 6

WARRINGTON WIZARDS 52
BRADFORD-DUDLEY HILL DEMONS 38

GROUP 3

LONDON SKOLARS 16 KEIGHLEY COUGARS 41

SKOLARS: 1 Ashley Tozer; 2 Austin Aggrey; 3 Joe Price; 4 Stuart Singleton; 5 Oran D'Arcy; 6 Tim Gee; 7 Gareth Honor; 8 Alex Smits; 9 Kurt Pittman; 10 Toby Hall; 11 Andrew Gourlay; 12 Matt Pitman; 13 Brett Blaker. Subs (all used): 14 James Sullivan; 15 Matt Ryan; 16 Nathan Gee; 17 Ben Joyce.
Tries: Aggrey (11), Honor (49), Tozer (56);
Goals: T Gee 2/3.
COUGARS: 1 Matt Bramald; 2 Sam Gardner; 3 David Foster; 4 Matt Foster; 5 Andrew Jackson; 6 Paul Ashton; 7 Matt Firth; 8 Phil Stephenson; 9 Jonny Wainhouse; 10 Danny Murgatroyd; 11 Lewis Taylor; 12 Matthew Steel; 13 Daniel Harvey. Subs (all used): 14 Adam Mitchell; 15 Andy Robinson; 16 Richard Mervill; 17 Jason Clegg.
Tries: M Foster (2, 7), D Foster (21), Bramald (30), Mervill (38), Ashton (40, 76);
Goals: Ashton 6/8; **Field goal:** Ashton.
Sin bin: Taylor (67) – holding down.
Rugby Leaguer & League Express Men of the Match: *Skolars:* Austin Aggrey; *Cougars:* Paul Ashton.
Penalty count: 7-7; **Half-time:** 4-32;
Referee: Peter Taberner (Wigan); **Attendance:** 353.

WEEK 6

Sunday 20th March 2005

GROUP 1

BARROW RAIDERS 2 WHITEHAVEN 42

RAIDERS: 1 Joel Osborn; 2 Jason Roach; 3 Alex Muff; 4 Freddie Zitter; 5 James Nixon; 6 Richard Colley; 7 Darren Holt; 8 Andy Fisher; 9 Dave Clark; 10 Paul Wilcock; 11 Glenn Osborn; 12 Mike Whitehead; 13 Phil Atkinson. Subs (all used): 14 Jon Williamson; 15 Darren Fisher; 16 Paul Jones; 17 Adrian Mulcahy.
Goals: Holt 1/1.
WHITEHAVEN: 1 Gary Broadbent; 2 Steven Wood; 3 Wesley Wilson; 4 Mick Nanyn; 5 Jamie Marshall; 6 Leroy Joe; 7 Joel Penny; 8 Marc Jackson; 9 Aaron Lester; 10 David Fatialofa; 11 Brett McDermott; 12 Ryan Campbell; 13 Carl Rudd. Subs (all used): 14 Steve Kirkbride; 15 Garry Purdham; 16 Carl Sice; 17 Craig Chambers.
Tries: Penny (12, 20), Wood (35), Nanyn (37), Sice (45, 65), Broadbent (55, 68); **Goals:** Penny 0/2, Nanyn 5/6.
Rugby Leaguer & League Express Men of the Match: *Raiders:* Freddie Zitter; *Whitehaven:* Gary Broadbent.
Penalty count: 4-5; **Half-time:** 2-18;
Referee: Mike Dawber (Wigan); **Attendance:** 877.

GROUP 6

BRAMLEY BUFFALOES 26
HEMEL HEMPSTEAD STAGS 12

GROUP 1

WORKINGTON TOWN 44 GATESHEAD THUNDER 14

TOWN: 1 Lusi Sione; 2 Matthew Woodcock; 3 Neil Frazer; 4 Jon Roper; 5 Matthew Johnson; 6 James Robinson; 7 Lee Kiddie; 8 Dean Burgess; 9 Jonny Limmer; 10 Dean Vaughan; 11 Ricky Wright; 12 John Tuimaualuga; 13 Brett Smith. Subs (all used): 14 Martyn Wilson; 15 Taani Lavulavu; 16 Jamie Beaumont; 17 Dean Bragg.
Tries: Frazer (14, 59), Woodcock (18, 50), Kiddie (28, 52), Johnson (38), Beaumont (62);
Goals: Smith 3/5, Roper 3/3.
THUNDER: 1 Kevin Neighbour; 2 Steve Elms; 3 Nigel Arizmendez; 4 Craig Firth; 5 Robin Peers; 6 Phil Carleton; 7 Chris Birch; 8 Selwyn St Bernard; 9 John Tomes; 10 Liam Garside; 11 Tabua Cakacaka; 12 Steven Bradley; 13 Steve Rutherford. Subs (all used): 14 Phil Pitt; 15 Tony Doherty; 16 Damian Martinez; 17 Rob Line.
Tries: Bradley (44), Birch (75); **Goals:** Birch 3/4.
Rugby Leaguer & League Express Men of the Match: *Town:* Lusi Sione; *Thunder:* Tabua Cakacaka.
Penalty count: 5-6; **Half-time:** 22-4;
Referee: Craig Halloran (Dewsbury); **Attendance:** 888.

GROUP 2

BLACKPOOL PANTHERS 16 OLDHAM 35

PANTHERS: 1 Danny Arnold; 2 Gary Rourke; 3 Eddie Kilgannon; 4 Glen Godbee; 5 Eric Andrews; 6 Liam McGovern; 7 Willie Swann; 8 Mike Callan; 9 Chris Ramsdale; 10 John Hill; 11 Gary Smith; 12 Matt Leigh; 13 Danny Barton. Subs (all used): 14 Martin Gambles; 15 Gareth Jones; 16 Steve Molloy; 17 Chris Hough.
Tries: Godbee (21), Andrews (32); **Goals:** McGovern 4/5.
OLDHAM: 1 Jon Goddard; 2 Gavin Dodd; 3 Will Cowell; 4 Alex Wilkinson; 5 Nick Johnson; 6 Simon Svabic; 7 Marty Turner; 8 Ricky Bibey; 9 John Hough; 10 Danny Nanyn; 11 Simon Haughton; 12 Martin Elswood; 13 Mark Roberts. Subs (all used): 14 Keith Brennan; 15 Dana Wilson; 16 Paul Norman; 17 Carlos Mataora.
Tries: Wilkinson (8), Svabic (28), Goddard (42, 51), Turner (73), Norman (75);
Goals: Turner 5/7; **Field goal:** Svabic.
Sin bin: Roberts (68) - dissent.
Rugby Leaguer & League Express Men of the Match: *Panthers:* Mike Callan; *Oldham:* Jon Goddard.
Penalty count: 14-13; **Half-time:** 14-10;
Referee: Paul Carr (Castleford);
Attendance: 250 *(at Lightfoot Green, Preston).*

ROCHDALE HORNETS 54 SWINTON LIONS 20

HORNETS: 1 Paul Owen; 2 Chris Campbell; 3 Mark McCully; 4 Richard Varkulis; 5 Chris Giles; 6 Radney Bowker; 7 John Braddish; 8 Tommy Hodgkinson; 9 Dave McConnell; 10 Dave Newton; 11 Dave Cunliffe; 12 Lee Doran; 13 Andy Gorski. Subs (all used): 14 Sam Butterworth; 15 Phil Farrell; 16 Phil Cantillon; 17 Lee Hansen.
Tries: McCully (15, 34), Gorski (26, 61), Braddish (40, 46, 64), Campbell (70), Bowker (76); **Goals:** McCully 9/12.
LIONS: 1 Wayne English; 2 Stuart Oldham; 3 Lee Patterson; 4 Chris Maye; 5 Chris Irwin; 6 Warren Ayres; 7 Ian Watson; 8 Danny Heaton; 9 Andy Crabtree; 10 Wes Rogers; 11 Lee Gardner; 12 Ian Sinfield; 13 Lee Marsh. Subs (all used): 14 Safraz Patel; 15 Ian Hodson; 16 Darren Speakman; 17 Rob Whittaker.
Tries: Patterson (7), Irwin (50, 80), Patel (52), Maye (74); **Goals:** Marsh 0/6.
Sin bin: Watson (25) - interference;
Irwin (66) - professional foul.
Rugby Leaguer & League Express Men of the Match: *Hornets:* John Braddish; *Lions:* Lee Patterson.
Penalty count: 12-9; **Half-time:** 24-4; **Referee:** Steve Nicholson (Whitehaven); **Attendance:** 967.

GROUP 3

HALIFAX 34 HULL KINGSTON ROVERS 26

HALIFAX: 1 Damian Gibson; 2 James Haley; 3 James Bunyan; 4 Anthony Blackwood; 5 Rikki Sheriffe; 6 Dean Lawford; 7 Ben Black; 8 Chris Birchall; 9 Ben Fisher; 10 Jason Boults; 11 David Larder; 12 Andy Spink; 13 Pat Weisner. Subs (all used): 14 Jamie Bloem; 15 Wayne Corcoran; 16 Jode Sheriffe; 17 Fereti Tuilagi.
Tries: Blackwood (2), Spink (31), Haley (52), Gibson (62), R Sheriffe (69, 75); **Goals:** Lawford 4/5, Bloem 1/2.
Sin bin: Bloem (58) - dissent.
ROVERS: 1 Craig Poucher; 2 Jon Steel; 3 Paul Parker; 4 Kane Epati; 5 Byron Ford; 6 Dwayne Barker; 7 James Webster; 8 James Garmston; 9 Andy Ellis; 10 David Tangata-Toa; 11 Andy Raleigh; 12 Dale Holdstock; 13 Paul Mansson. Subs (all used): 14 Jimmy Walker; 15 Phil Hasty; 16 Jamie Bovill; 17 Makali Aizue.
Tries: Mansson (8), Epati (14), Holdstock (21), Poucher (25); **Goals:** Poucher 5/7.
Rugby Leaguer & League Express Men of the Match: *Halifax:* Dean Lawford; *Rovers:* Paul Mansson.
Penalty count: 8-5; **Half-time:** 12-24; **Referee:** Colin Morris (Huddersfield); **Attendance:** 2,095.

GROUP 4

FEATHERSTONE ROVERS 28 HUNSLET HAWKS 18

ROVERS: 1 Craig Moss; 2 Bryn Powell; 3 Danny Maun; 4 Richard Newlove; 5 Matthew Wray; 6 Andy McNally; 7 Josh Weeden; 8 Andy Jarrett; 9 Andy Kay; 10 Nathan Sykes; 11 James Houston; 12 Adam Hayes; 13 Carl Hughes. Subs (all used): 14 James Ford; 15 Greg Nicholson; 16 Ian Tonks; 17 Jim Carlton.
Tries: Jarrett (17), Moss (26), Tonks (32), Newlove (50), Maun (66, 79); **Goals:** Weeden 2/6.
HAWKS: 1 George Rayner; 2 Jeremy Dyson; 3 Anthony Gibbons; 4 Chris Redfearn; 5 Chris North; 6 Mark Cass; 7 Mark Moxon; 8 Nick Staveley; 9 Joe Hawley; 10 Neil Mears; 11 Wayne Freeman; 12 Paul Cummins; 13 Anthony Gibbons. Subs (all used): 14 Andy Shickell; 15 Marc Shickell; 16 Danny Cook; 17 Gareth Naylor.
Tries: A Shickell (38), North (55), Moxon (71);
Goals: Dyson 3/4.
Sin bin: W Freeman (30) - obstruction.
Rugby Leaguer & League Express Men of the Match: *Rovers:* Josh Weeden; *Hawks:* Mark Moxon.
Penalty count: 9-6; **Half-time:** 16-8;
Referee: Phil Bentham (Warrington); **Attendance:** 1,150.

YORK CITY KNIGHTS 16 CASTLEFORD TIGERS 24

CITY KNIGHTS: 1 Lee Lingard; 2 Peter Fox; 3 Darren Callaghan; 4 Neil Law; 5 Calvin Watson; 6 Scott Rhodes; 7 Paul Thorman; 8 John Smith; 9 Jimmy Elston; 10 Adam Sullivan; 11 James Ward; 12 Simon Friend; 13 Jon Liddell. Subs (all used): 14 Lee Jackson; 15 Neil Thorman; 16 Yusuf Sozi; 17 Craig McDowell.
Tries: Watson (6), Lingard (29); **Goals:** P Thorman 4/4.
Sin bin: Smith (61) - holding down.
TIGERS: 1 Stuart Kain; 2 Waine Pryce; 3 Damien Reid; 4 Jon Hepworth; 5 Michael Shenton; 6 Andy Kain; 7 Paul Handforth; 8 Adam Watene; 9 Andrew Henderson; 10 Frank Watene; 11 Tom Haughey; 12 Steve Crouch; 13 Aaron Smith. Subs (all used): 14 Shaun Lunt; 15 Leigh Cooke; 16 Jordan James; 17 Byron Smith.
Tries: Haughey (9, 65), Shenton (17), Henderson (55), A Kain (76); **Goals:** Handforth 1/4, A Kain 1/1.
Dismissal: A Watene (79) - high tackle.
Sin bin: A Kain (52) - dissent.
On report: A Watene (21) - high tackle.
Rugby Leaguer & League Express Men of the Match: *City Knights:* Adam Sullivan; *Tigers:* Tom Haughey.
Penalty count: 11-9; **Half-time:** 16-8;
Referee: Ben Thaler (Wakefield); **Attendance:** 2,340.

GROUP 5

DEWSBURY RAMS 40 SHEFFIELD EAGLES 8

RAMS: 1 Ian Preece; 2 Oliver Fairbank; 3 Wayne McHugh; 4 Kevin Crouthers; 5 Darren Rogers; 6 Francis Maloney; 7 Ryan Sheridan; 8 Paul Hicks; 9 Chris Woolford; 10 Jonlee Lockwood; 11 Anthony Thewliss; 12 Warren Jowitt; 13 Alex Bretherton. Subs (all used): 14 Richard Chapman; 15 Mark Stubley; 16 James Walker; 17 Mark Hawksley.
Tries: McHugh (14), Chapman (19, 33, 45), Maloney (37), Jowitt (71), Bretherton (79); **Goals:** Maloney 6/8.
EAGLES: 1 John Crawford; 2 Kieron Collins; 3 Alex Dickinson; 4 Adrian Veamatahau; 5 Carl De Chenu; 6 Ryan Dickinson; 7 Gavin Brown; 8 Damien Lynch; 9 Liam Brentley; 10 Chris Molyneux; 11 Joseph Pitt; 12 Nick Turnbull; 13 Sean Dickinson. Subs (all used): 14 Peter Moore; 15 Simon Morton; 16 Greg Hurst; 17 Rob North.
Try: Crawford (2); **Goals:** G Brown 2/2.
Dismissal: Lynch (58) - high tackle.
Rugby Leaguer & League Express Men of the Match: *Rams:* Ryan Sheridan; *Eagles:* Liam Brentley.
Penalty count: 12-9; **Half-time:** 22-8;
Referee: Robert Hicks (Oldham); **Attendance:** 862.

DONCASTER DRAGONS 54 BATLEY BULLDOGS 0

DRAGONS: 1 Craig Horne; 2 Dean Colton; 3 Craig Farrell; 4 Dale Cardoza; 5 Craig Miles; 6 Graham Holroyd; 7 Latham Tawhai; 8 Gareth Handford; 9 Craig Cook; 10 Martin Ostler; 11 Andy Hay; 12 Peter Green; 13 Martin Moana. Subs (all used): 14 Aaron Wood; 15 Dean O'Loughlin; 16 Craig Lawton; 17 Kirk Netherton.
Tries: Hay (3, 65), Holroyd (6), Cardoza (24, 43), Colton (58), Netherton (71), Wood (75), Miles (80);
Goals: Holroyd 9/10.
BULLDOGS: 1 Craig Lingard; 2 Adrian Flynn; 3 Iain Marsh; 4 Shad Royston; 5 Gary O'Regan; 6 Neil Roden; 7 Barry Eaton; 8 Craig Wright; 9 Kris Lythe; 10 David Rourke; 11 Sean Richardson; 12 Dane Morgan; 13 Mark Toohey. Subs (all used): 14 Ryan Horsley; 15 Tim Spears; 16 Will Cartledge; 17 Gary Shillabeer.
Dismissal: Richardson (65) - use of the elbow.
Sin bin: Lingard (6) - high tackle.
Rugby Leaguer & League Express Men of the Match: *Dragons:* Dean O'Loughlin; *Bulldogs:* Dane Morgan.
Penalty count: 14–8; **Half-time:** 20-0;
Referee: Gareth Hewer (Whitehaven); **Attendance:** 804.

Thursday 24th March 2005

GROUP 1

GATESHEAD THUNDER 20 BARROW RAIDERS 29

THUNDER: 1 Wade Liddell; 2 Joe Brown; 3 Craig Firth; 4 Ian Brown; 5 Robin Peers; 6 Phil Carleton; 7 Chris Birch; 8 Rob Line; 9 John Tomes; 10 Liam Garside; 11 Tabua Cakacaka; 12 Steven Bradley; 13 Joe Burley. Subs (all used): 14 Tony Doherty; 15 Nigel Arizmendez; 16 Paul Dodsworth; 17 Selwyn St Bernard.
Tries: Liddell (12), Bradley (16), Peers (76), Arizmendez (78); **Goals:** Birch 2/5.
RAIDERS: 1 Joel Osborn; 2 Nick Beech; 3 Paul Jones; 4 Freddie Zitter; 5 James Nixon; 6 Richard Colley; 7 Darren Holt; 8 Andy Fisher; 9 Dave Clark; 10 Paul Wilcock; 11 Mike Whitehead; 12 Glenn Osborn; 13 Phil Atkinson. Subs (all used): 14 Jon Williamson; 15 Darren Fisher; 16 Adrian Mulcahy; 17 Anthony Horton.
Tries: Zitter (21, 27), Atkinson (55), A Fisher (61), Mulcahy (71); **Goals:** Holt 4/6; **Field goal:** Holt.

Rugby Leaguer & League Express Men of the Match: *Thunder:* Selwyn St Bernard; *Raiders:* Andy Fisher.
Penalty count: 5-6; **Half-time:** 10-10;
Referee: Paul Carr (Castleford); **Attendance:** 268.

Friday 25th March 2005

GROUP 1

WHITEHAVEN 58 WORKINGTON TOWN 10

WHITEHAVEN: 1 Gary Broadbent; 2 Craig Calvert; 3 Wesley Wilson; 4 Mick Nanyn; 5 John Lebbon; 6 Leroy Joe; 7 Joel Penny; 8 Neil Baynes; 9 Aaron Lester; 10 David Fatialofa; 11 Craig Chambers; 12 Howard Hill; 13 Carl Rudd. Subs (all used): 14 Steve Kirkbride; 15 Paul Davidson; 16 Carl Sice; 17 Marc Jackson.
Tries: Nanyn (2, 16, 38), Calvert (8, 72, 76), Penny (34, 45), Broadbent (48), Sice (57, 67), Wilson (79);
Goals: Nanyn 5/12.
TOWN: 1 Matthew Johnson; 2 Matthew Woodcock; 3 Kevin Hetherington; 4 Neil Frazer; 5 Andrew Fearon; 6 Martyn Wilson; 7 Scott Chilton; 8 Dean Burgess; 13 Brett Smith; 10 Dean Bragg; 11 Ricky Wright; 12 Jamie Beaumont; 9 James Robinson. Subs (all used): 14 Lee Burns; 15 Taani Lavulavu; 16 Tom Armstrong; 17 Malcolm Caton.
Try: Bragg (50); **Goals:** Hetherington 2/2, Bragg 1/1.
Rugby Leaguer & League Express Men of the Match: *Whitehaven:* Mick Nanyn; *Town:* Kevin Hetherington.
Penalty count: 7-7; **Half-time:** 22-4;
Referee: Colin Morris (Huddersfield); **Attendance:** 3,439.

GROUP 2

SWINTON LIONS 14 BLACKPOOL PANTHERS 14

LIONS: 1 Lee Patterson; 2 Chris Irwin; 3 Ben Cramant; 4 Chris Maye; 5 Marlon Billy; 6 Mick Coates; 7 Ian Watson; 8 Paul Southern; 9 Phil Joseph; 10 Darren Speakman; 11 Rob Russell; 12 Ian Hodson; 13 Lee Marsh. Subs (all used): 14 Neil Hayden; 15 Andy Crabtree; 16 Lee Gardner; 17 Rob Whittaker.
Tries: Irwin (20), Coates (40), Maye (54);
Goals: Marsh 1/3.
On report: Watson (26) - alleged biting.
PANTHERS: 1 Chris Ramsdale; 2 Gary Rourke; 3 Tommy Grundy; 4 Eddie Kilgannon; 5 Jake Johnstone; 6 Liam McGovern; 7 Martin Gambles; 8 Gus Martin; 9 Dave Rowland; 10 Lee Rowley; 11 Steve Ormesher; 12 James Lomax; 13 John Chamberlain. Subs (all used): 14 Craig Tipeny; 15 Ian Parry; 16 Gareth Jones; 17 Jamie Stenhouse.
Tries: Gambles (3), Rourke (17), Stenhouse (49);
Goals: Johnstone 1/3.
Rugby Leaguer & League Express Men of the Match: *Lions:* Mick Coates; *Panthers:* Liam McGovern.
Penalty count: 8-8; **Half-time:** 8-10;
Referee: Peter Taberner (Wigan); **Attendance:** 541.

OLDHAM 10 ROCHDALE HORNETS 54

OLDHAM: 1 Jon Goddard; 2 Gavin Dodd; 3 Mark Roberts; 4 Alex Wilkinson; 5 Nick Johnson; 6 Simon Svabic; 7 Marty Turner; 8 Paul Norman; 9 John Hough; 10 Ricky Bibey; 11 Simon Haughton; 12 Tere Glassie; 13 Carlos Mataora. Subs (all used): 14 Danny Nanyn; 15 Dana Wilson; 16 Craig Farrimond; 17 James Kirkland.
Tries: Johnson (64), Wilkinson (68); **Goals:** Turner 1/2.
Dismissal: Bibey (26) - high tackle.
HORNETS: 1 Chris Giles; 2 Chris Campbell; 3 Mark McCully; 4 Richard Varkulis; 5 Andy Saywell; 6 Radney Bowker; 7 Lee Birdseye; 8 Rob Ball; 9 Dave McConnell; 10 Dave Cunliffe; 11 Andy Gorski; 12 Lee Doran; 13 Phil Farrell. Subs (all used): 14 Sam Butterworth; 15 Tommy Hodgkinson; 16 Phil Cantillon; 17 Lee Hansen.
Tries: (Saywell 8, 38, 40, 61), Campbell (15, 22), McConnell (34), Gorski (51), Doran (55), Cunliffe (72);
Goals: McCully 1/1, Birdseye 6/9.
Dismissal: McCully (12) - head-butt.
Rugby Leaguer & League Express Men of the Match: *Oldham:* Mark Roberts; *Hornets:* Radney Bowker.
Penalty count: 6-9; **Half-time:** 0-32;
Referee: Ben Thaler (Wakefield); **Attendance:** 1,544.

GROUP 3

HULL KINGSTON ROVERS 78 LONDON SKOLARS 20

ROVERS: 1 Loz Wildbore; 2 Jon Steel; 3 Kane Epati; 4 Jimmy Walker; 5 Byron Ford; 6 Paul Mansson; 7 Phil Hasty; 8 Neil Harmon; 9 Paul Pickering; 10 Jamie Bovill; 11 Andy Raleigh; 12 Dale Holdstock; 13 Dwayne Barker. Subs (all used): 14 James Webster; 15 Paul Parker; 16 Mark Blanchard; 17 Makali Aizue.
Tries: Raleigh (4, 25, 50), Bovill (13), Hasty (18, 22), Ford (35), Wildbore (39), Barker (42, 44, 66), Webster (52), Epati (57), Blanchard (61); **Goals:** Wildbore 11/14.
SKOLARS: 1 Oran D'Arcy; 2 Austin Aggrey; 3 Joe Price; 4 Ben Joyce; 5 Ade Aderiye; 6 Tim Gee; 7 Nathan Meischke; 8 Wayne Parillon; 9 Kurt Pittman; 10 Rubert Jonker; 11 Dave Brown; 12 Matt Pitman; 13 Brett Blaker. Subs (all used): 14 Gareth Honor; 15 Keir Bell; 16 Matt Ryan; 17 Toby Hall.
Tries: Aggrey (32, pen), Jonker (70), Blaker (79);
Goals: T Gee 2/2, K Pittman 2/2.
Sin bin: Meischke (24) - interference.
Rugby Leaguer & League Express Men of the Match: *Rovers:* Loz Wildbore; *Skolars:* Rubert Jonker.
Penalty count: 7-13; **Half-time:** 40-8;
Referee: Robert Hicks (Oldham); **Attendance:** 2,009.

KEIGHLEY COUGARS 24 HALIFAX 50

COUGARS: 1 Matt Bramald; 2 Sam Gardner; 3 David Foster; 4 Matt Foster; 5 Andrew Jackson; 6 Paul Ashton; 7 Matt Firth; 8 Phil Stephenson; 14 Adam Mitchell; 10 Danny Murgatroyd; 11 Lewis Taylor; 12 Matthew Steel; 13 Daniel Harvey. Subs (all used): 9 Chris Beever; 15 Andy Robinson; 16 Chris Parker; 17 Richard Mervill.
Tries: Steel (2, 64), Gardner (16), Bramald (27);
Goals: Ashton 4/4.
Sin bin: Stephenson (8) - fighting; Ashton (78) - dissent.
HALIFAX: 1 Jamie Bloem; 2 James Haley; 3 Damian Gibson; 4 Anthony Blackwood; 5 Rikki Sheriffe; 6 Dean Lawford; 7 Ben Black; 8 Chris Birchall; 9 Andy Boothroyd; 10 Ryan McDonald; 11 David Larder; 12 Andy Spink; 13 Pat Weisner. Subs (all used): 14 Ben Fisher; 15 Wayne Corcoran; 16 Jon Simpson; 17 Fereti Tuilagi.
Tries: Weisner (9), Birchall (12), Haley (22, 72), Gibson (42), Spink (45), Black (52, 57), Tuilagi (76);
Goals: Bloem 7/9.
Sin bin: McDonald (8) - fighting.
Rugby Leaguer & League Express Men of the Match: *Cougars:* Matthew Steel; *Halifax:* Ben Black.
Penalty count: 9-12; **Half-time:** 18-16;
Referee: Phil Bentham (Warrington); **Attendance:** 1,404.

GROUP 4

CASTLEFORD TIGERS 35 FEATHERSTONE ROVERS 16

TIGERS: 1 Stuart Kain; 2 Waine Pryce; 3 Damien Reid; 4 Michael Shenton; 5 Tim Robinson; 6 Andy Kain; 7 Dominic Brambani; 8 Byron Smith; 9 Shaun Lunt; 10 Alex Rowe; 11 Leigh Cooke; 12 Lance Hamilton; 13 Jordan James. Subs (all used): 14 Tom Haughey; 15 Rob Worrincy; 16 Paul Handforth; 17 Frank Watene.
Tries: Pryce (15, 19, 45), S Kain (22), Robinson (52), Shenton (54); **Goals:** A Kain 5/8; **Field goal:** A Kain.
ROVERS: 1 Nathan Batty; 2 Bryn Powell; 3 Danny Maun; 4 Richard Newlove; 5 Matthew Wray; 6 Andy McNally; 7 Josh Weeden; 8 Ian Tonks; 9 Andy Kay; 10 Nathan Sykes; 11 James Houston; 12 Neil Lowe; 13 Greg Nicholson. Subs (all used): 14 Craig Moss; 15 Danny Evans; 16 Carl Hughes; 17 Jim Carlton.
Tries: Newlove (8), Lowe (11), McNally (67), C Hughes (70); **Goals:** Weeden 0/4.
Sin bin: Tonks (78) - dissent.
Rugby Leaguer & League Express Men of the Match: *Tigers:* Waine Pryce; *Rovers:* Andy McNally.
Penalty count: 13-7; **Half-time:** 19-8; **Referee:** Gareth Hewer (Whitehaven); **Attendance:** 7,338.

HUNSLET HAWKS 18 YORK CITY KNIGHTS 12

HAWKS: 1 Gary McLelland; 2 Jeremy Dyson; 3 Anthony Gibbons; 4 Paul Cummins; 5 Chris North; 6 Andy Bastow; 7 Mark Moxon; 8 Nick Staveley; 9 Jamaine Wray; 10 Matt Carbutt; 11 Wayne Freeman; 12 Craig Cawthray; 13 Gareth Naylor. Subs (all used): 14 Glen Freeman; 15 Marc Shickell; 16 Andy Shickell; 17 Shaun Ibbetson.
Tries: Wray (28, 65), North (40); **Goals:** Dyson 3/6.
CITY KNIGHTS: 1 Matt Blaymire; 2 Peter Fox; 3 Calvin Watson; 4 Neil Law; 5 Chris Ross; 6 Scott Rhodes; 7 Chris Levy; 8 Tom Buckenham; 9 Neil Thorman; 10 Yusuf Sozi; 11 Mick Ramsden; 12 Darren Callaghan; 13 Lee Patterson. Subs (all used): 14 Mark Cain; 15 James Ward; 16 Craig McDowell; 17 Craig Forsyth.
Tries: Blaymire (15), Ramsden (79);
Goals: Ross 1/1, Cain 1/1.
Rugby Leaguer & League Express Men of the Match: *Hawks:* Jamaine Wray; *City Knights:* Tom Buckenham.
Penalty count: 9-7; **Half-time:** 10-6;
Referee: Jamie Leahy (Dewsbury); **Attendance:** 657.

GROUP 5

SHEFFIELD EAGLES 20 DONCASTER DRAGONS 38

EAGLES: 1 Greg Hurst; 2 Danny Mills; 3 Alex Dickinson; 4 Adrian Veamatahau; 5 Kieron Collins; 6 Ryan Dickinson; 7 Peter Moore; 8 Damien Lynch; 9 Gareth Stanley; 10 Simon Morton; 11 Joseph Pitt; 12 Jaymes Chapman; 13 Simon Tillyer. Subs (all used): 14 Jimmy Pearson; 15 Sean Dickinson; 16 Jon Breakingbury; 17 Rob North.
Tries: Veamatahau (3), Chapman (6), Mills (44), Pitt (66); **Goals:** Moore 0/2, Pearson 2/3.
DRAGONS: 1 Wayne Green; 2 Dean Colton; 3 Chris Langley; 4 Aaron Wood; 5 Craig Miles; 6 Shaun Leaf; 7 Ben Cockayne; 8 Dean O'Loughlin; 9 Kirk Netherton; 10 Jonathan Jones; 11 Lee Harland; 12 Dean Andrews; 13 Craig Lawton. Subs (all used): 14 Gareth Handford; 15 Martin Ostler; 16 Dale Cardoza; 17 Peter Green.
Tries: Cockayne (11, 18, 74), Langley (14), Colton (47, 58), Netherton (55), Andrews (78);
Goals: Cockayne 1/3, W Green 2/5.
Rugby Leaguer & League Express Men of the Match: *Eagles:* Danny Mills; *Dragons:* Ben Cockayne.
Penalty count: 7-6; **Half-time:** 10-14;
Referee: Mike Dawber (Wigan);
Attendance: 1,003 *(at Clifton Lane, Rotherham).*

BATLEY BULLDOGS 12 DEWSBURY RAMS 10

BULLDOGS: 1 Craig Lingard; 2 Jamie Stokes; 3 Iain Marsh; 4 Shad Royston; 5 Adrian Flynn; 6 Neil Roden; 7 Barry Eaton; 8 Craig Wright; 9 Joe Berry; 10 Will Cartledge; 11 Sean Richardson; 12 Dane Morgan; 13 Mark Toohey. Subs (all used): 14 Mark Sibson; 15 Kris Lythe; 16 Gary Shillabeer; 17 Paul Harrison.
Tries: Roden (32), Eaton (65); **Goals:** Eaton 2/4.
Sin bin: Marsh (21) - fighting.
RAMS: 1 Ian Preece; 2 Oliver Fairbank; 3 Wayne McHugh; 4 Kevin Crouthers; 5 Darren Rogers; 6 Francis Maloney; 7 Ryan Sheridan; 8 Paul Hicks; 9 Richard Chapman; 10 Jonlee Lockwood; 11 Anthony Thewliss; 12 Warren Jowitt; 13 Alex Bretherton. Subs (all used): 14 David Mycoe; 15 Mark Stubley; 16 James Walker; 17 Mark Hawksley.
Try: Preece (52); **Goals:** Maloney 3/5.
Sin bin: Preece (21) - fighting; Sheridan (65) - striking.
Rugby Leaguer & League Express Men of the Match: *Bulldogs:* Neil Roden; *Rams:* Ian Preece.
Penalty count: 18-19; **Half-time:** 6-0;
Referee: Steve Nicholson (Whitehaven), replaced by Brandon Robinson (Dewsbury) (40); **Attendance:** 1,234.

Saturday 26th March 2005

GROUP 6

BRADFORD-DUDLEY HILL DEMONS 76
BRAMLEY BUFFALOES 0

HEMEL HEMPSTEAD STAGS 30
WARRINGTON WIZARDS 20

WEEK 7

Wednesday 6th April 2005

GROUP 1

GATESHEAD THUNDER 4 WHITEHAVEN 44

THUNDER: 1 Kevin Neighbour; 2 Phil Pitt; 3 James Hauxwell; 4 Ian Ball; 5 Joe Brown; 6 Phil Carleton; 7 Steve Elms; 8 Selwyn St Bernard; 9 Scott Collins; 10 Damian Martinez; 11 Nigel Arizmendez; 12 Liam Garside; 13 Steve Rutherford. Subs (all used): 14 Robin Peers; 15 Rob Line; 16 Paul Dodsworth; 17 Brandon Fall.
Try: Neighbour (15); **Goals:** Elms 0/1.
WHITEHAVEN: 1 Paul O'Neil; 2 Jamie Marshall; 3 David Seeds; 4 Derry Eilbeck; 5 John Lebbon; 6 Steven Wood; 7 Steve Kirkbride; 8 Neil Baynes; 9 Carl Sice; 10 Chris McKinney; 11 Ryan Campbell; 12 Graeme Morton; 13 Carl Rudd. Subs (all used): 14 Aaron Summers; 15 Mark Deans; 16 Mick Nanyn; 17 Mark Cox.
Tries: Seeds (3, 52), Lebbon (5), Marshall (28), Eilbeck (46, 63), Rudd (74), Kirkbride (76); **Goals:** Kirkbride 6/8.
Rugby Leaguer & League Express Men of the Match: *Thunder:* Scott Collins; *Whitehaven:* John Lebbon.
Penalty count: 7-6; **Half-time:** 4-18;
Referee: Craig Halloran (Dewsbury); **Attendance:** 266.

Saturday 9th April 2005

GROUP 6

BRADFORD-DUDLEY HILL DEMONS 66
HEMEL HEMPSTEAD STAGS 8

FINAL TABLES

GROUP 1

	P	W	D	L	F	A	Diff	Pts
Whitehaven	6	5	0	1	238	56	182	10
Workington	6	4	0	2	184	140	44	8
Gateshead	6	2	0	4	115	207	-92	4
Barrow	6	1	0	5	89	223	-134	2

GROUP 2

	P	W	D	L	F	A	Diff	Pts
Rochdale	6	5	0	1	288	118	170	10
Swinton	6	4	1	1	171	150	21	9
Oldham	6	2	0	4	137	241	-104	4
Blackpool	6	0	1	5	116	203	-87	1

GROUP 3

	P	W	D	L	F	A	Diff	Pts
Halifax	6	5	0	1	240	95	145	10
Hull KR	6	5	0	1	244	104	140	10
Keighley	6	2	0	4	147	181	-34	4
London Skolars	6	0	0	6	62	313	-251	0

GROUP 4

	P	W	D	L	F	A	Diff	Pts
Castleford	6	6	0	0	237	50	187	12
Featherstone	6	3	1	2	123	127	-4	7
York	6	1	1	4	104	141	-37	3
Hunslet	6	1	0	5	60	206	-146	2

GROUP 5

	P	W	D	L	F	A	Diff	Pts
Doncaster	6	5	0	1	244	105	139	10
Batley	6	4	0	2	124	140	-16	8
Dewsbury	6	2	0	4	135	137	-2	4
Sheffield	6	1	0	5	93	214	-121	2

GROUP 6

	P	W	D	L	F	A	Diff	Pts
Bradford-Dudley Hill	6	5	0	1	327	96	231	10
Warrington Wizards	6	2	2	2	146	167	-21	6
Hemel Hempstead	6	2	1	3	100	190	-90	5
Bramley	6	1	1	4	80	200	-120	3

Group 1-5 winners progressed to Quarter Finals. Group 1-5 runners-up and Group 6 winners progressed to Quarter Final Qualifiers.

National League Cup 2005 - Round by Round

QUARTER FINAL QUALIFIERS

Sunday 1st May 2005

FEATHERSTONE ROVERS 44 WORKINGTON TOWN 20

ROVERS: 1 Nathan Batty; 2 Danny Kirmond; 3 Danny Maun; 4 Richard Newlove; 5 Bryn Powell; 6 Josh Weeden; 7 Liam Finn; 8 Jason Southwell; 9 Carl Hughes; 10 Nathan Sykes; 11 Steve Dooler; 12 Neil Lowe; 13 Adam Hayes. Subs (all used): 14 Stephen Jones; 15 James Houston; 16 Ian Tonks; 17 Jim Carlton.
Tries: Finn (2), Powell (35), Newlove (36, 51), Lowe (67, 79), C Hughes (75); **Goals:** Finn 8/10.
TOWN: 1 Lusi Sione; 2 Matthew Woodcock; 3 Neil Frazer; 4 Kevin Hetherington; 5 Matthew Johnson; 6 Lee Kiddie; 7 Scott Chilton; 8 Taani Lavulavu; 9 Jonny Limmer; 10 John Tuimaualuga; 11 James Robinson; 12 Jon Roper; 13 Brett Smith. Subs (all used): 14 Martyn Wilson; 15 Jamie Beaumont; 16 Dean Vaughan; 17 Malcolm Caton.
Tries: Limmer (4, 41), Lavulavu (16), Sione (71);
Goals: Hetherington 2/4.
Rugby Leaguer & League Express Men of the Match: *Rovers:* Liam Finn; *Town:* Jonny Limmer.
Penalty count: 8-2; **Half-time:** 20-10;
Referee: Colin Morris (Huddersfield); **Attendance:** 836.

HULL KINGSTON ROVERS 64 BRADFORD-DUDLEY HILL DEMONS 14

ROVERS: 1 Leroy Rivett; 2 Loz Wildbore; 3 Paul Parker; 4 Kane Epati; 5 Byron Ford; 6 Phil Hasty; 7 Paul Pickering; 8 Neil Harmon; 9 Andy Ellis; 10 David Tangata-Toa; 11 James Garmston; 12 Dale Holdstock; 13 Mark Blanchard. Subs (all used): 14 Jon Steel; 15 Jamie Bovill; 16 Paul Fletcher; 17 Makali Aizue.
Tries: Hasty (18, 54), Parker (21), Ford (24), Rivett (28), Blanchard (39, 58), Pickering (48), Aizue (61), Wildbore (74), Steel (79); **Goals:** Wildbore 9/10, Steel 1/1.
DEMONS: 1 Lewis Evans; 2 Michael Piper; 3 Paul Gleadhill; 4 Chris Marsh; 5 Jack Bradbury; 6 Victor Tordoff; 7 Liam Jarvis; 8 Richard Bingley; 9 Gareth Walker; 10 John Vaicekauskas; 11 Sam Broadley; 12 Liam Jordan; 13 Anthony Huby. Subs (all used): 14 Craig Tyman; 15 Martin Brannan; 16 Lee O'Connor; 17 Neil Wall.
Tries: Piper (12), Jordan (66);
Goals: Jarvis 2/2, Piper 1/1.
Rugby Leaguer & League Express Men of the Match: *Rovers:* Paul Pickering; *Demons:* Liam Jordan.
Penalty count: 12-5; **Half-time:** 28-8;
Referee: Jamie Leahy (Dewsbury); **Attendance:** 1,133.

SWINTON LIONS 40 BATLEY BULLDOGS 24

LIONS: 1 Wayne English; 2 Stuart Oldham; 3 Lee Patterson; 4 Chris Maye; 5 Marlon Billy; 6 Mick Coates; 7 Ian Watson; 8 Rob Whittaker; 9 Phil Joseph; 10 Wes Rogers; 11 Danny Heaton; 12 Ian Sinfield; 13 Lee Marsh. Subs (all used): 14 Andy Crabtree; 15 Kris Smith; 16 Danny Barton; 17 Ian Parry.
Tries: Patterson (5, 17, 26), Sinfield (8), Heaton (20, 67), Billy (38), Maye (71); **Goals:** Marsh 2/6, Smith 2/2.
BULLDOGS: 1 Craig Lingard; 2 Jamie Stokes; 3 Mark Sibson; 4 Steve Beard; 5 Adrian Flynn; 6 Neil Roden; 7 Barry Eaton; 8 Craig Wright; 9 Kris Lythe; 10 Joe Berry; 11 Sean Richardson; 12 Dane Morgan; 13 Mark Toohey. Subs (all used): 14 Darren Robinson; 15 Will Cartledge; 16 Paul Harrison; 17 Gary Shillabeer.
Tries: Lingard (12), Toohey (24), Sibson (32, 76);
Goals: Eaton 4/4.
Rugby Leaguer & League Express Men of the Match:

Lions: Ian Watson; *Bulldogs:* Neil Roden.
Penalty count: 10-9; **Half-time:** 28-18;
Referee: Julian King (St Helens); **Attendance:** 689.

QUARTER FINALS

Sunday 29th May 2005

DONCASTER DRAGONS 54 HALIFAX 38

DRAGONS: 1 Ben Cockayne; 2 Dean Colton; 3 Craig Lawton; 4 Craig Farrell; 5 Craig Miles; 6 Graham Holroyd; 7 Latham Tawhai; 8 Gareth Handford; 9 Craig Cook; 10 Martin Ostler; 11 Lee Harland; 12 Peter Green; 13 Martin Moana. Subs (all used): 14 Wayne Green; 15 Karl Mills; 16 Dean O'Loughlin; 17 Tom Buckenham.
Tries: Colton (3), Lawton (16, 53), Cockayne (46), Harland (63), Handford (67, 73), Tawhai (70), W Green (77); **Goals:** Holroyd 3/4, W Green 6/6.
HALIFAX: 1 Damian Gibson; 2 James Haley; 3 James Bunyan; 4 Jamie Bloem; 5 Rikki Sheriffe; 6 Dean Lawford; 7 Ben Black; 8 Andy Hobson; 9 Ben Fisher; 10 Jason Boults; 11 David Larder; 12 Andy Spink; 13 Pat Weisner. Subs (all used): 14 Damian Ball; 15 Chris Morley; 16 Ryan McDonald; 17 Fereti Tuilagi.
Tries: Gibson (7, 39, 56), Larder (12), Fisher (28), Haley (49), Spink (60); **Goals:** Bloem 5/7.
Rugby Leaguer & League Express Men of the Match: *Dragons:* Wayne Green; *Halifax:* Ben Black.
Penalty count: 11-5; **Half-time:** 12-22; **Referee:** Steve Nicholson (Whitehaven); **Attendance:** 1,008.

FEATHERSTONE ROVERS 14 CASTLEFORD TIGERS 38

ROVERS: 1 Nathan Batty; 2 Danny Kirmond; 3 Dean Ripley; 4 Richard Newlove; 5 Bryn Powell; 6 Liam Finn; 7 Andrew Georgiadis; 8 Danny Evans; 9 Carl Hughes; 10 Nathan Sykes; 11 Adam Hayes; 12 Neil Lowe; 13 Josh Weeden. Subs (all used): 14 Andy McNally; 15 Ian Tonks; 16 Steve Dooler; 17 Jim Carlton.
Tries: Georgiadis (13), Newlove (52); **Goals:** Finn 3/5.
Sin bin: Newlove (61) - holding down.
TIGERS: 1 Michael Platt; 2 Craig Huby; 3 Deon Bird; 4 Jon Hepworth; 5 Michael Shenton; 6 Paul Handforth; 7 Brad Davis; 8 Adam Watene; 9 Andrew Henderson; 10 Richard Fletcher; 11 Tom Haughey; 12 Steve Crouch; 13 Aaron Smith. Subs (all used): 14 Andy Kain; 15 Andy Bailey; 16 Byron Smith; 17 Jordan James.
Tries: Platt (2, 31, 69, 79), Davis (7), Bird (74);
Goals: Huby 3/4, Handforth 4/4.
Rugby Leaguer & League Express Men of the Match: *Rovers:* Andrew Georgiadis; *Tigers:* Michael Platt.
Penalty count: 12-10; **Half-time:** 8-18;
Referee: Peter Taberner (Wigan); **Attendance:** 3,418.

HULL KINGSTON ROVERS 62 SWINTON LIONS 0

ROVERS: 1 Leroy Rivett; 2 Alasdair McClarron; 3 Paul Parker; 4 Dwayne Barker; 5 Kane Epati; 6 Paul Mansson; 7 Phil Hasty; 8 Makali Aizue; 9 James Webster; 10 David Tangata-Toa; 11 Andy Raleigh; 12 Michael Smith; 13 Gareth Morton. Subs (all used): 14 Andy Ellis; 15 Loz Wildbore; 16 Mark Blanchard; 17 Jason Netherton.
Tries: Hasty (1, 52, 70), Aizue (4), Raleigh (11), Smith (21), Mansson (26), Morton (57), Blanchard (63), Ellis (66), Rivett (74); **Goals:** Morton 9/11.
LIONS: 1 Wayne English; 2 Chris Irwin; 3 Lee Patterson; 4 Chris Maye; 5 Marlon Billy; 6 Mick Coates; 7 Warren Ayres; 8 Paul Southern; 9 Phil Joseph; 10 Wes Rogers; 11 Danny Heaton; 12 Ian Sinfield; 13 Danny Barton. Subs (all used): 14 Stuart Oldham; 15 Andy Crabtree; 16 Rob Russell; 17 Rob Whittaker.

On report: Sinfield (32) - alleged high tackle on Epati.
Rugby Leaguer & League Express Men of the Match: *Rovers:* Gareth Morton; *Lions:* Wayne English.
Penalty count: 11-6; **Half-time:** 30-0;
Referee: Phil Bentham (Warrington); **Attendance:** 1,506.

WHITEHAVEN 28 ROCHDALE HORNETS 22

WHITEHAVEN: 1 Gary Broadbent; 2 Craig Calvert; 3 Wesley Wilson; 4 Howard Hill; 5 Paul O'Neil; 6 Leroy Joe; 7 Joel Penny; 8 Aaron Summers; 9 Aaron Lester; 10 David Fatialofa; 11 Mick Nanyn. Subs: 14 Carl Sice; 15 Paul Davidson; 16 Graeme Morton (not used); 17 Steve Kirkbride.
Tries: Joe (26), Calvert (29), Broadbent (44), Lester (73); **Goals:** Nanyn 6/8.
Sin bin: Nanyn (64) - fighting.
HORNETS: 1 Chris Giles; 2 Andy Saywell; 3 Mark McCully; 4 David Alstead; 5 Chris Campbell; 6 Radney Bowker; 7 John Braddish; 8 Tommy Hodgkinson; 9 Phil Cantillon; 10 Gareth Price; 11 Dave Newton; 12 Lee Doran; 13 Andy Gorski. Subs (all used): 14 Richard Varkulis; 15 Rob Ball; 16 Paul Anderson; 17 Darren Shaw.
Tries: Cantillon (50, 64), Alstead (69, 77);
Goals: McCully 3/5.
Sin bin: Anderson (64) - fighting.
Rugby Leaguer & League Express Men of the Match: *Whitehaven:* Gary Broadbent; *Hornets:* Phil Cantillon.
Penalty count: 13-9; **Half-time:** 16-2;
Referee: Colin Morris (Huddersfield); **Attendance:** 1,748.

SEMI FINALS

Sunday 19th June 2005

HULL KINGSTON ROVERS 34 DONCASTER DRAGONS 26

ROVERS: 1 Loz Wildbore; 2 Alasdair McClarron; 3 Paul Parker; 4 Kane Epati; 5 Byron Ford; 6 Paul Mansson; 7 James Webster; 8 Jason Netherton; 9 Andy Ellis; 10 David Tangata-Toa; 11 Dale Holdstock; 12 Michael Smith; 13 Gareth Morton. Subs (all used): 14 Phil Hasty; 15 Dwayne Barker; 16 Jamie Bovill; 17 Makali Aizue.
Tries: Bovill (27), Parker (32), Mansson (42), Ford (52), Epati (55), Morton (58); **Goals:** Morton 5/6.
DRAGONS: 1 Ben Cockayne; 2 Danny Mills; 3 Marvin Golden; 4 Craig Farrell; 5 Craig Miles; 6 Graham Holroyd; 7 Latham Tawhai; 8 Gareth Handford; 9 Craig Cook; 10 Dean O'Loughlin; 11 Lee Harland; 12 Craig Lawton; 13 Martin Moana. Subs (all used): 14 Shaun Leaf; 15 Karl Mills; 16 Martin Ostler; 17 Dean Colton.
Tries: Moana (5), Cockayne (14), Golden (17), Colton (65, 79, 89); **Goals:** Holroyd 3/6.
Rugby Leaguer & League Express Men of the Match: *Rovers:* James Webster; *Dragons:* Ben Cockayne.
Penalty count: 9-6; **Half-time:** 10-18;
Referee: Ian Thaler (Wakefield); **Attendance:** 2,474.

CASTLEFORD TIGERS 42 WHITEHAVEN 14

TIGERS: 1 Michael Platt; 2 Waine Pryce; 3 Deon Bird; 4 Jon Hepworth; 5 Michael Shenton; 6 Paul Handforth; 7 Brad Davis; 8 Adam Watene; 9 Andrew Henderson; 10 Richard Fletcher; 11 Tom Haughey; 12 Steve Crouch; 13 Aaron Smith; 14 Andy Kain; 17 Frank Watene.
Tries: Haughey (6), Handforth (14), Crouch (21), Bird (31), Platt (40), F Watene (41), A Kain (56);
Goals: Fletcher 1/2, Huby 5/6, Davis 1/1.
WHITEHAVEN: 1 Gary Broadbent; 2 Craig Calvert; 3 David Seeds; 4 Mick Nanyn; 5 Wesley Wilson; 6 Leroy Joe; 7 Joel Penny; 8 Aaron Summers; 9 Aaron Lester; 10 David Fatialofa; 11 Brett McDermott; 12 Howard Hill; 13 Carl Rudd. Subs (all used): 14 Spencer Miller; 15 Paul Davidson; 16 Carl Sice; 17 Graeme Morton.
Tries: Fatialofa (45), Nanyn (50), Calvert (59);
Goals: Nanyn 1/3.
Sin bin: Hill (6) - late tackle on Davis.
Rugby Leaguer & League Express Men of the Match: *Tigers:* Paul Handforth; *Whitehaven:* Aaron Lester.
Penalty count: 8-10; **Half-time:** 24-0;
Referee: Phil Bentham (Warrington); **Attendance:** 5,019.

FINAL

Sunday 17th July 2005

CASTLEFORD TIGERS 16 HULL KINGSTON ROVERS 18

TIGERS: 1 Michael Platt; 2 Waine Pryce; 3 Deon Bird; 4 Jon Hepworth; 5 Michael Shenton; 6 Paul Handforth; 7 Brad Davis; 8 Adam Watene; 9 Andrew Henderson; 10 Andy Bailey; 11 Tom Haughey; 12 Steve Crouch. Subs (all used): 14 Andy Kain; 15 Richard Fletcher; 16 Byron Smith; 17 Frank Watene.
Tries: Platt (32), Hepworth (73); **Goals:** Huby 4/4.
On report: Platt (50) - spear tackle on Ford.
ROVERS: 1 Leroy Rivett; 2 Jon Steel; 3 Kane Epati; 4 Gareth Morton; 5 Byron Ford; 6 Paul Mansson; 7 James Webster; 8 James Garmston; 9 Andy Ellis; 10 David Tangata-Toa; 11 Andy Raleigh; 12 Jason Netherton; 13 Dale Holdstock. Subs (all used): 14 Paul Pickering; 15 Dwayne Barker; 16 Jamie Bovill; 17 Makali Aizue.
Tries: Raleigh (46), Ford (68); **Goals:** Morton 5/5.
Rugby Leaguer & League Express Men of the Match: *Tigers:* Andrew Henderson; *Rovers:* Andy Raleigh.
Penalty count: 7-10; **Half-time:** 10-2;
Referee: Ben Thaler (Wakefield);
Attendance: 9,400 *(at Bloomfield Road, Blackpool).*

Whitehaven's David Fatialofa offloads during his side's semi-final defeat at Castleford

Hull Kingston Rovers fullback Leroy Rivett tackled by Castleford's Craig Huby during the Northern Rail Cup Final

CHALLENGE CUP 2005
Round by Round

ROUND 3

Friday 11th March 2005

SHARLSTON ROVERS 14 OLDHAM 46

ROVERS: 1 Lee Lingard; 2 Jamie Cox; 3 Gareth Davies; 4 Keith Brodie; 5 Lee Maskill; 6 Jon Agar; 7 Danny Grimshaw; 8 Carl Sayer; 9 Lee Bettinson; 10 Andy Booth; 11 Dale Potter; 12 James Ward; 13 Adam Thaler. Subs (all used): 14 Gordon Long; 15 Stan Smith; 16 David Lee; 17 Stuart Bailey.
Tries: Cox (27), Ward (45); **Goals:** Lingard 3/4.
OLDHAM: 1 Gavin Dodd; 2 Will Cowell; 3 Damian Munro; 4 Gareth Barber; 5 Nick Johnson; 6 Simon Svabic; 7 Marty Turner; 8 Paul Norman; 9 John Hough; 10 Dana Wilson; 11 Simon Haughton; 12 Martin Elswood; 13 Mark Roberts. Subs (all used): 14 Carlos Mataora; 15 Tere Glassie; 16 James Kirkland; 17 Andy Gorey.
Tries: Roberts (12), Haughton (17, 22, 37, 79), Elswood (56), Barber (58), Gorey (63), Dodd (69), Cowell (74);
Goals: Turner 1/5, Svabic 2/5.
Rugby Leaguer & League Express Men of the Match: *Rovers:* Gareth Davies; *Oldham:* Simon Svabic.
Penalty count: 7-4; **Half-time:** 8-18;
Referee: Colin Morris (Huddersfield);
Attendance: 852 *(at Lionheart Stadium, Featherstone).*

CASTLEFORD LOCK LANE 0 HALIFAX 76

LOCK LANE: 1 Carl Robinson; 2 John Paul Briers; 3 Carl Saville; 4 Matt Bateman; 5 Andy Tillett; 6 Mark Spears; 7 Paul Gough; 8 Mark Kear; 9 Darren Simms; 10 Kalum Senior; 11 Chris Stockton; 12 Richard Potts; 13 Paul Birdsall. Subs (all used): 14 Steve Thickbroom; 15 Stuart Arundel; 16 Jamie Price; 17 Wayne Hardy.
HALIFAX: 1 Damian Gibson; 2 James Haley; 3 James Bunyan; 4 Anthony Blackwood; 5 Rikki Sheriffe; 6 Danny Jones; 7 Dean Lawford; 8 Jode Sheriffe; 9 Todd O'Brien; 10 Jason Boults; 11 Wayne Corcoran; 12 Andy Spink; 13 Pat Weisner. Subs (all used): 14 Ben Fisher; 15 Gareth Greenwood; 16 Chris Birchall; 17 David Larder.
Tries: Jones (11), Lawford (17), Blackwood (22, 42, 71), O'Brien (35), Haley (37, 50), R Sheriffe (39, 76, 79), Gibson (46), Weisner (65), J Sheriffe (68);
Goals: Jones 8/11, Corcoran 2/3.
Rugby Leaguer & League Express Men of the Match: *Lock Lane:* Mark Spears; *Halifax:* Dean Lawford.
Penalty count: 8-7; **Half-time:** 0-36;
Referee: Steve Nicholson (Whitehaven);
Attendance: 747 *(at The Shay, Halifax).*

Saturday 12th March 2005

WATH BROW HORNETS 32 DEWSBURY RAMS 30

HORNETS: 1 Gavin Curwen; 2 Stewart Sanderson; 3 Ian Rooney; 4 Gary Clarke; 5 Johnny Lopez; 6 Craig Johnstone; 7 Andrew Hocking; 8 Mark Troughton; 9 Graeme Mattinson; 10 Dave Currie; 11 Paul Davidson; 12 Andrew Stables; 13 Gary Elliott. Subs (all used): 14 Matthew Whalley; 15 Micky McAllister; 16 Neil Stewart; 17 Scott Teare.
Tries: Hocking (3), Rooney (17), Johnstone (21), Sanderson (39), Teare (45); **Goals:** Curwen 6/6.
RAMS: 1 Ian Preece; 2 Richard Tillotson; 3 Wayne McHugh; 4 Darren Rogers; 5 Oliver Fairbank; 6 Francis Maloney; 7 Ryan Sheridan; 8 James Walker; 9 Richard Chapman; 10 Paul Hicks; 11 Alex Bretherton; 12 Warren Jowitt; 13 Kevin Crouthers. Subs (all used): 14 David Mycoe; 15 Anthony Thewliss; 16 Jonlee Lockwood; 17 Mark Hawksley.
Tries: McHugh (10), Maloney (29), Preece (49), Hicks (53), Crouthers (56); **Goals:** Maloney 5/5.
Rugby Leaguer & League Express Men of the Match: *Hornets:* Graeme Mattinson; *Rams:* Kevin Crouthers.
Penalty count: 7-7; **Half-time:** 24-12;
Referee: Ben Thaler (Wakefield);
Attendance: 741 *(at Recreation Ground, Whitehaven).*

Sunday 13th March 2005

HAYDOCK 4 HUNSLET HAWKS 46

HAYDOCK: 1 Matt Cunliffe; 2 Simon Tickle; 3 Sean Appleton; 4 Mark Rigby; 5 Darrell Rotherham; 6 Mark Forber; 7 Mark Boland; 8 Ash Carroll; 9 Peter Cahalin; 10 Matt Reynolds; 11 Neil Ireland; 12 Mark Pickering; 13 Wayne Bloor. Subs (all used): 14 Craig Haughey; 15 Martin Hardman; 16 Chris Pearson; 17 Lee Cooper.
Goals: Forber 2/2.
Sin bin: Pearson (69) - high tackle.
On report: Pearson (68) - high tackle.
HAWKS: 1 George Rayner; 2 Jeremy Dyson; 3 Anthony Gibbons; 4 Chris Redfearn; 5 Steve Morton; 6 Mark Cass; 7 Mark Moxon; 8 Nick Staveley; 9 Joe Hawley; 10 Neil Mears; 11 Wayne Freeman; 12 Paul Cummins; 13 David Gibbons. Subs (all used): 14 Matt Carbutt; 15 Danny Cook; 16 David Norcross; 17 Chris North.
Tries: G Rayner (5), Mears (22), Cook (30), Moxon (36, 71), Morton (43, 65), Dyson (53), Staveley (80);
Goals: Dyson 5/9.
Rugby Leaguer & League Express Men of the Match: *Haydock:* Peter Cahalin; *Hawks:* Mark Moxon.
Penalty count: 12-10; **Half-time:** 4-24;
Referee: Peter Taberner (Wigan);
Attendance: 971 *(at Knowsley Road, St Helens).*

BARROW RAIDERS 42 EAST HULL 22

RAIDERS: 1 Joel Osborn; 2 Jason Roach; 3 Paul Jones; 4 Freddie Zitter; 5 James Nixon; 6 Adrian Mulcahy; 7 Darren Holt; 8 Andy Fisher; 9 Dave Clark; 10 Stuart Dancer; 11 Mike Whitehead; 12 Simon Knox; 13 Phil Atkinson. Subs (all used): 14 Richard Colley; 15 Paul Wilcock; 16 Glenn Osborn; 17 Alex Muff.
Tries: Mulcahy (2), A Fisher (15), J Osborn (25), Zitter (37, 49), Nixon (60), Knox (65), Roach (72);
Goals: Holt 5/8.
Sin bin: Roach (78) - dissent.
EAST HULL: 1 Jason Abdul; 2 John McCracken; 3 Jordan Precious; 4 Gary Noble; 5 Danny Lakeman; 6 Gary Blanchard; 7 Shaun Cooke; 8 Mick Docherty; 9 Gary Weymes; 10 Paul Roberts; 11 Ian Madley; 12 Mark Woodcock; 13 Craig Bassett. Subs (all used): 14 Mark Moore; 15 Dale Blakeley; 16 Lee Roberts; 17 Martin Johnson.
Tries: Precious (10, 77), Weymes (23), Abdul (77);
Goals: Docherty 3/4.
Rugby Leaguer & League Express Men of the Match: *Raiders:* Freddie Zitter; *East Hull:* Gary Weymes.
Penalty count: 4-4; **Half-time:** 20-12;
Referee: Colin Morris (Huddersfield); **Attendance:** 564.

BATLEY BULLDOGS 40 ST GAUDENS 14

BULLDOGS: 1 Craig Lingard; 2 Aiden Lister; 3 Iain Marsh; 4 Shad Royston; 5 Gary O'Regan; 6 Neil Roden; 7 Barry Eaton; 8 Craig Wright; 9 Joe Berry; 10 David Rourke; 11 Sean Richardson; 12 Dane Morgan; 13 Mark Toohey. Subs (all used): 14 Kris Lythe; 15 Tim Spears; 16 Will Cartledge; 17 Gary Shillabeer.
Tries: Royston (20), O'Regan (38, 42, 73), Roden (60), Richardson (72), Marsh (78); **Goals:** Eaton 6/8.
ST GAUDENS: 1 Adam Inness; 2 Thibault Surre; 3 Claude Sirvent; 4 Russell Bussian; 5 Fourcade Abasse; 6 Arnaud Dulac; 7 Thomas Fertoux; 8 Brad Middlebosch; 9 Julien Sous; 10 Jean Christophe Borlin; 11 Boutros Coulibaly; 12 Eric Anselme; 13 Richard Bell. Subs (all used): 14 Julien Dariaux; 15 Frederic Chanfreau; 16 Cedric Vivian; 17 Christophe Caligari.
Tries: Surre (28), Sirvent (33), Caligari (65);
Goals: Dulac 1/3.
Rugby Leaguer & League Express Men of the Match: *Bulldogs:* Gary O'Regan;
St Gaudens: Jean Christophe Borlin.
Penalty count: 12-8; **Half-time** 10-10;
Referee: Ian Smith (Oldham); **Attendance:** 569.

BLACKPOOL PANTHERS 18 TOULOUSE 58

PANTHERS: 1 Liam Bretherton; 2 Danny Arnold; 3 Jake Johnstone; 4 Glen Godbee; 5 Eric Andrews; 6 Liam McGovern; 7 Chris Hough; 8 Steve Molloy; 9 Martin Roden; 10 Ian Parry; 11 Mick Redford; 12 Gary Smith; 13 Willie Swann. Subs (all used): 14 Martin Gambles; 15 John Hill; 16 Danny Barton; 17 Matt Leigh.
Tries: Andrews (3), Hill (32), Godbee (60);
Goals: Johnstone 3/3.
TOULOUSE: 1 Sam Murphy; 22 Mickael Cousseau; 23 Damien Couturier; 4 Cedric Estebanez; 5 Cedric Olieu; 6 Dave Mulhall; 7 James Wynne; 8 Sebastien Amigas; 9 Cedric Gay; 10 Tommy Gallagher; 11 David Delpoux; 12 Sebastien Raguin; 20 Trent Robinson. Subs (all used): 15 Adrien Viala; 17 Fabrice Estebanez; 16 Eric Frayssinet; 19 Cedric Prizzon.
Tries: Gay (7, 77), Raguin (22), Gallagher (26), Olieu (41, 44, 72, 80), Wynne (64), F Estebanez (75);
Goals: Couturier 4/4, Murphy 5/6.
Rugby Leaguer & League Express Men of the Match: *Panthers:* John Hill; *Toulouse:* Tommy Gallagher.
Penalty count: 13-10; **Half-time:** 12-18;
Referee: Karl Kirkpatrick (Warrington); **Attendance:** 410.

CASTLEFORD TIGERS 72 HULL DOCKERS 10

TIGERS: 1 Stuart Kain; 2 Waine Pryce; 3 Damien Reid; 4 Jon Hepworth; 5 Michael Shenton; 6 Andy Kain; 7 Paul Handforth; 8 Adam Watene; 9 Andrew Henderson; 10 Frank Watene; 11 Jordan James; 12 Steve Crouch; 13 Aaron Smith. Subs (all used): 14 Leigh Cooke; 15 Anthony England; 16 Michael Knowles; 17 Dean Sampson.
Tries: A Kain (10, 37), Reid (14, 61, 75), James (16), Hepworth (20, 33, 49), Pryce (39), F Watene (58), A Watene (68), Shenton (77); **Goals:** Handforth 10/13.
DOCKERS: 1 Mike Hall; 2 Andrew Walker; 3 Paul Taylor; 4 Gavin Molloy; 5 Glyn Jones; 6 Chris Stephenson; 7 Scott Yeaman; 8 Matthew Emerson; 9 Stephen Sellars; 10 Danny Jay; 11 Craig Henry; 12 John Eccles; 13 Andrew Taylor. Subs (all used): 14 Chris Gardner; 15 Danny Ulyatt; 16 Dean Walker; 17 Nick Caldwell.
Tries: P Taylor (5), Henry (65); **Goals:** Stephenson 1/2.
Sin bin: Stephenson (32) – holding down.
Rugby Leaguer & League Express Men of the Match: *Tigers:* Damien Reid; *Dockers:* Paul Taylor.
Penalty count: 10-8; **Half-time:** 38-4;
Referee: Jamie Leahy (Dewsbury); **Attendance:** 3,331.

DONCASTER DRAGONS 54 STANNINGLEY 6

DRAGONS: 1 Wayne Green; 2 Craig Farrell; 3 Chris Langley; 4 Aaron Wood; 5 Craig Miles; 6 Graham Holroyd; 7 Latham Tawhai; 8 Gareth Handford; 9 Craig Cook; 10 Dean O'Loughlin; 11 Peter Green; 12 Craig Lawton; 13 Martin Moana. Subs (all used): 14 Kirk Netherton; 15 Dean Andrews; 16 Jonathan Jones; 17 Ben Cockayne.
Tries: W Green (19, 49, 67), Wood (24, 42), Handford (29), Farrell (33), Cockayne (55), Netherton (58), Andrews (60); **Goals:** Holroyd 6/9, Cockayne 1/1.
STANNINGLEY: 1 Paul Murray; 2 Paul Smith; 3 Steve McGeechie; 4 Matthew Wilson; 5 Paul Robinson; 6 Rob Kirk; 7 Ian Summers; 8 Lee Taylor; 9 Daniel Berrell; 10 Philip Wartley; 11 Ross Barnard; 12 Darren Woods; 13 Chris Rouse. Subs (all used): 14 Eddie Norfolk; 15 Martin Wood; 16 Michael Banks; 17 Andrew Parkinson.
Try: Smith (69); **Goals:** Kirk 1/4.
Rugby Leaguer & League Express Men of the Match: *Dragons:* Craig Lawton; *Stanningley:* Paul Smith.
Penalty count: 14-12; **Half-time:** 20-2; **Referee:** Steve Nicholson (Whitehaven); **Attendance:** 839.

ELLAND 12 YORK CITY KNIGHTS 50

ELLAND: 1 Philip Taylor; 2 Steve Brocklehurst; 3 Dean Bishop; 4 James Fairbank; 5 David Holmes; 6 Hayden Bailey; 7 Adam Oldroyd; 8 Marc Shickell; 9 Paul Shaw; 10 Mark Bailey; 11 Simon Gray; 12 Andy Shickell; 13 Lee Shackleton. Subs (all used): 14 Alan Chapman; 15 Steve Wood; 16 Neil Walton; 17 Thomas Horsfall.
Tries: Bishop (51, 76); **Goals:** Oldroyd 2/2, Taylor 0/1.
Sin bin: Bishop (31) - holding down;
A Shickell (62) - interference.
On report: Fairbank (61) - dangerous tackle.
CITY KNIGHTS: 1 Matt Blaymire; 2 Peter Fox; 3 Calvin Watson; 4 Darren Callaghan; 5 Chris Ross; 6 Neil Thorman; 7 Paul Thorman; 8 Tom Buckenham; 9 Jimmy Elston; 10 Adam Sullivan; 11 John Smith; 12 Ian Kirke; 13 Mark Cain. Subs (all used): 14 Scott Rhodes; 15 Lee Jackson; 16 Yusuf Sozi; 17 Craig Forsyth.
Tries: Fox (2, 24), Smith (10), Watson (12), Rhodes (53), P Thorman (56), Callaghan (68), Elston (70), N Thorman (72); **Goals:** Ross 7/9.
Rugby Leaguer & League Express Men of the Match: *Elland:* Dean Bishop; *City Knights:* Matt Blaymire.
Penalty count: 8-12; **Half-time:** 2-20;
Referee: Matthew Thomasson (Warrington);
Attendance: 930 *(at Huntington Stadium, York).*

FEATHERSTONE ROVERS 48 THORNHILL TROJANS 10

ROVERS: 1 Craig Moss; 2 Bryn Powell; 3 Danny Maun; 4 Richard Newlove; 5 Matthew Wray; 6 Josh Weeden; 7 Jon Presley; 8 Andy Jarrett; 9 Andy Kay; 10 Nathan Sykes; 11 James Houston; 12 Adam Hayes; 13 Carl Hughes. Subs (all used): 14 Andy McNally; 15 Steve Dooler; 16 James Ford; 17 Jim Carlton.
Tries: Wray (3, 33, 47, 77), Powell (18), Sykes (22), McNally (44), Newlove (56), Moss (64);
Goals: Weeden 6/9.
TROJANS: 1 Craig Holmes; 2 Danny Ratcliffe; 3 Shane Davies; 4 Jason Firth; 5 Scott Redgwick; 6 Scott Dyson; 7 Luke Haigh; 8 Ian Rayner; 9 Anthony Broadhead; 10 Rob Carruthers; 11 Matthew Roberts; 12 Rob Kelly; 13 Scott Woodcock. Subs (all used): 14 Danny Lee; 15 Neil Ratcliffe; 16 Rob Hoyle; 17 Lee Schofield.
Tries: Firth (41), D Ratcliffe (62); **Goals:** Holmes 1/3.
Dismissal: Hoyle (69) - punching.
Sin bin: Schofield (67) - dissent.
Rugby Leaguer & League Express Men of the Match: *Rovers:* Matthew Wray; *Trojans:* Scott Dyson.
Penalty count: 8-10; **Half-time:** 22-0;
Referee: Robert Hicks (Oldham); **Attendance:** 774.

GATESHEAD THUNDER 6
UNION TREIZISTE CATALANE 56

THUNDER: 1 Kevin Neighbour; 2 Graham Stephenson; 3 Ian Brown; 4 Wade Liddell; 5 Robin Peers; 6 Chris Birch; 7 Phil Carleton; 8 Damian Martinez; 9 John Tomes; 10 Tabua Cakacaka; 11 Steven Bradley; 12 Joe Burley; 13 Steve Rutherford. Subs (all used): 14 Rob Line; 15 Craig Firth; 16 Selwyn St Bernard; 17 Liam Garside.
Try: Peers (77); **Goals:** Birch 1/2.
UTC: 1 Thomas Bosc; 2 Justin Murphy; 3 Sean Rudder; 4 Matt Bickerstaff; 5 Bruno Verges; 6 Laurent Frayssinous; 7 Julien Rinaldi; 8 Chris Beattie; 9 David Berthezene; 10 Adel Fellous; 11 Aurelien Cologni; 12 Djamel Fakir; 13 Gregory Mounis. Subs (all used): 14 Romain Gagliazzo; 15 Sebastien Martins; 16 Pascal Jampy; 17 Julien Touxagas.
Tries: Berthezene (11, 33), Fellous (16), Fakir (22), Martins (27, 71), Murphy (40), Touxagas (42), Bosc (46), Rudder (55); **Goals:** Frayssinous 8/10.
Rugby Leaguer & League Express Men of the Match: *Thunder:* Robin Peers; *UTC:* Julien Rinaldi.
Penalty count: 13-7; **Half-time:** 2-32; **Referee:** Richard Silverwood (Dewsbury); **Attendance:** 296.

KEIGHLEY COUGARS 62 STRELA KAZAN 14

COUGARS: 1 Matt Bramald; 2 Chris Beever; 3 David Foster; 4 Matt Foster; 5 Andy Robinson; 6 Paul Ashton; 7 Matt Firth; 8 Phil Stephenson; 9 Jonny Wainhouse; 10 Danny Murgatroyd; 11 Jordan Ross; 12 Matthew Steel; 13 Daniel Harvey. Subs (all used): 14 Adam Mitchell; 15 James Rushforth; 16 Lewis Taylor; 17 Jason Clegg.
Tries: Bramald (6, 50, 64, 76), Robinson (10), Firth (16, 24), Stephenson (20), Taylor (35, 57), Wainhouse (55);
Goals: Ashton 8/10, Mitchell 1/1.
STRELA: 1 Oleg Sokolov; 2 Radif Safin; 3 Ramil Yusupov; 4 Artem Artemenko; 5 Maxim Keller; 6 Rinat Chamsoutdinov; 7 Denis Makarov; 8 Alexander Chulkov; 9 Alexander Napalkov; 10 Lenar Zaynutdinov; 11 Aidar Akhmetshin; 12 Andrey Kuzovkov; 13 Maxim Romanov. Subs (all used): 14 Marat Gabdullazyanov; 15 Azat Musin; 16 Ramil Valiullin; 17 Nikolay Bulanki.
Tries: Keller (28, 72), Napalkov (33);
Goals: Chamsoutdinov 1/2, Napalkov 0/1.
Sin bin: Sokolov (18) - interference.
Rugby Leaguer & League Express Men of the Match: *Cougars:* Matt Bramald; *Strela:* Oleg Sokolov.
Penalty count: 6-10; **Half-time:** 34-10; **Referee:** Jean Pierre Boulagnon (France); **Attendance:** 1,176.

LONDON SKOLARS 14 PIA 58

SKOLARS: 1 Nathan Meischke; 2 Oran D'Arcy; 3 Austin Aggrey; 4 Tim Gee; 5 Ashley Tozer; 6 Joe Price; 7 Gareth Honor; 8 Alan Barker; 9 Kurt Pittman; 10 Toby Hall; 11 Brett Blaker; 12 Andrew Gourlay; 13 Stuart Singleton.

Subs (all used): 14 James Sullivan; 15 Wayne Parillon; 16 Matt Pitman; 17 Alex Smits.
Tries: Tozer (7), Blaker (18), K Pittman (53);
Goals: T Gee 1/3.
Sin bin: Parillon (32) - fighting.
PIA: 1 Craig West; 2 Nicholas Athiel; 3 Gilles Mendez; 4 Florien Chaubet; 5 Patrice Gomez; 6 Tom O'Reilly; 7 Maxime Greseque; 8 Franck Rovira; 9 Mathias Garrabe; 10 Brett O'Farrell; 11 Emmanuel Bansept; 12 David Romero; 13 Aaron Smith. Subs (all used): 14 Patrick Cala; 15 Yannick Brousse; 16 Dean Bosnich; 17 Franck Traversa.
Tries: Greseque (1, 48, 70, 73), Athiel (3), Chaubet (20), Mendez (33), O'Reilly (44), Garabe (58, 63);
Goals: Greseque 9/10.
Sin bin: O'Farrell (32) - fighting; Cala (32) - fighting.
Rugby Leaguer & League Express Men of the Match: *Skolars:* Matt Pitman; *Pia:* Maxime Greseque.
Penalty count: 10-6; **Half-time:** 8-22;
Referee: Mike Dawber (Wigan); **Attendance:** 209.

OLDHAM ST ANNES 30 WHITEHAVEN 62

ST ANNES: 1 Kevin Fitzpatrick; 2 John Gillam; 3 Danny Tyrell; 4 Paul Garrett; 5 Ryan Knight; 6 Rick Badby; 7 David Sweeney; 8 Jason Akeroyd; 9 Andy Wallace; 10 Andy Sands; 11 Chris Worth; 12 Chris Carter; 13 Mick Martindale. Subs (all used): 14 Eric Johnson; 15 Dave Harris; 16 Ken Kerr; 17 Peter Deakin.
Tries: Fitzpatrick (16, 55), Wallace (24), Tyrell (48), Kerr (75); **Goals:** Tyrell 5/5.
WHITEHAVEN: 1 Gary Broadbent; 2 Craig Calvert; 3 Wesley Wilson; 4 Howard Hill; 5 Paul O'Neil; 6 Leroy Joe; 7 Joel Penny; 8 Mark Cox; 9 Aaron Lester; 10 David Fatialofa; 11 Brett McDermott; 12 Spencer Miller; 13 Carl Rudd. Subs (all used): 14 Steve Kirkbride; 15 Paul Davidson; 16 Carl Sice; 17 Aaron Summers.
Tries: Fatialofa (2), Broadbent (6, 60), Calvert (11, 30, 65), Penny (20, 47), Lester (27), O'Neil (51), Wilson (69); **Goals:** Penny 7/7, Kirkbride 2/4.
Rugby Leaguer & League Express Men of the Match: *St Annes:* Danny Tyrell; *Whitehaven:* Joel Penny.
Penalty count: 7-7; **Half-time:** 12-36;
Referee: Julian King (St Helens);
Attendance: 968 *(at Recreation Ground, Whitehaven).*

ROCHDALE HORNETS 120 ILLINGWORTH 4

HORNETS: 1 Paul Owen; 2 Andy Saywell; 3 Mark McCully; 4 Paul Anderson; 5 Chris Giles; 6 John Braddish; 7 Lee Birdseye; 8 Lee Hansen; 9 Dave McConnell; 10 Tommy Hodgkinson; 11 Kris Ratcliffe; 12 Lee Doran; 13 Andy Gorski. Subs (all used): 14 Phil Cantillon; 15 Gareth Price; 16 Radney Bowker; 17 Rob Ball.
Tries: Braddish (1), Doran (5, 65), Giles (8, 13), McConnell (18, 72, 74), Cantillon (25, 41, 55), Birdseye (35, 45), Gorski (38, 42), Owen (40, 48), Saywell (53), McCully (57), Bowker (59), Ball (79);
Goals: Birdseye 18/21.
ILLINGWORTH: 1 Peter Noel; 2 Paul Ackroyd; 3 Daley Williams; 4 Dean Williams; 5 Aaron Brown; 6 David Roberts; 7 Graham Dobson; 8 Andrew Greenway; 9 Wayne Casswell; 10 Ryan Jepson; 11 Ashley Ainley; 12 Paul Carter; 13 Andrew Laheney. Subs (all used): 14 Chris Reeves; 15 Gareth Halliday; 16 Nicholas Cahill; 17 Dale Taylor.
Try: Dean Williams (68); **Goals:** Taylor 0/1.
Rugby Leaguer & League Express Men of the Match: *Hornets:* Lee Birdseye; *Illingworth:* Dale Taylor.
Penalty count: 5-2; **Half-time:** 52-0;
Referee: Craig Halloran (Dewsbury); **Attendance:** 654.

SIDDAL 6 HULL KINGSTON ROVERS 50

SIDDAL: 1 Darren Phillips; 2 Andy Rose; 3 Steve Lewis; 4 Lee Gudor; 5 Steve Hope; 6 Chris Harding; 7 Liam Walsh; 8 Gary Lewis; 9 Martin Scrimshaw; 10 Jamie Wrigley; 11 Nick Smith; 12 Peter Howard; 13 Gareth Hooson. Subs (all used): 14 Paul Phillips; 15 Jon Bruce; 16 Matthew Smith; 17 Richard Wilde.
Try: Gudor (14); **Goals:** Walsh 1/1.
Sin bin: N Smith (78) - interference.
ROVERS: 1 Loz Wildbore; 2 Jon Steel; 3 Paul Parker; 4 Kane Epati; 5 Byron Ford; 6 Paul Mansson; 7 Phil Hasty; 8 Jamie Bovill; 9 Andy Ellis; 10 Makali Aizue; 11 Dale Holdstock; 12 Andy Raleigh; 13 Mark Blanchard. Subs (all used): 14 Jimmy Walker; 15 Craig Poucher; 16 David Tangata-Toa; 17 Neil Harmon.
Tries: Mansson (5), Epati (11, 20, 27), Bovill (18), Steel (29, 42), Aizue (68), Parker (78); **Goals:** Wildbore 7/9.
Rugby Leaguer & League Express Men of the Match: *Siddal:* Liam Walsh; *Rovers:* Kane Epati.
Penalty count: 5-13; **Half-time:** 6-34;
Referee: Gareth Hewer (Whitehaven);
Attendance: 1,705 *(at Craven Park, Hull).*

SWINTON LIONS 70 LOKOMOTIV MOSCOW 10

LIONS: 1 Wayne English; 2 Stuart Oldham; 3 Lee Patterson; 4 Chris Maye; 5 Marlon Billy; 6 Mick Coates; 7 Ian Watson; 8 Danny Heaton; 9 Phil Joseph; 10 Wes Rogers; 11 Rob Russell; 12 Ian Sinfield; 13 Lee Marsh. Subs (all used): 14 Warren Ayres; 15 Andy Crabtree; 16 Lee Gardner; 17 Rob Whittaker.
Tries: Maye (7, 27, 50, 54), Marsh (13), Joseph (19), Russell (37), Patterson (44, 70), Billy (61, 64), Oldham (75), Watson (79); **Goals:** Marsh 9/13.
LOKOMOTIV: 5 Valentin Baskakov; 2 Nikolay Zagoskin; 7 Artem Grigoryan; 4 Andrey Cherevichnyy; 17 Denis Korolev; 6 Viktor Nechaev; 19 Igor Gavrilin; 21 Philipp Romanov; 9 Roman Ovchinnikov; 22 Andrey Dumalkin; 11 Rouslan Izmailov; 12 Andrey Koltykhov; 13 Evgeny Bouzhukov. Subs (all used): 1 Oleg Logunov; 3 Alexander Klebanov; 14 Vladimir Odnosumov; 18 Vitally Gusev.
Tries: Cherevichnyy (21), Bouzhukov (57);
Goals: Cherevichnyy 0/1, Grigoryan 1/1.
Rugby Leaguer & League Express Men of the Match: *Lions:* Chris Maye; *Lokomotiv:* Roman Ovchinnikov.
Penalty count: 10-5; **Half-time:** 26-4;
Referee: Thierry Alibert (France); **Attendance:** 544.

WATERHEAD 16 SHEFFIELD EAGLES 22

WATERHEAD: 1 Kieran Grennan; 2 Paul Joyce; 3 Michael Foggerty; 4 Darren Nixon; 5 Carlton Campbell; 6 Ryan Collins; 7 Lee Charlesworth; 8 Thomas Howe; 9 Liam Coates; 10 Daniel Parkin; 11 Matthew Barren; 12 Tony Pemberton; 13 Warren Druggitt. Subs (all used): 14 Terence Fitzgerald; 15 James Campbell; 16 Rory Freek; 17 David Byrns.
Tries: Grennan (15), Nixon (50), Coates (75);
Goals: Collins 2/3.
Dismissal: Pemberton (59) - off the ball tackle.
EAGLES: 1 John Crawford; 2 Danny Mills; 3 Jon Breakingbury; 4 Alex Dickinson; 5 Carl De Chenu; 6 Aled James; 7 Gavin Brown; 8 Damien Lynch; 9 Liam Brentley; 10 Simon Morton; 11 Andy Rice; 12 Craig Brown; 13 Simon Tillyer. Subs (all used): 14 Ryan Dickinson; 15 Nick Turnbull; 16 Sean Dickinson; 17 Rob North.
Tries: Breakingbury (20), Crawford (38), R Dickinson (45), De Chenu (56), C Brown (64); **Goals:** G Brown 1/6.
Rugby Leaguer & League Express Men of the Match: *Waterhead:* Darren Nixon; *Eagles:* Craig Brown.
Penalty count: 7-7; **Half time:** 4-8;
Referee: Phil Bentham (Warrington);
Attendance: 390 *(at Castleton Gabriels AFC, Rochdale).*

WORKINGTON TOWN 44 WIGAN ST JUDES 20

TOWN: 1 Lusi Sione; 2 Martyn Wilson; 3 Neil Frazer; 4 Jon Roper; 5 Matthew Johnson; 6 James Robinson; 7 Lee Kiddie; 8 Dean Burgess; 9 Jonny Limmer; 10 Dean Vaughan; 11 John Tuimaualuga; 12 Ricky Wright; 13 Brett Smith. Subs (all used): 14 Matthew Tunstall; 15 Taani Lavulavu; 16 Allan McGuiness; 17 Dean Bragg.
Tries: Roper (7), McGuiness (21, 48), Limmer (44), Kiddie (60, 73), Tuimaualuga (62), Johnson (70);
Goals: Smith 6/8.
ST JUDES: 1 John Whalley; 2 Scott Robinson; 3 Gavin Corfield; 4 Kevin Oakes; 5 Ian Thompson; 6 Shaun Spowart; 7 John McMullen; 8 Brendan Barr; 9 Shaun Hilton; 10 Paul Olurkinse; 11 Lee Maiden; 12 Danny O'Mara; 13 Dave Peel. Subs (all used): 14 Peter Cain; 15 Lee Pilling; 16 Phil Roby; 17 Craig Walsh.
Tries: Spowart (14), Walsh (52, 76);
Goals: Robinson 4/5, O'Mara 0/1.
Rugby Leaguer & League Express Men of the Match: *Town:* Jonny Limmer; *St Judes:* Danny O'Mara.
Penalty count: 17-7; **Half-time:** 12-10;
Referee: Paul Carr (Castleford); **Attendance:** 899.

ROUND 4

Saturday 2nd April 2005

LEEDS RHINOS 26 WARRINGTON WOLVES 22

RHINOS: 1 Richard Mathers; 2 Mark Calderwood; 3 Chev Walker; 4 Keith Senior; 5 Marcus Bai; 13 Kevin Sinfield (C); 7 Rob Burrow; 8 Ryan Bailey; 14 Andrew Dunemann; 15 Danny Ward; 18 Jamie Jones-Buchanan; 12 Chris McKenna; 20 Gareth Ellis. Subs (all used): 22 Nick Scruton; 16 Willie Poching; 21 Liam Botham; 6 Danny McGuire.
Tries: Burrow (4, 46), McKenna (10), Calderwood (39), Walker (53); **Goals:** Sinfield 3/5.
WOLVES: 1 Brent Grose; 2 Henry Fa'afili; 3 Martin Gleeson; 25 Chris Bridge; 5 Dean Gaskell; 6 Lee Briers (C); 7 Nathan Wood; 10 Mark Hilton; 14 Mark Gleeson; 15 Ben Westwood; 16 Paul Wood; 12 Mike Wainwright; 9 Jon Clarke. Subs (all used): 8 Chris Leikvoll; 17 Danny Lima; 20 Warren Stevens; 18 Graham Appo.
Tries: N Wood (17, 55), Clarke (37), Westwood (64);
Goals: Bridge 3/5.
Rugby Leaguer & League Express Men of the Match: *Rhinos:* Andrew Dunemann; *Wolves:* Jon Clarke.
Penalty count: 9-7; **Half-time:** 16-12;
Referee: Steve Ganson (St Helens); **Attendance:** 8,215.

PIA 53 KEIGHLEY COUGARS 26

PIA: 1 Craig West; 2 Gilles Mendez; 3 Dayne Neirinckx; 4 Florien Chaubet; 5 Nicholas Athiel; 6 Tom O'Reilly; 7 Maxime Greseque; 8 Dean Bosnich; 9 Mathias Garrabe; 10 Brett O'Farrell; 11 Nathan McMillan; 12 David Romero; 13 Aaron Smith. Subs (all used): 14 Mathieu Ambert; 15 Yannick Brousse; 16 Franck Rovira; 17 Gregory Tiquet.
Tries: Greseque (3, 18, 45), Ambert (14), Brousse (27), Smith (37), Chaubet (48), Neirinckx (67), Bosnich (69);
Goals: Greseque 8/9; **Field goal:** Greseque.
COUGARS: 1 Matt Bramald; 2 Sam Gardner; 3 David Foster; 4 Matt Foster; 5 Andy Robinson; 6 Paul Ashton; 7 Matt Firth; 8 Phil Stephenson; 9 Jonny Wainhouse; 10 Danny Murgatroyd; 11 Chris Parker; 12 Matthew Steel; 13 Daniel Harvey. Subs (all used): 14 Adam Mitchell; 15 James Rushforth; 16 Richard Mervill; 17 Jason Clegg.
Tries: Bramald (11), Robinson (20, 31), Gardner (55), Mitchell (76); **Goals:** Ashton 2/4, Mitchell 1/1.
Rugby Leaguer & League Express Men of the Match: *Pia:* Maxime Greseque; *Cougars:* Danny Murgatroyd.
Penalty count: 6-9; **Half-time:** 31-16;
Referee: Richard Silverwood (Dewsbury);
Attendance: 300 *(at Salanque Mediterranae).*

TOULOUSE 60 WATH BROW HORNETS 12

TOULOUSE: 1 Sam Murphy; 22 Damien Couturier; 23 Fabrice Estebanez; 4 Cedric Estebanez; 5 Olivier Janzac; 6 Dave Mulhall; 7 James Wynne; 8 Nicolas Faure; 9 Cedric Gay; 10 Justin Morgan; 11 Peter Lima; 12 Sebastien Raguin; 20 Trent Robinson. Subs (all used): 15 Eric Frayssinet; 16 Gael Sans; 17 Adrien Viala; 19 Sebastien Amigas.
Tries: Couturier (3, 36, 73), F Estebanez (11, 76), Robinson (18), Gay (26), Raguin (47), Wynne (61, 78), Murphy (63); **Goals:** Couturier 8/11.
HORNETS: 1 Gavin Curwen; 2 Johnny Lopez; 3 Ian Rooney; 4 Gary Clarke; 5 Stewart Sanderson; 6 Craig Johnstone; 7 Andrew Hocking; 8 Mark Troughton; 9 Graeme Mattinson; 10 Dave Currie; 11 Paul Davidson; 12 Andrew Stables; 13 Gary Elliott. Subs (all used): 14 Matthew Whalley; 15 Micky McAllister; 16 Neil Stewart; 17 Scott Teare.
Tries: Clarke (23), McAllister (38), Sanderson (54);
Goals: Curwen 0/3.
Rugby Leaguer & League Express Men of the Match: *Toulouse:* Damien Couturier; *Hornets:* Micky McAllister.
Penalty count: 10-10; **Half-time:** 28-8;
Referee: Phil Bentham (Warrington);
Attendance: 500 *(at Stade des Minimes).*

Sunday 3rd April 2005

UNION TREIZISTE CATALANE 32
HULL KINGSTON ROVERS 18

UTC: 1 Renaud Guigue; 2 Justin Murphy; 17 Teddy Saddaoui; 15 Matt Bickerstaff; 5 Bruno Verges; 6 Laurent Frayssinous; 7 Julien Rinaldi; 8 Chris Beattie; 9 David Berthezene; 20 Adel Fellous; 12 Djamel Fakir; 13 Aurelien Cologni; 16 Sean Rudder. Subs: 19 Gregory Mounis; 11 Pascal Jampy; 21 Julien Touxagas; 14 Steve Hall (not used).
Tries: Murphy (1), Mounis (25), Jampy (31), Fakir (34), Berthezene (78); **Goals:** Frayssinous 6/6.
ROVERS: 1 Loz Wildbore; 2 Jon Steel; 3 Paul Parker; 4 Kane Epati; 5 Byron Ford; 6 Paul Mansson; 7 James Webster; 8 Neil Harmon; 9 Andy Ellis; 10 David Tangata-Toa; 11 Andy Raleigh; 12 Dale Holdstock; 13 Michael Smith. Subs (all used): 14 Phil Hasty; 15 Dwayne Barker; 16 Jamie Bovill; 17 Makali Aizue.
Tries: Epati (15, 63), Smith (49); **Goals:** Wildbore 3/4.
On report: Parker (70) - high tackle.
Rugby Leaguer & League Express Men of the Match: *UTC:* Sean Rudder; *Rovers:* James Webster.
Penalty count: 11-8; **Half-time:** 24-6;
Referee: Ashley Klein (Keighley);
Attendance: 3,000 *(at Stade Municipal).*

BARROW RAIDERS 33 SHEFFIELD EAGLES 26

RAIDERS: 1 Joel Osborn; 2 Jason Roach; 3 Adrian Mulcahy; 4 Freddie Zitter; 5 James Nixon; 6 Richard Colley; 7 Darren Holt; 8 Andy Fisher; 9 Dave Clark; 10 Paul Wilcock; 11 Mike Whitehead; 12 Glenn Osborn; 13 Phil Atkinson. Subs: 14 Jon Williamson (not used); 15 Alex Muff; 16 Darren Fisher; 17 Adam Pate.
Tries: Whitehead (13), Mulcahy (31, 51), A Fisher (39), Clark (55); **Goals:** Holt 5/6; **Field goals:** Holt 3.
EAGLES: 1 Lynton Stott; 2 Danny Mills; 3 Aled James; 4 Adrian Veamatahau; 5 Carl De Chenu; 6 John Crawford; 7 Gavin Brown; 8 Damien Lynch; 9 Gareth Stanley; 10 Chris Molyneux; 11 Andy Rice; 12 Craig Brown; 13 Nick Turnbull. Subs (all used): 14 Jimmy Pearson; 15 Sean Dickinson; 16 Simon Morton; 17 Simon Tillyer.
Tries: Turnbull (19), Crawford (25), James (27), Morton (44), S Dickinson (73); **Goals:** G Brown 2/4, Stott 1/1.
Sin bin: Pearson (46) - holding down.
On report: Molyneux (10) - off the ball challenge on Holt.
Rugby Leaguer & League Express Men of the Match: *Raiders:* Andy Fisher; *Eagles:* Gavin Brown.
Penalty count: 10-3; **Half-time:** 16-16;
Referee: Craig Halloran (Dewsbury); **Attendance:** 893.

BATLEY BULLDOGS 8 LEIGH CENTURIONS 25

BULLDOGS: 1 Craig Lingard; 2 Jamie Stokes; 3 Iain Marsh; 4 Shad Royston; 5 Adrian Flynn; 6 Mark Toohey; 7 Barry Eaton; 8 Craig Wright; 9 Kris Lythe; 10 Joe Berry; 11 Sean Richardson; 12 Dane Morgan; 13 Ryan Horsley. Subs (all used): 14 Mark Sibson; 15 Tim Spears; 16 Gary Shillabeer; 17 Paul Harrison.
Tries: Flynn (8, 42); **Goals:** Eaton 0/2.
CENTURIONS: 22 Neil Turley; 24 John Wilshere; 1 Ben Cooper; 8 Rob Jackson; 14 Steve Maden; 10 Jason Kent; 2 John Duffy; 21 Matt Sturm; 5 Mick Govin; 4 Darren Fleary (C); 20 Craig Stapleton; 23 Ian Knott; 13 Mark Leafa. Subs (all used): 15 Richard Marshall; 19 Rob Smyth; 11 James King; 29 James Taylor.
Tries: Turley (17), Knott (38), King (51, 67), Wilshere (77); **Goals:** Turley 1/1, Wilshere 1/4;
Field goal: Marshall.
Rugby Leaguer & League Express Men of the Match: *Bulldogs:* Barry Eaton; *Centurions:* John Duffy.
Penalty count: 10-9; **Half-time:** 4-8;
Referee: Ian Smith (Oldham); **Attendance:** 1,661.

DONCASTER DRAGONS 54 WORKINGTON TOWN 18

DRAGONS: 1 Wayne Green; 2 Dean Colton; 3 Craig Farrell; 4 Chris Langley; 5 Craig Miles; 6 Martin Moana; 7 Latham Tawhai; 8 Gareth Handford; 9 Craig Cook; 10 Martin Ostler; 11 Andy Hay; 12 Peter Green; 13 Dale Cardoza. Subs (all used): 14 Aaron Wood; 15 Dean Andrews; 16 Dean O'Loughlin; 17 Lee Harland.
Tries: Langley (10), Farrell (22), W Green (25), Colton (30, 57), P Green (54, 74), Wood (59), Cardoza (70), Moana (78); **Goals:** W Green 7/10.

TOWN: 1 Scott Chilton; 2 Matthew Woodcock; 3 Neil Frazer; 4 Jon Roper; 5 Martyn Wilson; 6 Lee Kiddie; 7 Tane Manihera; 8 Taani Lavulavu; 9 Jonny Limmer; 10 Dean Vaughan; 11 John Tuimaualuga; 12 Jamie Beaumont; 13 James Robinson. Subs (all used): 14 Matthew Johnson; 15 Dean Burgess; 16 Brett Smith; 17 Dean Bragg.
Tries: Lavulavu (50), Manihera (62), Limmer (66);
Goals: Manihera 3/4.
Rugby Leaguer & League Express Men of the Match: *Dragons:* Andy Hay; *Town:* Taani Lavulavu.
Penalty count: 7-3; **Half-time:** 22-2;
Referee: Peter Taberner (Wigan); **Attendance:** 770.

FEATHERSTONE ROVERS 14 BRADFORD BULLS 80

ROVERS: 1 Craig Moss; 2 Nathan Batty; 3 Danny Maun; 4 Richard Newlove; 5 Matthew Wray; 6 Andy McNally; 7 Josh Weeden; 8 Ian Tonks; 9 Carl Hughes; 10 Nathan Sykes; 11 James Houston; 12 Neil Lowe; 13 Dean Ripley. Subs (all used): 14 Bryn Powell; 15 Danny Evans; 16 Greg Nicholson; 17 Jim Carlton.
Tries: Newlove (2, 60), Tonks (24); **Goals:** Ripley 1/3.
BULLS: 3 Leon Pryce; 15 Karl Pratt; 17 Stuart Reardon; 22 Karl Pryce; 32 Andy Smith; 18 Iestyn Harris; 7 Paul Deacon; 8 Joe Vagana; 1 Robbie Paul (C); 29 Stuart Fielden; 27 Rob Parker; 11 Lee Radford; 19 Jamie Langley. Subs (all used): 14 Andy Lynch; 25 Brett Ferres; 20 Matt Cook; 23 Ryan Atkins (D).
Tries: Paul (7, 9, 11), Parker (17), Fielden (20), L Pryce (35), I Harris (39, 49), Smith (63, 71, 75), Ferres (64, 77), Pratt (68); **Goals:** Deacon 11/13, Vagana 1/2.
Rugby Leaguer & League Express Men of the Match: *Rovers:* Danny Maun; *Bulls:* Robbie Paul.
Penalty count: 7-8; **Half time:** 10-42;
Referee: Ben Thaler (Wakefield); **Attendance:** 3,355.

HALIFAX 23 CASTLEFORD TIGERS 14

HALIFAX: 1 Damian Gibson; 2 James Haley; 3 James Bunyan; 4 Anthony Blackwood; 5 Alan Hadcroft; 6 Wayne Corcoran; 7 Ben Black; 8 Chris Morley; 9 Ben Fisher; 10 Chris Birchall; 11 David Larder; 12 Jamie Bloem; 13 Pat Weisner. Subs (all used): 14 Brad Attwood; 15 Jode Sheriffe; 16 Ryan McDonald; 17 Jason Boults.
Tries: Weisner (28), Fisher (32), Bunyan (43), Black (51); **Goals:** Bloem 3/4, Corcoran 0/1;
Field goal: Weisner.
TIGERS: 1 Michael Platt; 2 Waine Pryce; 3 Damien Reid; 4 Jon Hepworth; 5 Michael Shenton; 6 Brad Davis; 7 Paul Handforth; 8 Adam Watene; 9 Andrew Henderson; 10 Byron Smith; 11 Tom Haughey; 12 Steve Crouch; 13 Aaron Smith. Subs (all used): 14 Dominic Brambani; 15 Jordan James; 16 Lance Hamilton; 17 Alex Rowe.
Tries: Shenton (37, 80); **Goals:** Davis 3/3.
Rugby Leaguer & League Express Men of the Match: *Halifax:* Ben Fisher; *Tigers:* Andrew Henderson.
Penalty count: 10-10; **Half-time:** 14-8;
Referee: Jamie Leahy (Dewsbury); **Attendance:** 3,925.

HUDDERSFIELD GIANTS 22 ST HELENS 26

GIANTS: 1 Paul Reilly; 2 Hefin O'Hare; 3 James Evans; 4 Michael De Vere; 34 Marcus St Hilaire; 13 Stanley Gene; 7 Paul March; 21 Paul Jackson; 9 Brad Drew; 10 Jim Gannon; 11 Chris Nero; 17 Paul Smith; 12 Ben Roarty (C). Subs (all used): 8 Mick Slicker; 14 Stuart Jones; 20 Paul White; 18 Eorl Crabtree.
Tries: Gene (9), St Hilaire (35), Nero (44), White (66);
Goals: De Vere 3/4.
SAINTS: 1 Paul Wellens; 5 Darren Albert; 11 Lee Gilmour; 3 Jamie Lyon; 2 Ade Gardner; 21 James Roby; 7 Sean Long (C); 8 Nick Fozzard; 9 Keiron Cunningham; 17 Paul Anderson; 15 Mike Bennett; 27 Vinnie Anderson; 12 Jon Wilkin. Subs (all used): 14 Mick Higham; 19 James Graham; 16 Keith Mason; 24 Maurie Fa'asavalu.
Tries: Gilmour (16), Albert (50, 55), V Anderson (53);
Goals: Lyon 5/6.
On report: Fa'asavalu (30) - high tackle.
Rugby Leaguer & League Express Men of the Match: *Giants:* Stanley Gene; *Saints:* Keiron Cunningham.
Penalty count: 7-6; **Half-time:** 12-8; **Referee:** Ronnie Laughton (Barnsley); **Attendance:** 7,105.

OLDHAM 28 YORK CITY KNIGHTS 32

OLDHAM: 1 Jon Goddard; 2 Gavin Dodd; 3 Will Cowell; 4 Alex Wilkinson; 5 Nick Johnson; 6 Marty Turner; 7 Gareth Barber; 8 Ricky Bibey; 9 John Hough; 10 Dana Wilson; 11 Simon Haughton; 12 Mark Roberts; 13 Simon Svabic. Subs: 14 James Kirkland; 15 Danny Nanyn; 16 Andy Gorey (not used); 17 Tere Glassie.
Tries: Haughton (3), Dodd (35, 47, 58), Johnson (74);
Goals: Turner 4/6.
CITY KNIGHTS: 1 Jon Liddell; 2 Peter Fox; 3 Dan Potter; 4 Darren Callaghan; 5 Neil Law; 6 Lee Patterson; 7 Scott Rhodes; 8 John Smith; 9 Lee Jackson; 10 Adam Sullivan; 11 James Ward; 12 Simon Friend; 13 Ian Kirke. Subs (all used): 14 Jimmy Elston; 15 Mark Cain; 16 Yusuf Sozi; 17 Tom Buckenham.
Tries: Potter (22, 25), Liddell (32), Fox (42), Friend (63), Ward (71); **Goals:** Patterson 0/1, Liddell 4/5.
Rugby Leaguer & League Express Men of the Match: *Oldham:* Gavin Dodd; *City Knights:* Mark Cain.
Penalty count: 8-5; **Half-time:** 14-16; **Referee:** Gareth Hewer (Whitehaven); **Attendance:** 1,282.

ROCHDALE HORNETS 24 SALFORD CITY REDS 30

HORNETS: 1 Chris Giles; 2 Chris Campbell; 3 Mark McCully; 4 Richard Varkulis; 5 Andy Saywell; 6 Radney Bowker; 7 Lee Birdseye; 8 Tommy Hodgkinson; 9 Dave McConnell; 10 Gareth Price; 11 Andy Gorski; 12 Lee Doran; 13 Phil Farrell. Subs (all used): 14 Phil Cantillon; 15 Dave Cunliffe; 16 David Alstead; 17 Dave Newton.
Tries: McCully (16), Bowker (25, 68), Saywell (35);
Goals: McCully 4/5.
CITY REDS: 15 Karl Fitzpatrick; 2 David Hodgson; 3 Stuart Littler; 12 Ian Sibbit; 5 Anthony Stewart; 33 Kevin McGuinness; 7 Luke Robinson; 10 Sean Rutgerson; 9 Malcolm Alker (C); 18 Stuart Dickens; 11 Mark Shipway; 8 Andy Coley; 13 Chris Charles. Subs (all used): 4 Junior Langi (D); 24 Andy Johnson; 20 Tim Jonkers; 22 Simon Baldwin.
Tries: Sibbit (6, 73), Dickens (11), Baldwin (39), Alker (46), Robinson (48); **Goals:** Charles 3/6.
Rugby Leaguer & League Express Men of the Match: *Hornets:* Radney Bowker; *City Reds:* Luke Robinson.
Penalty count: 9-6; **Half-time:** 18-16;
Referee: Julian King (St Helens); **Attendance:** 1,971.

WIDNES VIKINGS 32 SWINTON LIONS 18

VIKINGS: 24 Tim Holmes; 19 Steve Rowlands; 5 Andrew Emelio; 3 Aaron Moule (C); 2 Misili Manu (D); 27 Paul Crook; 14 Gary Hulse; 15 Matt Whitaker; 20 Mark Smith; 17 David Mills; 11 Mick Cassidy; 16 Daniel Frame; 13 Simon Finnigan. Subs (all used): 25 Stephen Nash (D); 18 Sala Fa'alogo; 31 Paul Alcock; 32 Michael Gill (D).
Tries: Frame (2, 58), Manu (23, 50), Cassidy (26), Holmes (77); **Goals:** Crook 3/5, Rowlands 1/1.
LIONS: 1 Wayne English; 2 Stuart Oldham; 3 Lee Patterson; 4 Chris Maye; 5 Marlon Billy; 6 Mick Coates; 7 Ian Watson; 8 Paul Southern; 9 Phil Joseph; 10 Wes Rogers; 11 Danny Heaton; 12 Rob Russell; 13 Lee Marsh. Subs (all used): 14 Warren Ayres; 15 Chris Irwin; 16 Lee Gardner; 17 Rob Whittaker.
Tries: Billy (7, 68), Joseph (32); **Goals:** Marsh 3/4.
Rugby Leaguer & League Express Men of the Match: *Vikings:* Aaron Moule; *Lions:* Lee Patterson.
Penalty count: 10-7; **Half-time:** 16-12;
Referee: Mike Dawber (Wigan); **Attendance:** 2,263.

WIGAN WARRIORS 42 WHITEHAVEN 4

WARRIORS: 1 Kris Radlinski (C); 3 Martin Aspinwall; 19 Stephen Wild; 4 David Vaealiki; 2 Brett Dallas; 14 Kevin Brown; 25 James Coyle; 8 Jerry Seuseu; 18 Wayne Godwin; 10 Jerome Guisset; 20 Harrison Hansen; 12 Danny Tickle; 24 Bob Beswick. Subs (all used): 21 Chris Melling; 22 David Allen; 23 Liam Colbon; 27 Bryn Hargreaves.
Tries: Godwin (16), Radlinski (25), Wild (31, 77), Dallas (35), Allen (46, 70); **Goals:** Tickle 5/5, Melling 2/2.
WHITEHAVEN: 1 Gary Broadbent; 5 John Lebbon; 3 Wesley Wilson; 4 Mick Nanyn; 2 Craig Calvert; 6 Leroy Joe; 7 Joel Penny; 8 Aaron Summers; 9 Carl Sice; 10 David Fatialofa; 11 Brett McDermott; 12 Craig Chambers; 13 Carl Rudd. Subs (all used): 14 Steve Kirkbride; 15 Paul Davidson; 16 Garry Purdham; 17 Chris McKinney.
Try: Joe (11); **Goals:** Nanyn 0/1.
Rugby Leaguer & League Express Men of the Match: *Warriors:* Bob Beswick; *Whitehaven:* Craig Chambers.
Penalty count: 6-5; **Half-time:** 24-4; **Referee:** Colin Morris (Huddersfield); **Attendance:** 6,974.

WAKEFIELD TRINITY WILDCATS 12 HULL FC 36

WILDCATS: 21 Mark Field; 1 Colum Halpenny; 3 Jason Demetriou (C); 24 Sylvain Houles; 5 Semi Tadulala; 6 Jamie Rooney; 7 Ben Jeffries; 8 Darrell Griffin; 9 David March; 10 Michael Korkidas; 15 David Wrench; 18 Olivier Elima; 22 Mark Applegarth. Subs (all used): 12 Jamie Field; 16 Steve Snitch; 26 Julian O'Neill; 27 Chris Feather.
Tries: Halpenny (36), Snitch (67); **Goals:** Rooney 2/2.
Sin bin: Rooney (11) - deliberate offside.
HULL: 1 Shaun Briscoe; 2 Nathan Blacklock; 30 Richard Whiting; 3 Kirk Yeaman; 5 Gareth Raynor; 13 Paul Cooke (C); 6 Richard Horne; 8 Ewan Dowes; 21 Danny Brough; 15 Jamie Thackray; 17 Chris Chester; 12 Stephen Kearney; 11 Shayne McMenemy. Subs (all used): 24 Graeme Horne; 14 Motu Tony; 23 Paul McNicholas; 20 Garreth Carvell.
Tries: Raynor (4), McMenemy (14), Briscoe (17, 77), Yeaman (28), Thackray (58), Tony (73);
Goals: Brough 2/4, Cooke 2/3.
Rugby Leaguer & League Express Men of the Match: *Wildcats:* Michael Korkidas; *Hull:* Paul Cooke.
Penalty count: 11-4; **Half-time:** 6-20; **Referee:** Karl Kirkpatrick (Warrington); **Attendance:** 4,866.

HUNSLET HAWKS 4 LONDON BRONCOS 70

HAWKS: 1 George Rayner; 2 Jeremy Dyson; 3 Anthony Gibbons; 4 Paul Cummins; 5 Chris North; 6 Mark Cass; 7 Mark Moxon; 8 Matt Carbutt; 9 Jamaine Wray; 10 Neil Mears; 11 Wayne Freeman; 12 Shaun Ibbetson; 13 Andy Bastow. Subs (all used): 14 Joe Hawley; 15 Glen Freeman; 16 Danny Cook; 17 Steve Morton.
Try: Cass (33); **Goals:** Dyson 0/1.
BRONCOS: 2 Jon Wells; 23 Lee Greenwood; 4 Mark O'Halloran; 3 Nick Bradley-Qalilawa; 5 John Kirkpatrick; 1 Paul Sykes; 6 Mark McLinden (C); 8 Francis Stephenson; 19 David Highton; 20 Filimone Lolohea; 11 Solomon Haumono; 14 Danny Williams; 16 Joe Mbu. Subs (all used): 12 Lee Hopkins; 17 Mark Tookey; 18 Anthony Armour; 21 Luke Dorn.
Tries: Kirkpatrick (3, 22, 38), O'Halloran (6, 78), Haumono (16), Sykes (42), Wells (49), Hopkins (52), Greenwood (54, 70, 72, 80), Dorn (77);
Goals: Sykes 7/14.
Rugby Leaguer & League Express Men of the Match: *Hawks:* Mark Cass; *Broncos:* John Kirkpatrick.
Penalty count: 7-6; **Half-time:** 4-24;
Referee: Thierry Alibert (France); **Attendance:** 450.

ROUND 5

Friday 6th May 2005

LEEDS RHINOS 70 PIA 0

RHINOS: 1 Richard Mathers; 2 Mark Calderwood; 12 Chris McKenna; 4 Keith Senior; 23 Lee Smith; 13 Kevin Sinfield (C); 7 Rob Burrow; 8 Ryan Bailey; 14 Andrew Dunemann; 15 Danny Ward; 18 Jamie Jones-Buchanan; 16 Willie Poching; 20 Gareth Ellis. Subs (all used): 10 Barrie McDermott; 11 Ali Lauitiiti; 21 Liam Botham; 22 Nick Scruton.
Tries: Calderwood (3, 43, 61), Burrow (11, 68), Ellis (14), Mathers (29, 75), McKenna (35), Smith (39, 65), Scruton (54), Jones-Buchanan (73);
Goals: Sinfield 4/7, Burrow 5/6.
PIA: 1 Patrice Gomez; 2 Nicholas Athiel; 3 Gilles Mendez; 4 Florien Chaubet; 5 Nicolas Piguelmal; 6 Tom O'Reilly; 7 Maxime Greseque; 8 Brett O'Farrell; 9 Dean Bosnich; 10 Mathias Garrabe; 11 Emmanuel Bansept; 12 Nathan McMillan; 13 Yannick Brousse. Subs (all used): 14 Franck Rovira; 15 Marc Humbert; 16 Franck Traversa; 17 Mathieu Ambert.
Rugby Leaguer & League Express Men of the Match: *Rhinos:* Mark Calderwood; *Pia:* Brett O'Farrell.
Penalty count: 5-4; **Half-time:** 30-0; **Referee:** Karl Kirkpatrick (Warrington); **Attendance:** 7,705.

ST HELENS 62 YORK CITY KNIGHTS 0

SAINTS: 1 Paul Wellens; 20 Ian Hardman; 5 Darren Albert; 11 Lee Gilmour; 2 Ade Gardner; 6 Jason Hooper; 7 Sean Long; 17 Paul Anderson; 9 Keiron Cunningham; 16 Keith Mason; 12 Jon Wilkin; 15 Mike Bennett; 13 Paul Sculthorpe (C). Subs (all used): 14 Mick Higham; 10 Mark Edmondson; 24 Maurie Fa'asavalu; 19 James Graham.
Tries: P Anderson (3), Gardner (6), Long (21, 66), Wellens (24), Hardman (33, 69), Hooper (36, 49), Wilkin (53), Albert (56), Graham (59); **Goals:** Long 7/12.
CITY KNIGHTS: 1 Jon Liddell; 2 Matt Blaymire; 3 Dan Potter; 4 Neil Law; 5 Peter Fox; 6 Scott Rhodes; 7 Chris Levy; 8 John Smith; 9 Lee Jackson; 10 Adam Sullivan; 11 Darren Callaghan; 12 Ian Kirke; 13 Lee Patterson. Subs (all used): 14 Jimmy Elston; 15 Mick Ramsden; 16 David Bates; 17 Yusuf Sozi.
Rugby Leaguer & League Express Men of the Match: *Saints:* Paul Anderson; *City Knights:* Jimmy Elston.
Penalty count: 3-2; **Half-time:** 30-0; **Referee:** Colin Morris (Huddersfield); **Attendance:** 6,640.

WIGAN WARRIORS 16 UNION TREIZISTE CATALANE 10

WARRIORS: 4 David Vaealiki; 3 Martin Aspinwall; 19 Stephen Wild; 21 Chris Melling; 2 Brett Dallas; 14 Kevin Brown; 7 Dennis Moran; 8 Jerry Seuseu; 9 Terry Newton (C); 16 Danny Sculthorpe; 20 Harrison Hansen; 10 Jerome Guisset; 22 David Allen. Subs (all used): 23 Liam Colbon; 24 Bob Beswick; 18 Wayne Godwin; 27 Bryn Hargreaves.
Tries: Melling (43), Wild (72), Brown (80);
Goals: Melling 2/3.
UTC: 1 Renaud Guigue; 2 Justin Murphy; 15 Matt Bickerstaff; 3 Steve Hall; 14 Thomas Bosc; 6 Laurent Frayssinous; 7 Julien Rinaldi; 8 Chris Beattie; 9 David Berthezene; 20 Adel Fellous; 13 Aurelien Cologni; 12 Djamel Fakir; 16 Sean Rudder. Subs (all used): 14 Pascal Jampy; 19 Gregory Mounis; 16 Julien Touxagas; 10 Romain Gagliazzo.
Try: Mounis (51); **Goals:** Frayssinous 3/3.
Rugby Leaguer & League Express Men of the Match: *Warriors:* Dennis Moran; *UTC:* Chris Beattie.
Penalty count: 8-7; **Half-time:** 0-2; **Referee:** Richard Silverwood (Dewsbury); **Attendance:** 5,906.

Saturday 7th May 2005

HULL FC 26 BRADFORD BULLS 24

HULL: 1 Shaun Briscoe; 2 Nathan Blacklock; 3 Kirk Yeaman; 30 Richard Whiting; 5 Gareth Raynor; 13 Paul Cooke; 6 Richard Horne (C); 8 Ewan Dowes; 14 Motu Tony; 15 Jamie Thackray; 17 Chris Chester; 12 Stephen Kearney; 11 Shayne McMenemy. Subs (all used): 10 Paul King; 24 Graeme Horne; 20 Garreth Carvell; 21 Danny Brough.
Tries: Blacklock (10), Whiting (15), Cooke (22), Chester (40), Tony (60); **Goals:** Cooke 3/4, Brough 0/1.
BULLS: 3 Leon Pryce; 15 Karl Pratt; 17 Stuart Reardon; 19 Jamie Langley; 5 Lesley Vainikolo; 18 Iestyn Harris; 1 Robbie Paul; 12 Jamie Peacock (C); 7 Paul Deacon; 29 Stuart Fielden; 27 Rob Parker; 10 Brad Meyers; 11 Lee Radford. Subs (all used: 22 Karl Pryce; 8 Joe Vagana; 25 Brett Ferres; 14 Andy Lynch.
Tries: Peacock (41), Vainikolo (64, 71), K Pryce (79);
Goals: Deacon 4/4.
Rugby Leaguer & League Express Men of the Match: *Hull:* Paul Cooke; *Bulls:* Lesley Vainikolo.
Penalty count: 5-7; **Half-time:** 20-0;
Referee: Ashley Klein (Keighley); **Attendance:** 11,350.

TOULOUSE 32 DONCASTER DRAGONS 18

TOULOUSE: 1 Olivier Janzac; 2 Mickael Cousseau; 3 Damien Couturier; 4 Fabrice Estebanez; 5 Cedric Olieu; 6 Dave Mulhall; 7 James Wynne; 8 Sebastien Amigas; 9 Cedric Gay; 10 Tommy Gallagher; 11 David Delpoux; 12 Sebastien Raguin; 20 Trent Robinson. Subs (all used): 14 Adrien Viala; 15 Jerome Vincent; 16 Nicolas Faure; 17 Eric Frayssinet.
Tries: F Estebanez (22, 33, 62), Couturier (41, 68), Wynne (47); **Goals:** Couturier 4/6.
Dismissal: Cousseau (80) - striking.

Sin bin: Mulhall (65) - holding down;
F Estebanez (73) - striking.
DRAGONS: 1 Ben Cockayne; 2 Dean Colton; 3 Craig Farrell; 4 Shaun Leaf; 5 Craig Miles; 6 Graham Holroyd; 7 Latham Tawhai; 8 Gareth Handford; 9 Craig Cook; 10 Dean O'Loughlin; 11 Peter Green; 12 Lee Harland; 13 Martin Moana. Subs (all used): 14 Craig Lawton; 15 Martin Ostler; 16 Dean Andrews; 17 Aaron Wood.
Tries: Cockayne (9), Tawhai (15), Colton (80);
Goals: Holroyd 3/5.
Sin bin: Harland (62) - holding down.
Rugby Leaguer & League Express Men of the Match:
Toulouse: Fabrice Estebanez; *Dragons:* Graham Holroyd.
Penalty count: 10-11; **Half-time:** 8-12;
Referee: Ronnie Laughton (Barnsley);
Attendance: 1,200 *(at Stade des Minimes).*

Sunday 8th May 2005

BARROW RAIDERS 8 WIDNES VIKINGS 50

RAIDERS: 1 Joel Osborn; 2 Jason Roach; 3 Adrian Mulcahy; 4 Freddie Zitter; 5 James Nixon; 6 Richard Colley; 7 Darren Holt; 8 Darren Fisher; 9 Dave Clark; 10 Paul Wilcock; 11 Mike Whitehead; 12 Glenn Osborn; 13 Phil Atkinson. Subs (all used): 14 Chris Archer; 15 Stuart Dancer; 16 Jon Williamson; 17 Nick Beech.
Tries: Nixon (37), Whitehead (50); **Goals:** Holt 0/2.
VIKINGS: 24 Tim Holmes; 2 Misili Manu; 3 Aaron Moule; 4 Adam Hughes; 5 Andrew Emelio; 6 Owen Craigie; 7 Stephen Myler; 17 David Mills; 9 Shane Millard (C); 10 Julian O'Neill; 18 Sala Fa'alogo; 16 Daniel Frame; 13 Simon Finnigan. Subs: 14 Gary Hulse; 15 Matt Whitaker; 20 Mark Smith; 19 Steve Rowlands (not used).
Tries: Mills (13), Myler (16), Holmes (22), Whitaker (24, 45), Manu (40), Hughes (43), Fa'alogo (58), Hulse (74); **Goals:** Myler 7/9.
Rugby Leaguer & League Express Men of the Match:
Raiders: Joel Osborn; *Vikings:* Owen Craigie.
Penalty count: 7-7; **Half-time:** 4-28;
Referee: Ian Smith (Oldham); **Attendance:** 2,599.

LEIGH CENTURIONS 40 HALIFAX 20

CENTURIONS: 24 John Wilshere; 14 Steve Maden; 8 Rob Jackson; 9 Phil Jones; 1 Ben Cooper; 10 Jason Kent; 2 John Duffy; 21 Matt Sturm; 18 Paul Rowley; 4 Darren Fleary (C); 20 Craig Stapleton; 13 Mark Leafa; 23 Ian Knott. Subs (all used): 16 Steve McCurrie; 15 Richard Marshall; 27 Dom Feaunati (D); 11 James King.
Tries: Cooper (40, 80), Wilshere (49), Rowley (55, 60), P Jones (63), Fleary (73); **Goals:** P Jones 6/7.
HALIFAX: 1 Damian Gibson; 2 James Haley; 3 James Bunyan; 4 Anthony Blackwood; 5 Rikki Sheriffe; 6 Wayne Corcoran; 7 Danny Jones; 8 Chris Morley; 9 Ben Fisher; 10 Jason Boults; 11 David Larder; 12 Andy Spink; 13 Pat Weisner. Subs (all used): 14 Andy Boothroyd; 15 Ryan McDonald; 16 Andy Hobson; 17 Jon Simpson.
Tries: Bunyan (8), Haley (24), Fisher (42), Spink (70);
Goals: Jones 2/4.
Rugby Leaguer & League Express Men of the Match:
Centurions: John Wilshere; *Halifax:* Ben Fisher.
Penalty count: 10-7; **Half-time:** 6-8;
Referee: Julian King (St Helens); **Attendance:** 3,255.

SALFORD CITY REDS 12 LONDON BRONCOS 26

CITY REDS: 2 David Hodgson; 5 Anthony Stewart; 3 Stuart Littler; 33 Kevin McGuinness; 16 Nathan McAvoy; 1 Cliff Beverley; 7 Luke Robinson; 8 Andy Coley; 9 Malcolm Alker (C); 10 Sean Rutgerson; 11 Mark Shipway; 12 Ian Sibbit; 13 Chris Charles. Subs (all used): 26 Darren Bamford; 22 Simon Baldwin; 20 Tim Jonkers; 17 Gareth Haggerty.
Tries: McGuinness (28), Bamford (73);
Goals: Charles 2/2, Robinson 0/1.
BRONCOS: 6 Mark McLinden (C); 2 Jon Wells; 1 Paul Sykes; 4 Mark O'Halloran; 3 Nick Bradley-Qalilawa; 21 Luke Dorn; 7 Thomas Leuluai; 20 Filimone Lolohea; 19 David Highton; 10 Steve Trindall; 12 Lee Hopkins; 13 Rob Purdham; 11 Solomon Haumono. Subs (all used): 14 Danny Williams; 17 Mark Tookey; 8 Francis Stephenson; 24 Tyrone Smith.
Tries: Sykes (11), Leuluai (37), McLinden (55), Smith (61); **Goals:** Sykes 5/6.
On report: Williams (33) - use of the elbow.
Rugby Leaguer & League Express Men of the Match:
City Reds: Kevin McGuinness; *Broncos:* Paul Sykes.
Penalty count: 6-9; **Half-time:** 8-12;
Referee: Steve Ganson (St Helens); **Attendance:** 2,339.

QUARTER FINALS

Friday 24th June 2005

LEEDS RHINOS 32 LONDON BRONCOS 12

RHINOS: 1 Richard Mathers; 2 Mark Calderwood; 3 Chev Walker; 4 Keith Senior; 5 Marcus Bai; 6 Danny McGuire; 7 Rob Burrow; 8 Ryan Bailey; 14 Andrew Dunemann; 18 Jamie Jones-Buchanan; 20 Gareth Ellis; 12 Chris McKenna; 13 Kevin Sinfield (C). Subs (all used): 16 Willie Poching; 11 Ali Lauitiiti; 10 Barrie McDermott; 22 Nick Scruton.
Tries: McGuire (11, 66), Walker (36), Burrow (55), Senior (70), Bai (76); **Goals:** Sinfield 4/6.
BRONCOS: 25 Zebastian Luisi; 2 Jon Wells; 1 Paul Sykes; 24 Tyrone Smith; 3 Nick Bradley-Qalilawa; 21 Luke Dorn; 7 Thomas Leuluai; 10 Steve Trindall; 19 David Highton; 8 Francis Stephenson; 13 Rob Purdham; 12 Lee Hopkins (C); 16 Joe Mbu. Subs (all used): 14 Danny Williams; 17 Mark Tookey; 4 Mark O'Halloran; 11 Solomon Haumono.
Tries: Bradley-Qalilawa (23), Haumono (50);
Goals: Sykes 2/2.
Sin bin: Smith (76) – late challenge on Dunemann.
Rugby Leaguer & League Express Men of the Match:
Rhinos: Kevin Sinfield; *Broncos:* Lee Hopkins.
Penalty count: 7-5; **Half-time:** 10-6;
Referee: Steve Ganson (St Helens); **Attendance:** 9,444.

Saturday 25th June 2005

HULL FC 46 LEIGH CENTURIONS 14

HULL: 1 Shaun Briscoe; 2 Nathan Blacklock; 3 Kirk Yeaman; 16 Tom Saxton; 26 Richie Barnett; 13 Paul Cooke; 6 Richard Horne (C); 8 Ewan Dowes; 21 Danny Brough; 20 Garreth Carvell; 24 Graeme Horne; 12 Stephen Kearney; 11 Shayne McMenemy. Subs (all used): 15 Jamie Thackray; 10 Paul King; 14 Motu Tony; 22 Kirk Dixon.
Tries: McMenemy (8), Saxton (14), R Horne (20, 28), Thackray (35), Blacklock (39), Barnett (56), Cooke (58);
Goals: Cooke 7/7, Brough 0/1.
CENTURIONS: 24 John Wilshere; 1 Ben Cooper; 6 Danny Halliwell; 8 Rob Jackson; 14 Steve Maden; 9 Phil Jones; 2 John Duffy; 4 Darren Fleary (C); 18 Paul Rowley; 20 Craig Stapleton; 16 Steve McCurrie; 13 Mark Leafa; 10 Jason Kent. Subs (all used): 5 Mick Govin; 15 Richard Marshall; 21 Matt Sturm; 34 Matthew Bottom.
Tries: Marshall (45), Jackson (62), Halliwell (76);
Goals: Wilshere 1/3.
Rugby Leaguer & League Express Men of the Match:
Hull: Richard Horne; *Centurions:* Danny Halliwell.
Penalty count: 13-13; **Half-time:** 34-0;
Referee: Ian Smith (Oldham); **Attendance:** 10,447.

Sunday 26th June 2005

TOULOUSE 40 WIDNES VIKINGS 24

TOULOUSE: 1 Sam Murphy; 2 Peter Lima; 3 Damien Couturier; 4 Fabrice Estebanez; 5 Cedric Olieu; 6 Dave Mulhall; 7 James Wynne; 8 Nicolas Faure; 9 Cedric Gay; 10 Tommy Gallagher; 11 David Delpoux; 12 Sebastien Raguin; 20 Trent Robinson. Subs (all used): 14 Cedric Prizzon; 15 Adrien Viala; 16 Jerome Vincent; 17 Vincent Almuzara.
Tries: Murphy (4), F Estebanez (12), Gay (22, 53), Faure (43), Gallagher (72); **Goals:** Couturier 8/8.
VIKINGS: 14 Gary Hulse; 2 Misili Manu; 1 Gary Connolly; 4 Adam Hughes; 5 Andrew Emelio; 6 Owen Craigie; 7 Stephen Myler; 8 Terry O'Connor; 9 Shane Millard (C); 10 Julian O'Neill; 11 Mick Cassidy; 15 Matt Whitaker; 16 Daniel Frame. Subs (all used): 20 Mark Smith; 17 David Mills; 24 Tim Holmes; 34 Bruce Johnson.
Tries: Emelio (34), Johnson (39), Smith (50), Manu (58); **Goals:** Myler 4/4.
Rugby Leaguer & League Express Men of the Match:
Toulouse: Dave Mulhall; *Vikings:* Mark Smith.
Penalty count: 5-8; **Half-time:** 20-12;
Referee: Karl Kirkpatrick (Warrington);
Attendance: 4,500 *(at Stade des Minimes).*

ST HELENS 75 WIGAN WARRIORS 0

SAINTS: 1 Paul Wellens; 5 Darren Albert; 3 Jamie Lyon; 4 Willie Talau; 2 Ade Gardner; 6 Jason Hooper; 12 Jon Wilkin; 8 Nick Fozzard; 9 Keiron Cunningham; 17 Paul Anderson; 27 Vinnie Anderson; 11 Lee Gilmour; 13 Paul Sculthorpe (C). Subs (all used): 10 Mark Edmondson; 15 Mike Bennett; 21 James Roby; 19 James Graham.
Tries: Gilmour (11), V Anderson (18), Fozzard (23, 60), Hooper (27), Talau (30), Wellens (36), Edmondson (51, 64, 66), Lyon (61), Gardner (77), Graham (79); **Goals:** Sculthorpe 9/12, Lyon 2/2;
Field goal: Sculthorpe.
WARRIORS: 30 Sean Gleeson; 5 Brian Carney; 19 Stephen Wild; 3 Martin Aspinwall; 2 Brett Dallas; 14 Kevin Brown; 7 Dennis Moran; 8 Jerry Seuseu; 9 Terry Newton (C); 16 Danny Sculthorpe; 22 David Allen; 12 Danny Tickle; 24 Bob Beswick. Subs (all used): 10 Jerome Guisset; 18 Wayne Godwin; 20 Harrison Hansen; 27 Bryn Hargreaves.
Rugby Leaguer & League Express Men of the Match:
Saints: Nick Fozzard; *Warriors:* Sean Gleeson.
Penalty count: 6-8; **Half-time:** 35-0;
Referee: Ashley Klein (Keighley); **Attendance:** 17,100.

Paul Sculthorpe on the charge during St Helens' 75-0 quarter final win over Wigan

SEMI FINALS

Saturday 30th July 2005

HULL FC 34 ST HELENS 8

HULL: 1 Shaun Briscoe; 26 Richie Barnett; 3 Kirk Yeaman; 30 Richard Whiting; 5 Gareth Raynor; 6 Richard Horne; 21 Danny Brough; 8 Ewan Dowes; 9 Richard Swain (C); 20 Garreth Carvell; 11 Shayne McMenemy; 12 Stephen Kearney; 13 Paul Cooke. Subs (all used): 10 Paul King; 14 Motu Tony; 15 Jamie Thackray; 24 Graeme Horne.
Tries: McMenemy (9, 58), Cooke (54), Tony (71), R Horne (79); **Goals:** Cooke 5/6, Brough 2/2.
SAINTS: 1 Paul Wellens; 5 Darren Albert; 3 Jamie Lyon; 4 Willie Talau; 2 Ade Gardner; 6 Jason Hooper; 7 Sean Long; 8 Nick Fozzard; 9 Keiron Cunningham; 17 Paul Anderson; 11 Lee Gilmour; 27 Vinnie Anderson; 13 Paul Sculthorpe (C). Subs (all used): 12 Jon Wilkin; 19 James Graham; 21 James Roby; 24 Maurie Fa'asavalu.
Try: Lyon (45); **Goals:** Sculthorpe 2/2.
On report: Wilkin and P Anderson (36) - alleged spear tackle on Carvell.
Rugby Leaguer & League Express Men of the Match:
Hull: Paul Cooke; *Saints:* Paul Wellens.
Penalty count: 10-6; **Half-time:** 8-2;
Referee: Ashley Klein (Keighley);
Attendance: 16,171 *(at Galpharm Stadium, Huddersfield).*

Sunday 31st July 2005

LEEDS RHINOS 56 TOULOUSE 18

RHINOS: 1 Richard Mathers; 2 Mark Calderwood; 3 Chev Walker; 4 Keith Senior (C); 5 Marcus Bai; 6 Danny McGuire; 7 Rob Burrow; 15 Danny Ward; 9 Matt Diskin; 10 Barrie McDermott; 11 Ali Lauitiiti; 12 Chris McKenna; 20 Gareth Ellis. Subs (all used): 16 Willie Poching; 14 Andrew Dunemann; 22 Nick Scruton; 8 Ryan Bailey.
Tries: McKenna (5), Ellis (17), McGuire (33, 64), Lauitiiti (36), Bai (42), Calderwood (52), Burrow (61), Walker (74), Poching (80); **Goals:** Burrow 8/9, McDermott 0/1.
TOULOUSE: 1 Sam Murphy; 5 Olivier Janzac; 4 Fabrice Estebanez; 3 Damien Couturier; 2 Peter Lima; 6 Dave Mulhall; 7 James Wynne; 8 Nicolas Faure; 9 Cedric Gay; 10 Tommy Gallagher; 11 David Delpoux; 12 Sebastien Raguin; 13 Adrien Viala. Subs (all used): 14 Cedric Prizzon; 15 Jerome Vincent; 16 Eric Frayssinet; 17 Vincent Almuzara.
Tries: Viala (2), Wynne (14), Raguin (38);
Goals: Couturier 3/4.
Rugby Leaguer & League Express Men of the Match:
Rhinos: Matt Diskin; *Toulouse:* Dave Mulhall.
Penalty count: 9-8; **Half-time:** 22-18;
Referee: Richard Silverwood (Dewsbury);
Attendance: 10,553 *(at Galpharm Stadium, Huddersfield).*

FINAL

Saturday 27th August 2005

HULL FC 25 LEEDS RHINOS 24

HULL: 2 Nathan Blacklock; 14 Motu Tony; 30 Richard Whiting; 3 Kirk Yeaman; 5 Gareth Raynor; 6 Richard Horne; 21 Danny Brough; 8 Ewan Dowes; 9 Richard Swain (C); 20 Garreth Carvell; 11 Shayne McMenemy; 12 Stephen Kearney; 13 Paul Cooke. Subs (all used): 10 Paul King for Carvell (19); 17 Chris Chester for Kearney (25); 15 Jamie Thackray for Dowes (28); Carvell for King (32); Dowes for Carvell (50); Kearney for McMenemy (50); King for Thackray (50); McMenemy for Chester (61); 16 Tom Saxton for Kearney (70); Thackray for King (71); Carvell for Dowes (72).
Tries: Tony (20), Raynor (46), Whiting (53), Cooke (77);
Goals: Brough 4/4; **Field goal:** Brough.
RHINOS: 1 Richard Mathers; 2 Mark Calderwood; 3 Chev Walker; 4 Keith Senior; 5 Marcus Bai; 13 Kevin Sinfield (C); 7 Rob Burrow; 8 Ryan Bailey; 9 Matt Diskin; 15 Danny Ward; 11 Ali Lauitiiti; 12 Chris McKenna; 20 Gareth Ellis. Subs (all used): 18 Jamie Jones-Buchanan for Ward (17); 16 Willie Poching for McKenna (19); 6 Danny McGuire for Ellis (25); 14 Andrew Dunemann for Diskin (27); Ward for Bailey (30); McKenna for Senior (41); Bailey for Jones-Buchanan (47); Diskin for Burrow (54); Ellis for Lauitiiti (56); Jones-Buchanan for Poching (58); Lauitiiti for McKenna (64); Poching for Lauitiiti (78).
Tries: Calderwood (12, 65), Ward (50), Bai (68);
Goals: Sinfield 4/4.
Rugby Leaguer & League Express Men of the Match:
Hull: Richard Swain; *Rhinos:* Kevin Sinfield.
Penalty count: 3-3; **Half-time:** 6-6;
Referee: Steve Ganson (St Helens);
Attendance: 74,213 *(at Millennium Stadium, Cardiff).*

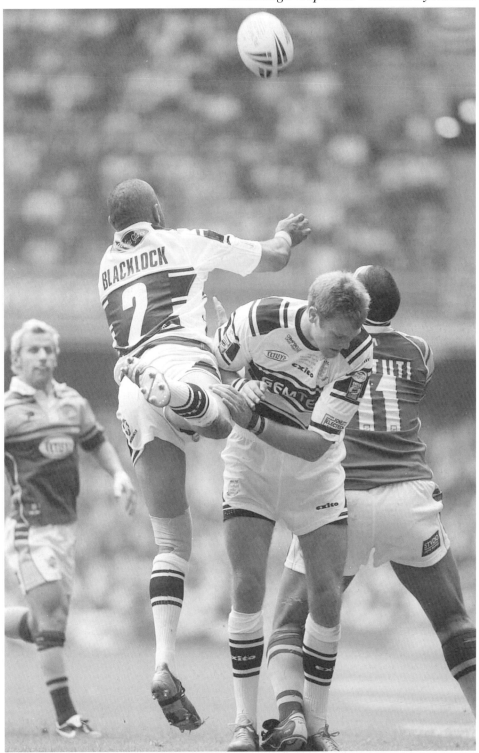

Hull duo Nathan Blacklock and Richard Whiting compete for a high ball with Leeds' Ali Lauitiiti during the Challenge Cup Final

NATIONAL LEAGUE THREE

FINAL TABLE

	P	W	D	L	F	A	D	PTS
Bradford-Dudley H	18	17	0	1	844	237	607	34
Bramley	18	16	0	2	832	228	604	32
St Albans	18	14	0	4	770	349	421	28
Warrington W	18	10	1	7	683	382	301	21
Sheffield-H'boro	18	9	1	8	444	514	-70	19
Hemel Hempstead	18	8	0	10	406	523	-117	16
Coventry	18	7	0	11	525	645	-120	14
Huddersfield-U'bank	18	5	0	13	466	679	-213	10
Gateshead S	18	3	0	15	369	769	-400	6
Essex	18	0	0	18	181	1194	-1013	0

Carlisle & Birmingham records expunged

ELIMINATION PLAY-OFFS
Saturday 17th September 2005
St Albans Centurions 40 ....Hemel Hempstead Stags 6
Warrington Wizards 48...........Sheffield-Hillsborough 12

QUALIFYING SEMI-FINAL
Saturday 24th September 2005
Bradford-Dudley Hill Demons 18 ..Bramley Buffaloes 19

ELIMINATION SEMI-FINAL
Saturday 24th September 2005
St Albans Centurions 46.............Warrington Wizards 24

FINAL ELIMINATOR
Saturday 1st October 2005
Bradford-Dudley Hill Demons 63 ..St Albans Centurions 10

GRAND FINAL
Sunday 9th October 2005
Bradford-Dudley Hill Demons 28 ..Bramley Buffaloes 26
at Halton Stadium, Widnes

PLAYER OF THE YEAR
Harry Gee (Gateshead Storm)

COACH OF THE YEAR
Colin Baker (St Albans Centurions)

YOUNG PLAYER OF THE YEAR
Shaun Flynn (Bramley Buffaloes)

RUGBY LEAGUE WORLD ALL-STARS TEAM
1 Barry John Swindells (Hemel Hempstead Stags)
2 Shaun Flynn (Bramley Buffaloes)
3 Dene Miller (St Albans Centurions)
4 Paul Drake (Bramley Buffaloes)
5 Mark Roughneen (Warrington Wizards)
6 Scott Pendlebury (Bramley Buffaloes)
7 Tony Williams (Bradford-Dudley Hill Demons)
8 Tim Orr (Bramley Buffaloes)
9 Gareth Walker (Bradford-Dudley Hill Demons)
10 Richard Bingley (Bradford-Dudley Hill Demons)
11 Dave Birchall (Huddersfield-Underbank Rangers)
12 Harry Gee (Gateshead Storm)
13 Alan Kilshaw (Warrington Wizards)

NATIONAL CONFERENCE

PREMIER DIVISION

	P	W	D	L	F	A	D	PTS
Leigh Miners R	26	18	2	6	657	467	190	38
Wath Brow Hornets	26	18	0	8	671	452	219	36
Thornhill Trojans	26	17	1	8	550	428	122	35
Hull Dockers	26	16	0	10	547	441	106	32
Wigan St Patricks	26	14	2	10	515	388	127	30
Wigan St Judes	26	13	0	13	518	487	31	26
Oldham St Annes	26	12	0	14	514	498	16	24
Siddal	26	12	0	14	479	514	-35	24
Leigh East	26	11	1	14	540	610	-70	23
Skirlaugh *	26	13	0	13	492	521	-29	22
Oulton Raiders	26	11	0	15	481	559	-78	22
West Hull	26	10	0	16	512	532	-20	20
West Bowling	26	9	0	17	354	581	-227	18
Thatto Heath C	26	5	0	21	335	687	-352	10

* *Denotes four points deducted*

ELIMINATION PLAY-OFFS
Saturday 30th April 2005
Thornhill Trojans 36 ....Wigan St Judes 14
Hull Dockers 17 ....Wigan St Patricks 4

QUALIFYING SEMI-FINAL
Saturday 7th May 2005
Leigh Miners Rangers 48 ....Wath Brow Hornets 18

ELIMINATION SEMI-FINAL
Saturday 7th May 2005
Thornhill Trojans 22................................Hull Dockers 24

FINAL ELIMINATOR
Saturday 14th May 2005
Wath Brow Hornets 36 ....Hull Dockers 30

GRAND FINAL
Saturday 21st May 2005
Leigh Miners Rangers 30 ....Wath Brow Hornets 22
at Orrell RUFC

DIVISION ONE

	P	W	D	L	F	A	D	PTS
Shaw Cross Sharks	24	21	1	2	586	296	290	43
Eccles & Salford J	24	19	0	5	655	423	232	38
East Hull	24	19	0	5	604	381	223	38
Rochdale Mayfield	24	13	0	11	611	496	115	26
Walney Central	24	12	0	12	547	478	69	24
Askam	24	11	0	13	482	501	-19	22
Milford Marlins	24	10	1	13	570	619	-49	21
Castleford LL	24	10	1	13	472	539	-67	21
Hunslet Warriors	24	10	0	14	438	507	-69	20
East Leeds	24	8	3	13	386	492	-106	19
Ideal Isberg	24	9	0	15	406	538	-132	18
Castleford Panthers	24	8	0	16	469	553	-84	16
Featherstone Lions	24	3	0	21	342	736	-394	6

DIVISION TWO

	P	W	D	L	F	A	D	PTS
Ince Rosebridge	26	20	1	5	766	380	386	41
Eastmoor Dragons	26	20	0	6	805	429	376	40
York Acorn	26	18	1	7	752	429	323	37
Stanningley	26	16	1	9	636	473	163	33
Waterhead	26	16	0	10	671	467	204	32
Ovenden	26	16	0	10	616	543	73	32
Crosfields	26	15	0	11	603	622	-19	30
Widnes St Maries	26	13	1	12	590	499	91	27
Millom	26	11	0	15	545	557	-12	22
Normanton Knights	26	9	0	17	518	668	-150	18
Cottingham Tigers	26	8	0	18	385	754	-369	16
Saddleworth R	26	6	1	19	481	785	-304	13
Heworth	26	6	0	20	484	861	-377	12
Huddersfield S	26	5	1	20	365	778	-413	11

NATIONAL CUP

QUARTER FINALS
Saturday 9th April 2005
Castleford Panthers 17................................Crosfields 18
Sharlston 22 ....Skirlaugh 29
Wath Brow Hornets 35 ....Leigh Miners Rangers 18
Wigan St Patricks 8 ....Wigan St Judes 10

SEMI-FINALS
Saturday 23rd April 2005
Skirlaugh 36..Crosfields 26
Wath Brow Hornets 56 ....Wigan St Judes 28

FINAL
Saturday 28th May 2005
Skirlaugh 6 ....Wath Brow Hornets 16
at Bloomfield Road, Blackpool

TOTALRL.COM CONFERENCE

NORTH PREMIER

	P	W	D	L	F	A	D	PTS
West Cumbria C	12	12	0	0	582	138	444	24
Copeland Athletic	12	6	2	4	380	326	54	14
Penrith Pumas	12	5	1	6	340	335	5	11
Jarrow Vikings	12	3	0	9	296	432	-136	6
Peterlee Pumas	12	3	0	9	244	504	-260	6
Sunderland City	12	3	0	9	172	610	-438	6

CENTRAL PREMIER

	P	W	D	L	F	A	D	PTS
Leeds Akkies	12	11	0	1	428	137	291	22
Hull Phoenix	12	8	0	4	410	215	195	16
Bolton Le Moors	12	7	0	5	317	299	18	14
Dewsbury Celtic	12	6	1	5	395	294	101	13
Nottingham O	12	3	0	9	296	438	-142	6
Telford Raiders	12	1	0	11	156	517	-361	2

SOUTH PREMIER

	P	W	D	L	F	A	D	PTS
South London S	12	11	0	1	726	110	616	22
West London S	12	11	0	1	588	176	412	22
Ipswich Rhinos	12	7	0	5	370	346	24	14
London Skolars A	12	4	0	8	206	434	-228	8
Luton Vipers	12	3	1	8	199	480	-281	7
Greenwich A	12	1	1	10	116	430	-314	3

WELSH PREMIER

	P	W	D	L	F	A	D	PTS
Bridgend Blue Bulls	12	11	0	1	606	210	396	22
Aberavon Fighting I	12	10	0	2	584	322	262	20
Torfaen Tigers	12	6	1	5	352	369	-17	13
Newport Titans	12	5	0	7	397	400	-3	10
Valley Cougars	12	5	0	7	304	526	-222	10
Cardiff Demons	12	3	1	8	349	436	-87	7
Swansea Valley M	12	1	0	11	259	588	-329	2

HARRY JEPSON TROPHY - PLAY-OFFS

Saturday 30th July 2005
Bolton Le Moors 34 ....Dewsbury Celtic 26
Ipswich Rhinos 24...........................London Skolars A 0
Leeds Akkies 42...Hull Phoenix 10
Penrith Pumas 34....................................Jarrow Vikings 4
South London Storm 70.............West London Sharks 6
West Cumbria Crusaders 42.............Copeland Athletic 4

Saturday 6th August 2005
Aberavon Fighting Irish 44 ....Torfaen Tigers 45
Copeland Athletic 64..............................Penrith Pumas 6
Hull Phoenix 28................................Bolton Le Moors 16
London Sharks 50..............................Ipswich Rhinos 26

Saturday 13th August 2005
Leeds Akkies 40...Hull Phoenix 0
South London Storm 24 ....West London Sharks 6
West Cumbria Crusaders 48............Copeland Athletic 12

Sunday 21st August 2005
Bridgend Blue Bulls 34 ....South London Storm 18
West Cumbria Crusaders 18 ....Leeds Akkies 19

HARRY JEPSON TROPHY - GRAND FINAL

Sunday 28th August 2005
Bridgend Blue Bulls 60 ....Leeds Akkies 10
at Brewery Field, Bridgend

WELSH PREMIER DIVISION - GRAND FINAL

Sunday 14th August 2005
Bridgend Blue Bulls 56 ....Torfaen Tigers 16
at Brewery Field, Bridgend

WELSH PREMIER DIVISION - SHIELD FINAL

Sunday 14th August 2005
Newport Titans 42 ....Valley Cougars 41
at Brewery Field, Bridgend

TRL.COM REGIONAL LEAGUES

NORTH EAST

	P	W	D	L	F	A	D	PTS
Durham Tigers	10	8	1	1	541	168	373	17
Newcastle Knights	10	7	0	3	354	201	153	14
Scarborough P	10	6	0	4	386	264	122	12
Catterick	10	5	1	4	360	234	126	11
Winlaton Vulcans	10	2	0	8	224	438	-214	4
Whitley Bay B	10	1	0	9	92	652	-560	2

WEST MIDLANDS

	P	W	D	L	F	A	D	PTS
Wolverhampton W	10	8	1	1	364	152	212	17
Leicester Phoenix	10	8	0	2	513	180	333	16
Birmingham B	10	4	0	6	278	310	-32	8
Coventry Bears 'A'	10	2	1	7	288	388	-100	5
Redditch Ravens	10	2	0	8	166	598	-432	4

SOUTH WEST

	P	W	D	L	F	A	D	PTS
Gloucestershire W	10	9	0	1	400	196	204	18
Somerset Vikings	10	7	1	2	454	195	259	15
Bristol Sonics	10	6	1	3	386	280	106	13
Plymouth	10	2	0	8	188	352	-164	4
Oxford Cavaliers	10	0	0	10	104	490	-386	0

EAST

	P	W	D	L	F	A	D	PTS
St Albans C	8	8	0	0	424	170	254	16
South Norfolk S	8	6	0	2	348	190	158	12
Cambridge Eagles	8	3	0	5	146	312	-166	6
St Ives Roosters	8	2	0	6	202	256	-54	4
Bedford Tigers	8	1	0	7	164	356	-192	2

LONDON & SOUTH

	P	W	D	L	F	A	D	PTS
Kingston Warriors	6	5	1	0	303	118	185	11
Haringey Hornets	6	3	1	2	202	126	76	7
Hemel Stags A	6	2	2	2	176	218	-42	6
South London S	6	0	0	6	108	327	-219	0

NORTH WEST

	P	W	D	L	F	A	D	PTS
Warrington Wizards	10	8	0	2	375	172	203	16
Liverpool B	10	8	0	2	381	255	126	16
Rochdale S R	10	6	0	4	344	214	130	12
Widnes Saints	10	6	0	4	305	187	118	12
Crewe Wolves	10	6	0	4	338	303	35	12
Blackpool S E	10	5	0	5	268	314	-46	10
Wigan & Leigh C	10	4	0	6	302	301	1	8
Ormskirk Heelers	10	3	0	7	240	380	-140	6
North Wales C	10	2	0	8	236	416	-180	4
Runcorn Vikings	10	2	0	8	221	444	-223	4

YORKSHIRE

	P	W	D	L	F	A	D	PTS
Wetherby Bulldogs	10	10	0	0	684	73	611	20
Bramley Buffaloes	10	9	0	1	390	176	214	18
Huddersfield U'bank	10	6	0	4	284	394	-110	12
Bridlington Bulls	10	5	0	5	320	294	26	10
South Wakefield S	10	5	0	5	239	271	-32	10
Bradford-Dudley H	10	2	0	8	254	402	-148	4
Hull Phoenix	10	2	0	8	168	464	-296	4
Leeds Akkies	10	1	0	9	194	459	-265	2

NORTH MIDLANDS

	P	W	D	L	F	A	D	PTS
Derby City	10	8	0	2	353	235	118	16
Thorne Moor M	10	7	0	3	389	160	229	14
Lincoln City Knights	10	6	1	3	271	253	18	13
Worksop Sharks	10	4	0	6	198	288	-90	8
Mansfield Storm	10	2	1	7	240	364	-124	5
Sheffield-H'boro	10	2	0	8	231	384	-153	4

REGIONAL LEAGUES - GRAND FINAL

Sunday 4th September 2005
Gloucestershire Warriors 16 ....Wetherby Bulldogs 32
at Butts Park Arena, Coventry

REGIONAL LEAGUES - SHIELD FINAL

Sunday 4th September 2005
Blackpool Sea Eagles 74 ....St Ives Roosters 10
at Butts Park Arena, Coventry

Hull FC - Senior Academy Champions

ACADEMY

SENIOR ACADEMY UNDER-21 CHAMPIONSHIP

	P	W	D	L	F	A	D	PTS
Wigan Warriors	14	11	0	3	468	296	172	22
Hull FC	14	10	0	4	458	247	211	20
Bradford Bulls	14	9	0	5	471	316	155	18
Wakefield T W'cats	14	7	1	6	350	382	-32	15
St Helens	14	7	0	7	424	378	46	14
Warrington Wolves	14	5	0	9	312	383	-71	10
Halifax	14	4	1	9	277	390	-113	9
Leigh Centurions	14	2	0	12	234	602	-368	4

ELIMINATION PLAY-OFFS
Thursday 8th September 2005
Bradford Bulls 32...........................Warrington Wolves 12
Wakefield Trinity Wildcats 12 ....St Helens 15

ELIMINATION SEMI-FINAL
Thursday 15th September 2005
Bradford Bulls 32 ....St Helens 18

QUALIFYING SEMI-FINAL
Sunday 18th September 2005
Wigan Warriors 16 ....Hull FC 40

FINAL ELIMINATOR
Saturday 24th September 2005
Wigan Warriors 32 ....Bradford Bulls 26

GRAND FINAL
Sunday 2nd October 2005
Hull FC 36 ....Wigan Warriors 34
at Kingston Communications Stadium, Hull

SENIOR ACADEMY UNDER-21 DIVISION ONE

	P	W	D	L	F	A	D	PTS
Leeds Rhinos	14	13	0	1	801	145	656	26
Widnes Vikings	14	12	0	2	736	178	558	24
Castleford Tigers	14	10	0	4	486	358	128	20
Salford City Reds	14	10	0	4	414	375	39	20
Huddersfield Giants	14	6	1	7	368	459	-91	13
Keighley Cougars	14	4	1	9	309	547	-238	9
Featherstone R	14	3	0	11	246	525	-279	6
Dewsbury Rams	14	2	0	12	250	614	-364	4
Doncaster Dragons	14	2	0	11	169	582	-413	4

ELIMINATION PLAY-OFFS
Wednesday 31st August 2005
Salford City Reds 22 ....Huddersfield Giants 27
Tuesday 6th September 2005
Castleford Tigers 28 ....Keighley Cougars 16

QUALIFYING SEMI-FINAL
Thursday 8th September 2005
Leeds Rhinos 20 ....Widnes Vikings 30

ELIMINATION SEMI-FINAL
Tuesday 13th September 2005
Castleford Tigers 56 ....Huddersfield Giants 22

FINAL ELIMINATOR
Friday 16th September 2005
Leeds Rhinos 42 ....Castleford Tigers 16

GRAND FINAL
Thursday 22nd September 2005
Leeds Rhinos 42 ....Widnes Vikings 12
at Headingley, Leeds

JUNIOR ACADEMY UNDER-18 CHAMPIONSHIP

	P	W	D	L	F	A	D	PTS
Wigan Warriors	14	13	0	1	515	260	255	26
Widnes Vikings	14	9	1	4	419	318	101	19
Warrington Wolves	14	9	0	5	491	316	175	18
Leeds Rhinos	14	9	0	5	414	306	108	18
Huddersfield Giants	14	6	1	7	379	369	10	13
Hull FC	14	5	0	9	298	372	-74	10
Castleford Tigers	14	2	0	12	282	465	-183	4
Salford City Reds	14	2	0	12	218	604	-386	4

ELIMINATION PLAY-OFFS
Saturday 17th September 2005
Leeds Rhinos 25 ....Huddersfield Giants 14
Warrington Wolves 66 ....Hull FC 28

QUALIFYING SEMI-FINAL
Saturday 24th September 2005
Wigan Warriors 24 ....Widnes Vikings 12

ELIMINATION SEMI-FINAL
Saturday 24th September 2005
Warrington Wolves 26 ....Leeds Rhinos 38

FINAL ELIMINATOR
Sunday 2nd October 2005
Widnes Vikings 16 ....Leeds Rhinos 28

GRAND FINAL
Sunday 9th October 2005
Leeds Rhinos 22 ....Wigan Warriors 33
at Headingley, Leeds

JUNIOR ACADEMY UNDER-18 DIVISION ONE

	P	W	D	L	F	A	D	PTS
Hull KR	14	13	0	1	582	124	458	26
St Helens	14	12	1	1	640	224	416	25
Wakefield T W'cats	14	12	0	2	596	226	370	24
Bradford Bulls	14	9	1	4	540	305	235	19
Hunslet Hawks	14	8	0	6	410	329	81	16
London Broncos	14	5	0	9	274	407	-133	10
Whitehaven	14	3	2	9	193	514	-321	8
Leigh Centurions	14	3	0	11	234	581	-347	6
Featherstone R	14	2	0	11	244	538	-294	4
Keighley Cougars	14	1	0	13	169	646	-477	2

ELIMINATION PLAY-OFFS
Friday 2nd September 2005
Bradford Bulls 44 ....Hunslet Hawks 24
Sunday 4th September 2005
Wakefield Trinity Wildcats 12...........London Broncos 24

QUALIFYING SEMI-FINAL
Sunday 11th September 2005
Hull Kingston Rovers 12..............................St Helens 25

ELIMINATION SEMI-FINAL
Sunday 11th September 2005
Bradford Bulls 20.............................London Broncos 12

FINAL ELIMINATOR
Saturday 17th September 2005
Hull Kingston Rovers 38 ....Bradford Bulls 12

GRAND FINAL
Saturday 24th September 2005
Hull Kingston Rovers 12..............................St Helens 52
at New Craven Park, Hull

Wigan Warriors - Junior Academy Champions

SUPER LEAGUE 2006 FIXTURES

ROUND 1

FRIDAY 10 FEBRUARY 2006
Castleford Tigers v Hull FC 8:00
SATURDAY 11 FEBRUARY 2006
Catalans Dragons v Wigan Warriors 7:05
Harlequins v St Helens 3:00
SUNDAY 12 FEBRUARY 2006
Leeds Rhinos v Huddersfield Giants 3:00
Wakefield T Wildcats v Bradford Bulls..3:30
Warrington Wolves v Salford City Reds ..3:00

ROUND 2

FRIDAY 17 FEBRUARY 2006
Salford City Reds v Catalans Dragons ..8:00
St Helens v Castleford Tigers................8:00
Wigan Warriors v Leeds Rhinos 8:00
SATURDAY 18 FEBRUARY 2006
Bradford Bulls v Harlequins..................6:05
SUNDAY 19 FEBRUARY 2006
Huddersfield Giants v Warrington Wolves ..3:00
Hul FC v Wakefield Trinity Wildcats 3:15

ROUND 3

FRIDAY 24 FEBRUARY 2006
Bradford Bulls v Salford City Reds 8:00
St Helens v Leeds Rhinos.................... 8:00
Wigan Warriors v Huddersfield Giants..8:00
SATURDAY 25 FEBRUARY 2006
Harlequins v Wakefield T Wildcats........3:00
Warrington Wolves v Hull FC................6:05
SUNDAY 26 FEBRUARY 2006
Castleford Tigers v Catalans Dragons ..3:30

ROUND 4

FRIDAY 3 MARCH 2006
Hul FC v Harlequins 8:00
Leeds Rhinos v Castleford Tigers 8:00
Salford City Reds v Wigan Warriors 8:00
Warrington Wolves v St Helens............8:00
SATURDAY 4 MARCH 2006
Catalans Dragons v Bradford Bulls 6:00
Wakefield T Wildcats v Huddersfield Giants..6:05

ROUND 5

FRIDAY 10 MARCH 2006
Bradford Bulls v Hull FC 8:00
Wigan Warriors v Warrington Wolves ..8:00
SATURDAY 11 MARCH 2006
Catalans Dragons v Leeds Rhinos 6:00
Salford City Reds v Wakefield T Wildcats ..6:05
SUNDAY 12 MARCH 2006
Harlequins v Castleford Tigers..............3:00
Huddersfield Giants v St Helens 3:00

**POWERGEN CHALLENGE CUP
- THIRD ROUND**

ROUND 6

FRIDAY 17 MARCH 2006
Leeds Rhinos v Salford City Reds 8:00
St Helens v Bradford Bulls....................8:00
SATURDAY 18 MARCH 2006
Warrington Wolves v Catalans Dragons..6:05
SUNDAY 19 MARCH 2006
Castleford Tigers v Wigan Warriors......3:30
Huddersfield Giants v Harlequins 3:00
Wakefield Trinity Wildcats v Hull FC 3:30

ROUND 7

FRIDAY 24 MARCH 2006
Bradford Bulls v Wigan Warriors 8:00
Hull FC v St Helens 8:00
SATURDAY 25 MARCH 2006
Catalans Dragons v Salford City Reds ..6:00
Harlequins v Leeds Rhinos 6:05
SUNDAY 26 MARCH 2006
Castleford Tigers v Huddersfield Giants ..3:30
Wakefield T Wildcats v Warrington Wolves ..3:30

**SUNDAY 2 APRIL 2006
POWERGEN CHALLENGE CUP
- FOURTH ROUND**

ROUND 8

FRIDAY 7 APRIL 2006
Hull FC v Leeds Rhinos 8:00
Salford City Reds v Huddersfield Giants ..8:00
St Helens v Harlequins 8:00
Wakefield T Wildcats v Wigan Warriors ..8:00
SATURDAY 8 APRIL 2006
Bradford Bulls v Warrington Wolves 6:00
Catalans Dragons v Castleford Tigers ..6:00
at Figueres

ROUND 9

THURSDAY 13 APRIL 2006
Leeds Rhinos v Bradford Bulls.............TBA
FRIDAY 14 APRIL 2006
Harlequins v Catalans Dragons 3:00
Huddersfield Giants v Hull FC 7:30
St Helens v Wigan Warriors ....TBA
Wakefield T Wildcats v Castleford Tigers ..7:30
Warrington Wolves v Salford City Reds ..3:00

ROUND 10

MONDAY 17 APRIL 2006
Castleford Tigers v Warrington Wolves..TBA
Catalans Dragons v St Helens 6:00
Hull FC v Wakefield Trinity Wildcats 3:15
Salford City Reds v Leeds Rhinos 3:00
Wigan Warriors v Harlequins................8:00
TUESDAY 18 APRIL 2006
Bradford Bulls v Huddersfield Giants ....TBA

ROUND 11

FRIDAY 21 APRIL 2006
Leeds Rhinos v Castleford Tigers 8:00
Salford City Reds v St Helens 8:00
SATURDAY 22 APRIL 2006
Catalans Dragons v Hull FC 6:00
Huddersfield Giants v Wigan Warriors..6:05
SUNDAY 23 APRIL 2006
Wakefield Trinity Wildcats v Harlequins..3:30
Warrington Wolves v Bradford Bulls 3:00

ROUND 12

FRIDAY 28 APRIL 2006
Bradford Bulls v Catalans Dragons 8:00
St Helens v Wakefield Trinity Wildcats..8:00
SATURDAY 29 APRIL 2006
Harlequins v Huddersfield Giants 6:05
SUNDAY 30 APRIL 2006
Castleford Tigers v Salford City Reds ..3:30
Hull FC v Wigan Warriors 3:15
MONDAY 1 MAY 2006
Warrington Wolves v Leeds Rhinos ......TBA

ROUND 13

FRIDAY 5 MAY 2006
Hull FC v Bradford Bulls 8:00
Leeds Rhinos v Harlequins 8:00
Salford City Reds v Wakefield T Wildcats ..8:00
Wigan Warriors v Castleford Tigers 8:00
SATURDAY 6 MAY 2006
Catalans Dragons v Warrington Wolves..6:00
Huddersfield Giants v St Helens 6:05

ROUND 14

FRIDAY 12 MAY 2006
Leeds Rhinos v Hull FC 8:00
St Helens v Warrington Wolves............8:00
SATURDAY 13 MAY 2006
Harlequins v Bradford Bulls..................3:00
Wakefield T Wildcats v Wigan Warriors..6:05
SUNDAY 14 MAY 2006
Castleford Tigers v Catalans Dragons ..3:30
Huddersfield Giants v Salford City Reds ..3:00

**SUNDAY 21 MAY 2006
POWERGEN CHALLENGE CUP
- FIFTH ROUND**

ROUND 15

FRIDAY 26 MAY 2006
Bradford Bulls v Leeds Rhinos 8:00
SATURDAY 27 MAY 2006
Catalans Dragons v Wakefield T Wildcats..6:00
at Narbonne
Wigan Warriors v St Helens..................6:05
SUNDAY 28 MAY 2006
HullFC v Huddersfield Giants 3:15
Warrington Wolves v Castleford Tigers ..3:00
MONDAY 29 MAY 2006
Salford City Reds v Harlequins..............TBA

SUNDAY 4 JUNE 2006
POWERGEN CHALLENGE CUP
- QUARTER FINALS

ROUND 16

FRIDAY 9 JUNE 2006
Leeds Rhinos v Wigan Warriors 8:00
St Helens v Hull FC 8:00
SATURDAY 10 JUNE 2006
Harlequins v Warrington Wolves 6:05
SUNDAY 11 JUNE 2006
Castleford Tigers v Bradford Bulls 3:30
Huddersfield Giants v Catalans Dragons ..3:00
Wakefield T Wildcats v Salford City Reds ..3:30

ROUND 17

FRIDAY 16 JUNE 2006
Bradford Bulls v St Helens...................8:00
HullFC v Harlequins 8:00
Salford City Reds v Leeds Rhinos 8:00
SATURDAY 17 JUNE 2006
Wigan Warriors v Catalans Dragons 6:05
SUNDAY 18 JUNE 2006
Castleford Tigers v Huddersfield Giants ..3:30
Warrington Wolves v Wakefield T Wildcats ..3:00

ROUND 18

FRIDAY 23 JUNE 2006
Bradford Bulls v Huddersfield Giants....8:00
Leeds Rhinos v Wakefield T Wildcats ..8:00
Wigan Warriors v Warrington Wolves ..8:00
SATURDAY 24 JUNE 2006
Catalans Dragons v Harlequins 6:00
at Narbonne
St Helens v Salford City Reds 6:05
SUNDAY 25 JUNE 2006
Hull FC v Castleford Tigers 3:15

ROUND 19

FRIDAY 30 JUNE 2006
Salford City Reds v Bradford Bulls 8:00
SATURDAY 1 JULY 2006
Castleford Tigers v Warrington Wolves ..6:05
Catalans Dragons v Hull FC 6:00
at Narbonne
Harlequins v Wigan Warriors................3:00
SUNDAY 2 JULY 2006
Huddersfield Giants v Leeds Rhinos 3:00
Wakefield Trinity Wildcats v St Helens..3:30

ROUND 20

FRIDAY 7 JULY 2006
Leeds Rhinos v Bradford Bulls 8:00
St Helens v Catalans Dragons 8:00
Wigan Warriors v Wakefield T Wildcats ..8:00
SATURDAY 8 JULY 2006
Harlequins v Castleford Tigers..............3:00
Salford City Reds v Hull FC 6:05
SUNDAY 9 JULY 2006
Warrington Wolves v Huddersfield Giants ..3:00

ROUND 21

FRIDAY 14 JULY 2006
Bradford Bulls v Catalans Dragons 8:00
St Helens v Harlequins 8:00
Wigan Warriors v Salford City Reds 8:00
SATURDAY 15 JULY 2006
Hull FC v Warrington Wolves 6:05
SUNDAY 16 JULY 2006
Castleford Tigers v Leeds Rhinos 3:30
Huddersfield Giants v Wakefield T Wildcats ..3:00

ROUND 22

SATURDAY 22 JULY 2006
Catalans Dragons v Salford City Reds ..6:00
at Narbonne
Harlequins v Hull FC 3:00
Leeds Rhinos v St Helens 6:05
SUNDAY 23 JULY 2006
Huddersfield Giants v Castleford Tigers ..3:00
Wakefield T Wildcats v Bradford Bulls..3:30
Warrington Wolves v Wigan Warriors ..3:00

SUNDAY 30 JULY 2006
POWERGEN CHALLENGE CUP
- SEMI FINALS

ROUND 23

FRIDAY 4 AUGUST 2006
Bradford Bulls v Warrington Wolves 8:00
Hull FC v Leeds Rhinos 8:00
Salford City Reds v Harlequins 8:00
St Helens v Huddersfield Giants 8:00
Wigan Warriors v Catalans Dragons 8:00
SUNDAY 6 AUGUST 2006
Castleford Tigers v Wakefield T Wildcats ..3:30

ROUND 24

FRIDAY 11 AUGUST 2006
Leeds Rhinos v Wigan Warriors 8:00
Salford City Reds v Warrington Wolves ..8:00
SATURDAY 12 AUGUST 2006
Harlequins v Bradford Bulls..................3:00
SUNDAY 13 AUGUST 2006
Castleford Tigers v St Helens...............3:30
Huddersfield Giants v Hull FC 3:00
Wakefield T Wildcats v Catalans Dragons ..3:30

ROUND 25

FRIDAY 18 AUGUST 2006
Bradford Bulls v Castleford Tigers 8:00
Wakefield T Wildcats v Leeds Rhinos ..8:00
Wigan Warriors v Huddersfield Giants..8:00
SATURDAY 19 AUGUST 2006
Catalans Dragons v St Helens 6:00
at Narbonne
SUNDAY 20 AUGUST 2006
Hull FC v Salford City Reds 3:15
Warrington Wolves v Harlequins 3:00

SATURDAY 26 AUGUST 2006
POWERGEN CHALLENGE CUP - FINAL

ROUND 26

FRIDAY 1 SEPTEMBER 2006
Leeds Rhinos v Warrington Wolves......8:00
St Helens v Wakefield Trinity Wildcats..8:00
Wigan Warriors v Bradford Bulls..........8:00
SUNDAY 3 SEPTEMBER 2006
Castleford Tigers v Harlequins..............3:30
Huddersfield Giants v Salford City Reds ..3:00
Hull FC v Catalans Dragons 3:15

ROUND 27

FRIDAY 8 SEPTEMBER 2006
Bradford Bulls v Wakefield T Wildcats..8:00
Salford City Reds v Castleford Tigers ..8:00
St Helens v Leeds Rhinos....................8:00
SATURDAY 9 SEPTEMBER 2006
Catalans Dragons v Huddersfield Giants ..6:00
at Narbonne
Harlequins v Wigan Warriors................3:00
SUNDAY 10 SEPTEMBER 2006
Warrington Wolves v Hull FC................3:00

ROUND 28

FRIDAY 15 SEPTEMBER 2006
Leeds Rhinos v Catalans Dragons 8:00
Wigan Warriors v Hull FC 8:00
SATURDAY 16 SEPTEMBER 2006
Harlequins v Salford City Reds 3:00
SUNDAY 17 SEPTEMBER 2006
Huddersfield Giants v Bradford Bulls....3:00
Wakefield T Wildcats v Castleford Tigers ..3:30
Warrington Wolves v St Helens 3:00

PLAY-OFFS

WEEKEND COMMENCING
FRIDAY 22 SEPTEMBER 2006
ELIMINATION PLAY-OFFS

WEEKEND COMMENCING
FRIDAY 29 SEPTEMBER 2006
QUALIFYING SEMI-FINAL
ELIMINATION SEMI-FINAL

WEEKEND COMMENCING
FRIDAY 6 OCTOBER 2006
FINAL ELIMINATOR

SATURDAY 14 OCTOBER 2006
SUPER LEAGUE XI GRAND FINAL

KEY DATES FOR THE
2006 AUSTRALIAN CALENDAR

NRL PREMIERSHIP OPENING ROUND

FRIDAY 10 / SATURDAY 11 /
SUNDAY 12 MARCH 2006
Brisbane Broncos v
North Queensland Cowboys
Bulldogs v Penrith Panthers
Manly Sea Eagles v Canberra Raiders
New Zealand Warrriors v Melbourne Storm
Newcastle Knights v Parramatta Eels
South Sydney Rabbitohs v Sydney Roosters
Wests Tigers v St George-Illawarra Dragons
Bye - Cronulla Sharks

STATE OF ORIGIN SERIES

WEDNESDAY 24 MAY 2006
Game 1 *(Sydney)*

WEDNESDAY 14 JUNE 2006
Game 2 *(Brisbane)*

WEDNESDAY 5 JULY 2006
Game 3 *(Melbourne)*

NRL PREMIERSHIP FINALS SERIES

FRIDAY 8 / SATURDAY 9 /
SUNDAY 10 SEPTEMBER 2006
Opening round

NRL GRAND FINAL

SUNDAY 1 OCTOBER 2006
(Telstra Stadium, Sydney)

CATALANS DRAGONS HOME FIXTURES -
All kick-offs central european time, and at Stade Aime Giral (Perpignan) unless stated

NATIONAL LEAGUE 2006 FIXTURES

NATIONAL LEAGUE ONE

SUNDAY 2 APRIL 2006
POWERGEN CHALLENGE CUP
- FOURTH ROUND

SUNDAY 9 APRIL 2006
Doncaster Lakers v Rochdale Hornets 3:00
Halifax v Leigh Centurions...........................3:00
Oldham v Hull Kingston Rovers 3:00
Whitehaven v Batley Bulldogs 3:00
Widnes Vikings v York City Knights 3:00

FRIDAY 14 APRIL 2006
Batley Bulldogs v Halifax 7:30
Doncaster Lakers v Whitehaven 7:30
Leigh Centurions v Widnes Vikings............3:00
Rochdale Hornets v Oldham 3:00
York City Knights v Hull Kingston Rovers ..6:00

MONDAY 17 APRIL 2006
Halifax v York City Knights 3:00
Hull Kingston Rovers v Leigh Centurions ..3:00
Oldham v Doncaster Lakers 3:00
Whitehaven v Rochdale Hornets 3:00
Widnes Vikings v Batley Bulldogs 3:00

SUNDAY 30 APRIL 2006
Batley Bulldogs v Doncaster Lakers 3:00
Hull Kingston Rovers v Halifax 3:00
Leigh Centurions v Oldham 3:00
Rochdale Hornets v York City Knights........3:00
Whitehaven v Widnes Vikings 3:00

SUNDAY 14 MAY 2006
Doncaster Lakers v Batley Bulldogs 3:00
Halifax v Rochdale Hornets 3:00
Oldham v Whitehaven 3:00
Widnes Vikings v Hull Kingston Rovers 3:00
York City Knights v Leigh Centurions 3:00

SUNDAY 21 MAY 2006
POWERGEN CHALLENGE CUP - FIFTH ROUND

SUNDAY 28 MAY 2006
Batley Bulldogs v York City Knights 3:00
Hull Kingston Rovers v Oldham 3:00
Leigh Centurions v Doncaster Lakers 3:00
Rochdale Hornets v Widnes Vikings 3:00
Whitehaven v Halifax 3:00

SUNDAY 4 JUNE 2006
Batley Bulldogs v Leigh Centurions............3:00
Doncaster Lakers v Hull Kingston Rovers ..3:00
Halifax v Oldham 3:00
Rochdale Hornets v Whitehaven 3:00
York City Knights v Widnes Vikings 3:00

POWERGEN CHALLENGE CUP
- QUARTER FINALS

SUNDAY 11 JUNE 2006
Halifax v Batley Bulldogs 3:00
Hull Kingston Rovers v Whitehaven 3:00
Leigh Centurions v Rochdale Hornets 3:00
Oldham v York City Knights........................3:00
at TBA
Widnes Vikings v Doncaster Lakers 3:00

SUNDAY 25 JUNE 2006
Batley Bulldogs v Widnes Vikings 3:00
Doncaster Lakers v Halifax 3:00
Rochdale Hornets v Hull Kingston Rovers 3:00
Whitehaven v Leigh Centurions...................3:00
York City Knights v Oldham........................3:00

SUNDAY 2 JULY 2006
Hull Kingston Rovers v Batley Bulldogs 3:00
Leigh Centurions v Halifax 3:00
Oldham v Rochdale Hornets 3:00
at TBA
Widnes Vikings v Whitehaven 3:00
York City Knights v Doncaster Lakers 3:00

SUNDAY 9 JULY 2006
Batley Bulldogs v Rochdale Hornets 3:00
Doncaster Lakers v Leigh Centurions 3:00
Halifax v Hull Kingston Rovers 3:00
Whitehaven v York City Knights 3:00
Widnes Vikings v Oldham 3:00

FRIDAY 21 JULY 2006
Oldham v Batley Bulldogs 7:45

SUNDAY 23 JULY 2006
Hull Kingston Rovers v Widnes Vikings 3:00
Leigh Centurions v Whitehaven..................3:00
Rochdale Hornets v Doncaster Lakers 3:00
York City Knights v Halifax 3:00

SUNDAY 30 JULY 2006
Batley Bulldogs v Whitehaven 3:00
Doncaster Lakers v Oldham 3:00
Halifax v Widnes Vikings 3:00
Hull Kingston Rovers v York City Knights ..3:00
Rochdale Hornets v Leigh Centurions 3:00

POWERGEN CHALLENGE CUP - SEMI-FINALS

SUNDAY 6 AUGUST 2006
Leigh Centurions v Hull Kingston Rovers ..3:00
Oldham v Halifax 3:00
Whitehaven v Doncaster Lakers 3:00
Widnes Vikings v Rochdale Hornets 3:00
York City Knights v Batley Bulldogs 3:00

SUNDAY 13 AUGUST 2006
Batley Bulldogs v Oldham 3:00
Halifax v Doncaster Lakers 3:00
Hull Kingston Rovers v Rochdale Hornets ..3:00
Widnes Vikings v Leigh Centurions 3:00
York City Knights v Whitehaven 3:00

SUNDAY 20 AUGUST 2006
Doncaster Lakers v York City Knights 3:00
Leigh Centurions v Batley Bulldogs 3:00
Oldham v Widnes Vikings 3:00
Rochdale Hornets v Halifax 3:00
Whitehaven v Hull Kingston Rovers 3:00

SATURDAY 26 AUGUST 2006
POWERGEN CHALLENGE CUP - FINAL

SUNDAY 3 SEPTEMBER 2006
Batley Bulldogs v Hull Kingston Rovers 3:00
Doncaster Lakers v Widnes Vikings 3:00
Halifax v Whitehaven 3:00
Oldham v Leigh Centurions 3:00
York City Knights v Rochdale Hornets.......3:00

SUNDAY 10 SEPTEMBER 2006
Hull Kingston Rovers v Doncaster Lakers ..3:00
Leigh Centurions v York City Knights 3:00
Rochdale Hornets v Batley Bulldogs 3:00
Whitehaven v Oldham 3:00
Widnes Vikings v Halifax 3:00

SUNDAY 17 SEPTEMBER 2006
ELIMINATION PLAY-OFFS

SUNDAY 24 SEPTEMBER 2006
QUALIFYING SEMI-FINAL
ELIMINATION SEMI-FINAL

SUNDAY 1 OCTOBER 2006
FINAL ELIMINATOR

SUNDAY 8 OCTOBER 2006
GRAND FINAL

NATIONAL LEAGUE TWO

SUNDAY 2 APRIL 2006
POWERGEN CHALLENGE CUP
- FOURTH ROUND

FRIDAY 7 APRIL 2006
Sheffield Eagles v Keighley Cougars 8:00

SUNDAY 9 APRIL 2006
Blackpool Panthers v Hunslet Hawks 3:00
Featherstone Rovers v Gateshead Thunder ..3:00
London Skolars v Dewsbury Rams 3:00
Swinton Lions v Barrow Raiders 3:00
Workington Town v Celtic Crusaders 3:00

FRIDAY 14 APRIL 2006
Celtic Crusaders v London Skolars 6:00
Dewsbury Rams v Keighley Cougars..........7:30
Featherstone Rovers v Sheffield Eagles......7:30
Hunslet Hawks v Gateshead Thunder 7:30
Swinton Lions v Blackpool Panthers 3:00
Workington Town v Barrow Raiders 3:00

MONDAY 17 APRIL 2006
Barrow Raiders v Featherstone Rovers 3:00
Blackpool Panthers v Dewsbury Rams 3:00
Gateshead Thunder v Workington Town 3:00
Keighley Cougars v Hunslet Hawks 3:00
London Skolars v Swinton Lions................3:00
Sheffield Eagles v Celtic Crusaders 12:00

FRIDAY 28 APRIL 2006
Sheffield Eagles v Workington Town 8:00

SUNDAY 30 APRIL 2006
Barrow Raiders v Celtic Crusaders 3:00
Dewsbury Rams v Featherstone Rovers 3:00
Hunslet Hawks v London Skolars 3:30
Keighley Cougars v Blackpool Panthers 3:00
Swinton Lions v Gateshead Thunder..........3:00

SATURDAY 6 MAY 2006
Gateshead Thunder v Keighley Cougars 4:00

SUNDAY 7 MAY 2006
Celtic Crusaders v Hunslet Hawks 3:00
Dewsbury Rams v Sheffield Eagles............3:00
Featherstone Rovers v Blackpool Panthers ..3:00
London Skolars v Barrow Raiders..............3:00
Workington Town v Swinton Lions 3:00

FRIDAY 12 MAY 2006
Sheffield Eagles v Gateshead Thunder 8:00

SUNDAY 14 MAY 2006
Barrow Raiders v Swinton Lions 3:00
Blackpool Panthers v London Skolars........3:00
Hunslet Hawks v Featherstone Rovers 3:30
Keighley Cougars v Celtic Crusaders..........3:00
Workington Town v Dewsbury Rams 3:00

SUNDAY 21 MAY 2006
Celtic Crusaders v Blackpool Panthers 3:00
Featherstone Rovers v Workington Town ..3:00
Gateshead Thunder v Barrow Raiders........3:00
Hunslet Hawks v Keighley Cougars 3:30
London Skolars v Sheffield Eagles 3:00
Swinton Lions v Dewsbury Rams 3:00

POWERGEN CHALLENGE CUP - FIFTH ROUND

FRIDAY 26 MAY 2006
Sheffield Eagles v Hunslet Hawks 8:00

SUNDAY 28 MAY 2006
Barrow Raiders v London Skolars...............3:00
Blackpool Panthers v Swinton Lions 3:30
Dewsbury Rams v Celtic Crusaders 3:00
Keighley Cougars v Featherstone Rovers ..3:00
Workington Town v Gateshead Thunder 3:00

SUNDAY 4 JUNE 2006
Barrow Raiders v Workington Town 3:00
Celtic Crusaders v Keighley Cougars..........3:00
Featherstone Rovers v Dewsbury Rams 3:00
Gateshead Thunder v Sheffield Eagles 3:00
London Skolars v Blackpool Panthers........3:00
Swinton Lions v Hunslet Hawks 3:00

**POWERGEN CHALLENGE CUP
- QUARTER FINALS**

FRIDAY 9 JUNE 2006
Sheffield Eagles v Barrow Raiders..............8:00

SUNDAY 11 JUNE 2006
Dewsbury Rams v London Skolars 3:00
Hunslet Hawks v Blackpool Panthers 3:30
Keighley Cougars v Gateshead Thunder 3:00
Swinton Lions v Celtic Crusaders 3:00
Workington Town v Featherstone Rovers ..3:00

SUNDAY 18 JUNE 2006
Barrow Raiders v Hunslet Hawks 3:00
Blackpool Panthers v Keighley Cougars 3:00
Celtic Crusaders v Sheffield Eagles 3:00
Featherstone Rovers v Swinton Lions 3:00
Gateshead Thunder v Dewsbury Rams 3:00
London Skolars v Workington Town 3:00

FRIDAY 23 JUNE 2006
Sheffield Eagles v Featherstone Rovers......8:00

SUNDAY 25 JUNE 2006
Blackpool Panthers v Gateshead Thunder ..3:00
Hunslet Hawks v Dewsbury Rams..............3:30
Keighley Cougars v Barrow Raiders 3:00
London Skolars v Celtic Crusaders 3:00
Swinton Lions v Workington Town 3:00

SUNDAY 2 JULY 2006
Barrow Raiders v Sheffield Eagles..............3:00
Celtic Crusaders v Swinton Lions 3:00
Dewsbury Rams v Blackpool Panthers 3:00
Featherstone Rovers v Keighley Cougars ..3:00
Gateshead Thunder v London Skolars.........3:00
Workington Town v Hunslet Hawks...........3:00

FRIDAY 7 JULY 2006
Sheffield Eagles v Swinton Lions 8:00

SUNDAY 9 JULY 2006
Barrow Raiders v Gateshead Thunder 3:00
Blackpool Panthers v Workington Town 3:00
Featherstone Rovers v London Skolars.......3:00
Hunslet Hawks v Celtic Crusaders.............3:30
Keighley Cougars v Dewsbury Rams..........3:00

SUNDAY 16 JULY 2006
Celtic Crusaders v Barrow Raiders 3:00
Dewsbury Rams v Hunslet Hawks..............3:00
Gateshead Thunder v Blackpool Panthers ..3:00
London Skolars v Keighley Cougars 3:00
Swinton Lions v Featherstone Rovers 3:00
Workington Town v Sheffield Eagles 3:00

FRIDAY 21 JULY 2006
Sheffield Eagles v London Skolars 8:00

SUNDAY 23 JULY 2006
Blackpool Panthers v Celtic Crusaders 3:00
Dewsbury Rams v Gateshead Thunder 3:00
Featherstone Rovers v Barrow Raiders 3:00
Hunslet Hawks v Swinton Lions 3:30
Keighley Cougars v Workington Town........3:00

SUNDAY 30 JULY 2006
Barrow Raiders v Keighley Cougars 3:00
Celtic Crusaders v Dewsbury Rams 3:00
Gateshead Thunder v Featherstone Rovers ..3:00
London Skolars v Hunslet Hawks 3:00
Swinton Lions v Sheffield Eagles 3:00
Workington Town v Blackpool Panthers 3:00

POWERGEN CHALLENGE CUP - SEMI-FINALS

SUNDAY 6 AUGUST 2006
Blackpool Panthers v Sheffield Eagles........3:00
Celtic Crusaders v Gateshead Thunder 3:00
Dewsbury Rams v Barrow Raiders 3:00
Hunslet Hawks v Workington Town............3:30
Keighley Cougars v Swinton Lions 3:00
London Skolars v Featherstone Rovers.......3:00

FRIDAY 11 AUGUST 2006
Sheffield Eagles v Dewsbury Rams.............8:00

SUNDAY 13 AUGUST 2006
Barrow Raiders v Blackpool Panthers 3:00
Featherstone Rovers v Celtic Crusaders ...3:00
Gateshead Thunder v Hunslet Hawks 3:00
Swinton Lions v London Skolars................3:00
Workington Town v Keighley Cougars 3:00

SUNDAY 20 AUGUST 2006
Blackpool Panthers v Featherstone Rovers ..3:00
Celtic Crusaders v Workington Town..........3:00
Dewsbury Rams v Swinton Lions 3:00
Hunslet Hawks v Barrow Raiders 3:30
Keighley Cougars v Sheffield Eagles 3:00
London Skolars v Gateshead Thunder........3:00

SATURDAY 26 AUGUST 2006
POWERGEN CHALLENGE CUP - FINAL

FRIDAY 1 SEPTEMBER 2006
Sheffield Eagles v Blackpool Panthers........8:00

SUNDAY 3 SEPTEMBER 2006
Barrow Raiders v Dewsbury Rams 3:00
Featherstone Rovers v Hunslet Hawks 3:00
Gateshead Thunder v Celtic Crusaders 3:00
Swinton Lions v Keighley Cougars 3:00
Workington Town v London Skolars 3:00

SUNDAY 10 SEPTEMBER 2006
Blackpool Panthers v Barrow Raiders 3:00
Celtic Crusaders v Featherstone Rovers ...3:00
Dewsbury Rams v Workington Town 3:00
Gateshead Thunder v Swinton Lions 3:00
Hunslet Hawks v Sheffield Eagles 3:30
Keighley Cougars v London Skolars 3:00

SUNDAY 17 SEPTEMBER 2006
ELIMINATION PLAY-OFFS

SUNDAY 24 SEPTEMBER 2006
QUALIFYING SEMI-FINAL
ELIMINATION SEMI-FINAL

SUNDAY 1 OCTOBER 2006
FINAL ELIMINATOR

SUNDAY 8 OCTOBER 2006
GRAND FINAL

NATIONAL LEAGUE CUP

SUNDAY 12 FEBRUARY 2006
Blackpool Panthers v Leigh Centurions......3:00
Celtic Crusaders v Hemel Hempstead Stags ..12:00
Dewsbury Rams v Batley Bulldogs 3:00
Doncaster Lakers v Hunslet Hawks 3:00
Featherstone Rovers v Sheffield Eagles......3:00
Gateshead Thunder v Barrow Raiders 3:00
Halifax v Keighley Cougars 3:00
Rochdale Hornets v Oldham 3:00
St Albans Centurions v London Skolars 2:30
Whitehaven v Workington Town 3:00
Widnes Vikings v Swinton Lions 3:00
York City Knights v Hull Kingston Rovers ..3:00

FRIDAY 17 FEBRUARY 2006
Hunslet Hawks v Dewsbury Rams..............7:30
Sheffield Eagles v York City Knights 8:00

SUNDAY 19 FEBRUARY 2006
Barrow Raiders v Whitehaven 3:00
Batley Bulldogs v Doncaster Lakers 3:00
Hemel Hempstead v St Albans 2:30
Hull Kingston Rovers v Featherstone Rovers..3:00
Keighley Cougars v Rochdale Hornets 3:00
Leigh Centurions v Widnes Vikings............3:00
London Skolars v Celtic Crusaders 3:00
Oldham v Halifax 3:00
Swinton Lions v Blackpool Panthers 3:00
Workington Town v Gateshead Thunder 3:00

FRIDAY 24 FEBRUARY 2006
Sheffield Eagles v Hull Kingston Rovers 8:00

SUNDAY 26 FEBRUARY 2006
Batley Bulldogs v Hunslet Hawks 3:00
Doncaster Lakers v Dewsbury Rams...........3:00
Featherstone Rovers v York City Knights ..3:00
Halifax v Rochdale Hornets 3:00
London Skolars v Hemel Hempstead Stags ..3:00
Oldham v Keighley Cougars 3:00
St Albans Centurions v Celtic Crusaders ...2:30
Swinton Lions v Leigh Centurions..............3:00
Whitehaven v Gateshead Thunder 3:00
Widnes Vikings v Blackpool Panthers 3:00
Workington Town v Barrow Raiders 3:00

SUNDAY 5 MARCH 2006
Blackpool Panthers v Swinton Lions 3:00
Celtic Crusaders v London Skolars 3:00
Dewsbury Rams v Hunslet Hawks..............3:00
Doncaster Lakers v Batley Bulldogs...........3:00
Featherstone Rovers v Hull Kingston Rovers ..3:00
Gateshead Thunder v Workington Town ...3:00
Halifax v Oldham 3:00
Rochdale Hornets v Keighley Cougars 3:00
St Albans v Hemel Hempstead 2:30
Whitehaven v Barrow Raiders 3:00
Widnes Vikings v Leigh Centurions............3:30
York City Knights v Sheffield Eagles 3:00

SUNDAY 12 MARCH 2006
**POWERGEN CHALLENGE CUP
- THIRD ROUND**

SUNDAY 19 MARCH 2006
Barrow Raiders v Gateshead Thunder 3:00
Batley Bulldogs v Dewsbury Rams 3:00
Hemel Hempstead Stags v Celtic Crusaders ..2:30
Hull Kingston Rovers v York City Knights ..3:00
Hunslet Hawks v Doncaster Lakers 3:30
Keighley Cougars v Halifax 3:00
Leigh Centurions v Blackpool Panthers 3:00
London Skolars v St Albans Centurions 3:00
Oldham v Rochdale Hornets 3:00
Sheffield Eagles v Featherstone Rovers......2:00
at TBA
Swinton Lions v Widnes Vikings 3:00
Workington Town v Whitehaven 3:00

SUNDAY 26 MARCH 2006
Barrow Raiders v Workington Town 3:00
Blackpool Panthers v Widnes Vikings 3:00
Celtic Crusaders v St Albans Centurions ...3:00
Dewsbury Rams v Doncaster Lakers...........3:00
Gateshead Thunder v Whitehaven 3:00
Hemel Hempstead Stags v London Skolars ..2:30
Hull Kingston Rovers v Sheffield Eagles 3:00
Hunslet Hawks v Batley Bulldogs 3:30
Keighley Cougars v Oldham 3:00
Leigh Centurions v Swinton Lions..............3:00
Rochdale Hornets v Halifax 3:00
York City Knights v Featherstone Rovers ..3:00

313

Grand Finals 1998-2004

1998

DIVISION ONE GRAND FINAL

Saturday 26th September 1998

FEATHERSTONE ROVERS 22 WAKEFIELD TRINITY 24

ROVERS: 1 Steve Collins; 2 Carl Hall; 3 Shaun Irwin; 4 Danny Baker; 5 Karl Pratt; 6 Jamie Coventry; 7 Ty Fallins; 8 Chico Jackson; 9 Richard Chapman; 10 Stuart Dickens; 11 Gary Price; 12 Neil Lowe; 13 Richard Slater. Subs: 14 Paddy Handley for Coventry (70); 15 Asa Amone for Lowe (50); 16 Micky Clarkson for Jackson (50); 17 Steve Dooler (not used). **Tries:** Baker (15), Jackson (45), Collins (49), Hall (69); **Goals:** Chapman 3.
TRINITY: 1 Martyn Holland; 2 Josh Bostock; 3 Adam Hughes; 4 Martin Law; 5 Kevin Gray; 6 Garen Casey; 7 Roger Kenworthy; 8 Francis Stephenson; 9 Roy Southernwood; 10 Gary Lord; 11 Ian Hughes; 12 Sonny Whakarau; 13 Matt Fuller. Subs: 14 Sean Richardson for I Hughes (32); 15 Andy Fisher for Lord (26); 16 David Mycoe (not used); 17 Wayne McDonald for Whakarau (70); Lord for Stephenson (40); Stephenson for Lord (70).
Tries: Southernwood (2), Bostock (7, 25), Casey (58), Stephenson (76); **Goals:** Casey 2.
League Express Men of the Match:
Rovers: Richard Chapman; *Trinity:* Garen Casey.
Penalty count: 8-3; **Half time:** 6-12; **Referee:** Nick Oddy (Halifax); **Attendance:** 8,224 *(at McAlpine Stadium, Huddersfield).*

SUPER LEAGUE GRAND FINAL

Saturday 24th October 1998

LEEDS RHINOS 4 WIGAN WARRIORS 10

RHINOS: 1 Iestyn Harris (C); 22 Leroy Rivett; 3 Richie Blackmore; 4 Brad Godden; 5 Francis Cummins; 13 Daryl Powell; 7 Ryan Sheridan; 8 Martin Masella; 21 Terry Newton; 25 Darren Fleary; 11 Adrian Morley; 17 Anthony Farrell; 12 Marc Glanville. Subs: 20 Jamie Mathiou for Masella (25); 24 Marcus St Hilaire for Powell (40); 14 Graham Holroyd for Newton (27); 27 Andy Hay for Fleary (54); Powell for Godden (58); Masella for Mathiou (71).
Try: Blackmore (20).
WARRIORS: 1 Kris Radlinski; 2 Jason Robinson; 3 Danny Moore; 4 Gary Connolly; 5 Mark Bell; 6 Henry Paul; 7 Tony Smith; 16 Terry O'Connor; 9 Robbie McCormack; 10 Tony Mestrov; 20 Lee Gilmour; 17 Stephen Holgate; 13 Andy Farrell (C). Subs: 8 Neil Cowie for O'Connor (18BB, rev 48); 14 Mick Cassidy for McCormack (19BB, rev 27); 25 Paul Johnson for Moore (37); 12 Simon Haughton for Gilmour (27BB, rev 33); Haughton for Holgate (33); Cowie for Mestrov (54); Cassidy for Haughton (64); Holgate for Cowie (68); Haughton for Gilmour (71BB, rev 75); Mestrov for O'Connor (75BB).
Try: Robinson (37); **Goals:** Farrell 3.
League Express Men of the Match:
Rhinos: Iestyn Harris; *Warriors:* Jason Robinson.
Penalty count: 7-13; **Half-time:** 4-6; **Referee:** Russell Smith (Castleford); **Attendance:** 43,553 *(at Old Trafford, Manchester).*

1999

NORTHERN FORD PREMIERSHIP GRAND FINAL

Saturday 25th September 1999

DEWSBURY RAMS 11 HUNSLET HAWKS 12

RAMS: 1 Nathan Graham; 2 Alex Godfrey; 3 Paul Evans; 4 Brendan O'Meara; 5 Adrian Flynn; 6 Richard Agar; 7 Barry Eaton; 8 Alan Boothroyd; 9 Paul Delaney; 10 Matthew Long; 11 Andy Spink; 12 Mark Haigh; 13 Damian Ball. Subs: 14 Brendan Williams for Eaton (5BB, rev 15); 15 Sean Richardson for Haigh (50); 16 Simon Hicks for Long (25); 17 Paul Medley for Spink (50); Williams for Evans (61); Long for Boothroyd (71); Spink for Long (78).
Tries: Flynn (27), Ball (54); **Goal:** Eaton; **Field goal:** Agar.
HAWKS: 1 Abraham Fatnowna; 2 Chris Ross; 3 Shaun Irwin; 4 Paul Cook; 5 Iain Higgins; 6 Marcus Vassilakopoulos; 7 Latham Tawhai; 8 Richard Hayes; 9 Richard Pachniuk; 10 Steve Pryce; 11 Rob Wilson; 12 Jamie Leighton; 13 Lee St Hilaire. Subs: 14 Mick Coyle for Wilson (57); 15 Phil Kennedy for Pryce (35); 16 Jamie Thackray for St Hilaire (25); 17 Richard Baker for Higgins (55); Higgins for Fatnowna (62); Pryce for Kennedy (65).
Tries: Cook (31), Higgins (46);
Goal: Ross; **Field goals:** Tawhai, Leighton.
League Express Men of the Match:
Rams: Barry Eaton; *Hawks:* Latham Tawhai.
Penalty count: 8-5; **Half-time:** 7-7; **Referee:** Steve Ganson (St Helens); **Attendance:** 5,783 *(at Headingley Stadium, Leeds).*

SUPER LEAGUE GRAND FINAL

Saturday 9th October 1999

BRADFORD BULLS 6 ST HELENS 8

BULLS: 28 Stuart Spruce; 2 Tevita Vaikona; 20 Scott Naylor; 5 Michael Withers; 17 Leon Pryce; 6 Henry Paul; 1 Robbie Paul (C); 10 Paul Anderson; 9 James Lowes; 29 Stuart Fielden; 15 David Boyle; 23 Bernard Dwyer; 13 Steve McNamara. Subs: 14 Paul Deacon for R Paul (53); 4 Nathan McAvoy (not used); 12 Mike Forshaw for McNamara (18); 22 Brian McDermott for Anderson (18); Anderson for Fielden (61); Fielden for Dwyer (65); R Paul for Deacon (72).
Try: H Paul (18); **Goal:** H Paul.
SAINTS: 1 Paul Atcheson; 14 Chris Smith; 3 Kevin Iro; 4 Paul Newlove; 5 Anthony Sullivan; 13 Paul Sculthorpe; 20 Tommy Martyn; 8 Apollo Perelini; 9 Keiron Cunningham; 10 Julian O'Neill; 2 Fereti Tuilagi; 21 Sonny Nickle; 11 Chris Joynt (C). Subs: 26 Paul Wellens for Martyn (52); 6 Sean Hoppe for Newlove (43); 16 Vila Matautia for O'Neill (20); 7 Sean Long for Perelini (24); Perelini for Matautia (46); O'Neill for Perelini (69).
Tries: Iro (65); **Goals:** Long 2.
League Express Men of the Match:
Bulls: Henry Paul; *Saints:* Kevin Iro.
Penalty count: 4-7; **Half-time:** 6-2; **Referee:** Stuart Cummings (Widnes); **Attendance:** 50,717 *(at Old Trafford, Manchester).*

1998...Andy Farrell and coach John Monie toast Wigan's victory

1999...Shaun Irwin brought to ground by Paul Evans

2000

NORTHERN FORD PREMIERSHIP GRAND FINAL

Saturday 29th July 2000

DEWSBURY RAMS 13 LEIGH CENTURIONS 12

RAMS: 1 Nathan Graham; 2 Richard Baker; 4 Dan Potter; 3 Brendan O'Meara; 5 Adrian Flynn; 6 Richard Agar; 7 Barry Eaton; 8 Shayne Williams; 9 David Mycoe; 10 Mark Haigh; 11 Sean Richardson; 12 Daniel Frame; 13 Damian Ball. Subs: 14 Gavin Wood (not used); 15 Paul Delaney for Mycoe (53); 16 Ryan McDonald for Haigh (30); 17 Matthew Long for Williams (23); Haigh for McDonald (64).
Tries: Eaton (2), Long (23); **Goals:** Eaton 2; **Field goal:** Agar.
Sin bin: Williams (66) - use of the elbow.
On report: Richardson (20) - high tackle on Donlan.
CENTURIONS: 1 Stuart Donlan; 5 David Ingram; 3 Paul Anderson; 4 Andy Fairclough; 2 Alan Cross; 6 Liam Bretherton; 7 Kieron Purtill; 8 Tim Street; 9 Mick Higham; 10 Andy Leatham; 11 Simon Baldwin; 12 Heath Cruckshank; 13 Adam Bristow. Subs: 14 James Arkwright for Cross (68); 15 Paul Norman for Street (36); 16 Radney Bowker (not used); 17 David Whittle for Leathem (24); Street for Norman (62).
Tries: Higham (29, 69); **Goals:** Bretherton 2.
Sin bin: Whittle (66) - retaliation.
League Express Men of the Match:
Rams: Richard Agar; *Centurions:* Mick Higham.
Penalty count: 4-4; **Half-time:** 10-6; **Referee:** Robert Connolly (Wigan); **Attendance:** 8,487 *(at Gigg Lane, Bury).*

SUPER LEAGUE GRAND FINAL

Saturday 14th October 2000

ST HELENS 29 WIGAN WARRIORS 16

SAINTS: 17 Paul Wellens; 24 Steve Hall; 3 Kevin Iro; 15 Sean Hoppe; 5 Anthony Sullivan; 20 Tommy Martyn; 7 Sean Long; 8 Apollo Perelini; 9 Keiron Cunningham; 10 Julian O'Neill; 11 Chris Joynt (C); 22 Tim Jonkers; 13 Paul Sculthorpe. Subs: 14 Fereti Tuilagi for O'Neill (20); 12 Sonny Nickle for Perelini (28); 26 John Stankevitch for Jonkers (50); 23 Scott Barrow (not used); Perelini for Nickle (52); Jonkers for Stankevitch (66); Stankevitch for Perelini (67BB); O'Neill for Hall (74).
Tries: Hoppe (7), Joynt (28, 50), Tuilagi (69), Jonkers (80); **Goals:** Long 4; **Field goal:** Sculthorpe.
WARRIORS: 5 Jason Robinson; 2 Brett Dallas; 1 Kris Radlinski; 3 Steve Renouf; 26 David Hodgson; 4 Tony Smith; 7 Willie Peters; 8 Terry O'Connor; 9 Terry Newton; 10 Neil Cowie; 11 Mick Cassidy; 12 Denis Betts; 13 Andy Farrell (C). Subs: 23 Brady Malam for Cowie (30); 17 Tony Mestrov for O'Connor (43); 19 Chris Chester for Cassidy (47BB, rev 69); 14 Lee Gilmour for Betts (51); O'Connor for Mestrov (61); Cowie for Malam (67); Chester for Newton (75).
Tries: Farrell (13), Hodgson (58), Smith (61); **Goals:** Farrell 2.
League Express Men of the Match:
Saints: Chris Joynt; *Warriors:* Andy Farrell.
Penalty count: 10-6; **Half-time:** 11-4; **Referee:** Russell Smith (Castleford); **Attendance:** 58,132 *(at Old Trafford, Manchester).*

2001

NORTHERN FORD PREMIERSHIP GRAND FINAL

Saturday 28th July 2001

OLDHAM 14 WIDNES VIKINGS 24

OLDHAM: 1 Mark Sibson; 2 Joey Hayes; 3 Anthony Gibbons; 4 Pat Rich; 5 Joe McNicholas; 6 David Gibbons; 7 Neil Roden; 8 Leo Casey; 9 Keith Brennan; 10 Paul Norton; 11 Phil Farrell; 12 Bryan Henare; 13 Kevin Mannion. Subs: 14 Mike Ford for Mannion (27); 15 Jason Clegg for Casey (18); 16 John Hough for Brennan (44); 17 Danny Guest for Norton (40BB, rev 54); Mannion for Henare (66); Guest for Clegg (73).
Tries: Brennan (9), Ford (74), Mannion (80); **Goal:** Rich.
VIKINGS: 1 Paul Atcheson; 2 Damian Munro; 3 Craig Weston; 4 Jason Demetriou; 5 Chris Percival; 6 Richard Agar; 7 Martin Crompton; 8 Simon Knox; 9 Phil Cantillon; 10 Stephen Holgate; 11 Steve Gee; 12 Sean Richardson; 13 Tommy Hodgkinson. Subs: 14 Andy Craig for Percival (65); 15 Chris McKinney for Gee (41); 16 Joe Faimalo for Knox (32); 17 Matthew Long for Holgate (23); Knox for Long (49BB, rev 61); Holgate for Long (74).
Tries: Gee (17), Demetriou (38, 60), Cantillon (50), Munro (69); **Goals:** Weston 2.
League Express Men of the Match:
Oldham: Jason Clegg; *Vikings:* Phil Cantillon.
Penalty count: 8-5; **Half-time:** 4-10; **Referee:** Steve Ganson (St Helens); **Attendance:** 8,974 *(at Spotland, Rochdale).*

SUPER LEAGUE GRAND FINAL

Saturday 13th October 2001

BRADFORD BULLS 37 WIGAN WARRIORS 6

BULLS: 5 Michael Withers; 2 Tevita Vaikona; 20 Scott Naylor; 23 Graham Mackay; 3 Leon Pryce; 6 Henry Paul; 1 Robbie Paul (C); 8 Joe Vagana; 9 James Lowes; 22 Brian McDermott; 11 Daniel Gartner; 19 Jamie Peacock; 12 Mike Forshaw. Subs: 29 Stuart Fielden for McDermott (21BB, rev 65); 10 Paul Anderson for Vagana (22); 15 Shane Rigon for Pryce (40); 7 Paul Deacon for R Paul (69); Vagana for Anderson (53); Fielden for Gartner (72); Anderson for Vagana (74).
Tries: Lowes (9), Withers (11, 27, 31), Fielden (65), Mackay (72); **Goals:** H Paul 5, Mackay; **Field goal:** H Paul.
WARRIORS: 1 Kris Radlinski; 2 Brett Dallas; 4 Gary Connolly; 3 Steve Renouf; 5 Brian Carney; 6 Matthew Johns; 7 Adrian Lam; 8 Terry O'Connor; 9 Terry Newton; 20 Harvey Howard; 11 Mick Cassidy; 14 David Furner; 13 Andy Farrell (C). Subs: 15 Paul Johnson for Carney (12BB); 10 Neil Cowie for Howard (17); 12 Denis Betts for O'Connor (32); 19 Chris Chester for Farrell (59); O'Connor for Cowie (55); Howard for Newton (64); Cowie for Cassidy (72).
Try: Lam (63); **Goal:** Furner.
League Express Men of the Match:
Bulls: Michael Withers; *Warriors:* Adrian Lam.
Penalty count: 6-7; **Half-time:** 26-0; **Referee:** Stuart Cummings (Widnes); **Attendance:** 60,164 *(at Old Trafford, Manchester).*

2000... Fereti Tuilagi bursts past Tony Smith

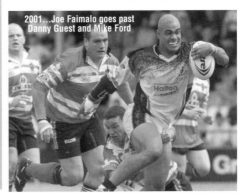

2001...Joe Faimalo goes past Danny Guest and Mike Ford

Grand Finals 1998-2004

2002

NORTHERN FORD PREMIERSHIP GRAND FINAL

Saturday 12th October 2002

HUDDERSFIELD GIANTS 38 LEIGH CENTURIONS 16

GIANTS: 1 Ben Cooper; 2 Hefin O'Hare; 3 Eorl Crabtree; 4 Graeme Hallas; 5 Marcus St Hilaire; 6 Stanley Gene; 7 Chris Thorman; 8 Michael Slicker; 9 Paul March; 10 Jeff Wittenberg; 11 David Atkins; 12 Robert Roberts; 13 Steve McNamara. Subs: 14 Heath Cruckshank for Roberts (24BB); 15 Chris Molyneux for Slicker (53); 16 Darren Turner for March (21); 17 Andy Rice for Cruckshank (57); Roberts for Wittenberg (34); Wittenberg for Roberts (74).
Tries: O'Hare (12, 78), St Hilaire (34, 53), Thorman (46), Gene (57); **Goals:** McNamara 7.
Sin bin: Roberts (47) - fighting.
CENTURIONS: 1 Neil Turley; 2 Leon Felton; 4 Jon Roper; 3 Dale Cardoza; 5 Oliver Marns; 6 Willie Swann; 7 Bobbie Goulding; 8 Vila Matautia; 9 Paul Rowley; 10 David Bradbury; 11 Simon Baldwin; 12 Andrew Isherwood; 13 Adam Bristow. Subs: 14 Gareth Price for Bradbury (24BB, rev 35); 15 John Duffy for Swann (32); 16 John Hamilton for Bristow (46BB, rev 57); 17 David Whittle for Matautia (22); Matautia for Bradbury (53BB); Swann for Goulding (58); Hamilton for Whittle (67); Bradbury for Turley (72); Goulding for Swann (75).
Tries: Cardoza (9), Marns (18), Hamilton (70); **Goals:** Turley 2.
Sin bin: Whittle (47) - fighting; Bristow (74) - interference.
On report: Isherwood (66) - high tackle on Roberts.
Rugby Leaguer & League Express Men of the Match:
Giants: Chris Thorman; *Centurions:* Adam Bristow.
Penalty count: 11-11; **Half-time:** 14-10; **Referee:** Karl Kirkpatrick (Warrington); **Attendance:** 9,051 *(at Halton Stadium, Widnes).*

SUPER LEAGUE GRAND FINAL

Saturday 19th October 2002

BRADFORD BULLS 18 ST HELENS 19

BULLS: 6 Michael Withers; 2 Tevita Vaikona; 20 Scott Naylor; 15 Brandon Costin; 5 Lesley Vainikolo; 1 Robbie Paul (C); 7 Paul Deacon; 8 Joe Vagana; 9 James Lowes; 29 Stuart Fielden; 11 Daniel Gartner; 12 Jamie Peacock; 13 Mike Forshaw. Subs: 14 Lee Gilmour for Gartner (21); 10 Paul Anderson for Vagana (25); 22 Brian McDermott for Fielden (34); 3 Leon Pryce for Vainikolo (53); Fielden for Anderson (55); Vainikolo for Paul (77).
Tries: Naylor (3), Paul (44), Withers (47); **Goals:** Deacon 3.
SAINTS: 1 Paul Wellens; 5 Darren Albert; 3 Martin Gleeson; 4 Paul Newlove; 19 Anthony Stewart; 13 Paul Sculthorpe; 7 Sean Long; 8 Darren Britt; 9 Keiron Cunningham; 10 Barry Ward; 23 Mike Bennett; 15 Tim Jonkers; 11 Chris Joynt (C). Subs: 2 Sean Hoppe for Wellens (3); 12 Peter Shiels for Ward (27); 14 John Stankevitch for Britt (31BB, rev 58); 17 Mick Higham for Joynt (54); Stankevitch for Shiels (58); Joynt for Britt (75); Shiels for Jonkers (77).
Tries: Bennett (24), Long (32), Gleeson (56); **Goals:** Long 3; **Field goal:** Long.
Rugby Leaguer & League Express Men of the Match:
Bulls: Paul Deacon; *Saints:* Mike Bennett.
Penalty count: 5-4; **Half-time:** 12-8; **Referee:** Russell Smith (Castleford); **Attendance:** 61,138 *(at Old Trafford, Manchester).*

2002...Martin Gleeson slides over to score as Robbie Paul looks on

2003

NATIONAL LEAGUE TWO GRAND FINAL

Sunday 5th October 2003

KEIGHLEY COUGARS 13 SHEFFIELD EAGLES 11

COUGARS: 1 Matt Foster; 2 Max Tomlinson; 3 David Foster; 4 James Rushforth; 5 Andy Robinson; 6 Paul Ashton; 7 Matt Firth; 8 Phil Stephenson; 9 Simeon Hoyle; 10 Danny Ekis; 11 Oliver Wilkes; 12 Ian Sinfield; 13 Lee Patterson. Subs (all used): 14 Chris Wainwright; 15 Richard Mervill; 16 Mick Durham; 17 Jason Ramshaw.
Tries: M Foster (7), Robinson (74); **Goals:** Ashton 2;
Field goal: Firth.
EAGLES: 1 Andy Poynter; 2 Tony Weller; 3 Richard Goddard; 4 Tom O'Reilly; 5 Greg Hurst; 6 Gavin Brown; 7 Mark Aston; 8 Jack Howieson; 9 Gareth Stanley; 10 Dale Laughton; 11 Andy Raleigh; 12 Craig Brown; 13 Wayne Flynn. Subs (all used): 14 Peter Reilly; 15 Simon Tillyer; 16 Nick Turnbull; 17 Mitchell Stringer.
Try: O'Reilly (51); **Goals:** G Brown 3; **Field goal:** Reilly.
Rugby Leaguer & League Express Men of the Match:
Cougars: Simeon Hoyle; *Eagles:* Andy Raleigh.
Penalty count: 6-8; **Half-time:** 9-4; **Referee:** Peter Taberner (Wigan). *(At Halton Stadium, Widnes).*

NATIONAL LEAGUE ONE GRAND FINAL

Sunday 5th October 2003

LEIGH CENTURIONS 14 SALFORD CITY REDS 31

CENTURIONS: 1 Neil Turley; 2 Damian Munro; 3 Alan Hadcroft; 4 Danny Halliwell; 5 Leroy Rivett; 6 John Duffy; 7 Tommy Martyn; 8 Sonny Nickle; 9 Patrick Weisner; 10 Paul Norman; 11 Sean Richardson; 12 Willie Swann; 13 Adam Bristow. Subs (all used): 14 David Bradbury; 15 Lee Sanderson; 16 Bryan Henare; 17 Ricky Bibey.
Tries: Richardson (33), Halliwell (38), Swann (65); **Goal:** Turley.
On report: Nickle (60) - late tackle on Clinch.
CITY REDS: 1 Jason Flowers; 2 Danny Arnold; 3 Stuart Littler; 4 Alan Hunte; 5 Andy Kirk; 6 Cliff Beverley; 7 Gavin Clinch; 8 Neil Baynes; 9 Malcolm Alker; 10 Andy Coley; 11 Simon Baldwin; 12 Paul Highton; 13 Chris Charles. Subs (all used): 14 Steve Blakeley; 15 David Highton; 16 Martin Moana; 17 Gareth Haggerty.
Tries: Hunte (3, 52), Beverley (23), Littler (73); **Goals:** Charles 6, Blakeley; **Field goal:** Blakeley.
Rugby Leaguer & League Express Men of the Match:
Centurions: Willie Swann; *City Reds:* Gavin Clinch.
Penalty count: 10-10; **Half-time:** 10-16; **Referee:** Richard Silverwood (Dewsbury); **Attendance:** 9,186 *(at Halton Stadium, Widnes).*

SUPER LEAGUE GRAND FINAL

Saturday 18th October 2003

BRADFORD BULLS 25 WIGAN WARRIORS 12

BULLS: 17 Stuart Reardon; 2 Tevita Vaikona; 6 Michael Withers; 4 Shontayne Hape; 5 Lesley Vainikolo; 15 Karl Pratt; 7 Paul Deacon; 8 Joe Vagana; 9 James Lowes; 29 Stuart Fielden; 11 Daniel Gartner; 12 Jamie Peacock; 13 Mike Forshaw. Subs (all used): 10 Paul Anderson; 18 Lee Radford; 3 Leon Pryce; 1 Robbie Paul (C).
Tries: Reardon (51), Hape (59), Lowes (75);
Goals: Deacon 6/6; **Field goal:** Deacon.
WARRIORS: 1 Kris Radlinski; 5 Brian Carney; 18 Martin Aspinwall; 14 David Hodgson; 2 Brett Dallas; 15 Sean O'Loughlin; 20 Luke Robinson; 30 Quentin Pongia; 9 Terry Newton; 10 Craig Smith; 11 Mick Cassidy; 12 Danny Tickle; 13 Andy Farrell (C). Subs (all used): 4 Paul Johnson; 8 Terry O'Connor; 23 Gareth Hock; 17 Mark Smith.
Tries: Tickle (17), Radlinski (72); **Goals:** Farrell 2/3.
Rugby Leaguer & League Express Men of the Match:
Bulls: Stuart Reardon; *Warriors:* Kris Radlinski.
Penalty count: 7-6; **Half-time:** 4-6; **Referee:** Karl Kirkpatrick (Warrington); **Attendance:** 65,537 *(at Old Trafford, Manchester).*

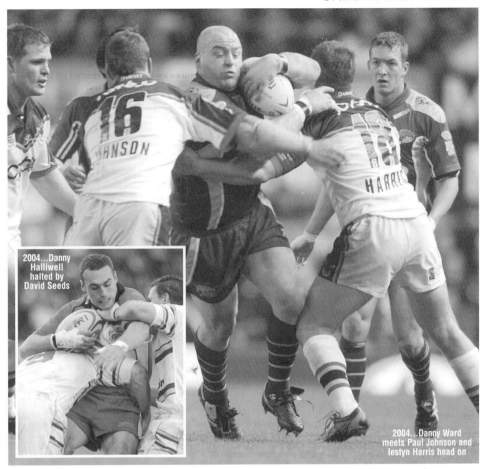

2004...Danny Halliwell halted by David Seeds

2004...Danny Ward meets Paul Johnson and Iestyn Harris head on

2004

NATIONAL LEAGUE ONE GRAND FINAL

Sunday 10th October 2004

LEIGH CENTURIONS 32 WHITEHAVEN 16
(After extra time)

CENTURIONS: 1 Neil Turley; 2 Rob Smyth; 3 Danny Halliwell; 4 Ben Cooper; 5 David Alstead; 6 John Duffy; 7 Tommy Martyn; 8 Simon Knox; 9 Paul Rowley; 10 Matt Sturm; 11 David Larder; 12 Oliver Wilkes; 13 Ian Knott. Subs (all used): 14 Dave McConnell; 15 Heath Cruckshank; 16 Richard Marshall; 17 Willie Swann.
Tries: Cooper (27, 83), Martyn (61), Turley (87);
Goals: Turley 6/8; **Field goals:** Turley 2, Rowley, Martyn.
WHITEHAVEN: 1 Gary Broadbent; 2 Craig Calvert; 3 David Seeds; 4 Mick Nanyn; 5 Wesley Wilson; 6 Leroy Joe; 7 Sam Obst; 8 Marc Jackson; 9 Aaron Lester; 10 David Fatialofa; 11 Paul Davidson; 12 Howard Hill; 13 Craig Walsh. Subs (all used): 14 Spencer Miller; 15 Carl Sice; 16 Chris McKinney; 17 Ryan Tandy.
Tries: Wilson (2, 71), Calvert (45); **Goals:** Nanyn 2/6.
Rugby Leaguer & League Express Men of the Match:
Centurions: Neil Turley; *Whitehaven:* Aaron Lester.
Penalty count: 5-9; **Half-time:** 7-6; **Referee:** Ronnie Laughton (Barnsley); **Attendance:** 11,005 *(at Halton Stadium, Widnes).*

SUPER LEAGUE GRAND FINAL

Saturday 16th October 2004

BRADFORD BULLS 8 LEEDS RHINOS 16

BULLS: 6 Michael Withers; 17 Stuart Reardon; 16 Paul Johnson; 4 Shontayne Hape; 5 Lesley Vainikolo; 18 Iestyn Harris; 7 Paul Deacon; 8 Joe Vagana; 1 Robbie Paul (C); 29 Stuart Fielden; 12 Jamie Peacock; 13 Logan Swann; 11 Lee Radford. Subs: 10 Paul Anderson for Vagana (14); 15 Karl Pratt for Paul (23); 27 Rob Parker for Anderson (24); 19 Jamie Langley for Peacock (32); Paul for Withers (ht); Peacock for Radford (48); Radford for Swann (54); Vagana for Parker (56); Parker for Fielden (63); Fielden for Vagana (67); Swann for Langley (68).
Tries: Vainikolo (7), Hape (43); **Goals:** Deacon 0/2.
RHINOS: 21 Richard Mathers; 18 Mark Calderwood; 5 Chev Walker; 4 Keith Senior; 22 Marcus Bai; 13 Kevin Sinfield (C); 6 Danny McGuire; 19 Danny Ward; 9 Matt Diskin; 8 Ryan Bailey; 3 Chris McKenna; 29 Ali Lauitiiti; 11 David Furner. Subs: 16 Willie Poching for Furner (19); 10 Barrie McDermott for Ward (22); Ward for Bailey (29); 7 Rob Burrow for Lauitiiti (30); Bailey for McDermott (41); 20 Jamie Jones-Buchanan for McKenna (48); Lauitiiti for Ward (50); Furner for Sinfield (60); McKenna for Poching (63); Sinfield for Diskin (67); Poching for McKenna (72); Ward for Bailey (73).
Tries: Diskin (15), McGuire (75); **Goals:** Sinfield 4/4.
Rugby Leaguer & League Express Men of the Match:
Bulls: Lesley Vainikolo; *Rhinos:* Richard Mathers.
Penalty count: 5-5; **Half-time:** 4-10; **Referee:** Steve Ganson (St Helens); **Attendance:** 65,547 *(at Old Trafford, Manchester).*

SUPER LEAGUE

(Play-offs in brackets, inc. in totals)

TRIES
1. Lesley Vainikolo
   Bradford 32 (7)
2. Mark Calderwood
   Leeds 27 (0)
3. Darren Albert
   St Helens 25 (0)
4. Keith Senior
   Leeds 24 (0)
5. Luke Dorn
   London 23 (0)
   Henry Fa'afili
   Warrington 23 (0)
7. Jamie Lyon
   St Helens 22 (2)
8. Rob Burrow
   Leeds 21 (0)
9. Nathan Blacklock
   Hull 20 (3)
   Ben Jeffries
   Wakefield . . . . .20 (-)

GOALS
1. Paul Deacon
   Bradford 153 (16)
2. Kevin Sinfield
   Leeds 129 (4)
3. Paul Sykes
   London 119 (3)
4. Danny Tickle
   Wigan . . . . .103 (-)
5. Chris Thorman
   Huddersfield . . . . .99 (-)
6. Jamie Rooney
   Wakefield . . . . .69 (-)
7. Chris Charles
   Salford . . . . .65 (-)
8. Paul Cooke
   Hull 61 (0)
9. Danny Brough
   Hull 60 (6)
10. Sean Long
    St Helens 59 (0)

POINTS
1. Paul Deacon
   Bradford 359 (33)
2. Paul Sykes
   London 288 (6)
3. Kevin Sinfield
   Leeds 283 (9)
4. Chris Thorman
   Huddersfield . . . . .274 (-)
5. Danny Tickle
   Wigan . . . . .259 (-)
6. Jamie Rooney
   Wakefield . . . . .182 (-)
7. Sean Long
   St Helens 180 (0)
8. Jamie Lyon
   St Helens 172 (18)
9. Chris Bridge
   Warrington 147 (0)
10. Paul Cooke
    Hull 146 (0)

NATIONAL LEAGUE 1

(Play-offs in brackets, inc. in totals)

TRIES
1. Mick Nanyn
   Whitehaven 24 (3)
2. Waine Pryce
   Castleford 23 (1)
3. Ben Black
   Halifax 20 (3)
4. Rikki Sheriffe
   Halifax 17 (3)
   Carl Sice
   Whitehaven 17 (2)
6. Byron Ford
   Hull KR 16 (4)
7. Craig Calvert
   Whitehaven 15 (2)
8. Pat Weisner
   Halifax 14 (2)
9. Tom Haughey
   Castleford 13 (1)
   Michael Shenton
   Castleford 13 (0)
   Ben Fisher
   Halifax 13 (2)

GOALS
1. Mick Nanyn
   Whitehaven 78 (4)
2. Gareth Morton
   Hull KR 71 (11)
3. Liam Finn
   Featherstone . . . . .69 (-)
4. Barry Eaton
   Batley 68 (10)
5. Marty Turner
   Oldham . . . . .62 (-)
6. Graham Holroyd
   Doncaster 59 (1)
7. Craig Huby
   Castleford 58 (8)
8. Jamie Bloem
   Halifax 52 (4)
9. Mark McCully
   Rochdale 46 (0)
10. Darren Holt
    Barrow . . . . .44 (-)

POINTS
1. Mick Nanyn
   Whitehaven 252 (20)
2. Liam Finn
   Featherstone . . . . .166 (-)
3. Gareth Morton
   Hull KR 154 (26)
4. Marty Turner
   Oldham . . . . .153 (-)
5. Craig Huby
   Castleford 152 (20)
6. Barry Eaton
   Batley 149 (28)
7. Graham Holroyd
   Doncaster 138 (2)
8. Pat Weisner
   Halifax 135 (36)
9. Mark McCully
   Rochdale 120 (0)
10. Jamie Bloem
    Halifax 108 (8)

NATIONAL LEAGUE 2

(Play-offs in brackets, inc. in totals)

TRIES
1. Darren Rogers
   Dewsbury 21 (5)
   Peter Fox
   York . . . . .21 (-)
3. Wayne English
   Swinton 19 (1)
   Lusi Sione
   Workington 19 (2)
5. Marlon Billy
   Swinton 18 (1)
   Jonny Limmer
   Workington 18 (1)
7. Lee Marsh
   Swinton 16 (1)
8. George Rayner
   Hunslet 15 (0)
9. Lee Patterson
   Swinton 14 (1)
10. Wade Liddell
    Gateshead 13 (0)
    Dan Potter
    York . . . . .13 (-)

GOALS
1. Lee Marsh
   Swinton 84 (10)
2. Chris Birch
   Gateshead 77 (0)
3. Francis Maloney
   Dewsbury 70 (10)
4. Paul Thorman
   York . . . . .64 (-)
5. Jamaine Wray
   Hunslet 48 (4)
6. Jake Johnstone
   Blackpool . . . . .46 (-)
   Tane Manihera
   Workington 46 (0)
8. John Crawford
   Sheffield . . . . .37 (-)
9. Paul Ashton
   Keighley . . . . .35 (-)
10. Tim Gee
    London Skolars . . . . .31 (-)

POINTS
1. Lee Marsh
   Swinton 233 (24)
2. Chris Birch
   Gateshead 202 (0)
3. Francis Maloney
   Dewsbury 169 (24)
4. Tane Manihera
   Workington 136 (8)
5. Paul Thorman
   York . . . . .129 (-)
6. Jake Johnstone
   Blackpool . . . . .120 (-)
7. John Crawford
   Sheffield . . . . .115 (-)
8. Jamaine Wray
   Hunslet 112 (8)
9. Paul Ashton
   Keighley . . . . .91 (-)
10. Darren Rogers
    Dewsbury 84 (20)
    Peter Fox
    York . . . . .84 (-)

Lesley Vainikolo

Mick Nanyn

Peter Fox

NAT LEAGUE CUP

TRIES
1 John Braddish
   Rochdale 9
2 Michael Platt
   Castleford 8
   Damian Gibson
   Halifax 8
   James Haley
   Halifax 8
   Rikki Sheriffe
   Halifax 8
   Phil Hasty
   Hull KR 8
   Mark Roughneen
   Warrington Wizards 8
8 Michael Shenton
   Castleford 7
   Andy Raleigh
   Hull KR 7
   Phil Cantillon
   Rochdale 7
   Carl Sice
   Whitehaven 7

GOALS
1 Graham Holroyd
   Doncaster 35
2 Craig Huby
   Castleford 28
3 Barry Eaton
   Batley 26
4 Loz Wildbore
   Hull KR 24
5 Mark McCully
   Rochdale 21
6 Chris Birch
   Gateshead 19
   Francis Maloney
   Dewsbury 19
   Gareth Morton
   Hull KR 19
9 Lee Marsh
   Swinton 18
   Craig Poucher
   Hull KR 18

POINTS
1 Graham Holroyd
   Doncaster 90
2 Craig Huby
   Castleford 72
3 John Braddish
   Rochdale 62
4 Barry Eaton
   Batley 60
   Loz Wildbore
   Hull KR 60
6 Mark McCully
   Rochdale 58
7 Mick Nanyn
   Whitehaven 54
8 Francis Maloney
   Dewsbury 50
9 Lee Marsh
   Swinton 49
10 Gareth Morton
   Hull KR 46

CHALLENGE CUP

TRIES
1 Mark Calderwood
   Leeds 7
   Maxime Greseque
   Pia .7
   Fabrice Estebanez
   Toulouse 7
4 Rob Burrow
   Leeds 6
5 Kane Epati
   Hull KR 5
   Matt Bramald
   Keighley 5
   Simon Haughton
   Oldham 5
   Damien Couturier
   Toulouse 5
   Cedric Gay
   Toulouse 5
   James Wynne
   Toulouse 5

GOALS
1 Damien Couturier
   Toulouse 27
2 Lee Birdseye
   Rochdale 18
3 Paul Cooke
   Hull 17
   Laurent Frayssinous
   UTC 17
   Maxime Greseque
   Pia .17
6 Paul Deacon
   Bradford 15
   Kevin Sinfield
   Leeds 15
8 Paul Sykes
   London 14
9 Rob Burrow
   Leeds 13
10 Lee Marsh
   Swinton 12

POINTS
1 Damien Couturier
   Toulouse 74
2 Maxime Greseque
   Pia .63
3 Rob Burrow
   Leeds 50
   Paul Cooke
   Hull 50
5 Lee Birdseye
   Rochdale 44
6 Paul Sykes
   London 36
7 Laurent Frayssinous
   UTC 34
8 Paul Deacon
   Bradford 30
   Wayne Green
   Doncaster 30
   Kevin Sinfield
   Leeds 30

ALL COMPETITIONS

TRIES
1 Mark Calderwood
   Leeds 35
2 Lesley Vainikolo
   Bradford 34
3 Waine Pryce
   Castleford 30
4 Mick Nanyn
   Whitehaven 29
5 Rikki Sheriffe
   Halifax 28
   Rob Burrow
   Leeds 28
   Darren Albert
   St Helens 28
8 Ben Black
   Halifax 26
   Marlon Billy
   Swinton 26
10 Keith Senior
   Leeds 25
   Wayne English
   Swinton 25
   Jonny Limmer
   Workington 25
   Peter Fox
   York 25

GOALS
1 Paul Deacon
   Bradford 168
2 Kevin Sinfield
   Leeds 149
3 Paul Sykes
   London 133
4 Lee Marsh
   Swinton 114
5 Danny Tickle
   Wigan 108
6 Graham Holroyd
   Doncaster 103
7 Barry Eaton
   Batley 100
8 Chris Thorman
   Huddersfield 99
9 Chris Birch
   Gateshead 97
10 Mick Nanyn
   Whitehaven 95

POINTS
1 Paul Deacon
   Bradford 389
2 Kevin Sinfield
   Leeds 324
   Paul Sykes
   London 324
4 Lee Marsh
   Swinton 310
5 Mick Nanyn
   Whitehaven 306
6 Chris Thorman
   Huddersfield 274
7 Danny Tickle
   Wigan 269
8 Chris Birch
   Gateshead 246
   Graham Holroyd
   Doncaster 246
10 Francis Maloney
   Dewsbury 233

Damien Couturier

Mark Calderwood

Graham Holroyd

319

FINAL TABLES

SUPER LEAGUE

	P	W	D	L	F	A	D	PTS
St Helens	28	23	1	4	1028	537	491	47
Leeds	28	22	0	6	1152	505	647	44
Bradford	28	18	1	9	1038	684	354	37
Warrington	28	18	0	10	792	702	90	36
Hull	28	15	2	11	756	670	86	32
London	28	13	2	13	800	718	82	28
Wigan	28	14	0	14	698	718	-20	28
Huddersfield	28	12	0	16	742	791	-49	24
Salford	28	11	0	17	549	732	-183	22
Wakefield	28	10	0	18	716	999	-283	20
Widnes	28	6	1	21	598	1048	-450	13
Leigh	28	2	1	25	445	1210	-765	5

NATIONAL LEAGUE ONE

	P	W	D	L	F	A	D	PTS
Whitehaven	18	16	0	2	648	307	341	32
Castleford	18	15	0	3	683	368	315	30
Hull KR	18	13	0	5	589	389	200	26
Halifax	18	10	0	8	604	467	137	20
Doncaster	18	10	0	8	485	470	15	20
Rochdale	18	9	1	8	468	506	-38	19
Oldham	18	6	1	11	455	545	-90	13
Batley	18	5	0	13	417	574	-157	10
Featherstone	18	3	2	13	454	648	-194	8
Barrow	18	1	0	17	303	832	-529	2

NATIONAL LEAGUE TWO

	P	W	D	L	F	A	D	PTS
York	18	15	0	3	683	356	327	30
Dewsbury	18	13	1	4	526	350	176	27
Workington	18	13	1	4	507	442	65	27
Swinton	18	11	0	7	623	434	189	22
Hunslet	18	11	0	7	476	385	91	22
Gateshead	18	8	1	9	516	508	8	17
Sheffield	18	8	0	10	414	529	-115	16
Keighley	18	4	1	13	359	471	-112	9
Blackpool	18	3	0	15	356	623	-267	6
London S	18	2	0	16	258	620	-362	4

FIELD GOALS

1	Darren Holt	
	Barrow	5
	Paul Deacon	
	Bradford	5
3	Chris Birch	
	Gateshead	4
	Gavin Brown	
	Sheffield	4
	Jamie Rooney	
	Wakefield	4
6	James Webster	
	Hull KR	3
	Lee Kiddie	
	Workington	3

ATTENDANCES

SUPER LEAGUE

	2005 Avg	2004 Avg	Diff
Leeds	17,006	16,608	+398
Wigan	13,894	13,333	+561
Bradford	13,090	13,500	-410
Warrington	11,085	9,889	+1,196
St Helens	10,817	9,507	+1,310
Hull	10,639	11,397	-758
Widnes	6,794	6,167	+627
Huddersfield	5,411	4,362	+1,049
Wakefield	5,099	4,804	+295
Leigh	4,750	2,166	+2,584
Salford	4,093	3,994	+99
London	4,038	3,458	+580

'05 Avg 8,977 / **'04 Avg** 8,833 / **Diff** +144

BEST CROWDS

65,537	Bradford v Leeds (GF)	15/10/05
	at Old Trafford, Manchester	
25,004	Wigan v St Helens (R7)	25/3/05
22,843	Bradford v Leeds (R7)	24/3/05
21,225	Leeds v St Helens (R2)	18/2/05
21,225	Leeds v Bradford (R19)	1/7/05
20,274	Wigan v St Helens (R27)	9/9/05
20,220	Leeds v Bradford (R25)	19/8/05
18,257	Leeds v Wakefield (R8)	28/3/05
18,177	Leeds v Wigan (R18)	18/6/05
17,619	Leeds v Wakefield (R28)	16/9/05

WORST CROWDS

2,682	Salford v Huddersfield (R19)	2/7/05
2,683	Salford v London (R27)	9/9/05
2,854	London v Wakefield (R3)	27/2/05
2,877	London v Huddersfield (R26)	3/9/05
2,997	London v Salford (R14)	22/5/05
3,005	Salford v Wakefield (R25)	19/8/05
3,201	Leigh v London (R8)	28/3/05
3,213	Leigh v Wakefield (R12)	30/4/05
3,221	London v Huddersfield (R22)	24/7/05
3,234	Wakefield v Widnes (R26)	4/9/05

NATIONAL LEAGUE ONE

	2005 Avg	2004 Avg	Diff
Castleford	5,573	7,035	-1,462
Hull KR	2,502	2,186	+316
Whitehaven	2,404	1,763	+641
Featherstone	2,001	1,419	+582
Halifax	1,825	1,953	-128
Oldham	1,272	1,352	-80
Rochdale	1,084	1,010	+74
Doncaster	1,061	874	+187
Batley	1,037	914	+123
Barrow	907	925	-18

'05 Avg 1,967 / **'04 Avg** 1,482 / **Diff** +485

BEST CROWDS

13,300	Whitehaven v Castleford (GF)	9/10/05
	at Halton Stadium, Widnes	
8,078	Castleford v Hull KR (W5)	15/5/05
7,323	Castleford v Whitehaven (W7)	5/6/05
6,197	Castleford v Halifax (FE)	2/10/05
6,154	Whitehaven v Castleford (QSF)	25/9/05
5,943	Castleford v Featherstone (W18)	4/9/05
5,023	Hull KR v Castleford (W15)	7/8/05
5,005	Castleford v Doncaster (W11)	3/7/05
4,941	Castleford v Halifax (W17)	21/8/05
4,776	Castleford v Rochdale (W2)	10/4/05

WORST CROWDS

506	Barrow v Doncaster (W16)	14/8/05
584	Barrow v Hull KR (W19)	11/9/05
587	Batley v Rochdale (W11)	3/7/05
588	Batley v Barrow (W2)	10/4/05
630	Doncaster v Rochdale (W17)	21/8/05
646	Rochdale v Batley (W1)	29/3/05
653	Doncaster v Batley (W6)	15/5/05
653	Batley v Whitehaven (W8)	12/6/05
663	Rochdale v Featherstone (W15)	7/8/05
686	Doncaster v Barrow (W7)	5/6/05

NATIONAL LEAGUE TWO

	2005 Avg	2004 Avg	Diff
York	1,917	1,579	+338
Dewsbury	1,081	809	+272
Workington	1,067	862	+205
Keighley	910	1,184	-274
Sheffield	845	902	-57
Hunslet	677	544	+133
Swinton	612	580	+32
London S	432	407	+25
Blackpool	423	N/A	N/A
Gateshead	361	303	+58

'05 Avg 832 / **'04 Avg** 726 / **Diff** +106

BEST CROWDS

(Attendance figure unavailable for NL1QS-F)

3,224	York v Hunslet (W6)	22/5/05
2,177	York v Workington (W20)	4/9/05
2,056	York v Dewsbury (W4)	24/4/05
1,981	York v Blackpool (W7)	4/6/05
1,961	Batley v Dewsbury (NL1QS-QSF)	25/9/05
1,890	York v Swinton (W1)	28/3/05
1,884	Dewsbury v York (W15)	31/7/05
1,756	York v Keighley (W11)	3/7/05
1,610	York v London Skolars (W17)	14/8/05
1,596	York v Sheffield (W11)	17/4/05

WORST CROWDS

200	London S v Sheffield (W1)	28/3/05
240	London S v Blackpool (W20)	10/9/05
253	Gateshead v Blackpool (W3)	23/4/05
288	Gateshead v Hunslet (W3)	17/4/05
290	Blackpool v Keighley (W1)	28/3/05
	at Lightfoot Green, Preston	
295	Blackpool v Gateshead (W15)	31/7/05
319	Gateshead v Swinton (W17)	14/8/05
330	London S v Gateshead (W19)	3/9/05
335	Hunslet v London S (W2)	10/4/05
340	Hunslet v Workington (W15)	31/7/05

NATIONAL LEAGUE CUP

BEST CROWDS

9,400	Castleford v Hull KR (F)	17/7/05
	at Bloomfield Road, Blackpool	
7,338	Castleford v Featherstone (W6)	25/3/05
6,353	Featherstone v Castleford (W2)	20/2/05
5,768	Castleford v York (W1)	13/2/05
5,019	Castleford v Whitehaven (SF)	19/6/05
4,483	Castleford v Hunslet (W3)	27/2/05
3,439	Whitehaven v Workington (W6)	25/3/05
3,418	Featherstone v Castleford (QF)	29/5/05
3,012	Workington v Whitehaven (W1)	13/2/05
2,474	Hull KR v Doncaster (SF)	19/6/05

WORST CROWDS

220	Blackpool v Rochdale (W3)	27/2/05
	at Lightfoot Green, Preston	
250	Blackpool v Oldham (W6)	20/3/05
	at Lightfoot Green, Preston	
266	Gateshead v Whitehaven (W7)	6/4/05
268	Gateshead v Barrow (W6)	24/3/05
303	Gateshead v Workington (W5)	16/3/05
353	London S v Keighley (W5)	19/3/05
450	London S v Hull KR (W4)	6/3/05
492	Batley v Sheffield (W3)	27/2/05
512	London S v Swinton (W1)	18/2/05
541	Swinton v Blackpool (W6)	25/3/05

CHALLENGE CUP

BEST CROWDS

74,213	Hull v Leeds (F)	27/8/05
	at Millennium Stadium, Cardiff	
17,100	St Helens v Wigan (QF)	26/6/05
16,171	Hull v St Helens (SF)	30/7/05
	at Galpharm Stadium, Huddersfield	
11,350	Hull v Bradford (R5)	7/5/05
10,553	Leeds v Toulouse (SF)	31/7/05
	at Galpharm Stadium, Huddersfield	
10,447	Hull v Leigh (QF)	25/6/05
9,444	Leeds v London (QF)	24/6/05
8,215	Leeds v Warrington (R4)	2/4/05
7,705	Leeds v Pia (R5)	6/5/05
7,105	Huddersfield v St Helens (R4)	3/4/05

WORST CROWDS

209	London Skolars v Pia (R3)	13/3/05
296	Gateshead v UTC (R3)	13/3/05
300	Pia v Keighley (R4)	2/4/05
390	Waterhead v Sheffield (R3)	13/3/05
	at Castleton Gabriels AFC, Rochdale	
410	Blackpool v Toulouse (R3)	13/3/05
450	Hunslet v London (R4)	3/4/05
544	Swinton v L'motiv Moscow (R3)	13/3/05
564	Barrow v East Hull (R3)	13/3/05
569	Batley v St Gaudens (R3)	13/3/05
654	Rochdale v Illingworth (R3)	13/3/05